P9-DMZ-868

lonely planet

Northern California

Northern Mountains
p270

North Coast & Redwoods
p215

Gold Country
p305

Lake Tahoe
p330

Napa & Sonoma Wine Country
p159

Yosemite & the Sierra Nevada
p368

San Francisco
p68

Marin County & the Bay Area
p108

Central Coast
p424

Sacramento & Central Valley
p483

THIS EDITION WRITTEN AND RESEARCHED BY

John A Vlahides,

Sara Benson, Alison Bing, Celeste Brash, Tienlon Ho, Beth Kohn

Contents

SAN FRANCISCO P68

COASTAL HIGHWAY 1 P217

Contents

ON THE ROAD

NAGARAJU HANCHANAHAL PHOTOGRAPHY / GETTY IMAGES ©

TENAYA LAKE, YOSEMITE NATIONAL PARK P373

Contents

UNDERSTAND

SURVIVAL GUIDE

SPECIAL FEATURES

Welcome to Northern California

*Northern California has its own scale –
the world's biggest trees, the continent's
highest peaks – and to know it firsthand
is to change forever the way you
apprehend space and time.*

Natural Splendor

Mother Nature puts on a spectacular show
all across Northern California. In the
mighty Sierra Nevada Mountains, blue
Lake Tahoe is so deep that if drained it
would fill the entire state with 14 inches of
water. Across the Sierra's eastern escarpment, the mountains hang like curtains
above the vast high deserts of the Great
Basin. Even the region's major city, San
Francisco, gets in on the act, with the
towers of the Golden Gate Bridge playing
peekaboo in the fog, while eagles and osprey soar overhead.

National Parks

Northern California has an incredible
six national parks. At Yosemite National
Park see – and hear – some of the world's
highest waterfalls. The tallest trees on the
planet grow in Redwood National Park; the
world's most massive trees at Sequoia National Park. Lassen Volcanic National Park
showcases a bona fide volcano, while King's
Canyon has gorges deeper than even the
Grand Canyon. And the rock formations at
Pinnacles National Park look like the Desert Southwest plunked down in Northern
California.

Food & Drink

Expect to eat really well – this is a region at
the forefront of American culinary trends.
Everything grows here, from apple trees
to Zinfandel grapes, and great food and
wine are a collective fetish. You need not be
fancy. Locals wax poetic about the humble
burrito, or a platter of fresh cracked crab,
plucked that day from the sea. Napa and
Sonoma are the rural outposts of the Bay
Area's dynamic and progressive food scene,
with restaurants by celeb chefs, you-pick-
'em orchards and artisanal dairy farms
producing some of the highest-grade foods
anywhere in the nation.

Weekend Escapes

Idyllic escapes are never far away here –
just pick your theme. For road trips, it's
hard to beat coastal drives up fog-shrouded
Hwy 1 to Mendocino; or down the dramatic
Pacific Coast Highway to Big Sur, a thousand feet above the crashing surf. For history, head east to explore the foothills of the
Sierra Nevada and Old West towns dating
to the Gold Rush. For outdoor adventure,
go up, up, up the mighty Sierra Nevada
and hike granite domes and valleys made
famous by John Muir. And for world-class
art and culture, you need never leave San
Francisco's city limits.

Why I Love Northern California

By John A Vlahides, Author

Nature constantly pulls focus in Northern California. Even in San Francisco, I'm forever looking skyward, mouth agape, at flocks of wild parrots zipping overhead, or an approaching wall of fog tumbling over the hills. Unlike Southern California, where the coast has been subdivided to death, Northern California's coast mostly remains wild, preserved in parklands. We need wild places to restore us. Northern California restores me. When I need a real jolt, I head up high in the Sierra Nevada, and recall John Muir, who said, 'You will top arise and need the tongues of angels to tell what you see.' Indeed.

For more about our authors, see page 576.

Above: Yosemite Falls (p372), Yosemite National Park

Northern California

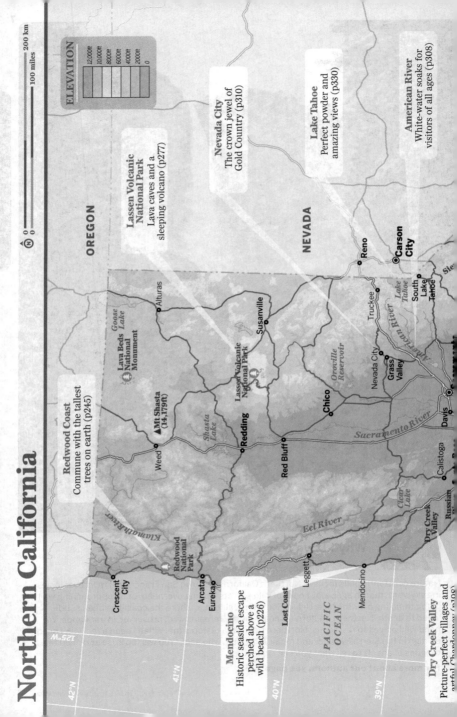

Redwood Coast
Commune with the tallest trees on earth (p245)

Mendocino
Historic seaside escape perched above a wild beach (p226)

Dry Creek Valley
Picture-perfect villages and artful Chardonnay (p198)

Lassen Volcanic National Park
Lava caves and a sleeping volcano (p277)

Nevada City
The crown jewel of Gold Country (p310)

Lake Tahoe
Perfect powder and amazing views (p330)

American River
White-water soaks for visitors of all ages (p308)

OREGON

NEVADA

PACIFIC OCEAN

ELEVATION

12,000ft
10,000ft
8000ft
6000ft
4000ft
2000ft
0

0 —— 100 miles
0 —— 200 km

Crescent City

Arcata
Eureka

Lost Coast

Leggett

Mendocino

Klamath River

Redwood National Park

Weed

▲Mt Shasta (14,179ft)

Shasta Lake

Lava Beds National Monument

Alturas

Goose Lake

Redding

Lassen Volcanic National Park

Susanville

Red Bluff

Eel River

Chico

Oroville Reservoir

Sacramento River

Clear Lake

Calistoga

Russian

Dry Creek Valley

Davis

Nevada City

Grass Valley

Truckee

Reno

Carson City

Lake Tahoe

South Lake Tahoe

American River

125°W
42°N
41°N
40°N
39°N

Yosemite National Park
A wonderland of carved granite peaks and waterfalls (p369)

Highway 395
Jaw-dropping drive through the Sierra Nevada (p402)

San Luis Obispo & Paso Robles
Rolling wine country that quietly rivals Napa (p469)

San Francisco
Bold, urbane and irreverent (p68)

Napa & Sonoma Valleys
America's most renowned wine region (p159)

Death Valley

Telescope Peak
(11,049ft) ▲

Death Valley
National
Park

Barstow

Mt Williamson
(14,375ft) ▲

Mt Whitney
(14,505ft) ▲

Sierra Nevada

Los Angeles

Bishop

Kings
Canyon
National Park

Sequoia
National
Park

Mojave

Mono
Lake

Mammoth
Lakes

Fresno

Bakersfield

ada

Yosemite
National
Park

Sonora

Santa
Barbara

Santa Ynez Mountains

Point
Conception

Channel
Islands
National Park

121°W

Paso Robles

San Luis Obispo

Stockton

San Joaquin River

Kings River

San Jose

Big Sur

Piedras
Blanco
Point

Cambria

Morro Bay

122°W

Berkeley
Oakland

Palo Alto

Santa Cruz
Mountains

Santa Cruz

Monterey
Bay

Monterey

Carmel-by-the-Sea

123°W

Point
Reyes

San
Rafael

San Francisco

PACIFIC
OCEAN

124°W

37°N

36°N

35°N

34°N

Northern California's
Top 25

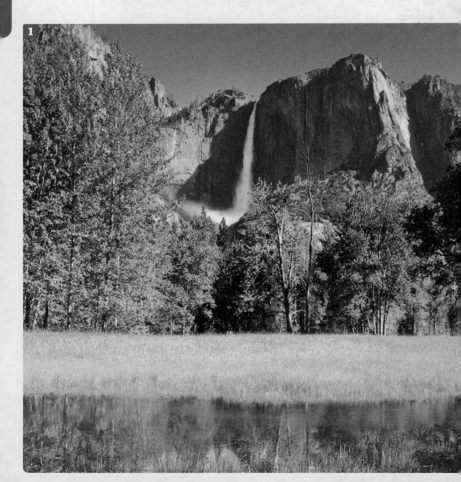

1

Yosemite National Park

1 Yosemite (p369) is arguably Northern California's greatest natural wonder. This beloved national park is gorgeous at any time, but especially so in spring, when several of the world's tallest waterfalls thunder and roar in the valley. Come summer, head up high to hike subalpine valleys ablaze with wildflowers, then cross the mile-high eastern escarpment and drop into vast desert landscapes where tumbleweeds blow. The leaves change colors in autumn, as the waterfalls start to dry up. In winter, snow blankets meadows, and jagged mountain peaks sparkle iridescent-white against an electric-blue sky. Bottom left: Yosemite Falls (p372)

San Francisco

2 SF (p68; say Ess-Eff, not Frisco) is the gateway to Northern California. The views are iconic – clanging cable cars rattling up impossibly high hills, sunsets through the towers of the Golden Gate Bridge – and so is the culture, high art and low, with a Grammy-winning symphony, weird underground performance art, and America's most dynamic food scene. Nature holds a special place in SF: keep your eye on the sky to spot flocks of wild green parrots, and head to the glittering blue bay to hear sea lions bark and bray. Bottom right: Transamerica Pyramid, designed by William Pereira

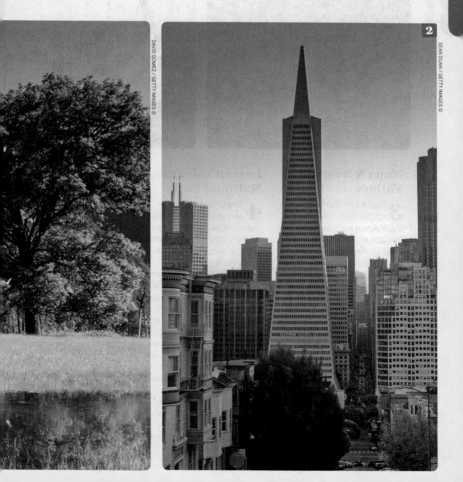

DAVID GOMEZ / GETTY IMAGES ©

SEAN DUAN / GETTY IMAGES ©

COSMO CONDINA / GETTY IMAGES ©

Napa & Sonoma Valleys

3 Napa and Sonoma (p159) not only produce America's best wines but are also beautiful areas to explore. Cruise hidden back roads by bicycle or convertible in search of that perfect bottle of wine; soak and swim at thermal-spring spas; feast on meals by celebrity chefs; and bed down at a country inn. The pastoral landscape provides a lovely backdrop for hedonism – a patchwork of vineyards on oak-dotted hillsides, rising from serpentine rivers flanked by redwoods.

Lassen Volcanic National Park

4 These days Mt Lassen volcano might be dormant, but its eruption a century ago created what's now Lassen Volcanic National Park (p277). Descend into the earth down a pitch-black lava tube, and explore bubbling thermal fields, where mud pots spew sulfur. This wildly alive geological area is visibly morphing itself into a new landscape. And it's remote: even at the peak of summer, it never feels crowded. Book ahead to stay at a classic dude ranch, and ride horseback into grassy meadows that fringe the high-mountain landscape.

Mono Lake

5 Spectacularly eerie Mono Lake (p402) sits on the floor of a vast high-mountain desert, surrounded by towering snow-covered peaks, its shores dense with pungent sagebrush. The ancient lake sprawls far and wide, with giant 'tufa' towers of calcium carbonate rising vertically from its salty black waters. Millions of migratory birds come to feast on brine shrimp, and 80% of all the seagulls in California begin life here. The scale of things is enormous. Instead of hiking, consider kayaking.

Skiing Tahoe

6 Epic snowfall, warm sunshine and panoramic vistas of blue, blue Lake Tahoe (p330) make skiing in Northern California unlike skiing anywhere else. In a good year, these mountains receive some of the deepest snowpack on the continent, and an average 300 annual days of sunshine mean you can work on your tan while you perfect your carves. The terrain varies wildly, from Olympic-caliber steeps and rocky chutes, to ballroom groomers and gentle baby bunny slopes. Book a cozy cabin to snuggle fireside and watch icicles drip from the eaves outside.

Mendocino

7 Perched atop a headland surrounded on three sides by the Pacific, Mendocino (p226) is *the* romantic weekend getaway. A former whaling village taken over by artists in the 1960s, Mendo appears frozen in time, with century-old New England–style saltbox cottages you don't see elsewhere in California. Amble wooden sidewalks and peek into galleries and shops inside rose-covered cottages and weathered wooden water towers. Leave time to kayak, watch for whales, linger over a romantic fireside dinner, and drift asleep in a quiet country inn. Bottom: Mendocino coast

Rafting the American River

8 It's a little unfair that the American River (p308) trumps so many other white-water destinations in California – it's actually three rivers in one. All three branches – the North Fork, Middle Fork and South Fork – are ready-made for family outings. River expeditions can be short and sweet, or full-on adrenaline-packed multiday adventures. And on the way home, it's a quick detour to one of several classic Gold Country towns, such as Nevada City, where you can immerse yourself in history.

Dry Creek & Russian River Valleys

9 There are three Sonomas – the town, the valley, and the county. The latter's remote western and northern valleys are among the least known – and far less busy than Sonoma Valley – but they produce some incredible wines. Plan to sample top-notch Pinot Noir and Chardonnay in the foggy Russian River Valley (p195); and Zinfandel in narrow and warm Dry Creek Valley (p198). During autumn, the leaves turn red and gold, and the smell of fermenting fruit lingers on the breeze. Bottom: Dry Creek Valley vineyard (p198)

Driving the Big Sur Coastline

10 Highway 1 around Big Sur (p449) is the most famous stretch of highway in all California. The road twists and turns a thousand feet above the vast blue Pacific, hugging the skirts of mile-high mountains. This is a drive that merits an upgraded rental car. Alas, passengers get the best views. Spend a night or two in a famous inn or cozy cottage, hike high peaks looking through the fog like islands in the sky, and take a late-night soak beneath the stars in seaside hot springs. Top left: Bixby Bridge (p451)

Highway 395

11 Hwy 395 (the Eastern Sierra Scenic Byway; p401) is California's ultimate road trip (sorry PCH): a north–south route tracing the eastern escarpment of the mighty Sierra Nevada Mountains, with offshoots to both the highest and lowest points in the continental US. Expect to lose all perspective on scale and distance as you drive beneath mountains rising nearly 3 miles high. Famous destinations include Yosemite National Park (summer only); eerie Mono Lake; Mt Whitney, the highest peak in the lower 48; Bodie, California's best-preserved ghost town; and the rugged Alabama Hills. Top right: Whitney Portal (p422)

Monterey

12 Monterey (p436) is home to the finest aquarium on the West Coast and the incredible marine reserve that is Monterey Bay. The former fishing and canning town, made famous by Steinbeck's *Cannery Row*, is now the Central Coast's most family-friendly destination. After you've checked off the aquarium, take the kids for saltwater taffy at Fisherman's Wharf, on a boat trip to spot whales, and to explore forts, missions and historic adobes from California's Mexican and Spanish past. Bottom right: Monterey Bay Aquarium

KARL WEATHERLY / GETTY IMAGES ©

San Luis Obispo & Paso Robles

13 Napa and Sonoma may be more famous, but the golden hills around San Luis Obispo (p471) and Paso Robles (p469) cover three times the ground of Napa. And they produce remarkably great wines, similar in style to France's Rhone Valley, most particularly Châteauneuf-du-Pape. Hard to believe so few people know it. The little city of San Luis Obispo anchors the region, with cute window-shopping and good restaurants that provide a lively counterpoint to the sleepy rural farms and wineries that sprawl everywhere outside town. Above left: Paso Robles vineyards

Swimming Holes

14 You're traveling California's back roads on a blazing July day when, in the middle of nowhere, you pass a cluster of cars parked at the side of the road. Don't ask questions – just park, strip and plunge. California's byways are dotted with swimming holes that provide welcome respite from summer's heat. Those who travel without a swimsuit will be sorry, unless of course you happen upon one of the nude spots. Look for a concentration of swimming holes along Hwy 49 in northern Gold Country, notably the Yuba River Bridge; or just ask locals – but you'll have to sweet-talk them into giving up their favorites. Top right: Yuba River

Klamath Basin National Wildlife Refuges

15 The Klamath Basin (p298) provides bird-watchers with a thrilling spectacle beneath the Pacific Flyway, the 'avian superhighway' of migrating north–south bird traffic. If spotting a semipalmated sandpiper doesn't quicken your pulse, take heart: birds are but a few of the fauna found everywhere in this remote northern mountain region. Head to the edges of Lava Beds National Monument, and you'll encounter ever more wildlife, from vesper bats and mule deer, to flying squirrels and marmot. Bottom right: Black-tailed deer

Sequoia & Kings Canyon National Parks

16 This is a landscape of superlatives (p391) – a cleft in high mountains deeper than the Grand Canyon, and pristine backcountry wilderness dominated by the highest peak in the continental US, Mt Whitney (14,497ft). But it's the trees that grab all the attention for being so immediately awe-inspiriing – find the granddaddy of them all, General Sherman, the largest tree on earth. Come wintertime, snow blankets the park: plan to snowshoe through the silent woods.

Top: Sequoia redwoods

Lost Coast

17 If you crave getting as far away as possible from the sound of civilization and internal combustion engines, you can't get further than the Lost Coast (p248), the longest stretch of undeveloped coastline in all California. The King Range rises so abruptly from the Pacific Ocean – a mile nearly straight up – that building a road on its flanks proved impossible. The only way to reach this windswept foggy shore is to hike your way in. Along the way, spot roaming herds of Roosevelt elk, rusted-out shipwrecks and wide-open vistas of the roaring sea.

Mt Shasta

18 No other mountain in California stirs the imagination quite like Mt Shasta (p286). Its conical summit rises over 14,000ft from the sea-level Central Valley flatlands, and stays shrouded by snow many months of the year. Native tribes believed a god left heaven to live on its summit. John Muir said it made his 'blood turn to wine.' An early-20th-century explorer reported a city of mummies 11 miles below its surface. New Agers claim it's an energy vortex in the earth. Find your own metaphor (and test your endurance) on a hike to the summit.

Redwood National & State Parks

19 A few minutes craning your neck at the world's tallest trees, contemplating what it means to be standing before a 2000-year-old living thing, and the day-to-day world feels far away. It is. Most people never make it to this northernmost edge of the state (p263), but consider this: there's no other place on the globe where coast redwoods grow. And the primordial forest – lush with spiky prehistoric ferns and hot-pink azalea flowers – is as biologically complex as the rainforests. *Carpe diem:* brave the drive.

JOHN ELK / GETTY IMAGES ©

JOHN ELK / GETTY IMAGES ©

Nevada City & Gold Country

20 Judging by a trip to the Gold Country's most famous town (p310), you might think that the '49ers stormed California in search of antiques shops, ice-cream parlors and frilly B&Bs. Nevada City may be the most famous, but it's not the only well-preserved town along winding Hwy 49, aka the Gold Country Highway. Plan to visit Columbia State Historic Park for a glimpse of the Wild West, complete with swinging saloon doors; and detour from the main road to find Murphys, which looks much as it always has (except for the horseless carriages).
Top right: Broad St, Nevada City

Point Reyes National Seashore

21 Only an hour from San Francisco, Point Reyes National Seashore (p127) juts 10 miles out to sea, a 1400ft-high peninsula atop an entirely different tectonic plate from the mainland. Its rugged natural beauty is dazzling. Seals colonize the rocky headlands, tide pools teem with life, grasslands burst into color with spring flowers, and herds of tule elk roam high bluffs above the crashing surf. Descend 300 steps – 30 stories – from the bluff tops to the Point Reyes Lighthouse for the best whale-watching in Northern California. Bottom right: Drakes Beach at sunrise

RON KOEBERER / GETTY IMAGES ©

Santa Cruz

22 Though surfers, hippies, college students and left-wing activists would totally disagree, Santa Cruz (p426) feels more like southern California than northern. Blame geography: Santa Cruz faces south, not west, and gets drenched in warm sunshine. The beach is every local's backyard. After exploring the park-like campus of USC, and shopping downtown for records and vintage clothing, hit the sand. No visit would be complete without a trip to the Boardwalk and a ride on the Giant Dipper, a wooden roller coaster and National Historic Landmark fronting Main Beach. Above left: Santa Cruz Beach Boardwalk (p427)

Muir Woods

23 Pictures don't do justice to Muir Woods National Monument (p123) – you simply can't appreciate the scale of the world's tallest trees until you're standing beneath them, watching fog swirl in the branches like evanescing ghosts. Muir Woods is tiny compared with the northern redwood parks but it's just a half-day trip from San Francisco, providing a glimpse of the trees without the long drive north. Get here first thing to beat crowds, and then make sure to ascend nearby Mt Tamalpais – by foot or car – for bird's-eye vistas of ocean and forest.

Wilderness Camping

24 Nowhere else in the US has such majestic natural beauty as Northern California. Whether the high-mountain forests of the Trinity Alps, the granite domes of Yosemite, the forgotten expanse of the Lost Coast, or lonely Angel Island right in San Francisco Bay, you'll find many breathtaking and beautiful places to sleep beneath the stars. For serious hiking, plan a backpacking trip along the epic Pacific Crest Trail, which runs all the way from Canada to Mexico.

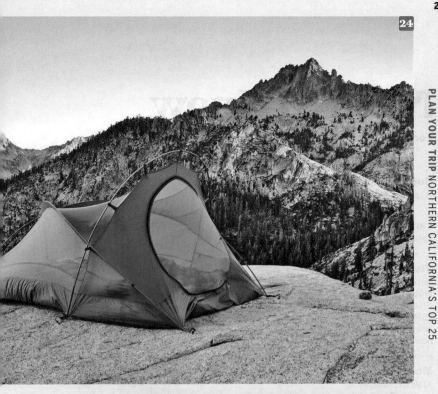

Hot Springs

25 Northern California's rugged terrain is alive with geothermal activity and hot water bubbles from the earth from mountains to coast – at undeveloped mud holes in the Eastern Sierra and by eerie Mono Lake; at old-fashioned spa resorts in Calistoga, where the local specialty is a volcanic-ash mud bath; and at rustic spas and retreat centers around Big Sur and Mendocino, places like Harbin Hot Springs, where nudists meditate in searingly hot water and yoga is the preferred sport.
Right: Old Faithful Geyser (p180), Calistoga

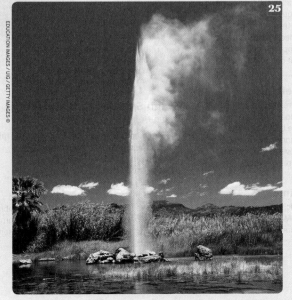

EDUCATION IMAGES / UIG / GETTY IMAGES ©

Need to Know

For more information, see Survival Guide (p545)

Currency
US dollars ($)

Language
English

Visas
Not required for citizens of Visa Waiver Program (VWP) countries with ESTA approval; apply online. Other travelers need a valid US visa.

Money
ATMs and banks widely available. Credit cards required for car and hotel reservations. Checks rarely accepted. Tipping is customary, not optional.

Cell Phones
Foreign GSM multiband phones will work in the USA. Prepaid cell phones widely available. Coverage can be spotty in remote areas.

Time
Pacific Time Zone (GMT/UTC minus eight hours)

When to Go

Redwood National Park
GO May–Oct

Lake Tahoe
GO Jun–Oct, Dec–Apr

San Francisco
GO Mar–Oct

Yosemite National Park
GO Mar–Oct

Big Sur
GO Apr–May, Sept–Oct

Desert, dry climate
Dry climate
Warm to hot summers, mild winters
Warm to hot summers, cold winters

High Season (Jun–Aug)

➡ Accommodations are at their most expensive; weekday rates are cheaper, especially at popular weekend destinations, such as Wine Country.

➡ During holiday weekends, prices for accommodations increase dramatically.

Shoulder (Sep–Oct, Mar–May)

➡ Prices drop in fall and spring.

➡ Best time to visit the national parks, as they're less crowded and generally accessible, especially in autumn, before snow season.

Low Season (Nov–Feb)

➡ Crowds vanish at national parks and in Wine Country, but not at ski towns.

➡ Prices and occupancy spike during holidays.

➡ Lake Tahoe has high-season pricing in wintertime (ski season); highest rates are around Christmastime.

Useful Websites

California Travel & Tourism Commission (www.visitcalifornia.com) Multilingual trip-planning guides.

SF Gate Travel (www.sfgate.com/travel) Travel features and Bay Area getaways.

Redwood Hikes (www.redwoodhikes.com) A guide to walking under old-growth redwood.

Lonely Planet (www.lonelyplanet.com/california) Destination info, travelers' forums and more.

California State Parks (www.parks.ca.gov) Outdoor activities and free e-guides.

Caltrans (www.dot.ca.gov) Highway information.

Important Numbers

Country code	☏1
International access code	☏011
Operator	☏0
Emergency (ambulance, fire & police)	☏911
Directory assistance (local)	☏411

Exchange Rates

Australia	A$1	$0.86
Canada	C$1	$0.88
Europe	€1	$1.24
Japan	¥100	$0.87
Mexico	MXN10	$0.74
UK	£1	$1.59

For current exchange rates see www.xe.com.

Daily Costs

**Budget:
Less than $100**

➡ Burrito for dinner: $6–10

➡ Campsites: $20–40; hostels: $25–40

➡ Museum admission: free (once per month) to $10

➡ Public transit in San Francisco: $2.25; cable cars: $6

**Midrange:
$100–$200**

➡ Two-star motel room: $75–150

➡ Car rental: from $30 per day, plus insurance and gas

➡ Short taxi trip: $8–15, plus tip

**Top End:
More than $200**

➡ Single-day rafting trip: $135

➡ Meal in top restaurant: $60–75, plus alcohol and tip

➡ Three-star lodging: from $150

Opening Hours

Banks 9am–5pm Monday to Thursday, to 6pm Friday, some 9am–12:30pm Saturday

Bars 5pm–2am daily, till midnight in rural areas

Business hours (general) 9am–5pm Monday to Friday

Nightclubs 9pm–2am Thursday to Saturday

Post offices 9am–5pm Monday to Friday, some 9am–noon Saturday

Restaurants 7–10:30am, 11:30am–2:30pm and 5–9:30pm daily, some later Friday and Saturday

Shops 10am–6pm or 7pm Monday to Saturday, noon–5pm Sunday (malls open later, usually 8pm or 9pm)

Arriving in Northern California

San Francisco International Airport (p106; SFO) BART to downtown ($8.65, 30 minutes); door-to-door shuttles ($15 to $20, one hour); find shuttles upstairs at departures level; taxis to downtown ($40 to $55, plus 15% tip, 30 to 50 minutes)

Oakland International Airport (p136; OAK) Trams ($6) connect airport with BART station; BART to downtown SF ($4.05, 25 minutes); taxis to downtown SF (about $65)

Sacramento International Airport (p491; SMF) Good for Yosemite, Gold Country and Sierra Nevada; Capitol Corridor (www.capitolcorridor.org) trains connect to the Bay Area; transfer to BART in Richmond

Getting Around

Apart from in San Francisco, a car is a necessity. Beyond the Bay Area, most towns do not provide public transit.

Car Essential for travel at your own pace. Drive on the right. For highway information, contact Caltrans (www.dot.ca.gov).

Train Amtrak serves many cities, using connecting bus services from main routes to lesser destinations. Look for the bus icon to determine which routes are served by bus, not train.

Bus Greyhound serves major cities, with very limited service on the coast. Other companies serve the suburbs and parts of Wine Country.

Air Because of the state's size, it's not unreasonable to consider flying between some cities.

For much more on **getting around**, see p556

If You Like...

Majestic Scenery

Northern California has some of America's most spectacular natural lands. Make time for at least one national park.

Yosemite National Park High meadows and granite domes, this was conservationist John Muir's wonderland. (p369)

Lassen Volcanic National Park Discover alien lava fields, sulfuric mud pots and a snowcapped dormant volcano. (p277)

Redwood National & State Parks The world's tallest trees date from prehistory at this patchwork of parks. (p263)

Sequoia & Kings Canyon National Parks Stand agape beneath the world's most massive living things; hike into California's wildest canyon wilderness. (p392)

Marin Headlands Across the Golden Gate from San Francisco, eagles and hawks circle above dramatic cliffs; find hiking trails and hidden beaches. (p110)

History

Gold Country Follow in the footsteps of Western pioneers and hardscrabble miners, or pan for real gold yourself. (p305)

Sutter's Fort State Historic Park The highest ground in Sacramento, this historic fort was California's first major settlement. (p486)

Alcatraz 'The Rock' – America's first military prison – rises just offshore from San Francisco. (p74)

Bodie State Historic Park California's creepiest, biggest ghost town, preserved in a state of arrested decay. (p405)

Manzanar National Historic Site Commemorates the Japanese Americans interned here during WWII. (p421)

Small Towns

Ferndale The North Coast's former dairy capital is home to grand Victorian-era 'butterfat mansions' – the entire town is listed on the National Register of Historic Places. (p252)

Mendocino The ocean is never out of earshot in this tiny New England–style town, on a fog-shrouded rocky peninsula jutting out to sea. (p226)

Angels Camp Mark Twain's big break came writing about a contest of jumping frogs here, and the town still buzzes with rowdy Gold Rush history. (p323)

Weaverville In the shadow of the majestic Trinity Alps, this tiny berg has an ancient Chinese temple, access to rugged outdoors and stunning nature in every direction. And there isn't a stoplight in the entire county. (p300)

Boonville Great food, stylish lodging, a killer brewery and dynamic wineries make for a brilliant escape from the Bay Area. Locals have their own language. (p239)

Lakes

Lake Tahoe America's second-deepest lake – and the world's tenth deepest – Tahoe never freezes. Come summer to swim and sail; come wintertime to ski with a big blue view. (p330)

Shasta Lake Party with your friends on a houseboat, or find tranquillity hiking endless miles of shoreline. (p275)

Eagle Lake Venture where few others tread, navigating gorgeous two-lane roads to the pristine area surrounding the state's third-largest natural lake. (p283)

Mono Lake The eerie rock formations of this otherworldly landscape include giant towers of calcium carbonate – plan to kayak and bird-watch, not swim. (p402)

Tenaya Lake This glittering blue lake is one of the prettiest in all California, along the high country summertime-only road through Yosemite National Park. (p373)

Museums

MH de Young Memorial Museum A copper-skinned temple to global art in San Francisco's Golden Gate Park. (p95)

California Academy of Sciences San Francisco's natural-history museum and aquarium breathes 'green' in its eco-certified design, with a four-story rainforest and living roof. (p95)

California Museum Sacramento's modern-history museum highlights famous people and lesser-known tales from the state's past. (p486)

Laws Railroad Museum Old West aficionados love Bishop's original 1883 train depot and museum. (p419)

Live Music

The Fillmore This is the house that Bill Graham built in the '60s. Dig those priceless concert posters on display upstairs, advertising past shows by The Dead, The Doors, Radiohead and Adele. (p103)

Yoshi's In Oakland's Jack London Sq, Yoshi's stages top talents in jazz and blues and serves delish Japanese food. (p136)

San Francisco Symphony Under the baton of famous conductor Michael Tilson Thomas, the SFS often wins Grammys – hear why at a concert of Mahler or Beethoven. (p104)

Buck Owens' Crystal Palace Shine your boots and don pressed denim at the premier country-music venue in the Central Valley, monument to the legendary king of the Bakersfield Sound. (p511)

High Sierra Music Festival Thank goodness this top-notch folk and jam band festival is in the middle of nowhere – if it were

Top: Shasta Lake (p275) and Mt Shasta (p286) at dawn
Bottom: View across Telegraph Hill (p79) to Alcatraz (p74) and the Marin Headlands (p110), San Francisco

any easier to get there it'd be mobbed. (p284)

Skinny Dippin'

Northern California has a remarkable variety of au naturel hot springs and swimming spots.

Orr Hot Springs Connect with your inner hippie, camp beneath the stars and soak in thermal waters, just a couple of hours from San Francisco. (p243)

Esalen Institute Big Sur's blissful retreat is spendy, but the memory of soaking in a bath on a ledge over the crashing Pacific will last a lifetime. (p454)

Finnish Country Sauna & Tubs Private open-air redwood tubs and a European coffeehouse vibe make this a unique North Coast soak. (p258)

Baker Beach Most days you'll need a sweater, but when the sun's out, head to the northern end of San Francisco's principal clothing-optional beach. (p83)

Mind-Bending Festivals

Northern California hosts some of the most wild, wacky and wonderful festivals in the nation. Not for the xenophobic, these festivals are a study in diversity.

Hardly Strictly Bluegrass San Francisco's best free music festival hosts three days of A-list folk, rock, bluegrass and country artists. (p93)

Reggae on the River In the heart of Humboldt County, this music event is all dreadlocks and Jamaican-influenced jams – and no, that's not a skunk you smell. (p247)

Burning Man The world's greatest experiment in culture and community, this trippy art party in the desert is an anything-goes affair, where commerce and advertising are prohibited, and creativity replaces cash as currency.

San Francisco Pride Month The last Sunday in June, a million people descend upon San Francisco to celebrate Gay Pride Day, which is preceded by a month of parties and a brilliant film festival. (p28)

Beautiful Coastline

Julia Pfeiffer Burns State Park It's tough to pick a favorite among Big Sur's coast sights, but this remote crescent-shaped beach is a stunner – and includes a waterfall that drains into the sea. (p452)

Point Reyes National Seashore Migrating whales, incredible birding, excellent hiking and kayaking on a pristine peninsula jutting 10 miles out to sea, just an hour from San Francisco. (p127)

Redwood Coast Mysterious and majestic, this wild coast of big trees and brooding surf feels lost in time. (p245)

Sonoma Coast State Beach A series of rocky coves and sandy beaches, these rugged beauties reveal the awesome power of nature. (p220)

Month by Month

January

Typically California's wettest month. Coastal regions go quiet. The hills turn green. Mountain ski resorts are packed on weekends, quiet on weekdays. Bay Area skies gray. Wine Country a bargain.

🎆 Chinese New Year

San Francisco's Chinatown sounds like a war zone, as firecrackers announce the lunar new year with parades, lion dancers and street vendors. Late January, early February.

February

Rain at the coast, heavy snow in the mountains – ski season is in full swing.

Beach towns and the Wine Country are quiet.

🏃 Wildlife-Watching

Don't let rain keep you indoors – February is prime time to spot whales migrating offshore, colonies of elephant seals mating and birthing, monarch butterflies roosting in the trees, and hundreds of bird species along the Pacific Flyway.

March

Following winter's rains, the entire state turns deep green, just for March – except the Sierra Nevada, which remains white. California poppies appear along the coast.

🎆 North Lake Tahoe SnowFest

Celebrating the peak of the winter season, this wild affair celebrates all things snow, with costume parties, ski competitions, parades and (of course) a snow queen contest.

🎆 Mendocino Coast Whale Festivals

As the northbound winter migration of gray whales peaks, Mendocino and Fort Bragg fill three weekends in

March with food and wine tasting, art shows, marine-mammal educational exhibits and naturalist-guided walks and talks.

April

Shoulder season on the coast and mountains brings hotel deals – except during spring break, around Easter. Wildflower season peaks at lower elevations. Gold Country wildflowers bloom. Tahoe spring skiing is at its best – as are Yosemite's waterfalls.

🎆 San Francisco International Film Festival

Since 1957, North America's longest-running film festival has been bringing independent-minded films to San Francisco, including provocative global premiers; held late April, early May.

☆ Perpetual Indulgence in Dolores Park

On Easter Sunday, the Sisters of Perpetual Indulgence (Catholic drag queens) stage an Easter egg hunt, bonnet contest and the notorious Hunky Jesus

Contest in San Francisco's Dolores Park.

May

Weather warms statewide, dry season begins: sea-level hills turn golden-brown. Coastal fog forms as the sun's now-hot rays hit the icy Pacific. Summer begins Memorial Day weekend – among the year's busiest travel weekends. Yosemite rangers install cables for climbers ascending Half Dome.

🏃 Bay to Breakers

Race across town in the wackiest costume you can dream up at San Francisco's annual ragtag run from the Embarcadero to Ocean Beach. Snarky locals call it 'Straight Pride Day.' Third Sunday in May.

🎏 Healdsburg Future Farmers Country Fair

Sonoma County's très chic capital of gastronomy reverts to its agrarian roots for this country fair, featuring the future farmers' parade, when little children display baby animals and the whole town cheers.

🏃 Kinetic Grand Championship

Over Memorial Day weekend, this 'triathlon of the art world' is a three-day, 38-mile race, from Arcata to Ferndale, of human-powered, self-propelled contraptions that defy definition. Competitors – all tinkerers and inventors – are hell-bent on outdoing one another.

June

School's out by the end of the month; family travel begins. Everywhere is busy. Coastal fog – 'June gloom' – thickens and spreads over San Francisco, drawn through the Golden Gate by the Central Valley's intense heat.

🎏 Pride Month

Out and proud since 1970, San Francisco's big, bawdy celebrations take place throughout June, with costumed parades, coming-out parties, live music, DJs and more. It's one of the city's most joyful events.

🎏 San Francisco International LGBT Film Festival

The world's largest LGBT film festival runs the last two weeks in June, ending on Pride weekend, in San Francisco.

July

At the peak of summer, the trails of Yosemite get crowded, and the Central Valley gets blazingly hot. July 4 is summer's busiest weekend; towns host fairs and fireworks. San Francisco's daily high is just 68°F (20°C). Lake Tahoe's high season begins.

🎏 California State Fair

A million people come to Sacramento's fairgrounds for two weeks in July to pet pigs and cheer horse races, browse blue ribbons, and sample California wines

and microbrews. Special events – like concerts and bull-riding – draw huge crowds.

☆ Reggae on the River

Come party with the 'Humboldt Nation' of hippies, Rastafarians, tree-huggers and other beloved NorCal eccentrics for two days of live reggae bands, arts and crafts, barbecue, juggling, unicycling, camping and swimming; mid-July.

August

Warm weather keeps Santa Cruz beaches crowded; non-south-facing coastal areas remain shrouded in fog three days out of four. Europeans throng San Francisco. Wildflowers peak in the High Sierra.

🎏 Strawberry Festival at Monterey Bay

The messy marquee event at this Watsonville festival is the pie-eating contest, but live music and tons of fruit keep families entertained. The berries are entirely local: Watsonville produces almost 90% of all the strawberries grown in the US.

🎏 Humboldt County Fair

Held annually since 1869, this is a classic county fair, with broad appeal to traditionalists, who throng the picturesque Victorian village of Ferndale.

🎏 Burning Man

Although Burning Man happens in Nevada's Black

Rock Desert, it began in San Francisco and draws tens of thousands of Northern Californians, who celebrate art's ephemeral nature, radical inclusion, self-reliance and self-expression. No commerce or advertising allowed. Make arrangements way ahead.

September

Summer's last hurrah is Labor Day weekend, when cities empty and parks get crowded. High Sierra aspens turn gold. School resumes. Resorts go quiet weekdays. Fog clears at the coast; San Francisco warms. Wine Country begins its harvest.

Monterey Jazz Festival

A roster of iconic artists and young jazz visionaries arrive to play one of the world's longest-running jazz festivals, featuring outdoor concerts and more intimate indoor shows

over a long weekend in mid-September.

October

Fog season concludes. The weather on the coast is sunny and warm. Fire season peaks. Mountain regions' hotel rates drop – Lake Tahoe is a bargain. Wine Country is in its high season.

Donner Party Hike

Retrace the steps of the ill-fated Donner Party on a hike, led by historians, between Lake Tahoe and Truckee.

Vineyard Festivals

California's wine regions celebrate their harvest with star-chef food-and-wine shindigs, grape-stomping 'crush' parties and barrel tastings; some events start in September.

Litquake

San Francisco's thrilling literary festival features

readings, storytelling hours, workshops, author appearances, guided walking tours and a 'LitCrawl' between Mission district pubs.

November

Rain and snow begin to fall. Coastal areas and cities quieten down. Thanksgiving is the year's busiest travel weekend – nationwide. Ski season begins at the end of the month. The weeks between Thanksgiving and Christmas are cold and dark; barely anyone travels at this time, and hotel rates plummet.

Día de los Muertos

Mexican communities honor ancestors on November 2 with costumed parades, sugar skulls, graveyard picnics and candlelight processions. Join the colorful festivities in San Francisco's Mission District.

Itineraries

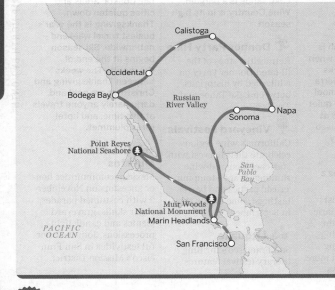

1 WEEK San Francisco, Marin County & Wine Country

This classic NorCal itinerary explores San Francisco, then heads north up the rugged coast, and inland to Wine Country. **San Francisco** begs exploration – its hills, cable cars, glorious bay and dynamic culture are unique in the world. Wander hidden alleyways in Chinatown, see Beat-poet hangouts in North Beach and ascend Telegraph Hill beneath flocks of wild parrots. Head to Golden Gate Park for gorgeous gardens and thrilling museums, then get off the beaten path in the Mission District to find colorful murals and great cheap eats. Cross the Golden Gate Bridge to the **Marin Headlands** and hike cliffs rising straight from the Pacific. Or wander among redwoods – the world's tallest trees – at cathedral-like **Muir Woods National Monument**. For a full-day trip, go whale-watching on the rugged coast of **Point Reyes National Seashore**. Stay the night.

Explore Sonoma Coast State Beach, near **Bodega Bay**, then cut inland to tiny **Occidental** and Wine Country to spend another night. Recharge in thermal springs and mud baths in **Calistoga** before sampling famous California vintages in the surrounding Napa Valley. Head to **Napa** and return to San Francisco via **Sonoma** to explore historic sights between visits to wine-tasting rooms, and picnic on the state's largest town square.

Up the Coast

The serpentine stretch of Hwy 1 (and Hwy 101) between San Luis Obispo and the Oregon border is among Northern California's most epic road trips, connecting cute beach towns, rugged coastline and majestic redwood forests.

From the college town of **San Luis Obispo**, head straight to jaw-dropping **Hearst Castle National Historic Monument** (reservations essential). Here begins one of America's most famous drives: the **Big Sur** coast, 1000ft above the Pacific. Spend at least one night between Hearst Castle and Santa Cruz. Choose your adventure: a romantic hideaway in Big Sur, the West's best aquarium at **Monterey**, or a classic beachside amusement park, complete with boardwalk and bone-rattling wooden roller coaster at **Santa Cruz**. Or combine them over several days.

Get an early start for **San Francisco**, the thrilling urban centerpiece of the trip – spend at least two days exploring the City by the Bay. Then continue north for a day to **Point Reyes National Seashore** and **Sonoma Coast State Beach**, where you can stop for picnicking, tide-pooling and whale-watching. Here the coast gets wild again, with windswept bluffs and nary a traffic light. Spend a couple of nights in a seaside cottage near **Gualala** and dawdle on hidden beaches; or book a B&B in moody **Mendocino** to gallery-hop, explore rocky headlands and fall asleep beside a crackling fire.

Highway 1 cuts inland and joins four-lane Hwy 101 at the **Lost Coast**, the North Coast's premier backpacking destination. Leave the main highway to follow the parallel-running **Avenue of the Giants**, flanked by towering redwoods. Most people turn around after the Avenue, but to see the depth of the redwood forests, keep going north. Detour from the main road for lunch in the cute-as-a-button Victorian village of **Ferndale**, or the wildly progressive college town of **Arcata**. Spend two days exploring the magnificent ancient groves of **Redwood National & State Parks** before returning south.

3 WEEKS Northern California Classics

To see Northern California's most spectacular scenery, plan to make a loop around the entire region. Begin with a dose of big-city culture in **San Francisco**. Get a taste of the California food scene at the Ferry Building market, then hop on a ferry to notorious Alcatraz. Plan to ride a cable car, wander the waterfront, and discover the spectacular gardens and museums of Golden Gate Park. Head north over the famous Golden Gate Bridge to **Marin County** and the windswept coastline of Point Reyes National Seashore. California's most famous grapes grow nearby in Wine Country – leave time to explore the over-the-top wineries of **Napa Valley** and historic **Sonoma**. If you've extra time, get lost on back roads in the **Russian River Valley**. Wine Country meets the boondocks in hidden **Anderson Valley**, on the way north to coastal **Mendocino**, a picture-perfect New England–like village on rocky Pacific headlands above the roaring surf.

Work your way north, past **Leggett**, where Hwy 1 cuts inland and joins Hwy 101; here begins the Redwood Coast, home to the world's tallest trees. In **Humboldt Redwoods State Park** drive beneath towering redwoods along the Avenue of the Giants. Stop for a night in conservative **Eureka**, with its pretty waterfront and candy-colored Victorians; or let your hair down with the college kids in Eureka's left-leaning neighbor, **Arcata**. Turn east on Hwy 299 for a mountainous scenic drive toward Gold Rush–era **Weaverville**, skirting the lake-studded Trinity Alps. Head north on I-5 to gape at stunning **Mt Shasta**, then head southeast on Hwy 89 to **Lassen Volcanic National Park** (p32), that hellishly beautiful volcanic landscape in the Cascade Range. Keep trucking southeast on Hwy 89 to **Lake Tahoe**, a four-season mountain resort. Spend a couple of nights. Afterward, cut south down the Eastern Sierra and Hwy 395 to the back-door entrance into **Yosemite National Park**, via summertime-only Tioga Rd.

If you've time, tack on a drive down spectacularly scenic Hwy 395, which passes between the highest and lowest points in the contiguous US: **Mt Whitney** and **Death Valley**. Otherwise, after a night or two in Yosemite Valley, go south to **Sequoia & Kings Canyon National Parks** and wander groves of giant sequoias – the world's most massive living things.

Top: Golden Gate
Bridge (p72)

Bottom: Lassen
Volcanic National Park
(p277)

California: Off the Beaten Track

LOST COAST

Tackle an epic backpacking route, take a day hike to Punta Gorda Lighthouse, or beachcomb in utterly remote Shelter Cove, an overnight escape. (p248)

SMITH RIVER NATIONAL RECREATION AREA

The state's last remaining undammed waterway tumbles out of the Siskiyou Mountains, into Redwood National and State Parks. Plan to hike or raft. (p266)

LAVA BEDS NATIONAL MONUMENT

A geological wonderland of lava flows, spatter cones, shield volcanoes and craters. Strap on a helmet and clamber inside two dozen lava tubes. (p297)

AMADOR COUNTY WINE REGION

Explore one of California's oldest but least-known wine countries up in the Sierra Nevada foothills, where old Zinfandel grapevines thrive in mineral-rich soil. (p320)

BODIE STATE HISTORIC PARK

High above Mono Lake, this Gold Rush-era mining camp has become a ghost town where 200 buildings stand eerily frozen in time. (p405)

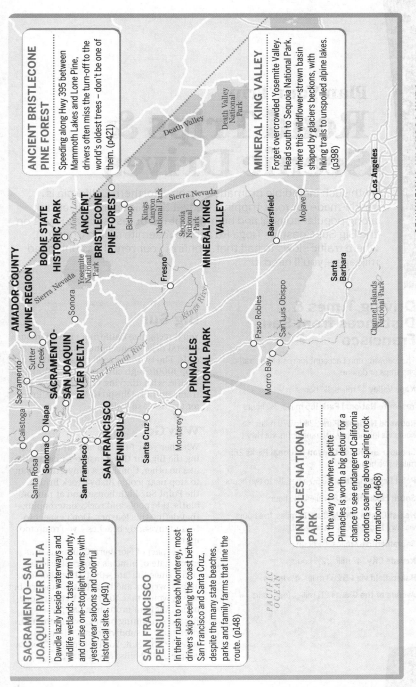

ANCIENT BRISTLECONE PINE FOREST

Speeding along Hwy 395 between Mammoth Lakes and Lone Pine, drivers often miss the turn-off to the world's oldest trees – don't be one of them. (p421)

MINERAL KING VALLEY

Forget overcrowded Yosemite Valley. Head south to Sequoia National Park, where this wildflower-strewn basin shaped by glaciers beckons, with hiking trails to unspoiled alpine lakes. (p398)

SACRAMENTO–SAN JOAQUIN RIVER DELTA

Dawdle lazily beside waterways and wildlife wetlands, taste farm bounty, and cruise one-stoplight towns with yesteryear saloons and colorful historical sites. (p491)

SAN FRANCISCO PENINSULA

In their rush to reach Monterey, most drivers skip seeing the coast between San Francisco and Santa Cruz, despite the many state beaches, parks and family farms that line the route. (p148)

PINNACLES NATIONAL PARK

On the way to nowhere, petite Pinnacles is worth a big detour for a chance to see endangered California condors soaring above spiring rock formations. (p468)

AMADOR COUNTY WINE REGION
BODIE STATE HISTORIC PARK
ANCIENT BRISTLECONE PINE FOREST
SACRAMENTO–SAN JOAQUIN RIVER DELTA
SAN FRANCISCO PENINSULA
MINERAL KING VALLEY
PINNACLES NATIONAL PARK

Mono Lake, Sierra Nevada, Sonora, Sutter Creek, Sacramento, Calistoga, Sonoma, Napa, Santa Rosa, San Francisco, Santa Cruz, Monterey, Morro Bay, San Luis Obispo, Paso Robles, Fresno, Bishop, Kings Canyon National Park, Sequoia National Park, Yosemite National Park, Bakersfield, Mojave, Santa Barbara, Los Angeles, Death Valley, Death Valley National Park, Channel Islands National Park, San Joaquin River, Kings River

PACIFIC OCEAN

Plan Your Trip

Road Trips & Scenic Drives

With such incredible dramatic scenery, Northern California is ready-made for road-tripping. Budget 50 miles per hour, except along popular coastal and high-mountain routes (such as Hwy 1 on the Big Sur Coast, or Tioga Rd across Yosemite's High Country), where traffic slows to half that. Confirm your rental has unlimited mileage – you'll need it!

Driving Times & Distances from San Francisco

The following don't account for rush-hour traffic, gas stops or detours.

Napa Valley 47 miles, 1¼ hours

Yosemite National Park 165 miles, 3½ hours

Redwood National Park 330 to 370 miles, six hours via inland Hwy 101, nine hours via Hwy 1

Sequoia and Kings Canyon National Parks 265 miles, five hours

Point Reyes Lighthouse 60 miles, 1½ to two hours

South Lake Tahoe 186 miles, 3½ hours

Hearst Castle via Big Sur 213 miles, five hours via Hwy 1, four hours via Hwy 101

Sacramento 87 miles, 1½ hours

Nevada City 147 miles, 2½ hours

Bakersfield via I-5 283 miles, 4½ hours

Avenue of the Giants 211 miles, four hours

Big Sur

You'll recognize California's most famous coastal drive from countless car commercials. The two-lane road twists and turns atop 1000ft-high cliffs over the roiling blue Pacific, with dizzying views all the way from San Luis Obispo to Monterey. Prep for traffic: take it slow.

Why Go

Whether your first trip or your 50th, driving the Big Sur Coast inspires imagination like no other. Consider a convertible. Plan to stop near iconic Bixby Creek Bridge, the Point Sur Lighthouse, and at random bluffs, tide pools and rocky outcroppings that define this journey. Don't expect to find many sandy beaches – you're up too high.

This part of Northern California is as much state of mind as geographic location – since the late '40s it's been home to artists, writers and back-to-the-landers, but now it would take 10 artists to afford one house. Vigilant protection has preserved Big Sur's stunning nature, with zero high-rise hotels or subdivisions. Cell-phone service? Forget it. You'll be lucky to coax a couple of $20 bills from a dial-up ATM.

Road Trips & Scenic Drives

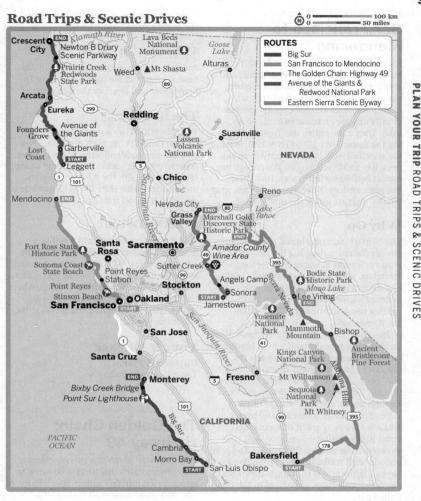

ROUTES
- Big Sur
- San Francisco to Mendocino
- The Golden Chain: Highway 49
- Avenue of the Giants & Redwood National Park
- Eastern Sierra Scenic Byway

When to Go

April, May, September and October – when skies are clearest. Summertime brings moody gray fog. Avoid during winter's heavy rains.

The Route

Although only 135 miles from San Luis Obispo to Monterey, it takes at least three hours, if not four. To dawdle and sightsee, budget a full day. North of Monterey, you can save time by cutting inland from Hwy 1 to faster-running Hwy 101 or I-280 –

provided it's not rush hour, when Bay Area freeways jam.

Worthy Detour

Stop in Santa Cruz for a wild ride on the Giant Dipper, a historic wooden roller coaster on a classic seaside boardwalk, overlooking a sandy beach packed with sunbathers and surfers.

Time & Mileage

Distance: 135 miles
Time: at least three hours

San Francisco to Mendocino

Everyone rushes to drive the Big Sur coast, but the trip north is almost as scenic and gets far less traffic. The terrain is more varied, with table bluffs, pastureland, redwood forests and long rocky beaches. Hardly anyone en route to Mendocino takes Hwy 1 the entire way (instead favoring the faster Hwy 101 to Hwy 128), leaving the winding road largely empty from Bodega Bay to Mendocino. In the springtime, expect brilliant wildflowers, including hot-pink azaleas. November to March, gray whales migrate along the misty coast.

Why Go

The North Coast provides a lower perspective on the coast than Big Sur. Here the road runs right at water level for long stretches, with access to low bluffs jutting like fingers into the sea, and to wide-open beaches where rolling breakers crash against the driftwood trunks of fallen giant redwoods.

Just over the Golden Gate Bridge, nature immediately reveals itself – high bluffs and coastal hills rise straight from the sea. Follow Hwy 1 to the ancient redwood forests of Muir Woods, and over the mountains to Stinson Beach for long walks on the sand. Further north, the little village of Point Reyes Station has good eats and pretty B&Bs within easy reach of spectacular Point Reyes National Seashore. Add time to explore the windswept beaches and hike seaside bluff trails; in wintertime Point Reyes Lighthouse is the hands-down best place to spot whales anywhere in Northern California.

North of Point Reyes Station, the road hugs ocean-side bluffs, darting up and down, in and out, along the headlands and coves of Sonoma Coast State Beach, where you'll need a sweater, not a bikini, most days of summer. At Fort Ross State Historic Park, glimpse a re-created Russian Fort. Ascend Point Arena lighthouse – the tallest in California that you can ascend – to better understand the geography, then find wild and windy Manchester State Beach, where the San Andreas Fault juts out to sea. End in Mendocino, a little village of New England–style saltbox cottages on a flat-topped headland surrounded on three sides by the roaring Pacific. Spend the night in a romantic B&B.

When to Go

April and May are greenest; June to August are foggy three days out of four. In September and October the sun returns.

The Route

Take Hwy 101/Hwy 1 north across the Golden Gate Bridge; turn north on Hwy 1 all the way to Mendocino. For a quicker return to San Francisco, cut inland along Hwy 128, through the Anderson Valley, and connect with Hwy 101 at Cloverdale to shave an hour off the trip.

Worthy Detour

Fort Bragg, the former mill town just north of Mendocino, looks more like the rest of America, with shopping strips and traffic lights. But it also has the gorgeous Mendocino Coast Botanical Garden, where the flora of different climatic zones is represented in gardens terraced on cliffs above the Pacific.

Time & Mileage

Distance: 170 miles
Time: two to four days

The Golden Chain: Highway 49

That highway number is no coincidence: it commemorates the '49ers who came to strike it rich during California's Gold Rush. The 300-some-mile road through the Sierra Nevada foothills connects historic towns leftover from the Wild West. Brush up on history, stop to taste wine and maybe run some Class III white water. Further north, the road cuts inland and ascends the mountains along the Yuba River, where you can pan for gold or cool off at hidden swimming holes.

Why Go

An adventure along Hwy 49 traces the turf of gold-rushing '49ers, who left behind them a series of historic towns, some of which remain largely unchanged. The

Top: Highway 1, Big Sur (p449)

Bottom: Yuba River (p312)

A K POTTS PHOTOGRAPHY / GETTY IMAGES ©

20 GREAT TRIPS FROM THE BAY AREA

DESTINATION	APPROXIMATE DISTANCE/ TIME FROM SAN FRANCISCO	GOOD FOR	BEST TIME TO GO
Arcata	280mi/5hr	Political radicals, college kids, redwood trees	Year-round
Bear Valley	180mi/4hr	Skiing, sledding, snowshoeing	Dec-Apr
Big Sur	150mi/3½hr	Picturesque coastline, amazing drive	Sep-Nov
Blossom Trail	200mi/3½hr	Blooming fruit trees, roadside farm stands, small towns	late Feb–mid-Mar
Gualala	155mi/3hr	B&Bs, beachcombing, whale-watching	Apr-Nov
Lake Tahoe	190mi/3½hr to Truckee	Swimming, boating, camping, hiking, casinos	Jun-Sep
Lake Tahoe ski resorts	186mi/4hr	Skiing, snowboarding, sledding, snowshoeing	Dec-Apr
Lost Coast	230mi/4½hr	Wilderness hiking, deserted beaches, sea lions	Jun-Oct
Mendocino	155mi/3½hr	Art, nature, wine tasting, B&Bs	Jun-Oct
Monterey	115mi/2½hr	Aquarium, boutiques, rugged coastline	Year-round
Mt Shasta	276mi/5hr	Climbing, camping, swimming, mysticism	Jul-Sep
Murphys	142mi/3hr	Old West town, wine tasting, caverns	Year-round
Nevada City	148mi/2½hr	Gold Rush town, wine tasting, swimming holes	May-Sep
Russian River Area	65mi/1½hr	Wine tasting, cycling, canoeing, coastline	Year-round
San Luis Obispo & Paso Robles	233mi/4hr	College town, rolling countryside, Hearst Castle, great wine	Sep-Nov
Santa Cruz	75mi/1½-2hr	Beaches, thrift-shopping, wine tasting, roller coasters	Jun-Oct
Sonoma Coast	45mi/1½hr	Misty coves, beachcombing, barking seals	Year-round
Sonoma Valley	45mi/1¼hr	History, wine tasting, small towns, hiking, cycling	Mar-Nov
Trinity Scenic Byway	217mi/4hr	Hiking, camping, mountain towns, scenic drives	Jun-Oct
Yosemite Valley	190mi/3½-4hr	Hiking, camping, snowshoeing, wildlife-watching	Year-round

route hovers around 2500ft to 3500ft elevation on the skirts of the mighty Sierra Nevada. When summer heat gets unbearable go white-water rafting on the American or Yuba Rivers, or take refuge in history museums that showcase jaw-dropping taxidermy and old mining equipment.

After gold came the railroads – get the story at Jamestown's Railtown 1897 State Historic Park. At nearby Angels Camp, the wooden sidewalks and Old West storefront provide the backdrop for the famous annual jumping-frog competition, made famous by Mark Twain. Add a stop at Columbia State Historic Park, where costumed docents play out 19th-century life. No Gold Country trip would be complete without seeing where James Marshall discovered gold, at Marshall Gold Discovery State Historic Park.

At the drive's northern end, gas lamps line Nevada City, the largest best-preserved Gold Country town, where historic storefronts house galleries, restaurants, saloons and ice-cream parlors. The gingerbread Victorians and Old West architecture look like a scene from beneath a Christmas tree. When it's hot, keep going north to the South Yuba Bridge to swim beneath giant white boulders where miners once panned for gold.

Bonus: Amador and El Dorado counties make pretty good wine. Head directly for heat-loving varietals, such as Zinfandel and Cabernet Sauvignon, which thrive in these rolling hills.

When to Go

Spring through fall. April and May are prettiest, with green grass and flowers. Summers are busy and hot: stick to the rivers. September and October are ideal, once the weather cools.

The Route

Start in Jamestown and follow Hwy 49, making detours to tiny old towns, such as Murphys, that were bypassed when the new highway was built. Continue all the way to Nevada City.

Time & Mileage

Distance: 127 miles
Time: one to two days

Avenue of the Giants & Redwood National Park

Driving beneath the canopy of the world's tallest trees is like driving nowhere else – cars look like tiny matchbox toys beneath the mighty giants. The 32-mile scenic route along the Avenue of the Giants is the old two-lane highway, which parallels modern four-lane Hwy 101, through Humboldt Redwoods State Park. After the Avenue, continue north through Redwood National Park to Prairie Creek Redwoods

ODDITIES OF THE NORTHERN COAST

➜ **Giant Paul Bunyan** A gargantuan lumberjack waves hello at Trees of Mystery. On weekends, Paul even wisecracks (via loudspeaker) at visitors ambling in the parking lot.

➜ **Drive-Thru Trees** Conflicted conservationists navigate Chevys through the bellies of redwood. There are – count 'em – *three* opportunities along the North Coast.

➜ **California's Smallest Licensed Bar** Order a martini on a cruise aboard the *Madaket,* America's oldest continuously operating passenger vessel, based in Eureka.

➜ **Confusion Hill** Clapper-trap complex of slanting floors, skewed perspectives and corny delights – pure roadside Americana.

State Park, where elk roam alongside the highway.

Why Go

Few road trips pack such a punch as this. The giant redwoods of Northern California are the largest trees in the world, as much as 2000 years old, and so big around their girth it takes 15 people with arms outstretched to encircle one single trunk. If you feel nothing in the face of such enormity, we suggest immediate counseling.

Begin the trip around Garberville, where right-wing loggers, left-wing hippies, pot farmers and back-to-the-landers coexist in a little main-street village. Heading north, take the first exit for the Avenue of the Giants – there are several – to commune with trees that were seedlings during the Roman Empire. The half-mile stroll through Founders' Grove provides a good glimpse. Head north along Hwy 101 to the Newton B Drury Scenic Parkway (once again, the old two-lane highway, bypassed by the modern four-lane freeway), which winds through ancient groves at Prairie Creek Redwoods State Park, and ends at the mouth of the Klamath River, where eagles and bears compete for salmon. The trips ends with a whimper in Crescent City, an otherwise nothing-special town, but a welcome sight after so many miles of driving through woods.

When to Go

April to October. For hiking, come May to September, when rangers re-open seasonal walking bridges that close during the rainy season. Contact Redwood National and State Parks for current details.

The Route

Take Hwy 101 to Garberville; look for signs to Phillipsville and the Avenue of the Giants/State Rte 254, which parallels Hwy 101. Rejoin Hwy 101 just south of Rio Dell, and follow it through Eureka and Arcata. Take exit 753 for the Newton B Drury Scenic Parkway to Klamath, reconnecting with Hwy 101 toward Crescent City.

Worthy Detour

The entire village of Ferndale is listed on the National Register of Historic Places for its jaw-dropping Victorian mansions. It's 5 miles west of Hwy 101, just north of the Avenue of the Giants.

Time & Mileage

Distance: 155 miles
Time: two days

Eastern Sierra Scenic Byway

The mountains hang like curtains from heaven along US Hwy 395, which rivals Hwy 1 for the title of the state's most spectacular drive. The highway flanks the high-mountain deserts of the Great Basin, hugging the vertically rising eastern escarpment of the Sierra Nevada, passing otherworldly tufa towers at Mono Lake, dense pine forests, crystalline alpine lakes, a Wild West ghost town and hidden hot springs.

Why Go

You'll lose all perspective on scale, size and distance as you drive this spectacular road along the backside of the Sierra Nevada. The mountains form a mile-high near-vertical wall, delineating the edge of the Great Basin's deserts from the escarpment of the High Sierra. The road passes near the highest and lowest points in the Continental US (Mt Whitney and Death Valley, respectively), plus three national parks, including the back entrance to Yosemite (summer only).

Along the way, spur roads lead to Bodie State Historic Park, California's best ghost town; Mammoth Mountain, where you can ride a year-round gondola up an 11,000ft peak; the Ancient Bristlecone Pine Forest, location of the world's oldest living trees (one named Methuselah has lived over 4750 years); the Alabama Hills, backdrop of John Wayne Hollywood westerns; and heartbreaking Manzanar National Historic Site, where 10,000 Japanese descendents were interned during WWII. To linger longer, spend time fly-fishing and hunting for hot springs.

When to Go

Unless you're skiing Mammoth Mountain, come during summer or fall, once summertime-only Tioga Rd/Hwy 120 opens over the mountains of Yosemite, usually July to October.

The Route

Connect with Hwy 395 east of Bakersfield, via CA 178, and travel north to reach CA 120 (summer only), west across Yosemite National Park; if it's closed for winter, continue north to year-round CA 88 to cross the mountains. Or do it in reverse.

Worthy Detour

Instead of ending at Yosemite, continue north to Lake Tahoe.

Time & Mileage

Distance: 300 miles (Bakersfield to Lee Vining)
Time: one to three days

Plan Your Trip

Northern California Camping & Outdoors

Mountains, rivers and vast wildernesses provide a majestic backdrop for Northern California's all-seasons outdoor adventures. Hike among wildflowers at the coast in spring, explore sub-alpine meadows in summer, mountain-bike through fiery fall foliage, and schuss through deep snow in winter. And if you plan to surf, thank the heavens for Northern California: this was the birthplace of the wetsuit.

Camping

Northern California camping is among the best in America – what else would you expect of a state that covers both the highest and lowest places in the lower 48 states? Backcountry campers reap the biggest rewards – especially in the High Sierra, land of John Muir, where you can pitch a tent beside a hidden alpine lake, within view of jagged High Sierra peaks, and not see another soul. Car-campers and travelers in RVs (recreational vehicles) won't have that same solitude; California's state and national parks fill up every weekend in high season. Still, with such a diversity between the regional, state, county and federal campgrounds, there are campgrounds near and far to get you off the grid. Even RVs are (sometimes) accommodated at the super-basic (but often free!) national-forest campgrounds. If you didn't bring a tent, you can rent or buy camping gear in most cities – find good deals at **REI** (www.rei.com) in San Francisco and Sacramento.

Northern California's Ultimate Outdoor Experiences

Cycling Pacific Coast Hwy

Backpacking John Muir Trail and Mt Whitney

White-water rafting American River, and Cherry Creek on the Upper Tuolumne River

Mountain biking Around Downieville and Marin County

Rock climbing Yosemite Valley

Whale-watching Bodega Bay

Surfing Mavericks, Bolinas or Santa Cruz

Northern California's Best Places to Camp

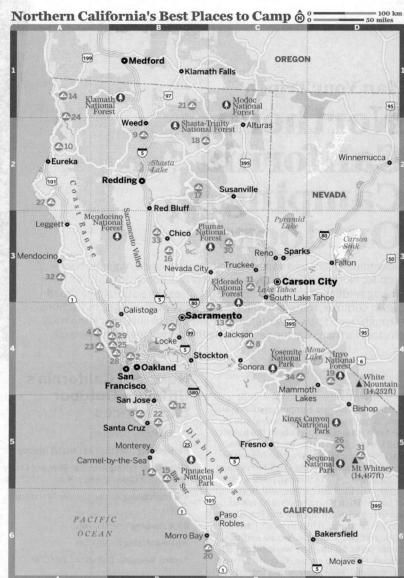

Campground Types & Amenities

➡ **Primitive campsites** The cheapest; many are seldom full. Usually have fire pits, picnic tables and access to drinking water and vault toilets.

Most common in USFS-managed national forests and on Bureau of Land Management (BLM) land.

➡ **Developed campgrounds** Typically found in state and national parks, with more amenities, including flush toilets, barbecue grills and

Northern California's Best Places to Camp

occasionally hot showers and a coin-op laundry. May need reservations.

➡ **RV hookups and dump stations** Available at many privately owned campgrounds, but only a few public-lands campgrounds.

➡ **Private campgrounds** Cater mainly to RVers. Offer hot showers, swimming pools, wi-fi and family camping cabins; tent sites may be few, exposed and uninviting. Typically more expensive than developed public campgrounds and usually not as nice.

➡ **Walk-in (environmental) sites** More peace and privacy; a few public-lands campgrounds reserve these for long-distance hikers and cyclists.

➡ **Hiker/biker sites** Along the coast the 'hiker/biker' sites are the best value for those traveling the slow way along Hwy 1. While occasionally crowded, they reward hikers and cyclists with excellent sites.

Seasons, Rates & Reservations

Many campgrounds, especially in the mountains, are closed late fall through early spring. Actual opening dates depend on weather. Private campgrounds are sometimes open year round, especially those nearest cities, beaches and major highways, but these often lack natural beauty.

Many public and private campgrounds accept reservations for all, or some, of their sites, but a few are strictly first-come, first-served. Overnight rates range from free for the most primitive campsites to $75 or more for pull-through RV sites with full hookups. The best deals are almost always with USFS campgrounds and in the national forests of the Northern Mountains. Check with a ranger station before setting up your tent, but an astonishing amount of land in the Plumas, Lassen, Mendocino, Modoc, Trinity and Shasta National Forests allows camping for no fee whatsoever. If you decide to go this route, always have a good supply of water on hand, and be prepared to pack out your waste.

ADVANCE RESERVATIONS WORTH MAKING
....

➡ **Wright's Beach Campground** (p220) Easy car-camping, right on a sandy stretch of the North Coast.

➡ **Angel Island State Park** (p118) Stunning views of the San Francisco skyline from an island in the bay.

➡ **Yosemite backcountry** (p380) Trailhead permits for popular backcountry camps fill months in advance.

➡ **Limekiln State Park** (p455) One of the best camping options on Big Sur, with only 24 sites.

These agencies let you search for campground locations and amenities, check availability and reserve campsites online:

Recreation.gov (☑877-444-6777, 518-885-3639; www.recreation.gov; most tent & RV sites $10-25) Camping and cabin reservations in national parks, national forests (USFS) and other federal recreational lands (eg BLM).

ReserveAmerica (☑916-638-5883, 800-444-7275; www.reserveamerica.com) Reservations for California state-park campgrounds and cabins that accept advance bookings, as well as East Bay and Orange County regional parks and some private campgrounds.

Hipcamp (www.hipcamp.com) Reviews, photographs, real-time availability and reservations at NorCal campgrounds.

Kampgrounds of America (KOA; ☑888-562-0000; www.koa.com) National chain of reliable but more expensive private campgrounds offering full facilities, including for RVs.

Cycling & Mountain Biking

Strap on that helmet! Northern California is outstanding cycling territory for a leisurely spin along the coast, an adrenaline-fueled mountain ride or a multiday bike-touring adventure. Cycling season runs year round in coastal areas, but expect cold rain in wintertime. The mountains are off limits, due to snow, late October through April.

Road Rules

➡ In national and state parks bicycles are usually limited to paved and dirt roads and are not allowed on trails or in designated wilderness areas.

➡ Most national forests and BLM lands are open to mountain bikers. Stay on established tracks and always yield to hikers and horseback riders.

Best Places to Cycle

➡ In the summer, Hwy 1 is a heavily traveled route for cycle tourism on the coast, especially the dizzying stretch through Big Sur.

➡ In Northern California's bike-friendly San Francisco, you can cruise through Golden Gate Park and over the Golden Gate Bridge, then hop on the ferry from Sausalito back across the bay.

➡ South along the Central Coast, the waterfront Monterey Peninsula Recreational Trail and the famously scenic 17-Mile Drive (p446) entice cyclists of all skill levels.

➡ NorCal's Wine Country offers some beautiful bike tours and wine tasting – just don't get too wobbly.

➡ Up north at Humboldt Redwoods State Park (p250), ride beneath the world's tallest trees on the winding Avenue of the Giants.

➡ In the Sierra Nevada, Yosemite National Park has mostly level, paved recreational paths through a glacier-carved valley overhung by waterfalls.

Best Mountain-Biking Areas

➡ Serious mountain bikers should prioritize a stop in Downieville, a little Gold Rush town that offers an enormous downhill sweep.

➡ Just north of San Francisco, the Marin Headlands offers a bonanza of trails for fat-tire fans – nearby Mt Tamalpais (p122) is the sport's birthplace.

➡ Top-rated single-track rides near Lake Tahoe include Mr Toad's Wild Ride and the Flume Trail.

➡ Speed freaks also sing the praises of the Eastern Sierra's Mammoth Mountain, whose summer-only bike park beckons with 70 miles of dirt singletrack.

➡ More ski areas that open trails and chairlifts to mountain bikers can be found at some resorts at Lake Tahoe.

➡ State parks especially popular with mountain bikers include NorCal's Prairie Creek Redwoods (p265), the Gold Country's Calaveras Big Trees (p406), Wilder Ranch outside Santa Cruz, Andrew Molera (p451) in Big Sur and San Luis Obispo's Montaña de Oro (p465).

Maps & Online Resources

Local bike shops can supply you with more cycling-route ideas, as well as maps and advice.

➡ **California Association of Bicycling Organizations** (www.cabobike.org) Offers free bicycle touring and freeway-access information.

➡ **California Bicycle Coalition** (www.calbike.org) Links to free online cycling maps, bike-sharing programs and community bike shops.

➡ **Adventure Cycling Association** (www.adventurecycling.org) Sells long-distance cycling route guides and touring maps, including the Pacific Coast Hwy (PCH).

➡ **League of American Bicyclists** (www.bikeleague.org) Find bicycle specialty shops, local cycling clubs, group rides and other special events.

➡ **MTBR.com** (www.mtbr.com) Online forums and reviews of mountain-biking trails in California.

Hiking

California's epic scenery and extensive parks provide many chances to hike, even in urban areas. No matter where you find yourself in California, you're never far from a trail. During spring, colorful wildflowers bloom on coastal hillsides; wildflower season in the Sierra happens in summer, after the snow melts. The deserts are best fall through spring, and the coastal forests and beaches are ideal year round.

Best Places to Hike

For jaw-dropping scenery, head to national and state parks to choose from a staggering variety of trails, from easy nature walks negotiable by wheelchairs and strollers, to multiday backpacking routes through rugged wilderness.

➡ **Sierra Nevada** In Yosemite, Sequoia and Kings Canyon National Parks, clamber toward waterfalls, wildflower meadows and alpine lakes, tackle mighty granite domes and peaks, or

wander among the world's biggest trees – giant sequoias.

➡ **North Coast** Redwood National & State Parks provide misty trails through groves of old-growth redwoods; or backpack the truly wild beaches of the challenging Lost Coast Trail.

➡ **San Francisco Bay Area** Marin Headlands, Muir Woods, Mt Tamalpais, Point Reyes National Seashore and Big Basin Redwoods State Park, all within a 90-minute drive of San Francisco, are crisscrossed by dozens of superb trails.

➡ **Northern Mountains** Summiting Mt Shasta is a spiritually uplifting experience; Lassen Volcanic National Park is a bizarre, raw world of smoking fumaroles, cinder cones and craters.

Fees & Wilderness Permits

➡ Most California state parks charge a daily parking fee of $5 to $15; there's often no charge if you walk or cycle into these parks.

➡ National-park entry averages $10 to $20 per vehicle for seven consecutive days; some national parks are free.

➡ For unlimited admission to national parks, national forests and other federal recreation lands, buy an 'America the Beautiful' annual pass for $80.

➡ Often required for overnight backpackers and extended day hikes, wilderness permits are issued at ranger stations and park visitor centers. Daily quotas may be in effect during peak periods, usually late spring through early fall.

➡ Some wilderness permits may be reserved ahead of time, and very popular trails (like the

---

TAKE A (REALLY LONG) HIKE

Famous long-distance trails that wind through California include the 2650-mile **Pacific Crest National Scenic Trail** (PCT; www.pcta.org), which runs all the way from Mexico to Canada. Following portions of the PCT, the 211-mile John Muir Trail links Yosemite Valley and Mt Whitney via the Sierra Nevada high country. The lake and mountain views are likewise thrilling along the 165-mile **Tahoe Rim Trail** (www.tahoerimtrail.org), portions of which trace the footsteps of early pioneers and Native Americans.

ascent to the top of Half Dome or Mt Whitney) may sell out months in advance.

➡ Buy passes from USFS ranger stations and local vendors, such as sporting-goods stores.

Maps & Online Resources

Find bulletin boards showing basic trail maps and other information at most major trailheads in national, state and regional parks. For short, well-established hikes, the free trail maps handed out at visitor centers and ranger stations are usually sufficient. A more detailed tear-proof topographical map may be necessary for longer backcountry hikes. Topo maps are sold at park bookstores, visitor centers, ranger stations and outdoor-gear shops including **REI** (www.rei.com). We especially like **Thom Harrison** (www.tomharrisonmaps.com) waterproof maps.

➡ **US Geological Survey** (USGS; www.store. usgs.gov) Offers its topographic maps as free downloadable PDFs, or order print copies online.

➡ **Trails.com** (www.trails.com) Lets you search for hundreds of multisport trails throughout California (trail overviews are free).

➡ **Coastwalk** (www.coastwalk.org) Advocates for a long-distance trail along California's entire 1271-mile shoreline. Join a group hike, or volunteer to do beach cleanup or trail maintenance.

➡ **Leave No Trace Center** (www.lnt.org) Learn how to minimize your impact on the environment while traipsing through the wilderness.

Rock Climbing

Climbers test their mettle on the granite monoliths, domes and boulders of Yosemite National Park, where climbing season runs April to October. Outfitters offer guided climbs and instruction.

Other prime spots for bouldering and rock climbing include Sequoia and Kings Canyon National Parks, south of Yosemite; around Bishop in the Eastern Sierra; outside Truckee, near Lake Tahoe; and at Pinnacles National Monument in central California.

SuperTopo (www.supertopo.com) is a one-stop shop for rock-climbing guidebooks, online forums, free topo maps and route descriptions across the state.

Beaches & Swimming

If you've come to Northern California expecting the idyllic scenes from a Beach Boys song, forget it. You'll get more use from a good sweater than a skimpy swimsuit. Northern California beaches are best for strolling, not swimming: the water is icy cold, with strong currents. If you must swim, bring or rent a wetsuit. The water warms around Santa Barbara and points south.

The mind-bogglingly detailed *California Coastal Access Guide* (University of California Press, 2014) has comprehensive beach driving directions and maps.

Water quality varies from beach to beach, and day to day. Stay out of the ocean for at least three days after major rainstorms, due to toxic pollutants flushing out to sea through storm drains. For current water-safety conditions statewide, check the **Beach Report Card** (http://brc. healthebay.org).

Scuba Diving & Snorkeling

All along the coast, rock reefs, shipwrecks and kelp beds teem with sea creatures. If you've already got your PADI certification, you can rent one-tank dive outfits for $65 to $100, while two-tank boat dives cost over $100; reserve either at least a day in advance. Snorkel kits can be rented from most dive shops for around $15 to $40 per day. If you're going to be taking the plunge more than once or twice, it's probably worth buying your own mask and fins. Remember to not touch anything while you're out snorkeling, and don't snorkel alone. Sunblock can hurt reefs; choose a 'reef-safe' brand, or better yet, wear a UV-protection suit.

Best Scuba-Diving & Snorkeling Spots

➡ With national marine sanctuary protection, Monterey Bay offers world-renowned diving and snorkeling – but you'll need a wetsuit.

➡ Further south, Point Lobos State Natural Reserve (p447) is another gem for scuba divers (snorkeling prohibited); permit reservations are required.

➡ North of San Francisco, dive boats depart from Bodega Bay.

Sea Kayaking

Few water sports are as accessible and fun for groups as kayaking. Most outfitters offer a choice between sit-upon (open) kayaks and sit-in (closed-hull) ones, the latter usually requiring some training before you head out. Kayak rentals average $40 to $70 per day, and you'll usually have a choice between single and tandem. A reputable outfitter will make sure you're aware of the tide schedule and wind conditions of your proposed route. Many also give lessons and lead guided paddles (from $50), including full-moon, sunset and sunrise trips. Try to make reservations at least a day ahead.

There are dozens of places to launch along the coast. If you're a beginner and the idea of kayaking on waves scares you, consider instead the calm water of Tomales Bay, in Point Reyes National Seashore, where you can spot incredible birds as you paddle the placid bay.

Surfing

Surf's up! – well for part of the year, at least. The most powerful swells arrive along the coast during late fall and winter. May and June are generally the flattest months, although they do bring warmer water. On the subject of temperature, don't believe all those images of hot blonds surfing in bikinis; without a wetsuit, you'll freeze your butt off, except maybe at the height of summer.

Crowds can be a problem at many surf spots, as can overly territorial surfers. Befriend a local surfer for an introduction before hitting the most famous waves. Sharks do inhabit California waters, but attacks are extremely rare. Most happen in the 'Red Triangle' between Monterey on the Central Coast, Tomales Bay north of San Francisco and the offshore Farallon Islands.

Generally speaking, Northern California is better for beginners than for hard-core

EVEN MORE IN THE OUTDOORS!

ACTIVITY	LOCATION	REGION
Bird-watching	Klamath Basin National Wildlife Refuges	Northern Mountains
	Mono Lake	Yosemite & the Sierra Nevada
	Marin Headlands	Marin County & the Bay Area
Caving	Lava Beds National Monument	Northern Mountains
	Crystal Cave	Yosemite & the Sierra Nevada
	Pinnacles National Monument	Central Coast
Fishing*	Shasta Lake	Northern Mountains
	Bodega Bay	North Coast & Redwoods
	Mammoth Lakes	Yosemite & the Sierra Nevada
Horseback riding	Yosemite National Park	Yosemite & the Sierra Nevada
	Wild Horse Sanctuary	Northern Mountains
	Point Reyes National Seashore	Marin County & the Bay Area
Kiteboarding & Windsurfing	San Francisco Bay	San Francisco
	Bodega Bay	North Coast & Redwoods
	Lake Tahoe	Lake Tahoe

*For fishing licenses, regulations and location information, consult the **California Department of Fish & Game** (www.dfg.ca.gov).

pros, who find greater challenges down south. There are notable exceptions: Santa Cruz' Steamers Lane, with glassy point breaks and rocky reef breaks, and Half Moon Bay's **Mavericks** (www.maverickssurf. com), world-famous for big-wave surfing. Mavericks tops 50ft when the most powerful winter swells arrive.

Best Breaks for Beginners

The best spots to learn to surf are at the beach breaks of long, shallow bays where waves are small and rolling, including:

➡ **Central Coast** Santa Cruz, Cayucos

➡ **San Francisco Area** Pacifica

➡ **North Coast** Bolinas, Stinson Beach

Rentals & Lessons

➡ You'll find board rentals on just about every patch of sand where surfing is possible. Expect to pay about $25 per day for a board, with wetsuit rental another $15.

➡ Two-hour group lessons for beginners start at around $75 per person, while private, two-hour instruction costs over $100 per hour. If you're ready to jump in the deep end, many surf schools offer pricier weekend surf clinics and week-long 'surfari' camps.

➡ Stand-up paddle surfing (SUP) is easier to learn, and it's skyrocketing in popularity. You'll find similarly priced board-and-paddle rentals and lessons all along the coast.

Books, Maps & Online Resources

➡ Plan a coastal surfing adventure using **Surfline** (www.surfline.com), which details seasonal weather and water temperatures.

➡ Enlightened surfers can join up with **Surfrider** (www.surfrider.org), a nonprofit organization that seeks to protect the coastal environment.

White-Water Rafting

California has dozens of kick-ass rivers, which flow heavily in spring, then diminish as the snowpack disappears at higher elevation. Like ski season, rafting season depends entirely upon winter's snow depth. Paddling giant, ice-cold white-water rapids, ripping through sheer canyons, it can be a challenge to overcome fear. Sometimes it's all you can do to hang on for dear life. Too much for you? Fret not: beginner paddlers will find many places to develop their skills – in a safe environment – and in little time can become river rats.

California Whitewater Rafting (www.c-w-r.com) covers all of California's prime river-running spots, with links to outfitters and river-conservation groups. Most of the premier river runs are in the Sierra Nevada and the Gold Country, but the Northern Mountains also offer rides, including on the Klamath, Trinity, Sacramento, Smith and California Salmon Rivers.

White-water trips are not without danger, and it's not unusual for participants to fall out of the raft in rough conditions. Serious injuries are rare, however, and most trips are without incident. No prior experience is needed for guided river trips up to Class III, but for Class IV you want to be healthy, active, in good shape and an excellent swimmer, plus have some paddling experience under your life-jacket belt. As for Class V, you'd better know what the hell you're doing or stay away.

Seasons, Rates & Reservations

Commercial outfitters run a variety of trips, from short, inexpensive morning or afternoon floats to overnight outings and multiday expeditions. Expect to pay from $100 for a guided all-day trip. Reservations are recommended, especially for overnight trips.

The main river-running season is from April to August, although the exact months depend on which river you're rafting and how much snow accumulated during the preceding winter. During drought years, the season can end mid-summer. You'll either take a large raft, with a captain at the motor and a dozen or more passengers; or a small motorless raft, which seats only a half dozen people, all of whom paddle. Be sure to inquire whether or not you will be expected to paddle.

Whale-Watching

During their annual migration, gray whales can be spotted off the California coast from December to April, while blue, humpback and sperm whales pass by in summer and fall. You can try your luck whale-watching (eg from lighthouses) while staying shore-bound – it's free, but you're less likely to see whales and you'll be removed from all the action.

➡ Just about every port town worth its sea salt offers whale-watching boat excursions, especially during winter. Be sure to bring binoculars!

➡ Half-day boat trips cost from $30 to $50, while all-day trips average $65 to $100; make reservations at least a day ahead.

➡ Better tour boats limit the number of people and have a trained naturalist or marine biologist on board. Ask before booking about the credentials of the person leading the tour.

➡ Some tour companies will let you go again for free if you don't spot any whales on your first trip.

➡ Choppy seas can be nauseating. To avoid seasickness, sit outside on the boat's second level – but not too close to the diesel fumes in back – and watch the horizon line. Crystallized ginger helps settle queasy stomachs. We've also had good success wearing motion-sickness pressure-point bracelets.

Snow Sports

In a good snow year, the Sierra Nevada gets the deepest snowpack anywhere in North America. Most resorts are above 6000ft elevation, with the best topping out over 10,000ft. This is the roof of California, and the scenery is breathtaking. However, powder days are rare. It's just too warm for fluffy, dry snow – they call it 'Sierra cement' for a reason. But with an annual average of 300 sunny days, and midday temperatures above freezing, you can work on your tan while schussing down the slopes.

Season, Rates & Lessons

Ski season runs late November or early December until the end of April, depending upon resorts' specific elevations and

CALIFORNIA'S BEST WHITE-WATER RAFTING

NAME	CLASS	SEASON	DESCRIPTION
American River	Class II-IV	Apr-Oct	The South Fork is ideal for families and rafting virgins looking to get their feet wet, while the more challenging Middle and North Forks carve through deep gorges in the Gold Country.
Kaweah River	Class IV+	Apr-Jul	After steeply dropping through Sequoia National Park, this fast, furious ride is for experienced paddlers craving hair-raising white water.
Kern River	Class II-V	Apr-Sep	Staged near Bakersfield, the Upper and Lower Forks offer some of the Southern Sierra's best white water.
Kings River	Class III-IV	Apr-Jul	One of California's most powerful rivers cuts a groove deeper than the Grand Canyon; trips begin outside Kings Canyon National Park.
Merced River	Class III-IV	Apr-Jul	Starting outside Yosemite National Park, this canyon run is the Sierra's best one-day intermediate trip.
Stanislaus River	Class II-IV	Apr-Oct	In the Gold Country, the North Fork provides rafting trips for novices and the more adventure-minded.
Truckee River	Class II-IV	Apr-Aug	Near Lake Tahoe, this is a great beginners' run, with a white-water park for kayakers on the river in downtown Reno.
Tuolumne River	Class IV-V	Apr-Sep	Experienced paddlers may prefer a ferocious run on 'the T'; in summer, experts-only Cherry Creek is a legendary Sierra Nevada run.

weather conditions. The higher the resort, the drier the snow and longer the season. The best months are typically January to March. All resorts have ski schools and equipment-rental facilities and offer a variety of lift tickets, including half-day and multiday. Prices vary wildly, from $25 to $95 per day for adults. Discounts for children, teens, students and seniors are usually available. 'Ski and stay' lodging packages offer good value, as do learn-to-ski packages geared toward families.

Best Places for Snow Sports

The triumvirate of California's top ski resorts is Mammoth Mountain, Squaw Valley USA, and Heavenly Lake Tahoe. Mammoth is highest, Heavenly biggest, Squaw steepest.

The highest concentration of resorts is around Lake Tahoe, which is within four hours of San Francisco and manageable as a long day trip – but it's better to stay a night or two. Mammoth Mountain is seven hours from the Bay Area, making it more popular among Southern California skiers; it often stays open until June.

The highest-elevation resorts (read: drier snow) are Kirkwood, Mt Rose and Mammoth. For the best views of Lake Tahoe, choose Homewood, Heavenly or Diamond Peak. In a storm, the best-protected Tahoe resorts are Homewood and Northstar.

West of Donner Pass, near Truckee, a handful of tiny family resorts have prices half those of the big resorts. They're ideal for beginners, but may not open in bad snow years. Also nearby is Royal Gorge (p335), the largest cross-country resort in North America, but again, conditions depend on snowfall.

Skiing in Yosemite National Park, at Badger Pass (p379), is more novelty than sport, but lovely for beginners – and where else can you ski with a view of Half Dome? But low elevations and warm temps mean a short season. For another only-in-California winter wonderland, consider Sequoia and Kings Canyon National Parks, in the Southern Sierra, where you can tramp or cross-country among giant sequoia trees.

If you just want to play in the snow, California's family-friendly sno-parks (p362) offer sledding and snow play. To find them, visit www.parks.ca.gov.

Plan Your Trip
Travel with Children

Kids love Northern California. It's an adventurous destination, and it's also safe for family travel. Because of the coast's mild climate, you can cycle, hike or beachcomb February to November. In winter, there's great skiing at Tahoe. And year round, you'll find family-friendly museums and indoor entertainment galore in the region's cities.

Northern California for Kids

Children's discounts are available for everything from museum admissions to bus fares. The definition of a 'child' varies – in some places anyone under 18 is eligible, while at others the cut-off is age six.

Kids are welcomed at casual restaurants, which often have high chairs, children's menus, and paper place mats and crayons for drawing. On the road, several chain supermarkets, such as Trader Joe's and Whole Foods, have wholesome, ready-to-eat take-out dishes.

Most women are discreet about breast-feeding in public. Many public toilets have a change table, while places such as airports and museums may have gender-neutral, private 'family' bathrooms.

Children's Highlights

Northern California has ample services and attractions geared toward kids. National and state parks often have ranger-led activities and self-guided 'Junior Ranger' programs, in which kids earn a

Best Regions for Kids

San Francisco Bay Area

Explore hands-on, whimsical and 'wow!' science museums, hear the barking sea lions at Pier 39, traipse through Golden Gate Park and along that famous bridge, and make new friends at the city's many playgrounds.

Sierra Nevada

Kids will gawk at Yosemite's waterfalls and granite domes, and can hike through ancient groves of giant sequoias. Mammoth Lakes is a four-seasons family adventure base camp, as are some of the resorts at Lake Tahoe, notably Squaw Valley, Heavenly and Northstar.

Gold Country

Young imaginations run wild in Gold Country, ignited by tall tales of rough-n-tumble '49ers, gun-slinging bandits and treasure hunters. Connect with the Wild West in historic towns such as Columbia State Historic Park and Nevada City. In late summer and fall, pick apples together at you-pick-'em orchards.

HOW OLD IS OLD ENOUGH?

Naturally some outdoor activities will be easier to master than others. Those as young as five can take part in paddling and skiing. Horseback riding is a good choice for kids aged seven and up, and there are plenty of pleasant hikes easy enough for little legs. Teens will love the challenge of rock climbing, white-water rafting and surfing.

badge after completing learning-based scavenger hunts.

Aquariums & Museums

➡ **San Francisco** (p68) The Bay Area is a mind-bending classroom for kids of all ages, especially the hands-on Exploratorium, the multimedia Children's Creativity Museum and the eco-friendly California Academy of Sciences.

➡ **Monterey Bay Aquarium** (p436) Get acquainted with the denizens of the deep next door to the Central Coast's biggest marine sanctuary.

➡ **Seymour Marine Discovery Center** (p427) Santa Cruz' university-run aquarium makes interactive science fun, with nearby tide pools for exploring at the beach.

➡ **Turtle Bay Exploration Park** (p272) In Redding, this indoor/outdoor attraction combines an eco-museum with arboretum, botanical and butterfly gardens.

Beaches

➡ **Central Coast** (p424) Beach towns line the coast, from Pismo Beach all the way north to Santa Cruz, famous for its beachside boardwalk and pier.

➡ **Lake Tahoe** (p330) In summer, it's California's favorite high-altitude beach escape, a sparkling jewel in the Sierra Nevada mountains.

➡ **North Coast** (p215) No swimming – the water is too rough – but plenty of chances for beachcombing, collecting shells and building sandcastles on uncrowded beaches. The giant driftwood trunks of redwood trees strewn on the sand are ready-made climbing structures.

Parks

➡ **Yosemite National Park** (p369) The ultimate in Sierra Nevada scenery, with gushing waterfalls, alpine lakes, glacier-carved valleys and 2-mile-high peaks.

➡ **Golden Gate Park** (p95) The giant green swath in the heart of San Francisco has grassy areas for lounging, strolling ice-cream vendors, a carousel, children's playgrounds, model boating and plenty of space to fly a kite.

➡ **Redwood National & State Parks** (p269) On the fog-shrouded North Coast, a patchwork of nature reserves protect magnificent wildlife, beaches and the world's tallest trees.

➡ **Lassen Volcanic National Park** (p277) An off-the-beaten-path destination in the Northern Mountains, with otherworldly volcanic scenery and lakeside camping and cabins.

Planning

When to Go

Family travel is viable year round in Northern California, but some family-centric attractions close during winter – check individual listings. Explore the coast from spring through fall. Once winter's rains arrive, consider a ski trip to the mountains.

Accommodations

Motels and hotels often have rooms with two beds or an extra sofa bed, ideal for families. Many hotels have roll-away beds or cots, sometimes for a surcharge. Most offer 'kids stay free' promotions, provided the kids are under 18 and traveling with their parents. Some B&Bs don't allow children; ask when booking.

Resorts may have drop-off day camps for kids or on-call babysitting services. At other hotels, the front-desk staff or concierge may be able to help you make babysitting arrangements, whereby the sitter comes to your hotel room. Make sure the sitter is licensed, bonded and fully insured.

Transportation

Airlines usually allow infants (up to age two) to fly for free, while older children requiring a seat of their own qualify for reduced fares. Children receive substantial discounts on Amtrak and Greyhound. In cars, any child under age eight must be buckled up in the back seat in a child or infant safety seat, unless they're over 4ft 9in tall, in which case they may ride in front with a seat belt.

Most car-rental agencies rent safety seats for about $10 per day or up to $80 per trip, but you must book them in advance. Hertz offers AAA members one free child seat. Take note: rest stops on freeways are few and far between, and gas stations and fast-food bathrooms are frequently icky.

A word of advice: don't pack your schedule too tightly. Navigating metro areas, such as San Francisco, and the winding back roads to Northern California's natural areas always takes longer than expected.

What to Pack

There are two magic words for traveling in Northern California: sunscreen and layers.

The first of these is always necessary, even where cool, high-altitude climates and overcast skies lull visitors into a false sense of security – the higher the elevation, the thinner the atmosphere, especially in the High Sierra. The second is an absolute must: a day that is blisteringly hot in the Gold Country can be chilly in the Sierra and downright bone-chilling on the coast. This is particularly true in San Francisco, where the weather changes fast.

For outdoor vacations, bring broken-in shoes and your own camping equipment. Alternatively, outdoors gear can be purchased or often rented from outdoor stores. But remember that brand-new hiking shoes often result in blisters, and setting up a new tent in the dark ain't easy.

If you forget some critical piece of equipment, **Baby's Away** (www.babysaway.com) rents cribs, strollers, car seats, high chairs, backpacks, beach gear and more.

Before You Go

➡ Lonely Planet's *Travel with Children* is loaded with valuable tips and amusing anecdotes, especially for new parents and those with kids who haven't traveled before.

➡ **Lonelyplanet.com** (www.lonelyplanet.com) lets you ask questions and get advice from other travelers on the Thorn Tree's 'Kids to Go' and 'USA' forums.

➡ **California Travel & Tourism** (www. visitcalifornia.com), the state's official visitor website, lists family-friendly attractions, activities and more – just search for 'Family Fun' and 'Events.'

➡ **Family Travel Files** (www. thefamilytravelfiles.com/locations/california) is an info-packed site with vacation-planning articles, tips and discounts.

➡ **Parents Connect** (www.parentsconnect. com/family-travel) is a virtual encyclopedia of everything first-time family travelers need to know.

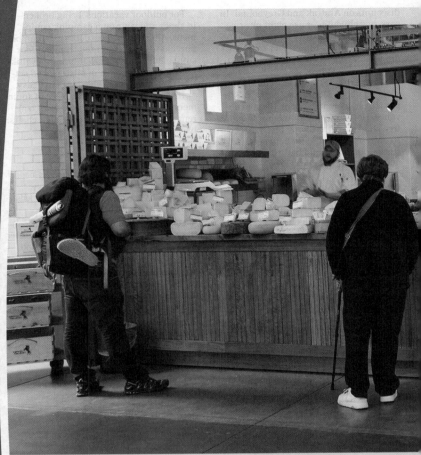

Cheese store, Ferry Building (p99), San Francisco

Plan Your Trip
Eat & Drink Like a Local

At the vanguard of culinary invention, Northern California determines the way America eats – or will eat, eventually. The current national trends of sustainable, local food originated here, and lately farmers and small-batch producers have achieved superstar status. Great food is available (almost) everywhere – if you know where to look.

WENDY CONNETT / GETTY IMAGES ©

Top Five Annual Food & Drink Festivals

Pebble Beach Food & Wine (www.pbfw.com) Near Monterey on the Central Coast in February.

Gilroy Garlic Festival (www.gilroygarlicfestival.com) Near Santa Cruz, on the Central Coast, July.

Eat Drink SF (www.eatdrink-sf.com) In San Francisco, late July or early August.

Gravenstein Apple Fair (www.gravensteinapplefair.com) In Sonoma County in mid-August.

Savor the Central Coast (www.savorcentralcoast.com) On the Central Coast in late September.

California Cuisine: Then & Now

'Let the ingredients speak for themselves!' is the rallying cry of California cuisine. With such incredibly fresh fruit, vegetables, seafood and meats, there's no need for heavy sauces or fussy molecular-gastronomy foams to make meals memorable. That said, Northern California's food fixations are easily exaggerated: not everyone demands grass-fed-beef burgers with heirloom-tomato ketchup.

Even so, when New York chefs David Chang and Anthony Bourdain mocked California cuisine as merely putting an organic fig on a plate, Californian chefs turned the tables, saying that New York needs to get out more often and actually try some Mission figs – one of hundreds of heirloom varietals preserved or developed by California horticulturalists and farmers since the late 18th century. By sheer numbers, New York may have more great chefs, but Northern California has – by far – America's best raw ingredients.

California's 20th-Century Food Revolution

Seasonal, locavorian eating has become mainstream, but Northern California started the movement more than 40 years ago. As the turbulent 1960s wound down, many disillusioned idealists conceded that the revolution was not about to be delivered on a platter, yet Northern California's pioneering organic farmers weren't about to give up.

In 1971, Alice Waters opened her now legendary restaurant Chez Panisse in a converted house in Berkeley with the then-radical notion of making the most of Northern California's seasonal, all-natural, sustainably produced food. Waters combined French flourishes with home-grown ingredients, and diners tasted the difference.

Today Waters' credo of organic, seasonal, sustainably sourced and locally grown ingredients aligns perfectly with the worldwide Slow Food movement. In Northern California today, farmers markets are popular weekly gathering places for local communities, where artisanal producers of foodstuffs, such as honey and cheese, and local farmers come to sell their best, often picking it that day and trucking it in themselves from the fields.

Global Fusion Cooking

Beyond its exceptionally fertile farmland, Northern California has another culinary advantage: an experimental attitude toward food that dates from its Wild West days. Most Gold Rush miners were men not accustomed to cooking for themselves, which resulted in such doomed mining-camp experiments as jelly omelets. But the era also introduced the world to the hangtown fry (a scramble of eggs, bacon and deep-fried cornbread-battered oysters),

Cantonese dim sum, and the USA's first Italian restaurant, which opened in San Francisco in 1886.

Some 150 years later, fusion is not fad, but second nature in Northern California, where chefs can hardly resist adding international twists to local flavors. Menus often combine ingredients and kitchen-craft borrowed from neighbors across the Pacific in Asia, from south of the border and all across Latin America, and from Europe's distant Mediterranean, where the climate and soil are similar to Northern California's.

Keep in mind that California belonged to Mexico before it became a US state in 1850, and Latinos make up almost 40% of the entire state's population today. It's no surprise that Californianized versions of Mexican classics remain go-to comfort foods, especially for takeout. Culinary cross-pollination has yielded the California burrito – a mega-meal bursting out of a giant flour tortilla – and the Korean taco (grilled marinated beef and spicy, pickled kimchi atop small corn tortillas).

Burrito

California's Regional Specialties

Calculate the distance between your tomato's origin and your fork: in Northern California, chances are it's shorter than you might think. So what are your best bets on local menus? That depends on where you are and the time of year; for example, winter can bring slim pickings even in the fertile Central Valley, but it's the ideal moment for citrus and squashes.

Remember, the ground never freezes in Northern California – there's always *something* in season.

San Francisco Bay Area

For miners converging here for the Gold Rush, San Francisco offered an unrivaled variety of novelties and cuisines, from cheap Chinese street food to French fine dining for those who struck it rich. Today, San Francisco's adventurous eaters support the most restaurants per capita of

FOOD TRUCKS & POP-UP RESTAURANTS

Weekday lunches may last only 30 minutes for Californians, and every minute counts. Rolling along the streets of many cities, creative food trucks deliver gourmet options on the go, anything from Indian curry-and-naan wraps to Chinese buns packed with roast duck and fresh mango. To find trucks coming soon to a curb near you, search for 'food truck' and your location on Twitter. Come prepared with cash and sunblock: most trucks don't accept plastic cards, and lines can be long.

Lately, dinner has also been popping up in unexpected urban spaces, including galleries, warehouses and storefronts. Chefs at pop-up restaurants prepare wildly creative meals around a theme, like street food or winemakers' dinners. Foodies seek out these overnight sensations via Twitter and websites like www.eater.com. Bring cash and arrive early, as popular dishes run out fast.

Cioppino

any US city – five times more than NYC, ahem – and over two dozen farmers markets, notably the spectacular Ferry Building Marketplace (p99).

Some of San Francisco's novelty dishes have had extraordinary staying power, including ever-popular cioppino (Dungeness crab stew), chocolate bars invented by the Ghirardelli family, and sourdough bread, with original Gold Rush–era mother dough still yielding local loaves with a distinctive tang.

Today no star Bay Area chef's tasting menu would be complete without a few foraged ingredients – wild chanterelles found beneath California oaks, miner's lettuce from Berkeley hillsides or stinging nettles from SF backyards.

Napa & Sonoma Wine Country

With international acclaim for local wines in the 1970s came woozy wine-country visitors in need of food, and Sonoma cheese makers and Napa restaurateurs graciously obliged. In 1994, chef Thomas Keller transformed a 1900s Yountville saloon into an international foodie landmark called the French Laundry (p173), showcasing garden-grown organic produce in elegant multicourse feasts. Other chefs eager to make their names and fortunes among free-spending wine-tasters soon moved to the area. To plug into the locavorian and artisanal food scene, make time for Napa's Oxbow Public Market (p169).

North Coast

San Francisco hippies headed back to the land here in the 1970s to find a more self-sufficient lifestyle, reviving traditions of making breads and cheeses from scratch and growing their own *everything*. Early adopters of pesticide-free farming, these hippie homesteaders innovated hearty, organic cuisine that was health-minded yet still satisfied the pot-smoking munchies.

On the North Coast today, you can taste the influence of Ohlone and Miwok tribes. Alongside traditional abalone-hunting grounds, sustainable oyster farms have sprung up. Way up north, local tribes sell fresh-smoked salmon and jerky at roadside stands. Nature has been generous, yielding bonanzas of blackberries and wildflower honey. Fearless foragers have identified

IAIN BAGWELL / GETTY IMAGES ©

Tofu and mushroom dish

Sacramento, but road-tripping foodies tend to bolt through the sunny farmlands, if only to make it past stinky cattle feedlots without losing their appetites. Much of the region remains dedicated to large-scale agribusiness, but valley farms that have converted to organic methods have helped make California the top US producer of organic foods. Get off the freeway and find roadside farm stands selling walnuts, almonds and seasonal fruits and veggies.

Over on the Central Coast, some of California's freshest seafood is harvested from Monterey Bay (visit www.seafoodwatch.org for help choosing the most sustainable catch on restaurant menus). There's great wine too. In the fog-shrouded Santa Cruz Mountains, wineries make cool-climate Burgundian-style wines, notably Pinot Noir and Chardonnay. In the hills around Paso Robles and San Luis Obispo, winemakers favor Rhône and Bordeaux varietals, such as Syrah and Cabernet Sauvignon, which thrive in the heat. Along the coast, farm stands galore sell locally grown artichokes, strawberries and avocados. In San Luis Obispo, the weekly farmers market features Santa Maria–style barbecue – a specialty from down south in Santa Barbara County.

every edible plant from wood sorrel to Mendocino sea vegetables, but key spots for wild mushrooms remain closely guarded local secrets.

Central Valley & Central Coast

Most of California's produce is grown in the hot, irrigated Central Valley south of

---

STEAM BREWING

Blowing off steam took on new meaning during the Gold Rush when entrepreneurs trying to keep up with the demand for drink started brewing beer at higher temperatures. The result was an amber color, a rich, malted flavor and such powerful effervescence that when a keg was tapped a mist would rise like steam. San Francisco's Anchor Brewing Company has made its signature Anchor Steam amber ale this way since 1896, using copper distilling equipment.

Wine, Beer & Beyond

Powerful drink explains a lot about Northern California. Mission vineyards planted in the 18th century gave Northern California a taste for wine, and the mid-19th-century Gold Rush brought a rush on the bar. By 1850 San Francisco had one woman per 100 men, but 500 saloons shilling hooch. Now the traditions of wine, beer and cocktails are being reinvented by cult winemakers, craft brewers and microdistillers – and, for the morning after, there are specialty coffee roasters.

Wine

When imported French wine was slow to arrive in California via Australia during the Gold Rush, three brothers from Bohemia named Korbel started making their own bubbly in 1882. Today, the Russian River winery they founded has become the biggest US maker of traditional sparkling wines.

Top: Californian seafood bounty

Bottom: Craft beer tasting

FUMIAKI YAMAZAKI / GETTY IMAGES ©

Some California vines survived federal scrutiny during Prohibition (1920–33) on the grounds that the grapes were needed for sacramental wines back east – a bootlegging bonanza that kept West Coast speakeasies well supplied and saved old vine stock from being torn out by the authorities.

By 1976 California had an established reputation for mass-market plonk and bottled wine spritzers when upstart Napa Valley and Santa Cruz Mountains wineries suddenly gained international status. At a landmark blind tasting by international critics, their Cabernet Sauvignon and Chardonnay beat venerable French wines to take top honors. This event became known as the Judgment of Paris, as amusingly retold in the movie *Bottle Shock* (2008).

During the internet bubble of the late '90s, owning a vineyard became the ultimate Silicon Valley status symbol. It seemed like a comparatively solid investment – until phylloxera insects made a catastrophic comeback and acres of infected vines across the state had to be dug out from the roots. But disaster brought breakthroughs: winemakers rethought their approach, using organic and biodynamic methods to keep the soil healthy and pests at bay.

Beer

In California, which claims almost 400 craft breweries (more than any other US state), beer geeks fuss over their triple Belgians and debate relative hoppiness levels. You won't get attitude for ordering beer with fancy food here, and many sommeliers are happy to suggest beer pairings with your five-star meal.

Any self-respecting California city has at least one brewery or brewpub of note, serving quality small-batch brews you won't find elsewhere. The well-established craft beer scenes in San Diego and on the North Coast are remarkably robust, but you're just as likely to find memorable microbrews on the Central Coast, especially around Santa Cruz and Santa Barbara, and in the San Francisco Bay Area.

California's craft breweries are increasingly canning craft beer to make it cheaper, more ecofriendly and more widely distributable across California. There's nothing as satisfying as popping the tab of a cold one on a hot California day at the beach.

Cocktails

Cocktails have been shaken in Northern California since San Francisco's Barbary Coast days, when they were used to sedate sailors and kidnap them onto outbound ships. Now hip bartenders all across the state are researching old recipes and inventing new cocktail traditions. Don't be surprised to see absinthe poured into cordial glasses of Sazerac, or holiday eggnog spiked with tequila and organic orange peel. Originally made in Mexico, margaritas (made with tequila, lime, Cointreau, ice

---

WINE-TASTING TIPS

➡ Swirl. Before tasting, swirl your glass to oxygenate the wine and release flavors.

➡ Sniff. Dip your nose (without getting it wet!) into the glass for a good whiff.

➡ Swish. Take a swig, leave it on your tongue and bubble air through it as you roll it over the front of your teeth and tongue; this releases complex flavors. After you spit or swallow, exhale through your nose and count how long the flavor evolves to appreciate 'the finish.'

➡ If you're driving or cycling, don't swallow. Sips are hard to track, so perfect your graceful arc into the spit bucket.

➡ You don't have to buy anything. No one expects you to buy, especially if you're paying to taste or tour; but if you plan to picnic and haven't paid to taste, it's customary to buy a bottle. Most wineries don't mind if two people share one tasting.

➡ Take it slow and easy. Plan to visit no more than three wineries a day, four maximum.

➡ Don't wear cologne. And don't smoke, not in the gardens either – wait until you're off-property.

Cup of joe: California's coffee culture is booming

and salt) have refreshed Californians since the 1940s.

Legend has it that the martini was invented when a boozehound walked into an SF bar and demanded something to tide him over until he reached Martinez across the bay – a likely story, but we'll drink to that. The original was made with vermouth, gin, bitters, lemon, maraschino cherry and ice, although by the days of Sinatra's Rat Pack, the recipe was reduced to gin with vermouth vapors and an olive or two. The tropical mai tai (with rum, Orgeat, Curaçao and lime juice) is another cocktail allegedly invented in the Bay Area at Trader Vic's tiki bar in Oakland during the 1940s.

Coffee

California has become a hub for 'third wave' coffee. Pulitzer Prize–winning critic Jonathan Gold defines this as coffee directly sourced from farms instead of countries and roasted to maximize the bean's unique characteristics. LA's third-wave coffee shops tend not to roast their own, but cherry-pick the best beans from micro-roasters along the West Coast and Chicago. San Francisco's Blue Bottle Coffee added a 'fourth wave' element of showmanship to coffee geekery, introducing a $20,000 Japanese coffee siphon to filter its brews. Meanwhile, SF's Ritual Coffee Roasters has become the latest object of coffee cult worship with beans roasted in-house in small batches and hand-poured specialty coffees.

Regions at a Glance

Considering it's only half a state, Northern California is huge. To comprehend the geography, think of it as a giant bathtub, ringed by mountains. To the west, the Coastal Range rises straight from the Pacific Ocean, a wall unbroken except at the Golden Gate – mouth of San Francisco Bay. To the east, the Sierra Nevada makes another unbroken wall, only much higher, comprising the tallest peaks in the Continental US. To the north, the Cascade and Siskiyou ranges bleed into Oregon. To the south, the Transverse Ranges anomalously run east–west, separating Northern California from Southern California – geographically, if not culturally. And in the middle – the floor of the bathtub – extends the vast sea-level Central Valley, which drains into San Francisco Bay. The dramatic scenery is in the hills and mountains.

San Francisco

Food
Culture
Museums

Markets

SF has glorious markets, especially the Ferry Building. This 19th-century ferry terminal was converted into a covered market and showcases the best of Northern California's food producers.

New Perspectives

Northern California's 'Left Coast' reputation rests on SF, where self expression is a high virtue. Free-thinkers, techies, foodies and renegade artists set the city's creative tone.

Arts & Sciences

SF loves its museums. Recent expansions include a glass-walled pier for the hands-on Exploratorium, and a building with living roof and indoor rainforest at the Academy of Sciences. The Museum of Modern Art reopens in 2016.

p68

Marin County & the Bay Area

Outdoor Sports
Nature
Cities

Mountain Biking

Discover the birthplace of mountain biking at Mt Tamalpais, which rises from the Pacific. Trails reveal jaw-dropping vistas of the entire Bay Area.

Wildlife-Spotting

Across the San Andreas Fault, Point Reyes National Seashore juts 10 miles to sea, with towering cliffs and spectacular vistas. Plan to hike high bluffs among wild elk, while watching for rare birds and migrating whales.

Oakland & Berkeley

Oakland fosters a dynamic arts scene, notable for live music. Berkeley remains at the forefront of social change, thanks to its university, whose campus you should explore.

p108

Napa & Sonoma Wine Country

Wine
Food
Recreation

Wineries

Napa is famous for Cabernet Sauvignon and side-by-side wineries. Sonoma County has more history, and retains its folksy roots. Lucky for you, they're neighbors: see both.

Farm-to-Table Dining

Napa's top-end restaurants are the rural outpost of San Francisco's dining scene, but the raw ingredients often come from Sonoma County, where you can tour farms and orchards.

Cycling & Canoeing

Sonoma County's back roads are made for cycling, with few cars and gorgeous scenery. The Russian River is ideal for kayaking and canoeing.

p159

North Coast & Redwoods

Forests
Beaches
Small Towns

Redwood Trees

Redwood trees, the tallest trees on earth, rise like giants along the North Coast, the only place in the entire world that they grow. Plan on a six-hour drive from San Francisco, and a two-night stay.

State Beaches

The North Coast's wild and rugged beaches are shrouded in fog and littered with giant driftwood of fallen redwoods. Bring a warm sweater and plan to beachcomb, not swim.

Mendocino Coast

This wild stretch of coast, four hours from San Francisco, remains largely undeveloped, with side-by-side state parks and tiny towns built by whalers and loggers. Consider a night in a romantic B&B.

p215

Northern Mountains

Mountains
Lakes
Road Trips

Famous Peaks

Mount Shasta rises to over 11,000ft, drawing Native Americans, ice-axe-wielding alpinists, poets and painters. At Lassen Volcanic National Park, the otherworldly landscape includes a volcano and steaming vents from the earth's mantle.

Fishing & Boating

The wild lands of far northeastern California comprise spectacular lakes and reservoirs. Consider renting a houseboat and fishing pole, and fry your own trout for dinner.

Scenic Drives

Make a loop around the dramatic volcanic landscape, and if time permits, also find the cute-as-a-button, lesser-known, Gold Rush–era town of Weaverville.

p270

Gold Country

History
Museums
Outdoor Activities

Gold Rush

Glimpse back in time at 19th-century towns that line Hwy 49. Stop at Sutter's Mill to see where gold was first discovered. Consider panning for gold with the kids.

Living-History Parks

The region has incredible outdoor history parks on gold and the railroads – head directly to Jamestown and Columbia for the best.

White-Water Rafting

Gold Country is in the foothills of the mighty Sierra Nevada Mountains, which get pummeled by deep snow. When the snow melts, the American River runs wild, producing incredible rapids you can experience firsthand on a single- or multiday rafting trip.

p305

Lake Tahoe

Snow Sports
Water Sports
Rustic Lodging

Skiing

Some of the deepest snow in America falls around Lake Tahoe, and the skiing is incredible at over a dozen resorts. And this being California, most days are sunny and it's never bitterly cold.

Swimming & Boating

Lake Tahoe is so deep that it never freezes, but the surface temperature changes with the seasons. By July it's warm enough for swimming. Boating is popular spring through fall.

Cabins & Campgrounds

Tahoe's accommodations, including cottages, knotty-pine cabins and campgrounds, sit beneath towering pines on the lake's shore – they're ideal for a romantic weekend.

p330

Yosemite & the Sierra Nevada

Scenery
Wildlife
Hiking

Waterfalls & Granite

Yosemite's incredible waterfalls run heaviest in spring, roaring over rock and casting rainbows. Rising above, Yosemite's famous granite domes include Half Dome.

Flora & Fauna

Wildflowers carpet the valley in spring, the High Country in summer. You probably won't see a bear – provided you properly store food – but you will see incredible birds, deer and – if you're lucky – the elusive bighorn sheep.

Valley Walks

Many brilliant hiking trails originate in Yosemite Valley, including waterfall walks to Vernal and Nevada Falls, and the near-vertical ascent of famous Yosemite Falls. Follow the watercourses for maximum drama.

p368

Central Coast

Wildlife
Beaches
Scenic Drives

Elephant Seals & Whales

Elephant seals breed along the Central Coast, splitting time between Año Nuevo State Park, near Santa Cruz, and Point Piedras Blancas, near Hearst Castle. To spot whales, board a cruise in Monterey.

Surfing

Learn to surf and try your new skill along the coast at the many various surf breaks. Explore the history of the sport at Santa Cruz' tiny surfing museum.

Coastal Highway 1

The most famous drive in California – if not all America – hugs the coastline north of San Simeon, atop 1000ft cliffs, to moody Big Sur. Passengers get the best view southbound, drivers northbound.

p424

Sacramento & Central Valley

History
Museums
Farms & Fairs

History Parks

When early American settlers ventured west to California, they were aiming for Sutter's Fort in Sacramento, the otherwise-flat city's highest point. Today the fort is a state park.

Then & Now

Sacramento has fantastic museums, which focus on various periods in state history. Look for the exceptional California Museum, California State Railroad Museum and California Indian Museum.

Agricultural Bounty

The Valley is devoted almost entirely to farming, and you'll spot roadside stands selling walnuts, almonds, honey and fresh fruit. Time your visit to attend the California State Fair in July.

p483

On the Road

San Francisco

Best Places to Eat

➡ Coi (p98)

➡ Benu (p99)

➡ La Taqueria (p99)

➡ Rich Table (p100)

➡ Aziza (p101)

Best Places to Stay

➡ Hotel Drisco (p96)

➡ Hotel Vitale (p96)

➡ Hotel Bohème (p94)

➡ Inn San Francisco (p96)

➡ Argonaut Hotel (p94)

Why Go?

Get to know the world capital of weird from the inside out, from mural-lined alleyways named after poets to clothing-optional beaches on a former military base. But don't be too quick to dismiss San Francisco's wild ideas. Biotech, gay rights, personal computers, cable cars and organic fine dining were once considered outlandish too, before San Francisco introduced these underground ideas into the mainstream decades ago. San Francisco's morning fog erases the boundaries between land and ocean, reality and infinite possibility.

Rules are never strictly followed here. Golden Gate Bridge and Alcatraz are entirely optional – San Franciscans mostly admire them from afar – leaving you free to pursue inspiration through Golden Gate Park, past flamboyantly painted Victorian homes and through Mission galleries. Just don't be late for your sensational, sustainable dinner: in San Francisco, you can find happiness and eat it too.

When to Go
San Francisco

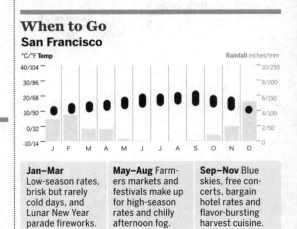

Jan–Mar Low-season rates, brisk but rarely cold days, and Lunar New Year parade fireworks.

May–Aug Farmers markets and festivals make up for high-season rates and chilly afternoon fog.

Sep–Nov Blue skies, free concerts, bargain hotel rates and flavor-bursting harvest cuisine.

Bay Bridge

San Francisco's other landmark bridge was inspired by a madman. Joshua Norton lost his shirt and his mind in the Gold Rush before proclaiming himself 'Emperor of these United States and Protector of Mexico,' and ordering construction of a trans-bay bridge in 1872. Taxpayers took some convincing: the Bay Bridge was completed in 1936. But the eastern span collapsed in the 1989 Loma Prieta earthquake, taking 12 years and $6.4 billion to repair.

Emperor Norton's idea seemed not quite so bright anymore – until artist Leo Villareal installed 25,000 LED lights along the western span, mesmerizing commuters with a 1.8-mile-long light show that shimmers and pulses in never-repeating patterns. The show runs from dusk until 2am nightly until March 2015 – but a crowdfunding campaign may keep the lights twinkling through 2026. For more, see thebaylights.org.

DON'T MISS...

➡ **Saloons** The Barbary Coast is roaring back to life with historically researched whiskey cocktails and staggering gin concoctions in San Francisco's great Western saloon revival (p101).

➡ **Rooftop-garden cuisine** SF chefs are raising the roof on hyperlocal fare with ingredients raised right upstairs: city-bee honey at Jardinière (p100), edible pansies at Coi (p98), herbs at farm:table (p97) and salad greens to feed the homeless at Glide Memorial (p72).

➡ **Green everything** Recent reports rank San Francisco as the greenest city in North America, with its pioneering parklets, citywide composting laws and America's biggest stretch of urban greenery: Golden Gate Park (p95).

SF's Best Free...

➡ **Music** Golden Gate Park hosts free concerts summer through fall, from opera and reggae to Hardly Strictly Bluegrass.

➡ **Speech** City Lights Bookstore (p72) won a landmark free-speech case in 1957 over the publication of Allen Ginsberg's magnificent, incendiary *Howl*; take a seat in the designated Poet's Chair and celebrate your right to read freely.

➡ **Love** Pride fills San Francisco streets with free candy, free condoms and over a million people freely smooching total strangers under rainbow flags.

➡ **Spirits** Anywhere within city limits – and you're free to join in anytime.

DID YOU KNOW?

Despite slacker reputations cultivated at 30 medical marijuana clubs, San Franciscans hold more patents and earn more degrees per capita than residents of any other US city.

Fast Facts

➡ **Population** 839,336

➡ **Area** 47 sq miles

➡ **Telephone area code** 415

Planning Your Trip

➡ **Three weeks before** Book Alcatraz trips and dinner at Coi or Benu.

➡ **Two weeks before** Build stamina for downtown hills, Golden Gate Park adventures and Mission bars.

➡ **One week before** Score tickets to San Francisco Symphony or Opera, and assemble your costume – SF throws parades whenever.

Resources

➡ **SF Bay Guardian** (www.sfbg.com) Hot tips on local entertainment, arts, politics.

➡ **SFGate** (www.sfgate.com) News and event listings.

History

Oysters and acorn bread were prime dinner options in the Mexico-run Ohlone settlement of San Francisco circa 1848 – but a year and some gold nuggets later, Champagne and chow mein were served by the bucket. Gold found in nearby Sierra Nevada foothills turned a sleepy 800-person village into a port city of 100,000 prospectors, con artists, prostitutes and honest folk – good luck telling them apart in the city's 200 saloons.

Panic struck when Australia glutted the market with gold in 1854. Rioters burned waterfront 'Sydney-Town' before turning on SF's Chinese community, who from 1877 to 1945 were restricted to living and working in Chinatown by anti-Chinese exclusion laws. Chinese laborers were left with few employment options besides dangerous work building railroads for San Francisco's robber barons, who dynamited, mined and clear-cut their way across the Golden West, and built Nob Hill mansions above Chinatown.

But the city's grand ambitions came crashing down in 1906, when earthquake and fire reduced the city to rubble. Theater troupes and opera divas performed for free amid smoldering ruins, and reconstruction hummed along at an astounding rate of 15 buildings per day.

During WWII, soldiers accused of insubordination and homosexuality were dismissed in San Francisco, as though that would teach them a lesson. Instead San Francisco's counterculture thrived, with North Beach jazz and Beat poetry. When the Central Intelligence Agency (CIA) tested LSD on the willing volunteer and *One Flew Over the Cuckoo's Nest* author Ken Kesey, he slipped some into Kool-Aid and kicked off the psychedelic '60s.

The Summer of Love brought free food, love and music to the Haight, and pioneering gay activists in the Castro helped elect Harvey Milk as San Francisco supervisor – America's first out gay official. When San Francisco witnessed devastating losses from HIV/AIDS in the 1980s, the city rallied to become a global model for epidemic treatment and prevention.

San Francisco's unconventional thinking spawned the web in the 1990s, until the dot-com bubble burst in 2000. But risk-taking SF continues to float outlandish new ideas –

NEIGHBORHOODS IN A NUTSHELL

North Beach & the Hills Poetry and parrots, top-of-the-world views, Italian gossip and opera on the jukebox.

Embarcadero & the Piers Weird science, sea-lion antics, gourmet treats, and getaways to and from Alcatraz.

Downtown & the Financial District The notorious Barbary Coast has gone legit with banks and boutiques, but shows its wild side in redwood parks and provocative art.

Chinatown Pagoda roofs, mahjong games, revolutionary plots, and fortunes made and lost in historic alleyways.

Hayes Valley, Civic Center & the Tenderloin Grand buildings and great performances, dive bars and cable cars, foodie finds and local designs.

SoMa South of Market; where high technology meets higher art, and everyone gets down and dirty on the dance floor.

Mission A book in one hand, a burrito in the other, and murals all around.

Castro Out and proud with samba whistles, rainbow sidewalks and history-making policy platforms.

Haight Flashbacks and fashion-forwardness, free thinking, free music and pricey skateboards.

Japantown, the Fillmore & Pacific Heights Sushi in the fountains, John Coltrane over the altar, and rock at the Fillmore.

Marina & the Presidio Boutiques, organic dining, peace and public nudity at a former army base.

Golden Gate Park & the Avenues SF's great green streak, surrounded by gourmet hangouts for hungry surfers.

San Francisco Highlights

1 Follow your bliss through SF's mile-wide wild streak: **Golden Gate Park** (p95).

2 See how real life is cooler than science fiction at the **Exploratorium** (p73).

3 Watch fog dance atop the deco towers of the **Golden Gate Bridge** (p72).

4 Explore SF's colorful history, captured in renegade **Mission murals** (p89).

5 Plot your escape from **Alcatraz** (p76), SF's notorious island prison.

6 Wander through 150 years of California history in pagoda-topped **Chinatown** (p72).

7 Come out and celebrate GLBT history in **the Castro** (p85), the center of the gay universe.

8 Get breathless from the climb, freshly restored murals and panoramic views at **Coit Tower** (p79).

9 Graze at the **Ferry Building** (p99), SF's local, sustainable food destination.

social media, mobile apps, biotech. Congratulations: you're just in time for San Francisco's next wild ride.

◉ Sights

◉ Union Square, Civic Center & the Tenderloin

★ **Asian Art Museum**   MUSEUM
(Map p76; ☑ 415-581-3500; www.asianart.org; 200 Larkin St; adult/student/child $12/8/free, 1st Sun of month free; ☺ 10am-5pm Tue-Sun, to 9pm Thu; 🚹; Ⓜ Civic Center, Ⓑ Civic Center) Imaginations race from ancient Persian miniatures to cutting-edge Japanese architecture through three floors spanning 6000 years of Asian arts. Besides the largest Asian art collection outside Asia – 18,000 works – the Asian offers excellent programs for all ages, from shadow-puppet shows and yoga for kids to weeknight Artist's Drawing Club mixers with crosscultural DJ mashups.

City Hall   HISTORIC BUILDING
(Map p76; ☑ art exhibit line 415-554-6080, tour info 415-554-6139; http://sfgsa.org/index.aspx?page=1085; 400 Van Ness Ave; ☺ 8am-8pm Mon-Fri, tours 10am, noon & 2pm; 🚹; Ⓜ Civic Center, Ⓑ Civic Center) FREE That mighty beaux-arts dome has covered San Francisco's greatest civic ambitions and setbacks, from marriage equality to McCarthy hearings. Designed in 1915 to outstyle Paris and outsize the capitol in Washington, DC, the dome was unsteady until its retrofit after the 1989 earthquake, when ingenious technology enabled it to swing on its base.

Glide Memorial United Methodist Church   CHURCH
(Map p76; ☑ 415-674-6090; www.glide.org; 330 Ellis St; ☺ celebrations 9am & 11am Sun; Ⓜ Powell, Ⓑ Powell) The rainbow-robed, 100-strong Glide gospel choir kicks off Sunday celebrations with a warm welcome for whomever comes through the door. Between celebrations, volunteers help Glide provide a million free meals a year and housing for formerly homeless families. Thursdays from 10am to 2pm, volunteers head upstairs to Glide's sunny Graze the Roof garden, harvesting organic vegetables for its free meals.

Luggage Store Gallery   ART GALLERY
(Map p76; ☑ 415-255-5971; www.luggagestoregallery.org; 1007 Market St; ☺ noon-5pm Wed-Sat; Ⓜ Civic Center, Ⓑ Civic Center) Bringing signs of life to one of SF's toughest blocks for two decades, this nonprofit gallery has launched renowned SF graffiti-art stars including Barry McGee and Clare Rojas. Don't miss the door camouflaged by spray paint, or the new rooftop mural by Brazilian street-art-duo Os Gemeos.

Union Square   SQUARE
(Map p76; intersection of Geary, Powell, Post & Stockton Sts; 🚋 Powell-Mason, Powell-Hyde, Ⓜ Powell, Ⓑ Powell) Free spirits and socialites converge on Union Square, named after pro-Union Civil War rallies, ringed by department stores and presided over by bare-breasted bronze socialite (and Legion of Honor founder) Alma Spreckels as the Goddess of Victory. Public outcry obliged Apple to revise its Union Square flagship plans in order to preserve SF sculptor Ruth Asawa's beloved Stockton St fountain, featuring SF icons by 250 contributors.

◉ Chinatown & North Beach

★ **City Lights Bookstore**   BUILDING
(Map p82; ☑ 415-362-8193; www.citylights.com; 261 Columbus Ave; ☺ 10am-midnight) When founder and Beat poet Lawrence Ferlinghetti and manager Shigeyoshi Murao defended their right to 'willfully and lewdly print' Allen Ginsberg's magnificent *Howl and Other Poems* in 1957, City Lights became a free-

---

> **DON'T MISS**

GOLDEN GATE BRIDGE

Hard to believe the Navy almost nixed SF's signature art-deco landmark (Map p71; www.goldengatebridge.org/visitors; off Lincoln Blvd; northbound free, southbound toll $6, billed electronically to vehicle's license plate; 🚌 28, all Golden Gate Transit buses) by architects Gertrude and Irving Murrow and engineer Joseph B Strauss. Photographers, take your cue from Hitchcock: seen from Fort Point (Map p114; ☑ 415-556-1693; www.nps.gov/fopo; Marine Dr; admission free; ☺ 10am-5pm Fri-Sun; 🅿; 🚌 28) FREE, the 1937 bridge induces a thrilling case of vertigo. Fog aficionados prefer Marin's Vista Point, watching gusts billow through bridge cables like dry ice at a Kiss concert. For the full effect, hike or bike the 2-mile span.

THREE CHINATOWN ALLEYS THAT MADE HISTORY

→ **Waverly Place** (Map p82; 🚇 30, 🚋 California St, Powell-Mason) After the 1906 earthquake and fire devastated Chinatown, developers schemed to relocate Chinatown residents left homeless to less-desirable real estate outside the city. But representatives from the Chinese consulate and several gun-toting merchants marched back to Waverly Place, holding temple services amid the rubble at still-smoldering altars. The alley is the namesake of the main character in Amy Tan's bestselling *The Joy Luck Club*.

→ **Spofford Alley** (Map p82; 🚇 1, 15, 30, 45) Sun Yat-sen plotted the overthrow of China's last emperor at No 36, and the 1920s brought bootleggers' gun battles to this alley – but Spofford has mellowed with age. In the evenings you'll hear shuffling mahjong tiles and *erhu* (two-stringed Chinese fiddle) players warming up at local senior centers.

→ **Ross Alley** (Map p82; 🚇 1, 30, 45) Alternately known as Manila, Spanish and Mexico St after the working girls who once worked this block, mural-lined Ross Alley is occasionally pimped out for Hollywood productions, including *Karate Kid II* and *Indiana Jones and the Temple of Doom*. Duck into the alley's **Golden Gate Fortune Cookie Factory** (56 Ross Alley; admission free; ⊙ 8am-7pm) for custom cookies hot off the press (50¢ each), and write your own fortune.

---

speech landmark. Celebrate your freedom to read freely in the designated Poet's Chair upstairs overlooking Jack Kerouac Alley, load up on 'zines on the mezzanine and entertain radical ideas downstairs in the Muckracking and Stolen Continents sections.

Beat Museum   MUSEUM
(Map p82; 🕿 1-800-537-6822; www.kerouac.com; 540 Broadway; adult/student $8/5; ⊙ 10am-7pm; 🚇 10, 12, 30, 41, 45, 🚋 Powell-Hyde, Powell-Mason) Grab a ramshackle theater seat redolent with the accumulated odors of literary giants, pets and pot to watch fascinating films about the SF Beat literary scene c 1950–69. Upstairs are shrines to Beat achievements, including *On the Road* and other books that expanded America's outlook to include the margins. Two-hour guided tours at 1pm Wednesday, Saturday and Sunday cover the museum and Beat hangouts (adult/student $30/25).

Chinese Historical Society of America   MUSEUM
(CHSA; Map p82; 🕿 415-391-1188; www.chsa.org; 965 Clay St; ⊙ noon-5pm Tue-Fri, 11am-4pm Sat; 🚇 1, 30, 45, 🚋 California St) **FREE** Picture what it was like to be Chinese in America during the gold rush, transcontinental railroad construction or the Beat heyday in this 1932 landmark, built as Chinatown's YWCA by Julia Morgan (also chief architect of Hearst Castle). The nation's largest Chinese American historical institute is a treasury of artifacts and personal stories, tracing journeys from China that made American history.

◉ Fisherman's Wharf

★**Exploratorium**   MUSEUM
(Map p84; 🕿 415-528-4444; www.exploratorium. edu; Pier 15; adult/child $25/19, Thu evening $15; ⊙ 10am-5pm Tue-Sun, over-18yr only Thu 6-10pm; 🅿👶; Ⓜ F) 🚲 Is there a science to skateboarding? Do toilets flush conterclockwise in Australia? Find out first-hand with 600-plus fascinating, freaky exhibits. In under an hour you can star in psychedelic fractal music videos, make art from bacteria, and grope your way in total darkness through the Tactile Dome. Founded in 1969 by atom-bomb physicist Frank Oppenheimer, the newly relocated, expanded Exploratorium shows how life is cooler than science fiction.

★**Musée Mécanique**   AMUSEMENT PARK
(Map p84; 🕿 415-346-2000; www.museemechanique.org; Pier 45, Shed A; ⊙ 10am-7pm Mon-Fri, to 8pm Sat & Sun; 👶; 🚇 47, 🚋 Powell-Mason, Powell-Hyde, Ⓜ F) Where else can you guillotine a man for a quarter? Creepy, 19th-century arcade games like the macabre French Execution compete for your spare change with the diabolical Ms Pac-Man.

USS Pampanito   HISTORIC SITE
(Map p84; 🕿 415-775-1943; www.maritime.org/ pamphome.htm; Pier 45; adult/child $12/6; ⊙ 9am-8pm Thu-Tue, to 6pm Wed; 👶; 🚇 19, 30, 47, 🚋 Powell-Hyde, Ⓜ F) Explore a restored WWII submarine that survived six tours of duty, while you listen to submariner sailors' tales of stealth mode and sudden attacks in a riveting

Alcatraz

Book a ferry from Pier 33 and ride 1.5 miles across the bay to explore America's most notorious former prison. The trip itself is worth the money, providing stunning views of the city skyline. Once you've landed at the **Ferry Dock & Pier 1**, you begin the 580-yard walk to the top of the island and prison; if you're out of shape, there's a twice-hourly tram.

As you climb toward the **Guardhouse 2**, notice the island's steep slope; before it was a prison, Alcatraz was a fort. In the 1850s, the military quarried the rocky shores into near-vertical cliffs. Ships could then only dock at a single port, separated from the main buildings by a sally port (a drawbridge and moat in what became the guardhouse). Inside, peer through floor grates to see Alcatraz' original prison.

Volunteers tend the brilliant **Officer's Row Gardens 3** – an orderly counterpoint to the overgrown rose bushes surrounding the burned-out shell of the **Warden's House 4**. At the top of the hill, by the front door of the **Main Cellhouse 5**, beauty shots unfurl all around, including a **view of the Golden Gate Bridge 6**. Above the main door of the administration building, notice the **historic signs & graffiti 7**, before you step inside the dank, cold prison to find the **Frank Morris cell 8**, former home to Alcatraz' most notorious jail-breaker.

TOP TIPS

➡ Book at least two weeks prior for self-guided daytime visits, longer for ranger-led night tours. For info on garden tours, see www.alcatraz gardens.org.

➡ Be prepared to hike; a steep path ascends from the ferry landing to the cell block. Most people spend two to three hours on the island. You need only reserve for the outbound ferry; take any ferry back.

➡ There's no food (just water) but you can bring your own; picnicking is allowed at the ferry dock only. Dress in layers as weather changes fast and it's usually windy.

JOHN A VLAHIDES ©

Historic Signs & Graffiti
During their 1969–71 occupation, Native Americans graffitied the water tower: 'Home of the Free Indian Land.' Above the cellhouse door, examine the eagle-and-flag crest to see how th red-and-white stripes were changed to spell 'Free.'

Warden's House
Fires destroyed the warden's house and other structures during the Indian Occupation. The government blamed the Native Americans; the Native Americans blamed agents provocateurs acting on behalf of the Nixon Administration to undermine public sympathy.

Parade Grounds

DAVID CLAPP / GETTY IMAGES ©

Ferry Dock & Pier
A giant wall map helps you get your bearings. Inside nearby Bldg 64, short films and exhibits provide historical perspective on the prison and details about the Indian Occupation.

View of Golden Gate Bridge
The Golden Gate Bridge stretches wide on the horizon. Best views are from atop the island at Eagle Plaza, near the cellhouse entrance, and at water level along the Agave Trail (September to January only).

Main Cellhouse
During the mid-20th century, the maximum-security prison housed the day's most notorious troublemakers, including Al Capone and Robert Stroud, the 'Birdman of Alcatraz' (who actually conducted his ornithology studies at Leavenworth).

Power House

Recreation Yard

Water Tower

Officers' Club

Lighthouse

Guard Tower

Frank Morris Cell
Peer into cell 138 on B-Block to see a re-creation of the dummy's head that Frank Morris left in his bed as a decoy to aid his notorious – and successful – 1962 escape from Alcatraz.

Guardhouse
Alcatraz' oldest building dates to 1857 and retains remnants of the original drawbridge and moat. During the Civil War the basement was transformed into a military dungeon – the genesis of Alcatraz as prison.

Officer's Row Gardens
In the 19th century soldiers imported topsoil to beautify the island with gardens. Well-trusted prisoners later gardened – Elliott Michener said it kept him sane. Historians, ornithologists and archaeologists choose today's plants.

Downtown San Francisco & SoMa

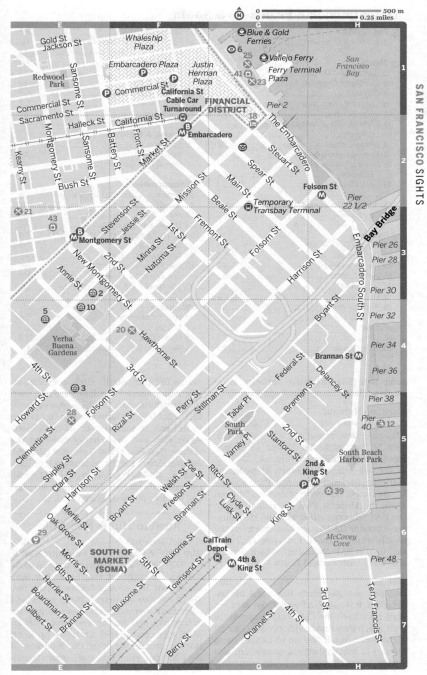

Downtown San Francisco & SoMa

audio tour ($3) that makes surfacing afterwards a relief (caution claustrophobes).

**Maritime National
Historic Park** HISTORIC SITE
(Map p84; www.nps.gov/safr; 499 Jefferson St, Hyde St Pier; adult/child $5/free; ⊙9:30am-5pm Oct-May, to 5:30pm Jun-Sep; 🚹; 🚌19, 30, 47, 🚋Powell-Hyde, MF) Historic ships at the Maritime National Historical Park are the Wharf's most authentic attraction. Moored along the Hyde St Pier, standouts include the 1891 schooner *Alma* and the 1895 lumber schooner *CA Thayer*. Also check out the paddle-wheel tugboat *Eppleton Hall* and the iron-hulled *Balclutha*, which hauled coal from Australia and Wales.

Pier 39 PIER
(Map p84; www.pier39.com; Beach St & the Embarcadero; P 🚹; 🚌47, 🚋Powell-Mason, MF) Sea lions have lived the California dream since 1989, when they first bellyflopped on Pier 39 yacht docks. You'll find up to 1300 of them January to July, sunbathing, canoodling, and setting SF standards for beach-bumming.

Across the pier, sharks circle overhead inside **Aquarium of the Bay** (Map p84; www.aquariumofthebay.com; Pier 39; adult/child/family $21.95/12.95/64; ⊙10am-7pm Mon-Thu, to 8pm Fri-Sun, daily in summer; 🚹; 🚌49, 🚋Powell-Mason, MF), and your chariot awaits at the vintage **San Francisco Carousel** (Map p84; www.pier39.com; Pier 39; admission $3; ⊙11am-7pm; 🚹; 🚌47, 🚋Powell-Mason, MF). The visitors' center rents strollers, stores luggage, and has free phone-charging stations.

Russian Hill & Nob Hill

Grace Cathedral CHURCH
(Map p76; ☎415-749-6300; www.gracecathedral.org; 1100 California St; suggested donation adult/child $3/2, Sun services free; ⊙8am-6pm Mon-Sat, to 7pm Sun, services 8:30am & 11am Sun; 🚌1, 🚋California St) Rebuilt three times and completed over 40 years, Grace celebrates community and human endeavor with an AIDS memorial chapel altarpiece by Keith Haring, murals honoring the founding of the UN in San Francisco, and Gothic stained-

glass windows featuring Albert Einstein up-lifted in swirling atomic particles. Check the website for choral performances with Grace's splendid acoustics.

San Francisco Art Institute ART GALLERY
(Map p84; www.sfai.edu; 800 Chestnut St; admission free; ⊙ Walter & McBean Galleries 11am-7pm Tue, to 6pm Wed-Sat, Diego Rivera Gallery 9am-5pm; ⊠ Powell-Mason) FREE Founded in the 1870s, SFAI was the vanguard for 1960s Bay Area Abstraction, 1970s conceptual art, and 1990s new-media art – glimpse what's next in contemporary art here at the Walter & McBean Gallery. Diego Rivera's 1931 *The Making of a Fresco Showing a Building of a City* sprawls across Diego Rivera Gallery, showing the artist pausing to admire the constant work-in-progress that is San Francisco.

Lombard Street STREET
(Map p84; 900 block of Lombard St; ⊠ Powell-Hyde) You've seen Lombard's eight downhill switchbacks on postcards, movies (*Vertigo*), TV (*The Real World*), even video games (Tony Hawk's *Pro Skater*). Billed incorrectly as 'the world's crookedest street' – SF's Vermont St deserves the honor – scenic Lombard St earns street cred with zigzagging flowerbeds. The street often closes to traffic on busy summer weekends, accommodating pedestrians who brave 250 steps for Sterling Park sunsets with Golden Gate Bridge views.

Japantown

Japan Center BUILDING
(www.sfjapantown.org; 1737 Post St; ⊙10am-midnight; ⊠2, 3, 22, 38, 38L) Welcome to *kawaii* (cuteness) – this 1968 mall is a vintage gem, with rock gardens, wooden bridges and *maneki-neko* (waving cat) figurines atop sushi-bar counters. Lose track of time in photo-sticker booths, karaoke lounges, *ukiyo-e* (woodblock print) galleries and Japanese video-game arcades – then take a breather under the cherry trees by the Peace Plaza pagoda.

Cottage Row STREET
(off Bush St btwn Webster & Fillmore Sts; ⊠2, 3, 22, 38) Detour to the 1860s and '70s via this National Historic Landmark promenade formerly known as 'Japan Street,' where Japanese Americans lived in clapboard cottages, farmed tiny backyard plots and socialized under plum trees until their forced internment in WWII. Forty-five years later, San Francisco's Japanese American Citizens League won a presidential apology for internees – and today, Cottage Row's public mini-park remains a point of community pride.

The Marina & Presidio

★**Crissy Field** PARK
(Map p84; www.crissyfield.org; 1199 East Beach; ⊠30, PresidioGo Shuttle) The Presidio's army airstrip has been stripped of asphalt and

SAN FRANCISCO SIGHTS

WORTH A TRIP

COIT TOWER

Adding an exclamation mark to San Francisco's landscape, Coit Tower (Map p82; ✆415-362-0808; http://sfrecpark.org/destination/telegraph-hill-pioneer-park/coit-tower; Telegraph Hill Blvd; elevator entry (nonresident) adult/child $7/5; ⊙10am-5:30pm Mar-Sep, 9am-4:30pm Oct-Feb; ⊠39) offers views worth shouting about – especially after you climb the giddy, steep Filbert St or Greenwich St steps to the top of Telegraph Hill. This 210ft, peculiar projectile is a monument to San Francisco firefighters financed by eccentric heiress Lillie Hitchcock Coit. Lillie could drink, smoke and play cards as well as any off-duty firefighter, rarely missed a fire or a firefighter's funeral, and even had the firehouse emblem embroidered on her bedsheets.

Even before it opened in 1934, Lillie's tower became a lightning-rod for controversy. Federally funded lobby murals show San Franciscans during the Great Depression at speakeasies, soup kitchens, and dock-workers' unions. Authorities denounced Coit Tower's 25 muralists as communists, but San Franciscans rallied to protect their artwork as a national landmark.

Newly restored in 2014, the bright, bold murals broaden world views just as surely as the 360-degree views from the tower-top viewing platform. To glimpse murals inside Coit Tower's spiral stairwell, join free guided tours at 11am on Saturdays.

San Francisco by Cable Car

Carnival rides can't compare to cable cars, San Francisco's vintage public transit. Novices slide into strangers' laps but regular commuters just grip leather hand-straps, lean back and ride downhill slides like pro surfers. On this trip, you'll master the San Francisco stance and conquer SF hills without breaking a sweat.

At the **❶ Powell St Cable Car Turnaround** operators turn the car atop a revolving wooden platform and a vintage kiosk; buy an all-day Muni Passport for $14 instead of paying $6 per ride. Board the Powell-Hyde cable car and begin your journey up Nob Hill.

As your cable car lurches uphill, you can imagine 19th-century horses struggling up this slippery crag. Inventor Andrew Hallidie's cable cars survived the 1906 earthquake and fire that destroyed 'Snob Hill' mansions, returning the faithful to rebuilt **❷ Grace Cathedral** (p78).

Back on the Powell-Hyde car, careen past crooked, flower-lined **❸ Lombard Street** (p79) toward **❹ Fisherman's Wharf** (p73). The waterfront terminus is named for Friedel Klussman, who saved cable cars from mayoral modernization plans in 1947. She did the math: cable cars brought in more tourism dollars than they cost in upkeep. The mayor demanded a vote – and lost to 'the Cable Car Lady' by a landslide.

At the wharf you can see SF as sailors did as they emerged from the submarine **❺ USS Pampanito** (p73). Witness Western saloon brawls in vintage arcade games at the **❻ Musée Mécanique** (p73) before hitching the Powell-Mason cable car to North Beach.

Hop off to see Diego Rivera's 1934 cityscape at the **❼ San Francisco Art Institute** (p79) or follow your rumbling stomach directly to **❽ Liguria Bakery** (p97). Stroll through North Beach and Chinatown alleyways or take the Powell-Mason line to time-travel through the **❾ Chinese Historical Society of America** (p73). Nearby, catch a ride on the city's oldest line: the California St cable car. The terminus is near the **❿ Ferry Building** (p99), where champagne-and-oyster happy hour awaits.

Top: Cable Car Turnaround; Bottom: Cable car on Hyde St, heading toward Fisherman's Wharf

DAVID CLAPP / GETTY IMAGES ©

SABRINA DALBESIO / GETTY IMAGES ©

Chinatown & North Beach

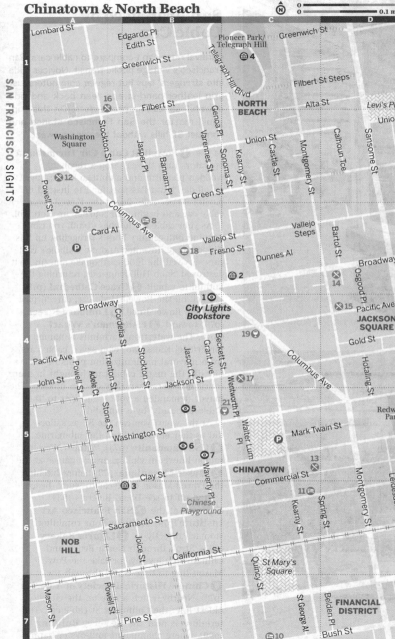

SAN FRANCISCO SIGHTS

N 0   200 m
0   0.1 miles

Lombard St

Edgardo Pl
Edith St

Greenwich St

Pioneer Park/
Telegraph Hill

☑ 4

Greenwich St

Battery St

Greenwich St

Filbert St Steps

Telegraph Hill Blvd

Alta St

Levi's Plaza

Union St

**NORTH
BEACH**

Filbert St

⊗ 16

Genoa Pl

Union St

Castle St

Montgomery St

Calhoun Tce

Sansome St

Washington
Square

Stockton St

Jasper Pl

Bannam Pl

Varennes St

Sonoma St

Kearny St

⊗ 12

Powell St

Green St

Columbus Ave

☆ 23

Card Al

☐ 8

Vallejo St
Fresno St

Dunnes Al

Vallejo
Steps

Bartol St

Broadway

Ⓟ

☐ 18

☐ 2

⊗ 14

Osgood Pl

Broadway

Cordelia St

City Lights
Bookstore

☉ 1

⊗ 15

Pacific Ave

**JACKSON
SQUARE**

☐ 19

Gold St

Pacific Ave

Powell St

Trenton St

Stockton St

Jason Ct

Grant Ave

Beckett St

Columbus Ave

Hotaling St

John St

Adele Ct

Jackson St

Wentworth Pl

⊗ 17

Stone St

◉ 5

☐ 21

Redwood
Park

Washington St

◉ 6

◉ 7

Walter Lum Pl

Ⓟ

Mark Twain St

Clay St

Waverly Pl

CHINATOWN

⊗ 13

Montgomery St

Leidesdorff St

☐ 3

Commercial St

Chinese
Playground

☐ 11

Kearny St

Spring St

Sacramento St

**NOB
HILL**

Joice St

California St

St Mary's
Square

Quincy St

St George Al

**FINANCIAL
DISTRICT**

Mason St

Powell St

Pine St

Belden Pl

Bush St

☐ 10

☐ 9

☐ 20

☐ 22

Chinatown & North Beach

reinvented as a haven for coastal birds, kite-fliers and windsurfers enjoying sweeping views of Golden Gate Bridge.

★ **Baker Beach**   BEACH
(☉ sunrise-sunset; ☐ 29, PresidiGo Shuttle) Unswimmable waters (except when the tide's coming in) but unbeatable views of the Golden Gate make this former Army beachhead SF's tanning location of choice, especially the clothing-optional north end – at least until the afternoon fog rolls in.

Presidio Visitors Center   TOURIST INFORMATION
(www.presidio.gov; Montgomery St & Lincoln Blvd, Bldg 105; ☉ 10am-4pm Thu-Sun; ☐ PresidiGo Shuttle) San Francisco's official motto is 'Oro in Paz, Fierro in Guerra' (Gold in Peace, Iron in War), but it hasn't seen much military action since 1776, when its Spanish *presidio* (military post) was built by conscripted Ohlone. Today the revamped Officers Club features archaeological displays and California cuisine from celebrity chef Traci des Jardins. Cultural institutions including the Walt Disney Family Museum (Map p84; ☑ 415-345-6800; www.waltdisney.org; 104 Montgomery St, Presidio; adult/student/child $20/15/12; ☉ 10am-6pm Wed-Mon, last entry 5pm; ℙ ♠; ☐ 43, PresidiGo Shuttle) line the former parade grounds, and a Yoda statue fronts George Lucas' Letterman Digital Arts Center.

◎ SoMa

Contemporary Jewish Museum   MUSEUM
(Map p76; ☑ 415-344-8800; www.thecjm.org; 736 Mission St; adult/child $12/free, after 5pm Thu $5, 1st Tue of month free; ☉ 11am-5pm Mon-Tue & Fri-Sun, to 8pm Thu; Ⓜ Montgomery, Ⓑ Montgomery) A blue-steel box balancing on one corner brings signs of life to San Francisco's commercial downtown – literally. Architect Daniel Libeskind based his landmark design for the Contemporary Jewish Museum on the shape of the Hebrew word *l'chaim* – 'to life.' Galleries inside a converted power substation illuminate Jewish life and ideals through artists as diverse as Andy Warhol, Maurice Sendak, Marc Chagall and the Bay Area's own Gertrude Stein.

Cartoon Art Museum   MUSEUM
(Map p76; ☑ 415-227-8666; www.cartoonart.org; 655 Mission St; adult/student $8/6, 1st Tue of month free; ☉ 11am-5pm Tue-Sun; ♠; ☐ 14, 15, 30, 45, Ⓜ Montgomery, Ⓑ Montgomery) Introducing this place to comics fans would be an insult. Of course you know it was funded by *Peanuts*' Charles M Schultz. Naturally you recognize Mike Zeck's *Captain America* covers, own R Crumb's underground classic *Mr Natural,* and can recite Edward Gorey's alphabet ('A is for Amy who fell down the stairs/B is for Basil assaulted by bears...') But even diehard fans learn something new here, from lectures by Pixar animators to celebrations of women cartoonists with SF comics legend Trina Robbins.

Museum of the African Diaspora   MUSEUM
(MoAD; Map p76; ☑ 415-358-7200; www.moadsf.org; 685 Mission St; adult/student/child $10/5/free; ☉ 11am-6pm Wed-Sat, noon-5pm Sun; ℙ ♠; ☐ 14, 15, 30, 45, Ⓜ Montgomery, Ⓑ Montgomery) MoAD tells the epic story of diaspora across three floors with an international cast of artists, writers and historians. Quarterly exhibits

Fisherman's Wharf, The Marina & Russian Hill

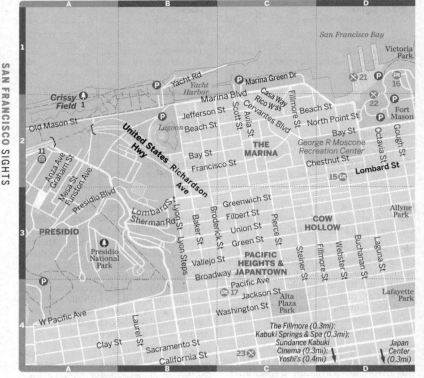

Fisherman's Wharf, The Marina & Russian Hill

have showcased glittering royals by Nigerian British sensation Chris Ofili, Romare Bearden's Harlem jazz portraits, and Siddi family quilts by South Indians descended from African slaves. Don't miss the moving video narrated by Maya Angelou.

The Mission & the Castro

★ 826 Valencia
CULTURAL SITE

(Map p86; ☑ 415-642-5905; www.826valencia.org; 826 Valencia St; ⊕ noon-6pm; ♠; ☐ 14, 33, 49, ⓑ 16th St Mission, ⓜ J) Avast, ye scurvy scalawags! If ye be shipwrecked without yer eye patch or McSweeney's literary anthology, lay down yer dubloons and claim yer booty at this here nonprofit Pirate Store. Below decks, kids be writing tall tales for dark nights asea, and ye can study making video games and magazines and suchlike, if that be yer dastardly inclination…arrrr!

Mission Dolores
CHURCH

(Misión San Francisco de Asís; Map p86; ☑ 415-621-8203; www.missiondolores.org; 3321 16th St; adult/child $5/3; ⊕ 9am-4pm Nov-Apr, to 4:30pm May-Oct; ☐ 22, 33, ⓑ 16th St Mission, ⓜ J) The city's oldest building was founded in 1776 and rebuilt in 1782 with conscripted Ohlone and Miwok labor – a graveyard memorial hut commemorates 5000 Native laborers who died of hardship and measles epidemics. Today the original adobe is overshadowed by the ornate 1913 Churrigueresque basilica, featuring stained-glass windows of California's 21 missions.

GLBT History Museum
MUSEUM

(Map p86; ☑ 415-621-1107; www.glbthistory.org/museum; 4127 18th St; admission $5, 1st Wed of month free; ⊕ 11am-7pm Mon & Wed-Sat, noon-5pm Sun; ⓜ Castro) America's first gay-history museum captures proud moments and historic challenges: Harvey Milk's campaign literature, interviews with trailblazing bisexual author Gore Vidal, matchbooks from long-gone bathhouses and 1950s penal codes banning homosexuality.

Harvey Milk & Jane Warner Plazas
SQUARE

(Market & Castro Sts; ⓜ Castro) A huge rainbow flag welcomes arrivals to Harvey Milk

The Mission & The Castro

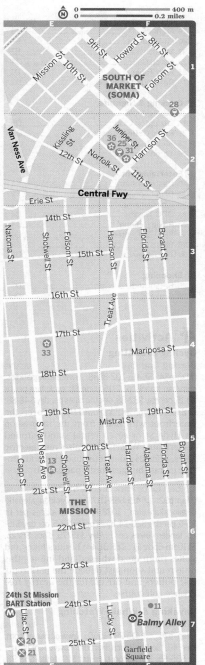

Plaza (Map p86; 24, 33, F, Castro St), where a display honors the Castro camera-store owner who was assassinated not long after becoming America's first out gay official – but who remains an icon of civil rights and civic pride. By the F-train terminus is Jane Warner Plaza (Map p86), named for the Castro's trailblazing lesbian police officer. The community converges here for sun and local color – including thong-clad protestors of SF's 2013 nudity ban.

Human Rights Campaign Action Center
HISTORIC SITE

(Map p86; 415-431-2200; http://shop.hrc.org/san-francisco-hrc-store; 575 Castro St; 10am-8pm Mon-Sat, to 7pm Sun) You may recognize Harvey Milk's former camera storefront, featured in the Oscar-winning movie *Milk*. Now it's home to the civil rights advocacy group, where supporters converge to sign petitions, shop for 'Equality' wedding rings, and admire the mural featuring Milk's famous words: 'If a bullet should enter my brain, let that bullet shatter every closet door.'

The Haight

Haight & Ashbury
LANDMARK

(Map p90; 6, 33, 37, 43, 71) This legendary intersection was the epicenter of the psychedelic '60s and remains a counterculture magnet. On average Saturdays here you can sign Green Party petitions, commission a poem, hear Hare Krishna on keyboards and Bob Dylan on banjo. The clock overhead always reads 4:20 – better known in herbal circles as International Bong-Hit Time. A local clockmaker recently fixed it; within a week it was stuck at 4:20.

Alamo Square Park
PARK

(Map p86; Hayes & Scott Sts; ; 5, 21, 22, 24) FREE The pastel Painted Ladies of famed Postcard Row on Alamo Square's east side pale in comparison to colorful characters along the park's north side. Here you'll spot Barbary Coast baroque, with facades bedecked with fish-scale shingles and gingerbread trim dripping from peaked roofs. On the northwest corner, the 1889 Westerfield mansion miraculously survived tenancies by czarist Russian bootleggers, Fillmore jazz musicians, and hippie communes – plus watchtower rituals by Church of Satan founder Anton LaVey.

The Mission & The Castro

👁 The Richmond

Coastal Trail   TRAIL

(Map p92; www.californiacoastaltrail.info; Fort Funston to Lincoln Park; ☉sunrise-sunset; 🚍1, 18, 38) Hit your stride on the 9-mile stretch of Coastal Trail starting near former nuclear bunkers at Fort Funston, crossing 4 miles of sandy Ocean Beach, wrapping around the Presidio and ending at the Golden Gate Bridge. Casual strollers can pick up the trail near the ruins of Sutro Baths, head around cliffside Land's End for end-of-the-world views, then duck into the Legion of Honor at Lincoln Park.

**California Palace of the
Legion of Honor**   MUSEUM

(Map p92; ☎415-750-3600; http://legionofhonor. famsf.org; 100 34th Ave; adult/child $10/free, $2 discount with Muni ticket, 1st Tue of month free; ☉9:30am-5:15pm Tue-Sun; 🅿👫; 🚍18) Larger-than-life sculptor's model 'Big Alma' Spreckels gifted this museum to lift San Francisco's spirits and pay tribute to Californians killed in WWI. Featured artworks range from Monet waterlilies to John Cage soundscapes, Iraqi ivories to R Crumb comics – part of the Legion's stellar Achenbach Collection of 90,000 graphic artworks.

🏃 Activities

Cycling & Skating

Blazing Saddles   CYCLING

(Map p84; ☎415-202-8888; www.blazingsaddles. com/san-francisco; 2715 Hyde St; cycle hire per hr $8-15, per day $32-88, electric bikes per day $48-88; ☉8am-7:30pm; 👫; 🚃Powell-Hyde) Cover the waterfront with bikes from the main shop on Hyde St or seven rental stands around Fisherman's Wharf. They also rent electric bikes, offer 24-hour return service and provide extras (bungee cords, packs etc).

Golden Gate Park Bike & Skate   BICYCLING

(Map p92; ☎415-668-1117; www.goldengatepark-bikeandskate.com; 3038 Fulton St; skates per hr $5-6, per day $20-24, bikes per hr $3-5, per day $15-25, tandem bikes per hr/day $15/75, discs $6/25; ☉10am-6pm; 👫; 🚍5, 31, 44) Besides bikes and skates (both quad-wheeled and inline), this little rental shop just outside the park rents disc putters and drivers for the nearby free Frisbee golf course.

Kayaking & Whale-Watching

City Kayak   KAYAKING

(Map p76; ☎415-294-1050; www.citykayak.com; Pier 40, South Beach Harbor; kayak rentals per hr $35-65, 3hr lesson & rental $59, tours $58-98;

M Brannan) Newbies to kayaking can take lessons and venture calm waters near the Bay Bridge, and experienced paddlers can brave choppy currents beneath the Golden Gate (conditions permitting) – but romantics prefer calm-water moonlight tours.

Oceanic Society WHALE-WATCHING
(☑ reservations 415-256-9941; www.oceanic-society.org; tours per person $125; ☺ reservations 8:30am-5pm Mon-Fri, trips Sat & Sun) Whale sightings aren't a fluke on naturalist-led, ocean-going, weekend boat trips during mid-October through December migrations. In the off-season, trips run to the Farallon Islands, 27 miles west of San Francisco.

Spas

★ Kabuki Springs & Spa SPA
(☑ 415-922-6000; www.kabukisprings.com; 1750 Geary Blvd; admission $25; ☺ 10am-9:45pm, co-ed Tue, women-only Wed, Fri & Sun, men-only Mon, Thu & Sat; ☐ 22, 38) Unwind in these Japanese baths. Scrub down with salt in the steam room, soak in the hot pool, take the cold plunge and reheat in the sauna. Most days are clothing-optional, but bathing suits are required on co-ed Tuesdays. Silence is mandatory – if you hear the gong, it means *Shhhh!*

☞ Tours

Day visits to Alcatraz (www.nps.gov/alca) include captivating audio tours with prisoners and guards recalling cellhouse life, while creepy twilight tours are led by park rangers; book tickets at least two weeks ahead. See also p76.

Alcatraz Cruises BOAT TOUR
(Map p84; ☑ 415-981-7625; www.alcatrazcruises.com; day tours adult/child/family $30/18/92, night adult/child $37/22) Ferries depart Pier 33 half-hourly 9am to 3:55pm, night tours leave at 6:10pm and 6:45pm.

★ Precita Eyes Mission Mural Tours TOUR
(Map p86; ☑ 415-285-2287; www.precitaeyes.org; adult $15-20, child $3; ☺ see website calendar for tour dates; ☙) Muralists lead two-hour tours on foot or bike covering 60 to 70 murals in a six- to 10-block radius of mural-bedecked Balmy Alley; proceeds fund mural upkeep at this community arts nonprofit.

Chinatown Alleyway Tours TOUR
(☑ 415-984-1478; www.chinatownalleywaytours.org; adult/student $18/12; ☺ 11am Sat; ☙; ☐ 8X, 8AX, 8BX) Neighborhood teens lead two-hour community nonprofit tours for up-close-and-personal peeks into Chinatown's past (weather permitting). Book five days ahead or pay double for Saturday walk-ins; cash only.

Public Library City Guides TOUR
(☑ 415-557-4266; www.sfcityguides.org; donations/tips welcome) **FREE** Volunteer historians lead nonprofit tours organized by neighborhood

---

MISSION MURALS

Inspired by Diego Rivera's San Francisco Works Progress Administration (WPA) murals and outraged by US foreign policy in Central America, Mission *muralistas* set out in the 1970s to transform the political landscape, one alley at a time. Today, 400-plus murals line Mission streets, including:

➡ ★ **Balmy Alley** (Map p86; ☑ 415-285-2287; www.precitaeyes.org; btwn 24th & 25th Sts; ☐ 10, 12, 27, 33, 48, **B** 24th St Mission) Between Treat Ave and Harrison St, murals spanning 35 years transform garage doors into artistic and political statements, from an early memorial for El Salvador activist Archbishop Òscar Romero to a homage to the golden age of Mexican cinema.

➡ **Clarion Alley** (Map p86; btwn 17th & 18th Sts, off Valencia St; ☐ 14, 22, 33, **B** 16th St Mission, **M** J) Only the strongest street art survives in Clarion, where lesser works are peed on or painted over. Very few pieces survive for years, such as Megan Wilson's daisy-covered *Capitalism Is Over (If You Want It)* or Jet Martinez' view of Clarion Alley within a man standing in a forest.

➡ **Women's Building** (Map p86; 3543 18th St; ☙; **M** 18th St, **B** 16th St Mission) San Francisco's biggest mural is the 1994 *MaestraPeace*, a show of female strength painted by 90 *muralistas* that hugs the Women's Building. Featured icons range from ancient Mayan and Chinese goddesses to modern trailblazers, including Nobel Prize–winner Rigoberta Menchu, poet Audre Lorde and artist Georgia O'Keeffe.

The Haight

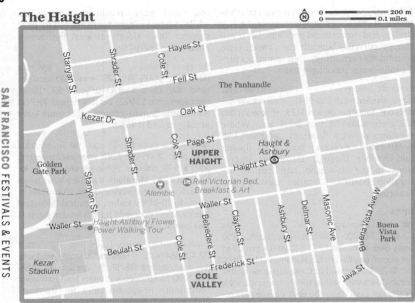

0 — 200 m
0 — 0.1 miles

Hayes St
Stanyan St
Shrader St
Cole St
Fell St
The Panhandle
Kezar Dr
Oak St
Shrader St
Cole St
Page St
Haight &
Ashbury
UPPER
HAIGHT
Haight St
Golden
Gate Park
Stanyan St
Alembic
Red Victorian Bed,
Breakfast & Art
Ashbury St
Delmar St
Masonic Ave
Buena Vista Ave W
Waller St
Waller St
Haight-Ashbury Flower
Power Walking Tour
Belvedere St
Clayton St
Buena
Vista
Park
Kezar
Stadium
Beulah St
Cole St
Frederick St
Java St
COLE
VALLEY

and theme: Art Deco Marina, Gold Rush Downtown, Secrets of Fisherman's Wharf, Telegraph Hill Stairway Hike and more.

Sea Foraging Adventures　　TOUR
(www.seaforager.com; tours from $42 per person; ⊙calendar & reservations online) California sealife expert Kirk Lombard leads guided adventures to secret foraging spots around San Francisco's waterfront, finding urban edibles ranging from bullwhip seaweed to eels under the Golden Gate Bridge.

Emperor Norton's Fantastic Time Machine　　TOUR
(http://emperornortontour.com/; tours depart from Union Square; tours $20; ⊙tours 11am & 2:30pm Tue & Sun; ☒2,38, ⒷPowell) Gold Rush through Wild West legends in a 2¾-hour walking tour led by SF's self-proclaimed Emperor Norton, the eccentric schemer and Bay Bridge dreamer reincarnated by SF historian Joseph Amster.

Haight-Ashbury Flower Power Walking Tour　　WALKING
(Map p90; ☎415-863-1621; www.haightashburytour. com; adult/child under 9yr $20/free; ⊙10:30am Tue & Sat, 2pm Thu, 11am Fri; ☒6, 71, ⓂN) Take a long, strange trip through 12 blocks of hippie history in two hours, following the steps of

Jimi, Jerry and Janis – if you have to ask for last names, you totally need this tour. Tours meet at the corner of Stanyan and Waller Sts; reservations required.

★ Festivals & Events

February
Lunar New Year　　CULTURAL
(www.chineseparade.com) Firecrackers, legions of tiny-tot martial artists and a 200ft dancing dragon make this parade the highlight of San Francisco winters.

April & May
SF International Film Festival　　FILM
(www.sffs.org) Stars align and directors launch premieres each April at the nation's oldest film festival.

Bay to Breakers　　SPORT
(www.baytobreakers.com; race registration $58-89.50) Run costumed from Embarcadero to Ocean Beach (7.5 miles) on the third Sunday in May, while joggers dressed as salmon run upstream.

June
SF Pride Celebration　　CULTURAL
A day isn't enough to do SF proud: June begins with International LGBT Film Festival (www.frameline.org; ⊙mid-Jun) and goes out in

City Walk
San Francisco Hilltops

START DRAGON GATE
FINISH GRACE CATEHDRAL
LENGTH 2.3 MILES; 2½ HOURS

Conquer San Francisco's three most famous hills – Telegraph, Russian and Nob – for views that are pure poetry.

Enter Chinatown's **❶ Dragon Gate** and walk up dragon-lantern-lined Grant Ave to Sacramento St. Turn left half a block up, then right onto **❷ Waverly Place** (p73), where prayer flags grace painted temple balconies. At Clay St, jog left and right again onto **❸ Spofford Alley** (p73), where Sun Yat-sen plotted revolution. At the end of the block on Washington, take a right and an immediate left onto mural-lined **❹ Ross Alley** (p73), once San Francisco's bordello byway.

Turn right down Jackson to Grant, then turn right onto **❺ Jack Kerouac Alley**, where the pavement echoes Kerouac's ode to San Francisco: 'The air was soft, the stars so fine, and the promise of every cobbled alley so great...' Ahead is literary landmark

❻ City Lights (p72), where you'll pause to read a poem upstairs in the designated Poet's Chair.

Head left up Columbus and veer right up Vallejo to fuel up with an espresso at **❼ Caffe Trieste** (p101), where Francis Ford Coppola drafted his script for *The Godfather*. Continue up Vallejo and scale the steps to Montgomery St. Go left three blocks, and turn left onto cottage-lined **❽ Greenwich Street Steps** to summit Telegraph Hill. Inside **❾ Coit Tower** (p79), enjoy 1934 city views in newly restored murals downstairs and panoramic Bay views up top.

Head downhill, past wild parrots and tai-chi masters at **❿ Washington Square**. Turn left on Columbus, right on Vallejo, and up three blocks to take another picturesque stairway path to flower-lined **⓫ Ina Coolbrith Park**. Any breath you have left will be taken away by sweeping views to Alcatraz. Summit your last hill of the day the easy way: catch the **⓬ Powell-Mason cable car** up Nob Hill to walk the meditation labyrinth at **⓭ Grace Cathedral** (p78).

SAN FRANCISCO

The Richmond, The Sunset & Golden Gate Park

1 km
0.5 miles

Iris Ave
Cook St
Spruce St
Parker Ave
Commonwealth Ave
Palm Ave
Arguello Blvd
2nd Ave
3rd Ave
4th Ave
5th Ave
6th Ave
7th Ave
8th Ave
9th Ave
10th Ave
11th Ave
12th Ave
Funston Ave
14th Ave
15th Ave
16th Ave
17th Ave
18th Ave
19th Ave
20th Ave
21st Ave

University of San Francisco
Turk Blvd
Rossi Playground
Balboa St
Cabrillo St
Funston Ave
14th Ave
15th Ave
16th Ave
17th Ave
18th Ave
19th Ave
20th Ave
21st Ave
22nd Ave
23rd Ave
24th Ave

Park Presidio Blvd

Lake St
California St
Clement St
Geary Blvd
Anza St
25th Ave

Fulton St

Frederick St
Stanyan St
John F Kennedy Dr
Lawn Bowling Club
Children's Playground
Kezar Dr
Lincoln Way
Hugo St
Carl St
Parnassus Ave
3rd Ave
4th Ave
5th Ave
6th Ave
7th Ave
8th Ave
9th Ave
10th Ave
11th Ave
12th Ave
Funston Ave
14th Ave
15th Ave
16th Ave
17th Ave
18th Ave

California Academy of Sciences
Lily Pond
Bowling Green Dr

MH de Young Museum

Strawberry Hill
Stow Lake

Crossover Dr

Lloyd Lake
Golden Gate Park
Elk Glen Lake
Mersey Lake
Martin Luther King Dr

THE RICHMOND

26th Ave
27th Ave
28th Ave
29th Ave
30th Ave
31st Ave
32nd Ave
33rd Ave
34th Ave
35th Ave
36th Ave
37th Ave
38th Ave

Irving St
24th Ave
25th Ave
26th Ave
27th Ave
28th Ave
29th Ave
30th Ave
31st Ave
32nd Ave
33rd Ave
34th Ave
35th Ave

THE SUNSET

Sunset Blvd
38th Ave

Lincoln Park Golf Course
Camino del Mar
34th Ave
Lincoln Park
Fort Miley
Clement St

Spreckels Lake
Golden Gate Park Stables
John F Kennedy Dr
Middle Dr W

39th Ave
40th Ave
41st Ave
42nd Ave

Point Lobos Ave
Balboa St
Cabrillo St
Anza St
Fulton St
45th Ave
47th Ave
48th Ave
La Playa St

North Lake
Middle Lake
South Lake

Lincoln Way
Irving St
Judah St
44th Ave
45th Ave
46th Ave
47th Ave
48th Ave

OCEAN BEACH

Point Lobos

Lincoln Park
Sutro Heights Park
Windmills
47th Ave
Upper Great Hwy
Great Hwy

PACIFIC OCEAN

Point Lobos
Seal Rocks

The Richmond, The Sunset & Golden Gate Park

style the last weekend with Pink Saturday's **Dyke March** (www.dykemarch.org) and **Pride Parade** (www.sfpride.org).

August & September

Outside Lands   MUSIC
(www.sfoutsidelands.com/; 1-/3-day $115/375) Three days of major acts – such as Kanye West, Macklemore, The Killers, The Flaming Lips – and outlandish debauchery at Wine Land, Beer Lands and Taste of the Bay.

Folsom Street Fair   STREET FAIR
(www.folsomstreetfair.com) Work that leather look and enjoy public spankings for local charities the last weekend of September.

October & November

Litquake   LITERATURE
(www.litquake.org) Score signed books and grab drinks with authors in October.

Hardly Strictly Bluegrass   MUSIC
(www.strictlybluegrass.com) Three days of free Golden Gate Park concerts and headliners ranging from Elvis Costello to Gillian Welch; early October.

Día de los Muertos   FESTIVAL
(Day of the Dead; www.dayofthedeadsf.org) Party to wake the dead with a spooky costume parade, sugar skulls and fabulous altars in the Mission on November 2.

🛏 Sleeping

🛏 Union Square & the Tenderloin

Hotel des Arts   HOTEL $
(Map p82; ☎ 415-956-3232, 800-956-4322; www.sfhoteldesarts.com; 447 Bush St; r with bath $129-

199, without bath $99; ☜; Ⓜ Montgomery, Ⓑ Montgomery) A budget hotel for art freaks, with jaw-dropping murals by underground artists – it's like sleeping inside a painting. Rooms with private bath require seven-night stays. Bring earplugs.

Pacific Tradewinds Hostel   HOSTEL $
(Map p82; ☎ 415-433-7970, 888-734-6783; www.sanfranciscohostel.org; 680 Sacramento St; dm $35; @ ☜; ☒ 1, ⬚ California St, Ⓑ Montgomery) San Francisco's smartest-looking all-dorm hostel has a blue-and-white nautical theme, fully equipped kitchen, spotless glass-brick showers, no lockout time and great staff. No elevator means hauling bags up three flights.

Hotel Carlton   DESIGN HOTEL $$
(Map p76; ☎ 415-673-0242, 800-922-7586; www.hotelcarltonsf.com; 1075 Sutter St; r $175-245; @ ☜ ☒; ☒ 2, 3, 19, 38, 47, 49) ◉ World travelers fit right into this freshly renovated hotel off the beaten track – a 10-minute walk to Union Square. Spotless rooms have an upbeat, worldly vibe, with colorful bedspreads and tapestry pillows. Rooftop solar panels help keep the hotel carbon neutral; downstairs is a top-notch Middle Eastern restaurant.

Phoenix Hotel   MOTEL $$
(Map p76; ☎ 415-776-1380, 800-248-9466; www.thephoenixhotel.com; 601 Eddy St; r $209-244; Ⓟ ☜ ☒; ☒ 19, 31, 47, 49) The ultimate rocker crash pad earns street cred with courtyard pool parties (bring earplugs), rooms packed with pop art, and a long list of California rebels (Red Hot Chili Peppers, Joan Jett, Keanu Reeves) who frequent this cool converted midcentury motel in the gritty Tenderloin. Free parking and admission to Kabuki Springs & Spa (p89).

WORTH A TRIP

OCEAN BEACH

Bundle up for strolls along the blustery 4-mile stretch of Ocean Beach (Map p92; ☑415-561-4323; www.parksconservancy.org; Great Hwy; ☉sunrise-sunset; ☐5, 18, 31, Ⓜ N), where Golden Gate Park greenery ends and the great blue Pacific Ocean begins. Dedicated sand-castle architects dot the water's edge year-round, but only hardcore surfers brave these riptides (casual swimmers beware). Beachcombers may spot sand dollars and 19th-century shipwrecks along the south end – but stick to paths in fragile dunes, where skittish snowy plover shorebirds shelter in winter. Bonfires are permitted in artist-designed fire pits only; no alcohol allowed. For drinks, stop by oceanfront Beach Chalet (Map p92; ☑415-386-8439; www.beachchalet.com; 1000 Great Hwy; ☉9am-10pm Mon-Thu, to 11pm Fri, 8am-11pm Sat, 8am-10pm Sun; ☝; ☐5, 18, 31) for house-brewed beer on the heated patio and 1930s lobby murals.

Golden Gate Hotel HOTEL $$
(Map p76; ☑415-392-3702, 800-835-1118; www.goldengatehotel.com; 775 Bush St; r with/without bath $190/135; @☎; ☐2, 3, ☐Powell-Hyde, Powell-Mason) Like an old-fashioned *pensione*, this 1913 Edwardian inn has kindly owners and homey mismatched furniture. Rooms are simple and cozy, most with private baths – request an antique claw-foot tub. Homemade cookies and a resident cat provide comfort after sightseeing.

★**Orchard Garden Hotel** BOUTIQUE HOTEL $$$
(Map p82; ☑415-399-9807, 888-717-2881; www.theorchardgardenhotel.com; 466 Bush St; r $295-370; ✳@☎; ☐2, 3, 30, 45, ⒷMontgomery) ✎ San Francisco's first all-green-practices hotel features sustainable wood furnishings, chemical-free cleaning products, and a sunny rooftop terrace. Luxe touches include fluffy down pillows and Egyptian-cotton sheets in soothingly quiet rooms.

Hotel Rex BOUTIQUE HOTEL $$$
(Map p76; ☑415-433-4434, 800-433-4434; www.thehotelrex.com; 562 Sutter St; r $287-309; ✳@☎✳; ☐Powell-Hyde, Powell-Mason, ⓂPowell, ⒷPowell) ✎ French gramophone music evokes New York's Algonquin in the

1920s, and handsome guestrooms feature hand-painted lampshades, local art and plush beds piled with crisp linens and down pillows. Street-facing rooms are bright but noisy; request air-con.

🛏 North Beach

San Remo Hotel HOTEL $$
(Map p84; ☑415-776-8688, 800-352-7366; www.sanremohotel.com; 2237 Mason St; r with shared bath $99-139; @☎✳; ☐30, 47, ☐Powell-Mason) One of the city's best-value stays, this 1906 inn is an old-fashioned charmer with antique furnishings. Bargain rooms have windows facing the corridor; family suites accommodate up to five. No elevator.

★**Hotel Bohème** BOUTIQUE HOTEL $$$
(Map p82; ☑415-433-9111; www.hotelboheme.com; 444 Columbus Ave; r $214-275; @☎; ☐10, 12, 30, 41, 45) A love letter to the Beat era, with vintage photos, parasol lights and moody 1950s color schemes. Rooms are smallish and some face noisy Columbus Ave – but the vibrant North Beach neighborhood scene could inspire your next novel.

🛏 Fisherman's Wharf

★**HI San Francisco Fisherman's Wharf** HOSTEL $
(Map p84; ☑415-771-7277; www.sfhostels.com; Bldg 240, Fort Mason; dm incl breakfast $30-42, r $75-109; 🅿@☎; ☐28, 30, 47, 49) A former army hospital building offers bargain-priced private rooms and dorms (some co-ed) with four to 22 beds and a huge kitchen. No curfew, but no heat during the day – bring warm clothes. Limited free parking.

★**Argonaut Hotel** BOUTIQUE HOTEL $$$
(Map p84; ☑415-563-0800, 800-790-1415; www.argonauthotel.com; 495 Jefferson St; r $389-449, with view $489-529; ✳☎✳; ☐19, 47, 49, ☐Powell-Hyde) ✎ Built as a cannery in 1908, Fisherman's Wharf's best inn has century-old wooden beams, exposed brick walls and an over-the-top nautical theme that includes porthole-shaped mirrors. Ultra-comfy beds and iPod docks are standard, though some rooms are small and dark – pay extra for mesmerising bay views.

🛏 The Marina & Pacific Heights

Coventry Motor Inn MOTEL $$
(Map p84; ☑415-567-1200; www.coventrymotorinn.com; 1901 Lombard St; r $155-165; 🅿✳☎;

GOLDEN GATE PARK

When San Franciscans refer to 'the park,' there's only one that gets the definite article. Everything they hold dear is in Golden Gate Park (Map p92; http://sfrecpark.org; 🚻 🚳; 🚌 5, 18, 21, 28, 29, 33, 44, 71, Ⓜ N) 🐾, including free spirits, free music, Frisbee and bison.

At the east end you can join year-round drum circles at Hippie Hill, sweater-clad athletes at the historic Lawn Bowling Club, toddlers clinging for dear life onto the 100-year-old carousel and meditators in the contemplative AIDS Memorial Grove (Map p92). To the west, turtles paddle past model yachts at Spreckels Lake, offerings are made at pagan altars behind the baseball diamond and free concerts are held in the Polo Fields, site of 1967's hippie Human Be-In.

This scenery seems far-fetched now, but impossible when proposed in 1866. When New York's Central Park architect Frederick Law Olmsted balked at transforming 1017 acres of dunes into the world's largest developed park, San Francisco's green scheme fell to tenacious young civil engineer William Hammond Hall. He insisted that instead of casinos, resorts, race tracks and an igloo village, park features should include botanical gardens (Strybing Arboretum; Map p92; 🖉 415-661-1316; www.strybing.org; 1199 9th Ave; adult/child $7/5, 2nd Tue of month free; ☺ 9am-6pm Apr-Oct, to 5pm Nov-Mar, bookstore 10am-4pm; 🚻; 🚌 6, 43, 44, 71, Ⓜ N) 🐾, a dedicated bison paddock (Map p92) and waterfalls at Stow Lake.

Today the park offers 7.5 miles of bicycle trails, 12 miles of equestrian trails, an archery range, fly-casting pools, four soccer fields and 21 tennis courts. Sundays, when JFK Dr closes to traffic around 9th Ave, don't miss roller disco and lindy-hopping in the park. Other times, catch these park highlights:

MH de Young Museum (Map p92; 🖉 415-750-3600; http://deyoung.famsf.org/; 50 Hagiwara Tea Garden Dr; adult/child $10/6, discount with Muni ticket $2, 1st Tue of month free, online booking fee $1 per ticket; ☺ 9:30am-5:15pm Tue-Sun, to 8:45pm Fri Apr-Nov; 🚌 5, 44, 71, Ⓜ N) Follow sculptor Andy Goldsworthy's artificial earthquake fault in the sidewalk into Herzog + de Meuron's faultlessly sleek, copper-clad building that's oxidizing green to blend into the park. Don't be fooled by the de Young's camouflaged exterior: shows here boldly broaden artistic horizons, from Oceanic ceremonial masks and Bulgari jewels to California photographer Anthony Friedkin's 1970s portraits of gay liberation.

California Academy of Sciences (Map p92; 🖉 415-379-8000; www.calacademy.org; 55 Music Concourse Dr; adult/child $34.95/24.95, discount with Muni ticket $3; ☺ 9:30am-5pm Mon-Sat, 11am-5pm Sun; 🅿 🚻; 🚌 5, 6, 31, 33, 44, 71, Ⓜ N) Architect Renzo Piano's landmark, LEED-certified green building houses 38,000 weird and wonderful animals, with a four-story rainforest and split-level aquarium under a 'living roof' of California wildflowers. After the penguins nod off to sleep, the wild rumpus starts at kids'-only Academy Sleepovers and over-21 NightLife Thursdays, when rainforest-themed cocktails encourage strange mating rituals among shy first dates.

Japanese Tea Garden (Map p92; 🖉 tea ceremony reservations 415-752-1171; www.japanese-teagardensf.com; 75 Hagiwara Tea Garden Dr; adult/child $7/2, before 10am Mon, Wed & Fri free; ☺ 9am-6pm Mar-Oct, to 4:45pm Nov-Feb; 🅿 🚻; 🚌 5, 44, 71, Ⓜ N) Since 1894, this 5-acre garden has blushed with cherry blossoms in spring, turned flaming red with maple leaves in fall, and lost all track of time in the meditative Zen Garden. The 100-year-old bonsai grove is the legacy of founder Makoto Hagiwara, who tended them until his family's forced deportation to WWII Japanese American internment camps, and spent decades afterwards restoring these priceless miniature evergreens. Don't miss green tea and fortune cookies (invented for the garden's opening) at the tea pavilion.

Conservatory of Flowers (Map p92; 🖉 info 415-831-2090; www.conservatoryofflowers.org; 100 John F Kennedy Dr; adult/child $7/2, 1st Tue of month free; ☺ 10am-4:30pm Tue-Sun; 🚌 5, Ⓜ N) Flower power thrives inside this restored 1878 Victorian greenhouse, where orchids dangle from the ceiling like trapeze artists, lilies float contemplatively and creepy carnivorous plants make lunch of passing insects.

❶ DEALS & HIDDEN COSTS

San Francisco is the birthplace of the boutique hotel, offering stylish rooms for a price: $150-plus for most midrange rooms, plus 16% hotel tax (hostels exempt) and $35 to $50 for overnight parking. For last-minute vacancies and deals, check Lonely Planet (http://hotels.lonelyplanet.com) and San Francisco–based accommodations specialists HotelTonight (www.hotel tonight.com), Airbnb (www.airbnb. com), Bed & Breakfast SF (www. bbsf.com), Hipmunk (www.hipmunk. com) and Hotwire (www.hotwire.com).

🖼22, 28, 30, 43) Of the many motels lining Lombard St (Hwy 101), the generic Coventry has the highest quality-to-value ratio with spacious, plain, well-maintained rooms and extras like air-con and covered parking.

⭐**Hotel Drisco**　　BOUTIQUE HOTEL $$$
(Map p84; ☎415-346-2880, 800-634-7277; www.hoteldrisco.com; 2901 Pacific Ave; r incl breakfast $375-425; @🛜; 🖼3, 24) A stately apartment-hotel tucked between Pacific Heights mansions, with elegant architecture, attentive service and understated-chic room decor. At this lofty ridgeline location, spring for city-view rooms and taxis.

🛌 SoMa

Hotel Vitale　　BOUTIQUE HOTEL $$$
(Map p76; ☎415-278-3700, 888-890-8688; www.hotelvitale.com; 8 Mission St; r $419-509; ❋@🛜❉; Ⓜ Embarcadero, Ⓑ Embarcadero) Behind that tinted glass is a laid-back luxury waterfront hotel. The clever Vitale has thought of everything: 450-thread-count sheets, on-site spa with two rooftop hot tubs and a sleek downstairs lounge. Get bayfront rooms for spectacular Bay Bridge views.

Good Hotel　　MOTEL $$$
(Map p76; ☎415-621-7001, 800-444-5819; www. thegoodhotel.com; 112 7th St; r $199-279; @🛜❉; Ⓜ Civic Center, Ⓑ Civic Center) 🏖 SF's hip green motel, with reclaimed-wood headboards, upcycled-bottle chandeliers, and fleece bedspreads made from recycled soda bottles. Drawbacks are the sketchy neighborhood and street noise; book rooms in back.

🛌 The Mission & the Castro

Inn San Francisco　　B&B $$
(Map p86; ☎800-359-0913, 415-641-0188; www. innsf.com; 943 S Van Ness Ave; r incl breakfast $185-310, with shared bath $135-200; 🅿@🛜; 🖼14, 49) 🏖 An impeccably maintained 1872 Italianate-Victorian mansion, this inn has period antiques, fresh-cut flowers, and fluffy featherbeds; some have Jacuzzi tubs. There's also a freestanding garden cottage that sleeps up to six. Outside there's an English garden and redwood hot tub. Limited parking: reserve ahead.

Inn on Castro　　GLBT, B&B $$
(Map p86; ☎415-861-0321; www.innoncastro.com; 321 Castro St; r incl breakfast $165-185, without bath $125-145, self-catering apt $165-210; 🛜; Ⓜ Castro) Flashback to the Castro's disco heyday inside this Edwardian townhouse with '70s-mod furnishings. Rooms are retro-cool and breakfasts exceptional – the owner is a chef. Ask about nearby apartments also available for rental.

Parker Guest House　　B&B $$$
(Map p86; ☎415-621-3222, 888-520-7275; www. parkerguesthouse.com; 520 Church St; r incl breakfast $209-259; @🛜; 🖼33, ⒿJ) Welcome to the Castro's stateliest gay digs, inside twin Edwardian mansions sharing a garden and steam room. Elegant rooms have cushy beds with down duvets; bath fixtures gleam.

🛌 The Haight & Hayes Valley

Metro Hotel　　HOTEL $
(Map p86; ☎415-861-5364; www.metrohotelsf. com; 319 Divisadero St; r $88-100; @🛜; 🖼6, 24, 71) A central Haight hotel providing cheap, clean rooms with private bath, 24-hour reception, a garden patio and excellent pizza downstairs. No elevator.

Chateau Tivoli　　B&B $$
(☎415-776-5462, 800-228-1647; www.chateau-tivoli.com; 1057 Steiner St; r incl breakfast $175-215, with shared bath $115-135; 🛜; 🖼5, 22) This glorious chateau off Alamo Sq once hosted Isadora Duncan and Mark Twain, and shows plenty of character with turrets, carved woodwork and (rumor has it) the ghost of a Victorian opera diva. No elevator, no TV.

Red Victorian Bed, Breakfast & Art　　B&B $$
(Map p90; ☎415-864-1978; www.redvic.net; 1665 Haight St; r incl breakfast $179-189, without bath $119-149; 🛜; 🖼33, 43, 71) 🏖 The trippy '60s

live on inside this 1904 Victorian, with theme rooms like Sunshine, Flower Children and Summer of Love. Only four of 18 rooms have baths, but all include breakfast in the organic Peace Café downstairs. Reduced rates for longer stays; no elevator.

Hayes Valley Inn
HOTEL **$$**

(Map p76; ☑ 415-431-9131, 800-930-7999; www.hayesvalleyinn.com; 417 Gough St; d incl breakfast $93-115, queen $103-126; @ 🛜 🐾; 🚇 21, Ⓜ Van Ness) Amid tempting boutiques and bistros, this amazingly reasonable find has simple, small rooms with shared baths, kindly staff and a good-natured resident dog. Bring ear plugs and expect a walk to the nearest bathroom; no elevator.

Parsonage
B&B **$$$**

(Map p86; ☑ 415-863-3699; www.theparsonage.com; 198 Haight St; r $220-270; @ 🛜; 🚇 6, 71, streetcar F) The charming owners are justly proud of their 23-room Italianate-Victorian's gorgeous original details, including brass chandeliers and Carrara-marble fireplaces. Airy rooms are bedecked with oriental rugs and period antiques. Take breakfast in the formal dining room, and nightcaps of brandy and chocolate by the fire.

✗ Eating

✗ Union Square

farm:table
AMERICAN **$**

(Map p76; ☑ 415-292-7089; www.farmtablesf.com; 754 Post St; dishes $6-9; ⊘ 7:30am-2pm Tue-Fri, 8am-3pm Sat & Sun; 🚇 2, 3, 27, 38) 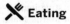 A tiny storefront with one wooden communal table inside, two tables and a stand-up outdoor counter, farm:table uses local organics and rooftop-grown herbs in daily menus posted on Twitter (@farmtable). Cash only.

Sweet Woodruff
CAFE, CALIFORNIAN **$**

(Map p76; ☑ 415-292-9090; www.sweetwoodruffsf.com; 798 Sutter St; dishes $8-14; ⊘ 8am-9:30pm Mon-Fri, 9:30am-9:30pm Sat & Sun; 🚇 2, 3, 27) Little sister to neighboring Michelin-starred Sons & Daughters, this storefront features top-end, seasonal-regional ingredients in small plates like roasted padron peppers with fromage blanc and sea-urchin baked potatoes with bacon. No waiters, no frills, just tasty.

Cafe Claude
FRENCH **$$**

(Map p76; ☑ 415-392-3505; www.cafeclaude.com; 7 Claude Lane; mains $15-23; ⊘ 11:30am-10:30pm Mon-Sat, 5:30pm-10:30pm Sun; Ⓜ Montgomery)

Montgomery) Hidden in an alleyway, Cafe Claude is a sweet downtown retreat with outdoor tables and effortlessly charming staff. Lunch is served until 5pm, jazz combos play weekends, and coq au vin and a stellar wine list make dream dates.

✗ Chinatown & North Beach

★ Liguria Bakery
BAKERY **$**

(Map p82; ☑ 415-421-3786; 1700 Stockton St; focaccia $4-5; ⊘ 8am-1pm Tue-Fri, from 7am Sat; 🅿 🚼; 🚇 8X, 30, 39, 41, 45, 🚋 Powell-Mason) Bleary-eyed art students and Italian grandmothers line up by 8am for cinnamon-raisin focaccia hot from the 100-year-old oven, leaving 9am dawdlers a choice of tomato or classic rosemary. Take yours in wax paper or boxed for picnics; cash only.

City View
CHINESE **$**

(Map p82; ☑ 415-398-2838; 662 Commercial St; dishes $3-8; ⊘ 11am-2:30pm Mon-Fri, from 10am Sat & Sun; 🚇 8X, 10, 12, 30, 45, 🚋 California St) Order off the menu or hail carts loaded with shrimp dumplings, garlicky Chinese broccoli, tangy spare ribs and other tantalizing dim sum. Arrive before noon for first picks from fragrant bamboo steamers.

★ Cotogna
ITALIAN **$$**

(Map p82; ☑ 415-775-8508; www.cotognasf.com; 490 Pacific Ave; mains $17-29; ⊘ 11:30am-11pm Mon-Thu, 11:30am-midnight Fri & Sat, 5-9:30pm Sun; 🅿; 🚇 10, 12) Rustic Italian pastas, woodfired pizzas and rotisserie meats spiked with rooftop-grown herbs show chef Michael Tusk's finesse with well-chosen, balanced ingredients. Book ahead or plan a late lunch.

Z & Y
CHINESE **$$**

(Map p82; ☑ 415-981-8988; www.zandyrestaurant.com; 655 Jackson St; mains $9-20; ⊘ 11am-9:30pm Mon-Thu, to 10:30pm Fri-Sun; 🚇 8X, 🚋 Powell-Mason, Powell-Hyde) Graduate from so-so sweet-and-sour and middling *mu-shu* pork to sensational Szechuan dishes that go down in a blaze of glory: spicy pork dumplings, heat-blistered string beans, housemade noodles, and fish poached in flaming chili oil. Go early; expect a wait.

Cinecittà
PIZZA **$$**

(Map p82; ☑ 415-291-8830; www.cinecittarestaurant.com; 663 Union St; pizza $12-15; ⊘ noon-10pm Sun-Thu, to 11pm Fri & Sat; 🅿 🚼; 🚇 8X, 30, 39, 41, 45, 🚋 Powell-Mason) Squeeze in at the counter for thin-crust pizza served with local brews on tap and sass by Roman owner Romina.

ℹ SF MEALS & DEALS

Hope you're hungry: there are more restaurants per capita in San Francisco than in any other US city. Scan for deals at www.blackboardeats.com and www.opentable.com – and since SF's top restaurants are quite small, reserve now. Some restaurants brazenly tack on a 4% surcharge to cover city-mandated healthcare for SF food workers. Factor in 9.5% tax on top of your meal price, plus 15% to 25% for the tip.

North Beach loyalties are divided between the Roman Travestere (mozzarella, arugula and prosciutto) and Neapolitan O Sole Mio (capers, olives, mozzarella and anchovies).

★ Coi   CALIFORNIAN $$$

(Map p82; ☑ 415-393-9000; www.coirestaurant.com; 373 Broadway; set menu $195; ⊙5:30-10pm Tue-Sat; 🚍8X, 30, 41, 45, 🚠Powell-Mason) 🍴 Chef Daniel Patterson's restlessly imaginative eight-course tasting menu is like licking California's coastline: rooftop-raised pansies grace Sonoma duck's tongue, and wild-caught abalone surfaces in pea-shoot tidepools. Settle in among the shaggy cushions and spot-lit stoneware to enjoy only-in-California wine pairings ($115; generous enough for two).

✕ Fisherman's Wharf & Russian Hill

Fisherman's Wharf Crab Stands   SEAFOOD $

(Map p84; foot of Taylor St; mains $5-15; Ⓜ F) Brawny-armed men stir steaming cauldrons of Dungeness crab at takeaway crab stands at the foot of Taylor St. Crab season runs winter through spring, but you'll find shrimp and seafood year-round. Take your haul to Pier 43 Promenade benches, or duck through glass doors marked 'Passageway to the Boats' at 8/9 Fisherman's Wharf for dockside lunches.

★ Gary Danko   CALIFORNIAN $$$

(Map p84; ☑ 415-749-2060; www.garydanko.com; 800 North Point St; 3-/5-course menu $76/111; ⊙5:30-10pm; 🚍19, 30, 47, 🚠Powell-Hyde) The true test of SF romance is whether you're willing to share Gary Danko's crèmes brûlée trio. Smoked-glass windows prevent passersby from tripping over their tongues at roast lobster with trumpet mushrooms, duck breast with rhubarb compote, and the lavish cheese cart. Reservations required.

✕ The Marina, Japantown & Pacific Heights

Off the Grid   FOOD TRUCK $

(Map p84; www.offthegridsf.com; 2 Marina Blvd; dishes $5-10; ⊙5-11pm Fri; 🚻; 🚍22, 28) Some 30 food trucks converge Fridays for SF's largest mobile-gourmet hootenanny (other nights/locations attract fewer trucks; see website). Arrive before 6:30pm or expect 20-minute waits for Chairman Bao's roast duck buns, Roli Roti's free-range herbed roast chicken, and Crème Brûlée Man desserts. Cash only; enjoy takeout dockside with Golden Gate Bridge sunsets.

★ Greens   VEGETARIAN, CALIFORNIAN $$

(Map p84; ☑ 415-771-6222; www.greensrestaurant.com; Bldg A, Fort Mason Center, cnr Marina Blvd & Laguna St; lunch $15-18, dinner $18-25; ⊙11:45am-2:30pm & 5:30-9pm Tue-Fri, from 11am Sat, 10:30am-2pm & 5:30-9pm Sun, 5:30-9pm Mon; 🍴🚻; 🚍28) 🍴 Career carnivores won't realize there's zero meat in hearty roasted-eggplant panini and black-bean chili with crème fraîche and pickled jalapeños – they're packed with flavor-bursting ingredients grown on a Zen farm in Marin. Make reservations on weekends, or get take-out to enjoy on a wharf-side bench.

State Bird Provisions   CALIFORNIAN $$

(☑415-795-1272; statebirdsf.com; 1529 Fillmore St; ⊙5:30-10pm Sun-Thu, to 11pm Fri & Sat; 🚍22, 38) James Beard dubbed State Bird America's best new restaurant in 2013 for its wildly inventive take on dim sum, with esoteric local ingredients like fennel pollen and garum (fish extract). Book ahead, or arrive by 5pm for a coveted walk-in bar spot. Prices are deceptive; all those small plates add up.

Tataki   JAPANESE $$

(Map p84; ☑ 415-931-1182; www.tatakisushibar.com; 2815 California St; dishes $12-20; ⊙11:30am-2pm & 5:30-10pm Mon-Thu, 11:30am-2pm & 5:30-10:30pm Fri, 5-10:30pm Sat, 5-9:30pm Sun; 🚍1, 24) 🍴 Pioneering sustainable sushi chefs Kin Lui, Raymond Ho and Kenny Zhu rescue dinner and the oceans with silky farmed Arctic char with yuzu-citrus and the Golden State Roll – a California dream of spicy, line-caught scallop, Pacific tuna, organic avocado and apple slivers.

✕ SoMa

Zero Zero   PIZZA **$$**

(Map p76; ☎415-348-8800; www.zerozerosf.com;
826 Folsom St; pizzas $12-19; ⏱11:30am-2:30pm
& 4-10pm Mon-Thu, to 11pm Fri, 11:30am-11pm Sat,
11:30am-10pm Sun; Ⓜ Powell, Ⓑ Powell) The
name is a throw-down of Neapolitan pizza
credentials – '00' flour is used for Naples'
famous puffy-edged crust – and these pies
deliver on that promise, with inspired SF-
themed toppings. The Geary is a crossover
hit with Manila clams, bacon and chilies,
but the real crowd-pleaser is the Castro,
turbo-loaded with housemade sausage.

★ Benu   CALIFORNIAN, FUSION **$$$**

(Map p76; ☎415-685-4860; www.benusf.com; 22
Hawthorne St; tasting menu $195; ⏱5:30-8:30pm
Tue-Sat; ☐10, 12, 14, 30, 45) SF has refined fusion cuisine over 150 years, but no one rocks
it quite like chef/owner Corey Lee (formerly of Napa's French Laundry), who remixes
local, sustainable, fine-dining staples and
Pacific Rim flavors with a SoMa DJ's finesse.
Dungeness crab and truffle bring such outsize flavor to his faux-shark's-fin soup, you'll
swear there's Jaws in there.

✕ The Mission & the Castro

★ La Taqueria   MEXICAN **$**

(Map p86; ☎415-285-7117; 2889 Mission St; burritos $6-8; ⏱11am-9pm Mon-Sat, to 8pm Sun; ♿;
☐12, 14, 48, 49, Ⓑ24th St Mission) SF's definitive
burrito has no debatable saffron rice, spin-
ach tortilla or mango salsa – just perfectly
grilled meats, slow-cooked beans and classic
tomatillo or mesquite salsa wrapped in flour
tortillas.

★ Ichi Sushi   SUSHI **$$**

(☎415-525-4750; www.ichisushi.com; 3282 Mis-
sion St; sushi $4-8; ⏱5:30-10pm Mon-Thu, to 11pm
Fri & Sat; ☐14, 49, Ⓑ24th St Mission, Ⓜ J) Ichi
Sushi is a sharp cut above other fish joints.
Silky, sustainably sourced fish is sliced with
a jeweler's precision, balanced atop well-
packed rice, and topped with powerfully
tangy dabs of gelled yuzu and microscopi-
cally diced chili daikon that make soy sauce
unthinkable.

★ Namu Gaji   KOREAN, CALIFORNIAN **$$**

(Map p86; ☎415-431-6268; www.namusf.com; 499
Dolores St; small plates $10-21; ⏱11:30am-4pm
Wed-Fri, from 10:30am Sat & Sun, 5-10pm Tue-Thu
& Sun, 5-11pm Fri & Sat; ☐22, 33, Ⓜ J, Ⓑ16th St
Mission) 🌱 SF's culinary advantages are

THE FERRY BUILDING

San Francisco's monument to food, the **Ferry Building** (Map p76; ☎415-983-8000;
www.ferrybuildingmarketplace.com; Market St & the Embarcadero; ⏱10am-6pm Mon-Fri, 9am-
6pm Sat, 11am-5pm Sun; Ⓟ♿; Ⓜ Embarcadero, Ⓑ Embarcadero) still doubles as a trans-bay
transit hub – but with dining options like these, you may never leave.

Ferry Plaza Farmers Market (Map p76; ☎415-291-3276; www.cuesa.org; Market St &
the Embarcadero; ⏱10am-2pm Tue & Thu, 8am-2pm Sat; Ⓜ Embarcadero, Ⓑ Embarcadero)
Star chefs troll farmers-market stalls for rare heirloom varietals, foodie babies blissfully
teethe on organic apricots, and organic tamale trucks have rock-star fan bases. Pass
time in line exchanging recipe tips, then haul your picnic to Pier 2.

Slanted Door (Map p76; ☎415-861-8032; www.slanteddoor.com; 1 Ferry Bldg; lunch $16-36,
dinner $18-45; ⏱11am-4:30pm & 5:30-10pm Mon-Sat, 11:30am-4:30pm & 5:30-10pm Sun;
Ⓜ Embarcadero, Ⓑ Embarcadero) Charles Phan earns his 2014 James Beard Outstanding
Chef title with California-fresh, Vietnamese-inspired fare that rivals the sparkling Bay
views – especially five-spice duck with figs. Reserve ahead or hit the takeout window.

Hog Island Oyster Company (Map p76; ☎415-391-7117; www.hogislandoysters.com; 1
Ferry Bldg; 4 oysters $13; ⏱11:30am-9pm Mon-Thu, to 10pm Fri, 11am-10pm Sat, 11am-9pm Sun;
Ⓜ Embarcadero, Ⓑ Embarcadero) 🌱 Slurp sustainably farmed Tomales Bay oysters as you
please: drizzled with tangy caper buerre blanc, spiked with bacon and paprika, or au
naturel with Sonoma bubbly.

Mijita (Map p76; ☎415-399-0814; www.mijitasf.com; 1 Ferry Bldg; dishes $4-10; ⏱10am-7pm
Mon-Thu, to 8pm Fri, 9am-8pm Sat, 8:30am-3pm Sun; ⊘♿; Ⓜ Embarcadero, Ⓑ Embarcadero)
Sustainable fish tacos reign supreme and *agua fresca* (fruit punch) is made with fresh
juice at chef-owner Traci des Jardin's bayfront Cal-Mex joint.

showcased in Namu's Korean-inspired soul food. Menu standouts include ultra-savory shiitake mushroom dumplings, meltingly tender marinated beef tongue, and a sizzling stone pot of rice with organic vegetables, grass-fed steak and a Sonoma farm egg.

★**Frances** CALIFORNIAN $$$
(Map p86; ☑ 415-621-3870; www.frances-sf. com; 3870 17th St; mains $20-27; ⏱ 5-10pm Sun-Thu, to 10:30pm Fri & Sat; Ⓜ Castro) Chef/ owner Melissa Perello ditched downtown fine dining to start this bistro showcasing bright, seasonal flavors and luxurious textures: cloudlike sheep's-milk ricotta gnocchi with crunchy broccolini, grilled calamari with preserved Meyer lemon, and artisan wine served by the ounce, directly from Wine Country.

✕ The Haight & Hayes Valley

Second Act FOOD ARTISANS $
(http://secondactsf.com/; 1727 Haight St; dishes $5-12; ⏱ 8am-6pm, to 8pm Fri) When collectively run Red Vic movie house ended its 30-year run, neighbors demanded an encore – now Second Act Marketplace houses local

food makers and a neighborhood events space. Stop by for dumplings at Anda Piroshki, High Cotton Kitchen soul food, and the cherry-lavender ice cream at Eatwell Farm – and stay for Friday happy hours and indie-movie premieres (see website).

★**Rich Table** CALIFORNIAN $$$
(Map p86; ☑ 415-355-9085; http://richtablesf. com; 199 Gough St; meals $17-30; ⏱ 5:30-10pm Sun-Thu, to 10:30pm Fri & Sat; ☐ 5, 6, 21, 47, 49, 71, Ⓜ Van Ness) ✐ Licking plates is the obvious move after finishing chilled apricot soup with pancetta or rabbit cannelloni with nasturtium cream. Married co-chefs/co-owners Sarah and Evan Rich invent playful, exquisite Californian food like the Dirty Hippie: silky goat-buttermilk pannacotta topped with nutty sunflower seeds and hemp. Book two to four weeks ahead (call the restaurant directly) or arrive early for bar seating.

★**Jardinière** CALIFORNIAN $$$
(Map p76; ☑ 415-861-5555; www.jardiniere.com; 300 Grove St; mains $18-32; ⏱ 5-10:30pm Tue-Sat, to 10pm Sun & Mon; ☐ 5, 21, 47, 49, Ⓜ Van Ness) ✐ *Iron Chef, Top Chef* Master and James Beard Award–winner Traci Des Jardins

---

TOP SAN FRANCISCO TREATS

Life is sweet in San Francisco, where chocolate bars were invented in the Gold Rush and velvet ropes keep ice-cream lines from getting ugly. Before you dismiss dessert, consider these temptations.

➡ ★**Craftsman & Wolves** (Map p86; ☑ 415-913-7713; http://craftsman-wolves.com; 746 Valencia St; pastries $3-7; ⏱ 7am-7pm Mon-Thu, to 8pm Fri, 8am-8pm Sat, 8am-7pm Sun; ☐ 14, 22, 33, 49, Ⓑ 16th St Mission, Ⓜ J) A sleek counter fit to showcase diamonds offers something far better: exquisite salted-caramel eclairs and black-sesame checkered cake.

➡ **Bi-Rite Creamery** (Map p86; ☑ 415-626-5600; www.biritecreamery.com; 3692 18th St; ice cream $3-7; ⏱ 11am-10pm Sun-Thu, to 11pm Fri & Sat; ☻ ; ☐ 33, Ⓑ 16th St Mission, Ⓜ J) ✐ Organic ice cream worth the line even in foggy weather – especially salted caramel and balsamic strawberry.

➡ **Tout Sweet** (Map p76; ☑ 415-385-1679; www.toutsweetsf.com; Geary & Stockton Sts, Macy's, 3rd fl; baked goods $2-8; ⏱ 10am-8pm Mon-Wed, until 9pm Thu-Sat, 11am-7pm Sun; ☐ 2, 38, ☐ Powell-Mason, Powell-Hyde, Ⓑ Powell St) Bypass sales and head directly to Macy's 3rd floor, where *Top Chef* winner Yigit Pura reinvents French macarons in irreverent SF flavors like sour cherry/bourbon and peanut butter and jelly.

➡ **Benkyodo** (☑ 415-922-1244; www.benkyodocompany.com; 1747 Buchanan St; mochi $1.25-2; ⏱ 8am-5pm Mon-Sat; ☐ 2, 3, 22, 38) Legendary *mochi* (rice cakes) made in-house daily – come early for perennially popular green tea, peanut butter, and chocolate-filled strawberry flavors.

➡ **Mission Pie** (Map p86; ☑ 415-282-1500; www.missionpie.com; 2901 Mission St; pie slices $3.50-4; ⏱ 7am-10pm Mon-Fri, from 8am Sat, from 9am Sun; ☎ ✐ ☻ ; ☐ 12, 14, 48, 49, Ⓑ 24th St Mission) ✐ Warm, flaky, heirloom apple pie served with free organic whipped cream in a sunny, certified-green Victorian storefront with toys for kids.

champions sustainable, salacious California cuisine. She lavishes housemade tagliatelle with bone marrow and tops velvety scallops with satiny sea urchin. Go Mondays, when $55 scores three decadent courses with wine pairings.

The Richmond & the Sunset

★ Outerlands   CALIFORNIAN $$
(Map p92; ☑ 415-661-6140; www.outerlandssf. com; 4001 Judah St; sandwiches & small plates $7-14, mains $18-22; ⏲ 10am-3pm Tue-Fri, from 9am Sat & Sun, 5:30-10pm Tue-Sun; 🖱; 🚍 18, Ⓜ N) 🍴 When windy Ocean Beach leaves you feeling shipwrecked, drift into this beach-shack bistro for organic, seed-to-table California comfort food. Brunch demands Dutch pancakes in iron skillets with housemade ricotta, and lunch brings grilled artisan-cheese combos with farm-inspired soup. Reserve ahead or enjoy wine while you wait.

Nopalito   MEXICAN $$
(Map p92; ☑ 415-233-9966; www.nopalitosf.com; 1224 9th Ave; ⏲ 11:30am-10pm; 🖱; 🚍 6, 43, 44, 71, Ⓜ N) 🍴 Head south of Golden Gate Park's border for upscale, sustainably sourced Cal-Mex, including tasty *tortas* (flatbread sandwiches), tender *carnitas* (braised pork) tacos and cinnamon-laced Mexican hot chocolate. No reservations; call one to two hours ahead to join the wait list.

★ Aziza   MOROCCAN, CALIFORNIAN $$$
(Map p92; ☑ 415-752-2222; www.aziza-sf.com; 5800 Geary Blvd; mains $19-29; ⏲ 5:30-10pm Wed-Mon; 🚍 1, 29, 31, 38) *Iron Chef* champ Mourad Lahlou's inspiration is Moroccan and his ingredients organic Californian, but the flavors are out of this world: Sonoma duck confit and caramelized onion fill flaky pastry *basteeya*, and slow-cooked Marin lamb tops saffron-infused barley. Pastry chef Melissa Chou's apricot bavarian is a goodnight kiss.

🍷 Drinking & Nightlife

🍸 Union Square

★ Rickhouse   BAR
(Map p82; ☑ 415-398-2827; www.rickhousebar. com; 246 Kearny St; ⏲ 5pm-2am Mon, 3pm-2am Tue-Fri, 6pm-2am Sat; Ⓜ Montgomery, Ⓑ Montgomery) Like a shotgun shack plunked downtown, Rickhouse is lined with bourbon casks and shelving from an Ozark Mountains nunnery that once secretly brewed

hooch. The emphasis is on rare bourbon, but groups guzzle authentic Pisco Punch by the garage-sale punchbowl.

Irish Bank   PUB
(Map p82; ☑ 415-788-7152; www.theirishbank.com; 10 Mark Lane; ⏲ 11:30am-2am; Ⓜ Montgomery, Ⓑ Montgomery) Perfectly pulled pints, thick-cut fries with malt vinegar, and sausages with lashings of mustard are staples at this genuinely friendly Irish pub. Cozy snugs are great for conversation, but tables under alley awnings appeal to smokers.

Chinatown & North Beach

★ Caffe Trieste   CAFE
(Map p82; ☑ 415-392-6739; www.caffetrieste.com; 601 Vallejo St; ⏲ 6:30am-11pm Sun-Thu, to midnight Fri & Sat; 🛜; 🚍 8X, 10, 12, 30, 41, 45) Poetry on bathroom walls, opera on the jukebox, live accordion jams weekly and sightings of Beat poet laureate Lawrence Ferlinghetti: Trieste has been a North Beach landmark since the 1950s. Sip espresso under the Sicilian mural, where Francis Ford Coppola drafted *The Godfather*. Cash only.

★ Comstock Saloon   BAR
(Map p82; ☑ 415-617-0071; www.comstocksaloon. com; 155 Columbus Ave; ⏲ noon to 2am Mon-Fri, from 4pm Sat, 4pm-midnight Sun; 🚍 8X, 10, 12, 30, 45, 🚃 Powell-Mason) Cocktails at this Victorian saloon remain period-perfect: Pisco Punch is made with pineapple gum and martini-precursor Martinez features gin, vermouth, bitters and maraschino liqueur. Call ahead for booths or tufted-velvet parlor seating and to get dates when ragtime-jazz bands play.

Specs'   BAR
(☑ 415-421-4112; 12 William Saroyan Pl; ⏲ 4:30pm-2am Mon-Fri, from 5pm Sat & Sun) Order pitchers of Anchor Steam, admire walls plastered with merchant-marine memorabilia and join salty old-timers plotting mutinies against last call.

Li Po   BAR
(Map p82; ☑ 415-982-0072; www.lipolounge. com; 916 Grant Ave; ⏲ 2pm-2am; 🚍 8X, 30, 45, 🚃 Powell-Mason, Powell-Hyde) Beat a hasty retreat to red vinyl booths where Allen Ginsberg and Jack Kerouac debated the meaning of life alongside a bemused golden Buddha. Enter the 1937 faux-grotto doorway and dodge red lanterns to order beer or a sweet, sneaky-strong Chinese mai tai made with *baiju* (rice liquor). Bathrooms and random DJ appearances are in the basement.

🍸 Downtown & SoMa

★ Bar Agricole   BAR
(Map p86; ☎ 415-355-9400; www.baragricole.com; 355 11th St; ⊗ 6-10pm Tue-Thu & Sun, 5:30-11pm Fri & Sat; 🚌 9, 12, 27, 47) Drink your way to a history degree with these cocktails: Bellamy Scotch Sour with egg whites passes the test, but Tequila Fix with lime, pineapple gum and hellfire bitters earns honors. Don't miss the sea-urchin deviled eggs.

Blue Bottle Coffee Company   CAFE
(www.bluebottlecoffee.net; 66 Mint St; ⊗ 7am-7pm Mon-Fri, 8am-6pm Sat & Sun) The mad-scientist $20,000 coffee siphon yields superior fair-trade, organic drip coffee, rivaled only by bittersweet mochas and an off-menu invention called the Gibraltar.

Local Edition   LOUNGE
(☎ 415-795-1375; www.localeditionsf.com; 691 Market st; ⊗ 5pm-2am Mon-Fri, from 7pm Sat) Get the scoop on SF's cocktail scene at this new speakeasy in the historic Hearst newspaper building's basement. Lights are so dim you might bump into typewriters, but all is forgiven when you get the Pulitzer – a scotch-sherry cocktail that goes straight to your head.

DNA Lounge   CLUB
(Map p86; www.dnalounge.com; 375 11th St; admission $3-25; ⊗ 9pm-3am Fri & Sat, other nights vary; 🚌 12, 27, 47) One of SF's last megaclubs hosts live bands, mash-up dance party Bootie, epic drag at Trannyshack, and Monday's 18-plus Goth Death Guild.

🍸 The Mission

Ritual Coffee Roasters   CAFE
(Map p86; ☎ 415-641-1011; www.ritualroasters.com; 1026 Valencia St; ⊗ 6am-8pm Mon-Thu, to 10pm Fri, 7am-10pm Sat, 7am-8pm Sun; 📶; 🚌 14, 49, 🅱 24th St Mission) Cults wish they inspired the same devotion as Ritual, where devotees queue for house-roasted espresso drinks and specialty drip coffees with genuinely bizarre flavor profiles – believe descriptions of beans with cashew and grapefruit-peel notes.

GAY/LESBIAN/BI/TRANS SAN FRANCISCO

Singling out the best places to be queer in San Francisco is almost redundant. Though the Castro is a gay hub and the Mission is a magnet for lesbians, dancing queens and party bois head to SoMa for thump-thump clubs. Top GLBT venues include:

➡ The Stud (Map p86; www.studsf.com; 399 9th St; admission $5-8; ⊗ noon-2am Tue, from 5pm Wed & Sat, 5pm-3am Thu & Fri, 5pm to midnight Sun; 🚌 12, 19, 27, 47) Rocking the gay scene since 1966, and branching out beyond leather daddies with rocker-grrrl Mondays, Tuesday drag variety shows, raunchy comedy/karaoke Wednesdays, Friday art-drag dance parties, and performance-art cabaret whenever hostess/DJ Anna Conda gets it together.

➡ Lexington Club (Map p86; ☎ 415-863-2052; www.lexingtonclub.com; 3464 19th St; ⊗ 5pm-2am Mon-Thu, from 3pm Fri-Sun; 🚌 14, 33, 49, 🅱 16th St Mission) Odds are eerily high you'll develop a crush on your ex-girlfriend's hot new girlfriend over strong drinks, pinball and tattoo comparisons; live dangerously at SF's most famous/notorious full-time lesbian bar.

➡ Aunt Charlie's (Map p76; ☎ 415-441-2922; www.auntcharlieslounge.com; 133 Turk St; admission $2-5; ⊗ noon-2am Mon-Fri, from 10am Sat, 10am-midnight Sun; Ⓜ Powell, 🅱 Powell) Total dive, with the city's best classic drag show Fridays and Saturdays at 10pm. Thursday nights, art-school boys freak for bathhouse disco at Tubesteak ($5).

➡ Endup (Map p76; ☎ 415-646-0999; www.theendup.com; 401 6th St; admission $5-20; ⊗ 10pm Thu-4am Fri, 11pm Fri-11am Sat, 10pm Sat-4am Mon, 10pm Mon-4am Tue; 🚌 12, 27, 47) Home of Sunday 'tea dances' since 1973, though technically the party starts Saturday, EndUp watching the sunrise Monday over the freeway on-ramp.

➡ Rickshaw Stop (Map p76; ☎ 415-861-2011; www.rickshawstop.com; 155 Fell St; admission $5-35; ⊗ variable, check online; Ⓜ Van Ness) Freak beats keep sweaty 18-plus crowds up past their bedtimes at this all-ages, all-orientations, all-fabulous shoebox club; lesbian go-go and bhangra nights rule.

➡ Sisters of Perpetual Indulgence (Map p76; www.thesisters.org) For guerrilla antics and wild fundraisers, check the website of the self-described 'leading-edge order of queer nuns,' a charitable organization and San Francisco institution.

El Rio
CLUB

(📞415-282-3325; www.elriosf.com; 3158 Mission St; admission $3-8; ⏰1pm-2am; 🚌12,14,27,49, 🚇24th St Mission) The DJ mix takes its cue from El Rio regulars: eclectic, funky and internationally sexy, no matter your orientation. Margaritas get crowds bopping to disco-punk mashups and flirting shamelessly in the back garden. Come for shuffleboard and free oysters Fridays at 5:30pm. Cash only.

🍴 The Haight & Hayes Valley

★ Smuggler's Cove
BAR

(Map p76; 📞415-869-1900; www.smugglerscovesf.com; 650 Gough St; ⏰5pm-1:15am; 🚌5, 21, 49, 🚇Van Ness) Yo-ho-ho and a bottle of rum...or perhaps a Dead Reckoning with bitters, Nicaraguan rum, tawny port and vanilla liqueur. Pirates are bedeviled by choice at this shipwreck tiki speakeasy – with 400 rums and 70 cocktails, you won't be dry-docked long.

★ Toronado
PUB

(Map p86; 📞415-863-2276; www.toronado.com; 547 Haight St; ⏰11:30am-2am; 🚌6, 22, 71, 🚇N) Glory hallelujah, beer lovers: your prayers are answered with 50-plus brews on tap and hundreds more bottled. Bring cash and pair seasonal ales with sausages from Rosamunde (Map p86; 📞415-437-6851; http://rosamundesausagegrill.com; 545 Haight St; sausages $6.50-7; ⏰11:30am-10pm Sun-Wed, to 11pm Thu-Sat; 🚌6, 22, 71, 🚇N) next door – it may get too loud to hear your date, but you'll hear angels sing.

Alembic
BAR

(Map p90; 📞415-666-0822; www.alembicbar.com; 1725 Haight St; ⏰noon-2am Mon-Fri, from noon Sat & Sun; 🚌6,33,37,43,71, 🚇N) The floors are well-stomped and the tin ceilings hammered – and you will be too, if you gulp Alembic's potent concoctions made with 250 specialty spirits. Honor the Haight with a Lava Lamp (rosé bubbly with walnut bitters) or be rendered speechless by Charlie Chaplin (sloe gin, lime and apricot liqueur).

☆ Entertainment

Live Music

★ SFJAZZ Center
JAZZ

(Map p86; 📞866-920-5299; www.sfjazz.org; 201 Franklin St; ⏰showtimes vary; 🚌5, 7, 21, 🚇Van Ness) America's newest, largest jazz center draws legendary artists-in-residence like Wynton Marsalis, Regina Carter and Tony Bennett (who left his heart here, after all) – but the real thrills are experimental performances, like pianist Jason Moran's jam session with SF skateboarders pounding a ramp inside the auditorium. Upper-tier cheap seats are more like stools, but offer clear stage views and ledges for drinks.

★ The Chapel
LIVE MUSIC

(Map p86; 📞415-551-5157; www.thechapelsf.com; 777 Valencia St; tickets $15-22; 🚌14, 33, 🚇J, 🚇16th St Mission) Musical prayers are answered in a 1914 California Craftsman landmark with heavenly acoustics. The 40ft roof is raised by shows like Preservation Hall Jazz Band jams with Nick Lowe, Polyphonic Spree's full-choir ruckus and Radiohead's *OK Computer* lipsynched by an all-star drag revue. Many shows are all-ages, except when comedians like W Kamau Bell test edgy material.

The Fillmore
CONCERT VENUE

(📞415-346-3000; www.thefillmore.com; 1805 Geary Blvd; tickets from $20; ⏰shows nightly) Hendrix, Zeppelin, Janis – they all played the Fillmore. The legendary venue that launched the psychedelic era has the posters to prove it upstairs, and hosts arena acts in a 1250-seat venue where you can squeeze in next to the stage.

Slim's
LIVE MUSIC

(Map p86; 📞415-255-0333; www.slimspresents.com; 333 11th St; tickets $12-30; ⏰box office 10:30am-6pm Mon-Fri & show nights; 🚌9, 12, 27, 47) Guaranteed good times by Gogol Bordello, the Expendables and the Mekons fit the bill at this midsized club, where Prince and Elvis Costello have played sets unannounced. Shows are all-ages, though shorties may have a hard time seeing once the floor starts bouncing. Reserve dinner ($25) to score balcony seats.

Great American Music Hall
LIVE MUSIC

(Map p76; 📞415-885-0750; www.gamh.com; 859 O'Farrell St; admission $12-35; ⏰box office 10:30am-6pm Mon-Fri & show nights; 🚌19, 38, 47, 49) Once a bordello, the Great American Music Hall is full of surprises: Black Rebel Motorcycle Club playing acoustic, hardcore bluegrass jams, and burly bouncers swaying to Vetiver. Arrive early to claim balcony seats, or find standing room near the stage.

Independent
LIVE MUSIC

(Map p86; 📞415-771-1421; www.theindependentsf.com; 628 Divisadero St; tickets $12-45; ⏰box office 11am-6pm Mon-Fri, to 9:30pm show nights; 🚌5, 6, 21, 71) Shows earn street cred here, featuring indie dreamers (Magnetic Fields, Rogue Wave), rock legends (Courtney Love, Marky Ramone), alterna-pop (Imagine Dragons, Vampire Weekend) and wacky events like the US Air Guitar Championships.

Yoshi's
JAZZ, LIVE MUSIC

(☑415-655-5600; www.yoshis.com; 1330 Fillmore St; ☺shows 8pm &/or 10pm Tue-Sun, dinner 5:30-9pm Tue & Wed, 5:30-10pm Thu, 5:30-10:30pm Fri & Sat, 5-9pm Sun; ☒22, 31) The Fillmore Jazz District was once called 'the Harlem of the West,' and Yoshi's still draws top global talent like guitarist Leon Redbone, singer Nancy Wilson and Sufi electronica artist Niyaz – and it throws Black Panther reunions and serves mean sushi besides.

Mezzanine
LIVE MUSIC

(Map p76; ☑415-625-8880; www.mezzaninesf. com; 444 Jessie St; admission $10-40; Ⓜ Powell, Ⓑ Powell) Beats boom off brick walls at shows by Wyclef Jean, Quest Love, Method Man, Nas and Snoop Lion (aka Dogg), plus throwback alt-classics like the Dandy Warhols and Psychedelic Furs.

Theater

★American Conservatory Theater THEATER

(ACT; Map p76; ☑415-749-2228; www.act-sf.org; 415 Geary St; ☺box office noon-6pm Mon, to curtain Tue-Sun; ☒38, Ⓟ Powell-Mason, Powell-Hyde) Breakthrough shows destined for Broadway premiere at ACT's Geary Theater, including Tony Kushner's *Angels in America* and Robert Wilson's *Black Rider*, with a libretto by William S Burroughs and music by the Bay Area's Tom Waits.

Beach Blanket Babylon
CABARET

(BBB; Map p82; ☑415-421-4222; www.beachblanketbabylon.com; 678 Green St; admission $25-100; ☺shows 8pm Wed, Thu & Fri, 6:30pm & 9:30pm Sat, 2pm & 5pm Sun; ☒8X, Ⓟ Powell-Mason) Snow White searches for Prince Charming in San Francisco: what could possibly go wrong? SF's signature musical-comedy cabaret since 1974 stays fresh with topical comedy and

ⓘ HOT TICKETS

At TIX Bay Area (www.tixbayarea.org), half-price tickets are sold on show day for cash only. For advance tickets to concerts and Broadway shows, check Ticketmaster (www.ticketmaster.com) and SHN (www.shnsf.com).

wigs big as parade floats. Pop icons and heads of state are spoofed mercilessly – even when President Obama, Queen Elizabeth and the SF Giants attended.

Cobb's Comedy Club
COMEDY

(Map p84; ☑415-928-4320; www.cobbscomedyclub.com; 915 Columbus Ave; admission $12.50-45, plus 2-drink minimum; ☺showtimes vary; ☒8X, 30, 39, 41, 45, Ⓟ Powell-Mason) Bumper-to-bumper shared tables make an intimate audience for breakthrough talent and big-name acts from Dave Chappelle to Louis CK. Check the website for shows and comically twisted events – Father's Day Burlesque Brunch, anyone?

AsiaSF
DRAG CABARET

(Map p76; ☑415-255-2742; www.asiasf.com; 201 9th St; per person from $39; ☺7:15-11pm Wed, Thu & Sun, 7:15pm-2am Fri, 5pm-2am Sat; Ⓜ Civic Center, Ⓑ Civic Center) Cocktails and Asian-inspired dishes are served with surplus sass and one little secret: your servers are drag stars. Hostesses rock the bar/runway hourly, but once drinks kick in, everyone mingles on the downstairs dance floor. Bring cash for tips.

Classical Music, Opera & Dance

★Davies Symphony Hall
CLASSICAL MUSIC

(Map p76; ☑rush tickets 415-503-5577, 415-864-6000; www.sfsymphony.org; 201 Van Ness Ave; Ⓜ Van Ness, Ⓑ Civic Center) SF Symphony has racked up nine Grammys, and you can see why: conductor Michael Tilson Thomas keeps the audience rapt through Beethoven, Mahler, even Metallica. The season runs September to July; call the rush-ticket hotline for $20 next-day tickets, and don't miss free pre-show talks.

★San Francisco Opera
OPERA

(Map p76; ☑415-864-3330; www.sfopera.com; War Memorial Opera House, 301 Van Ness Ave; tickets $10-350; Ⓑ Civic Center, Ⓜ Van Ness) SF Opera rivals New York's Met with original operas like Stephen King's *Dolores Claiborne* and Verdi and Puccini revivals by acclaimed Tuscan director Nicola Luisotti. Book ahead, or score $10 same-day, standing-room tickets at 10am and two hours before curtain.

★ODC Theater
DANCE

(Map p86; ☑415-863-9834; www.odctheater.org; 3153 17th St; ☺box office noon-3pm Mon-Fri) For 40 years, ODC has redefined dance with risky, raw performances September through December – plus year-round guest performers and 200 dance classes a week.

San Francisco Ballet
DANCE

(Map p76; ☑ 415-861-5600, tickets 415-865-2000; www.sfballet.org; War Memorial Opera House, 301 Van Ness Ave; tickets $10-120; Ⓜ Van Ness, Ⓑ Civic Center) SF Ballet performs 100 gloriously staged shows annually at the War Memorial Opera House January to May; check website for dates and ticket deals.

Cinemas

★ Castro Theatre
CINEMA

(Map p86; ☑ 415-621-6120; www.castrotheatre.com; 429 Castro St; adult/child $11/8.50; ☺ show-times vary; Ⓜ Castro) The crowd sings along to pre-show Mighty Wurlitzer organ tunes, especially the theme song to the 1936 classic *San Francisco*. Don't miss silver-screen revivals, and cult classics preceded by live re-enactments – in drag. Cash only.

★ Roxie Cinema
CINEMA

(Map p86; ☑ 415-863-1087; www.roxie.com; 3117 16th St; regular screening/matinee $10/7; ☐ 14, 22, 33, 49, Ⓑ 16th St Mission) A little neighborhood nonprofit cinema with major international clout for indie premieres, controversial films and documentaries banned elsewhere. No ads, plus personal introductions to every film.

Sundance Kabuki Cinema
CINEMA

(☑ 415-346-3243; www.sundancecinemas.com; 1881 Post St; adult $9.75-15, child $9.50-12; ☐ 2, 3, 22, 38) ✒ Robert Redford's Sundance Institute runs this innovative green multiplex with first-run flicks, festival premieres and no ads – get comfortable in reserved recycled-fiber seating and booze in 21-plus screenings.

Sports

San Francisco Giants
BASEBALL

(Map p76; ☑ 415-972-2000; www.sfgiants.com; AT&T Park, 24 Willie Mays Plaza; tickets $5-135) Watch and learn how the World Series is won.

🔒 Shopping

San Francisco has big department stores and name-brand boutiques around Union Sq, including Macy's (Map p76; www.macys.com; 170 O'Farrell St; ☺ 10am-9pm Mon-Sat, 11am-7pm Sun; ☐ Powell-Mason, Powell-Hyde, Ⓜ Powell, Ⓑ Powell) and Westfield San Francisco Centre (Map p76; www.westfield.com/sanfrancisco; 865 Market St; ☺ 10am-8:30pm Mon-Sat, to 7pm Sun; ♿; ☐ Powell-Mason, Powell-Hyde, Ⓜ Powell, Ⓑ Powell) – but only-in-SF scores are found in the Haight, Castro, Mission and Hayes Valley.

SAN FRANCISCO FOR CHILDREN

Imaginations come alive in this story-book city, with wild parrots squawking around Coit Tower (p79) and sunning sea lions gleefully nudging one another off the docks at Pier 39 (p78). For thrills, try rickety, seatbelt-free cable cars. Kids will find playmates at Golden Gate Park (p95) and Crissy Field (p79). The Children's Creativity Museum (Map p76; ☑ 415-820-3320; www.zeum.org; 221 4th St; admission $11; ☺ 10am-4pm Wed-Sun Sep-May, Tue-Sun Jun-Aug; ♿; Ⓜ Powell, Ⓑ Powell) features technology that's too cool for school: robots, live-action video games, and 3D animation workshops.

See also: Exploratorium (p73), California Academy of Sciences (p95), Cartoon Art Museum (p83), Musée Mécanique (p73), Japan Center (p79), and 826 Valencia (p85).

★ Under One Roof
GIFTS

(Map p76; ☑ 415-503-2300; www.underoneroof.org; Crocker Galleria, 50 Post St; ☺ 10am-6pm Mon-Fri) AIDS service organizations receive 100% of the proceeds from goods donated by local designers and retailers, so show volunteer salespeople some love.

★ Gravel & Gold
HOUSEWARES, GIFTS

(Map p86; ☑ 415-552-0112; www.gravelandgold.com; 3266 21st St; ☺ noon-7pm Mon-Sat, to 5pm Sun; Ⓜ 24th St Mission, Ⓑ 24th St Mission) Get back to the land and in touch with California roots with Gravel & Gold's trippy silkscreened totes, hippie homesteader smock-dresses, 1960s Osborne/Woods ecology posters, and rare books on '70s beach-shack architecture.

★ Park Life
ART, GIFTS

(Map p92; ☑ 415-386-7275; www.parklifestore.com; 220 Clement St; ☺ noon-8pm Mon-Thu, from 11am Fri & Sat, 11am-7pm Sun; ☐ 1, 2, 33, 38, 44) Design store, indie publisher and art gallery in one. Park Life presents are too good to wait for birthdays, including Golden State pendants, Sean O'Dell utopia catalogs, and Ian Johnson's portrait of John Coltrane radiating rainbow vibes.

★ Heath Ceramics
HOUSEWARES

(Map p76; ☑ 415-399-9284; www.heathceramics.com; 1 Ferry Bldg; ☺ 10am-7pm Mon-Fri, 8am-6pm Sat, 11am-5pm Sun; Ⓜ Embarcadero,

B Embarcadero) No SF tablescape is complete without handmade modern Heath stoneware, thrown by potters in Heath's Sausalito studio since 1948. Pieces are priced for fine dining except studio seconds, sold on weekends.

★**Betabrand** CLOTHING
(Map p86; ☏800-694-9491; www.betabrand.com; 780 Valencia St; ◷11am-7pm Mon-Fri, to 8pm Sat, noon-6pm Sun; ▣14, 22, 33, 49, B 16th St Mission) Experimental designs are put to online votes and winners produced in limited editions. Recent designs include lunch-meat-patterned socks, reversible smoking jackets, and bike-to-work pants with reflective-strip cuffs.

ℹ Information

DANGERS & ANNOYANCES
Keep your city smarts and wits sharp, especially at night in SoMa, the Mission and the Haight. Unless you know where you're going, avoid the seedy, depressing Tenderloin (bordered east–west by Powell and Polk Sts and north–south by O'Farrell and Market Sts), Skid Row (6th St between Market and Folsom Sts) and Bayview–Hunters Point. Panhandlers and homeless people are part of San Francisco's community. People will probably ask you for spare change, but donations to local nonprofits stretch further. Don't engage with panhandlers at night or around ATMs. A simple 'I'm sorry,' is a polite response.

EMERGENCY & MEDICAL SERVICES
Haight Ashbury Free Clinic (☏415-762-3700; www.healthright360.org; 558 Clayton St; ◷by appointment; ▣6, 33, 37, 43, 71, Ⓜ N) Provides substance abuse and mental health services by appointment.

San Francisco General Hospital (☏emergency 415-206-8111, main hospital 415-206-8000; www.sfdph.org; 1001 Potrero Ave; ◷24hr; ▣9, 10, 33, 48) Provides care to uninsured patients; no documentation required.

Walgreens (☏415-861-3136; www.walgreens.com; 498 Castro St, cnr 18th St; ◷24hr; ▣24, 33, 35, Ⓜ F, K, L, M) Pharmacy and over-the-counter meds; locations citywide (see website).

INTERNET ACCESS
SF has free wi-fi hot spots citywide – locate one nearby with www.openwifispots.com.

Apple Store (☏415-392-0202; www.apple.com/retail/sanfrancisco; 1 Stockton St; ◷9am-9pm Mon-Sat, 10am-8pm Sun; ☎; Ⓜ Powell St) Free wi-fi and internet terminal usage.

San Francisco Main Library (☏415-871-4294; www.sfpl.org; 100 Larkin St; ◷10am-6pm Mon & Sat, 9am-8pm Tue-Thu, noon-6pm Fri, noon-5pm Sun; ☎; Ⓜ Civic Center) Free 15-minute internet terminal usage; spotty wi-fi access.

MONEY
Bank of America (www.bankamerica.com; 1 Market Plaza; ◷9am-5pm Mon-Thu, to 6pm Fri)

POST
Rincon Center Post Office (Map p76; www.usps.gov; 180 Steuart St; ◷7:30am-5pm Mon-Fri, 9am-2pm Sat; Ⓜ Embarcadero, B Embarcadero)

US Post Office (Map p76; www.usps.gov; Macy's, 170 O'Farrell St; ◷10am-5pm Mon-Sat; ▣ Powell-Mason & Powell-Hyde, Ⓜ Powell St, B Powell St) At Macy's department store.

TOURIST INFORMATION
California Welcome Center (Map p84; ☏415-981-1280; www.visitcwc.com; Pier 39, Bldg P, Suite 241b; ◷9am-7pm)

San Francisco Visitor Information Center (Map p76; ☏415-391-2000, events hotline 415-391-2001; www.onlyinsanfrancisco.com; lower level, Hallidie Plaza, Market & Powell Sts; ◷9am-5pm Mon-Fri, to 3pm Sat & Sun; ▣ Powell-Mason, Powell-Hyde, Ⓜ Powell St, B Powell St) Provides practical information and runs a 24-hour events hotline.

USEFUL WEBSITES
Craig's List (http://sfbay.craigslist.org) Events, activities, partners, freebies and dates.

Eater (http://sf.eater.com) Food and bars.

Flavorpill (www.flavorpill.com) Live music, lectures, art openings and movie premieres.

The Bold Italic (www.thebolditalic.com) SF trends, openings and opinions.

Urban Daddy (www.urbandaddy.com) Bars, shops, restaurants and events.

ℹ Getting There & Away

AIR
San Francisco is served by three major airports:

➡ **San Francisco International Airport** Most international flights arrive/depart SFO, 14 miles south of downtown SF off Hwy 101.

➡ **Oakland International Airport** Travelers from other US cities may find flights that arrive across the Bay on discount airlines such as JetBlue and Southwest.

➡ **Norman Y Mineta San Jose International Airport** Just 50 miles south of San Francisco along Hwy 101, and accessible via Caltrain.

BUS
Until the new terminal is completed in 2017, SF's intercity hub remains the **Temporary Transbay Terminal** (Map p76; Howard & Main Sts), where you can catch buses on **AC Transit** (www.actransit.org) to the East Bay, **Golden Gate Transit** (http://goldengatetransit.org) north to Marin and Sonoma, and **SamTrans** (www.

samtrans.com) south to Palo Alto and the Pacific coast. **Greyhound** (☑ 800-231-2222; www. greyhound.com) buses leave daily for Los Angeles ($59, eight to 12 hours), Truckee near Lake Tahoe ($31, 5½ hours), and other destinations.

CAR & MOTORCYCLE

Major car-rental operators have offices at airports and downtown.

FERRY

Blue & Gold Ferries (Map p76; ☑ 415-705-8200; www.blueandgoldfleet.com; one-way $6.25) Runs the Alameda–Oakland ferry from Pier 41 and the Ferry Building.

Golden Gate Ferry (☑ 415-455-2000; www. goldengateferry.org; adult/child $9.75/4.75; ⊘ 6am-9:30pm Mon-Fri, 10am-6pm Sat & Sun) Ferry service from the Ferry Building to Sausalito and Larkspur.

Vallejo Ferry (Map p76; ☑ 877-643-3779; www.baylinkferry.com; adult/child $13/6.50) Get to Napa car-free via Vallejo Ferry with departures from Ferry Building docks 6:30am to 7pm weekdays and 11am to 7:30pm weekends; bikes permitted. From Vallejo Ferry Terminal, take Napa Valley Vine bus 10.

TRAIN

Amtrak (☑ 800-872-7245; www.amtrakcalifornia.com) Serves San Francisco via Oakland stations, with free shuttle buses to San Francisco. Scenic routes with sleeping cars include the 35-hour Los Angeles–Seattle run via Oakland on the *Coast Starlight*, and the 51-hour Chicago–Oakland journey on the *California Zephyr*.

CalTrain (www.caltrain.com; cnr 4th & King Sts) Links San Francisco to the South Bay, ending in San Jose.

❶ Getting Around

For Bay Area transit options, departures and arrivals, check ☑ 511 or www.511.org.

TO/FROM THE AIRPORT

➡ **BART** Direct 30-minute ride to/from downtown.

➡ **SuperShuttle** (☑ 800-258-3826; www. supershuttle.com) Door-to-door vans depart baggage-claim areas, taking 45 minutes to most SF locations; $17.

➡ **Taxis** To/from downtown costs $35 to $50.

BART

Bay Area Rapid Transit (Bay Area Rapid Transit; www.bart.gov; one way $8.25) links SFO, the Mission, downtown and the East Bay. Within SF, one-way fares start at $1.75.

BICYCLE

Bicycling is safest in Golden Gate Park and along the waterfront; rentals are readily available.

CAR

Avoid driving in San Francisco: street parking is rare and meter readers ruthless. Convenient downtown parking lots are at 5th and Mission Sts, Union Sq, and Sutter and Stockton Sts. Daily rates run $25 to $50.

If your car is towed for parking violations, retrieve it from **Autoreturn** (☑ 415-865-8200; www.autoreturn.com; 450 7th St, SoMa; ⊘ 24hr; ⓜ 27, 42). Fines run $73, plus towing and storage ($453.75 for the first four hours).

Members of **American Automobile Association** (AAA; ☑ 800-222-4357, 415-773-1900; www.aaa.com; 160 Sutter St; ⊘ 8:30am-5:30pm Mon-Fri) can call anytime for emergency service.

MUNI

MUNI (Municipal Transit Agency; www.sfmuni. com) operates bus, streetcar and cable-car lines. The standard fare for buses and streetcars is $2, and tickets are good for transfers for 90 minutes; hang onto your ticket to avoid a $100 fine. The cable-car fare is $6 per ride.

MUNI Passport (1-/3-/7-days $14/22/28) allows unlimited travel on all MUNI transport, including cable cars; it's sold at San Francisco Visitor Information Center and many hotels.

Key routes include:

➡ **California cable car** California St between Market St and Van Ness Ave

➡ **F** Fisherman's Wharf to Castro

➡ **J** Downtown to Mission

➡ **K, L, M** Downtown to Castro

➡ **N** Caltrain to Haight and Ocean Beach

➡ **Powell-Mason** and **Powell-Hyde cable cars** Powell and Market Sts to Fisherman's Wharf

➡ **T** Embarcadero to Caltrain

RIDESHARE & TAXI

SF-based rideshare companies including **Uber** (www.uber.com) and **Lyft** (www.lyft.com) offer rides from mostly non-professional drivers at set rates, starting around $15 for in-city rides. Expect fast dispatch and fares charged to your account; signup and/or app download required.

San Francisco taxi fares run $2.75 per mile, plus 10% tip ($1 minimum); meters start at $3.50. SF taxis have their own app to hail and pay cabs, downloadable at www.flywheel.com. Major cab companies include:

DeSoto Cab (☑ 415-970-1300; www.desotogo. com)

Green Cab (☑ 415-626-4733) Fuel-efficient hybrids; worker-owned collective.

Luxor (☑ 415-282-4141; www.luxorcab.com)

Yellow Cab (☑ 415-333-3333; www.yellow-cabsf.com)

Marin County & the Bay Area

Why Go?

The region surrounding San Francisco encompasses a bonanza of natural vistas and wildlife. Cross the Golden Gate Bridge to Marin and visit wizened ancient redwoods body-blocking the sun and herds of elegant tule elk prancing along the bluffs of Tomales Bay. Gray whales show some fluke off the cape of wind-scoured Point Reyes, and hawks surf the skies in the pristine hills of the Marin Headlands.

On the cutting edge of intellectual thought, Stanford University and the University of California at Berkeley draw academics and students from around the world. The city of Berkeley sparked the locavore food movement and continues to be on the forefront of environmental and left-leaning political causes. South of San Francisco, Hwy 1 traces miles of undeveloped coastline and sandy pocket beaches.

Best Places to Eat

➜ Chez Panisse (p143)
➜ Sushi Ran (p117)
➜ Lake Chalet (p133)
➜ Duarte's Tavern (p157)
➜ Ippuku (p143)

Best Places to Stay

➜ HI Pigeon Point Lighthouse Hostel (p157)
➜ Cavallo Point (p115)
➜ Mountain Home Inn (p121)
➜ Hotel Shattuck Plaza (p143)

When to Go
Berkeley

Dec–Mar Elephant seal pupping season and the peak of gray whale migrations.

Mar–Apr Wildflowers hit their peak on trails throughout the region.

Jun–Sep Farmers markets overflow with sweet seasonal fruit.

Marin County & the Bay Area Highlights

① Gazing up at the majestic redwood canopy at **Muir Woods National Monument** (p123).

② Cavorting with elk and gray whales at the **Point Reyes National Seashore** (p127).

③ Touring the beach-cove coastline along **Hwy 1** from Pacifica to Santa Cruz.

④ Feasting your way through the delectable **Gourmet Ghetto** (p140) in Berkeley.

⑤ Kayaking **Tomales Bay** (p127) amid harbor seals and splendid shorelines.

⑥ Hiking or cycling the perimeter of panoramic **Angel Island** (p118).

⑦ Spying on the elephant seals at **Año Nuevo State Reserve** (p157).

⑧ Cooling off with a cannonball splash at blissful **Bass Lake** (p125).

⑨ Heading to Oakland's **Chabot Space & Science Center** (p132) to marvel at the stars.

MARIN COUNTY

If there's a part of the Bay Area that consciously attempts to live up to the California dream, it's Marin County. Just across the Golden Gate Bridge from San Francisco, the region has a wealthy population that cultivates a seemingly laid-back lifestyle. Towns may look like idyllic rural hamlets, but the shops cater to cosmopolitan and expensive tastes. The 'common' folk here eat organic, vote Democrat and drive hybrids.

Geographically, Marin County is a near mirror image of San Francisco. It's a south-pointing peninsula that nearly touches the north-pointing tip of the city, and is surrounded by ocean and bay. But Marin is wilder, greener and more mountainous. Redwoods grow on the coast side of the hills, the surf crashes against cliffs, and hiking and cycling trails crisscross the blessed scenery of Point Reyes, Muir Woods and Mt Tamalpais. Nature is what makes Marin County such an excellent day trip or weekend escape from San Francisco.

ⓘ Information

The **Marin Convention & Visitors Bureau** (☑ 866-925-2060, 415-925-2060; www.visitmarin.org; 1 Mitchell Blvd, San Rafael; ⊙9am-5pm Mon-Fri) provides tourist information for the entire county.

ⓘ Getting There & Around

Busy Hwy 101 heads north from the Golden Gate Bridge ($7 toll when heading back into San Francisco), spearing through Marin's middle; quiet Hwy 1 winds its way along the sparsely populated coast. In San Rafael, Sir Francis Drake Blvd cuts across west Marin from Hwy 101 to the ocean.

Hwy 580 comes in from the East Bay over the Richmond–San Rafael bridge ($5 toll for westbound traffic) to meet Hwy 101 at Larkspur.

ⓘ **GETTING AROUND**

Visitors taking multiple forms of public transportation throughout the Bay Area should note that the regional **Clipper card** (www.clippercard.com) can be used on the Caltrain, BART, SamTrans, VTA, Golden Gate Transit and the Golden Gate Ferry systems. It can be a handy way to avoid buying multiple tickets, and offers some small discounts, plus almost 50% off on the Golden Gate Ferry system.

Frequent **Marin Airporter** (☑ 415-461-4222; www.marinairporter.com; fare $20) buses connect from Marin stops to the San Francisco International Airport (SFO) from 4am until about 10:30pm; SFO–Marin service departs every 30 minutes.

Marin Headlands

The headlands rise majestically out of the water at the north end of the Golden Gate Bridge, their rugged beauty all the more striking given the fact that they're only a few miles from San Francisco's urban core. A few forts and bunkers are left over from a century of US military occupation – which is, ironically, the reason they are protected parklands today and free of development. It's no mystery why this is one of the Bay Area's most popular hiking and cycling destinations. As the trails wind through the headlands, they afford stunning views of the sea, the Golden Gate Bridge and San Francisco, leading to isolated beaches and secluded spots for picnics.

◉ Sights

After crossing the Golden Gate Bridge, exit immediately at Alexander Ave, then dip left under the highway and head out west for the expansive views and hiking trailheads. Conzelman Rd snakes up into the hills, where it eventually forks. Conzelman Rd continues west, becoming a steep, one-lane road as it descends to Point Bonita. From here it continues to Rodeo Beach and Fort Barry. McCullough Rd heads inland, joining Bunker Rd toward Rodeo Beach.

Hawk Hill   HILL
About 2 miles along Conzelman Rd is Hawk Hill, where thousands of migrating birds of prey soar along the cliffs from late summer to early fall.

Point Bonita Lighthouse   LIGHTHOUSE
(www.nps.gov/goga/pobo.htm; off Field Rd; ⊙12:30-3:30pm Sat-Mon) **FREE** At the end of Conzelman Rd, this lighthouse is a breathtaking half-mile walk from a small parking area. From the tip of Point Bonita, you can see the distant Golden Gate Bridge and beyond it the San Francisco skyline. It's an uncommon vantage point of the bay-centric city, and harbor seals haul out nearby in season. To reserve a spot on one of the free monthly full-moon tours of the promontory, call ☑ 415-331-1540.

WHY IS IT SO FOGGY?

When the summer sun's rays warm the air over the chilly Pacific, fog forms and hovers offshore; to grasp how it moves inland requires an understanding of California's geography. The vast agricultural region in the state's interior, the Central Valley, is ringed by mountains like a giant bathtub. The only substantial sea-level break in these mountains occurs at the Golden Gate, to the west, which happens to be the direction from which prevailing winds blow. As the inland valley heats up and the warm air rises, it creates a deficit of air at surface level, generating wind that gets sucked through the only opening it can find: the Golden Gate. It happens fast and it's unpredictable. Gusty wind is the only indication that the fog is about to roll in. But even this is inconsistent: there can be fog at the beaches south of the Golden Gate and sun a mile to the north. Hills block fog – especially at times of high atmospheric pressure, as often happens in summer. Because of this, weather forecasters speak of the Bay Area's 'microclimates.' In July it's not uncommon for inland areas to reach 100°F (38°C), while the mercury at the coast barely reaches 70°F (21°C).

Nike Missile Site SF-88   HISTORIC SITE
(☎415-331-1453; www.nps.gov/goga/nike-missile-site.htm; off Field Rd; ⏰12:30pm-3:30pm Thu-Sat) FREE File past guard shacks with uniformed mannequins to witness the area's not-too-distant military history at this fascinating Cold War museum staffed by veterans. Watch them place a now-warhead-free missile into position, then ride a missile elevator to the cavernous underground silo to see the multikeyed launch controls that were thankfully never set in motion.

Marine Mammal Center   ANIMAL RESCUE CENTER
(☎415-289-7325; www.marinemammalcenter.org; ⏰10am-5pm; ♿) FREE Set on the hill above Rodeo Lagoon, the Marine Mammal Center rehabilitates injured, sick and orphaned sea mammals before returning them to the wild, and has educational exhibits about these animals and the dangers they face. During the spring pupping season the center can have up to several dozen orphaned seal pups on site and you can often see them before they're set free.

Headlands Center for the Arts   GALLERY
(☎415-331-2787; www.headlands.org; 944 Simmonds Rd; ⏰noon-5pm Sun-Thu) FREE In Fort Barry, refurbished barracks converted into artist work spaces host open studios with its artists-in-residence, as well as talks, performances and other events.

🏃 Activities

Hiking
At the end of Bunker Rd sits Rodeo Beach, protected from wind by high cliffs. From here the Coastal Trail meanders 3.5 miles inland, past abandoned military bunkers, to the Tennessee Valley Trail. It then continues 6 miles along the blustery headlands all the way to Muir Beach.

All along the coastline you'll find cool old battery sites – abandoned concrete bunkers dug into the ground with fabulous views. Evocative Battery Townsley, a half-mile walk or bike ride up from the Fort Cronkite parking lot, opens for free subterranean tours from noon to 4pm on the first Sunday of the month.

Tennessee Valley Trail   HIKING
This trail offers beautiful views of the rugged coastline and is one of the most popular hikes in Marin (expect crowds on weekends), especially for families. It has easy, level access to the cove beach and ocean, and is a short 3.8-mile round trip. From Hwy 101, take the Mill Valley–Stinson Beach–Hwy 1 exit and turn left onto Tennessee Valley Rd from the Shoreline Hwy; follow it to the parking lot and trailhead.

ℹ️ GOLDEN GATE BRIDGE TOLL

The bridge toll ($7) crossing from Marin to San Francisco is now all electronic; drivers can no longer stop to pay. Rental-car drivers may use their car company's toll program or pay in advance online, and motorists in private vehicles are billed by mail if they haven't prepaid online. See www.goldengate.org/tolls/tolltipsforvisitors.php for payment information.

Marin County

Ross (1mi);
San Anselmo (2mi);
Fairfax (4mi)

Bon
Tempe
Lake

Phoenix
Lake

Lake
Lagunitas

Alpine
Lake

Marin Municipal
Water District

Rocky Ridge Rd

Rock Springs Lagunitas Rd

Fairfax Bolinas Rd

East
Peak
(2571m) **3**

Middle
Peak
(2490m) **8**

Mt Tamalpais
Interpretative
Association

7

Cataract Creek

Cataract Trail

Coastal Trail

West Peak
(2560m)

Old Railroad Grade

Matt Davis Trail

Cascade
Creek

Ridgecrest Blvd

Bolinas Ridge Rd

Old Stage Rd

13

43

38

Old Mill Creek

Mt Tamalpais
State Park

Shoreline Hwy

46

Audubon
Canyon
Ranch (1mi)

**STINSON
BEACH**

Matt Davis Trail

14

Bootjack Trail

Alice Eastwood Camp Rd

Redwood Trail

18

52

30

Four
Corners

49 **40**

Stinson
Beach **25**

Panoramic Hwy

Cardiac
Hill

39

Sun Trail

16

Bolinas
Bay

Webb Creek

Dipsea Trail

Lone Tree Creek

Kent Canyon Creek

Coastal Trail

Muir Woods Rd

Redwood Creek

Diaz Ridge Trail

Panoramic Hwy

22

Red Rock
Beach
Rocky Point

41

Cold Stream

Shoreline Hwy

15

Redwood Creek

50

33

Coyote Ridge Trail

Muir
Beach

Coastal Trail

Tennessee
Beach

Tennessee
Point

2
*Sausalito
Houseboats*

**MARIN
CITY**

44

47

Bridgeway Blvd

Richardson
Bay

0 _____ 1 km
0 _____ 0.5 miles

6

28

Spring St

Caledonia St

Oakwood Trail

Redwood Hwy

51

Sausalito
Visitor Center **35**

27 **32**

SAUSALITO

Bobcat Trail

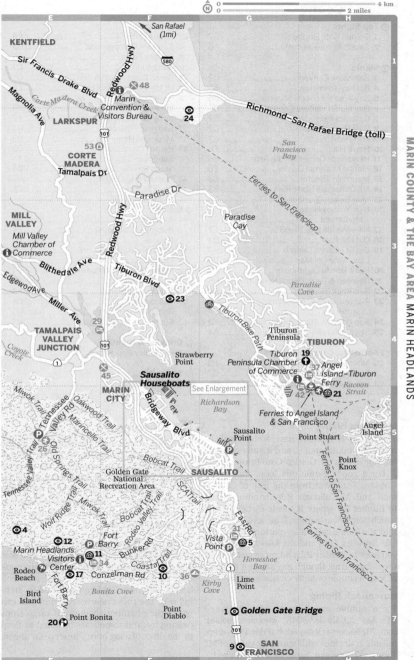

N ↑ 0 —————————— 4 km
0 —————————— 2 miles

KENTFIELD

San Rafael (1mi)

Sir Francis Drake Blvd

Magnolia Ave

Redwood Hwy

580

Corte Madera Creek

⊗ 48

Marin Convention & Visitors Bureau

◉ 24

Richmond–San Rafael Bridge (toll)

San Francisco Bay

LARKSPUR

101

CORTE MADERA

53 🔒

Tamalpais Dr

Paradise Dr

Ferries to San Francisco

MILL VALLEY

Mill Valley Chamber of Commerce

Blithedale Ave

Edgewood Ave

Miller Ave

Redwood Hwy

Tiburon Blvd

Paradise Cay

◉ 23

Tiburon Bike Path

Paradise Cove

TAMALPAIS VALLEY JUNCTION

101

29

Coyote Creek

1

45

Strawberry Point

Tiburon Peninsula

TIBURON

Peninsula Chamber of Commerce

Tiburon 🔟 19

37

Sausalito Houseboats

See Enlargement

MARIN CITY

Bridgeway Blvd

Richardson Bay

Angel Island–Tiburon Ferry

42 🏦 21

Racoon Strait

Ferries to Angel Island & San Francisco

Miwok Trail

Tennessee Valley Rd

Oakwood Trail

Marincello Trail

P 26

Old Springs Trail

Tennessee Valley Trail

Wolf Ridge Trail

Miwok Trail

Bobcat Trail

Rodeo Valley Trail

Golden Gate National Recreation Area

Bobcat Trail

SAUSALITO

SCA Trail

Sausalito Point

P

Point Stuart

Angel Island

Point Knox

Ferries to San Francisco

◉ 4

◉ 12

Marin Headlands Visitors Center 🛈 11

34

Fort Barry

P

Bunker Rd

Coastal Trail

◉ 17

Conzelman Rd

◉ 10

36

East Rd

31

🏦 5

Vista Point

P

Horseshoe Bay

1

Ferries to San Francisco

Rodeo Beach

Bird Island

Fort Barry

Bonita Cove

Point Diablo

Kirby Cove

Lime Point

20 ♿ Point Bonita

1 ◉ **Golden Gate Bridge**

101

9 ◉ **SAN FRANCISCO**

Marin County

◎ Top Sights
1	Golden Gate Bridge	G7
2	Sausalito Houseboats	A6

◎ Sights
3	Baltimore Canyon	D2
4	Battery Townsley	E6
5	Bay Area Discovery Museum	G6
6	Bay Model Visitors Center	B6
7	Cataract Falls	B2
8	East Peak (2571m)	C2
9	Fort Point	G7
10	Hawk Hill	F6
11	Headlands Center for the Arts	E6
12	Marine Mammal Center	E6
13	Mountain Theater	B3
14	Mt Tamalpais State Park	B3
15	Muir Beach Overlook	C5
16	Muir Woods National Monument	C3
17	Nike Missile Site SF-88	E7
18	Old Mill Park	D3
19	Old St Hilary's Church	H4
	Plaza Viña Del Mar	(see 35)
20	Point Bonita Lighthouse	E7
21	Railroad & Ferry Depot Museum	H5
22	Red Rock Beach	B4
23	Richardson Bay Audubon Center	F4
24	San Quentin State Penitentiary	F2
25	Stinson Beach	A4

◎ Activities, Courses & Tours
26	Miwok Livery Stables	E5
27	Sausalito Bike Rentals	C7
28	Sea Trek Kayak & SUP	B6

◎ Sleeping
29	Acqua Hotel	E4
30	Bootjack Campground	C3
31	Cavallo Point	G6
32	Gables Inn	C7
33	Green Gulch Farm & Zen Center	D5
34	HI Marin Headlands Hostel	E6
35	Hotel Sausalito	C7
	Inn Above Tide	(see 35)
36	Kirby Cove Campground	F7
37	Lodge at Tiburon	H4
38	Mountain Home Inn	C3
39	Pantoll Campground	C3
40	Sandpiper	A3
41	Steep Ravine	B4
42	Water's Edge Hotel	H5
43	West Point Inn	C3

◎ Eating
44	Avatar's	A6
45	Buckeye Roadhouse	F4
	Caprice	(see 21)
46	Depot Bookstore & Cafe	D3
47	Fish	B6
48	Marin Brewing Company	F1
	Murray Circle	(see 31)
49	Parkside Cafe	A3
50	Pelican Inn	D5
	Sam's Anchor Cafe	(see 42)
51	Sushi Ran	B7

◎ Drinking & Nightlife
52	Mill Valley Beerworks	D3

◎ Shopping
53	Book Passage	E2

Mountain Biking

The Marin Headlands have some excellent mountain-biking routes, and it's an exhilarating ride across the Golden Gate Bridge.

For a good 12-mile dirt loop, choose the Coastal Trail west from the fork of Conzelman and McCullough Rds, winding down to Bunker Rd where it meets Bobcat Trail, which joins Marincello Trail and descends into the Tennessee Valley parking area. The Old Springs Trail and the Miwok Trail take you back to Bunker Rd a bit more gently than the Bobcat Trail, though any attempt to avoid at least a couple of hefty climbs is futile.

Horseback Riding

For a ramble on all fours, Miwok Livery Stables (☎415-383-8048; www.miwokstables. com; 701 Tennessee Valley Rd; trail ride $75) offers hillside trail rides with stunning views of Mt Tam and the ocean. Reservations required.

🛏 Sleeping

There are four small campgrounds in the headlands, and two involve hiking (or cycling) in at least 1 mile from the nearest parking lot. Hawk, Bicentennial and Haypress campgrounds are inland, with free camping, but sites must be reserved through the Marin Headlands Visitors Center. None have water available.

Kirby Cove Campground   CAMPGROUND $
(☎877-444-6777; www.recreation.gov; tent sites $25; ◎Apr–Oct) In a closely shady nook near the entrance to the bay, there's a small beach with the Golden Gate Bridge arching over the rocks nearby. At night you can watch the phantom shadows of cargo ships passing by (and sometimes be lulled to sleep by the dirge of a fog horn). Reserve far ahead.

HI Marin Headlands Hostel   HOSTEL $

(☑415-331-2777; www.norcalhostels.org/marin; Fort Barry, Bldg 941; dm $26-30, r $72-92, all with shared bath; @) ✎ Wake up to grazing deer and dew on the ground at this spartan 1907 military compound snuggled in the woods. It has comfortable beds and two well-stocked kitchens, and guests can gather round a fireplace in the common room, shoot pool or play ping-pong. Hiking trails beckon outside.

Cavallo Point   HOTEL $$$

(☑888-651-2003, 415-339-4700; www.caval-lopoint.com; 601 Murray Circle; r from $359; ✳@🐾🐕🐾🐕) ✎ Spread out over 45 acres of the Bay Area's most scenic parkland, Cavallo Point is a buzz-worthy lodge that flaunts a green focus, a full-service spa and easy access to outdoor activities. Choose from richly renovated rooms in the landmark Fort Baker officers' quarters or more contemporary solar-powered accommodations with exquisite bay views (including a turret of the Golden Gate Bridge).

❶ Information

Information is available from the **Golden Gate National Recreation Area** (GGNRA; ☑415-561-4700; www.nps.gov/goga) and the **Marin Headlands Visitors Center** (☑415-331-1540; www.nps.gov/goga/marin-headlands.htm; Fort Barry; ⊙9:30am-4:30pm), in an old chapel off Bunker Rd near Fort Barry.

❶ Getting There & Away

By car, take the Alexander Ave exit just after the Golden Gate Bridge and dip left under the freeway. Conzelman Rd, to the right, takes you up along the bluffs; you can also take Bunker Rd, which leads to the headlands through a one-way tunnel. It's also a snap to reach these roads from the bridge via bicycle.

On weekdays, **Golden Gate Transit** (☑415-455-2000, 511; www.goldengatetransit.org) buses 2, 4 and 92 service Sausalito ($4.75) and the eastern Headlands. On Saturday, Sunday and holidays, **MUNI** (☑511, 415-701-2311; www.sfmta.com) bus 76X runs hourly from San Francisco's Financial District to the Marin Headlands Visitors Center and Rodeo Beach. Both lines are equipped with bicycle racks.

Sausalito

Perfectly arranged on a secure little harbor on the bay, Sausalito is undeniably lovely. Named for the tiny willows that once populated the banks of its creeks, it's a small settlement of pretty houses that tumble neatly down a green hillside into a well-heeled downtown. Much of the town affords the visitor uninterrupted views of San Francisco and Angel Island, and due to the ridgeline at its back, fog generally skips past it.

Sausalito began as a 19,000-acre land grant to an army captain in 1838. When it became the terminus of the train line down the Pacific Coast, it entered a new stage as a busy lumber port with a racy waterfront. Dramatic changes came in WWII when Sausalito became the site of Marinship, a huge shipbuilding yard. After the war a new bohemian period began, with a resident artists' colony living in 'arks' (houseboats moored along

---

HIKING & CYCLING THE GOLDEN GATE BRIDGE

Walking or cycling across the Golden Gate Bridge to Sausalito is a fun way to avoid traffic, get some great ocean views and bask in that refreshing Marin County air. It's a fairly easy journey, mostly flat or downhill when heading north from San Francisco (cycling back to the city involves one big climb out of Sausalito). You can also simply hop on a ferry back to SF.

The trip is about 4 miles from the south end of the bridge and takes less than an hour. Pedestrians have access to the bridge's east walkway between 5am and 9pm daily (until 6pm in winter). Cyclists generally use the west side, except on weekdays between 5am and 3:30pm, when they must share the east side with pedestrians (who have the right-of-way). After 9pm (6pm in winter), cyclists can still cross the bridge on the east side through a security gate. Check the bridge website (www.goldengatebridge.org/bikes-bridge/bikes.php) for changes.

For more ambitious cyclists, the Cal Park Hill Tunnel is a safe subterranean passage from Larkspur (another ferry terminus) to San Rafael.

More information and resources are available at the websites of the San Francisco Bicycle Coalition (www.sfbike.org) and the Marin County Bicycle Coalition (www.marinbike.org).

the bay). Hundreds of these floating abodes remain.

Sausalito today is a major tourist haven, jam-packed with souvenir shops and costly boutiques. It's the first town you encounter after crossing the Golden Gate Bridge, so daytime crowds turn up in droves and make parking difficult. Ferrying from San Francisco makes a more relaxing excursion.

⊙ Sights

Sausalito is actually on Richardson Bay, a smaller bay within San Francisco Bay. The commercial district is mainly one street, Bridgeway Blvd, on the waterfront.

★ Sausalito Houseboats ARCHITECTURE

Bohemia still thrives along the shoreline of Richardson Bay, where free spirits inhabit hundreds of quirky homes that bobble in the waves amongst the seabirds and seals. Structures range from psychedelic mural-splashed castles to dilapidated salt-sprayed shacks and immaculate three-story floating mansions. It's a tight-knit community, where residents tend sprawling dockside gardens and stop to chat on the creaky wooden boardwalks as they wheel their groceries home.

You can poke around the houseboat docks located off Bridgeway between Gate 5 and Gate 6½ Rds.

Bay Model Visitors Center MUSEUM

(☑ 415-332-3871; www.spn.usace.army.mil/Missions/Recreation/BayModelVisitorCenter.aspx; 2100 Bridgeway Blvd; ⊙9am-4pm Tue-Sat, plus 10am-5pm Sat & Sun in summer; 📶) One of the coolest things in town, fascinating to both kids and adults, is the Army Corps of Engineers' solar-powered visitor center. Housed in one of the old (and cold!) Marinship warehouses, it's a 1.5-acre hydraulic model of San Francisco Bay and the delta region. Self-guided tours take you over and around it as the water flows.

Bay Area Discovery Museum MUSEUM

(☑ 415-339-3900; www.baykidsmuseum.org; 557 McReynolds Rd; admission $11, free 1st Wed each month; ⊙9am-5pm Tue-Sun; 📶) Just under the north tower of the Golden Gate Bridge, at East Fort Baker, this excellent hands-on activity museum is specifically designed for children. Permanent (multilingual) exhibits include a wave workshop, a small underwater tunnel and a large outdoor play area

with a shipwreck to romp around. A small cafe has healthy nibbles.

Plaza Viña Del Mar PARK

Near the ferry terminal, the plaza has a fountain flanked by 14ft-tall elephant statues from the 1915 Panama–Pacific Exposition in San Francisco.

🏃 Activities

Sausalito is great for bicycling, whether for a leisurely ride around town, a trip across the Golden Gate Bridge or a longer-haul journey. From the ferry terminal, an easy option is to head south on Bridgeway Blvd, veering left onto East Rd toward the Bay Area Discovery Museum. Another nice route heads north along Bridgeway Blvd, then crosses under Hwy 101 to Mill Valley. At Blithedale Ave, you can veer east to Tiburon; a bike path parallels parts of Tiburon Blvd.

Sea Trek Kayak & SUP KAYAKING

(☑ 415-332-8494; www.seatrek.com; Schoonmaker Point Marina; single/double kayaks per hr $20/35) On a nice day, Richardson Bay is irresistible. Kayaks and stand-up paddleboards can be rented here, near the Bay Model Visitor Center. No experience is necessary, and lessons and group outings are also available.

Also on offer are guided kayaking excursions around Angel Island from $75 per person, including overnight camping ($125). Tours include equipment and instructions. May through October is the best time to paddle.

Sausalito Bike Rentals BICYCLE RENTAL

(☑ 415-331-2453; www.sausalitobikerentals.com; 34a Princess St; bicycle per hour $10; ⊙10am-6pm) Rent road, mountain, tandems ($25 per hour) and electric ($20 per hour) bicycles to explore the area.

🛏 Sleeping

All of the lodgings below charge an additional $15 to $20 per night for parking.

Hotel Sausalito HISTORIC HOTEL $$

(☑ 415-332-0700; www.hotelsausalito.com; 16 El Portal; r $180-225, ste $305-320; ❀🛜) Steps away from the ferry in the middle of downtown, this grand 1915 hotel has loads of period charm, paired with modern touches like MP3-player docking stations. Each guest room is decorated in Mediterranean hues, with sumptuous bathrooms and park or partial bay views.

Inn Above Tide
INN **$$$**

(☑ 415-332-9535, 800-893-8433; www.in-nabovetide.com; 30 El Portal; r incl breakfast $345-625, ste $735-1100; ❋@☎) Next to the ferry terminal, ensconce yourself in one of the 31 modern and spacious rooms – most with private decks and wood-burning fireplaces – that practically levitate over the water. With envy-inducing bay views from your window, scan the horizon with the in-room binoculars. Free loaner bicycles available.

Gables Inn
INN **$$$**

(☑ 415-289-1100; www.gablesinnsausalito.com; 62 Princess St; r incl breakfast $199-545; @☎) Tranquil and inviting, this inn has nine guest rooms in a historic 1869 home, and six in a newer building. The more expensive rooms have spa baths, fireplaces and balconies with spectacular views, but even the smaller, cheaper rooms are stylish and tranquil. Evening wine and cheese is included.

✗ Eating

Bridgeway Blvd is packed with moderately priced cafes, a few budget ethnic food options and some more expensive bay-view restaurants.

Avatar's
INDIAN **$$**

(www.enjoyavatars.com; 2656 Bridgeway Blvd; mains $10-17; ⊙11am-3pm & 5-9:30pm Mon-Sat; ☑🖐) Boasting a cuisine of 'ethnic confusion,' the Indian fusion dishes here incorporate Mexican, Italian and Caribbean ingredients and will bowl you over with their flavor and creativity. Think Punjabi enchilada with curried sweet potato or spinach and mushroom ravioli with mango and rose petal alfredo sauce. All diets (vegan, gluten-free, etc) are graciously accommodated.

Fish
SEAFOOD **$$**

(☑ 415-331-3474; www.fish311.com; 350 Harbor Dr; mains $14-28; ⊙11:30am-8:30pm; 🖐) ✹ Chow down on seafood sandwiches, oysters and Dungeness crab roll with organic local butter at redwood picnic tables facing Richardson Bay. A local leader in promoting fresh and sustainably caught fish, this place has wonderful wild salmon in season, and refuses to serve the farmed stuff. Cash only.

Sushi Ran
JAPANESE **$$$**

(☑ 415-332-3620; www.sushiran.com; 107 Caledonia St; sushi $4-33; ⊙11:45am-2:30pm Mon-Fri, 5-10pm Sun-Thu, to 11pm Fri & Sat; ☑) Many Bay Area residents claim this place is the best sushi spot around. If you didn't reserve ahead, the wine and sake bar next door eases the pain of the long wait for a table.

Murray Circle
MODERN AMERICAN **$$$**

(☑ 415-339-4750; www.cavallopoint.com/dine.html; 601 Murray Circle, Fort Baker; dinner mains $23-34; ⊙7-11am & 11:30am-2pm Mon-Fri, to 2:30pm Sat & Sun, 5:30-10pm Sun-Thu, to 11pm Fri & Sat) At the Cavallo Point lodge, dine on locally sourced meats, seafood and produce, like grass-fed organic beef burgers or Dungeness crab BLT, in a clubby dining room topped by a pressed-tin ceiling. Reservations recommended for dinner.

ⓘ Information

The **Sausalito Visitors Center** (☑ 415-332-0505; www.sausalito.org; 780 Bridgeway Blvd; ⊙11:30am-4pm Tue-Sun) has local information. There's also an information kiosk at the ferry terminal.

ⓘ Getting There & Away

Driving to Sausalito from San Francisco, take the Alexander Ave exit (the first exit after the Golden Gate Bridge) and follow the signs into Sausalito. There are five municipal parking lots in town, and street parking is difficult to find.

Golden Gate Transit (☑ 415-455-2000; www.goldengatetransit.org) bus 10 runs daily to Sausalito from downtown San Francisco ($4.75). On weekends and holidays from late May through early September, the **West Marin Stagecoach** (☑ 415-526-3239; www.marintransit.org/stage.html) bus 61 extends to Sausalito and Fort Baker, with six daily departures for Mt Tamalpais State Park, Stinson Beach and Bolinas.

The ferry is a fun and easy way to travel to Sausalito. **Golden Gate Ferry** (☑ 415-455-2000; www.goldengateferry.org; one-way $10.25) operates to and from the San Francisco Ferry Building six to nine times daily and takes 30 minutes. The **Blue & Gold Fleet** (☑ 415-705-8200; www.blueandgoldfleet.com; Pier 41, Fisherman's Wharf; one-way $11) sails to Sausalito four to five times daily from the Fisherman's Wharf area in San Francisco. Both ferries operate year-round and transport bicycles for free.

Tiburon

At the end of a small peninsula pointing out into the center of the bay, Tiburon is blessed with gorgeous views. The name comes from the Spanish *Punta de Tiburon* (Shark Point). Take the ferry from San Francisco, browse the shops on Main St, grab a bite to eat and you've seen Tiburon. The town

WORTH A TRIP

ANGEL ISLAND

Angel Island (📞 415-435-5390; www.parks.ca.gov/?page_id=468), in San Francisco Bay, has a mild climate with fresh bay breezes, which makes it pleasant for hiking and cycling. For a unique treat, picnic in a protected cove overlooking the close but distant urban surroundings. The island's varied history – it was a hunting and fishing ground for the Miwok people, served as a military base, an immigration station, a WWII Japanese internment camp and a Nike missile site – has left it with some evocative old forts and bunkers to poke around in. There are 12 miles of roads and trails around the island, including a hike to the summit of 781ft Mt Livermore (no bicycles) and a 5-mile perimeter trail.

The Immigration Station (📞 415-435-5537; www.aiisf.org/visit; ⊙ 11am-3pm Mon-Fri, 11am-4pm Sat & Sun), which operated from 1910 to 1940, was the Ellis Island of the West Coast. But this facility was primarily a screening and detention center for Chinese immigrants, who were at that time restricted from entering the US under the Chinese Exclusion Act. Many detainees were held here for long periods before ultimately being returned home, and one of the most unusual sights on the island is the sad and longing Chinese poetry etched into the barrack walls. The site is now a museum with excellent interpretive exhibits; more extensive tours (adult/child $7/5) include admission fees and can be reserved ahead or purchased first-come first-served on-site.

Sea Trek (www.seatrek.com) runs kayaking excursions around the island. You can rent bicycles at Ayala Cove (per hour/day $12.50/40), and there are tram tours ($15) around the island. Two-hour tours on Segway scooters ($68) and electric scooters ($50) are another option, and should be booked in advance. Tour schedules vary seasonally; go to www.angelisland.com for more information.

You can camp on the island, and when the last ferry sails off for the night, the place is your own – except for the very persistent raccoons. The dozen hike-, bicycle- or kayak-in campsites (📞 800-444-7275; www.reserveamerica.com; tent sites $30) are usually reserved months in advance. Near the ferry dock, there's a cafe serving sandwiches and snacks.

Getting There & Away

From San Francisco, take a Blue & Gold Fleet ferry (Map p86; 📞 415-773-1188; www.blueandgoldfleet.com; round-trip adult/child $17/9.50) from Pier 41. From May to September there are three ferries a day on weekends and two on weekdays; during the rest of the year the schedule is reduced.

From Tiburon, take the Angel Island–Tiburon (📞 415-435-2131; www.angelislandferry.com; round-trip adult/child/bike $13.50/11.50/1) ferry.

From Oakland, San Francisco Bay Ferry (📞 415-705-8291; www.sanfranciscobayferry.com; round-trip adult/child $14.50/8.50) has one round-trip on summer weekends.

---

is also a jumping-off point for nearby Angel Island.

◉ Sights & Activities

The central part of town is comprised of Tiburon Blvd, with Juanita Lane and charming Main St arcing off. Main St, which is also known as Ark Row, is where the old houseboats have taken root on dry land and metamorphosed into classy shops and boutiques.

Railroad & Ferry Depot Museum MUSEUM
(www.landmarkssociety.com; 1920 Paradise Dr; suggested donation $5; ⊙ 1-4pm Wed-Sun Apr-Oct) Formerly the terminus for a 3000-person ferry to San Francisco and a railroad that once reached north to Ukiah, this late-19th-century building showcases a scale model of Tiburon's commercial hub, circa 1909. The restored stationmaster's quarters can be visited upstairs.

Old St Hilary's Church CHURCH
(201 Esperanza; ⊙ 1-4pm Sun Apr-Oct) There are great views from the lovely hillside surrounding this fine 19th-century example of Carpenter Gothic.

Richardson Bay Audubon Center NATURE RESERVE
(📞 415-388-2524; http://richardsonbay.audubon.org/; 376 Greenwood Beach Rd; ⊙ 9am-5pm Mon-Sat; 🅿) Off Tiburon Blvd, this center is home to a huge variety of water birds.

Angel Island–Tiburon Ferry   BOAT TOUR
(☑415-435-2131; www.angelislandferry.com; round-trip adult/child/bike $13.50/11.50/1, sunset cruise adult/child 6-12/child 3-5 $20/10/5) Also runs sunset cruises on Friday and Saturday evenings from May through October. Reservations recommended.

🛏 Sleeping

Lodge at Tiburon   HOTEL $$
(☑415-435-3133; www.lodgeattiburon.com; 1651 Tiburon Blvd; r from $179; ❋❅@🤖❄) 🅿 Now a stylish and comfortable contemporary hotel with a grill restaurant, the concrete hallways and staircases testify to the more basic motel it once was. The best value in town, it's a short stroll to anywhere – including the ferry – and there's a pool, DVD library, rental bikes, free parking and a rooftop deck with fireplace and heady Mt Tamalpais views.

Water's Edge Hotel   HOTEL $$$
(☑415-789-5999; www.watersedgehotel.com; 25 Main St; r incl breakfast $249-539; ❋@🤖) 🅿 This hotel, with its deck extending over the bay, is exemplary for its tasteful modernity. Rooms have an elegant minimalism that combines comfort and style, and all afford an immediate view of the bay. The rooms with rustic, high wood ceilings are quite romantic. Perks include complimentary bicycles and evening wine and cheese.

✗ Eating

Sam's Anchor Cafe   SEAFOOD $$
(☑415-435-4527; www.samscafe.com; 27 Main St; mains $14-32; ☺11am-9:30pm Mon-Fri, 9:30am-10pm Sat & Sun; 👪) Sam's has been slinging seafood and burgers since 1920, and though the entrance looks like a shambling little shack, the area out back has unbeatable views. On a warm afternoon, you can't beat a cocktail or a tasty plate of sautéed prawns on the deck.

Caprice   AMERICAN $$$
(☑415-435-3400; www.thecaprice.com; 2000 Paradise Dr; mains $17-58; ☺5-10pm Tue-Sun, plus 11am-3pm Sun) Splurge-worthy and romantic, book a table here at sunset for riveting views of Angel Island, the Golden Gate Bridge and San Francisco. Caprice mostly features seafood, though other standouts include the artichoke bisque and the filet mignon. Take a peek at the fireplace downstairs – it's constructed into the coast bedrock. A three-course midweek dinner ($30) is easier on the wallet.

ⓘ Information

The **Tiburon Peninsula Chamber of Commerce** (☑415-435-5633; www.tiburonchamber.org; 96b Main St) can provide information about the area.

ⓘ Getting There & Away

Golden Gate Transit (☑415-455-2000; www.goldengatetransit.org) commute bus 8 runs directly between San Francisco and Tiburon ($4.75) during the week.

On Hwy 101, look for the off-ramp for Tiburon Blvd, E Blithedale Ave and Hwy 131; driving east, it leads into town and intersects with Juanita Lane and Main St.

Blue & Gold Fleet (☑415-705-8200; one-way $11) sails daily from Pier 41 or the Ferry Building (weekdays commute times only) in San Francisco to Tiburon. You can transport bicycles for free. From Tiburon, ferries also connect regularly to Angel Island.

Sir Francis Drake Blvd & Around

The towns along and nearby the Sir Francis Drake Blvd corridor – including Larkspur, Corte Madera, Ross, San Anselmo and Fairfax – evoke charmed small-town life, even though things get busy around Hwy 101.

Starting from the eastern section in Larkspur, window-shop along Magnolia Ave or explore the redwoods in nearby Baltimore Canyon. On the east side of the freeway is the hulking mass of San Quentin State Penitentiary, California's oldest and most notorious prison, founded in 1852. Johnny Cash recorded an album here in 1969 after scoring a big hit with his live At Folsom Prison album a few years earlier.

Take the bicycle and pedestrian bridge from the ferry terminal across the road to the Marin Country Mart, a shopping center with a dozen excellent eateries and comfortable outdoor seating. One favorite is the Marin Brewing Company (www.marinbrewing.com; 1809 Larkspur Landing Cir, Marin Country Mart, Bldg 2, Larkspur; mains $12-19; ☺11:30am-midnight Sun-Thu, to 1am Fri & Sat; 🤖) brewpub, where you can see the glassed-in kettles behind the bar. The head brewer, Arne Johnson, has won many awards, and the Mt Tam Pale Ale complements the menu of pizza, burgers and hearty sandwiches.

Just south, Corte Madera is home to one of the Bay Area's best bookstores, Book Passage (☑415-927-0960; www.bookpassage.com;

51 Tamal Vista Blvd; ⊕9am-9pm), in the Marketplace shopping center. It has a strong travel section, plus frequent author appearances.

Continuing west along Sir Francis Drake, San Anselmo has a cute, small downtown area along San Anselmo Ave, including several antique shops. The attractive center of neighboring Fairfax has ample dining and shopping options, and cyclists congregate at Gestalt Haus Fairfax (28 Bolinas Rd, Fairfax; ⊕11:30am-11pm Sun & Mon, 11:30am-midnight Tue & Wed, 11:30am-2am Thu-Sat) for the indoor bicycle parking, board games, European draft beers and sausages of the meaty or vegan persuasion.

Arti (www.articafe.com; 7282 Sir Francis Drake Blvd, Lagunitas; mains $10-14; ⊕noon-9pm; 🖉), between Hwys 1 and 101 in the tiny hamlet of Lagunitas, is a tempting stop for organic Indian fare. There's a cozy, casual dining room and an outdoor patio for warm days, and folks from miles around adore its sizzling chicken tikka platter.

Six miles east of Olema on Sir Francis Drake Blvd, Samuel P Taylor State Park (☑415-488-9897; www.parks.ca.gov/?page_id=469; parking $8, tent & RV sites $35, cabin $100) has beautiful, secluded campsites in redwood groves and a coveted handful of new five-person cabins with electricity and wood stoves. The park's also located on the paved Cross Marin Trail, with miles of creekside landscape to explore along a former railroad grade.

ℹ️ Getting There & Around

Golden Gate Ferry (☑415-455-2000; www.goldengateferry.org) runs a daily ferry service ($9.50, 50 minutes) from the Ferry Building in San Francisco to Sir Francis Drake Blvd in Larkspur, directly east of Hwy 101. You can take bicycles on the ferry.

San Rafael

The oldest and largest town in Marin, San Rafael is slightly less upscale than most of its neighbors but doesn't lack atmosphere. It's a common stop for travelers on their way to Point Reyes. Just north of San Rafael, Lucas Valley Rd heads west to Point Reyes Station, passing George Lucas' Skywalker Ranch. Fourth St, San Rafael's main drag, is lined with cafes and shops. If you follow it west out of downtown San Rafael, it meets Sir Francis Drake Blvd and continues west to the coast.

👁️ Sights

China Camp State Park PARK
(☑415-456-0766; www.parks.ca.gov/?page_id=466; per car $5) About 4 miles east of San Rafael, this is a pleasant place to stop for a picnic or short hike. From Hwy 101, take the N San Pedro Rd exit and continue 3 miles east. A Chinese fishing village once stood here, and a small museum exhibits interesting artifacts from the settlement.

Mission San Rafael Arcángel MISSION
(www.saintraphael.com; 1104 5th Ave) The town began with this mission, founded in 1817, which served as a sanatorium for Native Americans suffering from European diseases. The present building is a replica from 1949.

🛏️ Sleeping & Eating

China Camp State Park CAMPGROUND $
(☑800-444-7275; www.reserveamerica.com; tent sites $35) The park has 30 walk-in campsites with showers and pleasant shade.

Panama Hotel B&B $$
(☑415-457-3993; www.panamahotel.com; 4 Bayview St; s/d with shared bath $75/90, r $120-195; ✴️ 🛜 🐾) The 10 artsy rooms at this B&B, in a building dating from 1910, each have their own unique style and charming decor – such as crazy quilts and vibrant accent walls. The hotel restaurant has an inviting courtyard patio.

★ Sol Food Puerto Rican Cuisine PUERTO RICAN $$
(☑415-451-4765; www.solfoodrestaurant.com; cnr Lincoln Ave & 3rd St; mains $7.50-16; ⊕7am-midnight Mon-Thu, to 2am Fri, 8am-2am Sat, to midnight Sun) 🌿 Lazy ceiling fans, a profusion of tropical plants and the pulse of Latin rhythms create a soothing atmosphere for delicious dishes such as a *jíbaro* sandwich and other meals concocted with plantains, organic veggies and free-range meats.

☆ Entertainment

Rafael Film Center CINEMA
(☑415-454-1222; www.cafilm.org/rfc; 1118 4th St) A restored downtown cinema offering innovative art-house programming on three screens in state-of-the-art surroundings.

ℹ️ Getting There & Away

Numerous **Golden Gate Transit** (☑415-455-2000, 511; www.goldengatetransit.org) buses operate between San Francisco and the San Rafael Transit Center at 3rd and Hetherton Sts ($5.75, one hour).

Mill Valley

Nestled under the redwoods at the base of Mt Tamalpais, tiny Mill Valley is one of the Bay Area's most picturesque hamlets. Mill Valley was originally a logging town, its name stemming from an 1830s sawmill – the first in the Bay Area to provide lumber. Though the 1892 Mill Valley Lumber Company still greets motorists on Miller Ave, the town's a vastly different place today, packed with wildly expensive homes, fancy cars and pricey boutiques.

Mill Valley also served as the starting point for the scenic railway that carried visitors up Mt Tamalpais. The tracks were removed in 1940, and today the Depot Bookstore & Cafe occupies the space of the former station.

◉ Sights & Activities

Old Mill Park   PARK
Several blocks west of downtown along Throckmorton Ave is Old Mill Park, perfect for a picnic. Here you'll also find a replica of the town's namesake sawmill. Just past the bridge at Old Mill Creek, the **Dipsea Steps** mark the start of the Dipsea Trail.

★ Dipsea Trail   HIKING
A beloved though demanding hike is the 7-mile Dipsea Trail, which climbs over the coastal range and down to Stinson Beach, cutting through a corner of Muir Woods. This classic trail starts at Old Mill Park with a climb up 676 steps in three separate flights, and includes a few more ups and downs before reaching the ocean. **West Marin Stagecoach** (www.marintransit.org/stage.html) route 61 runs from Stinson Beach to Mill Valley, making it a doable one-way day hike.

The few slaloms between staircases aren't well-signed, but locals can point the way.

⚞ Festivals & Events

Mill Valley Film Festival   FILM
(www.mvff.com; ⊙Oct) Each October the Mill Valley Film Festival presents an innovative, internationally regarded program of independent films.

⊨ Sleeping

Acqua Hotel   BOUTIQUE HOTEL $$
(☑415-380-0400, 888-662-9555; www.marinhotels.com; 555 Redwood Hwy; r incl breakfast from $159; ⊕@⊚⊚) 🖉 With views of the bay and Mt Tamalpais, and a lobby with a soothing fireplace and fountain, the Acqua doesn't lack for pleasant eye candy. Contemporary rooms are sleekly designed with beautiful fabrics.

Mountain Home Inn   INN $$$
(☑415-381-9000; www.mtnhomeinn.com; 810 Panoramic Hwy; r incl breakfast $195-345; ⊚) Set amid redwood, spruce and pine trees on a ridge of Mt Tamalpais, this retreat is both modern and rustic. The larger (more expensive) rooms are rugged beauties, with unfinished timbers forming columns from floor to ceiling, as though the forest is shooting up through the floor. Smaller rooms are cozy dens for two. The positioning of a good local trail map on the dresser makes it clear that it's a place to breathe and unwind.

✕ Eating & Drinking

Depot Bookstore & Cafe   CAFE $
(www.depotbookstore.com; 87 Throckmorton Ave; mains under $10; ⊙7am-7pm; ⊚) Smack in the town center, Depot serves cappuccinos, sandwiches and light meals. The bookstore sells lots of local publications, including trail guides.

Buckeye Roadhouse   AMERICAN $$
(☑415-331-2600; www.buckeyeroadhouse.com; 15 Shoreline Hwy; mains $18-37; ⊙11:30am-10:30pm Mon-Sat, 10:30am-10pm Sun) Originally opened as a roadside stop in 1932, the Buckeye is a Marin County gem, and its upscale American cuisine is in no danger of being compared to truck-stop fare. Stop off for chili-lime 'brick' chicken, baby back ribs or oysters Bingo and a devilish wedge of s'more pie before getting back on Hwy 101.

Mill Valley Beerworks   PUB
(www.millvalleybeerworks.com; 173 Throckmorton Ave; mains $18-32; ⊙5:30-10:30pm Mon-Fri, 11:30am-10:30pm Sat & Sun, kitchen closed 3-5:30pm) 🖉 With 60 bottled varieties of brew and a few of its own (from the Fort Point Brewing Company in San Francisco) amongst the dozen or so on tap, beer lovers can pair their favorites with the kitchen's delicious farm-to-table cuisine. The unsigned setting is stark and stylish, with unfinished wood tables and a pressed-tin wall.

❶ Information

Visitor information is available from the **Mill Valley Chamber of Commerce** (☑415-388-9700; www.millvalley.org; 85 Throckmorton Ave; ⊙10am-4pm Tue-Fri).

ⓘ Getting There & Away

From San Francisco or Sausalito, take Hwy 101 north to the Mill Valley–Stinson Beach–Hwy 1 exit. Follow Hwy 1 (also called the Shoreline Hwy) to Almonte Blvd (which becomes Miller Ave), then follow Miller Ave into downtown Mill Valley.

From the north, take the E Blithedale Ave exit from Hwy 101, then head west into Mill Valley.

Golden Gate Transit (☑ 415-455-2000; www.goldengatetranist.org) bus 4 runs directly from San Francisco to Mill Valley ($4.75) on weekdays; route 17 ($2) runs between there from the Sausalito ferry terminal daily.

Mt Tamalpais State Park

Standing guard over Marin County, majestic Mt Tamalpais (Mt Tam) has breathtaking 360-degree views of ocean, bay and hills rolling into the distance. The rich, natural beauty of the 2571ft mountain and its surrounding area is inspiring – especially considering it lies within an hour's drive from one of the state's largest metropolitan areas.

Mt Tamalpais State Park (☑ 415-388-2070; www.parks.ca.gov/mttamalpais; parking $8) was formed in 1930, partly from land donated by congressman and naturalist William Kent (who also donated the land that became Muir Woods National Monument in 1907). Its 6300 acres are home to deer, foxes, bobcats and many miles of hiking and cycling trails.

Mt Tam was a sacred place to the coastal Miwok people for thousands of years before the arrival of European and American settlers. By the late 19th century, San Franciscans were escaping the bustle of the city with all-day outings on the mountain, and in 1896 the 'world's crookedest railroad' (281 turns) was completed from Mill Valley to the summit. Though the railroad was closed in 1930, Old Railroad Grade is today one of Mt Tam's most popular and scenic hiking and cycling paths.

⊙ Sights

Panoramic Hwy climbs from Mill Valley through the park to Stinson Beach. From Pantoll Station, it's 4.2 miles by car to East Peak Summit; take Pantoll Rd and then panoramic Ridgecrest Blvd to the top. A 10-minute hike leads to a fire lookout at the very top and awesome sea-to-bay views.

Mountain Theater   THEATER
(☑ 415-383-1100; www.mountainplay.org; adult/child $40/20) The park's natural-stone, 4000-seat theater hosts the annual 'Mountain Play' series on a half dozen weekend afternoons between mid-May and late June. Free shuttles are provided from Mill Valley. Free monthly astronomy programs (www.friendsofmttam.org/astronomy.html; ⊙ Apr-Oct) also take place here on Saturday nights around the new moon.

🏃 Activities

Hiking

The park map is a smart investment, as there are a dozen worthwhile hiking trails in the area. From Pantoll Station, the Steep Ravine Trail follows a wooded creek on to the coast (about 2.1 miles each way). For a longer hike, veer right (northwest) after 1.5 miles onto the Dipsea Trail, which meanders through trees for 1 mile before ending at Stinson Beach. Grab some lunch, then walk north through town and follow signs for the Matt Davis Trail, which leads 2.7 miles back to Pantoll Station, making a good loop. The Matt Davis Trail continues on beyond Pantoll Station, wrapping gently around the mountain with superb views.

Another worthy option is Cataract Trail, which runs along Cataract Creek from the end of Pantoll Rd; it's approximately 3 miles to Alpine Lake. The last mile is a spectacular rooty staircase as the trail descends alongside Cataract Falls.

Mountain Biking

Cyclists must stay on the fire roads (and off the single-track trails) and keep to speeds under 15mph. Rangers are prickly about these rules, and a ticket can result in a steep fine.

The most popular ride is the Old Railroad Grade. For a sweaty, 6-mile, 2280ft climb, start in Mill Valley at the end of W Blithedale Ave and cycle up to East Peak. It takes about an hour to reach the West Point Inn from Mill Valley. For an easier start, begin part way up at the Mountain Home Inn and follow the Gravity Car Grade to the Old Railroad Grade and the West Point Inn. From the inn, it's an easy half-hour ride to the summit.

From just west of Pantoll Station, cyclists can either take the Deer Park fire road, which runs close to the Dipsea Trail, through giant redwoods to the main entrance of Muir Woods, or the southeastern extension of the Coastal Trail, which has breathtaking views of the coast before joining Hwy 1 about 2 miles north of Muir

Beach. Either option requires a return to Mill Valley via Frank Valley/Muir Woods Rd, which climbs steadily (800ft) to Panoramic Hwy and then becomes Sequoia Valley Rd as it drops toward Mill Valley. A left turn on Wildomar and two right turns at Mill Creek Park lead to the center of Mill Valley.

For further information on bicycle routes and rules, contact the Marin County Bicycle Coalition (p115), whose Marin Bicycle Map is the gold standard for local cycling.

🛏 Sleeping & Eating

⭐ **Steep Ravine** CAMPGROUND, CABIN $
(Map p48; ☑ 800-444-7275; www.reserveamerica. com; Nov-Sep; tent site $25, cabin $100) Just off Hwy 1, about 1 mile south of Stinson Beach, this jewel has seven beachfront campsites and nine rustic five-person cabins with wood stoves overlooking the ocean. Both options are booked out months in advance and reservations can be made up to seven months ahead.

Bootjack Campground CAMPGROUND $
(Panoramic Hwy; tent sites $25) Recently re-opened after decades of closure, its 15 first-come, first-served walk-in sites are right on two of the park's best hiking trails and adjacent to Redwood Creek, with open vistas to the south. It's a half-mile northeast of Pantoll Station.

Pantoll Campground CAMPGROUND $
(Panoramic Hwy; tent sites $25) From the parking lot it's a 100yd walk or bicycle ride to the campground, with 16 first-come, first-served tent sites but no showers.

West Point Inn LODGE, CABIN $
(☑info 415-388-9955, reservations 415-646-0702; www.westpointinn.com; 100 Old Railroad Grade Fire Rd, Mill Valley; r per adult/child $50/25) Load up your sleeping bag and hike in to this rustic 1904 hilltop hideaway built in as a stopover for the Mill Valley and Mt Tamalpais Scenic Railway. It also hosts monthly pancake breakfasts ($10) on Sundays during the summer.

ℹ Information

Pantoll Station (☑ 415-388-2070; www.parks. ca.gov/?page_id=471; 801 Panoramic Hwy; ☺ variable hours; 🚻) is the park headquarters. Detailed park maps are sold here. The **Mt Tamalpais Interpretative Association** (www.mttam. net; ☺ 11am-4pm Sat & Sun) staffs a small visitor center at East Peak.

ℹ Getting There & Away

To reach Pantoll Station by car, take Hwy 1 to the Panoramic Hwy and look for the Pantoll signs. **West Marin Stagecoach** (☑ 415-526-3239; www.marintransit.org/stage.html) route 61 runs daily minibuses ($2) from Marin City (via Mill Valley; plus weekend and holiday service from the Sausalito ferry) to both the Pantoll Station and Mountain Home Inn.

Muir Woods National Monument

Walking through an awesome stand of the world's tallest trees is an experience to be had only in Northern California and a small part of southern Oregon. The old-growth redwoods at Muir Woods (☑ 415-388-2595; www.nps.gov/muwo; Muir Woods Rd, Mill Valley; adult/child $7/free; ☺ 8am-sunset), just 12 miles north of the Golden Gate Bridge, is the closest redwood stand to San Francisco. The trees were initially eyed by loggers, and Redwood Creek, as the area was known, seemed ideal for a dam. Those plans were halted when congressman and naturalist William Kent bought a section of Redwood Creek and, in 1907, donated 295 acres to the federal government. President Theodore Roosevelt made the site a national monument in 1908, the name honoring John Muir, naturalist and founder of environmental organization the Sierra Club.

Muir Woods can become quite crowded, especially on weekends. Try to come midweek, early in the morning or late in the afternoon, when tour buses are less of a problem. Even at busy times, a short hike will get you out of the densest crowds and onto trails with huge trees and stunning vistas. A lovely cafe serves local and organic goodies and hot drinks that hit the spot on foggy days.

🏃 Activities

The 1-mile Main Trail Loop is a gentle walk alongside Redwood Creek to the 1000-year-old trees at Cathedral Grove; it returns via Bohemian Grove, where the tallest tree in the park stands 254ft high. The Dipsea Trail is a good 2-mile hike up to the top of aptly named Cardiac Hill.

You can also walk down into Muir Woods by taking trails from the Panoramic Hwy, such as the Bootjack Trail from the Bootjack picnic area, or from Mt Tamalpais' Pantoll Station campground, along the Ben Johnson Trail.

ⓘ Getting There & Away

The parking lot is insanely full during busy periods, so consider taking the seasonal **Muir Woods Shuttle** (Route 66F; www.marintransit. org; round trip adult/child $5/free; ⊙ weekends & holidays late-Mar–Oct). The 40-minute shuttle connects with Sausalito ferries arriving from San Francisco before 3pm.

To get there by car, drive north on Hwy 101, exit at Hwy 1 and continue north along Hwy 1/ Shoreline Hwy to the Panoramic Hwy (a right-hand fork). Follow that for about 1 mile to Four Corners, where you turn left onto Muir Woods Rd (there are plenty of signs).

Muir Beach

The turnoff to Muir Beach from Hwy 1 is marked by the longest row of mailboxes on the north coast. Muir Beach is a quiet little town with a nice beach, but it has no direct bus service. Just north of Muir Beach there are superb views up and down the coast from the Muir Beach Overlook; during WWII, watch was kept from the surrounding concrete lookouts for invading Japanese ships.

⌂ Sleeping & Eating

Green Gulch Farm & Zen Center LODGE $$
(☏415-383-3134; www.sfzc.org; 1601 Shoreline Hwy; s $90-155, d $160-225, d cottage $350-400, all with 3 meals; @☎) ◢ Green Gulch Farm & Zen Center is a Buddhist retreat in the hills above Muir Beach. The center's accommodations are elegant, restful and modern, and delicious buffet-style vegetarian meals are included. A hilltop retreat cottage is 25 minutes away by foot.

Pelican Inn PUB $$$
(☏415-383-6000; www.pelicaninn.com; 10 Pacific Way; mains $14-34; ▣) The oh-so-English Tudor-style Pelican Inn is Muir Beach's only commercial establishment. Hikers, cyclists and families come for pub lunches inside its timbered restaurant and cozy bar, perfect for a pint, a game of darts and warming up beside the open fire. The British fare is respectable, but it's the setting that's magical. Upstairs are seven luxe rooms (from $206) with cushy half-canopy beds.

Stinson Beach

Just 5 miles north of Muir Beach, Stinson Beach is positively buzzing on warm weekends. The town flanks Hwy 1 for about three blocks and is densely packed with galleries, shops, eateries and B&Bs. The beach itself is often blanketed with fog, and when the sun's shining it's blanketed with surfers, families and gawkers. There are views of Point Reyes and San Francisco on clear days, and the beach is long enough for a vigorous stroll.

◉ Sights

Stinson Beach BEACH
Three-mile-long Stinson Beach is a popular surf spot, but swimming is advised from late May to mid-September only; for updated weather and surf conditions call ☏415-868-1922. The beach is one block west of Hwy 1.

Red Rock Beach BEACH
Around 1 mile south of Stinson Beach is Red Rock Beach. It's a clothing-optional beach that attracts smaller crowds, probably because it can only be accessed by a steep trail from Hwy 1.

★ **Audubon Canyon Ranch** WILDLIFE RESERVE
(☏415-868-9244; www.egret.org; donations requested; ⊙ usually 10am-4pm Sat, Sun & holidays mid-Mar–mid-Jul) Audubon Canyon Ranch is about 3.5 miles north of Stinson Beach on Hwy 1, in the hills above the Bolinas Lagoon. A major nesting ground for great blue herons and great egrets, viewing scopes are set up on hillside blinds where you can watch these magnificent birds congregate to nest and hatch their chicks in tall redwoods. At low tide, harbor seals often doze on sand bars in the lagoon. Confirm hours, as a recent nesting failure may alter future public access.

⌂ Sleeping & Eating

Sandpiper MOTEL, CABINS $$
(☏415-868-1632; www.sandpiperstinsonbeach. com; 1 Marine Way; r $145-225; ☎) Just off Hwy 1 and a quick stroll to the beach, the ten comfortable rooms and cabins of the Sandpiper have gas fireplaces and kitchenettes, and are ensconced in a lush garden and picnic area. Prices dip from November through March; two-night minimum stay on weekends.

Parkside Cafe AMERICAN $$
(☏415-868-1272; www.parksidecafe.com; 43 Arenal Ave; mains $9-25; ⊙7:30am-9pm, coffee from 6am) ◢ Parkside Cafe is famous for its hearty breakfasts and lunches, and noted far and wide for its excellent coastal cuisine. Reservations are recommended for dinner.

ℹ️ Getting There & Away

West Marin Stagecoach (☏ 415-526-3239; www.marintransit.org/stage.html) route 61 runs daily minibuses ($2) from Marin City, and weekend and holiday services to the Sausalito ferry. By car from San Francisco, it's nearly an hour's drive, though on weekends plan for toe-tapping traffic delays.

Bolinas

For a town that is so famously unexcited about tourism, Bolinas offers some fairly tempting attractions for the visitor. Known as Jugville during the Gold Rush days, the sleepy beachside community is home to writers, musicians and fisherfolk, and deliberately hard to find. The highway department used to put signs up at the turnoff from Hwy 1; locals kept taking them down, so the highway department finally gave up.

◎ Sights & Activities

★ Point Blue Conservation Science   BIRD OBSERVATORY
(☏ 415-868-0655; www.pointblue.org) Off Mesa Rd west of downtown and formerly known as the Point Reyes Bird Observatory, its Palomarin Field Station has bird-banding and netting demonstrations, a visitors center and nature trail. Banding demonstrations are held in the morning every Tuesday to Sunday from May to late November, and on Wednesday, Saturday and Sunday the rest of the year.

Bolinas Museum   MUSEUM
(☏ 415-868-0330; www.bolinasmuseum.org; 48 Wharf Rd; ◎ 1-5pm Fri, noon-5pm Sat & Sun) **FREE** This courtyard complex of five galleries exhibits local artists and showcases the region's history. Look for the weathered Bolinas highway sign affixed to the wall, since you certainly didn't see one on your way into town.

Agate Beach   BEACH
There are tide pools along some 2 miles of coastline at Agate Beach, around the end of Duxbury Point.

2 Mile Surf Shop   SURFING
(☏ 415-868-0264; www.2milesurf.com; 22 Brighton Ave; ◎ 9am-6pm May-Oct, 10am-5pm Nov-Apr) Surfing's popular in these parts, and this shop behind the post office rents boards and wetsuits and also gives lessons. Call ☏ 415-868-2412 for the surf report.

Hiking

Beyond the observatory is the Palomarin parking lot and access to various walking trails in the southern part of the Point Reyes National Seashore, including the easy (and popular) 3-mile trail to lovely Bass Lake. A sweet inland spot buffered by tall trees, this small lake is perfect for a pastoral swim on a toasty day. You can dive in wearing your birthday suit (or not), bring an inner tube to float about, or do a long lap all the way across.

If you continue 1.5 miles northwest, you'll reach the unmaintained trail to Alamere Falls, a fantastic flume plunging 50ft off a cliff and down to the beach. But sketchy beach access makes it more enjoyable to walk another 1.5 miles to Wildcat Beach and then backtrack a mile on sand.

🛏️ Sleeping & Eating

Smiley's Schooner Saloon & Hotel MOTEL $$ (☏ 415-868-1311; www.smileyssaloon.com; 41 Wharf Rd; r $104-124; 🐾 ❄️) A crusty old place dating back to 1851, Smiley's has simple but decent rooms, and last-minute weekday rates can be a bargain. The bar, which serves some food, has live bands Thursday through Saturday and is frequented by plenty of salty dogs and grizzled deadheads.

Bolinas People's Store   CAFE, MARKET $ (14 Wharf Rd; ◎ 8:30am-6:30pm; 🖊️) 🍴 An awesome little co-op grocery store hidden behind the community center, the People's Store serves Fair Trade coffee and sells organic produce, fresh soup and excellent tamales. Eat at the tables in the shady courtyard, and have a rummage through the Free Box, a shed full of clothes and other waiting-to-be-reused items.

Coast Café   AMERICAN $$ (www.bolinascoastcafe.com; 46 Wharf Rd; mains $10-22; ◎ 11:30am-3pm & 5-8pm Tue-Thu, to 9pm Fri, 8am-3pm & 5-9pm Sat, to 8pm Sun; 🖊️🖐️) 🍴 The only 'real' restaurant in town, everyone jockeys for outdoor seats among the flowerboxes for fish and chips, barbecued oysters, or buttermilk pancakes with damn good coffee. Live music Thursday and Sunday nights.

ℹ️ Getting There & Away

Route 61 of the **West Marin Stagecoach** (☏ 415-526-3239; www.marintransit.org/stage.html) goes daily ($2) from the Marin City transit hub (weekend and holiday service from the Sausalito ferry) to downtown Bolinas. By car, follow Hwy

1 north from Stinson Beach and turn west for Bolinas at the first stop sign. At the first stop sign, take another left onto Olema–Bolinas Rd and follow it 2 miles to town.

Olema & Nicasio

About 10 miles north of Stinson Beach near the junction of Hwy 1 and Sir Francis Drake Blvd, Olema was the main settlement in west Marin in the 1860s. Back then, there was a stagecoach service to San Rafael and there were *six* saloons. In 1875, when the railroad was built through Point Reyes Station instead of Olema, the town's importance began to fade. In 1906 it gained distinction once again as the epicenter of the Great Quake.

The Bolinas Ridge Trail, a 12-mile series of ups and downs for hikers or bikers, starts about 1 mile west of Olema, on Sir Francis Drake Blvd. It has great views.

In the former Olema Inn, a creaky 1876 building, hyper-local Sir & Star (☑415-663-1034; www.sirandstar.com; cnr Sir Francis Drake Blvd & Hwy 1; mains $20, prix fixe Sat/other nights $75/48; ⊙5-9pm Wed-Sun, plus earlier hours in summer; ☎) 🍴 restaurant delights with Marin-sourced seasonal bounty such as Tomales Bay oysters, Dungeness crab and duck 'faux' gras. Reservations recommended.

About a 15-minute drive inland from Olema, at the geographic center of Marin County, is Nicasio, a tiny town with a low-key rural flavor. In the town center, its music venue, Rancho Nicasio (☑415-662-2219; www.ranchonicasio.com; 1 Old Rancheria Rd; ⊙11:30am-3pm & 5-9pm Mon-Thu, to 10pm Fri, 11am-3pm & 5-10pm Sat, to 9pm Sun), is a rustic saloon that regularly attracts local and national blues, rock and country performers.

ⓘ Getting There & Away

Route 68 of the **West Marin Stagecoach** (☑415-526-3239; www.marintransit.org/stage.html) runs daily to Olema and Samuel P Taylor State Park from the San Rafael Transit Center ($2).

Nicasio is located at the west end of Lucas Valley Rd, 10 miles from Hwy 101.

Point Reyes Station

Though the railroad stopped coming through in 1933 and the town is small, Point Reyes Station is nevertheless the hub of west Marin. Dominated by dairies and ranches, the region was invaded by artists in the 1960s. Today it's an interesting blend of art galleries and tourist shops. The town has a rowdy saloon and the occasional smell of cattle on the afternoon breeze.

🛏 Sleeping & Eating

Cute little cottages, cabins and B&Bs are plentiful in and around Point Reyes. The West Marin Chamber of Commerce (☑415-663-9232; www.pointreyes.org) has numerous listings, as does the Point Reyes Lodging Association (☑415-663-1872, 800-539-1872; www.ptreyes.com).

Windsong Cottage Guest Yurt   YURT **$$**
(☑415-663-9695; www.windsongcottage.com; 25 McDonald Lane; d yurt $185-210; ☎) A wood-burning stove, private outdoor hot tub, comfy king bed and kitchen stocked with breakfast supplies make this round sky-lighted abode a cozy slice of heaven.

Bovine Bakery   BAKERY **$**
(www.thebovinebakery.com; 11315 Hwy 1; pastry $3; ⊙6:30am-5pm Mon-Fri, 7am-5pm Sat & Sun) 🍴 Don't leave town without sampling something buttery from possibly the best bakery in Marin. A sweet bear-claw pastry and an organic coffee are a good way to kick off your morning.

Tomales Bay Foods & Cowgirl Creamery   DELI, MARKET **$**
(www.cowgirlcreamery.com; 80 4th St; sandwiches $6-12; ⊙10am-6pm Wed-Sun; ☑) 🍴 A market in an old barn selling picnic items, including gourmet cheeses and organic produce. Reserve a spot in advance for the small-scale artisanal cheesemaker's demonstration and tasting ($5); watch the curd-making and cutting, then sample a half dozen of the fresh and aged cheeses. All of the milk is local and organic, with vegetarian rennet in the soft cheeses.

Osteria Stellina   ITALIAN **$$**
(☑415-663-9988; www.osteriastellina.com; 11285 Hwy 1; mains $15-24; ⊙11:30am-2:30pm & 5-9pm; ☑) 🍴 This place specializes in rustic Italian cuisine made from locally sourced produce, including pizza and pasta dishes and Niman Ranch meats. For dessert, the water-buffalo-milk gelato is the way to go.

Pine Cone Diner   DINER **$$**
(www.pineconediner.com; 60 4th St; mains $9-13; ⊙8am-2:30pm; ☑) 🍴 The Pine Cone serves big breakfasts and lunches inside a cute

retro dining room and at shaded al fresco picnic tables. Try the buttermilk biscuits, the chorizo or tofu scramble, or the fried oyster sandwich.

☆ Entertainment

Old Western Saloon   LIVE MUSIC, BAR
(☑415-663-1661; cnr Shoreline Hwy & 2nd St; ☉10am-midnight or 2am) A rustic 1906 saloon with live bands and cool tables emblazoned with horseshoes. Prince Charles stopped in here for an impromptu pint during a local visit in 2006.

❶ Getting There & Away

Hwy 1 becomes Main St in town, running right through the center. Route 68 of the **West Marin Stagecoach** (☑415-526-3239; www.marintransit.org/stage.html) runs here daily from the San Rafael Transit Center ($2).

Inverness

This tiny town, the last outpost on your journey westward, is spread along the west side of Tomales Bay. It's got good places to eat and, among the surrounding hills and picturesque shoreline, multiple rental cottages and quaint B&Bs. Several great beaches are only a short drive north.

🏃 Activities

Blue Waters Kayaking   KAYAKING
(☑415-669-2600; www.bluewaterskayaking.com; rentals/tours from $50/68; ▥) At the Tomales Bay Resort and across the bay in Marshall (on Hwy 1, eight miles north of Point Reyes Station), this outfit offers various Tomales Bay tours, or you can rent a kayak and paddle around secluded beaches and rocky crevices on your own; no experience necessary.

🛏 Sleeping

Cottages at Point Reyes Seashore   BUNGALOW $$
(☑800-416-0405, 415-669-7250; www.invernessvalleyinn.com; 13275 Sir Francis Drake Blvd; r $139-219; ❀▥) 🖋 Cottages at Point Reyes Seashore is a family-friendly place hidden away in the woods, just a mile from town. It offers clean, modern kitchenette rooms in A-frame structures, and has a tennis court, hot tub, horseshoe pitches, barbecue pits and in-room DVD players. There's also a large garden and private nature trail. It's

past the town, on the way down the Point Reyes peninsula.

Tomales Bay Resort   MOTEL $$
(☑415-669-1389; www.tomalesbayresort.com; 12938 Sir Francis Drake Blvd; r $125-275; ❀▥) The bayside Tomales Bay Resort has 36 motel rooms and a pool (unheated). When rates drop – Sunday through Thursday and in the winter – it's one of the best bargains around.

Dancing Coyote Beach Cottages   BUNGALOW $$$
(☑415-669-7200; www.dancingcoyotebeach.com; 12794 Sir Francis Drake Blvd; cottages $200-260; ❀▥) Serene and comfortable, these four modern cottages back right onto Tomales Bay, with skylights and decks extending the views in all directions. Full kitchens contain tasty breakfast foods and fireplaces are stocked with firewood for foggy nights.

❶ Getting There & Away

From Hwy 1, Sir Francis Drake Blvd leads straight into Inverness. Route 68 of the **West Marin Stagecoach** (☑415-526-3239; www.marintransit.org/stage.html) makes daily stops here from San Rafael ($2).

Point Reyes National Seashore

The windswept peninsula Point Reyes (Map p48; www.nps.gov/pore) FREE is a rough-hewn beauty that has always lured marine mammals and migratory birds as well as scores of shipwrecks. It was here in 1579 that Sir Francis Drake landed to repair his ship, the *Golden Hind*. During his five-week stay he mounted a brass plaque near the shore claiming this land for England. Historians believe this occurred at Drakes Beach and there is a marker there today. In 1595 the first of scores of ships lost in these waters, the *San Augustine,* went down. She was a Spanish treasure ship out of Manila laden with luxury goods, and to this day bits of her cargo wash up on shore. Despite modern navigation, the dangerous waters here continue to claim the odd boat.

Point Reyes National Seashore has 110 sq miles of pristine ocean beaches, and the peninsula offers excellent hiking and camping opportunities. Be sure to bring warm clothing, as even the sunniest days can quickly turn cold and foggy.

ℹ POINT REYES SHUTTLE

On good-weather weekends and holidays from late December through mid-April, the road to Chimney Rock and the lighthouse is closed to private vehicles. Instead you must take a shuttle ($5, children under 17 free) from Drakes Beach.

◉ Sights & Activities

For an awe-inspiring view, follow the Earthquake Trail from the park headquarters at Bear Valley. The trail reaches a 16ft gap between the two halves of a once-connected fence line, a lasting testimonial to the power of the 1906 earthquake that was centered in this area. Another trail leads from the visitors center a short way to Kule Loklo, a reproduction of a Miwok village.

Limantour Rd, off Bear Valley Rd about 1 mile north of Bear Valley Visitor Center, leads to the Point Reyes Hostel and Limantour Beach, where a trail runs along Limantour Spit with Estero de Limantour on one side and Drakes Bay on the other. The Inverness Ridge Trail heads from Limantour Rd up to Mt Vision (1282ft), from where there are spectacular views of the entire national seashore. You can drive almost to the top of Mt Vision from the other side.

About 2 miles past Inverness, Pierce Point Rd splits off to the right from Sir Francis Drake Blvd. From here you can get to two nice swimming beaches on the bay: Marshall Beach requires a mile-long hike from the parking area, while Hearts Desire, in Tomales Bay State Park, is accessible by car.

Pierce Point Rd continues to the huge windswept sand dunes at Abbotts Lagoon, full of peeping killdeer and other shorebirds. At the end of the road is Pierce Point Ranch, the trailhead for the 3.5-mile Tomales Point Trail through the Tule Elk Reserve. The plentiful elk are an amazing sight, standing with their big horns against the backdrop of Tomales Point, with Bodega Bay to the north, Tomales Bay to the east and the Pacific Ocean to the west.

★Point Reyes Lighthouse   LIGHTHOUSE
(☺lighthouse 10am-4:30pm Fri-Mon, lens room 2:30-4pm Fri-Mon) FREE At the very end of Sir Francis Drake Blvd, with wild terrain and ferocious winds, this spot feels like the end of the earth and offers the best whale-watching along the coast. The lighthouse sits below the headlands; to reach it requires descending more than 300 stairs. Nearby Chimney Rock is a fine short hike, especially in spring when the wildflowers are blossoming. A nearby viewing area allows you to spy on the park's elephant seal colony.

Keep back from the water's edge at the exposed North Beach and South Beach, as people have been dragged in and drowned by frequent rogue waves.

Five Brooks Stables   HORSEBACK RIDING
(☏415-663-1570; www.fivebrooks.com; trail rides from $40; ▣) Explore the landscape on horseback with a trail ride. Take a slow amble through a pasture or ascend more than 1000ft to Inverness Ridge for views of the Olema Valley. If you can stay in the saddle for six hours, ride along the coastline to Alamere Falls via Wildcat Beach.

🛏 Sleeping

Wake up to deer nibbling under a blanket of fog at one of Point Reyes' four very popular hike-in campgrounds (☏877-444-6777; www.recreation.gov; tent sites $20), each with pit toilets, water and tables. Reservations are accepted up to six months in advance, and weekends go fast. Reaching the campgrounds requires a 2- to 6-mile hike or bicycle ride, or you can try for a permit to camp on the beach in Tomales Bay. Check with the Bear Valley Visitor Center for same-day permits.

★HI Point Reyes Hostel   HOSTEL $
(☏415-663-8811; www.norcalhostels.org/reyes; 1390 Limantour Spit Rd; dm $25, r $82-120, all with shared bath; @) ⌾ Just off Limantour Rd, this rustic HI property has bunkhouses with warm and cozy front rooms, big-view windows and outdoor areas with hill vistas, and a newer LEED-certified building with four private rooms (two-night minimum stay on weekends) and a stunning modern kitchen. It's in a secluded valley 2 miles from the ocean and surrounded by lovely hiking trails.

ℹ Information

The park headquarters, Bear Valley Visitor Center (☏415-464-5100; www.nps.gov/pore; ☺10am-5pm Mon-Fri, from 9am Sat & Sun), is near Olema and has information and maps. You can also get information at the Point Reyes Lighthouse and the Kenneth Patrick Center (☏415-669-1250; ☺9:30am-4:30pm Sat, Sun & holidays) at Drakes Beach. All visitor centers have slightly longer hours in summer.

HIKING & CYCLING THE BAY BRIDGE

Why should the Golden Gate get all the outdoor action? Inaugurated in 2013, the Bay Bridge Trail (www.baybridgeinfo.org/path) is a separated pedestrian and bicycle path along the new Bay Bridge span between Oakland and Yerba Buena Island. The path has two access points: from outside the Ikea store on Shellmound St in Emeryville (1.5 miles from the MacArthur BART station), and from the corner of Maritime St and Burma Rd in West Oakland. One-way distances are about 5 miles from Emeryville and 3.5 miles from West Oakland, and a number of benches line the trail so you can drink in the open vistas.

Steps from the ferry in Jack London Square, Bay Area Bikes (☎510-836-2311; www. bayareabikerentals.net; 427 Water St; rentals per day from $25; ⊙10am-5pm Mon-Fri, 9am-6pm Sat & Sun) rents bikes with helmets and locks.

❶ Getting There & Away

By car you can get to Point Reyes a few different ways. The curviest is along Hwy 1, through Stinson Beach and Olema. More direct is to exit Hwy 101 in San Rafael and follow Sir Francis Drake Blvd all the way to the tip of Point Reyes. For the latter route, take the central San Rafael exit and head west on 4th St, which turns into Sir Francis Drake Blvd. By either route, it's about 1½ hours to Olema from San Francisco.

Just north of Olema, where Hwy 1 and Sir Francis Drake Blvd come together, is Bear Valley Rd; turn left to reach the Bear Valley Visitor Center. If you're heading to the further reaches of Point Reyes, follow Sir Francis Drake Blvd through Point Reyes Station and out onto the peninsula (about an hour's drive).

West Marin Stagecoach (www.marintransit. org/stage.html) route 68 makes daily stops at the Bear Valley Visitor Center from San Rafael ($2).

EAST BAY

Berkeley and Oakland are what most San Franciscans think of as the East Bay, though the area includes numerous other suburbs that swoop up from the bayside flats into exclusive enclaves in the hills. While many residents of the 'West Bay' would like to think they needn't ever cross the Bay Bridge or take a BART train under water, a wealth of museums, universities, excellent restaurants, woodsy parklands and better weather are just some of attractions that lure travelers from San Francisco.

Oakland

Named for the grand oak trees that once lined its streets, Oakland is to San Francisco what Brooklyn is to Manhattan. To some degree a less expensive alternative to the nearby city of hills, it's often where people have fled to escape pricey San Francisco housing costs. An ethnically diverse city, Oakland has a strong African American community and a long labor union history. Urban farmers raise chickens in their backyard or occupy abandoned lots to start community gardens, families find more room to stretch out, and self-satisfied residents thumb their noses at San Francisco's fog while basking in a sunnier Mediterranean climate.

◉ Sights & Activities

Broadway is the backbone of downtown Oakland, running from Jack London Sq at the waterfront all the way north to Piedmont and Rockridge. Telegraph Ave branches off Broadway at 15th St and heads north straight to Berkeley via the Temescal neighborhood (located between 40th St and 51st St). San Pablo Ave also heads north from downtown into Berkeley. Running east from Broadway is Grand Ave, leading to the Lake Merritt commercial district.

Downtown BART stations are on Broadway at both 12th and 19th Sts; other stations are near Lake Merritt, Rockridge and Temescal (MacArthur station).

◉ Downtown

Oakland's downtown is full of historic buildings and a growing number of colorful local businesses. With such easy access from San Francisco via BART and the ferry, it's worth spending part of a day exploring here – and nearby Chinatown and Jack London Sq – on foot or by bicycle.

The pedestrianized City Center, between Broadway and Clay St, 12th and 14th Sts, forms the heart of downtown Oakland. The twin towers of the Ronald Dellums Federal Building are on Clay St, just behind it.

Oakland

Oakland

MARIN COUNTY & THE BAY AREA OAKLAND

City Hall, at 14th & Clay Sts, is a beautifully refurbished 1914 beaux arts hall.

Old Oakland, along Washington St between 8th and 10th Sts, is lined with historic buildings dating from the 1860s to the 1880s. The buildings have been restored and the area has a lively restaurant and after-work scene. The area also hosts a lively **farmers market** every Friday morning.

East of Broadway and bustling with commerce, **Chinatown** centers on Franklin and Webster Sts, as it has since the 1870s. It's much smaller than the San Francisco version.

◉ Uptown

Continuing north of Oakland's City Center, the Uptown district contains many of the city's art-deco beauties and a proliferating arts and restaurant scene. The area stretches roughly between Telegraph and Broadway, bounded by Grand Ave to the north.

Great Western Power Company CLIMBING, GYM
(📞510-452-2022; www.touchstoneclimbing.com; 520 20th St; day pass $15-20; ⏰6am-10pm Mon-Thu, to 11pm Tue & Thu, 10am-6pm Sat & Sun) Work up a sweat in the belly of this former power plant – you can't miss the smokestack – where climbers can scale a 48-foot-high wall (full gear rental $5), conquer their problems in the 1500-square-foot bouldering area, take yoga classes or use the gym.

◉ Jack London Square

The area where writer and adventurer Jack London once raised hell now bears his name, and recent spasms of redevelopment have added a new cinema complex, condo development, excellent restaurants and some eclectic watering holes. The pretty waterfront location is worth a stroll, especially when the Sunday **farmers market** (⏰10am-2pm) takes over, or get off your feet and kayak around the harbor. Catch a ferry from San Francisco – a worthwhile excursion in and of itself – and you'll land just paces away.

Jack London's Yukon Cabin LANDMARK
A replica of Jack London's Yukon cabin stands at the eastern end of the square. It's partially built from the timbers of a cabin London lived in during the Yukon Gold Rush. Oddly, people throw coins inside as if it's a fountain. Another interesting stop, adjacent to the tiny cabin, is Heinold's First & Last Chance Saloon.

USS Potomac HISTORIC SITE
(📞510-627-1215; www.usspotomac.org; admission $10; ⏰11am-3pm Wed, Fri & Sun) Franklin D Roosevelt's 'floating White House,' the 165ft USS *Potomac*, is moored at Clay and Water Sts by the ferry dock, and is open for dockside tours. Two-hour history cruises (adult/child $55/35) are also held several times a month from May through October.

Lake Merritt

An urban respite, Lake Merritt is a popular place to stroll or go running (a 3.5-mile track circles the lake). The two main commercial streets skirting Lake Merritt are Lakeshore Ave on the eastern edge of the lake and Grand Ave, running along the north shore.

★**Oakland Museum of California**   MUSEUM
(OMCA; ☑ 888-625-6873, 510-318-8400; www.museumca.org; 1000 Oak St; adult/child 9-17yr $15/6, 1st Sun each month free; ☺ 11am-5pm Wed-Sun, to 9pm Fri; ⊕) Near the southern end of the lake and one block from the Lake Merritt BART station, this museum has rotating exhibitions on artistic and scientific themes, and excellent permanent galleries dedicated to the state's diverse ecology and history, as well as California art. Admission is half-off on Friday nights, when DJs, food trucks and free kids' art workshops made it a fun hangout spot.

Children's Fairyland   AMUSEMENT PARK
(☑ 510-452-2259; www.fairyland.org; 699 Bellevue Ave; admission $8; ☺ 10am-4pm Mon-Fri, to 5pm Sat & Sun Jun-Aug, off-season hours vary; ⊕) Lakeside Park, at the northern end of the saltwater lake, includes this 10-acre attraction, which dates from 1950 and has charming fairy-tale-themed train, carousel and mini Ferris-wheel rides.

Lake Merritt Boating Center   WATER SPORTS
(☑ 510-238-2196; www2.oaklandnet.com; 568 Bellevue Ave; boat rentals per hour $12-24; ☺ daily Mar-Oct, Sat & Sun only Nov-Feb) Rents canoes, rowboats, kayaks, pedal boats and sailboats.

Piedmont Ave & Rockridge

North of downtown Oakland, Broadway becomes a lengthy strip of car dealerships called Broadway Auto Row. Just past that is Piedmont Ave, wall-to-wall with antique stores, coffeehouses, fine restaurants and an art cinema.

One of Oakland's most popular shopping areas is Rockridge, a lively, upscale neighborhood. It is centered on College Ave, which runs from Broadway all the way to the UC Berkeley Campus. College Ave is lined with clothing boutiques, good bookstores, several pubs and cafes, and quite a few upscale restaurants – maybe the largest concentration in the Bay Area. BART at the Rockridge station puts you in the thick of things.

Mountain View Cemetery   CEMETERY
(www.mountainviewcemetery.org; 5000 Piedmont Ave; ☺ 6:30am-7pm) At the end of Piedmont Ave, this is perhaps the most serene and lovely artificial landscape in all the East Bay. Designed by Frederick Law Olmstead, the architect of New York City's Central Park, it's great for walking and the views are stupendous.

Oakland Hills

The large parks of the Oakland Hills are ideal for day hiking and challenging cycling, and the East Bay Regional Parks District (www.ebparks.org) manages more than 1200 miles of trails in 65 regional parks, preserves and recreation areas in the Alameda and Contra Costa counties.

Off Hwy 24, Robert Sibley Volcanic Regional Preserve is the northernmost of the Oakland Hills parks. It has great views of the Bay Area from its Round Top Peak (1761ft). From Sibley, Skyline Blvd runs south past Redwood Regional Park and adjacent Joaquin Miller Park to Anthony Chabot Regional Park. A hike or mountain-bike ride through the groves and along the hilltops of any of these sizable parks will make you forget you're in an urban area. At the southern end of Chabot Park is the enormous Lake Chabot, with an easy trail along its shore and canoes, kayaks and other boats for rent from the Lake Chabot marina (☑ 510-247-2526; www.norcalfishing.com/chabot).

Chabot Space & Science Center   SCIENCE CENTER
(☑ 510-336-7300; www.chabotspace.org; 10000 Skyline Blvd; adult/child $16/12; ☺ 10am-5pm Wed & Thu, to 10pm Fri & Sat, 10am-5pm Sun, plus 10am-5pm Tue summer; ⊕) Stargazers will go gaga over this science and technology center in the Oakland Hills with loads of exhibits on subjects such as space travel and eclipses, as well as cool planetarium shows. When the weather's good, check out the free Friday and Saturday evening viewings (7:30pm to 10:30pm) using a 20in refractor telescope.

🛏 Sleeping

If you like B&Bs, the Berkeley and Oakland Bed & Breakfast Network (www.bbonline.com/ca/berkeley-oakland) lists private homes that rent rooms, suites and cottages; prices start from $100 per night and many have a two-night-minimum stay. Reservations recommended.

Anthony Chabot Regional Park
CAMPGROUND $

(📞510-639-4751, reservations 888-327-2757; www.ebparks.org/parks/anthony_chabot; tent sites $25, RV sites with hookups $25-35; 🐕) This 5000-acre park has 75 campsites open year-round and hot showers. Reservations ($8 service charge) at www.reserveamerica.com.

Waterfront Hotel
BOUTIQUE HOTEL $$

(📞510-836-3800; www.waterfronthoteloakland.com; 10 Washington St; r $149-279; ✳@🛜☕🐕) Paddle-printed wallpaper and lamps fashioned from faux lanterns round out the playful nautical theme of this bright, cheerful harborside hotel. A huge brass-topped fireplace warms the foyer, and comfy rooms include MP3-players and coffeemakers, plus microwaves and fridges. Unless you're an avid trainspotter, water-view rooms are preferred, as trains rattle by on the city side.

Washington Inn
HISTORIC HOTEL $$

(📞510-452-1776; www.thewashingtoninn.com; 495 10th St; r incl breakfast $99-140; ✳@🛜) Small and modern with a boutique feel, this historic downtown lodging offers guest rooms with character and efficient sophistication. The dramatic high-ceilinged lobby is a wasted opportunity, outfitted with random chairs instead of velvet divans. Still, the carved lobby bar is perfect for a predinner cocktail, and you're spoiled for choice with several fine restaurants within a few blocks' radius.

Claremont Resort & Spa
RESORT $$$

(📞800-551-7266, 510-843-3000; www.claremontresort.com; 41 Tunnel Rd; r $215-309, plus $26 nightly resort fee; ✳@🛜☕🐕) Oakland's classy crème de la crème, the Claremont is a glamorous white 1915 building with elegant restaurants, a fitness center, swimming pools, tennis courts and a full-service spa (room/spa packages are available). The bay view rooms are superb. It's located at the foot of the Oakland Hills, off Hwy 13 (Tunnel Rd) near Claremont Ave on the Berkeley border.

✗ Eating

Oakland's fun and sophisticated eateries rival those of its neighbor San Francisco.

✗ Uptown, Downtown & Jack London Square

Ratto's
DELI $

(www.rattos.com; 821 Washington St; sandwiches from $6; ⏰8:30am-4:30pm Mon-Fri, 9:30am-3:30pm Sat; 🚫) If you want to eat outside on a sunny day, grab a sandwich from Ratto's, a vintage Oakland grocery (since 1897) with a deli counter (and a few sidewalk tables) that attracts a devoted lunch crowd.

Rudy's Can't Fail Cafe
AMERICAN $$

(www.iamrudy.com; 1805 Telegraph Ave; mains $9-13; ⏰7am-1am; 🚫👶) A modern diner with tables crafted from board games and strange toys under glass, it has a goofy punk rock feel, possibly because an owner is the bassist from Green Day. Show up for huevos or tofu rancheros all day, or just chow down on a big burger under the gaze of an army of Barbie dolls. Right next to the Fox Theater.

Bocanova
LATIN AMERICAN $$

(📞510-444-1233; www.bocanova.com; 55 Webster St; mains $12-28; ⏰11:30am-9:30pm Mon-Thu, 11am-10:30pm Fri & Sat, to 9:30pm Sun) Facing the water at sun-drenched Jack London Sq, you can people-watch from the outdoor patio or eat inside the chic industrial dining room lit by hanging glass lamps. The focus here is Pan-American cuisine, and standouts include the Dungeness crab deviled eggs and scallops in Brazilian curry sauce. Reservations recommended on Wednesday – when wine bottles are half-price – and weekends.

✗ Lake Merritt

Arizmendi
BAKERY $

(http://lakeshore.arizmendi.coop; 3265 Lakeshore Ave; pizza slices $2.50; ⏰7am-7pm Tue-Sat, to 6pm Sun, to 3pm Mon; 🚫) Great for breakfast or lunch but beware – this bakery co-op is not for the weak-willed. The gourmet vegetarian pizza, yummy fresh breads and amazing scones are mouthwateringly addictive.

Boot & Shoe Service
PIZZERIA $$

(📞510-763-2668; www.bootandshoeservice.com; 3308 Grand Ave; pizza from $10; ⏰5:30-10pm Tue-Thu, 5-10:30pm Fri & Sat, to 10pm Sun) 🚫 The name plays off its former identity as a cobbler shop, but the current patrons pack this brick-walled place for its wood-fired pizzas, original cocktails and creative antipasti made from sustainably sourced fresh ingredients.

Lake Chalet
SEAFOOD $$$

(📞510-208-5253; www.thelakechalet.com; 1520 Lakeside Dr; mains $17-36; ⏰11am-10pm Mon-Thu, to 11pm Fri, 10am-11pm Sat, 10am-10pm Sun) Whether you stop by the long pump house

BAY AREA BACKPACKING

For an overnight experience in the wilds just outside the city, grab your gear and set off to one of these local jewels. Sports Basement (http://community.sportsbasement.com/rentals/camping) and REI (www.rei.com) rent all gear.

➡ **Point Reyes National Seashore** (877-444-6777; www.recreation.gov; tent sites $20) Established hike- and bike-in campgrounds near the ocean; toilets and potable water.

➡ **Henry W Coe State Park** (p152) Where local backpackers set out when snow engulfs the Sierra, this enormous park has miles of hilly backcountry with seasonal ponds and creeks.

➡ **Hawk Camp** (www.nps.gov/goga/planyourvisit/outdooractivities.htm) Remote Marin Headlands' campsite with the requisite bird's-eye views; toilets but no water.

➡ **Angel Island** (p118) So close to the city and yet so far, you can watch the cargo ships thread under the Golden Gate Bridge.

➡ **Ohlone Wilderness Trail** (www.ebparks.org/parks/ohlone) A 28-mile adventure through mountains and canyons in the East Bay.

---

view bar for a martini and oysters during the buzzing happy hour (3pm to 6pm and 9pm to close), feast on a whole roasted crab by a window seat in the formal dining room, or cruise Lake Merritt on a Venetian-style gondola (www.gondolaservizio.com; per couple from $60), this 100-year-old former park office and boathouse is an enjoyable destination restaurant. Weekend reservations recommended.

Piedmont Ave & Rockridge

À Côté MEDITERRANEAN $$
(510-655-6469; www.acoterestaurant.com; 5478 College Ave; dishes $8-20; 5:30-10pm Sun-Tue, to 11pm Wed & Thu, to midnight Fri & Sat) This small-plates eatery with individual and friendly communal tables is one of the best restaurants along College Ave. What the menu calls 'flatbread' is actually pizza for the gods. Mussels with Pernod is a signature dish.

Commis CALIFORNIAN $$$
(510-653-3902; www.commisrestaurant.com; 3859 Piedmont Ave; 8-course dinner $95; 5:30pm Wed-Sat, from 5pm Sun) The only Michelin-starred restaurant in the East Bay, the signless and discreet dining room counts a minimalist decor and some coveted counter real estate (reservable by phone only) where patrons can watch chef James Syhabout and his team piece together creative and innovative dishes. Reservations highly recommended.

Temescal & Emeryville

Emeryville is a separate bite-sized city, wedged between Oakland and south Berkeley on I-80.

Bakesale Betty SANDWICHES, BAKERY $
(www.bakesalebetty.com; 5098 Telegraph Ave; sandwiches $8; 11am-2pm Tue-Sat;) An Aussie expat and Chez Panisse alum, Betty Barakat (in signature blue wig) has patrons licking their lips and lining up out the door for her heavenly strawberry shortcake and scrumptious fried-chicken sandwiches. Rolling pins dangle from the ceiling, and blissed-out locals sit down at ironing-board sidewalk tables.

Emeryville Public Market INTERNATIONAL $
(www.publicmarketemeryville.com; 5959 Shellmound St, Emeryville; mains under $10; 7am-9pm Mon-Sat, 7am-8pm Sun;) To satisfy a group of finicky eaters, cross the Amtrak tracks to the indoor area and choose from dozens of ethnic food stalls dishing out a huge range of international cuisines.

Homeroom AMERICAN $$
(510-597-0400; www.homeroom510.com; 400 40th St; mains $9-16; 11am-10pm Tue-Sun;) Mac-n-cheese, the ultimate in American comfort food, gets a long-overdue ovation at this quirky restaurant modeled after a school. A menu of regionally focused options – including the Ivy Leaguer Truffle, Dungeness crab, vegan and the spicy Exchange Student Sriracha – are more gour-

met than anything Mom packed for your lunchbox. Six rotating beers on tap.

Drinking & Nightlife

★ Café Van Kleef
BAR

(📞 510-763-7711; www.cafevankleef.com; 1621 Telegraph Ave; ⊙ noon-2am Tue-Fri, 4pm-2am Sat-Mon) Order a greyhound (with fresh-squeezed grapefruit juice) and take a gander at the profusion of antique musical instruments, fake taxidermy heads, sprawling formal chandeliers and bizarro ephemera clinging to every surface possible here. Quirky, kitschy and evocative even *before* you get lit, it features live blues, jazz and the occasional rock band on weekends plus DJs and a drag show other nights.

Awaken Cafe
CAFE

(www.awakencafe.com; 1429 Broadway; ⊙ 7:30am-10pm Mon-Thu, to midnight Fri, 8:30am-midnight Sat, to 7pm Sun; 📶) The laptop brigade camps out at this central downtown cafe by day, munching wood-fired bagels and drinking fairly traded Four Barrel coffee. But they get sidelined at 5pm, with live Afro-Cuban, folk, R&B and other events (cover free to $15) taking center stage after 7pm.

Beer Revolution
BEER HALL

(www.beer-revolution.com; 464 3rd St; ⊙ noon-11pm Mon-Sat, to 9pm Sun) Go ahead and drool. With almost 50 beers on tap, and more than 500 in the bottle, there's a lifetime of discovery ahead, so kick back on the sunny deck or park yourself at that barrel table embedded with bottle caps. Bonuses include no distracting TVs and a punk soundtrack played at conversation-friendly levels. Check Facebook for meet-the-brewer sessions and Sunday barbecues.

Blue Bottle Coffee Company
CAFE

(www.bluebottlecoffee.net; 300 Webster St; ⊙ 7am-5:30pm Mon-Fri, from 8am Sat & Sun) 🍴 The java gourmands queue up here for single-origin espressos and what some consider the best coffee in the country, and the very origin-specific beans are roasted on site. Its newer cafe (4270 Broadway; ⊙ 7am-6pm Mon-Fri, 8am-6pm Sat & Sun) in the historic WC Morse Building (a 1920s truck showroom) has two communal tables, lofty ceilings and a minimalist white decor for drinking an espresso or an Oji cold-drip coffee.

Trappist
PUB

(www.thetrappist.com; 460 8th St; ⊙ noon-12:30am Sun-Thu, noon-1:30am Fri & Sat) So popular that it busted out of its original brick-and-wood-paneled shoebox and expanded into a second storefront and back terrace, the specialty here is Belgian ales. More than two dozen drafts rotate through the taps, and tasty stews and sandwiches, and seasonal beer-friendly cuisine ($8.50 to $12) make it easy to linger.

Make Westing
COCKTAIL BAR

(www.makewesting.com; 1741 Telegraph Ave; ⊙ 4pm-2am) Named for a Jack London story, the free indoor bocce ball courts and eclectic cocktails pack this Uptown hotspot on weekends. Toss back a garden gimlet and satiate the munchies with some cilantro and habañero-infused popcorn.

Heinold's First & Last Chance
BAR

(www.heinolds.com; 48 Webster St; ⊙ 3-11pm Mon, noon-11pm Tue-Sun, to midnight Fri & Sat) An 1883 bar constructed from wood scavenged from an old whaling ship, you really have to hold on to your beer here. Keeled to a severe slant during the 1906 earthquake, the building's 20% grade might make you feel self-conscious about stumbling before you even order. Its big claim to fame is that author Jack London was a regular patron.

Tribune Tavern
BAR

(www.tribunetavern.com; 401 13th St; ⊙ 11:30am-10pm Mon-Fri, 10:30am-11pm Sat & Sun) For sophisticated downtown drinks under a pressed-tin ceiling and Edison lights, head to the 1923 Tribune Tower, an Oakland icon with a red-neon clock and former home of the *Oakland Tribune* newspaper.

MARIN COUNTY & THE BAY AREA OAKLAND

PINBALL WIZARDS, UNITE!

Put down that video game console, cast aside your latest phone app, and return to the bygone days of pinball play. Lose yourself in bells and flashing lights at **Pacific Pinball Museum** (📞 510-769-1349; www.pacificpinball.org; 1510 Webster St, Alameda; adult/child under 16 $15/7.50; ⊙ 2-9pm Tue-Thu, to midnight Fri, 11am-midnight Sat, to 9pm Sun; 🚐), a pinball parlor with almost 100 games dating from the 1930s to the present, and vintage jukeboxes playing hits from the past. Take AC Transit bus 51A from downtown Oakland.

☆ Entertainment

A monthly street festival, Oakland First Fridays (www.oaklandfirstfridays.org) takes place between 5pm and 9pm on the first Friday of the month. Telegraph Ave between 27th St and W Grand Ave closes to car traffic, with thousands turning out for food vendors, live music and performances. There's a concurrent gallery-hop called Oakland Art Murmur (www.oaklandartmurmur.com; ⊙6-9pm), which also coordinates a more low-key Saturday Stroll in the afternoons every week.

Music

Uptown LIVE MUSIC
(☑510-451-8100; www.uptownnightclub.com; 1928 Telegraph Ave; admission free-$20; ⊙Tue-Sun) For an eclectic calendar of indie, punk and experimental sounds, burlesque shows and fun DJ dance parties, this club hits the spot. Come for a good mix of national acts and local talent, and the easy two-block walk to BART.

Yoshi's JAZZ
(☑510-238-9200; www.yoshis.com/oakland; 510 Embarcadero West; admission $15-49) Yoshi's has a solid jazz calendar, with talent from around the world passing through on a near-nightly basis. Often, touring artists will stop in for a stand of two or three nights. It's also a Japanese restaurant, so you might enjoy a sushi plate before the show. Some events have half-price tickets for students and seniors.

Luka's Taproom & Lounge DJ
(www.lukasoakland.com; 2221 Broadway; ⊙DJs Wed-Sun) Go Uptown to get down. DJs spin nightly at this popular restaurant and lounge, with a soulful mix of hip-hop, reggae, funk and house. There's generally a $10 cover on Fridays and Saturdays after 11pm.

Theaters & Cinemas

The Fox Theater is the nucleus of evening activity in the Uptown district, with hip restaurants and bars clustered nearby.

Fox Theater THEATER
(www.thefoxoakland.com; 1807 Telegraph Ave) A phoenix arisen from the urban ashes, this restored 1928 art-deco stunner adds dazzle to downtown and is a cornerstone of the happening Uptown theater district. It's a popular concert venue for national and international acts.

Paramount Theatre THEATER
(☑510-465-6400; www.paramounttheatre.com; 2025 Broadway) This massive 1931 art-deco masterpiece shows classic films a few times each month and is also home to the Oakland East Bay Symphony (www.oebs.org) and Oakland Ballet (www.oaklandballet.org). It periodically books big-name concerts. Tours ($5) are given at 10am on the first and third Saturdays of the month.

Grand Lake Theatre CINEMA
(☑510-452-3556; www.renaissancerialto.com; 3200 Grand Ave) In Lake Merritt, this 1926 beauty lures you in with its huge corner marquee (which sometimes displays left-leaning political messages) and keeps you coming back with a fun balcony and a Wurlitzer organ playing the pipes on weekends.

New Parkway Theater CINEMA
(☑510-658-7900; www.thenewparkway.com; 474 24th St) This great, laid-back moviehouse shows quality second-run films in a comfy couch setting, and serves reasonably priced beer, wine, sandwiches and pizza, with delivery to your seat.

Sports

Sports teams play at the (insert most recent and ever-changing corporate branding) Coliseum or the Oracle Arena off I-880 (Coliseum/Oakland Airport BART station). Cheer on the Golden State Warriors, the Bay Area's NBA basketball team, the Oakland A's, the Bay Area's American League baseball team, and the Raiders, Oakland's NFL team; see www.coliseum.com for listings of upcoming events.

ⓘ Information

Oakland's daily newspaper is the *Oakland Tribune* (www.insidebayarea.com/oakland-tribune). The free weekly *East Bay Express* (www.eastbayexpress.com) has good Oakland and Berkeley listings.

Visit Oakland Visitor Center (☑510-839-9000; www.visitoakland.org; 481 Water St; ⊙9:30am-4pm Tue-Sun) At Jack London Sq.

ⓘ Getting There & Away

AIR

Oakland International Airport is directly across the bay from San Francisco International Airport, and it's usually less crowded and less expensive to fly here. Southwest Airlines has a large presence.

BART

Within the Bay Area, the most convenient way to get to Oakland and back is by **BART** (☑ 510-465-2278, 511; www.bart.gov). Trains run on a set schedule from 4am to midnight on weekdays, 6am to midnight on Saturday and 8am to midnight on Sunday, and operate at 15- or 20-minute intervals on average.

To get to downtown Oakland, catch a Richmond or Pittsburg/Bay Point train. Fares to the 12th or 19th St stations from downtown San Francisco are $3.30. From San Francisco to Lake Merritt or the Oakland Coliseum/Airport station, catch a BART train that is heading for Fremont or Dublin/Pleasanton. Rockridge is on the Pittsburg/Bay Point line. Between Oakland and downtown Berkeley you can catch a Fremont-Richmond train.

For AC Transit bus connections, take a transfer from the white AC Transit machines in the BART station to save 25¢ off the bus fare.

BUS

Regional company **AC Transit** (☑ 511, 510-817-1717; www.actransit.org; day pass $5) runs convenient buses from San Francisco's Transbay Temporary Terminal at Howard and Main Streets to downtown Oakland and Berkeley, and between the two East Bay cities. Scores of buses go to Oakland from San Francisco during commute hours ($4.20), but only the 'O' line runs both ways all day and on weekends; you can catch the 'O' line at the corner of 5th and Washington Sts in downtown Oakland.

After BART trains stop, late-night transportation between San Francisco and Oakland is with the 800 line, which runs hourly from downtown Market St and the Transbay Temporary Terminal in San Francisco to the corner of 14th St and Broadway.

Between Berkeley and downtown Oakland ($2.10) on weekdays, take the fast and frequent 1R bus along Telegraph Ave between the two city centers. Alternatively, take bus 18 that runs via Martin Luther King Jr Way daily.

Greyhound (☑ 510-832-4730; www.greyhound.com; 2103 San Pablo Ave) operates direct buses from Oakland to Vallejo, San Jose, Santa Rosa and Sacramento. The station is pretty seedy. Discount carrier **Megabus** (across from the south entrance to W Oakland BART station) has daily service to Los Angeles (seven hours), departing from opposite the south entrance to W Oakland BART station.

CAR & MOTORCYCLE

From San Francisco by car, cross the Bay Bridge and enter Oakland via one of two ways: I-580, which leads to I-980 and drops you near the City Center; or I-880, which curves through West Oakland and lets you off near the south end of Broadway. I-880 then continues to the Coliseum, the Oakland International Airport and, eventually, San Jose.

Driving to San Francisco, the bridge toll is $4 to $6, depending on the time and day of the week.

FERRY

With splendid bay views, ferries are the most enjoyable way of traveling between San Francisco and Oakland, though also the slowest and most expensive. From San Francisco's Ferry Building, the **Alameda–Oakland ferry** (☑ 510-522-3300; www.sanfranciscobayferry.com) sails to Jack London Sq (one-way $6.25, 30 minutes, about a dozen times a day, and also departing from Pier 41 on weekends). Ferry tickets include a free transfer, which you can use on AC Transit buses from Jack London Sq.

TRAIN

Oakland is a regular stop for Amtrak trains operating up and down the coast. From Oakland's **Amtrak station** (☑ 800-872-7245; www.amtrak.com; 245 2nd St) in Jack London Sq, you can catch AC Transit bus 72 to downtown Oakland (and the free Broadway Shuttle on weekdays and Saturday night), or take a ferry across the bay to San Francisco.

Amtrak passengers with reservations on to San Francisco need to disembark at the Emeryville Amtrak station, one stop away from Oakland. From there, an Amtrak bus shuttles you to San Francisco's Ferry Building stop. The free **Emery Go Round** (www.emerygoround.com) shuttle runs a circuit that includes the **Emeryville Amtrak station** (☑ 800-872-7245; www.amtrak.com; 5885 Horton St) and MacArthur BART. Emeryville is also the terminus for the California Zephyr (9:10am, one daily departure) to Chicago via Reno, Salt Lake City and Denver.

🛈 Getting Around

TO/FROM THE AIRPORT

BART is the cheapest and easiest transportation option. From the Coliseum/Oakland Airport BART, the new Oakland Airport Connector train ($6, 15 minutes) runs directly to the airport every five minutes during BART hours.

SuperShuttle (☑ 800-258-3826; www.supershuttle.com) is one of many door-to-door shuttle services operating out of Oakland International Airport. One-way service to San Francisco destinations costs about $27 for the first person and $15 for the second. East Bay service destinations are also served. Reserve ahead.

A taxi from Oakland International Airport to downtown Oakland costs about $30; to downtown San Francisco about $60.

BUS

AC Transit (p137) has a comprehensive bus network within Oakland. Fares are $2.10 and exact change is required.

The free **Broadway Shuttle** (www.meetdown-townoak.com/shuttle.php; ⊙7am-7pm Mon-Fri, to 1am Fri, 6pm-1am Sat) runs down Broadway between Jack London Sq and Lake Merritt, stopping at Old Oakland/Chinatown, the downtown BART stations and the Uptown district. The lime-green buses arrive every 10 to 15 minutes.

Berkeley

As the birthplace of the free speech and disability rights movements, and the home of the hallowed halls of the University of California, Berkeley is no bashful wallflower. A national hotspot of (mostly left-of-center) intellectual discourse and one of the most vocal activist populations in the country, this infamous college town has an interesting mix of graying progressives and idealistic undergrads. It's easy to stereotype 'Beserkeley' for some of its recycle-or-else PC crankiness, but the city is often on the forefront of environmental and political issues that eventually go mainstream.

Berkeley is also home to a large South Asian community, as evidenced by an abundance of sari shops on University Ave and a large number of excellent Indian restaurants.

☉ Sights & Activities

Approximately 13 miles east of San Francisco, Berkeley is bordered by the bay to the west, the hills to the east and Oakland to the south. I-80 runs along the town's western edge, next to the marina; from here University Ave heads east to downtown and the campus.

Shattuck Ave crosses University Ave one block west of campus, forming the main crossroads of the downtown area. Immediately to the south is the downtown shopping strip and the downtown Berkeley BART station.

◉ University of California, Berkeley

The Berkeley campus of the University of California (UCB, called 'Cal' by both students and locals) is the oldest university in the state. The decision to found the college was made in 1866, and the first students

arrived in 1873. Today UCB has more than 35,000 students, more than 1500 professors and more Nobel laureates than you could point a particle accelerator at.

From Telegraph Ave, enter the campus via Sproul Plaza and Sather Gate, a center for people-watching, soapbox oration and pseudotribal drumming. Or you can enter from Center St and Oxford Lane, near the downtown BART station.

★ UC Berkeley Art Museum   MUSEUM
(☎510-642-0808; www.bampfa.berkeley.edu; 2626 Bancroft Way; adult/child $10/7; ⊙11am-5pm Wed-Sun) The museum has 11 galleries showcasing a huge range of works, from ancient Chinese to cutting-edge contemporary. The complex also houses a bookstore, cafe and sculpture garden. The museum and the much-loved Pacific Film Archive are scheduled to move to a new home on Oxford St between Addison and Center Streets in 2016.

★ Campanile   LANDMARK
(Sather Tower; adult/child $3/2; ⊙10am-3:45pm Mon-Fri, to 4:45pm Sat, 10am-1:30pm & 3-4:45pm Sun; 🖐) Officially called Sather Tower, the Campanile was modeled on St Mark's Basilica in Venice. The 328ft spire offers fine views of the Bay Area, and at the top you can stare up into the carillon of 61 bells, ranging from the size of a cereal bowl to that of a Volkswagen. Recitals take place daily at 7:50am, noon and 6pm, with a longer piece performed at 2pm on Sunday.

Museum of Paleontology   MUSEUM
(☎510-642-1821; www.ucmp.berkeley.edu; ⊙8am-10pm Mon-Thu, to 5pm Fri, 10am-5pm Sat, 1-10pm Sun) **FREE** Housed in the ornate Valley Life Sciences Building (and primarily a research facility that's closed to the public), you can see a number of fossil exhibits in the atrium, including a *Tyrannosaurus rex* skeleton.

Bancroft Library   LIBRARY
(☎510-642-3781; www.bancroft.berkeley.edu; ⊙10am-5pm Mon-Fri) The Bancroft houses, among other gems, the papers of Mark Twain, a copy of Shakespeare's First Folio and the records of the Donner Party. Its small public exhibits of historical Californiana include the surprisingly small gold nugget that sparked the 1849 Gold Rush. To register to use the library, you must be 18 years or older (or a high school graduate) and present two forms of identification (one with a photo). The registration desk is on your way in.

Phoebe A Hearst Museum of Anthropology   MUSEUM
(☎510-643-7648; http://hearstmuseum.berkeley.edu; Kroeber Hall) South of the Campanile in Kroeber Hall, this museum includes exhibits from indigenous cultures around the world, including ancient Peruvian, Egyptian and African items. There's also a large collection highlighting native Californian cultures. Closed for renovations until 2015.

South of Campus

Telegraph Ave   STREET
Telegraph Ave has traditionally been the throbbing heart of studentville in Berkeley, the sidewalks crowded with undergrads, postdocs and youthful shoppers squeezing their way past throngs of vendors, buskers and homeless people. Numerous cafes and budget food options cater to students, and most of them are very good.

The frenetic energy buzzing from the university's Sather Gate on any given day is a mixture of youthful posthippies reminiscing about days before their time and young hipsters and punk rockers who sneer at tie-dyed nostalgia. Panhandlers press you for change, and street stalls hawk everything from crystals to bumper stickers to self-published tracts.

People's Park   PARK
This park, just east of Telegraph, between Haste St and Dwight Way, is a marker in local history as a political battleground between residents and the city and state government in the late 1960s. The park has since served mostly as a gathering spot for Berkeley's homeless. A publicly funded restoration spruced it up a bit, and occasional festivals do still happen here, but it's rather run-down.

Elmwood District   NEIGHBORHOOD
South along College Ave is the Elmwood District, a charming nook of shops and restaurants that offers a calming alternative to the frenetic buzz around Telegraph Ave. Continue further south and you'll be in Rockridge.

First Church of Christ Scientist   CHURCH
(www.friendsoffirstchurch.org; 2619 Dwight Way; ⊙services Sun) Bernard Maybeck's impressive 1910 church uses concrete and wood in its blend of Arts and Crafts, Asian and Gothic influences. Maybeck was a professor of architecture at UC Berkeley and designed San Francisco's Palace of Fine Arts, plus many landmark homes in the Berkeley Hills. Free tours happen the first Sunday of every month at 12:15pm.

Julia Morgan Theatre   THEATER
(☎510-845-8542; 2640 College Ave) To the southeast of People's Park is this beautifully understated, redwood-infused 1910 theater, a performance space (formerly a church) created by Bay Area architect Julia Morgan. She designed numerous Bay Area buildings and, most famously, the Hearst Castle.

Downtown

Berkeley's downtown, centered on Shattuck Ave between University Ave and Dwight Way, has far fewer traces of the city's tie-

---

WATER SPORTS ON THE BAY

The San Francisco Bay makes a lovely postcard or snapshot, and there are myriad outfits to help you play in it.

California Canoe & Kayak (☎510-893-7833; www.calkayak.com; 409 Water St, Oakland; rental per hour single/double kayak $20/30, canoe $30, stand-up paddleboard $20; ⊙10am-6pm) Rents kayaks, canoes and stand-up paddleboards at Oakland's Jack London Sq.

Cal Adventures (☎510-642-4000; www.recsports.berkeley.edu; 124 University Ave, Berkeley; ⊞) Run by the UC Berkeley Aquatic Center and located at the Berkeley Marina, Cal offers sailing, windsurfing and sea-kayaking classes and rentals for adults and youth.

Cal Sailing Club (www.cal-sailing.org; Berkeley Marina) An affordable membership-based and volunteer-run nonprofit with sailing and windsurfing programs, based at the Berkeley Marina.

Boardsports School & Shop (www.boardsportsschool.com) Offers lessons and rentals for kiteboarding, windsurfing and stand-up paddleboarding from its three locations in San Francisco, Alameda (East Bay) and Coyote Point.

Sea Trek Kayak & SUP (p116) Located in Sausalito, it has kayaking and stand-up paddleboards, and a fabulous full moon paddle tour.

Central Berkeley

MARIN COUNTY & THE BAY AREA BERKELEY

dyed reputation. The area has emerged as an exciting arts district with numerous shops and restaurants and restored public buildings. At the center are the acclaimed thespian stomping grounds of the Berkeley Repertory Theatre and the Aurora Theatre Company and live music at the Freight & Salvage Coffeehouse; a few good movie houses are also nearby.

North Berkeley

Not too far north of campus is a neighborhood filled with lovely garden-front homes,

parks and some of the best restaurants in California. The popular Gourmet Ghetto stretches along Shattuck Ave north of University Ave for several blocks, anchored by Chez Panisse. Northwest of here, Solano Ave, which crosses from Berkeley into Albany, is lined with lots of funky shops and more good restaurants.

On Euclid Ave just south of Eunice St is the Berkeley Rose Garden and its eight terraces of colorful explosions. Here you'll find quiet benches and a plethora of almost perpetually blooming roses arranged by hue. Across the street is a picturesque park with a

Central Berkeley

children's playground (including a very fun concrete slide, about 100ft long).

◉ The Berkeley Hills

Tilden Regional Park PARK
(www.ebparks.org/parks/tilden) This 2079-acre park, in the hills east of town, is Berkeley's crown jewel. It has more than 30 miles of trails of varying difficulty, from paved paths to hilly scrambles, including part of the magnificent Bay Area Ridge Trail. There's also a miniature steam train ($3), a children's farm, a wonderfully wild-looking botanical garden, an 18-hole **golf course** (☑510-848-7373) and environmental education center. **Lake Anza** is good for picnics, and from spring through late fall you can swim ($3.50).

AC Transit bus 67 runs to the park on weekends and holidays from the downtown BART station, but only stops at the entrances on weekdays.

UC Botanical Garden at Berkeley GARDENS
(☑510-643-2755; www.botanicalgarden.berkeley.edu; 200 Centennial Dr; adult/child $10/2; ⊗9am-5pm, closed 1st Tue each month) With 34 acres and more than 12,000 species of plants in the Strawberry Canyon hills, the garden is one of the most varied collections in the USA.

A fire trail is a woodsy walking loop around Strawberry Canyon that has great views of town and the off-limits Lawrence Berkeley National Laboratory. Enter at the trailhead at the parking lot on Centennial Dr just southwest of the Botanical Garden; you'll emerge near the Lawrence Hall of Science.

The garden can be reached via the Bear Transit shuttle H line.

Lawrence Hall of Science SCIENCE CENTER
(☑510-642-5132; www.lawrencehallofscience.org; Centennial Dr; adult/senior & child 7-8/child 3-6 $12/9/6; ⊗10am-5pm daily; ⊞) Near Grizzly Peak Blvd, the science hall is named after Ernest Lawrence, who won the Nobel Prize for his invention of the cyclotron particle accelerator. He was a key member of the WWII Manhattan Project, and he's also the name behind the Lawrence Berkeley and Lawrence Livermore laboratories. The Hall of Science has interactive exhibits for kids and adults (many closed on weekdays) on subjects ranging from earthquakes to nanotechnology, and outside there's a 60ft model of a DNA molecule.

AC Transit bus 65 runs to the hall from the downtown BART station. You can also catch the university's Bear Transit shuttle (H line) from the Hearst Mining Circle.

West Berkeley

Berkeley Marina
MARINA

At the west end of University Ave is the marina, frequented by squawking seagulls, silent types fishing from the pier, unleashed dogs and, especially on windy weekends, lots of colorful kites. First construction began in 1936, though the pier has much older origins. It was originally built in the 1870s, then replaced by a 3-mile-long ferry pier in 1920 (its length dictated by the bay's extreme shallowness). Part of the original pier is now rebuilt, affording visitors sweeping bay views.

Adventure Playground
PLAYGROUND

(☎510-981-6720; www.cityofberkeley.info/adventureplayground; ◷11am-5pm Sat & Sun & daily mid-Jun–mid-Aug, closed last week of year; ⊕) At the Berkeley Marina, this is one of the coolest play spaces in the country – a free outdoor park encouraging creativity and cooperation where supervised kids of any age can help build and paint their own structures. There's an awesome zip line too. Dress the tykes in play clothes, because they *will* get dirty.

San Pablo Ave
STREET

Formerly US Rte 40, this was the main thoroughfare from the east before I-80 came along. The area north of University Ave is still lined with a few older motels, diners and atmospheric dive bars with neon signs. South of University Ave are pockets of trendiness, such as the short stretch of gift shops and cafes around Dwight Way.

4th St Shopping District
NEIGHBORHOOD

Hidden within an industrial area near I-80 lies a three-block area offering shaded sidewalks for upscale shopping or just strolling, and a few good restaurants.

Takara Sake
MUSEUM

(www.takarasake.com; 708 Addison St; ◷noon-6pm) FREE Stop in to see the traditional wooden tools used for making sake and a short video of the brewing process. Tours of the factory aren't offered, but you can view elements of modern production and bottling through a window. Flights ($5) are available in a spacious tasting room constructed with reclaimed wood and floor tiles fashioned from recycled glass.

Sleeping

Lodging rates spike during special university events such as graduation (mid-May) and home football games. A number of older motels along University Ave can be handy during peak demand. For B&B options, look up the Berkeley & Oakland Bed & Breakfast Network (www.bbonline.com).

YMCA
HOSTEL $

(☎510-848-6800; www.ymca-cba.org/locations/downtown-berkeley-hotel; 2001 Allston Way; s/d with shared bath from $49/81; @⊛⊛⊛) The 100-year-old downtown Y building is still the best budget option in town. Rates for the austere private rooms (all with shared bathroom) include use of the sauna, pool and fitness center, and kitchen facilities, and wheelchair-accessible rooms are available as well. Corner rooms 310 and 410 boast enviable bay views. Entrance on Milvia St.

Berkeley City Club
HISTORIC HOTEL $$

(☎510-848-7800; www.berkeleycityclub.com; 2315 Durant Ave; r/ste incl breakfast from $165; @⊛⊛⊛) Designed by Julia Morgan, the architect of Hearst Castle, the 35 rooms and dazzling common areas of this refurbished 1929 historic landmark building (which is also a private club) feel like a glorious time warp into a more refined era. The hotel contains lush and serene Italianate courtyards, gardens and terraces, and a stunning indoor pool.

Elegant Old World rooms contain no TVs, and those with numbers ending in 4 and 8 have to-die-for views of the bay and the Golden Gate Bridge.

Bancroft Hotel
HISTORIC HOTEL $$

(☎800-549-1002, 510-549-1000; www.bancrofthotel.com; 2680 Bancroft Way; r incl breakfast $135-179; @⊛) ⊘ A gorgeous 1928 Arts and Crafts building that was originally a women's club, the Bancroft is just across the street from campus and two blocks from Telegraph Ave. It has 22 comfortable, beautifully furnished rooms (number 302 boasts a lovely balcony) and a spectacular bay-view rooftop, though no elevator.

Rose Garden Inn
INN $$

(☎800-922-9005, 510-549-2145; www.rosegardeninn.com; 2740 Telegraph Ave; r incl breakfast from $138; @⊛) The decor flirting with flowery, this cute place is a few blocks south from the Telegraph Ave action and very peaceful, with two old houses surrounded by pretty gardens.

Downtown Berkeley Inn
MOTEL **$$**

(📞510-843-4043; www.downtownberkeleyinn.com; 2001 Bancroft Way; r $79-129; ❄️ 🛜) A 27-room budget boutique-style motel with good-sized rooms and correspondingly ample flat-screen TVs.

★Hotel Shattuck Plaza
HOTEL **$$$**

(📞510-845-7300; www.hotelshattuckplaza.com; 2086 Allston Way; r from $195; ❄️ @ 🛜) Peace is quite posh following a $15-million renovation and greening of this 100-year-old downtown jewel. A foyer of red Italian glass lighting, flocked Victorian-style wallpaper – and yes, a peace sign tiled into the floor – leads to comfortable rooms with down comforters, and an airy, columned restaurant serving all meals. Accommodations off Shattuck are quietest; cityscape rooms boast bay views.

Hotel Durant
BOUTIQUE HOTEL **$$$**

(📞510-845-8981; www.hoteldurant.com; 2600 Durant Ave; r from $209; @ 🐾) 🐾 Located a block from campus, this classic 1928 hotel has been cheekily renovated to highlight the connection to the university. The lobby is adorned with embarrassing yearbook photos and a ceiling mobile of exam books, and smallish rooms have dictionary-covered shower curtains and bongs repurposed into bedside lamps.

✖ Eating

Telegraph Ave is packed with cafes, pizza counters and cheap restaurants, and Berkeley's Little India runs along the University Ave corridor. Many more restaurants can be found downtown along Shattuck Ave near the BART station. The section of Shattuck Ave north of University Ave is the 'Gourmet Ghetto,' with lots of excellent eating.

✖ Downtown & Around Campus

Berkeley Farmers Market
MARKET **$**

(cnr Center St & MLK Way; ⏰10am-3pm Sat) Pick up some organic produce or tasty prepared food at the downtown farmers market, operating year-round, and sit down to munch at MLK Park across from city hall.

Au Coquelet Café
CAFE **$**

(www.aucoquelet.com; 2000 University Ave; mains $7-13; ⏰6am-1:30am Sun-Thu, to 2am Fri & Sat; 🛜) Open till late, Au Coquelet is a popular stop for postmovie meals or late-night studying. The front section serves coffee and pastries while the skylit and spacious back room does a big range of omelets, pastas, sandwiches, burgers and salads.

★Ippuku
JAPANESE **$$**

(📞510-665-1969; www.ippukuberkeley.com; 2130 Center St; small plates $5-18; ⏰Sun-Thu 5-10pm, to 11pm Fri & Sat) Specializing in *shochu* (flights $12), a distilled alcohol made from rice, barley or sweet potato, Japanese expats gush that Ippuku reminds them of *izakayas* (pub-style restaurants) back in Tokyo. Choose from a menu of skewered meats and settle in at one of the traditional wood platform tables (no shoes, please) or cozy booth perches. Reservations essential.

Gather
CALIFORNIAN **$$**

(📞510-809-0400; www.gatherrestaurant.com; 2200 Oxford St; mains lunch $11-19, dinner $15-25; ⏰11:30am-2pm Mon-Fri, from 10am Sat & Sun, & 5-10pm daily; 🐾) 🐾 When vegan foodies and passionate farm-to-table types dine out together, they often end up here. Inside a salvaged wood interior punctuated by green vines streaking down over an open kitchen, patrons swoon over dishes created from locally sourced ingredients and sustainably raised meats. Reserve for dinner.

La Note
FRENCH **$$**

(📞510-843-1535; www.lanoterestaurant.com; 2377 Shattuck Ave; breakfast mains $10-14, dinner $15-20; ⏰8am-2:30pm Mon-Fri, to 3pm Sat & Sun, & 6-10pm Thu-Sat) A rustic country-French bistro downtown, La Note serves excellent breakfasts. Wake up to a big bowl of café au lait, paired with oatmeal raspberry pancakes or lemon gingerbread pancakes with poached pears. Anticipate a wait on weekends.

✖ North Berkeley

Cheese Board Pizza
PIZZERIA **$**

(www.cheeseboardcollective.coop; 1512 Shattuck Ave; slice/half-pizza $2.50/10; ⏰7am-8pm Tue-Sat; 🐾) Stop in to take stock of the more than 300 cheeses available at this worker-owned business, and scoop up some fresh bread to make a picnic lunch. Or sit down for a slice of the fabulously crispy one-option-per-day veggie pizza just next door, where live music's often featured.

★Chez Panisse
CALIFORNIAN **$$$**

(📞cafe 510-548-5049, restaurant 510-548-5525; www.chezpanisse.com; 1517 Shattuck Ave; cafe dinner mains $22-30, restaurant prix-fixe dinner $65-100; ⊙ cafe 11:30am-2:45pm & 5-10:30pm Mon-Thu, to 3pm & to 11:30pm Fri & Sat; restaurant seatings 5:30-6pm & 8-8:45pm Mon-Thu & half hour later Fri & Sat) 🍃 Foodies come to worship here at the church of Alice Waters, the inventor of California cuisine. It's in a lovely Arts and Crafts house in the Gourmet Ghetto, and you can choose to pull all the stops with a prix-fixe meal downstairs, or go less expensive and a tad less formal in the cafe upstairs. Reservations accepted one month ahead.

The restaurant is as good and popular as it ever was, and despite its fame, the place has retained a welcoming atmosphere.

🔪 West Berkeley

Vik's Chaat Corner   INDIAN $
(📞 644 4432; www.vikschaatcorner.com; 2390 4th St, at Channing Way; dishes $5-8; ⊙11am-6pm Mon-Thu, to 8pm Fri-Sun; 🚗) 🍃 This longtime and very popular *chaat* house has moved to a larger space but still gets mobbed at lunchtime by regulars that include an equal number of hungry office workers and Indian families. Try a *cholle* (spicy garbanzo curry) or one of the many filling *dosas* (savory crepes) on the weekend menu. It's one block east of the waterfront.

Bette's Oceanview Diner   DINER $$
(www.bettesdiner.com; 1807 4th St; mains $6-13; ⊙6:30am-2:30pm Mon-Fri, to 4pm Sat & Sun) A buzzing breakfast spot, especially on the weekends, serving yummy baked soufflé pancakes and German-style potato pancakes with applesauce, plus eggs and sandwiches. Superfresh food and a nifty diner interior make it worth the wait. It's about a block north of University Ave.

🍸 Drinking & Nightlife

Caffe Strada   CAFE
(2300 College Ave; ⊙6am-midnight; 🛜) A popular, student-saturated hangout with an inviting shaded patio and strong espressos. Try the signature white-chocolate mocha.

Torpedo Room   BEER HALL
(www.sierranevada.com/brewery/california/torpedoroom; 2031 4th St; ⊙11am-8pm Tue-Sat, noon-5pm Sun) Sample a flight of 4 oz pours ($2 each) from the sixteen rotating drafts on tap at Sierra Nevada brewery's new tasting room. No pints are served, but growlers are available to go, and a small selection of bar snacks helps keep you fortified. It's one block south of University Ave.

Jupiter   PUB
(www.jupiterbeer.com; 2181 Shattuck Ave; ⊙11:30am-1am Mon-Thu, 11:30am-1:30am Fri, noon-1:30am Sat, noon-midnight Sun) This downtown pub has loads of regional microbrews, a beer garden, good pizza and live bands most nights. Sit upstairs for a bird's-eye view of bustling Shattuck Ave.

Albatross   PUB
(www.albatrosspub.com; 1822 San Pablo Ave; ⊙6pm-2am Sun-Tue, 4:30pm-2am Wed-Sat) A block north of University Ave, Berkeley's oldest pub is one of the most inviting and friendly in the entire Bay Area. Some serious darts are played here, and boardgames will be going on around many of the worn-out tables. Sunday is Pub Quiz night.

Triple Rock Brewery & Ale House   BREWERY
(www.triplerock.com; 1920 Shattuck Ave; ⊙11:30am-1am Mon-Wed, to 2am Thu-Sat, to midnight Sun) Opened in 1986, Triple Rock was one of the country's first brewpubs. The house beers and pub grub are quite good, and the antique wooden bar and rooftop sun deck are delightful.

Guerilla Café   CAFE
(📞 510-845-2233; www.guerillacafe.com; 1620 Shattuck Ave; ⊙7am-2pm Mon, 7am-4:30pm Tue-Fri, 8am-4:30pm Sat & Sun) 🍃 Exuding a 1970s flavor, this small and sparkling cafe has a creative political vibe, with polka-dot tiles on the counter handmade by one of the artist-owners, and order numbers spotlighting guerillas and liberation revolutionaries. Organic and Fair Trade ingredients feature in the breakfasts and panini sandwiches, and locally roasted Blue Bottle coffee is served.

⭐ Entertainment

The arts corridor on Addison St between Milvia and Shattuck Sts anchors a lively downtown entertainment scene.

Live Music
Berkeley has plenty of intimate live-music venues. Cover charges range from $5 to $20, and a number of venues are all-ages or 18-and-over.

Freight & Salvage Coffeehouse   FOLK, WORLD
(📞510-644-2020; www.thefreight.org; 2020 Addison St; 🎫) This legendary club has almost 50 years of history and is conveniently located

in the downtown arts district. It features great traditional folk and world music and welcomes all ages, with half-price tickets for patrons under 21.

La Peña Cultural Center · WORLD
(☎ 510-849-2568; www.lapena.org; 3105 Shattuck Ave) A few blocks east of the Ashby BART station, this cultural center and Chilean cafe presents dynamic musical and visual arts programming with a peace and justice bent. Look for the vibrant mural on its facade.

Ashkenaz · FOLK, WORLD
(☎ 510-525-5054; www.ashkenaz.com; 1317 San Pablo Ave; ♿) Ashkenaz is a 'music and dance community center' attracting activists, hippies and fans of folk, swing and world music who love to dance (lessons offered).

924 Gilman · PUNK ROCK
(www.924gilman.org; 924 Gilman St; ☺ Fri-Sun) This volunteer-run and booze-free all-ages space is a West Coast punk rock institution. From Berkeley BART, take AC Transit bus 25 to Gilman and 8th Sts.

Cinemas

Pacific Film Archive · CINEMA
(PFA; ☎ 510-642-5249; www.bampfa.berkeley.edu; 2575 Bancroft Way; adult/child $9.50/6.50) A renowned film center with an ever-changing schedule of international and classic films, cineastes should seek this place out. The spacious theater has seats that are comfy enough for hours-long movie marathons.

Theater & Dance

Zellerbach Hall · PERFORMING ARTS
(☎ 510-642-9988; http://tickets.berkeley.edu) On the south end of campus near Bancroft Way and Dana St, Zellerbach Hall features dance events, concerts and performances of all types by national and international artists. The on-site Cal Performances Ticket Office sells tickets without a handling fee.

Berkeley Repertory Theatre · THEATER
(☎ 510-647-2949; www.berkeleyrep.org; 2025 Addison St; tickets $35-100) This highly respected company has produced bold versions of classical and modern plays since 1968. Most shows have half-price tickets for patrons under 30.

California Shakespeare Theater · THEATER
(☎ 510-548-9666; www.calshakes.org; box office 701 Heinz Ave) Headquartered in Berkeley, with a fantastic outdoor amphitheater further east in Orinda, 'Cal Shakes' is a warm-weather tradition of al fresco Shakespeare (and other classic) productions, with a season that lasts from about June through September.

Aurora Theatre Company · THEATER
(☎ 510-843-4822; www.auroratheatre.org; 2081 Addison St) An intimate downtown theater, it performs contemporary and thought-provoking plays staged with a subtle chamber-theater aesthetic.

Marsh · PERFORMING ARTS
(☎ 510-704-8291; www.themarsh.org; 2120 Allston Way) The 'breeding ground for new performance' in Berkeley has eclectic solo and comedy acts.

Shotgun Players · THEATER
(☎ 510-841-6500; www.shotgunplayers.org; 1901 Ashby Avenue) The country's first all-solar-powered theater company stages exciting

WHERE THE EARTH MOVED

Curious to find a few places where the earth shook? Visit these notorious spots in and around the Bay Area:

➡ Earthquake Trail, at Point Reyes National Seashore, shows the effects of the big one in 1906.

➡ Cypress Freeway Memorial Park, at 14th St and Mandela Parkway, commemorates the forty-two people that died and those who helped rescue survivors when the Cypress Freeway collapsed in West Oakland, one of the most horrifying and enduring images of the 1989 Loma Prieta quake.

➡ In the Forest of Nisene Marks State Park (☎ 831-763-7062; www.parks.ca.gov/?page_id=666; parking $8), near Aptos in Santa Cruz County, a sign on the Aptos Creek Trail marks the actual epicenter of the Loma Prieta quake, and on the Big Slide Trail a number of fissures can be spotted.

➡ At UC Berkeley, the Hayward Fault runs just beneath Memorial Stadium.

and provocative work in an intimate space. Across from the Ashby BART station.

Sports

Memorial Stadium, which dates from 1923, is the university's 63,000-seat sporting venue, and the Hayward Fault runs just beneath it. On alternate years, it's the site of the famous football frenzy between the UC Berkeley and Stanford teams.

The Cal Athletic Ticket Office (☑800-462-3277; www.calbears.com; 2223 Fulton St) on campus has ticket information on all UC Berkeley sports events. Keep in mind that some sell out weeks in advance.

🔒 Shopping

Branching off the UC campus, Telegraph Ave caters mostly to students, hawking a steady dose of urban hippie gear, handmade jewelry and head-shop paraphernalia. Audiophiles will swoon over the music stores. Other shopping corridors include College Ave in the Elmwood District, 4th St (north of University Ave) and Solano Ave.

Amoeba Music   MUSIC
(☑510-549-1125; 2455 Telegraph Ave; ☉10:30am-8pm Mon-Thu, to 10pm Fri & Sat, 11am-8pm Sun) If you're a music junkie, you might plan on spending a few hours at the original Berkeley branch of Amoeba Music, packed with massive quantities of new and used CDs, DVDs, tapes and records (yes, lots of vinyl).

Moe's   BOOKS
(☑510-849-2087; 2476 Telegraph Ave; ☉10am-10pm) A longstanding local favorite, Moe's offers four floors of new, used and remaindered books for hours of browsing.

University Press Books   BOOKS
(☑510-548-0585; 2430 Bancroft Way; ☉10am-8pm Mon-Fri, to 6pm Sat, noon-5pm Sun) Across

the street from campus, this academic and scholarly bookstore stocks works by UC Berkeley professors and other academic and museum publishers.

Down Home Music   MUSIC
(☑510-525-2129; www.downhomemusic.com; 10341 San Pablo Ave, El Cerrito; ☉11am-7pm Thu-Sun) North of Berkeley in El Cerrito, this world-class store for roots, blues, folk, Latin and world music is affiliated with the Arhoolie record label, which has been issuing landmark recordings since the early 1960s.

Rasputin   MUSIC
(☑800-350-8700; www.rasputinmusic.com; 2401 Telegraph Ave; ☉11am-7pm Mon-Thu, to 8pm Sat, noon-7pm Sun) A large music store full of new and used releases.

North Face Outlet   OUTDOOR EQUIPMENT
(☑510-526-3530; cnr 5th & Gilman Sts; ☉10am-7pm Mon-Sat, 11am-5pm Sun) Discount store for the well-respected Bay Area-based brand of outdoor gear. It's a few blocks west of San Pablo Ave.

REI   OUTDOOR EQUIPMENT
(☑510-527-4140; 1338 San Pablo Ave; ☉10am-9pm Mon-Fri, to 8pm Sat, to 7pm Sun) This large and busy co-op lures in active folks for camping and mountaineering rentals, sports clothing and all kinds of nifty outdoor gear.

ℹ Information

Alta Bates Summit Medical Center (☑510-204-4444; www.altabatessummit.org; 2450 Ashby Ave) 24-hour emergency services.
Visit Berkeley (☑800-847-4823, 510-549-7040; www.visitberkeley.com; 2030 Addison St; ☉9am-1pm & 2-5pm Mon-Fri, 10am-1pm & 2-4pm Sat) The helpful Berkeley Convention & Visitors Bureau has a free visitors guide.
UC Berkeley Visitor Services Center (☑510-642-5215; http://visitors.berkeley.edu; 101

EAST BROTHER LIGHT STATION

East Brother Light Station (☑510-233-2385; www.ebls.org; d incl breakfast & dinner $295-415; ☉Thu-Sun) Most Bay Area residents have never heard of this speck of an island off the East Bay city of Richmond, and even fewer know that the East Brother Light Station is an extraordinary five-room Victorian B&B. Spend the night in the romantic lighthouse or fog signal building (the foghorn is used from October through March), where every window has stupendous bay views and harbor seals frolic in the frigid currents.

Resident innkeepers serve afternoon hors d'oeuvres and champagne, and between gourmet meals you can stroll around the breezy one-acre islet and rummage through historical photos and artifacts.

Sproul Hall; ⊙ tours usually 10am Mon-Sat & 1pm Sun) Campus maps and information available. Free 90-minute campus tours are given at 10am Monday to Saturday and 1pm Sunday; reservations required.

❶ Getting There & Away

BART

The easiest way to travel between San Francisco, Berkeley, Oakland and other East Bay points is on **BART** (☑ 511, 510-465-2278; www.bart.gov). Trains run approximately every 10 minutes from 4am to midnight on weekdays, with limited service from 6am on Saturday and from 8am on Sunday.

To get to Berkeley, catch a Richmond-bound train to one of three BART stations: Ashby (Adeline St and Ashby Ave), Downtown Berkeley (Shattuck Ave and Center St) or North Berkeley (Sacramento and Delaware Sts). The fare ranges from $3.75 to $4 between Berkeley and San Francisco; $1.85 between Berkeley and downtown Oakland. After 8pm on weekdays, 7pm on Saturday and all day Sunday, there is no direct service operating from San Francisco to Berkeley; instead, catch a Pittsburg/Bay Point train and transfer at 19th St station in Oakland.

A **BART-to-Bus** transfer ticket, available from white AC Transit machines near the BART turnstiles, reduces the connecting bus fare by 25¢.

BUS

The regional company **AC Transit** (☑ 511, 510-817-1717; www.actransit.org) operates a number of buses from San Francisco's Transbay Temporary Terminal to the East Bay. The F line leaves from the Transbay Temporary Terminal to the corner of University and Shattuck Aves approximately every half-hour ($4.20, 30 minutes).

Between Berkeley and downtown Oakland ($2.10) on weekdays, take the fast and frequent 1R bus along Telegraph Ave between the two city centers, or bus 18 that runs daily via Martin Luther King Jr Way. Bus 51B travels along University Ave from Berkeley BART to the Berkeley Marina.

CAR & MOTORCYCLE

With your own wheels you can approach Berkeley from San Francisco by taking the Bay Bridge and then following either I-80 (for University Ave, downtown Berkeley and the UCB campus) or Hwy 24 (for College Ave and the Berkeley Hills).

Driving to San Francisco, the bridge toll is $4 to $6, depending on the time and day of the week.

TRAIN

Amtrak does stop in Berkeley, but the shelter is not staffed and direct connections are few. More convenient is the nearby **Emeryville Amtrak**
station (☑ 800-872-7245; www.amtrak.com; 5885 Horton St), a few miles south.

To reach the Emeryville station from downtown Berkeley, take a Transbay F bus or ride BART to the MacArthur station and then take the free Emery Go Round bus (Hollis route) to Amtrak.

❶ Getting Around

Public transportation, cycling and walking are the best options for getting around central Berkeley.

BICYCLE

Cycling is a popular means of transportation, and safe and well-marked 'bicycle boulevards' with signed distance information to landmarks make crosstown journeys very easy. Just north of Berkeley, **Wheels of Justice** (☑ 510-524-1094; www.wheelsofjustice.com; 1554 Solano Ave, Albany; ⊙ 11am-7pm Thu, 10am-6pm Fri-Wed, to 5pm Sun) has 24-hour mountain-bike rentals for $35.

BUS

AC Transit operates public buses in and around Berkeley, and UC Berkeley's **Bear Transit** (http://pt.berkeley.edu/around/beartransit) runs a shuttle from the downtown BART station to various points on campus ($1). From its stop at the Hearst Mining Circle, the H Line runs along Centennial Dr to the higher parts of the campus.

CAR & MOTORCYCLE

Drivers should note that numerous barriers have been set up to prevent car traffic from traversing residential streets at high speeds, so zigzagging is necessary in some neighborhoods.

Mt Diablo State Park

◉ Sights

Mt Diablo State Park   PARK
(☑ 925-837-2525; www.mdia.org; per vehicle $6-10; ⊙ 8am-sunset) Collecting a light dusting of snowflakes on the coldest days of winter, at 3849ft Mt Diablo is more than 1000ft higher than Mt Tamalpais in Marin County. On a clear day (early on a winter morning is a good bet) the views from Diablo's summit are vast and sweeping. To the west you can see over the bay and out to the Farallon Islands; to the east you can see over the Central Valley to the Sierra Nevada.

The park has more than 50 miles of hiking trails, and can be reached from Walnut Creek, Danville or Clayton. You can also drive to the top, where there's a visitors center.

MARIN COUNTY & THE BAY AREA MT DIABLO STATE PARK

🛏 Sleeping

Mt Diablo Campgrounds CAMPGROUND $
(☑ 800-444-7275; www.reserveamerica.com; tent & RV sites $30) Of the three campgrounds, Juniper and Live Oak have showers, though the campgrounds can be closed during high fire danger and water may be turned off throughout the park if water restrictions are in effect.

ℹ Information

Mt Diablo State Park Visitors Center
(☉ 10am-4pm) The park office is at the junction of the two entry roads.

John Muir National Historic Site

John Muir Residence HISTORIC SITE
(☑ 925-228-8860; www.nps.gov/jomu; 4202 Alhambra Ave, Martinez; ☉ 10am-5pm Wed-Sun) **FREE** Just 15 miles north of Walnut Creek, the John Muir residence sits in a pastoral patch of farmland in bustling, modern Martinez. Though Muir wrote of sauntering the High Sierra with a sack of tea and bread, it may be a shock for those familiar with the iconic Sierra Club founder's ascetic weather-beaten appearance that the house (built by his father-in-law) is a model of Victorian Italianate refinement, with a tower cupola, a daintily upholstered parlor and splashes of white lace.

Muir's 'scribble den' has been left as it was during his life, with crumpled papers overflowing from wire wastebaskets and dried bread balls – his preferred snack – resting on the mantelpiece.

Acres of his fruit orchard still stand, and visitors can enjoy seasonal samples. The grounds include the 1849 Martinez Adobe, part of the rancho on which the house was built, and the oak-speckled hiking trails on nearby Mt Wanda.

ℹ Getting There & Away

The park is just north of Hwy 4, and accessible by **County Connection** (www.cccta.org) buses from Amtrak and BART.

Vallejo

For one week in 1852 Vallejo was officially the California state capital – but the fickle legislature changed its mind. It tried Vallejo a second time in 1853, but after a month moved on again (to Benicia). That same year, Vallejo became the site of the first US naval installation on the West Coast (Mare Island Naval Shipyard, now closed).

👁 Sights

Six Flags Discovery Kingdom AMUSEMENT PARK
(☑ 707-643-6722; www.sixflags.com/discovery-kingdom; adult/child under 4ft $63/43; ☉ approx 10:30am-6pm Fri-Sun spring & fall, to 8pm or 9pm daily summer, variable weekend & holiday hours Dec) The town's biggest tourist draw, this modern wildlife and theme park offers mighty coasters and other rides alongside animal shows featuring sharks and a killer whale. Significant discounts are available on the park's website. Exit I-80 at Hwy 37 westbound, 5 miles north of downtown Vallejo. Parking is $20.

Vallejo Naval & Historical Museum MUSEUM
(☑ 707-643-0077; www.vallejomuseum.org; 734 Marin St; admission $5; ☉ noon-4pm Tue-Sat) This museum tells the story of Vallejo's shortlived history as California's state capital and West Coast naval site.

ℹ Getting There & Away

San Francisco Bay Ferry (☑ 415-705-8291; www.sanfranciscobayferry.com; one way adult/child $13/6.50) runs ferries from San Francisco's Pier 41 at Fisherman's Wharf and the Ferry Building to Vallejo; the journey takes one hour. Discount admission and transportation packages are available from San Francisco. The ferry is also a gateway to the Wine Country, with connections via the **Napa Valley Vine** (www.ridethevine.com) buses and the **Napa Valley Wine Train** (www.winetrain.com/ferry).

THE PENINSULA

South of San Francisco, squeezed tightly between the bay and the coastal foothills, a vast swath of suburbia continues to San Jose and beyond. Dotted within this area are Palo Alto, Stanford University and Silicon Valley, the center of the Bay Area's immense tech industry. West of the foothills, Hwy 1 runs down the Pacific Coast via Half Moon Bay and a string of beaches to Santa Cruz. Hwy 101 and I-280 both run to San Jose, where they connect with Hwy 17, the quickest route to Santa Cruz. Any of these routes can be combined into an interesting loop or extended to the Monterey Peninsula.

And don't bother looking for Silicon Valley on the map – you won't find it. Because silicon chips form the basis of modern microcomputers, and the Santa Clara Valley – stretching from Palo Alto down through Mountain View, Sunnyvale, Cupertino and Santa Clara to San Jose – is thought of as the birthplace of the microcomputer, it's been dubbed 'Silicon Valley.' The Santa Clara Valley is wide and flat, and its towns are essentially a string of shopping centers and industrial parks linked by a maze of freeways. It's hard to imagine that even after WWII this area was still a wide expanse of orchards and farms.

San Francisco to San Jose

South of the San Francisco peninsula, I-280 is the dividing line between the densely populated South Bay area and the rugged and lightly populated Pacific Coast. With sweeping views of hills and reservoirs, I-280 is a more scenic choice than crowded Hwy 101, which runs through miles of boring business parks. Unfortunately, these parallel north–south arteries are both clogged with traffic during commute times and often on weekends.

A historic site where European explorers first set eyes on San Francisco Bay, Sweeney Ridge (www.nps.gov/goga/planyourvisit/upload/ sb-sweeney-2008.pdf) straddles a prime spot between Pacifica and San Bruno, and offers hikers unparalleled ocean and bay views. From I-280, exit at Sneath Lane and follow it 2 miles west until it dead ends at the trailhead.

Right on the bay at the northern edge of San Mateo, 4 miles south of San Francisco International Airport, is Coyote Point Recreation Area (parking $6; [icon]), a popular park (its playground sports a huge castle) and windsurfing destination. The main attraction – formerly known as the Coyote Point Museum – is CuriOdyssey ([icon]650-342-7755; www.curiodyssey.org; adult/child $9/7; ⊙10am-5pm Tue-Sat, noon-5pm Sun; [icon]), with innovative exhibits for kids and adults highlighting science and wildlife. Exit Hwy 101 at Coyote Point Dr.

Stanford University

Sprawled over 8200 leafy acres in Palo Alto, Stanford University (www.stanford.edu) was founded by Leland Stanford, one of the Central Pacific Railroad's 'Big Four' founders and a former governor of California. When the Stanfords' only child died of typhoid during a European tour in 1884, they decided to build a university in his memory. Stanford University was opened in 1891, just two years before Leland Stanford's death, but the university grew to become a prestigious and

NERDS' NIRVANA

Touted as the largest computer history exhibition in the world, the Computer History Museum ([icon]650-810-1010; www.computerhistory.org; 1401 N Shoreline Blvd, Mountain View; adult/student & senior $15/12; ⊙10am-5pm Wed-Sun) has rotating exhibits drawn from its 100,000-item collection. Artifacts range from the abacus to the iPod, including Cray-1 supercomputers, a Babbage Difference Engine (a Victorian-era automatic computing engine) and the first Google server.

Don't come looking to ogle the latest iPhone or get a Genius Bar consultation. At Apple Headquarters (www.apple.com/companystore; 1 Infinite Loop, Cupertino; ⊙10am-5:30pm Mon-Fri), hardcore fans can load up on Apple-branded clothing and ephemera from its company store and commiserate that, yes, Steve Jobs has left the building.

Though there are no official tours of the Googleplex (www.google.com/about/company/facts/locations; 1600 Amphitheatre Pkwy, Mountain View), visitors can stroll the campus and gawk at the public art on the leafy grounds, where scads of Googlers zoom about on primary-colored bicycles. Don't miss the 'dessert yard' outside Building 44, with lawn sculptures of Android operating systems (a cupcake! a donut! a robot!), and across the street, a toothy T-Rex festooned in pink flamingos next to the volleyball court.

At the company's headquarters, the Intel Museum ([icon]408-765-5050; www.intel.com/museum; 2200 Mission College Blvd, Santa Clara; ⊙9am-6pm Mon-Fri, 10am-5pm Sat) FREE has displays on the birth and growth of the computer industry with special emphasis, not surprisingly, on microchips and Intel's involvement. Reserve ahead if you want to schedule a guided tour.

wealthy institution. The campus was built on the site of the Stanfords' horse-breeding farm and, as a result, Stanford is still known as 'The Farm.'

◉ Sights

Main Quad
PLAZA

Auguste Rodin's *Burghers of Calais* bronze sculpture marks the entrance to the university's Main Quad, an open plaza where the original 12 campus buildings, a mix of Romanesque and Mission revival styles, were joined by the Memorial Church (also called MemChu) in 1903. The church is noted for its beautiful mosaic-tiled frontage, stained-glass windows and four organs with more than 8000 pipes.

Hoover Tower
TOWER

(adult/child $2/1; ⊙10am-4pm, closed during final exams, breaks btwn sessions & some holidays) A campus landmark at the east of the Main Quad, the 285ft-high Hoover Tower offers superb views. The tower houses the university library, offices and part of the right-wing Hoover Institution on War, Revolution & Peace (where Donald Rumsfeld caused a university-wide stir by accepting a position after he resigned as Secretary of Defense).

Cantor Center for Visual Arts
MUSEUM

(http://museum.stanford.edu; 328 Lomita Dr; ⊙11am-5pm Wed & Fri-Sun, to 8pm Thu) FREE The Cantor Center for Visual Arts is a large museum originally dating from 1894. Its collection spans works from ancient civilizations to contemporary art, sculpture and photography, and rotating exhibits are eclectic in scope.

Rodin Sculpture Garden
SCULPTURE GARDEN

Immediately south of the Cantor Center is the open-air Rodin Sculpture Garden, which boasts the largest collection of bronze sculptures by Auguste Rodin outside of Paris, including reproductions of his towering *Gates of Hell*. More sculpture can be found around campus, including pieces by Andy Goldsworthy and Maya Lin.

ⓘ Information

Stanford Visitor Center (www.stanford.edu/dept/visitorinfo; 295 Galvez St) The Stanford Visitor Center offers free one-hour walking tours of the campus daily at 11am and 3:15pm, except during the winter break (mid-December through early January) and some holidays. Specialized tours are also available.

ⓘ Getting There & Away

Stanford University's free public shuttle, **Marguerite** (http://transportation.stanford.edu/marguerite), provides service from Caltrain's Palo Alto and California Ave stations to the campus, and has bicycle racks. Parking on campus is expensive and trying.

San Jose

Though culturally diverse and historic, San Jose has always been in San Francisco's shadow, awash in Silicon Valley's suburbia. Founded in 1777 as El Pueblo de San José de Guadalupe, San Jose is California's oldest Spanish civilian settlement. Its downtown is small and scarcely used for a city of its size, though it does bustle with 20-something clubgoers on the weekends. Industrial parks, high-tech computer firms and look-alike

---

WINCHESTER MYSTERY HOUSE

Winchester Mystery House (☎408-247-2101; www.winchestermysteryhouse.com; 525 S Winchester Blvd; adult/senior/child 6-12 $33/30/25; ⊙9am-5pm Oct-Mar, 9am-7pm Apr-Sep) An odd structure purposefully commissioned to be so by the heir to the Winchester rifle fortune, the Winchester Mystery House is a ridiculous Victorian mansion with 160 rooms of various sizes and little utility, with dead-end hallways and a staircase that runs up to a ceiling all jammed together like a toddler playing architect. Apparently, Sarah Winchester spent 38 years constructing this mammoth white elephant because the spirits of the people killed by Winchester rifles told her to.

No expense was spared in the construction and the extreme results sprawl over 4 acres. Tours start every 30 minutes, and the standard hour-long guided mansion tour includes a self-guided romp through the gardens as well as entry to an exhibition of guns and rifles.

It's west of central San Jose and just north of I-280, across the street from Santana Row.

housing developments have sprawled across the city's landscape, taking over where farms, ranches and open spaces once spread between the bay and the surrounding hills.

◎ Sights

Downtown San Jose is at the junction of Hwy 87 and I-280. Hwy 101 and I-880 complete the box. Running roughly north–south along the length of the city, from the old port town of Alviso on the San Francisco Bay all the way downtown, is 1st St; south of I-280, its name changes to Monterey Hwy.

San Jose State University is immediately east of downtown, and the SoFA district, with numerous nightclubs, restaurants and galleries, is on a stretch of S 1st St south of San Carlos St.

★ History Park   PARK

(☑ 408-287-2290; www.historysanjose.org; cnr Senter Rd & Phelan Ave; ⊙ 11am-5pm Tue-Sun, closed 1st Mon of month) Historic buildings from all over San Jose have been brought together in this open-air history museum, southeast of the city center in Kelley Park. The centerpiece is a dramatic half-scale replica of the 237ft-high 1881 Electric Light Tower. The original tower was a pioneering attempt at street lighting, intended to illuminate the entire town center. It was a complete failure but was left standing as a central landmark until it toppled over in 1915 because of rust and wind. Other buildings include an 1888 Chinese temple and the Pacific Hotel, which has rotating exhibits inside. The Trolley Restoration Barn restores historic trolley cars to operate on San Jose's light-rail line, and on weekends you can ride a trolley along the park's own short line.

Tech Museum of Innovation   MUSEUM

(The Tech; ☑ 408-294-8324; www.thetech.org; 201 S Market St; adult/child 3-17 $15/10; ⊙ 10am-5pm; ⌨) This excellent technology museum, opposite Plaza de Cesar Chavez, examines subjects from robotics to space exploration to genetics. The museum also includes an IMAX dome theater (additional $5 admission), which screens different films throughout the day.

San Jose Museum of Art   MUSEUM

(☑ 408-271-6840; www.sjmusart.org; 110 S Market St; adult/student & senior $8/5; ⊙ 11am-5pm Tue-Sun) With a strong permanent collection of 20th-century works and a variety of imaginative changing exhibits, the city's central art museum is one of the Bay Area's finest. The main building started life as the post office in 1892, was damaged by the 1906 earthquake and became an art gallery in 1933. A modern wing was added in 1991.

Rosicrucian Egyptian Museum   MUSEUM

(☑ 408-947-3635; www.egyptianmuseum.org; 1342 Naglee Ave; adult/child/student $9/5/7; ⊙ 9am-5pm Wed-Fri, 10am-6pm Sat & Sun) West of downtown, this unusual and educational Egyptian Museum is one of San Jose's more interesting attractions, with an extensive collection that includes statues, household items and mummies. There's even a two-room, walk-through reproduction of an ancient subterranean tomb. The museum is the centerpiece of Rosicrucian Park (cnr Naglee & Park Aves), west of downtown San Jose.

MACLA   GALLERY

(Movimiento de Arte y Cultura Latino Americana; ☑ 408-998-2783; www.maclaarte.org; 510 S 1st St; ⊙ noon-7pm Wed & Thu, noon-5pm Fri & Sat) FREE A cutting-edge gallery highlighting themes by both established and emerging Latino artists, MACLA is one of the best community arts spaces in the Bay Area, with open-mic performances, hip-hop and other live-music shows, experimental theater and well-curated and thought-provoking visual arts exhibits. It's also a hub for the popular South First Fridays (www.southfirstfridays.com) art walk and street fair.

Plaza de Cesar Chavez   PLAZA

This leafy square in the center of downtown, which was part of the original plaza of El Pueblo de San José de Guadalupe, is the oldest public space in the city. It's named after Cesar Chavez – founder of the United Farm Workers, who lived part of his life in San Jose – and is surrounded by museums, theaters and hotels.

Cathedral Basilica of St Joseph   CHURCH

(80 S Market St) At the top of the Plaza de Cesar Chavez, the pueblo's first church. Originally constructed of adobe brick in 1803, it was replaced three times due to earthquakes and fire; the present building dates from 1877.

Santana Row   MALL

(www.santanarow.com; Stevens Creek & Winchester Blvds) An upscale Main St-style mall, Santana Row is a mixed-use space west of downtown with shopping, dining and entertainment

SAN JOSE FOR CHILDREN

Children's Discovery Museum (☎408-298-5437; www.cdm.org; 180 Woz Way; admission $12; ⊙10am-5pm Tue-Sat, from noon Sun; ⊕) Downtown, this science and creativity museum has hands-on displays incorporating art, technology and the environment, with plenty of toys, and very cool play-and-learn areas. The museum is on Woz Way, which is named after Steve Wozniak, the cofounder of Apple.

Great America (☎408-986-5886; www.cagreatamerica.com; 4701 Great America Pkwy, Santa Clara; adult/child under 4ft $60/40; ⊙Apr-Oct; ⊕) If you can handle the shameful product placements, kids love the roller coasters and other thrill rides. Note that online tickets cost much less than walk-up prices; parking costs $15 but it's also accessible by public transportation.

Raging Waters (☎408-238-9900; www.rwsplash.com; 2333 South White Rd; adult/child under 4ft $39/29, parking $6; ⊙May-Sep; ⊕) A water park inside Lake Cunningham Regional Park, Raging Waters has fast water slides, a tidal pool and a nifty water fort. Online discounts.

along with a boutique hotel, lofts and apartments. Restaurants spill out onto sidewalk terraces, and public spaces have been designed to invite loitering and promenading. On warm evenings, the Mediterranean-style area swarms with an energetic crowd.

🛏 Sleeping

Conventions and trade shows keep the downtown hotels busy year-round, and midweek rates are usually higher than weekends.

Henry W Coe State Park CAMPGROUND $
(☎408-779-2728, reservations 800-444-7275; www.reserveamerica.com; sites $20; ☻) Southeast of San Jose near Morgan Hill, this huge state park has 20 drive-in campsites at the top of an open ridge overlooking the hills and canyons of the park's backcountry. There are no showers. You can't make reservations less than two days in advance, though it rarely fills up except on spring and summer holidays and weekends.

Hikers (permit $5) can overnight in the park's vast wilderness.

Westin San Jose HISTORIC HOTEL $$
(☎866-870-0726, 408-295-2000; www.thesainteclaire.com; 302 S Market St; r weekend/midweek from $129/179; ✻@ হ☻) Formerly the Sainte Claire, this atmospheric 1926 landmark hotel overlooking Plaza de Cesar Chavez has a drop-dead beautiful lobby with stretched leather ceilings. Guest rooms are smallish, and were being completely remodeled at research time.

Hotel De Anza HOTEL $$
(☎800-843-3700, 408-286-1000; www.hoteldeanza.com; 233 W Santa Clara St; r Sun-Thu/Fri & Sat $149/239; ✻@ হ☻) This downtown hotel is a restored art-deco beauty, although contemporary stylings overwhelm the place's history. Guest rooms offer plush comforts (the ones facing south are a tad larger) and full concierge service is available.

Hotel Valencia BOUTIQUE HOTEL $$$
(☎866-842-0100, 408-551-0010; www.hotelvalencia-santanarow.com; 355 Santana Row; r incl breakfast $199-309; ✻@ হ☻) A burbly lobby fountain and deep-red corridor carpeting set the tone for this tranquil 212-room contemporary hotel in the Santana Row shopping complex. In-room minibars and bathrobes and a pool and hot tub create an oasis of luxury with European and Asian design accents.

🍴 Eating

Tofoo Com Chay VEGETARIAN, VIETNAMESE $
(☎408-286-6335; 388 E Santa Clara St; mains $6.50; ⊙9am-9pm Mon-Fri, 10am-6pm Sat; ☑) Conveniently located on the border of the San Jose State University campus, students and vegetarians queue up for the Vietnamese dishes such as the fake-meat *pho* and the heaped combo plates.

Original Joe's ITALIAN $$
(www.originaljoes.com; 301 S 1st St; mains $15-37; ⊙11am-11pm Sun-Thu, 11am-midnight Fri & Sat) Waiters flit about this busy 1950s San Jose landmark, serving standard Italian dishes to locals and conventioneers. The dining room is a curious but tasteful hodgepodge of '50s

brick, contemporary wood paneling and 5ft-tall Asian vases. Expect a wait.

Arcadia
STEAK $$$

(☎408-278-4555; www.michaelmina.net/restaurants; 100 W San Carlos St; mains lunch $12-19, dinner $28-50; ☻6:30am-2pm daily, 5:30-10pm Mon-Sat) This fine New American steakhouse restaurant in the Marriott Hotel is run by Chef Michael Mina, one of San Francisco's biggest celebrity chefs. It's not the daring, cutting-edge style Mina is known for, but it's slick, expensive and, of course, very good.

🍷 Drinking & Nightlife

The biggest conglomeration of clubs is on S 1st St, aka SoFA, and around S 2nd at San Fernando. Raucous young clubgoers pack the streets on Friday and Saturday nights.

★ Singlebarrel
COCKTAIL BAR

(www.singlebarrelsj.com; 43 W San Salvador St; ☻5pm-midnight Sun & Tue, 5pm-1:30am Wed-Sat) A speakeasy-style lounge, where bartenders sheathed in tweed vests artfully mix custom cocktails ($12) tailored to customer's preferences, with some recipes dating back to before Prohibition. There's often a line out the door, but you'll be whisked downstairs as soon as they're ready to craft you a drink.

Caffe Frascati
CAFE

(www.caffefrascati.com; 315 S 1st St; ☻7am-10pm Mon-Thu, to midnight Fri, 8am-midnight Sat, to 9pm Sun; 🛜) Photos of local theater folks line the walls at this high-ceilinged hangout a few doors down from the California Theatre. Linger over a cappuccino with a pastry or panini, and stop by for live music on Friday and Saturday nights. Opera performances rattle the cups the first Friday of each month.

Trials Pub
PUB

(www.trialspub.com; 265 N 1st St; ☻from 5pm) If you seek a well-poured pint in a supremely comfortable atmosphere, Trials Pub, north of San Pedro Sq, has many excellent ales on tap (try a Fat Lip), all served in a warm and friendly room with no TVs. There's good pub food and a fireplace in the back room.

Hedley Club
LOUNGE

(www.hoteldeanza.com/hedley_club.asp; 233 W Santa Clara St) Inside the elegant 1931 Hotel De Anza, the Hedley Club is a good place for a quiet drink in swanky art-deco surroundings. Jazz combos play Thursday through Saturday night.

South First Billiards
BAR, POOL HALL

(www.facebook.com/420southfirst; 420 S 1st St; ☻4pm-midnight Mon-Thu, 4pm-2am Fri & Sat) It's a great place to shoot some stick, and a welcoming club to boot. Check its Facebook page for live music and DJ nights.

☆ Entertainment

Live Music

Blank Club
LIVE MUSIC

(www.theblankclub.com; 44 S Almaden; ☻Tue-Sat) A small club near the Greyhound station and off the main party streets. Live bands jam on a stage cascading with silver tinsel, and a glittering disco ball presides over fun retro dance parties.

Theaters

California Theatre
THEATER

(☎408-792-4111; www.sanjosetheaters.org/theaters/california-theatre; 345 S 1st St) The absolutely stunning Spanish interior of this landmark entertainment venue is cathedral-worthy. The theater is home to Opera San José, Symphony Silicon Valley, and is a venue for the city's annual film festival, Cinequest (www.cinequest.org), held in late February or early March.

Sports

SAP Center
STADIUM

(☎408-287-9200; www.sapcenteratsanjose.com; cnr Santa Clara & N Autumn Sts) Formerly the HP Pavilion, the fanatically popular San Jose Sharks, the city's NHL (National Hockey League) team, plays at this massive glass-

---

PSYCHO DONUTS? QU'EST QUE C'EST?

Who knew that a sugary confection with a hole could induce such devious giggles and fiendish delight? Saunter on over to Psycho Donuts (www.psycho-donuts.com; 288 S 2nd St; ☻7am-10pm Mon-Thu, to midnight Fri, 8am-midnight Sat, to 10pm Sun; 🛜), where counter staff dressed in saucy medical garb hand out bubble wrap to pop as patrons choose from twisted flavors such as Cereal Killer (topped with marshmallows and Cap'n Crunch breakfast cereal), Headbanger (death-metal visage oozing red jelly) and the tantalizing square S'mores (campfire not included).

and-metal stadium. The NHL season runs from September to April.

San Jose Earthquakes SOCCER
(www.sjearthquakes.com) San Jose's Major League Soccer team plays from February through October. Until 2015, when the Quakes' new stadium opens nearby just west of San Jose airport, catch the action at Santa Clara University's Buck Shaw Stadium (500 El Camino Real, Santa Clara).

ℹ Information

To find out what's happening and where, check out the free weekly *Metro* (www.metroactive.com) newspaper or the Friday 'eye' section of the daily *San Jose Mercury News* (www.mercurynews.com).

San Jose Convention & Visitors Bureau (☎800-726-5673, 408-295-9600; www.sanjose.org)

Santa Clara Valley Medical Center (☎408-885-5000; 751 S Bascom Ave; ⊗24hr)

ℹ Getting There & Away

AIR

Two miles north of downtown, between Hwy 101 and I-880, Mineta San José International Airport has free wi-fi and numerous domestic flights from two terminals.

BART

To access the BART system in the East Bay, **VTA** (☎408-321-2300; www.vta.org) bus 181 runs daily between the Fremont BART station and downtown ($4).

BUS

Greyhound buses to Los Angeles ($22 to $59, seven to 10 hours) leave from the **Greyhound station** (☎408-295-4151; www.greyhound.com; 70 Almaden Ave). The super-cheap new carrier **Megabus** (us.megabus.com) boasts electrical outlets and free wi-fi, with fares to Los Angeles averaging $10 to $40; departures from Diridon Station.

The VTA Hwy 17 Express bus (route 970) plies a handy daily route between Diridon Station and Santa Cruz ($5, one hour).

CAR & MOTORCYCLE

San Jose is right at the bottom end of the San Francisco Bay, about 40 miles from Oakland (via I-880) or San Francisco (via Hwy 101 or I-280). Expect lots of traffic at all times of the day on Hwy 101. Although I-280 is slightly longer, it's much prettier and usually less congested. Heading south, Hwy 17 leads over the hill to Santa Cruz.

Many downtown retailers offer two-hour parking validation, and on weekends until 6pm parking is free in city-owned lots and garages downtown. Check www.sjdowntownparking.com for details.

TRAIN

A double-decker commuter rail service that operates up and down the Peninsula between San Jose and San Francisco, **Caltrain** (☎800-660-4287; www.caltrain.com) makes more than three dozen trips daily (fewer on weekends); the 60-minute (on the Baby Bullet commuter trains) to 90-minute journey costs $9 each way and bicycles can be brought on designated cars. It's definitely your best bet, as traffic can be crazy any day of the week. San Jose's terminal, **Diridon Station** (off 65 Cahill St), is just south of the Alameda.

Diridon Station also serves as the terminal for **Amtrak** (☎408-287-7462; www.amtrak.com), serving Seattle, Los Angeles and Sacramento, and **Altamont Commuter Express** (www.acerail.com), which runs to Great America, Livermore and Stockton.

VTA runs a free weekday shuttle (known as the Downtown Area Shuttle or DASH) from the station to downtown.

ℹ Getting Around

VTA buses run all over Silicon Valley. From the airport, free VTA Airport Flyer shuttles (route 10) run every 10 to 15 minutes to the Metro/Airport Light Rail station, where you can catch the San Jose light rail to downtown San Jose. The route also goes to the Santa Clara Caltrain station. Fares for buses (except express lines) and light-rail trains are $2 for a single ride and $6 for a day pass.

The main San Jose light-rail line runs 20 miles north–south from the city center. Heading south gets you as far as Almaden and Santa Teresa. The northern route runs to the Civic Center, the airport and Tasman, where it connects with another line that heads west past Great America to downtown Mountain View.

San Francisco to Half Moon Bay

One of the real surprises of the Bay Area is how fast the urban landscape disappears along the rugged and largely undeveloped coast. The 70-mile stretch of coastal Hwy 1 from San Francisco to Santa Cruz is one of the most beautiful motorways anywhere. For the most part a winding two-lane blacktop, it passes small farmstands and beach after beach, many of them little sandy coves hidden from the highway. Most beaches along Hwy 1 are buffeted by wild and un-predictable wind, making them more suitable for sunbathing (weather permitting) than swimming. The state beaches along the coast don't charge an access fee, but parking can cost a few dollars.

A cluster of isolated and supremely scenic HI hostels, at Point Montara (22 miles south of San Francisco) and Pigeon Point (36 miles), make this an interesting route for cyclists, though narrow Hwy 1 itself can be stressful, if not downright dangerous, for the inexperienced.

Pacifica & Devil's Slide

Pacifica and Point San Pedro, 15 miles from downtown San Francisco, signal the end of the urban sprawl. South of Pacifica is Devil's Slide, a gorgeous coastal cliff area now by-passed by a car tunnel, though hikers and cyclists can sightsee on the adjacent Devil's Slide Coastal Trail, a paved 1.3-mile section of old Hwy 1.

In Pacifica, the main attractions are Rock-away Beach and the more popular Pacifica State Beach (also known as Linda Mar Beach; per car $3), where the nearby Nor-Cal Surf Shop (☑ 650-738-9283; 5440 Coast Hwy; ☺ 9am-6pm Sun-Fri, 8am-6pm Sat) rents surf-boards ($19 per day) and wetsuits ($16.50).

Gray Whale Cove to Half Moon Bay

One of the coast's popular 'clothing-optional' beaches is Gray Whale Cove State Beach, just south of Point San Pedro. Park across the road and cross Hwy 1 to the beach *very* carefully. Montara State Beach is just a half-mile south. From the town of Montara, 22 miles from San Francisco, trails climb up from the Martini Creek parking lot into Mc-Nee Ranch, which has hiking and cycling trails aplenty, including a strenuous ascent to the panoramic viewpoint of Montara Mountain, and access to the new 4000-acre park of Ranch Corral de Tierra (www.nps.gov/goga/rcdt.htm).

Starting life as a fog station in 1875, the Point Montara Lighthouse Hostel (☑ 650-728-7177; www.norcalhostels.org/montara; cnr Hwy 1 & 16th St; dm $27, r $75; @ 🖥) 🚭 is adjacent to the current lighthouse, which dates from 1928. This very popular hostel has a living room, kitchen facilities and an international clientele. There are a few private rooms for couples or families. Reservations are a good idea, especially on weekends during summer. SamTrans bus 17 stops outside.

The Fitzgerald Marine Reserve (☑ 650-728-3584; www.fitzgeraldreserve.org; 🖥), south of the lighthouse at Moss Beach, is an extensive area of natural tidal pools and a habitat for harbor seals. Walk out among the pools at low tide – wearing shoes that you can get wet – and explore the myriad crabs, sea stars, mollusks and rainbow-colored sea anemone. Note that it's illegal to remove any creatures, shells or even rocks from the marine reserve. From Hwy 1 in Moss Beach, turn west onto California Ave and drive to the end. SamTrans bus 17 stops along Hwy 1.

Overlooking the ocean, the Moss Beach Distillery (☑ 650-728-5595; www.mossbeach-distillery.com; cnr Beach Way & Ocean Blvd; mains $15-36; ☺ noon-9pm Mon-Sat, from 11am Sun; 🖥) is a 1927 landmark. In fair weather the restaurant's deck is the best place for miles around to have a leisurely cocktail or glass of vino. Reservations recommended.

South of here is a hamlet named Prince-ton, with a stretch of coast called Pillar Point. Fishing boats bring in their catch at the Pillar Point Harbor, some of which gets cooked up in a bevy of seafront restaurants. In the harbor, Half Moon Bay Kayak (☑ 650-773-6101; www.hmbkayak.com; ☺ 10am-4pm Wed-Mon) rents kayaks and offers guided trips of Pillar Point and the Fitzgerald Marine Reserve. Half Moon Bay Brewing Compa-ny (www.hmbbrewingco.com; 390 Capistrano Rd; mains $15-23; ☺ 11:30am-9pm Mon-Thu, to 10pm Fri, 9:30am-10pm Sat & Sun; 🖥) 🚭 serves sea-food, burgers and a tantalizing menu of local brews from a sheltered and heated outdoor patio looking out over the bay, complement-ed by live music on the weekends.

At the western end of Pillar Point is Mav-ericks, a serious surf break that attracts the world's top big-wave riders to battle its huge, steep and very dangerous waves. The annual Mavericks surf contest, called on a few days' notice when the swells get huge, is usually held between December and March.

Half Moon Bay

Developed as a beach resort back in the Victorian era, Half Moon Bay is the main coastal town between San Francisco (28 miles north) and Santa Cruz (40 miles south). Its long stretches of beach still attract rambling week-enders and hearty surfers. Half Moon Bay spreads out along Hwy 1 (called Cabrillo Hwy in town), but despite the development, it's

SCENIC DRIVE: HIGHWAY 84

Inland, large stretches of the hills are protected in a patchwork of parks that, just like the coast, remain remarkably untouched despite the huge urban populations only a short drive to the north and east. Heading east toward Palo Alto, Hwy 84 winds its way through thick stands of redwood trees and several local parks with mountain biking and hiking opportunities.

A mile in from San Gregorio State Beach (per car $8) on Hwy 1, kick off your shoes and stomp your feet to live bluegrass, Celtic and folk music on the weekends at the landmark San Gregorio General Store (www.sangregoriostore.com), and check out the wooden bar singed by area branding irons.

Eight miles east is the tiny township of La Honda, former home to *One Flew Over the Cuckoo's Nest* author Ken Kesey, and the launching spot for his 1964 psychedelic bus trip immortalized in Tom Wolfe's *The Electric Kool-Aid Acid Test*. Housed in an old blacksmith's shop, Apple Jack's (☑ 650-747-0331) is a rustic, down-home bar with lots of local color.

To stretch your legs in the redwoods, Sam McDonald Park (☑ 650-879-0238; http://parks.smcgov.org/sam-mcdonald-park; ⊘ parking $6), two miles south of La Honda on Pescadero Rd, has a number of worthy trails and a secluded hike-to cabin (http://lp.sierra-club.org/hikers_hut/hikers_hut.asp; ⊘ adult $25-30, child 2-10 $10) available for rent.

still relatively small. The main drag is a five-block stretch called Main St lined with shops, cafes, restaurants and a few upscale B&Bs. Visitor information is available from the Half Moon Bay Coastside Visitors Bureau (☑ 650-726-8380; www.halfmoonbaychamber.org).

Pumpkins are a major deal around Half Moon Bay, and the pre-Halloween harvest is celebrated in the annual Art & Pumpkin Festival (www.pumpkinfest.miramarevents.com). The mid-October event kicks off with the World Championship Pumpkin Weigh-Off, where the bulbous beasts can bust the scales at more than 1000lb.

Around 1 mile north of the Hwy 92 junction, Sea Horse Ranch (☑ 650-726-9903; www.seahorseranch.org) offers daily horseback rides along the beach. A two-hour ride is $75; an early-bird special leaves at 8am and costs just $50.

SamTrans (☑ 800-660-4287; www.samtrans.com) bus 294 operates from the Hillsdale Caltrain station in San Mateo to Half Moon Bay; bus 17 connects up the coast to Moss Beach and Pacifica and has very limited weekday service to Pescadero.

Half Moon Bay to Santa Cruz

With its long coastline, mild weather and abundant fresh water, this area has always been prime real estate. When Spanish missionaries set up shop along the California coast in the late 1700s, it had been Ohlone Native American territory for thousands of years. Pescadero was formally established in 1856, when it was mostly a farming and dairy settlement, although its location along the stagecoach route – now called Stage Rd – transformed it into a popular vacation destination. The Pigeon Point promontory was an active whaling station until 1900, when Prohibition-era bootleggers favored the isolated regional beaches for smuggling booze.

Pescadero

A foggy speck of coastside crossroads between the cities of San Francisco and Santa Cruz, 150-year-old Pescadero is a close-knit rural town of sugar-lending neighbors and community pancake breakfasts. But on weekends the tiny downtown strains its seams with long-distance cyclists panting for carbohydrates and day trippers dive-bombing in from the ocean-front highway. They're all drawn to the winter vistas of emerald-green hills parched to burlap brown in summer, the wild Pacific beaches populated by seals and pelicans, and the food at a revered destination restaurant. With its cornucopia of tide-pool coves and parks of sky-blotting redwood canopy, city dwellers come here to slow down and smell the sea breeze wafting over fields of bushy artichokes.

◉ Sights & Activities

A number of pretty sand beaches speckle the coast, though one of the most interesting places to stop is Pebble Beach, a tide-pool jewel a mile and a half south of Pescadero Creek Rd (and part of Bean Hollow State Beach). As the name implies, the shore is awash in bite-sized eye candy of agate, jade and carnelians, and sandstone troughs are pockmarked by groovy honeycombed formations called tafoni. Bird-watchers enjoy Pescadero Marsh Reserve, across the highway from Pescadero State Beach, where numerous species feed year-round.

★Pigeon Point Light Station   LIGHTHOUSE
(☑650-879-2120; www.parks.ca.gov/?page_id=533) Five miles south along the coast, the 115ft Light Station is one of the tallest lighthouses on the West Coast. The 1872 landmark had to close access to the upper tower when chunks of its cornice began to rain from the sky (restoration is in progress), but the beam still flashes brightly and the bluff is a prime though blustery spot to scan for breaching gray whales. The hostel here is one of the best in the state.

Butano State Park   PARK
(☑650-879-2040; per car $10, camping $35 Apr-Nov) About 5 miles south of Pescadero, bobcats and full-throated coyotes reside discreetly in 2800 acres of dense redwood canyon. From Hwy 1, take Gazos Creek Rd.

🛏 Sleeping & Eating

★HI Pigeon Point Lighthouse
Hostel   HOSTEL $
(☑650-879-0633; www.norcalhostels.org/pigeon; 210 Pigeon Point Rd; dm $26-27, r/t/6-bed $75/101/162, all with shared bath; @⑧) ⚑ Not your workaday HI outpost, this highly coveted coastside hostel is all about location. Check in early to snag a spot in the outdoor hot tub, and contemplate roaring waves as the lighthouse beacon races through a starburst sky.

Costanoa   CABIN, CAMPGROUND $$
(☑877-262-7848, 650-879-1100; www.costanoa.com; 2001 Rossi Rd; tent/cabin with shared bath from $89/179, lodge r $203-291; ⑧) Even though the resort includes a campground (☑800-562-9867; www.koa.com/campgrounds/santa-cruz-north; tent site $30-34, RV site from $69; ⑧⑧), no one can pull a straight face to declare they're actually roughing it here. Down bedding swaddles guests in cushy canvas tent cabins, and chill-averse tent campers can use communal 'comfort stations' with 24-hour dry saunas, fireside patio seating, heated floors and hot showers.

Lodge rooms with private fireplaces and hot tub access fulfill the whims of those without such spartan delusions. There's a restaurant (dinner mains $17 to $36) and spa on site; bicycle rentals and horseback riding are available as well.

Pescadero Creek Inn B&B   INN $$
(☑888-307-1898; www.pescaderocreekinn.com; 393 Stage Rd; r $155-225; ⑧) ⚑ Unwind in the private two-room cottage or one of the spotless Victorian rooms in a restored 100-year-old farmhouse with a tranquil creekside garden.

★Duarte's Tavern   AMERICAN $$
(☑650-879-0464; www.duartestavern.com; 202 Stage Rd; mains $11-45; ⊙7am-9pm) You'll rub shoulders with fancy-pants foodies, spandex-swathed cyclists and dusty cowboys at this casual, surprisingly unpretentious fourth-generation family restaurant. Duarte's is the culinary magnet of Pescadero – for many the town and eatery are synonymous. Feast on crab cioppino and a half-and-half split of the cream of artichoke and green chili soups, and bring it home with a wedge of olallieberry pie.

Except for the unfortunate lull of Prohibition, the wood-paneled bar has been hosting the locals and their honored guests since 1894. Reservations recommended.

❶ Getting There & Away

By car, the town is 3 miles east from Hwy 1 on Pescadero Creek Rd, south of San Gregorio State Beach. On weekdays, SamTrans (www.samtrans.com) bus 17 runs once a day to/from Half Moon Bay.

Año Nuevo State Reserve

More raucous than a full-moon beach rave, thousands of boisterous elephant seals party down year-round on the dunes of Año Nuevo point, their squeals and barks reaching fever pitch during the winter pupping season. The beach is 5 miles south of Pigeon Point and 27 miles north of Santa Cruz.

Elephant seals were just as fearless two centuries ago as they are today, but unfortunately, club-toting seal trappers were not in the same seal-friendly category as camera-toting tourists. Between 1800 and

THE CULINARY COAST

Pescadero is renowned for Duarte's Tavern, but loads of other tidbits are very close by.

Arcangeli Grocery/Norm's Market (Norm's Market; www.normsmarket.com; 287 Stage Rd, Pescadero; sandwiches $6.50-8.75; ☉10am-6pm Mon-Thu, 9am-6pm Sat & Sun) Create a picnic with made-to-order deli sandwiches, homemade artichoke salsa and a chilled bottle of California wine. And don't go breezing out the door without nabbing a crusty loaf of the famous artichoke garlic herb bread, fresh-baked almost hourly.

Harley Farms Cheese Shop (☑650-879-0480; www.harleyfarms.com; 250 North St, Pescadero; ☉10am-5pm Wed-Sun; 🖶) Follow the cool wooden cut-outs of the goat and the Wellington-shod girl with the faraway eyes. Another local food treasure with creamy artisanal goat cheeses festooned with fruit, nuts and a rainbow of edible flowers. Weekend farm tours by reservation, and a new shop selling goat-milk body products and non-toxic paint. Splurge for a seat at one of the monthly five-course farm dinners in the restored barn's airy hayloft.

Pie Ranch (www.pieranch.org; 2080 Cabrillo Hwy, Pescadero; ☉noon-6pm Thu & Fri, 10am-6pm Sat & Sun; 🖶) 🖊 Hit the brakes for this roadside farmstand in a wooden barn, and pick up fresh produce, eggs and coffee, plus amazing pies made with the fruit grown here. The historic pie-slice-shaped farm is a nonprofit dedicated to leadership development and food education for urban youth. Check the website for details on its monthly farm tours and barn dances. Located 11 miles south of Pescadero Creek Rd.

Swanton Berry Farm (☑650-469-8804; www.swantonberryfarm.com; Coastways Ranch, 640 Cabrillo Hwy, Pescadero; ☉10am-4pm Fri-Sun) To get a better appreciation of the rigors and rewards of farm life, smoosh up your shirtsleeves and harvest some fruit at this organic pick-your-own farm near Año Nuevo. It's a union outfit (operated by Cesar Chavez's United Farm Workers), with buckets of seasonal kiwis and olallieberries ripe for the plucking. Its **farm stand and strawberry u-pick** (☉8am-5pm) is 8.5 miles further south near Davenport.

Bonnie Doon Vineyard (☑831-471-8031; www.bonnydoonvineyard.com; 450 Hwy 1, Davenport; ☉11am-5pm Thu-Mon) Round out your palate with a flight ($10 to $20) at the new roadside tasting room of Randall Grahm's acclaimed winery, where Edison lights and rough-hewn wooden tables entice you to sample a Cigare Volant (yes, that's a flying cigar) and other bottles made with lesser-known varietals.

1850, the elephant seal was driven to the edge of extinction. Only a handful survived around the Guadalupe Islands off the Mexican state of Baja California. With the availability of substitutes for seal oil and the conservationist attitudes of more recent times, the elephant seal has made a comeback, reappearing on the Southern California coast from around 1920. In 1955 they returned to Año Nuevo Beach.

In the midwinter peak season, during the mating and birthing time from December 15 to the end of March, you must plan well ahead if you want to visit the reserve, because visitors are only permitted access through heavily booked guided tours. For the busiest period, mid-January to mid-February, it's recommended you book eight weeks ahead. If you haven't booked, bad weather can sometimes lead to last-minute cancellations.

The rest of the year, advance reservations aren't necessary, but visitor permits from the entrance station are required; arrive before 3pm from September through November and by 3:30pm from April through August.

Although the **park office** (☑650-879-2025, recorded information 650-879-0227; www.parks.ca.gov/?page_id=523) can answer general questions, high-season tour bookings must be made at ☑800-444-4445 or http://anonuevo.reserveamerica.com. When required, these tours cost $7, and entry is $10 per car year-round. From the ranger station it's a 3- to 5-mile round-trip hike on sand, and a visit takes two to three hours. No dogs are allowed on-site, and visitors aren't permitted for the first two weeks of December.

There's another, more convenient viewing site further south in Piedras Blancas.

Napa & Sonoma Wine Country

Best Places to Eat

➜ The Shed (p212)

➜ Oxbow Public Market (p169)

➜ Fremont Diner (p191)

➜ Madrona Manor (p213)

Best Places to Stay

➜ Beltane Ranch (p194)

➜ Cottages of Napa Valley (p168)

➜ Mountain Home Ranch (p181)

➜ El Bonita (p175)

Why Go?

America's premier viticulture region has earned its reputation among the world's best. Despite hype about Wine Country style, it's from the land that all Wine Country lore springs. Rolling hills, dotted with century-old oaks, turn the color of lion's fur under the summer sun and swaths of vineyards carpet hillsides as far as the eye can see. Where they end, lush redwood forests follow serpentine rivers to the sea.

There are over 600 wineries in Napa and Sonoma Counties, but it's quality, not quantity, that sets the region apart – especially in Napa, which competes with France and doubles as an outpost of San Francisco's top-end culinary scene. Sonoma prides itself on agricultural diversity, with goat-cheese farms, you-pick-'em orchards and roadside fruit stands. Plan to get lost on back roads, and, as you picnic atop sun-dappled hillsides, grab a hunk of earth and know firsthand the thing of greatest meaning in Wine Country.

When to Go

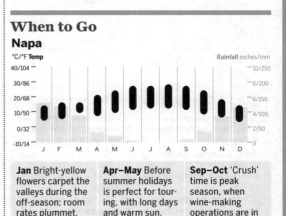

Jan Bright-yellow flowers carpet the valleys during the off-season; room rates plummet.

Apr–May Before summer holidays is perfect for touring, with long days and warm sun.

Sep–Oct 'Crush' time is peak season, when wine-making operations are in full force.

ℹ️ Getting There & Away

Napa and Sonoma counties each have an eponymous city and valley. So, the town of Sonoma is in Sonoma County, at the southern end of Sonoma Valley. The same goes for the city, county and valley of Napa.

From San Francisco, public transportation gets you to the valleys, but it's insufficient for vineyard-hopping. For public-transit informa-

tion, ⌨ dial 511 from Bay Area telephones, or look online at www.transit.511.org.

Both valleys are 90 minutes' drive from San Francisco. Napa, the further inland, has over 400 wineries and attracts the most visitors (expect heavy traffic on summer weekends). Sonoma County has 260 wineries, 40 in Sonoma Valley, which is less commercial and less congested than Napa. If you have time to visit only one, for ease choose Sonoma.

Napa & Sonoma Wine Country Highlights

① Sample California's greatest red wines in **Napa Valley** (p162).

② Picnic in sun-dappled shade on the state's largest town square, **Sonoma Plaza** (p188).

③ Bite into the artisanal food scene at Napa's **Oxbow Public Market** (p169).

④ Get lost on West County Sonoma back roads, like **Coleman Valley Road** (p202).

⑤ Submerge yourself in a volcanic-ash mud bath in **Calistoga** (p179).

⑥ Meet kooky locals at the **Occidental Farmers Market** (p202).

⑦ Pedal between wineries along pastoral **West Dry Creek Road** (p198), in the Dry Creek Valley.

⑧ Float in a canoe or kayak down the **Russian River** (p195).

BUS

Evans Transportation (☎707-255-1559; www.evanstransportation.com) Shuttles ($29) to Napa from San Francisco and Oakland Airports.

Golden Gate Transit (☎415-923-2000; www.goldengate.org) Bus 70/80 from downtown San Francisco to Petaluma ($10.25) and Santa Rosa ($11.25); board at 1st and Mission Sts. Connects with Sonoma County Transit buses.

Greyhound Buses (☎800-231-2222; www.greyhound.com) San Francisco to Santa Rosa ($22 to $30); transfer to local buses.

Napa Valley Vine (☎707-251-2800, 800-696-6443; www.nctpa.net) Operates local bus 10 daily from downtown Napa to Calistoga ($1.50); express bus 29 Monday to Friday from the Vallejo Ferry Terminal ($3.25) and El Cerrito del Norte BART station ($5.50), via Napa, to Calistoga; and local bus 11 daily from the Vallejo Ferry Terminal to downtown Napa ($1.50).

Sonoma County Airport Express (☎800-327-2024, 707-837-8700; www.airportexpressinc.com) Shuttles ($34) between Sonoma County Airport (Santa Rosa) and San Francisco and Oakland Airports.

CAR

From San Francisco, take Hwy 101 north over the Golden Gate Bridge, then Hwy 37 east to Hwy 121 north; continue to the junction of Hwy 12/121. For Sonoma Valley, take Hwy 12 north; for Napa Valley, take Hwy 12/121 east. Plan 70 minutes in light traffic, two hours during the weekday commute.

Hwy 12/121 splits south of Napa: Hwy 121 turns north and joins with Hwy 29 (aka St Helena Hwy); Hwy 12 merges with southbound Hwy 29 toward Vallejo. Hwy 29 backs up weekdays 3pm to 7pm, slowing returns to San Francisco.

From the East Bay (or downtown San Francisco), take I-80 east to Hwy 37 west (north of Vallejo), then northbound Hwy 29.

From Santa Rosa, take Hwy 12 east to access the northern end of Sonoma Valley. From Petaluma and Hwy 101, take Hwy 116 east.

FERRY

Baylink Ferry (☎877-643-3779; sanfranciscobayferry.com) Downtown San Francisco to Vallejo (adult/child $13/6.50, 60 minutes); connect with Napa Valley Vine bus 29 (weekdays) or bus 11 (daily).

TRAIN

Amtrak (☎800-872-7245; www.amtrak.com) Trains travel to Martinez (south of Vallejo), with connecting buses to Napa (45 minutes), Santa Rosa (1¼ hours) and Healdsburg (1¾ hours).

BART trains (☎415 989-2278; www.bart.gov) Run from San Francisco to El Cerrito del Norte ($4.40, 30 minutes). Napa Valley Vine bus 29 runs weekdays from BART to Calistoga, via Napa; on Saturdays take **SolTrans** (☎707-648-4666; www.soltransride.com) from BART to Vallejo ($5, 30 minutes), then connect with Napa Valley Vine bus 11 to Napa and Calistoga; on Sundays there's no connecting bus service from BART.

🄾 Getting Around

You'll need a car or bike to winery-hop. Alternatively visit tasting rooms in downtown Napa or downtown Sonoma.

BICYCLE

Touring Wine Country by bicycle is unforgettable. Stick to back roads. We most love pastoral West Dry Creek Rd, northwest of Healdsburg, in Sonoma County. Through Sonoma Valley, take Arnold Dr instead of Hwy 12; through Napa Valley, take the Silverado Trail instead of Hwy 29.

Cycling between wineries isn't demanding – the valleys are mostly flat – but crossing between the Napa and Sonoma Valleys is intense, particularly via steep Oakville Grade and Trinity Rd (between Oakville and Glen Ellen).

Bicycles, in boxes, can be checked on Greyhound buses for $30 to $40; bike boxes cost $10 (call ahead). You can transport bicycles on Golden Gate Transit buses, which usually have free racks available (first-come, first-served).

CAR

Napa Valley is 30 miles long and 5 miles across at its widest point (city of Napa), 1 mile at its narrowest (Calistoga). Two roads run north–south: Hwy 29 (St Helena Hwy) and the more scenic Silverado Trail, a mile east. Drive up one, down the other.

The American Automobile Association ranks Napa Valley among America's most congested rural vacation destinations. Summer and fall weekend traffic is unbearable, especially on Hwy 29 between Napa and St Helena. Plan accordingly.

Cross-valley roads linking Silverado Trail with Hwy 29 – including Yountville, Oakville and Rutherford crossroads – are bucolic and get less traffic. For scenery, the Oakville Grade and rural Trinity Rd (which leads southwest to Hwy 12 in Sonoma Valley) are narrow, curvy and beautiful – but treacherous in rainstorms. Mt Veeder Rd leads through pristine countryside west of Yountville.

Note: Police watch like hawks for traffic violators. *Don't drink and drive.*

There are a number of shortcuts between the Napa and Sonoma Valleys: from Oakville, take Oakville Grade to Trinity Rd; from St Helena, take Spring Mountain Rd into Calistoga Rd; from Calistoga, take Petrified Forest Rd to Calistoga Rd.

PUBLIC TRANSPORTATION

Napa Valley Vine (707-251-2800, 800-696-6443; www.nctpa.net) Bus 10 runs daily from downtown Napa to Calistoga ($1.50, 1¼ hours).

Sonoma County Transit (800-345-7433, 707-576-7433; www.sctransit.com) Buses from Santa Rosa to Petaluma ($2.45, 70 minutes), Sonoma ($3.05, 1¼ hours) and western Sonoma County, including Russian River Valley towns ($3.05, 30 minutes).

NAPA VALLEY

The birthplace of modern-day Wine Country is famous for regal Cabernet Sauvignons, château-like wineries and fabulous food, attracting more than four million visitors a year, many planning to wine and dine themselves into a stupor, maybe get a massage, and sleep somewhere swell with fine linens and a pool.

A few decades ago, this 5-by-35-mile strip of former stagecoach stops seemed forgotten by time, a quiet agricultural valley dense with orchards. Grapes had grown here since the Gold Rush, but grape-sucking phylloxera bugs, Prohibition and the Great Depression reduced 140 wineries in the 1890s, to around 25 by the 1960s.

In 1968, Napa was declared the 'Napa Valley Agricultural Preserve,' effectively blocking future valley development for non-ag purposes. The law stipulated no subdivision of valley-floor land under 40 acres. This succeeded in preserving the valley's natural beauty, but when Napa wines earned top honors at a 1976 blind tasting in Paris, the wine-drinking world noticed and land values skyrocketed. Only the very rich could afford to build. Hence, so many architecturally jaw-dropping wineries. Independent, family-owned wineries still exist – we highlight a number of them – but much of Napa Valley is now owned by global conglomerates.

The city of Napa anchors the valley, but the real work happens up-valley. Napa isn't as pretty as other towns, but has some noteworthy sights, among them Oxbow Public Market. Scenic towns include St Helena, Yountville and Calistoga – the latter more famous for water than wine.

Napa Valley Wineries

Cab is king in Napa. No varietal captures imaginations like the fruit of the Cabernet Sauvignon vine – Bordeaux is the French equivalent – and no wine fetches a higher price. Napa farmers can't afford *not* to grow Cabernet. Other heat-loving varietals, such as Sangiovese and Merlot, also thrive here.

Napa's wines merit their reputation among the world's finest – complex, with luxurious finishes. Napa wineries sell many 'buy-and-hold' wines, versus Sonoma's 'drink-now' wines.

Artesa Vineyards & Winery WINERY

(707-254-2126; www.artesawinery.com; 1345 Henry Rd, Napa; glass $12, tasting $15-20, incl tour $30; 10am-4:30pm) Begin or end the day with a glass of bubbly or Pinot at Artesa, southwest of Napa. Built into a mountainside, the ultra-modern Barcelona-style architecture is stunning, and you can't beat the top-of-the-world vistas over San Pablo Bay. Tours run at 11am and 2pm. Bottles cost $20 to $60.

Vintners' Collective TASTING ROOM

(Map p167; 707-255-7150; www.vintnerscollective.com; 1245 Main St, Napa; tasting $10-30; 11am-6pm) Ditch the car and chill in downtown Napa at this tasting bar, inside a former 19th-century brothel, representing 20 high-end boutique wineries too small to have their own tasting rooms.

Twenty Rows WINERY

(707-265-7750; www.twentyrows.com; 880 Vallejo St, Napa; tasting $10; 11am-5pm Tue-Sat, by appointment Sun & Mon) Downtown Napa's only working winery crafts light-on-the-palate Cabernet Sauvignon for just $20 a bottle. Taste in a chilly garage, on plastic furniture, with fun dudes who know their wines. Good Sauvignon Blanc, too.

★ Hess Collection WINERY, GALLERY

(707-255-1144; www.hesscollection.com; 4411 Redwood Rd, Napa; tasting $15, gallery free; 10am-5:30pm) ✐ Art lovers: don't miss Hess Collection, whose galleries display mixed-media and large-canvas works, including pieces by Francis Bacon and Louis Soutter. In the cave-like tasting room, find well-known Cabernet and Chardonnay, but also try the Viognier. Hess overlooks the valley: be prepared to drive a winding road. Reservations recommended. Bottles: $20 to $60. (NB: Don't confuse Hess Collection with Hess Select, the grocery-store brand.)

Darioush WINERY

(707-257-2345; www.darioush.com; 4240 Silverado Trail, Napa; tasting $18-40; 10:30am-5pm)

TOURING NAPA & SONOMA WINE COUNTRY

You have the most flexibility by driving your own vehicle, but to drink and not drive, here are some tour options. Note that some wineries do not allow limousines (because the people in them are often obnoxious and don't buy anything); and limousine companies have set itineraries with little flexibility (ie, you'll have few choices about which wineries you visit).

Bicycle Tours & Rentals

Guided tours start around $90 per day including bikes, tastings and lunch. Daily rentals cost $25 to $85; make reservations.

Backroads (☎800-462-2848; www.backroads.com) All-inclusive guided biking and walking.

Calistoga Bike Shop (☎707-942-9687; www.calistogabikeshop.com; 1318 Lincoln Ave, Calistoga; ⊙10am-6pm) Wine-tour rental package ($90) includes wine pickup.

Getaway Adventures (☎800-499-2453, 707-568-3040; http://getawayadventures.com; tours $149) Great guided tours, some combined with kayaking, of Napa, Sonoma, Calistoga, Healdsburg and Russian River. Single- and multiday trips.

Good Time Touring (☎888-525-0453, 707-938-0453; www.goodtimetouring.com) Tours of Sonoma Valley, Dry Creek and West County Sonoma.

Napa River Velo (Map p167; ☎707-258-8729; www.napariververlo.com; 680 Main St, Napa; ⊙10am-7pm Mon-Fri, 9am-6pm Sat, 10am-5pm Sun) Daily rentals and weekend tours with wine pickup.

Napa Valley Adventure Tours (☎707-224-9080, 707-259-1833; www.napavalleyadventuretours.com; 1147 1st St, Napa) Guides tours between wineries, off-road trips, hiking and kayaking. Daily rentals.

Napa Valley Bike Tours (☎707-944-2953; www.napavalleybiketours.com; 6500 Washington St, Yountville; ⊙8:30am-5pm) Daily rentals; easy and moderately difficult tours.

Spoke Folk Cyclery (☎707-433-7171; www.spokefolk.com; 201 Center St, Healdsburg; ⊙10am-6pm Mon-Fri, to 5pm Sat & Sun) Rents touring, racing and tandem bicycles.

Wine Country Bikes (☎707-473-0610, toll free 866-922-4537; www.winecountrybikes.com; 61 Front St, Healdsburg; rentals per day from $39, multiday guided tours from $595; ⊙9am-5pm) Rents bikes in downtown Healdsburg and guides multiday Sonoma County tours.

Other Tours

Wine Country Jeep Tours (☎800-539-5337, 707-546-1822; www.jeeptours.com; 3hr tour $75) Tour Wine Country's back roads and boutique wineries by Jeep, year-round at 10am and 1pm. Also operates tours of Sonoma Coast.

Antique Tours Limousine (☎707-761-3949; www.antiquetours.net) Drive in style in a 1947 Packard convertible; tours cost $120 to $170 per hour.

Beau Wine Tours (☎800-387-2328, 707-938-8001; www.beauwinetours.com) Winery tours in sedans and stretch limos; charges $60 to $95 per hour (four- to six-hour minimum).

Beyond the Label (☎707-363-4023; www.btlnv.com; per couple $995) Personalized tours, including lunch at home with a vintner, guided by a Napa native.

Flying Horse Carriage Company (☎707-849-8989; www.flyinghorse.org; 4hr tour per person $150; ⊙Fri-Mon) Trot through Alexander Valley by horse-drawn carriage. Includes picnic.

Magnum Tours (☎707-753-0088; www.magnumwinetours.com) Sedans and specialty limousines from $65 to $125 per hour (four-hour minimum, five hours Saturdays). Exceptional service.

Like a modern-day Persian palace, Darioush ranks high on the fabulosity scale, with towering columns, Le Corbusier furniture, Persian rugs and travertine walls. Though known for Cabernet, Darioush also bottles Chardonnay, Merlot and Shiraz, all made with 100% of their respective varietals. Call about wine-and-cheese pairings. Bottles cost $40 to $95.

Regusci
WINERY

(☑707-254-0403; www.regusciwinery.com; 5584 Silverado Trail, Napa; tasting $25-30, incl tour $30-60; ☺10am-5pm) One of Napa's oldest, unfussy Regusci dates to the late 1800s, with 173 acres of vineyards unfurling around a century-old stone winery that makes Bordeaux-style blends on the valley's quieter eastern side – good when traffic up-valley is bad. No appointment necessary; lovely oak-shaded picnic area. Bottles cost $36 to $140.

★Robert Sinskey
WINERY

(☑707-944-9090; www.robertsinskey.com; 6320 Silverado Trail, Napa; tasting $25, incl tour $50-75; ☺10am-4:30pm) ✎ Chef-owned Robert Sinskey's dramatic hilltop tasting room, constructed of stone, redwood and teak, resembles a small cathedral – fitting, given the sacred status bestowed upon food and wine here. Sinskey specializes in bright-acid organic Pinot, Merlot and Cabernet, and exceptional Alsatian varietals, Vin Gris, Cabernet Franc and dry Rosé, specifically designed to pair well with food. Tasting fee waived with two-bottle purchase – a rarity. Small bites accompany tastings. Call about culinary tours. Bottles cost $28 to $100.

Robert Mondavi
WINERY

(☑888-766-6328; www.robertmondaviwinery.com; 7801 Hwy 29, Oakville; tasting & tour $20-55; ☺10am-5pm; ♿) Tour buses flock to this corporate-owned winery, but if you know nothing about wine and can cope with crowds, the worthwhile tours provide excellent insight into winemaking. Otherwise, skip it unless you're considering one of its glorious outdoor summer concerts; call for schedules. Bottles cost $25 to $150.

Elizabeth Spencer
TASTING ROOM

(☑707-963-6067; www.elizabethspencerwines.com; 1165 Rutherford Rd, Rutherford; tasting $20; ☺10am-5:30pm) Taste inside an 1872 railroad depot or the outdoor garden at this inviting small winery, featuring monster-sized Pinot Noir, grapefruity Sauvignon Blanc, structured light-body Grenache, and signature Cabernet. Bottles cost $30 to $95.

Mumm Napa
WINERY, GALLERY

(☑800-686-6272; www.mummnapa.com; 8445 Silverado Trail, Rutherford; glass $8; tasting $18-40, tour $25; ☺10am-4:45pm) Valley views are spectacular at Mumm, which makes respectable sparkling wines you can sample while seated on a vineyard-view terrace – ideal when you want to impress conservative parents-in-law. Dodge crowds by coming early, or paying $40 for the reserve-tasting Oak Terrace (reservations advised).

★Frog's Leap
WINERY

(☑707-963-4704; www.frogsleap.com; 8815 Conn Creek Rd, Rutherford; tasting $15, incl tour $20; ☺by appointment; ♿❀) ✎ Meandering paths wind through magical gardens and

---

NAPA OR SONOMA?

Napa and Sonoma Valleys run parallel, separated by the narrow, imposing Mayacamas Mountains. The two couldn't be more different. It's easy to mock aggressively sophisticated Napa, its monuments to ego, trophy homes and trophy wives, $1000-a-night inns, $50-plus tastings and wine-snob visitors, but Napa makes some of the world's best wines. Constrained by its geography, it stretches along a single valley, making it easy to visit. Drawbacks are high prices and heavy traffic, but there are 400 nearly side-by-side wineries. And the valley is gorgeous.

There are three Sonomas: the town of Sonoma, which is in Sonoma Valley, which is in Sonoma County. Think of them as Russian dolls. Sonoma County is much more down-to-earth and politically left-leaning. Though it's becoming gentrified, Sonoma lacks Napa's chic factor (Healdsburg notwithstanding), and locals like it that way. The wines are more approachable, but the county's 260 wineries are spread out. If you're here on a weekend, head to Sonoma (County or Valley), which gets less traffic, but on a weekday, see Napa, too. Ideally schedule two to four days: one for each valley, and one or two additional for western Sonoma County.

Spring and fall are the best times to visit. Summers are hot, dusty and crowded. Fall brings fine weather, harvest time and the 'crush,' the pressing of the grapes, but lodging prices skyrocket.

fruit-bearing orchards – pick peaches in July – surrounding an 1884 barn and farmstead with cats and chickens. The vibe is casual and down-to-earth, with a major emphasis on *fun*. Sauvignon Blanc is its best-known wine, but the Merlot merits attention. There's also a dry, restrained Cabernet, atypical of Napa.

All are organic. Appointments required. Bottles cost $22 to $42.

★ **Tres Sabores** WINERY

(☎ 707-967-8027; www.tressabores.com; 1620 South Whitehall Lane, St Helena; tour & tasting $20; ☺ by appointment; 🔊) 🍴 At the valley's westernmost edge, where sloping vineyards meet wooded hillsides, Tres Sabores is a portal to old Napa – no fancy tasting room, no snobbery, just great wine in a spectacular setting. Bucking the Cabernet custom, Tres Sabores crafts elegantly structured, Burgundian-style Zinfandel, and spritely Sauvignon Blanc, which the *New York Times* dubbed a top 10 of its kind in California. Reservations essential.

Guinea fowl and sheep control pests on the 35-acre estate, while golden labs chase butterflies through gnarled old vines. After your tour, linger at olive-shaded picnic tables and drink in gorgeous valley views. Bottles cost $22 to $80.

Hall WINERY

(Map p176; ☎ 707-967-2626; www.hallwines.com; 401 St Helena Hwy, St Helena; tasting $30, tour $50; ☺ 10am-5:30pm; 🔊) Owned by Bill Clinton's former ambassador to Austria, Hall specializes in Sauvignon Blanc, Merlot and Cabernet Sauvignon, crafted in big-fruit California style. Its dramatic tasting room has a stand-up bar with 180-degree views of vineyards and mountains through floor-to-ceiling glass, and the glorious art collection includes a giant chrome rabbit leaping over the vines. Bottles cost $22 to $80.

Long Meadow Ranch TASTING ROOM

(Map p176; ☎ 707-963-4555; www.longmeadow-ranch.com; 738 Main St, St Helena; tasting $15-25; ☺ 11am-6pm) 🍴 Long Meadow stands out for olive-oil tastings (free), plus good estate-grown Cabernet, Sauvignon Blanc, Chardonnay and Pinot noir (bottles $20 to $47), served inside an 1874 farmhouse surrounded by lovely gardens.

Pride Mountain WINERY

(Map p176; ☎ 707-963-4949; www.pridewines. com; 3000 Summit Trail, St Helena; tasting incl tour

$20-25; ☺ by appointment) High atop Spring Mountain, cult-favorite Pride straddles the Napa–Sonoma border and bottles vintages under both appellations. The well-structured Cabernet and heavy-hitting Merlot are the best-known but there's also an elegant Viognier (perfect with oysters) and standout Cab Franc, available only here. Picnicking here is spectacular: choose Viewpoint for drop-dead vistas or Ghost Winery for shade and the historic ruins of a 19th-century winery, but you must first reserve a tasting. Bottles cost $38 to $70.

Titus WINERY

(Map p176; ☎ 707-963-3235; www.titusvineyards. com; 2971 Silverado Trail North, St Helena; tasting $20; ☺ by appointment; 🔊) Unfussy Titus occupies a tiny oak-shaded 1910 farmhouse, surrounded by white-picket fence and roses. Call ahead to sample good-value, fruit-forward Cabernet Sauvignon and old-vine Zinfandel, which you taste in an old-fashioned kitchen overlooking the vineyards. Afterward, take your glass outside and wander the vineyards. The tasting fee is waived with a purchase and bottles are $20 to $70.

Casa Nuestra WINERY

(Map p176; ☎ 866-844-9463; www.casanuestra. com; 3451 Silverado Trail North, St Helena; tasting $10; ☺ by appointment) 🍴 A peace flag and portrait of Elvis greet you at this old-school, mom-and-pop winery, which produces unusual blends and interesting varietals (including good Chenin Blanc) and 100% Cabernet Franc. Vineyards are all-organic; the sun provides power. Picnic free (call ahead and buy a bottle) beneath weeping willows shading happy goats. Bottles are $20 to $60.

Cade WINERY

(Map p176; ☎ 707-965-2746; www.cadewinery.com; 360 Howell Mountain Rd S, Angwin; tasting $40-70; ☺ by appointment) 🍴 Ascend Mt Veeder for drop-dead vistas, 1800ft above the valley, at Napa's oh-so-swank, first-ever organically farmed, LEED-gold-certified winery, partly owned by former San Francisco mayor Gavin Newsom. Hawks ride thermals at eye level as you sample bright Sauvignon Blanc and luscious Cabernet Sauvignon that's more Bordelaise in style than Californian. Reservations required. Bottles cost $44 to $80.

Ladera WINERY

(Map p176; ☎707-965-2445, 866-523-3728; www. laderavineyards.com; 150 White Cottage Rd S, Angwin; tasting $25; ⊗ by appointment) 🖋 High atop Howell Mountain, Ladera makes wonderful, little-known, estate-grown Cabernet Sauvignon and Sauvignon Blanc in a well-off-the-beaten-path, 1886, stone-walled winery, one of Napa's oldest – ideal when you want to escape the crowds. Bottle are $28 to $85.

Schramsberg WINERY

(Map p176; ☎707-942-2414; www.schramsberg. com; 1400 Schramsberg Rd, off Peterson Dr; tour & tasting $50; ⊗ by appointment 10am, 11:30am, 12:30pm, 1:30pm & 2:30pm) Napa's second-oldest winery, Schramsberg makes some of California's best brut sparkling wines, and in 1972 was the first domestic wine served at the White House. Blanc de Blancs is the signature. The appointment-only tasting and tour (book well ahead) is expensive, but you'll sample all the *tête de cuvées*, not just the low-end wines. Tours include a walk through the caves; bring a sweater. Bottles cost $22 to $100.

Castello di Amorosa WINERY, CASTLE

(Map p176; ☎707-967-6272; www.castellodiamorosa.com; 4045 Hwy 29, Calistoga; admission & tasting $19-29, incl guided tour $34-75; ⊗9:30am-6pm, to 5pm Nov-Feb) It took 14 years to build this perfectly replicated, 12th-century Italian castle, complete with moat, hand-cut stone walls, ceiling frescoes by Italian artisans, Roman-style cross-vault brick catacombs, and a torture chamber with period equipment. You can taste without an appointment, but this is one tour worth taking. Oh, the wine? Some respectable Italian varietals, including a velvety Tuscan blend, and a Merlot blend that goes great with pizza. Bottles are $20 to $125.

Lava Vine WINERY

(Map p176; ☎707-942-9500; www.lavavine.com; 965 Silverado Trail; tasting $10; ⊗10am-5pm; 👶🐾) 🖋 Breaking ranks with Napa snobbery, the party kids at Lava Vine take a light-hearted approach to their seriously good

wines – don't be surprised if they bust out musical instruments and start jamming. Children and dogs play outside, while you tap your toe to uptempo tunes in the tiny tasting room. Picnicking allowed. Reservations recommended. Bottles cost $25 to $55.

Vincent Arroyo WINERY

(Map p176; ☎707-942-6995; www.vincentarroyo. com; 2361 Greenwood Ave, Calistoga; ⊗by appointment) FREE The tasting room is a garage, where you may even meet Mr Arroyo, known for his all-estate-grown petite Syrah and Cabernet Sauvignon. They're distributed nowhere else and are so consistently good that 75% of production is sold before it's bottled. Tastings are free, but appointments are required. Bottles are $22 to $45.

Napa

The valley's workaday hub was once a nothing-special city of storefronts, Victorian cottages and riverfront warehouses, but booming real-estate values caused an influx of new money that's transforming downtown into a hub of arts and food.

◉ Sights

Napa lies between Silverado Trail and St Helena Hwy/Hwy 29. For downtown, exit Hwy 29 at 1st St and drive east. Napa's main drag, 1st St, is lined with shops and restaurants.

★ Oxbow Public Market MARKET

(Map p167; ☎707-226-6529; www.oxbowpublicmarket.com; 610 1st St; ⊗9am-7pm Mon, Wed & Thu, to 8pm Tue, Fri & Sat, 10am-6pm Sun; 🍴) 🖋 Produce stalls, kitchen shops, and everywhere something to taste – Oxbow is foodie central, with emphasis on seasonal eating and sustainability. Come hungry.

★ di Rosa Art + Nature Preserve GALLERY, GARDENS

(☎707-226-5991; www.dirosaart.org; 5200 Hwy 121; admission $5, tours $12-15; ⊗10am-4pm Wed-Sun) West of downtown, scrap-metal sheep graze Carneros vineyards at 217-acre di Rosa Preserve, a stunning collection of Northern California art, displayed indoors in galleries and outdoors in sculpture gardens. Reservations recommended for tours.

☞ Tours

Napa Valley Wine Train TRAIN TOUR

(☎800-427-4124, 707-253-2111; www.winetrain. com; adult/child from $109/74) A cushy, if tour-

Napa

0 — 400 m
0 — 0.2 miles

Napa

isty, way to see Wine Country, the Wine Train offers three-hour daily trips in vintage Pullman dining cars, from Napa to St Helena and back, with an optional winery tour. Trains depart from McKinstry St, near 1st St.

🛏 Sleeping

Summer demand exceeds supply. Weekend rates skyrocket. Also consider staying in Calistoga.

Chablis Inn MOTEL $$
(☏ 707-257-1944; www.chablisinn.com; 3360 Solano Ave; r Mon-Fri $89-109, Sat & Sun $169-189; ❋@🛜🏊) Good-value, well-kept motel near Napa's only stretch of freeway. Hot tub.

★**Carneros Inn** RESORT $$$
(☏ 707-299-4900; www.thecarnerosinn.com; 4048 Sonoma Hwy; r Mon-Fri $485-570, Sat & Sun $650-900; ❋@🛜🏊🐾) Carneros Inn's contemporary aesthetic and retro, small-town

agricultural theme shatter the predictable Wine Country mold. The semi-detached, corrugated-metal cottages look like itinerant housing, but inside they're snappy and chic, with cherry-wood floors, ultrasuede headboards, wood-burning fireplaces, heated-tile bathroom floors, giant tubs and indoor-outdoor showers. Linger by day at the hilltop pool, by night at the outdoor fireplaces. Two excellent on-site restaurants.

Milliken Creek Inn INN $$$

(☎888-622-5775, 707-255-1197; www.millikencreek-inn.com; 1815 Silverado Trail; r incl breakfast $295-750; ✳@🕸) Understatedly elegant Milliken Creek combines small-inn charm, fine-hotel service and B&B intimacy. Rooms are impeccably styled in English-Colonial style, and have top-flight amenities, fireplaces and ultra-high-thread-count linens. Breakfast is delivered. Book a river-view room.

Cottages of Napa Valley BUNGALOW $$$

(☎707-252-7810; www.napacottages.com; 1012 Darns Lane; d $395-500, q $475-575; ✳🕸) Eight pristine cottages of quality construction – made for romantic hideaways, with extra-long soaking tubs, indoor gas fireplaces and outdoor campfire pits – surround a big garden shaded by towering pines. Cottages 4 and 8 have private porches and swinging chairs. The only drawback is white noise from traffic, but interiors are silent.

Andaz Hotel HOTEL $$$

(☎707-224-3900; napa.andaz.hyatt.com; 1450 1st St; r $289-389; ✳@🕸) Smack downtown, the Andaz was constructed in 2009, and feels like a big-city hotel, with business-class-fancy rooms, styled in sexy retro-70s style. Walkable to restaurants and bars.

Napa River Inn HOTEL $$$

(Map p167; ☎877-251-8500, 707-251-8500; www.napariverinn.com; 500 Main St; r incl breakfast $249-549; ✳@🕸🕸) Beside the river, in the 1884 Hatt Building, the inn has upper-mid-range rooms, Victoriana to modern, in three satellite buildings. Walkable to restaurants and bars. Dogs get special treatment.

River Terrace Inn HOTEL $$$

(☎707-320-9000, 866-627-2386; www.riverterra-ceinn.com; 1600 Soscol Ave; r $189-360; ✳🕸🕸) Upmarket, business-class, chain-style hotel with shopping-mall-bland architecture fronting on the Napa River. Heated outdoor pool.

Casita Bonita BUNGALOW $$$

(☎707-321-4853, 707-259-1980; www.lacasitabon-ita.com; q $395; ✳🕸) Well decorated two-bedroom cottage with full kitchen and veggie garden – kids love the chickens. Perfect for two couples or a family. Two-night minimum. Check the website for location details.

Best Western Ivy Hotel HOTEL $$$

(☎800-253-6272, 707-253-9300; www.ivyhotelnapa.com; 4195 Solano Ave; r $180-295; ✳@🕸🕸) Redone in 2011, this colorful, smart-looking, two-story hotel, on the suburban strip north of Napa, has extras like fridge, microwave and on-site laundry. Good value when under $250.

Napa Winery Inn HOTEL $$$

(☎800-522-8999, 707-257-7220; www.napawine-ryinn.com; 1998 Trower Ave; r incl breakfast Mon-Fri $179-279, Sat & Sun $229-339; ✳@🕸🕸🕸) Request a remodeled room at this good-value hotel, north of downtown, decorated with generic. Hot tub, good service.

Blackbird Inn B&B $$$

(Map p167; ☎888-567-9811, 707-226-2450; www.blackbirdinnnapa.com; 1775 1st St; r incl breakfast $185-300; ✳🕸) Gorgeous, eight-room Arts and Crafts–style B&B, but anticipate street noise.

Best Western Elm House INN $$$

(☎707-255-1831; www.bestwesternelmhouseinn.com; 800 California Blvd; r incl breakfast $199-299; ✳@🕸) Impeccably kept rooms with generic furnishings in soft pastels. Ideal for conservative travelers. Fifteen-minute walk to downtown; easy highway access. Hot tub.

ℹ CUTTING COSTS IN NAPA

To avoid overspending on tasting fees, it's perfectly acceptable to pay for one tasting to share between two people. Ask in advance if fees are applicable to purchase (they usually aren't). Tour fees cannot be split. Ask at your hotel, or at visitors centers, for free- or discounted-tasting coupons, or download from napatouristguide.com. If you can't afford the hotels, try western Sonoma County, but if you want to be nearer Napa, try the suburban towns of Vallejo and American Canyon, about 20 minutes from downtown Napa. Both have motels for $75 to $125 in high season. Also find chains 30 minutes away in Fairfield, off I-80 exits 41 (Pittman Rd) and 45 (Travis Blvd).

🍴 Eating

Make reservations whenever possible. July to mid-August, look for the peach stand at Deer Park Rd and Silverado Trail (across Deer Park Rd from Stewart's farmstand) for juicy-delicious heirloom varieties.

⭐ **Oxbow Public Market**   MARKET $
(☏707-226-6529; www.oxbowpublicmarket.com; 644 1st St; dishes from $3; ☉9am-7pm Mon, Wed & Thu-Sat, to 8pm Tue, 10am-5pm Sun) 🍴 Graze this gourmet market and plug into the Northern California food scene. Standouts: Hog Island oysters (six for $16); comfort cooking at celeb-chef Todd Humphries' Kitchen Door (mains $14 to $24); Venezuelan cornbread sandwiches ($9) at Pica Pica; great Cal-Mexican at C Casa (tacos $5 to $9); pastries at Ca'Momi ($2); and Three Twins certified-organic ice cream ($3.75 for a single cone).

Tuesday is locals' night (5pm to 8pm), with many discounts. Tuesday and Saturday mornings, there's a farmers market. Some stalls remain open till 9pm, even on Sundays, but many close earlier.

Alexis Baking Co   CAFE $
(Map p167; ☏707-258-1827; www.alexisbakingcompany.com; 1517 3rd St; dishes $7-13; ☉7am-3pm Mon-Fri, 7:30am-3pm Sat, 8am-2pm Sun; 🚗🐕) Our fave spot for quality scrambles, granola, focaccia, big cups of joe and boxed lunches to go.

Taqueria Maria   MEXICAN $
(☏707-257-6925; www.taqueriamaria.com; 640 3rd St; mains $8-13; ☉9am-8:30pm Sun-Thu, to 9pm Fri & Sat; 🚗🐕) Reliably good Mexican cooking that won't break the bank. Also serves breakfast.

Buttercream Bakery   DINER $
(☏707-255-6700; www.buttercreambakery.com; 2297 Jefferson St; breakfast $5; ☉5:30am-3pm) For a retro-flashback: this pink-striped diner, favored by Napa's little old ladies, has all-day breakfasts and white-bread lunches, served by matrons in heavy eye shadow.

Soda Canyon Store   DELI $
(☏707-252-0285; www.sodacanyonstore.com; 4006 Silverado Trail; ☉6am-5:30pm Mon-Sat, 7:30am-5pm Sun) This roadside deli, with shaded picnic area, makes an easy stop while winery-hopping north of town.

Oenotri   ITALIAN $$
(Map p167; ☏707-252-1022; www.oenotri.com; 1425 1st St; dinner mains $17-29, lunch $13-15; ☉11:30am-2:30pm & 5:30-9pm Sun-Thu, to 10pm Fri & Sat) 🍴 Housemade salumi and pastas, and wood-fired Naples-style pizzas are the stars at always-busy Oenotri, which draws crowds for daily-changing, locally sourced, rustic-Italian cooking, served in a cavernous brick-walled space.

Carpe Diem Wine Bar   CALIFORNIAN $$
(☏707-224-0800; www.carpediemwinebar.com; 1001 2nd St; mains $17-19; ☉4-9pm Mon-Thu, to 10pm Fri & Sat) This busy storefront wine bar and restaurant makes inventive, flavorful small plates, from simple skewers and flatbreads, to elaborate ostrich burgers, salumi platters and – wait for it – duck confit 'quack and cheese.'

Pearl Restaurant   NEW AMERICAN $$
(☏707-224-9161; www.therestaurantpearl.com; 1339 Pearl St; mains $15-23; ☉11:30am-2pm & 5:30-9pm Tue-Sat; 🐕) Meet locals at this dog-friendly bistro with pinewood tables and open-rafter ceilings, whose winning down-to-earth cooking includes double-cut pork chops, chicken-verde polenta, steak tacos, and oysters – the specialty.

Pizza Azzuro   PIZZA $$
(Map p167; ☏707-255-5552; www.azzurropizzeria.com; 1260 Main St; mains $13-16; ☉11:30am-9pm Sun-Thu, to 9:30pm Fri & Sat; 🚗🐕) This Napa classic gets deafeningly loud, but it's worth bearing for tender-crusted pizzas, salad-topped 'manciata' bread, good Caeser salads and pastas.

Norman Rose Tavern   PUB FOOD $$
(Map p167; ☏707-258-1516; www.normanrosenapa.com; 1401 1st St; mains $10-24; ☉11:30am-9pm Sun-Thu, to 10pm Fri & Sat; 🐕) This happening gastropub, styled with reclaimed wood and tufted-leather banquettes, is good for a burger and beer. Great fries. Beer and wine only.

HIGH SEASON VS LOW SEASON

Many Wine Country restaurants and hotels diminish operations in wintertime. Make reservations, especially in summertime, or you may not eat. Hotel rates jump during September and October's grape-crushing season – the most popular time.

Bounty Hunter Wine Bar & Smokin' BBQ

BARBECUE $$

(Map p167; ☎707-226-3976; www.bountyhunter-winebar.com; 975 1st St; mains $13-24; ⊙11am-10pm Sun-Thu, to midnight Fri & Sat; 🖲) Inside an 1888 grocery store, Bounty Hunter has an Old West vibe and superb barbecue, made with house-smoked meats. The standout whole chicken is roasted over a can of Tecate. Ten local beers and 40 wines by the glass.

Torc

CALIFORNIAN $$$

(☎707-252-3292; www.torcnapa.com; 1140 Main St; mains $26-29; ⊙5-9:30pm daily, 10:30am-2:30pm Sat & Sun) Wildly popular Torc plays off the seasons with dynamic combinations of farm-fresh ingredients, such as springtime white asparagus with black-truffle toasts, and squab with artichoke and licorice. Well-arranged for people-watching, the big stone dining room has an open-truss ceiling, and exposed pinewood tables that downplay formality. Reservations essential.

Bistro Don Giovanni

ITALIAN $$$

(☎707-224-3300; www.bistrodongiovanni.com; 4110 Howard Lane; mains $16-28; ⊙11:30am-10pm Sun-Thu, to 11pm Fri & Sat) This long-running favorite roadhouse serves modern-Italian pastas, crispy pizzas and wood-roasted meats. Reservations essential. Weekends get packed – and loud. Request a vineyard-view table (good luck).

Angèle

FRENCH $$$

(Map p167; ☎707-252-8115; www.angelerestaurant.com; 540 Main St; lunch mains $14-27, dinner $26-34; ⊙11:30am-10pm) Stalwart Angèle serves reliable provincial-French cooking –

A LOVELY SPOT FOR A PICNIC

Unlike Sonoma, there aren't many places to picnic legally in Napa. Here's a short list, in south-to-north order, but call ahead and remember to buy a bottle (or glass, if available) of your host's wine. If you don't finish it, California law forbids driving with an uncorked bottle in the car (keep it in the trunk).

➡ Regusci (p164)

➡ Napa Valley Museum (p171)

➡ Pride Mountain (p165)

➡ Casa Nuestra (p165)

➡ Lava Vine (p166)

Niçoise salads and *croques messieurs* at lunch, duck confit and beef Bourguignon at dinner – on a river-view deck or cozy dining room, both perfect for lingering with a good bottle of wine.

🍷 Drinking & Nightlife

Empire

LOUNGE

(☎707-254-8888; www.empirenapa.com; 1400 1st St; ⊙5:30pm-midnight Tue-Thu, to 2am Fri & Sat) Moody and dark, with candlelight and a jellyfish tank, Empire mimics big-city lounges, with good cocktails and uptempo music. Alas, no dance floor.

Billco's Billiards & Darts

SPORTS BAR

(Map p167; www.billcos.com; 1234 3rd St; ⊙noon-midnight) Dudes in khakis swill craft beers and throw darts inside this polite pool hall.

Downtown Joe's

SPORTS BAR, BREWERY

(Map p167; www.downtownjoes.com; 902 Main St at 2nd St; 🖲) Live music Thursday to Sunday, TV-sports nightly. Often packed, usually messy.

☆ Entertainment

Silo's Jazz Club

LIVE MUSIC

(Map p167; ☎707-251-5833; www.silosjazzclub.com; 530 Main St; cover varies; ⊙6-10pm Wed-Thu, 7pm-midnight Fri & Sat, varied hrs Sun) A cabaret-style wine-and-beer bar, Silo's hosts jazz and rock acts Friday and Saturday nights; Wednesday and Thursday it's good for drinks. Reservations recommended weekends.

City Winery at Napa Valley Opera House

THEATER

(Map p167; ☎707-260-1600; www.citywinery.com/napa; 1030 Main St) Napa's vintage-1880s opera theater houses a happening wine bar and restaurant downstairs, and 300-seat cabaret upstairs, hosting acts like Ginger Baker and Graham Nash. Opening hours vary, though it's usually open Thursday to Sunday evenings.

Uptown Theatre

THEATER

(Map p167; ☎707-259-0333; www.uptowntheatrenapa.com; 1350 3rd St) Big-name acts play this restored 1937 theater.

🛍 Shopping

Betty's Girl

WOMEN'S CLOTHING, VINTAGE

(Map p167; ☎707-254-7560; www.bettysgirlnapa.com; 968 Pearl St; ⊙11am-6pm Thu & Fri, 10am-2pm Sat) Expert couturier Kim Northrup fits women with fabulous vintage cocktail dresses and custom-made designs, altering and shipping for no additional charge. Open extra hours by appointment.

Napa Valley Olive Oil Mfg Co FOOD
(nvoliveoil.com; 1331 1st St; ⊘10am-5:30pm) Sample 30 varieties of fine olive oil and vinegar at this downtown specialty-food boutique, which also carries fancy salts and local jam.

Napa General Store GIFTS
(Map p167; ☑707-259-0762; www.napageneralstore.com; 540 Main St; ⊘8am-6pm) Finally, cutesy Wine Country souvenirs reasonably priced. The on-site wine bar is convenient for non-shopping spouses.

ℹ️ Information

Napa Library (☑707-253-4241; www.countyofnapa.org/Library; 580 Coombs St; ⊘10am-9pm Mon-Thu, to 6pm Fri & Sat; 🛜) Free internet access.

Napa Valley Welcome Center (Map p167; ☑707-251-5895, lodging assistance 707-251-9188, toll free 855-847-6272; www.visitnapavalley.com; 600 Main St; ⊘9am-5pm; 🏼) Lodging assistance, wine-tasting passes, spa deals and comprehensive winery maps.

Queen of the Valley Medical Center (☑707-252-4411; www.thequeen.org; 1000 Trancas St; ⊘24hr) Emergency medical.

ℹ️ Getting Around

Pedi cabs park outside downtown restaurants – especially at the foot of Main St, near the Napa Valley Welcome Center – in summertime. The car-sharing service **Uber** (www.uber.com) also operates in Napa.

Yountville

This onetime stagecoach stop, 9 miles north of Napa, is now a fine-food destination playing to the haute bourgeoisie, with more Michelin stars per capita than any other American town. There are some good inns here, but it's deathly boring by night. You stay in Yountville to drink at dinner without having to drive afterward. Napa, St Helena and Calistoga are more interesting bases. Most businesses are on Washington St.

👁️ Sights

Ma(i)sonry GALLERY, TASTING ROOM
(☑707-944-0889; www.maisonry.com; 6711 Washington St; ⊘10am-6pm Sun-Thu, to 7pm Fri & Sat) Ma(i)sonry occupies a free-to-browse 1904

stone house and garden, transformed into a fussy winery-collective and gallery of over-priced rustic-modern *meubles* and art, some quite cool. Wine-tasting (by reservation) ranges from $25 to $45.

Napa Valley Museum MUSEUM
(☑707-944-0500; www.napavalleymuseum.org; 55 Presidents Circle, off California Drive; adult/child $5/2.50; ⊘10am-5pm Wed-Mon) Yountville's modernist 40,000-sq-ft museum chronicles cultural history and showcases local paintings. From town, it's across Hwy 29.

🛏️ Sleeping

Napa Valley Railway Inn INN $$
(☑707-944-2000; www.napavalleyrailwayinn.com; 6523 Washington St; r $125-260; ✳️@🛜🏊) Sleep in a converted railroad car, part of two short trains parked at a central platform. They've little privacy, but come moderately priced. Bring earplugs.

Maison Fleurie B&B $$$
(☑800-788-0369, 707-944-2056; www.maison-fleurienapa.com; 6529 Yount St; r incl breakfast $160-295; ✳️@🛜🏊) Rooms at this ivy-covered country inn are in a century-old home and carriage house, decorated in French-provincial style. Big breakfasts, afternoon wine and *hors d'oeuvres,* hot tub.

Bardessono LUXURY HOTEL $$$
(☑877-932-5333, 707-204-6000; www.bardessono.com; 6524 Yount St; r $600-800, ste from $800; ✳️@🛜🏊) 🌿 The outdoors flows indoors at California's first-ever (for what it's worth) LEED-platinum-certified green hotel, made of recycled everything, styled in Japanese-led austerity, with neutral tones and hard angles that are exceptionally

urban for farm country. Glam pool deck and on-site spa. Tops for a splurge.

Poetry Inn INN $$$
(☎707-944-0646; www.poetryinn.com; 6380 Silverado Trail; r incl breakfast $650-1400; ❋🐾≋) There's no better valley view than from this contemporary three-room inn, high on the hills east of Yountville. Decorated with posh restraint, rooms have private balconies, wood-burning fireplaces, 1000-thread-count linens and enormous baths with indoor-outdoor showers. Bring a ring.

Napa Valley Lodge HOTEL $$$
(☎707-944-2468, 888-944-3545; www.napavalleylodge.com; 2230 Madison St; r $300-475; ❋🐾≋) It looks like a condo complex, but rooms are spacious and modern; some have fireplaces. Hot tub, sauna and exercise room.

Petit Logis INN $$$
(☎707-944-2332, 877-944-2332; www.petitlogis.com; 6527 Yount St; r Mon-Fri $195-285, Sat & Sun $265-295; ❋🐾) Simple, cozy and comfortable, this cedar-sided inn has five correct rooms, each with jetted tub and gas fireplace.

✕ Eating

Make reservations or you may not eat. **Yountville Park** (cnr Washington & Madison Sts) has picnic tables and barbecue grills. Find groceries across from the post office. There's a great **taco truck** (6764 Washington St) parked in town.

Bouchon Bakery BAKERY $
(☎707-944-2253; http://bouchonbakery.com; 6528 Washington St; items from $3; ⊙7am-7pm) Bouchon makes as-good-as-in-Paris French pastries and strong coffee. There's always a line and rarely a seat: get it to go.

Napa Style Paninoteca CAFE $
(☎707-945-1229; www.napastyle.com; 6525 Washington St; dishes $8-10; ⊙11am-3pm) TV-chef Michael Chiarello's cafe (inside his store, Napa Style) makes camera-ready salads and paninos – try the slow-roasted pork – that pair nicely with his organic wines.

Redd Wood ITALIAN $$
(☎707-299-5030; www.redd-wood.com; 6755 Washington St; pizzas $12-16, mains $24-28; ⊙11:30am-3pm & 5-10pm, to 11pm Fri & Sat) Celeb-chef Richard Reddington's casual Italian trattoria serves outstanding homemade

Napa Valley South

Napa Valley South

pastas, salumi, and tender-to-the-tooth pizzas from a wood-fired oven.

★ **French Laundry**   CALIFORNIAN **$$$**
(☎707-944-2380; www.frenchlaundry.com; 6640 Washington St; prix-fixe dinner $295; ⊙ seatings 11am-1pm Fri-Sun, 5:30pm-9:15pm daily) The pinnacle of California dining, Thomas Keller's French Laundry is epic, a high-wattage culinary experience on par with the world's best. Book two months ahead at 10am sharp, or log onto OpenTable.com precisely at midnight. Avoid tables before 7pm; first-service seating moves a touch quickly.

Ad Hoc   CALIFORNIAN **$$$**
(☎707-944-2487; www.adhocrestaurant.com; 6476 Washington St; prix-fixe dinner from $52; ⊙5-10pm Mon & Thu-Sat, 10am-1pm & 5-10pm Sun) A winning formula by Yountville's culinary patriarch, Thomas Keller, Ad Hoc serves the master's favorite American home cooking in four-course family-style menus, with no variations (dietary restrictions notwithstanding). Monday is fried-chicken night, which you can also sample weekend lunchtime, takeout only, behind the restaurant at Keller's latest venture, Addendum (⊙11am-

2pm Thu-Sat), which serves to-go boxed-lunch barbecue (order ahead).

Bouchon   FRENCH **$$$**
(☎707-944-8037; www.bouchonbistro.com; 6354 Washington St; mains $19-45; ⊙11am-midnight Mon-Fri, from 10am Sat & Sun) Details are celeb-chef Thomas Keller's French brasserie are so impeccable you'd swear you were in Paris. Only the Bermuda-shorts-clad Americans look out of place. On the menu: oysters, onion soup, roasted chicken, leg of lamb, trout with almonds, runny cheeses and perfect profiteroles.

Bistro Jeanty   FRENCH **$$$**
(☎707-944-0103; www.bistrojeanty.com; 6510 Washington St; mains $19-30; ⊙11:30am-10:30pm) French bistros by classical definition serve comfort food to weary travelers, and that's what French-born chef-owner Philippe Jeanty does, with succulent cassoulet, coq au vin, *steak-frites*, braised pork with lentils, and scrumptious tomato soup.

Mustards Grill   CALIFORNIAN **$$$**
(☎707-944-2424; www.mustardsgrill.com; 7399 St Helena Hwy; mains $25-30; ⊙11:30am-9pm

Mon-Thu & Sun, to 10pm Fri & Sat; ⊞) The valley's original and always-packed roadhouse makes platters of crowd-pleasing, wood-fired, California comfort food – roasted meats, lamb shanks, pork chops, hearty salads and sandwiches.

Étoile CALIFORNIAN $$$
(☎707-944-8844; www.chandon.com; 1 California Dr, Chandon Winery; lunch mains $28-36, dinner mains $29-39; ⊙11:30am-2:30pm & 6-9pm Thu-Mon) At Chandon winery, Étoile is perfect for a top-shelf lunch, an ideal one-stop destination when you want to visit a winery, eat a good meal and minimize driving.

♉ Drinking & Entertainment

Pancha's DIVE BAR
(6764 Washington St; ⊙noon-2am) Swill tequila with vineyard-workers early, waiters later.

Lincoln Theater THEATER
(☎box office 707-949-9900; www.lincolntheater.org; 100 California Dr) Various artists, including Napa Valley Symphony, play this theater.

⬛ Shopping

Napa Style FOOD
(☎707-945-1229; www.napastyle.com; 6525 Washington St; ⊙10am-6pm) The only worthwhile store at Yountville's V Martketplace is this

---

FLYING & BALLOONING

Wine Country is stunning from the air – a multihued tapestry of undulating hills, deep valleys and rambling vineyards. Make reservations.

The **Vintage Aircraft Company** (Map p186; ☎707-938-2444; www.vintageaircraft.com; 23982 Arnold Dr, Sonoma) flies over Sonoma in a vintage biplane with an awesome pilot who'll do loop-de-loops on request (add $50). Twenty-minute tours cost $175/260 for one/two adults.

Napa Valley's signature hot-air balloon flights leave early, around 6am or 7am, when the air is coolest; they usually include a champagne breakfast on landing. Adults pay about $200 to $250, and kids $150 to $175. Call **Balloons above the Valley** (☎800-464-6824, 707-253-2222; www.balloonrides.com) or **Napa Valley Balloons** (☎800-253-2224, 707-944-0228; www.napavalleyballoons.com), both in Yountville.

---

fancy cookware shop by celeb-chef Michael Chiarello.

Oakville & Rutherford

But for its famous grocery, you'd drive through Oakville (pop 71) and never know you'd missed it. Vineyards sprawl everywhere. Rutherford (pop 164) is more conspicuous.

🛏 Sleeping & Eating

There's no budget lodging.

★ Auberge du Soleil LUXURY HOTEL $$$
(☎800-348-5406, 707-963-1211; www.aubergedusoleil.com; 180 Rutherford Hill Rd, Rutherford; r $850-1200, ste $1500-4000; ❀🐾🛜🏊) The top splurge for a no-holds-barred romantic weekend. A meal in its dining room (breakfast mains $16 to $19, lunch $31 to $42, three-/four-/six-course prix-fixe dinner $105/125/150) is an iconic Napa experience: come for a fancy breakfast, lazy lunch or will-you-wear-my-ring dinner; valley views are mesmerizing – *don't* sit inside. Make reservations; arrive before sunset.

Rancho Caymus HOTEL $$$
(☎800-845-1777, 707-963-1777; www.rancho-caymus.com; 1140 Rutherford Rd, Rutherford; r $179-299; ❀@🛜🏊) Styled after California's missions, this hacienda-like inn scores high marks for its fountain courtyard, kiva fireplaces, oak-beamed ceilings, and comparitively great rates.

La Luna Market & Taqueria MARKET $
(☎707-963-3211; 1153 Rutherford Rd, Rutherford; dishes $4-6; ⊙9am-5pm May-Nov) Vineyard workers flock here for burrito lunches and homemade hot sauce.

Oakville Grocery DELI, MARKET $$
(☎707-944-8802; www.oakvillegrocery.com; 7856 Hwy 29, Oakville; sandwiches $9-15; ⊙6:30am-5pm) The definitive Wine Country deli: excellent cheeses, charcuterie, bread, olives and wine – however pricy. Find tables outside or ask where to picnic nearby.

Rutherford Grill AMERICAN $$
(☎707-963-1792; www.rutherfordgrill.com; 1180 Rutherford Rd, Rutherford; mains $15-30) Yes, it's a chain, but its bar provides a chance to rub shoulders with winemakers at lunchtime. The food is consistent – ribs, rotisserie chicken, grilled artichokes – and there's no corkage, so bring that bottle you just bought.

WINE TASTING

The best way to discover the real Wine Country is to avoid factory wineries and visit family-owned boutique houses (producing fewer than 20,000 annual cases) and mid-sized houses (20,000 to 60,000 annual cases). Why does it matter? Think of it. If you were to attend two dinner parties, one for 10 people, one for 1000, which would have the better food? Small wineries maintain tighter control. Also, you won't easily find these wines elsewhere.

Tastings are called 'flights' and include four to six different wines. Napa wineries charge $10 to $50. In Sonoma Valley, tastings cost $5 to $20, often refundable with purchase. In Sonoma County, tastings are free or $5 to $10. You must be 21 to taste.

Do not drink and drive. The curvy roads are dangerous, and police monitor traffic, especially on Napa's Hwy 29.

To avoid burnout, visit no more than three wineries per day. Most open daily 10am or 11am to 4pm or 5pm, but call ahead if your heart's set, or you absolutely want a tour, especially in Napa, where law requires that some wineries accept visitors only by appointment. If you're buying, ask if there's a wine club, which is free to join and provides discounts, but you'll have to agree to buy a certain amount annually.

St Helena

You'll know you're here when traffic halts. St Helena (ha-*lee*-na) is the Rodeo Dr of Napa. Fancy boutiques line the historic downtown's Main St (Hwy 29) and provide excellent window-shopping. Parking, however, is next-to-impossible summer weekends (tip: look behind the visitors center).

◉ Sights

Silverado Museum   MUSEUM
(Map p176; ☑707-963-3757; www.silveradomuseum.org; 1490 Library Lane; ⊙noon-4pm Tue-Sat) FREE Contains a fascinating collection of Robert Louis Stevenson memorabilia. In 1880, the author – then sick, penniless and unknown – stayed in an abandoned bunkhouse at the old Silverado Mine on Mt St Helena with his wife, Fanny Osbourne; his novel *The Silverado Squatters* is based on his time there. Turn east off Hwy 29 at the Adams St traffic light and cross the railroad tracks.

Farmers Market   MARKET
(Map p176; www.sthelenafarmersmkt.org; ⊙7:30am-noon Fri May-Oct) Meets at Crane Park, half a mile south of downtown.

◈ Courses

Culinary Institute of America at Greystone   COOKING COURSE
(Map p176; ☑707-967-2320; www.ciachef.edu/california; 2555 Main St; mains $25-29, cooking demonstration $20; ⊙restaurant 11:30am-9pm, cooking demonstrations 1:30pm Sat & Sun) Inside an 1889 stone chateau, now a cooking school, there's a gadget- and cookbook-filled culinary shop; fine restaurant; weekend cooking demonstrations; and wine-tasting classes by luminaries including Karen MacNeil, author of *The Wine Bible*.

🛏 Sleeping

El Bonita   MOTEL $$
(Map p176; ☑707-963-3216; www.elbonita.com; 195 Main St; r $169-239; ❀@🛜🏊🐾) Book in advance to secure this sought-after motel, with up-to-date rooms (quietest are in back), attractive grounds, hot tub and sauna.

Wydown Hotel   BOUTIQUE HOTEL $$$
(Map p176; ☑707-963-5100; www.wydownhotel.com; 1424 Main St; r Mon-Fri $269-380, Sat & Sun $379-475; ❀🛜) Opened 2012, this fashion-forward boutique hotel, with good service, sits smack downtown, its 12 oversized rooms smartly decorated with tufted-velvet, distressed leather, subway-tile baths, and California-king beds with white-on-white high-thread-count linens.

Harvest Inn   INN $$$
(Map p176; ☑707-963-9463, 800-950-8466; www.harvestinn.com; 1 Main St; r incl breakfast $369-569; ❀@🛜🏊🐾) 🌿 A former estate, this 74-room resort has rooms in satellite buildings on sprawling manicured grounds. The newest building's generic; choose the vineyard-view rooms, which have private hot tubs.

Meadowood   RESORT $$$
(Map p176; ☑800-458-8080, 707-963-3646; www.meadowood.com; 900 Meadowood Lane; r from

Napa Valley North

0 ____ 2 km
0 ____ 1 mile

Tubbs Ln

Grant St

16

10

Meadowlark Country House (0.3mi); Safari West (1mi); Petrified Forest (3.5mi); Santa Rosa (12mi); Guerneville (26mi)

29

28

24

See Calistoga Enlargement

Lake St

CALISTOGA

21

37

Washington St

Grant St

Silverado Trail

Brannan

30

20

31

22

26

25

Cedar St

13

54

23

56

55

35

St Helena Hwy

41

42

27

39

17

53

Chamber of Commerce & Visitors Center

18

Washington St

Napa River

Calistoga

5

12

57

33

Lommel Rd

Larkmead

Bothe Napa Valley State Park

11

2

Silverado Trail

Santa Rosa (12mi)

1

St Helena Hwy

29
128

Napa River

4

8

3

Lodi La

Sanitarium Rd

St Helena

38

61

49

52

15

Oak Ave

48

43

40

44

45

60

Deer Park Rd

36

Spring St

46

51

58

Pope St

19

Spring Mountain Rd

29

ST HELENA

See St Helena Enlargement

14

Pope St

50

ST HELENA

47

Spring St

6

32

34

Charter Oak Ave

St Helena Welcome Center

St Helena Hwy

7

9

59

Napa Valley North

$600; ❉@🛜❉) Hidden in a wooded dell with towering pines and miles of hiking, Napa's grandest resort has cottages and rooms in satellite buildings surrounding a croquet lawn. We most like the hillside fireplace cottages; lawn-view rooms lack privacy but are good for families. The vibe is Republican country club: wear linen and play *Great Gatsby*. Kids love the mammoth pool.

✗ Eating

Make reservations where possible.

Napa Valley Olive Oil Mfg Co MARKET $
(Map p176; ☎707-963-4173; www.oliveoilsainthe-lena.com; 835 Charter Oak Ave; ⊙8am-5:30pm) Before the advent of fancy-food stores, this ramshackle market introduced Napa to Italian delicacies – real prosciutto and salami, meaty olives, fresh bread, nutty cheeses and, of course, olive oil. Ask nicely and the owner

will lend you a knife and a board to picnic at the rickety tables in the grass outside. Cash only.

Sunshine Foods
MARKET, DELI $

(Map p176; www.sunshinefoodsmarket.com; 1115 Main St; 7:30am-8:30pm) Town's best grocery store; excellent deli.

Model Bakery
CAFE $

(Map p176; 707-963-8192; www.themodelbakery. com; 1357 Main St; dishes $5-10; 6:30am-6pm Mon-Sat, 7am-5pm Sun) Good bakery with scones, muffins, salads, pizzas, sandwiches and exceptional coffee.

Gillwood's Cafe
AMERICAN $

(Map p176; www.gillwoodscafe.com; 1313 Main St; dishes $8-13; 7am-3pm;) Convenient for breakfast and lunch, Gillwood's serves good diner fare – scrambles, pancakes, sandwiches, burgers and salads. Beer and wine, too.

Gott's Roadside
AMERICAN $$

(Map p176; 707-963-3486; http://gotts.com; 933 Main St; mains $10-15; 7am-9pm, to 10pm May-Sep;) Wiggle your toes in the grass and feast on quality burgers – of beef or ahi tuna – plus Cobb salads and fish tacos at this classic roadside drive-in, whose original name, 'Taylor's Auto Refresher,' remains on the sign. Avoid weekend waits by phoning ahead or ordering online. There's another at Oxbow Public Market (p169).

Cindy's Backstreet Kitchen
NEW AMERICAN $$

(Map p176; 707-963-1200; www.cindysbackstreetkitchen.com; 1327 Railroad Ave; mains $16-28; 11:30am-9:30pm) The inviting retro-homey decor complements the Cal-American comfort food, such as avocado-and-papaya salad, wood-fired duck, steak with French fries and burgers. The bar makes mean mojitos.

Cook
CAL-ITALIAN $$

(Map p176; 707-963-7088; www.cooksthelena. com; 1310 Main St; lunch $14-23, dinner $16-28; 11:30am-10pm Mon-Sat, 10am-9pm Sun) Locals crowd this tiny storefront bistro, beloved for its earthy Cal-Italian cooking – homemade pasta and risotto, melt-off-the-bone ribs and simple-delicious burgers. Expect a wait, even with reservations.

Armadillo's
MEXICAN $$

(Map p176; www.armadillosnv.com; 1304 Main St; mains $8-12; 11am-9pm Sun-Thu, to 10pm Fri & Sat) Respectable, reasonably priced Mexican cooking.

Restaurant at Meadowood
CALIFORNIAN $$$

(Map p176; 707-967-1205; www.meadowood. com; 900 Meadowood Lane; 9-course menu $225; 5:30-10pm Mon-Sat) If you couldn't score reservations at French Laundry (p173), fear not: Meadowood – the valley's only other Michelin-three-star restaurant – has a slightly more sensibly priced menu, elegantly unfussy dining room, and lavish haute cuisine that's not too esoteric. Auberge (p174) has better views, but Meadowood's food and service far surpass it.

Terra
CALIFORNIAN $$$

(Map p176; 707-963-8931; www.terrarestaurant. com; 1345 Railroad Ave; 4-/5-/6-course menus $78/93/105; 6-9pm Wed-Sun) Seamlessly blending Japanese, French and Italian culinary styles, Terra is one of Wine Country's top tables – the signature is broiled sake-marinated black cod with shrimp dumplings in shiso broth. The adjoining bar serves small bites without reservations, but the dining room's the thing.

Goose & Gander
NEW AMERICAN $$$

(Map p176; 707-967-8779; www.gooseegander. com; 1245 Spring St; mains $23-32; 5-10pm Sun-Thu, noon-midnight Fri & Sat) Inside a converted Craftsman house, with cathedral ceiling and gorgeous woodwork, Goose & Gander has a clubby vibe conducive to drinking, excellent craft cocktails, and an imaginative (sometimes heavy) menu with some standouts, like the summertime-only shrimp-and-watermelon salad. Consider the garden. Boozy locals favor the basement pub.

Farmstead
NEW AMERICAN $$$

(Map p176; 707-963-9181; www.farmsteadnapa. com; 738 Main St; mains $16-27; 11:30am-9pm) An enormous open-truss barn with big leather booths and rocking-chair porch, Farmstead draws a youthful crowd and grows many of its own ingredients – including grass-fed beef – for an earthy menu highlighting wood-fired cooking.

Market
NEW AMERICAN $$$

(Map p176; 707-963-3799; www.marketsthelena. com; 1347 Main St; mains $18-27; 11:30am-9pm) We love Market's big portions of simple, fresh American cooking, including hearty salads of local produce, and soul-satisfying mains like buttermilk fried chicken. The stone-walled dining room dates to the 19th century, as does the ornate backbar, where cocktails get muddled to order. Free corkage.

🔒 Shopping

Main St is lined with high-end boutiques (think $100 socks), but some mom-and-pop shops remain.

Woodhouse Chocolates FOOD
(Map p176; www.woodhousechocolate.com; 1367 Main St; ⊙10:30am-5:30pm) Woodhouse looks more like Tiffany than a candy shop, with housemade chocolates similarly priced, but their quality is beyond reproach.

Napa Soap Company BEAUTY
(Map p176; www.napasoap.com; 651 Main St; ⊙10am-5:30pm) 🍃 Eco-friendly bath products, locally produced.

Baksheesh HOMEWARES
(Map p176; www.baksheeshfairtrade.com; 1327 Main St; ⊙10am-6pm) 🍃 Handcrafted fair-trade home decor from 38 countries.

Lolo's Consignment VINTAGE
(Map p176; www.lolosconsignment.com; 1120 Main St; ⊙10:30am-4pm Mon, to 5:30pm Tue-Sat, 11am-4pm Sun) Groovy cheap dresses and cast-off cashmere.

Vintage Trunk VINTAGE
(Map p176; http://vintagetrunkonline.com; 1210 Main St; ⊙10:30am-5:30pm) High-end women's designer consignment; prices from $90.

Main Street Books BOOKS
(Map p176; 1315 Main St; ⊙10am-5:30pm Mon-Sat, 11am-3pm Sun) Good used books.

ℹ️ Information

St Helena Welcome Center (Map p176; 🖉707-963-4456; www.sthelena.com; 657 Main St; ⊙9am-5pm Mon-Fri, plus 10am-4pm Sat-Sun May-Nov) The visitor center has information and lodging assistance.

Calistoga & Around

The least gentrified town in Napa Valley feels refreshingly simple, with an old-fashioned main street lined with shops, not boutiques, and diverse characters wandering the sidewalks. Bad hair? No problem. Fancy-pants St Helena couldn't feel further away. Many don't go this far north. You should.

Famed 19th-century author Robert Louis Stevenson said of Calistoga: 'the whole neighborhood of Mt St Helena is full of sulfur and boiling springs…Calistoga itself seems to repose on a mere film above a boiling, subterranean lake.'

Indeed, it does. Calistoga is synonymous with mineral water bearing its name, bottled here since 1924. Its springs and geysers have earned it the nickname the 'hot springs of the West.' Plan to visit a spa to indulge in the local specialty: hot-mud baths, made with volcanic ash from nearby Mt St Helena.

The town's odd name comes from Sam Brannan, who founded Calistoga in 1859, believing it would develop like the New York spa town of Saratoga. Apparently Sam liked his drink and at the founding ceremony tripped on his tongue, proclaiming it the 'Cali-stoga' of 'Sara-fornia.' The name stuck.

◉ Sights

Hwys 128 and 29 run together from Rutherford through St Helena; in Calistoga, they split. Hwy 29 turns east and becomes Lincoln Ave, continuing across Silverado Trail, toward Clear Lake. Hwy 128 continues north as Foothill Blvd (not St Helena Hwy). Calistoga's shops and restaurants line Lincoln Ave.

Sharpsteen Museum MUSEUM
(Map p176; 🖉707-942-5911; www.sharpsteen-museum.org; 1311 Washington St; suggested donation $3; ⊙11am-4pm; 🖈) **FREE** Across from the picturesque 1902 City Hall (originally an opera house), the Sharpsteen Museum was created by an ex-Disney animator (whose Oscar is on display) and houses a fantastic diorama of town in the 1860s, big Victorian dollhouse, full-size horse-drawn carriage, cool taxidermy and a restored cottage from Brannan's original resort. (The only Brannan cottage still at its original site is at 106 Wappo Ave).

Bale Grist Mill & Bothe-Napa Valley State Parks HISTORIC PARK
(🖉707-942-4575; parks.ca.gov; 🖈) Both these parks have picnic areas and admission to one includes the other. **Bale Grist Mill State Historic Park** (Map p176; 🖉707-963-2236; adult/child $5/2; 🖈) features a 36ft-high water-powered mill wheel dating to 1846 – the largest still operating in North America; Saturdays and Sundays (and sometimes Fridays and Mondays) from 10am to 4pm, it grinds flour. A mile-long trail leads to adjacent **Bothe-Napa Valley State Park** (Map p176; 🖉707-942-4575; parking $8; ⊙8am-sunset; 🖈), where there's a swimming pool ($5), and camping (p181), plus hiking through redwood groves.

NAPA & SONOMA WINE COUNTRY CALISTOGA & AROUND

If you're two or more adults, go first to Bothe and pay $8, instead of the per-head charge at Bale Grist. The mill and both parks are on Hwy 29/128, midway between St Helena and Calistoga. In early October, look for living-history festival Old Mill Days.

Old Faithful Geyser
GEYSER

(Map p176; ☑707-942-6463; www.oldfaithfulgeyser.com; 1299 Tubbs Lane; adult/child/under 5yr $14/8/free; ☉9am-6pm, to 5pm Nov-Mar; ⊕) Calistoga's mini-version of Yellowstone's Old Faithful shoots boiling water 60ft to 100ft into the air, every 30 minutes. The vibe is pure roadside Americana, with folksy hand-painted interpretive exhibits, picnicking and a little petting zoo, where you can come nose-to-nose with llamas. It's 2 miles north of town, off Silverado Trail. Find discount coupons online.

Petrified Forest
FOREST

(☑707-942-6667; www.petrifiedforest.org; 4100 Petrified Forest Rd; adult/child $10/5; ☉9am-7pm summer, to 5pm winter) Three million years ago at this now roadside-Americana attraction, a volcanic eruption at Mt St Helena blew down a stand of redwoods. The trees fell in the same direction, away from the blast, and over the millennia the mighty giants' trunks turned to stone. Discover them on a short interpretive trail through the woods. The first stumps were discovered in 1870. A monument marks Robert Louis Stevenson's 1880 visit, which he described in *The Silverado Squatters*.

It's 5 miles northwest of town, off Hwy 128.

Safari West
WILDLIFE RESERVE

(☑707-579-2551; www.safariwest.com; 3115 Porter Creek Rd; adult $70-80, child 3-12yr $32; ⊕) Giraffes in Wine Country? Whadya know. Safari West sprawls over 400 acres and protects zebras, cheetahs and other exotic animals, which mostly roam free. See them on a guided two-and-a-half-hour safari in open-sided jeeps; reservations required, no kids under three. If you're feeling adventurous, stay overnight in nifty canvas-sided tent cabins (cabin including breakfast $225 to $305) inside the preserve.

Robert Louis Stevenson State Park
PARK

(☑707-942-4575; www.parks.ca.gov; Hwy 29; ☉sunrise-sunset) FREE At this undeveloped state park 8 miles north of Calistoga, the long-extinct volcanic cone of Mt St Helena marks Napa Valley's end and often gets snow

TOP KID-FRIENDLY WINERIES

➡ Kaz (p187) Play-Doh, playground and grape juice.

➡ Benziger (p187) Open-air tram rides.

➡ Frog's Leap (p164) Cats, chickens and croquet.

➡ Casa Nuestra (p165) Playful goats.

➡ Castello di Amorosa (p166) Bona-fide castle.

➡ Lava Vine (p166) Mellow vibe, grassy play area.

in winter. It's a strenuous 5-mile climb to the peak's 4343ft summit, but what a view – 200 miles on a clear winter's day. Check conditions before setting out. Also consider 2.2-mile one-way Table Rock Trail (go south from the summit parking area) for drop-dead valley views.

Temperatures are best in wildflower season, February to May; fall is prettiest, when the vineyards change colors. The park includes the site of the Silverado Mine where Stevenson and his wife honeymooned in 1880.

🏃 Activities

Oat Hill Mine Trail
CYCLING, HIKING

(Map p176) One of Northern California's most technically challenging trails, OHM Trail draws hardcore mountain bikers and hikers. Softcore walkers, take heart: a moderately strenuous half-mile up from town, there's a bench with incredible valley views. The trailhead is at the intersection of Hwy 29 and Silverado Trail.

Calistoga Bike Shop
BICYCLE RENTAL

(Map p176; ☑707-942-9687, 866-942-2453; www.calistogabikeshop.com; 1318 Lincoln Ave; ☉10am-6pm) Rents full-suspension mountain bikes ($75 per day) and hybrids ($12/39 per hour/day), and provides reliable trail information. Wine-touring packages ($90 per day) include wine-rack baskets and free wine pickup.

Spas

Calistoga is famous for hot-spring spas and mud-bath emporiums, where you're buried in hot mud and emerge feeling supple, detoxified and enlivened. (The mud is made with volcanic ash and peat; the higher the ash content, the better the bath.)

Packages take 60 to 90 minutes and cost $70 to $90. You start semi-submerged in hot mud, then soak in hot mineral water. A steam bath and blanket-wrap follow. A massage increases the cost to $130 and up.

Baths can be taken solo or, at some spas, as couples. Variations include thin, painted-on clay-mud wraps (called 'fango' baths, good for those uncomfortable sitting in mud), herbal wraps, seaweed baths and various massage treatments. Discount coupons are sometimes available from the visitors center. Book ahead, especially on summer weekends. Reservations are essential everywhere.

Most spas offer multi-treatment packages. Some offer discounted spa-lodging packages.

★ **Indian Springs Spa**   SPA
(Map p176; ☎707-942-4913; www.indiansprings-calistoga.com; 1712 Lincoln Ave; ☺by appointment 9am-8pm) California's longest continually operating spa, and original Calistoga resort, has concrete mud tubs and mines its own ash. Treatments include use of the huge, hot-spring-fed pool. Great cucumber body lotion.

Spa Solage   SPA
(Map p176; ☎707-226-0825; www.solagecalistoga.com/spa; 755 Silverado Trail; ☺by appointment 8am-8pm) Chichi, austere, top-end spa, with couples' rooms and a fango-mud bar for DIY paint-on treatments. Also has zero-gravity chairs for blanket wraps, and a clothing-optional pool.

Dr Wilkinson's Hot Springs Resort   SPA
(Map p176; ☎707-942-4102; www.drwilkinson.com; 1507 Lincoln Ave; ☺by appointment 10am-3:30pm) Fifty years running; 'the doc' uses more peat in its mud.

Mount View Spa   SPA
(Map p176; ☎707-942-5789, 800-816-6877; www.mountviewhotel.com; 1457 Lincoln Ave; ☺by appointment 9am-9pm) Traditional full-service, eight-room spa, good for clean-hands people who prefer painted-on mud to submersion.

Lavender Hill Spa   SPA
(Map p176; ☎707-341-6002, 800-528-4772, 707-942-4495; http://lavenderhillspa.com; 1015 Foothill Blvd; ☺by appointment 9am-9pm Thu-Mon, to 7pm Tue & Wed) Small, cute spa that uses much-lighter, less-icky lavender-infused mud; offers couples' treatments.

Golden Haven Hot Springs   SPA
(Map p176; ☎707-942-8000; www.goldenhaven.com; 1713 Lake St; ☺by appointment 8am-8pm) Old-school and unfussy; offers couples' mud baths and couples' massage.

Calistoga Spa Hot Springs   SPA, SWIMMING
(Map p176; ☎866-822-5772, 707-942-6269; www.calistogaspa.com; 1006 Washington St; ☺by appointment 8:30am-4:30pm Tue-Thu, to 9pm Fri-Mon, swimming pools 10am-9pm; ⊕) Traditional mud baths and massage at a motel complex with two huge swimming pools where kids can play while you soak (pool passes $25).

🛏 Sleeping

Bothe-Napa Valley State Park
Campground   CAMPGROUND $
(Map p48; ☎800-444-7275; www.reserveamerica.com; 3801 Hwy 128; camping & RV sites $35; ⊕⊕) Three miles south, Bothe has shady camping near redwoods, coin-operated showers, and gorgeous hiking (p179). Sites 28 to 36 are most secluded.

★ **Mountain Home Ranch**   RESORT $$
(☎707-942-6616; www.mountainhomeranch.com; 3400 Mountain Home Ranch Rd; r $111-121, cabins $71-156; ⊕⊛⊕⊕) ⌁ In continuous operation since 1913, this 340-acre homestead outside town is a flashback to old California. Doubling as a retreat center, the ranch has simple lodge rooms and rustic freestanding cabins, some with kitchens and fireplaces, ideal for families, but you may be here during someone else's family reunion or spiritual quest.

No matter. With miles of oak-woodland trails, a hilltop swimming pool, private lake with canoeing and fishing, and a hike to warm springs in a magical fault-line canyon, you may hardly notice – and you may never make it to a single winery. Breakfast is included, but you'll have to drive 15 minutes to town for dinner. Pack hiking boots, not high heels.

Dr Wilkinson's Motel &
Hideaway Cottages   MOTEL, COTTAGES $$
(Map p176; ☎707-942-4102; www.drwilkinson.com; 1507 Lincoln Ave; r $149-255, cottages $165-270; ⊛⊕⊕⊕) This good-value vintage-1950s motel has well-kept rooms facing a swimming-pool courtyard with hot tub, three pools (one indoors), and mud baths. Also rents simple, great-value stand-alone cottages with kitchens at the affiliated Hideaway Cottages, also with pool and hot tub.

EuroSpa & Inn
MOTEL $$

(Map p176; ☑707-942-6829; www.eurospa.com; 1202 Pine St; r incl breakfast $145-199; ✳🔊✹) Immaculate single-story motel on a quiet side street, with extras like gas-burning fireplaces, afternoon wine and small on-site spa. Excellent service, but tiny pool.

Golden Haven Hot Springs
MOTEL $$

(Map p176; ☑707-942-8000; www.goldenhaven. com; 1713 Lake St; r $165-239; ✳🔊✹) This motel-spa has mudbath-lodging packages and good-value well-kept rooms, some with Jacuzzis.

Best Western Stevenson Manor
HOTEL $$

(Map p176; ☑800-528-1238, 707-942-1112; www. stevensonmanor.com; 1830 Lincoln Ave; r weekday $159-189, weekend $249-289; ✳@🔊✹) This entry-level business-class hotel feels generic, but has good extras, including full hot breakfast. Upstairs rooms are quietest. No elevator.

Calistoga Spa Hot Springs
MOTEL $$

(Map p176; ☑707-942-6269, 866-822-5772; www. calistogaspa.com; 1006 Washington St; r $187-235; ✳🔊✹) Great for families, who jam the place weekends, this motel-resort has slightly scuffed generic rooms (request one that's been remodeled) with kitchenettes, and fantastic pools – two full-size, a kiddie-pool with miniwaterfall and a huge adults-only Jacuzzi. Outside are barbecues and snack bar. Wi-fi in lobby.

Calistoga Inn
INN $$

(Map p176; ☑707-942-4101; www.calistogainn.com; 1250 Lincoln Ave; r with shared bath incl breakfast $129-169; 🔊) Upstairs from a busy bar, this inn has 18 clean, basic rooms with shared bath, ideal for no-fuss bargain-hunters. No TVs, no elevator. Bring earplugs.

Solage
RESORT $$$

(Map p176; ☑866-942-7442, 707-226-0800; www. solagecalistoga.com; 755 Silverado Trail; r $530-675; ✳🔊✹✹) 🖉 Calistoga's top spa-hotel ups the style factor, with Cali-chic semidetached cottages and a glam palm-tree-lined pool. Rooms are austere, with vaulted ceilings, zillion-thread-count linens and pebble-floor showers. Cruiser bikes included.

Indian Springs Resort
RESORT $$$

(Map p176; ☑707-942-4913; www.indiansprings-calistoga.com; 1712 Lincoln Ave; lodge r $229-359, cottage $259-429, 2-bedroom cottage $359-499; ✳🔊✹) The definitive old-school Calistoga resort, Indian Springs has cottages facing a central lawn with palm trees, shuffleboard, bocce, hammocks and Weber grills – not unlike a vintage Florida resort. Some sleep six. There are also top-end, motel-style lodge rooms (adults only). Huge hot-springs-fed swimming pool.

Chateau De Vie
B&B $$$

(Map p176; ☑877-558-2513, 707-942-6446; www. cdvnapavalley.com; 3250 Hwy 128; r incl breakfast $229-429; ✳🔊✹✹) Surrounded by vineyards, with gorgeous views of Mt St Helena, CDV has five modern, elegantly decorated B&B rooms with top-end amenities and zero froufrou. Charming owners serve wine on the sun-dappled patio, then leave you alone. Hot tub, big pool. Gay-friendly.

Meadowlark Country House
B&B $$$

(☑800-942-5651, 707-942-5651; www.meadow-larkinn.com; 601 Petrified Forest Rd; r incl breakfast $210-265, ste $285; ✳🔊✹✹) On 20 acres west of town, Meadowlark has homey rooms decorated in contemporary style, most with decks and Jacuzzis. Outside there's a hot tub, sauna and clothing-optional pool. The truth-telling innkeeper lives elsewhere, offers helpful advice, then vanishes when you want privacy. There's a fabulous cottage for $465. Gay-friendly.

Mount View Hotel & Spa
HISTORIC HOTEL $$$

(Map p176; ☑707-942-6877, 800-816-6877; www. mountviewhotel.com; 1457 Lincoln Ave; r Mon-Fri $209-429, Sat & Sun $279-459; ✳🔊✹) Smack in the middle of town, this 1917 Mission Revival hotel is decorated in vaguely mod-Italian style at odds with the vintage building, but rooms are clean and fresh-looking nonetheless. Gleaming bathrooms, on-site spa, year-round heated pool. No elevator.

Chanric
B&B $$$

(Map p176; ☑707-942-4535; www.thechanric. com; 1805 Foothill Blvd; r incl breakfast $249-439; ✳🔊✹) A converted Victorian near the road, this cushy B&B has small, but smartly furnished rooms, plus many free extras including champagne on arrival and lavish three-course breakfasts. Gay-friendly. No elevator.

Hotel d'Amici
HOTEL $$$

(Map p176; ☑707-942-1007; www.hoteldamici. com; 1436 Lincoln Ave; r incl breakfast $200-300; ✳@🔊) All four rooms at this 2nd-floor hotel are remarkably spacious and include continental breakfast, but they're up two flights of stairs (no elevator) and there's no on-site staff.

Cottage Grove Inn
BUNGALOW $$$

(Map p176; ☑707-942-8400, 800-799-2284; www.cottagegrove.com; 1711 Lincoln Ave; cottages $315-450; ✳🐾) Romantic cottages for over-40s, with wood-burning fireplaces, two-person tubs and rocking-chair front porches.

Aurora Park Cottages
COTTAGES $$$

(Map p176; ☑877-942-7700, 707-942-6733; www.aurorapark.com; 1807 Foothill Blvd; cottages incl breakfast $269-299; ✳🐾) Six immaculately kept, sunny-yellow cottages – with polished-wood floors, featherbeds and sundeck – stand in a row beside flowering gardens. Though close to the road, they're quiet by night. The innkeeper couldn't be nicer.

Sunburst Calistoga
MOTEL $$$

(Map p176; ☑707-942-0991; www.thesunburstcalistoga.com; 1880 Lincoln Ave; r $229-289; @🐾🏊) This single-story 1950s motor lodge got a makeover in 2013, with mid-century-modern-led aesthetics, but it's basically still a drive-to-the-door motel, only with nicer-than-average furnishings and thin walls.

Chelsea Garden Inn
B&B $$$

(Map p176; ☑707-942-0948; www.chelseagardeninn.com; 1443 2nd St; r incl breakfast $195-350; ✳🐾🏊) On a quiet sidestreet, this single-story inn has five floral-print rooms, with private entrances, facing pretty gardens. Never mind the pool's rust spots.

Wine Way Inn
B&B $$$

(Map p176; ☑800-572-0679, 707-942-0680; www.winewayinn.com; 1019 Foothill Blvd; r $189-299; ✳🐾) A small B&B, in a 1910-era house, close to the road; friendly owners.

🍴 Eating

Buster's Southern BBQ
BARBECUE $

(Map p176; ☑707-942-5605; www.busterssouthernbbq.com; 1207 Foothill Blvd; dishes $8-12; ⊙10am-7:30pm Mon-Sat, 10:30am-6pm Sun; 🖐) The sheriff dines at this indoor-outdoor barbecue joint, which serves smoky ribs, chicken, tri-tip steak and burgers, but closes early at dinnertime. Beer and wine.

Calistoga Inn & Brewery
AMERICAN $$

(Map p176; ☑707-942-4101; www.calistogainn.com; 1250 Lincoln Ave; lunch mains $11-15, dinner $15-30; ⊙11:30am-3pm & 5:30-9pm) Locals crowd the outdoor beer garden Sundays. Midweek we prefer the country dining room's big oak-

wood tables – a homey spot for simple American cooking. Live music summer weekends.

Solbar
CALIFORNIAN $$$

(☑707-226-0850; www.solagecalistoga.com; 755 Silverado Trail; lunch mains $17-20, dinner $24-34; ⊙7am-11am, 11:30am-3pm & 5:30-9pm) We like the spartan ag-chic look of this Michelin-starred resort restaurant, whose menu maximizes seasonal produce in elegant dishes, playfully composed. And this being a spa (p181), too, the menu is split for calorie-counters into light and hearty dishes. Reservations essential.

JoLé
CALIFORNIAN $$$

(Map p176; ☑707-942-5938; www.jolerestaurant.com; 1457 Lincoln Ave; mains $25-30; ⊙5-9pm) The inventive farm-to-table plates at chef-owned Jolé evolve seasonally, and may include such dishes as local sole with tangy miniature Napa grapes, caramelized brussels sprouts with capers, and organic Baldwin apple strudel with burnt-caramel ice cream. Four courses cost $55. Reservations essential.

Calistoga Kitchen
CALIFORNIAN $$$

(Map p176; ☑707-942-6500; www.calistogakitchen.com; 1107 Cedar St; lunch mains $12-18, dinner $18-29; ⊙5:30-9pm Thu, 11:30am-3pm & 5:30-9pm Fri & Sat, 9:30am-3pm Sun) A sparsely decorated cottage surrounded by a white-picket fence, Calistoga Kitchen is especially good for lunch in the garden. The chef-owner favors simplicity, focusing on quality ingredients in a half-dozen changing dishes, such as a delicious lamb stew. Reservations advised.

All Seasons Bistro
NEW AMERICAN $$$

(Map p176; ☑707-942-9111; www.allseasonsnapavalley.net; 1400 Lincoln Ave; lunch mains $12-18, dinner $18-27; ⊙noon-2pm & 5:30-8:30pm Tue-Sun) 🍃 It looks like a white-tablecloth soda fountain, but All Seasons makes very fine meals, from simple *steak-frites* to composed dishes like cornmeal-crusted scallops with summer succotash.

🍷 Drinking & Nightlife

Yo El Rey
CAFE

(Map p176; ☑707-942-1180; www.yoelreyroasting.com; 1217 Washington St; ⊙6:30am-6pm) 🍃 Hip kids favor this micro-roastery, which serves stellar small-batch, fair-trade coffee.

Hydro Grill
BAR

(Map p176; ☑707-942-9777; 1403 Lincoln Ave; ⊙8:30am-midnight Sun-Thu, to 2am Fri & Sat)

OUTLET SHOPPING

Max out your credit cards on last season's close-outs.

Napa Premium Outlets (☎707-226-9876; www.premiumoutlets.com; 629 Factory Stores Dr, Napa; ☺10am-9pm Mon-Sat, to 7pm Sun) Fifty stores.

Petaluma Village Premium Outlets (☎707-778-9300; www.premiumoutlets.com; 2200 Petaluma Blvd North, Petaluma; ☺10am-9pm Mon-Sat, to 7pm Sun) Sixty stores, Sonoma County.

Vacaville Premium Outlets (☎707-447-5755; www.premiumoutlets.com/vacaville; 321 Nut Tree Rd, Vacaville; ☺10am-9pm Mon-Sat, to 7pm Sun) 120 stores, northeast of the Wine Country on I-80.

Live music plays weekend evenings at this hoppin' corner bar-restaurant.

Solbar　　　　BAR
(Map p176; ☎707-226-0850; www.solagecalistoga.com; 755 Silverado Trail; ☺11am-9pm) Sip craft cocktails beside outdoor fireplaces and a palm-lined pool at this swank resort bar.

Brannan's Grill　　　　BAR
(Map p176; ☎707-942-2233; www.brannanscalistoga.com; 1374 Lincoln Ave; ☺11am-11pm) The mahogany bar at Calistoga's handsomest restaurant is great for martinis and microbrews, especially weekends when jazz combos play.

Susie's Bar　　　　DIVE BAR
(Map p176; ☎707-942-6710; 1365 Lincoln Ave) Turn your baseball cap sideways, swill beer and shoot pool to a soundtrack of classic rock.

🔒 Shopping

Calistoga Pottery　　　　CERAMICS
(Map p176; ☎707-942-0216; www.calistogapottery.com; 1001 Foothill Blvd; ☺9am-5pm) Artisanal pottery, hand-thrown on site.

Coperfield's Bookshop　　　　BOOKS
(Map p176; ☎707-942-1616; 1330 Lincoln Ave; ☺10am-7pm Mon-Sat, 10am-6pm Sun) Indie bookshop, with local maps and guides.

❶ Information

Chamber of Commerce & Visitors Center (Map p176; ☎707-942-6333, 866-306-5588; www.calistogavisitors.com; 1133 Washington St; ☺9am-5pm)

SONOMA VALLEY

We have a soft spot for Sonoma's folksy ways. Unlike in fancy Napa, nobody cares if you drive a clunker and vote Green. Locals call it 'Slow-noma.' Anchoring the bucolic 17-mile-long Sonoma Valley, the town of Sonoma makes a great jumping-off point for exploring Wine Country – it's an hour from San Francisco – and has a marvelous sense of place, with storied 19th-century historical sights surrounding the state's largest town square. Halfway up-valley, tiny Glen Ellen is straight from a Norman Rockwell painting – in stark contrast to the valley's northernmost town, Santa Rosa, the workaday urban center best known for traffic. If you have more than a day, explore Sonoma's quiet, rustic western side, along the Russian River Valley, and continue to the sea.

Sonoma Hwy/Hwy 12 is lined with wineries, and runs from Sonoma to Santa Rosa, to western Sonoma County; Arnold Dr has less traffic (but few wineries) and runs parallel, up the valley's western side, to Glen Ellen.

Sonoma Valley Wineries

Rolling grass-covered hills rise from 17-mile-long Sonoma Valley. Its 40-some wineries get less attention than Napa's, but many are equally good. If you love Zinfandel and Syrah, you're in for a treat.

Picnicking is allowed at Sonoma wineries. Get maps and discount coupons in the town of Sonoma or, if you're approaching from the south, the Sonoma Valley Visitors Bureau (p190) at Cornerstone Gardens.

Plan at least five hours to visit the valley from bottom to top.

Homewood　　　　WINERY
(Map p186; ☎707-996-6353; www.homewoodwinery.com; 23120 Burndale Rd, at Hwy 121/12; tasting $5; ☺10am-4pm; 🐾) Barn cats dart about at this down-home winery, where the tasting room is a garage, and the winemaker crafts standout ports and Rhône-style Grenache, Mourvèdre and Syrah – 'Da redder, da better' – plus some late-harvest dessert wines, including excellent Viognier and Albariño. Bottles are $22 to $42, the tasting fee is waived with a purchase.

Robledo　　　　WINERY
(Map p186; ☎707-939-6903; www.robledofamilywinery.com; 21901 Bonness Rd, off Hwy 116; tasting $10-15; ☺by appointment 10am-5pm Mon-Sat,

11am-4pm Sun) Sonoma Valley's feel-good winery, Robledo was founded by a former grape-picker from Mexico who worked his way up to vineyard manager, then land owner, now vintner. His kids run the place. The wines – served at hand-carved furniture in a garage – include a no-oak Sauvignon Blanc, jammy Syrah, spicy Cabernet, and bright-fruit Pinot Noir. Bottles cost $18 to $60.

Gundlach-Bundschu Winery   WINERY
(Map p186; ☑ 707-939-3015; www.gunbun.com; 2000 Denmark St, Sonoma; tasting $10-15, incl tour $20-50; ⊙ 11am-4:30pm, to 5:30pm Jun–mid-Oct; ▣) 🖉 California's oldest family-run winery looks like a castle, but has a down-to-earth vibe. Founded 1858 by a Bavarian immigrant, its signatures are Gewürztraminer

and Pinot Noir, but 'Gun-Bun' was the first American winery to produce 100% Merlot. Down a winding lane, it's a terrific bike-to winery, with picnicking, hiking and a lake. Tour the 2000-barrel cave ($20) by reservation only. Bottles are $22 to $45.

★**Bartholomew Park Winery**   WINERY
(☑ 707-939-3026; www.bartpark.com; 1000 Vineyard Lane, Sonoma; tasting $10, incl tour $20; ⊙ 11am-4:30pm) 🖉 A great bike-to winery, Bartholomew Park occupies a 375-acre preserve, with oak-shaded picnicking and valley-view hiking. The vineyards were originally cultivated in 1857 and now yield certified-organic Sauvignon Blanc, Cabernet Sauvignon softer in style than Napa, and lush Zinfandel. Tours (reservations

A WINE COUNTRY PRIMER

When people talk about Sonoma, they're referring to the *whole* county which, unlike Napa, is huge. It extends all the way from the coast, up the Russian River Valley, into Sonoma Valley and eastward to Napa Valley; in the south it stretches from San Pablo Bay (an extension of San Francisco Bay) to Healdsburg in the north. It's essential to break Sonoma down by district.

West County refers to everything west of Hwy 101 and includes the Russian River Valley and the coast. Sonoma Valley stretches north–south along Hwy 12. In northern Sonoma County, Alexander Valley lies east of Healdsburg, and Dry Creek Valley lies north of Healdsburg. In the south, Carneros straddles the Sonoma–Napa border, north of San Pablo Bay. Each region has its own particular wines; what grows where depends upon the weather.

Inland valleys get hot; coastal regions stay cool. In West County and Carneros, nighttime fog blankets the vineyards. Burgundy-style wines do best, particularly Pinot Noir and Chardonnay. Further inland, Alexander, Sonoma and much of Dry Creek Valleys (as well as Napa Valley) are fog-protected. Here, Bordeaux-style wines thrive, especially Cabernet Sauvignon, Sauvignon Blanc, Merlot and other heat-loving varieties. For California's famous cabernets, head to Napa. Zinfandel and Rhône-style varieties, such as Syrah and Viognier, grow in both regions, warm and cool. In cooler climes, wines are lighter and more elegant; in warmer areas they are heavier and more rustic. As you explore, notice the bases of grapevines: the fatter they are, the older. 'Old vine' grapes yield color and complexity not found in grapes from younger vines.

Some basics: wineries and vineyards aren't the same. Grapes grow in a vineyard, then get fermented at a winery. Wineries that grow their own grapes are called estates, as in 'estate-grown' or 'estate-bottled,' but estates, too, ferment grapes from other vineyards. When vintners speak of 'single-vineyard' or 'vineyard-designate' wines, they mean the grapes all originated from the same vineyard; this allows for tighter quality-control. 'Single varietal' means all the grapes are the same variety (such as 100% merlot), but may come from different vineyards. Reserves are the vintner's limited-production wines; they're usually available only at the winery.

Don't be afraid to ask questions. Vintners love to talk. If you don't know how to taste wine, or what to look for, ask the person behind the counter to help you discover what you like. Just remember to spit out the wine; the slightest buzz will diminish your capacity to taste.

For a handy-dandy reference on the road, pick up a copy of Karen MacNeil's *The Wine Bible* (2001, Workman Publishing) or Jancis Robinson's *The Oxford Companion to Wine* (2006, Oxford University Press) to carry in the car.

required) Friday to Sunday. Bottles are $22 to $45.

Hawkes
TASTING ROOM

(Map p189; ☎707-938-7620; www.hawkeswine. com; 383 1st St W, Sonoma; tasting $10; ⊘11am-6pm) When you're in downtown Sonoma and don't feel like fighting traffic, Hawke's refreshingly unfussy tasting room showcases meaty Merlot and Cabernet Sauvignon, never blended with other varietals. Bottles are $30 to $70, the tasting fee is waived with a purchase over $30.

Little Vineyards
WINERY

(Map p186; ☎707-996-2750; www.littlevineyards. com; 15188 Sonoma Hwy, Glen Ellen; tasting $15; ⊘11am-4:30pm Thu-Mon; ⊕⊛) The name fits at this family-owned small-scale winery surrounded by grapes, with a lazy dog to greet you and a weathered, cigarette-burned tasting bar, at which Jack London formerly drank (before it came here). The big reds include Syrah, petite Syrah, Zin, Cab and several delish blends. Good picnicking on the vineyard-view terrace. Also rents a cottage in the vines. Bottles cost $20 to $45.

BR Cohn
WINERY

(Map p186; ☎800-330-4064, 707-938-4064; www. brcohn.com; 15000 Sonoma Hwy, Glen Ellen; tasting $10; ⊘10am-5pm) Picnic like a rock star at always-busy BR Cohn, whose founder managed '70s-superband the Doobie Brothers before moving on to make outstanding organic olive oils and fine wines – including excellent Cabernet Sauvignon, atypical in Sonoma. The little gourmet shop offers lots to taste, plus limited picnic supplies. In autumn, benefit concerts showcase bands like Skynyrd and the Doobies. Bottles are $16 to $56.

Arrowood
WINERY

(Map p186; ☎707-935-2600; www.arrowood-vineyards.com; 14347 Sonoma Hwy; tasting $20; ⊘10am-4:30pm) 🍃 Arrowood's hilltop tasting room has postcard-perfect valley views and a bourgeois vibe, fussy for Sonoma, but the excellent Chardonnay and Cabernet Sauvignon merit the hype. Tasting fee refunded with two-bottle purchase. Bottles are $25 to $90.

Imagery Estate
WINERY

(Map p186; ☎707-935-4515; www.imagerywinery.com; 14335 Sonoma Hwy; tasting $10-20; ⊘10am-4:30pm; ⊕⊛) 🍃 Imagery produces lesser-known varietals, biodynamically

NAPA & SONOMA WINE COUNTRY SONOMA VALLEY WINERIES

Sonoma Valley

Sonoma Valley

grown, that you can't buy anywhere else – Cabernet Franc and Sangiovese are standouts. Each bottle sports an artist-designed label, with originals on display in the on-site gallery. Lovely gardens include a grassy picnic area with horseshoes and bocce. Limited picnic supplies available. Bottles are $24 to $45.

Benziger   WINERY
(Map p186; ☑707-935-4527, 888-490-2739; www.benziger.com; 1883 London Ranch Rd, Glen Ellen; tasting $15-20, tram tour adult/under 21yr $25/10; ⊙10am-5pm, tram tours 11:30am-3:30pm; 🚗🐾) 🌿 If you're new to wine, make Benziger your first stop for Sonoma's best crash course in winemaking. The worthwhile, non-reservable tour includes an open-air tram ride (weather permitting) through biodynamic vineyards, and a five-wine tasting. Great picnicking, plus a playground, make it tops for families. The large-production wine's OK (head for the reserves); the tour's the thing. Bottles are $15 to $80.

Wellington   WINERY
(Map p186; ☑800-816-9463; www.wellingtonvine-yards.com; 11600 Dunbar Rd, Glen Ellen; tasting $10; ⊙10:30am-4:30pm) 🌿 Known for port (including a white) and meaty reds, Welling-ton makes great Zinfandel, one from vines planted in 1892 – wow, what color! The noir de noir is a cult favorite. Alas, servers have vineyard views, while you face the warehouse. Bottles are $15 to $30 and the tasting fee is refundable with a purchase.

Loxton   WINERY
(Map p186; ☑707-935-7221; www.loxtonwines.com; 11466 Dunbar Rd, Glen Ellen; ⊙11am-5pm) **FREE** Say g'day to Chris the Aussie winemaker at Loxton, a no-frills winery with million-dollar views and free tastings. The 'tasting room' is actually a small warehouse, where you can taste wonderful Syrah and Zinfandel; non-oaky, fruit-forward Chardonnay; and good port. Bottles cost $16 to $30.

★ Kaz   WINERY
(Map p186; ☑707-833-2536; www.kazwinery.com; 233 Adobe Canyon Rd, Kenwood; tasting $5; ⊙11am-5pm Fri-Mon; 🚗🐾) 🌿 Sonoma's cult favorite, supercool Kaz is about blends: whatever's in the organic vineyards goes into the wine – and they're blended at crush, not during fermentation. Expect lesser-known varietals like Alicante Bouschet and Lenoir, and a worthwhile Cabernet-Merlot blend. Kids can sample grape juice, then run

around the playground outside. Bottles cost $20 to $48.

Sonoma & Around

Fancy boutiques may be replacing hardware stores lately, but Sonoma still retains an old-fashioned charm, thanks to the plaza and its surrounding frozen-in-time historic buildings. You can legally drink on the plaza – a rarity in California parks – but only between 11:30am and sunset.

Sonoma has rich history. In 1846 it was the site of a second American revolution, this time against Mexico, when General Mariano Guadalupe Vallejo deported all foreigners from California, prompting outraged frontiersmen to occupy the Sonoma Presidio and declare independence. They dubbed California the Bear Flag Republic after the battle flag they'd fashioned.

The republic was short-lived. The Mexican-American War broke out a month later, and California was annexed by the US. The revolt gave California its flag, which remains emblazoned with the words 'California Republic' beneath a muscular brown bear. Vallejo was initially imprisoned, but ultimately returned to Sonoma and played a major role in its development.

Sonoma Hwy (Hwy 12) runs through town. Sonoma Plaza, laid out by Vallejo in 1834, is the heart of downtown, lined with hotels, restaurants, tasting rooms and shops. The visitors bureau has a walking-tour brochure. Immediately north along Hwy 12, expect a brief suburban landscape before the valley's pastoral gorgeousness begins.

◎ Sights

★Sonoma Plaza   SQUARE
(Map p189; btwn Napa, Spain & 1st Sts) Smack in the center of the plaza, the Mission-revival-style city hall, built between 1906 and 1908, has identical facades on four sides, reportedly because plaza businesses all demanded City Hall face their direction. At the plaza's northeast corner, the Bear Flag Monument marks Sonoma's moment of revolutionary glory. The weekly farmers market (5:30pm to 8pm Tuesday, April to October) showcases Sonoma's incredible produce.

Sonoma State Historic Park   HISTORIC SITE
(☑707-938-9560; www.parks.ca.gov; adult/child $3/2; ☺10am-5pm) The park is comprised of multiple sites, most side-by-side. The 1823

Mission San Francisco Solano de Sonoma anchors the plaza, and was the final California mission. Sonoma Barracks houses exhibits on 19th-century life. The 1886 Toscano Hotel lobby is beautifully preserved – peek inside. The 1852 Vallejo Home lies a half-mile northwest. One ticket allows admission to all, including Petaluma Adobe (☑707-762-4871; www.petalumaadobe.com; 3325 Adobe Rd, Petaluma; ☺10am-5pm Sat & Sun), Vallejo's ranch, 15 miles away.

➡ Mission San Francisco Solano de Sonoma
(Map p189; ☑707-938-9560; 114 E Spain St) At the plaza's northeast corner, the mission was built in 1823, partly to forestall Russians at Fort Ross from moving inland. This was the 21st and final California mission – the northernmost point on El Camino Real – and the only one built during the Mexican period (the rest were founded by the Spanish). Five original rooms remain. The not-to-be-missed chapel dates to 1841.

➡ Sonoma Barracks
(Map p189; ☑707-939-9420; parks.ca.gov; 20 E Spain St; adult/child $3/2; ☺10am-5pm) The adobe Sonoma Barracks was built by Vallejo between 1836 and 1840 to house Mexican troops. Today, interpretive displays describe life during the Mexican and American periods. The Barracks became the capital of a rogue nation on June 14, 1846, when American settlers, of varying sobriety, surprised guards and declared an independent 'California Republc' [sic] with a homemade flag featuring a blotchy bear.

The US took over a month later, but abandoned the barracks during the Gold Rush, leaving Vallejo to turn them into (what else?) a winery, in 1860.

➡ Toscano Hotel
(Map p189; ☑707-938-9560; 20 E Spain St) FREE Toscano Hotel opened as a store and library in the 1850s, then became a hotel in 1886. Peek into the lobby from 10am to 5pm; except for the traffic outside, you'd swear you were peering back in time. There are free tours 1pm through 4pm Saturdays and Sundays.

➡ General Vallejo Home
(☑707-938-9559; 363 3rd St W) A half-mile from the plaza, the lovely Vallejo Home, aka Lachryma Montis (Latin for 'Tears of the Mountain'), was built between 1851 and 1852 for General Vallejo and named for the on-site spring; the Vallejo family made good

Sonoma

money piping water to town. The property remained in the family until 1933, when the state of California purchased it, along with its original furnishings. Docents lead tours Saturdays and Sundays at 1pm, 2pm and

3pm. A bike path leads to the house from downtown.

La Haye Art Center
ARTS CENTER

(Map p189; ☏707-996-9665; 148 E Napa St; ⊙11am-5pm) **FREE** At this collective in a converted foundry, you can tour a storefront gallery and meet the artists – sculptor, potter and painters – in their studios.

Sonoma Valley Museum of Art
MUSEUM

(Map p189; ☏707-939-7862; www.svma.org; 551 Broadway; adult/family $5/8; ⊙11am-5pm Wed-Sun) Though this museum presents compelling work by local and international artists, such as David Hockney, the annual standout is October's Día de los Muertos exhibition.

Bartholomew Park
PARK

(☏707-938-2244; www.bartholomewpark.org; 1000 Vineyard Lane; ⊙10am-6pm) **FREE** The top near-town outdoors destination is 375-acre Bartholomew Park, off Castle Rd, where you can picnic beneath giant oaks and hike 2 miles of trails, with hilltop vistas to San Francisco. The Palladian Villa, at the park's entrance, is a re-creation of Count Haraszthy's original residence, open noon to 3pm Saturdays and Sundays. There's also a good winery, independently operated.

Cornerstone Sonoma
GARDENS

(Map p186; ☏707-933-3010; www.cornerstone-gardens.com; 23570 Arnold Dr, Hwy 121; ⊙10am-4pm; ⊞) **FREE** There's nothing traditional about Cornerstone Gardens, which showcases 25 walk-through gardens by renowned avant-garde landscape designers who explore the intersection of art and nature. Let the kids run free while you explore top-notch garden shops, taste wine and gather information from the on-site Sonoma Valley Visitors Bureau (Map p186; ☏707-935-4747; www.sonomavalley.com; Cornerstone Gardens, 23570 Hwy 121; ⊙10am-4pm); there's also a good, if pricy, on-site cafe. Look for the enormous blue Adirondack chair at road's edge.

We especially love Pamela Burton's 'Earth Walk,' which descends into the ground; and Planet Horticulture's 'Rise,' which exaggerates space.

🏃 Activities

Many local inns provide bicycles.

Traintown
AMUSEMENT PARK

(Map p186; ☏707-938-3912; www.traintown.com; 20264 Broadway; ⊙10am-5pm daily late May–mid-Sep, Fri-Sun mid-Sep–late May; ⊞) Little kids adore Traintown, 1 mile south of the plaza. A miniature steam engine makes 20-minute loops ($5.75), and six other vintage amusement-park rides ($2.75 per ride) include a carousel and Ferris wheel.

Sonoma Valley Cyclery
BICYCLE RENTAL

(Map p186; ☏707-935-3377; www.sonomacyclery.com; 20091 Broadway/Hwy 12; bikes per day from $30; ⊙10am-6pm Mon-Sat, to 4pm Sun; ⊞) Sonoma is ideal for cycling – not too hilly – with multiple wineries near downtown. Book ahead for weekends.

Willow Stream Spa at
Sonoma Mission Inn
SPA

(Map p186; ☏707-938-9000; www.fairmont.com/sonoma; 100 Boyes Blvd; ⊙7:30am-8pm) Few Wine Country spas compare with glitzy Sonoma Mission Inn, where two treatments on the weekend – or $89 on a weekday (make reservations) – allow use of three outdoor and two indoor mineral pools, gym, sauna, and herbal steam room at the Romanesque bathhouse. No under 18s.

🍴 Courses

Ramekins Sonoma
Valley Culinary School
COOKING COURSE

(Map p189; ☏707-933-0450; www.ramekins.com; 450 W Spain St; ⊞) Offers demonstrations and hands-on classes for home chefs. Also runs weekend 'culinary camps' for adults and kids.

🛏 Sleeping

Off-season rates plummet. Reserve ahead. Ask about parking; some historic inns have no lots. Also consider Glen Ellen and, if counting pennies, Santa Rosa.

Sonoma Chalet
B&B $$

(☏800-938-3129, 707-938-3129; www.sonomachalet.com; 18935 5th St W; r $160-180, with shared bath $140, cottages $195-225; ☏) A historic farmstead surrounded by rolling hills, Sonoma Chalet has rooms in a Swiss chalet–style house adorned with little balconies and country-style bric-a-brac. We love the free-standing cottages; Laura's has a wood-burning fireplace. All rooms come with breakfast, which is served on a deck overlooking a nature preserve. No air-con in rooms with shared bath. No phones, no internet.

Sonoma Hotel
HISTORIC HOTEL $$

(Map p189; ☏800-468-6016, 707-996-2996; www.sonomahotel.com; 110 W Spain St; r incl breakfast $170-200, ste $250; ❄☏) Long on charm, this good-value, vintage-1880s hotel, decorated with country-style willow-wood furnishings, sits right on the plaza. Double-pane glass blocks the noise, but there's no elevator or parking lot.

Swiss Hotel HISTORIC HOTEL **$$**
(Map p189; ☎707-938-2884; www.swisshotelsono-ma.com; 18 W Spain St; r incl breakfast Mon-Fri $150-170, Sat & Sun $200-240; ❀♠) It opened in 1905, so you'll forgive the wavy floors. The floral prints are likewise dated, but rooms are large, good value and share a plaza-view balcony. Downstairs there's a raucous bar and restaurant. No parking lot or elevator.

Windhaven Cottage COTTAGE **$$**
(Map p186; ☎707-483-1856, 707-938-2175; www.windhavencottage.com; 21700 Pearson Ave; cottage $155-165; ❀♠) Great-bargain Windhaven has two units: a hideaway cottage with vaulted wooden ceilings and a fireplace, and a handsome 800-sq-ft studio. We prefer the romantic cottage. Both have hot tubs. Tennis facilities, bicycles and barbecues sweeten the deal.

Sonoma Creek Inn MOTEL **$$**
(Map p186; ☎888-712-1289, 707-939-9463; www.sonomacreekinn.com; 239 Boyes Blvd; r $116-225; ❀♠♣) This cute-as-a-button motel has spotless, cheery, retro-Americana rooms, but it's not downtown. Valley wineries are a short drive. When available, last-minute bookings cost just $89.

El Dorado Hotel BOUTIQUE HOTEL **$$$**
(Map p189; ☎707-996-3220; www.eldoradosono-ma.com; 405 1st St W; r Mon-Fri $165-265, Sat & Sun $245-325; ❙❀♠♣) Stylish touches, such as high-end linens, justify rates and compensate for the rooms' compact size, as do private balconies, which overlook the plaza or rear courtyard (we prefer the plaza view, despite noise). No elevator.

El Pueblo Inn MOTEL **$$$**
(Map p186; ☎707-996-3651, 800-900-8844; www.elpuebloinn.com; 896 W Napa St; r incl breakfast $189-239; ❀@♠♣) One mile west of downtown, family-owned El Pueblo has surprisingly cushy rooms with great beds. The big lawns and the heated pool are perfect for kids; parents appreciate the 24-hour hot tub.

Sonoma's Best Guest Cottages COTTAGES **$$$**
(Map p186; ☎800-291-8962, 707-933-0340; www.sonomasbestcottages.com; 1190 E Napa St; cottages $199-349, q $279-395; ❀♠) Each of these four colorful, inviting cottages has a bed-room, living room, kitchen and barbecue, with comfy furniture, stereos, DVDs and bicycles. One mile east of the plaza.

Hidden Oak Inn B&B **$$$**
(Map p189; ☎707-996-9863; www.hiddenoakinn.com; 214 E Napa St; r incl breakfast $195-245; ❀♠♣) Three-room, 1914 Craftsman B&B with lovely service.

MacArthur Place INN **$$$**
(☎800-722-1866, 707-938-2929; www.macar-thurplace.com; 29 E MacArthur St; r from $350, ste from $499; ❀@♠♣) Sonoma's top full-service inn occupies a former estate with century-old gardens.

✘ Eating

There's creek-side picnicking, with barbecue grills, up-valley at Sugarloaf Ridge State Park (p193). Find late-night taco trucks on Hwy 12, between Boyes Blvd and Aqua Caliente.

Angelo's Wine Country Deli DELI **$**
(Map p186; ☎707-938-3688; 23400 Arnold Dr; sandwiches $7; ☉9am-5:30pm) Look for the cow on the roof of this roadside deli, south of town, a fave for fat sandwiches and home-made jerky. In springtime, little lambs graze outside.

Pearl's Diner DINER **$**
(☎707-996-1783; 561 5th St W; mains $7-10; ☉7am-2:30pm; ♣) Across from Safeway's west-facing wall, greasy-spoon Pearl's serves giant American breakfasts, including stand-out bacon and waffles with batter enriched by melted vanilla ice cream.

Sonoma Market DELI, MARKET **$**
(☎707-996-3411; www.sonoma-glenellenmkt.com; 500 W Napa St; sandwiches from $6; ☉5:30am-10pm) Sonoma's best groceries and deli sandwiches.

★ Fremont Diner AMERICAN **$$**
(Map p186; ☎707-938-7370; http://thefremontdin-er.com; 2698 Fremont Dr; mains $10-16; ☉8am-3pm Mon-Wed, to 9pm Thu-Sun; ♣) ✿ Lines snake out the door peak times at this farm-to-table roadside diner. We prefer the indoor tables, but will happily accept a picnic table in the big outdoor tent to feast on ricotta pancakes with real maple syrup, chicken and waffles, oyster po' boys, finger-licking barbecue and skillet-baked cornbread. Arrive early, or late, to beat queues.

Sunflower Caffé & Wine Bar
CAFE $$

(Map p189; 707-996-6845; www.sonomasunflower.com; 421 1st St W; dishes $8-15; 7am-4pm;) The big back garden at this local hangout is a great spot for breakfast, a no-fuss lunch or afternoon wine.

Red Grape
ITALIAN $$

(Map p189; 707-996-4103; http://theredgrape.com; 529 1st St W; mains $10-20; 11:30am-10pm;) A reliable spot for an easy meal, Red Grape serves good thin-crust pizzas and big salads in a cavernous, echoey space. Good for takeout, too.

Della Santina's
ITALIAN $$

(Map p189; 707-935-0576; www.dellasantinas.com; 135 E Napa St; mains $14-24; 11:30am-3pm & 5-9:30pm) The waiters have been here forever, and the 'specials' rarely change, but Della Santina's American-Italian cooking – linguini pesto, veal parmigiana, rotisserie chickens – is consistently good, and the brick courtyard is inviting on warm evenings.

Taste of the Himalayas
INDIAN, NEPALESE $$

(Map p189; 707-996-1161; 464 1st St E; mains $10-20; 11am-2:30 Tue-Sun, 5-10pm daily) Spicy curries, luscious lentil soup and sizzle-platter meats make a refreshing break from the usual French-Italian Wine Country fare.

★ Cafe La Haye
CALIFORNIAN $$$

(Map p189; 707-935-5994; www.cafelahaye.com; 140 E Napa St; mains $20-32; 5:30-9pm Tue-Sat) One of Sonoma's top tables for earthy New American cooking, La Haye only uses produce sourced from within 60 miles. Its dining room gets packed cheek-by-jowl and service can border on perfunctory, but the clean simplicity and flavor-packed cooking make it many foodies' first choice. Reserve well ahead.

the girl & the fig
FRENCH $$$

(Map p189; 707-938-3634; www.thegirlandthefig.com; 11 W Spain St; mains $20-27; 11:30am-10pm Mon-Fri, 11am-11pm Sat, 10am-10pm Sun) For a festive evening, book a garden table at this French-provincial bistro, with good small plates ($12 to $14) including steamed mussels with matchstick fries, and duck confit with lentils. Weekday three-course prix-fixe costs $36, add $12 for wine. Stellar cheeses. Reservations essential.

El Dorado Kitchen
CALIFORNIAN $$$

(Map p189; 707-996-3030; www.eldoradosonoma.com; 405 1st St W; lunch mains $12-17, dinner $24-31; 8-11am, 11:30am-2:30pm & 5:30-9:30pm) The swank plaza-side choice for contemporary California-Mediterranean cooking, El Dorado showcases seasonal-regional ingredients in dishes like duck-confit salad and housemade ravioli, served in a see-and-be-seen dining room with a big community table at its center. The happening lounge serves good small plates ($9 to $15) and craft cocktails. Make reservations.

La Salette
PORTUGUESE $$$

(Map p189; 707-938-1927; www.lasalette-restaurant.com; 452 1st St E; lunch mains $12-25, dinner $19-25; 11:30am-2pm & 5:30-9pm) Contemporary Portuguese cuisine is the focus at this restaurant that serves excellent-value, proper sit-down meals, including a standout seafood stew. Make reservations.

Harvest Moon Cafe
NEW AMERICAN $$$

(Map p189; 707-933-8160; www.harvestmooncafesonoma.com; 487 1st St W; mains $19-29; 5:30-9pm Wed-Mon) Inside a cozy 1836 adobe, this casual bistro uses local ingredients in its changing menu, with simple soul-satisfying dishes like duck risotto with Bellwether Farms ricotta. Book the patio in warm weather.

Drinking & Entertainment

Free jazz concerts happen on the plaza every second Tuesday, June to September, 6pm to 8:30pm; arrive early, bring a picnic.

Murphy's Irish Pub
PUB

(Map p189; 707-935-0660; www.sonomapub.com; 464 1st St E; noon-11pm) Don't ask for Bud – there're only *real* brews here. Good hand-cut fries and shepherd's pie, too. Live music Thursday through Sunday evenings.

Swiss Hotel
BAR

(Map p189; www.swisshotelsonoma.com; 18 W Spain St; 11:30am-midnight) Locals and tourists crowd the 1909 Swiss Hotel for cocktails. There's OK food, but the bar's the thing.

Hopmonk Tavern
BREWERY

(Map p189; 707-935-9100; www.hopmonk.com; 691 Broadway; 11:30am-10pm) This happening gastro-pub (dishes $10 to $20) and beer garden takes its brews seriously, with 16 on tap, served in type-appropriate glassware. Live music Friday through Sunday.

Enoteca Della Santina
WINE BAR

(Map p189; www.enotecadellasantina.com; 127 E Napa St; 4-10pm Mon-Thu, to 11pm Fri, 2-11pm Sat, 2-10pm Sun) Thirty global vintages by the glass let you compare what you're tasting in California with the rest of the world's wines.

Steiner's
BAR

(Map p189; www.steinerstavern.com; 465 1st St W; ⊙6am-2am; 🛜) Sonoma's oldest bar gets crowded Sunday afternoons with cyclists and motorcyclists.

Sebastiani Theatre
CINEMA

(Map p189; ☑707-996-2020; sebastianitheatre. com; 476 1st St E) The plaza's gorgeous 1934 Mission-revival cinema screens art-house and revival films, and sometimes live theater.

🛍 Shopping

Vella Cheese Co
FOOD

(Map p189; ☑707-938-3232; www.vellacheese.com; 315 2nd St E; ⊙9:30am-6pm Mon-Sat) Known for its dry-jack cheeses (made here since the 1930s), Vella also makes good Mezzo Secco with cocoa powder–dusted rind. Staff will vacuum-pack for shipping.

Tiddle E Winks
TOYS

(Map p189; ☑707-939-6933; www.tiddleewinks. com; 115 E Napa St; ⊙10:30am-5:30pm Mon-Sat, 11am-5pm Sun; 🛝) Vintage five-and-dime, with classic, mid-20th-century toys.

Sign of the Bear
HOMEWARES

(Map p189; ☑707-996-3722; 435 1st St W; ⊙10am-6pm) Kitchen-gadget freaks: make a beeline to this indie cookware store.

Chateau Sonoma
HOMEWARES, GIFTS

(Map p189; ☑707-935-8553; www.chateausonoma. com; 153 W Napa St; ⊙10:30am-6pm Mon-Sat, 11am-5pm Sun) France meets Sonoma in one-of-a-kind gifts and arty home decor.

Readers' Books
BOOKS

(Map p189; ☑707-939-1779; readers.indiebound. com; 130 E Napa St; ⊙10am-7pm Mon-Sat, to 6pm Sun) Independent bookseller.

ℹ Information

Sonoma Post Office (Map p189; ☑800-275-8777; www.usps.com; 617 Broadway; ⊙9am-5pm Mon-Fri)

Sonoma Valley Hospital (☑707-935-5000; www.svh.com; 347 Andrieux St) Twenty-four-hour emergency room.

Sonoma Valley Visitors Bureau (Map p189; ☑707-996-1090; www.sonomavalley.com; 453 1st St E; ⊙9am-5pm Mon-Sat, 10am-5pm Sun) Arranges accommodations; has a good walking-tour pamphlet and events information. There's another at Cornerstone Gardens (p190).

Glen Ellen & Kenwood

Sleepy Glen Ellen is a snapshot of old Sonoma, with white-picket fences and tiny cottages beside a poplar-lined creek. When downtown Sonoma is jammed, you can wander quiet Glen Ellen and feel far away. It's ideal for a leg-stretching stopover between wineries or a romantic overnight – the nighttime sky blazes with stars. Arnold Dr is the main drag and the valley's back-way route. Kenwood lies just north, along Hwy 12, but has no town center like Glen Ellen's. For services, drive 8 miles south to Sonoma. Glen Ellen's biggest draws are Jack London State Historic Park and Benziger winery (p187).

👁 Sights & Activities

Jack London State Historic Park
PARK

(Map p186; ☑707-938-5216; www.jacklondon-park.com; 2400 London Ranch Rd, Glen Ellen; per car $10, tour adult/child $4/2; ⊙9:30am-5pm) Napa has Robert Louis Stevenson, but Sonoma's got Jack London. This 1400-acre park frames the author's last years; don't miss the excellent on-site museum. Miles of hiking trails (some open to mountain bikes) weave through oak-dotted woodlands, between 600ft and 2300ft elevations; an easy 2-mile loop meanders to a lake, great for picnicking. Watch for poison oak.

Changing occupations from Oakland fisherman to Alaska gold prospector to Pacific yachtsman – and novelist on the side – London (1876–1916) ultimately took up farming. He bought 'Beauty Ranch' in 1905 and moved here in 1910. With his second wife, Charmian, he lived and wrote in a small cottage while his mansion, Wolf House, was under construction. On the eve of its completion in 1913, it burned down. The disaster devastated London, and although he toyed with rebuilding, he died before construction got underway. His widow, Charmian, built the House of Happy Walls, which has been preserved as a museum. It's a half-mile walk from there to the remains of Wolf House, passing London's grave along the way. Other paths wind around the farm to the cottage where he lived and worked.

Sugarloaf Ridge State Park
HIKING

(Map p186; ☑707-833-5712; www.parks.ca.gov; 2605 Adobe Canyon Rd, Kenwood; per car $8) There's fantastic hiking – when it's not blazingly hot. On clear days, Bald Mountain has drop-dead views to the sea; Bushy Peak

ℹ WHAT'S CRUSH?

Crush is autumn harvest, the most atmospheric time of year, when the vine's leaves turn brilliant colors and you can smell fermenting fruit on the breeze. Farmers throw big parties for the vineyard workers to celebrate their work. Everyone wants to be here. That's why room rates skyrocket. If you can afford it, come during autumn. To score party invitations, join your favorite winery's wine club.

Trail peers into Napa Valley. Both are moderately strenuous; plan four hours round-trip.

Morton's Warm Springs SWIMMING
(Map p186; ☎707-833-5511; www.mortonswarmsprings.com; 1651 Warm Springs Rd, Glen Ellen; adult/child $15/5; ⏰10am-6pm Sat, Sun & holidays May & Sep, Tue-Sun Jun-Aug; 🏊) This old-fashioned family swim club has two mineral pools, limited hiking, volleyball and BBQ facilities. No credit cards Tuesday to Friday: exact change required. From Sonoma Hwy in Kenwood, turn west on Warm Springs Rd.

Triple Creek Horse Outfit HORSEBACK RIDING
(☎707-887-8700; www.triplecreekhorseoutfit.com; 60/90min rides $75/95; ⏰Wed-Mon) Explore Jack London State Park by horseback for stunning vistas over Sonoma Valley. Reservations required.

🛏 Sleeping

Sugarloaf Ridge State Park CAMPGROUND $
(Map p186; ☎800-444-7275; www.reserveamerica.com; 2605 Adobe Canyon Rd, Kenwood; tent & RV sites $35; 🅿) Sonoma's nearest camping is north of Kenwood at this lovely hilltop park, with 50 drive-in sites, clean coin-operated showers and great hiking.

Jack London Lodge MOTEL $$
(Map p186; ☎707-938-8510; www.jacklondonlodge.com; 13740 Arnold Dr, Glen Ellen; r Mon-Fri $124, Sat & Sun $189; 🅿🛜🏊) An old-fashioned wood-sided motel, with well-kept rooms decorated with antique repros, this is a weekday bargain – and the manager will sometimes negotiate rates. Outside there's a hot tub; next door, a saloon.

Glen Ellen Cottages BUNGALOW $$
(Map p186; ☎707-996-1174; www.glenelleninn.com; 13670 Arnold Dr, Glen Ellen; cottage Mon-Fri $139-159, Sat & Sun $209-249; 🅿🛜) Hidden behind Glen Ellen Inn, these five creek-side cottages are designed for romance, with oversized jetted tubs, steam showers and gas fireplaces.

★Beltane Ranch B&B $$$
(Map p186; ☎707-996-6501; www.beltaneranch.com; 11775 Hwy 12, Glen Ellen; d incl breakfast $160-285; 🛜) 🐾 Surrounded by horse pastures and vineyards, Beltane is a throwback to 19th-century Sonoma. The cheerful, lemon-yellow, 1890s ranch house has double porches, lined with swinging chairs and white wicker. Though it's technically a B&B, each country-Americana-style room has a private entrance – nobody will make you pet the cat. Breakfast in bed. No phones or TVs mean zero distraction from pastoral bliss.

Gaige House Inn B&B $$$
(Map p186; ☎707-935-0237, 800-935-0237; www.gaige.com; 13540 Arnold Dr, Glen Ellen; d incl breakfast from $275, ste from $425; @🛜🏊) Among the valley's most chic inns, Gaige has 23 rooms, five inside an 1890 house decked out in Euro-Asian style. Best are the Japanese-style 'Zen suites,' with requisite high-end bells and whistles, including freestanding tubs made from hollowed-out granite boulders. Fabulous.

Kenwood Inn & Spa INN $$$
(Map p186; ☎800-353-6966, 707-833-1293; www.kenwoodinn.com; 10400 Sonoma Hwy, Kenwood; r incl breakfast $450-825; ❄@🛜🏊) Lush gardens surround ivy-covered bungalows at this sexy 25-room inn, designed to resemble a Mediterranean château. Two hot tubs (one with a waterfall) and an on-site spa make it ideal for lovers, boring for singles. No kids. Book an upstairs balcony room.

🍴 Eating

Glen Ellen Village Market DELI, MARKET $
(Map p186; www.sonoma-glenellenmkt.com; 13751 Arnold Dr, Glen Ellen; ⏰6am-8pm) Fantastic market with huge deli, ideal for picnickers.

Garden Court Cafe CAFE $
(Map p186; ☎707-935-1565; www.gardencourtcafe.com; 13647 Arnold Dr, Glen Ellen; mains $9-12; ⏰8:30am-2pm Wed-Mon) Basic breakfasts, sandwiches and salads.

fig cafe & winebar FRENCH, CALIFORNIAN $$
(Map p186; ☎707-938-2130; www.thefigcafe.com; 13690 Arnold Dr, Glen Ellen; mains $18-22; ⏰10am-3pm Sat & Sun, 5:30-9pm daily) The fig's earthy California–Provençal comfort food includes flash-fried calamari with spicy-lemon aioli,

duck confit and *moules-frites* (mussels and French fries). Good wine prices and weekend brunch give reason to return.

Yeti
INDIAN $$

(Map p186; ☎707-996-9930; www.yetirestaurant.com; 14301 Arnold Dr, Glen Ellen; mains $12-22; ⊙11:30am-2:30pm & 5-9pm) Surprisingly good Indian and Nepalese cooking, served on a creek-side patio at a converted mill, make Yeti worth seeking out. Great value.

Glen Ellen Inn
AMERICAN $$

(Map p186; ☎707-996-6409; www.glenelleninn.com; 13670 Arnold Dr, Glen Ellen; mains $16-25; ⊙11:30am-9pm Thu-Tue, 5:30-9pm Wed) Oysters, martinis and grilled steaks. Lovely garden, full bar.

Mayo Winery Reserve
WINERY $$

(Map p186; ☎707-833-5504; www.mayofamilywinery.com; 9200 Sonoma Hwy, Kenwood; 7-course menu $35; ⊙by appointment 11am-5pm) Feast on a seven-course small-plates menu, paired with seven wines, for just $35 at this unatmospheric roadside wine-tasting room.

Cafe Citti
ITALIAN $$

(Map p186; ☎707-833-2690; www.cafecitti.com; 9049 Sonoma Hwy, Kenwood; mains $8-15; ⊙11am-3:30pm & 5-9pm; 🖩) Locals favor this order-at-the-counter Italian-American deli, with standout roasted chicken, homemade gnocchi and ravioli; lunchtime, there's pizza and house-baked focaccia-bread sandwiches.

Kenwood Restaurant & Bar
CALIFORNIAN $$$

(Map p186; ☎707-833-6326; www.kenwoodrestaurant.com; 9900 Sonoma Hwy, Kenwood; mains $22-30; ⊙11:30am-8:30pm Wed-Sun) 🍷 A stone patio flanks vineyards and flowering gardens at this roadhouse restaurant, lovely for a lingering lunch. The chef showcases quality ingredients by local producers in simple-delicious dishes like pork chops with bacon or roasted chicken. The small-plates menu ($10 to $16) is ideal for a quick bite between wineries. Reservations advised.

Aventine
ITALIAN $$$

(Map p186; ☎707-934-8911; http://glenellen.aventinehospitality.com; 14301 Arnold Dr, Glen Ellen; mains $14-28; ⊙4:30-10pm Tue-Fri, 11am-10pm Sat & Sun) The Sonoma outpost of the popular San Francisco and Hollywood restaurants occupies an atmospheric former grist mill with a sun-dappled outdoor patio, and serves Italian-derived dishes, including mozzarella-stuffed meatball with pesto over polenta. Make reservations.

Olive & Vine
NEW AMERICAN $$$

(Map p186; ☎707-996-9152; oliveandvinerestaurant.com; 14301 Arnold Dr, Glen Ellen; mains $23-36; ⊙5:30-9pm Wed-Sun) 🍷 Inside a repurposed grist mill with mismatched shabby-chic furniture, Olive & Vine showcases seasonal flavors in its cooking. Reservations essential.

🛍 Shopping

Wine Country Chocolates Tasting Bar
FOOD

(Map p186; ☎707-996-1010; www.winecountrychocolates.com; 14301 Arnold Dr, Glen Ellen; ⊙10am-5pm) Sample fine chocolates of varying degrees of cacao.

Figone's Olive Oil
FOOD

(Map p186; ☎707-282-9092; www.figoneoliveoil.com; 9580 Sonoma Hwy, Kenwood; ⊙11am-5pm) Figone's presses its own extra-virgin olive oil, and infuses some with flavors like Meyer-lemon, all free to sample.

RUSSIAN RIVER AREA

Lesser-known western Sonoma County was formerly famous for its apple farms and vacation cottages. Lately vineyards are replacing orchards, and the Russian River has taken its place among California's important wine appellations, especially for pinot noir.

'The River,' as locals call it, has long been a summertime-weekend destination for Northern Californians, who come to canoe, wander country lanes, taste wine, hike redwood forests and live at a lazy pace. In winter the river floods, and nobody's here.

The Russian River begins in the mountains north of Ukiah, in Mendocino County, but the most-known sections lie southwest of Healdsburg, where the river cuts a serpentine course toward the sea. Just north of Santa Rosa, River Rd, the lower valley's main artery, connects Hwy 101 with coastal Hwy 1 at Jenner. Hwy 116 heads northwest from Cotati through Sebastopol, then at Guerneville joins River Rd and cuts west to the sea. Westside Rd connects Guerneville and Healdsburg. West County's winding roads get confusing and there's limited cell service; carry a proper map.

Russian River Area Wineries

Sonoma County's wine-growing regions encompass several diverse areas, each famous

Russian River Area

for different reasons (p185). Pick up the free, useful *Russian River Wine Road* map (www. wineroad.com) in tourist-brochure racks.

Russian River Valley

Nighttime coastal fog drifts up the Russian River Valley, then usually clears by midday. Pinot Noir does beautifully, as does Chardonnay, which also grows in hotter regions, but prefers the longer 'hang time' of cooler climes. The highest concentration of wineries is along Westside Rd, between Guerneville and Healdsburg.

Hartford Family Winery WINERY
(☏707-887-8030; www.hartfordwines.com; 8075 Martinelli Rd, Forestville; tasting $15; ⏰10am-4:30pm) 🍷 Surprisingly upscale for West County, Hartford sits in a pastoral valley surrounded by redwood-forested hills, on one of the area's prettiest back roads. It specializes in fine single-vineyard Pinot (12 kinds), Chardonnay and Zinfandel from old-vine fruit. Umbrella-shaded picnic tables dot the garden. Bottles are $38 to $90 and the tasting fee is waived with purchase.

Korbel

WINERY

(☎707-824-7000, 707-824-7316; www.korbel.com; 13250 River Rd, Guerneville; ⏰10am-5pm; 🎫) **FREE**
Gorgeous rose gardens (April to October) and an on-site deli make Korbel worth a stop for free tasting; the sparking wine's just OK.

Iron Horse Vineyards

WINERY

(☎707-887-1507; www.ironhorsevineyards.com; 9786 Ross Station Rd, Sebastopol; tasting $20; ⏰10am-4:30pm) Atop a hill with drop-dead views over the county, Iron Horse is known for Pinot Noir and sparkling wines, which the White House often pours. The outdoor tasting room is refreshingly unfussy; when you're done with your wine, pour it in the grass. Sunday noon to 4pm, April to October, they serve oysters ($3). Located off Hwy 116. Bottles cost $27 to $85.

Marimar

WINERY

(☎707-823-4365; www.marimarestate.com; 11400 Graton Rd, Sebastopol; tasting $10-15; ⏰11am-4pm; 🎫) 🍷 Middle-of-nowhere Marimar specializes in all-organic Pinot – seven different kinds – and Spanish varietals. The hacienda-style hilltop tasting room has a knockout vineyard-view terrace, good for picnics. Also consider tapas-and-wine pairings ($45). Bottles are $29 to $57.

Gary Farrell

WINERY

(☎707-473-2900; www.garyfarrellwines.com; 10701 Westside Rd, Healdsburg; tasting $15-25; ⏰10:30am-4:30pm; 🎫) High on a hilltop, overlooking the Russian River, Gary Farrell's tasting room sits perched among second-growth redwoods. The elegant Chardonnay and long-finish Pinot, made by a big-name winemaker, score high marks for consistency. Bottles are $32 to $60.

Porter Creek

WINERY

(☎707-433-6321; www.portercreekvineyards.com; 8735 Westside Rd, Healdsburg; ⏰10:30am-4:30pm; 🎫) 🍷 **FREE** Inside a vintage-1920s garage, Porter Creek's tasting bar is a former bowling-alley lane, plunked atop barrels. Porter is old-school Northern California, an early pioneer in biodynamic farming. High-acid, food-friendly Pinot Noir and Chardonnay are specialties, but there's silky Zinfandel and other Burgundian- and Rhône-style wines, too. Check out the aviary. Bottles cost $20 to $72 and tastings are free.

Hop Kiln Winery

WINERY

(☎707-433-6491; www.hopkilnwinery.com; 6050 Westside Rd, Healdsburg; tasting $7; ⏰10am-5pm) This photogenic, historic landmark, has a busy tasting room inside a former hop kiln; we especially like the flavored vinegars, which make great $10 gifts.

De La Montanya

WINERY

(☎707-433-3711; www.dlmwine.com; 999 Foreman Lane, Healdsburg; tasting $10; ⏰by appointment Mon-Thu, 11am-4:30pm Fri-Sun; 🎫) This tiny winery, tucked amid vineyards, is known for 17 small-batch varieties made with estate-grown fruit. Viognier, Primitivo, Pinot and Cabernet are signatures; the 'summer white' and Gewürtztraminer are great back-porch wines. Apple-shaded picnic area, bocce ball and horseshoes add to the fun. Bottles are $20 to $60 and the tasting fee is refundable with a purchase.

J Winery

WINERY

(☎707-431-3646; www.jwine.com; 11447 Old Redwood Hwy, Healdsburg; tasting $20, tour $30; ⏰11am-5pm) 🍷 J crafts crisp sparkling wines, among Sonoma's best, but it's pricy. Splurge on seated food-and-wine pairings ($45; Friday to Sunday, May to October, call ahead). Bottles cost $20 to $90.

Dry Creek Valley

Hemmed in by 2000ft-high mountains, Dry Creek Valley is relatively warm, ideal for Sauvignon Blanc and Zinfandel, and in some places Cabernet Sauvignon. It's west of Hwy 101, between Healdsburg and Lake Sonoma. Dry Creek Rd is the fast-moving main thoroughfare. Parallel-running West Dry Creek Rd is an undulating country lane with no center stripe – one of Sonoma's great back roads, ideal for cycling.

Quivira

WINERY

(☎707-431-8333; www.quivirawine.com; 4900 West Dry Creek Rd; tasting $10; ⏰11am-5pm; 👶🎫) 🍷 Sunflowers, lavender and crowing roosters greet your arrival at this winery and biodynamic farm, with self-guided garden tours and a picnic grove beside the vines. Kids can giggle with pigs and chickens, while you sample Rhône varietals, unusual blends, and lip-smacking Sauvignon Blanc. Bottles are $22 to $45; the tasting fee is refundable with purchase.

Unti Vineyards

WINERY

(☎707-433-5590; www.untivineyards.com; 4202 Dry Creek Rd; tasting $5; ⏰by appointment 10am-4pm; 🎫) 🍷 Inside a vineyard-view tasting room, Unti pours all estate-grown reds –

Châteauneuf-du-Pape–style grenache, compelling Syrah, and superb Sangiovese – favored by oenophiles for their structured tannins and concentrated fruit. If you love small-batch wines, don't miss Unti. Bottles are $23 to $40 and the tasting fee is refundable with a purchase.

Family Wineries
WINERY

(☎707-433-0100; familywines.com; 4791 Dry Creek Rd; tasting $10; ◷10:30am-4:30pm) Sample multiple varietals at this cooperative, which showcases six boutique wineries too small to have their own tasting rooms. Tasting fee is refundable with a purchase.

Truett Hurst Vineyards
WINERY

(☎707-433-9545; www.truetthurst.com; 5610 Dry Creek Rd; tasting $5-10; ◷10am-5pm) 🍴 Pull up an Adirondack chair and picnic creekside at Truett Hurst, Dry Creek's newest biodynamic winery. Sample terrific old-vine zins, standout petite Syrah and Russian River Pinots at the handsome contemporary tasting room, then meander through fragrant butterfly gardens to the creek, where salmon spawn in autumn. Saturdays there are snacks, Sundays live music (1pm to 4:30pm). Bottles are $18 to $50.

Bella Vineyards
WINERY

(☎707-473-9171; www.bellawinery.com; 9711 West Dry Creek Rd; tasting $10; ◷11am-4:30pm) Atop the valley's north end, always-fun Bella has caves built into the hillside. The estate-grown grapes include 110-year-old vines from Alexander Valley. The focus is on big reds – Zin and Syrah – but there's terrific rosé (good for barbecues), and late-harvest Zin (great with brownies). The wonderful vibe and dynamic staff make Bella special. Bottles are $25 to $42.

Preston Vineyards
WINERY

(www.prestonvineyards.com; 9282 West Dry Creek Rd; tasting $5; ◷11am-4:30pm; 🚻) 🍴 An early leader in organics, Lou Preston's 19th-century farm is old Sonoma. Weathered picket fencing frames the 19th-century farmhouse-turned-tasting room, with candy-colored walls and tongue-in-groove ceilings setting a country mood. The signature is citrusy Sauvignon Blanc, but try the Rhône varietals and small-lot wines: Mourvèdre, Viognier, Cinsault and cult-favorite Barbera. Preston also bakes good bread; picnic in the shade of a walnut tree. Monday to Friday, there's bocce ball. Bottles are $24 to $38, and the tasting fee is refundable with a purchase.

Alexander Valley

Bucolic Alexander Valley flanks the Mayacamas Mountains, with postcard-perfect vistas and wide-open vineyards. Summers are hot, ideal for Cabernet Sauvignon, Merlot and warm-weather Chardonnays, but there's also fine Sauvignon Blanc and Zinfandel. For events info, visit www.alexandervalley.org.

Hanna
WINERY

(☎800-854-3987, 707-431-4310; http://hannawinery.com; 9280 Hwy 128, Healdsburg; tasting $10-20; ◷10am-4pm; 🚻) Abutting oak-studded hills, Hanna's tasting room has lovely vineyard views and good picnicking. At the bar, find estate-grown Merlot and Cabernet, and big-fruit Zins and Syrah. Sit-down wine-and-cheese tastings are available ($25). Bottles cost $18 to $56.

Hawkes
TASTING ROOM

(☎707-433-4295; www.hawkeswine.com; 6734 Hwy 128, Healdsburg; tasting $10; ◷10am-5pm; 🚻) Friendly Hawkes' makes an easy stopover while you're exploring the valley. The single-vineyard Cab is damn good, as is the blend; there's also a clean-and-crisp, non-malolactic Chardonnay. Bottles are $30 to $70 and the tasting fee is refundable with a purchase.

Stryker Sonoma
WINERY

(☎707-433-1944; www.strykersonoma.com; 5110 Hwy 128, Geyserville; tasting $10; ◷10:30am-5pm; 🚻) 🍴 Wow, what a view from the hilltop concrete-and-glass tasting room at Stryker Sonoma. The standouts are fruit-forward Zinfandel and Sangiovese, which you can't buy anywhere else. Good picnicking. Bottles are $20 to $50; tasting fee is refundable with purchase.

Trentadue
WINERY

(☎888-332-3032, 707-433-3104; www.trentadue.com; 19170 Geyserville Ave, Geyserville; tasting $5-10; ◷10am-5pm; 🚻) Specializes in ports (ruby, not tawny); the chocolate port makes a great gift.

Sebastopol

Grapes have replaced apples as the new cash crop, but Sebastopol's farm-town identity remains rooted in the apple – evidence the much-heralded summertime Gravenstein

Apple Fair. The town center feels suburban because of traffic, but a hippie tinge gives it color. This is the refreshingly unfussy side of Wine Country, and makes a good-value base for exploring the area.

Hwy 116 splits downtown; southbound traffic uses Main St, northbound traffic Petaluma Ave. North of town, it's called Gravenstein Hwy N and continues toward Guerneville; south of downtown, it's Gravenstein Hwy S, which heads toward Hwy 101 and Sonoma.

◎ Sights

Around Sebastopol, look for family-friendly farms, gardens, animal sanctuaries and pick-your-own orchards. For a countywide list, check out the Sonoma County Farm Trails Guide (www.farmtrails.org).

★ The Barlow   MARKET
(☑ 707-824-5600; thebarlow.net; 6770 McKinley St; ☺ 8:30am-9:30pm; ⓟ) The Barlow occupies a former apple processing plant, covering 12 acres, re-purposed into a village of food producers, artists, winemakers, coffee roasters, spirits distillers and indie restaurateurs, who showcase West County's culinary and artistic diversity. Wander shed to shed, sample everything from house-brewed beer to nitrogen flash-frozen ice cream, and meet artisanal producers in their workshops. Thursdays 4pm to 8pm, mid-June to mid-October, the Barlow hosts a 'street fair,' with live music and local vendors.

Spirit Works Distillery   DISTILLERY
(☑ 707-634-4793; www.spiritworksdistillery.com; 6790 McKinley St, 100, The Barlow; tasting $5, tour $15; ☺ 11am-4pm Thu-Sun) ⬤ A bracing alternative to wine-tasting, Spirit Works crafts superb small-batch spirits – vodka, gin, sloe gin and (soon) whiskey – of organic California red-winter wheat. Sample and buy in the warehouse. Tours (by reservation) happen Friday to Sunday at 4pm. Bottles are $27 to $36.

California Carnivores   GARDENS
(☑ 707-824-0433; www.californiacarnivores.com; 2833 Old Gravenstein Hwy S; ☺ 10am-4pm Thu-Mon) Even vegans can't help admiring these incredible carnivorous plants – the largest collection in the US – including specimens from around the globe.

Farmers Market   MARKET
(www.sebastopolfarmmarket.org; cnr Petaluma & McKinley Aves; ☺ 10am-1:30pm Sun) Meets at the downtown plaza.

✿ Festivals & Events

Apple Blossom Festival   CULTURAL
(appleblossomfest.com) Live music, food, drink, wine, a parade and exhibits in April.

Gravenstein Apple Fair   FOOD
(www.gravensteinapplefair.com) Arts, crafts, food, wines and brews, games, live entertainment and farm-life activities in August.

🛏 Sleeping

Staying in Sebastopol is convenient to Russian River Valley, the coast, and Sonoma Valley.

Sebastopol Inn   MOTEL $$
(☑ 800-653-1082, 707-829-2500; www.sebastopolinn.com; 6751 Sebastopol Ave; r $119-209; ✳ ⬤ ⬛) We like this independent, non-cookie-cutter motel for its quiet, off-street location, usually reasonable rates and good-looking if basic rooms. Outside are grassy areas for kids and a hot tub.

Fairfield Inn & Suites   HOTEL $$
(☑ 800-465-4329, 707-829-6677; www.winecountryhi.com; 1101 Gravenstein Hwy S; r $134-249; ✳ @ ⬤ ⬛) Generic but modern, this hotel has little extras, such as in-room refrigerators and coffee makers, plus a hot tub.

🍴 Eating

Fiesta Market   MARKET $
(Pacific Market; ☑ 707-823-9735; fiestamkt.com; 550 Gravenstein Hwy N; ☺ 8am-8pm) Excellent for groceries and picnics; north of downtown.

East-West Cafe   MEDITERRANEAN $
(☑ 707-829-2822; www.eastwestcafesebastopol.com; 128 N Main St; meals $9-13; ☺ 8am-9pm Mon-Sat, to 8pm Sun; ⬤ ⓟ) ⬤ This unfussy cafe serves everything from grass-fed burgers to macrobiotic wraps, stir-fries to huevos rancheros (corn tortilla with fried egg and chili-tomato sauce). Good blue-corn pancakes at breakfast.

Slice of Life   VEGETARIAN $
(☑ 707-829-6627; www.thesliceoflife.com; 6970 McKinley St; mains under $10; ☺ 11am-9pm Tue-Fri, 9am-9pm Sat & Sun; ⬤) ⬤ This vegan-vegetarian kitchen doubles as a pizzeria. Breakfast all day. Great smoothies and date shakes.

Screamin' Mimi   ICE CREAM $
(☑ 707-823-5902; www.screaminmimisicecream.com; 6902 Sebastopol Ave; ☺ 11am-10pm) Delish homemade ice cream.

Mom's Apple Pie
DESSERTS **$**

(☎707-823-8330; www.momsapplepieusa.com; 4550 Gravenstein Hwy N; whole pies $7-17; ⏰10am-6pm; 🅿🐾) Pie's the thing at this roadside bakery – and yum, that flaky crust. Apple is predictably good, especially in autumn, but the blueberry is our fave, made better with vanilla ice cream.

Forchetta Bastoni
ITALIAN, SOUTHEAST ASIAN **$$**

(☎707-829-9500; www.forchettabastoni.com; 6948 Sebastopol Ave; ⏰11am-9pm Sun-Thu, to 10pm Fri & Sat; 🐾) Inside a converted brick-walled warehouse, Forchetta Bastoni has two kitchens that make wildly different food – Southeast Asian and Italian. Pick a cuisine, then be seated on one side or the other for wood-fired pizzas, pastas and roasted meats; or noodles, rice bowls and curries. If you can't decide, sit at the happening bar.

Red's Apple Roadhouse
AMERICAN **$$**

(☎707-861-9338; www.redsappleroadhouse.com; 4550 Gravenstein Hwy N; mains $9-15; ⏰8am-9:30pm Tue-Sat, to 5pm Sun) 🍃 A rustic roadhouse and tavern north of downtown (next door to Mom's Apple Pie), Red's smokes its own bacon and pastrami, bakes its own bread and serves simple, quality American cooking, using locally sourced ingredients in dishes like fried chicken and waffles, pulled-pork sandwiches, biscuits and gravy, and classic mac-n-cheese. Local beer and wine. Live music Wednesday and Friday evenings.

Hopmonk Tavern
PUB FOOD **$$**

(☎707-829-9300; www.hopmonk.com; 230 Petaluma Ave; mains $12-23; ⏰11:30am-9pm Sun-Wed, to 9:30pm Thu-Sat, bar to 1:30am; 🐾) Inside a converted 1903 railroad station, Hopmonk's serves 76 varieties of beer – served in type-specific glassware – that pair with a good menu of burgers, fried calamari, charcuterie platters and salads.

K&L Bistro
FRENCH **$$$**

(☎707-823-6614; www.klbistro.com; 119 S Main St; lunch $14-20, dinner $19-29; ⏰11am-9pm) K&L serves earthy provincial Cal-French bistro cooking in a convivial bar-and-grill space with sidewalk patio. Expect classics like mussels and French fries, and grilled steaks with red-wine reduction. Reservations essential.

Zazu Kitchen & Farm
ITALIAN, NEW AMERICAN **$$$**

(☎707-523-4814; zazukitchen.com; 6770 McKinley St, 150, The Barlow; lunch mains $13-18, dinner $24-29; ⏰11:30am-10pm Wed & Thu, to midnight Fri, from 9am Sat & Sun, from 5pm Mon) 🍃 We love the farm-to-table ethos of Zazu – they raise their own pigs and source everything locally – but some dishes miss, and the industrial-style space gets crazy loud. Still, we love their pizzas, salads, housemade salumi and bacon. Good breakfasts, too.

🍷 Drinking & Entertainment

Woodfour Brewing Co.
BREWERY

(☎707-823-3144; www.woodfourbrewing.com; 6780 Depot St, The Barlow; ⏰11am-9pm Sun-Thu, to 11pm Fri & Sat) 🍃 Woodfour's solar-powered brewery serves 12 housemade beers, light on alcohol and hops, plus several sours (high-acid beer). It has an exceptionally good menu of small plates, designed to pair with beer, from simple snacks to refined, technique-driven dishes better than any we've had at a California brewery.

Taylor Maid Farms
CAFE

(☎707-634-7129; www.taylormaidfarms.com; 6790 Depot St, The Barlow; ⏰6am-7pm Sun-Thu, to 9pm Fri & Sat) 🍃 Choose your brew method (drip, press, etc) at this third-wave coffeehouse that roasts its own organic beans. Exceptional seasonal drinks include lavender lattes.

Hardcore Espresso
CAFE

(☎707-823-7588; 1798 Gravenstein Hwy S; ⏰6am-7pm; 🛜) 🍃 Meet local hippies and art freaks over coffee and smoothies at this classic Nor-Cal, off-the-grid, indoor-outdoor coffeehouse, south of downtown, that's essentially a corrugated-metal-roofed shack surrounded by umbrella tables.

Jasper O'Farrell's
BAR

(☎707-823-1389; 6957 Sebastopol Ave; ⏰noon-2am) Busy bar with billiards and live music most nights; good drink specials.

Hopmonk Tavern
LIVE MUSIC

(☎707-829-7300; www.hopmonk.com; 230 Petaluma Ave; ⏰11:30am-11pm Sun-Wed, to midnight Thu-Sat) This always-busy tavern and beer garden has town's most diverse live-music calendar, and sometimes hosts the likes of Jonathan Richman.

🔒 Shopping

Antique shops line Gravenstein Hwy S toward Hwy 101.

Aubergine
VINTAGE

(☎707-827-3460; 755 Petaluma Ave; ⏰10am-6pm) Vast vintage emporium, specializing in cast-off European thrift-shop clothing.

Sumbody BEAUTY
(707-823-2053; www.sumbody.com; 118 N Main St; ⊗10am-7pm Mon-Wed, to 8pm Thu-Sat, to 6pm Sun) Eco-friendly bath products made with all-natural ingredients. Also offers well-priced facials ($49) and massages ($85) at its small on-site spa.

Toyworks TOYS
(707-829-2003; www.sonomatoyworks.com; 6940 Sebastopol Ave; ⊗10am-6pm Mon-Sat, 11am-5pm Sun;) Indie toy-seller with phenomenal selection of quality games for kids.

Funk & Flash CLOTHING
(707-829-1142; www.funkandflash.com; 228 S Main St; ⊗11am-7pm) Disco-glam party clothes, inspired by Burning Man.

Antique Society ANTIQUES
(707-829-1733; www.antiquesociety.com; 2661 Gravenstein Hwy S; ⊗10am-5pm) One-hundred-and-twenty-five antiques vendors under one roof.

Beekind FOOD, HOMEWARES
(707-824-2905; www.beekind.com; 921 Gravenstein Hwy S; ⊗10am-6pm Mon-Sat, to 4pm Sun) Local honey and beeswax candles.

Copperfield's Books BOOKS
(707-823-2618; www.copperfields.net; 138 N Main St; ⊗10am-7pm Mon-Sat, to 6pm Sun) Indie bookshop with literary events.

Midgley's Country Flea Market MARKET
(707-823-7874; mfleamarket.com; 2200 Gravenstein Hwy S; ⊗6:30am-4:30pm Sat & Sun) The region's largest flea market.

ⓘ Information

Sebastopol Area Chamber of Commerce & Visitors Center (877-828-4748, 707-823-3032; www.visitsebastopol.org; 265 S Main St; ⊗10am-4pm Mon-Fri) Maps, information and exhibits.

Occidental & Around

Our favorite West County town is a haven of artists, back-to-the-landers and counter-culturalists. Historic 19th-century buildings line a single main street, easy to explore in an hour; continue north by car and you'll hit the Russian River, in Monte Rio. At Christmastime, Bay Area families flock to Occidental to buy trees. The town decorates to the nines, and there's weekend cookie-decorating and caroling at the Union Hotel's Bocce Ballroom.

◉ Sights & Activities

Occidental Farmers Market MARKET
(www.occidentalfarmersmarket.com; ⊗4pm-dusk Fri Jun-Oct) Meet the whole community at Occidental's detour-worthy farmers market, with musicians, craftspeople and – the star attraction – **Gerard's Paella** (www.gerardspa-ella.com) of TV-cooking-show fame.

Sonoma Canopy Tours OUTDOORS
(888-494-7868; www.sonomacanopytours.com; 6250 Bohemian Hwy; adult $99-109, child $69) North of town, fly through the redwood canopy on seven interconnected ziplines, ending with an 80ft-rappel descent; reservations required.

Osmosis SPA
(707-823-8231; www.osmosis.com; 209 Bohemian Hwy, Freestone; ⊗by appointment) Three miles south in Freestone, tranquility prevails at this Japanese-inspired spa, which indulges patrons with dry-enzyme baths of aromatic cedar fibers (bath-and-blanket wrap $89

WORTH A TRIP

SCENIC DRIVE: COLEMAN VALLEY ROAD

Wine Country's most scenic drive isn't through the grapes, but along these 10 miles of winding West County byway, from Occidental to the sea. It's late morning, after the fog has cleared. Drive west, not east, with the sun behind you and the ocean ahead. First you'll pass through redwood forests and lush valleys where Douglas firs stand draped in sphagnum moss – an eerie sight in the fog. The real beauty shots lie further ahead, when the road ascends 1000ft hills, dotted with gnarled oaks and craggy rock formations, with the vast blue Pacific unfurling below. The road ends at coastal Hwy 1, where you can explore Sonoma Coast State Beach (p220), then turn left and find your way to the tiny town of Bodega (not Bodega Bay) to see locales where Hitchcock shot his 1963 classic, *The Birds*.

to $99), lovely tea-and-meditation gardens, plus outdoor massages. Make reservations.

🛏 Sleeping

Occidental Hotel
MOTEL $$
(☎877-867-6084, 707-874-3623; www.occidentalhotel.com; 3610 Bohemian Hwy; r $120-160, 2-bedroom q $200-240; ❋🛜🅿🐾) Rates are sometimes negotiable for these well-kept motel rooms

Valley Ford Hotel
INN $$
(☎707-876-1983; www.vfordhotel.com; r $115-175) Surrounded by pastureland 8 miles south in Valley Ford, this 19th-century, six-room inn has good beds, great rates and a terrific roadhouse restaurant.

Inn at Occidental
INN $$$
(☎707-874-1047, 800-522-6324; www.innatoccidental.com; 3657 Church St; r incl breakfast $249-339; 🐾) One of Sonoma's finest, this beautifully restored 18-room Victorian inn is filled with collectible antiques; rooms have gas fireplaces and cozy feather beds.

🍴 Eating

Howard Station Cafe
AMERICAN $
(☎707-874-2838; www.howardstationcafe.com; 3811 Bohemian Hwy; mains $6-12; ⏱7am-2:30pm Mon-Fri, to 3pm Sat & Sun; 🚼🐾) Big plates of comfort cooking and fresh-squeezed juices. Cash only.

Wild Flour Bread
BAKERY $
(www.wildflourbread.com; 140 Bohemian Hwy, Freestone; items from $3; ⏱8:30am-6:30pm Fri-Mon) Organic brick-oven sourdough breads, giant sticky buns and good coffee.

Bohemian Market
DELI $
(☎707-874-3312; 3633 Main St; ⏱8am-9pm) Occidental's best grocery store has an OK deli.

Rocker Oysterfeller's
NEW AMERICAN $$
(☎707-876-1983; www.rockeroysterfellers.com; 14415 Hwy 1, Valley Ford; mains $13-24; ⏱5pm-8:30pm Thu & Fri, from 3pm Sat, from 10am Sun) We love the flavor-rich cooking at this Valley Ford roadhouse, which features barbecued oysters, local crab cakes, steaks and fried chicken. Great wine bar, too. Sundays there's brunch.

Barley & Hops
PUB FOOD $$
(☎707-874-9037; www.barleynhops.com; 3688 Bohemian Hwy; mains $10-15; ⏱4-9:30pm Mon-Thu, from 11am Fri-Sun) Serves over 100 beers, sandwiches, giant salads and shepherd's pie.

Union Hotel
ITALIAN $$
(☎707-874-3555; www.unionhoteloccidental.com; 3703 Bohemian Hwy; meals $15-25; ⏱11am-9pm; 🚼) Occidental has two old-school American-Italian restaurants that serve family-style meals. The Union is slightly better (neither is great), and has a hard-to-beat lunch special in its 1869 saloon – whole pizza, salad and soda for $12. At dinner, sit in the fabulous Bocce Ballroom.

Bistro des Copains
FRENCH-CALIFORNIAN $$$
(☎707-874-2436; www.bistrodescopains.com; 3728 Bohemian Hwy; mains $24-26, 3-course menu $40-45; ⏱5-9pm Wed-Mon) 🌿 Worth a special trip, this convivial bistro draws bon vivants for Cal-French country cooking, like *steakfrites* and roast duck. Great wines; $10 corkage for Sonoma vintages. Make reservations.

🔒 Shopping

Verdigris
HOMEWARES
(☎707-874-9018; www.1lightartlamps.com; 72 Main St; ⏱11am-6pm Thu-Mon) Crafts gorgeous art lamps.

Hand Goods
CERAMICS
(☎707-874-2161; www.handgoods.net; 3627 Main St; ⏱10am-6pm) Collective of ceramicists and potters.

Guerneville & Around

The Russian River's biggest vacation-resort town, Guerneville gets busy summer weekends with party-hardy gay boys, sun-worshipping lesbians and long-haired, beer-drinking Harley riders, earning it the nickname 'Groin-ville.' Though the town is slowly gentrifying, it hasn't lost its honky-tonk vibe – fun-seeking crowds still come to canoe, hike redwoods and hammer cocktails poolside.

Downriver, some areas are sketchy (due to drugs). The local chamber of commerce has chased most of the tweakers from Main St in Guerneville, but if some off-the-beaten-path areas feel creepy – especially campgrounds – they probably are.

Four miles downriver, tiny Monte Rio has a sign over Hwy 116 declaring it 'Vacation Wonderland' – an overstatement, but the dog-friendly beach is a hit with families. Further west, idyllic Duncans Mills is home to a few dozen souls and has picture-ready historic buildings, now converted into cute shops. Upriver, east of Guerneville, Forestville is where agricultural country resumes.

⊙ Sights & Activities

Look for sandy beaches and swimming holes along the river; there's good river access east of town at Sunset Beach (www.sonoma-county.org/parks; 11060 River Rd, Forestville; per car $7; ⊙7am-sunset). Fishing and watercraft outfitters operate mid-May to early October, after which winter rains dangerously swell the river. A farmers market meets downtown on Wednesdays, June through September, from 3pm to 7pm. On summer Saturdays, there's also one at Monte Rio Beach, 11am to 2pm.

Armstrong Redwoods
State Natural Reserve FOREST
(☑information 707-869-2015, office 707-869-9177, visitor center 707-869-2958; www.parks.ca.gov; 17000 Armstrong Woods Rd; per car $8; ⊙8am-sunset; ▣) A magnificent redwood forest 2 miles north of Guerneville, the 805-acre Armstrong Redwoods State Reserve was saved from the saw by a 19th-century lumber magnate. Short interpretive trails lead into magical forests, with trees 30-stories high. Beyond lie 20 miles of backcountry trails, through oak woodlands, in adjoining Austin Creek State Recreation Area, one of Sonoma County's last-remaining wilderness areas. Walk or cycle in for free; pay only to park.

Burke's Canoe Trips CANOEING
(☑707-887-1222; www.burkescanoetrips.com; 8600 River Rd, Forestville; canoe/kayak rental incl shuttle $65/45; ⊙10am-6pm Mon-Fri, 9am-6pm Sat & Sun) You can't beat Burke's for a day on the river. Self-guided canoe and kayak trips include shuttle back to your car. Make reservations; plan four hours. Camping in its riverside redwood grove costs $10 per person.

R3 Hotel Pool SWIMMING
(Triple R; ☑707-869-8399; www.ther3hotel.com; 16390 4th St, Guerneville; ⊙9am-midnight) FREE The gay, adults-only, party-scene swimming pool at the Triple R is free, provided you buy drinks. Bring your own towel. Bathing suits mandatory, but only because state liquor-license laws require them.

Pee Wee Golf & Arcade GOLF, CYCLING
(☑707-869-9321; 16155 Drake Rd at Hwy 116, Guerneville; 18/36 holes $8/12; ⊙11am-10pm Jun-Aug, to 5pm Sat & Sun May & Sep; ▣) Flashback to 1948 at this impeccably kept, retro-kitsch, 36-hole miniature golf course, just south of the Hwy 116 bridge, with brilliantly painted obstacles, including T Rex and Yogi Bear.

Bring your own cocktails; also rents gas barbecue grills ($20).

King's Sport &
Tackle FISHING, KAYAKING, CANOEING
(☑707-869-2156; www.kingsrussianriver.com; 16258 Main St, Guerneville; ⊙8am-6pm) *The* local source for fishing and river-condition information. Also rents kayaks ($35 to $55), canoes ($55) and fishing gear.

River Rider BICYCLE RENTAL
(☑707-483-2897; www.riverridersrentals.com; half-/full-day rental $25/45; ⊙7am-7pm) Delivers bicycles, along with wine-tasting passes on request; discounts for multiday rentals.

Johnson's Beach WATER SPORTS
(☑707-869-2022; www.johnsonsbeach.com; 16241 First St, Guerneville; kayak & canoe per hr/day $10/30; ⊙10am-6pm May-Sep; ▣) Canoe, paddleboat and watercraft rental (from $30). Beach admission free, and you can camp here.

Northwood Golf Course GOLF
(☑707-865-1116; www.northwoodgolf.com; 19400 Hwy 116, Monte Rio; walking $25-27, riding $33-35, 9 holes $25-35, 18 holes $35-53; ⊙7:30am-sunset) Vintage-1920s Alistair MacKenzie–designed, par-36, nine-hole course.

✯ Festivals & Events

Monte Rio Variety Show MUSIC
(www.monterioshow.org) Members of the elite, secretive Bohemian Grove (Google it) perform publicly, sometimes showcasing unannounced celebrities, in July.

Lazy Bear Weekend CULTURAL
(www.lazybearweekend.com) Read: heavy, furry gay men; August.

Russian River Jazz & Blues Festival MUSIC
(www.russianriverfestivals.com) A day of jazz, followed by a day of blues in September, with occasional luminaries like BB King.

⊨ Sleeping

Russian River has few budget sleeps; prices drop midweek. For weekends and holidays, book ahead. Many places have no TVs. Because the river sometimes floods, some lodgings have cold linoleum floors: pack slippers.

Guerneville

Staying downtown means you can walk to restaurants and bars.

Guerneville Lodge
CAMPGROUND $

(707-869-0102; www.guernevillelodge.com; 15905 River Rd; tent sites $40) The prettiest place to camp in downtown Guerneville is behind this retreat-center lodge, on sprawling grassy lawns fronting on the river. Amenities: hot clean showers, big campsites, refrigerator access, fire pits with grills. When available, lodge rooms cost $189 to $229.

Bullfrog Pond Campground
CAMPGROUND $

(Mon-Fri reservations & information 707-869-9177, Sat & Sun ranger kiosk 707-869-2015; www.stewardscr.org; sites reserved/non-reserved $35/25;) Reached via a steep road from Armstrong Redwoods State Natural Reserve, 4 miles from the entrance kiosk, Bullfrog Pond has forested campsites, with cold water, and primitive hike-in and equestrian backcountry campsites. Reserve via www.hipcamp.com or by phone.

Schoolhouse Canyon Campground
CAMPGROUND $

(707-869-2311; www.schoolhousecanyon.com; 12600 River Rd; tent sites $30;) Two miles east of Guerneville, Schoolhouse's well-tended sites lie beneath tall trees, across the main road from the river. Coin-operated hot showers, clean bathrooms, quiet by night.

Johnson's Beach Resort
CABIN, CAMPGROUND $

(707-869-2022; www.johnsonsbeach.com; 16241 1st St; tent sites $25, RV sites $25-35, cabins $75, per week $400) On the river in Guerneville, Johnson's has rustic, but clean, thin-walled cabins on stilts; all have kitchens. Bring earplugs. There's camping, too, but it's loud. No credit cards.

Fern Grove Cottages
CABIN $$

(707-869-8105; www.ferngrove.com; 16650 River Rd; cabins incl breakfast $159-219, with kitchen $199-269; @) Downtown Guerneville's cheeriest resort, Fern Grove has vintage-1930s pine-paneled cabins, tucked beneath redwoods and surrounded by lush flowering gardens. Some have Jacuzzis and fireplaces. The pool uses salt, not chlorine; the lovely English innkeeper provides concierge services; and breakfast includes homemade scones.

Highlands Resort
CABIN, CAMPGROUND $$

(707-869-0333; www.highlandsresort.com; 14000 Woodland Dr; tent sites $20-30, r with bath $90-100, without $70-80, cabins $120-205;) Guerneville's mellowest all-gay resort sits on a wooded hillside, walkable to town, and has simply furnished rooms, little cottages with porches and good camping. The large pool and hot tub are clothing-optional (weekday/weekend day use $10/15).

R3 Hotel
RESORT $$

(Triple R; 707-869-8399; www.ther3hotel.com; 16390 4th St; r Mon-Fri $80-150, Sat & Sun $105-215;) Ground zero for party-hardy gay lads and lesbians, Triple-R (as it's known) has plain-Jane, motel-style rooms surrounding a bar and pool deck that get so crowded summer weekends, management won't allow guests to bring pets because 'they get hurt' (actual quote). Come for the scene, not for quiet (light sleepers: bring ear plugs). Midweek it's mellow, wintertime dead.

Riverlane Resort
CABIN $$

(707-869-2323, 800-201-2324; www.riverlaneresort.com; 16320 1st St; cabins $90-140;) Right downtown, Riverlane has basic cabins with kitchens, decorated with mismatched furniture, but they're very clean and have decks with barbecues. Best for no-frills travelers or campers wanting an upgrade. Heated pool, private beach and hot tub.

Applewood Inn
INN $$$

(800-555-8509, 707-869-9093; www.applewoodinn.com; 13555 Hwy 116; r incl breakfast $215-345; @) A hideaway estate on a wooded hilltop south of town, cushy Applewood has marvelous 1920s-era detail, with dark wood and heavy furniture that echo the forest. Rooms have Jacuzzis, couples' showers and top-end linens; some have fireplaces. Small on-site spa.

Boon Hotel + Spa
BOUTIQUE HOTEL $$$

(707-869-2721; www.boonhotels.com; 14711 Armstrong Woods Rd; r $165-275;) Rooms surround a swimming-pool courtyard (with Jacuzzi) at this mid-century-modern, 14-room motel-resort, gussied up in minimalist style. The look is austere but fresh, with organic-cotton linens and spacious rooms; most have wood-burning fireplaces. Drive to town, or ride the free bicycles.

Santa Nella House
B&B $$$

(707-869-9488; www.santanellahouse.com; 12130 Hwy 116; r incl breakfast $199-219; @) All four spotless rooms at this 1871 Victorian, south of town, have wood-burning fireplaces and frilly Victorian furnishings. Upstairs rooms are biggest. Outside there's a hot tub and sauna. Best for travelers who appreciate the B&B aesthetic.

Forestville

Raford Inn B&B $$$
(☑800-887-9503, 707-887-9573; http://rafordinn.
com; 10630 Wohler Rd, Healdsburg; r $185-270;
※@☎🐾) 🐾 We love this 1880 Victorian
B&B's secluded hilltop location, surround-
ed by tall palms and rambling vineyards.
Rooms are big and airy, done with lace and
antiques; some have fireplaces. And wow,
those sunset views.

Farmhouse Inn INN $$$
(☑800-464-6642, 707-887-3300; www.farm-
houseinn.com; 7871 River Rd; r $445-795;
※@☎🐾) Think love nest. The area's premier inn has spacious rooms and cottages,
styled with cushy amenities like saunas,
steam-showers and wood-burning fireplaces. Small on-site spa and top-notch restaurant. Check in early to maximize time.

Monte Rio

Village Inn INN $$
(☑707-865-2304; www.villageinn-ca.com; 20822
River Blvd; r $145-235; ☎) 🐾 A retired con-
cierge owns this cute, old-fashioned, 11-room
inn, beneath towering trees, right on the
river. Some rooms have river views; all have
fridge and microwave. No elevator.

Rio Villa Beach Resort INN $$
(☑877-746-8455, 707-865-1143; www.riovilla.com;
20292 Hwy 116; r with kitchen $149-209, without
$139-189; ※☎🐾) Landscaping is lush at this
small riverside resort with excellent sun exposure (you see redwoods, but you're not under them). Rooms are well kept but simple
(request a quiet room, not by the road); the
emphasis is on the outdoors, evident by the
large riverside terrace, outdoor fireplace and
barbecues. Some air-con.

Highland Dell INN $$
(☑707-865-2300; highlanddell.com; 21050 River
Blvd; r $109-179; ☺Apr-Nov; ※☎) 🐾 Built in
1906 in grand lodge style, redone in 2007,
the inn fronts right on the river. Above
the giant dining room are 12 bright, fresh-
looking rooms with comfy beds. No elevator.

Duncans Mills

Casini Ranch CAMPGROUND $
(☑800-451-8400, 707-865-2255; www.casin-
iranch.com; 22855 Moscow Rd; tent sites $45-52,
RV sites partial hookups $47-58, full hookups $53-
56; ☎※) In quiet Duncans Mills, beautifully

set on riverfront ranchlands, Casini is an
enormous, well-run campground. Amenities
include kayaks and paddleboats (day use $5
to $10); bathrooms are spotless.

🍴 Eating

Guerneville

There's a good taco truck, in the Safeway
parking lot at 16451 Main St.

Big Bottom Market MARKET, CAFE $
(☑707-604-7295; www.bigbottommarket.com;
16228 Main St; sandwiches $7-10; ☺8am-5pm
Sun-Thu, to 6pm Fri & Sat) 🐾 Gourmet deli and
wine shop with scrumptuous pastries and
grab-and-go picnic supplies.

Coffee Bazaar CAFE $
(☑707-869-9706; www.mycoffeeb.com; 14045
Armstrong Woods Rd; dishes $5-9; ☺6am-8pm;
☎) Happening cafe with salads, sandwiches
and all-day breakfasts; adjoins a good used
bookstore.

Taqueria La Tapatia MEXICAN $
(☑707-869-1821; 16632 Main St; mains $7-14;
☺11am-9pm) Reasonable choice for tradi-
tional Mexican.

Garden Grill BARBECUE $
(☑707-869-3922; www.gardengrillbbq.com; 17132
Hwy 116, Guerneewood Park; mains $6-12; ☺8am-
8pm) One mile west of Guerneville, this road-
house barbecue joint, with redwood-shaded
patio, serves good house-smoked meats, but
the fries could be better. Breakfast till 3pm.

Food for Humans MARKET $
(☑707-869-3612; 16385 1st St; ☺9am-8pm; 🐾)
🐾 Organic groceries; better alternative than
neighboring Safeway, but no meat.

Seaside Metal Oyster Bar SEAFOOD $$
(☑707-604-7250; seasidemetal.com; 16222 Main
St; dishes $11-16; ☺5-10pm Wed-Sun) Unexpect-
edly urban for Guerneville, this storefront
raw bar is an offshoot of San Francisco's Bar
Crudo – one of the city's best – and showcases oysters, clams, lobster and exquisitely
prepared raw-fish dishes. There's limited hot
food, but it's overwrought: stick to raw.

**Dick Blomster's
Korean Diner** KOREAN, AMERICAN $$
(☑707-896-8006; 16236 Main St; mains $15-20;
☺5-10pm Sun-Thu, to 2am Fri & Sat Jun-Aug, to
11pm Fri & Sat Sep-May) By day a vintage-1940s
coffee shop, by night a Korean-American

diner with full bar, Dick Blomster's serves playfully tongue-in-cheek dishes, including fried PB&J sandwiches and 'the other KFC – Korean fried crack' – fried chicken with sugary-sweet brown sauce, which sure hits the spot after a night's drinking.

Boon Eat + Drink CALIFORNIAN $$$
(☑707-869-0780; http://eatatboon.com; 16248 Main St; lunch mains $14-18, dinner $15-26; ⊙11am-3pm Mon, Tue, Thu & Fri, 5-9pm Mon-Fri, 10am-3pm & 5-10pm Sat & Sun) Locally sourced ingredients inform the seasonal, Cali-smart cooking at this tiny, always-packed, New American bistro, with cheek-by-jowl tables that fill every night. Make reservations or expect to wait.

Applewood Inn Restaurant CALIFORNIAN $$$
(☑707-869-9093; www.applewoodinn.com; 13555 Hwy 116; mains $20-28; ⊙5:30-8:30pm Wed-Sun) Cozy up by the fire in the treetop-level dining room and sup on quality Euro-Cal cooking that maximizes seasonal produce, with dishes like rack of lamb with minted *chimichuri* (garlic-parsley vinaigrette) and smoked trout with corn and crayfish. Sunday nights there's a $35 prix-fixe menu. Reservations essential.

Forestville

Canneti Roadhouse ITALIAN $$
(☑707-887-2232; http://cannetirestaurant.com; 6675 Front St; lunch mains $12-24, dinner $15-28; ⊙11:30am-3pm Wed-Sat, to 5pm Sun, 5:30-9pm Tue-Sun) 🍴 A Tuscan-born chef makes bona fide *cucina Italiana*, using quality ingredients from local farms, at this austere restaurant in downtown Forestville, worth the 15-minute drive from Guerneville. The menu ranges from simple brick-oven pizzas to an all-Tuscan, five-course tasting menu ($55, dinner only). When it's warm, sit on the patio beneath a giant redwood. Make reservations.

Farmhouse Inn NEW AMERICAN $$$
(☑707-887-3300; www.farmhouseinn.com; 7871 River Rd; 3-/4-course dinner $69/84; ⊙from 5.30pm Thu-Mon) 🍴 Special-occasion worthy, Michelin-starred Farmhouse changes its seasonal Euro-Cal menu daily using locally raised, organic ingredients like Sonoma lamb, wild salmon and rabbit – the latter is the house specialty. Details are impeccable, from aperitifs in the garden to tableside cheese service, but detractors call it precious. Make reservations.

Monte Rio

Don's Dogs FAST FOOD $
(☑707-865-4190; cnr Bohemian Hwy & Hwy 116; sandwiches $4-12; ⊙9am-4pm Thu-Mon Oct-May, to 7pm daily Jun-Sep; ☎) Gourmet hot dogs, wine, beer, simple breakfasts and coffee, behind the Rio Theater.

Highland Dell GERMAN $$$
(☑707-865-2300; http://highlanddell.com; 21050 River Blvd; mains $20-22; ⊙4-10pm Fri-Tue Apr-Nov) A dramatic, three-story-high, chalet-style dining room with a river-view deck, Highland Dell makes pretty good German-inspired cooking, including steaks and schnitzel. Full bar.

Village Inn AMERICAN $$$
(☑707-865-2304; www.villageinn-ca.com; 20822 River Blvd; mains $19-26; ⊙5-8pm Wed-Sun) The straightforward steaks-and-seafood menu is basic American and doesn't distract from the wonderful river views. Great local wine list, full bar.

Duncans Mills

Cape Fear Cafe AMERICAN $$
(☑707-865-9246; 25191 Main St; lunch mains $9-15, dinner $15-25; ⊙10am-8pm Mon & Thu, to 3pm Tue & Wed, to 9pm Fri-Sun) A country-Americana diner in a 19th-century grange, Cape Fear is visually charming, but it's erratic – except at weekend brunch, when the kitchen makes excellent Benedicts. Good stopover en route to the coast.

🍷 Drinking & Nightlife

Stumptown Brewery BREWERY
(www.stumptown.com; 15045 River Rd, Guerneville; ⊙11am-midnight Sun-Thu, to 2am Fri & Sat) Guerneville's best straight bar, 1 mile east of downtown, is gay-friendly and has a foot-stompin' jukebox, billiards, riverside beer garden, and several homemade brews. Pretty-good pub grub includes house-smoked barbecue.

Rainbow Cattle Company GAY
(www.queersteer.com; 16220 Main St, Guerneville; ⊙noon-midnight Sun-Thu, to 2am Fri & Sat) The stalwart gay watering hole has pinball and shuffleboard.

Sophie's Cellars WINE BAR
(☑707-865-1122; www.sophiescellars.com; 25179 Main St/Hwy 116, Duncans Mills; glasses $7-15; ⊙11am-5pm Mon, Thu, Sat & Sun, to 7pm Fri) The

perfect stopover between river and coast, Sophie's rural wine bar, in Duncans Mills, pours glasses and tastes of local wine, and carries cheese, salami and a well-curated selection of bottles. Friday's 'locals happy hour' (4pm to 7pm) brings hors d'oeuvres, drink specials and a big crowd.

☆ Entertainment

Rio Theater   CINEMA
(☎707-865-0913; www.riotheater.com; cnr Bohemian Hwy & Hwy 116, Monte Rio; adult/child $8/5; 👪) Dinner and a movie take on new meaning at this vintage-WWII Quonset hut converted to a cinema in 1950, with a concession stand serving gourmet hot dogs with a drink and chips for just $7. In 2014 they finally added heating, but still supply blankets. Only in Monte Rio. Shows nightly (and sometimes Sunday afternoons), but call ahead, especially off-season.

Main Street Station   CABARET
(☎707-869-0501; www.mainststation.com; 16280 Main St, Guerneville; ⊙7-10pm or 11pm; 👪) FREE Hosts live acoustic-only jazz, blues and cabaret nightly in summer (weekends in winter), and families are welcome because the cabaret doubles as an American-Italian restaurant (stick to pizza).

Rio Nido Roadhouse   LIVE MUSIC
(☎707-869-0821; www.rionidoroadhouse.com; 14540 Canyon Two, Rio Nido) Raucous roadhouse bar, off River Rd, 4 miles east of Guerneville, with eclectic lineup of live bands. Shows start 6pm Saturday and sometimes Friday and Sunday, too; check website.

🛍 Shopping

Eight miles west of Guerneville, tiny Duncans Mills (pop 85) has good shopping in a handful of side-by-side businesses within weathered 19th-century cottages.

Mr Trombly's Tea & Table   FOOD & DRINK
(www.mrtromblystea.com; 25185 Main St, Duncans Mills; ⊙10am-5pm Sun-Thu, to 6pm Sat & Sun) Different kinds of tea and teapots, plus quality kitchen gadgets and well-priced tableware.

Pig Alley   JEWELRY
(☎707-865-2698; www.pigalleyshop.com; 25193 Main St, Duncans Mills; ⊙10:30am-5:30pm) Vast selection of handcrafted American-made jewelry, notable for gorgeous earrings.

ℹ Information

Russian River Chamber of Commerce & Visitors Center (☎707-869-9000, 877-644-9001; www.russianriver.com; 16209 1st St, Guerneville; ⊙10am-4:45pm Mon-Sat, plus 10am-3pm Sun May-Sep) For information and lodging referrals.

Russian River Visitors Center (☎707-869-4096; ⊙10am-3pm Oct-Apr, to 4pm May-Sep) At Korbel Cellars.

Santa Rosa

Wine Country's biggest city and the Sonoma County seat, Santa Rosa claims two famous native sons – a world-renowned cartoonist and a celebrated horticulturalist – whose legacies include museums and gardens enough to keep you busy for an afternoon. Otherwise, there ain't much to do, unless you need your car fixed or you're here in July during the Sonoma County Fair (www.sonomacountyfair.com), at the fairgrounds on Bennett Valley Rd. Santa Rosa is mostly known for traffic and suburban sprawl. It generally lacks charm (except downtown, where redwood trees serve as landscaping and tower over buildings), but has reasonably priced accommodations and easy access to Sonoma County and Valley.

◉ Sights & Activities

The main shopping stretch is 4th St, which abruptly ends at Hwy 101, but re-emerges across the freeway at historic Railroad Sq. Downtown parking garages (75¢ hour, $8 max) are cheaper than street parking. East of town, 4th St becomes Hwy 12 into Sonoma Valley.

Luther Burbank Home & Gardens   GARDENS
(☎707-524-5445; www.lutherburbank.org; cnr Santa Rosa & Sonoma Aves; ⊙8am-dusk) FREE Pioneering horticulturist Luther Burbank (1849–1926) developed many hybrid plant species, including the Shasta daisy, here at his 19th-century, Greek-revival home. The extensive gardens are lovely. The house and adjacent Carriage Museum (guided tour adult/child $7/free; ⊙10am-3:30pm Tue-Sun Apr-Oct) have displays on Burbank's life and work, you can take a self-guided cell phone tour for free. Across the street from Burbank's home, Julliard Park has a playground.

Charles M Schulz Museum
MUSEUM

(📞707-579-4452; www.schulzmuseum.org; 2301 Hardies Lane; adult/child $10/5; ⏰11am-5pm Mon & Wed-Fri, 10am-5pm Sat & Sun; 🚻) Charles Schulz, Santa Rosa resident and creator of *Peanuts* cartoons, was born in 1922, published his first drawing in 1937, introduced Snoopy and Charlie Brown in 1950, and produced *Peanuts* cartoons until his death in 2000. This modern museum honors his legacy with a Snoopy labyrinth, *Peanuts*-related art, and a re-creation of Schulz's studio. Skip Snoopy's Gallery gift shop; the museum has the good stuff.

Farmers Markets
MARKET

(4th & B Sts; ⏰5-8:30pm Wed mid-May–Aug) Sonoma County's largest farmers market. Another year-round market meets 8:30am to 1pm Saturdays at Santa Rosa Veterans Building, 1351 Maple Ave.

Redwood Empire Ice Arena
SKATING

(📞707-546-7147; www.snoopyshomeice.com; 1667 West Steele Lane; adult incl skates $9-12, child $7-10; 🚻) This skating rink was formerly owned and deeply loved by Schulz. It's open most afternoons (call for schedules). Bring a sweater.

Children's Museum of Sonoma County
SCIENCE CENTER

(📞707-546-4069; www.cmosc.org; 1835 Steele Lane; admission $7; ⏰9am-4pm Tue-Sat, noon-4pm Sun; 🚻) Geared to little children 10 and under, this happy learning center inspires discovery, exploration and creativity with hands-on exhibits, most outdoors, focused on nature and science. Picnicking welcome. No adults without kids.

🛌 Sleeping

Find chain hotels near Railroad Sq. Nothing-special motels line Cleveland Ave, fronting Hwy 101's western side, between the Steele Lane and Bicentennial Lane exits; skip Motel 6. Nearby Windsor has two chain hotels (Hampton Inn and Holiday Inn) off Hwy 101 at exit 'Central Windsor.'

Spring Lake Park
CAMPGROUND $

(📞707-539-8092, reservations 707-565-2267; www.sonomacountyparks.org; 5585 Newanga Ave; sites $32; 🛁) 🍴 Lovely lakeside park, 4 miles from downtown; make reservations ($8.50 fee) online or 10am to 3pm weekdays by phone. The park is open year-round, with lake swimming in summer; the campground operates May to September, weekends Oc-

---

OLIVE-OIL TASTING

When you weary of wine-tasting, pop by one of the following olive-oil makers and dip some crusty bread – it's free. Harvest and pressing happen in November.

➡ BR Cohn (p186)

➡ Napa Valley Olive Oil Mfg Co (p171)

➡ Long Meadow Ranch (p165)

➡ Figone's Olive Oil (p195)

tober to April. Take 4th St eastbound, turn right on Farmer's Lane, pass the first Hoen St and turn left on the second Hoen St, then left on Newanga Ave.

Hillside Inn
MOTEL $

(📞707-546-9353; www.hillside-inn.com; 2901 4th St; s/d Nov-Mar $70/82, Apr-Oct $74/86; 📶🛁) Santa Rosa's best-value motel, Hillside is close to Sonoma Valley; add $4 for kitchens. Furnishings are dated and service peculiar, but everything is scrupulously maintained. Adjoins an excellent breakfast cafe.

Hotel La Rose
HISTORIC HOTEL $$

(📞707-579-3200; www.hotellarose.com; 308 Wilson St; r Mon-Fri $139-199, Sat & Sun $159-229; ❄📶) 🍴 At Railroad Sq, Hotel La Rose has rooms in a well-kept historic 1907 brick hotel, and across the street in a 1980s-built 'carriage house,' which feels like a small condo complex with boxy, spacious rooms. All are decorated in out-of-fashion pastels, but have excellent beds with quality linens and down duvets; some have jetted tubs.

Flamingo Resort Hotel
HOTEL $$

(📞800-848-8300, 707-545-8530; www.flamingoresort.com; 2777 4th St; r $159-269; ❄@📶🛁🐕) 🍴 Sprawling over 11 acres, this mid-century modern hotel doubles as a conference center. Rooms are business-class-generic, but the pool is gigantic – and kept 82°F year-round. Kids love it. On-site health-club and gym. Prices double summer weekends.

Best Western Garden Inn
MOTEL $$

(📞888-256-8004, 707-546-4031; www.thegarden-inn.com; 1500 Santa Rosa Ave; r Mon-Fri $119-139, Sat & Sun $199-229; ❄@📶🛁🐕) Well-kept motel, south of downtown, with two pools. Rear rooms open to grassy gardens, but you may hear kids in the pool; book up front for quiet. The street gets seedy by night, but the hotel is secure, clean and comfortable.

Vintners Inn　　　　　　　　INN $$$
(☎ 800-421-2584, 707-575-7350; www.vintnersinn.com; 4350 Barnes Rd; r $245-495; ❋@☎) 🍴 Surrounded by vineyards north of town (near River Rd), Vintner's Inn caters to the gated-community crowd with business-classy amenities. Jacuzzi, no pool. Check for last-minute specials.

🍴 Eating

Jeffrey's Hillside Cafe　　　　AMERICAN $
(www.jeffreyshillsidecafe.com; 2901 4th St; dishes $8-12; ⏱ 7am-2pm; 🏠) 🍴 East of downtown, near Sonoma Valley, chef-owned Jeffrey's is excellent for breakfast or brunch before wine-tasting.

Rosso Pizzeria & Wine Bar　　PIZZA $$
(☎ 707-544-3221; www.rossopizzeria.com; 53 Montgomery St, Creekside Shopping Centre; pizzas $13-17; ⏱ 11am-10pm; 🏠) 🍴 Fantastic wood-fired pizzas, inventive salads and standout wines make Rosso worth seeking out.

Naked Pig　　　　　　　　CAFE $$
(☎ 707-978-3231; 435 Santa Rosa Ave; mains $11-14; ⏱ 8am-3pm Wed-Sun) 🍴 This tiny cafe in a former bus depot makes everything from scratch and serves simple-delicious, farm-to-table breakfasts and lunches at communal tables.

El Coqui　　　　　　　CARIBBEAN $$
(☎ 707-542-8868; http://elcoqui2eat.com; 400 Mendocino Ave; lunch mains $10-14, dinner $14-19; ⏱ 11am-10pm Mon-Sat, noon-9pm Sun) Unique in Wine Country, El Coqui serves yummy Puerto Rican food, including stuffed plantains. Beer and wine.

Spinster Sisters　　　　CALIFORNIAN $$$
(☎ 707-528-7100; www.thespinstersisters.com; 401 South A St; lunch mains $10-16, dinner $23-26; ⏱ 8am-3pm Mon, to 10pm Tue-Fri, 9am-10pm Sat & Sun) 🍴 At Santa Rosa's culinary vanguard, this casual market-driven restaurant makes its own bagels, cheese and charcuterie meats. The diverse tapas-like small plates ($7 to $14) pair well with the extensive wine list.

🍷 Drinking & Nightlife

⭐ **Russian River Brewing Co**　　BREWERY
(www.russianriverbrewing.com; 729 4th St; ⏱ 11am-midnight Sun-Thu, to 1am Fri & Sat) Santa Rosa's justly famous brewery crafts outstanding double IPA, called Pliny the Elder,

plus top-grade sour beer aged in wine barrels. Good pizza and pub grub, too.

ℹ️ Information

California Welcome Center & Santa Rosa Visitors Bureau (☎ 800-404-7673, 707-577-8674; www.visitsantarosa.com; 9 4th St; ⏱ 9am-5pm Mon-Sat, 10am-5pm Sun) Same-day lodging assistance. At Railroad Sq, west of Hwy 101; take downtown exit from Hwy 12 or 101.

Santa Rosa Memorial Hospital (☎ 707-546-3210; 1165 Montgomery St)

Healdsburg & Around

Once a sleepy ag town best known for its Future Farmers of America parade, Healdsburg has emerged as northern Sonoma County's culinary capital. Foodie-scenester restaurants and cafes, wine-tasting rooms and fancy boutiques line Healdsburg Plaza, the town's sun-dappled central square (bordered by Healdsburg Ave and Center, Matheson and Plaza Sts). Traffic grinds to a halt summer weekends, when second-home-owners and tourists jam downtown. Old-timers aren't happy with the Napa-style gentrification, but at least Healdsburg retains its historic look, if not its once-quiet summers. It's best visited weekdays – stroll tree-lined streets, sample locavore cooking and soak up the NorCal flavor.

👁 Sights

Tasting rooms surround the plaza. Free summer concerts play Tuesday afternoons.

Healdsburg Museum　　　　　MUSEUM
(☎ 707-431-3325; www.healdsburgmuseum.org; 221 Matheson St, Healdsburg; donation requested; ⏱ 11am-4pm Wed-Sun) Exhibits include compelling installations on northern Sonoma County history, with an emphasis on Healdsburg. Pick up the walking-tour pamphlet.

Healdsburg Public Library　　LIBRARY
(☎ 707-433-3772; sonomalibrary.org; cnr Piper & Center Sts; ⏱ 10am-6pm Tue, Thu & Fri, to 8pm Wed, to 4pm Sat) Wine Country's leading oenology-reference library.

Healdsburg Veterans Memorial Beach　　　　　BEACH
(☎ 707-433-1625; www.sonomacountyparks.org; 13839 Healdsburg Ave, Healdsburg; parking $7; ⏱ 7am-sunset; 🏠) You can swim at this beach – lifeguards are on duty summer weekends –

but if you're squeamish, confirm current water quality online (www.sonoma-county.org/health/services/freshwater.asp).

Locals Tasting Room
TASTING ROOM

(☎707-857-4900; www.tastelocalwines.com; Geyserville Ave & Hwy 128, Geyserville; ☺11am-6pm) **FREE** Eight miles north of Healdsburg, tiny Geyserville is home to this indie tasting room, which represents 12 small-production wineries with free tastings.

Farmers Markets
MARKET

(www.healdsburgfarmersmarket.org; Healdsburg) Discover Healdsburg's agricultural abundance at the **Tuesday market** (cnr Vine & North Sts; ☺3:30pm-6pm Wed Jun-Oct) and **Saturday market** (☺9am-noon Sat May-Nov), the latter held one block west of the plaza.

🏃 Activities

After you've walked around the plaza, there isn't much to do in town. Go wine-tasting in Dry Creek Valley or Russian River Valley (p195). Bicycling on winding West Dry Creek Rd is brilliant, as is paddling the Russian River, which runs through town. Rent bikes from Spoke Folk Cyclery (p163).

Coppola Winery Swimming Pool
SWIMMING, WINERY

(☎707-857-1400, 877-590-3329; www.francisfordcoppolawinery.com; 300 Via Archimedes, Geyserville; adult/child $30/15; ☺11am-6pm daily Jun-Sep, Fri-Sun Apr, May & Oct; ⊕) The two huge interconnected pools at Francis Ford Coppola Winery are a glam way to spend a hot day with kids. To ensure admission, reserve in advance a cabine ($135), which includes chairs for four and wine-tasting passes; day passes include towel and lawn seating, not chairs; summer weekends sell out immediately – arrive before 10:45am.

Russian River Adventures
CANOEING

(☎707-433-5599; russianriveradventures.com; 20 Healdsburg Ave, Healdsburg; adult/child $50/25; ⊕⊛) Paddle a secluded stretch of river in quiet inflatable canoes, stopping for rope swings, swimming holes, beaches and bird-watching. This ecotourism outfit points you in the right direction and shuttles you back at day's end. Or they'll guide your kids downriver while you go wine-tasting (guides $125 per day). Reservations required.

Getaway Adventures
CYCLING, KAYAKING

(☎800-499-2453, 707-763-3040; www.getawayadventures.com) Guides spectacular morning

vineyard cycling in Dry Creek Valley, followed by lunch and optional kayaking on Russian River ($150 to $175).

River's Edge Kayak & Canoe Trips
BOATING

(☎707-433-7247; www.riversedgekayakandcanoe.com; 13840 Healdsburg Ave, Healdsburg) Rents hard-sided canoes ($90/110 per half/full day) and kayaks ($40/55). Self-guided rentals include shuttle.

🎓 Courses

The Shed
COURSE

(☎707-431-7433; healdsburgshed.com; 25 North St, Healdsburg) 🍴 Healdsburg's culinary center (p212) leads classes and workshop on topics related to food and sustainability, from seed-saving and bee-keeping, to home-brewing and kombucha-fermenting. Also hosts important lecturers, such as Michael Pollan.

Relish Culinary Adventures
COOKING COURSE

(☎707-431-9999, 877-759-1004; www.relishculinary.com; 14 Matheson St, Healdsburg; ☺by appointment) Plug into the locavore food scene with culinary day trips, demo-kitchen classes or winemaker dinners.

✨ Festivals & Events

Russian River Wine Road Barrel Tasting
WINE

(www.wineroad.com) Sample wine, directly from the cask, before it's bottled or released for sale, in March.

Future Farmers Parade
CULTURAL

(www.healdsburgfair.org) The whole town shows up for this classic-Americana farm parade in May.

Wine & Food Affair
FOOD

(www.wineroad.com/events) Special food and wine pairings at over 100 wineries in November.

🛏 Sleeping

Healdsburg is expensive: demand exceeds supply. Rates drop winter to spring, but not significantly. Guerneville is much less expensive, and just 20 minutes away. Most Healdsburg inns are within walking distance of the plaza; several B&Bs are in surrounding countryside. Find motels at Hwy 101's Dry Creek exit.

Cloverdale Wine Country KOA
CAMPGROUND $

(☎800-368-4558, 707-894-3337; www.winecountrykoa.com; 1166 Asti Ridge Rd, Cloverdale; tent/RV sites from $50/65, 1-/2-bedroom cabins $85/95;

🛜 🚰 🐕) Six miles from central Cloverdale (exit 520) off Hwy 101; hot showers, pool, hot tub, laundry, paddleboats and bicycles.

L&M Motel
MOTEL **$$**

(☎707-433-6528; www.landmmotel.com; 70 Healdsburg Ave, Healdsburg; r $150-180; ❄🛜🚰🐕) Simple, clean, old-fashioned motel, with big lawns and barbecue grills, great for families. Dry sauna and Jacuzzi. Winter rates plummet.

Geyserville Inn
MOTEL **$$**

(☎877-857-4343, 707-857-4343; www.geyservilleinn.com; 21714 Geyserville Ave, Geyserville; r Mon-Fri $129-169, Sat & Sun $269-289; ❄🛜🚰🐕) Eight miles north of Healdsburg, this immaculately kept upmarket motel is surrounded by vineyards. Rooms have unexpectedly smart furnishings and quality extras, like feather pillows. Request a remodeled room. Hot tub.

Best Western Dry Creek
MOTEL **$$**

(☎707-433-0300; www.drycreekinn.com; 198 Dry Creek Rd, Healdsburg; r Mon-Fri $109-149, Sat & Sun $219-319; ❄@🛜🚰) This generic midrange motel has good service and an outdoor hot tub. New rooms have jetted tubs and gas fireplaces.

Hotel Healdsburg
HOTEL **$$$**

(☎707-431-2800, 800-889-7188; www.hotelhealdsburg.com; 25 Matheson St, Healdsburg; r incl breakfast from $450; ❄@🛜🚰) Smack on the plaza, the fashion-forward HH has a coolly minimalist style of concrete and velvet, with requisite top-end amenities, including sumptuous beds and extra-deep tubs. Full-service spa.

H2 Hotel
HOTEL **$$$**

(☎707-431-2202, 707-922-5251; www.h2hotel.com; 219 Healdsburg Ave, Healdsburg; r incl breakfast Mon-Fri $289-389, Sat & Sun $409-509; ❄@🛜🚰) 🌿 Little sister to Hotel Healdsburg, H2 has the same angular concrete style, but was built LEED-gold-certified from the ground up, with a living roof, reclaimed everything, and fresh-looking rooms with cush organic linens. Tiny pool, free bikes.

Madrona Manor
HISTORIC HOTEL **$$$**

(☎800-258-4003, 707-433-4231; www.madronamanor.com; 1001 Westside Rd, Healdsburg; r incl breakfast Mon-Fri $260-305, Sat & Sun $385-515; ❄🛜🚰) The first choice of lovers of country inns and stately manor homes, the regal 1881 Madrona Manor exudes Victorian elegance. Surrounded by 8 acres of woods and gorgeous century-old gardens, the hilltop mansion is decked out with many original furnishings. A mile west of downtown, it's convenient to Westside Rd wineries.

Belle de Jour Inn
B&B **$$$**

(☎707-431-9777; www.belledejourinn.com; 16276 Healdsburg Ave, Healdsburg; r $225-295, ste $355; ❄🛜) Charming Belle de Jour's sunny, uncluttered rooms have American-country furnishings, with extras like private entrances, sun-dried sheets and jetted tubs. The manicured gardens are ready-made for a moonlight tryst.

Healdsburg Inn on the Plaza
INN **$$$**

(☎800-431-8663, 707-433-6991; www.healdsburginn.com; 110 Matheson St, Healdsburg; r $295-375; ❄🛜🚰) The spiffy, clean-lined rooms, conservatively styled in khaki and beige, feel bourgeois summer-house casual, with fine linens and gas fireplaces; some have jetted double tubs. The plaza-front location explains the price.

Honor Mansion
INN **$$$**

(☎707-433-4277, 800-554-4667; www.honormansion.com; 891 Grove St, Healdsburg; r incl breakfast $330-595; ❄🛜🚰) Elegant 1883 Victorian mansion with spectacular resort-like grounds, cushy rooms and great service.

Camellia Inn
B&B **$$$**

(☎707-433-8182, 800-727-8182; www.camelliainn.com; 211 North St, Healdsburg; r $139-395; ❄🛜🚰) Elegantly furnished 1869 mansion, with (among others) one budget room ($139), plus a two-bed family room ($259).

Haydon Street Inn
B&B **$$$**

(☎707-433-5228, 800-528-3703; www.haydon.com; 321 Haydon St, Healdsburg; r $195-325, cottage $425; ❄🛜) Two-story Queen Anne with big front porch and separate cottage.

Piper Street Inn
INN **$$$**

(☎707-433-8721, 877-703-0370; www.piperstreetinn.com; 402 Piper St, Healdsburg; r $295; ❄🛜🚰) Cozy garden cottage.

🍴 Eating

Healdsburg is the gastronomic capital of Sonoma County. Your hardest decision will be choosing where to eat. Reservations essential.

★ The Shed
CAFE, MARKET **$**

(☎707-431-7433; healdsburgshed.com; 25 North St, Healdsburg; dishes $3-15; ⊙8am-7pm Wed-Mon; 🚗) 🌿 At the vanguard of locavore eating, the Shed integrates food at all stages of production, milling its own locally sourced flours, pressing olive oils, fermenting vinegars and kombucha from local fruit, and growing its own produce. It comprises a cafe with wood-fired dishes, fermentation bar with housemade shrubs, coffee bar with stellar pastries, and a market with prepared to-go foods.

Healdsburg Bar & Grill
PUB FOOD $$

(2 707-433-3333; www.healdsburgbarandgrill.com; 245 Healdsburg Ave, Healdsburg; mains $9-15; 8am-9pm) 'Top Chef Masters' winner Doug Keane's gastropub is perfect when you're famished, but don't want to fuss. Expect simple classics – mac-n-cheese, pulled-pork sandwiches, top-end burgers and truffle-parmesan fries. At breakfast, look for homemade bagels and waffles. Sit in the garden.

Oakville Grocery
DELI $$

(2 707-433-3200; www.oakvillegrocery.com; 124 Matheson St, Healdsburg; sandwiches $10; 8am-7pm) Luxurious smoked fish and caviar, fancy sandwiches and grab-and-go gourmet picnics. It's overpriced, but the plaza-view fireside terrace is ever-fun for scouting Botox blonds, while nibbling cheese and sipping vino.

Scopa
ITALIAN $$

(2 707-433-5282; www.scopahealdsburg.com; 109A Plaza St, Healdsburg; mains $15-24; 5:30-10pm Tue-Sun) Space is tight inside this converted barbershop, but it's worth cramming in for perfect thin-crust pizza and rustic Italian home cooking, like Nonna's slow-braised chicken, with sautéed greens, melting into toasty polenta. A lively crowd and good wine prices create a convivial atmosphere.

Diavola
ITALIAN $$

(2 707-814-0111; www.diavolapizzera.com; 21021 Geyserville Ave, Geyserville; pizzas $15-18; 11:30am-9pm;) Ideal for lunch while wine-tasting in Alexander Valley, Diavola makes oustanding salumi and thin-crust pizzas, served in an Old West, brick-walled space, loud enough to drown out the kids.

Ravenous
NEW AMERICAN $$

(2 707-431-1302; 117 North St, Healdsburg; lunch mains $12-17, dinner $20-24) Chalkboard-scrawled menu, with California comfort cooking and excellent burgers, served in a tiny eight-table dining room inside a former theater lobby.

Costeaux French Bakery & Cafe
CAFE $$

(2 707-433-1913; www.costeaux.com; 417 Healdsburg Ave, Healdsburg; mains $10-13; 7am-3pm Mon-Sat, to 1pm Sun;) This cavernous bakery-cafe is good for an easy lunch of salads and sandwiches on house-baked bread, plus all-day breakfast dishes including omelets and scrambles.

★ Madrona Manor
CALIFORNIAN $$$

(800-258-4003, 707-433-4231; www.madronamanor.com; 1001 Westside Rd, Healdsburg; 6-/11-course menu $106/$129; 6-9pm Wed-Sun) You'd be hard-pressed to find a lovelier place to propose than this retro-formal Victorian mansion's garden-view verandah – though there's nothing old-fashioned about the artful haute cuisine: the kitchen churns its own butter, each course comes with a different variety of just-baked bread, lamb and cheese originate down the road, and desserts include ice cream flash-frozen tableside. Reserve a pre-sunset table on the verandah.

Mateo's Cucina Latina
MEXICAN $$$

(2 707-433-1520; www.mateoscocinalatina.com; 214 Healdsburg Ave, Healdsburg; small plates $11-15, mains $21-25; 11:30am-9pm Thu-Tue, 4-9pm Wed, closed Tue Nov-Apr) This is not Mexican food as you may know it. Here the upmarket Yucatan-inspired cooking integrates fine technique and all-local ingredients for standout small plates, such as wild-nettle empanadas and slow-roasted suckling pig, whose subtle flavors shine through the spice. The full bar showcases rare tequilas and mescals. Make reservations; request a garden table.

Barndiva
CALIFORNIAN $$$

(2 707-431-0100; www.barndiva.com; 231 Center St, Healdsburg; lunch mains $15-22, dinner $28-38; noon-2:15 & 5:30pm-9pm Wed-Sat, from 11am Sun) Impeccable seasonal-regional cooking, happening bar, beautiful garden, but service sometimes misses.

Self-Catering

Dry Creek General Store
DELI $

(2 707-433-4171; www.drycreekgeneralstore1881.com; 3495 Dry Creek Rd, Healdsburg; sandwiches $8-10; 6:30am-6pm) Stop at this vintage general store, where locals and cyclists gather for coffee on the creaky front porch. Perfect picnic supplies include Toscano-salami-and-manchego sandwiches on chewy-dense ciabatta.

Cheese Shop
FOOD $

(☎707-433-4998; www.sharpandnutty.com; 423 Center St, Healdsburg; ☺11am-6pm Mon-Sat) Top-notch imported and local cheeses.

Shelton's Natural Foods
MARKET, DELI $

(☎707-431-0530; www.sheltonsmarket.com; 428 Center St, Healdsburg; ☺8am-8pm) Indie alternative for groceries and picnic supplies; reasonably priced.

Moustache Baked Goods
BAKERY $

(☎707-395-4111; moustachebakedgoods.com; 381 Healdsburg Ave, Healdsburg; cupcakes $3; ☺11am-7pm) Incredible locavore small-batch sweets (some gluten-free), including scrumptious cupcakes in unusual combos like maple-bacon.

Noble Folk Ice Cream & Pie Bar
DESSERTS $

(☎707-395-4426; 116 Matheson St, Healdsburg; slice $5.25, single cone $3.25; ☺noon-9pm) Handcrafted ice cream and classic American pie, made with top-quality, all-local ingredients.

Downtown Bakery & Creamery
BAKERY $

(☎707-431-2719; www.downtownbakery.net; 308A Center St, Healdsburg; ☺7am-5:30pm) Healdsburg's classic bakery makes perfect breakfast pastries and specialty breads.

Jimtown Store
DELI, MARKET $$

(☎707-433-1212; www.jimtown.com; 6706 Hwy 128; sandwiches $6-14; ☺7:30am-3pm Mon, Wed & Thu, to 5pm Fri-Sun) One of our favorite Alexander Valley stopovers, Jimtown is great for picnic supplies and sandwiches made with housemade condiment spreads.

Drinking & Entertainment

Flying Goat Coffee
CAFE

(www.flyinggoatcoffee.com; 324 Center St, Healdsburg; ☺7am-7pm) See ya later, Starbucks. Flying Goat is what coffee should be – fairtrade and house-roasted – and locals line up for it every morning.

Bear Republic Brewing Company
BREWERY

(☎707-433-2337; www.bearrepublic.com; 345 Healdsburg Ave, Healdsburg; ☺11am-9:30pm Sun-Thu, to 11pm Fri & Sat) Bear Republic features handcrafted award-winning ales, non-award-winning pub grub, and live music weekends.

Alexander Valley Bar
COCKTAIL BAR

(AVB; ☎707-431-1904; 3487 Alexander Valley Rd, Medlock Ames Winery; ☺5-9pm Sun-Thu, to 11pm Fri & Sat) Vineyard sunsets are incredible at this speakeasy-style bar in Alexander Valley, which crafts cocktails ($10) using whatever's growing in the garden outside.

Raven Theater & Film Center
THEATER

(☎707-433-5448; www.raventheater.com; 115 N Main St, Healdsburg) Hosts concerts, events and first-run art-house films.

🔒 Shopping

The Shed
GARDEN, CULINARY

(☎707-431-7433; healdsburgshed.com; 25 North St, Healdsburg; ☺8am-7pm Wed-Mon) 'Tools and supplies for growing, preparing and sharing food,' including heritage seeds by local farmers, house-milled California flour, and practical cookware.

Jimtown Store
GIFTS

(☎707-433-1212; www.jimtown.com; 6706 Hwy 128) Forage antique bric-a-brac, candles and Mexican oilcloths at this roadside deli and store in Alexander Valley.

Gardener
GARDENS

(☎707-431-1063; www.thegardener.com; 516 Dry Creek Rd, Healdsburg) Garden-shop lovers: don't miss this rural beauty.

One World
GIFTS, HOMEWARES

(☎707-473-0880; www.oneworldfairtrade.net; 104 Matheson St, Healdsburg; ☺10am-6pm Mon-Sat, to 5:30pm Sun) Household goods from fairtrade collectives.

Options Gallery
CRAFTS, JEWELRY

(☎707-431-8861; www.optionsgallery.com; 126 Matheson St, Healdsburg; ☺10:30am-5:30pm Mon-Sat, 11am-4pm Sun) Gifts, crafts and jewelry by local artists, including lovely earrings.

Copperfield's Books
BOOKS

(☎707-433-9270; copperfieldsbooks.com; 104 Matheson St, Healdsburg; ☺9am-6pm Sun-Thu, to 7pm Fri & Sat) Good general-interest books.

Levin & Company
BOOKS, MUSIC

(☎707-433-1118; 306 Center St, Healdsburg; ☺9am-9pm Mon-Sat, 10am-6pm Sun) Fiction and CDs; co-op art gallery.

❶ Information

Healdsburg Chamber of Commerce & Visitors Bureau (☎707-433-6935, 800-648-9922; www.healdsburg.com; 217 Healdsburg Ave, Healdsburg; ☺9am-5pm Mon-Fri, to 3pm Sat, 10am-2pm Sun) A block south of the plaza. Has winery maps and information on ballooning, golf, tennis, spas and nearby farms (get the *Farm Trails* brochure); 24-hour walk-up booth.

North Coast & Redwoods

Why Go?

There's a stretch of the coast with no road access called the 'Lost Coast,' but even the rest of the region, reached by a circuitous two-lane blacktop, feels far from the world's radar. The North Coast is no Beach Boys' song; there are no bikinis and few surfboards. The jagged edge of the continent is wild, scenic and even slightly foreboding, where spectral fog and an outsider spirit have fostered the world's tallest trees, most potent weed and a string of idiosyncratic two-stoplight towns. Explore hidden coves with a blanket and a bottle of local wine, scan the horizon for migrating whales and retreat at night to fire-warmed Victorians. As you travel further north, find valleys of redwood, wide rivers and mossy, overgrown forests. Befitting this dramatic clash of land and water are its unlikely mélange of residents: timber barons and tree huggers, pot farmers and political radicals of every stripe.

Best Places to Eat

➡ Café Beaujolais (p230)
➡ Brick & Fire (p256)
➡ Café Aquatica (p221)
➡ Mario's Lost Coast Cafe (p253)
➡ Table 128 (p240)

Best Places to Stay

➡ Mar Vista Cottages (p224)
➡ Philo Apple Farm (p240)
➡ Benbow Inn (p247)
➡ Alegria (p229)
➡ Gold Bluffs Beach (p265)

When to Go
Eureka

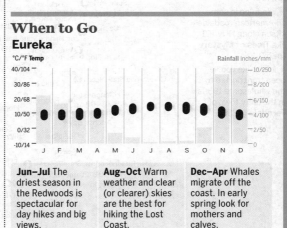

Jun–Jul The driest season in the Redwoods is spectacular for day hikes and big views.

Aug–Oct Warm weather and clear (or clearer) skies are the best for hiking the Lost Coast.

Dec–Apr Whales migrate off the coast. In early spring look for mothers and calves.

North Coast & Redwoods Highlights

1 Explore the gargantuan forests and dramatic coast of **Redwood National & State Parks** (p263).

2 Feel small amongst the standing and fallen giants in **Humboldt Redwoods State Park** (p250).

3 Hike the lush, remote and wild **Lost Coast** (p248).

4 Find a hidden cove on the **Sonoma Coast** (p220).

5 Get pampered at the B&Bs of **Mendocino** (p226).

6 Drink the sampler at McKinleyville's **Six Rivers Brewery** (p260), NorCal's best brewpub.

7 Climb to the top of **Point Arena Lighthouse** (p224) for views over the jagged coast.

8 Tour the laid-back vineyards of the **Anderson Valley** (p239).

9 Indulge in some all-American roadside kitsch along Hwy 101 like **Trees of Mystery** (p267).

10 Feel like you've been transported to the wholesome 1950s in the dairy town of **Ferndale** (p252).

ⓘ Getting Around

Although Hwy 1 is popular with cyclists and there are bus connections, you will almost certainly need a car to explore this region. Those headed to the far north and on a schedule should take Hwy 101, the faster, inland route and then cut over to the coast. Windy Hwy 1 hugs the coast, then cuts inland and ends at Leggett, where it joins Hwy 101. Neither Amtrak nor Greyhound serve cities on coastal Hwy 1.

Amtrak (☑ 800-872-7245; www.amtrakcal-ifornia.com) operates the *Coast Starlight* between Los Angeles and Seattle. From LA, Amtrak buses connect to several North Coast towns including Leggett ($85, 11 hours, two daily) and Garberville ($87, 11½ hours, two daily).

Brave souls willing to piece together bus travel through the region will face a time-consuming headache, but connections are possible to almost every town in the region. **Greyhound** (☑ 800-231-2222; www.greyhound.com) runs buses between San Francisco and Ukiah, ($44, three hours, one daily) Willits ($44, 3½ hours, one daily), Rio Dell (near Fortuna, $57, six hours, one daily), Eureka ($57, 6¾ hours, one daily) and Arcata ($57, seven hours, one daily).

The **Mendocino Transit Authority** (MTA; ☑ 800-696-4682, 707-462-1422; www.4mta. org; fares $3.25-7.75) operates bus 65, which travels between Mendocino, Fort Bragg, Willits, Ukiah and Santa Rosa daily, with an afternoon return. Bus 95 runs between Point Arena and Santa Rosa, via Jenner, Bodega Bay and Sebastopol. Bus 75 heads north every weekday from Gualala to the Navarro River junction at Hwy 128, then runs inland through the Anderson Valley to Ukiah, returning in the afternoon. The North Coast route goes north between Navarro River junction and Albion, Little River, Mendocino and Fort Bragg, Monday to Friday. The best long-distance option is a daily ride between Fort Bragg and Santa Rosa via Willits and Ukiah ($21, three hours).

North of Mendocino County, the **Redwood Transit System** (☑ 707-443-0826; www.hta. org) operates buses ($3) Monday through Saturday between Scotia and Trinidad (2½ hours), stopping en route at Eureka (1¼ hours) and Arcata (1½ hours). **Redwood Coast Transit** (☑ 707-464-9314; www.redwoodcoasttransit. org) runs buses Monday to Saturday between Crescent City, Klamath ($1.50, one hour, five daily) and Arcata ($30, two hours, three daily), with numerous stops along the way.

COASTAL HIGHWAY 1

Down south it's called the 'PCH,' or Pacific Coast Hwy, but North Coast locals simply call it 'Hwy 1.' However you label it, get ready for a fabulous coastal drive, which cuts a winding course on isolated cliffs high above the crashing surf. Compared to the famous Big Sur coast, the serpentine stretch of Hwy 1 up the North Coast is more challenging, more remote and more *real*; passing farms, fishing towns and hidden beaches. Drivers use roadside pull-outs to scan the hazy Pacific horizon for migrating whales and explore a coastline dotted with rock formations that are relentlessly pounded by the surf. The drive between Bodega Bay and Fort Bragg takes four hours of daylight driving without stops. At night in the fog, it takes steely nerves and much, much longer. The most popular destination is the cliffside charmer of Mendocino.

Considering their proximity to the Bay Area, Sonoma and Mendocino counties remain unspoiled, and the austere coastal bluffs are some of the most spectacular in the country. But the trip north gets more rewarding and remote with every mile. By the time Hwy 1 cuts inland to join Hwy 101, the land along the Pacific – called the Lost Coast – the highway disappears and offers the state's best-preserved natural gifts.

Coastal accommodations (including campgrounds) can fill from Memorial Day to Labor Day (late May to early September) and on fall weekends, and often require two-night stays, so reserve ahead. Try to visit during spring or fall, especially in September and October; when the fog lifts, the ocean sparkles and most other visitors have gone home.

Bodega Bay

Bodega Bay is the first pearl in a string of sleepy fishing towns that line the North Coast and was the setting of Hitchcock's terrifying 1963 avian psycho-horror flick *The Birds*. The skies are free from bloodthirsty gulls today (though you best keep an eye on the picnic); it's Bay Area weekenders who descend en masse for extraordinary beaches, tide pools, whale-watching, fishing, surfing and seafood. Mostly a few restaurants, hotels and shops on both sides of Hwy 1, the downtown is not made for strolling, but it is a great base for exploring the endless nearby coves of the Sonoma Coast State Beach (p220).

Originally inhabited by the Pomo people, the bay takes its name from Juan Francisco de la Bodega y Quadra, captain of the Spanish sloop *Sonora*, which entered the bay in 1775. The area was then settled by Russians in the early 19th century, and farms were established to grow wheat for the Russian fur-trapping empire, which stretched from Alaska all the way down the coast to Fort Ross. The Russians pulled out in 1842, abandoning fort and farms, and American settlers moved in.

Hwy 1 runs through town and along the east side of Bodega Bay. On the west side, a peninsula juts out to sea, forming the entrance to Bodega Harbor.

⊙ Sights & Activities

Surfing, beach combing and sportfishing are the main activities here – the latter requires advance booking. From December to April, the fishing boats host whale-watching trips, which are also good to book ahead. Just about everyone in town sells kites which are great for flying at Bodega Head. The excellent *Farm Trails* (www.farmtrails.org) guide at the Sonoma Coast Visitor Center (p220) has suggestions for tours of local ranches, orchards, farms and apiaries.

Bodega Head   LOOKOUT
At the peninsula's tip, Bodega Head rises 265ft above sea level. To get there (and see the open ocean), head west from Hwy 1 onto Eastshore Rd, then turn right at the stop sign onto Bay Flat Rd. It's great for whale-watching. Landlubbers enjoy hiking above the surf, where several good trails include a 3.75-mile trek to Bodega Dunes Campground and a 2.2-mile walk to Salmon Creek Ranch.

Bodega Marine
Laboratory & Reserve   SCIENCE CENTER
(☏707-875-2211; www.bml.ucdavis.edu; 2099 Westside Rd; ⊙2-4pm Fri) **FREE** Run by University of California (UC) Davis, this spectacularly diverse teaching and research reserve surrounds the research lab, which has studied Bodega Bay since the 1920s. The 263-acre reserve hosts many marine environments, including rocky intertidal coastal areas, mudflats and sandflats, salt marsh, sand dunes and freshwater wetlands. On most Friday afternoons docents give tours of the lab and surrounds.

Ren Brown Collection Gallery   GALLERY
(www.renbrown.com; 1781 Hwy 1; ⊙10am-5pm Wed-Sun) The renowned collection of modern Japanese prints and California works at this small gallery is a tranquil escape from the elements. Check out the Japanese garden at the back.

Chanslor Ranch   HORSEBACK RIDING
(☏707-785-8849; www.chanslorranch.com; 2660 N Hwy 1; rides from $40) Just north of town, this friendly outfit leads horseback expeditions along the coastline and the rolling inland hills. Ron, the trip leader, is an amiable, sun-weathered cowboy straight from central casting; he recommends taking the Salmon Creek ride or calling ahead for weather-permitting moonlight rides. The 90-minute beach rides are donation based, and support a horse-rescue program.

Overnight trips in simple platform tents, which are excellent for families, can also be arranged. If you book a ride, you can park your RV at the ranch for free.

BLOODTHIRSTY BIRDS OF BODEGA BAY

Bodega Bay has the enduring claim to fame as the setting for Alfred Hitchcock's *The Birds*. Although special effects radically altered the actual layout of the town, you still get a good feel for the supposed site of the farm owned by Mitch Brenner (played by Rod Taylor). The once-cozy Tides Restaurant, where much avian-caused havoc occurs in the movie, is still there but since 1962 it has been transformed into a vast restaurant complex. Venture 5 miles inland to the tiny town of Bodega and you'll find two icons from the film: the schoolhouse and the church. Both stand just as they did in the movie – a crow overhead may make the hair rise on your neck. The **Bodega Country Store** (⊙8am-8pm) claims to have more *The Birds* artifacts than anywhere else in the world.

The movie's star Tipi Hedren, now in her 80s, visits Bodega Bay at least once a year to help with local events and fundraisers. She also was in town for the movie's 50th anniversary festival in 2013 and there are hopes that the event will become annual.

Coincidentally, right after production of *The Birds* began, a real-life bird attack occurred in Capitola, the sleepy seaside town south of Santa Cruz. Thousands of seagulls ran amok, destroying property and attacking people.

Bodega Bay

Sportfishing Center FISHING, WHALE-WATCHING
(☑ 707-875-3344; www.bodegacharters.com; 1410
Bay Flat Rd) Beside the Sandpiper Cafe, this
outfit organizes full-day fishing trips ($135)
and whale-watching excursions (three hours
adult/child $50/35). It also sells bait, tackle
and fishing licenses. Call ahead to ask about
recent sightings.

Bodega Bay Surf Shack SURFING
(☑ 707-875-3944; http://bodegabaysurf.com; 1400
N Hwy 1; surfboard/wetsuit/kayak rentals from
$17/17/45) If you want to get on the water,
this easygoing one-stop shop has all kinds of
rentals, lessons and good local information.

🎇 Festivals & Events

**Bodega Seafood, Art &
Wine Festival** FOOD, WINE
(www.winecountryfestivals.com; 🖼) In late August, this festival of food and drink brings
together the best beer- and wine-makers of
the area, tons of seafood and activities for
kids. It takes place in the town of Bodega.

Bodega Bay Fishermen's Festival CULTURAL
(www.bbfishfest.org) At the end of April, this
festival culminates in a blessing of the fleet,
a flamboyant parade of vessels, an arts-and-
crafts fair, kite-flying and feasting.

🛏 Sleeping

There's a wide spread of options – RV and
tent camping, quaint motels and fancy hotels. All fill up early during peak seasons.
Campers should consider heading just north
of town to the state-operated sites.

**Sonoma County
Regional Parks** CAMPGROUND $
(☑ 707-565-2267; www.parks.sonomacounty.
ca.gov; tent sties $7, RV sites without hookups $32)
There are a few walk-in sites at the Doran
Regional Park (201 Doran Beach Rd), at the
quiet Miwok Tent Campground, and Westside Regional Park (2400 Westshore Rd),
which is best for RVs. It caters primarily to
boaters and has windy exposures, beaches,
hot showers, fishing and boat ramps. Both
are heavily used. Excellent camping is also
available at the Sonoma Coast State Beach
(p220).

Bodega Harbor Inn MOTEL $$
(☑ 707-875-3594; www.bodegaharborinn.com;
1345 Bodega Ave; r $80-155, cottages $135-175;
🛜🐾) Half a block inland from Hwy 1, sur-
rounded by grassy lawns and furnished with

both real and faux antiques, this modest yet
adorable blue-and-white shingled motel is
the town's most economical option. Pets are
allowed in some rooms for a fee of $15 plus
a security deposit of $50. They also offer a
variety of cottages and rentals around town.

Chanslor Guest Ranch RANCH $$
(☑ 707-875-2721; www.chanslorranch.com; 2660
Hwy 1; campsites $40, furnished tents from $80, r
from $175) A mile north of town, this working
horse ranch has rooms and options for upscale camping. Wildlife programs and guided horse tours make this one sweet place,
with sweeping vistas across open grasslands
to the sea.

Bodega Bay Lodge & Spa LODGE $$$
(☑ 888-875-2250, 707-875-3525; www.bodegabay-
lodge.com; 103 Hwy 1; r $190-470; @🛜🐾) Bode-
ga's plushest option, this small oceanfront
resort has an ocean-view swimming pool,
golf course, a Jacuzzi and a state-of-the-art
fitness club. In the evenings it hosts wine
tastings. The more expensive rooms have
commanding views, but all have balconies.
The other pluses on-site include Bodega
Bay's best spa and the Duck Club (☑ 707-
875-3525; mains $16-37; ⊙ 7:30-11am & 6-9pm),
which is the fanciest dining in town.

Bay Hill Mansion B&B $$$
(☑ 877-468-1588; www.bayhillmansion.com; 3919
Bay Hill Rd; d $279-299; 🛜🐾) A luxe B&B in
a spacious, modern mansion. The decor is
tasteful without much imagination but the
cleanliness and comfort standards here are
some of the best we've ever seen. Get a private yoga class or massage then the helpful
hosts can direct you to the area's best spots.
Views overlook trees with just a peek at the
bay.

🍴 Eating & Drinking

For the old-fashioned thrill of seafood by the
docks there are two options: Tides Wharf &
Restaurant (835 Hwy 1; breakfast $8-22, lunch
$13-28, dinner $16-28; ⊙ 7:30am-9:30pm Mon-
Thu, 7:30am-10pm Fri, 7am-10pm Sat, 7am-9:30pm
Sun; 🖼) and Lucas Wharf Restaurant &
Bar (595 Hwy 1; mains $9-28; ⊙ 11:30am-9pm
Mon-Fri, 11am-10pm Sat; 🖼). Both have views
and similar menus of clam chowder, fried
fish and coleslaw, and markets for picnic
supplies. Tides boasts a great fish market,
though Lucas Wharf feels less like a factory.
Don't be surprised if a bus pulls up outside
either of them.

Spud Point Crab Company
SEAFOOD $

(www.spudpointcrab.com; 1910 Westshore Rd; dishes $4-11; ⏰9am-5pm; 🚗) In the classic tradition of dockside crab shacks, Spud Point serves salty-sweet crab cocktails and *real* clam chowder, served at picnic tables overlooking the marina. Take Bay Flat Rd to get here.

The Birds Cafe
MEXICAN, AMERICAN $

(1407 Hwy 1; meals $6-14; ⏰11:30am-5pm) The menu consists of just a few things – usually fish tacos, fish 'n' chips, chowder and a few salads. Barbecued oysters are available seasonally. Order at the bar then take it to an outdoor picnic table overlooking the harbor. There's beer and wine available. Bliss.

Terrapin Creek Cafe & Restaurant
CALIFORNIAN $$

(📞707-875-2700; www.terrapincreekcafe.com; 1580 Eastshore Dr; lunch mains $12-19, dinner mains $23-30; ⏰11am-2:30pm & 4:30-9pm Thu-Sun; 🖊) 🍴 Bodega Bay's most exciting upscale restaurant is run by a husband-wife team who espouse the slow food movement and serve local dishes sourced from the surrounding area. Comfort-food offerings like black cod roasted in lemon grass and coconut broth are artfully executed, while the Dungeness crab salad is fresh, briny and perfect. Jazz and warm light complete the atmosphere.

Gourmet Au Bay
WINE BAR

(913 Hwy 1; ⏰11am-6pm Thu-Tue) The back deck of this wine bar offers a salty breeze with wine tasting.

ⓘ Information

Sonoma Coast Visitor Center (📞707-875-3866; www.bodegabay.com; 850 Hwy 1; ⏰9am-5pm Mon-Thu & Sat, to 6pm Fri, 10am-5pm Sun) Opposite the Tides Wharf. Stop by for the best help on the coast and for a copy of the *North Coaster*, a small-press indie newspaper of essays and brilliant insights on local culture.

Sonoma Coast State Beach

Stretching 17 miles north from Bodega Head to Vista Trail, the glorious Sonoma Coast State Beach (📞707-875-3483) is actually a series of beaches separated by several beautiful rocky headlands. Some beaches are tiny, hidden in little coves, while others stretch far and wide. Most of the beaches are connected by vista-studded coastal hiking trails that wind along the bluffs. Exploring this area makes an excellent day-long adventure, so bring a picnic. Be advised however: the surf is often too treacherous to wade, so keep an eye on children. While this system of beaches and parks has some camping, you can't just pitch a tent anywhere; most are for day-use only.

⊙ Sights & Activities

Beaches

Salmon Creek Beach
BEACH

Situated around a lagoon, this has 2 miles of hiking and good waves for surfing.

Portuguese Beach & Schoolhouse Beach
BEACHES

Both are very easy to access and have sheltered coves between rocky outcroppings.

Duncan's Landing
BEACH

Small boats unload near this rocky headland in the morning. A good place to spot wildflowers in the spring.

Shell Beach
BEACH

A boardwalk and trail leads out to a stretch perfect for tide-pooling and beachcombing.

Goat Rock
BEACH

Famous for its colony of harbor seals, lazing in the sun at the mouth of the Russian River.

🛏 Sleeping

Bodega Dunes
CAMPGROUND $

(📞800-444-7275; www.reserveamerica.com; 3095 Hwy 1, Bodega Bay; tent & RV sites $35, day use $8) The largest campground in the Sonoma Coast State Beach system of parks, it is also closest to Bodega Bay. It gets a lot of use. Sites are in high dunes and have hot showers but be warned – the fog horn sounds all night.

Wright's Beach Campground
CAMPGROUND $

(📞800-444-7275; www.reserveamerica.com; tent & RV sites $35, day use $8) Of the few parks that allow camping along Sonoma Coast State Beach, this is the best, even though sites lack privacy. Sites can be booked six months in advance, and numbers 1–12 are right on the beach. There are BBQ pits for day use and it's a perfect launch for sea kayakers.

Everyone else, stay out of the water; according to camp hosts the treacherous rip tides claim a life every season.

Jenner

Perched on the hills looking out to the Pacific and above the mouth of the Russian River, tiny Jenner offers access to the coast and the Russian River wine region. A harbor-seal colony sits at the river's mouth and pups are born here from March to August. There are restrictions about getting too close to the chubby, adorable pups – handling them can be dangerous and cause the pups to be abandoned by their mothers. Volunteers answer questions along the roped-off area where day trippers can look on at a distance. The best way to see them is by kayak and most of the year you will find Water Treks Ecotours (☑707-865-2249; 2hr rental from $25; ☺10am-3pm) renting kayaks on the highway. Heading north on Hwy 1 you will begin driving on one of the most beautiful, windy stretches of California highway. You'll also probably lose cell-phone service – possibly a blessing.

🛏 Sleeping & Eating

Jenner Inn & Cottages
INN $$

(☑707-865-2377; www.jennerinn.com; 10400 Hwy 1; r incl breakfast creekside $118-278, cottages $228-298; @) It's difficult to sum up this collection of properties dispersed throughout Jenner – some are in fairly deluxe ocean-view cottages with kitchen and ready-to-light fireplaces, others are small and upland near a creek. All have the furnishings of a stylish auntie from the early 1990s.

★Café Aquatica
CAFE $

(www.cafeaquatica.com; 10439 Hwy 1; sandwiches $10-13; 🖤) This is the kind of North Coast coffee shop you've been dreaming of: fresh pastries, organic coffee and chatty locals. The view of the Russian River from the patio and gypsy sea-hut decor make it hard to leave.

★River's End
CALIFORNIAN $$$

(☑707-865-2484; www.rivers-end.com; 11048 Hwy 1; lunch mains $14-26, dinner mains $25-39; ☺noon-3pm & 5-8:30pm Thu-Mon; 🚗) Unwind in style at this picture-perfect restaurant that overlooks the river's mouth and the grand sweep of the Pacific Ocean. It serves world-class meals at world-class prices, but the real reward is the view. Its ocean-view cottages (rooms and cottages $159 to $229) are wood paneled and have no TVs, wi-fi or phones. Children under 12 are not recommended.

Fort Ross State Historic Park

A curious glimpse into Tsarist Russia's exploration of the California coast, the salt-washed buildings of Fort Ross State Historic Park (☑707-847-3286; www.fortrossstatepark.org; 19005 Hwy 1; per car $8; ☺10:30am-4pm Sat & Sun) offer a fascinating insight into the pre-American Wild West. It's a quiet, picturesque place with a riveting past.

In March 1812, a group of 25 Russians and 80 Alaskans (including members of the Kodiak and Aleutian tribes) built a wooden fort here, near a Kashaya Pomo village. The southernmost outpost of the 19th-century Russian fur trade on America's Pacific Coast, Fort Ross was established as a base for sea-otter hunting operations and trade with Alta California, and for growing crops for Russian settlements in Alaska. The Russians dedicated the fort in August 1812 and occupied it until 1842, when it was abandoned because the sea otter population had been decimated and agricultural production had never taken off.

Fort Ross State Historic Park, an accurate reconstruction of the fort, is 11 miles north of Jenner on a beautiful point. The original buildings were sold, dismantled and carried off to Sutter's Fort during the Gold Rush. The visitor center (☑707-847-3437) has a great museum with historical displays and an excellent bookshop on Californian and Russian history. Ask about hikes to the Russian cemetery.

On Fort Ross Heritage Day, the last Saturday in July, costumed volunteers bring the fort's history to life; check the website www.parks.ca.gov or call the visitor center for other special events.

If you pass by on a weekday when the fort is closed (due to budget cuts), you still may be able to walk down and have a peek inside if a school group is there.

🛏 Sleeping

Stillwater Cove Regional Park
CAMPGROUND $

(☑reservations 707-565-2267; www.sonoma-county.org/parks; 22455 N Hwy 1; tent & RV sites $28) Two miles north of Timber Cove, this park has hot showers and hiking under Monterey pines. Sites 1, 2, 4, 6, 9 and 10 have ocean views.

Timber Cove Inn
INN $$

(☑800-987-8319, 707-847-3231; www.timbercoveinn.com; 21780 N Hwy 1; r from $155, ocean view from $183) A dramatic and quirky '60s-modern seaside inn that was once a top-of-the-line luxury lodge. Though the price remains high, it has slipped a bit. The rustic architectural shell is still stunning, though, and a duet of tinkling piano and crackling fire fills the lobby. The quirky rooms facing the ocean have a treehouse feel, with rustic redwood details, balconies, fireplaces and lofted beds. Even those who don't bunk here should wander agape in the shadow of Benny Bufano's 93ft peace statue, a spectacular totem on the edge of the sea. The expensive restaurant on-site is nothing to write home about and the staff were grumpy when we passed by.

Salt Point State Park

Stunning 6000-acre Salt Point State Park (☎707-847-3321; per car $8; ☺visitor center 10am-3pm Sat & Sun Apr-Oct) has sandstone cliffs that drop dramatically into the kelp-strewn sea and hiking trails that crisscross windswept prairies and wooded hills, connecting pygmy forests and coastal coves rich with tidepools. The 6-mile-wide park is bisected by the San Andreas Fault – the rock on the east side is vastly different from that on the west. Check out the eerily beautiful *tafonis*, honeycombed-sandstone formations, near Gerstle Cove. For a good roadside photo op, there's a pullout at mile-marker 45, with views of decaying redwood shacks, grazing goats and headlands jutting out to the sea.

Though many of the day use areas have been closed off due to budget cuts, trails lead off Hwy 1 pull-outs to views of the pristine coastline. The platform overlooking Sentinel Rock is just a short stroll from the Fisk Mill Cove parking lot at the park's north end. Further south, seals laze at Gerstle Cove Marine Reserve, one of California's first underwater parks. Tread lightly around tidepools and don't lift the rocks: even a glimpse of sunlight can kill some critters. If you're here between April and June, you *must* see Kruse Rhododendron State Reserve. Growing abundantly in the forest's filtered light, magnificent, pink rhododendrons reach heights of over 30ft, making them the tallest species in the world; turn east from Hwy 1 onto Kruse Ranch Rd and follow the signs. Be sure to walk the short Rhododendron Loop Trail.

🛏 Sleeping

Woodside & Gerstle Cove Campgrounds   CAMPGROUND $
(☎800-444-7275; www.reserveamerica.com; tent & RV sites $35; ☺Woodside Apr-Sep) Two camp-grounds, Woodside and Gerstle Cove, both signposted off Hwy 1, have campsites with cold water. Inland Woodside is well protected by the Monterey pines. Gerstle Cove's trees burned over a decade ago and have only grown halfway back, giving the gnarled, blackened trunks a ghostly look when the fog twirls between the branches.

Ocean Cove Lodge Bar & Grill   MOTEL $
(☎707-847-3158;   www.oceancovelodge.com; 23255 Hwy 1; r from $69; ❄ 🐾) Just a few minutes south of Salt Point State Park is Ocean Cove Lodge Bar & Grill, a godsend for those on a budget. It's just a basic motel but the location is fabulous, there's a hot tub and a surprisingly good American-style restaurant on the premises.

Stuart Point Store & Retreat   TENT CABINS, GROCERY $$
(32000 Hwy 1; d tents Mon-Fri $155, Sat & Sun $225-250; ☺8am-5pm) For snacks, coffee and photo ops, don't miss a stop at Stuart Point Store just north of Salt Point State Park. This may be the oldest continuously family-run business west of the Mississippi (it opened in 1868), and while the decor has stayed true to its heritage, the gourmet fare on offer is deliciously modern. The owner's house is in the antique-looking ranch next door and about a quarter of a mile south down Hwy 1 are the eerie remains of the old schoolhouse.

'Glamping' is now available on the wild, 1200-acre property with canvas tents perched 400ft over stunning sea cliffs, all equipped with queen-sized beds and luxury linens. It's a bit pricey considering there's no electricity (tents are lit by battery-powered lanterns) and showers are outdoors, but the setting is unparalleled.

Sea Ranch

Though not without its fans, the exclusive community of Sea Ranch is a sort of weather-beaten Stepford-by-the-Sea. The ritzy subdivision that sprawls 10 miles along the coast is connected with a well-watched network of private roads. Approved for construction prior to the existence of the watchdog Coastal Commission, the community was a precursor to the concept of 'slow growth,' with strict zoning laws requiring that houses be constructed of weathered wood only. According to *The Sea Ranch Design Manual:* 'This is not a place for the grand architectural statement; it's a place

to explore the subtle nuances of fitting in...'
Indeed. Though there are some lovely and
recommended short-term rentals here, don't
break any community rules – like throwing
wild parties – or security will come knockin'.
For supplies and gasoline, go to Gualala.

After years of litigation, public through-
ways onto private beaches have been legally
mandated and are now well marked. Hiking
trails lead from roadside parking lots to the
sea and along the bluffs, but don't dare tres-
pass on adjacent lands. Stengel Beach (Hwy
1, Mile 53.96) has a beach-access staircase.
Walk-On Beach (Hwy 1, Mile 56.53) provides
wheelchair access and Shell Beach (Hwy 1,
Mile 55.24) also has beach-access stairs; parking at all three areas costs $6. For hiking
details, including maps, contact the Sea
Ranch Association (www.tsra.org).

Sea Ranch Lodge (☑ 707-785-2371; www.
searanchlodge.com; 60 Sea Walk Dr; r incl breakfast
$199-369; 🕾) 🖋, a marvel of '60s-modern
California architecture, has spacious, luxurious, minimalist rooms, many with dramatic views to the ocean; some have hot tubs
and fireplaces. The fine contemporary restaurant (lunch mains $12-18, dinner mains $22-
38; ☉ 8am-9pm) has a menu for discerning
guests; expect everything from duck breast
to local fish tacos. North of the lodge you'll
see Sea Ranch's iconic nondenomination-
al chapel; it's on the inland side of Hwy 1,
mileage marker 55.66. For those short on
time or on a budget, this is the best reason
to pull over in Sea Ranch.

Depending on the season, it can be surprisingly affordable to rent a house in Sea
Ranch; contact Rams Head Realty (www.
ramshead-realty.com), Sea Ranch Rentals
(www.searanchrentals.com), or Sea Ranch Escape (www.searanchescape.com).

Gualala & Anchor Bay

At just 2½ hours north of San Francisco,
Gualala – pronounced by most locals as
'Wah-la-la' – is northern Sonoma coast's hub
for a weekend getaway as it sits square in the
middle of the 'Banana Belt,' a stretch of coast
known for unusually sunny weather. Founded as a lumber town in the 1860s, the downtown stretches along Hwy 1 with a bustling
commercial district that has a great grocery
store and some cute, slightly upscale shops.

Just north, quiet Anchor Bay has several
inns, a tiny shopping center and, heading
north, a string of secluded, hard-to-find

ANNAPOLIS WINERY

Just south of Sea Ranch on Hwy 1,
you'll see signs for Annapolis Winery
(☑ 707-886-5460; www.annapoliswinery.
com; 26055 Soda Springs Rd; tasting fee
$5; ☉ 12-5pm daily). Swing a right onto
Annapolis Rd and drive a winding,
scenic 7½ miles to this small, remote,
yet utterly charming winery. This
super-friendly, mom-and-pop place
produces highly regarded small-batch
wines. The Gewürztraminer, Pinot Noir
and Zinfandel Port get the most raves
but all the varieties are worth sampling.
A few picnic supplies are available or
bring your own to enjoy the views over
the vines and coastal mountains.

beaches. Both are excellent jumping-off
points for exploring the area.

◉ Sights & Activities

Seven miles north of Anchor Bay, pull off
at mile-marker 11.41 for Schooner Gulch.
A trail into the forest leads down cliffs to a
sandy beach with tidepools. Bear right at the
fork in the trail to reach iconic Bowling Ball
Beach, where low tide reveals rows of big,
round rocks resembling bowling balls. Consult tide tables for Arena Cove. The forecast
low tide must be lower than +1.5ft on the
tide chart for the rocks to be visible.

Gualala Arts Center   ARTS CENTER
(☑ 707-884-1138; www.gualalaarts.org; ☉ 9am-
4pm Mon-Fri, noon-4pm Sat & Sun) Inland along
Old State Rd, at the south end of town and
beautifully built entirely by volunteers, this
center hosts changing exhibitions, organizes
the Art in the Redwoods Festival in late
August and has loads of info on local art.

Adventure Rents   KAYAKING
(☑ 888-881-4386, 707-884-4386; www.adventur-
erents.com) In the summer, a sand spit forms
at the mouth of the river, cutting it off from
the ocean and turning it into a warm-water
lake. This outfit rents canoes (two hours/
half-day/full day $70/80/90) and kayaks
(two hours/half-day/full day $35/40/45) out
of a van and provides instruction.

🛌 Sleeping & Eating

Of the two towns, Gualala has more services
and is a more practical hub for exploring –

there are a bunch of good motels and a pair of nice grocery stores. Get fresh veggies at the **farmers market** (Gualala Community Center; ⊙10am-12:30pm Sat Jun-Oct) and organic supplies and local wine at the **Anchor Bay Village Market** (35513 S Hwy 1).

Gualala Point Regional Park   CAMPGROUND $
(http://parks.sonomacounty.ca.gov; 42401 Highway 1, Gualala; campsites $32) Shaded by a stand of redwoods and fragrant California Bay laurel trees, a short trail connects this creekside campground to the windswept beach. The quality of sites, including several secluded hike-in spots, makes it the best drive-in camping on this part of the coast.

Gualala River Redwood Park   CAMPGROUND $
(⊠707-884-3533; www.gualalapark.com; day use $6, tent & RV sites $42-49) Another excellent Sonoma County Park. Inland along Old State Rd, you can camp and do short hikes along the river.

★ St Orres Inn   INN $$
(⊠707-884-3303; www.saintorres.com; 36601 Hwy 1, Gualala; B&B $95-135, cottages $140-445; 🐾🐕) Famous for its striking Russian-inspired architecture: dramatic rough-hewn timbers, stained glass and burnished copper domes, there's no place quite like St Orres. On the property's fairytale-like, wild-mushroom-strewn 90 acres, hand-built cottages range from rustic to luxurious. The inn's fine **restaurant** (⊠707-884-3335; dinner mains $40-50) serves worth-the-splurge, inspired Californian cuisine in one of the coast's most romantic rooms.

North Coast Country Inn   B&B $$
(⊠800-959-4537, 707-884-4537; www.northcoastcountryinn.com; 34591 S Hwy 1, Gualala; r incl breakfast $185-235; 🐾🐕) Perched on an inland hillside beneath towering trees, surrounded by lovely gardens, the perks of this adorable place begin with the gregarious owner and a hot tub. The six spacious, country-style rooms are decorated with lovely prints and boast exposed beams, fireplaces, board games and private entrances.

★ Mar Vista Cottages   CABIN $$$
(⊠877-855-3522, 707-884-3522; www.marvistamendocino.com; 35101 S Hwy 1, Gualala; cottages $175-305; 🐾🐕) ✍ The elegantly renovated 1930s fishing cabins offer a simple, stylish seaside escape with a vanguard commitment to sustainability. The harmonious environment is the result of pitch-perfect details: linens are line-dried over lavender, guests browse the organic vegetable garden to harvest their own dinner and chickens cluck around the grounds laying the next morning's breakfast. It often requires two-night stays.

Laura's Bakery & Taqueria   MEXICAN $
(⊠707-884-3175; 38411 Robinson Reef Rd, at Hwy 1, Gualala; mains $7-12; ⊙7am-7pm Mon-Sat; 🐕) Laura's is a refreshing, low-key break from Hwy 1 upscale dining. The menu's taqueria staples are fantastic (the Baja-style fish tacos are a steal) but the fresh *mole* dishes and distant ocean view are the real surprises.

Bones Roadhouse   BARBECUE $$
(www.bonesroadhouse.com; 39350 S Hwy 1, Gualala; mains $9-20; ⊙11:30am-9pm Sun-Thu, to 10pm Fri & Sat) Savory smoked meats and a busy biker bar vibe make this Gualala's most fun lunch stop. On weekends a codgerly blues outfit may be growling out 'Mustang Sally.'

ℹ Information

Redwood Coast Visitors Center (www.redwoodcoastchamber.com; 39150 Hwy 1, Gualala; ⊙12-5pm Thu-Sat) Has local information.

Point Arena

This laid-back little town combines creature comforts with relaxed, eclectic California living and is the first town up the coast where the majority of residents don't seem to be retired Bay Area refugees. Sit by the docks a mile west of town at **Arena Cove** and watch surfers mingle with fishermen and hippies.

◉ Sights

Point Arena Lighthouse   LIGHTHOUSE
(⊠707-882-2777; www.pointarenalighthouse.com; 45500 Lighthouse Rd; adult/child $7.50/1; ⊙10am-3:30pm, to 4:30pm late May-early Sep) Two miles north of town, this 1908 lighthouse (the tallest on the US West Coast) stands 10 stories high and is the only lighthouse in California you can ascend. Check in at the museum, then climb the 145 steps to the top and see the Fresnel lens and the jaw-dropping view. You an stay on-site (p225).

Stornetta Public Lands   NATURE RESERVE
For fabulous bird-watching, hiking on terraced rock past sea caves and access to hidden coves, head 1 mile down Lighthouse Rd from Hwy 1 and look for the Bureau of Land Management (BLM) signs on the left

indicating these 1132-acre public lands. The best, most dramatic walking trail leads along the coast and also begins on Lighthouse Rd from a small parking area about a quarter-mile before the Lighthouse parking area.

🛏 Sleeping & Eating

Wharf Master's Inn   HOTEL **$$**
(📞800-932-4031, 707-882-3171; www.wharfmasters.com; 785 Iversen Ave; r $100-195; 🛜🐾) This is a cluster of small, modern rooms on a cliff overlooking fishing boats and a stilt pier. Tidy and very clean, rooms have the character of a chain hotel.

Coast Guard House Inn   INN **$$**
(📞707-882-2442; www.coastguardhouse.com; 695 Arena Cove; r $165-265; 🛜) Come here if you want to soak up old-world oceanside charm and are willing to deal with historic plumbing. It's a 1901 Cape Cod–style house and cottage, with water-view rooms.

Coast Guard Homes   VACATION RENTAL **$$**
(📞877-725-4448; 45500 Lighthouse Rd; houses $135-235) True lighthouse buffs should look into staying at the plain three-bedroom, kitchen-equipped former Coast Guard homes at the Lighthouse. They're quiet, wind-swept retreats.

Franny's Cup & Saucer   BAKERY **$**
(www.frannyscupandsaucer.com; 213 Main St; items from $2; ⏰8am-4pm Wed-Sat) The cutest patisserie on this stretch of coast is run by Franny and her mother, Barbara (a veteran of Chez Panisse). The fresh berry tarts and creative housemade chocolates seem too beautiful to eat, until you take the first bite and immediately want to order another. Several times a year they pull out all the stops for a Sunday garden brunch ($25).

Arena Market   ORGANIC, DELI **$**
(www.arenaorganics.org; 183 Main St; ⏰7:30am-7pm Mon-Sat, 8:30am-6pm Sun; 🛜🍴) 🌿 The deli in front of this fully stocked organic grocer makes excellent to-go veg and gluten-free options, often sourced from local farms. The serve-yourself soup is delish.

Pizzas N Cream   PIZZA **$$**
(www.pizzasandcream.com; 790 Port Rd; pizzas $10-18; ⏰11:30am-9pm; 🛜🖐) In Arena Cove, this friendly place whips up exquisite pizzas and fresh salads, and serves beer and ice cream.

🍷 Drinking & Entertainment

215 Main   BAR
(www.facebook.com/215Main; 215 Main St; ⏰2pm-2am Tue-Sun) Head to this open, renovated historic building to drink local beer and wine. There's jazz on the weekends.

Arena Cinema   CINEMA
(www.arenatheater.org; 214 Main St) Shows mainstream, foreign and art films in a beautifully restored movie house. Sue, the ticket seller, has been in that booth for 40 years. Got a question about Point Arena? Ask Sue.

Manchester

Follow Hwy 1 for about 7 miles north of Point Arena, through gorgeous rolling fields dropping down from the hills to the blue ocean, and a turnoff leads to Manchester State Beach, a long, wild stretch of sand. The area around here is remote and beautiful (only one grocery store), but it's a quick drive to Point Arena for more elaborate provisions.

Ross Ranch (📞707-877-1834; www.rossranch.biz) at Irish Beach, another 5 miles to the north, arranges two-hour horseback beach ($60) and mountain ($50) rides; reservations recommended.

Mendocino Coast KOA (📞707-882-2375; www.manchesterbeachkoa.com; tent/RV sites from $29/49, cabins $64-78; 🛜🐾) is an impressive private campground with tightly packed campsites beneath enormous Monterey pines, a cooking pavilion, hot showers, a hot tub and bicycles. The cabins are a great

TOP WHALE-WATCHING SPOTS

Watch for spouts, sounding and breaching whales and pods. Anywhere coastal will do, but the following are some of the north coast's best:

➡ Bodega Head (p218)

➡ Mendocino Headlands State Park (p227)

➡ Jug Handle State Reserve (p231)

➡ MacKerricher State Park (p235)

➡ Shelter Cove & Lost Coast (p248)

➡ Trinidad Head Trail (p261)

➡ Klamath River Overlook (p266)

option for families who want to get the camping experience without roughing it.

A quarter-mile west, the sunny, exposed campground at Manchester State Park (www.parks.gov.ca; tent & RV sites $29-39) has cold water and quiet sites right by the ocean. Sites are nonreservable. Budget cuts have all but eliminated ranger service.

Elk

Thirty minutes north of Point Arena, itty-bitty Elk is famous for its stunning cliff-top views of 'sea stacks,' towering rock formations jutting out of the water. Otherwise, it's one of the cutest yet gentrified-looking villages before Mendocino. There is *nothing* to do after dinner, so bring a book if you're a night owl. And you can forget about the cell phone, too; reception here is nonexistent. Elk's visitor center (5980 Hwy 1; ⊙11am-1pm Sat & Sun mid-Mar–Oct) has exhibits on the town's logging past. At the southern end of town, Greenwood State Beach sits where Greenwood Creek meets the sea.

Tucked into a tiny house looking across the road to the ocean, the Elk Studio Gallery & Artist's Collective (www.artists-collective.net; 6031 S Hwy 1; ⊙10am-5pm) is cluttered with local art – everything from carvings and pottery to photography and jewelry.

🛏 Sleeping & Eating

Griffin House   INN $$
(☑707-877-3422; www.griffinn.com; 5910 S Hwy 1; cottages incl breakfast $138-260; 🐾🖧🐕) This is the most affordable choice, with an adorable cluster of simple, powder-blue bluffside cottages with wood-burning stoves.

Elk Cove Inn & Spa   INN $$$
(☑800-725-2967; www.elkcoveinn.com; 6300 S Hwy 1; r $100-375, cottages $275-355; 🐾🖧🐕) Several upmarket B&Bs take advantage of the views. You simply can't beat those from Elk Cove Inn & Spa, located on a bluff with steps leading down to the driftwood-strewn beach below. Prices in the wide selection of rooms and cottages include breakfast, wine, champagne and cocktails plus you can relax even further at their deluxe spa.

Harbor House Inn   INN $$$
(☑800-720-7474, 707-877-3203; www.theharborhouseinn.com; 5600 S Hwy 1; r & cottages incl breakfast & dinner $360-490; 🐕) Harbor House Inn, located in a 1915 Arts and Crafts–style mansion (closed for renovations when we passed), has gorgeous cliff-top gardens and a private beach. Rates include a superb four-course dinner for two in the ocean-view room with a lauded wine list.

Queenie's Roadhouse Cafe   CAFE $
(☑707-877-3285; 6061 S Hwy 1; dishes $6-10; ⊙8am-3pm Thu-Mon; 🚗) Everyone swears by excellent, retro-chic Queenie's Roadhouse Cafe for a creative range of breakfast (try the wild-rice waffles) and lunch treats.

Bridget Dolan's   AMERICAN $$
(☑707-877-1820; 5910 S Hwy 1; mains $10-15; ⊙4:30-8pm) Sweet, little Bridget Dolan's serves straight-forward cookin' like pot pies, and bangers and mash.

Van Damme State Park

Three miles south of Mendocino, this gorgeous 1831-acre park (☑707-937-5804; www.parks.ca.gov; per car $8) draws divers, beach-combers and kayakers to its easy-access beach. It's also known for its pygmy forest, where the acidic soil and an impenetrable layer of hardpan just below the surface create a bonsai forest with decades-old trees growing only several feet high. A wheelchair-accessible boardwalk provides access to the forest. Turn east off Hwy 1 onto Little River Airport Rd, a half-mile south of Van Damme State Park, and drive for 3 miles. Alternatively, hike or bike up from the campground on the 3.5-mile Fern Canyon Scenic Trail, which crosses back and forth over Little River.

The visitor center (☑707-937-4016; ⊙10am-3pm Fri-Sun) has nature exhibits, videos and programs; a half-hour Marsh Loop Trail starts nearby.

Two pretty campgrounds (☑800-444-7275; www.reserveamerica.com; tent & RV sites $35; 🐕) are excellent for family car camping. They both have hot showers: one is just off Hwy 1, the other is in a highland meadow, which has lots of space for kids to run around. Nine environmental campsites (tent sites $25) lie just a 1¼-mile hike up Fern Canyon; there's untreated creek water.

For sea-cave kayaking tours ($60), contact Kayak Mendocino (☑707-937-0700; www.kayakmendocino.com).

Mendocino

Leading out to a gorgeous headland, Mendocino is the North Coast's salt-washed perfect village, with B&Bs surrounded by rose gardens, white-picket fences and New England–style redwood water towers. Bay Area weekenders walk along the headland among berry bramble and wildflowers, where cypress trees stand over dizzying cliffs. Nature's power is evident everywhere, from driftwood-littered fields and cave tunnels to the raging surf. The town itself is full of cute shops – no chains – and has earned the nickname 'Spendocino,' for its upscale goods. In summer, fragrant bursts of lavender and jasmine permeate the foggy wind, tempered by salt air from the churning surf, which is never out of earshot.

Built by transplanted New Englanders in the 1850s, Mendocino thrived late into the 19th century, with ships transporting redwood timber from here to San Francisco. The mills shut down in the 1930s, and the town fell into disrepair until it was rediscovered in the 1950s by artists and bohemians. Today the culturally savvy, politically aware, well-traveled citizens welcome visitors, but eschew corporate interlopers – don't look for a Big Mac or Starbucks. To avoid crowds, come midweek or in the low season, when the vibe is mellower – and prices more reasonable.

⦿ Sights

Mendocino is lined with all kinds of interesting galleries, which hold openings on the second Saturday of each month from 5pm to 8pm.

Mendocino Art Center GALLERY
(☑707-937-5818, 800 653 3328; www.mendocinoartcenter.org; 45200 Little Lake St; ⊙10am-5pm Apr-Oct, to 4pm Tue-Sat Nov-Mar) Behind a yard of twisting iron sculpture, the city's art center takes up a whole tree-filled block, hosting exhibitions, the 81-seat Helen Schonei Theatre and nationally renowned art classes. This is also where to pick up the *Mendocino Arts Showcase* brochure, a quarterly publication listing all the happenings and festivals in town.

Kelley House Museum MUSEUM
(www.mendocinohistory.org; 45007 Albion St; admission $2; ⊙11am-3pm Thu-Tue Jun-Sep, Fri-Mon Oct-May) With a research library and changing exhibits on early California and Mendocino, the 1861 museum hosts seasonal, two-hour walking tours for $10; call for times.

Kwan Tai Temple TEMPLE
(www.kwantaitemple.org; 45160 Albion St) Peering in the window of this 1852 temple reveals an old altar dedicated to the Chinese god of war. Tours are available by appointment.

Point Cabrillo Lighthouse LIGHTHOUSE
(www.pointcabrillo.org; Point Cabrillo Dr; ⊙11am-4pm Sat & Sun Jan & Feb, daily Mar-Oct, Fri-Mon Nov & Dec) **FREE** Restored in 1909, this stout lighthouse stands on a 300-acre wildlife preserve north of town, between Russian Gulch and Caspar Beach. Guided walks of the preserve leave at 11am on Sundays from May to September. You can also stay in the lighthouse keeper's house and cottages which are now vacation rentals (p229).

🏃 Activities

Wine tours, whale-watching, shopping, hiking, cycling: there's more to do in the area than a thousand long weekends could accomplish. For navigable river and ocean kayaking, launch from tiny Albion, which hugs the north side of the Albion River mouth, 5 miles south of Mendocino.

Catch A Canoe & Bicycles Too! CANOEING, KAYAKING
(☑707-937-0273; www.catchacanoe.com; Stanford Inn by the Sea, 44850 Comptche-Ukiah Rd; kayak & canoe rental adult/child from $28/14; ⊙9am-5pm) This friendly outfit at the Stanford Inn south of town rents bikes, kayaks and stable outrigger canoes for trips up the 8-mile Big River tidal estuary, the longest undeveloped estuary in Northern California. No highways or buildings, only beaches, forests, marshes, streams, abundant wildlife and historic logging sites. Bring a picnic and a camera to enjoy the ramshackle remnants of century-old train trestles and majestic blue herons.

Mendocino Headlands State Park OUTDOORS
A spectacular park surrounds the village, with trails crisscrossing the bluffs and rocky coves. Ask at the visitor center about guided weekend walks, including spring wildflower walks and whale-watching.

🎭 Festivals & Events

For a complete list of Mendocino's many festivals, check with the visitor center or www.gomendo.com.

Mendocino Whale Festival WILDLIFE
(www.mendowhale.com) Early March, with wine and chowder tastings, whale-watching and music.

Mendocino

Mendocino

⊙ Sights
1	Kelley House Museum	C2
2	Kwan Tai Temple	A3
3	Mendocino Art Center	A2
4	Mendocino Headlands State Park	A1

⊜ Sleeping
5	Alegria	D2
6	Headlands Inn	C2
7	MacCallum House Inn	B2
8	Mendocino Coast Reservations	B2
9	Mendocino Hotel	B3
10	Packard House	B2
11	Raku House	D2
12	Sea Gull Inn	C2

⊗ Eating
13	955 Ukiah Street	C2
14	Café Beaujolais	D2
15	Farmers Market	C2
16	Flow	B3
17	GoodLife Cafe & Bakery	C2
	MacCallum House Restaurant	(see 7)
	Mendocino Cafe	(see 12)
18	Mendocino Market	B2
19	Mendosa's	C2
20	Patterson's Pub	C2

⊖ Drinking & Nightlife
21	Dick's Place	B3

⊚ Shopping
22	Compass Rose Leather	B3
23	Gallery Bookshop	B3
24	Moore Used Books	D2
25	Out Of This World	B3
26	Twist	A3
27	Village Toy Store	C2

Mendocino Music Festival   MUSIC
(www.mendocinomusic.com; ♦) Mid-July, with orchestral and chamber music concerts on the headlands, children's matinees and open rehearsals.

Mendocino Wine & Mushroom Festival   FOOD, WINE
(www.mendocino.com) Early November, guided mushroom tours and symposia.

⊨ Sleeping

Standards are high and so are prices; two-day minimums often crop up on weekends. Fort Bragg, 10 miles north, has cheaper lodgings. All B&B rates include breakfast; only a few places have TVs. For a range of cottages and B&Bs, contact **Mendocino Coast Reservations** (☎800-262-7801, 707-937-5033; www.mendocinovacations.com; 45084 Little Lake St; ☺9am-5pm).

Russian Gulch State Park
CAMPGROUND **$**

(✉ reservations 800-444-7275; www.reserveamerica.com; tent & RV sites $35) In a wooded canyon 2 miles north of town, with secluded drive-in sites, hot showers, a small waterfall and the Devil's Punch Bowl (a collapsed sea arch).

Andiron
CABIN **$$**

(☎ 800-955-6478, 707-937-1543; http://theandiron.com; 6051 N Hwy 1, Little River; most cabins $109-299; ☎ ☎) ✈ Styled with hip vintage decor, this cluster of 1950s roadside cottages is a refreshingly playful option amid the cabbage-rose and lace aesthetic of Mendocino. Each cabin houses two rooms with complementing themes: 'Read' has old books, comfy vintage chairs and hip retro eyeglasses, while the adjoining 'Write' features a huge chalk board and a ribbon typewriter.

A favorite for travelers? 'Here' and 'There,' themed with old maps, 1960s airline paraphernalia and collectables from North Coast's yesteryear.

MacCallum House Inn
B&B **$$**

(☎ 800-609-0492, 707-937-0289; www.maccallumhouse.com; 45020 Albion St; r & cottages from $149, water tower from $225; @☎☎) ✈ The finest B&B option in town with gardens in a riot of color. There are cheerful cottages, and a modern luxury home, but the most memorable space is within one of Mendocino's iconic historic water towers – living quarters fill the ground floor, a sauna is on the 2nd floor and there's a view of the coast from the top.

All accommodations have cushy extras like robes, DVD players, stereos and plush linens.

Packard House
B&B **$$**

(☎ 888-453-2677, 707-937-2677; www.packardhouse.com; 45170 Little Lake St; r $175-225; ☎) Decked out in contemporary style, this place is Mendocino's most chic and sleek B&B choice, with beautiful fabrics, colorful minimalist paintings and limestone bathrooms.

Headlands Inn
B&B **$$**

(☎ 707-937-4431; www.headlandsinn.com; cnr Albion & Howard Sts; r $139-249; ☎) Homey saltbox with featherbeds, English gardens and fireplaces. Quiet rooms have sea views and staff will bring you the gourmet breakfast in bed.

Sea Gull Inn
B&B **$$**

(☎ 888-937-5204, 707-937-5204; www.seagullbb.com; 44960 Albion St; r $130-198, barn $200; ☎) With pristine white bedspreads, organic breakfasts and a flowering garden, this cute,

converted motel is extremely comfortable, fairly priced, and right in the thick of the action.

Lighthouse Inn at Point Cabrillo
HISTORIC B&B **$$**

(☎ 866-937-6124, 707-937-6124; www.pointcabrillo.org; Point Cabrillo Dr; lightkeeper's house from $461, cottages from $132; ☎) On 300 acres, in the shadow of Point Cabrillo Lighthouse, the stately lightkeeper's house and the staff's two turn-of-the-century cottages have been turned into vacation rentals. All options have verandahs and lush period decor but are not very private.

★ Alegria
B&B **$$$**

(☎ 800-780-7905, 707-937-5150; www.oceanfrontmagic.com; 44781 Main St; r $239-299; ☎) A perfect romantic hideaway, beds have views over the coast, decks have ocean views and all rooms have wood-burning fireplaces. Outside a gorgeous path leads to a big, amber-grey beach. Ever-so-friendly innkeepers whip up amazing breakfasts served in the sea-view dining area. Less expensive rooms are available across the street at bright and simple Raku House (www.rakuhouse.com; r from $159).

Glendeven
B&B **$$$**

(☎ 707-937-0083; www.glendeven.com; 8205 N Hwy 1; r $165-320; ☎) ✈ This elegant estate 2 miles south of town has organic gardens, grazing llamas (with daily feedings at dusk), forest and oceanside trails, and a wine bar serving only Mendocino wines – and that's just the start. Romantic rooms have neutral-toned, soothing decor, fireplaces and top-notch linens. Farm-to-table dinners are available at the bistro.

Brewery Gulch Inn
B&B **$$$**

(☎ 800-578-4454, 707-937-4752; www.brewerygulchinn.com; 9401 N Hwy 1; d incl breakfast $245-495; ☎) ✈ Just south of Mendocino, this bright, woodsy place has 10 modern rooms (all with flat-screen televisions, gas fireplaces and spa bathtubs), and guests enjoy touches like feather beds and leather reading chairs. The hosts pour heavily at the complimentary wine hour and leave out sweets for midnight snacking. Made-to-order breakfast is served in a small dining room overlooking the distant water.

Stanford Inn by the Sea
INN **$$$**

(☎ 800-331-8884, 707-937-5615; www.stanfordinn.com; cnr Hwy 1 & Comptche-Ukiah Rd; r $211-299;

@⎙☷☷) 🏊 This masterpiece of a lodge standing on 10 lush acres has wood-burning fireplaces, knotty pine walls, original art, stereos and top-quality mattresses in every room. Figure in a stroll in the organic gardens, where they harvest food for the excellent on-site restaurant Ravens (p230), the solarium-enclosed pool and the hot tub, and it's a sublime getaway.

Mendocino Hotel   HISTORIC HOTEL **$$$**
(☎800-548-0513, 707-937-0511; www.mendocinohotel.com; 45080 Main St; r with/without bath from $261/186, ste $475; P☎) Built in 1878 as the town's first hotel, this is like a piece of the Old West. The modern garden suites sit behind the main building and don't have a shade of old-school class, but are modern and serviceable. As gorgeous as it is, the prices are inflated, especially for the rooms with shared bathrooms.

✖️ Eating

With quality to rival Napa Valley, the influx of Bay Area weekenders have fostered an excellent dining scene that enthusiastically espouses organic, sustainable principles. Make reservations. Gathering picnic supplies is easy at **Mendosa's** (☑8am-9pm; www.harvestmarket.com; 10501 Lansing St) 🏊 organic grocery store (with deli) and the **farmers market** (cnr Howard & Main St; ☺noon-2pm Fri May-Oct).

GoodLife Cafe & Bakery   CAFE **$**
(http://goodlifecafemendo.com; 10485 Lansing St; light meals $6-10; ☺8am-4pm) 🏊 Here's where locals and tourists mingle in an unpretentious, noisy and cozy cafe setting. Get bakery goods and fair-trade coffee for breakfast and comfort food like mac and cheese or curry bowls at lunch. Lots of gluten-free options are available.

Mendocino Market   DELI **$**
(45051 Ukiah St; sandwiches $6-9; ☺11am-5pm Mon-Fri, to 4pm Sat & Sun; ☎) Pick up huge deli sandwiches and picnics here.

Mendocino Cafe   CALIFORNIAN, FUSION **$$**
(www.mendocinocafe.com; 10451 Lansing St; lunch mains $12-16, dinner mains $21-33; ☺11:30am-8pm; ☑) One of Mendocino's few fine dinner spots that also serves lovely alfresco lunches on its ocean-view deck surrounded by roses. Try the fish tacos or the 'Healing Bowl' of soba noodles, miso, shitake mushrooms and choice of meat or seafood. At dinner there's grilled steak and seafood.

Ledford House   MEDITERRANEAN **$$**
(☎707-937-0282; www.ledfordhouse.com; 3000 N Hwy 1, Albion; mains $14-30; ☺5-8pm Wed-Sun; ☑) Watch the water pound the rocks and the sun set out of the Mendocino hubbub (8 miles south) at this friendly Cal-Med bistro. Try the cassoulet or the gnocchi. It's a local hangout and gets hoppin' with live jazz most nights.

Flow   CALIFORNIAN **$$**
(45040 Main St; mains $10-25; ☺8am-10pm; ☎☑) Run by the Mendocino Cafe, this new, very busy place has the best views of the ocean in town from its 2nd-story perch. Brunch is a specialty as are Mexican-inspired small plates, artisanal pizzas and a sublime local dungeness crab chowder. Gluten-free and vegan options are available.

Patterson's Pub   PUB FOOD **$$**
(www.pattersonspub.com; 10485 Lansing St; mains $13-16; ☺food till 11pm) If you pull into town late and hungry, you'll thank your lucky stars for this place; it serves quality pub grub – fish and chips, burgers and dinner salads – with cold beer. The only traditional Irish pub ambience spoiler is the plethora of flat-screen TVs. A busy brunch is served on Saturday and Sunday mornings from 10am to 2pm.

★ **Café Beaujolais**   CALIFORNIAN **$$$**
(☎707-937-5614; www.cafebeaujolais.com; 961 Ukiah St; dinner mains $23-35; ☺11:30am-2:30pm Wed-Sun, dinner from 5:30pm daily) 🏊 Mendocino's iconic, beloved country-Cal–French restaurant occupies an 1896 house restyled into a monochromatic urban-chic dining room, perfect for holding hands by candlelight. The refined, inspired cooking draws diners from San Francisco, who make this the centerpiece of their trip. The locally sourced menu changes with the seasons, but the Petaluma duck breast served with crispy skin is a gourmand's delight.

Ravens   CALIFORNIAN **$$$**
(☎707-937-5615; www.ravensrestaurant.com; Stanford Inn, Comptche-Ukiah Rd; breakfast $11-15, mains $24-30; ☺8-10:30am Mon-Sat, to noon Sun, dinner 5:30-10pm; ☑) 🏊 Ravens brings haute-contemporary concepts to a completely vegetarian and vegan menu. Produce comes from the idyllic organic gardens of the Stanford Inn (p229), and the bold menu takes on everything from sea-palm strudel and portabella sliders to decadent (guilt-free) desserts.

MacCallum House Restaurant
CALIFORNIAN **$$$**

(🏠707-937-0289; www.maccallumhouse.com; 45020 Albion St; cafe dishes $12-18, mains $25-42; ⊘8:15-10am Mon-Fri, to 11am Sat & Sun, 5:30-9pm daily; 🐾) 🍴 Sit on the verandah or fireside for a romantic dinner of all-organic game, fish or risotto primavera. Chef Alan Kantor makes *everything* from scratch and his commitment to sustainability and organic ingredients is nearly as visionary as his menu. The cafe menu, served at the Grey Whale Bar, is one of Mendocino's few four-star bargains.

955 Ukiah Street
CALIFORNIAN **$$$**

(🏠707-937-1955; www.955restaurant.com; 955 Ukiah St; mains $18-37; ⊘from 6pm Thu-Sun) One of those semi-secret institutions, the menu here changes with what's available locally. When we passed that meant wonderous things like yogurt and scallion marinated wild jumbo prawns. The dimly lit, bohemian setting overlooks rambling gardens. Check the website for the excellent-value, three-course meal with wine for $25 and other events.

🍸 Drinking & Nightlife

Have cocktails at the Mendocino Hotel or the Grey Whale Bar at the MacCallum House Restaurant. For boisterousness and beer head straight to Patterson's Pub.

Dick's Place
DIVE BAR

(45080 Main St) A bit out of place among the fancy-pants shops downtown, but an excellent spot to check out the *other* Mendocino and do shots with rowdy locals.

🔒 Shopping

Mendocino's walkable streets are great for shopping, and the ban on chain stores ensures unique, often upscale gifts. There are many small galleries in town where one-of-a-kind artwork is for sale.

Compass Rose Leather
LEATHER GOODS

(45150 Main St) From hand-tooled belts and leather-bound journals to purses and peg-secured storage boxes, the craftsmanship here is unquestionable.

Out Of This World
OUTDOOR EQUIPMENT

(45100 Main St) Birders, astronomy buffs and science geeks head directly to this telescope, binocular and science-toy shop.

Village Toy Store
TOYS

(10450 Lansing St) Get a kite or browse the old-world selection of wooden toys and games that you won't find in the chains – hardly anything requires batteries.

Gallery Bookshop
BOOKS

(www.gallerybookshop.com; 319 Kasten St) Stocks a great selection of books on local topics, titles from California's small presses and specialized outdoor guides.

Twist
CLOTHING

(45140 Main St) 🍴 Twist stocks ecofriendly, natural-fiber clothing and lots of locally made clothing and toys.

Moore Used Books
BOOKS

(990 Main St) An excellent bad-weather hideout, the stacks here have over 10,000 used titles. The shop is in an old house at the far east end of Main St.

❶ Information

Ford House Museum & Visitor Center (🏠707-537-5397; http://mendoparks.org; 735 Main St; ⊘11am-4pm) Maps, books, information and exhibits, including a scale model of 1890 Mendocino.

Jug Handle State Reserve

Between Mendocino and Fort Bragg, Jug Handle preserves an ecological staircase that you can view on a 5-mile (round-trip) self-guided nature trail. Five wave-cut terraces ascend in steps from the seashore, each 100ft and 100,000 years removed from the previous one, and each with its own distinct geology and vegetation. One of the terraces has a pygmy forest, similar to the better-known example at Van Damme State Park. Pick up a printed guide detailing the area's geology, flora and fauna from the parking lot. The reserve is also a good spot to stroll the headlands, whale-watch or lounge on the beach. It's easy to miss the entrance; watch for the turnoff, just north of Caspar.

Jug Handle Creek Farm & Nature Center (🏠707-964-4630; www.jughandlecreekfarm.com; tent sites $14, r & cabins adult $45, student $38; ⛺) is a nonprofit 39-acre farm with rustic cabins and hostel rooms in a 19th-century farmhouse. Call ahead about work-stay discounts. Drive 5 miles north of Mendocino to Caspar; the farm is on the east side of

Hwy 1. Take the second driveway after Fern Creek Rd.

Fort Bragg

In the past, Fort Bragg was Mendocino's ugly stepsister, home to a lumber mill, a scrappy downtown and blue-collar locals who gave a cold welcome to outsiders. Since the mill closure in 2002, the town has started to reinvent itself, slowly warming to a tourism-based economy. What to do with the seaside mill site is the talk of the town, running the gamut from ideas like a marine research center or university to commercial ones like a condo development. The town itself has little say since, including projected acquisitions, it will hold under 100 acres of the 415-acre site; the rest is owned by Georgia Pacific, which is owned by Koch Industries, which is majority owned by the Koch brothers.

In the meantime, Fort Bragg's downtown continues to develop as a wonderfully unpretentious alternative to Mendocino, even if the southern end of town is hideous. Unlike the *entire* franchise-free 180-mile stretch of Coastal Hwy 1 between here and the Golden Gate, in Fort Bragg you can get a Big Mac, grande latte or any of a number of chain store products whose buildings blight the landscape. Don't fret. In downtown you'll find better hamburgers and coffee, old-school architecture and residents eager to show off their little town.

Twisting Hwy 20 provides the main access to Fort Bragg from the east, and most facilities are near Main St, a 2-mile stretch of Hwy 1. Franklin St runs parallel, one block east.

◉ Sights & Activities

Fort Bragg has the same banner North Coast activities as Mendocino – beach combing, surfing, hiking – but basing yourself here is much cheaper and arguably less quaint and pretentious. The wharf lies at Noyo Harbor – the mouth of the Noyo River – south of downtown where you can find whale-watching cruises and deep-sea fishing trips.

Mendocino Coast Botanical
Gardens   GARDENS
(📞707-964-4352; www.gardenbythesea.org; 18220 N Hwy 1; adult/child/senior $14/5/10; ⊙9am-5pm Mar-Oct, to 4pm Nov-Feb) 🖉 This gem of

Northern California displays native flora, rhododendrons and heritage roses. The succulent display alone is amazing and the organic garden is harvested by volunteers to feed area residents in need. The serpentine paths wander along 47 seafront acres south of town. Primary trails are wheelchair-accessible.

Glass Beach   BEACH
Named for (what's left of) the sea-polished glass in the sand, remnants of its days as a city dump, this beach is now part of MacKerricher State Park (p235) where visitors comb the sand for multicolored glass. Take the headlands trail from Elm St, off Main St, but leave the glass; as a part of the park system, visitors are not supposed to pocket souvenirs.

Northcoast Artists Gallery   GALLERY
(www.northcoastartists.org; 362 N Main St; ⊙10am-6pm) An excellent local arts cooperative that has the useful *Fort Bragg Gallery & Exhibition Guide*, which directs you to other galleries around town. Openings are the first Fridays of the month. Antique and book stores line Franklin St, one block east.

Triangle Tattoo & Museum   MUSEUM
(www.triangletattoo.com; 356B N Main St; ⊙noon-7pm) FREE Shows multicultural, international tattoo art.

Guest House Museum   MUSEUM
(📞707-964-4251; www.fortbragghistory.org; 343 N Main St; admission $2; ⊙1-3pm Mon, 11am-2pm Tue-Fri, 10am-4pm Sat & Sun May-Oct, 11am-2pm Thu-Sun) A majestic Victorian structure built in 1892 displays historical photos and relics of Fort Bragg's history. As hours vary, call ahead.

★ Skunk Train   HISTORIC TRAIN
(📞866-866-1690, 707-964-6371; www.skunktrain. com; adult/child $54/34; 🐾) Fort Bragg's pride and joy, the vintage train got its nickname in 1925 for its stinky gas-powered steam engines, but today the historic steam and diesel locomotives are odorless. Passing through redwood-forested mountains, along rivers, over bridges and through deep mountain tunnels, the trains run from both Fort Bragg and Willits (p243) to the midway point of Northspur, where they turn around.

If you want to go to Willits, plan to spend the night. The rain depot is downtown at the foot of Laurel St, one block west of Main St.

All-Aboard Adventures FISHING, WHALE-WATCHING
(☑707-964-1881; www.allaboardadventures.com;
32400 N Harbor Dr) Captain Tim leads crab-
bing and salmon-fishing trips (five hours,
$80) and whale-watching during the whale
migration (two hours, $35).

Pudding Creek Trestle BOARDWALK
(📷) The walk along the Pudding Creek Trestle, north of downtown, is fun for the whole
family.

⭐ Festivals & Events

Fort Bragg Whale Festival WILDLIFE
(www.mendowhale.com) Held on the third
weekend in March, with microbrew tastings,
crafts fairs and whale-watching trips.

Paul Bunyan Days CARNIVAL
(www.paulbunyandays.com) Held on Labor Day
weekend in September, celebrate California's logging history with a logging show,
square dancing, parade and fair.

🛏 Sleeping

Fort Bragg's lodging is cheaper than Mendocino's, but most of the motels along noisy
Hwy 1 don't have air-conditioning, so you'll
hear traffic through your windows. Most
B&Bs do not have TVs and they all include
breakfast. The usual chains abound. The
best-value bland motel is **Colombi Motel**
(☑707-964-5773; www.colombimotel.com; 647
Oak St; 1-/2-bedroom units with kitchenette from
$60/70; 🖧) which is in town, not on the
highway.

Country Inn B&B $
(☑707-964-3737; www.beourguests.com; 632
N Main St; r $80-220; 🖧🐾) This cute-as-a-
button, gingerbread-trimmed B&B is right in
the middle of town and is an excellent way
to dodge the chain motels for a good-value
stay. The lovely family hosts are welcoming
and easygoing, and can offer good local tips.
Breakfast can be delivered to your room and
at night you can soak in a hot tub out back.

**California Department of
Forestry** CAMPGROUND $
(☑707-964-5674; 802 N Main St; ⊘8am-4:30pm
Mon, to noon Tue-Thu) Come here for maps,
permits and camping information for the
Jackson State Forest, east of Fort Bragg,
where camping is free – which attracts all
sorts so this isn't recommended for families
or solo women.

NORTH COAST BEER TOUR

The craft breweries of the North Coast
don't mess around – bold hop profiles,
Belgian-style ales and smooth lagers
are regional specialties, and they're
produced with flair. Some breweries are
better than others, but the following
tour makes for an excellent long weekend of beer tasting in the region.

➡ Ukiah Brewing Co (p242), Ukiah

➡ Anderson Valley Brewing Company
(p239), Boonville

➡ North Coast Brewing Company
(p234), Fort Bragg

➡ Six Rivers Brewery (p260),
McKinleyville

➡ Eel River Brewing (p252), Fortuna

Shoreline Cottages MOTEL, COTTAGE $$
(☑707-964-2977; www.shoreline-cottage.com;
18725 Shoreline Hwy, Fort Bragg; d $95-165; 🖧🐾)
Low-key, four-person rooms and cottages
with kitchens surround a central, tree-filled
lawn. The family rooms are a good bargain,
and suites feature modern artwork and
clean sight lines. All rooms have docks for
your iPod, snacks and access to a library of
DVDs and there's a communal hot tub.

Grey Whale Inn B&B $$
(☑800-382-7244, 707-964-0640; www.greywha-
leinn.com; 615 N Main St; r $110-195; 🖧) Situated
in a historic building on the north side of
town (walking distance from downtown and
Glass Beach), this comfortable, family-run
inn has simple, straightforward rooms that
are good value – especially for families.

Weller House Inn B&B $$$
(☑877-893-5537, 707-964-4415; www.wellerhouse.
com; 524 Stewart St; r $200-310; 🖧) Rooms in
this beautifully restored 1886 mansion have
down comforters, good mattresses and fine
linens. The water tower is the tallest struc-
ture in town – and it has a hot tub at the
top! Breakfast is in the massive redwood
ballroom.

🍴 Eating

Similar to the lodging scene, the food in
Fort Bragg is less spendy than Mendocino,
but there are a number of truly excellent op-
tions. Self-caterers should try the **farmers
market** (cnr Laurel & Franklin Sts; ⊘3:30-6pm

Wed May-Oct) downtown or the Harvest Market (📞 707-964-7000; cnr Hwys 1 & 20; ⊙ 5am-11pm) for the best groceries.

Cowlick's Handmade Ice Cream   ICE CREAM $
(250B N Main St; scoops from $1.85; ⊙ 11am-9pm) Just great ice cream in fun flavors from classics like mocha almond fudge to the very unusual like candy cap mushroom (tastes like maple syrup but better), ginger or blackberry chocolate chunk. The sorbets (try the grapefruit Campari) are also delish.

Los Gallitos   MEXICAN $
(130 S Main St; burritos $5.25-6.25; ⊙ 11am-8pm Mon-Sat, from 10am Sun) A packed hole-in-the-wall that serves the best Mexican on the coast. Chips are homemade, the guacamole is chunky and the dishes, from the fresh fish tacos to homemade pork tamales and generous *sopas*, are consistently flavorful and well beyond the standard glob of refried beans. It's located across the parking lot from the CVS.

Living Light Café   VEGAN $
(📞 707-964-2420; 301 N Main St; mains $5-11; ⊙ 8am-5:30pm Mon-Sat, to 4pm Sun; 🖉) 🍽 As an extension of the renowned Living Light Culinary Institute, one of the nation's leading raw food schools, this bright cafe serves a tasty to-go menu that can rival cooked food at even some of the better restaurants. Try the Sicilian-style pizza on a sprouted-seed crust, raw desserts (the brownies are amazing), salads and fresh juices.

Headlands Coffeehouse   CAFE $
(www.headlandscoffeehouse.com; 120 E Laurel St; dishes $4-8; ⊙ 7am-10pm Mon-Sat, to 7pm Sun; 📶🖉) The town's best cafe is in the middle of the historic downtown, with high ceilings and lots of atmosphere. The menu gets raves for the Belgian waffles, homemade soups, veggie-friendly salads, panini and lasagna.

Eggheads   BREAKFAST $
(www.eggheadsrestaurant.com; 326 N Main St; mains $8-15; ⊙ 7am-2pm) Enjoy the *Wizard of Oz* theme as you tuck into one of 50 varieties of omelet, crepe or burrito, some with local Dungeness crab.

★Piaci Pub & Pizzeria   ITALIAN $$
(www.piacipizza.com; 120 W Redwood Ave; mains $8-18; ⊙ 11am-9:30pm Mon-Thu, to 10pm Fri & Sat, 4-9:30pm Sun) Fort Bragg's must-visit pizzeria is known for its sophisticated wood-fired, brick-oven pies as much as for its long list of microbrews. Try the 'Gustoso' – with chèvre, pesto and seasonal pears – all carefully orchestrated on a thin crust. It's tiny, loud and fun, with much more of a bar atmosphere than a restaurant. Expect to wait at peak times.

Mendo Bistro   AMERICAN $$
(📞 707-964-4974; www.mendobistro.com; 301 N Main St; mains $14-28; ⊙ 5-9pm; 👶) This dining option gets packed with a young crowd on the weekend, offering a choose-your-own-adventure menu, where you select a meat, a preparation and an accompanying sauce from a litany of options. The loud, bustling 2nd-story room is big enough for kids to run around and nobody will notice.

North Coast Brewing Company   BREWERY $$
(www.northcoastbrewing.com; 455 N Main St; mains $8-25; ⊙ 7am-9:30pm Sun-Thu, to 10pm Fri & Sat) Though thick, rare slabs of steak and a list of specials demonstrate that they take the food as seriously as the bevvies, it's burgers and garlic fries that soak up the fantastic selection of handcrafted brews. A great stop for serious beer lovers.

☆ Entertainment

Gloriana Opera Company   THEATER
(www.gloriana.org; 721 N Franklin St) Stages musical theater and operettas.

🛍 Shopping

There's plenty of window-shopping in Fort Bragg's compact downtown, including a string of antique shops along Franklin St.

Outdoor Store   OUTDOOR EQUIPMENT
(www.mendooutdoors.com; 247 N Main St) If you're planning on camping on the coast or exploring the Lost Coast, this is the best outfitter in the region, stocking detailed maps of the region's wilderness areas, fuel for stoves and high-quality gear.

Mendocino Vintage   ANTIQUES
(www.mendocinovintage.com; 344 N Franklin St) Of the antique shops on Franklin, this is the hippest by a long shot, with a case full of vintage estate jewelry, antique glassware and old local oddities.

ℹ Information

Fort Bragg-Mendocino Coast Chamber of Commerce (www.fortbragg.com; 332 N Main St; per 15min $1; ⊙ 9am-5pm Mon-Fri, to 3pm Sat) Internet access.

Mendocino Coast District Hospital (☏707-961-1234; 700 River Dr; ⊕24hr) Emergency room.

ⓘ Getting There & Around

Fort Bragg Cyclery (☏707-964-3509; www.fortbraggcyclery.com; 221a N Main St; bike rental per day from $32) Rents bicycles.

Mendocino Transit Authority (MTA; ☏800-696-4682, 707-462-1422; www.mendocinotransit.org) Runs local route 5 'BraggAbout' buses between Noyo Harbor and Elm St, north of downtown ($2). Service runs throughout the day.

MacKerricher State Park

Three miles north of Fort Bragg, the MacKerricher State Park (☏707-964-9112; www.parks.ca.gov) preserves 9 miles of pristine rocky headlands, sandy beaches, dunes and tidepools.

The visitor center (⊕10am-4pm Mon-Fri, 9am-6pm Sat & Sun Jun-Aug, 9am-3pm Sep-May) sits next to the whale skeleton at the park entrance. Hike the Coastal Trail along dark-sand beaches and see rare and endangered plant species (tread lightly). Lake Cleone is a 30-acre freshwater lake stocked with trout and visited by over 90 species of birds. At nearby Laguna Point an interpretive disabled-accessible boardwalk overlooks harbor seals and, from December to April, migrating whales. Ricochet Ridge Ranch (☏707-964-7669; www.horse-vacation.com; 24201 N Hwy 1) offers horseback-riding trips through redwoods or along the beach ($50 for 90 minutes).

Just north of the park is Pacific Star Winery (33000 Hwy 1; tastings $5; ⊕11am-5pm), in a dramatic, rub-your-eyes-in-disbelief-beautiful location on a bluff over the sea. The wines don't get pros excited but they are very drinkable, the owners are supremely friendly and you're encouraged to picnic at one of the many coast-side tables, stroll some of the short coastal trails along the cliffs and generally enjoy yourself (which isn't hard).

Popular campgrounds (☏800-444-2725; www.reserveamerica.com; tent & RV sites $35), nestled in pine forest, have hot showers and water; the first-choice reservable tent sites are numbers 21 to 59. Ten superb, secluded walk-in tent sites (numbers 1 to 10) are first-come, first-served.

Westport

If sleepy Westport feels like the peaceful edge of nowhere, that's because it is. The last hamlet before the Lost Coast, on a twisting 15-mile drive north of Fort Bragg, it is the last town before Hwy 1 veers inland on the 22-mile ascent to meet Hwy 101 in Leggett.

Head 1.5 miles north of town for the ruggedly beautiful Westport-Union Landing State Beach (☏707-937-5804; tent sites $25), which extends for 3 miles on coastal bluffs. A rough hiking trail leaves the primitive campground and passes by tidepools and streams, accessible at low tide. Bring your own water.

🛏 Sleeping & Eating

Westport Inn INN $
(☏707-964-5135; www.westportinnca.com; 37040 N Hwy 1; r incl breakfast from $70; 🖥) Simple accommodations in town include the blue-and-red, plastic-flower-festooned Westport Inn.

★ **Westport Hotel & Old Abalone Pub** INN $$
(☏877-964-3688; www.westporthotel.us; Hwy 1; r $150-225; 🕸) Westport Hotel & Old Abalone Pub is quiet enough to have a motto which brags 'You've finally found nowhere.' The rooms are bright and beautiful – feather duvets, hardwood furniture, simple patterns – and enjoy excellent views. The classy historic pub downstairs is the only option for dinner, so be thankful it's a delicious sampling of whimsical California fusions (like turduken sausage and buttermilk potatoes, and rock shrimp mac and cheese) and hearty, expertly presented pub food.

Howard Creek Ranch RANCH $$
(☏707-964-6725; www.howardcreekranch.com; 40501 N Hwy 1; r $90-198, cabins $105-198; 🕸🐕) Howard Creek Ranch, sitting on 60 stunning acres of forest and farmland abutting the wilderness, has accommodations in an 1880s farmhouse or a few cabins including a carriage barn, whose way-cool redwood rooms have been expertly handcrafted by the owner. Rates include full breakfast. Bring hiking boots, not high heels.

ALONG HIGHWAY 101

To get into the most remote and wild parts of the North Coast on the quick, eschew winding Hwy 1 for inland Hwy 101, which runs north from San Francisco as a freeway, then as a two- or four-lane highway north of Sonoma County, occasionally pausing under the traffic lights of small towns.

Know that escaping the Bay Area at rush hour (weekdays between 4pm and 7pm) ain't easy. You might sit bumper-to-bumper through Santa Rosa or Willits, where trucks bound for the coast turn onto Hwy 20.

Although Hwy 101 may not look as enticing as the coastal route, it's faster and less winding, leaving you time along the way to detour into Sonoma and Mendocino counties' wine regions (Mendocino claims to be the greenest wine region in the country), explore pastoral Anderson Valley, splash about Clear Lake or soak at hot-springs resorts outside Ukiah – time well spent indeed!

Hopland

Cute Hopland is the gateway to Mendocino County's wine country and flaunts its eco-minded, green-living ways at every turn. Hops were first grown here in 1866, but Prohibition brought the industry temporarily to a halt. Today, booze drives the local economy again with wine tasting as the primary draw.

◉ Sights

For an excellent weekend trip, use Hopland as a base for exploring the regional wineries. More information about the constantly growing roster of wineries is available at www.destinationhopland.com. Find a map to the wine region at www.visitmendocino.com.

Real Goods Solar Living Center
ENVIRONMENT CENTER
(www.solarliving.org; 13771 S Hwy 101; ◷9am-6pm; ▣) ❀ This progressive, futuristic 12-acre campus is largely responsible for the area's bold green initiates. The Real Goods Store, which sold the first solar panel in the US, is an impressive straw-bale house showroom that also has free Frey Wine tastings. The suggested donation for tours of the center (11am and 3pm Friday to Sunday, April through October) is $3 to $5.

Sip! Mendocino
WINERY
(www.sipmendocino.com; 13420 S Hwy 101; tastings $5; ◷11am-6pm) In central Hopland, this is a friendly place to get your bearings, pick up a map to the region and taste several wines without navigating all the back roads.

Amiable proprietors guide you through a tour of 18 wines with delectable appetizer pairings and a blossom-filled courtyard.

Saracina
WINERY
(www.saracina.com; 11684 S Hwy 101; ◷10am-5pm) ❀ The highlight of a tour here is the descent into the cool caves. Sensuous whites are all biodynamcially and sustainably farmed.

Fetzer Vineyards Organic Gardens
WINERY
(www.fetzer.com; 13601 Eastside Rd; ◷9am-5pm) ❀ Fetzer's sustainable practices have raised the bar, and their gardens are lovely. The wines are excellent value.

Brutocao Schoolhouse Plaza
TASTING ROOM
(www.brutocaoschoolhouseplaza.com; 13500 S Hwy 101; ◷10am-5pm) In central Hopland, this place has bocce courts and bold reds – a perfect combo.

Graziano Family of Wines
WINERY
(www.grazianofamilyofwines.com; 13251 S Hwy 101; ◷10am-5pm) Specializes in 'Cal-Ital' wines – nebbiolo, dolcetto, barbera and Sangiovese – at some great prices.

🛏 Sleeping & Eating

Piazza de Campovida
INN $$$
(☎707-744-1977; www.piazzadecampovida.com; 13441 S Hwy 101; ste $250-285; ☎) Modern Californian meets Italian at this very comfortable spot where all the spacious suites have Jacuzzi tubs, fireplaces and private balconies. The homey pizzeria in front has big tables for communal dining and fantastic artisanal pizzas – there's no corkage fee either so bring your wine find of the day.

Hopland Tap House
PUB FOOD $
(13351 S Hwy 101; mains $6-9; ◷11:30am-9pm Wed-Mon) Friendly locals, good sandwiches and selection of local beers all served in a bright brick building (plus shuffleboard). What more could you want?

Bluebird Cafe
AMERICAN $
(☎707-744-1633; 13340 S Hwy 101; breakfast & lunch $5-15, dinner $12-22; ◷7am-2pm Mon-Thu, to 7pm Fri-Sun; ☎) For conservative tastes, this classic American diner serves hearty breakfasts, giant burgers and homemade pie (the summer selection of peach-blueberry pie is dreamy). For a more exciting culinary adventure, try the wild game burgers, including boar with apple chutney and elk with a bite of horseradish.

Clear Lake

With over 100 miles of shoreline, Clear Lake is the largest naturally occurring freshwater lake in California (Tahoe is bigger, but crosses the Nevada state line). In summer the warm water thrives with algae, giving it a murky green appearance and creating a fabulous habitat for fish – especially bass – and tens of thousands of birds. Mt Konocti, a 4200ft-tall dormant volcano, lords over the scene. Alas, the human settlements don't always live up to the grandeur and thousands of acres near the lake remain scarred from wildfires in 2008.

⊙ Sights & Activities

Locals refer to the northwest portion as 'upper lake' and the southeast portion as 'lower lake.' Likeable and well-serviced Lakeport (population 4695) sits on the northwest shore, a 45-minute drive east of Hopland along Hwy 175 (off Hwy 101); tiny, Old West style Kelseyville (population 3353) is 7 miles south. Clearlake, off the southeastern shore, is the biggest (and ugliest) town.

Hwy 20 links the relatively bland northshore hamlets of Nice (the northernmost town) and Lucerne, 4 miles southeast. Middletown, a cute village, lies 20 miles south of Clearlake at the junction of Hwys 175 and 29, 40 minutes north of Calistoga.

Clear Lake State Park   STATE PARK
(☑707-279-4293; 5300 Soda Bay Rd, Kelseyville; per car $8) Six miles from Lakeport, on the lake's west shore, the park is idyllic and gorgeous, with hiking trails, fishing, boating and camping. The bird-watching is extraor-dinary. The visitor center has geological and historical exhibits.

Redbud Audubon Society   BIRD WATCHING
(www.redbudaudubon.org) In lower lake, this conservation group leads birding walks.

🛏 Sleeping & Eating

Make reservations on weekends and during summer, when people flock to the cool water.

🛏 Lakeport & Kelseyville

There are a number of motels along the main drag in Keleysville and Lakeport, but if you want fresh air, Clear Lake State Park has four campgrounds (☑800-444-7275; www.reserveamerica.com; tent & RV sites $35) with showers. The weekly farmers market (Hwy 29 & Thomas Rd; ⊙8:30am-noon Sat May-Oct) is in Kelseyville.

Mallard House   MOTEL $
(☑707-262-1601; www.mallardhouse.com; 970 N Main St, Lakeport; r with kitchen $69-149, without $55-99; ✳️🛜) Waterfront motels with boat slips include this good-value, cottage-style place. There's a tiny beach in front half covered with reeds.

★Lakeport English Inn   B&B $$
(☑707-263-4317; www.lakeportenglishinn.com; 675 N Main St, Lakeport; r $185-210, cottages $210; ✳️🛜) The finest B&B at Clear Lake is an 1875 Carpenter Gothic with 10 impeccably furnished rooms, styled with a nod to the English countryside. Weekends take high tea (nonguests welcome by reservation) – with real Devonshire cream.

NORTH COAST & REDWOODS CLEAR LAKE

TOP CLEAR LAKE WINERIES

From north to south, the following four wineries are the best; some offer tours by appointment. Tastings generally cost $5 to $10.

Ceago Vinegarden (www.ceago.com; 5115 E Hwy 20, Nice; ⊙noon-5pm) Ceago (cee-*ay*-go) occupies a spectacular spot on the north shore, and pours biodynamic, fruit-forward wines.

Brassfield Estate (www.brassfieldestate.com; 10915 High Valley Rd, Clearlake Oaks; ⊙11am-5pm Mar-Nov, from noon Dec-Apr) A stunning, unique property in the remote High Valley appellation, try the Eruption and Serenity blends.

Wildhurst Vineyards (www.wildhurst.com; 3855 Main St, Kelseyville; ⊙10am-5pm) The best wine on the lake, but the place lacks atmosphere. Try the Sauvignon Blanc.

Langtry Estate Vineyards (21000 Butts Canyon Rd, Middletown; ⊙11am-5pm) The most beautiful vineyard. Try the port.

Skylark Shores Resort INN $$

(☎800-675-6151; www.lakeportskylarkshores.com; 1120 N Main St, Lakeport; r $84-145; ❄ 🛜 🏊) There's a 1960s holiday-camp feel here with a sprawl of well-maintained older units, many of which overlook the lakeside full of wading ducks and splashing kids and a big lawn dotted with smoking barbecues. Some units also have kitchens and there's a public launch boat dock.

Park Place AMERICAN $

(50 3rd St, Lakeport; mains $7-11; ⊙11am-9pm Tue-Sun, to 3pm Mon) 🌿 Simple but right on the waterfront, come to this bright and completely unpretentious eatery for basics like pasta, burgers and pizza made from sustainable, local produce at great prices. A local favorite.

Studebaker's Coffee House DELI $

(3990 Main St, Kelseyville; sandwiches from $6; ⊙6am-4pm Mon-Fri, 7am-4pm Sat, 7am-2pm Sun) A friendly, old-style diner/fountain place with plenty of character from black-and-white checker linoleum floors to old photos on the wall. Great sandwiches including vegetarian options and the coffee's good too.

★Saw Shop Gallery Bistro CALIFORNIAN $$$

(☎707-278-0129; www.sawshopbistro.com; 3825 Main St, Kelseyville; small plates $10-16, mains $15-26; ⊙from 3pm Tue-Sat) The best restaurant in Lake County serves a Californian-cuisine menu of wild salmon and rack of lamb, as well as a small plates menu of sushi, lobster tacos, Kobe-beef burgers and flatbread pizzas. Laid-back atmosphere, too.

🛏 North Shore

Tallman Hotel HISTORIC HOTEL $$

(☎888-880-5253, 707-274-0200; www.tallmanhotel.com; 9550 Main St, Nice; cottages $169-274; ❄ 🛜 🏊🐾) 🌿 The centerpiece may be the smartly renovated historic hotel – tile bathrooms, warm lighting, thick linens – but the rest of the property's lodging, including several modern, sustainably built cottages, are equally peaceful. The shaded garden, walled-in swimming pool, brick patios and porches exude timeless elegance. Garden rooms come with Japanese soaking tubs heated by an energy-efficient geothermal-solar system.

Featherbed Railroad Co HOTEL $$

(☎800-966-6322, 707-274-8378; www.featherbedrailroad.com; 2870 Lakeshore Blvd, Nice; cabooses incl breakfast $175-220; ❄🏊) A treat for train buffs and kids, Featherbed has 10 comfy, real cabooses on a grassy lawn. Some of the cabooses straddle the border between kitschy and tacky (the 'Easy Rider' has a Harley Davidson headboard and a mirrored ceiling), but they're great fun if you keep a sense of humor. There's a tiny beach across the road.

Sea Breeze Resort COTTAGES $$

(☎707-998-3327; www.seabreezeresort.net; 9595 Harbor Dr, Glenhaven; cottages $125-180; ⊙Apr-Oct; ❄🛜) Just south of Lucerne on a small peninsula, gardens surround seven spotless lakeside cottages. All have barbecues.

🛏 Middletown

★Harbin Hot Springs SPA $$

(☎800-622-2477, 707-987-2377; www.harbin.org; Harbin Hot Springs Rd; tent & RV sites midweek/weekend $30/40, dm $40/60, s $50-75, d $100-190) Harbin is classic Northern California. Originally a 19th-century health spa and resort, it now has a retreat-center vibe and people come to unwind in silent, clothing-optional hot- and cold-spring pools. This is the birthplace of Watsu (floating massage) and there are wonderful body therapies as well as yoga, holistic-health workshops and 1160 acres of hiking.

Accommodations are in Victorian buildings (which could use sprucing up) and share a common vegetarian-only kitchen. Food is available at the market, cafe and restaurant. Day-trippers are welcome Monday through Thursday only; day rates are $20.

The springs are 3 miles off Hwy 175. From Middletown, take Barnes St, which becomes Big Canyon Rd, and head left at the fork.

🍷 Drinking & Entertainment

Library Park, in Lakeport, has free lakeside Friday-evening summer concerts, with blues and rockabilly tunes to appeal to middle-aged roadtrippers. Harbin Hot Springs presents a surprising line-up of world music and dances.

Kelsey Creek Brewing BREWERY

(3945 Main St, Kelseyville; ⊙2-8pm Tue-Fri, noon-8pm Sat, noon-5pm Sun) A 'hop'-ping fun local's scene with excellent craft beer, peanut shells on the floor and a bring-your-own-food, bring-your-dog kind of laid-back vibe.

Lakeport Auto Movies CINEMA

(www.lakeportautomovies.com; 52 Soda Bay Rd, Lakeport; 1/2/3 people per car $10/18/25)

Lakeport is home to one of the few surviving drive-in movie theaters, with showings on Friday and Saturday nights.

ℹ Information

Lake County Visitor Information Center (www.lakecounty.com; 6110 E Hwy 120, Lucerne; ⊙9am-5pm Mon-Sat, noon-4pm Sun) Has complete information and an excellent website, which allows potential visitors to narrow their focus by interests.

ℹ Getting Around

Lake Transit (☑707-994-3334, 707-263-3334; www.laketransit.org) operates weekday routes between Middletown and Calistoga ($3, 35 minutes, three daily); on Thursday it connects through to Santa Rosa. Buses serve Ukiah ($5, two hours, four daily), from Clearlake via Lakeport ($3, 1¼ hours, seven daily). Since piecing together routes and times can be difficult, it's best to phone ahead.

Anderson Valley

Rolling hills surround rural Anderson Valley, famous for apple orchards, vineyards, pastures and quiet. Visitors come primarily to winery-hop, but there's good hiking and bicycling in the hills, and the chance to escape civilization. Traveling through the valley is the most common route to Mendocino from San Francisco.

◎ Sights & Activities

Boonville (population 1488) and **Philo** (population 349) are the valley's principal towns. From Ukiah, winding Hwy 253 heads 20 miles south to Boonville. Equally scenic Hwy 128 twists and turns 60 miles between Cloverdale on Hwy 101, south of Hopland, and Albion on coastal Hwy 1.

Philo Apple Farm FARM (www.philoapplefarm.com; 18501 Greenwood Rd, Philo; ⊙dawn-dusk) For the best fruit, skip the obvious roadside stands and head to this gorgeous farm for organic preserves, chutneys, heirloom apples and pears. It also hosts cooking classes with some of the Wine Country's best chefs. You can make a weekend out of it by staying in one of the orchard cottages (p240).

Anderson Valley Brewing Company BREWERY (☑707-895-2337; www.avbc.com; 17700 Hwy 253; ⊙11am-6pm) ⌀ East of the Hwy 128 crossroads, this solar-powered brewery crafts

---

> ### BOONTLING
>
> Boonville is famous for its unique language, 'Boontling,' which evolved about the turn of the 20th century when Boonville was very remote. Locals developed the language to *shark* (stump) outsiders and amuse themselves. You may hear *codgie kimmies* (old men) asking for a horn of *zeese* (a cup of coffee) or some *bahl gorms* (good food). If you are really lucky, you'll spot the tow truck called Boont Region De-arkin' Moshe (literally 'Anderson Valley Un-wrecking Machine'). Find a fun dictionary at www.andersonvalleymuseum.org.

award-winning beers in a Bavarian-style brewhouse. You can also toss around a disc on the Frisbee-golf course while enjoying the brews, but, be warned, the sun can take its toll. Tours leave at 1:30pm and 3pm daily (only Tuesday and Wednesday in winter); call ahead.

Anderson Valley Historical Society Museum MUSEUM (www.andersonvalleymuseum.org; 12340 Hwy 128; ⊙1-4pm Sat & Sun Feb-Nov) In a recently renovated little red schoolhouse west of Boonville, this museum displays historical artifacts.

✯ Festivals & Events

Pinot Noir Festival WINE (www.avwines.com) One of Anderson Valley's many wine celebrations; held in May.

Sierra Nevada World Music Festival MUSIC (www.snwmf.com) In June, the sounds of reggae and roots fill the air, co-mingling with the scent of Mendocino County's *other* cash crop.

Mendocino County Fair FAIR (www.mendocountyfair.com) A county classic in mid-September.

⊨ Sleeping

Accommodations fill on weekends.

Hendy Woods State Park CAMPGROUND $ (☑707-937-5804, reservations 800-444-7275; www.reserveamerica.com; tent & RV sites $40, cabins $60) Bordered by the Navarro River on Hwy 128, west of Philo, the park has hiking,

TOP ANDERSON VALLEY WINERIES

The valley's cool nights yield high-acid, fruit-forward, food-friendly wines. Pinot Noir, Chardonnay and dry Gewürztraminer flourish. Most wineries (www.avwines.com) sit outside Philo. Many are family-owned and offer free tastings, some give tours. The following are particularly noteworthy:

Navarro (www.navarrowine.com; 5601 Hwy 128; ◷10am-6pm) The best option with award-winning Pinot Noir and a delicious Riesling, picnicking is encouraged.

Esterlina (www.esterlinavineyards.com) For big reds, pack a picnic and head high up the rolling hills; call ahead.

Husch (www.huschvineyards.com; 4400 Hwy 128; ◷10am-5pm) The oldest vineyard in the valley serves exquisite tastings inside a rose-covered cottage.

Bink (9000 Hwy 128; ◷11am-5pm Wed-Mon) Small-batch artisanal wines that get rave reviews are served in the Madrones complex.

picnicking and a forested campground with hot showers.

The Other Place　　　　COTTAGES $$
(✆707-895-3979; www.sheepdung.com; Boonville; cottages $150-350; ⊛⊠) Outside of town, 500 acres of ranch land surrounds private, fully equipped hilltop cottages.

★**Philo Apple Farm**　　　COTTAGES $$$
(✆707-895-2333; www.philoapplefarm.com; 18501 Greenwood Rd, Philo; r Mon-Thu $200, Fri-Sun $275) Set within the orchard (p239), guests of Philo's bucolic apple Farm choose from four exquisite cottages, each built with reclaimed materials. With bright, airy spaces, polished plank floors, simple furnishings and views of the surrounding trees, each one is an absolute dream.

Red Door cottage is a favorite because of the bathroom – you can soak in the slipper tub, or shower on the private deck under the open sky. The cottages often get booked with participants of the farm's cooking classes, so book well in advance. For a swim, the Navarro River is within walking distance.

Boonville Hotel　　　BOUTIQUE HOTEL $$$
(✆707-895-2210; www.boonvillehotel.com; 14050 Hwy 128, Boonville; r $150-360; ⊛) Decked out in a contemporary American-country style with sea-grass flooring, pastel colors and fine linens that would make Martha Stewart proud, this historic hotel's rooms are safe for urbanites who refuse to abandon style just because they've gone to the country.

The Madrones　　　HOTEL $$$
(www.themadrones.com; 9000 Hwy 28, Philo; r $160-325; ⊛) Tucked off the back of the Madrones Mediterranean-inspired complex

that includes a restaurant and the wonderful Bink Wines tasting room (p240), the spacious 'guest quarters' here are as modern-country-luxe, with a tinge of Tuscany, as you'd hope they'd be.

✗ Eating

Boonville restaurants seem to open and close as they please, so expect hours to vary based on season and whimsy. There are several places along Hwy 128 which can supply a picnic with fancy local cheese and fresh bread.

Paysenne　　　ICE CREAM $
(14111 Hwy 128, Boonville; cone $2; ◷10am-3pm Thu-Mon) Booneville's fantastic ice-cream shop serves the innovative flavors of Three Twins Ice Cream, whose delightful choices include Lemon Cookie and Strawberry Je Ne Sais Quoi (which has a hint of balsamic vinegar).

Boonville General Store　　　DELI $
(17810 Farrer Larie, Boonville; dishes $5-12; ◷7:30am-3pm Mon-Thu, 7:30am-3pm & 5:30-8pm Fri, 8:30am-3pm Sat & Sun) Opposite the Boonville Hotel, this deli is good to stock up for picnics, offering sandwiches on homemade bread, thin-crust pizzas and organic cheeses.

★**Table 128**　　　CALIFORNIAN $$
(14050 Hwy 128, Boonville; lunch mains $10-14, dinner mains $19-31; ◷6:30-8:15pm Fri-Sun) Food-savvy travelers love the constantly changing New American menu here, featuring simple dishes done well, like roasted chicken, grilled local lamb, and cheesecake. The family-style service makes dinner here a freewheeling, elegant social affair, with big

farm tables and soft lighting. It also has great wines, craft beers, fine scotch and cocktails.

Lauren's   AMERICAN $$
(www.laurensgoodfood.com; 14211 Hwy 128, Boonville; mains $13-16; ⊙ 5-9pm Tue-Sat; ☑ ⛁) Locals pack Lauren's for eclectic homemade cookin' and a good wine list. Musicians sometimes jam on the stage by the front window.

❶ Information

Anderson Valley Chamber of Commerce
(☑ 707-895-2379; www.andersonvalleychamber.com; 9800 Hwy 128, Boonville) Has tourist information and a complete schedule of annual events.

Ukiah

As the county seat and Mendocino's largest city, Ukiah is mostly a utilitarian stop for travelers to refuel the car and get a bite. But, if you have to stop here for the night, you could do much worse: the town is a friendly place that's gentrifying. There are a plethora of cookie-cutter hotel chains, some cheaper midcentury motels and a handful of very good dining options. The coolest attractions, thermal springs and a sprawling campus for Buddhist studies, lie outside the city limits. Ukiah has a pleasant, walkable shopping district along School St near the courthouse.

❍ Sights

Germain-Robin   DISTILLERY
(☑ 707-462-0314; unit 35, 3001 S State St; ⊙ by appointment) Makes some of the world's best brandy, which is handcrafted by a fifth-generation brandy-maker from the Cognac region of France. It's by appointment only, but if you're into cognac, you gotta come.

Grace Hudson Museum & Sun House   MUSEUM
(www.gracehudsonmuseum.org; 431 S Main St; admission $4; ⊙ 10am-4:30pm Wed-Sat, from noon Sun) One block east of State St, the collection's mainstays are paintings by Grace Hudson (1865–1937). Her sensitive depictions of Pomo people complement the ethnological work and Native American baskets collected by her husband, John Hudson.

✯✯ Festivals & Events

Redwood Empire Fairs   FAIR
(www.redwoodempirefair.com) At the end of July through early August.

Ukiah Country PumpkinFest   CULTURAL
(www.cityofukiah.com; ⛁) In late October, with an arts-and-crafts fair, children's carnival and fiddle contest.

🛏 Sleeping

Every imaginable chain resort is here, just off the highway – the best of these is the **Hampton Inn** (☑ 707-462-6555; hamptoninn3.hilton.com; 1160 Airport Blvd; r $143-209; ❂ �)。 For something with more personality, hot-spring resorts and campgrounds cluster around Ukiah.

Discovery Inn Motel   MOTEL $
(☑ 707-462-8873; www.discoveryinnukiahca.com; 1340 N State St; r $51-95; ❂ ⚎ ☒) Clean, but dated with a 75ft pool and several Jacuzzis.

✗ Eating

It'd be a crime to eat the fast-food junk located off the highway; Ukiah has a burgeoning food scene that pairs nicely with the surrounding wine country.

★ Schat's Courthouse Bakery & Cafe   CAFE $
(www.schats.com; 113 W Perkins St; lunch mains $3-7, dinner mains $8-14; ⊙ 5:30am-6pm Mon-Fri, to 5pm Sat) Founded by Dutch bakers, Schat's makes a dazzling array of chewy, dense breads, sandwiches, wraps, big salads, delish hot mains, full breakfasts and homemade pastries.

Ukiah Farmers Market   MARKET $
(cnr School & Clay Sts; ⊙ 9am-noon Sat) The market offers farm-fresh produce, crafts and entertainment.

Kilkenny Kitchen   CAFE $
(www.kilkennykitchen.com; 1093 S Dora St; sandwiches $8; ⊙ 10am-3pm Mon-Fri; ☑ ⛁) Tucked into a neighborhood south of downtown, county workers love this chipper yellow place for the fresh rotation of daily soups and sandwich specials (a recent visit on a blazing-hot day found a heavenly, cold cucumber dill soup). The salads – like the pear, walnut and blue cheese – are also fantastic, and there's a kid's menu.

★ Saucy   PIZZA $$
(☑ 707-462-7007; 108 W Satandley St; pizzas $11-19; ⊙ 11:30am-9pm Mon-Thu, to 10pm Fri, noon-10pm Sat) Yes there are arty pizzas with toppings like Calabrian love sausage (really), fennel pollen and almond basil pesto but there are also amazing soups, salads,

pastas and starters – Nana's meatballs are to die for and the 'kicking' minestrone lives up to its name. The small-town ambience is slightly chic but also boistrous at the same time.

Oco Time JAPANESE $$
(☑707-462-2422; www.ocotime.com; 111 W Church St; lunch mains $7-10, dinner mains $8-19; ⏱11:15am-2:30pm Tue-Fri, 5:30-8:30pm Mon-Sat; ✐) Shoulder your way through the locals to get Ukiah's best sushi, noodle bowls and *oco* (a delicious mess of seaweed, grilled cabbage, egg and noodles). The 'Peace Café' has a great vibe, friendly staff and interesting special rolls. Downside? The place gets mobbed, so reservations are a good idea.

Patrona NEW AMERICAN $$
(☑707-462-9181; www.patronarestaurant.com; 130 W Standley St; lunch mains $10-16, dinner mains $15-34; ⏱11am-9pm; ✐) ✐ Foodies flock to excellent Patrona for earthy, flavor-packed, seasonal and regional organic cooking. The unfussy menu includes dishes like roasted chicken, brined-and-roasted pork chops, housemade pasta and local wines. Make reservations and ask about the prix fixe.

Himalayan Cafe HIMALAYAN $$
(www.thehimalayancafe.com; 1639 S State St; curries $15; ✐) South of downtown, find delicately spiced Nepalese cooking – tandoori breads and curries. Some Sundays there's a Nepalese buffet at 4pm.

🍷 Drinking & Entertainment

Ask at the chamber of commerce about cultural events, including **Sunday summer concerts** at Todd Grove Park, which have a delightfully festive atmosphere, and local **square dances**.

Dive bars and scruffy cocktail lounges line State St.

Ukiah Brewing Co BREWERY
(www.ukiahbrewingco.com; 102 S State St; 🛜) ✐ A great place to drink, this local brewpub makes organic beer and draws weekend crowds.

Black Oak Coffee Roasters CAFE
(476 N State St; lavender lattes from $4; ⏱6:30am-6pm) A big modern coffeehouse with some interesting and delicious choices like a local lavender latte or a matcha chia milkshake. Light breakfasts and lunches are also on offer.

ℹ Information

Running north–south, west of Hwy 101, State St is Ukiah's main drag. School St, near Perkins St, is also good for strolling.

Bureau of Land Management (☑707-468-4000; 2550 N State St) Maps and information on backcountry camping, hiking and biking in wilderness areas.

Greater Ukiah Chamber of Commerce (☑707-462-4705; www.gomendo.com; 200 S School St; ⏱9am-5pm Mon-Fri) One block west of State St; information on Ukiah, Hopland and Anderson Valley.

Around Ukiah

Ukiah Wineries

You'll notice the acres of grapes stretching out in every direction on your way into town. Winemakers around Ukiah enjoy much of the same climatic conditions that made Napa so famous. Pick up a wineries map from the Ukiah chamber of commerce. Tasting fees are generally around $5.

Parducci Wine Cellars WINERY
(www.parducci.com; 501 Parducci Rd, Ukiah; ⏱10am-5pm) ✐ Sustainably grown, harvested and produced, 'America's Greenest Winery' produces affordable, bold, earthy reds. The tasting room, lined in brick and soft light, is a perfect little cave-like environment to get out of the summer heat, sip wine and chat about sustainability practices.

Nelson Family Vineyards WINERY
(www.nelsonfamilyvineyards.com; 550 Nelson Ranch Rd, Ukiah; ⏱10am-5pm; 🐾) Just north of Ukiah, this winery, vineyard, pear, olive and Christmas-tree farm with wondrous views over the valley is a great place to picnic (in a redwood grove), make friends and sip not-too-sweet Chardonnay and luscious red blends.

Vichy Hot Springs Resort

Opened in 1854, Vichy is the oldest continuously operating mineral-springs spa in California. The water's composition perfectly matches that of its famous namesake in Vichy, France. A century ago, Mark Twain, Jack London and Robert Louis Stevenson traveled here for the water's restorative properties, which ameliorate everything from arthritis to poison oak.

Today, the beautifully maintained historic resort (☑ 707-462-9515; www.vichysprings.com; 2605 Vichy Springs Rd, Ukiah; lodge s/d $145/205, creekside r $205/255, cottages from $295; ✳ 🛜 ♨) has the only warm-water, naturally carbonated mineral baths in North America. Unlike others, Vichy requires swimsuits (rentals $2). Day use costs $30 for two hours, $50 for a full day.

Facilities include a swimming pool, outdoor mineral hot tub, 10 indoor and outdoor tubs with natural 100°F (38°C) waters, and a grotto for sipping the effervescent waters. Massages and facials are available. Entry includes use of the 700-acre grounds, abutting Bureau of Land Management (BLM) lands; hiking trails lead to a 40ft waterfall, an old cinnabar mine and 1100ft peaks – great for sunset views.

The resort's suite and two cottages, built in 1854, are Mendocino County's three oldest structures. The cozy rooms have wooden floors, top-quality beds, breakfast and spa privileges, and no TVs.

From Hwy 101, exit at Vichy Springs Rd and follow the state-landmark signs east for 3 miles. Ukiah is five minutes, but a world, away.

Orr Hot Springs

A clothing-optional resort that's beloved by locals, back-to-the-land hipsters, backpackers and liberal-minded tourists, springs (☑ 707-462-6277; tent sites $50-60, d $150-180, cottages $215-250; ♨) has private tubs, a sauna, spring-fed rock-bottomed swimming pool, steam, massage and magical gardens. Day use costs $30.

Accommodation includes use of the spa and communal kitchen; some of the rustic cottages have kitchens. Reservations are essential.

To get there from Hwy 101, take the N State St exit, go north a quarter of a mile to Orr Springs Rd, then 9 miles west. The steep, winding mountain road takes 30 minutes to drive.

Montgomery Woods State Reserve

Two miles west of Orr, this 1140-acre reserve (Orr Springs Rd) protects five old-growth redwood groves, and some of the best groves within a day's drive from San Francisco. A 2-mile loop trail crosses the creek, winding through the serene groves, starting near the picnic tables and toilets. It's out of the way, so visitors are likely to have it mostly to themselves. Day use only; no camping.

Lake Mendocino

Amid rolling hills, 5 miles northeast of Ukiah, this tranquil 1822-acre artificial lake fills a valley, once the ancestral home of the Pomo people. On the lake's north side, Pomo Visitor Center (☑ 707-467-4200) is modeled after a Pomo roundhouse, with exhibits on tribal culture and the dam. The center was closed indefinitely for upgrades at the time of update, but was still offering information via phone about camping.

Coyote Dam, 3500ft long and 160ft high, marks the lake's southwest corner; the lake's eastern part is a 689-acre protected wildlife habitat. The Army Corps of Engineers (www.spn.usace.army.mil/mendocino; 1160 Lake Mendocino Dr; ⏰ 8am-4pm Mon-Fri) built the dam, manages the lake and provides recreation information. Its office is inconveniently located on the lower lake.

There are 300 tent and RV sites (☑ 877-444-6777; www.reserveusa.com; sites $25-30), most with hot showers and primitive boat-in sites ($8).

City of Ten Thousand Buddhas

Three miles east of Ukiah, via Talmage Rd, the site (☑ 707-462-0939; www.cttbusa.org; 2001 Talmage Rd; ⏰ 8am-6pm) used to be a state mental hospital. Since 1976 it has been a lush, quiet 488-acre Chinese-Buddhist community. Don't miss the temple hall, which really does have 10,000 Buddhas. As this is a place of worship, please be respectful of those who use the grounds for meditating. Stay for lunch in the vegetarian Chinese restaurant (4951 Bodhi Way; mains $8-12; ⏰ noon-3pm; 🥗).

Willits

Twenty miles north of Ukiah, Willits mixes NorCal dropouts with loggers and ranchers (the high school has a bull-riding team). Lamp posts of the main drag are decorated with bucking broncos and cowboys, but the heart of the place is just as boho. Though ranching, timber and manufacturing may be its mainstays, tie-dye is de rigueur. For visitors, Willits' greatest claim to fame is as the eastern terminus of the Skunk Train. Fort

Bragg is 35 miles away on the coast; allow an hour to navigate twisty Hwy 20.

◉ Sights & Activities

Ten miles north of Willits, Hwy 162/Covelo Rd makes for a superb drive following the route of the Northwestern Pacific Railroad along the Eel River and through the Mendocino National Forest. The trip is only about 30 miles, but plan on taking at least an hour on the winding road, passing exquisite river canyons and rolling hills. Eventually, you'll reach Covelo, known for its unusual round valley.

Mendocino County Museum   MUSEUM
(www.mendocinomuseum.org; 400 E Commercial St; adult/child $4/1; ⊘10am-4:30pm Wed-Sun) Among the best community museums in this half of the state, this puts the lives of early settlers in excellent historical context – much drawn from old letters – and there's an entire 1920s soda fountain and barber shop inside. You could spend an hour perusing Pomo and Yuki basketry and artifacts, or reading about local scandals and countercultural movements.

Outside, the Roots of Motive Power (www.rootsofmotivepower.com) exhibit occasionally demonstrates steam logging and machinery.

Ridgewood Ranch   HISTORIC SITE
(☑reservations 707-459-7910; www.seabiscuitheritage.com; 16200 N Hwy 101; tours $20) Willits' most famous resident was the horse Seabiscuit, which grew up here. Ninety-minute tours operate on Monday, Wednesday and Friday (June to September) at 9:30am; three-hour tours for eight or more people are available by reservation and there are other events listed on the website. Reserve-in-advance, docent-led nature tours of the surrounding natural area are free.

Skunk Train   HISTORIC TRAIN
(☑866-866-1690, 707-964-6371; www.skunktrain.com; adult/child $54/34) The depot is on E Commercial St, three blocks east of Hwy 101. Trains run between Willits and Fort Bragg (p232).

Jackson Demonstration State Forest   HIKING
Fifteen miles west of Willits on Hwy 20, the forest offers day-use recreational activities, including educational hiking trails and mountain biking. You can also camp here.

✿ Festivals & Events

Willits Frontier Days & Rodeo   RODEO
(www.willitsfrontierdays.com) Dating from 1926, Willits has the oldest continuous rodeo in California, occurring in the first week in July.

⌂ Sleeping

Some of the in-town motels – and there seems to be about a hundred of them – are dumps, so absolutely check out the room before checking in. Ask about Skunk Train packages. There are a couple crowded, loud RV parks on the edges of town for only the most desperate campers.

Old West Inn   MOTEL $
(☑707-459-4201; www.theoldwestinn.com; 1221 S Main St; r $79; ✳♠) The facade looks like a mock up of an Old West main street and each room has a theme from the 'Stable' to the 'Barber Shop.' The decor is simple and comfy with just enough imagination to make it interesting. Besides that this is the cleanest, friendliest and most highly recommended place in town.

Jackson Demonstration State Forest   CAMPGROUND $
(☑707-964-5674; campsites $15) Campsites have barbecue pits and pit toilets, but no water. Get a permit from the on-site host, or from a self-registration kiosk.

Baechtel Creek Inn & Spa   BOUTIQUE HOTEL $$
(☑800-459-9911, 707-459-9063; www.baechtelcreekinn.com; 101 Gregory Lane; d incl breakfast $119-159; ✳♠✳✳) As Willits' only upscale option, this place draws an interesting mix: Japanese bus tours, business travelers and wine trippers. The standard rooms are nothing too flashy, but they have top-notch linens, iPod docks and tasteful art. Custom rooms come with local wine and more space. The immaculate pool and lovely egg breakfast on the patio are perks.

✗ Eating

Loose Caboose Cafe   SANDWICHES $
(10 Woods St; sandwiches $7-11; ⊘7:30am-3pm) People tend to get a bit flushed when talking about the sandwiches at the Loose Caboose, which gets jammed at lunch. The Reuben and Sante Fe Chicken sandwiches are two savory delights.

Aztec Grill   MEXICAN $
(781 S Main St; burritos $5-8; ⊘5am-9pm) Yes this is in the Chevron Gas Station but the

unanimous vote from locals is that this is, hands down, the best Mexican food in town. Cheap too.

Mariposa Market GROCERIES $
(600 S Main St) Willits' natural food outlet.

Ardella's Kitchen AMERICAN $
(35 E Commercial St; mains $5-11; ☺6am-noon Tue-Sat) For quick eats, this tiny place is tops for breakfast – and is *the* place for gossip. Prices are great, portions are big and fresh and there's an infectious, cheery vibe.

Adam's Restaurant MEDITERRANEAN $$$
(☑707-456-9226; 50 S Main St; mains $22-27) Willits' swankiest address is known for its crab cakes and special occasion-worthy mains like big New York steaks, lamb osso boco or bouillabaisse, perhaps finished off with a blueberry crème brûlée. The ambiance is simple and service stellar.

🍷 Drinking & Entertainment

Shanachie Pub BAR
(50 S Main St; ☺Mon-Sat) This is a friendly little garden-side dive with tons on tap.

Willits Community Theatre THEATER
(www.willitstheatre.org; 37 W Van Lane) Stages award-winning plays, readings and comedy.

🛍 Shopping

JD Redhouse & Co CLOTHING, HOMEWARES
(212 S Main St; ☺10am-6pm) Family-owned and operated, this central mercantile is a good reflection of Willits itself, balancing cowboy essentials – boots and grain, tools and denim – with treats for the weekend tourist. The Cowlick's counter (with excellent Mendocino-made ice cream) is a good place to cool off when the heat on the sidewalk gets intense.

Book Juggler BOOKS
(182 S Main St; ☺10am-7pm Mon-Thu, to 8pm Fri, to 6pm Sat, noon-5pm Sun) Has dense rows of new and used books, music books and local papers (pick up the weird, locally printed *Anderson Valley Advertiser* here).

SOUTHERN REDWOOD COAST

There's some real magic in the loamy soil and misty air 'beyond the redwood curtain'; it yields the tallest trees and most potent herb on the planet. North of Fort Bragg, Bay Area weekenders and antique-stuffed B&Bs give way to lumber wars, pot farmers and an army of carved bears. The 'growing' culture here is palpable and the huge profit it brings to the region has evident cultural side effects – an omnipresent population of transients who work the harvests, a chilling respect for 'No Trespassing' signs and a political culture that is an uneasy balance between gun-toting libertarians, ultra-left progressives and typical college-town chaos. Nevertheless, the reason to visit is to soak in the magnificent landscape, which runs through a number of pristine, ancient redwood forests.

ℹ Information

Redwood Coast Heritage Trails (www.redwoods.info) Gives a nuanced slant on the region with itineraries based around lighthouses, Native American culture, the timber and rail industries, and maritime life.

Leggett

Leggett marks the redwood country's beginning and Hwy 1's end. There ain't much but a creepy and expensive gas station (cash only), pizza joint and two markets (not always open).

Visit 1000-acre **Standish-Hickey State Recreation Area** (☑707-925-6482; www.parks.ca.gov; 69350 Hwy 101; per car $8; ♿), 1.5 miles to the north, for picnicking, swimming and fishing in the Eel River and hiking trails among virgin and second-growth redwoods. Year-round **campgrounds** (☑800-444-7275; www.reserveamerica.com; tent & RV sites $35) with hot showers book up in summer. Avoid highway-side sites.

Chandelier Drive-Thru Tree Park (www.drivethrutree.com; 67402 Drive Thru Tree Road, Leggett; per car $5; ☺8:30am-9pm; ♿) has 200 private acres of virgin redwoods with picnicking and nature walks. And yes, there's a redwood with a hole carved out, which cars can drive through. Only in America.

The 1949 tourist trap of **Confusion Hill** (www.confusionhill.com; 75001 N Hwy 101; adult/child Gravity House $5/4, train rides $8.50/6.50; ☺9am-6pm May-Sep, 10am-5pm Oct-Apr; ♿) is an enduring curiosity and the most elaborate of the old-fashioned stops that line the route north. The Gravity House challenges queasy visitors to keep their balance while standing at a 40-degree angle (a rad photo

Southern Redwood Coast

(☎707-925-6444; 69501 Hwy 101; ⊘8am-9pm)
north of Leggett on Hwy 101.

Richardson Grove State Park

Fifteen miles to the north of Leggett, and bisected by the Eel River, serene Richardson Grove (☎707-247-3318; www.parks.ca.gov; per car $8) occupies 1400 acres of virgin forest. Many trees are over 1000 years old and 300ft tall, but there aren't many hiking trails. In winter, there's good fishing for silver and king salmon. For the last few years, CalTrans has been considering widening the road through Richardson Grove, which has sparked an intense protest.

The visitor center (⊘9am-2pm) sells books inside a 1930s lodge, which often has a fire going during cool weather. The park is primarily a campground (☎reservations 800-444-7275; www.reserveamerica.com; tent & RV sites $35) with three separate areas with hot showers; some remain open year-round. Summer-only Oak Flat on the east side of the river is shady and has a sandy beach.

Benbow Lake

On the Eel River, 2 miles south of Garberville, the 1200-acre Benbow Lake State Recreation Area (☎summer 707-923-3238, winter 707-923-3318; per car $8) exists when a seasonal dam forms the 26-acre Benbow Lake, mid-June to mid-September. In mid-August avoid swimming in the lake or river until two weeks after the Reggae on the River festival, when 25,000 people use the river as a bathtub. The water is cleanest in early summer. You can avoid the day use fee by parking near the bridge and walking down to the river. According to a ranger, you can float from here all the way through the redwood groves along the Avenue of the Giants.

🛏 Sleeping

Campground   CAMPGROUND $
(☎reservations 800-444-7275; www.reserveamerica.com; tent & RV sites $35) The year-round riverside campground is subject to wintertime bridge closures due to flooding. This part of the Eel River has wide banks and is also excellent for swimming and sunbathing.

op). Kids and fans of kitsch go nuts for the playhouse quality of the space and the narrow-gauge train rides are exciting for toddlers.

For basic supplies, a burger and some good Americana visit Price's Peg House

★ **Benbow Inn** HISTORIC HOTEL **$$$**
(☑ 707-923-2124, 800-355-3301; www.benbowinn. com; 445 Lake Benbow Dr, Garberville; r $99-315, cottage $230-315; ✳ 🛜 ☒ 🐾) This inn is a monument to 1920s rustic elegance; the Redwood Empire's first luxury resort is a national historic landmark. Hollywood's elite once frolicked in the Tudor-style resort's lobby, where you can play chess by the crackling fire, and enjoy complimentary afternoon tea and evening hors d'oeuvres.

Rooms have top-quality beds, antique furniture and crystal sherry decanters (including complimentary sherry). The window-lined *dining room* (breakfast and lunch $10 to $15, dinner mains $22 to $32) serves excellent meals and the rib eye earns raves.

Garberville

The main supply center for southern Humboldt County is the primary jumping-off point for both the Lost Coast, to the west, and the Avenue of the Giants, to the north. There's an uneasy relationship between the old-guard loggers and the hippies, many of whom came in the 1970s to grow sinsemilla (potent, seedless marijuana) after the feds chased them out of Santa Cruz. At last count, the hippies were winning the culture wars, but it rages on: a sign on the door of a local bar reads simply: 'Absolutely NO patchouli oil!!!' Two miles west, Garberville's ragtag sister, Redway, has fewer services. Garberville is about four hours north of San Francisco, one hour south of Eureka.

✪✪ Festivals & Events

The **Mateel Community Center** (www. mateel.org), in Redway, is the nerve center for many of the area's long-running annual festivals, which celebrate everything from hemp to miming.

Reggae on the River MUSIC
(www.reggaeontheriver.com) In mid-July, this fest draws huge crowds for reggae, world music, arts and craft fairs, camping and swimming in the river.

Avenue of the Giants Marathon MARATHON
(www.theave.org) Among the nation's most picturesque marathons, held in May.

Harley-Davidson Redwood Run MOTORCYCLE RALLY
(www.redwoodrun.com) The redwoods rumble with the sound of hundreds of shiny bikes in June.

🛏 Sleeping

Garberville is lined with motels and many of them, although serviceable, rent out long-term and can house questionable characters. South of town, Benbow Inn blows away the competition. For cheaper lodging try **Humboldt Redwoods Inn** (☑ 707-923-2451; www.humboldtredwoodsinn.com; 987 Redwood Dr; r $65-110; ✳ 🛜 ☒), the least dodgy of the low-budget places.

Riverwood Inn INN **$**
(☑ 707-943-1766; www.riverwoodinn.info; 2828 Avenue of the Giants, Phillipsville; r $80-98; 🐾) Six miles north of Garberville is this rockin', vintage 1937, all-American roadhouse with a big bar at the front, an OK Mexican restaurant at the back and simple lodge rooms (some with lovely terraces) downstairs. There's live music most weekend nights when you can get rowdy with the locals and traveling motorbikers then sleep it off downstairs.

✗ Eating & Drinking

Woodrose Café BREAKFAST **$$**
(www.woodrosecafe.com; 911 Redwood Dr; meals $9-16; ⏲ 8am-12pm; 🖉 🖶) Garberville's beloved cafe serves organic omelets, veggie scrambles and buckwheat pancakes with *real* maple syrup in a cozy room. Lunch brings crunchy salads, sandwiches with all-natural meats and good burritos. Plenty of gluten-free options.

Cecil's New Orleans Bistro CAJUN **$$$**
(www.cecilsgarberville.com; 733 Redwood Dr; dinner mains $18-28; ⏲ 5-9pm Thu-Mon) This 2nd-story eatery overlooks Main St and serves ambitious dishes that may have minted the California-Cajun style. Start with fried green tomatoes before launching into the smoked boar gumbo. Check the website for music events.

Branding Iron Saloon BAR
(744 Redwood Dr) Craft beer, nice locals and a hopping pool table. We'll forgive the stripper pole in the middle of the room.

❶ Information

Find out what's really happening by tuning in to community radio **KMUD FM91** (www.kmud.org).

Lost Coast

The North Coast's superlative backpacking destination is a rugged, mystifying stretch of coast where narrow dirt trails ascend rugged coastal peaks. Here you'll find volcanic beaches of black sand and ethereal mist hovering above the roaring surf as majestic Roosevelt elk graze the forests. The rugged King Range boldly rises 4000ft within 3 miles of the coast between where Hwy 1 cuts inland north of Westport to just south of Ferndale. The coast became 'lost' when the state's highway system deemed the region impassable in the early 20th century.

The best hiking and camping is within the King Range National Conservation Area and the Sinkyone Wilderness State Park, which make up the central and southern stretch of the region. The area north of the King Range is more accessible, if less dramatic.

In autumn, the weather is clear and cool. Wildflowers bloom from April through May and gray whales migrate from December through April. The warmest, driest months are June to August, but days are foggy. Note that the weather can quickly change.

❶ Information

Aside from a few one-horse villages, Shelter Cove, the isolated unincorporated town 25 long miles west of Garberville, is the only option for services. Get supplies in Garberville, Fort Bragg, Eureka or Arcata. The area is a patchwork of government-owned land and private property; visit the Bureau of Land Management office for information, permits and maps. There are few circuitous routes for hikers, and rangers can advise on reliable (if expensive) shuttle services in the area.

A few words of caution: lots of weed is grown around here and it's wise to stay on trail and respect no trespassing signs, lest you find yourself at the business end of someone's right to bear arms. And pot farmers don't pose the only threat: you'll want to check for ticks (Lyme disease is common) and keep food in bear-proof containers, which are required for camping.

Bureau of Land Management (BLM; ☑707-825-2300, 707-986-5400; 768 Shelter Cove Rd; ⊘8am-4:30pm Mon-Sat Sep-May, 8am-4:30pm Mon-Fri Jun-Aug) Nine miles east of Shelter Cove, the Bureau of Land Management has maps and directions for trails and campsites; they're posted outside after hours.

Sinkyone Wilderness State Park

Named for the Sinkyone people who once lived here, this 7367-acre wilderness extends south of Shelter Cove along pristine coastline. The Lost Coast Trail passes through here for 22 miles, from Whale Gulch south to Usal Beach Campground, taking at least three days to walk as it meanders along high ridges, providing bird's-eye views down to deserted beaches and the crashing surf (side trails descend to water level). Near the park's northern end, you can register at the (haunted!) Needle Rock Ranch (☑707-986-7711; tent sites $35) for the adjacent campsites. This is the only source of potable water. For information on when the ranch is closed (most of the time), call Richardson Grove State Park (p246).

To get to Sinkyone, drive west from Garberville and Redway on Briceland-Thorn Rd, 21 miles through Whitethorn to Four Corners. Turn left (south) and continue for 3.5 miles down a very rugged road to the ranch house; it takes 1½ hours.

There's access to the Usal Beach Campground (tent sites $25) at the south end of the park from Hwy 1 (you can't make reservations). North of Westport, take the unpaved County Rd 431 beginning from Hwy 1's Mile 90.88 and travel 6 miles up the coast to the campground. The road is graded yearly in late spring and is passable in summer via 2WD vehicles. Most sites are past the message board by the beach. Use bear canisters or keep food in your trunk. Look for giant elk feeding on the tall grass – they live behind sites No 1 and 2 – and osprey by the creek's mouth.

North of the campground, Usal Rd (County Rd 431) is much rougher and recommended only if you have a high-clearance 4WD and a chainsaw. Seriously.

King Range National Conservation Area

Stretching over 35 miles of virgin coastline, with ridge after ridge of mountainous terrain plunging to the surf, the 60,000-acre area tops out at namesake King's Peak (4087ft). The wettest spot in California, the range receives over 120in – and sometimes as much as 240in – of annual rainfall, causing frequent landslides; in winter, snow falls

HIKING THE LOST COAST

The best way to see the Lost Coast is to hike, and the best hiking is through the southern regions within the Sinkyone and Kings Range Wilderness areas. Some of the best trails start from Mattole Campground, just south Petrolia, which is on the northern border of the Kings Range. It's at the ocean end of Lighthouse Rd, 4 miles from Mattole Rd (sometimes marked as Hwy 211), southeast of Petrolia.

Both Wailaki and Nadelos have developed **campgrounds** (tent sites $8) with toilets and water. There are another four developed campgrounds around the range, with toilets but no water (except Honeydew, which has purifiable creek water). There are multiple primitive walk-in sites. You'll need a bear canister and backcountry permit, both available from Bureau of Land Management (BLM) offices.

Lost Coast Trail The Lost Coast Trail follows 24.7 miles of coastline from Mattole Campground in the north to Black Sands Beach at Shelter Cove in the south. The prevailing northerly winds make it best to hike from north to south; plan for three or four days. In October and November, and April and May, the weather is iffy and winds can blow south to north, depending on whether there's a low-pressure system overhead. The best times to come are summer weekdays in early June, at the end of August, September and October. The trail is 'discovered' and will often have hikers; busiest times are Memorial Day, Labor Day and summer weekends. The only reliable shuttle with permits to transport backpackers through the area is pricey **Lost Coast Shuttle** (☎707-223-1547; www.lostcoastshuttle.com; 2 people $200-450, extra passenger $25). Transport prices depend on the distance you want to travel.

Highlights include an abandoned lighthouse at Punta Gorda, remnants of early shipwrecks, tidepools and abundant wildlife including sea lions, seals and some 300 bird species. The trail is mostly level, passing beaches and crossing over rocky outcrops. Along the Lost Coast Trail, **Big Flat** is the most popular backcountry destination. Carry a tide table, lest you get trapped: from Buck Creek to Miller Creek, you can only hike during an outgoing tide.

Punta Gorda Lighthouse Hike A good day hike starts at the Mattole Campground trailhead and travels 3 miles south along the coast to the Punta Gorda lighthouse (return against the wind).

Ridgeline Trails To ditch the crowds, take any of the (strenuous) upland trails off the beach toward the ridgeline. For a satisfying, hard, 21-mile-long hike originating at the Lost Coast Trail, take Buck Creek Trail to King Crest Trail to Rattlesnake Ridge Trail. The 360-degree views from **King Peak** are stupendous, particularly with a full moon or during a meteor shower. Note that if you hike up, it can be hellishly hot on the ridges, though the coast remains cool and foggy; wear removable layers. Carry a topographical map and a compass: signage is limited.

on the ridges. (By contrast, nearby sea-level Shelter Cove gets only 69in of rain and no snow.) Two-thirds of the area is awaiting wilderness designation.

See the Bureau of Land Management (BLM; p248) for information. For overnight hikes, you'll need a backcountry-use permit. Don't turn left onto Briceland-Thorn Rd to try to find the 'town' of Whitethorn; it doesn't exist. Whitethorn is the BLM's name for the general area. To reach the BLM office from Garberville/Redway, follow signs to Shelter Cove; look for the roadside information panel, a quarter mile past the post office. Information and permits are also available from the BLM in Arcata (p260).

Fire restrictions begin July 1 and last until the first soaking rain, usually in November. During this time, there are no campfires allowed outside developed campgrounds.

North of the King Range

Though it's less of an adventure, you can reach the Lost Coast's northern section year-round via paved, narrow Mattole Rd. Plan on three hours to navigate the sinuous 68 miles from Ferndale in the north to the coast at Cape Mendocino, then inland to Humboldt

Redwoods State Park (p250) and Hwy 101. Don't expect redwoods; the vegetation is grassland and pasture. It's beautiful in spots – lined with sweeping vistas and wildflowers that are prettiest in spring.

You'll pass two tiny settlements, both 19th-century stage-coach stops. Petrolia has an all-in-one store (☎707-629-3455; ⊙9am-5pm) which rents bear canisters and sells supplies for the trail, good beer and gasoline. Honeydew also has a general store. The drive is enjoyable, but the Lost Coast's wild, spectacular scenery lies further south in the more remote regions.

Shelter Cove

The only sizable community on the Lost Coast, Shelter Cove is surrounded by the King Range National Conservation Area and abuts a large south-facing cove. It's a tiny seaside subdivision with an airstrip in the middle – indeed, many visitors are private pilots. Fifty years ago, Southern California swindlers subdivided the land, built the airstrip and flew in potential investors, fast-talking them into buying seaside land for retirement. But they didn't tell buyers that a steep, winding, one-lane dirt road provided the *only* access and that the seaside plots were eroding into the sea.

Today, there's still only one route, but now it's paved. Cell phones don't work here: this is a good place to disappear. The town, though sleepy and bland, offers surfing (beginners to advanced), sea kayaking, fishing, whale-watching from the shore and fantastic tide pooling; a short drive brings you to the stunning Black Sands Beach stretching for miles northward. You can rent surf boards, kayaks, wetsuits and more at the Lost Coast Surf Shack (surfboards $25 per day, kayaks half/full-day $45/70; ⊙10:30am-4:30pm).

🛏 Sleeping

Shelter Cove RV Park, Campground & Deli   CAMPGROUND $
(☎707-986-7474; 492 Machi Rd; tent/RV sites $33/43) The services may be basic, but the fresh gusts of ocean air can't be beat – the deli has good fish and chips.

Oceanfront Inn & Lighthouse   INN $$
(☎707-986-7002; www.sheltercoveoceanfrontinn. com; 10 Seal Court; r $150-250; 🐾) It looks funky on the outside but the big, bright rooms have phenomenal sea views and are tidy and modern with microwaves, refrigerators and balconies. Plus Cove Restaurant downstairs is the best place to eat in town.

Tides Inn   HOTEL $$
(☎707-986-7900; www.sheltercovetidesinn.com; 59 Surf Pt; r $165, ste with kitchen $190-380; 🐾) Perched above tidepools teeming with starfish and sea urchins, the squeaky-clean rooms here offer excellent views (go for the mini-suites on the 3rd floor). The suite options are good for families, and kids are greeted warmly by the innkeeper with an activity kit.

Inn of the Lost Coast   INN $$
(☎888-570-9676, 707-986-7521; www.innofthelost-coast.com; 205 Wave Dr; r $160-250; 🐾🐾) This is the most family-friendly hotel in town with clean rooms with basic cooking facilities, breathtaking ocean views and fireplaces. Downstairs there's a serviceable take-out pizza place and coffeehouse as well as ping pong and a hot tub.

Spy Glass Inn   INN $$$
(☎707-986-4030; www.spyglassinnsheltercove. com; 118 Dolphin Dr; ste $295-335; 🐾) Up on a hill a short walk from town, the relatively new, luxurious suites here all have sea-view Jacuzzi tubs, full kitchens and windows lit up by the expansive shoreline beyond.

✖ Eating

Shelter Cove General Store   GROCERIES $
(☎707-986-7733; 7272 Shelter Cove Rd) For those who are self-catering, Shelter Cove General Store is 2 miles beyond town. Get groceries and gasoline here.

Cove Restaurant   AMERICAN $$
(☎707-986-1197; 10 Seal Ct; mains $8-25; ⊙10am-2pm & 5-9pm Thu-Sun) The first-choice place to eat, Cove has everything from veggie stir-fries to New York steaks.

Humboldt Redwoods State Park & Avenue of the Giants

Don't miss this magical drive through California's largest redwood park, Humboldt Redwoods State Park (www.humboldtredwoods.org), which covers 53,000 acres – 17,000 of which are old-growth – and contains some of the world's most magnificent trees. It also boasts three-quarters of the world's tallest 100 trees. Tree huggers take note: these groves rival (and some say surpass) those in Redwood National Park (p263), which is a long drive further north, although the landscapes here are less diverse.

Exit Hwy 101 when you see the 'Avenue of the Giants' sign, take this smaller alternative to the interstate; it's an incredible, 32-mile, two-lane stretch. You'll find free driving guides at roadside signboards at both the avenue's southern entrance, 6 miles north of Garberville, near Phillipsville, and at the northern entrance, south of Scotia, at Pepperwood; there are access points off Hwy 101.

Three miles north, the California Federation of Women's Clubs Grove is home to an interesting four-sided hearth designed by renowned San Franciscan architect Julia Morgan in 1931 to commemorate 'the untouched nature of the forest.'

Primeval Rockefeller Forest, 4.5 miles west of the avenue via Mattole Rd, appears as it did a century ago. It's the world's largest contiguous old-growth redwood forest, and contains about 20% of all such remaining trees. Walk the 2.5-mile Big Trees Loop (note that at the time of research a footbridge had been taken out and you'll have to walk across a fallen tree to cross the river where the trail starts). You quickly walk out of sight of cars and feel like you have fallen into the time of dinosaurs.

In Founders Grove, north of the visitor center, the Dyerville Giant was knocked over in 1991 by another falling tree. A walk along its gargantuan 370ft length, with its wide trunk towering above, helps you appreciate how huge these ancient trees are.

The park has over 100 miles of trails for hiking, mountain biking and horseback riding. Easy walks include short nature trails in Founders Grove and Rockefeller Forest and Drury-Chaney Loop Trail (with berry picking in summer). Challenging treks include popular Grasshopper Peak Trail, south of the visitor center, which climbs to the 3379ft fire lookout.

Sleeping & Eating

If you want to stay along the avenue, several towns have simple lodgings of varying calibers and levels of hospitality, but camping at Humboldt Redwoods is by far the best option.

Humboldt Redwoods State Park Campgrounds CAMPGROUND $
(☎800-444-7275; www.reserveamerica.com; campsites from $35) The park runs three

DRIVE-THRU TREES

Three carved-out (but living) redwoods await along Hwy 101, a bizarre holdover from a yesteryear road trip.

➜ Chandelier Drive-Thru Tree (p245) Fold in your mirrors and inch forward, then cool off in the über-kitschy gift shop; in Leggett and arguably the best one.

➜ Shrine Drive-Thru Tree (13078 Avenue of the Giants, Myers Flat; walk/drive through $3/6; ☻sunrise-sunset; 🚗) Look up to the sky as you roll through. The least impressive of the three.

➜ Tour Thru Tree (430 Highway 169, Klamath; ☻sunrise-sunset; 🚗) Take exit 769 in Klamath, squeeze through a tree and check out an emu.

campgrounds, with hot showers, two environmental camps, five trail camps, a hike/bike camp and an equestrian camp. Of the developed spots, Burlington Campground is open year-round beside the visitor center and near a number of trailheads. Hidden Springs Campground, 5 miles south, and Albee Creek Campground, on Mattole Rd past Rockefeller Forest, are open mid-May to early fall.

Miranda Gardens Resort RESORT $$
(☎707-943-3011; www.mirandagardens.com; 6766 Avenue of the Giants, Miranda; cottages with kitchen $165-300, without kitchen $115-200; 🎱🐕) The best indoor stay along the avenue. The slightly rustic cottages have redwood paneling, some with fireplaces, and are spotlessly clean. The grounds – replete with outdoor ping pong and a play area for kids and swaying redwoods – have wholesome appeal for families.

Chimney Tree AMERICAN $
(1111 Avenue of the Giants, Phillipsville; burgers $7-11; ☻10am-7pm May-Sep) If you're just passing through and want something quick, come here. It raises its own grass-fed beef. Alas, the fries are frozen, but those burgers... mmm-mmm!

Riverbend Cellars WINERY $$
(www.riverbendcellars.com; 12990 Avenue of the Giants, Myers Flat; ☻11am-5pm) For something a bit posh, pull over here. The El Centauro red – named for Pancho Villa – is an excellent estate-grown blend.

ℹ Information

Visitor Center (☏707-946-2263; ⊘9am-5pm May-Sep, 10am-4pm Oct-Apr) South of Weott, a volunteer-staffed visitor center shows videos and sells maps.

Scotia

For years, Scotia was California's last 'company town,' entirely owned and operated by the Pacific Lumber Company, which built cookie-cut houses and had an open contempt for long-haired outsiders who liked to get between their saws and the big trees. The company went belly up in 2006, sold the mill to another redwood company and, though the town still has a creepy *Twilight Zone* vibe, you no longer have to operate by the company's posted 'Code of Conduct.'

A history of the town awaits at the Scotia Museum & Visitor Center (www.townofscotia.com; cnr Main & Bridge Sts; ⊘8am-4:30pm Mon-Fri Jun-Sep), at the town's south end. The museum's fisheries center (admission free) is remarkably informative – ironic, considering that logging destroys fish habitats – and houses the largest freshwater aquarium on the North Coast.

There are dingy motels and diners in Rio Dell (aka 'Real Dull'), across the river but the best place to stay is Scotia itself at the historic but rather plain Scotia Inn (☏707-764-5338; www.thescotiainn.com; 100 Main St; r $75-150; ☎☷) with rooms that look like Grandma's house, with lace curtains and flowery wallpaper. Back in the day, Rio Dell is where the debauchery happened: because it wasn't a company town, Rio Dell had bars and hookers. In 1969, the freeway bypassed the town and it withered.

As you drive along Hwy 101 and see what appears to be a never-ending redwood forest, understand that this 'forest' sometimes consists of trees only a few rows deep – called a 'beauty strip' – a carefully crafted illusion for tourists. Most old-growth trees have been cut. Bay Area Coalition for Headwaters Forest (www.headwaterspreserve.org) helped preserve over 7000 acres of land with public funds through provisions in a long-negotiated agreement between the Pacific Lumber Company and state and federal agencies.

Up Hwy 101 there's a great pit stop at Eel River Brewing (www.eelriverbrewing.com; 1777 Alamar Way; ⊘11am-11pm Mon-Sun) where a breezy beer garden and excellent burgers accompany all-organic brews.

Ferndale

The North Coast's most charming town is stuffed with impeccable Victorians – known locally as 'butterfat palaces' because of the dairy wealth that built them. There are so many, in fact, that the entire place is a state and federal historical landmark. Dairy farmers built the town in the 19th century and it's still run by the 'milk mafia': you're not a local till you've lived here 40 years. A stroll down Main St offers a taste of super wholesome, small-town America from galleries to old-world emporiums and soda fountains. Although Ferndale relies on tourism, it has avoided becoming a tourist trap – and has no chain stores. Though a lovely place to spend a summer night, it's dead as a doornail in winter.

◉ Sights

Half a mile from downtown via Bluff St, enjoy short tramps through fields of wildflowers, beside ponds, past redwood groves and eucalyptus trees at 110-acre Russ Park. The cemetery, also on Bluff St, is amazingly cool with graves dating to the 1800s and expansive views to the ocean. Five miles down Centerville Rd, Centerville Beach is one of the few off-leash dog beaches in Humboldt County.

Kinetic Sculpture Museum　　　　MUSEUM
(580 Main St; ⊘10am-5pm Mon-Sat, noon-4pm Sun; ☷) This warehouse holds the fanciful, astounding, human-powered contraptions used in the town's annual Kinetic Grand Championship (p258). Shaped like giant fish and UFOs, these colorful piles of junk propel racers over roads, water and marsh in the May event.

Fern Cottage　　　　HISTORIC BUILDING
(☏707-786-4835; www.ferncottage.org; Centerville Rd; group tours per person $10; ⊘by appointment) This 1866 Carpenter Gothic grew to a 32-room mansion. Only one family ever lived here, so the interior is completely preserved.

✪ Festivals & Events

This wee town has a packed social calendar, especially in the summer. If you're planning a visit, check the events page at www.victorianferndale.com.

Tour of the Unknown Coast
BICYCLE RACE
(www.tuccycle.org) A challenging event in May, in which participants in the 100-mile race climb nearly 10,000ft.

Humboldt County Fair
FAIR
(www.humboldtcountyfair.org) Held mid-August, the longest-running county fair in California.

🛏 Sleeping

Francis Creek Inn
MOTEL $
(☑707-786-9611; www.franciscreekinn.com; 577 Main St; r from $85; 🖰) White picket balconies stand in front of this downtown motel, which is family owned and operated (check in at the Red Front convenience store, right around the corner). Rooms are basic, clean and furnished simply; the value is outstanding.

Humboldt County Fairgrounds
CAMPGROUND $
(☑707-786-9511; www.humboldtcountyfair.org; 1250 5th St; tent/RV sites $10/20) Turn west onto Van Ness St and go a few blocks for lawn camping with showers.

Hotel Ivanhoe
HISTORIC HOTEL $$
(☑707-786-9000; www.ivanhoe-hotel.com; 315 Main St; r $95-145; 🖰) Ferndale's oldest hostelry opened in 1875. It has four antique-laden rooms and an Old West–style, 2nd-floor gallery, perfect for morning coffee. The adjoining saloon, with dark wood and lots of brass, is an atmospheric place for a nightcap.

Shaw House
B&B $$
(☑800-557-7429, 707-786-9958; www.shawhouse.com; 703 Main St; r $110-159, ste $200-250; 🖰🐾) Shaw House, an emblematic 'butterfat palace,' was the first permanent structure in Ferndale, completed by founding father Seth Shaw in 1866. Today, it's California's oldest B&B, set back on extensive grounds. Original details remain, including painted wooden ceilings. Most of the rooms have private entrances, and three have private balconies over a large garden.

Victorian Inn
HISTORIC HOTEL $$
(☑888-589-1808, 707-786-4949; www.victorianvillageinn.com; 400 Ocean Ave; r $105-225; 🖰) The bright, sunny rooms inside this venerable, two-story former bank building (1890), are comfortably furnished with thick carpeting, good linens and antiques.

★ Gingerbread Mansion
HISTORIC B&B $$$
(☑707-786-4000; www.gingerbread-mansion.com; 400 Berding St; r $175-495; 🖰) This is the cream of dairyland elegance, an 1898 Queen Anne–Eastlake that's unsurprisingly the town's most photographed building. And the inside is no less extravagant with each room having its own unique (and complex) mix of floral wallpaper, patterned carpeting, grand antique furniture and perhaps a fireplace, wall fresco, stained glass window or Greek statue thrown in for kicks.

🍴 Eating

There is an abundance of great places to eat in Ferndale (mostly along Main St) – from pie shops and ice cream to a butcher/deli and chocolate shop – so take this list as a starting point only. A farmers market (400 Ocean Ave; ⊙10:30am-2pm Sat May-Oct) has locally grown veggies and locally produced dairy – including the freshest cheese you'll find anywhere.

★ Mario's Lost Coast Cafe
VEGETARIAN, VEGAN $
(468 Main St; sandwiches $7.25; ⊙10am-3:30pm; 🖰🐾) Step into Mario's homey kitchen and be blown away. This guy mills his own flour, bakes his own bread and is so passionate and well-versed in all things food that it's no wonder the soups, sandwiches, salads and baked goods are easily the best vegetarian choices north of Fort Bragg. Coffee is on the house. Cash only.

No Brand Burger Stand
BURGERS $
(989 Milton St; burgers $7; ⊙11am-5pm) Hiding near the entrance to town by an industrial building, this hole-in-the-wall turns out a juicy jalapeño double cheese burger that ranks easily as the North Coast's best burger. The shakes – so thick your cheeks hurt from pulling on the straw – are about the only other thing on the menu.

Poppa Joe's
AMERICAN $
(409 Main St; mains $5-7; ⊙11am-8:30pm Mon-Fri, 6am-noon Sat & Sun) You can't beat the atmosphere at this diner, where trophy heads hang from the wall, the floors slant at a precarious angle and old men play poker all day. The American-style breakfasts are good, too – especially the pancakes.

☆ Entertainment

Ferndale Repertory Theatre
THEATER
(☑707-786-5483; www.ferndale-rep.org; 447 Main St) This top-shelf community company produces excellent contemporary theater in the historic Hart Theatre Building.

🔒 Shopping

Main St is a great place to shop. Look for the handful of secondhand stores selling vintage cowboy boots and used designer jeans at reasonable prices.

Blacksmith Shop & Gallery   METAL GOODS
(☎ 707-786-4216; www.ferndaleblacksmith.com; 455 & 491 Main St) From wrought-iron art to hand-forged furniture, this is the largest collection of contemporary blacksmithing in America.

Abraxas Jewelry & Leather Goods   JEWELRY
(505 Main St) The pieces of locally forged jewelry here are extremely cool and moderately priced. The back room is filled with tons of hats.

Humboldt Bay National Wildlife Refuge

This pristine wildlife refuge (www.fws.gov/humboldtbay) protects wetland habitats for more than 200 species of birds migrating annually along the Pacific Flyway. Between the fall and early spring, when Aleutian geese descend en masse to the area, more than 25,000 geese might be seen in a cackling gaggle outside the visitor center.

The peak season for waterbirds and raptors runs September to March; for black brant geese and migratory shorebirds mid-March to late April. Gulls, terns, cormorants, pelicans, egrets and herons come year-round. Look for harbor seals offshore; bring binoculars. If it's open, drive out South Jetty Rd to the mouth of Humboldt Bay for a stunning perspective.

Pick up a map from the visitor center (1020 Ranch Rd; ☺ 8am-5pm). Exit Hwy 101 at Hookton Rd, 11 miles south of Eureka, turn north along the frontage road, on the freeway's west side. In April look for the Godwit Days festival, a celebration of the spring bird migration.

Eureka

One hour north of Garberville, on the edge of the giant Humboldt Bay, lies Eureka, the largest bay north of San Francisco. With strip-mall sprawl surrounding a lovely historic downtown, it wears its role as the county seat a bit clumsily. Despite a diverse and interesting community of artists, writers, pagans and other free-thinkers, Eureka's

wild side slips out only occasionally – the Redwood Coast Dixieland Jazz Festival (www.redwoodcoastmusicfestivals.org) is a rollicking festival with events all over town, and summer concerts rock out the F Street Pier – but mostly, Eureka goes to bed early. Make for Old Town, a small district with colorful Victorians, good shopping and a revitalized waterfront. For night life head to Eureka's trippy sister up the road, Arcata.

⊙ Sights

The free *Eureka Visitors Map*, available at tourist offices, details walking tours and scenic drives, focusing on architecture and history. Old Town, along 2nd and 3rd Sts from C St to M St, was once down-and-out, but has been refurbished into a buzzing pedestrian district. The F Street Plaza and Boardwalk run along the waterfront at the foot of F St. Gallery openings fall on the first Saturday of every month.

Blue Ox Millworks & Historic Park   HISTORIC BUILDING
(www.blueoxmill.com; adult/child 6-12yr $10/5; ☺ 9am-4pm Mon-Sat; 🚹) One of only seven of its kind in America, antique tools and mills are used to produce authentic gingerbread trim for Victorian buildings; one-hour self-guided tours take you through the mill and historical buildings, including a blacksmith shop and 19th-century skid camp. Kids love the oxen.

Romano Gabriel Wooden Sculpture Garden   GARDENS
(315 2nd St) The coolest thing to gawk at downtown is this collection of whimsical outsider art that's enclosed by aging glass. For 30 years, wooden characters in Gabriel's front yard delighted locals. After he died in 1977, the city moved the collection here.

Clarke Historical Museum   MUSEUM
(www.clarkemuseum.org; 240 E St; suggested donation $3; ☺ 11am-4pm Wed-Sat) The best community historical museum on this stretch of the coast houses a set of typically musty relics – needlework hankies and paintings of the area's history-making notables (in this case Ulysses Grant, who was once dismissed from his post at Fort Humboldt for drunkenness). Its best collection is that of intricately woven baskets from local tribes.

Carson Mansion   HISTORIC BUILDING
(143 M St) Of Eureka's fine Victorian buildings the most famous is the ornate 1880s

home of lumber baron William Carson. It took 100 men a full year to build. Today it's a private men's club. The pink house opposite, at 202 M St, is an 1884 Queen Anne Victorian designed by the same architects and built as a wedding gift for Carson's son.

Sequoia Park   PARK
(www.sequoiaparkzoo.net; 3414 W St; park free, zoo adult/child $5/3; ⊙ zoo 10am-5pm May-Sep, Tue-Sun Oct-Apr; ⊙) A 77-acre old-growth redwood grove is a surprising green gem in the middle of a residential neighborhood. It has biking and hiking trails, a children's playground and picnic areas, and a small zoo.

Morris Graves Museum of Art   MUSEUM
(www.humboldtarts.org; 636 F St; admission $5; ⊙ noon-5pm Thu-Sun) Across Hwy 101, the excellent museum shows rotating Californian artists and hosts performances inside the 1904 Carnegie library, the state's first public library.

Discovery Museum   MUSEUM
(www.discovery-museum.org; 517 3rd St; admission $4; ⊙ 10am-4pm Tue-Sat, from noon Sun; ⊙) A hands-on kids' museum.

🏃 Activities

Harbor Cruise   CRUISE
(www.humboldtbaymaritimemuseum.com; narrated cruise adult/child $18/10) Board the 1910 *Madaket*, America's oldest continuously operating passenger vessel, and learn the history of Humboldt Bay. Located at the foot of C St, it originally ferried mill workers and passengers until the Samoa Bridge was built in 1972. The $10 sunset cocktail cruise serves from the smallest licensed bar in the state; there's also a 75-minute narrated cruise.

Hum-Boats Sail, Canoe &
Kayak Center   BOAT RENTAL
(www.humboats.com; Startare Dr; ⊙ 9am-5pm Mon-Fri, to 6pm Sat & Sun Apr-Oct, to 2:30pm Nov-Mar) At Woodley Island Marina, this outfit rents kayaks and sailboats, offering lessons, tours, charters, sunset sails and full-moon paddles.

🛏 Sleeping

Every brand of chain hotel is along Hwy 101. Room rates run high midsummer; you can sometimes find cheaper in Arcata, to the north, or Fortuna, to the south. There are also a handful of motels which cost from $55 to $100 and have no air-conditioning; choose places set back from the road. The cheapest are south of downtown on the suburban strip.

Abigail's Elegant Victorian Mansion   INN $$
(☑ 707-444-3144; www.eureka-california.com; 1406 C St; r $115-145; ⊙) Inside this National Historic Landmark that's practically a living-history museum, the sweet-as-could-be innkeepers lavish guests with warm hospitality.

Eureka Inn   HISTORIC HOTEL $$
(☑ 877-552-3985, 707-497-6903; www.eurekainn.com; cnr 7th & F Sts; r from $109; ⊙) This magestic and enormous historic hotel is slowly being renovated. The style is cozy, in an early-20th-century-lodger, vagely Wild West sort of way. The staff are extremely friendly and there's a decent bar and restaurant on the premises.

Bayview Motel   MOTEL $$
(☑ 866-725-6813, 707-442-1673; www.bayviewmotel.com; 2844 Fairfield St; r $94-175; ⊙⊙) Spotless rooms are of the chain-motel standard; some have patios overlooking Humboldt Bay.

Eagle House Inn   HISTORIC INN $$
(☑ 707-444-3344; www.eaglehouseinn.com; 139 2nd St; r $105-250; ⊙) This hulking Victorian hotel in Old Town has 24 rooms above a turn-of-the-century ballroom that's used for everything from theater and movie performances to special events. Rooms and common areas are tastefully done with precious period decor. The coolest rooms are in the corner and have sitting areas in turrets looking over the street.

Daly Inn   B&B $$
(☑ 800-321-9656, 707-445-3638; www.dalyinn.com; 1125 H St; r with bath $170-185, without bath $130) This impeccably maintained 1905 Colonial Revival mansion has individually decorated rooms with turn-of-the-20th-century European and American antiques. Guest parlors are trimmed with rare woods; outside are century-old flowering trees.

Carter House Inns   B&B $$$
(☑ 800-404-1390, 707-444-8062; http://carterhouse.com; 301 L St, Eureka; r incl breakfast $179-385; ⊙⊙) Recently constructed in period style, this hotel is a Victorian lookalike, holding rooms with top-quality linens and modern amenities; suites have in-room Jacuzzis and marble fireplaces. The same owners operate three sumptuously decorated houses: a single-level 1900 house, a honeymoon-

hideaway cottage and a replica of an 1880s San Francisco mansion, which the owner built himself, entirely by hand.

Unlike elsewhere, you won't see the innkeeper unless you want to. Guests have an in-room breakfast or can eat at the understated, elegant restaurant.

✖ Eating

Eureka is blessed with two excellent natural food grocery stores – Eureka Co-op (cnr 5th & L Sts) and Eureka Natural Foods (1626 Broadway) – and two weekly farmers markets (cnr 2nd & F Sts; ⊙10am-1pm Tue Jun-Oct) and the Henderson Center (⊙10am-1pm Thu Jun-Oct). The vibrant dining scene is focused in the Old Town district.

Ramone's   BAKERY, DELI $
(2223 Harrison St; mains $6-10; ⊙7am-6pm Mon-Sat, 8am-4pm Sun) For grab-and-go sandwiches, fresh soups and wraps.

★ Brick & Fire   CALIFORNIAN $$
(☏707-268-8959; 1630 F St; pizzas from $14, mains $15-25; ⊙11:30am-8:30pm Mon, Wed & Thu, 11:30am-9pm Fri, 5-9pm Sat & Sun) Eureka's best restaurant is in an intimate, warm-hued, bohemian-tinged setting that is almost always busy. Choose from thin-crust pizzas, delicious salads (try the pear and blue cheese) and an ever-changing selection of appetizers and mains that highlight local produce and wild mushrooms. There's a weighty wine list and servers are well-versed in pairings.

Kyoto   JAPANESE $$
(☏707-443-7777; 320 F St; sushi $4-6, mains $15-27; ⊙11:30am-3pm & 5:30-9:30pm Wed-Sat) Renowned as the best sushi in Humboldt County, dine in a tiny, packed room, where conversation with the neighboring table is inevitable. A menu of sushi and sashimi is rounded out by grilled scallops and fern-tip salad. North Coast travelers who absolutely need sushi should phone ahead for a reservation.

Waterfront Café Oyster Bar   SEAFOOD $$
(102 F St; lunch $8-17, dinner $15-24; ⊙9am-9pm) With a nice bay view and baskets of steamed clams, fish and chips, oysters and chowder, this is a solid bayside lunch for the atmosphere more than anything. A top spot for Sunday brunch, with jazz and Ramos fizzes.

Restaurant 301   CALIFORNIAN $$$
(☏800-404-1390; www.carterhouse.com; 301 L St; dinner mains $23-32; ⊙6-9pm) Eureka's top table, romantic, sophisticated 301 serves a contemporary Californian menu, using produce from its organic gardens (tours available). Mains are pricey, but the prix-fixe menu is a good way to taste local food in its finest presentation. The eight-course Chef's Grand Menu ($96) is only worthy of *really* special occasions.

🍷 Drinking & Nightlife

Lost Coast Brewery   BREWERY
(☏707-445-4480; 617 4th St; 10 tasters for $12; ⊙11am-10pm Sun-Thu, to 11pm Fri & Sat; 🛜) The roster of the regular brews at Eureka's colorful brewery might not knock the socks off a serious beer snob (and can't hold a candle to some of the others on the coast), but highlights include the Downtown Brown Ale, Great White and Lost Coast Pale Ale. After downing a few pints, the fried pub grub starts to look pretty tasty.

2 Doors Down   WINE BAR
(1626 F St; glass/bottle from $5/19; ⊙4:40-9:30pm Wed-Mon) Wonderfully cozy and inviting, this Victorian-feeling wine bar lets you create your own flights and will open any bottle on their list of 80 plus wines if you're getting two or more glasses from it. Plenty of snacks are available or order from Brick & Fire (p256) next door.

Shanty   DIVE BAR
(213 2nd St; ⊙noon-2am; 🛜) The coolest spot in town is grungy and fun. Play pool, Donkey Kong, Ms Pac Man or ping pong, or kick it on the back patio with local 20- and 30-something hipsters.

Old Town Coffee & Chocolates   CAFE
(211 F St; ⊙7am-9pm) You'll smell roasting coffee blocks before you see this place. It's a local hang out with plenty of tables, baked goods and a board where you can give a cup of whatever to your favorite regular.

☆ Entertainment

For gay events, log onto www.queerhumboldt.com.

Morris Graves Museum of Art   PERFORMING ARTS
(www.humboldtarts.org; 636 F St; suggested donation $4; ⊙noon-5pm Thu-Sun) Hosts performing-arts events between September and May, usually on Saturday evenings and Sunday afternoons.

The Alibi CLUB
(www.thealibi.com; 744 9th St) Live music on
Wednesdays and Saturdays.

🔒 Shopping

Eureka's streets lie on a grid; numbered
streets cross lettered streets. For the best
window shopping, head to the 300, 400 and
500 blocks of 2nd St, between D and G Sts.
The town's low rents and cool old spaces
harbor lots of indie boutiques.

Shipwreck VINTAGE
(430 3rd St; ⊙ 10am-6pm Mon-Fri, noon-5pm Sun)
The quality of vintage goods here – *genuinely* distressed jeans and leather jackets,
1940s housedresses and hats – is compli-
mented by handmade local jewelry and paper products.

Going Places BOOKS
(328 2nd St; ⊙ 10:30am-5:30pm Mon-Sat, 11am-
5pm Sun) Guidebooks, travel gear and international goods are certain to give a thrill
to any vagabond. It's one of three excellent
bookshops in Old Town.

ℹ️ Information

Eureka Chamber of Commerce (☑ 800-356-
6381, 707-442-3738; www.eurekachamber.
com; 2112 Broadway; ⊙ 8:30am-5pm Mon-Fri;
🛜) The main visitor information center is on
Hwy 101.

Six Rivers National Forest Headquarters
(☑ 707-442-1721; 1330 Bayshore Way; ⊙ 8am-
4:30pm Mon-Fri) Maps and information.

ℹ️ Getting There & Around

The Arcata/Eureka Airport (ACV) is a small,
expensive airport which connects regionally. The
Greyhound station is in Arcata.

Eureka Transit Service (☑ 707-443-0826;
www.eurekatransit.org) operates local buses
($1.70), Monday to Saturday.

Samoa Peninsula

Grassy dunes and windswept beaches extend along the half-mile-wide, 7-mile long
Samoa Peninsula, Humboldt Bay's western
boundary. Stretches of it are spectacular,
particularly the dunes, which are part of a
34-mile-long dune system – the largest in
Northern California – and the wildlife viewing is excellent. The shoreline road (Hwy
255) is a backdoor route between Arcata and
Eureka.

At the peninsula's south end, Samoa
Dunes Recreation Area (⊙ sunrise-sunset) is
good for picnicking and fishing. For wildlife,
head to Mad River Slough & Dunes; from
Arcata, take Samoa Blvd west for 3 miles,
then turn right at Young St, the Manila turnoff. Park at the community center lot, from
where a trail passes mudflats, salt marsh
and tidal channels. There are over 200 species of birds: migrating waterfowl in spring
and fall, songbirds in spring and summer,
shorebirds in fall and winter, and waders
year-round.

These undisturbed dunes reach heights of
over 80ft. Because of the environment's fra-
gility, access is by guided tour only. Friends
of the Dunes (www.friendsofthedunes.org)
leads free guided walks; register via email
through the website and check online for
departure locations and information.

The lunch place on the peninsula is the
Samoa Cookhouse (☑ 707-442-1659; www.sa-
moacookhouse.net; 908 Vance Ave; breakfast $12,
lunch $13, dinner $16; ⊙ 7am-3pm & 5-8pm; 👪),
the last surviving lumber camp cookhouse
in the West, where you can shovel down
all-you-can-eat meals at long red-checkered
tables. Kids eat for half-price. The cookhouse is five minutes northwest of Eureka,
across the Samoa Bridge; follow the signs.
From Arcata, take Samoa Blvd (Hwy 255).

Arcata

The North Coast's most progressive town,
Arcata surrounds a tidy central square that
fills with college students, campers, tran-
sients and tourists. Sure, it occasionally
reeks of patchouli and its politics lean far
left, but its earnest embrace of sustainability
has fostered some of the most progressive
civic action in America. Here, garbage trucks
run on biodiesel, recycling gets picked up
by tandem bicycle, wastewater gets filtered
clean in marshlands and almost every street
has a bike lane.

Founded in 1850 as a base for lumber
camps, today Arcata is defined as a magnet for 20-somethings looking to expand
their minds: either at Humboldt State University (HSU), and/or on the highly potent
marijuana which grows around here like,
um, weeds. After a 1996 state proposition
legalized marijuana for medical purposes,
Arcata became what one *New Yorker* article
referred to as the 'heartland of high grade

marijuana.' The economy of the regions has become inexorably tied to the crop since.

Roads run on a grid, with numbered streets traveling east–west and lettered streets going north–south. G and H Sts run north and south (respectively) to HSU and Hwy 101. The plaza is bordered by G and H and 8th and 9th Sts.

◉ Sights

Around Arcata Plaza are two National Historic Landmarks: the 1857 Jacoby's Storehouse (cnr H & 8th Sts) and the 1915 Hotel Arcata (cnr G & 9th Sts). Another great historic building is the 1914 Minor Theatre (1013 10th St), which some local historians claim is the oldest theater in the US built specifically for showing films.

Humboldt State University UNIVERSITY
(HSU; www.humboldt.edu; 1 Harpst St) The University on the northeastern side of town holds the Campus Center for Appropriate Technology (CCAT), a world leader in developing sustainable technologies; on Fridays at 2pm you can take a self-guided tour of the CCAT House, a converted residence that uses only 4% of the energy of a comparably sized dwelling.

Arcata Marsh & Wildlife Sanctuary WILDLIFE RESERVE
On the shores of Humboldt Bay, this has 5 miles of walking trails and outstanding birding. The Redwood Region Audubon Society (📞 826 7031; www.rras.org; donation welcome) offers guided walks Saturdays at 8:30am, rain or shine, from the parking lot at I St's south end. Friends of Arcata Marsh offer guided tours Saturdays at 2pm from the Arcata Marsh Interpretive Center (📞 707-826-2359; 569 South G St; tours free; ⊙ 9am-5pm).

⚡ Activities

Finnish Country Sauna & Tubs DAY SPA, MASSAGE
(📞 707-822-2228; http://cafemokkaarcata.com; cnr 5th & J Sts; 30min per adult/child $9.50/2; ⊙ noon-11pm Sun-Thu, to 1am Fri & Sat) Like some kind of Euro-crunchy bohemian dream, these private, open-air redwood hot tubs (half-hour/hour $9/17) and sauna are situated around a small frog pond. The staff is easygoing, and the facility is relaxing, simple and clean. Reserve ahead, especially on weekends.

HSU Center Activities OUTDOORS
(www.humboldt.edu/centeractivities) An office on the 2nd floor of the University Center, beside the campus clock tower, sponsors myriad workshops, outings and sporting-gear rentals; nonstudents welcome.

Arcata Community Pool SWIMMING
(ww.arcatapool.com; 1150 16th St; adult/child $7/4.50; ⊙ 5:30am-9pm Mon-Fri, 9am-6pm Sat, 1-4pm Sun; 🏊) Has a co-ed hot tub, sauna and exercise room.

Adventure's Edge OUTDOORS
(www.adventuresedge.com; 650 10th St; ⊙ 9am-6pm Mon-Sat, 10am-5pm Sun) Rents, sells and services outdoor equipment.

🎉 Festivals & Events

Kinetic Grand Championship RACE
(www.kineticgrandchampionship.com) Arcata's most famous event is held Memorial Day weekend: people on amazing self-propelled contraptions travel 38 miles from Arcata to Ferndale.

Arcata Bay Oyster Festival FOOD
(www.oysterfestival.net) A magical celebration of oysters and beer happens in June.

North Country Fair FAIR
(www.sameoldpeopl.org) A fun September street fair, where bands with names like the Fickle Hillbillies jam.

🛏 Sleeping

Arcata has affordable but limited lodgings. A cluster of hotels – Comfort Inn, Hampton Inn, etc – is just north of town, off Hwy 101's Giuntoli Lane. There's cheap camping further north at Clam Beach.

Fairwinds Motel MOTEL $
(📞 707-822-4824; www.fairwindsmotelarcata.com; 1674 G St; s $70-75, d $80-90; 🐾) Serviceable rooms in a standard-issue motel, with some noise from Hwy 101. It's more expensive than the chain motels but has the advantage of being in town.

Hotel Arcata HISTORIC HOTEL $$
(📞 707-826-0217; www.hotelarcata.com; 708 9th St; r $89-156; 🐾) Anchoring the plaza, this renovated 1915 brick landmark has friendly staff, high ceilings and comfortable, old-world rooms of mixed quality. The rooms in front are an excellent perch for people-watching on the square, but the quietest face the back.

Lady Anne Inn
B&B $$

(☎707-822-2797; www.ladyanneinn.com; 902 14th St; r $115-140) Roses line the walkway to this 1888 mansion full of Victorian bric-a-brac. The frilly rooms are pretty, but there's no breakfast.

Arcata Stay
VACATION RENTALS $$

(☎877-822-0935, 707-822-0935; www.arcatastay. com; apt from $169) A network of excellent apartment and cottage rentals. There is a two-night minimum and prices go down the longer you stay.

✗ Eating

Great food abounds in restaurants throughout Arcata, almost all casual.

There are fantastic farmers markets, at the Arcata Plaza (☺9am-2pm Sat Apr-Nov) and in the parking lot of Wildberries Market. Just a few blocks north of downtown, there is a cluster of the town's best restaurants on G St.

Wildberries Marketplace
MARKET, DELI $

(www.wildberries.com; 747 13th St, Arcata; sandwiches $4-10; ☺6am-midnight; ☑) Wildberries Marketplace is Arcata's best grocery, with natural foods, a good deli, bakery and juice bar.

North Coast Co-op
GROCERIES $

(cnr 8th & I Sts; ☺6am-9pm) The gigantic North Coast Co-op carries organic foods and is a community staple; check the kiosk out front.

Japhy's Soup & Noodles
NOODLES $

(1563 G St; mains $5-9; ☺11:30am-8pm Mon-Fri) Big salads, tasty coconut curry, cold noodle salads and homemade soups – and cheap!

Stars Hamburgers
BURGERS $

(1535 G St; burgers $3-6; ☺11am-8pm Mon-Thu, to 9pm Fri, to 7pm Sat, noon-6pm Sun; ☑) Uses grass-fed beef to make fantastic burgers.

Los Bagels
BAGELS $

(1061 I St; bagels from $3.75; ☺6:30am-5pm Mon-Fri, 7am-5pm Sat, 7am-3pm Sun) Mixing 'traditional' Jewish food with the taste of Mexico.' Get all kinds of creative spreads and toppings on fresh bagels. Locals swear the Swedish dill sauce served here (from Trinidad's Larrapin Restaurant) is one of the best things on earth.

Don's Donuts
FAST FOOD $

(933 H St; donuts 80¢-$1.35, sandwiches from $6; ☺24hr) Tasty Southeast Asian sandwiches and doughnuts, even at 3am.

Arcata Scoop
ICE CREAM $

(1068 I St; cones from $3.50; ☺12-10:30pm) Creamy and wonderful flavors inspired by seasonal ingredients. Try the honey vanilla lavender. These are the same folks who run the ever-popular Fairfax Scoop in Marin County, California.

★ 3 Foods Cafe
FUSION $$

(www.cafeattheendoftheuniverse.com; 835 J St; dishes $4-14; ☺5:30am-10pm Tue-Thu, to 11pm Fri & Sat, to 9pm Sun; ☑) A perfect fit with the Arcata dining scene: whimsical, creative, worldly small plates (think Thai-style tacos or buttermilk fried chicken) at moderate prices (a prix fixe is sometimes available for $20). The lavender-infused cocktails start things off on the right foot. The 'uber' mac and cheese is the crowd favorite.

Wildflower Cafe & Bakery
CAFE $$

(☎707-822-0360; 1604 G St; breakfast & lunch $5-8, dinner mains $15-16; ☺8am-8pm Sun-Wed; ☑) Tops for vegetarians, this tiny storefront serves fab frittatas, pancakes and curries, and big crunchy salads.

Machine Works
CALIFORNIAN $$

(937 10th St; mains $10-20; ☺5-10pm Mon-Sun, 10am-2pm Sat & Sun) Inside the Robert Goodman Winery, this place gets raves from locals for its brunch (think: crab Benedict or

---

DON'T LEGALIZE IT: ECONOMICS OF HUMBOLDT HERB

With an estimated one-fifth of Humboldt County's population farming its world-famous weed, a good chunk of the economy here has run, for decades, as bank-less, tax-evading and cash only – but it's also been prosperous enough to strongly support many local businesses. Back in the 1990s farmers could expect to get around $6000 a pound for their crops but since medical marijauna has become legal the price has dropped radically, to just above $1000 per pound. So what happens if pot is legalized as it's expected to be by 2016? Prices may plummet even further and everything from local restaurants to clothing stores will suffer for it. So yeah, those 'Save Humboldt County Keep Pot Illegal' bumper stickers you may see around town, are serious.

eggs baked in chèvre mousse) and dinner fare from a killer French onion soup to burgers and hoisin-braised short ribs. It's also a fab spot for creative cocktails.

Folie Douce   MODERN AMERICAN **$$$**
(☑707-822-1042; www.foliedoucearcata.com; 1551 G St; dinner mains $24-37; ⊙5:30-9pm Tue-Thu, to 10pm Fri & Sat; ☑) *☞* Just a slip of a place, but with an enormous reputation. The short but inventive menu features seasonally inspired bistro cooking, from Asian to Mediterranean, with an emphasis on local organics. Wood-fired pizzas ($16 to $22) are renowned. Sunday brunch, too. Reservations essential.

☲ Drinking & Nightlife

Dive bars and cocktail lounges line the plaza's northern side. Arcata is awash in coffeehouses and brewpubs.

★ **Six Rivers Brewery**   BREWERY
(www.sixriversbrewery.com; 1300 Central Ave, McKinleyville; ⊙11:30am-midnight Tue-Sun, from 4pm Mon) One of the first female-owned breweries in California, the 'brew with a view' kills it in every category: great beer, amazing community vibe, occasional live music and delicious hot wings. The spicy chili-pepper ale is amazing. At first glance the menu might seem like ho-hum pub grub (mains $11 to $18), but portions are fresh and huge. They also make a helluva pizza.

Redwood Curtain Brewery   BREWERY
(550 S G St, suite 6; ⊙3-11pm Mon-Fri, 12-11pm Sat & Sun) A newer brewery (started in 2010), this tiny gem has a varied collection of rave-worthy craft ales and live music most Thursdays and Saturdays. Plus they offer free wheat thins and goldfish crackers to munch on.

Humboldt Brews   BAR
(www.humbrews.com; 856 10th St) This popular beer house has been elegantly remodeled and has a huge selection of carefully selected beer taps, fish tacos and buffalo wings (pub grub $5 to $10). Live music nightly.

Cafe Mokka   CAFE
(www.cafemokkaarcata.com; cnr 5th & J Sts) Bohos head to this cafe at Finnish Country Sauna & Tubs (p258) for a mellow, old-world vibe, good coffee drinks and homemade cookies (snacks $4).

☆ Entertainment

Arcata Theatre   CINEMA
(www.arcatatheater.com; 1036 G St) An exquisite remodeling has revived this classic movie house, which shows art films, rock documentaries, silent films and more. Serves beer.

Center Arts   PERFORMING ARTS
(☑tickets 707-826-3928; www.humboldt.edu/centerarts) Hosts events on campus and you'd be amazed at who shows up: from Diana Krall and Dave Brubeck to Ani DiFranco. The place to buy tickets is at the University Ticket Office in the HSU Bookstore on the 3rd floor of the University Center.

☖ Shopping

Tin Can Mailman   BOOKS
(www.tincanbooks.com; 1000 H St) Used volumes on two floors; excellent for hard-to-find books.

❶ Information

Arcata Eye (www.arcataeye.com) Free newspaper listing local events; the 'Police Log' column is hysterical.

Bureau of Land Management (BLM; ☑707-825-2300; 1695 Heindon Rd) Has information on the Lost Coast.

California Welcome Center (☑707-822-3619; www.arcatachamber.com; ⊙9am-5pm) At the junction of Hwys 299 and 101 is a California Welcome Center, with area info.

❶ Getting There & Around

United (www.united.com) makes regional connections (which are predictably expensive) to the Arcata/Eureka Airport.

Greyhound (www.greyhound.com) serves Arcata; from San Francisco budget $57 and seven hours. **Redwood Transit buses** (www.hta.org) serve Arcata and Eureka on the Trinidad–Scotia routes ($3, 2½ hours), which don't run on Sunday.

Arcata city buses (☑707-822-3775; ⊙Mon-Sat) stop at the **Arcata Transit Center** (☑707-825-8934; 925 E St at 9th St). For shared rides, read the bulletin board at the North Coast Co-op (p259).

Revolution Bicycle (www.revolutionbicycle.com; 1360 G St) and **Life Cycle Bike Shop** (www.lifecyclearcata.com; 1593 G St; ⊙Mon-Sat) rent, service and sell bicycles.

Only in Arcata: borrow a bike from **Library Bike** (www.arcata.com/greenbikes; 865 8th St) for a $20 deposit, which gets refunded when you return the bike – up to six months later! They're beaters, but they ride.

NORTHERN REDWOOD COAST

Congratulations, traveler, you've reached the middle of nowhere, or at least the top of the middle of nowhere. Here, the trees are so large that the tiny towns along the road seem even smaller. The scenery is pure drama: cliffs and rocks, native lore, legendary salmon runs, mammoth trees, redneck towns and RVing retirees. It's certainly the *weirdest* part of the California Coast. Leave time to dawdle and bask in the haunting grandeur of it all and, even though there are scores of mid-century motels, you simply must make an effort to sleep outdoors if possible.

Trinidad

Cheery, tiny Trinidad perches prettily on the side of the ocean, combining upscale homes with a mellow surfer vibe. Somehow it feels a bit off-the-beaten-path even though tourism augments fishing to keep the economy going. Trinidad gained its name when Spanish sea captains arrived on Trinity Sunday in 1775 and named the area La Santisima Trinidad (the Holy Trinity). It didn't boom, though, until the 1850s, when it became an important port for miners.

◉ Sights & Activities

Trinidad is small: approach via Hwy 101 or from the north via Patrick's Point Dr (which becomes Scenic Dr further south). To reach town, take Main St.

The free town map at the information kiosk (p263) shows several fantastic hiking trails, most notably the Trinidad Head Trail with superb coastal views; excellent for whale-watching (December to April). Stroll along an exceptionally beautiful cove at Trinidad State Beach; take Main St and bear right at Stagecoach, then take the second turn left (the first is a picnic area) into the small lot.

Scenic Dr twists south along coastal bluffs, passing tiny coves with views back toward the bay. It peters out before reaching the broad expanses of Luffenholtz Beach (accessible via the staircase) and serene white-sand Moonstone Beach. Exit Hwy 101 at 6th Ave/Westhaven to get there. Further south Moonstone becomes Clam Beach County Park.

Surfing is good year-round, but potentially dangerous: unless you know how to judge conditions and get yourself out of trouble – there are no lifeguards here – surf in better-protected Crescent City.

HSU Telonicher Marine Laboratory
AQUARIUM

(☑707-826-3671; www.humboldt.edu/marinelab; 570 Ewing St; self-guided tours $1; ☺9am-4:30pm Mon-Fri, 10am-5pm Sat & Sun mid-Sep–mid-May; ⚐) Near Edwards St, this marine lab has a touch tank, several aquariums (look for the giant Pacific octopus), an enormous whale jaw and a cool 3D map of the ocean floor. You can also join a naturalist on tidepooling expeditions (90 minutes, $3). All tours are by appointment only so call ahead and be sure to ask about conditions.

🛏 Sleeping

Many of the inns line Patrick's Point Dr, north of town. Trinidad Retreats (www.trinidadretreats.com) and Redwood Coast Vacation Rentals (www.redwoodcoastvacationrentals.com) handle local property rentals.

Clam Beach
CAMPGROUND $

(tent sites per car $15) South of town off Hwy 101, this beach has excellent camping, but can get very crowded and it's a favorite with traveling homeless folks. Pitch your tent in the dunes (look for natural windbreaks). Facilities include pit toilets, cold water, picnic tables and fire rings.

View Crest Lodge
LODGE $$

(☑707-677-3393; www.viewcrestlodge.com; 3415 Patrick's Point Dr; sites $27, 1-bedroom cottages $95-240; ☎) On a hill above the ocean on the inland side, some of the well-maintained, modern and terrific-value cottages have views and Jacuzzis; most have kitchens. There's also a good campground.

Trinidad Inn
INN $$

(☑707-677-3349; www.trinidadinn.com; 1170 Patrick's Point Dr; r $75-195; 🛜🐾) Sparklingly clean and attractively decorated rooms (many with kitchens) fill this upmarket, gray-shingled motel under tall trees. Most rooms have fully equipped kitchens.

★ Trinidad Bay B&B
B&B $$$

(☑707-677-0840; www.trinidadbaybnb.com; 560 Edwards St; r incl breakfast $200-300; 🛜) Opposite the lighthouse, this gorgeous light-filled Cape Cod–style place overlooks the harbor

Northern Redwood Coast

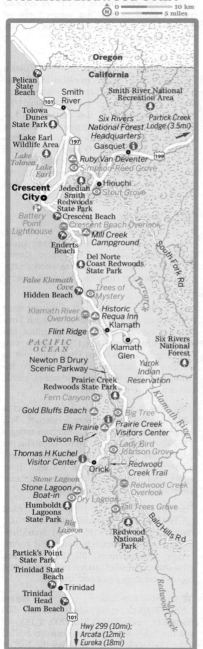

Oregon
California
Pelican State Beach
Smith River
Smith River National Recreation Area
Tolowa Dunes State Park
Six Rivers National Forest Headquarters
Patrick Creek Lodge (3.5mi)
Lake Earl Wildlife Area
Gasquet
Lake Tolowa
Lake Earl
Ruby Van Deventer
Simpson-Reed Grove
Crescent City
Jedediah Smith Redwoods State Park
Houchi
Stout Grove
Battery Point Lighthouse
Crescent Beach
Crescent Beach Overlook
Enderts Beach
Mill Creek Campground
Del Norte Coast Redwoods State Park
South Fork Rd
False Klamath Cove
Hidden Beach
Trees of Mystery
Turwar Rd
Klamath River Overlook
Historic Requa Inn
Klamath
Flint Ridge
PACIFIC OCEAN
Klamath Glen
Six Rivers National Forest
Newton B Drury Scenic Parkway
Yurok Indian Reservation
Prairie Creek Redwoods State Park
Fern Canyon
Big Tree
Gold Bluffs Beach
Prairie Creek Visitors Center
Elk Prairie
Davison Rd
Lady Bird Johnson Grove
Thomas H Kuchel Visitor Center
Orick
Redwood Creek Trail
Stone Lagoon
Redwood Creek Overlook
Stone Lagoon Boat-in
Dry Lagoon
Humboldt Lagoons State Park
Tall Trees Grove
Big Lagoon
Redwood National Park
Klamath River
Bald Hills Rd
Patrick's Point State Park
Trinidad State Beach
Trinidad
Trinidad Head
Clam Beach
Redwood Creek
Hwy 299 (10mi);
Arcata (12mi);
Eureka (18mi)

0 — 10 km
0 — 5 miles

NORTH COAST & REDWOODS TRINIDAD

and Trinidad Head. Breakfast is delivered to your uniquely styled room and in the afternoon the house fills with the scent of freshly baked cookies. The Trinity Alps room has a kitchenette and is well-set up for families.

Lost Whale Inn
B&B $$$

(☎707-677-3425; www.lostwhaleinn.com; 3452 Patrick's Point Dr; r incl breakfast $199-325, ste $408-750; ☎) Perched atop a grassy cliff, high above crashing waves and braying sea lions, this spacious, modern, light-filled B&B has jaw-dropping views out to the sea. The lovely gardens have a 24-hour hot tub. Kids under seven are not permitted.

Turtle Rocks Oceanfront Inn
B&B $$$

(☎707-677-3707; www.turtlerocksinn.com; 3392 Patrick's Point Dr; r incl breakfast $195-335) Enjoy truly stunning sea vistas from every room at this plush, modern place on three peaceful, windswept acres.

✖ Eating & Drinking

Lighthouse Café
FAST FOOD $

(☎707-677-0390; 355 Main St; mains $6-9; ☺11am-7pm Tue-Sun; ▣) ✐ Across from the Chevron, this fun little arty joint makes good food fast, using mostly organic ingredients – try the creative soups, fish and chips with hand-cut fries, local grass-fed beef burgers and homemade ice creams. Order at the counter and then sit inside or out.

Katy's Smokehouse & Fishmarket
SEAFOOD $

(www.katyssmokehouse.com; 740 Edwards St; ☺9am-6pm) ✐ Makes its own chemical-free and amazingly delicious smoked and canned fish, using line-caught sushi-grade seafood. There's no restaurant, just grab some for a picnic.

The Seascape
SEAFOOD $$

(1 Bay St; mains $12-35; ☺7am-8:30pm) Go to this old-school, diner-type place for a panoramic view of the sea more than the food. It's a lovely spot to watch the daily catch come in over a slice of pie or a bowl of yummy clam chowder.

Larrupin Cafe
CALIFORNIAN $$$

(☎707-677-0230; www.larrupin.com; 1658 Patrick's Point Dr; mains $20-37; ☺5-9pm) Everybody loves Larrupin, where Moroccan rugs, chocolate-brown walls, gravity-defying floral arrangements and deep-burgundy Oriental carpets create a moody atmosphere perfect for a lovers' tryst. On the menu expect consistently good mesquite-grilled seafood and meats – the smoked beef brisket is amazing. In the summer book a table on the garden patio for live music Wednesday and Friday nights.

Moonstone Grill   SEAFOOD **$$$**
(Moonstone Beach; mains $20-90; ⏱5:30-8:30pm Wed-Sun) Enjoy drop-dead sunset views over a picture-perfect beach while supping on the likes of oysters on the half-shell, Pacific wild king salmon or spice-rubbed rib eye. If the high price tag is a bit out-of-budget, drop in for a glass of wine.

Beachcomber Café   CAFE
(☑707-677-0106; 363 Trinity St; ⏱7am-4pm Mon-Fri, 8am-4pm Sat & Sun) Head here for the best homemade cookies and to meet locals. Bring your own cup if you want a drink to go. Friday rocks live music and beer's on tap.

ℹ Information

Information Kiosk (cnr Patrick's Point Dr & Main St) Just west of the freeway. The pamphlet *Discover Trinidad* has an excellent map.
Trinidad Chamber of Commerce (☑707-667-1610; www.trinidadcalif.com) Information on the web, but no visitor center.

Patrick's Point State Park

Coastal bluffs jut out to sea at 640-acre Patrick's Point (☑707-677-3570; www.parks.ca.gov; 4150 Patrick's Point Dr; per car $8), where sandy beaches abut rocky headlands. Five miles north of Trinidad, with supereasy access to dramatic coastal bluffs, it's a best-bet for families. Stroll scenic overlooks, climb giant rock formations, watch whales breach, gaze into tidepools, or listen to barking sea lions and singing birds from this manicured park.

Sumêg (⏱daily) FREE is an authentic reproduction of a Yurok village, with hand-hewn redwood buildings where Native Americans gather for traditional ceremonies. In the native plant garden you'll find species for making traditional baskets and medicines.

On Agate Beach look for stray bits of jade and sea-polished agate. Follow the signs to tidepools, but tread lightly and obey regulations. The 2-mile Rim Trail, a old Yurok trail around the bluffs, circles the point with access to huge rocky outcroppings. Don't miss Wedding Rock, one of the park's most romantic spots. Other trails lead around unusual formations like Ceremonial Rock and Lookout Rock.

The park's three well-tended campgrounds (☑reservations 800-444-7275; www.reserveamerica.com; tent & RV sites $35) have coin-operated hot showers and very clean bathrooms. Penn Creek and Abalone campgrounds are more sheltered than Agate Beach.

Humboldt Lagoons State Park

Stretching out for miles along the coast, Humboldt Lagoons has long, sandy beaches and a string of coastal lagoons. Big Lagoon and the even prettier Stone Lagoon are both excellent for kayaking and bird-watching. Sunsets are spectacular, with no artificial structures in sight. Picnic at Stone Lagoon's north end. The Stone Lagoon Visitor Center, on Hwy 101, has closed due to staffing shortages, but there's a toilet and a bulletin board displaying information.

A mile north, Freshwater Lagoon is also great for birding. South of Stone Lagoon, tiny Dry Lagoon (a freshwater marsh) has a fantastic day hike and good agate hunting. Park at Dry Lagoon's picnic area and hike north on the unmarked trail to Stone Lagoon; the trail skirts the southwestern shore and ends up at the ocean, passing through woods and marshland rich with wildlife. Mostly flat, it's about 2.5 miles one way – and nobody takes it because it's unmarked.

All campsites are first-come, first-served. The park runs two environmental campgrounds (tent sites $20; ⏱Apr-Oct); bring water. Stone Lagoon has six boat-in environmental campsites. Check in at Patrick's Point State Park, at least 30 minutes before sunset.

Humboldt County Parks (☑707-445-7651; tent sites $20) operates a lovely cypress-grove picnic area and campground beside Big Lagoon, a mile off Hwy 101, with flush toilets and cold water, but no showers.

Redwood National & State Parks

A patchwork of public lands jointly administered by the state and federal governments, the Redwood National & State Parks include Redwood National Park, Prairie Creek Redwoods State Park, Del Norte Coast Redwoods State Park and Jedediah Smith Redwoods State Park. A smattering

THE ENDANGERED MARBLED MURRELET: KEEPER OF THE FORESTS

Notice how undeveloped the Redwood National & State Parks have remained? Thank the marbled murrelet, a small white and brown-black auk that nests in old-growth conifers. Loss of nesting territory due to logging has severly depleted the bird's numbers but Redwood National Park scientists have discovered that corvid predators (ravens, jays etc) are also to blame. Because corvids are attracted to food scraps left by visitors, the number of snacking, picnicking or camping humans in the park greatly affects predation on the marbled murrelet. Restrictions on development to prevent food scraps and thus protect the birds are so strict that it's nearly impossible to build anything new.

of small towns break up the forested area, making it a bit confusing to get a sense of the parks as a whole. Prairie Creek and Jedediah Smith parks were originally land slated for clear-cutting, but in the '60s activists successfully protected them and today all these parks are an International Biosphere Reserve and World Heritage Site. At one time the national park was to absorb at least two of the state parks, but that did not happen, and so the cooperative structure remains.

Little-visited compared to their southern brethren, the world's tallest living trees have been standing here for time immemorial, predating the Roman Empire by over 500 years. Prepare to be impressed.

The small town of Orick (population 650), at the southern tip of the park, in a lush valley, is barely more than a few storefronts, the only gas station between Trinidad and Klamath, and a vast conglomeration of woodcarving.

Redwood National Park

Just north of the southern visitor center, turn east onto Bald Hills Rd and travel 2 miles to Lady Bird Johnson Grove, one of the park's most spectacular groves, and also one of the busiest, accessible via a gentle 1-mile loop trail. Continue for another 5 miles up Bald Hills Rd to Redwood Creek

Overlook. On the top of the ridgeline, at 2100ft, get views over the forest and the entire watershed – provided it's not foggy. Just past the overlook lies the gated turnoff for Tall Trees Grove, the location of several of the world's tallest trees. Rangers issue 50 vehicle permits. Pick one up, along with the gate-lock combination, from the visitor centers. Allow four hours for the round-trip, which includes a 6-mile drive down a rough dirt road (speed limit 15mph) and a steep 1.3-mile one-way hike, which descends 800ft to the grove.

Several longer trails include the awe-inspiring Redwood Creek Trail, which also reaches Tall Trees Grove. You'll need a free backcountry permit to hike and camp (highly recommended, as the best backcountry camping on the North Coast), but the area is most accessible from Memorial Day to Labor Day, when summer footbridges are up. Otherwise, getting across the creek can be perilous or impossible.

For hikes, kayaking, fishing or a slew of other tours, book with Redwood Adventures (☎866-733-9637; www.redwoodadventures.com; 7 Valley Green Camp Rd, Orick) whose guides know the area better than anyone and will get you to places you may not otherwise find on your own. For horseback riding from May to November call the Redwood Creek Bukarettes (☎707-499-2943; www.redwoodcreekbukarettes.com; 1000 Drydens Rd, Orick; 1½hr trail rides from $60).

🛏 Sleeping

Elk Meadow Cabins CABINS $$$
(☎866-733-9637; www.redwoodadventures.com; 7 Valley Green Camp Rd, Orick; cabins $179-279; 📶🐾) These spotless and bright cabins with equipped kitchens and all the mod-cons are in a perfect mid-parks location – they're great if you're traveling in a group and the most comfy choice even if you're not. Expect to see elk on the lawn in the mornings. Cabins sleep six to eight people and there's an additional $45 cleaning fee.

ℹ Information

Unlike most national parks, there are no fees and no highway entrance stations at Redwood National Park, so it's imperative to pick up the free map at the park headquarters in Crescent City (p269) or at the infomation center in Orick. Rangers here issue permits to visit Tall Trees Grove and loan bear-proof containers for backpackers.

For in-depth redwood ecology, buy the excellent official park handbook. The **Redwood Parks Association** (www.redwoodparksassociation.org) provides good information on its website, including detailed descriptions of all the parks hikes.

Redwood Information Center (Kuchel Visitor Center; ☎707-464-6101; www.nps.gov/redw; Hwy 101; ⊙9am-6pm June-Aug, to 5pm Sep-Oct & Mar-May, to 4pm Nov-Feb) On Hwy 101, a mile south of tiny Orick.

Prairie Creek Redwoods State Park

Famous for some of the world's best virgin redwood groves and unspoiled coastline, this 14,000-acre section of Redwood National & State Parks has spectacular scenic drives and 70 miles of hiking trails, many of which are excellent for children. Pick up maps and information and sit by the river-rock fireplace at Prairie Creek Visitor Center (☎707-464-6101; ⊙9am-5pm Mar-Oct, 10am-4pm Nov-Feb; ⓖ). Kids will love the taxidermy dioramas with push-button, light-up displays. Outside, elk roam grassy flats.

🏃 Activities

There are 28 mountain-biking and hiking trails through the park, from simple to strenuous. Only a few of these will appeal to hard-core hikers, who should take on the Del Norte Coast Redwoods State Park. Those tight on time or with mobility impairments should stop at Big Tree, an easy 100yd walk from the car park. Several other easy nature trails start near the visitor center, including Revelation Trail and Elk Prairie Trail. Stroll the recently reforested logging road on the Ah-Pah Interpretive Trail at the park's north end. The most challenging hike in this corner of the park is the truly spectacular 11.5-mile Coastal Trail which goes through primordial redwoods.

Just past the Gold Bluffs Beach Campground the road dead ends at Fern Canyon, the second busiest spot in the parks, where 60ft fern-covered sheer-rock walls can be seen from Steven Spielberg's *Jurassic Park 2: The Lost World*. This is one of the most photographed spots on the North Coast – damp and lush, all emerald green – and *totally* worth getting your toes wet to see.

Newton B Drury Scenic Parkway　DRIVING

Just north of Orick is the turn off for the 8-mile parkway, which runs parallel to Hwy 101 through untouched ancient redwood forests. This is a not-to-miss short detour off the freeway where you can view the magnificence of these trees. Numerous trails branch off from roadside pullouts, including family-friendly options and trails that fit ADA (American Disabilities Act) requirements, including Big Tree and Revelation Trail.

🛏 Sleeping

Welcome to the great outdoors: without any motels or cabins, the only choice here is to pitch a tent in the campgrounds at the southern end of the park.

⭐ Gold Bluffs Beach　CAMPGROUND $

(tent sites $35) This gorgeous campground sits between 100ft cliffs and wide-open ocean, but there are some windbreaks and solar-heated showers. Look for sites up the cliff under the trees. No reservations.

Elk Prairie Campground　CAMPGROUND $

(☎reservations 800-444-7275; www.reserveamerica.com; tent & RV sites $35) Elk roam this popular campground, where you can sleep under redwoods or at the prairie's edge. There are hot showers, some hike-in sites and a shallow creek to splash in. Sites 1–7 and 69–76 are on grassy prairies and get full sun; sites 8–68 are wooded. To camp in a mixed redwood forest, book sites 20–27.

Del Norte Coast Redwoods State Park

Marked by steep canyons and dense woods north of Klamath, half the 6400 acres of this park (☎707-464-6101, ext 5120; per car day-use $8) are virgin redwood forest, crisscrossed by 15 miles of hiking trails. Even the most cynical of redwood-watchers can't help but be moved.

Pick up maps and inquire about guided walks at the Redwood National & State Parks Headquarters (p269) in Crescent City or the Redwood Information Center in Orick.

Hwy 1 winds in from the coast at rugged, dramatic Wilson Beach, and traverses the dense forest, with groves stretching off as far as you can see.

Picnic on the sand at False Klamath Cove. Heading north, tall trees cling precipitously to canyon walls that drop to the rocky, timber-strewn coastline, and it's almost impossible to get to the water, except via the

SMITH RIVER NATIONAL RECREATION AREA

West of Jedediah Smith Redwoods State Park, the Smith River, the state's last remaining undammed waterway, runs right beside Hwy 199. Originating high in the Siskiyou Mountains, its serpentine course cuts through deep canyons beneath thick forests. Chinook salmon (October to December) and steelhead trout (December to April) annually migrate up its clear waters. Camp (there are four developed campgrounds), hike (75 miles of trails), raft (145 miles of navigable white water) and kayak here, but check regulations if you want to fish. Stop by the Six Rivers National Forest Headquarters (707-457-3131; www.fs.fed.us/r5/sixrivers; 10600 Hwy 199, Gasquet; 8am-4:30pm daily May-Sep, Mon-Fri Oct-Apr) to get your bearings. Pick up pamphlets for the Darlingtonia Trail and Myrtle Creek Botanical Area, both easy jaunts into the woods, where you can see rare plants and learn about the area's geology.

gorgeous but steep Damnation Creek Trail or Footsteps Rock Trail.

Between these two, serious hikers will be most greatly rewarded by the Damnation Creek Trail. It's only 4 miles long, but the 1100-ft elevation change and cliff-side redwood makes it the park's best hike. The unmarked trailhead starts from a parking area off Hwy 101 at Mile 16.

Crescent Beach Overlook and picnic area has superb wintertime whale-watching. At the park's north end, watch the surf pound at Crescent Beach, just south of Crescent City via Enderts Beach Rd.

Mill Creek Campground (800-444-7275; www.reserveamerica.com; tent & RV sites $35) has hot showers and 145 sites in a redwood grove, 2 miles east of Hwy 101 and 7 miles south of Crescent City. Sites 1-74 are woodsier; sites 75-145 sunnier. Hike-in sites are prettiest.

Jedediah Smith Redwoods State Park

The northernmost park in the system of Redwood National & State Parks, the dense stands at Jedediah Smith (707-464-6101, ext 5112; day use $8) are 10 miles northeast of Crescent City (via Hwy 101 east to Hwy 197). The redwood stands are so thick that few trails penetrate the park, but the outstanding 11-mile Howland Hill scenic drive cuts through otherwise inaccessible areas (take Hwy 199 to South Fork Rd; turn right after crossing two bridges). It's a rough road, impassable for RVs, but if you can't hike, it's the best way to see the forest.

Stop for a stroll under enormous trees in Simpson-Reed Grove. If it's foggy at the coast it may be sunny here. There's a swimming hole and picnic area near the park

entrance. An easy half-mile trail, departing from the far side of the campground, crosses the Smith River via a summer-only footbridge, leading to Stout Grove, the park's most famous grove. The visitor center (707-464-6101; 10am-4pm daily Jun-Aug, Sat & Sun Sep-Oct & Apr-May) sells hiking maps and nature guides. If you wade in the river, be careful in the spring when currents are swift and the water cold.

🛏 Sleeping

Campground   CAMPGROUND $
(reservations 800-444-7275; www.reserveamerica.com; tent & RV sites $35) The popular campground has gorgeous sites tucked through the redwoods beside the Smith River.

Hiouchi Motel   MOTEL $
(888-881-0819, 707-458-3041; www.hiouchimotel.com; 2097 Hwy 199; s $50, d $65-71;) If you don't camp, try the renovated Hiouchi Motel offering clean, straightforward motel rooms.

Klamath

Giant metal-cast golden bears stand sentry at the bridge across the Klamath River announcing Klamath, one of the tiny settlements that break up Redwood National & State Parks between Prairie Creek Redwoods State Park and Del Norte Coast Redwoods State Park. With a gas station/market, diner and a casino, Klamath is basically a wide spot in the road with some seriously great roadside kitsch at its edges. The Yurok Tribal Headquarters is in the town center and the entire settlement and much of the surrounding area is the tribe's ancestral land. Klamath is roughly an hour north of Eureka.

👁 Sights & Activities

The mouth of the Klamath River is a dramatic sight. Marine, riparian, forest and meadow ecological zones all converge and the birding is exceptional. For the best views, head north of town to Requa Rd and the Klamath River Overlook and picnic on high bluffs above driftwood-strewn beaches. On a clear day, this is one of the most spectacular viewpoints on the North Coast, and one of the best whale-watching spots in California (this is one of the mammal's first feeding stops as they come south from Alaska). For a good hike, head north along the Coastal Trail. You'll have the sand to yourself at Hidden Beach; access the trail at the northern end of Motel Trees.

Just south of the river, on Hwy 101, the scenic Coastal Drive, a narrow, winding country road traces extremely high cliffs over the ocean. Due to erosion a 3.3 mile section of the 9.5 mile loop (between Carruther's Cove trailhead and the intersection of the Coastal Drive with Alder Camp Rd) has been closed to motor traffic since 2011 but it's still walkable and bikeable. Though technically in Redwood National Park, this drive is much closer to Klamath.

Klamath Jet Boat Tours   BOAT TOURS
(www.jetboattours.com; 17635 US 101; 2hr tours adult/child $45/25) Book jet-boat excursions and fishing trips run by the Yukon Tribe.

🛏 Sleeping & Eating

Woodsy Klamath is cheaper than Crescent City, but there aren't as many places to eat or buy groceries, and there's nothing to do at night but play cards. There are ample private RV parks in the area.

Flint Ridge Campground   CAMPGROUND
(📞707-464-6101) FREE Four miles from the Klamath River Bridge via Coastal Drive, this tent-only, hike-in campground sits among a wild, overgrown meadow of ferns and moss. It's a 10-minute walk (half a mile) east, uphill from the parking area. There's no water, plenty of bear sightings (bear boxes on site) and you have to pack out trash. But, hey, it's free.

Ravenwood Motel   MOTEL $
(📞866-520-9875, 707-482-5911; www.ravenwood-motel.com; 131 Klamath Blvd; r/ste with kitchen $75/125; 🛜) The spotlessly clean rooms are better than anything in Crescent City and individually decorated with furnishings and flair you'd expect in a city hotel, not a small-town motel.

★ Historic Requa Inn   HISTORIC HOTEL $$
(📞707-482-1425; www.requainn.com; 451 Requa Rd, Klamath; r $119-199; 🛜) 🌿 A woodsy country lodge on bluffs overlooking the mouth of the Klamath, the creaky and bright 1914 Requa Inn is a North Coast favorite and – even better – it's a carbon-neutral facility. Many of the charming old-time-America–style rooms have mesmerizing views over the misty river, as does the dining room, which serves new Native American, organic cuisine.

Crescent City

Though Crescent City was founded as a thriving 1853 seaport and supply center for inland gold mines, the town's history was quite literally washed away in 1964, when half the town was swallowed by a tsunami. Of course, it was rebuilt (though mostly with the utilitarian ugliness of ticky-tacky buildings), but its marina was devastated by the 2011 Japan earthquake and tsunami, when the city was evacuated. Crescent City remains California's last big town north of Arcata, though the constant fog (and sounding fog horn) and damp, '60s sprawl makes it about as charming as a wet bag of dirty laundry. The economy depends heavily on shrimp and crab fishing, hotel tax and on Pelican Bay maximum-security prison, just

---

TREES OF MYSTERY

It's hard to miss the giant statues of Paul Bunyan and Babe the Blue Ox towering over the parking lot at Trees of Mystery (📞707-482-2251; www.treesofmystery.net; 15500 Hwy 101; adult/child & senior $14/7; ⊗8am-7pm Jun-Aug, 9am-4pm Sep-May; 🚹), a shameless tourist trap with a gondola running through the redwood canopy and a fun 'Tall Tales Forest' where chainsaw sculptures tell the tale of Paul Bunyan. It's perfect for families, anyone unable to take a strenuous hike or lovers of kitsch. The surprisingly wonderful End of the Trail Museum located behind the Trees of Mystery gift shop has an outstanding collection of Native American arts and artifacts, and it's free.

north of town, which adds tension to the air and lots of cops to the streets.

Hwy 101 splits into two parallel one-way streets, with the southbound traffic on L St, northbound on M St. To see the major sights, turn west on Front St toward the lighthouse. Downtown is along 3rd St.

◉ Sights & Activities

If you're in town in August, the Del Norte County Fair features a rodeo, and lots of characters. Jedediah Smith Redwoods State Park (p266) is 10 miles inland.

North Coast Marine Mammal Center   SCIENCE CENTER

(☎707-465-6265; www.northcoastmmc.org; 424 Howe Dr; admission by donation; ⊙10am-5pm; ☒) ◔ Just east of Battery Point, this is the ecologically minded foil to the garish Ocean World: the clinic treats injured seals, sea lions and dolphins and releases them back into the wild (donation requested).

Battery Point Lighthouse   LIGHTHOUSE

(☎707-467-3089; www.delnortehistory.org; adult/child $3/1; ⊙10am-4pm Wed-Sun Apr-Oct) The 1856 lighthouse, at the south end of A St, still operates on a tiny, rocky island that you can easily reach at low tide. You can also get a tour of the on-site museum for $3. Note that the listed hours are subject to change due to tides and weather.

Beachfront Park   PARK

(Howe Dr; ☒) Between B and H Sts, this park has a harborside beach with no large waves, making it perfect for little ones. Further east on Howe Dr, near J St, you'll come to Kidtown, with slides and swings and a make-believe castle.

🛏 Sleeping

Most people stop here for one night while traveling; motels are overpriced, but you'll pass a slew of hotels on the main arteries leading into and out of town. The county operates two excellent first-come, first-served campgrounds just outside of town.

★Curly Redwood Lodge   MOTEL $

(☎707-464-2137; www.curlyredwoodlodge.com; 701 Hwy 101 S; r $56-98; ☒☎) The Redwood Lodge is a marvel: it's entirely built and paneled from a single curly redwood tree which measured over 18in thick in diameter. Progressively restored and polished into a gem of mid-century kitsch, the inn is a delight

for retro junkies. Rooms are clean, large and comfortable (request one away from the road). For truly modern accommodations, look elsewhere.

Bay View Inn   HOTEL $

(☎800-742-8439; www.ccbvi.com; 2844 Fairfield; r $55-135; ☒☎) Bright, modern, updated rooms with microwaves and refrigerators fill this centrally located independent hotel. It may seem a bit like a better-than-average highway exit chain, but colorful bedspreads and warm hosts add necessary homespun appeal. The rooms upstairs in the back have views of the lighthouse and the harbor.

Crescent Beach Motel   MOTEL $

(☎707-464-5436; www.crescentbeachmotel.com; 1455 Hwy 101 S; r $84-136; ☒☎) Just south of town, this basic, old-fashioned motel is the only place in town to stay right on the beach, offering views that distract you from the somewhat plain indoor environs. Skip rooms without a view.

Florence Keller Park   CAMPGROUND $

(☎707-464-7230; http://www.co.del-norte.ca.us; 3400 Cunningham Lane; sites $10) County-run Florence Keller Park has 50 sites in a beautiful grove of young redwoods (take Hwy 101 north to Elk Valley Cross Rd and follow the signs).

Ruby Van Deventer Park   CAMPGROUND $

(4705 N Bank Rd; sites $15; ☒) The county's Ruby Van Deventer Park has 18 sites along the Smith River, off Hwy 197.

✕ Eating

Good Harvest Café   AMERICAN $

(575 Hwy 101 S; mains $7-14; ⊙7am-9pm Mon-Sat, from 8am Sun; ☒☒) This popular local cafe is in a spacious location across from the harbor. It's got a bit of everything – all pretty good – from soups and sandwiches to full meals and smoothies. Good beers, a crackling fire and loads of vegetarian options make this the best dining spot in town.

Tomasini's Enoteca   ITALIAN, AMERICAN $

(960 3rd St; mains $4-11; ⊙7:30am-2pm; ☒) Stop in for salads, sandwiches or jazz on weekend nights. Hands down the most happening place downtown.

Chart Room   SEAFOOD $$

(130 Anchor Way; dinner mains $10-28; ⊙6:30am-7pm Sun-Thu, to 8pm Fri & Sat; ☒) At the tip of the South Harbor pier, this joint is

renowned far and wide for its fish and chips: batter-caked golden beauties which deliver on their reputation. It's often a hive of families, retirees, Harley riders and local businessmen, so grab a beer at the small bar and wait for a table.

ℹ Information

Crescent City-Del Norte Chamber of Commerce (☑800-343-8300, 707-464-3174; www.northerncalifornia.net; 1001 Front St; ☻9am-5pm May-Aug, Mon-Fri Sep-Apr) Local information.

Redwood National & State Parks Headquarters (☑707-464-6101; 1111 2nd St; ☻9am-5pm Oct-May, to 6pm Jun-Sep) On the corner of K St; you'll find rangers here and information about all four parks under its jurisdiction.

ℹ Getting There & Around

United Express (☑800-241-6522) flies into tiny **Crescent City Airport** (CEC), north of town. **Redwood Coast Transit** (www.redwoodcoast-transit.org) serves Crescent City with local buses ($1), and runs buses Monday to Saturday to Klamath ($1.50, one hour, two daily) and Arcata ($30, two hours, two daily) with stops in between.

Tolowa Dunes State Park & Lake Earl Wildlife Area

Two miles north of Crescent City, this state park and wildlife area (☑707-464-6101, ext 5112; ☻sunrise-sunset) encompasses 10,000 acres of wetlands, dunes, meadows and two lakes, Lake Earl and Lake Tolowa. This major stopover on the Pacific Flyway route brings over 250 species of birds here. Listen for the whistling, warbling chorus. On land, look for coyotes and deer, angle for trout, or hike or ride 20 miles of trails; at sea, spot whales, seals and sea lions.

The park and wildlife area are a patchwork of lands administered by California State Parks and the Department of Fish and Game (DFG). The DFG focuses on single-species management, hunting and fishing; the State Parks' focus is on ecodiversity and recreation. You might be hiking a vast expanse of pristine dunes, then suddenly hear a shotgun or a whining 4WD. Strict regulations limit where and when you can hunt and drive; trails are clearly marked.

Register for two primitive, nonreservable campgrounds (tent sites $20) at Jedediah Smith (p266) or Del Norte Coast Redwoods State Park (p265) campgrounds. The mosquitoes are plentiful in the spring and early summer.

Pelican State Beach

Never-crowded Pelican State Beach (☑707-464-6101, ext 5151) occupies five coastal acres on the Oregon border. There are no facilities, but it's great for kite flying; pick one up at the shop just over the border in Oregon.

🛏 Sleeping

Clifford Kamph Memorial Park CAMPGROUND $ (☑707-464-7230; 15100 Hwy 101; tent sites $10) Pitch a tent by the ocean (no windbreaks) at Clifford Kamph Memorial Park; no RVs. It's a steal for the beachside location and, even though sites are exposed in a grassy area and there isn't much privacy, all have BBQs.

Casa Rubio BOUTIQUE HOTEL $$ (☑707-487-4313; www.casarubio.com; 17285 Crissey Rd; r $98-178; ☻❋) The best reason to visit Pelican State Beach is to stay at secluded, charming Casa Rubio, where three of the four ocean-view rooms have kitchens.

Northern Mountains

Best Places to Eat

→ Red Onion Grill (p282)
→ Trinity Café (p291)
→ Café Maddalena (p294)
→ La Grange Café (p301)
→ Pangaea Café & Pub (p285)

Best Places to Stay

→ McCloud River Mercantile Hotel (p296)
→ Houseboat on Shasta Lake (p276)
→ Quincy Courtyard Suites (p284)
→ Weaverville Hotel (p300)
→ Feather River Canyon Campgrounds (p284)

Why Go?

'Hidden California' gets bandied around fairly casually, but here you have an entire corner of the state that does seem forgotten. The coast and foggy redwood groves are far away, so prepare yourself for something completely different: vast expanses of wilderness – some 24,000 protected acres – divided by rivers and streams, dotted with cobalt lakes, horse ranches and alpine peaks; further east is a stretch of shrubby, high desert cut with amber gorges, caves and dramatic light that is a photographer's dream. Much of it doesn't look the way people envision California – the topography more resembles the older mountains of the Rockies than the relatively young granite Yosemite. The towns are hospitable but tiny, with few comforts; come to get lost in vast remoteness. Even the two principal attractions, Mt Shasta and Lassen Volcanic National Park, remain uncrowded (and sometimes snow-covered) at the peak of the summer.

When to Go
Lassen Volcanic National Park

Jul–Sep Warm weather and snow-free passes are ideal for backcountry camping.

Oct–Nov & Apr–May Shoulder seasons; scattered showers and snow at the high elevations.

Nov–Jan Skiing Mt Shasta is the main draw. Prices drop outside ski areas.

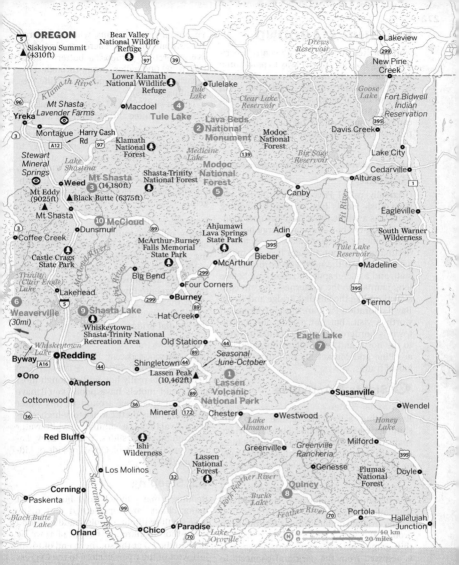

Northern Mountains Highlights

1 Gaping at geothermal spectacles in **Lassen Volcanic National Park** (p277).

2 Exploring the many caves of **Lava Beds National Monument** (p297).

3 Hiking and skiing **Mt Shasta** (p286).

4 Looking overhead at the bird superhighway at **Tule Lake** (p298).

5 Getting lost in **Modoc National Forest** (p298).

6 Hiding out in **Weaverville** and wading in the trout-filled water nearby (p300).

7 Camping along the shores of **Eagle Lake** (p283).

8 Chilling out in the mountain town of **Quincy** (p283).

9 Floating with a dozen pals on a **Shasta Lake houseboat** (p276).

10 Kicking up your heels at **McCloud's famous dance hall** (p296).

REDDING & AROUND

North of Red Bluff the dusty central corridor along I-5 starts to give way to panoramic mountain ranges on either side. Redding is the last major outpost before the small towns of the far north, and the surrounding lakes make for easy day trips or overnight camps. If you get off the highway – way off – this can be an exceptionally rewarding area of the state to explore.

Redding

Originally called Poverty Flats during the Gold Rush for its lack of wealth, Redding today has a whole lot of tasteless new money – malls, big-box stores and large housing developments surround its core. A tourist destination it is not, though it is the major gateway city to the northeast corner of the state and a useful spot for restocking before long jaunts into the wilderness. Recent constructions like the Sundial Bridge and Turtle Bay Exploration Park are enticing lures and worth a visit...but not a long one. Downtown is bordered by the Sacramento River to the north and east. Major thoroughfares are Pine and Market Sts and there's often lots of traffic.

◎ Sights & Activities

★ Sundial Bridge   BRIDGE

Resembling a beached cruise ship, the shimmering-white 2004 Sundial Bridge spans the river and is one of Redding's marquee attractions, providing an excellent photo op. The glass-deck pedestrian overpass connects the Turtle Bay Exploration Park to the north bank of the Sacramento River and was designed by renowned Spanish architect Santiago Calatrava.

The bridge/sundial attracts visitors from around the world who come to marvel at this unique feat of engineering artistry. It is accessed from the park and connects to the Sacramento River Trail system. The surrounding river scenery is beautiful.

Turtle Bay Exploration Park   MUSEUM, GARDENS
(☑ 800-887-8532; www.turtlebay.org; 844 Sundial Bridge Dr; adult/child $14/10, after 3:30pm $9/5; ◎ 9am-5pm Mon-Sat & 10am-5pm Sun, closing 1hr earlier Oct-Mar; 🚻) Situated on 300 meandering acres, this is an artistic, cultural and scientific center for visitors of all ages, with an emphasis on the Sacramento River watershed. The complex houses art and natural-science museums, with fun interactive exhibits for kids. There are also extensive arboretum gardens, a butterfly house and a 22,000-gallon, walk-through river aquarium full of regional aquatic life (yes, including turtles).

The on-site Café at Turtle Bay (meals $12) serves good coffee and decent light meals.

Cascade Theatre   HISTORIC BUILDING
(www.cascadetheatre.org; 1733 Market St) Try to catch some live music downtown at this refurbished 1935 art-deco theater. Usually it hosts second-tier national acts, but if nothing else, take a peek inside; this is a neon-lit gem.

Redding Trails   HIKING, CYCLING
Eighty miles of trails loop through parks, along rivers and up hills for strolling, hiking and mountain biking. Check out www.reddingtrails.com for maps or pick up the pamphlet at almost any hotel. The star is the Sacramento River Trail, which meanders along the river all the way to Shasta Dam. There are several access points, including the Sundial Bridge.

Waterworks Park   WATER PARK
(www.watersorkspark.com; 151 N Boulder Dr; day passes adult/child $20/16; ◎ late-May–Sep) Redding gets really hot, and although most hotels and motels have pools, you'll have more fun splashing around at this water park, including on the four-story-high, cliff-steep Avalanche, a simulated white-water river, giant waterslides, plus a 'Lazy Lagoon' and kiddie pool. Great for kids or kid-like adults.

🛏 Sleeping

Redding's many motels and hotels (most major chains are represented and many have small swimming pools) huddle around noisy thoroughfares. A couple of rows lie close to the I-5 at the southern end of town: just west of the freeway close to the Cypress Ave exit on Bechelli Lane, and on the east side of the freeway on Hilltop Dr. But aim for the ones on less-busy N Market St. The best tent camping is just up the road at Whiskeytown Lake or Shasta Lake.

Apples' Riverhouse B&B   B&B $$
(☑ 530-243-8440; www.applesriverhouse.com; 201 Mora Ct; r $99-115; 🐾) Just steps from the Sacramento River Trail, this modern, ranch-style home has three comfortable upstairs rooms, two with decks. It's a bit suburban, but it's

Redding

the best independent stay in Redding. In the evening the sociable hosts invite you for cheese and wine. Bikes are yours to borrow and the proximity to the trail is inviting.

Tiffany House B&B Inn   B&B **$$**

(☑ 530-244-3225; www.tiffanyhousebb.com; 1510 Barbara Rd; r $125-170; ☎ ☒) In a quiet cul-de-sac, a mile north of the river, this Victorian cottage has an expansive garden with sweeping views. Cozy rooms are packed with antiques, rosebuds and ruffles. Affable hosts make a big yummy to-do over breakfast.

✕ Eating & Drinking

If you want Redding's best food, it's essential that you get off the highway and into the downtown area.

Grilla Bites   SANDWICHES **$**

(www.grillabites.com; 1427 Market St; meals $5-11; ☺ 11am-8pm Mon-Thu, to 9pm Fri & Sat, to 4pm

Redding

◎ Top Sights
1 Sundial Bridge	D2

◎ Sights
2 Cascade Theatre	C3
3 Turtle Bay Exploration Park	D2

🛏 Sleeping
4 Apples' Riverhouse B&B	A1

✕ Eating
Café at Turtle Bay	(see 3)
5 Cafe Paradisio	C3
6 Grilla Bites	C3
7 Jack's Grill	C3
8 Wilda's Grill	B3

Sun; ☎ ☒) ✎ It doesn't get much simpler than this menu of grilled sandwiches and pay-by-the-pound salad bar, but the food is fresh, locally sourced and the sandwiches are punched up with fresh herbs and global fusions. The Thai Tuna is a local favorite. The restaurant was getting a full remodel when we passed.

Wilda's Grill
HOT DOGS, VEGETARIAN $

(1718 Placer St; mains $4.75-6; ⊙11am-4pm Mon-Fri; ⊘) The combo sounds weird but it works: Choose from big, excellent hot dogs with toppings from roasted garlic to homemade chili or blue cheese – or go vegetarian with falafal, breaded eggplant or the much-lauded Buddha Bowl, made from rice, veggies and yummy, spicy sauces. Expect a line at peak hours.

Cafe Paradisio
MEDITERRANEAN $$

(☑530-215-3499; 1270 Yuba St; lunch mains $6-10, dinner $8-25; ⊙11am-2pm Mon-Sat, 5-10pm Mon-Wed, 5pm-1am Thu-Sat; ⊘) Take Mediterranean food and give it a bit of Asian flair and you have the comforting fare of this casual and friendly little nook. Start with the baked brie platter then continue with salmon with coconut curry or three-cheese lasagne. The portions are huge and there are lots of vegetarian choices.

Moonstone Bistro
CALIFORNIAN $$$

(www.moonstonebistro.com; 3425 Placer St; lunch mains $13-18, dinner $24-36; ⊙11am-2pm & 5pm-late Tue-Sat, 10am-2pm Sun) ⊘ Organic, local, free range, line-caught, you name it, if the word is associated with sustainable food, you can use it to describe this place. Try the fish tacos at lunch and the hickory-smoked pork chops with mustard herb reduction for dinner, but don't skip dessert – the chocolate souffle in particular is to die for. Top it off with a microbrew.

Jack's Grill
STEAK $$$

(☑530 241 9705; www.jacksgrillredding.com; 1743 California St; mains $15-36; ⊙5-11pm, bar from 4pm Mon-Sat) This funky little old-time place doesn't look so inviting – the windows are blacked out and it's dark as a crypt inside – but the popularity with locals starts with its stubborn ain't-broke-don't-fix-it ethos and ends with its steak – a big, thick, charbroiled decadence.

Regulars start lining up for dinner at 4pm, when cocktail hour begins. There are no reservations, so it easily takes an hour to get a seat.

Alehouse Pub
BAR

(www.reddingalehouse.com; 2181 Hilltop Dr; mains $8-16; ⊙3pm-midnight Mon-Thu, to 1:30am Fri & Sat) Too bad for fans of the cheap stuff, this local pub keeps a selection of highly hopped beers on tap and sells T-shirts emblazoned with 'No Crap on Tap.' It's a fun local place that gets packed after Redding's young professionals get out of work.

ⓘ Information

California Welcome Center (☑530-365-1180; www.shastacascade.org; 1699 Hwy 273, Anderson; ⊙9am-6pm Mon-Sat, from 10am Sun) About 10 miles south of Redding, in Anderson's Prime Outlets Mall. It's an easy stop for northbound travelers, who are likely to pass it on the I-5 approach. It stocks maps for hiking and guides to outdoor activities, and the website has an excellent trip-planning section for the region.

Redding Convention & Visitor Center (☑530-225-4100; www.visitredding.com; 777 Auditorium Dr; ⊙9am-6pm Mon-Fri, 10am-5pm Sat) Near Turtle Bay Exploration Park.

Shasta-Trinity National Forest Headquarters (☑530-226-2500; 3644 Avtech Pkwy; ⊙8am-4:30pm Mon-Fri) South of town, in the USDA Service Center near the airport. Has maps and free camping permits for all seven national forests in Northern California.

ⓘ Getting There & Around

Redding Municipal Airport (RDD; http://ci.redding.ca.us/transeng/airports/rma.htm; 6751 Woodrum Circle, Redding) is 9.5 miles southeast of the city, just off Airport Rd. United Express flies to San Francisco.

The **Amtrak station** (www.amtrak.com; 1620 Yuba St), one block west of the Downtown Redding Mall, is not staffed. For the Coast Starlight service, make advance reservations by phone or via the website, then pay the conductor when you board the train. Amtrak travels once daily to Oakland ($48, six hours), Sacramento ($26, four hours) and Dunsmuir ($28, 1¾ hours).

The **Greyhound bus station** (1321 Butte St), adjacent to the Downtown Redding Mall, never closes. Destinations include San Francisco ($42, 8½ hours, four daily) and Weed ($23, 1½ hours, three daily). The **Redding Area Bus Authority** (RABA; www.rabaride.com) has a dozen city routes operating until around 6pm Monday to Saturday. Fares start at $1.50 (exact change only).

Around Redding

Shasta State Historic Park

On Hwy 299, 6 miles west of Redding, this state historic park (☑520-243-8194; www.parks.ca.gov; ⊙10am-5pm Fri-Sun) preserves the ruins of an 1850s Gold Rush mining town called Shasta – not to be confused with Mt Shasta City. When the Gold Rush was at its heady height, everything and everyone passed through this Shasta. But when the railroad bypassed it to set up in Poverty Flats (present-day Redding), poor Shasta lost its raison d'être. Shopkeepers packed up shingle and moved to Redding – literally. They moved many of Shasta's businesses brick by brick.

An 1861 courthouse contains the excellent museum (530-243-8194; admission $2; 10am-5pm Thu-Sun;), the best in this part of the state. With its amazing gun collection, spooky holograms in the basement and a gallows out back, it's a thrill ride. Pick up walking-tour pamphlets from the information desk and follow trails to the beautiful Catholic cemetery, brewery ruins and many other historic sites.

Whiskeytown Lake

Two miles further west on Hwy 299, sparkling Whiskeytown Lake (530-242-3400; www.nps.gov/whis; day use per vehicle $5) takes its name from an old mining camp. When the lake was created in the 1960s by the construction of a 263ft dam, designed for power generation and Central Valley irrigation, the few remaining buildings of old Whiskeytown were moved and the camp was submerged. John F Kennedy was present at the dedication ceremony, less than two months before his assassination. Today folks descend on the lake's serene 36 miles of forested shoreline to camp, swim, sail, mountain bike and pan for gold.

The visitors center (530-246-1225; 9am-6pm May-Sep, 10am-4pm Oct-Apr), on the northeast point of the lake, just off Hwy 299, provides free maps and information on Whiskeytown and Whiskeytown-Shasta-Trinity National Recreation Area from knowledgeable and agreeable staff. Look for ranger-led interpretive programs and guided walks. The hike from the visitors center to roaring Whiskeytown Falls (3.4 miles round-trip) follows a former logging road and is a good quick trip.

On the southern shore of the lake, Brandy Creek is ideal for swimming. Just off Hwy 299, on the northern edge of the lake, Oak Bottom Marina (530-359-2269; boat rental 2/8hr from $50/180) rents boats. On the western side of the lake, the Tower House Historic District contains the El Dorado

DETOUR AROUND THE I-5 DOLDRUMS

A good alternative for travelers heading north and south on I-5 is to drive along Hwy 3 through the Scott Valley, which rewards with world-class views of the Trinity Alps. Compared to rushing along the dull highway, this scenic detour will add an additional half a day of driving.

mine ruins and the pioneer Camden House, open for summer tours. In winter, when the trees are bare, it's an atmospheric, quiet place to explore.

Oak Bottom Campground (800-365-2267; tent/RV sites $20/22) is a privately run place with RV and tent camping. It's a bit tight, but nicer than most private campgrounds, with lots of manzanita shade. Most attractive are the walk-in sites right on the shore. Primitive campsites (summer/winter $10/5) surround the lake. The most accessible of these is the one at Crystal Creek, which doesn't have water, but has nice views.

Shasta Lake

About 15 minutes north of Redding, Shasta Lake (www.shastalake.com) was created in the 1940s when Shasta Dam flooded towns, railways and 90% of the local Wintu tribal lands to make the largest reservoir in California. Today it's home to the state's biggest population of nesting bald eagles. Surrounded by hiking trails and campgrounds, the lake gets packed in summer. The lake is also home to more than 20 different kinds of fish, including rainbow trout.

The ranger station (530-275-1589; 14250 Holiday Rd; 8am-4:30pm daily May-Sep, Mon-Fri Oct-Apr) offers free maps and information about fishing, boating and hiking. To get here, take the Mountaingate Wonderland Blvd exit off I-5, about 9 miles north of Redding, and turn right.

Sights & Activities

The lake is known as the 'houseboat capital of the world,' and is very popular with boaters of all kinds. Packer's Bay is the best area for leg-stretcher hikes with easy access off the I-5 (follow the Packer's Bay signs), but the prettiest trail (outside of summer months when the lack of shade can make it intensely hot) is the 7.5-mile loop of the Clikapudi Trail, which is also popular with mountain bikers and horse-back riders. To get there, follow Bear Mountain Rd several miles till it dead ends.

Shasta Dam
DAM

(☑ 530-275-4463; www.usbr.gov/mp/ncao/shasta/; 16349 Shasta Dam Blvd; ⊗ visitor center 8am-5pm, tours 9am-3pm) **FREE** On scale with the enormous natural features of the area, this colossal, 15-million-ton dam is second only in size to Grand Coolie Dam in Washington state (Hoover Dam in Nevada is the fourth biggest – but the tallest in the country). The dam is found at the south end of the lake on Shasta Dam Blvd.

Built between 1938 and 1945, its 487ft spillway is as high as a 60-story building – three times higher than Niagara Falls. Woody Guthrie wrote 'This Land Is Your Land' while he was here entertaining dam workers. The Shasta Dam visitors center (☑ 530-275-4463; ⊗ 8:30am-4:30pm) offers fascinating free guided tours at 9am, 11am, 1pm and 3pm daily of the structure's rumbling interior – but skip the movie.

Lake Shasta Caverns
CAVE TOUR

(www.lakeshastacaverns.com; adult/child 3-11yr $22/13; ⊗ tours 9am-4pm; ◉) High in the limestone megaliths at the north end of the lake hide these prehistoric caves. Tours of the crystalline caves operate daily and include a boat ride across Lake Shasta, and the office has a spacious play area for kids. The Cathedral Room is particularly stunning. Bring a sweater as the temperature inside is 58°F (14°C) year-round.

To get there, take the Shasta Caverns Rd exit from I-5, about 15 miles north of Redding, and follow the signs for 1.5 miles.

🛏 Sleeping & Eating

Hike-in camping and RV parks are sprinkled around the shores of the lake, and houseboats are a wildly popular option. Most houseboats require a two-night minimum stay. Make reservations as far in advance as possible, especially in the summer months. Houseboats usually sleep 10 to 16 adults and cost around $1600 to $8400 per week. The RV parks are often crowded and lack shade, but they have on-site restaurants. If you want to explore the area on a day trip, stay in Redding.

US Forest Service (USFS)
Campgrounds
CAMPGROUND $

(☑ 877-444-6777; www.reserveusa.com; tent sites $10-20) About half of the campgrounds around the lake are open year-round. The lake's many fingers have a huge range of camping, with lake and mountain views, and some of them are very remote. Free boat-in sites are first-come, first-served – sites without boat launches will be far less busy.

Camping outside organized campgrounds requires a campfire permit, available free from any USFS office.

Holiday Harbor
Resort
HOUSEBOATS, CAMPGROUND $

(☑ 530-238-2383; www.lakeshasta.com; Holiday Harbor Rd; tent & RV sites $38.50, houseboat for 2 nights from $920; 🐾) Primarily an RV campground, it also rents houseboats (note that off-season rates are almost 50% lower) and the busy marina offers parasailing and fishing-boat rentals. A little cafe (⊗ 8am-3pm) sits lakefront. It's off Shasta Caverns Rd, next to the lake.

Antlers RV Park &
Campground
CAMPGROUND, CABINS $

(☑ 530-238-2322; www.shastalakevacations.com; 20679 Antlers Rd; tent & RV sites $18-42, trailer rentals $88-105; 🐾 ⬛ 🐾) East of I-5 in Lakehead, at the north end of the lake, this very popular, family-oriented campground has cabins, a country store and a marina renting watercraft and houseboats.

Lakeshore Inn & RV
CAMPGROUND $

(☑ 530-238-2003; www.shastacamping.com; 20483 Lakeshore Dr; RV sites $20-37, cabins from $95; 🐾 ⬛) On the western side of I-5, this lakeside vacation park has a restaurant and tavern, horseshoes and basic cabins.

MT LASSEN & AROUND

The dramatic crags, volcanic formations and alpine lakes of Lassen Volcanic National Park seem surprisingly untrammeled when you consider they are only a few hours from the Bay Area. Snowed in through most of winter, the park blossoms in late spring. While it is only 50 miles from Redding, and thus close enough to be enjoyed on a day trip, to really do it justice you'll want to invest a few days exploring the area along its scenic, winding roads. From Lassen Volcanic National Park you can take one of two very picturesque routes: Hwy 36, which heads east past Chester, Lake Almanor and historic Susanville; or Hwy 89, which leads southeast to the cozy mountain town of Quincy.

Lassen Volcanic National Park

The dry, smoldering, treeless terrain within this 106,000-acre **national park** (☑530-595-4444; www.nps.gov/lavo; 7-day entry per car $10) stands in stunning contrast to the cool, green conifer forest that surrounds it. That's the summer; in winter tons of snow ensures you won't get too far inside its borders. Still, entering the park from the southwest entrance is to suddenly step into another world. The lavascape offers a fascinating glimpse into the earth's fiery core. In a fuming display the terrain is marked by roiling hot springs, steamy mud pots, noxious sulfur vents, fumaroles, lava flows, cinder cones, craters and crater lakes.

In earlier times the region was a summer encampment and meeting point for Native American tribes – namely the Atsugewi, Yana, Yahi and Maidu. They hunted deer and gathered plants for basket-making here. Some indigenous people still live nearby and work closely with the park to help educate visitors on their ancient history and contemporary culture.

◉ Sights & Activities

Lassen Peak, the world's largest plug-dome volcano, rises 2000ft over the surrounding landscape to 10,457ft above sea level. Classified as an active volcano, its most recent eruption was in 1917, when it spewed a giant cloud of smoke, steam and ash 7 miles into the atmosphere. The national park was created the following year to protect the newly formed landscape. Some areas destroyed by the blast, including the aptly named **Devastated Area** northeast of the peak, are recovering impressively.

Hwy 89, the road through the park, wraps around Lassen Peak on three sides and provides access to dramatic geothermal formations, pure lakes, gorgeous picnic areas and remote hiking trails.

In total, the park has 150 miles of **hiking trails**, including a 17-mile section of the Pacific Crest Trail. Experienced hikers can attack the **Lassen Peak Trail**; it takes at least 4½ hours to make the 5-mile round trip but the first 1.3 miles up to the Grandview viewpoint are suitable for families. The 360-degree view from the top is stunning, even if the weather is a bit hazy. Early in the season you'll need snow and ice-climbing equipment to reach the summit. Near the Kom Yah-mah-nee visitor facility, a gentler 2.3-mile trail leads through meadows and forest to **Mill Creek Falls**. Further north on Hwy 89 you'll recognize the roadside **sulfur works** by its bubbling mud pots, hissing steam vent, fountains and fumaroles. At **Bumpass Hell** a moderate 1.5-mile trail and boardwalk lead to an active geothermal area, with bizarrely colored pools and billowing clouds of steam.

The road and trails wind through cinder cones, lava and lush alpine glades, with views of Juniper Lake, Snag Lake and the plains beyond. Most of the lakes at higher elevations remain partially and beautifully frozen in summer. Leave time to fish, swim or boat on **Manzanita Lake**, a slightly lower emerald gem near the northern entrance.

🛏 Sleeping & Eating

If you're coming to Lassen Volcanic National Park from the north on Hwy 89, you won't see many gas/food/lodgings signs after Mt Shasta City. Your best option is to stock up en route and camp.

The park has eight developed **campgrounds** (☑877-444-6777; www.recreation.gov; tent & RV sites $10-18), and there are many more in the surrounding Lassen National Forest. Campgrounds in the park are open from late May to late October, depending on snow conditions. Manzanita Lake is the only one with hot showers, but the two Summit Lake campgrounds, in the middle of the park, are also popular. Reservations are permitted at Butte Lake in the northeast corner of the park, Manzanita Lake in the

> ### ❶ KNOW ABOUT THE SNOW
>
> Rangers tell rueful stories about people who drive across the country in their RVs to find the roads of Lassen Volcanic National Park impassable; don't let it happen to you. The road through the park is usually only open from June to October, though it has been closed due to snow (as much as 40ft of it) well into July at times. Travelers need to call ahead or check the park website (www.nps.gov/lavo; click 'Current Conditions') to get weather conditions before considering a visit during all but a couple of months of the year – the only safe bets are August and September. A slow melt or freak storm can close major parts of the park at any other time of year.

Lassen Volcanic National Park

Old Station (15mi);
Hat Creek (25mi);
Mt Shasta (95mi)

Shingletown (20mi);
Redding (50mi)

North Entrance Station

Manzanita Lake

Lassen National Forest

Reflection Lake

Crags

Manzanita Lake Visitors Center & Loomis Museum

Manzanita Lake Campground & Camping Cabins

Chaos Crags (8503ft)

Crescent Crater (8645ft)

Eagle Peak (9222ft)

Lassen Peak (10,457ft)

Mt Diller (9087ft)

Lake Helen

Brokeoff Mtn (9235ft)

Sulfur Works

Kom Yah-mah-nee Visitor Facility

Heart Lake Trail

Mill Creek Falls

Southwest Entrance Station

Seasonal June-October

Mt Conard (8204ft)

Mill Creek

Badger Mountain (7127ft)

Hat Creek

Seasonal June-October

Hot Rock (6145ft)

Devastated Area

Badger Flat

Lassen Volcanic National Park

Hat Mountain (7695ft)

Ranger Station

Summit Lake North

Summit Lake South

Shadow Lake

Bumpass Mtn (8753ft)

Bumpass Hell

Twin Meadows

Hot Springs Creek

Spencer Meadow Trail

Prospect Peak (8338ft)

Pacific Crest Trail

Cluster Lakes

Fairfield Peak (7272ft)

Twin Lakes

Rainbow Lake

Crater Butte (7267ft)

Horseshoe Lake

Pilot Mtn (7175ft)

Drakesbad Guest Ranch

Warner Valley

Ranger Station

Sifford Mountain (7408ft)

Saddle Mtn (7638ft)

Terminal Geyser

Kings Creek

Pacific Crest Trail

Lassen Park Rd

northwest, Summit Lake North and Summit Lake South.

If you don't want to camp, the nearest place to stay is Chester, which accesses the south entrance of the park. There are some basic services near the split of Hwy 89 and Hwy 44, in the north.

North Entrance of the Park

**Manzanita Lake
Camping Cabins** CABINS, CAMPGROUND $
(☑ summer 530-335-7557, winter 530-200-4578; www.lassenrecreation.com; Hwy 89, near Manzanita Lake; cabins $63-89; 🛜) These recently built log cabins enjoy a lovely position on one of Lassen's lakes, and they come in one- and two-bedroom options and slightly more basic eight-bunk configurations, which are a bargain for groups. They all have bear boxes, propane heaters and fire rings, but no bedding, electricity or running water.

Those who want to get a small taste of Lassen's more rustic comforts can call ahead to arrange a 'Camper Package,' which includes basic supplies for a night under the stars (starting at $100, it includes a s'mores kit).

**Manzanita Lake
Campground** CAMPGROUND, CABINS $
(☑ 877-444-6777; www.recreation.gov; campsites $10-18; 🛜) The biggest camping area in these parts has lake access, views of Lassen and 179 sites with fire rings, picnic tables and bear boxes. It has a store, hot showers and kayak rentals here as well.

**Hat Creek Resort &
RV Park** CABINS, CAMPGROUND $
(☑ 800-568-0109; www.hatcreekresortrv.com; 12533 Hwy 44/89; tent sites from $15, RV sites with/without hookups from $26/15, r $54-209, yurts $54-119; 🛜🐕) Outside the park, Old Station makes a decent stop before entering and is

a good second choice after Manzanita Lake Camping Cabins. It sits along a fast-moving, trout-stocked creek. Some simple motel rooms and cabins have full kitchens. Stock up at the convenience store and deli, then eat on a picnic table by the river.

South Entrance of the Park

Mt Lassen/Shingletown KOA CAMPGROUND $
(☑ 530-474-3133; www.koa.com; 7749 KOA Rd; tent sites $29, RV sites from $42, cabins $67-160; ⊙mid-Mar–Nov; 🛜🐕🏊) Enjoy all the standard KOA amenities: a playground, a deli and laundry facilities. It's off Hwy 44 in Shingletown, about 20 miles west of the park.

Childs Meadow Resort CABINS $
(☑ 530-595-3383; www.childsmeadowresort. com; 41500 E Hwy 36, Mill Creek; d $60-70, cabins $75-150) Rustic, run-down cabins – some of them more like permanently parked RV trailers – sit at the edge of a spectacularly lush mountain meadow 9 miles outside the park's southwest entrance. Don't expect the Ritz; it's an old-fashioned, fittingly grungy, mountain-resort experience, but it's very close to the park.

Drakesbad Guest Ranch RANCH $$$
(☑ 530-529-1512, ext 120; www.drakesbad.com; Warner Valley Rd; r per person $140-190; ⊙Jun-early Oct; 🏊) Seventeen miles northwest of Chester, this fabulously secluded place lies inside the park's boundary. Guests, many of whom are repeat visitors, use the hot-springs-fed swimming pool or go horseback riding. Except in the main lodge, there's no electricity (the kerosene lamps and campfires give things a lovely glow). Rates include country-style meals (vegetarian options available) and campfire barbecues every Wednesday.

This is one of the few places in the region to book up solidly, so make advance reservations as soon as possible.

❶ Information

Whether you enter at the north or southwest entrance, you'll be given a free map with general information.

Kom Yah-mah-nee Visitor Facility (☑ 530-595-4480; ⊙9am-6pm Jun-Sep, hours vary Oct-May) About half a mile north of the park's southwest entrance, this handsome center is certified at the highest standard by the US Green Building Council. Inside there are educational exhibits (including a cool topographical volcano), a bookstore, an auditorium, a gift shop and a restaurant. Visitor information and maps available.

Manzanita Lake Visitors Center & Loomis Museum (☑ 530-595-4480; ⊙9am-5pm Jun-Sep) Just past the entrance-fee station at the park's northern boundary, you can see exhibits and an orientation video inside this museum. During summer, rangers and volunteers lead programs on geology, wildlife, astronomy and local culture. Visitor information and maps available.

Park Headquarters (☑ 530-595-4444; www. nps.gov/lavo; 38050 Hwy 36; ⊙8am-4:30pm daily Jun-Sep, 8am-4:30pm Mon-Fri Oct-May) About a mile west of the tiny town of Mineral, it's the nearest stop for refueling and supplies.

❶ Getting There & Away

There's virtually no way to visit this park without a car, though all the two-lane roads around the park and the ample free national-forest camping options make for excellent, if fairly serious, cycle touring.

The park has two entrances. The northern entrance, at Manzanita Lake, is 50 miles east of

WORTH A TRIP

WILD HORSE SANCTUARY

Since 1978 the Wild Horse Sanctuary ([☎] 530-335-2241; www.wildhorsesanctuary.com; Shingletown; admission free; ◉ 9am-4pm Wed & Sat) FREE has been sheltering horses and burros that would otherwise have been destroyed. You can visit its humble visitors center on Wednesdays and Saturdays to see these lovely animals or even volunteer for a day, with advance arrangement. To see them on the open plains, take a two- to three-day weekend pack trip in spring or summer (from $435 per person). Shingletown lies 20 miles to the west of Lassen Volcanic National Park.

Redding via Hwy 44. The southwest entrance is on Hwy 89, about 5 miles north of the junction with Hwy 36. From this junction it is 5 miles west on Hwy 36 to Mineral and 44 miles west to Red Bluff. Heading east on Hwy 36, Chester is 25 miles away and Susanville about 60 miles. Quincy is 65 miles southeast from the junction on Hwy 89.

Lassen National Forest

The vast Lassen National Forest (www.fs.fed.us/r5/lassen), surrounding Lassen Peak and Lassen Volcanic National Park, is so big that it's hard to comprehend: it covers 1.2 million acres (1875 sq miles) of wilderness in an area called the Crossroads, where the granite Sierra, volcanic Cascades, Modoc Plateau and Central Valley meet. It's largely unspoiled land, though if you wander too far off the byways surrounding the park, you'll certainly see evidence of logging and mining operations that still happen within its borders.

The forest has some serious hikes, with 460 miles of trails, ranging from the brutally challenging (120 miles of the Pacific Crest Trail) to ambitious day hikes (the 12-mile Spencer Meadows National Recreation Trail), to just-want-to-stretch-the-legs-a-little trails (the 3.5-mile Heart Lake National Recreation Trail). Near the intersection of Hwys 44 and 89, visitors to the area will find one of the most spectacular features of the forest, the pitch-black 600yd Subway Cave lava tube. Other points of interest include the 1.5-mile volcanic Spattercone Crest Trail, Willow Lake and Crater Lake,

7684ft Antelope Peak, and the 900ft-high, 14-mile-long Hat Creek Rim escarpment.

For those seeking to get far off the beaten trail, the forest has three wilderness areas. Two high-elevation wilderness areas are the Caribou Wilderness and the Thousand Lakes Wilderness, best visited from mid-June to mid-October. The Ishi Wilderness, at a much lower elevation in the Central Valley foothills east of Red Bluff, is more comfortable in spring and fall, as summer temperatures often exceed 100°F (37°C). It harbors California's largest migratory deer herd, which can be upwards of 20,000 head.

The Lassen National Forest supervisor's office is in Susanville. Other ranger offices include Eagle Lake Ranger District ([☎] 530-257-4188; 477-050 Eagle Lake Rd, Susanville), Hat Creek Ranger District ([☎] 530-336-5521; 43225 E Hwy 299, Fall River Mills) and Almanor Ranger District ([☎] 530-258-2141; 900 E Hwy 36, Chester), about a mile west of Chester.

Lake Almanor Area

Calm, turquoise Lake Almanor lies south of Lassen Volcanic National Park via Hwys 89 and 36. This man-made lake is a crystalline example of California's sometimes awkward conservation and land-management policy: the lake was created by the now-defunct Great Western Power Company and is now ostensibly owned by the Pacific Gas & Electric Company. The lake is surrounded by lush meadows and tall evergreens and was once little-visited. Now, a 3000-acre ski resort sits on the hills above, with properties continually being developed near its shore and power boats zipping across its surface. The northeastern section in particular has become particularly ritzy and there are even a few gated communities. On the rugged southern end you'll find miles with nothing but pine trees.

The main town near the lake, Chester (population 2500, elevation 4528ft), isn't a looker. Though you could whiz right by and dismiss it as a few blocks of nondescript roadside storefronts, this little community, while outwardly drab, has a fledgling art scene hidden along the backroads for those willing to explore. It also offers some comfy places to stay but none as exciting or woodsy as you'll find along the lake.

🏃 Activities

Rent boats and water-sports equipment at many places around the lake.

Bodfish Bicycles & Quiet Mountain Sports   CYCLING, OUTDOORS

(☑530-258-2338; www.bodfishbicycles.com; 152 Main St, Chester; ⏰10am-5pm Tue-Sat, noon-4pm Sun) This outfit rents bicycles ($33 per day), cross-country skis and snowshoes, and sells canoes and kayaks. It's a great source of mountain-biking and bicycle-touring advice. If you want just a taste of the lovely rides possible in this part of the state, make this a priority stop.

🛏 Sleeping & Eating

The best sleeping options for campers are in the surrounding national forest.

🛏 Chester

Along Chester's main drag you'll find a scattering of '50s-style inns and a few chain lodgings (the nicest of which is the fairly overpriced Best Western Rose Quartz Inn). Many of these places keep seasonal hours, and when you live in a place where it can snow in mid-June, the season is short. Restaurants are of the burger-and-fries or mom-n-pop-diner variety – the best dining options are found a few miles out of town along the northeast shores of the lake.

St Bernard Lodge   B&B $$

(☑530-258-3382; www.stbernardlodge.com; 44801 E Hwy 36, Mill Creek; d with shared bath from $99; ☎) Located 10 miles west of Chester, this old-world charmer has seven B&B rooms with views to the mountains and forest. All have knotty-pine paneling and

quilted bedspreads. There are stables where those traveling with a horse can board them and have access to the nearby network of Lassen's trails. The tavern is good too – serving meaty American-style fare.

Bidwell House B&B   B&B $$

(☑530-258-3338; www.bidwellhouse.com; 1 Main St; r with shared bath $80-115, r with private bath $125-260, cottage $185-285; ☎) Set back from the street, this historic summer home of pioneers John and Annie Bidwell is packed with antiques. The classic accommodations come with all the modern amenities (including a spa in some rooms) – no roughing it here. Enjoy goodies like a three-course breakfast, home-baked cookies and afternoon sherry.

Knotbumper Restaurant   AMERICAN $

(274 Main St; meals $8-12; ⏰11am-8pm Tue-Sat) The Knotbumper is unlikely to dish up your most memorable meal, but it has a generous deli menu, including tamale pies, shrimp salad sandwiches and other eclectic selections. On summer days, eat on the lively front porch and watch the trucks rumble by. This place virtually closes down in winter.

Around the Lake

Book ahead for lakefront lodgings in summer. There are restaurants at the resorts.

PG&E Recreational Area Campgrounds   CAMPGROUND $

(☑916-386-5164; http://recreation.pge.com/Reserve-a-Campsite/; tent sites $16-22; ☎) A favorite for tents and RVs, Rocky Point Campground is right on the lake, with some sites

---

SCENIC DRIVE: LASSEN SCENIC BYWAY

Even in the peak of summer, you'll have the Lassen Scenic Byway mostly to yourself. The long loop though Northern California wilderness skirts the edge of Lassen Volcanic National Park and circles Lassen Peak, one of the largest dormant volcanoes on the planet. It mostly covers the big green patches on the map: expansive areas perfect for hiking, fishing, camping or just getting lost. This is a place where few people venture, and those who do come back with stories.

The launching point for this big loop could be either Redding or Sacramento, but there are few comforts for travelers along this course. The only cities in this neck of the woods – little places like Chester and Susanville – aren't all that exciting on their own; they're mostly just places to gas up, buy some beef jerky and enjoy the week's only hot meal. But the banner attractions are visible in every direction – the ominous, dormant volcanic peak of Lassen, the windswept high plains and the seemingly endless wilderness of the Lassen and Plumas National Forests.

This loop is formed by Hwy 36, Hwy 44 and Hwy 89. (You can see the map and some of the highlights at www.byways.org/explore/byways/2195.) Its best to do the drive between late June through mid-October. Other times of the year some of these roads close due to snow.

WESTWOOD & THE BIZZ JOHNSON TRAIL

A few miles east of Chester is Westwood, a tiny speck of a town that marks the beginning of the Bizz Johnson Trail, an extremely picturesque route that runs the remote 25.5 miles from Westwood to Susanville. Once part of the old Southern Pacific right-of-way, the wooden bridges and serenely crossing-free trail are traversable by foot, mountain bike, horseback or cross-country skis (no motorized vehicles allowed!). Do the trail in the Westwood–Susanville direction, as it's mostly downhill that way. Get trail guides at the chamber of commerce in Chester or at the Susanville Railroad Depot.

basically on the beach. For something more remote, try the Cool Springs Campground at the Butt Reservoir (try to say that with a straight face!). It's at the south end of the lake, at the end of Prattville Butt Reservoir Rd.

These campgrounds lie within the surrounding Lassen and Plumas National Forests on the lake's southwest shore. Sites tend to be more tranquil than the RV-centric private campgrounds that are right on the water.

North Shore Campground   CABINS, CAMPGROUND $
(☑ 530-258-3376; www.northshorecampground. com; tent sites $40, RV sites $45-56, cabins $119-269, pop-up trailer $89; ☏) Two miles east of Chester on Hwy 36, these expansive, forested grounds stretch for a mile along the water, and get filled up with mostly RVs. Ranch-style cabins have kitchens and are great for families. This place is fine if you want to spend all your time waterskiing on the lake, but those seeking the solitude of nature should look elsewhere.

Knotty Pine Resort & Marina   CABINS $$
(☑ 530-596-3348; www.knottypine.net; 430 Peninsula Dr; weekly RV sites $175, 2-bedroom cabins with kitchen $165, r $145; ☒) This lakeside option, 7 miles east of Chester, has simple cabins and rents boats, kayaks and canoes.

Tantardino's   ITALIAN $$
(☑ 530-596-3902; 401 Ponderosa Dr, Lake Almanor Peninsula; mains $9-19; ☉ 11:30am-9pm Tue-Sat) This is the locals' favorite place to eat in the

region hands down – even folks from Susanville drive the 32 miles to get here, with pleasure, for the excellent Sicillian-style lasagne, yummy pizzas and meatball or caprese sandwiches at lunch time. It's lively, friendly and you can eat and imbibe outside in summer. Reserve ahead for dinner.

★ Red Onion Grill   MODERN AMERICAN $$$
(www.redoniongrill.com; 384 Main St; meals $16-29; ☉ 11am-9pm) Head here for the finest dining on the lake with upscale Modern American, Italian-influenced cuisine (like the simply prepared rock shrimp and crab alfredo), and bar food that's executed with real panache. The setting is casual and fun – wall lanterns and a crackling fire – made all the more warm by the best wine list in town.

❶ Information

Chester & Lake Almanor Chamber of Commerce (☑ 530-258-2426; www.chester-lakealmanor.com; 529 Main St, Chester; ☉ 9am-4pm Mon-Fri) Get information about lodging and recreation around the lake, in Lassen National Forest and in Lassen Volcanic National Park.

Lassen National Forest Almanor Ranger Station (☑ 530-258-2141; 900 E Hwy 36; ☉ 8am-4:30pm Mon-Fri) About a mile west of Chester, with similar information to the chamber of commerce.

Susanville

Though it sits on a lovely high desert plateau, the Lassen County seat (population 16,616) isn't much of a charmer; it's a resupply post with a Wal-Mart, a few stop lights and two prisons. Although not a tourist destination in itself, it does provide good services for travelers passing through. It lies 35 miles east of Lake Almanor and 85 miles northwest of Reno – and is home to a couple of modest historic sites. The best event in town is the Lassen County Fair (☑ 530-251-8900; www.lassencountyfair.org), which swings into gear in July.

For local information about the town visit the Lassen County Chamber of Commerce (☑ 530-257-4323; www.lassencountychamber.org; 84 N Lassen St; ☉ 9am-4pm Mon-Fri), while the Lassen National Forest supervisor's office (☑ 530-257-2151; 2550 Riverside Dr; ☉ 8am-4:30pm Mon-Fri) has maps and recreation information for getting into the surrounding wilds.

The restored Susanville Railroad Depot, south of Main St, off Weatherlow St, sits beside the terminus of the Bizz Johnson Trail (p282). The visitors center (☎530-257-3252; 601 Richmond Rd; ☺10am-4pm May-Oct) rents bicycles and has brochures on mountain-biking trails in the area.

The town's oldest building, Roop's Fort (1853), is named after Susanville's founder, Isaac Roop. The fort was a trading post on the Nobles Trail, a California emigrant route. The town itself was named after Roop's daughter, Susan. Beside the fort is the freshly built Lassen Historical Museum (75 N Weatherlow St; admission by donation; ☺10am-4pm Mon-Fri May-Oct), which has well-presented displays of clothing and memorabilia from the area, which are worth a 20-minute visit.

Motels along Main St average $65 to $90 per night, High Country Inn (☎530-257-3450; www.high-country-inn.com; 3015 Riverside Dr; r $87-159; 🖥🚫) is the best of these. Try Roseberry House B&B (☎530-257-5675; www.roseberryhouse.com; 609 North St; r/ste $110/135; 🖥) for more character. This sweet 1902 Victorian house is two blocks north of Main St. Striking dark-wood antique headboards and armoires combine with rosebuds and frill. There are nice little touches, like bath salts and candy dishes. In the morning, expect homemade muffins and jam as part of the full breakfast.

To eat, head directly to the relatively new Lassen Ale Works (724 Main St; mains $9-21; ☺11am-10pm Mon-Thu, 11am-11pm Fri & Sat, 9am-10pm Sun) in the beautifully renovated circa 1862 Pioneer Saloon. It's known for its fish and chips, but everything from steaks to the Reuben sandwiches are fresh and as good as the service. Try one of the seven signature brews like the Pioneer Porter or Almanor Amber. Unfortunately for those traveling with kids, you must be 21 years old or over to eat here.

Sage Stage (☎530-233-6410; www.sage-stage.com) runs buses to Redding via Alturas ($18) and south to Reno ($22). Susanville City Buses (☎530-252-7433) makes a circuit around town (fare $2).

Eagle Lake

Those who have the time to get all the way out to Eagle Lake, California's second-largest natural lake, are rewarded with one of the most striking sites in the region: a stunningly blue jewel on the high plateau. From late spring until fall this lovely lake, about

15 miles northwest of Susanville, attracts a smattering of visitors who come to cool off, swim, fish, boat and camp. On the south shore, you'll find a pristine 5-mile recreational trail and several busy campgrounds (☎ reservations 877-444-6777; www.recreation.gov; tent sites $20, RV sites $30-60) administered by Lassen National Forest and the Bureau of Land Management (BLM; ☎530-257-5381). Campgrounds for tent camping include Merrill, Aspen, Christie and Eagle. Most of them are fairly scrubby, considering how lovely the lake is, though there are some highly sought-after lakeside sites in Merrill. Merrill and Eagle also have RV sites. Nearby Eagle Lake Marina (www.eaglelakerecreation-area.com) offers hot showers, laundry and boat rentals. It also can help you get out onto the lake with a fishing license.

Eagle Lake RV Park (☎530-825-3133; www.eaglelakeandrv.com; 687-125 Palmetto Way; tent/RV sites $25/36.50, cabins $37-100; 🖥🚫), on the western shore, and Mariners Resort (☎530-825-3333; Stones Landing; RV sites $37-40, cabins $110-190), on the quieter northern shore, both rent boats.

Quincy

Idyllic Quincy (population 1728) is one of the northern mountains' three mountain communities, which teeter on the edge of becoming an incorporated town (the other two are Burney, in Shasta County, and Weaverville). It's no metropolis, but it does have a large grocery store and even a Subway franchise. In 2013 *Budget Travel* named it one of the 'Coolest Small Towns in America,' and we have to agree. Nestled in a high valley in the northern Sierra, southeast of both Lassen Volcanic National Park and Lake Almanor via Hwy 89, it is a lovely little place, endowed with just enough edge by the student population of the local Feather River College. Nearby Feather River, Plumas National Forest, Tahoe National Forest and their oodles of open space make Quincy an excellent base from which to explore.

Once in town Hwy 70/89 splits into two one-way streets, with traffic on Main St heading east, and traffic on Lawrence St heading west. Jackson St runs parallel to Main St, one block south, and is another main artery. Just about everything you need is on, near or between these three streets, making up Quincy's low-key commercial district.

⊙ Sights & Activities

Pick up free walking and driving tour pamphlets from the visitors center to guide you through the gorgeous surrounding American Valley. The Feather River Scenic Byway (Hwy 70) leads into the Sierra. In summer the icy waters of county namesake Feather River (*plumas* is Spanish for feathers) are excellent for swimming, kayaking, fishing and floating in old inner tubes. The area is also a wonderland of winter activities, especially at Bucks Lake.

Plumas County Museum   MUSEUM
(☑ 530-283-6320; www.plumasmuseum.org; 500 Jackson St, at Coburn St; adult/child $2/1; ⊙ 9am-4:30pm Tue-Sat, 10am-3pm Sun; ⊕) In the block behind the courthouse, this multifloor county museum has flowering gardens, as well as hundreds of historical photos and relics from the county's pioneer and Maidu days, its early mining and timber industries, and construction of the Western Pacific Railroad. For the price, it's definitely worth the stop.

Plumas County Courthouse   HISTORIC BUILDING
(Main St) Pop into the 1921 Plumas County Courthouse, at the west end of Main St, to see enormous marble posts and staircases, and a bronze-and-glass chandelier in the lobby.

Sierra Mountain Sports   OUTDOORS
(www.sierramountainsports.net; 501 W Main St) Across from the courthouse, rent cross-country ski gear and snowshoes here.

Big Daddy's Guide Service   FISHING
(☑ 530-283-4103; www.bigdaddyfishing.com) Captain Bryan Roccucci is Big Daddy, the only fishing guide in Northeast California. He knows the lakes well and leads trips for all levels (starting at $175 per person).

⁂ Festivals & Events

★ High Sierra Music Festival   MUSIC
(www.highsierramusic.com) On the first weekend in July, quiet Quincy is host to this blowout festival, renowned statewide. The four-day extravaganza brings a five-stage smorgasbord of art and music from a spectrum of cultural corners (indie rock, classic blues, folk and jazz). Past acts include Thievery Corporation, Lauryn Hill, Primus, Ben Harper and Neko Case.

Sure, a curmudgeonly local might call it the Hippie Fest, but it's pretty tame in comparison to some of Northern California's fringe festivals. If you plan to attend, reserve a room or campsite a couple of months in advance. For those who don't want to camp in nearby national forest land, Susanville, one hour away, has the largest number of rooms.

🛏 Sleeping

Ranchito Motel   MOTEL $
(☑ 530-286-2265; www.ranchitomotel.com; 2020 E Main St; r from $79; ☎) With antique timber pillars, white-painted brick walls, old barn-style doors and the occasional wagon wheel for decoration, this friendly motel (in the eastern half of town) definitely has a Mexican ranch feel. Inside, rooms are modern, freshly painted and very comfortable for the price. The motel offers plenty more choices on the wooded land that extends back a few acres.

Pine Hill Motel   MOTEL $
(☑ 530-283-1670; www.pinehillmotel.com; 42075 Hwy 70; s/d/cabin from $69/75/150; ❄ ☎ ☺) A mile west of downtown Quincy, this little hotel is protected by an army of statues and surrounded by a big lawn. The units are nothing fancy, but they're clean and in a constant state of renovation. Each is equipped with microwave, coffeemaker and refrigerator; some cabins have full kitchens.

Feather River Canyon
Campgrounds   CAMPGROUND $
(☑ reservations 877-444-6777; www.fs.usda.gov; tent & RV sites $23) Area campgrounds are administered through the Mt Hough Ranger District Office. They are in a cluster along the north fork of the Feather River west of Quincy – five are no-fee, but also have no piped water. All are first come, first served.

★ Quincy Courtyard Suites   APARTMENT $$
(☑ 530-283-1401; www.quincycourtyardsuites.com; 436 Main St; apt $129-169; ☎) Staying in this beautifully renovated 1908 Clinch building, overlooking the small main drag of Quincy's downtown, feels just right, like renting the village's cutest apartment. The warmly decorated rooms are modern – no fussy clutter – and apartments have spacious, modern kitchens, claw-foot tubs and gas fireplaces.

Ada's Place   B&B $$
(☑ 530-283-1954; www.adasplace.com; 562 Jackson St; cottages $100-145; ☎) Even though it has the feel of a B&B, it's a bit of a misnomer. Without breakfast, Ada's is just an excellent B. No problem, as each of the three brightly painted garden units has a full kitchen. Ada's Cottage is worth the slight extra charge, as

its skylights offer an open feel. It's very quiet and private, yet right in town.

Greenhorn Guest Ranch
RANCH $$$

(☎ 800-334-6939; www.greenhornranch.com; 2116 Greenhorn Ranch Rd; per person per day incl trail rides from $258; ☺ May-Oct; 🔔🎽🏊) Not a 'dude' ranch but rather a 'guest' ranch: instead of shoveling stalls, guests are pampered with mountain-trail rides, riding lessons, even rodeo practice. Or you can just fish, hike, square dance and attend evening bonfires, cookouts and frog races – think of it like a cowboy version of the getaway resort in *Dirty Dancing*. Meals and riding included.

🍴 Eating & Drinking

Quincy is a good supply point for those headed into or out of the wilderness. There are some good restaurants, a big grocery store, and a sprawling farmers market (cnr Church & Main Sts; ☺ 5-8pm Thu mid-Jul–mid-Sep).

★ Pangaea Café & Pub
CAFE $$

(www.pangaeapub.com; 461 W Main St; mains $9-13; ☺ 11am-8pm Mon-Wed, 11am-9pm Thu & Fri; 🎫🔔🍴🚭) 🖊 Like a stranger you feel you've met before, this earthy spot feels warmly familiar, all the more lovable when you consider its commitment to serving local produce. Choose from regional beef burgers, salmon sushi, a slew of panini (many veggie) and rice bowls. It's hopping with locals drinking craft brews, kids running around and lots of hugging.

Morning Thunder Café
BREAKFAST $$

(557 Lawrence St; meals $9-16; ☺ 7am-2pm; 🚭) Homey and hip, this is the best place in town for breakfast, and the vine-shaded patio is a lovely way to start the day. The menu is mainly, though not exclusively, vegetarian. Try the vegetaters: roasted veg and potatoes smothered in cheese, the chicken avocado 'thunder melt,' or the 'drunken pig,' which brilliantly balances savory pork and pineapple.

Moon's
ITALIAN $$

(☎ 530-283-0765; 497 Lawrence St; mains $13-24; ☺ 5-9pm Tue-Sun) Follow the aroma of garlic to this welcoming little chalet with a charming ambience. Dig into choice steaks and Italian-American classics, including excellent pizza and rich lasagne.

Sweet Lorraine's
CALIFORNIAN $$

(384 Main St; meals $12-28; ☺ lunch Mon-Fri, dinner Mon-Sat) On a warm day – or, better yet, evening – the patio here is especially sweet. The menu features light Californian cuisine (fish, poultry, soups and salads), but it's also known for its award-winning St Louis ribs. Finish things off with the whiskey bread pudding.

Drunk Brush
WINE BAR

(www.facebook.com/TheDrunkBrush; 438 Main St; ☺ 2-7pm Mon-Wed, 2-10pm Thu & Fri, 2-8pm Sat) A sweet little courtyard wine bar that pours 25 wines and a few beers. Sample delicious appetizer pairings in a welcoming, arty atmosphere.

ℹ Information

Mt Hough Ranger District Office (☎ 530-283-0555; 39696 Hwy 70; ☺ 8am-4:30pm Mon-Fri) Five miles west of town. Has maps and outdoors information.

Plumas County Visitors Center (☎ 530-283-6345; www.plumascounty.org; 550 Crescent St; ☺ 8am-5pm Mon-Sat) Half a mile west of town.

Plumas National Forest Headquarters (☎ 530-283-2050; 159 Lawrence St; ☺ 8am-4:30pm Mon-Fri) For maps and outdoors information.

Bucks Lake

This clear mountain lake is cherished by locals in the know. Surrounded by pine forests, it's excellent for swimming, fishing and boating. It's about 17 miles southwest of Quincy, via the white-knuckle roads of Bucks Lake Rd (Hwy 119). The region is lined with beautiful hiking trails, including the Pacific Crest Trail, which passes through the adjoining 21,000-acre Bucks Lake Wilderness in the northwestern part of Plumas National Forest. In winter, the last 3 miles of Bucks Lake Rd are closed by snow, making it ideal for cross-country skiers.

Bucks Lake Lodge (☎ 530-283-2262; www.buckslakelodge.com; 16525 Bucks Lake Rd; d $99-109, cabins $145-195; 🔔🏊) is right on the lakeshore and rents boats and fishing tackle in summer and cross-country skis in winter. The restaurant (mains $8 to $16) is popular with locals. Haskins Valley Inn (☎ 530-283-9667; www.haskinsvalleyinn.com; 1305 Haskins Circle; r $129-149; 🔔) is actually a B&B across the street from the lake, with cozily overstuffed furnishings, woodsy paintings, Jacuzzis, fireplaces and a deck. The bold southwestern rugs and heavy rough timber bed posts of the Cowboy Room is a favorite.

Five first-come, first-served campgrounds (sites $20-25) are open from June to September. Get a map at the Plumas National Forest Headquarters (p285) or the Mt Hough Ranger District Office (p285), both in Quincy.

MT SHASTA & AROUND

'Lonely as God, and white as a winter moon, Mount Shasta starts up sudden and solitary from the heart of the great black forests of Northern California,' wrote poet Joaquin Miller on the sight of this lovely mountain. A sight of it is so awe-inspiring that the new age prattle about its power as an 'energy vortex' begins to sound plausible even after a first glimpse.

There are a million ways to explore the mountain and surrounding Shasta-Trinity National Forest, depending on the season – you can take scenic drives or get out and hike, mountain bike, raft, ski or snowshoe. At Mt Shasta's base sit three excellent little towns: Dunsmuir, Mt Shasta City and McCloud. Each community has a distinct personality, but all share a wild-mountain sensibility and first-rate restaurants and places to stay. In the same dramatic vicinity rise the snaggle-toothed peaks of Castle Crags, just 6 miles west of Dunsmuir.

Northeast of Mt Shasta, a long drive and a world away, is remote, eerily beautiful Lava Beds National Monument, a blistered badland of petrified fire. The contrasting cool wetlands of Klamath Basin National Wildlife Refuges are just west of Lava Beds.

Further east, high desert plateaus give way to the mountains of the northern Sierra. Folks in this remote area are genuinely happy to greet a traveler, even if they're a bit uncertain why you've come.

Mt Shasta

'When I first caught sight of it I was 50 miles away and afoot, alone and weary. Yet all my blood turned to wine, and I have not been weary since,' wrote naturalist John Muir of Mt Shasta in 1874. Mt Shasta's beauty is intoxicating, and the closer you get to her the headier you begin to feel. Dominating the landscape, the mountain is visible for more than 100 miles from many parts of Northern California and southern Oregon. Though not California's highest peak (at 14,162ft it ranks fifth), Mt Shasta is especially magnificent because it rises alone on the horizon, unrivaled by other mountains.

Mt Shasta is part of the vast volcanic Cascade chain that includes Lassen Peak to the south and Mt St Helens and Mt Rainier to the north in Washington state. The presence of thermal hot springs indicates that Mt Shasta is dormant, not extinct. Smoke was seen puffing out of the crater on the summit in the 1850s, though the last eruption was about 200 years ago. The mountain has two cones: the main cone has a crater about 200yd across; the younger, shorter cone on the western flank, called Shastina, has a crater about half a mile wide.

The mountain and surrounding Shasta-Trinity National Forest (www.fs.fed.us/r5/shastatrinity) are crisscrossed by trails and dotted with alpine lakes. It's easy to spend days or weeks here, camping, hiking, river rafting, skiing, mountain biking and boating.

The story of the first settlers here is a sadly familiar one: European fur trappers arrived in the area in the 1820s, encountering several Native American tribes, including the Shasta, Karuk, Klamath, Modoc, Wintu and Pit River people. By 1851, hordes of Gold Rush miners had arrived and steamrolled the place, destroying the tribes' traditional life and nearly causing their extinction. Later, the newly completed railroad began to import workers and export timber for the booming lumber industry. And since Mt Shasta City (called Sisson at the time) was the only non-dry town around, it became *the* bawdy, good-time hangout for lumberjacks.

The lumberjacks have now been replaced by middle-aged mystics and outdoor-sports enthusiasts. While the slopes have immediate appeal for explorers, spiritual seekers are attracted to the peak's reported cosmic properties. In 1987, about 5000 believers from around the world convened here for the Harmonic Convergence, a communal meditation for peace. Reverence for the mountain is nothing new; for centuries Native Americans have honored the mountain as sacred, considering it to be no less than the Great Spirit's wigwam.

Many use Redding as a base since there are plenty of chain options along the highway, but Mt Shasta City is the best balance of convenience, value and personality. For food, there are satisfying restaurants at all the mountain towns, though consider having snacks on hand in the car, as the winding drives from the woods to the lunch counter are time-consuming.

◉ Sights & Activities

The Mountain

You can drive almost the whole way up the mountain via the Everitt Memorial Hwy (Hwy A10) and see exquisite views at any time of year. Simply head east on Lake St from downtown Mt Shasta City, then turn left onto Washington Dr and keep going. Bunny Flat (6860ft), which has a trailhead for Horse Camp and the Avalanche Gulch summit route, is a busy place with parking spaces, information signboards and a toilet. The section of highway beyond Bunny Flat is only open from about mid-June to October, depending on snow, but if it's clear, it's worth the trouble. This road leads to Lower Panther Meadow, where trails connect the campground to a Wintu sacred spring, in the upper meadows near the Old Ski Bowl (7800ft) parking area. Shortly thereafter is the highlight of the drive, Everitt Vista Point (7900ft), where a short interpretive walk from the parking lot leads to a stone-walled outcrop affording exceptional views of Lassen Peak to the south, the Mt Eddy and Marble Mountains to the west and the whole Strawberry Valley below.

Climbing the summit is best done between May and September, preferably in spring and early summer, when there's still enough soft snow on the southern flank to make footholds easier on the nontechnical route. Although the elements are occasionally volatile and the winds are incredibly strong, the round-trip could conceivably be done in one day with 12 or more hours of solid hiking. A more enjoyable trip takes at least two days with one night on the mountain. How long it actually takes depends on the route selected, the physical condition of the climbers and weather conditions (for weather information call the recorded message of the Forest Service Mt Shasta climbing advisory on ☑ 530-926-9613).

The hike to the summit from Bunny Flat follows the Avalanche Gulch Route. Although it is only about 7 miles, the vertical climb is more than 7000ft, so acclimatizing to the elevation is important – even hearty hikers will be short of breath. Additionally this route requires crampons, an ice ax and a helmet, all of which can be rented locally. Rock slides, while rare, are also a hazard. If

Mt Shasta Area

you want to make the climb without gear, the only option is the Clear Creek Route to the top, which leaves from the east side of the mountain. In late summer, this route usually manageable in hiking boots, though there's still loose scree, and it should be done as an overnight hike. Novices should contact the Mt Shasta ranger station (p292) for a list of available guides.

There's a charge to climb beyond 10,000ft: a three-day summit pass costs $20, an annual pass is $30. Contact the ranger station for details. You must obtain a free wilderness permit any time you go into the wilderness, whether on the mountain or in the surrounding area.

Mt Shasta Board & Ski Park   SNOW SPORTS
(☑ snow reports 530-926-8686; www.skipark.com; full-day lift tickets adult/child $44/25; ⊙ 9am-9pm Thu-Sat, to 4pm Sun-Tue) On the south slope of Mt Shasta, off Hwy 89 heading toward McCloud, this winter skiing and snowboarding

park opens depending on snowfall. The park has a 1435ft vertical drop, 32 alpine runs and 18 miles of cross-country trails. These are all good for beginner and intermediate skiers, and are a less-crowded alternative to the slopes around Lake Tahoe.

Rentals, instruction and weekly specials are available. It's Northern California's largest night-skiing operation. There are lots of inexpensive options for skiing half a day or just at night, when hitting the slopes and taking in a full moon can be enchanting.

In summer, the park occasionally hosts mountain-biking events.

The Lakes

There are a number of pristine mountain lakes near Mt Shasta. Some of them are accessible only by dirt roads or hiking trails and are great for getting away from it all.

The closest lake to Mt Shasta City is lovely Lake Siskiyou (also the largest), 2.5 miles southwest on Old Stage Rd, where you can peer into Box Canyon Dam, a 200ft-deep chasm. Another 7 miles up in the mountains, southwest of Lake Siskiyou on Castle Lake Rd, lies Castle Lake, an unspoiled gem surrounded by granite formations and pine forest. Swimming, fishing, picnicking and free camping are popular in summer; in winter folks ice-skate on the lake. Lake Shastina, about 15 miles northwest of town, off Hwy 97, is another beauty.

ⓘ Information

Peak tourist season is from Memorial Day through Labor Day and weekends during ski season (late November to mid-April depending on snow fall). The ranger station (p292) and visitors center (p292) are in Mt Shasta City.

Mt Shasta City

Comfortable and practical Mt Shasta City (population 3330) glows in the shadow of the white pyramid of Mt Shasta. The downtown is charming; you can spend hours poking around bookstores, galleries and boutiques. Orienting yourself is easy with the mountain looming over the east side of town and you may get a kink in your neck from admiring it. The downtown area is a few blocks east of I-5. Take the Central Mt Shasta exit, then drive east on Lake St past the visitors center, up to the town's main intersection at Mt Shasta Blvd, the principal drag.

⊙ Sights & Activities

To head out hiking on your own, first stop by the ranger station or the visitors center for excellent free trail guides, including several access points along the Pacific Crest Trail. Gorgeous Black Butte, a striking, treeless, black volcanic cone, rises almost 3000ft. The 2.5-mile trail to the top takes at least 2½ hours for the round-trip. It's steep and rocky in many places, and there is no shade or water, so don't hike on a hot summer day. Wear good, thick-soled shoes or hiking boots and bring plenty of water. If you want an easier amble, try the 10-mile Sisson-Callahan National Recreation Trail, a partially paved trail that affords great views of Mt Shasta and the jagged Castle Crags, following a historic route established in the mid-1800s by prospectors, trappers and cattle ranchers to connect the mining town of Callahan with the town of Sisson, now called Mt Shasta City.

Mt Shasta City Park & Sacramento River Headwaters PARK
(Nixon Rd) Off Mt Shasta Blvd, about a mile north of downtown, the headwaters of the Sacramento River gurgle up from the ground in a large, cool spring. It's about as pure as water can get – so bring a bottle and have a drink. The park also has walking trails, picnic spots, sports fields and courts, and a children's playground.

Sisson Museum MUSEUM
(www.mountshastasissonmuseum.org; 1 Old Stage Rd; suggested donation $1; ☺10am-4pm Mon-Sat, 1-4pm Sun Jun-Sep, 1-4pm Fri-Sun Oct-Dec, 1-4pm daily Apr & May) A half-mile west of the freeway, this former hatchery headquarters is full of curious mountaineering artifacts and old pictures. The changing exhibitions highlight history – geological and human – but also occasionally showcase local artists. Next door, the oldest operating hatchery in the West maintains outdoor ponds teeming with rainbow trout that will eventually be released into lakes and rivers.

Shastice Park SKATING
(www.msrec.org; cnr Rockfellow & Adams Drs; adult/child $10/5; ☺10am-5pm Mon-Thu, to 9pm Fri & Sat, 1:30-5pm Sun) East of downtown, the immense outdoor skating rink is open to ice-skaters in winter and in-line skaters on summer weekends.

River Dancers Rafting & Kayaking RAFTING
(☏530-926-3517; www.riverdancers.com; 302 Terry Lynn Ave) Excellent outfit run by active

environmentalists who guide one- to five-day white-water-rafting excursions down the area's rivers: the Klamath, Sacramento, Salmon, Trinity and Scott. Prices start with a half-day on the nearby Sacramento River for $75.

Shasta Mountain Guides OUTDOORS
(☏ 530-926-3117; http://shastaguides.com) Offers two-day guided climbs of Mt Shasta between April and September, with all gear and meals included, for $650 per person. The experienced mountaineers have operated in Shasta for 30 years.

🗪 Courses

Osprey Outdoors Kayak School KAYAKING
(www.ospreykayak.com; 2925 Cantara Loop Rd) Owner and instructor Michael Kirwin has a reputation for quality classes on high mountain lakes and rivers. Expect to pay around $175 per adult per day.

**Mt Shasta
Mountaineering School** ADVENTURE SPORTS
(www.swsmtns.com; 210a E Lake St) Conducts clinics and courses for serious climbers, or those looking to get serious. A two-day summit climb of Mt Shasta costs $525.

☞ Tours

Note that hiking Mt Shasta doesn't require an operator, but those wanting one have plenty of options; ask at the visitor center.

**Shasta Vortex
Adventures** OUTDOORS, MEDITATION
(www.shastavortex.com; 400 Chestnut St) For a uniquely Mt Shasta outdoor experience, Shasta Vortex offers low-impact trips accented with the spiritual quest as much as the physical journey. The focus of the trips includes guided meditation and an exploration of the mountain's metaphysical power. Full-day tours for two people cost $474; larger groups get a slight discount.

🛏 Sleeping

Shasta really has it all – from free rustic camping to plush boutique B&Bs. If you are intent on staying at the upper end of the spectrum, you should make reservations well in advance, especially on weekends and holidays and during ski season.

Camping in the area is excellent and the visitors center has details on over two dozen campgrounds around Mt Shasta. Check with the Mt Shasta and McCloud ranger stations about USFS campgrounds in the area. As long as you set up camp at least 200ft from the water and get a free campfire permit from a ranger station, you can camp near many mountain lakes. Castle Lake (6450ft) and Gumboot Lake (6000ft) have free tent camping (purify your own drinking water), but are closed in winter. Lovely Toad Lake (7060ft), 18 miles from Mt Shasta City, isn't a designated camping area, but you may camp there if you follow regulations. To get there go down the 11-mile gravel road (4WD advised) and walk the last quarter-mile.

Many modest motels stretch along S Mt Shasta Blvd. All have hot tubs and wi-fi, and rooms cost between $60 and $140 in peak season. As many of them were built in the '50s, the cost difference is basically based on how recently they were remodeled. Many motels offer discount ski packages in winter and lower midweek rates year-round.

**★ Historic Lookout &
Cabin Rentals** CABIN $
(☏ 530-994-2184; www.fs.fed.us/r5/shastatrinity; r up to 4 people from $75) What better way to rough it in style than to bunk down in a fire lookout on forested slopes? Built from the 1920s to '40s, cabins come with cots, tables and chairs, have panoramic views and can accommodate four people. Details about Hirz Mountain, Little Mt Hoffman and Post Creek Lookouts can all be found on the national forest website.

Panther Meadows CAMPGROUND $
(tent sites free; ☺ usually Jul–Nov) Ten walk-in tent sites (no drinking water) sit at the timberline, right at the base of the mountain. They're a few miles from other options, but are still easily accessible from Everitt Memorial Hwy. No reservations; arrive early to secure a site.

Lake Siskiyou Camp-Resort CAMPGROUND $
(☏ 530-926-2618; www.lakesis.com; 4239 WA Barr Rd; tent/RV sites from $20/29, cabins $107-152; ☏ ⛱) Tucked away on the shore of Lake Siskiyou, this sprawling place has a summer-camp feel (there's an arcade and an ice-cream stand). Hardly rustic, it has a swimming beach, and kayak, canoe, fishing boat and paddle-boat rentals. Lots of amenities make it a good option for families on an RV trip.

Swiss Holiday Lodge MOTEL $
(☏ 530-926-3446; www.swissholidaylodge.com; 2400 S Mt Shasta Blvd; d from $60; ❋ 🛜 ⛱)

WEED & STEWART MINERAL SPRINGS

Just outside Weed, **Stewart Mineral Springs** (☏530-938-2222; www.stewartmineral-springs.com; 4617 Stewart Springs Rd; mineral baths $28, sauna $18; ☺10am-6pm Sun-Wed, to 7pm Thu-Sat) is a popular alternative (read clothing-optional) hangout on the banks of a clear mountain stream. Locals come for the day and visitors from afar come for weeks. Henry Stewart founded these springs in 1875 after Native Americans revived him from a near-death experience. He attributed his recovery to the healthful properties of the mineral waters, said to draw toxins out of the body.

Today you can soak in a private claw-foot tub or steam in the dry-wood sauna. Other perks include massage, body wraps, meditation, a Native American sweat lodge and a riverside sunbathing deck. You'll want to call ahead to be sure there is space in the steam and soaking rooms, especially on busy weekends. Dining and **accommodations** (tent & RV sites $35, tipis $50-55, r $70, cabins $90-100) are available. To reach the springs, go 10 miles north of Mt Shasta City on I-5, past Weed to the Edgewood exit, then turn left at Stewart Springs Rd and follow the signs.

While in the area, tickle your other senses at the **Mt Shasta Lavender Farms** (www.mtshastalavenderfarms.com; Harry Cash Rd, off Hwy A12; 100 stems $4; ☺9am-4pm mid-Jun–early Aug), 16 miles northwest of Weed. You can harvest your own sweet French lavender in the June and July blooming season. Or drink up the tasty porter at the **Weed Mt Shasta Brewing Company** (www.weedales.com; 360 College Ave, Weed). The rich, amber-colored Mountain High IPA is delicious, but watch out – at 7% ABV it has real kick.

Run by a friendly family and a small, energetic dog, you get a peek of the mountain from the back windows of these clean, well-priced rooms.

Horse Camp   HUT $
(www.sierraclubfoundation.org; per person with/without tent $5/3) This 1923 alpine lodge run by the Sierra Club is a 2-mile hike uphill from Bunny Flat, at 8000ft. The stone construction and natural setting are lovely. Caretakers staff the hut from May to September only.

McBride Springs   CAMPGROUND $
(tent sites $10; ☺Memorial Day-late Oct, depending on weather) Easily accessible from Everitt Memorial Hwy, this campground has running water and pit toilets, but no showers. It's near mile-marker 4, at an elevation of 5000ft. It's no beauty – a recent root disease killed many of the white fir trees that shaded the sites – but it's convenient. Arrive early in the morning to secure a spot (no reservations).

★ Shasta MountInn   B&B $$
(☏530-926-1810; www.shastamountinn.com; 203 Birch St; r with/without fireplace $185/135; 🛜) Only antique on the outside, this bright Victorian 1904 farmhouse is all relaxed minimalism, bold colors and graceful decor on the inside. Each airy room has a great bed and exquisite views of the luminous mountain.

Enjoy the expansive garden, wraparound deck, outdoor sauna and a complimentary foot massage. Not relaxed enough yet? Chill on the perfectly placed porch swings.

Dream Inn   B&B $$
(☏530-926-1536; www.dreaminnmtshastacity.com; 326 Chestnut St; r with shared bath $80-160, ste $120-160; 🛜❄) Made up of two houses in the center of town: one is a meticulously kept Victorian cottage stuffed with fussy knickknacks; the other a Spanish-style two-story with chunky, raw-wood furniture and no clutter. A rose garden with a koi pond joins the two properties. A hefty breakfast is included.

Finlandia Motel   MOTEL $$
(☏530-926-5596; www.finlandiamotel.com; 1612 S Mt Shasta Blvd; r $65-120, with kitchen $115-200) An excellent deal, the standard rooms are... standard – clean and simple. The suites get a little chalet flair with vaulted pine ceilings and mountain views. There's an outdoor hot tub and the Finnish sauna is available by appointment.

Strawberry Valley Inn   B&B $$
(☏530-926-2052; 1142 S Mt Shasta Blvd; d $99-159; 🛜) The understated rooms surround a garden courtyard, allowing you to enjoy the intimate feel of a B&B without the pressure of having to chat with the darling newlyweds around the breakfast table. A conti-

nental breakfast is included, guests can use the kitchen and the new owners are keen to please.

Mt Shasta Resort
RESORT **$$**

(☎530-926-3030; www.mountshastaresort.com; 1000 Siskiyou Lake Blvd; r from $109, 1-/2-bedroom chalets from $169/229; 🛜🛁) Divinely situated away from town, this upscale golf resort and spa has Arts and Crafts–style chalets nestled in the woods around the shores of Lake Siskiyou. They're a bit soulless, but they're immaculate, and each has a kitchen and gas fireplace. Basic lodge rooms are near the golf course, which boasts some challenging greens and amazing views of the mountain.

The restaurant has excellent views as well and serves Californian cuisine with a large selection of steaks.

✖ Eating

Trendy restaurants and cafes here come and go with the snowmelt, but there are still some tried-and-true places, favored by locals and visitors alike. For more options head 6 miles south to Dunsmuir, an unexpected hotspot for great food. A **farmers market** (⏱3:30-6pm Mon) sets up on Mt Shasta Blvd during summer.

Mount Shasta Pastry
BAKERY **$**

(610 S Mt Shasta Blvd; pastries from $1.95; ⏱6am-2:30pm Mon-Sat, 7am-1pm Sun) Walk in hungry and you'll be plagued with an existential breakfast crisis: the feta spinach quiche or the Tuscan scramble? The flaky croissants or a divine apricot turnover? It also serves terrific sandwiches, gourmet pizza and Peet's Coffee.

Poncho & Lefkowitz
MEXICAN, INTERNATIONAL **$**

(401 S Mt Shasta Blvd; meals $4-12; ⏱11am-4pm Tue-Sat; 🖊) Surrounded by picnic tables, this classy, wood-sided food cart – sort of a cafe on wheels – turns out juicy Polish sausage, big plates of nachos and veggie burritos. It's a good bet for food on the go.

Berryvale Grocery & Deli
MARKET **$**

(www.berryvale.com; 305 S Mt Shasta Blvd; mains $9; ⏱8:30am-7pm Mon-Sat, 10am-6pm Sun; 🖊) 🍃 This market sells groceries and organic produce to the health conscious. The excellent deli cafe serves good coffee and an array of tasty – mostly veggie – salads, sandwiches and burritos.

★ Trinity Café
CALIFORNIAN **$$**

(☎530-926-6200; 622 N Mt Shasta Blvd; mains $17-28; ⏱5-9pm Tue-Sat) Trinity has long ri-

valed the Bay Area's best. The owners, who hail from Napa, infuse the bistro with a Wine Country feel and an extensive, excellent wine selection. The organic menu ranges from delectable, perfectly cooked steaks, savory roast game hen to creamy-on-the-inside, crispy-on-the-outside polenta. The warm, mellow mood makes for an overall delicious experience.

Lily's
CALIFORNIAN **$$**

(www.lilysrestaurant.com; 1013 S Mt Shasta Blvd; breakfast & lunch mains $9-17, dinner mains $14-25; ⏱8am-4pm Mon-Fri, 4-10pm Sat & Sun; 🖊🐾) Enjoy quality Californian cuisine – Asian- and Mediterranean-touched salads, fresh sandwiches and all kinds of veg options – in a cute, white, clapboard house. Outdoor tables overhung by flowering trellises are almost always full, especially for breakfast. After closing and re-opening in a few variations, the old management is back, keeping this a Shasta classic.

Andaman Healthy Thai Cuisine
THAI **$$**

(313 N Mt Shasta Blvd; mains $12-23; ⏱11am-9pm Mon, Tue, Thu & Fri, from 4pm Sat & Sun) The food is great, but the kitchen and the staff can't keep up with the crowds. It also serves burgers if you're traveling with fussy folk.

🍸 Drinking & Nightlife

Goats Tavern
BAR

(www.thegoatmountshasta.com; 107 Chestnut St; ⏱7am-6pm; 🛜) Come here first to drink – it has 12 taps rotating some of the best microbrewed beer in the country – and then tuck into a 'wino burger,' which comes topped with peppered goat cheese, thick sliced bacon and a red-wine reduction sauce. It's a friendly place with an affable staff, surly regulars and a great summer patio.

Seven Suns Coffee & Cafe
CAFE

(1011 S Mt Shasta Blvd; light meals from $6.75; ⏱5:30am-7pm; 🛜) This snug little hangout serves organic, locally roasted coffee and is consistently busy. There's live acoustic music some evenings.

🔒 Shopping

Looking for an imported African hand drum, some prayer flags or a nice crystal? You've come to the right place. The downtown shopping district has a handful of cute little boutiques to indulge a little shopping for the spiritual seeker.

Village Books
BOOKS

(320 N Mt Shasta Blvd; ☉10am-6pm Mon-Sat, 11am-4pm Sun) Carries fascinating volumes about Mt Shasta, on topics ranging from geology and hiking to folklore and mysticism.

Fifth Season Sports
SPORTS

(☎530-926-3606; http://thefifthseason.com; 300 N Mt Shasta Blvd; ☉8am-5pm) A favorite outdoor store in Shasta, this place rents camping, mountain-climbing and backpacking gear and has staff familiar with the mountain. It also rents skis, snowshoes and snowboards.

❶ Information

Mt Shasta Ranger Station (☎530-926-4511; www.fs.usda.gov/stnf; 204 W Alma St; ☉8am-4:30pm Mon-Fri) One block west of Mt Shasta Blvd. Issues wilderness and mountain-climbing permits, good advice, weather reports and all you need for exploring the area. It also sells topographic maps.

Mt Shasta Visitors Center (☎530-926-4865; www.mtshastachamber.com; 300 Pine St; ☉9am-5:30pm Mon-Sat, to 4:30pm Sun summer, 10am-4pm daily winter) Detailed information on recreation and lodging across Siskiyou County.

❶ Getting There & Around

Greyhound (www.greyhound.com) buses heading north and south on I-5 stop opposite the Vet's Club (406 N Mt Shasta Blvd) and at the **depot** (628 S Weed Blvd) in Weed, 8 miles north on I-5. Services include Redding ($23, one hour and 20 minutes, three daily), Sacramento ($55, 5½ hours, three daily) and San Francisco ($68, 10½ hours, two or three times daily).

The **STAGE bus** (☎530-842-8295; www.co.siskiyou.ca.us) includes Mt Shasta City in its local I-5 corridor route (fares $1.75 to $8, depending on distance), which also serves McCloud, Dunsmuir, Weed and Yreka several times each weekday. Other buses connect at Yreka.

Dunsmuir

If you love railroad towns, stop here. Built by Central Pacific Railroad, Dunsmuir (population 1650) was originally named Pusher, for the auxiliary 'pusher' engines that muscled the heavy steam engines up the steep mountain grade. In 1886 Canadian coal baron Alexander Dunsmuir came to Pusher and was so enchanted that he promised the people a fountain if they would name the town after him. The fountain stands in the park today.

Stop there to quench your thirst; it could easily be – as locals claim – 'the best water on earth.'

Dunsmuir might have aptly been named Phoenix. Rising from the ashes, this town has survived one cataclysmic disaster after another – avalanche, fire, flood, even a toxic railroad spill in 1991. Long since cleaned up, the river has been restored to pristine levels and the community has a notably plucky spirit, though today a number of empty storefronts attest to the community's greatest challenge: the Global Economic Crisis.

Still, it's home to a spirited set of artists, naturalists, urban refugees and native Dunsmuirians, who are rightly proud of the fish-stocked rivers (yes, the fishing is great) around their little community. Its downtown streets – once a bawdy Gold Rush district of five saloons and three brothels – hold cafes, restaurants and galleries, and the town's reputation is still inseparable from the trains.

Split in two by the I-5, the southern half is where you'll find the bright and pleasant historic downtown.

❂ Sights & Activities

The chamber of commerce stocks maps of cycling trails and swimming holes on the Upper Sacramento River.

Ruddle Cottage
GALLERY

(www.ruddlecottage.net; 5815 Sacramento Ave; ☉10am-4pm May-Oct, 11am-4pm Nov-Apr) Behind a shaded garden, cluttered with eclectic sculptures, Jayne Bruck-Fryer's colorful gallery feels a bit like something from a fairy tale. Fryer makes each and every ingenious creation – from sculptures to jewelry – from recycled materials. The pretty fish hanging in the window? Dryer lint!

California Theater
HISTORIC BUILDING

(5741 Dunsmuir Ave) At downtown's north end stands what was once the town's pride. In a community effort, this once-glamorous venue is being restored to its original glory. First opened in 1926, the theater hosted stars such as Clark Gable, Carole Lombard and the Marx Brothers. Today the lineup includes second-run films, musical performances and yoga classes.

Dunsmuir City Park & Botanical Gardens
PARK

(www.dunsmuirparks.org; ☉dawn-dusk) **FREE** As you follow winding Dunsmuir Ave north over the freeway, look for this park with its local native gardens and a vintage steam engine in front. A forest path from the riverside gardens leads to a small waterfall, but Mossbrae Falls are the larger and more spectacular of Dunsmuir's waterfalls.

To reach the falls, park by the railroad tracks (there's no sign), then walk north along the right-hand side of the tracks for a half-hour until you reach a railroad bridge built in 1901. Backtracking slightly from the bridge, you'll find a little path going down through the trees to the river and the falls. Be extremely careful of trains as you walk by the tracks – the river's sound can make it impossible to hear them coming.

Shasta Valley Balloons BALLOONING
(📞 530-926-3612; www.hot-airballoons.com; 5304 Dunsmuir Ave, Dunsmuir; rides $200) Live a dream by seeing the area from a hot-air balloon. The office is in Dunsmuir but flights leave from Montague Municipal Airport, 6 miles east of Yreka.

🛏 Sleeping

Dunsmuir Lodge MOTEL $
(📞 530-235-2884; www.dunsmuirlodge.net; 6604 Dunsmuir Ave; r $79-153; 🐾🌐) Toward the south entrance of town, the simple but tastefully renovated rooms have hardwood floors, big chunky blond-wood bed frames and tiled baths. A grassy communal picnic area overlooks the canyon slope. It's a peaceful little place and very good value.

Cave Springs MOTEL, CABIN $
(📞 530-235-2721; www.cavesprings.com; 4727 Dunsmuir Ave; cabins from $76, r from $99; ❄🌐) These creekside cabins seem unchanged since the 1920s even though the interiors were recently updated. They are rustic – *very* rustic – but their location, nestled on a piney crag above the Sacramento River, is lovely and ideal for anglers. At night the sound of rushing water mingles with the haunting whistle of trains.

The motel rooms are bland, but they're up to modern standards and have amenities.

Dunsmuir Inn & Suites MOTEL $
(📞 530-235-4395; www.dunsmuirinn.com; 5400 Dunsmuir Ave; r $79-159; 🌐) Straightforward, immaculately clean motel rooms make a good, no-fuss option.

Railroad Park Resort INN, CAMPGROUND $$
(📞 530-235-4440, 800-974-7245; www.rrpark.com; 100 Railroad Park Rd; tent/RV sites from $29/37, d

$105-130; ❄🌐🌐🌐) About a mile south of town, off I-5, visitors can spend the night inside refitted vintage railroad cars and cabooses. The grounds are fun for kids, who can run around the engines and plunge in a centrally situated pool. The deluxe boxcars are furnished with antiques and claw-foot tubs, although the cabooses are simpler and a bit less expensive.

You get tremendous views of Castle Crags, a peaceful creekside setting and tall pines shading the adjoining campground.

🍴 Eating & Drinking

There's an impressive number of really good eating options for such a small town.

Cornerstone Bakery & Café CAFE $
(5759 Dunsmuir Ave; mains $8-9; ⏱8am-2pm Thu-Mon; ✏) Smack in the middle of town, it serves smooth, strong coffee, espresso and chai. All the baked goods – including thick, gooey cinnamon rolls – are warm from the oven. Creative omelets include cactus. The wine list is extensive, as is the dessert selection.

★ Dunsmuir Brewery Works PUB FOOD $$
(📞 530-235-1900; www.dunsmuirbreweryworks.info; 5701 Dunsmuir Ave; mains $11-20; ⏱11am-9pm Tue-Sun; 🌐) It's hard to describe this little microbrew pub without veering into hyperbole. Start with the beer: the crisp ales and chocolate porter are perfectly balanced, and the IPA is apparently pretty good, too, because patrons are always drinking it dry. Soak it up with awesome bar food – a warm potato salad, bratwurst or a thick Angus burger.

The atmosphere, with a buzzing patio and aw-shucks staff, completes a perfect picture.

**Brown Trout Gallery &
Dogwood Diner** CAFE $$
(📞 530-235-0754; 5841 Sacramento Ave; mains $10; ⏱11am-8pm Mon, Tue & Fri, 8am-9pm Sat & Sun; 🌐✏) This casual, high-ceilinged, brick-walled hangout (formerly the town mercantile) serves creative, internationally inspired dishes from burgers and salads to pasta and wild-caught salmon. Weekend breakfasts are a treat with mains like poached eggs and butter beans, pineapple French toast or peanut-butter-stuffed cinnamon rolls.

Railroad Park Dinner House CALIFORNIAN $$
(📞 530-235-4440; Railroad Park Resort, 100 Railroad Park Rd; mains $15-28; ⏱5-9pm Fri & Sat Apr, 5-9pm Wed-Sun May-Oct) Set inside a vintage

railroad car with views of Castle Crags, this popular restaurant-bar offers trainloads of dining-car ambience and Californian cuisine. Prime rib specials are on Friday and Saturdays.

YAKs

AMERICAN $$

(4917 Dunsmuir Ave; mains around $12; ⊙7:30am-7pm Mon-Sat, 7:30am-5pm Sun; 🛜) Hiding under the Hitching Post sign just off I-5, come here to blow your diet. Breakfast means Cuban peppersteak hash or perhaps home-baked cinnamon roll French toast with choice of house syrups like Baileys bourbon-butter. Lunch offers a huge range of burgers (try the one with the house-roasted coffee rub). There's also a take-out counter.

Sengthongs

THAI, VIETNAMESE $$

(📞530-235-4770; http://sengthongs.com; 5855 Dunsmuir Ave; mains $17-27; ⊙usually 5-8:30pm Thu-Sun) This funky joint serves up sizzling Thai, Lao and Vietnamese food and books first-rate jazz, reggae, salsa or blues most nights. Many dishes are simply heaping bowls of noodles, though the meat dishes – flavored with ginger, scallions and spices – are more complex and uniformly delicious.

★ Café Maddalena

EUROPEAN, NORTH AFRICAN $$$

(📞530-235-2725; www.cafemaddalena.com; 5801 Sacramento Ave; mains $22-25; ⊙5-10pm Thu-Sun Feb-Nov) Simple and elegant, this cafe put Dunsmuir on the foodie map. The menu was designed by chef Bret LaMott (of Trinity Café fame) and changes weekly to feature dishes from southern Europe and north Africa. Some highlights include pan-roasted king salmon with basil cream, or sauteed rabbit with carrots and morel sauce.

The wine bar is stocked with rare Mediterranean labels, including a great selection of Spanish varietals.

❶ Information

Dunsmuir Chamber of Commerce (📞530-235-2177; www.dunsmuir.com; Suite 100, 5915 Dunsmuir Ave; ⊙10am-3:30pm Tue-Sat) Free maps, walking-guide pamphlets and excellent information on outdoor activities.

❶ Getting There & Away

Amtrak Station (www.amtrak.com; 5750 Sacramento Ave) Dunsmuir's Amtrak station is the only train stop in Siskiyou County and it is not staffed. Buy tickets for the north–south Coast Starlight on board the train, but only after making reservations by phone or via the website. The Coast Starlight runs once daily to Redding ($28, 1¾ hours), Sacramento ($38, 5¾ hours) and Oakland ($42, eight hours).

STAGE Bus (📞530-842-8295) The STAGE bus includes Dunsmuir in its local I-5 corridor route, which also serves Mt Shasta City ($2.50, 20 minutes), Weed ($4, 30 minutes) and Yreka ($6, 1¼ hours) several times each weekday. The bus runs on Dunsmuir Ave.

Castle Crags State Park

The stars of this glorious state park alongside Castle Crags Wilderness Area are its soaring spires of ancient granite formed some 225 million years ago, with elevations ranging from 2000ft along the Sacramento River to more than 6500ft at the peaks. The crags are similar to the granite formations of the eastern Sierra, and Castle Dome resembles Yosemite's famous Half Dome.

Rangers at the park entrance station (📞530-235-2684; per car $8) have information and maps covering nearly 28 miles of hiking trails. There's also fishing in the Sacramento River at the picnic area on the opposite side of I-5.

If you drive past the campground, you'll reach Vista Point, near the start of the strenuous 2.7-mile Crags Trail, which rises through the forest past the Indian Springs spur trail, then clambers up to the base of Castle Dome. You're rewarded with unsurpassed views of Mt Shasta, especially if you scramble the last 100yd or so up into the rocky saddle gap. The park also has gentle nature trails and 8 miles of the Pacific Crest Trail, which passes through the park at the base of the crags.

The campground (📞reservations 800-444-7275; www.reserveamerica.com; tent & RV sites $35) is one of the nicer public campgrounds in this area, and very easily accessible from the highway. It has running water, hot showers, and three spots that can accommodate RVs but have no hookups. Sites are shady, but suffer from traffic noise. You can camp anywhere in the Shasta-Trinity National Forest surrounding the park if you get a free campfire permit, issued at park offices. At the time of writing, the future of this state park was uncertain because of budget issues.

McCloud

This tiny, historic mill town (population 1101) sits at the foot of the south slope of Mt Shasta, and is an alternative to staying in Mt Shasta City. Quiet streets retain a simple, easygoing charm. It's the closest settlement to Mt Shasta Board & Ski Park and is surrounded by abundant natural beauty. Hidden in the woods upriver are woodsy getaways for the Western aristocracy, including mansions owned by the Hearst and Levi Strauss estates.

The town made some press during a recent battle against the Nestlé corporation, which announced a plan for a water bottling facility on the site of the defunct mill. Fearing the damage to the local watershed, a cadre of residents organized to oppose the factory. By 2009 they had succeeded in entangling the multinational giant in red tape and bad publicity, and Nestlé scuttled the project.

◉ Sights & Activities

The McCloud River Loop, a gorgeous, 6-mile, partially paved road along the Upper McCloud River, begins at Fowlers Camp, 5.5 miles east of town on Hwy 89, and reemerges about 11 miles east of McCloud. Along the loop, turn off at Three Falls for a pretty trail that passes…yep, three lovely falls and a riparian habitat for bird-watching in the Bigelow Meadow. The loop can easily be done by car, bicycle or on foot, and has five first-come, first-served campgrounds.

Other good hiking trails include the Squaw Valley Creek Trail (not to be confused with the ski area near Lake Tahoe), an easy 5-mile loop trail south of town, with options for swimming, fishing and picnicking. Also south of town, Ah-Di-Na is the remains of a Native American settlement and historic homestead once owned by the William Randolph Hearst family. Sections of the Pacific Crest Trail are accessible from Ah-Di-Na Campground, off Squaw Valley Rd, and also up near Bartle Gap, offering head-spinning views.

Fishing and swimming are popular on remote Lake McCloud reservoir, 9 miles south of town on Squaw Valley Rd, which is signposted in town as Southern. You can also go fishing on the Upper McCloud River (stocked with trout) and at the Squaw Valley Creek.

The huge McCloud Mercantile anchors the downtown. There's a hotel upstairs and it hosts a couple of restaurants that warrant a longer stay, but those just passing though can get a bag of licorice at the old-world candy counter or browse the main floor. The collection of dry goods is very woodsy and very NorCal: Woolrich blankets, handmade soap and interesting gifts for the gardener, outdoors person or chef.

A tiny historical museum (⊙11am-3pm Mon-Sat, 1-3pm Sun) FREE sits opposite the depot and could use a bit of organization – it has the feel of a cluttered, messy thrift store – but tucked in the nooks and crannies are plenty of worthwhile curiosities from the town's past.

🛌 Sleeping

Lodging in McCloud is taken seriously – all are excellent and reservations are recommended. For camping go to the McCloud ranger district office for information on the

---

SKIING THE NORTHERN MOUNTAINS

Tahoe it ain't, but visitors in winter months will find a few small ski areas that lack the crowds and attitude of elsewhere in the state. These are also places for snowshoeing, sledding, cross-country skiing and general fun in the snow. Lassen Volcanic National Park (p277) doesn't have lifts or lodges but it does have over 150 miles of marked and unmarked trails for unmotorized winter sports. Through spring you'll see plenty of folks taking to the woods on skis.

Try the area's ski 'resorts':

Mt Shasta Board & Ski Park (p287) The biggest in this region, although some winters it doesn't snow enough for it to open at all.

Coppervale Ski Hill (Westwood; day passes $20-25; ⊙12:30-4:30pm Tue & Thu, 9:30am-4pm Sat & Sun) There's not even a website for this place (15 miles from Chester near Lake Almanor), but it does have one poma lift, a rope tow and a half pipe. Kids under six ski for free.

Cedar Pass Snow Park (p299) Way over in the Modoc National Forest, 20 minutes from Alturas, this tiny, community-run place has a rope tow, a T-bar and nice family vibe. Find specials and changing opening hours on its Facebook page: https://www.facebook.com/NCCPSP.

half-dozen campgrounds nearby. Fowlers Camp is the most popular. The campgrounds have a range of facilities, from primitive (no running water and no fee) to developed (hot showers and fees of up to $15 per site). Ask about nearby fire-lookout cabins for rent – they give amazing, remote views of the area.

Stoney Brook Inn HOTEL **$**
(☑530-964-2300; www.stoneybrookinn.com; 309 W Colombero Dr; s/d with shared bath $53/79, d with private bath $94, ste with kitchen $99-156; 🛜🞲) Smack in the middle of town, under a stand of pines, this alternative B&B also sponsors group retreats. Creature comforts include an outdoor hot tub, a sauna, a Native American sweat lodge and massage by appointment. Downstairs rooms are nicest. Vegetarian breakfast available.

McCloud Dance Country RV Park CAMPGROUND **$**
(☑530-964-2252; www.mccloudrvpark.com; 480 Hwy 89, at Southern Ave; tent sites $28, RV sites $36-45, cabins $140-175; 🛜🞲) Chock-full of RVs, with sites under the trees and a small creek, this is a good option for families. The view of the mountain is breathtaking and there's a large, grassy picnic ground. Cabins are basic but clean.

⭐**McCloud River Mercantile Hotel** INN **$$**
(☑530-964-2330; www.mccloudmercantile.com; 241 Main St; r incl breakfast $129-250; 🛜) Stoll up the stairs to the 2nd floor of McCloud's central Mercantile and try not to fall in love; it's all high ceilings, exposed brick and a perfect marriage of preservationist class and modern panache. The rooms are situated within open floor plans, and guests are greeted with fresh flowers and can drift to sleep on feather beds after soaking in claw-foot tubs.

McCloud Hotel HISTORIC HOTEL **$$**
(☑530-964-2822; www.mccloudhotel.com; 408 Main St; r $128-199; 🞲🛜) Regal, butter-yellow and a whole block long, the grand hotel opened in 1916 and has been a destination for Shasta's visitors ever since. The elegant historic landmark has been restored to a luxurious standard, and the included breakfast has gourmet flair. One room is accessible for travelers with disabilities.

McCloud River Inn B&B **$$**
(☑530-964-2130; www.mccloudriverinn.com; 325 Lawndale Ct; r incl breakfast $99-199; 🞲) Rooms in this rambling Victorian are fabulously big – the bathrooms alone could sleep two.

In the morning look out for the frittatas; in the evening enjoy a couple of glasses of wine in the cute downstairs wine bar. The atmosphere guarantees that it books up quickly.

✖ Eating

McCloud's eating options are few. For more variety, make the trip over to Mt Shasta City.

Mountain Star Cafe VEGETARIAN **$**
(241 Main St; mains $7-9; ⊗8am-3pm; 🖋) 🌱 Deep within the creaking Mercantile, this sweet lunch counter is a surprise, serving vegetarian specials made from locally sourced, organic produce. Some options on the menu during a recent visit included morale biscuits and gravy, a garlicky tempeh Ruben, roast vegetable salad and a homemade oat and veggie burger.

White Mountain Fountain Cafe AMERICAN **$**
(241 Main St; mains $8; ⊗8am-4pm) In the window-lined corner of the Mercantile, this old-fashioned little soda fountain serves burgers and shakes. The one coyly called 'Not the Dolly Varden' is an excellent vegetarian sandwich with roasted zucchini, red peppers and garlic aioli.

🍷 Drinking & Nightlife

McCloud Dance Country DANCE
(www.mcclouddancecountry.com; cnr Broadway & Pine Sts; per couple $20; ⊗7pm Fri & Sat) Dust it up on the 5000-sq-ft maple dance floor in the 1906 Broadway Ballroom. Square dancing, round dancing, ballroom dancing – they do it all. Starting at $299 per couple, multiday packages include lessons and evening dances. It's a worthwhile centerpiece to a weekend getaway. Visit the website to see what's on and whether you need a reservation for the event.

ⓘ Information

McCloud Chamber of Commerce (☑530-964-3113; www.mccloudchamber.com; 205 Quincy St; ⊗10am-4pm Mon-Fri)
McCloud Ranger District Office (☑530-964-2184; Hwy 89; ⊗8am-4:30pm Mon-Sat summer, 8am-4:30pm Mon-Fri rest of year) A quarter-mile east of town. Detailed information on camping, hiking and recreation.

McArthur-Burney Falls Memorial State Park

This beautiful state park (☑530-335-2777, summer reservations 800-444-7275; www.parks.

ca.gov; day-use/campsites $8/25; ⚓) lies southeast of McCloud, near the crossroads of Hwys 89 and 299 from Redding. The 129ft falls cascade with the same volume of water – 100 million gallons per day – and at the same temperature – 42°F (5°C) – year-round. Clear, lava-filtered water surges over the top and also from springs in the waterfall's face. Teddy Roosevelt loved this place; he called it the 'Eighth Wonder of the World.'

A lookout point beside the parking lot also has trails going up and down the creek from the falls. (Be careful of your footing here; in 2011 there was a fatality in the park when someone slipped on the rocks.) The nature trail heading downstream leads to Lake Britton; other hiking trails include a portion of the Pacific Crest Trail. The scenes in the film *Stand By Me* (1986) where the boys dodge the train were shot on the Lake Britton Bridge trestle in the park.

The park's **campgrounds** (☑530-335-2777, summer reservations 800-444-7275; www.reserveamerica.com; tent & RV sites $35) have hot showers and are open year-round.

About 10 miles northeast of McArthur-Burney Falls, the 6000-acre **Ahjumawi Lava Springs State Park** is known for its abundant springs, aquamarine bays, islets, and jagged flows of black basalt lava. It can only be reached by boats that are launched from Rat Farm, 3 miles north of the town of McArthur along a graded dirt road. Arrangements for primitive camping can be made by calling McArthur-Burney Falls Memorial State Park.

Lava Beds National Monument

A wild landscape of charred volcanic rock and rolling hills, this remote **national monument** (☑530-667-8113; www.nps.gov/labe; 7-day entry per car $10) is reason enough to visit the region. Off Hwy 139, immediately south of Tule Lake National Wildlife Refuge, it's a truly remarkable 72-sq-mile landscape of volcanic features – lava flows, craters, cinder cones, spatter cones, shield volcanoes and amazing lava tubes.

Lava tubes are formed when the surface of hot, spreading lava cools and hardens upon exposure to cold air. The lava inside is thus insulated and stays molten, flowing away to leave an empty tube of solidified lava. Nearly 400 such tubular caves have been found in the monument, and many

more are expected to be discovered. About two dozen or so are currently open for exploration by visitors.

On the south side of the park, the **visitors center** (☑530-667-2282, ext 230; ◷8am-6pm, shorter hours in winter) has free maps, activity books for kids and information about the monument and its volcanic features and history. Rangers loan mediocre flashlights (and rent helmets and kneepads in the summer season only) for cave exploration and lead summer interpretive programs, including campfire talks and guided cave walks. To explore the caves it's essential you use a high-powered flashlight, wear good shoes and long sleeves (lava is sharp), and do not go alone.

Near the visitors center, a short, one-way **Cave Loop** drive provides access to many lava-tube caves. **Mushpot Cave**, the one nearest the visitors center, has lighting and information signs and is beautiful, besides being a good introductory hike. There are a number of caves that are a bit more challenging, including Labyrinth, Hercules Leg, Golden Dome and Blue Grotto. Each one of these caves has an interesting history – visitors used to ice-skate by lantern light in the bottom of Merrill Cave, and when Ovls Cave was discovered, it was littered with bighorn sheep skulls. There are good brochures with details about each cave available from the visitors center. We found Sunshine Cave and Symbol Bridge caves (the latter is reached via an easy 0.8-mile hike) to be particularly interesting. Rangers are stern with their warnings for new cavers, though, so be sure to check in with the visitors center before exploring to avoid harming the fragile geological and biological resources in the park.

The tall black cone of **Schonchin Butte** (5253ft) has a magnificent outlook accessed via a steep 1-mile hiking trail. Once you reach the top, you can visit the fire-lookout staff between June and September. **Mammoth Crater** is the source of most of the area's lava flows.

The weathered Modoc **petroglyphs** at the base of a high cliff at the far northeastern end of the monument, called Petroglyph Point, are thousands of years old, but unfortunately the short interpretive trail has been closed due to vandalism – the rest is worth checking out anyway. At the visitors center, be sure to take the leaflet explaining the origin of the petroglyphs and their probable meaning. Look for the hundreds of nests in holes high up in the cliff face, which provide shelter for birds that sojourn at the wildlife refuges nearby.

Also at the north end of the monument, be sure to go to the labyrinthine landscape of Captain Jack's Stronghold, the Modoc Indians' very effective ancient wartime defense area. A brochure will guide you through the breathtaking Stronghold Trail.

Indian Well Campground (tent & RV sites $10), near the visitors center at the south end of the park, has water and flush toilets, but no showers. The campsites are lovely and have broad views of the surrounding valleys. The nearest place to buy food and camping supplies is on Hwy 139 in the nearby town of Tulelake, but the place is pretty bleak and rugged – just a couple of bars, a bunch of boarded-up buildings and a pair of gas stations. Don't count on finding food out of peak times besides the grocery store.

Klamath Basin National Wildlife Refuges

Of the six stunning national wildlife refuges in this group, Tule Lake and Clear Lake refuges are wholly within California, Lower Klamath refuge straddles the California–Oregon border, and the Upper Klamath, Klamath Marsh and Bear Valley refuges are across the border in Oregon. Bear Valley and Clear Lake (not to be confused with the Clear Lake just east of Ukiah) are closed to the public to protect their delicate habitats, but the rest are open during daylight hours.

These refuges provide habitats for a stunning array of birds migrating along the Pacific Flyway. Some stop over only briefly; others stay longer to mate, make nests and raise their young. The refuges are always packed with birds, but during the spring and fall migrations, populations can rise into the hundreds of thousands.

The Klamath Basin National Wildlife Refuges visitors center (☎530-667-2231; http://klamathbasinrefuges.fws.gov; 4009 Hill Rd, Tulelake; ☺8am-4:30pm Mon-Fri, 10am-4pm Sat & Sun) sits on the west side of the Tule Lake refuge, about 5 miles west of Hwy 139, near the town of Tule Lake. Follow the signs from Hwy 139 or from Lava Beds National Monument. The center has a bookstore and an interesting video program, as well as maps, information on recent bird sightings and updates on road conditions. It rents photo blinds. Be sure to pick up the excellent, free *Klamath Basin*

Birding Trail brochure for detailed lookouts, maps, color photos and a species checklist.

The spring migration peaks during March, and in some years more than a million birds fill the skies. In April and May the songbirds, waterfowl and shorebirds arrive, some to stay and nest, others to build up their energy before they continue north. In summer, ducks, Canada geese and many other waterbirds are raised here. The fall migration peaks in early November. In cold weather the area hosts the largest wintering concentration of bald eagles in the lower 48 states, with 1000 in residence at times from December to February. The Tule Lake and Lower Klamath refuges are the best places to see eagles and other raptors.

The Lower Klamath and Tule Lake refuges attract the largest numbers of birds year-round, and auto trails (driving routes) have been set up; a free pamphlet from the visitors center shows the routes. Self-guided canoe trails have been established in three of the refuges. Those in the Tule Lake and Klamath Marsh refuges are usually open from July 1 to September 30; no canoe rentals are available. Canoe trails in the Upper Klamath refuge are open year-round. Here, canoes can be rented at Rocky Point Resort (☎541-356-2287; 28121 Rocky Point Rd, Klamath Falls, OR; canoe, kayak & paddle boat rental per hr/half-day/day $15/30/40), on the west side of Upper Klamath Lake.

Camp at nearby Lava Beds National Monument. Alternatively, a couple of RV parks and budget motels cluster along Hwy 139 near the tiny town of Tulelake (4035ft), including the friendly, brightly painted Ellis Motel (☎530-667-5242; 2238 Hwy 139; d with/without kitchen $95/75) about a mile north of town. Comfortable Fe's B&B (☎877-478-0184; www.fesbandb.com; 660 Main St; s/d with shared bath $60/70) has four simple rooms right in 'downtown,' with a big breakfast included. There may or may not be restaurants open (everything was shut at 5pm on a Sunday when we passed). Another option is to drive 9 miles north to Merrill, OR, and stay at the backcountry-cute, good-value Wild Goose Lodge (☎541-331-2701; www.wild-gooselodge.webs.com; 105 E Court Dr, Merrill, OR; r $60, cabins $120; 🐾🐕). The closest real town is Klamath Falls, OR, 29 miles from Tulelake.

Modoc National Forest

It's nearly impossible to get your head around this enormous national forest

THE AVIAN SUPERHIGHWAY

California is on the Pacific Flyway, a migratory route for hundreds of species of birds heading south in winter and north in summer. There are birds to see year-round, but the best viewing opportunities are during the spring and fall migrations. Flyway regulars include everything from tiny finches, hummingbirds, swallows and woodpeckers to eagles, hawks, swans, geese, ducks, cranes and herons. Much of the flyway route corresponds with I-5 (or Fly-5 in the birds' case), so a drive up the interstate in spring or fall is a show: great Vs of geese undulate in the sky and noble hawks stare from roadside perches.

In Northern California, established wildlife refuges safeguard wetlands used by migrating waterfowl. The Klamath Basin National Wildlife Refuges offer extraordinary year-round bird-watching.

(www.fs.usda.gov/modoc) – it covers almost two million spectacular, remote acres of California's northeastern corner. Travelers through the remote northeast of the state will be passing in and out of its borders constantly. Fourteen miles south of Lava Beds National Monument, on the western edge of the forest, Medicine Lake is a stunning crater lake in a caldera (collapsed volcano), surrounded by pine forest, volcanic formations and campgrounds. The enormous volcano that formed the lake is the largest in area in California. When it erupted it ejected pumice followed by flows of obsidian, as can be seen at Little Glass Mountain, east of the lake.

Pick up the *Medicine Lake Highlands: Self-Guided Roadside Geology Tour* pamphlet from the McCloud ranger district office to find and learn about the glass flows, pumice deposits, lava tubes and cinder cones throughout the area. Roads are closed by snow from around mid-November to mid-June, but the area is still popular for winter sports, and accessible by cross-country skiing and snowshoeing.

Congratulations are in order for travelers who make it all the way to the Warner Mountains. This spur of the Cascade Range in the east of the Modoc National Forest is probably the least-visited range in California. With extremely changeable weather, it's also not so hospitable; there have been snowstorms here in every season of the year. The range divides into the North Warners and South Warners at Cedar Pass (elevation 6305ft), east of Alturas. Remote Cedar Pass Snow Park (530-233-3323; all day T-bar adult/child under 6yr/6-18yr $15/5/12, all-day rope tow $5; 10am-4pm Sat, Sun & holidays during ski season) offers downhill and cross-country skiing. The majestic South Warner Wilderness contains 77 miles of hiking and riding

trails. The best time to use them is from July to mid-October.

Maps, campfire permits and information are all available at the Modoc National Forest supervisor's headquarters (530-233-5811; 800 W 12th St; 8am-5pm Mon-Fri) in Alturas.

If you are heading east into Nevada from the forest, you'll pass through Alturas, the fairly uninspiring seat of Modoc County. The town was founded by the Dorris family in 1874 as a supply point for travelers, and it serves the same function today, providing basic services, motels and family-style restaurants. The best place to stay in town (which won't cost much more than the motels) is the newly re-opened, turn-of-the-century and beautifully period-decorated Niles Hotel (530-233-3773; www.nileshotel.com; 304 S Main St, Alturas; r from $80;), which also has a restaurant where the tables are lit by oil lamps.

WEST OF I-5

The wilderness west of I-5 is right in the sweet spot: here are some of the most rugged towns and seductive wilderness areas in the entire state of California – just difficult enough to reach to discourage big crowds.

The Trinity Scenic Byway (Hwy 299) winds spectacularly along the Trinity River and beneath towering cliffs as it makes its way from the plains of Redding to the coastal redwood forests around Arcata. It provides a chance to cut through some of the northern mountains' most pristine wilderness and passes through the vibrant Gold Rush town of Weaverville.

Heavenly Hwy 3 (a highly recommended – although slower and windier – alternative route to I-5) heads north from Weaverville.

NORTHERN MOUNTAINS MODOC NATIONAL FOREST

This mountain byway transports you through the Trinity Alps – a stunning granite range dotted with azure alpine lakes – past the shores of Lewiston and Trinity Lakes, over the Scott Mountains and finally into emerald, mountain-rimmed Scott Valley. Rough-and-ready Yreka awaits you at the end of the line.

Weaverville

In 1941 a reporter interviewed James Hilton, the British author of *Lost Horizon*. 'In all your wanderings,' the journalist asked, 'what's the closest you've found to a real-life Shangri-La?' Hilton's response? 'A little town in northern California. A little town called Weaverville.'

Cute as a button, Weaverville's streets are lined with flower boxes in the summer and banks of snow in the winter. The seat of Trinity County, it sits amid an endless tract of mountain and forest that's 75% federally owned. With its almost 3300 sq miles, the county is roughly the size of Delaware and Rhode Island together, yet has a total population of only 13,700 and not one freeway or parking meter.

Weaverville (population 3600) is a small gem of a town on the National Register of Historic Places and has a laid-back, gentle bohemian feel (thanks in part to the young back-to-landers and marijuana-growing subculture). You can easily spend a day here just strolling around the quaint storefronts and visiting art galleries, museums and historic structures. If you've got more time, there are 40 miles of hiking and mountain-biking trails in the Weaverville Basin Trail System, or you can cast a line along the Trinity River, Trinity Lake or Lewiston Lake for steelhead, salmon and trout.

◎ Sights & Activities

★ Weaverville Joss House State Historic Park   HISTORIC BUILDING
(☑530-623-5284; www.parks.ca.gov; cnr Hwy 299 & Oregon St; tour adult/child $4/2; ☉10am-5pm Thu-Sun, hourly tours until 4pm) The walls here actually talk – they're papered inside with 150-year-old donation ledgers from the once-thriving Chinese community, the immigrants who built Northern California's infrastructure, a rich culture that has all but disappeared. It's a surprise that the oldest continuously used Chinese temple in Cali-

fornia (and an exceptionally beautiful one at that), dating to the 1870s, is in Weaverville.

The blue-and-gold Taoist shrine contains an ornate altar, more than 3000 years old, which was brought here from China. The adjoining schoolhouse was the first to teach Chinese students in California. Even in Asia (let alone California) it's rare to see a Chinese temple with the all the ancient features so well preserved.

JJ Jackson Memorial Museum & Trinity County Historical Park   MUSEUM
(www.trinitymuseum.org; 508 Main St; donation requested; ☉10am-5pm daily May-Oct, noon-4pm daily Apr & Nov-Dec 24, noon-4pm Tue & Sat Dec 26-Mar) Next door to the Joss House you'll find gold-mining and cultural exhibits, plus vintage machinery, memorabilia, an old miner's cabin and a blacksmith shop.

Highland Art Center   GALLERY
(www.highlandartcenter.org; 691 Main St; ☉10am-5pm Mon-Sat, 11am-4pm Sun) Stroll through galleries showcasing local artists.

Coffee Creek Ranch   FISHING, HIKING
(☑530-266-3343; www.coffeecreekranch.com) In Trinity Center, these guys lead fishing and fully outfitted pack trips into the Trinity Alps Wilderness and week-long fishing excursions.

🛏 Sleeping

The ranger station (p301) has information on many USFS campgrounds in the area, especially around Trinity Lake. Commercial RV parks, some with tent sites, dot Hwy 299.

Red Hill Motel & Cabins   MOTEL $
(☑530-623-4331; www.redhillresorts.com; 116 Red Hill Rd; d $48, cabins with/without kitchen $64/52; 🐾📶) This very quiet and rustic motel is tucked under ponderosa pines at the west end of town, just off Main St, next to the library. It's a set of red wooden cabins built in the 1940s and they're equipped with kitchenettes and mini-fridges. The rooms are simple and good value. It sometimes fills with visiting groups, so book ahead.

Weaverville Hotel   HISTORIC HOTEL $$
(☑800-750-8957; www.weavervillehotel.com; 203 Main St; r $99-260; 🐾📶) Play like you're in the Old West at this upscale hotel and historic landmark, refurbished in grand Victorian style. It's luxurious but not stuffy, and the very gracious owners take great care in looking after you. Guests may use the local

gym, and $10 credit at local restaurants is included in the rates. Kids under 12 are not allowed.

Whitmore Inn HISTORIC HOTEL $$
(☎530-623-2509; www.whitmoreinn.com; 761 Main St; r $100-165; ❄☎) Settle into plush, cozy rooms in this downtown Victorian with a wraparound deck and abundant gardens. One room is accessible for travelers with disabilities. Only kids over five years old are welcome.

✖ Eating

Downtown Weaverville is ready to feed hungry hikers – in the summer the main drag has many cheap, filling options. There's also a fantastic farmers market (⊙4:30-7:30pm Wed May-Oct), which takes over Main St in the warmer months. In winter the tourist season dries up and opening hours get very short.

Trinideli DELI $
(201 Trinity Lakes Blvd, at Center St; sandwiches $5-9; ⊙6am-4pm Mon-Fri) Cheerful staff prepare decadent sandwiches stuffed with fresh goodness. The one-and-a-half-pound 'Trinideli' with four types of meat and three types of cheese will fill the ravenous, while simple turkey and ham standards explode with fresh veggies and tons of flavor. The suite of breakfast burritos is perfect for a quick pre-hike fill up.

Mountain Marketplace MARKET $
(222 S Main St; ⊙9am-6pm Mon-Fri, 10am-5pm Sat; ✐) Stock up on natural foods or hit its juice bar and vegetarian deli.

Johnny's Pizza PIZZA $$
(227 Main St; pizzas $9-26; ⊙11am-8pm) A small-town pizza joint with a good vibe, rock and roll on the stereo and friendly staff.

★La Grange Café CALIFORNIAN $$
(☎530-623-5325; 315 N Main St; mains $15-28; ⊙11:30am-9pm Mon-Thu, to 10pm Fri-Sun, with seasonal variations) Spacious yet intimate, this celebrated multistar restaurant serves exceptional light, fresh and satisfying fare. Chef and owner Sharon Heryford knows how to do dining without a whiff of pretention: apple-stuffed red cabbage in the fall, and brightly flavored chicken enchiladas in the summer, plus game dishes and seasonal vegetables.

Exposed brick and open sight lines complement the exceedingly friendly atmos-

phere. A seat at the bar is great when the tables are full, which they often are. The all-you-can-eat soup and salad is a stroke of genius.

🍷 Drinking & Entertainment

Mamma Llama CAFE
(www.mammallama.com; 490 Main St; breakfasts & sandwiches $4.50-10; ⊙6am-6pm Mon-Fri, 7am-6pm Sat, 7am-3pm Sun; ☎) A local institution, this coffeehouse is a roomy and relaxed chill spot. The espresso is well made, there's a selection of books and CDs, and there are couches for lounging. The small menu does breakfasts, wraps and sandwiches and there's microbrew beer available by the bottle. Live folk music (often including a hand drum) takes over occasionally.

Red House CAFE
(www.vivalaredhouse.com; 218 S Miner St; soup from $3; ⊙6:30am-5:30pm Mon-Fri, 7:30am-1pm Sun) ✐ This airy, light and bamboo-bedecked spot serves a wide selection of teas, light snacks and organic, fair-trade, shade-grown coffee. The daily food specials include a delicious chicken-and-rice soup on Mondays. If you're in a hurry (rare in Weaverville), there's a drive-through window.

Trinity Theatre CINEMA
(310 Main St) Plays first-run movies.

❶ Information

Trinity County Chamber of Commerce
(☎530-623-6101; www.trinitycounty.com; 215 Main St; ⊙10am-4pm) Knowledgeable staff with lots of useful information.
Weaverville Ranger Station (☎530-623-2121; www.fs.usda.gov/stnf; 360 Main St;

8am-4:30pm Mon-Fri) Maps, information and permits for all lakes, national forests and wilderness areas in and near Trinity County.

ℹ Getting There & Away

A local **Trinity Transit** (📞 530-623-5438; www.trinitytransit.org; fares from $1.50) bus makes a Weaverville–Lewiston loop via Hwy 299 and Hwy 3 from Monday to Friday. Another one runs between Weaverville and Hayfork, a small town about 30 miles to the southwest on Hwy 3.

Lewiston Lake

Pleasant little Lewiston is little more than a collection of buildings beside a crossroad, 26 miles west of Redding, around 5 miles off Hwy 299 on Trinity Dam Blvd and a few miles south of Lewiston Lake. It's right beside the Trinity River, and the locals here are in tune with the environment – they know fishing spots on the rivers and lakes, where to hike and how to get around.

The lake is about 1.5 miles north of town and is a serene alternative to the other area lakes because of its 10mph boat speed limit. The water is kept at a constant level, providing a nurturing habitat for fish and waterfowl. Migrating bird species sojourn here – early in the evening you may see ospreys and bald eagles diving for fish. The **Trinity River Fish Hatchery** (🕐 7am-3pm) **FREE** traps juvenile salmon and steelhead and holds them until they are ready to be released into the river. The only marina on the lake, **Pine Cove Marina** (www.pine-cove-marina.com; 9435 Trinity Dam Blvd), has free information about the lake and its wildlife, boat and canoe rentals, potluck dinners and guided off-road tours.

If you're just passing through town, make a stop at the Country Peddler (4 Deadwood Rd), a drafty old barn that sits behind a field of red poppies and is filled with cool antiques, rusting road signs and antique collectibles that seem like they were pulled out of some long-lost uncle's hunting cabin. The owners, avid outdoor enthusiasts, know the area like the back of their hand. It's often closed outside summer.

🛏 Sleeping & Eating

Several commercial campgrounds dot the rim of the lake. For information on USFS campgrounds, contact the ranger station in Weaverville. Two of these campgrounds are right on the lake: the wooded Mary Smith (📞 877-444-6777; tent sites $11; 🕐 May-Sep), which is more private; and the sunny Ackerman (sites $11), which has more grassy space for families. If there's no host, both have self-registration options. There are all kinds of RV parks, cabins for rent and motels in Lewiston.

★**Lewiston Hotel** HISTORIC HOTEL **$**
(📞 530-778-3823; 125 Deadwood Rd; r $60; 🛜) This 1862 rambling, ramshackle hotel has small, rustic rooms with quilts, historic photos and river views – all have tons of character but none have attached bathrooms. Ask (or don't ask) for the room haunted by George. Explore the building to find giant stuffed moose heads, old girly calendars, old rusty saws and so much more.

On-site are a friendly locals' bar, a dancehall, and a restaurant (with sporadic opening hours especially in winter) that specializes in prime rib.

Lakeview Terrace Resort CABIN, CAMPGROUND **$**
(📞 530-778-3803; www.lakeviewterraceresort.com; RV sites $30, cabins $80-155; ❄🛜🏊🐕) Five miles north of Lewiston, this is a woodsy Club Med, and rents boats.

Old Lewiston Bridge RV Resort CAMPGROUND **$**
(📞 530-778-3894; www.lewistonbridgerv.com; 8460 Rush Creek Rd, at Turnpike Rd; tent/RV sites $15/28, trailer $65; 🐕) A pleasant place to park your RV, with campsites beside the river bridge. This place also rents travel trailers that sleep four people (bed linens not included).

Old Lewiston Inn B&B B&B **$$**
(📞 530-778-3385; www.theoldlewistoninn.com; Deadwood Rd; r/ste $110/200; ❄🛜🐕) The prettiest place in town and right beside the river, this B&B is in an 1875 house and serves country-style breakfasts. Enjoy the hot tub, or ask about all-inclusive fly-fishing packages. There's one two-bedroom suite, which is great for families.

Trinity (Clair Engle) Lake

Placid Trinity Lake, California's third-largest reservoir, sits beneath dramatic snow-capped alps north of Lewiston Lake. In the off season it is serenely quiet, but it attracts multitudes in the summer, who come for swimming, fishing and other water sports.

Most of the campgrounds, RV parks, motels, boat rentals and restaurants line the west side of the lake.

The Pinewood Cove Resort (☑ 530-286-2201; www.pinewoodcove.com; 45110 Hwy 3; tent/RV sites $29/46, cabins $98-158; ❄), on the waterfront, is a popular place to stay, but doesn't provide bed linens.

The east side of the lake is quieter, with more secluded campgrounds, some accessible only by boat. The Weaverville ranger station (p301) has information on USFS campgrounds.

Klamath & Siskiyou Mountains

A dense conglomeration of rugged coastal mountains gives this region the nickname 'the Klamath Knot.' Coastal, temperate rainforest gives way to moist inland forest, creating an immense diversity of habitats for many species, some found nowhere else in the world. Around 3500 native plants live here. Local fauna includes the northern spotted owl, the bald eagle, the tailed frog, several species of Pacific salmon and carnivores like the wolverine and the mountain lion. One theory for the extraordinary biodiversity of this area is that it escaped extensive glaciation during recent ice ages. This may have given species refuge and longer stretches of relatively favorable conditions during which to adapt.

The region also includes the largest concentration of wild and scenic rivers in the US: the Salmon, Smith, Trinity, Eel and Klamath, to name a few. The fall color change is magnificent.

Five main wilderness areas dot the Klamath Knot. The Marble Mountain Wilderness in the north is marked by high rugged mountains, valleys and lakes, all sprinkled with colorful geological formations of marble and granite, and a huge array of flora. The Russian Wilderness is 8000 acres of high peaks and isolated, beautiful mountain lakes. The Trinity Alps Wilderness, west of Hwy 3, is one of the area's most lovely regions for hiking and backcountry camping, and has more than 600 miles of trails that cross passes over its granite peaks and head along its deep alpine lakes. The Yolla Bolly-Middle Eel Wilderness in the south is less visited, despite its proximity to the Bay Area, and so affords spectacular, secluded backcountry experiences. The Siskiyou Wilderness, closest to the coast, rises to heights of 7300ft, from where you can see the ocean. An extensive trail system crisscrosses the wilderness, but it is difficult to make loops.

The Trinity Scenic Byway (Hwy 299) follows the rushing Trinity River to the Pacific coast and is dotted with lodges, RV parks and blink-and-you'll-miss-'em burgs. There's river rafting at Willow Creek, 55 miles west of Weaverville. Bigfoot Rafting Company (☑ 530-629-2263; www.bigfootrafting.com; half/full-day trips per person $69/89) leads guided trips and also rents rafts and kayaks (from $40 per day).

Scott Valley

North of Trinity Lake, Hwy 3 climbs along the gorgeous eastern flank of the Trinity Alps Wilderness to Scott Mountain Summit (5401ft) and then drops gracefully down into verdant Scott Valley, a bucolic agricultural area nestled between towering mountains. There are good opportunities for hiking, cycling and mountain biking, or taking horse trips to mountain lakes. For a bit of history, pick up the *Trinity Heritage Scenic Byway* brochure from the Weaverville ranger station (p301) before taking this world-class drive.

Etna (population 737), toward the north end of the valley, is known by its residents as 'California's Last Great Place,' and they might be right. It hosts a fantastic Bluegrass Festival at the end of July and the tiny Etna Brewing Company (www.etnabrew.net; 131 Callahan St; brewery tours free; ☺ 11am-4pm Tue, to 8pm Wed & Thu, to 9pm Fri & Sat, to 7pm Sun, tours by appointment) offers delicious beers and pub grub. If you're sticking around, try the immaculate 10-room Motel Etna (☑ 530-467-5338; 317 Collier Way; s/d $50/60). Scott Valley Drug (www.scottvalleydrug.com; 511 Main St; ☺ Mon-Sat) serves up old-fashioned ice-cream sodas. If you're in town in summer and see lots of dirty people with backpacks, these are folks taking a break from hiking the nearby Pacific Crest Trail - Etna is a favorite pit stop.

Beyond Etna Fort Jones (population 839) is just 18 miles from Yreka. The visitors center (☑ 530-468-5442; 11943 Main St; ☺ 10am-5pm Tue-Sat, noon-4pm Sun) sits at the back of the Guild Shop mercantile. Down the street, a small museum (www.fortjonesmuseum.com; 11913 Main St; donation requested;

⊙ Mon-Sat Memorial Day-Labor Day) houses Native American artifacts.

Yreka

Inland California's northernmost town, Yreka (wy-*ree*-kah; population 7400) was once a booming Gold Rush settlement and has the gorgeous turn-of-the-century architecture to prove it. Most travelers only pass through en route to Oregon, but the new-age-tinged yet authentically Wild West–feeling historic downtown makes a good spot to stretch, eat and refuel before heading out into the hinterlands of the Scott Valley or the northeastern California wilderness.

◉ Sights & Activities

About 25 miles north of Yreka, on I-5, just across the Oregon border, Siskiyou Summit (elevation 4310ft) often closes in winter – even when the weather is just fine on either side. Call ☑ 530-842-4438 to check.

Siskiyou County Museum   MUSEUM
(www.siskiyoucountyhistoricalsociety.org; 910 S Main St; admission $3; ⊙ 9am-3pm Tue-Sat) Several blocks south of the downtown grid, this exceptionally well-curated museum brings together pioneer and Native American history. An outdoor section contains historic buildings brought from around the county.

Siskiyou County
Courthouse   HISTORIC BUILDING
(311 4th St) This hulking downtown building was built in 1857 and has a collection of gold nuggets, flakes and dust in the foyer.

Blue Goose Steam Excursion Train RAILWAY
(www.yrekawesternrr.com; adult/child 2-12yr $20/12) This train hisses and chugs along a 100-year-old track. The schedule is sporadic; look at the website for current information. It's one of the last remaining railroads of California's quickly vanishing historic rail network.

Yreka Creek Greenway   WALKING, CYCLING
(www.yrekagreenway.org) Behind the museum, the Yreka Creek Greenway has walking and cycling paths winding through the trees.

⌐ Sleeping & Eating

Motels, motels and more motels: budget travelers can do lots of comparison shopping along Yreka's Main St for mid-century motels galore. Klamath National Forest runs several campgrounds; the supervisor's office has information. RV parks cluster on the edge of town. Wander down W Miner St for more quirky places to eat.

Klamath Motor Lodge   MOTEL $
(☑ 530-842-2751; www.klamathmotorlodge.net; 1111 S Main St; d from $45; ☞ ⊠) Folks at this motor court are especially friendly, the rooms are clean and – bonus for those headed in from the wilderness – it has an on-site laundry. Of all the motels in Yreka, this is tops.

Klander's Deli   DELI $
(211 S Oregon St; sandwiches $6; ⊙ 8am-2pm Mon-Fri) Local to the core, this deli's long list of yummy sandwiches is named after regulars. Bob is a favorite, named for the first owner and stacked with ham, turkey, roast beef and Swiss.

Nature's Kitchen   HEALTH FOOD, BAKERY $
(☑ 530-842-1136; 412 S Main St; dishes $7; ⊙ 8am-5pm Mon-Sat; ☞) Friendly natural-foods store and bakery, serving healthy and tasty vegetarian dishes, fresh juices and good espresso. The adjoining store has all kinds of fairies, herbal supplements and new-agey trinkets.

ⓘ Information

Klamath National Forest Supervisor's Office
(☑ 530-842-6131; 1312 Fairlane Rd, at Oberlin Rd; ⊙ 8am-4:30pm Mon-Fri) At the south edge of town, with the lowdown on recreation and camping. This place is enormous; you can see it from the highway.

Yreka Chamber of Commerce (☑ 530-842-1649; www.yrekachamber.com; 117 W Miner St; ⊙ 9am-5pm, with seasonal variations; ☞)

ⓘ Getting There & Away

STAGE (☑ 530-842-8295; fares from $1.75) buses run throughout the region from a few different stops in Yreka. There are several daily services on weekdays along the I-5 corridor to Weed, Mt Shasta, McCloud and Dunsmuir. Other buses depart daily for Fort Jones (25 minutes), Greenview (35 minutes) and Etna (45 minutes) in the Scott Valley. On Monday and Friday only, buses go out to Klamath River (40 minutes) and Happy Camp (two hours).

Gold Country

Best Places to Eat

➜ New Moon Café (p312)

➜ Big Springs Gardens (p315)

➜ Argonaut Farm to Fork Cafe (p317)

➜ La Cocina de Oro Taqueria (p314)

➜ Taste (p320)

Best Places to Stay

➜ Outside Inn (p311)

➜ Lure Resort (p314)

➜ Camino Hotel (p323)

➜ Imperial Hotel (p320)

Why Go?

Hollywood draws the dreamers and Silicon Valley its fortune-hunters, but this isn't the first time droves of young folk looking to hit paydirt streamed into the Golden State. After a sparkle in the American River caught James Marshall's eye in 1848, more than 300,000 prospectors from America and abroad started digging for gold in the Sierra foothills. Soon California entered statehood with the official motto, 'Eureka,' solidifying its place as the land of discovery and opportunity.

The miner forty-niners are gone, but a ride along the aptly named Hwy 49 through sleepy hill towns, past clapboard saloons and oak-lined byways, is a journey back to modern California's founding. Between the quaint antique stores and sprawling wineries, historical markers still tell tales of Gold Rush violence and banditry. Many travelers hardly stop while rushing between California's coasts and mountains, but those who slow down will be rewarded with a taste of the helter-skelter era that first kick-started the heartbeat of this state.

When to Go

Nevada City

Apr–May Pan for gold after the snowmelt washes the treasure into Jamestown's hills.

Jul When temperatures are scorching, plunge into a refreshing South Yuba swimming hole.

Sep–Nov When crisp apples are ripe for the picking, head to Apple Hill's ranch lands.

Map legend / labels:

Lassen National Forest
Feather River
Plumas National Forest
Lake Oroville
Downieville 2
Oroville
Haskell Peak
Sierra Buttes ▲ Bassetts
Sierra City
Reno
NEVADA
Pyramid Lake
Middle Yuba River
Malakoff Diggins State Historic Park
Tahoe National Forest
Truckee
South Yuba River State Park
Nevada City 5
Empire Mine State Historic Park
Grass Valley
American River North Fork
Tahoe City
Lake Tahoe
Carson City
American River 6
Auburn
Auburn State Recreation Area
American River Middle Fork
Eldorado National Forest
Marshall Gold Discovery State Historic Park 1
Coloma
Placerville
CALIFORNIA
Roseville
Folsom Lake
Folsom Lake State Recreation Area
Woodland
Sacramento
Davis
Highway 49 8
Apple Hill ▲
Indian Grinding Rock State Historic Park
Daffodil Hill
Black Chasm
Volcano
Plymouth 3
Drytown
Amador City
Sutter Creek
Jackson
7
Mokelumne River
Mokelumne Hill
California Cavern
Arnold
Calaveras Big Trees State Park
Stanislaus National Forest
Camanche Reservoir
San Andreas
Murphys
Locke
Stanislaus River
Isleton
Lodi
Moaning Cavern
Angels Camp
Columbia State Historic Park 4
Yosemite National Park
Stockton
Sonora
Jamestown
San Joaquin River
Stanislaus River
Chinese Camp
Modesto
Yosemite Village

Gold Country Highlights

1 Seeing the birthplace of modern California at **Marshall Gold Discovery State Historic Park** (p316).

2 Rumbling down the premier single-track bike trails above **Downieville** (p313).

3 Tasting the wines made from grapes grown in the **Plymouth** (p319) hills.

4 Spotting the anachronisms in the living history of **Columbia State Historic Park** (p326).

5 Wandering the historic streets of **Nevada City** (p310), Gold Country's relaxing jewel of a town.

6 Riding the white water **American River** (p316).

7 Discovering traces left by the Miwoks who once thrived near **Indian Grinding Rock State Historic Park** (p322).

8 Driving down **Highway 49** (p316) through El Dorado & Amador Counties in pursuit of antiques and ice cream.

NEVADA COUNTY & NORTHERN GOLD COUNTRY

The forty-niners hit it big in Nevada County – the richest score in the region known as the Mother Lode – and their wealth built one of the most picturesque and well-preserved boomtowns, Nevada City. Get out of town and you'll find lovely, remote wilderness areas, a clutch of historic parks and rusting relics of the long-gone miners. This is also a magnet for adrenaline junkies looking to race down single-tracks on mountain bikes or plunge into icy swimming holes that are remote enough for skinny-dipping.

Auburn

Look for the big man: a 45-ton effigy of French gold panner Claude Chana marks your arrival in Placer County's Gold Country. Its hallmarks are all here – ice-cream shops, strollable historic districts and antiques. A major stop on the Central Pacific's transcontinental route, Auburn still welcomes trains on the Union Pacific's main line to the east and is a popular stop for those rushing along I-80 between the Bay Area and Lake Tahoe. You'll have to venture along Hwy 49 for a deeper taste of Gold Country, but those who want just a sample will enjoy this accessible town.

◉ Sights & Activities

The fact that Auburn minted itself the 'Endurance Sport Capital of the World' will give you a sense of how good the area is for cycling, trail running and other heart-pounding activities. See www.auburnendurancecapital.com for events.

Placer County Museum   MUSEUM
(www.placer.ca.gov; 101 Maple St; ⊙10am-4pm) **FREE** The 1st floor of the domed 1898 Placer County Courthouse (⊙8am-5pm) has Native American artifacts and displays of Auburn's transportation heritage. It's the easiest museum to visit and gives a good overview of area history; there's also the glitter of the museum's gold collection.

Bernhard Museum Complex   MUSEUM
(291 Auburn-Folsom Rd; entry by donation; ⊙11am-4pm Tue-Sun) This museum, built in 1851 as the Traveler's Rest Hotel, exhibits depictions of typical 19th-century-farm family life. Volunteers in period garb ham it up.

Gold Country Museum   MUSEUM
(1273 High St; ⊙11am-4pm Tue-Sun) **FREE** Toward the back of the fairgrounds, the Gold Rush history includes a reconstructed mine and gold panning, all great for kids.

Joss House   MUSEUM
(☏530-823-0373; 200 Sacramento St; entry by donation; ⊙10am-3pm 1st Sat of month) Built by the Yue family in the 1920s, this clapboard residence stands on what was known as Chinese Hill, one of many small-town Chinese communities established during the Gold Rush. After a 'mysterious' fire ripped through the Chinese settlement, the family converted their home into a public space for worship, seasonal boarders and a school. Grandson Richard is on hand to tell the full story.

⊨ Sleeping & Eating

Lincoln Way toward the chamber of commerce has several restaurants popular with locals, but there's plenty of sunny outdoor eating right off the highway around Sacramento St. For a place to sleep look to the highway exits where there's every brand of chain hotel.

Ikedas   MARKET $
(www.ikedas.com; 13500 Lincoln Way; sandwiches $6-9; ⊙8am-7pm Mon-Thu, to 8pm Fri-Sun; ⊘) If you're cruising this part of the state without time to explore, the best pit stop is this expanded farm stand off I-80 a few miles north of Auburn. Thick, grass-fed beef or veggie burgers, homemade pies and the seasonal fresh peach shake are deliriously good.

Tsuda   DELI $
(www.tsudabylina.com; 103 Sacramento St; mains $9; ⊙7am-5pm Mon-Thu, to 7pm Fri & Sat, 8am-6pm Sun; 🖥⊘🍴🐾) A bakery with crepes, a salad bar and something for every dietary consideration (gluten-free, veg, toddler etc). Eat outside on the adjacent public patio, which is open to pets.

Auburn Alehouse   BREWPUB $$
(www.auburnalehouse.com; 289 Washington; mains $8-21; ⊙11am-10pm Mon-Tue, to 11pm Wed-Thu, to midnight Fri, 9am-midnight Sat, 9am-10pm Sun) One of those rare brewpubs with both excellent craft beer *and* food; patrons dig into burgers, sweet potato fries, 'adult mac and cheese' and sweet-and-savory salads. The beer sampler is a great deal, as Auburn brings home tons of medals for their ales and pilsners. Hand over the keys before trying the PU240 Imperial

IPA, a 'weapons grade hop bomb.' Kitchen closes one hour before the bar.

Awful Annie's AMERICAN $$
(www.awfulannies.com; 160 Sacramento St; mains $9-13; ⏱8am-3pm) Huge breakfast scrambles and a sunny patio keep Annie's packed. Worth the wait.

Katrina's BREAKFAST $$
(www.katrinascafe.com; 456 Grass Valley Hwy; mains $10-15; ⏱7am-2:30pm Wed-Sat, to 2pm Sun) Lemon yogurt pancakes and all manner of sandwiches in a homey atmosphere; this place is legit.

🛍 Shopping

Pioneer Mining Supply OUTDOOR EQUIPMENT
(www.pioneermining.com; 878 High St; ⏱9am-6pm Mon-Fri, 10am-4pm Sat) Your one-stop prospecting shop. Don't mind the gruff salesfolk. They actually are happy to get you started, set up guided tours (from $100 per person), or if you're a pro, showcase the latest in sluicing technology.

ℹ Information

Auburn Area Chamber of Commerce
(☎530-885-5616; www.auburnchamber.net; 601 Lincoln Way; ⏱10am-4pm Tue-Fri) In the Southern Pacific railroad depot at the north end of Lincoln Way, it has lots of useful local info and a monument to the Transcontinental Railroad nearby.

California Welcome Center (Placer County Visitors Center; ☎530-887-2111; www.visitplacer.com; 1103 High St; ⏱9am-4:30pm Mon-Sat, 11am-4pm Sun) Great information on Gold Country and eastward.

ℹ Getting There & Away

Amtrak (☎800-872-7245; www.amtrak.com; 277 Nevada St) runs one bus a day along the

SUCTION DREDGING FOR GOLD

Floating down Gold Country's waterways, you may see someone trying to strike it rich with a suction dredge – a vacuum that sucks up the river bed and the gold in it. This method of prospecting was banned in California in 2009 for its destructive side effects, including disturbing riparian habitat and stirring up toxic quicksilver, the mercury that the forty-niners used to extract gold from ore.

Capital Corridor route (http://capitolcorridor.org) linking Auburn with Sacramento ($16, one hour), the rest require connecting to Bay Area and Central Valley trains. There is also one bus-train daily east to Reno ($61, six hours).

The **Gold Country Stage** (☎888-660-7433; www.goldcountrystage.com; adult$1.50-3, child free) links Auburn, including its Amtrak station, with Grass Valley and Nevada City five times a day on weekdays, no service weekends. It takes 30 to 50 minutes and kids and bikes ride free.

Amtrak's *California Zephyr* stops in Auburn on its daily run between the Bay Area and Chicago via Reno and Denver (to San Francisco takes three hours and costs $35).

Auburn State Recreation Area

This is a park (☎530-885-4527; www.parks.ca.gov; per car $10; ⏱8am-sunset) of deep gorges cut by the rushing waters of the North and Middle Forks of the American River that converge below a bridge on Hwy 49, about 4 miles south of Auburn. In the early spring, when waters are high, this is immensely popular for white-water rafting, as the rivers are class II to V runs. Late summer, calmer waters allow for sunning and swimming, especially around the confluence. Numerous trails are shared by hikers, mountain bikers and horses.

🏃 Activities

One of the most popular hikes is the **Western States Trail**, which connects Auburn State Recreation Area to **Folsom Lake State Recreation Area** and Folsom Lake. It's the site of the **Western States 100-Mile Endurance Run** (www.wser.org) and the **Tevis Cup** (www.teviscup.org), an endurance race on horseback. The **Quarry Trail** takes a level path from Hwy 49, just south of the bridge, along the Middle Fork of the American River. Several side trails reach the river.

All-Outdoors California Whitewater Rafting RAFTING
(☎800-247-2387; www.aorafting.com; from $139/person; ⏱9am-5pm Mon-Fri (seasonal)) The best tours of the American, Tuolumne and Stanislaus rivers are offered spring through fall by this family-run outfit. Their single- and multiday wilderness rafting excursions include breaks for hiking among the boulders and historically significant sights in the canyons. Plus they cook for you (the burrito

lunch might be worth the trip alone). Check online for discounts.

🛏 Sleeping

Auburn State Recreation Area CAMPGROUND $
(sites $25-35) There are basic sites on a sweeping bend of the Middle Fork at the blackberry-dotted Ford's Bar that are accessible only by a 2-mile hike from Rucky-A-Chucky Rd, or a half-day raft. Required permits for these sites are available from the **Ranger Office** (☑530-885-4527; 501 El Dorado St; ⊙9am-4pm Mon-Fri).

Grass Valley

From the margins, Grass Valley is the ugly utilitarian sister to Nevada City, a place to stock up on supplies and get an oil change, not necessarily vacation, but there are treasures if you dig.

Historic Mill and W Main Sts mark the town center. E Main St leads north to modern shopping centers and mini-malls and into Nevada City. On Thursday nights in late-June through August, Mill St closes to traffic to serve up farmstead food, arts and crafts, and music. In the town's outskirts are some of the state's oldest shaft mines. Being the first to exploit lode-mining (tunneling to find veins of gold in hard rock) rather than placer techniques (sifting debris carried by waterways), these were among the most profitable claims.

◉ Sights

Empire Mine State
Historic Park HISTORIC SITE
(www.empiremine.org; 10791 E Empire St; adult/child $7/3; ⊙10am-5pm) Atop 400 miles of mine shafts tunneling 11,000ft below is Gold Country's best-preserved gold quartz-mining operation – worth a solid half-day's exploration. The mine yard is littered with mining equipment and buildings constructed from waste rock. You can view main shaft's claustrophobic entry, next to the head frame (a tall structure used to haul ore and people from underground). By the visitor center are the country club–like manor home, gardener's cottage and rose garden of the Bourn family, who ran the mine.

From 1850 to 1956 the miners here, mostly Cornish, produced six million ounces of gold (worth about $4 billion today). Even if you don't have that kind of dough, hiking the trails that meander past abandoned

---

TRIBAL HISTORY IN GOLD COUNTRY

A few dedicated museums tell part of the stories of the Miwok, Maidu, Konkow, Monache, Nisenan, Tubatulabal, Washoe and Foothill Yokuts – the people who called this region home, even before the gold.

Maidu Museum & Historical Sight (www.roseville.ca.us; 1970 Johnson Ranch Dr, Roseville; adult/child $4.50/4; ⊙9am-4pm Mon-Fri, to 1pm Sat (extended hours every third Sat)) is built on the edge of an ancient Maidu village, where families thrived for over 3000 years.

The roundhouse-shaped museum in **Indian Grinding Rock State Historic Park** (p322) has a variety of artifacts representing different tribes of the area. Outside are more relics.

California State Indian Museum (p310) in Sacramento has the most extensive collections and regularly rotating exhibits on California's tribes.

---

mines and equipment is free. Trailheads are at the parking lots behind the visitor center and Penn Gate to its west. The visitors center leads guided tours (11am to 2pm) and has maps.

North Star Mining Museum MUSEUM
(Powerhouse and Pelton Wheel Museum; nevadacountyhistory.org; 10933 Allison Ranch Rd; entry by donation; ⊙11am-5pm Tue-Sat, noon-4pm Sun May-Oct) A museum for those who ache when they see machinery set aside to rust. The engineering-minded docents here have polished and oiled their extensive collection of 19th-century mining equipment to a shine. See stamp mills, dredges, dynamite packing machines, Cornish pumps and the largest Pelton wheel ever constructed in action. The grassy banks of the creek that once powered the North Star mine are perfect for a picnic.

🛏 Sleeping & Eating

The menus around here don't vary much but the quality is good. There are several good brunch spots and bars around downtown, and every imaginable chain among the strip malls by the highway.

Holbrooke Hotel
HISTORIC HOTEL **$$**

(☏530-273-1353, 800-933-7077; www.holbrooke.com; 212 W Main St; r $129-179, ste incl breakfast $249; ❋☀) The register in this 1862 hotel boasts the signatures of Mark Twain and Ulysses Grant. The rooms are aging but neat. The **restaurant and saloon** (mains $11 to $22) serves casual fare in the ornate dining room or on the shaded patio, but the best tables overlook the Main St action. Weekday rates drop by 15% to 30%.

Cousin Jack Pasties
BAKERY **$**

(100 S Auburn St; meals $5.25-9; ⊙10:30am-6pm Mon-Sat, 11am-5pm Sun; ☑) Cousin Jack and his kin have been serving flaky pasties – a meat-and-potato-stuffed pastry beloved by Cornish miners – for five generations. The pies – Basque lamb, pot roast and several vegetarian options – are all made from local ingredients.

Lazy Dog Ice Cream
ICE CREAM **$**

(www.spotlazydog.com; 111 Mill St; ice-cream bars $4; ⊙10am-9pm Sun-Thu, to 10pm Fri & Sat) This colorful ice-cream and candy shop explodes with sugar in all its forms. Besides scoops, there are hand-dipped bars, chocolates and old-timey candies from 'juicy wax sticks' to swirly suckers.

Tofanelli's
ITALIAN **$$**

(www.tofanellis.com; 302 W Main St; mains $8-23; ⊙8am-9pm Mon-Thu, to 10pm Fri & Sat) Hugely popular with locals in the know, this creative restaurant has everything from salads to hearty steaks with seasonal specials like summer squash ravioli. Portions are burly, prices low and the patio a treat.

❶ Information

Greater Grass Valley Visitor Center (☏530-273-4667; www.grassvalleychamber.com; 128 Main St; ⊙10am-5pm Mon-Fri, to 3pm Sat & Sun; ❋) In the thick of the historical sights stands this brick livery stable, which is stocked with maps and brochures covering the county and more. There's a very comprehensive walking-tour map.

❶ Getting There & Away

Transit in Grass Valley is by **Gold Country Stage** (☏888-660-7433; www.goldcountrystage.com), which links to Nevada City hourly from 7am to 6pm weekdays, 8am to 4pm Saturday. Fares are $1.50 to $3 for adults. Kids and bikes ride free. Check the website for connections to Auburn and schedule changes.

Amtrak (p308) bus connections are in Colfax, 12 miles south.

Nevada City

Nevada City knows it's charming, but it doesn't like to brag. Everything here is about balance. In the shops, there are prayer flags, chia smoothies and new-agey tchotchkes, while the drinking holes sling all manner of liquid enlightenment. The person browsing the local history museum with you is just as liable to be a crusty old-timer, a road-weary backpacker or a mystical folk artist. In the midst of all that are the requisite Victorian and Gold Rush tourist attractions – an elegantly restored town center and frilly B&Bs by the dozen.

This is the gateway to Tahoe National Forest, but linger a few days, and you'll experience a distinctly inviting NorCal culture. The theater companies, alternative film houses, bookstores and live music venues put on shows almost every night.

Nevada City's streets, best navigated on foot, are especially lively in the summer. In December the blankets of snow and twinkling lights are something out of a storybook. Broad St is the main drag and the hypotenuse of the Hwy 49 and Hwy 20 junction.

◉ Sights

The main attraction is the town itself – its restored buildings, all brick and wrought-iron trimmings, wear their history proudly. There are intriguing (if pricey) boutiques, galleries and places for food and drink everywhere, all with exhaustive posted histories.

Firehouse No. 1 Museum
MUSEUM

(www.nevadacountyhistory.org; 214 Main St; admission by donation; ⊙1-4pm Tue-Sun May-Oct) This small, painstakingly curated museum is run by the Nevada County Historical Society. From stunning Nisenan baskets to preserved Victorian bridal wear, its collections tell the story of the local people. The prize exhibit is relics from the Chinese settlers who often built but seldom profited from the mines. By 1880, miners of Chinese origin constituted more than a fifth of all engaged in the industry and were nearly exclusively subject to a hefty Foreign Miners Tax.

The altar was saved by a local merchant who hid the pieces around town to keep it from marauders. Open extra hours by appointment.

Nevada City Winery
WINERY

(☏530-265-9463; ncwinery.com; 321 Spring St; ⊙tasting room noon-5pm Sun-Thu, to 6pm Fri &

Sat) This popular winery excels with Syrah and Zinfandel varietals, which you can savor while touring the production facility in the old Miners Foundry Garage. It's a good place to get information on touring all of the surrounding wine region.

🛏 Sleeping

On weekends Nevada City fills up with urban refugees who inevitably weigh themselves down with real-estate brochures. There are B&Bs everywhere. The cheapest options are the National Forest campgrounds, just outside town in any direction.

⭐ Outside Inn
MOTEL, CABIN $$

(☑ 530-265-2233; www.outsideinn.com; 575 E Broad St; r $79-104, ste $129-145, cottage $155-200; ❋ ☎ ☷ 🐾) The best option for active explorers, this is an unusually friendly and fun motel, with 12 rooms and three cottages maintained by staff that loves the outdoors and has excellent information about area hiking. Some rooms have a patio overlooking a small creek; all have nice quilts and access to BBQ grills. It's a 10-minute walk from downtown.

Broad Street Inn
INN $$

(☑ 530-265-2239; www.broadstreetinn.com; 517 W Broad St; r incl breakfast $115-125; ❋ ☎ ☷) 🍴 This six-room inn is a favorite because it keeps things simple. (No weird old dolls, no yellowing lace doilies.) The rooms are modern, brightly furnished and elegant. A good value.

Red Castle Historic Lodgings
B&B $$

(☑ 530-265-5135; www.redcastleinn.com; 109 Prospect St; r $155-210; ❋ ☷) In a city of B&Bs this is the granddaddy – the first in Nevada City and one of the oldest in the state. The red-brick building sits atop a hill a short walk from town. Inside the Gothic Revival exterior are well-appointed Victorian details down to the elevated beds and the breakfast selection. Most private is the Garden Room.

Northern Queen Inn
MOTEL, CABINS $$

(☑ 530-265-5824; www.northernqueeninn.com; 400 Railroad Ave; r $90-140; ❋ @ ☎) With a wide range of options – from basic queen rooms to two-story chalets – this hotel might be a bit dated, but the cabins, with small kitchens, are a good deal for small groups and families.

🍴 Eating

In a town of holistic thinkers, it's no surprise most menus emphasize organic and seasonal ingredients. The options are mostly clustered in a three-block radius on Commercial and Broad Sts.

Café Mekka
CAFE $

(☑ 530-478-1517; 237 Commercial St; meals $5-15; ☉ 7am-10pm Mon-Thu, to midnight Fri, 8am-midnight Sat, to 10pm Sun) Decorated in a style best described as 'whorehouse baroque,' this charmer serves coffee and beer through the day, along with sandwiches, pizzas and delectable desserts. Listen for live folk music some nights.

Treats
DESSERT $

(http://treatsnevadacity.com; 110 York St; items $3.50-5; ☉ 1-5pm Mon-Thu, 1-9pm Fri, noon-9pm Sat, noon-5pm Sun; 🍴) It's a crowded contest for Gold Country's best ice-cream shop, but this cute little spot – the brilliant second career of avuncular scooper Bob Wright – wins in a walk. Many flavors are sourced from ripe local produce like the River Hill Red sorbet (sweet red peppers and strawberry), mint chip and pear ginger.

Ike's Quarter Cafe
CAJUN, BREAKFAST $$

(www.ikesquartercafe.com; 401 Commercial St; mains $11-23; ☉ 8am-3pm, closed Tue; 🍴) Ike's serves splendid brunch fare with a sassy charm that delights the blue hairs. There's banana and pecan flapjacks, jambalaya, Creole tempeh and more. It's an excellent place to get 'Hangtown Fry' – a cornmeal-crusted mess of oysters, bacon, caramelized onions and spinach. Right out of New Orleans' Garden District but with vegetarian options.

Fix for Foodies
CAFE $$

(www.superfoodfix.com; 205 York St; mains $8-14; ☉ 11am-8pm Tue-Sat, 12:30-4:30pm Sun; ☎ 🍴) You can't miss this old stable covered in corrugated steel. A favorite of raw, vegan enthusiasts and the generally health obsessed, it's the kind of place that makes its own almond milk, durian shakes, and sprouted breads.

Sopa Thai
THAI $$

(www.sopathai.net; 312 Commercial St; mains $10-15; ☉ 11am-3pm & 5-9:30pm Mon-Fri, noon-9:30pm Sat & Sun) Mango red curry, steamed mussels and springs rolls are all excellent in the region's best and most popular Thai restaurant. The interior is furnished with imported carvings and silk, and the patio seating in back is a busy scene midday. The $10.95 lunch special is a good value.

★ **New Moon Café** CALIFORNIAN $$$
(www.thenewmooncafe.com; 203 York St; mains $21-29.50; ⊗11:30-2pm Tue-Fri, 5-8:30pm Tue-Sun) ✐ Pure elegance, Peter Selaya's organic and local ingredient menu changes with the seasons. If you visit during the peak of the summer, go for the line-caught fish or their housemade, moon-shaped fresh ravioli.

☆ Entertainment

This little village has a vibrant art scene. The entertainment section of the *Union* newspaper (www.theunion.com) comes out on Thursday, and lists what's going on throughout the county.

Magic Theatre CINEMA
(www.themagictheatren.com; 107 Argall Way) This beloved theater screens a matchless line-up of unusual films and is about a mile south of downtown Nevada City. Plus bowls of fresh popcorn, coffee in real mugs and hot brownies.

Nevada Theatre THEATRE, CINEMA
(www.nevadatheatre.com; 401 Broad St) This brick fortress is one of California's first theaters (1865) and has welcomed the likes of Jack London, Emma Nevada, and Mark Twain to its stage. Now it's home to a number of small, top-notch theater companies and an off-beat film series.

① Information

Nevada City Chamber of Commerce (☏530-265-2692; www.nevadacitychamber.com; 132 Main St; ⊗9am-5pm Mon-Fri, 11am-4pm Sat, 11am-3pm Sun) Ideally located at the east end of Commercial St, this has two welcome traveler comforts – expert local advice and public toilets right next door.
Tahoe National Forest Headquarters (☏530-265-4531; www.fs.usda.gov/tahoe; 631 Coyote St; ⊗8am-4:30pm Mon-Fri) A useful and friendly resource for trail and campground information, covering the area from here to Lake Tahoe. They sell topographical maps.

① Getting There & Away

Nevada City is served by the **Gold Country Stage** (☏530-477-0103; www.goldcountrystage.com), which links it with Grass Valley (adult $1.50, 30 minutes) hourly from 6:30am to 5:30pm weekdays and 7:30am to 4:30pm Saturdays. Kids and bikes ride free. Check the website for connections to Auburn and schedule changes.

Amtrak (p308) bus connections are in Colfax, 15 miles south.

South Yuba River State Park

Brisk swimming holes are fed by rushing rapids in this 11,000-acre plot along the South Yuba River, a combination of state and federal lands. This area has a growing network of trails, including the wheelchair-accessible **Independence Trail**, which starts from the south side of the South Yuba River bridge on Hwy 49 and continues for a couple miles with canyon overlooks. June is the best time, when the rivers are rushing and the wildflowers are out.

The longest, single-span, wood-truss **covered bridge** in the USA, all 251ft of it, crosses the South Yuba River at Bridgeport (not to be confused with the Eastern Sierra town of the same name). It's easy to spend a whole day hiking and swimming in this wild area, where crowds can be left behind with little effort. The **Buttermilk Bend Trail** skirts the South Yuba for 1.4 miles, offering river access and bountiful wildflowers around April.

Maps and park information are available from the **state park headquarters** (☏530-432-2546; www.parks.ca.gov; 17660 Pleasant Valley Rd, Penn Valley; ⊗11am-4pm daily Mar-Nov, Thu-Sun Dec-Feb) in Bridgeport, or from the Tahoe National Forest Headquarters in Nevada City. The **South Yuba River Park Association** (www.southyubariverstatepark.org) is another great resource.

Malakoff Diggins State Historic Park

An otherworldly testament to the mechanical determination of the gold hunt, **Malakoff Diggins** (☏530-265-2740; 23579 North Bloomfield Rd; per car $8; ⊗sunrise-sunset) is a place to get lost on fern-lined trails and take in the raw beauty of a recovering landscape. The gold and crimson stratified cliffs and small mountains of tailings are curiously beautiful, and all part of the legacy of hydraulic mining.

In 1852, a French miner named Anthony Chabot channeled the Yuba through a canvas hose to blast away at the bedrock. To reach the veins of gold inside, miners eventually carved a canyon 600ft deep. To speed up the sorting process, they mixed

SWIMMING HOLE 101

Gold Country's rivers carved out precious metals as well as emerald pools perfect for late-summer dips. Check out http://swimmingholes.org for spots.

On the South Yuba, 8 miles northeast of Nevada City on Bloomfield Rd, under the Edwards Crossing bridge is a lively, popular pool. Just a mile hike downstream is the scenic cascade of waterfalls known as Mountain Dog, perfect for a more secluded skinny dip.

For an even more remote spot, head to the Stanislaus River, to Parrots Ferry Rd 7 miles south of Murphys, and then turn north on Camp Nine Rd. Near the end, where the river splits, a half mile hike up the right fork will lead you to Camp Nine, a peaceful, limestone-bordered pool and beach.

Some keys to swimming hole usage: always test rope swings and currents before jumping in. Never dive. Pack in your supplies and pack out your trash. No glass. And always stay at least 100yd from the water when nature calls.

the slurry of gravel with quicksilver (mercury) to recover the gold, and then washed all the leftovers into the Yuba River. When a few decades later, 20ft high glaciers of tailings and toxic waste choked the rivers and caused deadly flooding, farmers and miners collided in the courtroom. In 1884, the Sawyer Decision set a critical precedent: a profitable industry can be stopped for the public good. No longer able to reap profits by dumping in the Yuba, most fortune hunters moved on. North Bloomfield, the mining community at the center of Malakoff's operation, still stands as an eerie ghost town within the park's limits.

The Park Headquarters and Museum (☑530-265-2740; ◉9am-5pm, tour 1:30pm Fri-Sun May-Sep) offers a tour of the town and the chance to see some impressive gold nuggets. The one-mile Diggins Loop Trail is the quickest way to get a glimpse of the scarred moonscape. Reserve a campsite (☑800-444-7275; www.reserveamerica.com; tent sites $35, cabins $40; ◉May-Sep) at Chute Hill or a miner's cabin for not much more.

Access Tyler-Foote Crossing Rd, the turnoff for the park, 10 miles northwest of Nevada City on Hwy 49.

North Yuba River

The northernmost segment of Hwy 49 follows the North Yuba River through some stunning, remote parts of the Sierra Nevada, known for a tough, short season of white water and great fly-fishing. An entire lifetime outdoors could hardly cover the trail network that hikers, mountain bikers and skiers blaze every season. In summer, snow remains at the highest elevations and many places have roaring fireplaces year-round.

The best source of trail and camping information is the Yuba River Ranger Station (☑530-288-3231; 15924 Hwy 49, Camptonville; ◉8am-4:30pm Mon-Fri).

Downieville

Downieville, the biggest town in remote Sierra County, is located at the junction of the North Yuba and Downie rivers. With a reputation that quietly rivals Moab, Utah (before it got big), the town is one of the premier places for mountain-bike riding in the US, and a staging area for true wilderness adventures.

As with most Gold Rush towns, it wasn't always fun and games: the first justice of the peace was the local barkeep, and a placard tells the story of the racist mob that hanged a Chicana named Josefa on the town bridge in 1851, the only recorded lynching of a woman in California. The town retains a grisly affection for frontier justice and its ghosts; a reconstructed gallows is across the river, by the civic building.

🏃 Activities

The mountains and rivers in these parts beg to be explored. Favorite hikes include the Sierra Buttes Fire Lookout, a moderate 6 miler that joins the Pacific Crest Trail before a 1500ft elevation gain to epic views from the lookout tower, and North Yuba Trail, 12 miles along the canyon ridge, starting behind the courthouse in town. There are many more options. Pick up maps and a shuttle ride from the local outfitters. Downieville Visitors' Center (Main St), open seasonally next the mining equipment in Memorial Park, can also help.

Downieville Downhill
ADVENTURE SPORTS
(www.downievilleclassic.com) This world-class mountain-biking trail shoots riders over the Sierra Buttes and a molar-rattling 4000ft down into Downieville. There are plenty of other scenic biking trails to explore, including Chimney Rock, Empire Creek and Rattlesnake Creek, but this route is the reason why pro-riders arrive in August for the Downieville Classic, a mix of cross-country and downhill racing and general revelry.

Local outfitters run hourly shuttles to the start.

Yuba Expeditions
MOUNTAIN BIKING
(☑530-289-3010; www.yubaexpeditions.com; 208 Commercial St; bike rentals $65-85, shuttle $20; ⊙shuttles 9am-5pm May-Oct, reserve Nov-Apr) Yuba Expeditions is run by Sierra Buttes Trail Stewardship, a nonprofit in the center of the trail-bike scene. Non-bikers will find them helpful with maps and general trail advice.

Downieville Outfitters
BICYCLE RENTAL
(☑530-289-0155; www.downievilleoutfitters.com; 114 Main St; bike rentals from $60, shuttle $20; ⊙shuttles 8am-5pm May-Oct, reserve Nov-Apr) An option for bike rental and shuttles in Downieville.

🛏 Sleeping & Eating

In downtown Downieville, the soft roar of the rapids lull saddle-sore bikers to sleep in several small B&Bs. More secluded options are along Hwy 49 east of town. Find food at the intersection of Main and Commercial Sts. Most places are closed in winter.

Riverside Inn
HOTEL $
(☑530-289-1000; www.downieville.us; 206 Commercial St; r $90-120, ste incl breakfast $185; P🤖🛜🐾) There is a secluded, rustic charm to these 11 stove-warmed rooms overlooking the river. Five have kitchens and all have balconies for enjoying the river. Delightful innkeepers Nancy and Mike share excellent information about hiking and biking in the area, and in winter lend snowshoes.

Tahoe National Forest Campgrounds
CAMPGROUND $
(☑518-885-3639, reservations 877-444-6777; www.recreation.gov; tent sites $24) West of town on Hwy 49 are a string of beautiful campsites. Most have vault toilets, running water

and unreserved sites along the Yuba River. Of these, the prettiest is Fiddlecreek, which has tent-only sites right on the river.

★ Lure Resort
CABINS, CAMPGROUND $$
(☑800-671-4084; www.lureresort.com; camping cabins $80, housekeeping cabins $135-290; 🤖🛜🐾) A great option if you want to come with biking buddies or a family, this circle of tidy, modernized cabins is along a sublime stretch of river open to fly fishing with big lawns for the kids to play. The basic camping cabins, which are BYO sleeping bag and have shared bathrooms, sleep four tightly.

Carriage House Inn
INN $$
(☑530-289-3573; www.downievillecarriagehouse.com; 110 Commercial St; r incl basic breakfast $85-175; 🛜🐾) This renovated homey inn has country-style charms, which include rockers and river views. Two rooms share a shower.

Sierra Shangri-La
CABINS, HOTEL $$
(☑530-289-3455; www.sierrashangrila.com; r $115, cabins incl breakfast $168-273) Three miles east of Downieville on Hwy 49, in July and August these secluded, riverside cabins are usually booked with standing reservations, but rooms – each with a balcony overlooking the river – are often available.

★ La Cocina de Oro Taqueria
MEXICAN $
(☑530-289-9584; 322 Main St; tacos from $3.75, burritos $10; ⊙11am-9:30pm Apr-Dec; 🐾) Chef-owner Feather Ortiz uses herbs and peppers from her garden and sources everything else from local growers to make the freshest food around. The burritos are the size of chihuahuas. No credit cards.

Sierra City & the Lakes Basin

Sierra City is the primary supply station for people headed to the Sierra Buttes, a rugged, rocky shock of mountains that are probably the closest thing to the Alps you'll find in California without foisting a backpack. It's also the last supply point for people headed into the fishing paradise of the Lakes Basin. There's information about lodging and area activities at www.sierracity.com.

◉ Sights & Activities

There's a vast network of trails, including access to the famed Pacific Crest Trail. The Sierra Country Store (☑530-862-1560; 213 Main St/Hwy 49; ⊙8am-8pm summer, 10am-6pm winter; 🛜) is about the only consistently open place in town, and it welcomes Pacific Crest Trail refugees with its laundromat and deli.

To reach the Buttes, and many lakes and streams nearby, take Gold Lake Hwy north from Hwy 49 at Bassetts, 9 miles northeast of Sierra City. An excellent hiking trail leads 1.1 miles to Haskell Peak (8107ft), where you can see from the Sierra Buttes right to Mt Shasta and beyond. To reach the trailhead, turn right from Gold Lake Hwy at Haskell Peak Rd (Forest Rd 9) and follow it for 8.5 miles to the marked parking lot.

🛏 Sleeping & Eating

There's just one main drag in town, and that's the Golden Chain Highway (Hwy 49). All commerce happens here. The hotels often have the best restaurants – when they're open. Winter time is quiet.

USFS Campgrounds   CAMPING $
(☎530-993-1410; tent sites $24) The cheapest way to stay the night are in the USFS campgrounds east from Sierra City along Hwy 49. Wild Plum, Sierra, Chapman Creek and Yuba Pass all have vault toilets and running water (Sierra has river water only), and first-come, first-served sites. Wild Plum

(47 sites) is the most scenic. North of Hwy 49, 2 miles north of Bassetts on Gold Lake Hwy, Salmon Creek is one of several great USFS campgrounds. It has vault toilets, running water and first-come, first-served sites for RVs and tents, but no hook-ups. This site offers the most dramatic view of the Sierra Buttes with no crowds. Sites 16 and 20 are separated from the rest by a creek.

Buttes Resort   CABIN $$
(☎530-862-1170; www.buttesresort.citymax.com; 230 Main St; cabins $90-155) In the heart of Sierra City, the small Buttes Resort occupies a lovely spot overlooking the river and is a favorite with hikers looking to recharge. Most cabins have a private deck and barbecue, some have full kitchens. You can borrow bikes and games from the wilderness-loving owners.

★ Big Springs Gardens   AMERICAN $$$
(☎530-862-1333; bigspringgardens.com; 32163 Hwy 49; adult/child $15/10, entry incl buffet $35-39; ⊙brunch noon Wed-Sun mid-Jun–Sep) Offers the perfect brunch of berries from the surrounding hills and trout fresh from the pond, served in an open-air dining area (reservations re-

---

GOING FOR THE GOLD

California's Gold Rush started in 1848 when James Marshall was inspecting the fatefully sited lumber mill he was building for John Sutter near present-day Coloma. He saw a sparkle in the mill's tailrace water and pulled out a nugget 'roughly half the size of a pea.' Marshall hightailed it to Sacramento and consulted Sutter, who tested the gold by methods described in an encyclopedia. Sutter still wanted to finish his mill so he made a deal with his laborers, allowing them to keep gold they found after hours if they kept working. Before long, word of the find leaked out.

Sam Brannan was among those who went to Coloma to investigate the rumors shortly after Marshall's find. After finding 6oz of gold in one afternoon, he paraded through San Francisco's streets proclaiming, 'Gold on the American River!' Then he snapped up every piece of mining equipment – from handkerchiefs to shovels – in the area. When gold seekers needed equipment for their adventure, Brannan sold them goods at a 100% markup and was a rich man before the gold seekers even reached the foothills.

The mill's construction was finished in the spring of 1848 when the first wave of miners arrived from San Francisco. Only a few months later, the cities were depleted of able-bodied men, while towns near the 'diggins,' as the mines were called, swelled to thousands. News of the Gold Rush spread around the world, and by 1849 more than 60,000 people (who became widely known as forty-niners) rushed into California. Everyone was looking for the Mother Lode: the mythical deposit believed to be the source of all the gold washing into the streams and riverbeds.

Most prospectors didn't stick around after the initial diggings petered out; gold-extraction processes became increasingly equipment-dependent, culminating in the practice of hydraulic mining, by which miners drained lakes and rivers to power their water cannons and blast away entire hillsides. People downstream were inundated by the muck and finally sued in 1884. The Sawyer court held the environmental cost was too great to justify staying in business.

quired). Friday BBQ dinners in July and August as well. There are hiking trails through the 'Wild Garden,' a waterfall-laced natural area with pretty views. You have to call ahead to do any of the above.

EL DORADO & AMADOR COUNTIES

In the heart of the pine- and oak-covered Sierra foothills, this is where gold was first discovered – Spanish-speaking settlers named El Dorado County after a mythical city of riches.

Today, SUVs en route to South Lake Tahoe pull off Hwy 50 to find a rolling hillside dotted with the historic towns, sun-soaked terraces and the fertile soil of one of California's burgeoning wine-growing regions. If you make the stop, don't leave without toasting a glass of regional Zinfandel, which, like the locals, is packed with earthy attitude and regional character. It's also worth the detour to pause at the shore where a glint of gold caught James Marshall's eye.

Traveling through much of the central part of Gold Country requires a car, as the public transportation is unreliable between the towns, but this stretch of Hwy 49 makes an excellent road trip.

Coloma-Lotus

Coloma-Lotus Valley surrounds Sutter's Mill (the site of California's first gold discovery) and Marshall Gold Discovery State Historic Park. It is also a great launching pad for rafting operations. The South Fork of the American River gets the most traffic, since it features exciting rapids but is still manageable. Adrenaline junkies who have never rafted before should try the Middle Fork.

🏃 Activities

Half-day rafting trips usually begin at Chili Bar and end close to the state park. Full-day trips put in at the Coloma Bridge and take out at Salmon Falls, near Folsom Lake. The half-day options start in class III rapids and are action-packed (full-day trips start out slowly, then build up to class IV as a climax). Full-day trips include a lavish lunch. The season usually runs from May to mid-October, depending on water levels. Prices are generally lower on weekdays.

Don't want to get wet? Watch people navigate the Troublemaker Rapids, upstream from the bridge near Sutter's Mill in the state park.

Whitewater Connection RAFTING
(📞800-336-7238, 530-622-6446; www.whitewaterconnection.com; half-day trips $94-114, full-day $119-139; ☺Apr-Oct) Whitewater Connection is typical of the area's operators, with knowledgeable guides and excellent food.

🛏️ Sleeping & Eating

If you're looking for a basic hotel and don't mind the blandness of a highway motel, Auburn is a better bet. The food options around these parts pleasantly over-deliver.

American River Resort CAMPGROUND, CABINS $
(📞530-622-6700; www.americanriverresort.com; 6019 New River Rd; tent & RV sites $35-55, cabins $180-280; 🛜🏊) Only a quarter mile off Hwy 49, just south of the Marshall Gold Discovery State Historic Park, this site is more built-up than other area campgrounds: there's a small convenience store, free wi-fi, a playground, fishing pond and pool. The sites are basic, but some are right on the river. The most spacious and pretty oak-shaded sites are 14 to 29.

Coloma Club Cafe & Saloon BAR & GRILL $
(📞530-626-6390; colomaclub.com; 7171 Hwy 49, Coloma; mains from $9; ☺restaurant 6:30am-9pm, bar 10am-2am) The patio at this rowdy old saloon comes alive with guides and river rats when the water is high.

Cafe Mahjaic AMERICAN, GREEK $$
(Lotus Inn; 📞530-622-9587; www.cafemahjaic.com; 1006 Lotus Rd, Lotus; ☺from 5pm Wed-Sun; 🛜) House-baked breads and organic meats with a sense a humor: the sophisticated menu includes a Moody Soup (which changes per chef's daily whims). The four-course prix fixe for $28 is a great deal. The owners also run the three-room Lotus Inn (rooms $109 to $139) tucked in the brick house behind the restaurant.

Marshall Gold Discovery State Historic Park

Compared to the stampede of gun-toting, hill-blasting, hell-raising settlers that populate tall tales along Hwy 49, the Marshall Gold Discovery State Historic Park (📞530-622-3470; marshallgold.org; per car $8;

park 8am-5pm, to 7pm late May-early Sep, museum 10am-5pm;) is a place of bucolic tranquility, with two tragic protagonists in John Sutter and James Marshall.

Sutter, who had a fort in Sacramento, partnered with Marshall to build a sawmill on this swift stretch of the American River in 1847. It was Marshall who discovered gold here on January 24, 1848, and though the men tried to keep their findings secret, prospectors from around the world stampeded into town. In one of the tragic ironies of the Gold Rush, the men who made this discovery died nearly penniless. In another, many of the new immigrants who arrived seeking fortune were indentured, taxed and bamboozled out of anything they found.

In the rare moments there aren't a million school kids running around, the pastoral park by the river makes for a solemn stroll. Follow the trail to the bank where Marshall found gold and started the revolutionary birth of the 'Golden State.'

The park has been undergoing a restoration effort, which includes the mill itself and the Visitor Information Center & Museum (530-622-3470; 310 Back St, Coloma; tours adult/child $3/2; 10am-5pm Mar-Nov, to 4pm Dec-Feb, guided tours 11am & 1pm year-round), with historical dioramas and a shop with frontier-days trinkets.

On a hill overlooking the park is the James Marshall Monument, where he was buried in 1885, a ward of the state. You can drive the circuit but it's much better to meander the many trails around the park, past mining artifacts and pioneer cemeteries.

Panning for gold ($7, free if you have your own equipment) is popular. From 10am to 3pm in the summer, or by request, you get a quick training session and 45 minutes to pan.

Sleeping & Eating

Coloma Resort CAMPGROUND, CABINS $
(530-621-2267; www.colomaresort.com; 6921 Mt Murphy Rd; tent & RV sites $45-49, cabins & on-site RVs $100-295;) Another long-established riverside campground, this is better for RVs. It comes with a full range of activities and wi-fi. With lots of family activities, this has the feel of a summer camp.

★ Argonaut Farm to Fork Cafe AMERICAN $
(www.argonautcafe.com; 331 Hwy 49, Coloma; sandwiches $8; 8am-4pm) Truly delicious soups, sandwiches and coffee from well-known Sacramento and Coloma purveyors

find their way to this little wooden house between Sutter's Mill and the blacksmith's shop in Marshall Gold Discovery State Historic Park. The crowds of school kids waiting for gelato can slow things down.

Placerville

Placerville has always been a travelers' center: it was originally a destination for fortune hunters who reached California by following the South Fork of the American River. In 1857 the first stagecoach to cross the Sierra Nevada linked Placerville to Nevada's Carson Valley, which eventually became part of the nation's first transcontinental stagecoach route.

Today, Placerville is a place to explore while traveling between Sacramento and Tahoe on Hwy 50. It has a thriving and well-preserved downtown with antique shops and bars, and local wags who cherish the wild reputation of 'Hangtown' – a name earned when a handful of men swung from the gallows in the mid-1800s. Among the many awesome local legends is 'Snowshoe' John A Thompson, a postal carrier who regularly delivered 80lbs of mail on skis from Placerville over the Sierras to Carson Valley during the winter.

Sights

Main St is the heart of downtown Placerville and runs parallel to Hwy 50 between Canal St and Cedar Ravine Rd. Hwy 49 meets Main St at the west edge of downtown. Looking like a movie set, most buildings along Main St are false fronts and sturdy brick structures from the 1850s, dominated by the spindly Bell Tower, a relic from 1856 that once rallied volunteer firemen.

Gold Bug Park and Mine HISTORIC SITE
(www.goldbugpark.org; 2635 Goldbug Ln; adult/child $6/4; 10am-4pm Apr-Oct, noon-4pm Sat & Sun Nov-Mar) The best museum in Placerville, about 1 mile north of town on Bedford Ave. The park stands over the site of four mining claims that yielded gold from 1849 to 1888; you can descend into the self-guided Gold Bug Mine, do some gem panning ($2) and explore the grounds and picnic area for free. Guided tours cost $100 for up to 15 people.

El Dorado County Historical Museum MUSEUM
(http://museum.edcgov.us; 104 Placerville Dr; entry by donation; 10am-4pm Wed-Sun) On the El Dorado County Fairgrounds west of

PLACERVILLE WINERIES

The Placerville region's high heat and rocky soil produces excellent wines, which frequently appear on California menus. Oenophiles could spend a long afternoon rambling through the welcoming vineyards of El Dorado County alone (though a full weekend of tasting could be had if it was coupled with adjoining Amador County). Details can be found at the El Dorado Winery Association (☎800-306-3956; www.eldoradowines.org) or Wine Smith (☎530-622-0516; www.thewinesmith.com; 346 Main St, Placerville; ⏰11am-8pm Mon-Sat, from noon Sun), a local shop with just about everything grown in the area.

Some noteworthy wineries, all north of Hwy 50, include Lava Cap Winery (www.lavacap.com; 2221 Fruitridge Rd; ⏰11am-5pm), which has an on-hand deli for picnic supplies, and Boeger Winery (www.boegerwinery.com; 1709 Carson Rd; ⏰10am-5pm). Both have free tastings.

downtown (exit north on Placerville Dr from Hwy 50), is this complex of restored buildings, mining equipment and re-created businesses that tell the story of Old Hangtown.

🛏 Sleeping

Chain motels can be found at either end of the historic center of Placerville along Hwy 50.

National 9 Inn MOTEL $
(☎530-622-3884; www.national9inns.com; 1500 Broadway; r $50-89; ❄🐾) This mid-century motel, recently renovated by a young couple, is the best bargain in Placerville, even if it lies at the lonely north end of town. The building's exterior is ho-hum, but the rooms are sparkling with refrigerators, microwaves and remodeled baths. It's a great option for travelers who want a clean, no-frills stay and want to support independent businesses.

Cary House Hotel HISTORIC HOTEL $$
(☎530-622-4271; www.caryhouse.com; 300 Main St; r from $121; ❄@🐾) This historic hotel in the middle of downtown Placerville has a large, comfortable lobby with back-lit stained glass depicting scenes from the region's history. Once a bordello, it has up-

dated rooms (some with kitchenettes) with period decor. Ask for a room overlooking the courtyard to avoid street noise, or try room 212, a rumored supernatural haunt. Check online for deals.

Albert Shafsky House B&B B&B $$
(☎530-642-2776; www.shafsky.com; 2942 Coloma St; r $135-175; ❄🐾) Of all the Victorian bed-and-breakfast options in Placerville, Albert's proximity to downtown, ornate period furnishings and luxurious bedding make this cozy three-room option a favorite.

🍴 Eating

Z-Pie AMERICAN $
(www.z-pie.com; 3182 Center St; pies $7-8; ⏰11am-9pm) With its whimsical take on the all-American comfort-food staple, this casual stop stuffs flaky, butter-crusted pot pies with a gourmet flourish (steak cabernet! Thai chicken! tomatillo stew!). California beers are on tap. The four-beer sampler ($8) is ideal for the indecisive.

Sweetie Pie's BREAKFAST $
(www.sweetiepies.biz; 577 Main St; mains $5-12; ⏰6:30am-3pm Mon-Fri, 7am-3pm Sat, 7am-1pm Sun) Ski bunnies and bums fill this diner and bakery counter on the weekends en route to Lake Tahoe, filling up with egg dishes and top-notch homemade baked goods like heavenly cinnamon rolls. Breakfast is the specialty, but it also does a capable lunch.

Cozmic Café & Pub HEALTH FOOD $
(www.ourcoz.com; 594 Main St; items $4-10; ⏰7am-6pm Tue, Wed & Sun, to midnight Thu-Sat; 🐾♪) In the historic Placerville Soda Works building, the menu is organic and boasts vegetarian and healthy fare backed by fresh smoothies. There's a good selection of microbrews and live music on weekends, when it stays open late.

Heyday Café CAFE $$
(www.heydaycafe.com; 325 Main St; mains $9-25; ⏰11am-9pm Tue-Thu, to 10pm Fri & Sat, to 8pm Sun) Fresh and well-executed, the menu here leans toward simple Italian comfort food, made all the more comfortable by the wood-and-brick interior. The wine list is long on area vineyards. Locals rave about lunch.

🍷 Drinking & Nightlife

The profile of El Dorado County wines is rising, and several tasting rooms dot the main street offering earthy, elegant varietals of the region. Placerville's bars, on the other hand, are akin to the neighborhood watering holes in the Midwest: they open around 6am, get an annual cleaning at Christmas and are great for people who want to chew the fat with a colorful cast of locals.

Liar's Bench BAR
(📞 530-622-0494; 255 Main St; ⊙ 8am-1am) The Liar's Bench survives as the town's classic watering hole under a neon martini sign that beckons after dark.

🛍 Shopping

★ **Gothic Rose Antiques** ANTIQUES
(www.gothicroseantiques.com; 484 Main St; ⊙ 11am-5pm Thu-Sun) The most interesting antique and curiosity shop in Gold Country likely frightens the wigs off the other dealers in town with its collection of haute gothic house wares, antique occult goods and flawlessly macabre sensibility. Browsing the old medical instruments, taxidermy, 19th-century photos of corpses and the latest in latex and lace cemetery chic, is titillating.

Placerville Hardware HOMEWARES
(www.placervillehardware.com; 441 Main St; ⊙ 8am-6pm Mon-Sat, to 5pm Sun) The 1852 building, an anchor of Placerville's main drag, is the oldest continuously operating hardware store west of the Mississippi and a place to pick up a brochure for a self-guided tour of the town. The store has a smattering of Gold Country bric-a-brac but most of what clutters the place are bona-fide dry goods, like hammers and buckets.

Placerville Antiques & Collectibles ANTIQUES
(📞 530-626-3425; 448 Main St; ⊙ 10am-6pm) Of Placerville's many antique shops, the collective of dealers in this brightly lit space is a favorite. Reasonably priced mid-century dishware is a particular strength.

Bookery BOOKS
(326 Main St; ⊙ 10am-5:30pm Mon-Thu, to 7pm Fri & Sat, to 4pm Sun) A great used-book store to stock up on vacation pulp.

Placerville News Co BOOKS
(www.pvillenews.com; 409 Main St; ⊙ 8am-6:30pm Mon-Thu, to 7pm Fri & Sat, to 5:30pm Sun) This plank-floored bookshop has a wealth of excellent maps, history and local-interest books.

ℹ Information

El Dorado County Visitors Authority (Chamber of Commerce; 📞 530-621-5885; http://visit-el-

dorado.com; 542 Main St; ⊙ 9am-5pm Mon-Fri) Maps and local information on everything from farm trails to films, breweries and Tahoe.

ℹ Getting There & Away

Amtrak (📞 877-974-3322; www.capitolcorridor. org) Runs several buses daily to Sacramento ($20, 1½ hours), though some require train connections to points further along the Capital Corridor route.

El Dorado Transit (📞 530-642-5383; www. eldoradotransit.com; 6565 Commerce Way, Diamond Springs; adult/child $1.50/75¢) Operates hourly weekday commuter buses between 7am and 4pm to every corner of town out of the Placerville Station Transfer Center (2984 Mosquito Rd), a charming covered bus stop with benches and restrooms. It's about half a mile from downtown, on the north side of Hwy 50.

Plymouth & Amador City

Two small, sunny villages make equally good bases for exploring Amador County's wine region. The first, Plymouth, is where the region's Gold Rush history is evident in its original name, Pokerville. Few card sharks haunt the slumbering town today; it wakes late when the tiny main street fills with the smell of barbecue, a few strolling tourists and the odd rumble of a motorcycle posse. Amador City was once home to the Keystone Mine – one of the most prolific gold producers in California – but the town lay deserted from 1942 (when the mine closed) until the 1950s, when a family from Sacramento bought the dilapidated buildings and converted them into antique shops.

◉ Sights

Amador Whitney Museum MUSEUM
(📞 209-267-5250; www.amador-city.com; Main St, Amador City; ⊙ noon-4pm Fri-Sun) **FREE** This is the main thing going in town. Housed in an old Wells Fargo outpost, it has a covered wagon and a replica school house scene and mineshaft. It's worth the 15-minute stop.

Chew Kee Store Museum MUSEUM
(www.fiddletown.info; Fiddletown; entry by donation; ⊙ noon-4pm Sat Apr-Oct) Remnants of the bygone era are just outside of Plymouth. The Chew Kee Store Museum, 6 miles east in Fiddletown, is an old herbal shop that once served railroad workers. The dusty collection of artifacts frozen in time are *objets d'art*.

DON'T MISS

AMADOR COUNTY WINE REGION

Amador County might be something of an underdog among California's winemaking regions, but a thriving circuit of family wineries, Gold Rush history and local characters make for excellent imbibing without a whiff of pretension. The region lays claim to the oldest Zinfandel vines in the United States and the surrounding country has a lot in common with this celebrated variety – bold and richly colored, earthy and constantly surprising.

The region has two tiny towns, Plymouth and Amador City (p319). Start in Amador and follow Hwy 49 north through the blip known as Drytown and on to Plymouth by Hwy 49, and then follow Shenandoah Rd northeast, which takes you past rolling hills of neatly pruned vines. Most hosts are exceedingly welcoming and helpful, offering free tastes and whatever you want to know about their operations. In July, 38 wineries throw an annual 10-day tasting extravaganza.

Maps are available at the wineries, and from the **Amador Vintners Association** (www.amadorwine.com).

Deaver Vineyards (www.deavervineyards.com; 12455 Steiner Rd, Plymouth; ⊙10:30am-5pm) A true family affair where nearly everyone pouring has the last name on the bottles.

Drytown Cellars (www.drytowncellars.com; 16030 Hwy 49, Drytown; ⊙11am-5pm) This is the most fun tasting room in Amador County, thanks to vintner Allen Kreutzer, a gregarious host, and his array of stunning reds.

Sobon Estate (www.sobonwine.com; 14430 Shenandoah Rd, Plymouth; ⊙9:30am-5pm Apr-Oct, to 4:30pm Nov-Mar) Founded in 1856, it's also home to the free Shenandoah Valley Museum featuring wine-making memorabilia.

Wilderotter (www.wilderottervineyard.com; 19890 Shenandoah School Rd, Plymouth; ⊙10:30am-5pm) As if the award-winning Sauvignon Blanc weren't enough, tastings here are paired with Cowgirl Creamery cheeses.

Amador 360 Wine Collective (amador360.com; 18950 Hwy 49, Plymouth; ⊙11am-6pm) Run by the couple that organizes Amador's annual Barbera extravaganza (http://barberafestival.com), this expansive shop reserves special billing to boutique vintners who otherwise would not offer tastings.

🛏 Sleeping & Eating

★ **Imperial Hotel**   B&B $$
(☎209-267-9172; www.imperialamador.com; 14202 Main St, Amador City; r $105-155, ste $125-195; ✳🐾) The nicest place to stay in these parts. Built in 1879, it's one of the area's most inventive updates to the typical antique-cluttered hotels, with sleek deco touches accenting the usual gingerbread flourish, a genteel bar and a very good, seasonally minded restaurant (mains $13 to $28). On weekends during the summer, expect a two-night minimum.

★ **Taste**   CALIFORNIAN $$$
(☎209-245-3463; www.restauranttaste.com; 9402 Main St, Plymouth; mains $23-40; ⊙11:30am-2pm Sat & Sun, from 5pm Mon-Thu, from 4:30pm Fri-Sun) Book a table at Taste, where excellent Amador wines are paired with a fine menu of California-style cooking.

🍷 Drinking & Nightlife

Drytown Club   BAR
(www.drytownclub.com; 15950 Hwy 49; ⊙noon-midnight Wed-Fri, to 2am Sat, to 9pm Sun) Tired of wine? Hit the Drytown Club, the kind of rowdy roadhouse where people start drinking a little too early and soak it up with weekend BBQ. The bands on the weekend are bluesy, boozy and sometimes brilliant.

Sutter Creek

Perch on the balcony of one of the gracefully restored buildings on this particularly scenic Main St and view Sutter Creek, a gem of a Gold Country town with raised, arcade sidewalks and high-balconied buildings with false fronts that are perfect examples of California's 19th-century architecture. This is another option for staying the night when visiting Amador and El Dorado County wineries.

Begin the visit at volunteer-operated Sutter Creek Visitor Center (☏800-400-0305, 209-267-1344; www.suttercreek.org; 71a Main St) to collect a walking-tour map of historic traces left by Cornish, Yugoslavian and Italian arrivals, or pick up the excellent, free driving-tour guide to local gold mines.

⊙ Sights

Monteverde General Store   HISTORIC BUILDING
(☏209-267-0493; 11a Randolph St; entry by donation; ⊙by appointment) This building goes back in time to when the general store was the center of the town's social and economic life, represented by the chairs that circle the pot-belly stove and the detailed historic scale. Senior docents lead tours by appointment.

Knight Foundry   MINE
(www.knightfoundry.org; 81 Eureka St) In its prime, Sutter Creek was Gold Country's main supply center for all things forged. Three foundries operating in 1873 made pans and rock crushers, but only this one operated until 1996 — the last water-powered foundry and machine shop in the US. At press time, the interior was closed to visitors, but plans to reopen were in the works.

🛏 Sleeping

Eureka Street Inn   B&B $$
(☏209-267-5500; www.eurekastreetinn.com; 55 Eureka St; r incl breakfast $145; ❋🐾) Each of the four rooms in this 1914 Arts and Crafts–style home has unique decor and gas fireplaces. Once the home of a wealthy stagecoach operator, the inn is on a quiet side street.

Hotel Sutter   HOTEL $$
(☏209-267-0242; www.hotelsutter.com; 53 Main St; r $115-175; 🅿❋🐾) There was some controversy when they started gutting the beloved American Exchange, which had stood in repose for more than 150 years. The bricks and facade may be the only things left, but the modern rooms (some with en-suite bathrooms), and very fine restaurant (mains $14 to $25) and cool cellar bar seem to have quelled the protest.

Sutter Creek Inn   B&B $$
(☏209-267-5606; www.suttercreekinn.com; 75 Main St; r $120-210; ❋) The 17 rooms and cottages here vary in decor and amenities (antiques, fireplaces, sunny patios). All have private bathrooms. Guests can snooze in the hammock by the gardens or curl up with a book on a comfy chair on the sprawling lawn.

🍴 Eating

Sutter Creek Ice Cream Emporium   SWEETS $
(☏209-267-0543; 51 Main St; ⊙11am-6pm Thu-Sun) This sweet shop gets downright enchanting when town icon Stevens Price takes to the 1919 Milton piano and plays ragtime. The former proprietor still stops by in between organizing the Sutter Creek Ragtime Festival each August.

Pizza Plus   PIZZA $
(www.suttercreekpizzaplus.com; 20 Eureka St; pizzas $14; ⊙11am-9pm; 🍴) Crisp, chewy thin-crust pizza and pitchers of beer make this a favorite; it's the perfect place to hang out and chat up locals. Combinations like the BBQ pizza put it over the top.

Thomi's Coffee & Eatery   AMERICAN $
(www.thomissuttercreek.com; 40 Hanford St; mains $6-9; ⊙8am-3pm Fri-Wed; 🐾) A real star in a galaxy of lunch spots, Thomi serves classic griddle breakfasts, huge salads and a pot-roast melt. The brick dining room is welcoming in winter; in summer there's a sunny little patio.

Sutter Creek Cheese Shoppe   MARKET $
(☏209-267-5457; www.suttercreekcheese.com; 33b Main St; ⊙10am-5pm) A stop for cheeses from California and beyond. Call ahead for a picnic box of cheese, a baguette and even a little cutting board and knife to enjoy on your winery hop.

☆ Entertainment

Sutter Creek Theatre   PERFORMING ARTS
(www.suttercreektheater.com; 44 Main St) One of several excellent Gold Country arts groups, it has nearly a 100-year-long history of presenting live drama, films and other cultural events.

Volcano

One of the fading plaques in Volcano, 12 miles upstream from Sutter Creek, tellingly calls it a place of 'quiet history.' Even though the little L-shaped village on the bank of Sutter Creek yielded tons of gold and a Civil War battle, today it slumbers away in remote solitude. Only a smattering of patinated bronze monuments attest to Volcano's lively past.

Large sandstone rocks line Sutter Creek, which skirts the center of town. The rocks, now flanked by picnic tables, were blasted from surrounding hills by hydraulic mining before being scraped clean of their gold. The process had dire environmental consequences, but generated miners nearly $100 of booty a day.

◉ Sights & Activities

Daffodil Hill
FARM

(☏209-296-7048; 18310 Rams Horn Grade; donations accepted; ⊙10am-4pm mid-Mar–mid-Apr) This hilltop farm, 2 miles northeast of Volcano, is blanketed with more than 300,000 daffodil blooms in the spring. The McLaughlin and Ryan families have operated the farm since 1887 and keep hyacinths, tulips, violets, lilacs and the occasional peacock among the daffodils.

Indian Grinding Rock State Historic Park
HISTORIC SITE

(☏209-296-7488; parks.ca.gov; 14881 Pine Grove-Volcano Rd; per car $8; ⊙museum 11am-2:30pm Fri-Sun) Two miles southwest of Volcano is a sacred area for the local Miwok. There's a village site and a limestone outcrop covered with petroglyphs – 363 originals and a few modern additions – and over 1000 mortar holes called *chaw'se*, used for grinding acorns and seeds into meal.

Black Chasm
CAVE

(☏888-762-2837; www.caverntours.com; 15701 Pioneer Volcano Rd; adult/child $14.95/7.95; ⊙10am-5pm) A quarter of a mile east of Volcano, this has the whiff of a tourist trap, but one look at the array of helictite crystals – rare, sparkling white snowflakes – makes the crowd more sufferable. The tour guides are all experienced cavers. Reservations required for the adventurous Labyrinth tour ($79).

⊨ Sleeping & Eating

Indian Grinding Rock State Historic Park
CAMPGROUND $

(www.reserveamerica.com; tent & RV sites $30) The beautiful campground at Indian Grinding Rock State Historic Park has fresh water, plumbing and 22 unreserved sites set among the trees, with tent sites and hookups for RVs.

Volcano Union Inn
HISTORIC HOTEL $$

(☏209-296-7711; www.volcanounion.com; 21375 Consolation St; r incl breakfast $119-139; ❄☎) The preferred of two historic hotels in Volcano, there are four lovingly updated rooms with crooked floors: two have street-facing balconies. Flat-screen TVs and modern touches are a bit incongruous with the old building, but it's a comfortable place to stay. The on-site Union Pub has a superb menu and will host the occasional fiddler.

St George Hotel
HISTORIC HOTEL $$

(☏209-296-4458; www.stgeorgehotelvolcano.com; 16104 Main St; r $89-199) Up the crooked stairs of this charming, creaky hotel are 20 rooms that vary in size and amenity (most have shared bathrooms) and are free of clutter. The restaurant (open for dinner Thursday to Sunday, brunch Sunday) has a menu anchored by steak. Hang out in the saloon.

☆ Entertainment

Volcano Theatre Company
PERFORMING ARTS

(www.volcanotheatre.org; adult/child $16/11) On weekends between April and November, this highly regarded company produces live dramas in an outdoor amphitheater and the restored Cobblestone Theater.

Jackson

Jackson has some historic buildings and a small downtown, but it ain't much to look at. It stands at the junction of Hwy 49 and Hwy 88, which turns east from Hwy 49 here and heads over the Sierras near the Kirkwood ski resort.

◉ Sights

Kennedy Gold Mine
HISTORIC SITE

(☏209-223-9542; http://kennedygoldmine.com; 12594 Kennedy Mine Rd; adult/child $10/6) You can't miss the ominous steel headframe rising 125ft from the road. Its pulleys lifted ore and miners from the bowels of the earth. Once the deepest mine, this is now a peaceful park good for a stroll. Guided tours last about 1½ hours and take you past the stamp, gold recovery mill and massive tailing wheels. The parking lot is off of North Main St.

On-site Kennedy Tailing Wheels Park has marvelous examples of engineering and craftsmanship — four iron and wood wheels, 58ft in diameter, that transported tailings from neighboring Eureka Mine over two low hills. Be sure to climb to the top of the hill behind the wheels to see the impounding dam.

APPLE HILL

In 1860, a miner planted a Rhode Island Greening apple tree on a hill and with it established the foundation for bountiful Apple Hill, a 20-sq-mile area east of Placerville and north of Hwy 50 where there are more than 60 orchards. Apple growers sell directly to the public, usually from August to December, and some let you pick your own. Other fruits and Christmas trees are available during different seasons.

Maps of Apple Hill are available online through the **Apple Hill Association** (☑530-644-7692; www.applehill.com), or use the El Dorado **Farm Trails Guide** (www.visit-eldorado.com).

A great place to hunker down while touring the farms is the **Camino Hotel** (☑530-644-1800; www.caminohotel.com; 4103 Carson Rd, Camino; r incl breakfast $60-150), a former lumberjack bunkhouse – every bit as creaky as you'd hope – with rooms (some are very small) that have been recently redone. The rates are a steal (as low as $60 on weekdays) and room 4 is perfect for families with two rooms adjoined by a central sitting room. The breakfast is made to order.

Mokelumne Hill   HISTORIC SITE

(www.mokehill.org) The somewhat undiscovered settlement of Mokelumne Hill is 7 miles south of Jackson just off Hwy 49. Settled by French trappers in the early 1840s, it's a good place to see historic buildings without the common glut of antique stores and gift shops.

🛏 Sleeping & Eating

National Hotel   HISTORIC HOTEL **$$**

(☑209-223-0500; www.national-hotel.com; 2 Water St; r $125-165, ste $175-300) Jackson's historic hotel has had a serious upgrade from the Gold Rush era. While the restored building retains its historical details, all rooms are newly refurbished with luxurious details like gas fireplaces and heated floors. The top-notch steakhouse and bar downstairs complete the picture.

Mel's and Faye's Diner   AMERICAN **$$**

(www.melandfayesjackson.com; 31 N Hwy 49; meals $7-12; ⊙10am-11pm Sun-Thu, to 2am Fri & Sat) A local institution near Hwy 88, there's a takeout window but it's not meant for quick stops. Take a seat for solid diner fare that includes huge breakfasts, classic burgers (try the chili-soaked 'Miner') and – to balance the grease binge – a decent salad bar.

❶ Information

Amador County Chamber of Commerce

(☑209-223-0350; www.amadorcountychamber.com; 115 Main St; ⊙8am-4pm Mon-Fri, 10am-2pm Sat & Sun) Smack in the middle of Main St, has enough brochures to fill several recycling bins.

❶ Getting There & Away

The only way to easily travel through this area is with your own wheels. Placer County runs its bus system out of Jackson, but good luck catching it – the buses are few and far between. **Amador Transit** (☑209-267-9395; http://amadortransit.com; fares $1-2; ⊙Mon-Fri) is a bit better. It makes a weekday connection through Sutter Creek to Sacramento ($1, one hour) and, if you have enough patience, you can connect to Calaveras County and southern Gold Country. By car, Jackson is 2½ hours from San Francisco and just over one hour to the ski resorts of South Lake Tahoe.

CALAVERAS COUNTY & SOUTH GOLD COUNTRY

The southern region of Gold Country is hot as blazes in the summer so cruising through its historic Gold Rush hubs will demand more than one stop for ice cream. The tall tales of yesteryear come alive here through the region's infamous former residents: author Mark Twain, who got his start writing about a jumping frog contest in Calaveras County, and Joaquin Murrieta, a controversial symbol of the lawlessness of the frontier era who somehow seems to have frequented every old bar and hotel in the area.

Angels Camp

On the southern stretch of Hwy 49 one figure looms over all others: literary giant Mark Twain, who got his first big break with the story of *The Celebrated Jumping Frog of Calaveras County*, written and set in Angels

Camp. There are differing claims as to when or where Twain heard this tale, but Angels Camp makes the most of it. There are gentlemanly Twain impersonators and statues, and bronze frogs on Main St honoring the champions of the past 80 years. Look for the plaque of Rosie the Ribeter, who set an impressive 21ft record in 1986. Today the town is an attractive mix of buildings from the Gold Rush to art-deco periods.

Calaveras County Visitors Bureau (☑ 209-736-0049; www.gocalaveras.com; 1192 S Main St; ☺ 9am-5pm Mon-Sat, 11am-4pm Sun; 🖥) has a walking and driving tour of Angels Camp, history books and lots more beta for your trip.

🏃 Activities

Moaning Cavern   CAVE
(☑ 209-736-2708; www.caverntour.com; 5350 Moaning Cave Rd, Vallecito; adult/child $14.95/7.95; ☺ 10am-5pm) Perhaps not the greatest natural beauty, this cave does have the most thrills. Visitors can rappel 165ft to the bottom ($65). A pile of bones discovered here are some of the oldest human remains in the US. There's also above-ground zip lines and self-guided nature walk. Winter events like caroling utilize cave acoustics.

🎉 Festivals & Events

Angels Camp makes the most of the Twain connection; hosting the Jumping Frog Jubilee (www.frogtown.org) the third weekend in May (in conjunction with the county fair and something of a Harley rally) and Mark Twain impersonators make appearances at Gold Rush Day in the fall.

🍴 Eating

Strung out along Hwy 49 are a number of motels and diners to refill your gas tank or stomach.

Sidewinders   CALIFORNIAN, MEXICAN $
(http://eatatsidewinders.com; 1252 S Main St; mains $6.50-8.50; ☺ 11am-8pm Tue-Sat; 🚗) Choose from beef, chicken, pork, fish and veggie fillings for these tacos, bowls and wraps. The guacamole-dressed, panko-breaded fish tacos are excellent with a local brew.

Crusco's   ITALIAN $$
(www.cruscos.com; 1240 S Main St; mains $14-26; ☺ 11am-3pm & 5-9pm Thu-Mon) The class act in downtown Angels Camp puts out a serious, authentic northern Italian menu. The owners regularly hit Italy for more recipes, like the Polenta Antonella (creamy cornmeal with chicken and mushroom sauce).

ℹ️ Getting There & Away

Calaveras Transit (☑ 209-754-4450; http://transit.calaverasgov.us; fare $2; ☺ office 6am-5pm Mon-Fri) operates the most reliable public transportation system in the region from the Government Center (891 Mountain Ranch Rd, San Andreas) in downtown San Andreas. You can use it to connect to Angels Camp ($2, 30 minutes, several times daily) and other surrounding towns. You can catch it mid-route, just flag it down. To connect via public transportation to the rest of California you have to catch Route 1 to San Andreas, switch to Route 3 to Mokelumne Hill, and finally transfer to Amador County Transit.

Murphys

With its white picket fences and old-world charm, Murphys is one of the more scenic towns along the southern stretch of Gold Country, befitting its nickname as 'Queen of the Sierra.' It lies 8 miles east of Hwy 49 on Murphys Grade Rd, and is named for Daniel and John Murphy, who founded a trading post and mining operation on Murphy Creek in 1848. They employed the struggling local Miwok and Yokut people as laborers. While some settlers continued to persecute the tribes, John eventually married Pokela, a chieftain's daughter.

The town's Main St is refined with tons of wine-tasting rooms, boutiques, galleries and good strolling. For information and a town overview, look to www.visitmurphys.com.

👁 Sights & Activities

Even more than frogs, wine is a consistent draw in Calaveras County, and Murphys is at the center – a couple new tasting rooms seem to pop up downtown every summer.

Ironstone Vineyards   WINERY
(www.ironstonevineyards.com; 1894 Six Mile Rd; ☺ 8:30am-5pm; 🚗) 🌿 The unusually family-friendly atmosphere makes the wine feel secondary at Ironstone. There's a natural spring waterfall, a mechanical pipe organ, frequent exhibits by local artists, and blooming grounds. By the deli, the museum displays the world's largest crystalline gold leaf specimen (it weighs 44lb and was found in Jamestown in 1992). The enormous tasting room accommodates crowds.

WORTH A TRIP

CALAVERAS BIG TREES STATE PARK

From Angels Camp, Hwy 4 ascends into the High Sierra, eventually cresting at Ebbetts Pass (p406), at 8730ft, and then descending to junctions with Hwys 89 and 395. Along the way the road passes through the hardscrabble town of Arnold, which has a few cafes and motels strung along the roadside. But the real reason for taking Hwy 4 is 2 miles east of Arnold and 20 miles east of Murphys: a chance to commune with the largest living organisms on the planet.

Calaveras Big Trees State Park is home to giant sequoia redwood trees. Reaching as high as 325ft and with trunk diameters up to 33ft, these holdovers from the Mesozoic era are thought to weigh upwards of 3000 tons, or close to 20 blue whales.

The redwood giants are distributed in two large groves, one of which is easily viewed from the stroller-accessible North Grove Trail, a 1.7-mile self-guided loop, near the entrance, where the air is fresh with pine and rich soil. The River Canyon Trail, a challenging 8-mile hike out and back, climbs out of the North Grove, crosses a ridge and descends 1000ft to the Stanislaus River. Pack enough water for the return trip back up.

It's possible to find giant trees throughout the park's 6000 acres, though the largest are in fairly remote locations. The visitor center (☑209-795-7980; 1170 E Hwy 4, Arnold; ☺9am-5pm Sun-Thu, to 6pm Fri-Sat May-Sep, seasonal hrs Oct-Apr) has maps and good advice on the miles of trails. It's worth checking out the exhibits on sequoia biology and learning how a few dedicated individuals fought for decades to save them from becoming so many thousands of picnic tables.

Camping (☑800-444-7275; www.parks.ca.gov; off Hwy 4; tent & RV sites $35) is popular and reservations essential. North Grove Campground is near the park entrance; less crowded is Oak Hollow Campground, 4 miles farther on the park's main road. Most atmospheric are the hike-in environmental sites. Store food and toiletries in the provided bear lockers at all times.

Newsome-Harlow   WINERY
(www.nhvino.com; 403 Main St; tasting $5; ☺noon-5pm Mon-Thu, 11am-5:30pm Fri-Sun; 🎂🐾) This family-run winery pours the juicy red varietals that made them famous in their lively tasting lounge. At times, this place feels like the community social club. There's an on-site chef, fire pit, movie night, and kids and dogs are welcome.

Murphys Old Timers Museum   MUSEUM
(www.murphysoldtimersmuseum.com; 470 Main St; donation requested; ☺noon-4pm Fri-Sun) The name is a good hint that this place approaches history with a humorous touch. Housed in an 1856 building, it has an inscrutable tin type of the outlaw Joaquin Murrieta and the entertaining 'Wall of Comparative Ovations.' Guided tours of town leave from the museum every Saturday at 10am.

California Cavern   CAVE
(☑209-736-2708; www.caverntours.com; adult/child $14.95/7.95; ☺10am-5pm Apr-Oct; 🎂) In Cave City, 12 winding miles north of Murphys (take Main St to Sheep Ranch Rd to Cave City Rd), is a natural cavern, which John Muir described as 'graceful flowing

folds deeply placketed like stiff silken drapery.' Regular tours take 60 to 90 minutes.

Ages 16 and up can try the Middle Earth Expedition ($130), which lasts four hours and involves serious spelunking. The Trail of Lakes walking tour, available only toward both ends of wet season, is magical. Conditions are unpredictable, so call to plan.

🛏 Sleeping

Most accommodations in Murphys are top-end B&Bs. For the same price, there is a cluster of picturesque rental cottages (☑209-736-9372; www.murphysvacationrentals.com; 549 S Algiers St; cottages $115-160) just off Main St, or check nearby Angels Camp or Arnold for cheaper alternatives.

★Victoria Inn   B&B $$
(☑209-728-8933; www.victoriainn-murphys.com; 402 Main St; r $129-225, cottage $190-450; 🐾) This newly built B&B has elegant rooms with claw-foot slipper tubs, sleigh beds and balconies. The common spaces, like the long verandah for enjoying tapas and wine from the restaurant and bar (p326), have a chic country-mod appeal. Opi's Cabin ($158) –

with its iron bed and exposed beams – is the most interesting of the basic rooms.

Murphys Historic Hotel & Lodge
B&B, LODGE $$
(☏800-532-7684, 209-728-3444; www.murphyshotel.com; 457 Main St; d $129-149) Since either 1855 or 1856 (you have your pick of plaques out front), this hotel has anchored Main St. A must-stop on the Twain-slept-here tour, the original structure is a little rough around the edges. The adjoining buildings have bland, modern rooms that cost more. Make your way down to the dining room for fried chicken ($17).

Murphys Inn Motel
MOTEL $$
(☏888-796-1800, 209-728-1818; www.centralsierralodging.com; 76 Main St; r $129-149; ste $180; ❄@🛜🏊) Just off Hwy 4, half a mile from the center of town, this option has clean and modern motel rooms with a small pool. Not so much personality but a solid choice.

✕ Eating

Alchemy Market & Café
MARKET $$
(www.alchemymarket.com; 191 Main St; meals $12-24; ⊙market 11am-4:30pm Thu-Sun, cafe 11am-8pm Thu-Tue) For fancy picnic supplies. The cafe menu has many dishes great for sharing on the patio.

Firewood
CALIFORNIAN $$
(☏209-728-3248; www.firewoodeats.com; 420 Main St; mains $7-14; ⊙11am-9pm; 🦮) A rarity in a town with so much historical frill, Firewood's exposed concrete walls and corrugated metal offer a minimalist respite. When the weather's nice, they open the front wall for al-fresco dining. There are wines by the glass, half a dozen beers on tap and basic pub fare, but the wood-fired pizzas are the hallmark.

Grounds
BISTRO $$
(☏209-728-8663; www.groundsrestaurant.com; 402 Main St; meals $10-29; ⊙7am-10:30pm Mon-Fri, to 11:15pm Sat, 8am-11:15pm Sun; 🦮) Casually elegant Grounds does everything competently – expert breakfast foods, a roster of light lunch mains and weekend dinners of steaks and fresh fish. The herbal ice tea and fresh vegetarian options are key when the temperatures rise.

V Restaurant & Bar
MEDITERRANEAN $$
(☏209-728-0107; http://vrestaurantandbar-murphys.com; 402 Main St; mains $10-25; ⊙11:30am-8:30pm Sun-Thu, to 9:30pm Fri & Sat) Attached to the Victoria Inn, Murphys' most classic dinner spot offers Mediterranean small and large plates and a creative cocktail list. Options start with tapas (deep-fried anchovy-stuffed olives!) and end with a commanding rib eye. The dining room and patio fill up on weekends, so reserve ahead.

Columbia State Historic Park

More than any other place in Gold Country, Columbia blurs the lines between present and past with a carefully preserved Gold Rush town – complete with volunteers in period dress – at the center of a modern community. In 1850 Columbia was founded over the 'Gem of the Southern Mines;' as much as $150 million in gold was found here, and the center of the town (which was taken over by the state parks system) looks almost exactly as it did in its heyday. The authenticity of the old Main St is only shaken a bit by the sugared fragrance of the fudge and the occasional play-acting forty-niner who forgets to remove his digital watch. On the fringe of these blocks are homes and businesses that blend in so well that it becomes hard to tell what's park and what's not.

The blacksmith's shop, theater, old hotels and authentic bar are carefully framed windows into history, completed by easy gold panning (from $5) and breezy picnic spots.

Docents lead free hour-long tours on weekends at 11am from the Columbia Museum. After most shops and attractions close around 5pm, you can have the atmospheric town to yourself, which makes staying overnight an attractive option.

◉ Sights

Columbia Museum HISTORIC SITE
(☑general info 209-588-9128, museum 209-532-3184; cnr Main & State Sts; ◷9am-4:30pm spring & summer, 10am-4pm fall & winter) FREE Looking rather like dinosaur bones, limestone and granite boulders are noticeable around town. These were washed out of the surrounding hills by hydraulic mining and scraped clean by prospectors. There's a fascinating explanation of this technique at this renovated museum.

🛏 Sleeping & Eating

Fallon Hotel HOTEL $
(☑209-532-1470; parks.ca.gov; 11175 Washington St; r $50-115; ✳🤶) The historic Fallon Hotel hosts the most professional theater troupe in the region, the Sierra Repertory Theatre.

City Hotel HOTEL $$
(☑209-532-1479; parks.ca.gov/columbia; 22768 Main St; r $85-115; ✳🤶) Among the handful of restored Victorian hotels in the area, the City Hotel is the most elegant, with rooms that overlook a shady stretch of Main St and that open on lovely sitting rooms. The acclaimed restaurant (mains $15 to $30) is frequented by a Twain impersonator and the adjoining **What Cheer Saloon** is an atmospheric Gold Country joint with oil paintings of lusty ladies and stripped wallpaper.

Cottages COTTAGE $$
(☑209-532-1479; parks.ca.gov; 1-/2-/3-bedroom cottage $126.50/148.50/170.50) A cozy alternative to staying in a hotel are these cottages, two at the end of main street, and the largest with three bedrooms on Columbia St.

Columbia Mercantile MARKET $
(☑209-532-7511; cnr Main & Jackson Sts; ◷9am-6pm) For town gossip and snacks, stop at the friendly Columbia Mercantile, which also has a wide variety of groceries.

☆ Entertainment

Sierra Repertory Theatre THEATER
(☑209-532-3120; www.sierrarep.org; 11175 Washington St, Fallon Hotel) This theater mixes chestnuts of the stage (*Romeo & Juliet*, *South Pacific*) with popular reviews.

Sonora & Jamestown

Settled in 1848 by miners from Sonora, Mexico, this area was once a cosmopolitan center of commerce and culture with parks, elaborate saloons and the Southern Mines' largest concentration of gamblers and gold. Racial unrest drove the Mexican settlers out and their European immigrant usurpers got rich on the Big Bonanza Mine, where Sonora High School now stands. That single mine yielded 12 tons of gold in two years (including a 28lb nugget).

Today, people en route to Yosemite National Park use Sonora as a staging area, wandering through its pubs for refreshment or grabbing quick eats at the chain restaurants and stores that have cropped up on the periphery. Fortunately, the historic center is well preserved (so much so that it's a frequent backdrop in films).

The smaller **Jamestown** is 3 miles south of Sonora, just south of the Hwy 49/108 junction. Founded around the time of Tuolumne County's first gold strike in 1848, it has suffered the ups and downs of the region's roller-coaster development, and today it limps along on tourism and antiques. It has its charm but is only a few blocks long.

Two highways cross the Sierra Nevada east of Sonora and connect with Hwy 395 in the Eastern Sierra: Hwy 108 via Sonora Pass and Hwy 120 via Tioga Pass. Note that the section of Hwy 120 traveling through Yosemite National Park is only open in summer.

◉ Sights & Activities

The center of downtown Sonora is the T-shaped intersection of Washington and Stockton Sts, with Washington the main thoroughfare with boutiques, cafes and bars. If you're looking to get out of town, stroll the **Dragoon Gulch Trail**, a 2.5-mile loop through the oaks found just northwest of the main drag on Alpine Lane.

Sonora is also a base for white-water **rafting**: the Upper Tuolumne River is known for class IV and V rapids and its population of golden eagles and red-tailed hawks, while the Stanislaus River is more accessible with class III rapids. **Sierra Mac River Trips** (☑209-591-8027; www.sierramac.com; trips from $259) and **All-Outdoors** (☑800-247-2387; www.aorafting.com; from $164) both have good reputations and run trips of one day or more on multiple rivers.

Railtown 1897 State Historic Park HISTORIC SITE
(☑209-984-3953; www.railtown1897.org; 18115 5th Ave, Jamestown; adult/child $5/3, incl train ride $15/8; ◷9:30am-4:30pm Apr-Oct, 10am-3pm

JOAQUIN MURRIETA: VILLAIN OR ANTIHERO?

In a land where tall tales tower, none casts a darker shadow than Joaquin Murrieta's, the infamous Mexican miner long known by some as the Robin Hood of the Gold Rush. Stories of the vengeful Murrieta are as ubiquitous as they are incongruous: he was born in either Sonora, Mexico or Quillota, Chile and, after immigrating to California in 1850 to find gold or maybe trade horses, he became a treacherous villain – or was it, a heroic vigilante? In the soft focus of historical hindsight, his fiery vengeance – real or not – forged Gold Country's most intriguing antihero.

Much of his legend is shaped by dime novels written at the time, but from what historians can gather, his life might have gone like this: Murrieta and his brother had a claim near Hangtown (now known as Placerville). They had some luck but were either forced off by a mob of Anglo miners who beat him and raped his wife, or the land was stolen after he refused to pay the Foreign Miners Tax levied by the state against resourceful non-Anglo prospectors. Either way, with no hope for justice, Murrieta formed a posse to kill his assaulters and began a life of banditry that left a trail of slashed throats and purloined gold. His band of highwaymen, known as the Five Joaquins, terrorized miners (ironically, mostly Chinese) in the countryside between 1850 and 1853.

Governor John Bigler put a large price on Murrieta's head, and in July of 1853 a Texas bounty hunter named Harry Love produced a jar containing the severed head of a man he claimed was Murrieta. Love toured cities of Northern California charging audiences $1 to see his trophy but, even in death, Murrieta's legend grew: a woman claiming to be Murrieta's sister disputed the kill and sightings of the bandit continued long after his supposed death. Joaquin Murrieta was celebrated as a peoples' hero by many Mexican and Chileno people who were enraged by the oppressive, racist laws of the Gold Rush, which are largely unmentioned today.

Nov-Mar, train rides 11am-3pm Sat & Sun Apr-Oct; ♿) Five blocks south of Jamestown's Main St, this 26-acre, state-operated collection of trains and railroad equipment is the photogenic sister to Sacramento's rail museum. It's served as backdrop for countless films and TV shows including *Back to the Future III*, *Unforgiven* and *High Noon*. On some weekends and holidays (hourly from 11am to 3pm) you can ride the narrow-gauge railroad that once transported ore, lumber and miners.

Though today it has been shortened to a quick 3-mile circuit, it's still the best train ride in Gold Country. Ask the passionate volunteers to show you the roundhouse and restored station, or just wander. There's a lyrical romance to the place, where an explosion of orange poppies grow among the rusting shells of steel goliaths, and the air is spiced with creosote, campfire and pine.

Tuolumne County Museum MUSEUM
(www.tchistory.org; 158 W Bradford St, Sonora; ⊙10am-4pm Mon-Fri, to 3:30pm Sat) FREE In the former 1857 Tuolumne County Jail, two blocks west of Washington St is this interesting museum with a fortune's worth of gold on display.

California Gold Panning Lessons OUTDOORS
(☎209-694-6768; www.gold-panning-california. com; 17712 Harvard Mine Rd, Jamestown; from $60; ⊙9am-3pm Jun-Oct, or by appointment) Miner John and his experienced crew provide boots and all needed equipment for a genuine experience panning at Woods Creek and beyond. Be warned, real prospecting involves lots of digging. A couple hours in, you'll have gold fever, a blister or both. Take a right onto Harvard Mine Rd and drive to the parking lot with a 'Gold Panning' sign. Best to call ahead.

🛏 Sleeping & Eating

Bradford Place Inn B&B $$
(☎209-536-6075; www.bradfordplaceinn.com; 56 W Bradford St, Sonora; r $145-265; ❀@🛜) Gorgeous gardens and inviting porch seats surround this four-room B&B, which emphasizes green living. With a two-person claw-foot tub, the Bradford Suite is the definitive, romantic B&B experience.

Gunn House Hotel HISTORIC HOTEL $$
(☎209-532-3421; www.gunnhousehotel.com; 286 S Washington St, Sonora; r incl breakfast $79-125; ❀🛜☀) For a lovable alternative to Gold Country's cookie-cut chains, this historic

hotel hits the sweet spot. Rooms feature period decor and guests take to rocking chairs on the wide porches in the evening. Teddy bears, a nice pool and a big breakfast also make it a hit with families.

Legends Books, Antiques & Old-Fashioned Soda Fountain ANTIQUES $
(☑209-532-8120; 131 S Washington, Sonora; ☺11am-5pm) The place to sip sarsaparilla, snack on a polish dog, share a scoop of huckleberry ice cream, and then browse books downstairs in the old tunnel miners used to secret their stash directly into the former bank.

Lighthouse Deli & Ice Cream Shop DELI $
(www.thelighthousedeli.com; 28 S Washington, Sonora; sandwiches $8-9; ☺8am-4pm Mon-Sat) The flavors of N'Awlins make this unassuming deli an unexpected delight. The muffeletta – a toasted piece of Cajun paradise that's stacked with ham, salami, cheese and olive tapenade – is the best sandwich within 100 miles.

Diamondback Grill AMERICAN $
(www.thediamondbackgrill.com; 93 S Washington St, Sonora; meals $6-11; ☺11am-9:30pm Fri & Sat, to 8pm Sun) With exposed brick and modern fixtures, the fresh menu and contemporary details at this cafe are a reprieve from occasionally overbearing Victorian frill. Sandwiches dominate the menu (the salmon, and eggplant mozzarella are both great) and everything is homemade. For small bites, sample from the wine and cheese bar.

Drinking & Entertainment

The free and widely available weekend supplement of the *Union Democrat* comes out on Thursday and lists movies, music, performance art and events for Tuolumne County.

Iron Horse Lounge BAR
(☑209-532-4482; 97 S Washington St, Sonora; beer $3-6; ☺8:30am-2am) Sonora's classic hangout in the center of town. Bottles glitter like gold on the backlit bar.

Sierra Repertory Theatre THEATER
(☑209-532-3120; www.sierrarep.com; 13891 Hwy 108, Sonora; adult $26-32, child $18) In East Sonora, close to the Junction Shopping Center. This critically acclaimed company

also performs in the Fallon Hotel (p327) in Columbia.

Shopping

Sierra Nevada dventure Company OUTDOOR EQUIPMENT
(www.snacattack.com; 173 S Washington St, Sonora; ☺10am-6pm) This flagship is stocked with maps, equipment rental and sales, and offers friendly advice from guides with a passionate knowledge of ways to get outdoors in the area.

ℹ Information

Mi-Wok Ranger District Office (☑209-586-3234; 24695 State Hwy 108; ☺8am-4:30pm Mon-Fri) For information and permits for the Stanislaus National Forest.

Tuolumne County Visitors Bureau (☑209-533-4420; www.yosemitegoldcountry.com; 542 Stockton St, Sonora; ☺9am-6pm daily Jun-Sep, Mon-Sat Oct-May) More so than other brochure-jammed chamber of commerce joints, the staff here offers helpful trip planning advice throughout Gold Country as well as Yosemite National Park and Stanislaus National Forest up in the Sierras on Hwy 108.

ℹ Getting There & Away

Hwy 108 is the main access road here, and it links up with I-5, 55 miles west near Stockton. An entrance to Yosemite National Park is 60 scenic miles south on Hwy 120.

Navigating Southern Gold Country by public transportation can be tricky. Limited bus service is provided weekdays by **Tuolumne County Transit** (☑209-532-0404; www.tuolumnecountytransit.com; adult/child $1.50/free; ☺Mon-Fri) buses, which make the Sonora loop hourly from 7am to 7:46pm, and stops in Columbia and Jamestown less frequently. On summer weekends, look for air-conditioned **green trolleys** (☑209-532-0404; www.historic49trolleyservice.com; adult/child $1.50/free; ☺11am-9pm Sat, to 4pm Sun) that connect the historical sights in Columbia, Sonora and Jamestown hourly to Labor Day.

For Yosemite visitors staying in the Sonora area, **YARTS** (☑877-989-2878, 209-388-9589; www.yarts.com; adult/child return $25/18, one way $13/9) operates two round-trip buses connecting downtown Sonora, Jamestown's Main St and Yosemite from June 14 to September 1. There is just one round-trip bus in May and September. Ask nicely to be dropped off at unscheduled stops in Yosemite.

Lake Tahoe

Best Places to Eat

➡ Moody's Bistro & Lounge (p359)

➡ Cafe Fiore (p347)

➡ Fire Sign Cafe (p352)

➡ Rustic Lodge (p361)

➡ Old Granite Street Eatery (p366)

Best Places to Stay

➡ Cedar House Sport Hotel (p359)

➡ Hostel Tahoe (p362)

➡ PlumpJack Squaw Valley Inn (p356)

➡ Deerfield Lodge at Heavenly (p345)

➡ Clair Tappaan Lodge (p358)

Why Go?

Shimmering in myriad shades of blue and green, Lake Tahoe is the USA's second-deepest lake. Driving around the lake's spellbinding 72-mile scenic shoreline will give you quite a workout behind the wheel. Generally speaking, the north shore is quiet and upscale; the west shore, rugged and old-timey; the east shore, undeveloped; the south shore, busy and tacky, with aging motels and flashy casinos; and nearby Reno, the biggest little city in the region.

The horned peaks surrounding the lake, which straddles the California–Nevada state line, are year-round destinations. The sun shines on Tahoe three out of four days in the year. Swimming, boating, kayaking, windsurfing, stand-up paddleboarding and other water sports take over in summer, as do hiking, camping and wilderness backpacking adventures. Winter brings bundles of snow, perfect for those of all ages to hit the slopes at Tahoe's top-tier ski and snowboard resorts.

When to Go
South Lake Tahoe

| Jul & Aug Beach season; wildflowers bloom, and hiking and mountain-biking trails open. | Sep & Oct Cooler temperatures, colorful foliage and fewer tourists after Labor Day. | Dec–Mar Snow sports galore at resorts; storms bring hazardous roads. |

Lake Tahoe Highlights

❶ Survey the expanse of Lake Tahoe from aboard a kayak or from the sandy beach at **Zephyr Cove** (p339).

❷ Swoosh down the vertiginous double-black-diamond runs of **Heavenly ski resort** (p334).

❸ Trek the **Rubicon Trail** (p350) from Vikingsholm

Castle on sparkling Emerald Bay to DL Bliss State Park.

❹ Swim in an outdoor lagoon or ice-skate above 8000ft near the cable-car line in **Squaw Valley** (p355).

❺ Thunder down the **Flume Trail** (p364) on a mountain bike to tranquil Spooner Lake.

❻ Escape summer crowds with an overnight backpack to alpine lakes and high-country meadows in the **Desolation Wilderness** (p339).

❼ Cozy up with your family around a lakefront beach firepit or inside a comfortable cabin at **Tahoe Vista** (p360) on the no-fuss northern shore.

TAHOE SKI, SNOWBOARD & SNOWSHOE AREAS

Lake Tahoe has phenomenal skiing, with thousands of acres of the white stuff beckoning at more than a dozen resorts. Winter-sports complexes range from the giant, jet-set slopes of Squaw Valley, Heavenly and Northstar, to the no less enticing insider playgrounds like Sugar Bowl and Homewood. Tahoe's simply got a hill for everybody, from kids to kamikazes.

Ski season generally runs November to April, although it can start as early as October and last until the last storm whips through in May or even June. All resorts have ski schools, equipment rental and other facilities; check their websites for snow conditions, weather reports and free ski-season shuttle buses from area lodgings.

Downhill Skiing & Snowboarding

Tahoe's downhill resorts are usually open every day from December through April, weather permitting. All of these resorts rent equipment and have places to warm up slopeside and grab a quick bite or après-ski beer. Most offer group ski and snowboard lessons for adults and children (a surcharge applies, but usually no reservations are required).

Truckee & Donner Pass

Northstar California SKIING, SNOWBOARDING
(Map p336; ☎530-562-1010; www.northstarcalifornia.com; 5001 Northstar Dr, off Hwy 267, Truckee; adult/youth 13-22yr/child 5-12yr $116/96/69; ☺8:30am-4pm; ⊞) An easy 7 miles south of I-80, this hugely popular resort has great intermediate terrain. Northstar's relatively sheltered location makes it the second-best choice after Homewood when it's snowing, and the seven terrain parks and pipes are top-ranked. Advanced and expert skiers can look for tree-skiing challenges on the back of the mountain.

Recent additions to Northstar's 'Village' are making it look a lot more like amenity-rich Squaw. Weekends get superbusy. Stats: 20 lifts, 2280 vertical feet, 97 runs.

Sugar Bowl SKIING, SNOWBOARDING
(☎530-426-9000; www.sugarbowl.com; 629 Sugar Bowl Rd, off Donner Pass Rd, Norden; adult/youth

13-22yr/child 6-12yr $82/70/30; ☺9am-4pm; ⊞) Cofounded by Walt Disney in 1939, this is one of the Sierra's oldest ski resorts and a miniature Squaw Valley in terms of variety of terrain, including plenty of exhilarating gullies and chutes. Views are stellar on sunny days, but conditions go downhill pretty quickly, so to speak, during stormy weather.

The resort is 4 miles southeast of I-80 (exit Soda Springs/Norden). Stats: 13 lifts, 1500 vertical feet, 103 runs.

Boreal SKIING, SNOWBOARDING
(☎530-426-3666; www.rideboreal.com; 19659 Boreal Ridge Rd, off I-80 exit Castle Peak/Boreal Ridge Rd, Truckee; adult/child 5-12yr/youth 13-17yr $52/20/43, night-skiing adult/child $26/20, tubing $30; ☺9am-9pm; ⊞) Fun for newbies and intermediate skiers, Boreal is traditionally the first resort to open each year in the Tahoe area. For boarders, there are five terrain parks including a competition-level 450ft superpipe. Boreal is the only North Tahoe downhill resort besides Squaw that offers night skiing. Stats: seven lifts, 500 vertical feet, 33 runs.

Soda Springs SKIING, SNOWBOARDING
(☎530-426-3901; www.skisodasprings.com; 10244 Soda Springs Rd, off I-80 exit Soda Springs/Norden, Soda Springs; adult/child under 18yr $39/30, snow-

mobiling $12, tubing $30; ⊙10am-4pm Thu-Mon, daily during holidays; ⊛) This cute little resort is a winner with kids, who can snow-tube, ride around in pint-sized snowmobiles, or learn to ski and snowboard. Stats: two lifts, 650 vertical feet, 15 runs.

Donner Ski Ranch   SKIING, SNOWBOARDING
(☑530-426-3635; www.donnerskiranch.com; 19320 Donner Pass Rd, Norden; adult/child 7-12yr/youth 13-17yr $45/15/36; ⊙9am-4pm; ⊛) Generations of skiers have enjoyed this itty-bitty family-owned resort. It's a great place to teach your kids how to ski, or for beginners to build skills. Prices drop after 12:30pm. It's 3.5 miles southeast of I-80, exit Soda Springs/Norden. Stats: six lifts, 750 vertical feet, 52 runs.

Tahoe Donner   SKIING, SNOWBOARDING
(☑530-587-9444; www.tahoedonner.com; 11603 Snowpeak Way, off I-80 exit Donner Pass Rd, Truckee; adult/child 7-12yr/youth 13-17yr $45/21/40; ⊙9am-4pm; ⊛) Small, low-key and low-tech, Tahoe Donner is a darling resort with family-friendly beginner and intermediate runs only. Stats: five lifts, 600 vertical feet, 14 runs.

Tahoe City & Around

Squaw Valley   SKIING, SNOWBOARDING
(Map p336; ☑530-452-4331; www.squaw.com; 1960 Squaw Valley Rd, off Hwy 89, Olympic Valley; adult/youth 13-22yr/child under 13yr $114/94/66; ⊛) Few ski hounds can resist the siren call of this mega-sized, world-class, see-and-be-seen resort that hosted the 1960 Winter Olympic Games. Hardcore skiers thrill to white-knuckle cornices, chutes and bowls, while beginners practice their turns in a separate area on the upper mountain.

The valley turn-off is 5 miles northwest of Tahoe City. Stats: 29 lifts, 2850 vertical feet, over 170 runs.

Alpine Meadows   SKIING, SNOWBOARDING
(Map p336; ☑530-452-4356; www.skialpine. com; 2600 Alpine Meadows Rd, off Hwy 89, Tahoe City; adult/child under 13yr/youth 13-22yr $114/66/94; ⊙9am-4pm) Though now owned by neighboring Squaw (tickets are good at both resorts and a free shuttle connects them), Alpine remains a no-nonsense resort without the fancy village, attitude or crowds. It gets more snow than Squaw and its open-boundary policy makes it the most backcountry-friendly around. Boarders jib down the mountain in a terrain park designed by Eric Rosenwald. Also look for the supersmart and adorable ski patrol dogs.

The turn-off is 4 miles northwest of Tahoe City. Stats: 13 lifts, 1800 vertical feet, over 100 runs.

Homewood   SKIING, SNOWBOARDING
(Map p336; ☑530-525-2992; www.skihomewood. com; 5145 Westlake Blvd, off Hwy 89, Homewood; adult/child 5-12yr/youth 13-19yr $79/29/59; ⊙9am-4pm; ⊛) Larger than it looks from the road, this gem, 6 miles south of Tahoe City, proves that bigger isn't always better. Locals and in-the-know visitors cherish the awesome lake views, laid-back ambience,

LAKE TAHOE TAHOE SKI, SNOWBOARD & SNOWSHOE AREAS

ⓘ TOP WAYS TO SKI TAHOE FOR LESS MONEY

Midweek and half-day afternoon discounts on lift tickets are usually available, but expect higher prices on weekends and holidays. Lift-ticket rates go up incrementally almost every year, too. Parents should ask about the interchangeable 'Parent Predicament' lift tickets offered by some resorts, which let one parent ski while the other one hangs with the kids, then switch off later.

The **Bay Area Ski Bus** (☑925-680-4386; www.bayareaskibus.com) allows you to leave the headache of driving I-80 to others. Round-trips start at $109 including lift tickets, with various add-on packages available. Pick-up locations include San Francisco and Sacramento.

In San Francisco, **Sports Basement** (www.sportsbasement.com) sells deeply discounted lift tickets and has the best deals on multiday rental equipment because it doesn't charge for pick-up or drop-off days.

Handy money-saving websites:

Ski Lake Tahoe (www.skilaketahoe.com) Portal for the seven biggest Tahoe resorts, with deals covering all.

Sliding on the Cheap (www.slidingonthecheap.com) Homegrown website listing discounts and deals on lift tickets.

ℹ WINTER DRIVING AROUND LAKE TAHOE

From late fall through early spring, always pack snow chains in case a storm rolls in. Chains can also be purchased and installed in towns along I-80 and Hwy 50. Also stash some emergency supplies (eg blankets, water, flashlights) in the trunk, just in case your car breaks down, traffic gets tied up or roads close completely due to snowfall or avalanche danger.

Before hopping in the car, check road closures and conditions:

California Department of Transportation (CalTrans; ☎ 800-427-7623; www.dot.ca.gov)

Nevada Department of Transportation (NDOT; ☎ 877-687-6237, within Nevada 511; www.nevadadot.com)

smaller crowds, tree-lined slopes, open bowls (including the excellent but expert 'Quail Face') and a high-speed quad that gets things moving.

Families love the wide, gentle slopes. It's also the best place to ski during stormy weather. Stats: eight lifts, 1650 vertical feet, 64 runs.

South Lake Tahoe

Heavenly SKIING, SNOWBOARDING
(Map p340; ☎ 775-586-7000; www.skiheavenly.com; 3860 Saddle Rd, South Lake Tahoe; adult/youth 13-18yr/child 5-12yr $99/89/59; ◷ 9am-4pm Mon-Fri, 8:30am-4pm Sat, Sun & holidays; ⊕) The 'mother' of all Tahoe mountains boasts the most acreage, the longest run (5.5 miles) and the biggest vertical drop around. Follow the sun by skiing on the Nevada side in the morning, moving to the California side in the afternoon. Views of the lake and the high desert are heavenly indeed.

Five terrain parks won't strand snowboarders of any skill level, with the High Roller for experts only. Stats: 29 lifts, 3500 vertical feet, 97 runs.

Kirkwood SKIING, SNOWBOARDING
(☎ 209-258-6000; www.kirkwood.com; 1501 Kirkwood Meadows Dr, off Hwy 88, Kirkwood; adult/child 5-12yr/youth 13-18yr $89/61/76; ◷ 9am-4pm) Off-the-beaten-path Kirkwood, set in a high-elevation valley, gets great snow and

holds it longer than almost any other Tahoe resort. It has stellar tree-skiing, gullies, chutes and terrain parks, and is the only Tahoe resort with backcountry runs accessible by snowcats. Novice out-of-bounds skiers should sign up in advance for backcountry safety-skills clinics.

It's 35 miles southwest of South Lake Tahoe via Hwy 89; ski-season shuttles are available (from $15). Stats: 15 lifts, 2000 vertical feet, 72 runs.

Sierra-at-Tahoe SNOWBOARDING, SKIING
(☎ 530-659-7453; www.sierraattahoe.com; 1111 Sierra-at-Tahoe-Rd, off Hwy 50, Twin Bridges; adult/child 5-12yr/youth 13-22yr $84/25/74; ◷ 9am-4pm Mon-Fri, 8:30am-4pm Sat, Sun & holidays; ⊕) About 18 miles southwest of South Lake Tahoe, this is snowboarding central, with five raging terrain parks and a 17ft-high superpipe. A great beginners' run meanders gently for 2.5 miles from the summit, but there are also gnarly steeps and chutes for speed demons.

Kids get four 'adventure zones', while adults-only Huckleberry Gates tempts with steep-and-deep backcountry terrain for experts. Stats: 14 lifts, 2200 vertical feet, 46 runs.

Nevada

Mt Rose SKIING, SNOWBOARDING
(☎ 775-849-0704; www.mtrose.com; 22222 Mt Rose Hwy/Hwy 431, Reno; adult/child 6-12yr/youth 13-19yr $79/34/59; ◷ 9am-4pm) Conveniently the closest ski resort to Reno, Mt Rose has Tahoe's highest base elevation (8260ft) and offers four terrain parks and good snow

DON'T MISS

SNOWSHOEING UNDER THE STARS

A crisp quiet night with a blazing glow across the lake. What could be more magical than a full-moon snowshoe tour? Reserve ahead, as ramblings at these places are very popular:

➜ Ed Z'Berg Sugar Pine Point State Park (p351)

➜ Squaw Valley (p355)

➜ Tahoe Donner (p333)

➜ Northstar California (p332)

➜ Kirkwood (p334)

SLEDDING, TUBING & SNOW PLAY FOR KIDS

Major ski resorts such as Heavenly and Kirkwood around South Lake Tahoe, and Squaw Valley and Northstar California near Truckee, offer sledding hills for the kiddos, some with tubing rentals and thrilling rope tows. Smaller ski mountains including Sierra-at-Tahoe outside South Lake Tahoe, and Boreal, Soda Springs and Tahoe Donner, all near Truckee, also offer child-friendly slopes.

To avoid the crowds, bring your own sleds to designated local snow-play areas at North Tahoe Regional Park in Tahoe Vista on the north shore, or to Nevada's Incline Village, Tahoe Meadows off the Mt Rose Hwy (Hwy 431) or Spooner Summit on Hwy 50, all along the east shore. Back in California, DIY Sno-Parks (☑916-324-1222; www.parks.ca.gov; pass per day/yr $5/25) are found along Hwy 89 at Blackwood Canyon (Map p336), 3 miles south of Tahoe City on the west shore, and Taylor Creek, just north of Camp Richardson at South Lake Tahoe. Coming from Sacramento or the San Francisco Bay Area, two Sno-Parks are along I-80 at Yuba Gap (exit 161) and Donner Summit (exit 176 Castle Peak/Boreal Ridge Rd); their parking lots often fill by 11am on winter weekends. Buy required Sno-Park parking passes online or at local shops.

For private groomed sledding and tubing hills, swing by Hansen's Resort (Map p340; ☑530-544-3361; www.hansensresort.com; 1360 Ski Run Blvd; per person incl rental per hr $15; ⊙9am-5pm) in South Lake Tahoe or Adventure Mountain (☑530-577-4352; www.adventuremountaintahoe.com; 21200 Hwy 50; per car $20, tube/2-person sled rental per day $20/10; ⊙10am-4:30pm Mon-Fri, 9am-4:30pm Sat, Sun & holidays), south of town at Echo Summit.

conditions well into spring. 'The Chutes' expert terrain delivers some screamers along its north-facing steeps. Crowds aren't too bad, but the mountain's exposure means it gets hammered in a storm and avalanche control may intermittently close runs.

Excellent weekday deals online; round-trip Reno shuttle $15. Stats: eight lifts, 1800 vertical feet, 60 runs.

Diamond Peak　　　　SKIING, SNOWBOARDING
(Map p336; ☑775-832-1177; www.diamondpeak.com; 1210 Ski Way, off Tahoe Blvd/Hwy 28, Incline Village; adult/child 7-12yr/youth 13-23yr $59/120/49; ⊙9am-4pm; ⊛) This midsize mountain is a good place to learn, and boarders can romp around the terrain park, but experts get bored quickly. From the top you'll have a 360-degree panorama of desert, peaks and the lake. Free ski-season shuttle from Incline Village and Crystal Bay. Stats: six lifts, 1840 vertical feet, 30 runs.

Cross-Country Skiing & Snowshoeing

Tahoe's cross-country ski resorts are usually open daily from December through March, and sometimes into April. Most rent equipment and offer lessons; reservations typically aren't taken for either, so show up early in the morning for the best availability.

Truckee & Donner Pass

★ Royal Gorge　　　　SKIING, SNOWSHOEING
(☑530-426-3871; www.royalgorge.com; 9411 Pahatsi Rd, off I-80 exit Soda Springs/Norden, Soda Springs; adult/youth 13-22yr $29/22; ⊙9am-5pm; ⊛⊛) Nordic skiing aficionados won't want to pass up a spin around North America's largest cross-country resort (now operated by Sugar Bowl) with its mind-boggling 125 miles of groomed track crisscrossing 6000 acres of terrain. It has great skating lanes and diagonal stride tracks and also welcomes telemark skiers and snowshoers.

Group lessons are offered a few times daily, with ski camps for kids ages five to 12 (reservations recommended). For a twist, catch some air at the new on-site Sierra Snowkite Center (www.sierrasnowkite.com).

Tahoe Donner　　　　SKIING, SNOWSHOEING
(☑530-587-9484; www.tdxc.com; 15275 Alder Creek Rd, off I-80 exit Donner Pass Rd, Truckee; adult/child 7-12yr/youth 13-17yr $27/11/21; ⊙8:30am-5pm, night skiing 5-7pm Wed; ⊛) Occupying 4800 acres of thick forest north of Truckee, Tahoe Donner has lovely and varied terrain with over 62 miles of groomed tracks that cover three track systems and 51 trails. The most beautiful spot is secluded Euer Valley, where a warm hut serves food on weekends. A 1.5-mile loop stays open for night skiing, usually on Wednesdays.

Lake Tahoe

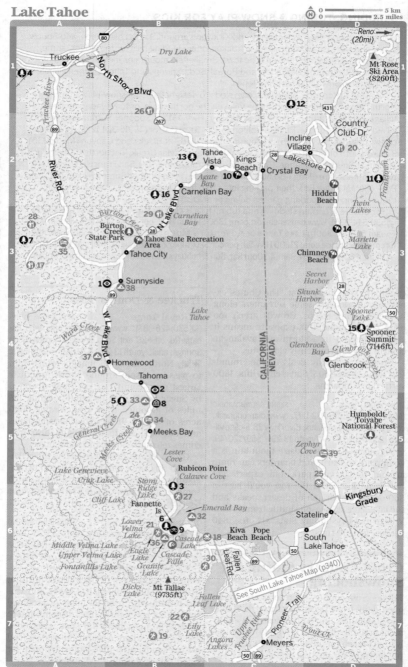

Lake Tahoe

Group lessons for beginners and 'Tiny Tracks', a supervised kids' ski and snow-play camp, are available; reserve ahead for intermediate skills clinics.

Northstar California   SKIING, SNOWSHOEING
(Map p336; ☎530-562-3270; www.northstarcalifornia.com; 5001 Northstar Dr, off Hwy 267; adult/child 5-12yr $31/17; ⊙9am-3pm Mon-Thu, 8:30am-4pm Fri-Sun & holidays) Seven miles southeast of I-80, this mega ski resort has a highly regarded Nordic and telemark school, making it a great choice for novices. A package, which includes the trail fee, ski rental and a group lesson, costs $75. Afterwards you can explore the nearly 25 miles of groomed trails. Moonlight snowshoe tours take place a few times per month.

Clair Tappaan Lodge   SKIING, SNOWSHOEING
(☎530-426-3632, hut reservations 800-679-6775; www.sierraclub.org/outings/lodges/ctl; adult/child under 12yr $7/3.50; ⊙9am-5pm; 🐾) You can ski right out the door if you're staying at this rustic mountain lodge near Donner Summit. Its 7 miles of groomed and tracked trails are great for beginners and intermediate skiers, and connect to miles of backcountry skiing. Stop by the lodge for ski and snowshoe rent-

als, and value-priced ski lessons at all skill levels (sign-up starts at 9am daily).

Tahoe City & Around

Tahoe Cross Country   SKIING, SNOWSHOEING
(Map p336; ☎530-583-5475; www.tahoexc.org; 925 Country Club Dr, off N Lake Blvd/Hwy 28, Tahoe City; adult/child under 12yr/youth 13-17yr $24/free/20; ⊙8:30am-5pm; 🐾🐕) Run by the nonprofit Tahoe Cross Country Ski Education Association, this center, about 3 miles north of Tahoe City, has 40 miles of groomed tracks (23 trails) that wind through lovely forest, suitable for all skill levels. Group lessons come with good-value equipment-rental packages; half-day and twilight trail-pass discounts are also available. Ask about free skate clinics and beginners' cross-country mid-week lessons.

Dogs are allowed on three trails.

Squaw Valley   SKIING, SNOWSHOEING
(Map p336; ☎530-583-6300; www.squaw.com; 1960 Squaw Valley Rd, off Hwy 89; trail pass/with ski or snowshoe rental $18/32) Although downhill rules the roost at this ex-Olympic resort, 11 miles of groomed track winding around an alpine meadow will keep beginner-level Nordic skiers

busy, too. Book ahead for monthly moonlight snowshoe tours high atop the mountain.

To reach the trailheads at the Resort at Squaw Creek, which supplies cross-country ski, snowshoe and sled rentals, grab a free shuttle from the downhill ski area parking lot.

South Lake Tahoe

Kirkwood   SKIING, SNOWSHOEING
(☎209-258-7248; www.kirkwood.com; 1501 Kirkwood Meadows Dr, off Hwy 88, Kirkwood; adult/child 5-12yr/youth 13-18yr $24/12/18; ⊙9am-4pm; 🐾) Definitely not a jogging trail, this cross-country network has sections that are very challenging and where you can actually gain some elevation. Groomed track stretches for 50 miles with separate skating lanes and three trailside warming huts; the views from the higher slopes are phenomenal.

Rentals, lessons and tours are all available. Dogs are welcome on two trails. It's at least an hour's drive south of Lake Tahoe.

Camp Richardson Resort   SKIING, SNOWSHOEING
(☎530-542-6584; www.camprichardson.com; 1900 Jameson Beach Rd, off Emerald Bay Rd/Hwy 89, South Lake Tahoe; trail pass $12; ⊙9am-4pm) At this woodsy resort with 6 miles of groomed track, you can ski lakeside or head for the solitude of the Desolation Wilderness. Locals turn out in droves for full-moon ski and snowshoe parties, which kick off at the resort's Beacon Bar & Grill (p348).

SOUTH LAKE TAHOE & STATELINE

Highly congested and arguably overdeveloped, South Lake Tahoe is a chockablock commercial strip bordering the lake and framed by picture-perfect alpine mountains. At the foot of the world-class Heavenly mountain resort, and buzzing from the gambling tables in the casinos just across the border in Stateline, NV, Lake Tahoe's south shore draws visitors with a cornucopia of activities, lodging and restaurant options, especially for summer beach access and tons of powdery winter snow.

⊙ Sights

Heavenly Gondola   CABLE CAR
(Map p340; www.skiheavenly.com; Heavenly Village; adult/child 5-12yr/youth 13-18yr from $45/27/37; ⊙10am-5pm Jun-Aug, reduced off-season hours; 🚠) Soar to the top of the world as you ride this gondola, which sweeps you from Heavenly Village some 2.4 miles up the mountain in just 12 minutes. From the observation deck at 9123ft, get gobstopping panoramic views of the entire Tahoe Basin, the Desolation Wilderness and Carson Valley.

From here jump on the Tamarack Express chairlift to go to the mountain summit and the Tamarack Lodge restaurant and bar.

Tallac Historic Site   HISTORIC SITE
(Map p340; www.tahoeheritage.org; Tallac Rd; optional tour adult/child $10/5; ⊙10am-4pm daily mid-Jun–Sep, Fri & Sat late May–mid-Jun; 🐾) FREE Sheltered by a pine grove and bordering a wide, sandy beach, this national historic site sits on the archaeologically excavated grounds of the former Tallac Resort, a swish vacation retreat for San Francisco's high society around the turn of the 20th century. Feel free to amble or cycle around the forested grounds, today transformed into a community arts hub, where leashed dogs are allowed.

Inside the 1921 Baldwin Estate, the museum has exhibits on the history of the resort and its founder, Elias 'Lucky' Baldwin, who made a bundle off Nevada's Comstock Lode. Nearby is the 1894 Pope Estate, now used for art exhibits and open for guided tours (daily except Wednesday). The boathouse of the Valhalla Estate functions as a theater venue. The 1923 Grand Hall contains an art gallery and gift shop. In summer, concerts, plays and other cultural events happen here, most notably the three-decade-old Valhalla Festival of Arts, Music & Film (☎530-541-4975; www.valhallatahoe.com; ⊙Jul-Aug).

The parking lot is about 3 miles north of the 'Y' junction of Hwys 89 and 50.

Lake Tahoe Historical Society Museum   MUSEUM
(Map p340; ☎530-541-5458; www.laketahoemuseum.org; 3058 Lake Tahoe Blvd; ⊙usually 11am-3pm weekends) FREE A small but interesting museum displays artifacts from Tahoe's pioneer past, including Washoe tribal baskets, vintage black-and-white films, hoary mining memorabilia and a model of a classic Lake Tahoe steamship. On summer Saturday afternoons, join a volunteer-led tour of the restored 1930s cabin out back.

🏃 Activities
Hiking
Many miles of summer hiking trails start from the top of the Heavenly Gondola

(p338), many with mesmerizing lake views. On the Nevada side of the state line, Lam Watah Nature Trail meanders for just over a mile each way across USFS land, winding underneath pine trees and beside meadows and ponds, on its way between Hwy 50 and Nevada Beach, starting from the community park off Kahle Dr.

Several easy kid- and dog-friendly hikes begin near the United States Forest Service (USFS) Taylor Creek Visitor Center (p348) off Hwy 89. The mile-long, mostly flat Rainbow Trail loops around a creekside meadow, with educational panels about ecology and wildlife along the way. On the opposite side of Hwy 89, the gentle, rolling one-mile Moraine Trail follows the shoreline of Fallen Leaf Lake; free trailhead parking is available near campsite No 75. Up at cooler elevations, the mile-long round-trip to Angora Lakes is another popular trek with kids, especially because it ends by a sandy swimming beach and a summer snack bar selling ice-cream treats. You'll find the trailhead on Angora Ridge Rd, off Tahoe Mountain Rd, accessed from Hwy 89.

For longer and more strenuous day hikes to alpine lakes and meadows, several major trailheads provide easy access to the evocatively named Desolation Wilderness: Echo Lakes (south of town); Glen Alpine (near Lily Lake, south of Fallen Leaf Lake), to visit a historic tourist resort and waterfall; and Tallac (opposite the entrance to Baldwin Beach). The latter two trailheads also lead to the peak of Mt Tallac (9735ft), a difficult 10- to 12-mile day hike. Self-serve wilderness permits for day hikers only are freely available at trailheads; overnight backpacking permits are subject to quotas.

Beaches & Swimming

On the California side, the nicest strands are Pope Beach (Map p340; per car $7), Kiva Beach (Map p340) and Baldwin Beach (Map p336; per car $7), each with picnic tables and barbecue grills; Kiva Beach offers free parking and allows leashed dogs, too. They're all found along Emerald Bay Rd (Hwy 89), running west and east of Tallac Historic Site. Nearby, Fallen Leaf Lake, where scenes from the Hollywood flicks *The Bodyguard* and *City of Angels* were filmed, is also good for summer swims. El Dorado Beach (Map p340) is a free public beach in town, just off Lake Tahoe Blvd.

Many folks prefer to head over to Stateline and keep driving north 2 miles to pretty Nevada Beach (Map p336; per car $7), where the wind really picks up in the afternoons, or always-busy Zephyr Cove (www.zephyr-cove.com; 760 Hwy 50; per car $8), which has

---

DON'T MISS

HIKING & BACKPACKING THE DESOLATION WILDERNESS

Sculpted by powerful glaciers aeons ago, this relatively compact wilderness area (Map p336; www.fs.usda.gov/eldorado/specialplaces) spreads south and west of Lake Tahoe and is the most popular in the Sierra Nevada. It's a 100-sq-mile wonderland of polished granite peaks, deep-blue alpine lakes, glacier-carved valleys and pine forests that thin quickly at the higher elevations. In summer wildflowers nudge out from between the rocks.

All this splendor makes for some exquisite backcountry exploration. Six major trailheads provide access from the Lake Tahoe side: Glen Alpine (Map p336), Tallac (Map p336), Echo Lakes (near Echo Summit on Hwy 50), Bayview (Map p336), Eagle Falls (Map p336) and Meeks Bay (Map p336). Tallac and Eagle Falls get the most traffic, but solitude comes quickly once you've scampered past the day hikers.

Wilderness permits are required year-round for both day and overnight explorations. Day hikers can self-register at the trailheads, but overnight permits must be either reserved online (fee $6) at www.recreation.gov and printed at home, or picked up in person at one of the three USFS offices in South Lake Tahoe and Pollack Pines. Permits cost $5 per person for one night, $10 per person for two or more nights.

Quotas are in effect from late May through the end of September. Over half of the permits for the season may be reserved online, usually starting in late March or April; the other permits are available on a first-arrival basis on the day of entry only.

Bearproof canisters are strongly advised in all wilderness areas (hanging your food in trees will not work – these bears are too smart!). Borrow canisters for free from the USFS offices. Bring bug repellent as the mosquitoes can be merciless. Wood fires are a no-no, but portable stoves are OK. Dogs must be leashed at *all* times.

South Lake Tahoe

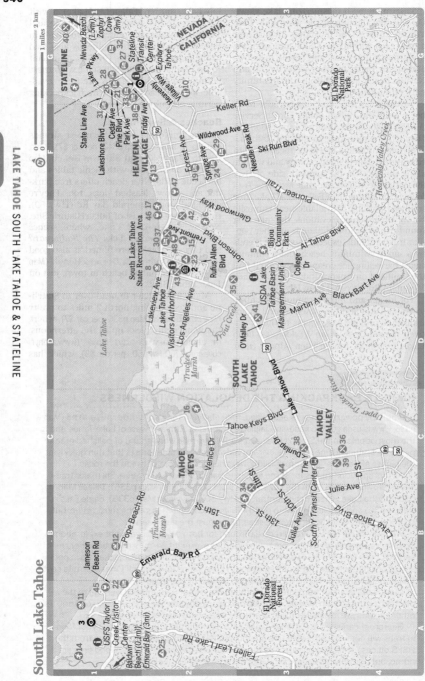

South Lake Tahoe

rustic resort and marina facilities along its sandy mile-long shoreline.

Boating & Water Sports

Ski Run Boat Company (Map p340; ☑530-544-0200; www.tahoesports.com; 900 Ski Run Blvd), at the Ski Run Marina (Map p340), and **Tahoe Keys Boat & Charter Rentals** (Map p340; ☑530-544-8888; www.tahoesports.com; 2435 Venice Dr), at the Tahoe Keys Marina (Map p340), both rent motorized powerboats, pontoons, sailboats and jet skis (rentals $110 to $235 per hour), as well as human-powered kayaks, canoes, hydro bikes, paddleboats and paddleboard sets (per hour $25 to $35). If you want to go parasailing up to 1200ft above Lake Tahoe's waves, the Ski Run Marina branch can hook you up (rides $55 to $80).

Kayak Tahoe KAYAKING, WATER SPORTS (☑530-544-2011; www.kayaktahoe.com; kayak single/double 1hr $20/32, 1 day $65/85, lessons & tours from $40; ☉10am-5pm Sat & Sun Jun-Sep) Rent a kayak or stand-up paddleboard, take a lesson or sign up for a guided tour, including sunset cove paddles, trips to Emerald Bay and explorations of the Upper Truckee River estuary and the eastern shore. Five seasonal locations at Timber Cove Marina (Map p340), Vikingsholm (Emerald Bay) and Baldwin, Pope and Nevada Beaches.

Zephyr Cove Resort & Marina WATER SPORTS (☑775-589-4901; www.zephyrcove.com; 760 Hwy 50, NV; ☉9am-5pm) Rents powerboats, pedal boats, waverunners, jet skis, canoes, kayaks and stand-up paddleboards; also offers single and tandem parasailing flights.

Camp Richardson Resort Marina   WATER SPORTS
(Map p340; ☑ 530-542-6570; www.camprichardson.com; 1900 Jameson Beach Rd) Rents powerboats, paddleboats, water skis, kayaks and stand-up paddleboarding gear.

Mountain Biking

For expert mountain bikers, the classic **Mr Toad's Wild Ride**, with its steep downhill sections and banked turns reminiscent of a Disneyland theme-park ride, should prove sufficiently challenging. Usually open from June until October, the one-way trail along Saxon Creek starts off Hwy 89 south of town near Grass Lake and Luther Pass.

Intermediate mountain bikers should steer toward the mostly single-track **Powerline Trail**, which traverses ravines and creeks. You can pick up the trail off Ski Run Blvd near the Heavenly mountain resort, from the western end of Saddle Rd. For a more leisurely outing over mostly level terrain, you can pedal around scenic **Fallen Leaf Lake**. Anyone with good lungs might try the **Angora Lakes Trail**, which is steep but technically easy and rewards you with sweeping views of Mt Tallac and Fallen Leaf Lake. It starts further east, off Angora Ridge and Tahoe Mountain Ridge Rds.

For shuttle service and mountain-bike rentals for Mr Toad's Wild Ride, the Tahoe Rim Trail (p349) and other downhill adventures, as well as family-friendly tours, talk to **Wanna Ride** (☑ 775-588-5800; www.wannaridetahoe.com; ☺ 8am-4pm Tue-Sat). For

mountain-biking trail conditions, race schedules, volunteer days and other special events, contact the **Tahoe Area Mountain Biking Association** (www.mountainbiketahoe.org).

Cycling

The **South Lake Tahoe Bike Path** is a level, leisurely ride suitable for anyone. It heads west from El Dorado Beach, eventually connecting with the **Pope-Baldwin Bike Path** past Camp Richardson, Tallac Historic Site and the USFS Taylor Creek Visitor Center. Visitor centers carry the excellent Lake Tahoe bike route map, also available online from the **Lake Tahoe Bicycle Coalition** (www.tahoebike.org), which has an info-packed website for cycling enthusiasts. **Anderson's Bike Rental** (Map p340; ☑ 877-720-2121, 530-541-0500; www.laketahoebikerental.com; 645 Emerald Bay Rd/Hwy 89; per hr $10; 🖪) rents hybrid bikes with helmets.

Golf & Disc Golf

Edgewood Tahoe Golf Course   GOLF
(Map p340; ☑ 775-588-3566; www.edgewood-tahoe.com; 100 Lake Pkwy, Stateline; green fee $110-240) Stunning lakeside scenery is a major distraction at this challenging championship 18-hole course designed by George Fazio, a favorite for celebrity golf tournaments. Tee-time reservations are required; cart and club rentals available.

Bijou Golf Course   GOLF
(Map p340; ☑ 530-542-6097; www.cityofslt.us; 3464 Fairway Ave; green fee $17-28, club/cart rental

---

SOUTH LAKE TAHOE FOR CHILDREN

With oodles of outdoor activities, families will never run out of mountains to explore and beaches to dig. If the kids start to get fractious though, try one of these local favorites to mix things up a little.

Stream Profile Chamber (Map p340; ☑ 530-543-2674; www.tahoeheritage.org; trailhead at USFS Taylor Creek Visitor Center, off Hwy 89; ☺ 8am-5pm late May-Sep, 8am-4pm Oct; 🖪) Along a family-friendly hiking trail, this submerged glass structure in a teeming creek lets you check out what plants and fish live below the waterline. The best time to visit is in October during the Kokanee salmon run, when the brilliant red beauties arrive to spawn. See the website for scheduled activities.

Tahoe Bowl (Map p340; ☑ 530-544-3700; www.tahoebowl.com; 1030 Fremont Ave; game per person $4.50, shoe rental $4; 🖪) For yucky-weather days or to tire out the tots by bedtime, this is a fun indoor haunt with 16 bowling lanes, a small diner and pizza joint, and an air hockey table. Call ahead for open-play schedules.

Shops at Heavenly Village (Map p340; www.theshopsatheavenly.com; 1001 Heavenly Village Way; ☺ seasonal hr vary; 🖪) If you don't feel like wandering far, this downtown outdoor mall sets up a little putt-putt golf course in summer, and opens an outdoor ice-skating rink in winter. Check website for current schedules and prices.

> ### ① NAVIGATING SOUTH LAKE TAHOE TRAFFIC
>
> South Lake Tahoe's main east–west thoroughfare is a 5-mile stretch of Hwy 50 called Lake Tahoe Blvd. Most hotels and businesses hover around the California–Nevada state line and Heavenly Village. Casinos are located in Stateline, which is officially a separate city.
>
> West of town, Hwy 50 runs into Hwy 89 at the 'Y' junction. Heavy snowfall sometimes closes Hwy 89 north of the Tallac Historic Site. The section of Hwy 89 between South Lake Tahoe and Emerald Bay is also known as Emerald Bay Rd.
>
> Traffic all along Hwy 50 between the 'Y' junction and Heavenly Village gets jammed around lunchtime and again by 5pm Monday to Friday in both summer and winter, but Sunday afternoons, when skiers head back down the mountain, are the worst.
>
> An alternate, less-crowded route through town is Pioneer Trail, which branches east off the Hwy 89/50 junction (south of the 'Y') and reconnects with Hwy 50 at Stateline.

$15/5; ☺ mid-Apr–Oct) So you don't know your putter from your 9-iron? That's OK at this laid-back, no-reservations municipal course with views of Heavenly Mountain. Built in the 1920s, it's got just 9 holes, which you can play twice around.

Kirkwood Disc-Wood DISC GOLF
(☎ 209-258-7210; www.kirkwood.com; 1501 Kirkwood Meadows Dr, Kirkwood) FREE Crazy terrain, tons of distance and high-elevation Sierra Nevada views from an epic 18 holes. Call ahead for directions and to check opening hours before making the hour-long drive southwest of South Lake Tahoe.

Zephyr Cove Park DISC GOLF
(www.douglascountynv.gov; Hwy 50 at Warrior Way, NV) FREE PDGA-approved 18-hole course is scenically set on the eastern shore, with kick-ass uphill and downhill shoots.

Bijou Community Park DISC GOLF
(Map p340; www.cityofslt.us; 1201 Al Tahoe Blvd) FREE In town, these 27 holes will taunt even experts with loooong greens on a mostly flat, forested course (ahoy, trees!).

Horseback Riding
Both **Camp Richardson Corral & Pack Station** (Map p340; ☎ 877-541-3113, 530-541-3113; www.camprichardsoncorral.com; Emerald Bay Rd/Hwy 89; trail rides $43-164; 🐎) and **Zephyr Cove Stables** (☎ 775-588-5664; www.zephyrcovestable.com; Hwy 50, NV; trail rides $40-80; 🐎), about 4 miles north of Stateline casinos, offer daily horseback rides in summer, varying from one-hour kid-friendly trips through the forest, to extended treks with meadow and lake views (reservations required).

Zip-Lining
Zip Tahoe ZIP-LINING
(☎ 209-258-7330; www.ziptahoe.com; 1501 Kirkwood Meadows Dr, Kirkwood; 2hr tour $125; ☺ Dec-mid-Apr & mid-Jun–mid-Sep) At Kirkwood, careen through the tree canopy over six zip lines and two suspension bridges, checking out the snowboarders below in winter or the wildflowers in summer. Kids aged eight and up permitted.

☞ Tours
Lake Tahoe Cruises CRUISE
(Map p340; ☎ 800-238-2463; www.zephyrcove.com; adult/child from $49/15) Two paddle wheelers ply Lake Tahoe's 'big blue' year-round with a variety of sightseeing, drinking, dining and dancing cruises, including a narrated two-hour daytime trip to Emerald Bay. The *Tahoe Queen* leaves from Ski Run Marina (summer parking fee $8) in town, while the MS *Dixie II* is based at Zephyr Cove Marina on the eastern shore in Nevada.

Woodwind Cruises CRUISE
(☎ 775-588-3000; www.tahoecruises.com; Zephyr Cove Marina, 760 Hwy 50, NV; 1hr cruise adult/child 2-12yr from $42/15) Champagne and happy-hour floats aboard this sailing catamaran are the perfect way to chill after an afternoon lazing on the beach. Five daily departures during summer; reservations recommended.

Action Watersports BOAT TOUR
(Map p340; ☎ 530-544-5387; www.action-watersports.com; Timber Cove Marina, 3411 Lake Tahoe Blvd; adult/child under 13yr $59/30) In a hurry to get to Emerald Cove? Wanna avoid those near-constant traffic jams on Hwy 89? Jump on board the *Tahoe Thunder* speedboat, which zips across the lake – watch out,

though, you'll get wet! Also offers parasailing rides ($55 to $80).

Lake Tahoe Balloons
BALLOONING

(Map p340; ☑ 530-544-1221; www.laketahoeballoons.com; per person $295) From May through October (weather permitting), you can cruise on a catamaran launched from Tahoe Keys Marina, then clamber aboard a hot-air balloon launched right from the boat's upper deck. The lake and Sierra Nevada mountain views may take away what little breath you have left at 10,000ft. Reservations required.

🛏 Sleeping

🏠 South Lake Tahoe

South Lake Tahoe has a bazillion choices for all budgets. Lodging options line Lake Tahoe Blvd (Hwy 50) between Stateline and Ski Run Blvd. Further west, closer to the 'Y' at the intersection of Hwys 50 and 89 is a string of mostly budget motels ranging from barely adequate to inexcusable. Peak season is generally winter ski season from December to March and summer from June to August. Some properties may impose minimum stays, especially on weekends and holidays. For more ski condos and hotel rooms near the slopes, contact Heavenly (☑ 775-586-7000; www.skiheavenly.com).

Camp Richardson Resort
CABINS, CAMPGROUND $

(Map p340; ☑ 530-541-1801; www.camprichardson.com; 1900 Jameson Beach Rd; tent sites from $35, RV sites with partial/full hookups from $40/45, r $95-215, cabins $125-263; 🛜) Removed from downtown's strip-mall aesthetic, this sprawling family camp is a hectic place offering seasonal camping (expect marauding bears all night long!), forested cabins rented by the week in summer, and so-so beachside hotel rooms. Sports gear and bicycle rentals are available, and there's a popular ice-cream parlor across the road. Wi-fi in lobby only.

Fallen Leaf Campground
CAMPGROUND $

(Map p340; ☑ 530-544-0426, reservations 877-444-6777; www.recreation.gov; Fallen Leaf Lake Rd; tent & RV sites $32-34, yurts $84; ⏱ mid-May–mid-Oct; 🛠) Near the north shore of stunning Fallen Leaf Lake, this is one of the biggest and most popular campgrounds on the south shore, with pay showers and approximately 200 wooded sites and six canvas-sided yurts that can sleep a family of five (bring your own sleeping bags).

Big Pines Mountain House
MOTEL $

(Map p340; ☑ 530-541-5155; www.thebigpines.com; 4083 Cedar Ave; r incl breakfast $50-129; 🌸@🛜🐾🏊) Choose from over 70 comfortable rooms in various sizes – some with blissful mountain views – and in summertime, stroll to the private beach nearby or take a dip in the heated pool. Gas fireplaces cozy up the king kitchenette rooms. Pet fee $15.

Blue Lake Inn
MOTEL $

(Map p340; ☑ 530-544-6459; www.thebluelakeinn.com; 944 Friday Ave; r incl breakfast $89-104; 🌸🛜🐾🏊) A good value choice near the Heavenly Gondola, these ample motel rooms have the core amenities: microwave, fridge, coffeemaker and flat-screen TV, plus a hot tub and outdoor pool. Pet fee $15.

Campground by the Lake
CAMPGROUND $

(Map p340; ☑ 530-542-6096; www.cityofslt.us; 1150 Rufus Allen Blvd; tent & RV sites with/without hookups from $40/29, cabins $49-80; ⏱ Apr-Oct; 🛜🏊) Highway noise can be an around-the-clock irritant, though proximity to the city pool and ice rink make this wooded in-town campground with an RV dump station a decent choice. Basic sleeping-platform cabins are available between Memorial Day (late May) and Labor Day (early September).

Alder Inn
INN $$

(Map p340; ☑ 530-544-4485; www.thealderinn.com; 1072 Ski Run Blvd; r $99-150; 🛜🏊) Even better than staying at your best friend's house by the lake, this hospitable inn on the Heavenly ski-shuttle route charms with color schemes that really pop, pillow-top mattresses, organic bath goodies, mini-fridges, microwaves and flat-screen TVs. Dip your toes in the kidney-shaped pool in summer. Continental breakfast included on weekends.

968 Park Hotel
BOUTIQUE HOTEL $$

(Map p340; ☑ 530-544-0968; www.968parkhotel.com; 968 Park Ave; r $109-309; @🛜🏊) 🌿 A refashioned motel with serious hipster edge, recycled, rescued and re-envisioned building materials have made this LEED-certified property an aesthetically pleasing ecohaven near the lake. A new lobby bar offers free wine tastings on Friday evenings, and in summer, unwind in a cabana by the sunny pool or in the zen garden before sinking into your dreamy Sterling bed.

Paradice Inn
MOTEL **$$**

(Map p340; ☎530-544-6800; www.paradice-moteltahoe.com; 953 Park Ave; r $148-218; ❄🌐) Harried travelers will appreciate the fabulous hospitality (turndown service!) at this small two-story motel. Step outside your minimalist room bordered by flower baskets, then stroll across the street to the Heavenly Gondola. Families should ask about the two-bedroom suites.

Fireside Lodge
INN **$$**

(Map p340; ☎530-544-5515; www.tahoefiresidelodge.com; 515 Emerald Bay Rd/Hwy 89; d incl breakfast $149-219; 🌐🐾) This woodsy cabin B&B wholeheartedly welcomes families, with free bikes, kayaks and snow shoes to borrow and evening s'mores and wine and cheese. Kitchenette rooms and suites have river-rock gas fireplaces, cozy patchwork quilts and pioneer-themed touches like wagon wheels or vintage skis. Pet fee $25.

Heavenly Valley Lodge
B&B **$$**

(Map p340; ☎530-564-1500; www.heavenlyvalleylodge.com; 1261 Ski Run Blvd; d incl breakfast $145-255; 🌐🐾) Located along the Heavenly shuttle route, this family-run place perfects the balance of old Tahoe – all-fireplace rooms of knotty pine and river rock – and great amenities, like DVD players and a huge movie library, a fire-pit patio and afternoon happy hour. Some kitchenette units; pet fee $25.

Basecamp Hotel
BOUTIQUE HOTEL **$$**

(Map p340; ☎530-208-0180; www.basecamphotels.com; 4143 Cedar Ave; d $109-229, 8-person bunkroom $209-299, all incl breakfast; 🌐🐾) 🐾 Recycled wood, original nature-themed canvases and artsy artifacts gussy up this stylish former motel. Lucky couples can rough it in the 'Great Indoors' room with a tented bed and faux campfire, and families can overnight in spacious bunk-bed rooms. A rooftop hot tub, beer and wine bar, and communal dinner nights sweeten the deal. Pet fee $40.

Spruce Grove Cabins
CABINS **$$**

(Map p340; ☎530-544-0549; www.sprucegrovetahoe.com; 3599-3605 Spruce Ave; 4-/6-person cabin $169/215; 🌐🐾) Away from the Heavenly hubbub, these tidy, private cabins are fenced off on a quiet residential street. The vintage look of the kitchen-equipped cabins, from knotty pine walls to the stone-bordered gas fireplaces, will make you feel like you're staying lakeside. Cleaning fee $30; refundable pet deposit $100.

Let your dogs cavort in the yard while you swing in the hammock or soak in outdoor hot tubs.

Inn by the Lake
HOTEL **$$$**

(Map p340; ☎530-542-0330; www.innbythelake.com; 3300 Lake Tahoe Blvd; r $180-300; ❄@🌐🐾) Rooms here are rather nondescript, although a bilevel outdoor hot tub, spa suites with kitchens, and bicycles and snowshoes to borrow are nifty. Rooms out back are cheaper and quieter, but then you'll miss the lake views. Pet fee $20.

Deerfield Lodge at Heavenly
BOUTIQUE HOTEL **$$$**

(Map p340; ☎530-544-3337; www.tahoedeerfieldlodge.com; 1200 Ski Run Blvd; r/ste incl breakfast from $179/229; ❄🌐) A small boutique hotel close to Heavenly ski resort, Deerfield has a dozen intimate rooms and spacious suites that each have a patio or balcony facing the green courtyard, along with a Jacuzzi, flickering gas fireplace and amusing coat racks crafted from skis and snowboards. Pet fee $25.

There's complimentary wine in the lobby, s'mores to be made over the fire pit, and barbecue grills appear in summer.

Timber Lodge
HOTEL **$$$**

(Map p340; ☎530-542-6600; www.marriott.com; 4100 Lake Tahoe Blvd; r $170-230, ste from $230; ❄@🌐🐾) Don't let the Marriott chaingang brand put you off this modern ski lodge with an enviable position, where you can watch the Heavenly Gondola whoosh by outside your window. Cookie-cutter hotel rooms have kitchenettes, while apartment-style 'vacation villa' suites come with full kitchens, gas fireplaces and deep soaking tubs for après-ski warm-ups. Parking fee $26.

Landing
LUXURY HOTEL **$$$**

(Map p340; ☎855-700-5263; www.thelandingtahoe.com; 4104 Lakeshore Blvd; d/ste from $319/619; ❄@🌐🐾) South Lake's newest and most luxurious lakeside resort dazzles with an in-house spa, marble bathrooms with toilet night lights and heated seats, Keurig coffeemakers, a private beach and the swank Jimmy's restaurant. Each room has a fireplace seating arrangement, and other perks include a complimentary town shuttle, a year-round outdoor pool and nightly wine tasting. Pet fee $100.

Stateline, NV

At Nevada's high-rise casino complexes, prices rise and fall like your luck at the slot machines. Season, day of the week and type of room are key. In winter ask about special ski-and-stay packages.

Nevada Beach Campground   CAMPGROUND $
(Map p336; ☎775-588-5562, reservations 877-444-6777; www.recreation.gov; off Hwy 50, NV; tent & RV sites $32-38; ☺mid-May–mid-Oct; ☒) Bed down on a carpet of pine needles at this tidy lakeside campground, about 3 miles north of Stateline, where 48 sites are nestled amid pines. Leashed dogs are allowed at campsites, but not the beach.

Zephyr Cove Resort   CABINS, CAMPGROUND $$
(Map p336; ☎775-589-4907; www.zephyrcove.com; 760 Hwy 50, NV; tent & RV sites with/without hookups from $73/41, cabins $160-389; ☺camping May-Sep, cabins year-round; ☎☒) In Nevada, about 4 miles north of Stateline, this family-oriented lakeside resort has historic cabins scattered among the pines and good facilities, including hot showers, barbecue grills and fire rings. Take your pick of 93 paved RV or 10 drive-in tent sites (some with lake views), or 47 walk-in tent sites tucked deeper into the shady forest.

Leashed dogs allowed, except on the main beach.

Harrah's   CASINO HOTEL $$
(Map p340; ☎775-588-6611; www.harrahslaketahoe.com; 15 Hwy 50, Stateline; r $80-369; ☒@☎☒) Clad in an oddly tasteful forest-green facade, this buzzing casino hotel is Stateline's top contender. Let yourself be swallowed up by even standard 'luxury' rooms, which each have two bathrooms with telephones, or spring for a luxury suite with panoramic lake-vista windows. For more eye-popping views, snag a window table at one of Harrah's upper-floor restaurants.

MontBleu   CASINO HOTEL $$
(Map p340; ☎775-588-3515; www.montbleuresort.com; 55 Hwy 50, Stateline; r $70-210, ste from $240; ☒@☎☒) The public areas may sport übercool modern boutique decor, but hallways are seriously dim. Recently remodeled rooms have fluffy duvets and art-deco-esque accents, and some of the marble-accented bathrooms sport hedonistic circular tubs. Rooms above the 5th floor are best, and the premier category have lake views. Unwind

in the lavish indoor pool lagoon, accented by a rockscape and mini waterfalls.

Harvey's   CASINO HOTEL $$
(Map p340; ☎775-588-2411; www.harveys-tahoe.com; 18 Hwy 50, Stateline; r $80-229; ☒@☎☒☒) Harvey's was South Lake Tahoe's first casino, and with 740 rooms, is also its biggest. Mountain Tower rooms have fancy marble bathrooms and oodles of space, but renovated Lake Tower rooms are more chic and design-savvy. The heated outdoor pool is open year-round, for beach and snow bunnies alike. Pet fee $75; wi-fi $11 daily.

🍴 Eating

For late-night cravings, each of the big casinos in Stateline has a 24-hour coffee shop for hangover-helper and night-owl breakfasts. If you're just looking for filling pub grub and après-ski appetizers and cocktails, most bars and cafes also serve just-OK food, some with waterfront views and live music, too.

Sprouts   VEGETARIAN $
(Map p340; 3123 Harrison Ave; mains $7-10; ☺8am-9pm; ☒☒) Cheerful chatter greets you at this energetic, mostly organic cafe that gets extra kudos for its smoothies. A healthy menu will have you noshing happily on satisfying soups, rice bowls, sandwiches, burrito wraps, tempeh burgers and fresh salads.

Sugar Pine Bakery   BAKERY $
(Map p340; 3564 Lake Tahoe Blvd; pastries $1-5; ☺8am-5pm Tue-Sat, to 4pm Sun) Crunchy baguettes, ooey-gooey cinnamon rolls, fruit tarts and choco-chunk cookies.

Cork & More   DELI $
(Map p340; www.thecorkandmore.com; 1032 Al Tahoe Blvd; sandwiches $5-10; ☺10am-7pm) Specialty foods, gourmet deli (sandwiches, soups, salads) and picnic baskets to go.

Ernie's Coffee Shop   DINER $
(Map p340; www.erniescoffeeshop.com; 1207 Hwy 50; mains $7.50-11; ☺6am-2pm; ☒) A sun-filled local institution, Ernie's dishes out filling four-egg omelets, hearty biscuits with gravy, fruity and nutty waffles and bottomless cups of locally roasted coffee. Toddlers can happily munch the ears off the Mickey Mouse pancake.

Burger Lounge   FAST FOOD $
(Map p340; ☎530-542-2010; www.burgerloungeintahoe.com; 717 Emerald Bay Rd; burgers $6-8; ☺10am-8pm daily Jun-Sep, 11am-7pm Wed-Sun

Oct-May; 🏵) You can't miss that giant beer mug standing outside a shingled cabin. Step inside for the south shore's tastiest burgers, including the crazy 'Jiffy burger' (with peanut butter and cheddar cheese), the zingy pesto fries or the knockout ice-cream shakes.

Freshie's FUSION **$$**
(Map p340; 📞530-542-3630; www.freshietahoe.com; 3330 Lake Tahoe Blvd; mains $14-28; ⏰11:30am-9pm; 🖋) From vegans to seafood lovers, everybody should be able to find a favorite on the extensive menu at this Hawaiian fusion joint with sunset upper-deck views. Most of the produce is local and organic, and the blackened fish tacos are South Lake Tahoe's best. Check the webcam to see if there's a wait.

Blue Angel Cafe CALIFORNIAN **$$**
(Map p340; 📞530-544-6544; www.theblueangelcafe.com; 1132 Ski Run Blvd; lunch $11-16, dinner $12-25; ⏰11am-9pm; 🔊🖋🏵🎨) Inside a cute wooden house on the way uphill to ski at Heavenly, this modern international-inspired kitchen churns out seafood, club sandwiches, elaborate salads, pastas and flank steaks to stuff your belly. Turn up for happy hour or the rotating lunch and dinner specials.

Off the Hook SUSHI **$$**
(Map p340; www.offthehooksushi.com; 2660 Lake Tahoe Blvd; mains $14-23; ⏰5-10pm) Sushi, so far from the ocean? Yup. Locals keep on coming back to this dynamite little sushi shack, where you can feast on bento boxes and *nigiri* combos, or big steaming bowls of floury udon noodles and pan-fried halibut steaks off the Japanese, Hawaiian and Californian menu.

Latin Soul LATIN AMERICAN **$$**
(Map p340; www.lakesideinn.com; 168 Hwy 50, Stateline; mains $9-28; ⏰8am-11pm) For something completely different, steal away to this little casino kitchen with a big, bold menu of spicy south-of-the-border flavors: Argentinean churrasco-grilled steak, Veracruz shrimp ceviche, goat *birria* (stew) and outrageously mixed mojitos.

Getaway Cafe AMERICAN **$$**
(www.getawaycafe.com; 3140 Hwy 50, Meyers; mains breakfast & lunch $8-13, dinner $10-19; ⏰7am-2:30pm Mon & Tue, to 9pm Wed-Sun Jun-Aug, reduced hours off-season; 🏵) On the outskirts of town, just south of the agriculture inspection checkpoint, this place really lives

up to its name; avoid the weekend crowds here. Friendly wait staff sling heaped-up buffalo chicken salads, barbecue burgers, chile rellenos, coconut-encrusted French toast and more.

Lake Tahoe Pizza Co PIZZA **$$**
(Map p340; 📞530-544-1919; www.laketahoepizzaco.com; 1168 Emerald Bay Rd/Hwy 89; pizzas $11-23; ⏰4-9:30pm; 🏵) Since the '70s, this classic pizza parlor has been hand rolling its housemade dough (cornmeal or whole wheat, anyone?), then piling the pizzas with crafty combos such as the meaty 'Barnyard Massacre' or vegan 'Green Giant.'

⭐**Cafe Fiore** ITALIAN **$$$**
(Map p340; 📞530-541-2908; www.cafefiore.com; 1169 Ski Run Blvd; mains $18-34; ⏰5:30-9pm) Upscale Italian without pretension, this tiny romantic eatery pairs succulent pasta, seafood and meats with an award-winning 300-vintage wine list. Swoon over the veal scaloppine, homemade white-chocolate ice cream and near-perfect garlic bread. With only seven tables (a baker's dozen in summer when the candle-lit outdoor patio opens), reservations are essential.

Self-Catering

Grass Roots Natural Foods GROCERY
(Map p340; 2030 Dunlap Dr; ⏰9am-8pm; 🖋) 🍃 Organic produce and home-baked muffins, sandwiches and fresh pizzas.

Safeway SUPERMARKET
(Map p340; www.safeway.com; 1020 Johnson Blvd; ⏰24hr) Standard supermarket fare, with an in-house deli and bakery.

🍷 Drinking & Entertainment

The siren song of blackjack and slot machines calls the masses over to Stateline. It's no Vegas, but there are plenty of ways to help you part with a bankroll. Each of the major casinos has live entertainment and several bars and lounges for you to while away the night. Published on Thursdays, the free alt-weekly newspaper *Reno News & Review* (www.newsreview.com/reno) has comprehensive Stateline entertainment and events listings. For what's going on around South Lake Tahoe, pick up a copy of the free weekly *Lake Tahoe Action*, published by the *Tahoe Daily Tribune* (www.tahoedailytribune.com).

Beacon Bar & Grill
BAR

(Map p340; www.camprichardson.com; Camp Richardson Resort, 1900 Jameson Beach Rd; ⊗ 11am-10pm) Imagine all of Lake Tahoe is your very own front yard when you and your buddies sprawl across this big wraparound wooden deck. If you want to get schnockered, order the signature Rum Runner cocktail. Bands rock here in summer.

Boathouse on the Pier
BAR

(Map p340; 3411 Lake Tahoe Blvd; ⊗ 11am-9pm, extended hours Jun-Sep) On the lake behind the Beach Retreat complex, this upstairs and upscale Timber Cove restaurant is the perfect spot for sunset cocktails, with outdoor tables to feel the summer breeze.

Brewery at Lake Tahoe
BREWERY

(Map p340; www.brewerylaketahoe.com; 3542 Lake Tahoe Blvd; ⊗ 11am-10:30pm) Crazy-popular brewpub pumps its signature Bad Ass Ale into grateful local patrons, who may sniff at bright-eyed out-of-towners. The barbecue is dynamite and a roadside patio opens in summer. Don't leave without a bumper sticker!

MacDuffs Pub
PUB

(Map p340; www.macduffspub.com; 1041 Fremont Ave; ⊗ 11:30am-10pm) With excellent beers rotating on tap, a dartboard on the wall, and fish-and-chips and shepherd's pie (as well as gourmet burgers and wood-fired pizzas) on the menu, this dark and bustling gastropub wouldn't look out of place in Edinburgh. Sports fans and beer drinkers, step right up.

Stateline Brewery
BREWERY

(Map p340; www.statelinebrewery.com; 4118 Lake Tahoe Blvd; ⊗ 11am-9pm Sun-Thu, to 10:30pm Fri & Sat) Seat yourself by the shiny industrial brewing vats at this subterranean eating and drinking spot. German and American-style ales taste mighty good after a day of sunning yourself on the lakeshore or skiing Heavenly (the gondola swings nearby).

Opal Ultra Lounge
CLUB

(Map p340; 775-586-2000; www.montbleuresort.com; MontBleu, 55 Hwy 50, Stateline; cover free-$10; ⊗ 10pm-4am Wed-Sat) With DJ booths and go-go dancers, this Top 40 and electro dance club draws a young party crowd that enjoys getting their bodies painted in-house. Ladies may get in free before midnight. On summer Sunday nights, hit up the casino's poolside DJ parties. Dress to impress.

Alpina Coffee Café
CAFE

(Map p340; 822 Emerald Bay Rd/Hwy 89; ⊗ 6am-5pm; 🛜) Internet-connected computers, plus locally roasted brews, toasted bagels and a summer garden patio.

Improv
COMEDY

(Map p340; www.harveystahoe.com; 18 Hwy 50, Stateline; tickets $25-30; ⊗ usually 9pm Wed, Fri & Sun, 8:30pm & 10:30pm Sat) Catch up-and-coming stand-up comedians doing their funny shtick at the intimate cabaret theater inside Harvey's old-school casino.

❶ Information

Barton Memorial Hospital (☎ 530-541-3420; www.bartonhealth.org; 2170 South Ave; ⊗ 24hr) Around-the-clock emergency room. Barton's urgent-care clinic is inside the Stateline Medical Center at 155 Hwy 50, Stateline, NV.

Explore Tahoe (Map p340; ☎ 530-542-4637; www.cityofslt.us; Heavenly Village Transit Center, 4114 Lake Tahoe Blvd; ⊗ 9am-5pm) Interpretive exhibits and recreational and transportation information at a multipurpose 'urban trailhead.'

Lake Tahoe Visitors Authority (Map p340; ☎ 530-544-5255; www.tahoesouth.com; 3066 Lake Tahoe Blvd; ⊗ 9am-5pm) Tourist information, maps, brochures and money-saving coupons, with a second center in Stateline (☎ 800-288-2463; www.tahoesouth.com; 169 Hwy 50, Stateline, NV; ⊗ 9am-5pm Mon-Fri).

South Lake Tahoe Library (☎ 530-573-3185; www.eldoradolibrary.org/tahoe.htm; 1000 Rufus Allen Blvd; ⊗ 10am-8pm Tue & Wed, to 5pm Thu-Sat; 🛜) First-come, first-served free internet terminals.

Tahoe Urgent Care (☎ 530-553-4319; www.tahoeurgentcare.com; 2130 Lake Tahoe Blvd; ⊗ 8am-6pm) Walk-in medical clinic for nonemergencies.

USDA Lake Tahoe Basin Management Unit (Map p340; ☎ 530-543-2600; www.fs.usda.gov/ltbmu; 35 College Dr; ⊗ 8am-4:30pm Mon-Fri) Wilderness permits and camping and outdoor recreation information.

USFS Taylor Creek Visitor Center (Map p340; ☎ 530-543-2674; www.fs.usda.gov/ltbmu; Visitor Center Rd, off Hwy 89; ⊗ 8am-5:30pm late May-Oct) Outdoor information, wilderness permits and daily ranger-led walks and talks during July and August.

❶ Getting There & Away

From Reno-Tahoe International Airport, **South Tahoe Express** (☎ 866-898-2463, 775-325-8944; www.southtahoeexpress.com; adult/child 4-12yr one way $30/17) operates several daily shuttle buses to Stateline casinos; the journey takes 75 minutes up to two hours.

Amtrak (☑ 800-872-7245; www.amtrak.com) has a daily Thruway bus service between Sacramento and South Lake Tahoe ($34, 2½ hours), stopping at the South Y Transit Center.

❶ Getting Around

South Lake Tahoe's main transportation hubs are the **South Y Transit Center** (Map p340; 1000 Emerald Bay Rd/Hwy 89), just south of the 'Y' intersection of Hwys 50 and 89; and the more central **Stateline Transit Center** (Map p340; 4114 Lake Tahoe Blvd).

BlueGO (☑ 530-541-7149; www.tahoetransportation.org; fare/day pass $2/5) local buses operate year-round from 6am to 11pm daily, stopping all along Hwy 50 between the two transit centers.

On summer weekends, BlueGo's **Emerald Bay Trolley** (www.tahoetransportation.org; fare $2) heads north from the South Y Transit Center to the Vikingsholm and Eagle Falls parking lot at Emerald Bay, but confirm the schedule as it changes from year to year. During winter ski season, BlueGO provides free and frequent shuttle service from Stateline and South Lake Tahoe to all Heavenly base operations every 30 minutes from stops along Hwy 50, Ski Run Blvd and Pioneer Trail.

WESTERN SHORE

Lake Tahoe's densely forested western shore, between Emerald Bay and Tahoe City, is idyllic. Hwy 89 sinuously wends past gorgeous state parks with swimming beaches, hiking trails, pine-shaded campgrounds and historic mansions. Several trailheads also access the rugged splendor of the Desolation Wilderness.

All campgrounds and many businesses shut down between November and May. Hwy 89 often closes after snowfall for plowing or due to imminent avalanche danger. Once you drive its tortuous slopeside curves, you'll understand why. The further south you are, the more of a roller coaster it is, no matter the season – so grip that steering wheel!

Emerald Bay State Park

Sheer granite cliffs and a jagged shoreline hem in glacier-carved Emerald Bay (Map p336; ☑ 530-541-6498; www.parks.ca.gov; per car $10; ☺ late May-Sep), a teardrop cove that

TAHOE RIM TRAIL

Partly paralleling the Pacific Crest Trail, the 165-mile Tahoe Rim Trail (www.tahoerimtrail.org) wraps around the lofty ridges and mountaintops of the Lake Tahoe Basin. Hikers, equestrians and – in some sections – mountain bikers can enjoy inspirational views of the lake and the snowcapped Sierra Nevada while tracing the footsteps of early pioneers, Basque shepherds and Washoe tribespeople. Dozens of marked trailheads all around the lakeshore provide easy access points for hikers, bikers and horseback riders.

Covering the entire basin, the Lake Tahoe Basin Trail Map (www.adventuremaps.net) is the best guide for hikers, bikers and cross-country skiers.

will have you digging for your camera. Its most captivating aspect is the water, which changes from cloverleaf green to light jade depending on the angle of the sun.

◉ Sights

You'll spy panoramic pullouts all along Hwy 89, including at Inspiration Point (Map p336), opposite USFS Bayview Campground. Just south, the road shoulder evaporates on both sides of a steep drop-off, revealing a postcard-perfect view of Emerald Bay to the north and Cascade Lake to the south.

The mesmerizing blue-green waters of the bay frame Fannette Island. This uninhabited granite speck, Lake Tahoe's only island, holds the vandalized remains of a tiny 1920s teahouse belonging to heiress Lora Knight, who would occasionally motorboat guests to the island from Vikingsholm Castle (Map p336; tour adult/child $10/8; ☺ 11am-4pm late May–Sep), her Scandinavian-style mansion on the bay. The focal point of the state park, Vikingsholm Castle is a rare example of ancient Scandinavian-style architecture. Completed in 1929, it has trippy design elements aplenty, including sod-covered roofs that sprout wildflowers in late spring. The mansion is reached by a steep 1-mile trail, which also leads to a visitors center.

🏃 Activities & Tours

Hiking

Vikingsholm Castle is the southern terminus of the famous Rubicon Trail (p350).

Two popular trailheads lead into the Desolation Wilderness. From the Eagle Falls parking lot ($5), the Eagle Falls Trail (Map p336) travels one steep mile to Eagle Lake, crossing by Eagle Falls along the way. This scenic short hike often gets choked with visitors, but crowds disappear quickly as the trail continues up to the Tahoe Rim Trail and Velma, Dicks and Fontanillis Lakes (up to 10 miles round-trip).

From the back of USFS Bayview Campground, it's a steep 1-mile climb to glacial Granite Lake or a moderate 1.5-mile round-trip to Cascade Falls, which rushes with snowmelt in early summer.

Boating

Fannette Island is accessible by boat, except during Canada goose nesting season (typically February to mid-June). Rent boats at Meeks Bay or South Lake Tahoe; from the latter, you can also catch narrated bay cruises or speedboat tours.

Scuba Diving

Divers prepared for chilly high altitude plunges can explore sunken barges, a submerged rockslide and artifacts at a historic dumping ground at the unique Underwater State Parks of Emerald Bay and DL Bliss State Park. Reno-based Sierra Diving Center (www.sierradive.com) and Adventure Scuba Center (www.renoscuba.com) offer classes and trips.

🛏 Sleeping

Eagle Point Campground CAMPGROUND $
(Map p336; ☑ 530-525-7277, reservations 800-444-7275; www.reserveamerica.com; Hwy 89; tent & RV sites $35; ⊙ mid-Jun–early Sep) With over 90 sites perched on the tip of Eagle Point, this state-park campground provides flush toilets, hot pay-showers, beach access and bay views. Another 20 scattered sites are reserved for boat-in campers.

USFS Bayview Campground CAMPGROUND $
(Map p336; Hwy 89; tent & RV sites $15; ⊙ Jun-Sep; 🐾) This rustic, nay, primitive forest-service campground has 13 no-reservation sites and vault toilets, but its potable water supplies are often exhausted sometime in July. It's opposite Inspiration Point.

DL Bliss State Park

Emerald Bay State Park spills over into DL Bliss State Park (Map p336; ☑ 530-525-7277;

www.parks.ca.gov; per car $10; ⊙ late May–Sep; 🐾), which has the western shore's most alluring beaches at Lester Cove and Calawee Cove. A half-mile round-trip nature trail leads to Balancing Rock, a 130-ton chunk of granite perched on a natural pedestal. Pick up an interpretive trail guide to park ecology and wildlife from the visitor center (⊙ 8am-5pm) near the entrance.

Near Calawee Cove is the northern terminus of the scenic one-way Rubicon Trail (Map p336), which ribbons along the lakeshore for 4.5 mostly gentle miles from Vikingsholm Castle (add one mile for the downhill walk to the castle from Hwy 89) in Emerald Bay State Park. It leads past small coves perfect for taking a cooling dip, and treats you to great views along the way. Add an extra mile to loop around and visit the restored historic lighthouse, a square wood-enclosed beacon (that looks a lot like an outhouse) constructed by the Coast Guard in 1916. Poised above 6800ft, it's the USA's highest-elevation lighthouse.

The park's campground (Map p336; ☑ 800-444-7275; www.reserveamerica.com; tent & RV sites $35-45, hike-and-bike sites $7; ⊙ mid-May–Sep; 🐾) has 145 sites, including some coveted spots near the beach, along with flush toilets, hot pay-showers, picnic tables, fire rings and an RV dump station.

The small visitor parking lot at Calawee Cove usually fills up by 10am, in which case it's a 2-mile walk from the park entrance to the beach. Alternatively, ask park staff at the entrance station about closer access points to the Rubicon Trail.

Meeks Bay

With a wide sweep of shoreline, sleek and shallow Meeks Bay has warm water by Tahoe standards and is fringed by a beautiful, but busy, sandy beach. On the west side of the highway, a few hundred feet north of the fire station, is another trailhead for the Desolation Wilderness. A moderate, mostly level and nicely shaded path parallels Meeks Creek before kicking off more steeply uphill through the forest to Lake Genevieve (9 miles round-trip), Crag Lake (10 miles round-trip) and other backcountry ponds, all surrounded by scenic Sierra peaks.

🛏 Sleeping & Eating

USFS Meeks Bay Campground CAMPGROUND $
(Map p336; ☑ 530-525-4733, reservations 877-444-6777; www.recreation.gov; tent & RV sites

$27-29; ☺mid-May–mid-Oct) This developed campground offers 36 reservable sites along the beach, along with flush toilets, picnic tables and fire rings. For pay showers, head to Meeks Bay Resort next door.

Meeks Bay Resort CABINS, CAMPGROUND **$$**
(Map p336; ☎530-525-6946; www.meeksbayresort.com; 7941 Emerald Bay Rd/Hwy 89; tent/RV sites with full hookups $30/50, cabins $125-400; ☺May-Oct) The Washoe tribe offers various lodging options (cabins require minimum stays) plus kayak, canoe and paddleboat rentals. If you're hungry, swing by the waterfront grill or small market, which stocks limited groceries and camping, fishing and beach gear, as well as Native American crafts and cultural books.

Ed Z'berg Sugar Pine Point State Park

About 10 miles south of Tahoe City, this woodsy **state park** (Map p336; ☎530-525-7982; www.parks.ca.gov; per car $10) occupies a promontory blanketed by a fragrant mix of pine, juniper, aspen and fir. It has a swimming beach, over a dozen miles of hiking trails and abundant fishing in General Creek. A paved cycling path travels north to Tahoe City. In winter, 12 miles of groomed cross-country trails await inside the park; book ahead for ranger-guided full-moon **snowshoe tours** (☎530-525-9920; adult/child under 12yr incl snowshoe rental $25/free). In summer, the park offers kayak and hiking tours through the **Sierra State Parks Foundation** (www.sierrastateparks.org).

Historic sights include the modest 1872 **cabin** (Map p336) of William 'General' Phipps, an early Tahoe settler, and the considerably grander 1903 Queen Anne–style **Hellman-Ehrman Mansion** (Map p336; tours adult/youth 7-17yr $10/8; ☺10:30am-3:30pm mid-Jun–Sep), an elegant lakefront house also known as Pine Lodge. Guided tours take in the richly detailed interior, including marble fireplaces, leaded-glass windows and period furnishings.

The park's secluded **General Creek Campground** (Map p336; ☎800-444-7275; www.reserveamerica.com; tent & RV sites $25-35; ☺late May–mid-Sep) has 120 fairly spacious, pine-shaded sites, plus flush toilets and hot pay-showers; a dozen sites stay open year-round (but without showers).

Tahoma

Another blink-and-you'll-miss-it lakeside outpost, Tahoma has a post office and a handful of places to stay and eat.

Cute but not too kitschy, the red cabins of **Tahoma Meadows Bed & Breakfast Cottages** (☎530-525-1553; www.tahomameadows.com; 6821 W Lake Blvd, Tahoma; cottages incl breakfast $99-389; ☎☀) dot a pine grove. Each has classy country decor, thick down comforters, a small TV, and bathrooms with clawfoot tubs. Pick up the in-room journal to record your impressions while you're toasting your feet by the gas-burning fireplace. Pet fee $20 per night.

Nearby, the **PDQ Market** (6890 W Lake Blvd; ☺6:30am-10pm) has groceries and a deli. Laying claim to being Tahoe's oldest bar, lakeside **Chamber's Landing** (☎530-525-9190; 6400 W Lake Blvd; ☺noon-8pm Jun-Sep) sees the biggest crowds descend for drinks and appetizers in the all-day bar, especially during happy hour. Do yourself a favor and skip the 'Chamber's Punch,' though.

Homewood

This quiet hamlet is popular with summertime boaters and, in winter, skiers and snowboarders. **West Shore Sports** (☎530-525-9920; www.westshoresports.com; 5395 W Lake Blvd; ☺8am-5pm) rents bicycles, kayaks, stand-up paddleboarding gear and snowsports equipment including skis, snowboards and snowshoes.

🛏 Sleeping & Eating

USFS Kaspian Campground CAMPGROUND **$**
(Map p336; ☎877-444-6777; www.recreation.gov; tent sites $19-21; ☺mid-May–mid-Oct) The closest campground is this nine-site, tent-only spot set among ponderosa and fir trees; amenities include flush toilets, picnic tables and fire rings.

West Shore Inn INN **$$$**
(☎530-525-5200; www.westshorecafe.com; 5160 W Lake Blvd; r/ste incl breakfast from $199/349; ❄☎) Oriental rugs and Arts and Crafts decor give this luxurious six-room inn a classic, aged ambience, and the lake's so close you feel like you could dive in. It's an upscale mountain lodge where crisp, modern suites feel decadent, and each has a fireplace and lake-view balcony. Rates include

complimentary use of bicycles, kayaks and stand-up paddleboards.

West Shore Café CALIFORNIAN, AMERICAN **$$$**
(☑530-525-5200; www.westshorecafe.com; 5160 W Lake Blvd; mains $12-33; ☺11am-9:30pm mid-Jun–Sep, 5-9:30pm Oct–mid-Jun) At the West Shore Inn's cozy destination restaurant, chef Mike Davis whips up worthy meals using fresh produce and ranched meats, from juicy burgers to Arctic char with spaghetti squash and hedgehog mushrooms. Dinner reservations recommended.

Sunnyside

Sunnyside is yet another lakeshore hamlet that may be just a dot on the map, but that has a couple of detour-worthy restaurants. To work off all that dang-good eating, rent a bicycle from another outpost of **West Shore Sports** (☑530-583-9920; www.westshoresports. com; 1785 W Lake Blvd), where you can get the scoop on all sorts of local outdoor information. You can pedal all the way north to Tahoe City along the paved bike path, or rent a stand-up paddleboarding set and hit the popular local beaches.

🛏 Sleeping & Eating

USFS William Kent Campground CAMPGROUND **$**
(Map p336; ☑877-444-6777; www.recreation.gov; Hwy 89; tent & RV sites $27-29; ☺mid-May–mid-Oct) About 2 miles south of Tahoe City, this roadside campground offers over 85 nicely shaded, but cramped, sites that often fill up. Amenities include flush toilets, picnic tables and fire rings, along with swimming beach access.

Sunnyside Lodge INN **$$$**
(☑530-583-7200; www.sunnysidetahoe.com; 1850 W Lake Blvd; d incl breakfast $150-380; 🛜🏊) This recently upgraded lodge features modern rooms with new bathrooms, pillowtop mattresses and flat-screen TVs, afternoon tea and cookies, and a guests-only sitting room overlooking the lake. The less expensive 'garden view' rooms lack good lake views. Note that there's lots of activity from the restaurant and boat dock and the marina next door. Pet fee $35.

★ Fire Sign Cafe AMERICAN **$**
(www.firesigncafe.com; 1785 W Lake Blvd; mains $7-13; ☺7am-3pm; 🚲🏊) For breakfast, everyone heads to the friendly Fire Sign for down-home omelets, blueberry pancakes, eggs Benedict with smoked salmon, fresh made-from-scratch pastries and other carbo-loading bombs, plus organic coffee. In summer, hit the outdoor patio. Lines are usually very long, so get there early.

Spoon AMERICAN **$$**
(☑530-581-5400; www.spoontakeout.com; 1785 W Lake Blvd; mains $9.50-15; ☺3-9pm, closed Tue & Wed Oct-May; 🍴) Call ahead for takeout, or squeeze yourselves into the cozy upstairs dining room at this little slat-sided cabin by the side of the highway. Barbecue tri-tip beef sandwiches, roasted veggies, soups, baked pastas and chicken enchiladas are the comfort-food staples, with brownies and ice cream for dessert.

Sunnyside Restaurant CALIFORNIAN **$$**
(☑530-583-7200; www.sunnysidetahoe.com; 1850 W Lake Blvd; mains lunch $9.50-13, dinner $16-35) Classic and innovative contemporary takes on steak and seafood – think porterhouse pork with cherry chutney or roasted chicken with braised fennel – pervade the lakeside dining room. In summer you'll probably have more fun doing lunch – or drinks with the signature zucchini sticks and a piece of hula pie – on the huge lakefront deck.

❶ Getting There & Around

From Tahoma, **Tahoe Area Rapid Transit** (TART; ☑530-550-1212; www.placer.ca.gov/tart; single/day pass $2/4; ☺7am-6pm) buses stop hourly at Ed Z'berg Sugar Pine Point State Park, Homewood and Sunnyside year-round, continuing north to Tahoe City and the north shore.

Also, in summertime, the **North Lake Tahoe Water Shuttle** (☑530-581-8707; www.northlaketahoewatershuttle.com; one way adult/child under 11yr $10/7) operates a half dozen daily trips between Tahoe Vista and Homewood/West Shore Café (30 minutes). Reserve ahead; bikes permitted.

TAHOE CITY

The north shore's commercial hub, Tahoe City straddles the junction of Hwys 89 and 28, making it almost inevitable that you'll find yourself breezing through here at least once during your round-the-lake sojourn. The town is handy for grabbing food and supplies and renting sports gear. It's also the closest lake town to Squaw Valley. The main drag, N Lake Blvd, is chockablock with outdoor outfitters, touristy shops and cafes.

◉ Sights

Gatekeeper's Museum & Marion Steinbach Indian Basket Museum   MUSEUM

(☑ 530-583-1762; www.northtahoemuseums.org; 130 W Lake Blvd/Hwy 89; adult/child under 13yr $5/ free; ☺ 10am-5pm daily late May-Sep, 11am-4pm Fri & Sat Oct-Apr) In a reconstructed log cabin close to town, this museum has a small but fascinating collection of Tahoe memorabilia, including Olympics history and relics from the early steamboat era and tourism explosion around the lake. In the museum's newer wing, uncover an exquisite array of Native American baskets collected from over 85 indigenous California tribes.

Fanny Bridge   BRIDGE

Just south of the always-jammed Hwy 89/28 traffic stoplight junction, the Truckee River flows through dam floodgates and passes beneath this bridge, cutely named for the most prominent feature of people leaning over the railings to look at fish (in American slang, 'fanny' means your rear end). The side facing the lake displays historical photos and hydrological facts.

Watson Cabin   MUSEUM

(☑ 530-583-8717; www.northtahoemuseums.org; 560 N Lake Tahoe Blvd; adult/child under 13yr $2/ free; ☺ noon-4pm Thu-Sun mid-Jun–early Sep) A few blocks east of the bridge over the Truckee River, this well-preserved 1908 settlers' cabin is one of the town's oldest buildings, built overlooking the beach.

⚡ Activities

Beaches & River Rafting

Though not an outstanding swimming area, Commons Beach is a small, attractive park with sandy and grassy areas, picnic tables, barbecue grills, a climbing rock and playground for kids, as well as free summer concerts (www.concertsatcommonsbeach.com) and outdoor movie nights. Leashed dogs welcome.

Truckee River Raft Rentals   RAFTING

(☑ 530-583-0123; www.truckeeriverraft.com; 185 River Rd; adult/child 6-12yr $30/25; ☺ 8:30am-3:30pm Jun-Sep; ⚐) The Truckee River here is gentle and wide as it flows northwest from the lake – perfect for novice paddlers. This outfit rents rafts for the 5-mile float from Tahoe City to the River Ranch Lodge, including transportation back to town. Reservations strongly advised.

Hiking

Explore the fabulous trails of the Granite Chief Wilderness (Map p336) north and west of Tahoe City. For maps and trailhead directions, stop by the visitors center. Recommended day hikes include the moderately strenuous Five Lakes Trail (over 4 miles round-trip), which starts from Alpine Meadows Rd off Hwy 89 heading toward Squaw Valley, and the easy trek to Paige Meadows, leading onto the Tahoe Rim Trail. Paige Meadows is also good terrain for novice mountain bikers and for snowshoeing. Wilderness permits are not required, even for overnight trips, but free campfire permits are needed, even for gas stoves. Leashed dogs are allowed on these trails.

Cycling

The paved 4-mile Truckee River Bike Trail runs from Tahoe City toward Squaw Valley, while the multi-use West Shore Bike Path heads 9 miles south to Ed Z'berg Sugar Pine Point State Park, including highway shoulder and residential street sections. Both are fairly easy rides, but expect crowds on summer weekends. The whole family can rent bicycles from any of several shops along N Lake Blvd. Park and head out from the 64 Acres Park trailhead behind the Tahoe City Transit Center. The excellent bike trail map of Lake Tahoe Bicycle Coalition (www.tahoebike.org) is also on its website.

Zip Lining

Tahoe Treetop Adventure Park   ZIP-LINING

(☑ 530-581-7563; www.tahoetreetop.com; 725 Granlibakken Rd, off Hwy 89; adult/child 5-12yr $45/35; ☺ 10am-5:30pm late May, 9am-7:30pm daily late May-Aug, reduced hours Sep-Dec; ⚐) At the Granlibakken resort, take a 2.5-hour monkey-like romp between tree platforms connected by zip lines and swinging bridges. Various courses are geared to everyone from little kids (no more than 10ft off the ground) to daredevils (two 100ft zip lines and one that's 300ft). Reserve ahead.

Winter Sports

Tahoe City is within easy reach of a half dozen downhill and cross-country skiing and snowboarding resorts.

Tahoe Dave's   OUTDOOR OUTFITTER

(☑ 530-583-0400, 530-583-6415; www.tahoedaves.com; 590 N Lake Tahoe Blvd; ski & snowboad rentals per day from $29) The main regional outfitter, with additional branches at Squaw Valley, Kings Beach and Truckee (rentals can be returned to any shop); reservations accepted.

Sleeping

If you show up without reservations, dingy, last-resort budget motels are along N Lake Blvd. For camping, head north to USFS campgrounds off Hwy 89 or south along Hwy 89 to state parks and small towns along the lake's western shore.

Mother Nature's Inn INN $$
(530-581-4278; www.mothernaturesinn.com; 551 N Lake Blvd; r $80-125;) Right in town behind Cabin Fever knickknack boutique, this good-value option offers quiet motel-style rooms with a tidy country look, fridges and coffeemaker, eclectic furniture and comfy pillow-top mattresses. It's within walking distance of Commons Beach. Pet fee $15.

Pepper Tree Inn MOTEL $$
(530-583-3711; www.peppertreetahoe.com; 645 N Lake Blvd; r incl breakfast $96-199;) The tallest building in town, this somberly painted establishment redeems itself with some birds-eye lake views. Fairly comfortable modern rooms with that familiar log-cabin decor each have a microwave and mini fridge. Top-floor rooms with hot tubs are most in demand.

River Ranch Lodge INN $$
(Map p336; 530-583-4264; www.riverranchlodge.com; Hwy 89 at Alpine Meadows Rd; r incl breakfast $115-190;) Though there's some noise from traffic outside and the bar downstairs, request a river-facing room so you can drift off to dreamland as the Truckee River tumbles below your window. Rooms bulge with lodgepole-pine furniture; those upstairs have wistful balconies. Pet-friendly rooms available in summer only.

Granlibakken LODGE $$
(530-583-4242; www.granlibakken.com; 725 Granlibakken Rd, off Hwy 89; r/ste from $150/242, 1-/2-/3-bedroom townhome from $330/409/516;) Sleep old-school at this cross-country ski area and kitschy wedding and conference venue. Basic lodge rooms are spacious, but timeshare townhomes with kitchens, fireplaces and lofts can be a decent deal for families and groups. Amenities include tennis, a full spa, year-round outdoor pool and hot tub and winter shuttle service to Homewood.

Eating & Drinking

Tahoe House Bakery BAKERY $
(www.tahoe-house.com; 625 W Lake Blvd; items $2-10; 6am-6pm;) Before you take off down the western shore for a bike ride or hike, drop by this mom-and-pop shop that opened in the 1970s. Their motto: 'While you sleep, we loaf.' Sweet cookies, European pastries, fresh-baked deli sandwiches and homemade salads and soups will keep you going all afternoon on the trail.

New Moon Natural Foods DELI, GROCERY $
(505 W Lake Blvd; mains $6-12; 9am-8pm Mon-Sat, 10am-7pm Sun;) A tiny but well-stocked natural-foods store, its gem of a deli concocts scrumptious ethnic food to go, all packaged in biodegradable and compostable containers. Try the Thai salad with organic greens and spicy peanut sauce.

Dam Cafe CAFE $
(55 W Lake Blvd; mains $6-11; 6am-3pm) Right by the Truckee River dam and the Fanny Bridge, stash your bikes in the racks outside this cute cottage and walk inside for a breakfast burrito, ice-cream fruit smoothie or pick-me-up espresso.

Syd's Bagelry and Espresso CAFE $
(550 N Lake Blvd; items $2-8.50; 7am-5pm;) A handy spot on the main drag serves bagels and locally roasted coffee, plus smoothies and breakfast burritos made with organic produce.

Dockside 700 Wine Bar & Grill AMERICAN $$
(530-581-0303; www.dockside700.com; 700 N Lake Blvd; lunch $10-17, dinner $14-32; 11:30am-8pm Mon-Thu, to 9pm Fri-Sun;) On a lazy summer afternoon, grab a table on the back deck that overlooks the boats bobbing at Tahoe City Marina. Barbecue chicken, ribs and steak light a fire under dinner (reservations advised), alongside seafood pastas and pizzas.

Fat Cat CALIFORNIAN $$
(www.fatcattahoe.com; 599 N Tahoe Blvd; mains $9-14; 11am-9pm, bar to 2am;) Hitting that happy Goldilocks median – not too expensive, but not too cheap – this casual, family-run restaurant with local art splashed on the walls does it all: from-scratch soups, heaped salads, sandwiches, pasta bowls and plenty of fried munchies for friends to share. Look for live indie music on Friday and Saturday nights.

Rosie's Cafe   DINER $$
(www.rosiescafe.com; 571 N Lake Blvd; breakfast & lunch $7-14, dinner $14-20; ⏰ 7:30am-9:30pm; 🅿) With antique skis, shiny bikes and lots of pointy antlers belonging to stuffed wildlife mounted on the walls, this quirky place serves breakfast until 2:30pm. The all-American hodge-podge menu is all right, but the convivial atmosphere is a winner.

River Ranch Lodge   NEW AMERICAN $$$
(☎ 530-583-4264; www.riverranchlodge.com; Hwy 89 at Alpine Meadows Rd; mains patio & cafe $8-13, restaurant $22-30; ⏰ lunch Jun-Sep, dinner year-round, call for seasonal hours) This riverside dining room is a popular stop, drawing rafters and bikers to its patio for summer barbecue lunches.

Bridgetender Tavern   PUB
(www.tahoebridgetender.com; 65 W Lake Blvd; ⏰ 11am-11pm, to midnight Fri & Sat) Après-ski crowds gather for beer, burgers and chili-cheese or garlic waffle fries (mains $8 to $14) at this woodsy bar. In summer, grab a seat on the open-air patio.

Tahoe Mountain Brewing Co.   BREWERY
(www.tahoebrewing.com; 475 N Lake Blvd; ⏰ 11:30am-10pm) Brewed in nearby Truckee, the Sugar Pine Porter, barrel-aged sours and award-winning Paddleboard Pale Ale here pair splendidly with sweet potato fries, burgers and other pub grub on the outdoor lake-facing patio.

ℹ Information

Tahoe City Downtown Association (www.visittahoecity.org) Tourist information and online events calendar.

Tahoe City Library (☎ 530-583-3382; Boatworks Mall, 740 N Lake Blvd; ⏰ 10am-5pm Tue & Thu, 11am-6pm Wed & Fri, 10am-2pm Sat; 📶) Free wi-fi and walk-in internet terminals.

Tahoe City Visitors Information Center (☎ 530-581-6900; www.gotahoenorth.com; 100 N Lake Blvd; ⏰ 9am-5pm) At the Hwy 89/28 split.

Truckee Tahoe Medical Group (☎ ext 3 530-581-8864; www.ttmg.net; Trading Post Center, 925 N Lake Blvd; ⏰ 9am-6pm Mon-Sat year-round, also 10am-5pm Sun Jul-early Sep) Walk-in clinic for nonemergencies.

ℹ Getting There & Around

Just south of the Hwy 28/89 split, the modern new **Tahoe City Transit Center** (www.nextbus.com/tahoe; 870 Cabin Creek Rd, off Hwy 89) is the main bus terminal, with a comfy waiting room. Behind it you'll find trailhead parking for the Tahoe Rim Trail and various bike path routes.

With a saucy acronym and reliable service, bike rack-equipped **Tahoe Area Rapid Transit** (TART; ☎ 530-550-1212; www.laketahoetransit.com; single/day pass $1.75/3.50) runs buses along the north shore as far as Incline Village, down the western shore to Ed Z'berg Sugar Pine Point State Park, and north to Squaw Valley and Truckee via Hwy 89. The main routes typically depart hourly from about 6am until 6pm daily.

Between June and September, TART also operates the **Night Rider**, a free local bus service connecting Squaw Valley, Tahoe City, Carnelian Bay, Tahoe Vista, Kings Beach, Crystal Bay and Incline Village hourly from 7pm until about 1am. Two more free nighttime summer-only trolley routes loop between Tahoe City and Tahoma via Sunnyside and Homewood, and between Northstar, Kings Beach and Crystal Bay, every hour from 6:30pm until midnight or 1am daily.

SQUAW VALLEY

The nirvana of the north shore, Squaw Valley played host to the 1960 Olympic Winter Games and still ranks among the world's top ski resorts. The stunning setting amid granite peaks, though, makes it a superb destination in any season, and this deluxe family-friendly resort stays almost as busy in summer as in winter.

◉ Sights & Activities

Much of the summertime action centers on 8200ft **High Camp** (☎ 800-403-0206; www.squaw.com; cable-car adult/child 5-12yr/youth 13-22yr $39/15/25, all-access pass $46/19/38; ⏰ 11am-4:30pm; 🎿), reached by a dizzying cable car (leashed dogs OK). At the top you'll find a heated seasonal outdoor swimming lagoon (adult/child $14/8), 18-hole disc-golf course (free), two high-altitude tennis courts (racquet rentals and ball purchase available), and a roller-skating rink (adult/child $14/8) that doubles as an ice-skating rink in winter. Cable-car tickets include admission to the **Olympic Museum**, which relives those magic moments from 1960.

Several hiking trails radiate out from High Camp, or try the lovely, moderate **Shirley Lake Trail** (round-trip 5 miles), which follows a sprightly creek to waterfalls, granite boulders and abundant wildflowers. It starts at the mountain base, near the end of Squaw Peak Rd, behind the cable-car building. Leashed dogs are allowed.

THE DOOMED DONNER PARTY

In the 19th century, tens of thousands of people migrated west along the Overland Trail with dreams of a better life in California. Among them was the ill-fated Donner Party.

When the families of George and Jacob Donner and their friend James Reed departed Springfield, IL, in April 1846 with six wagons and a herd of livestock, they intended to make the arduous journey as comfortable as possible. But the going was slow and, when other pioneers told them about a shortcut that would save 200 miles, they jumped at the chance.

However, there was no road for the wagons in the Wasatch Mountains, and most of the livestock succumbed under the merciless heat of the Great Salt Lake Desert. Arguments and fights broke out. James Reed killed a man, was kicked out of the group and left to trundle off to California alone. By the time the party reached the eastern foot of the Sierra Nevada, near present-day Reno, morale and food supplies ran dangerously low.

To restore their livestock's energy and reprovision, the emigrants decided to rest here for a few days. But an exceptionally fierce winter came early, quickly rendering what later came to be called Donner Pass impassable and forcing the pioneers to build basic shelter near today's Donner Lake. They had food to last a month and the fervent hope that the weather would clear by then. It didn't.

Snow fell for weeks, reaching a depth of 22ft. Hunting and fishing became impossible. In mid-December a small group of 15 made a desperate attempt to cross the pass. They quickly became disoriented and had to ride out a three-day storm that killed a number of them. One month later, less than half of the original group staggered into Sutter's Fort near Sacramento, having survived on one deer and their dead friends.

By the time the first rescue party arrived at Donner Lake in late February, the trapped pioneers were still surviving – barely – on boiled ox hides. But when the second rescue party, led by the banished James Reed, made it through in March, evidence of cannibalism was everywhere. Journals and reports tell of 'half-crazed people living in absolute filth, with naked, half-eaten bodies strewn about the cabins.' Many were too weak to travel.

When the last rescue party arrived in mid-April, only a sole survivor, Lewis Keseberg, was there to greet them. The rescuers found George Donner's body cleansed and wrapped in a sheet, but no sign of Tasmen Donner, George's wife. Keseberg admitted to surviving on the flesh of the dead, but denied charges that he had killed Tasmen for fresh meat. He spent the rest of his life trying to clear his name.

In the end, only 47 of the 89 members of the Donner Party survived. They settled in California, their lives forever changed by the harrowing winter at Donner Lake.

Other fun activities at the mountain base include a ropes course with zip lines, a climbing wall, mini golf and a Sky Jump (bungee trampoline), all operated by the Squaw Valley Adventure Center (☑530-583-7673; www.squawadventure.com). Golfers tee up at the 18-hole, par 71, Scottish-style links Resort at Squaw Creek Golf Course (☑530-583-6300; www.squawcreek.com; green fee incl cart $59-99); rental clubs are available.

🛏 Sleeping & Eating

For more resort hotel and condo lodging options, including ski-vacation packages, contact Squaw Valley (☑800-403-0206; www.squaw.com).

★ PlumpJack Squaw
Valley Inn   BOUTIQUE HOTEL $$$
(☑530-583-1576; www.plumpjacksquawvalleyinn.com; 1920 Squaw Valley Rd, Olympic Valley; r incl breakfast summer/winter $205-385/340-645; 🅿@🛜🐾♿🐕) Bed down at this artsy boutique hotel in the village, where every room has mountain views and extra-comfort factors like plush terry-cloth robes and slippers. Ski-in, ski-out access doesn't hurt either, but a $150 pet fee will. The chic PlumpJack Cafe (mains $24-45; ⊗7:30am-9:30pm), with its crisp linens and plush banquettes, serves seasonally inspired California cuisine with ace wines.

Wildflour Baking Company BAKERY $
(www.wildfloursquaw.com; items $2-12; ⏱7am-5pm) Fresh-baked bread sandwiches and bagels make great breakfasts or afternoon snacks in the basement level of Squaw's Olympic House building. Baristas whip up Scharffenberger hot chocolate and brew Peet's coffee and teas.

Le Chamois & Loft Bar PIZZERIA, PUB $$
(www.squawchamois.com; 1970 Squaw Valley Rd; mains $7-17; ⏱11am-6pm Mon-Fri, to 8pm Sat & Sun, bar open to 9pm or 10pm; 🐾🎵) For a social bite after shedding your bindings, this slopeside favorite is handily positioned between the cable-car building and the rental shop. Slide on over to devour a hot sammy or pizza and a beer with eye-pleasing mountain views.

ⓘ Getting There & Away

The village at Squaw Valley, at the base of the mountain cable-car, is about a 20-minute drive from Tahoe City or Truckee via Hwy 89 (turn off at Squaw Valley Rd).

Tahoe Area Rapid Transit (TART; ☏530-550-1212; www.laketahoetransit.com; single/day pass $1.75/3.50) buses between Truckee and Tahoe City, Kings Beach and Crystal Bay stop at Squaw Valley every hour or so between 6am and 5pm daily, with a free morning ski shuttle from December to April.

TRUCKEE & DONNER LAKE

Cradled by mountains and the Tahoe National Forest, Truckee is a thriving town steeped in Old West history. It was put on the map by the railroad, grew rich on logging and ice harvesting, and even had its brush with Hollywood during the 1924 filming of Charlie Chaplin's *The Gold Rush*. Today, tourism fills much of the city's coffers, thanks to a well-preserved historical downtown and its proximity to Lake Tahoe and no fewer than six downhill and four cross-country ski resorts.

⊙ Sights

The aura of the Old West still lingers over Truckee's teensy one-horse downtown, where railroad workers and lumberjacks once milled about in raucous saloons, bawdy brothels and shady gambling halls. Most of the late-19th-century buildings now contain restaurants and upscale boutiques. Donner Memorial State Park and Donner Lake, a busy recreational hub, are another 3 miles further west.

Donner Memorial State Park PARK
(Map p336; www.parks.ca.gov; Donner Pass Rd; per car $8; ⏱museum 10am-5pm, closed Tue & Wed Sep-May; 🅿) At the eastern end of Donner Lake, this state-run park occupies one of the sites where the doomed Donner Party got trapped during the fateful winter of 1846-47. Though its history is gruesome, the park is gorgeous and has a sandy beach, picnic tables, hiking trails and wintertime cross-country skiing and snowshoeing. The entry fee includes admission to the excellent **Emigrant Trail Museum**, which has fascinating, if admittedly macabre historical exhibits and a 25-minute film re-enacting the Donner Party's horrific plight.

The new and more multicultural **High Sierra Crossing Museum** sits completed across the parking lot; it's scheduled to replace the other museum when funding becomes available. Outside, the **Pioneer Monument** has a 22ft pedestal – the exact depth of the snow piles that horrendous winter. A short trail leads to a memorial at one family's cabin site.

Old Jail HISTORIC BUILDING
(www.truckeehistory.org; 10142 Jiboom St, cnr Spring St; suggested donation $2; ⏱11am-4pm Sat & Sun late May & mid-Jun–mid-Sep) Continuously in use until the 1960s, this 1875 red-brick building is filled with relics from the wild days of yore. George 'Machine Gun' Kelly was reportedly once held here for shoplifting at a local variety store, and 'Baby Face' Nelson and 'Ma' Spinelli and her gang did time here, too.

🏃 Activities

Northstar Mountain Bike Park MOUNTAIN BIKING
(www.northstarcalifornia.com; 5001 Northstar Drive, off Hwy 267; lift ticket adult/child 9-12yr $50/31; ⏱Jun-Sep) Sure, there's great cross-country here, but the downhill at this lift-serviced ski resort brings on the adrenaline with lots of intermediate and expert single-track and fire roads. Over 100 miles of trails; bikes and body armor rental available.

Back Country OUTDOOR OUTFITTER
(☏530-582-0909; www.thebackcountry.net; 11400 Donner Pass Rd; ⏱8am-6pm, call ahead in winter

LAKE TAHOE TRUCKEE & DONNER LAKE

& spring) Rents bicycles and snowshoes, and rents and sells new and used climbing gear, as well as backcountry ski gear.

Truckee Sports Exchange OUTDOOR OUTFITTER
(☎530-582-4510; www.truckeesportsexchange. com; 10095 W River St; ☺8am-8pm) Rents bicycles, kayaks and stand-up paddleboard gear as well as skis and winter backcountry gear.

Beaches & Water Sports
Warmer than Lake Tahoe, tree-lined Donner Lake is great for swimming, boating, fishing (license required), waterskiing and windsurfing.

West End Beach SWIMMING
(www.tdrpd.com; adult/child $4/3; ☻) This Donner Lake beach is popular with families for its roped-off swimming area, snack stand, volleyball nets, and kayak, paddleboat and stand-up paddleboard rentals.

Tributary Whitewater Tours RAFTING
(☎530-346-6812; www.whitewatertours.com; half-day trip per adult/child 7-17yr $69/62; ☻) From roughly mid-May through September, this long-running outfitter operates a 7-mile, half-day rafting run on the Truckee River over Class III+ rapids that will thrill kids and their nervous parents alike.

Hiking & Climbing
Truckee is a great base for treks in the Tahoe National Forest (Map p336), especially around Donner Summit. One popular 5-mile hike reaches the summit of 8243ft Mt Judah for awesome views of Donner Lake and the surrounding peaks. A longer, more strenuous ridge-crest hike (part of the Pacific Crest Trail) links Donner Pass to Squaw Valley (15 miles each way) skirting the base of prominent peaks, but you'll need two cars for this shuttle hike.

Donner Summit is also a major rock-climbing mecca, with over 300 traditional and sport-climbing routes. To learn the ropes, so to speak, take a class with Alpine Skills International (☎530-582-9170; www.alpineskills.com; 11400 Donner Pass Rd).

🖝 Tours

Tahoe Adventure Company ADVENTURE SPORTS
(☎530-913-9212; www.tahoeadventurecompany. com; tours per person from $55) A great option for guided Sierra adventures. Staff know the backcountry inside out and can customize any outing to your interest and skill level, from kayaking, hiking, mountain biking and

rock climbing to any combination thereof. They also offer full-moon snowshoe tours, and stand-up paddleboarding lessons and guided lake paddles.

🛏 Sleeping
A few dependable midrange chain motels and hotels are found off I-80 exits. A new hostel (www.truckeehostel.com) is in the works behind the train station.

Clair Tappaan Lodge HOSTEL $
(☎530-426-3632; www.sierraclub.org; 19940 Donner Pass Rd, Norden; dm incl meals adult/child from $65/45) ♠ About a mile west of Sugar Bowl, this cozy Sierra Club–owned rustic mountain lodge puts you near major ski resorts and sleeps up to 140 people in dorms and family rooms. Rates include family-style meals, but you're expected to do small chores and bring your own sleeping bag, towel and swimsuit (for the hot tub!).

In winter, go cross-country skiing or snowshoeing, or careen down the sledding hill out back.

Donner Memorial State Park Campground CAMPGROUND $
(Map p336; ☎530-582-7894, reservations 800-444-7275; www.reserveamerica.com; tent & RV sites $35, hike-and-bike sites $7; ☺late May-late Sep) Near Donner Lake, this family-oriented campground has 138 campsites with flush toilets and hot pay-showers.

USFS Campgrounds CAMPGROUND $
(☎518-885-3639; www.recreation.gov; campsites $17-48; ☻) Conveniently located along Hwy 89 (though with street noise) are three minimally developed riverside camping areas: Granite Flat, Goose Meadow and Silver Creek. All have potable water and vault toilets.

Truckee Hotel HISTORIC HOTEL $$
(☎530-587-4444; www.truckeehotel.com; 10007 Bridge St; r incl breakfast with shared bath $59-149, with private bath $129-179; ☎) Tucked behind an atmospheric four-story red-brick street front arcade, Truckee's most historic abode has welcomed weary travelers since 1873. A recent remodel has updated the carpets and furniture to genteel Victorian-infused modern luxury. Parking available across the street. Expect some train noise and no elevator.

Truckee Donner Lodge HOTEL $$
(☎530-582-9999; www.truckeedonnerlodge.com; 10527 Cold Stream Rd, off I-80 exit Donner Pass

Rd; r incl breakfast $84-204; ⚒ 📶 🏊) Just west of Hwy 89, this ex–Holiday Inn property gives you easy driving access to area ski resorts, shaving time off your morning commute to the slopes. No-nonsense, spacious hotel rooms come with microwaves and mini-fridges, and some have gas fireplaces. The hot-and-cold continental breakfast bar is complimentary.

River Street Inn
B&B $$

(📞 530-550-9290; www.riverstreetinntruckee.com; 10009 E River St; r incl breakfast $145-210; 📶) On the far side of the tracks, this sweet 1885 Victorian in Truckee's historic downtown has 11 rooms that blend nostalgic touches like clawfoot tubs with down comforters, but have few amenities other than TVs. Mingle with other guests over breakfast in the lounge. Bring earplugs to dull the occasional train noise.

★Cedar House Sport Hotel
BOUTIQUE HOTEL $$$

(Map p336; 📞 530-582-5655; www.cedarhousesporthotel.com; 10918 Brockway Rd; r incl breakfast $180-280; @ 📶 🏊) 🍴 This chic, environmentally conscious contemporary lodge aims at getting folks out into nature. It boasts countertops made from recycled paper, 'rain chains' that redistribute water from the green roof garden, low-flow plumbing and in-room recycling. However, it doesn't skimp on plush robes, sexy platform beds with pillow-top mattresses, flat-screen TVs or the outdoor hot tub. Pet fee $75.

Guided tours and multisport outdoor adventures can be arranged in-house.

Hotel Truckee-Tahoe
HOTEL $$$

(📞 530-587-4525; www.hoteltruckeetahoe.com; 11331 Brockway Rd; r incl breakfast $189-229; ⚒ @ 📶 🏊) Forget about retro ski-lodge kitsch as you cozy up inside these crisp, earth-toned and down-to-earth hotel rooms that abound in sunny, natural woods. Sink back onto the feather-topped mattresses, refresh yourself with spa-quality bath amenities or hit the seasonal outdoor heated pool by the hot tub. Pet fee $50.

🍴 Eating & Drinking

Coffeebar
CAFE $

(www.coffeebartruckee.com; 10120 Jiboom St; items $3-9; ⏰ 6am-10pm; 📶) 🍴 This beatnik, bare-bones industrial coffee shop serves Italian gelato, delectable pastries and home-brewed kombucha. Go for tantalizing breakfast crepes and overstuffed panini on herbed focaccia bread, or for a jolt of organic espresso or specialty tea blends.

Squeeze In
DINER $$

(www.squeezein.com; 10060 Donner Pass Rd; mains $8-15; ⏰ 7am-2pm; 🚼) Across from the Amtrak station, this snug locals' favorite dishes up breakfasts big enough to feed a lumberjack. Over 60 varieties of humungous omelets – along with burgers, burritos and big salads – are dished up in this funky place crammed with silly tchotchkes and colorful handwritten notes plastered on the walls.

Burger Me
BURGERS $$

(www.burgermetruckee.com; 10418 Donner Pass Rd; burgers $6.50-12.50; ⏰ 11am-9pm; 🚼) Getting two thumbs up from Food Network punk Guy Fieri may have gone to these guys' heads, but this fresh take on a burger shop still stocks all-natural meats and farm-fresh vegetables in the kitchen. Try the 'Trainwreck' – a beef patty topped with cheddar cheese, onion rings, turkey chili and a fried egg – if you dare. Gluten-free buns available.

★Moody's Bistro & Lounge
CALIFORNIAN $$$

(📞 530-587-8688; www.moodysbistro.com; 10007 Bridge St; lunch mains $12-18, dinner mains $13-32; ⏰ 11:30am-9:30pm) 🍴 With its sophisticated supper-club looks and live jazz (Thursday to Saturday evenings), this gourmet restaurant in the Truckee Hotel oozes urbane flair. Only fresh, organic and locally grown ingredients make it into the chef's perfectly pitched concoctions like pork loin with peach barbecue sauce, roasted beets with shaved fennel or pan-roasted Arctic char.

Stella
CALIFORNIAN $$$

(Map p336; 📞 530-582-5665; www.cedarhousesporthotel.com; 10918 Brockway Rd; mains $28-59; ⏰ 5:30-8:30pm Wed-Sun) 🍴 Housed at the trendy Cedar House Sport Hotel, this modern mountain-lodge dining room elevates Truckee's dining scene with Californian flair, harmonizing Asian and Mediterranean influences on its seasonal menu of housemade pastas, grilled meats and pan-roasted seafood. Bonuses: veggies grown on-site, housemade artisan bread and a killer wine list.

Fifty Fifty Brewing Co
BREWERY

(www.fiftyfiftybrewing.com; 11197 Brockway Rd; ⏰ 11:30am-11:30pm) Inhale the aroma of toasting grains at this brewpub south of downtown, near the Hwy 267 intersection. Sip the popular Donner Party Porter or Eclipse barrel-aged imperial stout while noshing a huge plate of nachos or other pub grub.

ℹ Information

Tahoe Forest Hospital (☎530-587-6011; www.tfhd.com; 10121 Pine Ave, cnr Donner Pass Rd; ⊙24hr) Emergency room, specializing in sports injuries.

Truckee Donner Chamber of Commerce (☎530-587-2757; www.truckee.com; 10065 Donner Pass Rd; computer access per 15 min $3; ⊙9am-6pm; ☎) Inside the Amtrak train depot; free walking-tour maps and wi-fi.

USFS Truckee District Ranger Station (☎530-587-3558; www.fs.usda.gov/tahoe; 10811 Stockrest Springs Rd, off I-80 exit 188; ⊙8am-5pm Mon-Sat, Mon-Fri in winter) Tahoe National Forest information.

ℹ Getting There & Around

Truckee straddles the I-80 and is connected to the lakeshore via Hwy 89 to Tahoe City or Hwy 267 to Kings Beach. The main drag through downtown Truckee is Donner Pass Rd, where you'll find the Amtrak train depot and metered on-street parking. Brockway Rd begins south of the river, connecting over to Hwy 267.

Though the Truckee Tahoe Airport has no commercial air service, **North Lake Tahoe Express** (☎866-216-5222; www.northlaketahoeexpress.com; one way/round-trip $45/85) shuttles to the closest airport at Reno. Buses make several runs daily from 3:30am to midnight, serving multiple northern and western shore towns and Northstar and Squaw Valley ski resorts. Make reservations in advance.

Greyhound (☎800-231-2222; www.greyhound.com) has twice-daily buses to Reno ($15, one hour), Sacramento ($40, 2½ hours) and San Francisco ($35, 5½ to six hours). Greyhound buses stop at the train depot, as do **Amtrak** (☎800-872-7245; www.amtrak.com) Thruway buses and the daily *California Zephyr* train to Reno ($16, 1½ hours), Sacramento ($41, 4½ hours) and Emeryville/San Francisco ($47, 6½ hours).

Truckee Transit (☎530-587-7451; www.laketahoetransit.com; single/day pass $2.50/5) links the Amtrak train depot with Donner Lake hourly from 9am to 5pm Monday through Saturday. For Tahoe City and other towns on the lake's north, west or east shores, hop on the TART bus at the train depot. Single-ride TART tickets cost $1.75 (day pass $3.50). During ski season, additional buses run to many area ski resorts.

NORTHERN SHORE

Northeast of Tahoe City, Hwy 28 cruises through a string of cute, low-key towns, many fronting superb sandy beaches, with reasonably priced roadside motels and hotels all crowded together along the lakeshore. Oozing old-fashioned charm, the north shore is a blissful escape from the teeming crowds of South Lake Tahoe, Tahoe City and Truckee, but still puts you within easy reach of winter ski resorts and snow parks, summertime swimming, kayaking, hiking trails and more.

The **North Lake Tahoe Visitors' Bureau** (☎888-434-1262; www.gotahoenorth.com) can help get you oriented, although their closest walk-in office is at Incline Village, NV.

Tahoe Vista

Pretty little Tahoe Vista has more **public beaches** (www.northtahoeparks.com) than any other lakeshore town. Sandy strands along Hwy 28 include small but popular **Moon Dunes Beach**, with picnic tables and firepits opposite the Rustic Cottages; **North Tahoe Beach** (7860 N Lake Blvd), near the Hwy 267 intersection, with picnic facilities, barbecue grills and beach volleyball courts; **Tahoe Vista Recreation Area** (7010 N Lake Blvd; parking $10), a locals' favorite with a small grassy area and marina; and the **Tahoe Adventure Company** (☎530-913-9212; www.tahoeadventurecompany.com) renting kayaks and stand-up paddleboarding gear ($15 to $80).

Away from all the maddening crowds, **North Tahoe Regional Park** (Map p336; www.northtahoeparks.com; 6600 Donner Rd, off National Ave; per car $3; ⊞) offers forested hiking and mountain-biking trails, an 18-hole disc-golf course, a children's playground and tennis courts lit-up for night play. In winter, a sledding hill (rentals available) and ungroomed cross-country ski and snowshoe tracks beckon. To find this hidden park, drive almost a mile uphill from Hwy 28 on National Ave, then go left on Donner Rd and follow the signs.

🛏 Sleeping

Cedar Glen Lodge CABINS, LODGE **$$**
(☎530-546-4281; www.tahoecedarglen.com; 6589 N Lake Blvd; r/ste/cottages incl breakfast $139-350; ◉ 🏊 ♨ 🐾) Completely renovated and

upgraded, and boasting an excellent new upscale restaurant, these gorgeous cabins and rustic-themed lodge rooms opposite the beach have knotty pine paneling, new mattresses and kitchenettes or full kitchens. Kids go nuts over all the freebies, from ping-pong tables, horseshoe pit and volleyball to an outdoor swimming pool, putting green and toasty firepit. Pet fee $30.

Franciscan Lakeside Lodge   CABINS $$
(☑530-546-6300; www.franciscanlodge.com; 6944 N Lake Blvd; cabin $93-399; 🛜🕸) Spend the day on a private sandy beach or in the outdoor pool, then light the barbecue grill after sunset – ah, now that's relaxation. All of the simple cabins, cottages and suites have kitchenettes. Lakeside lodgings have better beach access and views, but roomier cabins near the back of the complex tend to be quieter and will appeal to families with younger kids in tow.

Firelite Lodge   MOTEL $$
(☑530-546-7222; www.tahoelodge.com; 7035 N Lake Blvd; r incl breakfast $79-154; 🛜🕸) Recently rebuilt with thick walls, sound-proofed windows, and kitchenettes and gas fireplaces in every room, the family-run Firelite is a good-value stay in a prime walkable location, with the Tahoe Vista Recreation Area right across the street. The upstairs king-bed rooms have perfect lakeview balconies. Outside amenities include bikes to rent and a hot tub.

Rustic Cottages   CABIN $$
(☑530-546-3523; www.rusticcottages.com; 7449 N Lake Blvd; cottage incl breakfast $109-244; 🛜🕸) These cottages consist of a cluster of about 20 little storybook houses in the pines, with nametags fashioned from hand saws. They sport beautiful wrought-iron beds and a bevy of amenities. Most cabins have full kitchens, and some have gas or real wood-burning fireplaces.

Other perks: waffles and homemade muffins at breakfast, and free sleds and snowshoes to borrow in winter.

🍴 Eating & Drinking

Old Post Office Cafe   AMERICAN $
(5245 N Lake Blvd, Tahoe Vista; mains $6-12; ☺6:30am-2pm) Head west of town toward Carnelian Bay, where this always-packed, cheery wooden shack serves scrumptious breakfasts – buttery potatoes, crab-cake eggs Benedict, biscuits with gravy, fluffy omelets

with lotsa fillings and fresh-fruit smoothies. Waits for a table get long on summer and winter weekends, so roll up early.

El Sancho's   MEXICAN, TAKEOUT $
(7019 N Lake Blvd; items $4-10; ☺10am-9pm) Grab a big fat burrito or an order of *huaraches* – fried *masa* (cornmeal dough) topped with sauce, cheese and fried meat or beans – and a Mexican cane-sugar soda pop from this roadside *taqueria*.

★ Rustic Lodge   NEW AMERICAN $$$
(☑530-546-4281; www.tahoecedarglen.com/dining; 6589 N Lake Blvd; mains $19-36; ☺5-9pm Wed-Sun; 🍴) 🌱 Part of the va-va-va-vooming of Cedar Glen Lodge, this cozy wood-paneled restaurant and fireplace wine bar serve artisanal cheeses, locally-sourced produce and meats, free range chicken and hormone-free meats. Standouts include the truffle fries, roasted chicken breast, and absolutely anything made by the in-house pastry chef. Reservations recommended.

Gar Woods Grill & Pier   BAR
(☑530-546-3366; www.garwoods.com; 5000 N Lake Blvd; ☺11:30am-11:30pm) A shoreline hot spot judging by the rowdy crowds, Gar Woods pays tribute to the era of classic wooden boats. Don't show up for the lackadaisical grill fare, but instead to slurp a Wet Woody cocktail while watching the sunset over the lake. Be prepared to duke it out for a table on the no-reservations side of the beachfront deck out back.

Kings Beach

The utilitarian character of fetchingly picturesque Kings Beach lies in its smattering of back-to-basics retro motels all lined up along the highway. But in summer all eyes are on **Kings Beach State Recreation Area** (Map p336; www.parks.ca.gov; ☺dawn-10pm; 🅿🕸) **FREE**, a seductive 700ft-long beach that often gets deluged with sunseekers and leashed dogs. At the beach, you'll find picnic tables, barbecue grills and a fun kids' play structure, while nearby concessionaires rent kayaks, jet skis, paddleboats, stand-up paddleboarding (SUP) gear and more. **Adrift Tahoe** (☑530-546-1112; www.standuppaddletahoe.com; 8338 N Lake Blvd) is one of several local outfitters offering kayak, outrigger canoe and SUP rentals, private lessons and tours.

TIRED OF TAHOE?

To throw a few snowballs without blowing your family's budget or plodding along in weekend traffic, aim for some of California's 19 maintained sno-parks (☎916-324-1222; http://ohv.parks.ca.gov-/?page_id=1233; pass per day/year $5/25). Clustered along Sierra highways, these inexpensive winter activity parks offer opportunities for raucous sledding, serene cross-country ski touring or unhurried snowperson construction.

Or consider some of the smaller ski resorts. In addition to cheaper lift tickets, Bear Valley (www.bearvalley.com; Hwy 4) has its own snow play area, Dodge Ridge (www.dodgeridge.com; Hwy 108) has extensive get-to-know-the-snow lessons for kids, and China Peak (www.skichinapeak.com; Hwy 168) gets sparse crowds and is nowhere near the congested Tahoe-bound freeways.

Further inland, the nostalgic 1920s Old Brockway Golf Course (☎530-546-9909; www.oldbrockway.com; 400 Brassie Ave, nr cnr Hwy 267 & N Lake Blvd; greens fee $25-50, club/cart rental from $15/18) is a quick par-36, nine-hole diversion with peekaboo lake views from along pine tree-lined fairways where Hollywood celebs hobnobbed back in the day.

For drop-in yoga, Zumba and Jazzercise classes, check the schedule of the lakeside North Tahoe Event Center (www.northtahoeparks.com/ntec.php; 8318 N Lake Blvd).

🛏 Sleeping

★Hostel Tahoe   HOSTEL $
(☎530-546-3266; www.hosteltahoe.com; 8931 N Lake Blvd; dm $35, d/f $80/90; @🛜) 🚲
Minutes from Northstar and the beach, this former motel has private rooms and single-sex dorms with hand-painted murals and gauzy hanging textiles. A separate common building is the *pièce de résistance*, sunlight bathes the fireplace living room and a well-equipped honor kitchen stocks coffee, tea and food staples. Free loaner bikes, and breakfast included on Saturday and Sunday.

🍴 Eating & Drinking

Char-Pit   FAST FOOD $
(www.charpit.com; 8732 N Lake Blvd; items $3-11; ⊙11am-9pm; 👶) No gimmicks at this 1960s fast-food stand, which grills juicy burgers and St Louis–style baby back ribs, and also fries up crispy onion rings and breaded mozzarella sticks. Somebody call an ambulance!

Log Cabin Caffe   DINER $$
(☎530-546-7109; www.logcabinbreakfast.com; 8692 N Lake Blvd; mains $8-16; ⊙7am-2pm) Come early (especially on weekends) to join the queue for the North Shore's best breakfast. Eggs Benedict, whole-wheat pancakes with hot fresh fruit and cranberry-orange waffles are just a few highlights from the huge menu. Tip: call ahead to put your name on the waitlist if you'd rather not wait an hour for a table.

Lanza's   ITALIAN $$
(www.lanzastahoe.com; 7739 N Lake Blvd; mains $12-23; ⊙5-10pm, bar from 4:30pm) Next to the Safeway supermarket stands this beloved Italian trattoria where a tantalizing aroma of garlic, rosemary and 'secret' spices perfumes the air. Dinners, though undoubtedly not the tastiest you've ever had, are hugely filling and include salad and bread. Look for the owner's sepia-colored family photos in the entranceway.

Jason's Beachside Grille   BAR
(www.jasonsbeachsidegrille.com; 8338 N Lake Blvd; ⊙11am-10pm) Looking for the party around sundown? Hit this waterfront deck with a schooner of microbrew. Never mind the unexciting American fare, like smoked chicken pasta, alongside an overflowing salad bar (dinner mains $13 to $25). On colder days, red-velvet sofas orbiting a sunken fireplace are the coziest, but in summer it's all about sunset views.

Grid Bar & Grill   PUB
(www.thegridbarandgrill.com; 8545 N Lake Blvd; ⊙11am-2am) This locals' dive bar looks rough around the edges, but happy hours are super-cheap and you can catch live music, from bluegrass to punk, DJs, dancing or karaoke, or trivia nights.

❶ Getting There & Around

Tahoe Area Rapid Transit (TART; ☎530-550-1212; www.laketahoetransit.com; single/day pass $1.75/3.50) buses between Tahoe City and Incline Village make stops in Tahoe Vista, Kings Beach and Crystal Bay hourly from approximately 6am until 6pm daily. Another TART route connects Crystal Bay and Kings Beach with the Northstar resort every hour or so from 8am until 5pm daily; in winter, this bus continues to Truckee (between May and November, you'll have to detour via Tahoe City first).

In summer, the North Lake Tahoe Water Shuttle (p352) operates a half dozen daily trips between Tahoe Vista and Tahoe City (30 minutes). Reserve ahead; bikes permitted.

EASTERN SHORE

Lake Tahoe's eastern shore lies entirely within Nevada. Much of it is relatively undeveloped thanks to George Whittell Jr, an eccentric San Franciscan playboy who once owned a lot of this land, including 27 miles of shoreline. Upon his death in 1969, it was sold off to a private investor, who later wheeled and dealed most of it to the US Forest Service and Nevada State Parks. And lucky it was, because today the eastern shore offers some of Tahoe's best scenery and outdoor diversion. Hwy 28 rolls into Nevada at Crystal Bay and runs past Incline Village, heading along the eastern shore to intersect with Hwy 50, which rolls south to Zephyr Cove and Stateline casinos.

Crystal Bay

Crossing into Nevada, the neon starts to flash and old-school gambling palaces pant after your hard-earned cash. Though closed at research time for a multimillion-dollar remodel, historic Cal-Neva Resort literally straddles the California–Nevada border and has a colorful history involving ghosts, mobsters and Frank Sinatra, who once owned the joint. Ask about the guided secret tunnel tours once it's reopened.

Also on the main drag, the Tahoe Biltmore Lodge & Casino (800-245-8667; www.tahoebiltmore.com; 5 Hwy 28; r $84-129;), plays up its longevity with classic Tahoe photographs in the divey hotel rooms, though radiators give away the building's age. For greasy-spoon grill fare, duck under the mirrored ceilings into the artificial forest of the chintzy Cafe Biltmore (mains $8-15; 7am-4pm). Then catch a live-music show – often a tribute band – across the street at the Crystal Bay Club Casino (775-833-6333; www.crystalbaycasino.com; 14 Hwy 28).

For a breath of pine-scented air, flee the smoky casinos for the steep 1-mile hike up paved Forest Service Rd 1601 to Stateline Lookout. Sunset views over Lake Tahoe and the snowy mountains are all around.

A nature trail loops around the site of the former fire lookout tower – nowadays there's a split-level stone observation platform. To find the trailhead, drive up Reservoir Rd, just east of the Tahoe Biltmore parking lot, then take a quick right onto Lakeview Ave and follow it uphill just over a half-mile to the (usually locked) iron gate on your left.

Incline Village

One of Lake Tahoe's ritziest communities, Incline Village is the gateway to Diamond Peak and Mt Rose ski resorts. The latter is a 12-mile drive northeast via Hwy 431 (Mt Rose Hwy). During summer, the nearby Mt Rose Wilderness (Map p336; www.fs.usda.gov/ltbmu) offers miles of unspoiled terrain, including a strenuous 10-mile round-trip to the summit of majestic Mt Rose (10,776ft). The trail starts from the deceptively named Mt Rose Summit parking lot, 9 miles uphill from Incline Village. For a more mellow meadow stroll that even young kids can handle, pull over a mile or so earlier at wildflower-strewn Tahoe Meadows (). Stay on the nature loop trails to avoid trampling the fragile meadows; leashed dogs are allowed.

In summer, you can also visit George Whittell's mansion, Thunderbird Lodge (800-468-2463; www.thunderbirdlodge.org; adult/child 6-12yr $39/19; Tue-Sat May-Oct, reservations required), where he spent summers with his pet lion, Bill. Tours include a trip down a 600ft tunnel to the card house where George used to play poker with Howard Hughes and other famous recluses. The only way to get to the lodge is by shuttle bus, leaving from the helpful in-town Incline Village/Crystal Bay Visitors Bureau (775-832-1606; www.gotahoenorth.com; 969 Tahoe Blvd; 8am-5pm Mon-Fri, 10am-4pm Sat & Sun;), or on a boat cruise or kayak tour ($120 to $135).

Sleeping

Hyatt Regency Lake Tahoe RESORT $$$
(775-832-1234; www.laketahoe.hyatt.com; 111 Country Club Dr; r Sun-Thu/Fri & Sat from $199/379, ste & cottage Sun-Thu/Fri & Sat from $319/629;) Decorated like an Arts and Crafts–style mountain lodge, every room and lakeside cottage looks lavish, and the spa is even bigger than the casino. In summer you can sprawl on a private lakefront beach or in winter let the heated outdoor swimming lagoon warm you up after a day on the slopes.

✗ Eating & Drinking

Bite   CALIFORNIAN $$
(☑ 775-831-1000; www.bitetahoe.com; 907 Tahoe Blvd; shared plates $8-19; ⏱ 5-10pm, closed Wed Oct-May; 🅿) Don't let the strip-mall location stop you from rocking this creative, eclectic tapas and wine bar. Mix light, seasonal, veggie-friendly dishes with modern takes on rib-sticking comfort food like honeyed baby back ribs or green-chili mac 'n' cheese. An après-ski crowd turns up for happy hour.

Austin's   AMERICAN $$
(www.austinstahoe.com; 120 Country Club Dr; mains $9-17; ⏱ 11am-9pm; 🅿🔥) A hearty welcome for the whole family is what you'll find at this wood-cabin diner with an outdoor deck. Buttermilk fries with jalapeño dipping sauce, chicken-fried steak, classic meatloaf, burgers, huge salad bowls and sandwiches will fill you up – and so will mountain-sized martinis.

Lone Eagle Grille   COCKTAIL BAR
(www.laketahoe.hyatt.com; 111 Country Club Dr; ⏱ 11:30am-10pm Sun-Thu, to 11pm Fri & Sat) At the Hyatt's many-hearthed cocktail lounge, sip a divine orange-flavored margarita, then head outside for sunset and to flirt by the beach fire pit.

Lake Tahoe-Nevada State Park

Back on the lake, heading south, is Lake Tahoe-Nevada State Park (Map p336; www. parks.nv.gov; per car $7-12), which has beaches, lakes and miles of trails. Just 3 miles south of Incline Village is beautiful Sand Harbor (Map p336; ☑ 775-831-0494; www.parks. nv.gov/parks/sand-harbor; 2005 Hwy 28; per car $7-12), where two sand spits have formed a shallow bay with brilliant, warm turquoise water and white, boulder-strewn beaches. It gets very busy here, especially during July and August, when the Lake Tahoe Shakespeare Festival (☑ 800-747-4697; www.laketahoeshakespeare.com) is underway.

At the park's southern end, just north of the Hwy 50/Hwy 28 junction, Spooner Lake (Map p336; ☑ 775-749-5980; www.parks. nv.gov; per car $7-10) is popular for catch-and-release fishing, picnicking, nature walks, backcountry camping and cross-country skiing. Spooner Lake is also the start of the famous 13-mile Flume Trail, a holy grail for experienced mountain bikers. From the trail's end near Incline Village you can either backtrack 10 miles along the narrow, twisting shoulder of Hwy 28 or board a shuttle bus. Arrange shuttles and rent bikes by the trailhead inside the park at Spooner Summit Bike Rental Shop (☑ 775-749-1112; www. zephyrcove.com/flumetrail; mountain bike rental per day $40-60, shuttle $10-15; ⏱ 8:30am-5pm May-Oct) or in town at Flume Trail Bikes (☑ 775-298-2501; www.theflumetrail.com; 1115 Tunnel Creek Rd, Incline Village; mountain bike rental per day $35-85, shuttle $10-15).

RENO (NEVADA)

A city of big-time gambling and top-notch outdoor adventures, Reno resists pigeonholing. 'The Biggest Little City in the World' has something to raise the pulse of adrenaline junkies, hardcore gamblers and city people craving easy access to wide open spaces. The formerly gritty Midtown District – bordered by Liberty St (south of the river) to the north and Plumb Lane to the south, with S Virginia St running through it – has recently revitalized downtown with loads of exceptional new bars, restaurants and arts spaces.

◉ Sights

National Automobile Museum   MUSEUM
(☑ 775-333-9300; www.automuseum.org; 10 S Lake St; adult/child 6-18yr $10/4; ⏱ 9:30am-5:30pm Mon-Sat, 10am-4pm Sun; 🔥) Stylized street scenes illustrate a century's worth of automobile history at this engaging car museum. The collection is enormous and impressive, with one-of-a-kind vehicles – including James Dean's 1949 Mercury from *Rebel Without a Cause,* a 1938 Phantom Corsair and a 24-karat gold-plated DeLorean – and rotating exhibits bringing in all kinds of souped-up or fabulously retro rides.

Nevada Museum of Art   MUSEUM
(☑ 775-329-3333; www.nevadaart.org; 160 W Liberty St; adult/child 6-12yr $10/1; ⏱ 10am-5pm Wed & Fri-Sun, to 8pm Thu) In a sparkling building inspired by the geological formations of the Black Rock Desert north of town, a floating staircase leads to galleries showcasing temporary exhibits and eclectic collections on the American West, labor and contemporary landscape photography.

Fleischmann Planetarium & Science Center   MUSEUM
(☑ 775-784-4811; http://planetarium.unr.nevada. edu; 1650 N Virginia St; planetarium adult/child

under 12yr $7/5; ⊘ noon-7pm Mon-Thu, to 9pm Fri, 10am-9pm Sat, to 7pm Sun; ⏪) Pop into this flying-saucer-shaped building at the University of Nevada for a window on the universe during star shows and feature presentations.

Nevada Historical Society Museum MUSEUM (📞 775-688-1190; http://museums.nevadaculture. org; 1650 N Virginia St; adult/child under 17yr $4/ free; ⊘10am-5pm Tue-Sat) Near the University of Nevada Science Center, this museum includes permanent exhibits on neon signs, local Native American culture and the presence of the federal government.

Circus Circus CASINO (www.circusreno.com; 500 N Sierra St; ⊘24hr; ⏪) The most family-friendly of the bunch, Circus Circus has free circus acts to entertain kids beneath a giant big top, which also harbors a gazillion carnival and video games that look awfully similar to slot machines.

Silver Legacy CASINO (www.silverlegacyreno.com; 407 N Virginia St; ⊘24hr) A Victorian-themed place, the Silver Legacy is easily recognized by its white landmark dome, where a giant mock mining rig periodically erupts into a fairly tame sound-and-light spectacle.

Eldorado CASINO (www.eldoradoreno.com; 345 N Virginia St; ⊘24hr) The Eldorado has a kitschy Fountain of Fortune that probably has Italian sculptor Bernini spinning in his grave.

Harrah's CASINO (www.harrahsreno.com; 219 N Center St; ⊘24hr) Founded by Nevada gambling pioneer William Harrah in 1946, it's still one of the biggest and most popular casinos in town.

Atlantis CASINO (www.atlantiscasino.com; 3800 S Virginia St; ⊘24hr) Modeled on the legendary underwater city, with a mirrored ceiling and tropical flourishes like indoor waterfalls and palm trees.

🏃 Activities

Reno is a 30- to 60-minute drive from Lake Tahoe ski resorts, and many hotels and casinos offer special stay-and-ski packages.

For extensive information on regional hiking and mountain-biking trails, including the Mt Rose summit trail and the Tahoe-Pyramid Bikeway, download the **Truckee Meadows Trails guide** (www.washoecounty.us).

Mere steps from the casinos, the Class II and III rapids at the **Truckee River Whitewater Park** are gentle enough for kids riding inner tubes, yet sufficiently challenging for professional freestyle kayakers. Two courses wrap around Wingfield Park, a small island that hosts free concerts in summertime. **Tahoe Whitewater Tours** (📞775-787-5000; www. truckeewhitewaterrafting.com; rafting adult/child $68/58) and **Sierra Adventures** (📞866-323-8928; www.wildsierra.com; 11 N Sierra St; tubing $29) offer kayak trips and lessons.

👉 Tours

Historic Reno Preservation Society WALKING TOUR (📞775-747-4478; www.historicreno.org; tours $10) Dig deeper with a walking or biking tour of the city highlighting subjects including architecture, politics and literary history.

🎉 Festivals & Events

Reno River Festival SPORTS (www.renoriverfestival.com; ⊘May) The world's top freestyle kayakers compete in a mad paddling dash through Whitewater Park in mid-May. Free music concerts as well.

Hot August Nights CULTURAL (www.hotaugustnights.net; ⊘Aug) Catch the *American Graffiti* vibe during this seven-day celebration of hot rods and rock 'n' roll in early August. Hotel rates skyrocket to their peak.

🛏 Sleeping

Lodging rates vary widely depending on the day of the week and local events. Sunday through Thursday are generally the least

GREAT BALLS OF FIRE!

For one week at the end of August, **Burning Man** (www.burningman.com; admission $380-650) explodes onto the sunbaked Black Rock Desert, and Nevada sprouts a third major population center – Black Rock City. An experiential art party (and alternative universe) that climaxes in the immolation of a towering stick figure, Burning Man is a whirlwind of outlandish theme camps, dust-caked bicycles, bizarre bartering, costume-enhanced nudity and a general relinquishment of inhibitions.

WORTH A TRIP

PYRAMID LAKE

A piercingly blue expanse in an otherwise barren landscape, 25 miles north of Reno on the Paiute Indian Reservation, Pyramid Lake is popular for recreation. Permits for camping (primitive campsites per vehicle per night $9) on the beach on the west side of the lake and fishing (per person $9) are available online, at outdoor suppliers and CVS drugstore locations in Reno, and at the ranger station (📞 775-476-1155; http://plpt.nsn.us/rangers; 2500 Lakeview Dr; ⏰ 9am-1pm & 2-6pm Thu-Mon) east of SR 445 in Sutcliffe.

expensive; Friday is somewhat more expensive and Saturday can be as much as triple the midweek rate.

Mt Rose CAMPGROUND $
(📞 877-444-6777; www.recreation.gov; Hwy 431; RV & tent sites $17-50; ⏰ mid-Jun–Sep) In the summer months, there's gorgeous high-altitude camping here.

Sands Regency HOTEL $
(📞 775-348-2200; www.sandsregency.com; 345 N Arlington Ave; r Sun-Thu from $39, Fri & Sat from $85; P❋🛜⛱🐕) With some of the largest standard digs in town, rooms here are decked out in a cheerful tropical palette of upbeat blues, reds and greens – a visual relief from standard-issue motel decor. The 17th-floor gym and Jacuzzi are perfectly positioned to capture your eyes with drop-dead panoramic mountain views. An outdoor pool opens in summer. Empress Tower rooms are best.

Wildflower Village MOTEL, B&B $
(📞 775-747-8848; www.wildflowervillage.com; 4395 W 4th St; dm $34, motel $63, B&B $142; P❋@🛜) Perhaps more of a state of mind than a motel, this artists colony on the west edge of town has a tumbledown yet creative vibe. Individual murals decorate the facade of each room, and you can hear the freight trains rumble on by. Frequent live music and poetry readings at its cafe and pub, and bike rentals available.

Peppermill CASINO HOTEL $$
(📞 866-821-9996, 775-826-2121; www.peppermill-reno.com; 2707 S Virginia St; r Sun-Thu $59-129, Fri & Sat $79-209, resort fee $16; P❋@🛜⛱) 🐾

With a dash of Vegas-style opulence, the ever-popular Peppermill boasts Tuscan-themed suites in its newest 600-room tower, and plush remodeled rooms throughout the rest of the property. The three sparkling pools (one indoor) are dreamy, with a full spa on hand. Geothermal energy powers the resort's hot water and heat.

🍴 Eating

Reno's dining scene goes far beyond the casino buffets.

Pho 777 VIETNAMESE $
(201 E 2nd St; mains $6-8; ⏰ 10am-9pm) A no-frills Vietnamese noodle shop just off the casino strip that serves up bowls and bowls of steamy soup.

Peg's Glorified Ham & Eggs DINER $
(www.eatatpegs.com; 420 S Sierra St; mains $7-14; ⏰ 6:30am-2pm; ♿) Locally regarded as the best breakfast in town, Peg's offers tasty grill food that's not too greasy.

★ **Old Granite Street Eatery** NEW AMERICAN $$
(📞 775-622-3222; www.oldgranitestreeteatery.com; 243 S Sierra St; dinner mains $12-26; ⏰ 11am-10pm Mon-Thu, to 11pm Fri, 10am-11pm Sat, to 3pm Sun) A lovely well-lit place for organic and local comfort food, old-school artisanal cocktails and seasonal craft beers, this antique-strewn hotspot enchants diners with its stately wooden bar, water served in old liquor bottles and lengthy seasonal menu. Forgot to make a reservation? Check out the iconic rooster and pig murals and wait at a communal table fashioned from a barn door.

Silver Peak Restaurant & Brewery BREWPUB $$
(www.silverpeakrestaurant.com; 124 Wonder St; lunch $8.50-11, dinner $10-23; ⏰ restaurant 11am-10pm Sun-Thu, to 11pm Sat & Sun, pub open 1hr later) Casual and pretense-free, this place hums with the chatter of happy locals settling in for a night of microbrews and great eats, from pizza with barbecue chicken, to shrimp curry and filet mignon.

🍸 Drinking & Nightlife

Jungle CAFE, WINE BAR
(www.thejunglereno.com; 246 W 1st St; ⏰ coffee 6am-midnight, wine 3pm-midnight Mon-Thu, 3pm-2am Fri, noon-2am Sat, noon-midnight Sun; 🛜) A side-by-side coffee shop and wine bar with a cool mosaic floor and riverside patio all rolled into one. The wine bar has weekly

tastings, while the cafe serves breakfast bagels and lunchtime sandwiches ($6 to $8), and puts on diverse music shows.

Chapel Tavern COCKTAIL BAR
(www.chapeltavern.com; 1099 S Virgina St; ⊗ 2pm-2am Mon-Wed, 2pm-4am Thu-Sun) Midtown's cocktail mecca makes its own infusions – try the bourbon with fig – and a seasonal drinks menu attracts year-round interest to its antler-adorned bar and outdoor patio. DJs keep it jamming on Friday and Saturdays, and patrons comprise a diverse age mix.

Edge CLUB
(www.edgeofreno.com; 2707 S Virginia St, Peppermill; admission $20; ⊗ Thu & Sat from 10pm, Fri from 7pm) The Peppermill reels in the nighthounds with a big glitzy dance club, where go-go dancers, smoke machines and laser lights may cause sensory overload. If so, step outside to the lounge patio and relax in front of cozy fire pits.

☆ Entertainment

The free weekly *Reno News & Review* (www.newsreview.com) is your best source for listings.

Wedged between the I-80 and the Truckee River, downtown's N Virginia St is casino central. South of the river it continues as S Virginia St.

Knitting Factory LIVE MUSIC
(☑ 775-323-5648; http://re.knittingfactory.com; 211 N Virginia St) This midsized music venue books mainstream and indie favorites.

ℹ Information

An information center sits near the baggage claim at Reno-Tahoe International Airport, which also has free wi-fi.

Reno-Sparks Convention & Visitors Authority (☑ 800-367-7366; www.visitrenotahoe.com; 135 N Sierra St, inside Reno Envy; ⊗ 10am-6pm)

ℹ Getting There & Away

About 5 miles southeast of downtown, the **Reno-Tahoe International Airport** (RNO; www.

renoairport.com; ☎) is served by most major airlines.

The **North Lake Tahoe Express** (☑ 866-216-5222; www.northlaketahoeexpress.com; one-way $45) operates a shuttle (five daily, 3:30am to midnight) to and from the airport to multiple North Shore Lake Tahoe locations including Truckee, Squaw Valley and Incline Village. Reserve in advance.

The **South Tahoe Express** (☑ 866-898-2463; www.southtahoeexpress.com; adult/child one way $29.75/16.75, round-trip $53/30.25) operates several daily shuttle buses from the airport to Stateline casinos; the journey takes from 75 minutes up to two hours.

To reach South Lake Tahoe (weekdays only), take the wi-fi-equipped **RTC Intercity bus** (www.rtcwashoe.com; intercity $5) to the Nevada DOT stop in Carson City ($5, one hour, six daily Monday to Friday) and then the **BlueGo** (www.tahoetransportation.org/southtahoe) 21X bus ($2 with RTC Intercity transfer, one hour, five to six daily) to the Stateline Transit Center.

Greyhound (☑ 775-322-2970; www.greyhound.com; 155 Stevenson St) buses run daily service to Truckee, Sacramento and San Francisco ($35, five to seven hours), as does the once-daily westbound *California Zephyr* route operated by **Amtrak** (☑ 800-872-7245, 775-329-8638; www.amtrak.com; 280 N Center St). The train is slower and more expensive, but also more scenic and comfortable, with a bus connection from Emeryville for passengers to San Francisco ($51, 7½ hours). Discount bus company **Megabus** (www.megabus.com; ☎) has two daily departures from the Silver Legacy casino to San Francisco (from $15, 4½ hours) via Sacramento.

ℹ Getting Around

Casino hotels offer frequent free airport shuttles for their guests (and don't ask to see reservations).

The local **RTC Ride buses** (☑ 775-348-7433; www.rtcwashoe.com; per ride $2) blanket the city, and most routes converge at the RTC 4th St station downtown (between Lake St and Evans Ave). Useful routes include the RTC Rapid line for S Virginia St, 11 for Sparks and 19 for the airport.

The **Sierra Spirit bus** (50¢) loops around all major downtown landmarks – including the casinos and the university – every 15 minutes from 7am to 7pm.

Yosemite & the Sierra Nevada

Best Places to Eat

→ Evergreen Lodge (p384)

→ Lakefront Restaurant (p413)

→ Tioga Pass Resort (p407)

→ Narrow Gauge Inn (p386)

→ Mountain Room Restaurant (p384)

Best Places to Stay

→ High Sierra Camps (p382)

→ Ahwahnee Hotel (p381)

→ Evergreen Lodge Resort (p383)

→ Sierra Sky Ranch (p387)

→ Benton Hot Springs (p420)

Why Go?

An outdoor adventurer's wonderland, the Sierra Nevada is a year-round pageant of snow sports, white-water rafting, hiking, cycling and rock climbing. Skiers and snowboarders blaze through hushed pine-tree slopes, and wilderness seekers come to escape the stresses of modern civilization.

The eastern spine of California is a formidable but exquisite topographical barrier enclosing magnificent natural landscapes. And interspersed between its river canyons and 14,000ft peaks are the decomposing ghost towns left behind by California's early settlers, bubbling natural hot springs and Native American tribes that still call it home.

In the majestic national parks of Yosemite and Sequoia & Kings Canyon, visitors will be humbled by the groves of solemn giant sequoias, ancient rock formations and valleys, and the ever-present opportunity to see bears and other wildlife.

When to Go
Yosemite National Park

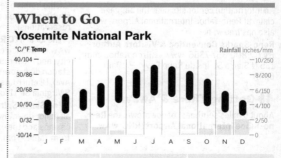

May & Jun The Yosemite waterfalls are gushing and spectacular in spring.

Jul & Aug Head for the mountains for wilderness adventures and glorious sunshine.

Dec–Mar Take a wintertime romp through snowy forests.

YOSEMITE NATIONAL PARK

The jaw-dropping head-turner of America's national parks, and a Unesco World Heritage Site, Yosemite (yo-*sem*-it-ee) garners the devotion of all who enter. From the waterfall-striped granite walls buttressing emerald-green Yosemite Valley to the skyscraping giant sequoias catapulting into the air at Mariposa Grove, the place inspires a sense of awe and reverence – four million visitors wend their way to the country's third-oldest national park annually. But lift your eyes above the crowds and you'll feel your heart instantly moved by unrivalled splendors: the haughty profile of Half Dome, the hulking presence of El Capitan, the drenching mists of Yosemite Falls, the gemstone lakes of the high country's subalpine wilderness and Hetch Hetchy's pristine pathways.

History

The Ahwahneechee, a group of Miwok and Paiute peoples, lived in the Yosemite area for around 4000 years before a group of pioneers, most likely led by legendary explorer Joseph Rutherford Walker, came through in 1833. During the Gold Rush era, conflict between the miners and native tribes escalated to the point where a military expedition (the Mariposa Battalion) was dispatched in 1851 to punish the Ahwahneechee, eventually forcing the capitulation of Chief Tenaya and his tribe.

Tales of thunderous waterfalls and towering stone columns followed the Mariposa Battalion out of Yosemite and soon spread into the public's awareness. In 1855 San Francisco entrepreneur James Mason Hutchings organized the first tourist party to the valley. Published accounts of his trip, in which he extolled the area's untarnished beauty, prompted others to follow, and it wasn't long before inns and roads began springing up. Alarmed by this development, conservationists petitioned Congress to protect the area – with success. In 1864 President Abraham Lincoln signed the Yosemite Grant, which eventually ceded Yosemite Valley and the Mariposa Grove of giant sequoias to California as a state park. This landmark decision paved the way for a national park system, of which Yosemite became a part in 1890, thanks to efforts led by pioneering conservationist John Muir.

Yosemite's popularity as a tourist destination continued to soar throughout the 20th century and, by the mid-1970s, traffic and congestion draped the valley in a smoggy haze. The General Management Plan (GMP), developed in 1980 to alleviate this and other problems, ran into numerous challenges and delays. Despite many improvements, and the need to preserve the natural beauty that draws visitors to Yosemite in the first place, the plan still hasn't been fully implemented.

◉ Sights

There are four main entrances to the park: South Entrance (Hwy 41), Arch Rock (Hwy 140), Big Oak Flat (Hwy 120 W) and Tioga Pass (Hwy 120 E). Hwy 120 traverses the park as Tioga Rd, connecting Yosemite Valley with the Eastern Sierra.

Visitor activity is concentrated in Yosemite Valley, especially in Yosemite Village, which has the main visitor center, a post office, a museum, eateries and other services. Curry Village is another hub. Notably less busy, Tuolumne (too-*ahl*-uh-*mee*) Meadows, toward the eastern end of Tioga Rd, primarily draws hikers, backpackers and climbers. Wawona, the park's southern focal point, also has good infrastructure. In the northwestern corner, Hetch Hetchy, which has no services at all, receives the smallest number of visitors.

◉ Yosemite Valley

The park's crown jewel, spectacular meadow-carpeted Yosemite Valley, stretches 7 miles long, bisected by the rippling Merced River and hemmed in by some of the most majestic chunks of granite anywhere on earth. The most famous are, of course, the monumental 7569ft El Capitan (El Cap), one of the world's largest monoliths and a magnet for rock climbers, and 8842ft Half Dome, the park's spiritual centerpiece – its rounded granite pate forms an unmistakable silhouette. You'll have great views of both from Valley View on the valley floor, but for the classic photo op head up Hwy 41 to Tunnel View, which boasts a new viewing area. With a little sweat you'll have even better postcard panoramas – sans the crowds – from Inspiration Point. The trail (2.6-mile round-trip) starts at the tunnel.

Yosemite's waterfalls mesmerize even the most jaded traveler, especially when the spring runoff turns them into thunderous

Yosemite & the Sierra Nevada Highlights

1 Marveling at the waterfall gush in spring at **Yosemite National Park** (p369).

2 Whooshing down the wintertime heights of snow-draped **Mammoth Mountain** (p409).

3 Gazing heavenward through the celestial sequoia canopies of **Sequoia & Kings Canyon National Parks** (p391).

4 Ambling around the evocative ghost town of **Bodie** (p405).

5 Canoeing or kayaking **Mono Lake** amid its haunting tufa (p407).

50 km
25 miles

NEVADA

Reno (45mi)

CARSON CITY

Lake Tahoe

Incline Village

Tahoe City

El Dorado National Forest

South Lake Tahoe

Walker Lake

Markleeville

Monitor Pass (8314ft)

Topaz Lake

Walker

Grover Hot Springs State Park

Ebbetts Pass (8730ft)

Lake Alpine

Bear Valley

Calaveras Big Trees State Park

Arnold

Murphys

Sonora

Sonora Pass (9624ft)

Dodge Ridge

Stanislaus National Forest

Groveland

Bridgeport

Bodie State Historic Park

Mono Lake

Lee Vining

Hoover Wilderness

Humboldt-Toiyabe National Forest

Tioga Pass (9945ft) (closed in winter)

Yosemite National Park

Ansel Adams Wilderness

Yosemite Village

El Portal

Briceburg

Briceburg

Humboldt-Toiyabe National Forest

Benton

Inyo National Forest

Inyo National Forest

White Mountain (14252ft)

Ancient Bristlecone

Inyo National Forest

Mammoth Lakes

Mammoth Mountain (11,053ft)

Devils Postpile

June Lake

Thornburg River

6 Viewing the bizarre volcanic formation of **Devils Postpile** (p418).

7 Soaking your troubles away at hot spring pools in **Bridgeport** (p402) and **Benton** (p420).

8 Visiting the **Manzanar National Historic Site** where one of the darkest events in US history is memorialized (p421).

ℹ️ VISITING YOSEMITE

From late June to September the entire park is accessible – all visitor facilities are open and everything from backcountry campgrounds to ice-cream stands are at maximum capacity. This is also when it's hardest – though not impossible – to evade the crush of humanity.

Crowds are smallest in winter but road closures (most notably of Tioga Rd but also of Glacier Point Rd beyond Badger Pass Ski Area) mean that activity is concentrated in the valley and on Badger Pass. Visitor facilities are scaled down to a bare minimum and most campgrounds are closed and other lodging options limited. Note that 'winter' in Yosemite starts with the first heavy snowfall, which can be as early as October, and often lasts until May.

Spring, when the waterfalls are at their best, is a particularly excellent time to visit. Fall brings fewer people, an enchanting rainbow of foliage and crisp, clear weather (although waterfalls have usually dried to a trickle by then).

cataracts. **Yosemite Falls** (west of Yosemite Village) is considered the tallest in North America, dropping 2425ft in three tiers. A slick wheelchair-accessible trail leads to the bottom of this cascade or, if you prefer solitude and different perspectives, you can also clamber up the **Yosemite Falls Trail**, which puts you atop the falls after a grueling 3.4 miles. No less impressive is nearby **Bridalveil Fall** and others scattered throughout the valley.

Any aspiring Ansel Adams should lug their camera gear along the 1-mile paved trail to **Mirror Lake** early or late in the day to catch the ever-shifting reflection of Half Dome in the still waters. The lake all but dries up by late summer.

South of here, where the Merced River courses around two small islands, lies **Happy Isles**, a popular area for picnics, swimming and strolls. It also marks the start of the **John Muir Trail** and **Mist Trail** to several waterfalls and Half Dome.

Yosemite Museum   MUSEUM
(📞209-372-0200; ⊗9am-5pm, often closed noon-1pm) **FREE** This museum has Miwok and Paiute artifacts, including woven baskets, beaded buckskin dresses and dance capes made from feathers. There's also an **art gallery** with paintings and photographs from the museum's permanent collection. Behind the museum, a self-guided interpretive trail winds past a reconstructed c 1870 **Indian village** with pounding stones, an acorn granary, a ceremonial roundhouse and a conical bark house.

Ahwahnee Hotel   HISTORIC BUILDING
About a quarter-mile east of Yosemite Village, the Ahwahnee Hotel is a graceful blend of rustic mountain retreat and elegant mansion dating back to 1927. You don't need to be a guest to have a gawk and a wander. Built from local granite, pine and cedar, the building is splendidly decorated with leaded glass, sculpted tiles, Native American rugs and Turkish kilims. You can enjoy a meal in the baronial dining room or a casual drink in the piano bar. Around Christmas, the Ahwahnee hosts the **Bracebridge Dinner** (📞801-559-5000; www.bracebridgedinners.com; per person $389), sort of a combination banquet and Renaissance fair. Book early.

Nature Center at Happy Isles   MUSEUM
(⊗9:30am-5pm late-May–Sep; 🚼) A great hands-on nature museum, the Nature Center displays explain the differences between the park's various pinecones, rocks, animal tracks and (everyone's favorite subject) scat. Out back, don't miss an exhibit on the 1996 rock fall, when an 80,000-ton rock slab plunged 2000ft to the nearby valley floor, killing a man and felling about 1000 trees.

👁 Glacier Point

A lofty 3200ft above the valley floor, 7214ft Glacier Point presents one of the park's most eye-popping vistas and practically puts you at eye level with Half Dome. To the left of Half Dome lies U-shaped, glacially carved **Tenaya Canyon**, while below you'll see Vernal and Nevada Falls. Glacier Point is about an hour's drive from Yosemite Valley via Glacier Point Rd off Hwy 41. Along the road, hiking trails lead to other spectacular viewpoints, such as **Dewey Point** and **Sentinel Dome**. You can also hike up from the valley floor to Glacier Point via the thigh-burning

Four Mile Trail. If you've driven up to Glacier Point and want to get away from the madding crowd, hiking down the Four Mile Trail for a bit will net you comparative solitude and more breathtaking views. Another way to get here is on the Glacier Point Hikers' Bus. Many hikers take the bus one way and hike the other. Drivers should go in the morning to avoid the afternoon backup from the parking lot.

◉ Tioga Road & Tuolumne Meadows

Tioga Rd (or Hwy 120 E), the only road through the park, travels through 56 miles of superb high country at elevations ranging from 6200ft at Crane Flat to 9945ft at Tioga Pass. Heavy snowfall keeps it closed from about November until May. Beautiful views await after many a bend in the road, the most impressive being Olmsted Point, where you can gawp all the way down Tenaya Canyon to Half Dome. Above the canyon's east side looms the aptly named 9926ft Clouds Rest. Continuing east on Tioga Rd snow drops you at Tenaya Lake, a placid blue basin framed by pines and granite cliffs.

Beyond here, about 55 miles from Yosemite Valley, 8600ft Tuolumne Meadows is the largest subalpine meadow in the Sierra. It provides a dazzling contrast to the valley, with its lush open fields, clear blue lakes, ragged granite peaks and domes, and cooler temperatures. If you come during July or August, you'll find a painter's palette of wildflowers decorating the shaggy meadows.

Tuolumne is far less crowded than the valley, though the area around the campground, lodge store and visitor center does get busy, especially on weekends. Some hiking trails, such as the one to Dog Lake, are also well traveled. Remember that the altitude makes breathing a lot harder than in the valley, and nights can get nippy, so pack warm clothes.

The main meadow is about 2.5 miles long and lies on the north side of Tioga Rd between Lembert Dome and Pothole Dome. The 200ft scramble to the top of the latter – preferably at sunset – gives you great views of the meadow. An interpretive trail leads from the stables to muddy Soda Springs, where carbonated water bubbles up in red-tinted pools. The nearby Parsons Memorial Lodge has a few displays.

Hikers and climbers will find a paradise of options around Tuolumne Meadows, which is also the gateway to the High Sierra Camps.

The Tuolumne Meadows Tour & Hikers' Bus makes the trip along Tioga Rd once daily in each direction, and can be used for one-way hikes. There's also a free Tuolumne Meadows Shuttle, which travels between the Tuolumne Meadows Lodge and Olmsted Point, including a stop at Tenaya Lake.

◉ Wawona

Wawona, about 27 miles south of Yosemite Valley, is the park's historical center, home to the park's first headquarters (supervised by Captain AE Wood on the site of the Wawona Campground) and its first tourist facilities. The park will soon restore part of the Mariposa Grove by removing summertime parking and creating a new trail system with improved signage; visitors will be shuttled from parking areas at Wawona and a new lot outside the South Entrance.

★ Mariposa Grove   FOREST
The main lure here is the biggest, most impressive cluster of giant sequoias in Yosemite. The star of the show – and what everyone comes to see – is the Grizzly Giant, a behemoth that sprang to life some 1800 years ago. You can't miss it – it's a half-mile walk along a well-worn path starting near the parking lot. Beyond here, crowds thin out a

IMPASSABLE TIOGA PASS

Hwy 120, the main route into Yosemite National Park from the Eastern Sierra, climbs through Tioga Pass, the highest pass in the Sierra at 9945ft. On most maps of California, you'll find a parenthetical remark – 'closed in winter' – printed on the map. While true, this statement is also misleading. Tioga Rd is usually closed from the first heavy snowfall in October to May, June or even July! If you're planning a trip through Tioga Pass in spring, you're likely to be out of luck. According to official park policy, the earliest date the road will be plowed is April 15, yet the pass has been open in April only once since 1980. Other mountain roads further north, such as Hwys 108, 4 and 88/89, may also be closed due to heavy snow, albeit only temporarily. Call ☎800-427-7623 for road and weather conditions.

Yosemite National Park

Yosemite National Park

⊙ Top Sights
1 Mariposa Grove	C7

⊙ Sights
2 Bridalveil Fall	C5
3 Chilnualna Falls	C7
4 Dewey Point Lookout	C5
5 Inspiration Point	B5
6 Mariposa Grove Museum	C7
7 McGurk Meadow	C5
8 Nevada Fall	D5
9 Olmsted Point	D4
10 Parsons Memorial Lodge	E4
11 Pioneer Yosemite History Center	C7
12 Tueeulala Falls	B3
13 Tunnel View	C5
14 Valley View	C5
15 Vernal Fall	C5
16 Wapama Falls	B3
17 Yosemite Falls	C5

☆ Activities, Courses & Tours
18 Badger Pass	C5
Badger Pass Cross-Country Center & Ski School	(see 18)
19 Ostrander Ski Hut	C6
20 Yosemite Ski School	C6
21 Yosemite Stables Wawona	C7

⊟ Sleeping
22 Bridalveil Creek Campground	C6
23 Crane Flat Campground	B5
24 Dimond O Campground	A4
25 Evergreen Lodge Resort	A4
26 Hodgdon Meadow Campground	A4
27 May Lake High Sierra Camp	D4
28 Porcupine Flat Campground	C4
29 Sunrise High Sierra Camp	D4
30 Tamarack Flat Campground	B5
31 Wawona Campground	C7
32 Wawona Hotel	C7
White Wolf Campground	(see 33)
33 White Wolf Lodge	C4
34 Yosemite Creek Campground	C4

⊗ Eating
Wawona Hotel Dining Room	(see 32)

bit, although for more solitude, arrive early in the morning or after 6pm.

Also nearby is the walk-through **California Tunnel Tree**, which continues to survive despite having its heart hacked out in 1895.

In the upper grove you'll find the **Fallen Wawona Tunnel Tree**, the famous drive-through tree that toppled over in 1969. For scenic views, take a 1-mile (round-trip) amble from the fallen tree to Wawona Point.

YOSEMITE & THE SIERRA NEVADA YOSEMITE NATIONAL PARK

Also in the upper grove, the **Mariposa Grove Museum** (☉10am-4pm May-Sep) `FREE` has displays about sequoia ecology. The full hike from the parking lot to the upper grove is about 2.5 miles.

Parking can be very limited, so come early or late, or take the free shuttle bus from the Wawona Store or the South Entrance. The grove can also be explored on a one-hour guided **tour** (☎209-375-1621; adult/child $26.50/19; ☉May-Sep) aboard a noisy open-air tram.

Pioneer Yosemite History Center MUSEUM (rides adult/child $5/4; ☉24hr, rides Wed-Sun Jun-Sep) `FREE` In Wawona itself, about 6 miles north of the grove, take in the manicured grounds of the elegant Wawona Hotel and cross a covered bridge to this rustic center, where some of the park's oldest buildings were relocated. It also features stagecoaches that brought early tourists to Yosemite, and offers short rides.

◉ Hetch Hetchy

In the park's northwestern corner, Hetch Hetchy, which is Miwok for 'place of tall grass,' gets the least amount of traffic yet sports waterfalls and granite cliffs that rival its famous counterparts in Yosemite Valley. The main difference is that Hetch Hetchy Valley is now filled with water, following a long political and environmental battle in the early 20th century. It's a lovely, quiet spot and well worth the 40-mile drive from Yosemite Valley, especially if you're tired of the avalanche of humanity rolling through that area. The 2013 Rim Fire charred a huge section of the forest in this region, but its beauty has not been significantly diminished.

The 8-mile long **Hetch Hetchy Reservoir**, its placid surface reflecting clouds and cliffs, stretches behind O'Shaughnessy Dam, the site of a parking lot and trailheads. An easy 5.4-mile (round-trip) trail leads to the

Yosemite Valley

YOSEMITE & THE SIERRA NEVADA YOSEMITE NATIONAL PARK

spectacular **Tueeulala** (*twee*-lala) **Falls** and **Wapama Falls**, which each plummet more than 1000ft over fractured granite walls on the north shore of the reservoir. **Hetch Hetchy Dome** rises up in the distance. This hike is best in spring, when temperatures are moderate and wildflowers poke out everywhere. Keep an eye out for rattlesnakes and the occasional bear, especially in summer.

There are bathrooms, but no other visitor services at Hetch Hetchy. The road is only open during daylight hours; specifics are posted at the Evergreen Rd turnoff.

🏃 Activities

Hiking

Over 800 miles of hiking trails cater to hikers of all abilities. Take an easy half-mile stroll on the valley floor; venture out all day on a quest for viewpoints, waterfalls and lakes; or go camping in the remote outer reaches of the backcountry.

Some of the park's most popular hikes start right in Yosemite Valley, including to the top of Half Dome (17-mile round-trip), the most famous of all. It follows a section of the John Muir Trail and is strenuous, difficult and best tackled in two days with an overnight in Little Yosemite Valley. Reaching the top can only be done after rangers have installed fixed cables. Depending on snow conditions, this may occur as early as late May or as late as July, and the cables usually come down in mid-October. To whittle down the cables' notorious human logjams, the park now requires permits for day hikers, but the route is still nerve-wracking as hikers must 'share the road.' The less ambitious or physically fit will still have a ball following the same trail as far as **Vernal Fall** (2.6-mile round-trip), the top of **Nevada Fall** (6.5-mile round-trip) or idyllic **Little Yosemite Valley** (8-mile round-trip). The Four Mile Trail (9.2-mile round-trip) to Glacier Point is a strenuous but satisfying climb to a glorious viewpoint.

Along Glacier Point Rd, **Sentinel Dome** (2.2-mile round-trip) is an easy hike to the crown of a commanding granite dome. And one of the most scenic hikes in the park, the **Panorama Trail** (8.5-mile one-way) descends to the Valley (joining the John Muir and Mist Trails) with nonstop views, including Half Dome and Illilouette Fall.

If you've got the kids in tow, nice and easy destinations include **Mirror Lake** (2-mile round-trip, or 4.5 miles via the **Tenaya Canyon Loop**) in the valley, the **McGurk Meadow Trail** (1.6-mile round-trip) on Glacier Point Rd, which has a historic log cabin to romp around in, and the trails meandering beneath the big trees of the Mariposa Grove in Wawona.

Also in the Wawona area has one of the park's prettiest (and often overlooked) hikes to **Chilnualna Falls** (8.6-mile round-trip). Best done between April and June, it follows a cascading creek to the top of the dramatic overlook falls, starting gently, then hitting you with some grinding switchbacks before sort of leveling out again.

The highest concentration of hikes lies in the high country of **Tuolumne Meadows** (p, which is only accessible in summer. A popular choice here is the hike to **Dog Lake** (2.8-mile round-trip), but it gets busy. You can also hike along a relatively flat part of the John Muir Trail into lovely **Lyell Canyon**

Yesemite Valley

◎ **Top Sights**
1 Glacier Point D4

◎ **Sights**
2 Ahwahnee Hotel D2
3 Happy Isles F4
4 Nature Center at Happy Isles F3
5 Sentinel Bridge C2
6 Sentinel Dome D4
7 Stoneman Bridge D2
8 Yosemite Museum C1

⊕ **Activities, Courses & Tours**
9 Curry Village Ice Rink E3
   Raft Rentals .... (see 9)
10 Yosemite Mountaineering School E3

⊟ **Sleeping**
11 Ahwahnee Hotel D2
12 Camp 4 .... A2
13 Curry Village E3
14 Housekeeping Camp D2
15 Lower Pines Campground E2
16 North Pines Campground E2

17 Upper Pines Campground E3
18 Yosemite Lodge at the Falls B2
19 Yosemite Valley Campground
    Reservation Office E3

⊗ **Eating**
   Ahwahnee Dining Room .... (see 11)
   Curry Village Coffee Corner .... (see 10)
   Curry Village Dining Pavilion ...... (see 10)
   Curry Village Pizza Patio .... (see 10)
   Degnan's Deli ....(see 20)
20 Degnan's Loft C1
   Meadow Grill .... (see 10)
   Mountain Room Restaurant ....(see 18)
21 Village Grill C1
   Yosemite Lodge Food Court ....(see 18)

⊝ **Drinking & Nightlife**
   Ahwahnee Bar .... (see 11)
   Mountain Room Lounge .... (see 18)

⊛ **Entertainment**
22 Yosemite Theater C1

(17.6-mile round-trip), following the Lyell Fork of the Tuolumne River.

Backpacks, tents and other equipment can be rented from the **Yosemite Mountaineering School** (☎ 209-372-8344; www.yosemitepark.com; Curry Village; ☺ Apr-Oct). The school also offers two-day Learn to Backpack trips for novices and all-inclusive three- and four-day guided backpacking trips ($375 to $500 per person), which are great for inexperienced and solo travelers. In summer the school operates a branch from Tuolumne Meadows.

Rock Climbing

With its sheer spires, polished domes and soaring monoliths, Yosemite is rock-climbing nirvana. The main climbing season runs from April to October. Most climbers, including some legendary stars, stay at Camp 4 (p381) near El Capitan, especially in spring and fall. In summer another base camp springs up at Tuolumne Meadows Campground (p382). Climbers looking for partners post notices on bulletin boards at either campground.

Yosemite Mountaineering School offers top-flight instruction for novice to advanced rock hounds, plus guided climbs and equipment rental. All-day group classes for beginners are $148 per person.

The meadow across from El Capitan and the northeastern end of Tenaya Lake (off

Tioga Rd) are good for watching climbers dangle from granite (you need binoculars for a really good view). Look for the haul bags first – they're bigger, more colorful and move around more than the climbers, making them easier to spot. As part of the excellent **'Ask a Climber' program**, climbing rangers set up telescopes at El Capitan Bridge from 11am to 3pm (mid-May through mid-October) and answers visitors' questions.

Cycling

Mountain biking isn't permitted within the park, but cycling along the 12 miles of paved trails is a popular and environmentally friendly way of exploring the valley. It's also the fastest way to get around when valley traffic is at a standstill. Many families bring bicycles, and you'll often find kids doing laps through the campgrounds. Hardcore cyclists brave the skinny shoulders and serious altitude changes of the trans-Sierra Tioga Rd.

Swimming

On a hot summer day, nothing beats a dip in the gentle Merced River, though if chilly water doesn't float your boat, you can always pay to play in the scenic outdoor swimming pools at Curry Village and Yosemite Lodge at the Falls (adult/child $5/4). With a sandy beach, Tenaya Lake is a frigid but interesting option, though White Wolf's Harden Lake warms up to a balmy temperature by mid summer.

Horseback Riding

Yosemite Stables (www.yosemitepark.com; trips 2hr/half-day $64/88) runs guided trips to such scenic locales as Mirror Lake, Chilnualna Falls and the Tuolumne River from three bases: Tuolumne Meadows (209-372-8427), Wawona (209-375-6502) and Yosemite Valley (209-372-8348). The season runs from May to October, although this varies slightly by location. No experience is needed, but reservations are advised, especially at the Yosemite Valley stables. Some mounts are horses, but most likely you'll be riding a sure-footed mule.

Rafting

From around late May to July, floating the Merced River from Stoneman Meadow, near Curry Village, to Sentinel Bridge is a leisurely way to soak up Yosemite Valley views. Four-person raft rentals (209-372-4386; per person $31) for the 3-mile trip are available from the concessionaire in Curry Village and include equipment and a shuttle ride back to the rental kiosk. Children must be over 50 pounds. Or bring your own equipment and pay $5 to shuttle back.

River rats are also attracted to the fierce Tuolumne River, a classic class IV run that plunges and thunders through boulder gardens and cascades. Outfitters OARS (209-736-2597; www.oars.com) and

Groveland-based Sierra Mac (209-591-8027, www.sierramac.com) offer guided trips.

Winter Sports

The white coat of winter opens up a different set of things to do, as the valley becomes a quiet, frosty world of snow-draped evergreens, ice-coated lakes and vivid vistas of gleaming white mountains sparkling against blue skies. Winter tends to arrive in full force by mid-November and peter out in early April.

Cross-country skiers can explore 350 miles of skiable trails and roads, including 90 miles of marked trails and 25 miles of machine-groomed track near Badger Pass. The scenic but grueling trail to Glacier Point (21-mile round-trip) also starts from here. More trails are at Crane Flat and the Mariposa Grove. The nongroomed trails can also be explored with snowshoes.

A free shuttle bus connects the Yosemite Valley and Badger Pass. Roads in the valley are plowed, and Hwys 41, 120 and 140 are usually kept open, conditions permitting. The Tioga Rd (Hwy 120 E), however, closes with the first snowfall. Be sure to bring snow chains with you, as prices for them double once you hit the foothills.

Badger Pass   SKIING, SNOWBOARDING
(209-372-8430; www.badgerpass.com; lift ticket adult/child $49/25; 9am-4pm mid-Dec–Mar) Most of the action converges on one of California's oldest ski resorts. The gentle slopes are perfect for families and beginner skiers and snowboarders. It's about 22 miles from

---

ⓘ MANDATORY HALF DOME PERMITS

To stem lengthy lines (and increasingly dangerous conditions) on the vertiginous cables of Half Dome, the park now requires that all-day hikers obtain an advance permit to climb the cables. There are currently three ways to do this, though check www.nps.gov/yose/planyourvisit/hdpermits.htm for the latest information. Rangers check permits at the base of the cables.

Preseason permit lottery (877-444-6777; www.recreation.gov; application fee online/by phone $4.50/6.50) Lottery applications for the 300 daily spots must be completed in March, with confirmation notification sent in mid-April; an additional $8 per person charge confirms the permit. Applications can include up to six people and seven alternate dates.

Daily lottery Approximately 50 additional permits are distributed by lottery two days before each hiking date. Apply online or by phone between midnight and 1pm Pacific Time; notification available late that same evening. It's easier to score weekday permits.

Backpackers Those with Yosemite-issued wilderness permits that reasonably include Half Dome can request Half Dome permits ($8 per person) without going through the lottery process. Backpackers with wilderness permits from a National Forest or another park can use that permit to climb the cables.

the valley on Glacier Point Rd. There are five chairlifts, 800 vertical feet and 10 runs, a full-service lodge, equipment rental ($27 to $37 for a full set of gear) and the excellent **Yosemite Ski School**, where generations of novices have learned how to get down a hill safely (group lessons from $47).

Badger Pass Cross-Country Center & Ski School
SKIING

(☑209-372-8444) Located in the Badger Pass Ski Area, this school offers beginner-lesson-plus-rental packages ($46), equipment rentals ($25), snow-camping rentals and guided tours. The center also runs overnight trips to **Glacier Point Ski Hut**, a rustic stone-and-log cabin. Rates, including meals, are $350/120 guided/self-guided for one night or $550/240 for two nights.

Ostrander Ski Hut
SKIING

(www.yosemiteconservancy.org) More experienced skiers can trek 10 miles out to the popular hut on **Ostrander Lake**, operated by Yosemite Conservancy. The hut is staffed all winter and open to backcountry skiers and snowshoers for $35 to $55 per person, per night on a lottery basis. See the website for details.

Curry Village Ice Rink
SKATING

(adult/child $10/9.50, skate rental $4) A delightful winter activity is taking a spin on the outdoor rink, where you'll be skating under the watchful eye of Half Dome.

👉 Tours

The nonprofit **Yosemite Conservancy** (☑209-379-2317; www.yosemiteconservancy.org) has scheduled tours of all kinds, plus custom trips available.

First-timers often appreciate the year-round, two-hour **Valley Floor Tour** (per adult/child $25/13) run by **DNC Parks & Resorts** (www.yosemitepark.com), which covers the valley highlights.

For other tour options stop at the tour and activity desks at Yosemite Lodge at the Falls, Curry Village or Yosemite Village, call ☑209-372-4386 or check www.yosemitepark.com.

🛏 Sleeping

Competition for campsites is fierce from May to September, when arriving without a reservation and hoping for the best is tantamount to getting someone to lug your Barcalounger up Half Dome. Even first-come,

---

WILDERNESS PERMITS FOR OVERNIGHT CAMPING

Shedding the high-season crowds is easiest when you set foot into Yosemite's backcountry wilderness. Start by identifying a route that matches your schedule, skill and fitness level. Then secure a **wilderness permit** (☑209-372-0740; www.nps.gov/yose/planyourvisit/wpres.htm; advance reservation fee $5, plus $5 per person, free for walk-ins; ⏱8:30am-4:30pm Mon-Fri Dec-Sep, extended hours late-May–early Sep), which is mandatory for overnight trips. To prevent tent cities sprouting in the woods, a quota system limits the number of people leaving from each trailhead each day. For trips between mid-May and September, 60% of the quota may be reserved by fax, phone, or mail from 24 weeks to two days before your trip. Faxes received between 5pm (the previous day) and 7:30am (the first morning you can reserve) get first priority.

The remainder are distributed by the office closest to the trailhead on a first-come, first-served basis (beginning at 11am one day before your planned hike) at Yosemite Valley Wilderness Center, Tuolumne Meadows Wilderness Center, the information stations at Wawona and Big Oak Flat, and the Hetch Hetchy Entrance Station. Hikers who turn up at the wilderness center nearest the trailhead get priority over those at another wilderness centers. For example, if a person who's been waiting for hours in the valley wants the last permit left for Lyell Canyon, the Yosemite Valley Wilderness Center calls the Tuolumne Meadows Wilderness Center to see if any hikers in Tuolumne want it. If a hiker waltzing into the Tuolumne office says 'yes!', they get priority over the person in the valley.

Reservations are not available from October to April, but you'll still need to get a permit by self-registering at the park.

At night you must be sure to store all scented items in bear-resistant containers, which may be rented for $5 per week at the wilderness and visitor centers. For locations and details, check www.nps.gov/yose/planyourvisit/bearcanrentals.htm.

first-served campgrounds tend to fill by noon, especially on weekends and around holidays. Campsites can be reserved up to five months in advance. **Reservations** (☎877-444-6777, 518-885-3639; www.recreation.gov) become available from 7am PST on the 15th of every month in one-month blocks, and often sell out within minutes.

Without a booking, your only chance is to hightail it to an open **first-come, first-served campground** or proceed to one of four **campground reservation offices** (☑information only 209-372-8502; Curry Village parking lot; ⊙8am-5pm) in **Yosemite Valley**, Wawona, Big Oak Flat and Tuolumne Meadows (the latter three are only open seasonally). Try to get there before they open at 8am (the valley office may open at 7:30am in summer), put your name on a waiting list and then hope for a cancellation or early departure. Return when the ranger tells you to (usually 3pm) and if you hear your name, consider yourself very lucky indeed.

All campgrounds have flush toilets, except for Tamarack Flat, Yosemite Creek and Porcupine Flat, which have vault toilets and no potable water. Those at higher elevations get chilly at night, even in summer, so pack accordingly. The Yosemite Mountaineering School (p378) rents camping gear.

If you hold a wilderness permit, you may spend the nights before and after your trip in the backpacker campgrounds at Tuolumne Meadows, Hetch Hetchy, White Wolf and behind North Pines in Yosemite Valley. The cost is $5 per person, per night and reservations aren't necessary.

Opening dates for seasonal campgrounds vary according to the weather.

All noncamping reservations within the park are handled by **DNC Parks & Resorts** (☎801-559-4884; www.yosemitepark.com) and can be made up to 366 days in advance; reservations are absolutely critical from May to early September. Rates – and demand – drop from October to April.

🏕 Yosemite Valley

Camp 4 CAMPGROUND $
(shared tent sites per person $5; ⊙year-round) Walk-in campground at 4000ft, popular with climbers; sites are shared.

North Pines Campground CAMPGROUND $
(tent & RV sites $20; ⊙Apr-Oct; 🐾) A bit off the beaten path (4000ft) with 81 sites near Mirror Lake; reservations required.

Upper Pines Campground CAMPGROUND $
(tent & RV sites $20; ⊙year-round; 🐾) Busy, busy, busy – and big (238 sites, 4000ft); reservations required mid-March through November.

Lower Pines Campground CAMPGROUND $
(tent & RV sites $20; ⊙Apr-Oct; 🐾) Crammed and noisy with 60 sites at 4000ft; reservations required.

Housekeeping Camp CABINS $
(q $98; ⊙Apr-Oct) This cluster of 266 cabins, each walled in by concrete on three sides and lidded by a canvas roof, is crammed and noisy, but the setting along the Merced River has its merits. Each unit can sleep up to six and has electricity, light, a table and chairs, and a covered patio with picnic tables.

Curry Village CABINS $$
(tent cabin $123-128, cabin without/with bath $146/195; 🐾🐕) Founded in 1899 as a summer camp, Curry has hundreds of units squished tightly together beneath towering evergreens. The canvas cabins are basically glorified tents, so for more comfort, quiet and privacy get one of the cozy wood cabins, which have bedspreads, drapes and vintage posters. There are also 18 attractive motel-style rooms in the **Stoneman House** (r $198), including a loft suite sleeping up to six.

Yosemite Lodge at the Falls MOTEL $$$
(r from $199; @🐾🐕) ✈ Situated a short walk from Yosemite Falls, this multibuilding complex contains a wide range of eateries, a lively bar, big pool and other handy amenities. Delightful rooms, thanks to a recent eco conscious renovation, now feel properly lodge-like, with rustic wooden furniture and striking nature photography. All have cable TV, telephone, refrigerator and coffeemaker, and great patio or balcony panoramas.

Ahwahnee Hotel HISTORIC HOTEL $$$
(r from $470; @🐾🐕) The crème de la crème of Yosemite's lodging, this sumptuous historic property dazzles with soaring ceilings, Turkish kilims lining the hallways and atmospheric lounges with mammoth stone fireplaces. It's the gold standard for upscale lodges, though if you're not blessed with bullion, you can still soak up the ambience during afternoon tea, a drink in the bar or a gourmet meal.

HIGH SIERRA CAMPS

In the backcountry near Tuolumne Meadows, the exceptionally popular High Sierra Camps provide shelter and sustenance to hikers who'd rather not carry food or a tent. The camps – called **Vogelsang**, **Merced Lake**, **Sunrise**, **May Lake** and **Glen Aulin** – are set 6 to 10 miles apart along a loop trail. They consist of dormitory-style canvas tent cabins with beds, blankets or comforters, plus showers (at May Lake, Sunrise and Merced Lake – subject to water availability) and a central dining tent. Guests bring their own sheets and towels. The rate is $161 per adult ($102 for children seven to twelve) per night, including breakfast and dinner. Organized hiking or saddle trips led by ranger naturalists are also available (from $928).

A short season (roughly late June to September) and high demand mean that there's a lottery for reservations. **Applications** (☑ 559-253-5672; www.yosemitepark.com) are currently accepted in September and October only. If you don't have a reservation, call from February to check for cancellations. Dates vary year to year, so watch the website for updates.

🛏 Tioga Road

Tuolumne Meadows campers should note that the closest pay showers are located at Mono Vista RV Park (p407) in Lee Vining.

Tuolumne Meadows Campground   CAMPGROUND $
(tent & RV sites $20; ☺ mid-Jul–late-Sep; 🐾) Biggest campground in the park (8600ft) with 304 fairly well-spaced sites; half of these can be reserved.

Porcupine Flat Campground   CAMPGROUND $
(tent & RV sites $10; ☺ Jul–Sep; 🐾) Primitive 52-site area, at 8100ft; some sites near the road.

Tamarack Flat Campground   CAMPGROUND $
(tent sites $10; ☺ Jul–Sep) Quiet, secluded, primitive at 6315ft; the 52 tent sites are a rough 3-mile drive off Tioga Rd.

White Wolf Campground   CAMPGROUND $
(tent & RV sites $14; ☺ Jul–mid-Sep; 🐾) Attractive setting at 8000ft, but the 74 sites are fairly boxed in.

Yosemite Creek Campground   CAMPGROUND $
(tent sites $10; ☺ Jul–mid-Sep; 🐾) The most secluded and quiet campground (7659ft) in the park, reached via a rough 4.5-mile road. There are 75 primitive sites.

Tuolumne Meadows Lodge   TENT CABINS $$
(tent cabin $123; ☺ mid-Jun–mid-Sep) In the high country, about 55 miles from the valley, this option attracts hikers to its 69 canvas tent cabins with four beds, a wood-burning stove and candles (no electricity). Breakfast and dinner are available.

White Wolf Lodge   CABINS, TENT CABINS $$
(tent cabin $123, cabin with bath $156; ☺ Jul–mid-Sep) This complex enjoys its own little world a mile up a spur road, away from the hubbub and traffic of Hwy 120 and the valley. There are 24 spartan four-bedded tent cabins without electricity and four very-in-demand hard-walled cabins that feel like rustic motel rooms. The generator cuts out at 11pm, so you'll need a flashlight until early morning.

There's also a dining room and a tiny counter-service store.

🛏 Hetch Hetchy & Big Oak Flat Road

Crane Flat Campground   CAMPGROUND $
(Big Oak Flat Rd; tent & RV sites $20; ☺ Jun–Sep) Large family campground at 6192ft, with 166 sites; reservations required.

Hodgdon Meadow Campground   CAMPGROUND $
(Big Oak Flat Rd; tent & RV sites $14-20; ☺ year-round) Utilitarian and crowded 105-site campground at 4872ft; reservations required mid-April to mid-October.

Dimond O Campground   CAMPGROUND $
(☑ 877-444-6777; www.recreation.gov; Evergreen Rd; tent & RV sites $24; ☺ May–mid-Sep) Four miles off Hwy 120, this reservable United States Forest Service (USFS) campground has 35 forested sites adjacent to the Tuolumne River. Arriving from the west, it's the last campground before the Big Oak Flat entrance, and a good fallback if you can't get a campsite inside the park.

★**Evergreen Lodge**
Resort CABINS, CAMPGROUND **$$$**
(☎209-379-2606; www.evergreenlodge.com;
33160 Evergreen Rd; tents $85-120, cabins $180-
415; @🌐🐾🏊) 🍴 Outside the park near
the entrance to Hetch Hetchy, this classic
90-year-old resort lets roughing-it guests
cheat with comfy, prefurnished tents and
rustic to deluxe mountain cabins with pri-
vate porches but no phone or TV. Outdoor
recreational activities abound, many of
them family-oriented, with equipment rent-
als available.

There's a general store, tavern with a
pool table and a fantastic restaurant serving
three hearty meals every day.

📷 **Wawona & Glacier Point Road**

Bridalveil Creek Campground CAMPGROUND **$**
(tent & RV sites $14; �
Jul–early Sep; 🐾) Quieter
than the valley campgrounds, with 110 sites
at 7200ft.

Wawona Campground CAMPGROUND **$**
(Wawona; tent & RV sites $14-20; ☉year-round;
🐾) Idyllic riverside setting at 4000ft with
93 well-spaced sites; reservations required
April to September.

Wawona Hotel HISTORIC HOTEL **$$$**
(r without/with bath incl breakfast $153/226;
☉mid-Mar–Dec; 🌐🏊) This National Historic Landmark, dating from 1879, is a collection of six graceful, whitewashed New
England-style buildings flanked by wide
porches. The 104 rooms – with no phone
or TV – come with Victorian-style furniture
and other period items, and about half the
rooms share bathrooms, with nice robes
provided for the walk there.

The grounds are lovely, with a spacious
lawn dotted with Adirondack chairs. Wi-fi
available in annex building only.

✖ **Eating**

You can find food options for all budgets and
palates within the park, from greasy slabs of
fast food to swanky cuts of top-notch steak.
All carry good vegetarian options.

Bringing in or buying your own food
saves money but remember that you *must*
remove it all from your car (or backpack or
bicycle) and store it overnight in a bear box
or canister. The Village Store in Yosemite
Village has the best selection (including toiletries, health-food items and some organic produce), while stores at Curry Village,
Wawona, Tuolumne Meadows, Housekeeping Camp and the Yosemite Lodge are more
limited.

★ **Yosemite Lodge Food Court** CAFETERIA **$**
(Yosemite Lodge; mains $7-12; ☉6:30am-8:30pm
Sun-Thu, to 9pm Fri & Sat; 🍴) This self-service
restaurant has several tummy-filling stations serving a large choice of pastas, burgers, pizza and sandwiches, either made to
order or served from beneath heat lamps.
Proceed to the cashier and find a table inside or on the patio.

Degnan's Loft PIZZA **$**
(mains $8-12; ☉5-9pm Mon-Fri, noon-9pm Sat &
Sun, late-May–Sep; 🍴♿) Head upstairs to this
convivial place with high-beamed ceilings
and a many-sided fireplace, and kick back
under the dangling lift chair for decent salads, veggie lasagna and pizza.

Degnan's Deli DELI **$**
(Yosemite Village; sandwiches $7-8; ☉7am-5pm;
🍴) Excellent made-to-order sandwiches,
breakfast items and snack foods.

Curry Village Coffee Corner CAFE **$**
(Curry Village; pastries $2-5; ☉6am-10pm, shorter
winter hours) For a coffee jolt or sugar fix.

Meadow Grill FAST FOOD **$**
(Curry Village; mains $5-8; ☉11am-5pm Apr-Oct)
Hot dogs, burgers and a few salads on a deck
near the parking area.

Tuolumne Meadows Grill FAST FOOD **$**
(Tioga Rd; mains $5-9; ☉8am-5pm mid-Jun–mid-
Sep) Scarf down burgers and grill items at
the outdoor picnic tables.

Village Grill FAST FOOD **$**
(Yosemite Village; mains $5-11; ☉11am-5pm Apr-
Oct) Fight the chipmunks for burgers and
tasty fries alfresco.

Curry Village Pizza Patio PIZZA **$**
(Curry Village; pizzas from $9; ☉noon-10pm, short-
er winter hours) Enjoy tasty pizza at this buzzing eatery that becomes a chatty après-hike
hangout in the late afternoon.

Curry Village Dining Pavilion CAFETERIA **$$**
(Curry Village; breakfast adult/child $10.50/6.50,
dinner adult/child $15.50/8; ☉7-10am & 5:30-8pm
Apr-Nov) Although the cafeteria-style setting
has all the charm of a train-station waiting
room, the mediocre all-you-can-eat break-
fast and dinner buffets are great for families,
gluttons and the undecided.

★ **Mountain Room Restaurant** AMERICAN $$$
(📞209-372-1403; www.yosemitepark.com; Yosemite Lodge; mains $21-35; ⊙5:30-9:30pm; 🖋🚼)
🖋 With a killer view of Yosemite Falls, the window tables at this casual and elegant contemporary steakhouse are a hot commodity. The chefs whip up the best meals in the park, with flat-iron steak and locally caught mountain trout wooing diners under a rotating display of nature photographs. Reservations accepted only for groups larger than eight; casual dress is OK.

★ **Evergreen Lodge** CALIFORNIAN $$
(📞209-379-2606; www.evergreenlodge.com; 33160 Evergreen Rd; breakfast & lunch $11-18, dinner $12-28; ⊙7-10:30am & noon-3pm & 5-9pm; 🖋🚼) Creative and satisfying, the Evergreen's restaurant serves some of the best meals around, with big and delicious breakfasts, three types of burgers (Black Angus beef, buffalo, and veggie) and dinner choices including dishes like rib-eye steak, grilled venison and braised seitan. The homey wooden tavern is a perennial favorite for evening cocktails, beers on tap over a game of pool and live music on select weekends. A general store fills the gaps with to-go sandwiches, snacks and dreamy gelato.

Wawona Hotel Dining Room AMERICAN $$$
(Wawona Hotel; breakfast & lunch $11-15, dinner $22-30; ⊙7:30-10am, 11:30am-1:30pm & 5:30-9pm Easter-Dec; 🖋🚼) Beautiful sequoia-painted lamps light this old-fashioned white-tablecloth dining room, and the Victorian detail makes it an enchanting place to have an upscale (though somewhat overpriced) meal. 'Tasteful, casual attire' is the rule for dinner dress, and there's a barbecue on the lawn every Saturday during summer.

The Wawona's wide, white porch makes a snazzy destination for evening cocktails, and listen for veteran pianist Tom Bopp in the lobby.

Ahwahnee Dining Room CALIFORNIAN $$$
(📞209-372-1489; Ahwahnee Hotel; breakfast $7-22, lunch $16-22, dinner $28-46; ⊙7-10am, 11:30am-3pm & 5:30-9pm; 🖋) 🖋 The formal ambience (mind your manners) may not be for everybody, but few would not be awed by the sumptuous decor, soaring beamed ceiling and palatial chandeliers. The menu is constantly in flux, but most dishes have perfect pitch and are beautifully presented. There's a dress code at dinner, but otherwise shorts and sneakers are OK.

Sunday brunch (adult/child $45/5; 7am to 3pm) is amazing. Reservations highly recommended for brunch and dinner.

🍷 **Drinking & Nightlife**

No one will mistake Yosemite for nightlife central, but there are some nice spots to relax with a Cabernet, cocktail or cold beer. Outside the park, the Yosemite Bug Rustic Mountain Resort (p390) and the Evergreen Lodge Resort (p383) both have lively lounges.

Mountain Room Lounge BAR
(Yosemite Lodge, Yosemite Valley; ⊙noon-11pm Sat & Sun, 4:30-11pm Mon-Fri) Catch up on the latest sports news while knocking back draft brews at this large bar that buzzes in wintertime. Order a s'mores kit (graham crackers, chocolate squares and marshmallows) to roast in the open-pit fireplace. Kids welcome until 10pm.

Ahwahnee Bar BAR
(Ahwahnee Hotel, Yosemite Valley; ⊙11:30am-11pm) The perfect way to experience the Ahwahnee without dipping too deep into your pockets; settle in for a drink at this cozy bar, complete with pianist. Appetizers and light meals ($10 to $25) provide sustenance.

☆ **Entertainment**

In addition to the Yosemite Theater, other activities scheduled year-round include campfire programs, children's photo walks, twilight strolls, night-sky watching, ranger talks and slide shows, and the tavern at the Evergreen Lodge has live bands some weekends. Scan the *Yosemite Guide* for full details.

Yosemite Theater THEATER
(performances adult/child $8/4; ⊙9am-7:30pm summer, shorter hours rest of year) Behind the visitor center, this theater screens two films: Ken Burns' *Yosemite: A Gathering of Spirit*, a celebration of the Yosemite Grant's 150th anniversary, and the painfully dramatic but beautifully photographed *Spirit of Yosemite*. The movies alternate, starting every half-hour between 9:30am and 4:30pm (from noon on Sundays), and offer a free, air-conditioned respite from the summer heat.

In the evening take your pick from a rotating cast of performers, including actor Lee Stetson, who portrays the fascinating life and philosophy of John Muir, and Park

Ranger Shelton Johnson, who re-creates the experiences of a Buffalo Soldier. There are also special children's shows.

ℹ Information

Yosemite's entrance fee is $20 per vehicle or $10 for those on bicycle or foot and is valid for seven consecutive days. Upon entering the park, you'll receive a National Park Service (NPS) map and a copy of the seasonal *Yosemite Guide* newspaper, which includes an activity schedule and current opening hours of all facilities.

For recorded park information, campground availability, and road and weather conditions, call ☏ 209-372-0200.

DANGERS & ANNOYANCES

Yosemite is prime black-bear habitat. Follow park rules on proper food storage and utilize bear-proof food lockers when parked overnight (see also p757). Mosquitoes can be pesky in summer, so bug spray's not a bad idea. And please don't feed those squirrels. They may look cute but they've got a nasty bite.

INTERNET ACCESS

Curry Village Lounge (Curry Village, behind registration office; 🛜) Free wi-fi.

Degnan's Cafe (Yosemite Village; per 3 min $1; ⏰ 7am-6pm) Pay terminals in this cafe adjacent to Degnan's Deli.

Mariposa County Public Library (🛜) Yosemite Valley (Girls Club Bldg, 58 Cedar Ct, Yosemite Valley; ⏰ 9am-noon Mon & Tue, 9am-1pm Wed & Thu); Bassett Memorial Library (Chilnualna Falls Rd, Wawona; ⏰ noon-5pm Mon, Wed & Fri, 10am-3pm Sat) Free internet terminals and wi-fi available.

Yosemite Lodge at the Falls (Yosemite Valley; per min 25¢; ⏰ 24hr) Pay terminals are in the lobby. Wi-fi costs $6 per day for nonguests.

INTERNET RESOURCES

Discussion forums with good local advice can be found at www.yosemite.ca.us/forum and www.yosemitenews.info.

Yosemite Conservancy (www.yosemiteconservancy.org) Information and educational programs offered by the nonprofit park-support organization.

Yosemite National Park (www.nps.gov/yose) Official Yosemite National Park Service site with the most comprehensive and current information. News and road closures/openings are often posted first on its Facebook page (www.facebook.com/YosemiteNPS).

Yosemite Park (www.yosemitepark.com) Online home of DNC Parks & Resorts, Yosemite's main concessionaire. Has lots of practical information and a lodging reservations function.

MEDICAL SERVICES

Yosemite Medical Clinic (☏ 209-372-4637; 9000 Ahwahnee Dr, Yosemite Village; ⏰ 9am-7pm daily late-May–late Sep, 9am-5pm Mon-Fri late-Sep–late-May) Twenty-four-hour emergency service available. A dental clinic (☏ 209-372-4200) is also available next door.

MONEY

Stores in Yosemite Village, Curry Village and Wawona all have ATMs, as does the Yosemite Lodge at the Falls.

POST

The main **post office** is in Yosemite Village, but Wawona and Yosemite Lodge also have year-round services. A seasonal branch operates in Tuolumne Meadows.

TELEPHONE

There are pay phones at every developed location throughout the park. Cell-phone reception is sketchy, depending on your location; AT&T, Verizon and Sprint have the only coverage.

TOURIST INFORMATION

Extended summer hours may apply.

Big Oak Flat Information Station (☏ 209-379-1899; ⏰ 8am-5pm late-May–Sep) Also has a wilderness permit desk.

Tuolumne Meadows Visitor Center (☏ 209-372-0263; ⏰ 9am-5pm Jun-Sep)

Tuolumne Meadows Wilderness Center (☏ 209-372-0309; ⏰ approx 8:30am-4:30pm spring & fall, 7:30am-5pm Jul & Aug) Issues wilderness permits.

Yosemite Valley Wilderness Center (☏ 209-372-0745; Yosemite Village; ⏰ 7:30am-5pm May-Sep) Wilderness permits, maps and backcountry advice.

Wawona Visitor Center (☏ 209-375-9531; ⏰ 8:30am-5pm May-Sep) Issues wilderness permits.

Yosemite Valley Visitor Center (☏ 209-372-0299; Yosemite Village; ⏰ 9am-6pm summer, shorter hours year-round) The main office, with exhibits and free film screenings in the theater.

ℹ Getting There & Away

CAR

Yosemite is accessible year-round from the west (via Hwys 120 W and 140) and south (Hwy 41), and in summer also from the east (via Hwy 120 E). Roads are plowed in winter, but snow chains may be required at any time. In 2006 a mammoth rockslide buried part of Hwy 140, 6 miles west of the park; traffic there is restricted to vehicles under 45ft.

Gas up year-round at Wawona and Crane Flat inside the park or at El Portal on Hwy 140 just outside its boundaries. In summer gas is also sold at Tuolumne Meadows. You'll pay dearly.

Yosemite is one of the few national parks that can be easily reached by public transportation. **Greyhound** (www.greyhound.com) buses and **Amtrak** (www.amtrak.com) trains serve Merced, west of the park, where they are met by buses operated by **Yosemite Area Regional Transportation System** (YARTS; ☏ 877-989-2787; www.yarts.com), and you can buy Amtrak tickets that include the YARTS segment all the way into the park. Buses travel to Yosemite Valley along Hwy 140 several times daily year-round, stopping along the way.

In summer (roughly June through September), another YARTS route runs from Mammoth Lakes along Hwy 395 to Yosemite Valley via Hwy 120. One-way tickets to Yosemite Valley are $13 ($9 child and senior, three hours) from Merced and $18 ($15 child and senior, 3½ hours) from Mammoth Lakes, less if boarding in between.

YARTS fares include the park-entrance fee, making them a super bargain, and drivers accept credit cards.

ⓘ Getting Around

BICYCLE

Bicycling is an ideal way to take in Yosemite Valley. You can rent a wide-handled cruiser (per hour/day $11.50/32) or a bike with an attached child trailer (per hour/day $19/59) at the Yosemite Lodge at the Falls or Curry Village. Strollers and wheelchairs are also rented here.

CAR

Roadside signs with red bears mark the many spots where bears have been hit by motorists, so think before you hit the accelerator, and follow the pokey posted speed limits. Valley visitors are advised to park and take advantage of the Yosemite Valley Shuttle Bus. Glacier Point and Tioga Rds are closed in winter.

PUBLIC TRANSPORTATION

The free, air-conditioned **Yosemite Valley Shuttle Bus** is a comfortable and efficient way of traveling around the park. Buses operate year-round at frequent intervals and stop at 21 numbered locations, including parking lots, campgrounds, trailheads and lodges. For a route map, see the *Yosemite Guide*.

Free buses also operate between Wawona and the Mariposa Grove (spring to fall), and Yosemite Valley and Badger Pass (winter only). The **Tuolumne Meadows Shuttle** runs between Tuolumne Lodge and Olmsted Point in Tuolumne Meadows (usually mid-June to early September), and the **El Capitan Shuttle** runs a summertime valley loop from Yosemite Village to El Capitan.

Two fee-based hikers' buses also travel from Yosemite Valley. For trailheads along Tioga Rd, catch the **Tuolumne Meadows Tour & Hikers' Bus** (☏ 209-372-4386; ⏱ Jul–early Sep), which runs once daily in each direction. Fares depend on distance traveled; the trip to Tuolumne Meadows costs $14.50/23 one way/round-trip. The **Glacier Point Hikers' Bus** (☏ 209-372-4386; one way/return $25/41; ⏱ mid-May–Oct) is good for hikers as well as for people reluctant to drive up the long, windy road themselves. Reservations are required.

YOSEMITE GATEWAYS

Fish Camp

Fish Camp, just south of the park on Hwy 41, is more of a bend in the road, but it does have some good lodging options as well as the ever-popular Sugar Pine Railroad (☏ 559-683-7273; www.ymsprr.com; rides adult/child $18/9; ⏱ Mar–Oct; ⊛), a historic steam train that chugs through the woods on a 4-mile loop.

🛌 Sleeping & Eating

Summerdale Campground CAMPGROUND $
(☏ 877-444-6677; www.recreation.gov; tent & RV sites $28; ⏱ May–Sep; ⊛) Has 28 well-dispersed United States Forest Service (USFS) sites along Big Creek.

White Chief Mountain Lodge MOTEL $$
(☏ 559-683-5444; www.whitechiefmountainlodge.com; 7776 White Chief Mountain Rd; r $145-155; ⏱ Apr–Oct) The cheapest and most basic option in town, this 1950s-era motel has simple kitchenette rooms. New owners have upgraded the exterior and some furniture, but the rooms are still pretty blah. It's located a few hundred yards east of Hwy 41; watch for the sign and go up the wooded country road. The on-site restaurant (mains $10-21) serves breakfast and a small dinner menu.

★ **Narrow Gauge Inn** INN $$$
(☏ 559-683-7720; www.narrowgaugeinn.com; 48571 Hwy 41; r incl breakfast Nov–Mar $89-134, Apr–Oct $229-369; ⊛🐾🛜) Next door to the Sugar Pine Railroad, this friendly, beautiful and supremely comfortable 26-room inn counts a hot tub, small bar, and the finest restaurant (☏ 559-683-6446; dinner mains $16-38; ⏱ 5-9pm Apr–Oct) in the area. Each tastefully appointed room features unique decor and a pleasant deck facing the trees and mountains, and all have flat-screen TVs.

Big Creek Inn B&B   B&B $$$

(☎559-641-2828; www.bigcreekinn.com; 1221 Hwy 41; r incl full breakfast $239-299; ☜) Each of the three white-palette rooms has peaceful creek views and a private balcony, and two have gas fireplaces. From the comfortable rooms or the back patio, you can often spot deer and beavers, or hummingbirds lining up at the patio feeder. Amenities include in-room DVD/Blu-Ray players and a large movie library, kitchenette use and big soaking tubs with bath salts.

Oakhurst

At the junction of Hwys 41 and 49, about 15 miles south of the park entrance, Oakhurst functions primarily as a service town. This is your last chance to stock up on reasonably priced groceries, gasoline and camping supplies. The lodgings listed are outside the center of town, where ho-hum chain motels abound.

🛏 Sleeping & Eating

★ Sierra Sky Ranch   LODGE $$

(☎559-683-8040; www.sierraskyranch. com; 50552 Rd 632; r incl breakfast $145-225; ❋☜⛱❋) This former ranch dates back to 1875 and has numerous outdoor activities available on 14 attractive acres. The homespun rooms are phone-free and pet-friendly, with oversized wooden headboards and double doors that open onto shady verandahs. The rambling and beautiful old lodge features a restaurant (dinner mains $12-45) and a rustic saloon, and has loads of comfortable lounging areas.

With a storied history including previous uses as a TB hospital and a bordello, its past guests include Marilyn Monroe and John Wayne. Many swear that it's cheerfully haunted by former residents.

Hounds Tooth Inn   B&B $$

(☎559-642-6600; www.houndstoothinn.com; 42071 Hwy 41; r incl breakfast $118-199; ❋☜) A few miles north of Oakhurst, this gorgeous B&B swims with rosebushes and Victorian-esque charm. Its airy rooms and cottages, some with spas and fireplaces, feel like an English manor house. Complimentary wine and hot drinks are available in the afternoon.

Château du Sureau   BOUTIQUE HOTEL $$$

(☎559-683-6860; www.chateaudusureau.com; r incl breakfast $385-585, 2-bedroom villa $2950; ❋@☜⛱) Never in a billion years would

---

SCENIC DRIVE: SIERRA VISTA SCENIC BYWAY

Set entirely within Sierra National Forest, this scenic route (www.sierravistascenicbyway.org) follows USFS roads in a 100-mile loop that takes you from 3000ft to nearly 7000ft. Along the way are dramatic vistas, excellent fishing, and camping almost anywhere you like (dispersed camping is allowed in most areas). It's a great way for car campers – and curious day trippers – to lose themselves within the mountains.

From its start in North Fork, the route takes a half-day to complete, emerging on Hwy 41 a few miles north of Oakhurst. Open from June to November, the road is paved most of the way, but narrow and laced with curves. See www.byways.org/explore/byways/2300 for a map and information on sights and the best overlooks.

---

you expect to find this in Oakhurst. A luxe and discreet full-service European-style hotel and world-class spa, this serene destination property boasts an exceptional level of service. With wall tapestries, oil paintings and ornate chandeliers, its restaurant (prix fixe dinner $108) could be a countryside castle.

Merced River Canyon

The approach to Yosemite via Hwy 140 is one of the most scenic, especially the section that meanders through Merced River Canyon. The springtime runoff makes this a spectacular spot for river rafting, with many miles of class III and IV rapids. Age minimums vary with water levels.

Outfitters include Zephyr Whitewater Expeditions (☎209-532-6249; www.zrafting.com; half-day/1-day trips per person from $109/135), a large, reputable outfitter with a seasonal office in El Portal, and OARS (☎209-736-2597; www.oars.com; 1-day trips per person $144-170), a worldwide rafting operator with a solid reputation.

Mariposa

About halfway between Merced and Yosemite Valley, Mariposa (Spanish for 'butterfly') is the largest and most interesting town near

California Wildlife

Unique creatures great and small inhabit the land, sky and waters of California's diverse ecosystems. Visit them at the ocean or in the forest, or just scan the skies.

1. Elephant seal
Equipped with a trunk-like nose, the enormous males noisily battle for dominance on the beach.

2. Black bear
The name is misleading, as bear fur can be shades of brown, black, cinnamon or tawny blonde.

3. California condor
A 10ft wingspan is the hallmark of these endangered carrion scavengers. Captive breeding has increased the population, though lead bullet poisoning remains its biggest threat.

4. Gray whale
Dramatic breaches and the puffs of water spouts mark the passage of these school-bus-sized mammals. Pods of whales migrate yearly between Mexico and Alaska, with peak viewing between December and April.

5. California sea lion
With dog-like faces and oversized flippers, vocal sea lions typically haul out in large social groups. The crowd-pleasing colony at San Francisco's Pier 39 mysteriously appeared soon after the 1989 Loma Prieta earthquake.

6. Mule deer
Ubiquitous throughout the state, mule deer are recognizable by their ample ears and black foreheads. Bucks wear forked antler racks.

7. Desert tortoise
Able to live for over half a century, these high desert reptiles burrow underground to survive extreme heat and cold.

8. Hawk
Frequently seen riding the thermal currents on windy ridges, a dozen types of hawks can be found in California. These speedy birds of prey are known for their keen eyesight and strong talons.

9. Mountain lion
Also known as cougars, panthers or pumas, these territorial big cats primarily stalk and feed on deer. They hunt from dusk to dawn, and can sprint at up to 50 miles per hour.

10. Banana slug
Tread carefully along the forest floor so you don't slip on these large and squishy bright yellow specimens.

11. Monarch butterfly
These orange and black beauties flutter thousands of miles to complete their annual migration.

12. Elk
Three subspecies of elk roam the state, with majestic males parading chandeliers of velvety antlers, and bugling dramatically during the fall rutting season.

JOHN LUND / GETTY IMAGES ©

3

STEVE JOHNSON / GETTY IMAGES ©

MICHAEL MIKE L. BAIRD / GETTY IMAGES ©

6

DAVID COURTENAY / GETTY IMAGES ©

BMSE / GETTY IMAGES ©

9

BRUCE LICHTENBERGER / GETTY IMAGES ©

MAUREEN P SULLIVAN / GETTY IMAGES ©

12

NOPPAWAT TOM CHARDENSINPHON / GETTY IMAGES ©

the park. Established as a mining and railroad town during the Gold Rush, it has the oldest courthouse in continuous use (since 1854) west of the Mississippi, loads of Old West pioneer character and a friendly feel.

Rock hounds should drive to the Mariposa County Fairgrounds, 2 miles south of town on Hwy 49, to see the 13-pound 'Fricot Nugget' – the largest crystallized gold specimen from the California Gold Rush era – and other gems and machinery at the **California State Mining & Mineral Museum** (209-742-7625; www.parks.ca.gov/?page_id=588; admission $4; 10am-5pm Thu-Sun May-Sep, to 4pm Oct-Apr). An exhibit on glow-in-the-dark minerals is also very cool.

🛏 Sleeping & Eating

⭐ River Rock Inn   MOTEL $$
(209-966-5793; www.riverrockmariposa.com; 4993 7th St; r incl breakfast $110-154; 🌐🎋🐾) A bold splash of psychedelic purple and dusty-orange paint spruces up what claims to be the oldest motel in town. Kitchenette rooms done up in artsy earth tones and have TVs but no phones, and calming ceiling fans resemble lily pads. A block removed from Hwy 140 on a quiet side street, it features a courtyard deck and deli cafe serving beer and wine, with live acoustic music some summer evenings.

Mariposa Historic Hotel   HISTORIC HOTEL $$
(209-966-7500; www.mariposahotelinn.com; 5029 Hwy 140; r incl breakfast $129-169; 🌐🎋) This creaky 1901 building has six king or queen rooms with old-time quilts and period-style furniture, and a corridor crammed with old town photos and newspaper clippings. Room 6 has an original clawfoot tub. Hummingbirds love the flowery back patio where breakfast is served.

Happy Burger   DINER $
(www.happyburgerdiner.com; Hwy 140 at 12th St; mains $7-11; 5:30am-9pm; 🎋🐾🛝) Boasting the largest menu in the Sierra, this buzzing roadside joint decorated with old LP album covers serves the cheapest meals in Mariposa. Its all-American cuisine means burgers, sandwiches, Mexican food and a ton of sinful ice-cream desserts. Free computer terminal, too.

Sugar Pine Cafe   AMERICAN $$
(www.sugarpinecafe.com; 5038 Hwy 140; breakfast $6-8, dinner $7-20; 7am-8:30pm Tue-Sat, to 3pm Sun & Mon) Gussied up with chrome soda counter stools and red circular booths, this 1940s-era diner serves yummy breakfast items, hot or cold sandwiches and burgers on whole-wheat buns. Dinner fare is pure comfort food like spaghetti and meatballs, and pork chops.

Savoury's   NEW AMERICAN $$
(209-966-7677; www.savouryrestaurant.com; 5034 Hwy 140; mains $17-32; 5-9pm, closed Wed winter; 🍴) Upscale yet casual Savoury's is still the best restaurant in town. Black lacquered tables and contemporary art create a tranquil window dressing for dishes like chipotle-and-orange-glazed chicken, hearty pastas and steak Diane.

ℹ Information

At the junction of Hwy 49s and 140 is the info-laden **Mariposa County Visitor Center** (866-425-3366, 209-966-7081; www.yosemiteexperience.com; 9am-6pm), which has friendly staff and racks of brochures.

ℹ Getting There & Away

YARTS (877-989-2787, 209-388-9589; www.yarts.com) buses run year-round along Hwy 140 into Yosemite Valley (adult/child $12/8 roundtrip, 1¾ hours one way) stopping at the Mariposa visitor center. Tickets include park admission.

Midpines

The highlight of this almost nonexistent town is the folksy **Yosemite Bug Rustic Mountain Resort** (866-826-7108, 209-966-6666; www.yosemitebug.com; 6979 Hwy 140, Midpines; dm $28, tent cabins $45-75, r without/with bath from $65/75; @🎋) 🐾, tucked away on a forested hillside about 25 miles from Yosemite National Park. It's more like a convivial mountain retreat than a hostel: at night, friendly folks of all ages and backgrounds share stories, music and delicious freshly prepared meals, and beer and wine in the woodsy **cafe** (mains $9-20; 7-10am, 11:30am-3pm & 6-9pm; 🍴) before retreating to their beds. Dorm dwellers have access to a communal kitchen, and the resort has a spa with a hot tub; yoga lessons and massages are also available. The YARTS bus stops a quarter mile up the driveway.

Briceburg

Some 20 miles outside the park, right where the Merced River meets Hwy 140, the town of Briceburg consists of a visitors center (☑209-379-9414; www.blm.gov/ca/st/en/fo/folsom/mercedriverrec.html; ⏱1-5pm Fri, from 9am Sat & Sun late-Apr–early-Sep) and three primitive Bureau of Land Management campgrounds (BLM; http://www.blm.gov/ca/st/en/fo/folsom/mercedriverrec.html; tent & RV sites $10; ▨) with a to-die-for location right on the river. To reach them you cross a beautiful 1920s wooden suspension bridge, so long trailers and large RVs are not recommended.

El Portal

Right outside the Arch Rock Entrance, and primarily inhabited by park employees, El Portal makes a convenient Yosemite base. YARTS buses run to Yosemite Valley (adult/child round-trip $7/5, one hour).

🛏 Sleeping & Eating

Indian Flat RV Park CAMPGROUND, CABINS $
(☑209-379-2339; www.indianflatrvpark.com; 9988 Hwy 140; tent sites $30, RV sites $42-47, tent cabins $79, cottages $129; ⏱year-round; ▨▨) Primarily an inexpensive private campground, Indian Flat RV Park also has a number of interesting housing options, including two pretty stone cabin cottages with air-conditioning and roomy tent cabins with ceiling fans and private porches. Guests can use the pool and wi-fi at its sister property next door, and nonguests can pay to shower.

Cedar Lodge MOTEL $$
(☑888-742-4371, 209-379-2612; www.stayyosemitecedarlodge.com; 9966 Hwy 140; r $149-189; ▨▩▨) Approximately 9 miles west of the Arch Rock Entrance, the Cedar is a sprawling establishment with more than 200 adequate rooms, an indoor pool, a seasonal outdoor pool and a couple of restaurants. Balcony rooms are the best of the bunch.

Yosemite View Lodge MOTEL $$$
(☑888-742-4371, 209-379-2681; www.stayyosemiteviewlodge.com; 11136 Hwy 140; r $189-269, ste $329-559; ▨▩▨▩▨) Less than 2 miles from the park entrance, Yosemite View Lodge is a big, modern complex with hot tubs, two restaurants and four pools. All the 336 rooms feature kitchenettes, some have gas fireplaces and views of the Merced River, and the ground-floor rooms have big patios. Wi-fi is $10 per day.

The souped-up 'majestic suites' are massive, with opulent bathrooms featuring waterfall showers and plasma-TV entertainment centers.

Groveland

From the Big Oak Flat entrance, it's 22 miles to Groveland, an adorable town with restored Gold Rush-era buildings and lots of visitor services. About 15 miles east of town, Rainbow Pool (www.fs.usda.gov/stanislaus) is a popular swimming hole with a small cascade; it's signed on the south side of Hwy 120.

🛏 Sleeping & Eating

Groveland Hotel HOTEL $$
(☑800-273-3314, 209-962-4000; www.groveland.com; 18767 Main St; r incl breakfast $169-319; ▨▩▨▩▨) The historic Groveland Hotel dates from 1850 and now houses a small bar, an upscale restaurant (mains $15-27) and 17 bright, lovingly decorated rooms with wraparound verandahs and resident teddy bears. Breakfast included May through September only.

Hotel Charlotte HOTEL $$
(☑209-962-6455; www.hotelcharlotte.com; 18736 Main St; r incl breakfast $149-225; ▨▩▨▩▨) A friendly, 12-room 1918 confection with beds adorned in patchwork quilts, the Hotel Charlotte keeps the vintage flair alive but still has modern conveniences. A sophisticated bistro (mains $12-20; ⏱6-9pm May-Sep) and bar serves a creative small-plates menu.

Mountain Sage CAFE $
(www.mtsage.com; 18653 Main St; snacks $2-6; ⏱7am-3pm, to 5pm Jun-Aug; ▩) 🌱 This popular cafe is also an art gallery, nursery and live-music venue all rolled into one, with organic and Fair Trade coffee, tasty baked treats and an excellent summer concert series (www.mountainsagemusic.org).

SEQUOIA & KINGS CANYON NATIONAL PARKS

The twin parks of Sequoia and Kings Canyon dazzle with superlatives, though they're often overshadowed by Yosemite, their smaller neighbor to the north (a three-hour drive away). With towering forests of giant sequoias containing some of the largest trees in the world, and the mighty Kings River

THE BUFFALO SOLDIERS

After the creation of the national parks in 1890, the US Army was called in to safeguard these natural resources. In the summer of 1903, troops from the 9th Cavalry – one of four well-respected (though segregated) African American regiments, known as the 'Buffalo Soldiers' – were sent to patrol here and in Yosemite. In Sequoia and what was then General Grant National Park, the troops had an impressively productive summer – building roads, creating a trail system and setting a high standard as stewards of the land.

The troops were commanded by Captain (later Colonel) Charles Young. At the time, Young was the only African American captain in the Army; his post as Acting Superintendent made him the first African American superintendent of a national park.

careening through the depths of Kings Canyon, one of the deepest chasms in the country, the parks are lesser-visited jewels where it's easier to find quiet and solitude. Throw in opportunities for caving, rock climbing and backcountry hiking through granite-carved Sierra landscapes, and backdoor access to Mt Whitney – the tallest peak in the lower 48 states – and you have all the ingredients for two of the best parks in the country.

The two parks (☎ 559-565-3341; www.nps.gov/seki; 7-day entry per car $20), though distinct, are operated as one unit with a single admission; for 24-hour recorded information, including road conditions, call the number listed or visit the parks' comprehensive website. At either entrance station (Big Stump or Ash Mountain), you'll receive an NPS map and a copy of the parks' *The Guide* newspaper, with information on seasonal activities, camping and special programs, including those in the surrounding national forests and the Giant Sequoia National Monument.

Cell-phone coverage is nonexistent except for limited reception at Grant Grove, and gas is available at Hume Lake and Stony Creek Lodge, both on USFS land.

History

In 1890 Sequoia became the second national park in the USA (after Yellowstone). A few days later, the 4 sq miles around Grant Grove were declared General Grant National Park and, in 1940, absorbed into the newly created Kings Canyon National Park. In 2000, to protect additional sequoia groves, vast tracts of land in the surrounding national forest became the Giant Sequoia National Monument.

❶ Dangers & Annoyances

Air pollution wafting up from the Sequoia Central Valley and Kings Canyon often thwarts long-range visibility, and people with respiratory problems should check with a visitor center about current pollution levels. Black bears are common and proper food storage is always required. Heed park instructions on wildlife procedures.

Kings Canyon National Park

With a dramatic cleft deeper than the Grand Canyon, Kings Canyon offers true adventure to those who crave seemingly endless trails, rushing streams and gargantuan rock formations. The camping, backcountry exploring and climbing here are all superb.

❂ Sights & Activities

Kings Canyon National Park has two developed areas with markets, lodging, showers and visitor information. Grant Grove Village is only 4 miles past the Big Stump entrance (in the park's west), while Cedar Grove Village is 31 miles east at the bottom of the canyon. The two are separated by the Giant Sequoia National Monument and are linked by Kings Canyon Scenic Byway/Hwy 180.

◉ Grant Grove

General Grant Grove   FOREST
This sequoia grove is nothing short of magnificent. The paved half-mile General Grant Tree Trail is an interpretive walk that visits a number of mature sequoias, including the 27-story General Grant Tree. This giant holds triple honors as the world's third-largest living tree, a memorial to US soldiers killed in war, and as the nation's Christmas tree. The nearby Fallen Monarch, a massive, fire-hollowed trunk that you can walk through, has been a cabin, hotel, saloon and stables for US Cavalry horses.

Panoramic Point
LOOKOUT

For a breathtaking view of Kings Canyon, head 2.3 miles up narrow, steep and winding Panoramic Point Rd (trailers and RVs aren't recommended), which branches off Hwy 180. Follow a short paved trail uphill from the parking lot to the viewpoint, where precipitous canyons and the snowcapped peaks of the Great Western Divide unfold below you. Snow closes the road to vehicles during winter, when it becomes a cross-country ski and snowshoe route.

Redwood Canyon
CANYON

South of Grant Grove Village, more than 15,000 sequoias cluster in this secluded and pristine corner of the park, making it the world's largest such grove. Relatively inaccessible, this area lets you enjoy the majesty of the giants away from the crowds on several moderate-to-strenuous trails. The trailhead is at the end of an unsigned, 2-mile bumpy dirt road across from the Hume Lake/Quail Flat sign on Generals Hwy, about 6 miles south of the village.

Cedar Grove & Roads End

At Cedar Grove Village, a simple lodge and snack bar provide the last outpost of civilization before the rugged grandeur of the backcountry takes over. Pretty spots around here include Roaring River Falls, where water whips down a sculpted rock channel before tumbling into a churning pool, and the easy, 1.5-mile Zumwalt Meadow nature trail, which loops around a verdant green meadow bordered by river and granite canyon. A short walk from Roads End, Muir Rock is a large flat river boulder where John Muir often gave talks during Sierra Club field trips. The rock now bears his name, and the lazy river abounds with gleeful swimmers in summer.

The trail to Mist Falls (8-mile roundtrip) is an easy to moderate hike to one of the park's larger waterfalls. The first 2 miles are fairly exposed, so start early to avoid the midday heat. Continuing past Mist Falls, the trail eventually connects with the John Muir/Pacific Crest Trail to form the 42-mile Rae Lakes Loop, the most popular long-distance hike in Kings Canyon National Park (a wilderness permit is required).

For guided horse trips, both day and overnight, check with Cedar Grove Pack Station (☎559-565-3464; Hwy 180, Cedar Grove; ☺May–mid-Oct).

🛏 Sleeping & Eating

Unless noted, all campsites are first-come, first-served. Pay showers are available at Grant Grove Village and Cedar Grove Village.

Potential campers should also keep in mind that there are great free uncrowded and undeveloped campgrounds off Big Meadows Rd in the Sequoia National Forest. They're some of the only empty campsites in the Sierra Nevada during peak summer season. Free roadside camping is also allowed in the forest, but no campfires without a permit (available from the Grant Grove Visitor Center).

Markets in Grant Grove Village and Cedar Grove Village have a limited selection of groceries.

🛏 Grant Grove

Crystal Springs Campground CAMPGROUND $
(tent & RV sites $18; ☺mid-May–mid-Sep; 🐾) Fifty wooded, well-spaced sites with flush toilets; the smallest campground in the Grant Grove area and generally very quiet.

Princess Campground CAMPGROUND $
(☎877-444-6777; www.recreation.gov; Giant Sequoia National Monument; tent & RV sites $18; ☺mid-May–late-Sep; 🐾) About 6 miles north of Grant Grove, with vault toilets and 88 reservable sites.

Azalea Campground CAMPGROUND $
(tent & RV sites $18; ☺year-round; 🐾) Flush toilets, 110 sites; the nicest sites border a

---

DON'T MISS

BUCK ROCK LOOKOUT

Built in 1923, this active fire lookout (www.buckrock.org; ☺9:30am-6pm Jul-Oct) is one of the finest restored watchtowers you could ever hope to visit. Staffed in fire season, its 172 stairs lead to a dollhouse-sized wooden cab on a dramatic 8500ft granite rise with panoramic forest views. To reach it from General Hwy, go about 1 mile north of the Montecito Sequoia Lodge and then east onto Big Meadows Rd (FS road 14S11). At approximately 2.5 miles, turn north on the signed dirt road (FS road 13S04) and follow signs another 3 miles to the lookout parking area.

Sequoia & Kings Canyon National Parks

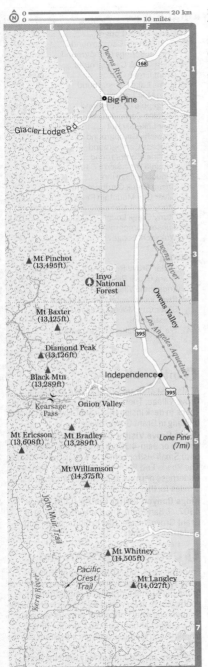

meadow. Close to Grant Grove Village (elevation 6500ft).

Sunset Campground
CAMPGROUND $
(tent & RV sites $18; ⊙late-May–early Sep; 🐾) Flush toilets, 157 sites, some overlooking the western foothills and the Central Valley. Close to Grant Grove Village.

Hume Lake Campground
CAMPGROUND $
(☑877-444-6777; www.recreation.gov; Hume Lake Rd, Giant Sequoia National Monument; tent & RV sites $20; ⊙late-May–early Sep; 🐾) Flush toilets, 74 reservable and uncrowded shady campsites, a handful with lake views; on the lake's northern shore about 10 miles northeast of Grant Grove.

Grant Grove Cabins
CABINS $$
(☑559-335-5500, 877-436-9615; www.visitsequoia.com; Hwy 180; cabins $63-140) Set amid towering sugar pines, around 50 cabins range from decrepit tent-top shacks (open from early June until early September) to rustic but comfortable heated duplexes (a few are wheelchair-accessible) with electricity, private bathrooms and double beds. For lovebirds, number 9 is the lone hard-sided, free-standing 'Honeymoon Cabin' with a queen bed, and books up fast.

John Muir Lodge
LODGE $$$
(☑877-436-9615, 559-335-5500; www.visitsequoia.com; Hwy 180; r $202-212; 🐾) An atmospheric wooden building hung with historical black-and-white photographs, this year-round hotel is a place to lay your head and still feel like you're in the forest. Wide porches have wooden rocking chairs, and homespun rooms contain rough-hewn wood furniture and patchwork bedspreads. Cozy up to the big stone fireplace on chilly nights with a board game.

Grant Grove Restaurant
AMERICAN $$
(Hwy 180; mains $9-18; ⊙7-10pm late-May–early Sep, reduced hours early Sep–late-May; 🐾🍴🖶) The only place to chow down in Grant Grove Village, its building will be torn down and rebuilt in 2015/2016, with plans for a temporary food area during construction. A new menu highlights seasonal dishes with rainbow trout or free-range chicken, but doesn't leave out comfort foods like pizza or fresh baked apple pie.

Cedar Grove

Cedar Grove's Sentinel campground, next to the village area, is open whenever Hwy

Sequoia & Kings Canyon National Parks

180 is open; Sheep Creek, Canyon View (tent only) and Moraine are opened as overflow when needed. These campgrounds are usually the last to fill up on busy summer weekends and are also good bets early and late in the season thanks to their comparatively low elevation (4600ft). All have flush toilets and $18 sites. Other facilities in the village don't start operating until mid-May.

Cedar Grove Lodge　　　　　LODGE $$
(☑866-522-6966, 559-335-5500; www.visitse-quoia.com; Hwy 180; r $129-135; ⊙mid-May–early Oct; ❋) The only indoor sleeping option in the canyon, the riverside lodge offers 21 un-exciting motel-style rooms, some with air-con. An in-progress remodel promises to dispel some of the frumpy decorations. Three ground-floor rooms with shady furnished patios have spiffy river views and kitchenettes. All rooms have phones and TVs.

Cedar Grove Restaurant　　　FAST FOOD $
(mains under $12; ⊙7am-8pm late-May–mid-Oct; ❢⊞) A basic counter service grill with hot and greasy fare.

ℹ Information

ATMs exist at Grant Grove Village and Cedar Grove Village. There's free wi-fi near the lodging check-in desk inside the Grant Grove Restaurant building in Grant Grove Village.

Cedar Grove Visitor Center (☑559-565-4307; ⊙8am or 9am-4:30pm or 5pm late-May–early Sep) Small visitor center in Cedar Grove Village. The Roads End Permit Station, which dispenses wilderness permits and rents bear canisters, is 6 miles further east.

Kings Canyon Visitor Center (☑559-565-4307; ⊙8am-5pm, shorter winter hours) In Grant Grove Village. Has exhibits, maps and wilderness permits.

ℹ Getting There & Around

From the west, Kings Canyon Scenic Byway (Hwy 180) travels 53 miles east from Fresno to the Big Stump entrance. Coming from the south, you're in for a long 46-mile drive through Sequoia National Park along sinuous Generals Hwy. Budget about two hours' driving time from the Ash Mountain entrance to Grant Grove Village. The road to Cedar Grove Village is only open from around April or May until the first snowfall.

Sequoia National Park

Picture unzipping your tent flap and crawling out into a 'front yard' of trees as high as a 20-story building and as old as the Bible. Brew some coffee as you plan your day in this extraordinary park with its soul-sustaining forests and gigantic peaks soaring above 12,000ft.

◉ Sights & Activities

Nearly all of the park's star attractions are conveniently lined up along the Generals Hwy, which starts at the Ash Mountain entrance and continues north into Kings Canyon. Tourist activity concentrates in the Giant Forest area and in Lodgepole Village, which has the most facilities, including a visitor center and market. The road to remote Mineral King veers off Hwy 198 in the town of Three Rivers, just south of the park's Ash Mountain entrance.

◉ Giant Forest

Named by John Muir in 1875, this area is the top destination in the park, and about 2 miles south of Lodgepole Village. By volume the largest living tree on earth, the massive General Sherman Tree rockets 275ft to the sky. Pay your respects via a short descent

from the Wolverton Rd parking lot, or join the Congress Trail, a paved 2-mile pathway that takes in General Sherman and other notable named trees, including the Washington Tree, the world's second-biggest sequoia, and the see-through Telescope Tree. To lose the crowds, set off on the 5-mile Trail of the Sequoias, which puts you into the heart of the forest.

Open in the warmer months, Crescent Meadow Rd heads east from the Giant Forest Museum for 3 miles to Crescent Meadow, a relaxing picnic spot, especially in spring when it's ablaze with wildflowers. Several short hikes start from here, including the 1-mile trail to Tharp's Log, where the area's first settler spent summers in a fallen tree. The road also passes Moro Rock, a landmark granite dome whose top can be reached via a quarter-mile carved staircase for breathtaking views of the Great Western Divide, a chain of mountains running north to south through the center of Sequoia National Park.

Giant Forest Museum   MUSEUM
(☎559-565-4480; Generals Hwy; ⊙9am-4:30pm or 6pm mid-May–mid-Oct; 🚹) FREE For a primer on the intriguing ecology, fire cycle and history of the 'big trees,' drop in at this excellent museum, then follow up your visit with a spin around the paved (and

---

SCENIC DRIVE: KINGS CANYON SCENIC BYWAY (HIGHWAY 180)

The 31-mile rollercoaster road connecting Grant Grove and Cedar Grove ranks among the most dazzling in all of California. It winds past the Converse Basin Grove, which once contained the world's largest grove of mature sequoias until loggers turned it into a sequoia cemetery in the 1880s. A half-mile loop trail leads to the 20ft-high Chicago Stump, the remains of the 3200-year-old tree that was cut down, sectioned and reassembled for the 1893 World Columbian Exposition in Chicago. North of here, a second side road goes to Stump Meadow, where stumps and fallen logs make good picnic platforms, and to the Boole Tree Trail, a 2.5-mile loop to the only 'monarch' left to live.

The road then begins its jaw-dropping descent into the canyon, snaking past chiseled rock walls, some tinged by green moss and red iron minerals, others decorated by waterfalls. Turnouts provide superb views, especially at Junction View.

Eventually the road runs parallel with the gushing Kings River, its thunderous roar ricocheting off granite cliffs soaring as high as 8000ft, making Kings Canyon even deeper than the Grand Canyon. Stop at Boyden Cavern (www.caverntours.com/BoydenRt.htm; Hwy 180; tours adult/child from $14.50/8.50; ⊙May–mid-Nov; 🚹) for a tour of its whimsical formations. While beautiful, they are smaller and less impressive than those in Crystal Cave in Sequoia National Park, but no advance tickets are required. Exciting canyoneering tours are also available by advance reservation. About 5 miles further east, Grizzly Falls can be torrential or drizzly, depending on the time of year.

On your return trip, consider a detour via Hume Lake, created in 1908 as a dam for logging operations and now offering boating, swimming and fishing. Facilities include a small market and a gas station.

wheelchair-accessible) 1.2-mile interpretive Big Trees Trail, which starts from the museum parking lot.

Foothills

From the Ash Mountain entrance in Three Rivers, the Generals Hwy ascends steeply through this southern section of Sequoia National Park. With an average elevation of about 2000ft, the Foothills are much drier and warmer than the rest of the park. Hiking here is best in spring when the air is still cool and wildflowers put on a colorful show. Summers are buggy and muggy, but fall again brings moderate temperatures and lush foliage.

The Potwisha people lived in this area until the early 1900s, relying primarily on acorn meal. Pictographs and grinding holes still grace the Hospital Rock picnic area, once a Potwisha village site. Swimming holes abound along the Marble Fork of the Kaweah River, especially near Potwisha Campground. Be careful, though – the currents can be deadly, especially when the river is swollen from the spring runoff.

Mineral King

A scenic, subalpine valley at 7500ft, Mineral King is Sequoia's backpacking mecca and a good place to find solitude. Gorgeous and gigantic, its glacially sculpted valley is ringed by massive mountains, including the jagged 12,343ft Sawtooth Peak. The area is reached via Mineral King Rd – a slinky, steep and narrow 25-mile road, not suitable for RVs or speed demons; the road is usually open from late May through October. Plan on spending the night unless you don't mind driving three hours round-trip.

Hiking anywhere from here involves a steep climb out of the valley along strenuous trails, so be aware of the altitude, even on short hikes. Enjoyable day hikes go to Crystal, Monarch, Mosquito and Eagle Lakes. For long trips, locals recommend the Little Five Lakes and, further along the High Sierra Trail, Kaweah Gap, surrounded by Black Kaweah, Mt Stewart and Eagle Scout Peak – all above 12,000ft.

In spring and early summer, hordes of hungry marmots terrorize parked cars at Mineral King, chewing on radiator hoses, belts and wiring of vehicles to get the salt they crave after their winter hibernation. If you're thinking of going hiking during that time, you'd be a fool not to protect your car by wrapping the underside with chicken wire or a diaper-like tarp.

From the 1860s to 1890s, Mineral King witnessed heavy silver mining and lumber activity. There are remnants of old shafts and stamp mills, though it takes some exploring to find them. A proposal by the Walt Disney Corporation to develop the area into a massive ski resort was thwarted when Congress annexed it to the national park in 1978. The website of the Mineral King Preservation Society (www.mineralking.org) has all kinds of info on the area, including its rustic and still-occupied historic mining cabins.

Sleeping & Eating

The market at Lodgepole Village is the best stocked in either park, but basic supplies are also available at the small store in Stony Creek Lodge (closed in winter).

Generals Highway

A handful of campgrounds line the highway and rarely fill up, although space may get tight on holiday weekends. Those in the Foothills area are best in spring and fall when the higher elevations are still chilly, but they get hot and buggy in summer. Unless noted, sites are available on a first-come, first-served basis. Free dispersed camping is possible in the Giant Sequoia National Monument. Stop by a visitor center or ranger station for details or a fire permit. Lodgepole Village and Stony Creek Lodge have pay showers.

Stony Creek Campground   CAMPGROUND $
(☎877-444-6777; www.recreation.gov; tent & RV sites $24; ☉mid-May–late-Sep; 🐾) USFS-operated with 49 comfortable wooded sites, including some right on the creek, and flush toilets. Smaller Upper Stony Creek campground is across the street and has vault toilets.

Lodgepole Campground   CAMPGROUND $
(☎877-444-6777; www.recreation.gov; tent & RV sites $22; ☉May-Nov) Closest to the Giant Forest area with over 200 closely packed sites and flush toilets; this place fills quickly because of proximity to Lodgepole Village amenities. A dozen or so walk-in sites are more private.

DON'T MISS

CRYSTAL CAVE

Discovered in 1918 by two fishermen, Crystal Cave (☎559-565-3759; www.sequoiahistory.org; Crystal Cave Rd; tours adult/child from $15/8; ⊗mid-May–Nov; ♠) was carved by an underground river and has formations estimated to be 10,000 years old. Stalactites hang like daggers from the ceiling, and milky white marble formations take the shape of ethereal curtains, domes, columns and shields. The cave is also a unique biodiverse habitat for spiders, bats and tiny aquatic insects that are found nowhere else on earth. The 45-minute tour covers a half-mile of chambers, though adults can also sign up for more in-depth lantern-lit cave explorations and full-day spelunking adventures.

Tickets are *only* sold at the Lodgepole and Foothills visitor centers and *not* at the cave. Allow about one hour to get to the cave entrance, which is a half-mile walk from the parking lot (restroom available) at the end of a twisty 7-mile road; the turnoff is about 3 miles south of the Giant Forest. Bring a sweater or light jacket, as it's a huddle-for-warmth 48°F (9°C) inside.

Potwisha Campground　CAMPGROUND $
(tent & RV sites $22; ⊗year-round; ☎) Also in the Foothills, and blazing in summertime, this campground has decent shade and swimming spots on the Kaweah River. It's 3 miles north of the Ash Mountain entrance, with 42 sites and flush toilets.

Dorst Creek Campground　CAMPGROUND $
(☎877-444-6777; www.recreation.gov; tent & RV sites $22; ⊗late-Jun–early Sep; ☎) Big and busy campground with 204 sites and flush toilets; quieter back sites are tent-only.

Buckeye Flat Campground　CAMPGROUND $
(tent sites $22; ⊗Apr-Sep; ☎) This campground is in the Foothills area, in an open stand of oaks about 6 miles north of the Ash Mountain entrance. There are 28 tent-only sites and flush toilets. Can be somewhat rowdy.

Stony Creek Lodge　LODGE $$
(☎559-565-3909; www.sequoia-kingscanyon.com; 65569 Generals Hwy; r $159-189; ⊗mid-May–mid-Oct; ☎) About halfway between Grant Grove Village and Giant Forest, this lodge has a big river-rock fireplace in its lobby and 12 aging but folksy motel rooms with telephone and flat-screen TVs.

Sequoia High Sierra Camp　CABINS $$$
(☎877-591-8982; www.sequoiahighsierracamp.com; r without bath incl all meals per adult/child $250/150; ⊗mid-Jun–early Oct) Accessed via a 1-mile hike deep into the Sequoia National Forest, off Generals Hwy, this off-the-grid, all-inclusive resort is nirvana for active, sociable people who don't think 'luxury camping' is an oxymoron. Canvas cabins are spiffed up by pillow-top mattresses, down pillows and

cozy wool rugs, with shared restrooms and a shower house. Reservations are required, with a two-night minimum stay.

Wuksachi Lodge　LODGE $$$
(☎866-807-3598, 559-565-4070; www.visitsequoia.com; 64740 Wuksachi Way, off Generals Hwy; r from $225; ☎) Built in 1999, the Wuksachi Lodge is the park's most upscale lodging and dining option. But don't get too excited – the wood-paneled atrium lobby has an inviting stone fireplace and forest views, but charmless motel-style kitchenette rooms with oak furniture and thin walls have an institutional feel. The lodge's location, however, just north of Lodgepole Village, can't be beat.

Lodgepole Village　MARKET $
(Generals Hwy; mains $6-10; ⊗market & snack bar 9am-6pm mid-Apr–late-May & early Sep–mid-Oct, 8am-8pm late-May–early Sep, deli 11am-6pm mid-Apr–mid-Oct; ♠) The park's most extensive market sells all kinds of groceries, camping supplies and snacks. Inside, a fast-food snack bar slings burgers and grilled sandwiches and dishes up breakfast. The adjacent deli is a tad more upscale and healthy, with focaccia sandwiches, veggie wraps and picnic salads.

Backcountry

Bearpaw High Sierra Camp　CABIN $$
(☎866-807-3598, 801-559-4930; www.visitsequoia.com; tent cabin incl breakfast & dinner $175; ⊗mid-Jun–mid-Sep) About 11.5 miles east of Giant Forest on the High Sierra Trail, this tent hotel is ideal for exploring the backcountry without lugging your own camping gear. Rates include showers, dinner and breakfast, as well as bedding and towels.

Bookings start at 7am every January 2 and sell out almost immediately, though you should always check for cancellations.

Mineral King

Mineral King's two pretty campgrounds, **Atwell Mill** (tent sites $12; ⊙late-May–mid-Oct; 🐻) and **Cold Springs** (tent sites $12; ⊙late-May–mid-Oct; 🐻), often fill up on summer weekends. Pay showers are available at the Silver City Mountain Resort.

Silver City Mountain Resort   CABINS $$
(📞559-561-3223;   www.silvercityresort.com; Mineral King Rd; cabins with/without bath from $195/120, chalets $250-395; ⊙late-May–late-Oct; 🛜) The only food and lodging option anywhere near these parts, this rustic, old-fashioned and family-friendly place rents everything from cute and cozy 1950s-era cabins to modern chalets that sleep up to eight. Its **restaurant** (mains $10-18; ⊙8am-8pm Thu-Mon, pie & coffee only 9am-4pm Tue-Wed) serves delicious homemade pies and simple fare on wooden picnic tables under the trees. It's located 3.5 miles west of the ranger station.

There's a ping-pong table, outdoor swings, and nearby ponds to splash around in. All guests should bring their own sheets and towels (rentals $25 to $50 per cabin). Most cabins don't have electricity, and the property's generator usually shuts off around 10pm.

Three Rivers

Named for the nearby convergence of three Kaweah River forks, Three Rivers is a friendly small town populated mostly by retirees and artsy newcomers. The town's main drag, Sierra Dr (Hwy 198), is sparsely lined with motels, eateries and shops.

Sequoia Village Inn   CABINS, COTTAGES $$
(📞559-561-3652;   www.sequoiavillageinn.com; 45971 Sierra Dr; d $129-319; ❄🛜🌊🐻) These 10 pretty modern cottages, cabins and chalets (most with kitchens and the rest with kitchenettes), border the park and are great for families or groups. Most have outdoor woodsy decks and barbecues, and the largest can sleep 12.

Buckeye Tree Lodge   MOTEL $$
(📞559-561-5900;   www.buckeyetreelodge.com; 46000 Sierra Dr; d incl breakfast $134-159; ❄🛜🌊🐻) 🍴 Sit out on your grassy back patio or perch on the balcony and watch the river ease through a maze of boulders. Modern white-brick motel rooms, one with a kitchenette, feel airy and bright.

We Three Bakery & Restaurant   BREAKFAST, BAKERY $
(43368 Sierra Dr; mains $7-15; ⊙7am-2:30pm, to 9pm Fri & Sat in summer; 🛜) Cinnamon French toast, biscuits with gravy and diner-style coffee lure in the breakfast crowd, while hot and cold sandwiches on blindingly bright Fiesta-ware make it a delish lunch spot. Chow down on the outdoor patio under a shady oak.

River View Restaurant & Lounge   AMERICAN $$
(42323 Sierra Dr; lunch $9-12, dinner $16-24; ⊙11am-9pm, to 10pm Fri & Sat, bar open late) Colorful honky-tonk with a great back patio; live music Fridays through Sundays.

BACKPACKING IN SEQUOIA & KINGS CANYON NATIONAL PARKS

With over 850 miles of marked trails, the parks are a backpacker's dream. Cedar Grove and Mineral King offer the best backcountry access. Trails are usually open by mid to late May.

For overnight backcountry trips you'll need a wilderness permit (per group $15), which is subject to a quota system in summer; permits are free and available by self-registration outside the quota season. About 75% of spaces can be reserved, while the rest are available in person on a first-come, first-served basis. Reservations can be made from March 1 until two weeks before your trip. For details see www.nps.gov/seki/planyourvisit/wilderness_permits.htm. There's also a dedicated wilderness desk at the Lodgepole Visitor Center.

All ranger stations and visitor centers carry topo maps and hiking guides. Note that you need to store your food in park-approved bearproof canisters, which can be rented at markets and visitor centers (from $5 per trip).

WINTER FUN

In winter a thick blanket of snow drapes over trees and meadows, the pace of activity slows and a hush falls over the roads and trails. Note that snow often closes Generals Hwy between Grant Grove and Giant Forest and that tire chains may be required at any time. These can usually be rented near the parks' entrances, although you're not supposed to put them on rental cars. For up-to-date road conditions call ☑559-565-3341 or check www.nps.gov/seki.

Snowshoeing and cross-country skiing are both hugely popular activities, with 50 miles of marked but ungroomed trails crisscrossing the Grant Grove and Giant Forest areas. Winter road closures also make for excellent cross-country skiing and snowshoeing on Sequoia's Moro Rock–Crescent Meadow Rd, Kings Canyon's Panoramic Point Rd and the Sequoia National Forest's Big Meadows Rd. Trail maps are available at the visitor centers, and park rangers lead free snowshoe tours (equipment included). Tree-marked trails connect with those in the Giant Sequoia National Monument and the 30 miles of groomed terrain maintained by the private Montecito Sequoia Lodge (☑559-565-3388; www.montecitosequoia.com; 8000 Generals Hwy). Equipment rentals are available at Grant Grove Village, the Wuksachi Lodge and the Montecito Sequoia Lodge. There are also snow-play areas near Columbine and Big Stump in the Grant Grove region and at Wolverton Meadow in Sequoia.

In winter cross-country skiers with reservations can sleep in one of the 10 bunks at Pear Lake Ski Hut (☑559-565-3759; www.sequoiahistory.org; dm $38-42; ☉mid-Dec–late Apr), a 1940-era pine-and-granite building run by the Sequoia Natural History Association. You'll be glad to see it after the strenuous 6-mile cross-country ski or snowshoe trek from Wolverton Meadow. Reservations are assigned by lottery in November. Call or check the website for details.

ℹ Information

Lodgepole Village has an ATM, and there's free wi-fi at Wuksachi Lodge.

Foothills Visitor Center (☑559-565-4212; ☉8am-4:30pm) One mile north of the Ash Mountain entrance.

Lodgepole Visitor Center (☑559-565-4436; ☉9am-4:30pm or 6pm daily, shorter winter hours) Maps, information, exhibits, Crystal Cave tickets and wilderness permits.

Mineral King Ranger Station (☑559-565-3768; ☉8am-4pm late-May–early Sep) Twenty-four miles east of Generals Hwy; wilderness permits and campground availability info.

ℹ Getting There & Around

Coming from the south, Hwy 198 runs north from Visalia through Three Rivers past Mineral King Rd to the Ash Mountain entrance. Beyond here the road continues as the Generals Hwy, a narrow and windy road snaking all the way into Kings Canyon National Park, where it joins the Kings Canyon Scenic Byway (Hwy 180) near the western Big Stump entrance. Vehicles over 22ft long may have trouble negotiating the steep road with its many hairpin curves. Budget about one hour to drive from the entrance to the Giant Forest/Lodgepole area and another hour from there to Grant Grove Village in Kings Canyon.

Sequoia Shuttle (☑877-287-4453; www.sequoiashuttle.com; one way/round-trip $7.50/15; ☉late-May–early Sep) buses run five times daily between Visalia and the Giant Forest Museum (2½ hours) via Three Rivers; reservations required.

Shuttle buses run every 15 minutes from the Giant Forest Museum to Moro Rock and Crescent Meadow or to the General Sherman Tree parking areas and Lodgepole Village. Another route links Lodgepole, Wuksachi Lodge and Dorst Creek Campground every 30 minutes. All routes are free and currently operate 9am to about 6pm from late May to early September.

EASTERN SIERRA

Cloud-dappled hills and sun-streaked mountaintops dabbed with snow typify the landscape of the Eastern Sierra, where slashing peaks – many over 14,000ft – rise abruptly upward from the arid expanses of the Great Basin and Mojave deserts. It's a dramatic juxtaposition that makes for a potent cocktail of scenery. Pine forests, lush meadows, ice-blue lakes, simmering hot springs and glacier-gouged canyons are only some of the beautiful sights you'll find in this region.

The Eastern Sierra Scenic Byway, officially known as Hwy 395, runs the entire length of the range. Turnoffs dead-ending at the foot of the mountains deliver you to pristine wilderness and countless trails, including the famous Pacific Crest Trail, John Muir Trail and main Mt Whitney Trail. The most important portals are the towns of Bridgeport, Mammoth Lakes, Bishop and Lone Pine. Note that in winter, when traffic thins, many facilities are closed.

ℹ Information

Locally produced and available throughout the region, Sierra Maps' *Eastern Sierra: Bridgeport to Lone Pine* recreation and road map shows hot springs, ghost towns, hiking trails and climbing areas. Check out www.thesierraweb.com for area events and links to visitor information, and *Sierra Wave* (www.sierrawave.net) for regional news.

ℹ Getting There & Around

The Eastern Sierra is easiest to explore under your own steam, although it's possible to access the area by public transportation. Buses operated by **Eastern Sierra Transit Authority** (☑ 760-872-1901; www.estransit.com/) make a round-trip between Lone Pine and Reno ($59, six hours) on Monday, Tuesday, Thursday and Friday, stopping at all Hwy 395 towns in between. Fares depend on distance, and reservations are recommended. There's also an express bus between Mammoth Lakes and Bishop ($7, one hour, three times daily) that operates Monday through Friday.

In the summer connect to Yosemite via YARTS bus in Mammoth Lakes or Lee Vining.

Mono Lake Area

Bridgeport

Barely three blocks long, set amid open high valley and in view of the peaks of Sawtooth Ridge, Bridgeport flaunts classic western flair with charming old storefronts and a homey ambience. Most everything shuts down or cuts back hours for the brutal winters, but the rest of the year the town is a magnet for anglers, hikers, climbers and hot-spring devotees.

⊙ Sights & Activities

Mono County Courthouse HISTORIC BUILDING
(☺ 9am-5pm Mon-Fri) The gavel has been dropped since 1880 at the courthouse, an all-white Italianate dreamboat surrounded by a gracious lawn and a wrought-iron fence. On the street behind it, look for the **Old County Jail**, a spartan facility fashioned with iron latticework doors and stone walls 2ft thick. Unlucky inmates overnighted in its six cells from 1883 until 1964.

Mono County Museum MUSEUM
(☑ 760-932-5281; www.monocomuseum.org; Emigrant St; adult/child $2/1; ☺ 9am-4pm Tue-Sat Jun-Sep) Two blocks away from the Mono County Courthouse, in a schoolhouse of the same age, this museum has mining artifacts on display from all the local ghost towns, plus a room of fine Paiute baskets.

★**Travertine Hot Spring** HOT SPRING
A bit south of town, head here to watch a panoramic Sierra sunset from three hot pools set amid impressive rock formations. To get there, turn east on Jack Sawyer Rd just before the ranger station, then follow the dirt road uphill for about 1 mile.

Ken's Sporting Goods FISHING
(☑ 760-932-7707; www.kenssport.com; 258 Main St; ☺ 7am-8pm Mon-Thu, to 9pm Fri & Sat mid-Apr–mid-Nov, 9am-4pm Tue-Sat mid-Nov–mid-Apr) Stop by Ken's for information and fishing gear. If you're trolling for trout, try the Bridgeport Reservoir and the East Walker River.

🍴 Sleeping & Eating

Redwood Motel MOTEL $
(☑ 760-932-7060; www.redwoodmotel.net; 425 Main St; d from $88-99; ☺ Apr-Nov; ✱🐾📶🐕) A bucking bronco, an ox in a Hawaiian shirt and other wacky farm animal sculptures provide a cheerful welcome to this little kitchenette motel. Rooms are spotless and your dog-friendly host is super helpful in dispensing local area tips.

Bodie Victorian Hotel HISTORIC HOTEL $
(☑ 760-932-7020; www.bodievictorianhotel.com; 85 Main St; r $60-125; ☺ May-Oct) Go back to the 1800s in this curious building transplanted from Bodie that's completely furnished with antiques and rumored to be haunted. The bold Victorian wallpaper and striking bordello accoutrements more than make up for the slightly run-down feel. If no one's there, poke your head inside the Sportsmens Bar & Grill next door to rustle up an employee.

Hays Street Cafe AMERICAN $
(www.haysstreetcafe.com; 21 Hays St; mains under $10; ☺ 6am-2pm May-Oct, 7am-1pm Nov-Apr) On

---

ℹ️ WILDERNESS PERMITS: EASTERN SIERRA

Free wilderness permits for overnight camping are required year-round in the Ansel Adams, John Muir, Golden Trout and Hoover Wilderness areas. For the first three, trailhead quotas are in effect frwilderom May through October and about 60% of the quota may be reserved online at www.recreation.gov for a $5 fee (per person). From November to April, you can pick up permits at most ranger stations. If you find the station closed, look for self-issue permits outside the office. Wilderness permits for the Inyo National Forest can be picked up in either Lone Pine, Bishop, Mammoth Lakes or its Mono Basin ranger stations. Yosemite's Tuolumne Meadows Wilderness Center can also issue permits for trips from Saddlebag Lake. For questions call the **Inyo National Forest Wilderness Permit Office** (📞 760-873-2483; www.fs.usda.gov/inyo).

Permits for the Hoover Wilderness that depart from the Humboldt-Toiyabe National Forest (seasonal quotas on some trails) are issued at the Bridgeport Ranger Station & Visitor Center.

The forums on **High Sierra Topix** (www.highsierratopix.com) are an excellent resource for planning trips.

---

the south end of town, this country-style place prides itself on its many homemade items, including its biscuits and gravy, and cinnamon rolls as big as bricks.

J's on the Corner   AMERICAN $
(247 Main St; mains $7-10; ⊘ 11am-9pm, variable hours Oct-Apr) Excellent hot and cold sandwiches and filling salads (no iceberg lettuce!) and great prices make this small grill a popular spot. Meat lovers should aim for the prime rib French dip.

Bridgeport Inn   AMERICAN $$
(www.thebridgeportinn.com; 205 Main St; mains $10-22; ⊘ 8am-8:30pm Thu-Tue Apr-Oct; 📶) Stop in at the country kitchen dining room of this whitewashed 1877 building for burgers, pot roast, steaks and seafood, and a dip into its modest wine list. Watch the world stream by from a classic soda fountain stool on the long front porch.

ℹ️ Information

Bridgeport Ranger Station & Visitor Center (📞 760-932-7070; www.fs.usda.gov/htnf; Hwy 395; ⊘ 8am-4:30pm daily Jun–mid-Sep, 8am-4:30pm Mon-Fri mid-Sep–May) Stop by this center for maps, information and Hoover Wilderness permits.

Twin Lakes

Eager anglers line the shoreline of Twin Lakes, a gorgeous duo of basins cradled by the fittingly named Sawtooth Ridge. The area's famous for its fishing – especially since some lucky guy bagged the state's largest ever brown trout here in 1987 (it weighed

in at a hefty 26lbs). Lower Twin is quieter, while Upper Twin allows boating and waterskiing. Other activities include mountain biking and, of course, hiking in the Hoover Wilderness Area and on into the eastern, lake-riddled reaches of Yosemite National Park.

◉ Sights & Activities

A stroll down a loose hillside brings you to out-of-the-way **Buckeye Hot Spring**, though it can get crowded. Water emerges piping hot from a steep hillside and cools as it trickles down into several rock pools right by the side of lively Buckeye Creek, which is handy for taking a cooling dip. One pool is partially tucked into a small cave made from a rock overhang. Clothing is optional. To get there from Hwy 395 via Twin Lakes Rd, turn right at Doc & Al's Resort (7 miles from Hwy 395), driving 3 miles on a (momentarily paved and then) graded dirt road. Cross the bridge at Buckeye Creek (at 2.5 miles), and bear right at the Y-junction, following signs to the hot spring. Go uphill a half mile until you see a flattish parking area on your right. Follow a trail down to the pools.

For hikers the main trailhead is at the end of Twin Lakes Rd just past Annett's Mono Village; weekly overnight parking is $10 per vehicle. From here hikers can set off along Robinson Creek for adventures in the stunning **Hoover Wilderness** and overnight backpacking trips (wilderness permit required) into northeastern Yosemite. The day hike to lovely **Barney Lake** (8 miles round-trip) takes in magnificent views of jagged granite spires in **Little Slide Canyon**, where

Mono Lake Area

rock climbers detour to scale a fierce wall called the **Incredible Hulk**, and steep boulder rockslides on the ridge to the north.

For a hike with great views of Twin Lakes, go south from Annett's on the **Horse Creek Trail**, which soon leads to the cascades of **Horsetail Falls**. It continues up to skirt the wilderness boundary and then descends back to Twin Lakes on the **Cattle Creek Trail**. Loop back along the lake for 7.5 miles in total. In *Dharma Bums*, Beat author Jack Kerouac describes an ascent he made from Horse Creek Canyon to nearby Matterhorn Peak (12,300ft) with poet Gary Snyder.

Twin Lakes Rd (Rte 420) runs through pastures and foothills for about 10 miles before reaching Lower Twin Lake. The road is a satisfying route for moderately fit cyclists, with mostly level terrain and heavenly scenery.

🛏 Sleeping & Eating

Past the bridge at Buckeye Creek, bear left at the signed Y-junction along a road for 2 miles to **Buckeye Campground** (tent & RV sites $15; ☺May–mid-Oct), with tables, fire grates, potable water and toilets. You can also camp for free in undeveloped spots

Mono Lake Area

along Buckeye Creek on both sides of the creek bridge.

Honeymoon Flat, Robinson Creek, Paha, Crags and Lower Twin Lakes USFS campgrounds (☎800-444-7275; www.recreation.gov; tent & RV sites $17-20; ⏲mid-May–Sep) set among Jeffrey pine and sagebrush along Robinson Creek and Lower Twin Lake. All have flush toilets except for Honeymoon Flat, which has vault toilets.

Twin Lakes Rd dead-ends at Annett's Mono Village (☎760-932-7071; www.monovillage.com; tent sites $20, RV sites with hookups $30, r $75, cabin $85-205; ⏲late Apr-Oct; ☎) a huge and rather chaotic tumbledown resort on Upper Twin Lake. It has cheap but cramped lodging, and a kitschy low-ceilinged cafe (mains $9-16) studded with taxidermied fish. Pay showers available.

Bodie State Historic Park

For a time warp back to the Gold Rush era, swing by Bodie (☎760-647-6445; www.parks.ca.gov/bodie; Hwy 270; adult/child $5/3; ⏲9am-6pm mid-May–Oct, to 4pm Nov–mid-May), one of the West's most authentic and best-preserved ghost towns. Gold was first discovered here in 1859, and within 20 years the place grew from a rough mining camp to an even rougher boomtown with a population of 10,000 and a reputation for unbridled lawlessness. Fights and murders took place almost daily, the violence no doubt fueled by liquor dispensed in the town's 65 saloons, some of which did double duty as brothels, gambling halls or opium dens. The hills disgorged some $35 million worth of gold and silver in the 1870s and '80s, but when production plummeted, so did the population, and eventually the town was abandoned to the elements.

About 200 weather-beaten buildings still sit frozen in time in this cold, barren and windswept valley heaped with tailing piles. Peering through dusty windows you'll see stocked stores, furnished homes, a schoolhouse with desks and books, and workshops filled with tools. The jail is still there, as are the fire station, churches, a bank vault and many other buildings.

The former Miners' Union Hall now houses a museum and visitors center (⏲9am to one hour before park closes). Rangers conduct free general tours. In summertime they also offer tours of the landscape and the cemetery; call for details. The second Saturday of August is Friends of Bodie Day (www.bodiefoundation.org), with stagecoach rides,

SCENIC DRIVE: EBBETTS PASS SCENIC BYWAY

For outdoor fanatics, a scenic 61-mile section of Hwys 4 and 89 called the **Ebbetts Pass Scenic Byway** (www.scenic4.org) is a road trip through paradise. Heading northeast from Arnold, gaze up at the giant sequoias of **Calaveras Big Trees State Park** (☑ 209-795-2334; www.parks.ca.gov; per car $10; ☼ sunrise-sunset) and in winter stop at the family-friendly ski resort of **Bear Valley** (☑ 209-753-2301; www.bearvalley.com; lift tickets adult/child $64/19; ♿). Continuing east the stunningly beautiful **Lake Alpine** is skirted by slabs of granite, several great beaches and a handful of campgrounds, and boasts excellent watersports, fishing and hiking.

The next stretch is the most dramatic, when the narrow highway continues past picturesque **Mosquito Lake** and the **Pacific Grade Summit** (8060ft) before slaloming through historic Hermit Valley and finally winding up and over the 8730ft summit of **Ebbetts Pass**. North on Hwy 89 and just west of **Markleeville**, visit the two developed pools and seasonal campground at **Grover Hot Springs State Park** (☑ 530-694-2249; www.parks.ca.gov/?page_id=508; per car $8; pool admission adult/child $7/5, tent & RV sites $35; ☼ variable hours year-round).

From San Francisco it's a three-hour drive east to Arnold, via Hwy 108 and Hwy 49. Ebbetts Pass closes after the first major snowfall and doesn't reopen until June, but Hwy 4 is usually plowed from the west as far as Bear Valley.

history presentations and lots of devotees in period costumes.

❶ Getting There & Away

Bodie is about 13 miles east of Hwy 395 via Rte 270; the last 3 miles are unpaved. Although the park is open year-round, the road is usually closed in winter and early spring, so you'd have to don snowshoes or cross-country skis to get there.

Virginia Lakes

South of Bridgeport, Hwy 395 gradually arrives at its highest point, **Conway Summit** (8143ft), where you'll be whipping out your camera to capture the awe-inspiring panorama of Mono Lake, backed by the Mono Craters, and June and Mammoth Mountains.

Also at the top is the turnout for Virginia Lakes Rd, which parallels Virginia Creek for about 6 miles to a cluster of lakes flanked by **Dunderberg Peak** (12,374ft) and **Black Mountain** (11,797ft). A trailhead at the end of the road gives access to the Hoover Wilderness Area and the **Pacific Crest Trail**. The trail continues down Cold Canyon through to Yosemite National Park. With a car shuttle, the excellent 10.5-mile hike to **Green Creek** visits a bevy of perfect lakes; an extra mile (each way) takes you to windswept – check out the mammoth tree blowdown – Summit Lake at the Yosemite border. Check with the folks at the **Virginia Lakes Resort** (☑ 760-647-6484; www.virgin-

ialakesresort.com; cabins from $112; ☼ mid-May–mid-Oct; ▣), opened in 1923, for maps and tips about specific trails. The resort itself has snug cabins, a cafe and a general store. Cabins sleep two to 12 people, and usually have a 3-day minimum stay.

There's also the option of camping at **Trumbull Lake Campground** (☑ 800-444-7275; www.recreation.gov; tent & RV sites $17; ☼ mid-Jun–mid-Oct). The shady sites here are located among lodgepole pines.

Nearby, **Virginia Lakes Pack Station** (☑ 760-937-0326; www.virginialakes.com) offers horseback riding trips.

Lundy Lake

After Conway Summit, Hwy 395 twists down steeply into the Mono Basin. Before reaching Mono Lake, Lundy Lake Rd meanders west of the highway for about 5 miles to Lundy Lake. This is a gorgeous spot, especially in spring when wildflowers carpet the canyon along Mill Creek, or in fall when it is brightened by colorful foliage. Before reaching the lake, the road skirts first-come, first-served **Lundy Canyon Campground** (tent & RV sites $12; ☼ mid-April–mid-Nov), with vault toilets; there's water available, but it must be boiled or treated. At the end of the lake, there's a ramshackle resort on the site of an 1880s mining town, plus a small store and boat rentals.

Past the resort a dirt road leads into **Lundy Canyon** where, in 2 miles, it dead-ends at the trailhead for the Hoover Wilderness Area. A fantastic 1.5-mile hike follows Mill Creek to the 200ft-high **Lundy Falls**. Industrious beavers define the landscape along the trail, with gnawed aspens scattered on the ground and a number of huge dams barricading the creek. Ambitious types can continue on via Lundy Pass to Saddlebag Lake and the Twenty Lakes Basin, though the final climb out of the canyon uses a very steep talus chute.

Lee Vining

Hwy 395 skirts the western bank of Mono Lake, rolling into the gateway town of Lee Vining where you can eat, sleep, gas up (for a pretty penny) and catch Hwy 120 to Yosemite National Park when the road's open. A superb base for exploring Mono Lake, Lee Vining is only 12 miles (about a 30-minute drive) from Yosemite's Tioga Pass entrance. **Lee Vining Canyon** is a popular location for ice climbing.

In town take a quick look at the **Upside-Down House**, a kooky tourist attraction created by silent film actress Nellie Bly O'Bryan. Originally situated along Tioga Rd, it now resides in a park in front of the tiny **Mono Basin Historical Society Museum** (www.monobasinhs.org; donation $2; ⊙10am-4pm Thu-Tue & noon-4pm Sun mid-May–early Oct). To find it, turn east on 1st St and go one block to Mattley Ave.

🛏 Sleeping

Lodging rates drop when Tioga Pass is closed. Psst, campers! **Mono Vista RV Park** (📞760-647-6401; www.monovistarvpark.net; Hwy 395; ⊙9am-6pm Apr-Oct) has the closest pay showers to Tuolumne Meadows.

El Mono Motel   MOTEL $
(📞760-647-6310; www.elmonomotel.com; 51 Hwy 395; r $69-99; ⊙mid-May–Oct; 🛜) Grab a board game or soak up some mountain sunshine in this friendly flower-ringed place attached to an excellent cafe. In operation since 1927, and often booked solid, each of its 11 simple rooms (a few share bathrooms) is unique, decorated with vibrant and colorful art and fabrics.

USFS Campgrounds   CAMPGROUND $
(www.fs.usda.gov/inyo; tent & RV sites $15-19; 🐾) Toward Yosemite, there are a handful of first-come, first-served campgrounds along Tioga Rd (Hwy 120) and Lee Vining Creek,

most with vault toilets and about half with potable water.

⭐**Yosemite Gateway Motel**   MOTEL $$
(📞760-647-6467; www.yosemitegatewaymotel.com; Hwy 395; r $119-159; 🛜) Think vistas. This is the only motel on the east side of the highway, and the views from some of the rooms are phenomenal. Recently remodeled, its boutique-style rooms have comfortable beds with thick duvets and swank new bathrooms.

Tioga Pass Resort   CABINS $$
(www.tiogapassresort.com; Hwy 120; r $125, cabin $190-250; ⊙Jun-Sep) Founded in 1914 and located 2 miles east of Tioga Pass, this resort attracts a fiercely loyal clientele to its basic and cozy cabins beside Lee Vining Creek. The thimble-sized cafe (lunch $8 to $11, dinner $20) serves excellent fare all day at a few tables and a broken horseshoe counter, with a house pastry chef concocting dozens of freshly made desserts.

Murphey's Motel   MOTEL $$
(📞760-647-6316; www.murpheysyosemite.com; Hwy 395; r $73-133; 🛜🐾) At the north end of town, this large and friendly motel offers comfy rooms with all mod cons.

🍴 Eating

Whoa Nellie Deli   CALIFORNIAN $$
(📞760-647-1088; www.whoanelliedeli.com; Tioga Gas Mart, Hwys 120 & 395; mains $10-20; ⊙6:30am-9pm late-Apr–early Nov; 🍴) After putting this unexpected gas station restaurant on the map, its famed chef has moved on to Mammoth Lake, but locals think the food is still damn good. Stop in for delicious fish tacos, wild buffalo meatloaf and other tasty morsels, and live bands two nights a week.

Historic Mono Inn   CALIFORNIAN $$
(📞760-647-6581; www.monoinn.com; 55620 Hwy 395; mains $10-28; ⊙5-9pm Apr–mid-Nov) A restored 1922 lodge owned by the family of photographer Ansel Adams, this is now an elegant lakefront restaurant with outstanding California comfort food, fabulous wine and views to match. Browse the 1000-volume cookbook collection upstairs, and stop in for the occasional live band on the creekside terrace. It's located about 5 miles north of Lee Vining. Reservations recommended.

Mono Lake

North America's second-oldest lake is a quiet and mysterious expanse of deep blue water, whose glassy surface reflects jagged Sierra peaks, young volcanic cones and the unearthly tufa (*too*-fah) towers that make the lake so distinctive. Jutting from the water like drip sand castles, tufas form when calcium bubbles up from subterranean springs and combines with carbonate in the alkaline lake waters.

In *Roughing It,* Mark Twain described Mono Lake as California's 'dead sea.' Hardly. The brackish water teems with buzzing alkali flies and brine shrimp, both considered delicacies by dozens of migratory bird species that return here year after year. So do about 85% of the state's nesting population of California gulls, which takes over the lake's volcanic islands from April to August. Mono Lake has also been at the heart of an environmental controversy.

⊙ Sights & Activities

South Tufa   NATURE RESERVE
(entry adult/child $3/free) Tufa spires ring the lake, but the biggest grove is on the south rim with a mile-long interpretive trail. Ask about ranger-led tours at the Mono Basin Scenic Area Visitor Center. To get to the reserve, head south from Lee Vining on Hwy 395 for 6 miles, then east on Hwy 120 for 5 miles to the dirt road leading to a parking lot.

Navy Beach   BEACH
The best place for swimming is at Navy Beach, just east of the South Tufa reserve. It's also the best place to put in canoes or kayaks. From late June to early September, the Mono Lake Committee (☑760-647-6595; www.monolake.org/visit/canoe; tours $25; ⊙8am, 9:30am & 11am Sat & Sun) operates one-hour canoe tours around the tufas. Half-day kayak tours along the shore or out to Paoha Island are also offered by Caldera Kayaks (☑760-934-1691; www.calderakayak.com; tours $75; ⊙mid-May–mid-Oct). Both require reservations.

Panum Crater   NATURAL FEATURE
Rising above the south shore, Panum Crater is the youngest (about 640 years old), smallest and most accessible of the craters that string south toward Mammoth Mountain. A panoramic trail circles the crater rim (about 30 to 45 minutes), and a short but steep 'plug trail' puts you at the crater's core. A dirt road leads to the trailhead from Hwy 120, about 3 miles east of the junction with Hwy 395.

Black Point Fissures   NATURAL FEATURE
On the north shore of Mono Lake are the Black Point Fissures, narrow crags that opened when lava mass cooled and contracted about 13,000 years ago. Access is from three places: east of Mono Lake County Park, from the west shore off Hwy 395, or south off Hwy 167. Check at the Mono Basin Scenic Area Visitor Center for specific directions.

ⓘ Information

Mono Basin Scenic Area Visitor Center
(☑760-647-3044; www.fs.usda.gov/inyo; ⊙8am-5pm Apr–Nov) Half a mile north of Lee Vining, this center has maps, interpretive displays, Inyo National Forest wilderness permits, bear-canister rentals, a bookstore and a 20-minute movie about Mono Lake.

Mono Lake Committee Information Center
(☑760-647-6595; www.monolake.org; cnr Hwy 395 & 3rd St; ⊙9am-5pm late-Oct–mid-Jun, 8am-9pm mid-Jun–Sep) Internet access ($2 per 15 minutes), maps, books, free 30-minute video about Mono Lake and passionate, preservation-minded staff. Public restroom too.

June Lake Loop

Under the shadow of massive Carson Peak (10,909ft), the stunning 14-mile June Lake Loop (Hwy 158) meanders through a picture-perfect horseshoe canyon, past the relaxed resort town of June Lake and four sparkling, fish-rich lakes: Grant, Silver, Gull and June. It's especially scenic in fall when the basin is ablaze with golden aspens. Catch the loop a few miles south of Lee Vining.

🏃 Activities

June Lake is backed by the Ansel Adams Wilderness area, which runs into Yosemite National Park. Rush Creek Trailhead has a day-use parking lot, posted maps and self-registration permits. Gem and Agnew Lakes make spectacular day hikes, while Thousand Island and Emerald Lake (both on the Pacific Crest/John Muir Trail) are stunning overnight destinations.

Boat and tackle rentals, as well as fishing licenses, are available at five marinas.

June Mountain Ski Area   SKIING
(☑888-586-3686, 24hr snow info 760-934-2224; www.junemountain.com; lift tickets adult/youth 13-18/child under 13 $72/48/free; ⊙8:30am-4pm) Winter fun concentrates in this area, which is smaller and less crowded than nearby Mammoth Mountain and perfect for beginner and intermediate skiers. Some 35 trails

crisscross 500 acres of terrain served by seven lifts, including two high-speed quads. Boarders can get their adrenaline flowing at three terrain parks with a kick-ass superpipe.

Ernie's Tackle & Ski Shop OUTDOOR EQUIPMENT
(☑760-648-7756; 2604 Hwy 158; ☺6am-7pm) One of the most established outfitters in June Lake village.

🛏 Sleeping & Eating

USFS Campgrounds CAMPGROUND $
(☑800-444-7275; www.recreation.gov; tent & RV sites $22; ☺mid-Apr–Oct) These include: June Lake, Oh! Ridge, Silver Lake, Gull Lake and Reversed Creek. The first three accept reservations; Silver Lake has gorgeous mountain views.

June Lake Motel MOTEL $$
(☑760-648-7547; www.junelakemotel.com; 2716 Hwy 158; r with/without kitchen $115/100; @ 🐾) Enormous rooms – most with full kitchens – catch delicious mountain breezes and sport attractive light-wood furniture. There's a fish-cleaning sink and barbecues, plus a book library.

Silver Lake Resort CABIN $$
(☑760-648-7525; www.silverlakeresort.com; Silver Lake; cabin $130-210; ☺late-Apr–mid-Oct) Across the road from Silver Lake and astride Alger Creek, this sweet cabin compound opened in 1916 and has a duck pond and boat rentals in addition to almost 20 rustic cabins with full kitchens. Its tiny old-time cafe (mains $8-11; ☺7am-2pm) displays antique winter sports equipment and serves diner fare like burgers, sandwiches and grilled chicken; it's most popular for excellent big breakfasts.

Double Eagle Resort & Spa RESORT $$$
(☑760-648-7004; www.doubleeagle.com; 5587 Hwy 158; r $229, cabins $349; 🐾 🖥 🛁) A swanky spot for these parts. The two-bedroom log cabins and balconied hotel rooms lack no comfort, while worries disappear at the elegant spa. Its restaurant (mains $15-25; ☺7:30am-9pm) exudes rustic elegance, with cozy booths, a high ceiling and a huge fireplace.

Tiger Bar AMERICAN $$
(www.thetigerbarcafe.com; 2620 Hwy 158; mains $8-19; ☺8am-10pm) After a day on slopes or trails, people gather at the long bar or around the pool table of this no-nonsense, no-attitude place. The kitchen feeds all appetites, with burgers, salads, tacos and other tasty grub, including homemade fries.

Carson Peak Inn AMERICAN $$$
(☑760-648-7575; Hwy 158 btwn Gull & Silver Lakes; meals $18-40; ☺5-10pm, shorter winter hours) Inside a cozy house with a fireplace, this restaurant is much beloved for its tasty old-time indulgences, such as fried chicken, pan-fried trout and chopped sirloin steak. Portion sizes can be ordered for regular or 'hearty' appetites.

Mammoth Lakes

This is a small mountain resort town endowed with larger-than-life scenery – active outdoorsy folks worship at the base of its dizzying 11,053ft Mammoth Mountain. Everlasting powder clings to these slopes, and when the snow finally fades, the area's an outdoor wonderland of mountain-bike trails, excellent fishing, endless alpine hiking and blissful hidden spots for hot-spring soaking. The Eastern Sierra's commercial hub and a four-season resort, outdoorsy Mammoth is backed by a ridgeline of jutting peaks, ringed by clusters of crystalline alpine lakes and enshrouded by the dense Inyo National Forest.

⊙ Sights

★**Earthquake Fault** NATURAL FEATURE
(Map p410) On Minaret Rd, about 1 mile west of the Mammoth Scenic Loop, detour to gape at Earthquake Fault, a sinuous fissure half a mile long gouging a crevice up to 20ft deep into the earth. Ice and snow often linger at the bottom until late summer, and Native Americans and early settlers used it to store perishable food.

Mammoth Museum MUSEUM
(Map p412; ☑760-934-6918; www.mammoth-museum.org; 5489 Sherwin Creek Rd; suggested donation $3; ☺10am-6pm mid-May–Sep; 🐾) For a walk down memory lane, stop by this little museum inside the historic Hayden log cabin.

🏃 Activities

The excellent website of the Mammoth Lakes Trail System (www.mammothtrails.org) contains a comprehensive guide to local hiking, biking and cross-country ski trails, with maps and information on services available.

Skiing & Snowboarding
There's free cross-country skiing along the more than 300 miles of nongroomed trails in town and in the Inyo National Forest. Pick

Mammoth Lakes Area

See Mammoth Lakes Map (p412)

up a free map at the Mammoth Lakes Welcome Center.

Tamarack Cross-Country Ski Center SKIING
(Map p412; ☎760-934-2442; 163 Twin Lakes Rd; all-day trail pass adult/child/senior $28/16/22; ⊙8:30am-5pm) Let the town shuttle take you to the Tamarack Lodge, which has almost 20 miles of meticulously groomed track around Twin Lakes and the Lakes Basin. The terrain is also great for snowshoeing. Rentals and lessons are available.

Hiking
Mammoth Lakes rubs up against the Ansel Adams Wilderness (Map p412) and John Muir Wilderness (Map p412) areas, both laced with fabulous trails leading to shimmering lakes, rugged peaks and hidden canyons. Major trailheads leave from the Mammoth Lakes Basin, Reds Meadow and Agnew Meadows; the latter two are accessible only by shuttle. Shadow Lake is a stunning 7-mile

day hike from Agnew Meadows, and Crystal Lake makes a worthy 2.5-mile round-trip trek from Lake George in the Lakes Basin.

From various spots along the Reds Meadow area, long-distance backpackers with wilderness permits and bear canisters can easily jump onto the John Muir Trail (to Yosemite to the north and Mt Whitney to the south) and the Pacific Crest Trail (fancy walking to Mexico or Canada?).

Cycling & Mountain Biking
Stop at the Mammoth Lakes Welcome Center for a free biking map with area route descriptions.

**Mammoth Mountain
Bike Park** MOUNTAIN BIKING
(☎800-626-6684; www.mammothmountain.com; day pass adult/child 7-12 $49/23; ⊙9am-4:30pm Jun-Sep) Come summer, Mammoth Mountain morphs into the massive Mammoth Mountain Bike Park, with more than 80 miles

of well-kept single-track trails. Several other trails traverse the surrounding forest. In general, Mammoth-style riding translates into plenty of hills and sandy shoulders, which are best navigated with big knobby tires.

But you don't need wheels (or a medic) to ride the vertiginous Village Gondola (Map p412) to the apex of the mountain, where there's a cafe and an interpretive center with scopes pointing toward the nearby peaks. And for kids 13 and under, a $39 Adventure Pass buys unlimited day access to a zip line, climbing wall, bungee trampoline and child's bike-park area.

When the park's open, it runs a free mountain-bike shuttle (☉ 9am-5:30pm) from the Village area to the main lodge. Shuttles depart every 30 minutes, and mountain bikers with paid mountain passes get priority over pedestrians.

Lakes Basin Path   CYCLING
One of Mammoth's fantastic new multi-use paths, the 5.3-mile Lakes Basin Path begins at the southwest corner of Lake Mary and Minaret Rds and heads uphill (1000ft, at a 5% to 10% grade) to Horseshoe Lake, skirting lovely lakes and accessing open views of the Sherwin Range. For a one-way ride, use the free Lakes Basin Trolley, which tows a 12-bicycle trailer.

Fishing & Boating
From the last Saturday in April, the dozens of lakes that give the town its name lure in fly and trout fishers from near and far. California fishing licenses are available at sporting goods stores throughout town. For equipment and advice, head to Troutfitter (Map p412; ☏ 760-934-2517; cnr Main St & Old Mammoth Rd; ☉ 8am-4pm) or Rick's Sports Center (Map p412; ☏ 760-934-3416; cnr Main & Center Sts; ☉ 6am-8pm).

The Pokonobe Store & Marina (Map p410; ☏ 760-934-2437; www.pokonoberesort. com), on the north end of Lake Mary, rents motor boats ($20 per hour), rowboats ($10), canoes ($20) and kayaks ($20 to $25). Caldera Kayaks (☏ 760-935-1691; www.calderakayak.com) has single ($30 for a half-day) and double kayaks ($50) for use on Crowley Lake.

Bowling

⭐ Mammoth Rock 'n' Bowl   BOWLING
(Map p412; ☏ 760-934-4200; www.mammothrocknbowl.com; 3029 Chateau Rd; per game adult $5-7/child under 13 $3-5, shoe rental adult/child $3/1; ☉ 11am-midnight; 🐾) A psychedelic

mural of Devils Postpile crowns this stylish and modern new 12-lane complex that has the locals raving. The ground floor has foosball, ping-pong and darts, plus a casual TV-surrounded restaurant with outdoor patio and cocktail bar. Upstairs you'll find its more upscale eatery Mammoth Rock Brasserie (p416), and a bank of high-def golf simulators ($30 to $40 per hour) let you whack real golf balls across 30 virtual courses.

🛏 Sleeping

Mammoth B&Bs and inns rarely sell out midweek, when rates tend to be lower. During ski season, reservations are a good idea on weekends and essential during holidays. Many properties offer ski-and-stay packages. Condo rentals often work out cheaper for groups.

Stop by the Mammoth Lakes Welcome Center or check its website for a full list of campgrounds, dispersed free camping locations (don't forget to pick up a free but mandatory fire permit) and public showers.

USFS Campgrounds   CAMPGROUND $
(☏ 877-444-6777; www.recreation.gov; tent & RV sites $20-21; ☉ approx mid-Jun–mid-Sep; 🐾) About 15 USFS campgrounds (see 'Recreation' at www.fs.usda.gov/inyo) are scattered in and around Mammoth Lakes, all with flush toilets but no showers. Many sites are available on a first-come, first-served basis, and some are reservable. Note that nights get chilly at these elevations, even in July. Campgrounds include New Shady Rest (Map p412), Old Shady Rest (Map p412), Twin Lakes (Map p410), Lake Mary (Map p410), Pine City (Map p410), Coldwater (Map p410), Lake George (Map p410), Reds Meadow (p418), Pumice Flat (Map p410), Minaret Falls (p417), Upper Soda Springs (Map p410) and Agnew Meadows (Map p410).

Davison Street Guest House   HOSTEL $
(Map p412; ☏ 760-924-2188, reservations 858-755-8648; www.mammoth-guest.com; 19 Davison St; dm $35-49, d $75-120; 🐾) A cute, five-room A-frame chalet hostel on a quiet residential street, this place has a stocked kitchen, plus mountain views from the living room with fireplace or sun deck. There's self-registration when the manager isn't around.

Tamarack Lodge   LODGE, CABINS $$
(Map p410; ☏ 760-934-2442; www.tamaracklodge.com; 163 Twin Lakes Rd; r incl breakfast with/

Mammoth Lakes

without bath $189/139, cabins from $229; @ 🤶)
🌿 In business since 1924, this charming year-round resort on Lower Twin Lake has a cozy fireplace lodge, a bar and excellent restaurant, 11 rustic-style rooms and 35 cabins. The cabins range from very simple to simply deluxe, and come with full kitchen, private bathroom, porch and wood-burning stove. Some can sleep up to 10 people. Daily resort fee $20.

Guests can use the pool and hot tub at the resort's Mammoth Mountain Inn.

Mammoth Creek Inn INN **$$**
(Map p412; 📞760-934-6162; www.mammoth-creekinn.com; 663 Old Mammoth Rd; r $119-135, with kitchen $179-199; @ 🤶) It's amenities galore at this pretty inn at the end of a commercial strip, with down comforters and fluffy terry robes, as well as a sauna, a hot tub and a fun pool table loft. The best rooms overlook the majestic Sherwin Mountains, and some have full kitchens and can sleep up to six.

Austria Hof Lodge LODGE **$$**
(Map p412; 📞760-934-2764; www.austriahof.com; 924 Canyon Blvd; r incl breakfast $109-215; 🤶) Close to Canyon Lodge, rooms here have modern knotty pine furniture, thick down duvets and DVD players. Ski lockers and a sundeck hot tub make winter stays here even

sweeter. The lodge restaurant (dinner mains $25 to $40) serves meaty gourmet German fare in a muraled cellar dining room.

Alpenhof Lodge HOTEL **$$**
(Map p412; 📞760-934-6330; www.alpen-hof-lodge.com; 6080 Minaret Rd; r incl breakfast $149-189; @ 🤶🐾🐕) A snowball's toss from the Village – and fresh from its star turn and teary Hollywood makeover in the TV reality show *Hotel Impossible* – this Euro-flavored inn has updated lodge rooms with tasteful accent walls and ski racks, plus more luxurious accommodations with gas fireplaces or kitchens.

Cinnamon Bear Inn B&B **$$**
(Map p412; 📞760-934-2873; www.cinnamon-bearinn.com; 133 Center St; r incl breakfast $119-179; @ 🤶) At this down-to-earth inn you'll sleep like a log in four-poster beds, and most rooms have cozy gas fireplaces. Swap stories about the day's adventures with other guests over homemade refreshments in the afternoon, or soak away soreness in the small outdoor Jacuzzi.

✗ Eating

Good Life Café CALIFORNIAN **$**
(Map p412; www.mammothgoodlifecafe.com; 126 Old Mammoth Rd; mains $9-15; ⏰ 6:30am-3pm, to

Mammoth Lakes

9pm Thu-Mon in winter; 🖉) Healthy food, generously filled veggie wraps and big bowls of salad make this a perennially popular place. The front patio is blissful for a long brunch on a warm day.

Stellar Brew
CAFE $
(Map p412; www.stellarbrewnaturalcafe.com; 3280b Main St; salads & sandwiches $5.50-10; ⏰5:30am-7pm, to 6pm Sep–mid-Jun; 🖥🖉🐾) 🖉 Proudly locavore and mostly organic, settle into a comfy sofa here for your daily dose of locally roasted coffee, homemade granola, breakfast burritos and scrumptious vegan (and some gluten-free) pastries.

Base Camp Café
AMERICAN $
(Map p412; www.basecampcafe.com; 3325 Main St; mains $7-15; ⏰7:30am-3pm Sun-Fri, to 9pm Sat; 🖥🖉) Fuel up with a bracing dose of organic tea or coffee and a filling breakfast, or comfort food like Tex-Mex jalapeño onion straws and pesto chicken fajitas. Decorated with various backpacking gear and beer mats, the bathroom has a hysterical photo display of backcountry outhouses.

Sierra Sundance Whole Foods
HEALTH FOOD $
(Map p412; 26 Old Mammoth Rd; ⏰9am-7pm Mon-Sat, to 5pm Sun; 🖉) Self-catering vegetarians can stock up on organic produce, bulk foods and tofu at this large store and deli.

Toomey's
NEW AMERICAN $$
(Map p412; www.toomeyscatering.com; 6085 Minaret Rd, The Village; mains $13-30; ⏰7am-9pm; 🍴) The legendary chef from Whoa Nellie Deli in Lee Vining has decamped here, along with his eclectic menu of wild-buffalo meatloaf, seafood jambalaya and lobster taquitos with mango salsa – plus a lifetime's worth of baseball paraphernalia. The central location's perfect for grabbing a to-go breakfast or a sit-down dinner near the Village Gondola or Mammoth Mountain bike-park shuttle.

Feeney's Starlight Cafe
FUSION $$
(Map p412; www.facebook.com/StarlightCafe-Mammoth; 452 Old Mammoth Rd, Sierra Center Mall; mains $10-22; ⏰11am-9pm Mon-Sat, variable hours in fall & spring; 🖉🎮) Harvesting the best of Vietnamese, Korean and Italian cuisine, chef-owner James Feeney rocks the house with dishes like Korean burritos, kimchi burgers, shrimp po'boy sandwiches, housemade pasta and Creole fried chicken.

Stove
AMERICAN $$
(Map p412; www.thestoverestaurantmammoth. com; 644 Old Mammoth Rd; breakfast $6-13, dinner $12-20; ⏰6:30am-2pm & 5-9pm) Great coffee and carbs; try the cinnamon-bread French toast. Dinner includes a choice of a dozen yummy side dishes.

★Lakefront Restaurant
NEW AMERICAN $$$
(📞760-934-3534; www.tamaracklodge.com/ lakefront_restaurant; 163 Twin Lakes Rd; mains $24-38; ⏰5-9:30pm year-round, plus 11am-2pm summer, closed Tue & Wed in fall & spring) The most atmospheric and romantic restaurant in Mammoth, this intimate dining room at Tamarack Lodge overlooks lovely Twin Lakes. A new chef crafts specialties like pork belly, oxtail risotto and braised beef short ribs, and the staff are superbly friendly. Reservations recommended.

1. Fall foliage, Lundy Canyon (p406) 2. May Lake, Yosemite National Park (p382) 3. Emerald Bay (p349) 4. John Muir Trail (p372)

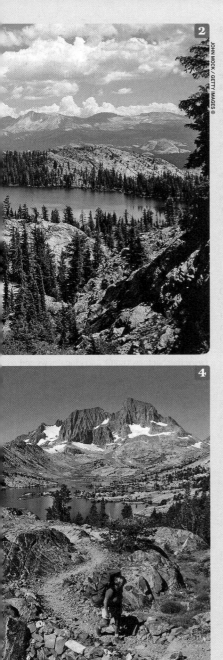

JOHN MOCK / GETTY IMAGES ©

Best Hikes of the Sierra Nevada

Packed with ancient granite peaks, icy blue lakes and serpentine stream meadows, the Sierra Nevada beckons mountain-worshippers. Though the sights may look lovely from the car, you need to stop, smell and touch to really experience the landscape. And once you witness its burning alpenglow, you'll understand why Sierra Club cofounder John Muir called it the 'Range of Light.'

Yosemite High Sierra Camps

Tour Yosemite's high country without a bulging backpack and share the sights with pudgy whistling marmots. Highlights include overnights at pristine May Lake, the waterfalls of Glen Aulin and lake-studded Vogelsang.

Lundy Canyon

In the Hoover Wilderness east of Yosemite, ambitious beavers gnaw and stack stands of leafy aspens, and frothy waterfalls draw you deeper and deeper into this stunning and solitary canyon.

John Muir Trail

Load up that pack and connect the dots from the heart of Yosemite to the pinnacle of Mt Whitney, the highest peak in the contiguous USA. This 200-plus mile trek goes step-by-step up and over six passes topping 11,000ft. Cross chilly rivers and streams between bumper-to-bumper Yosemite Valley, the roadless backcountry of Sequoia & Kings Canyon and the oxygen-scarce summit of Mt Whitney.

Little Lakes Valley

Marvel at this perfect chain of alpine lakes jostled between snow-tipped summits. With the Sierra's highest trailhead, there's no need to earn your elevation here.

Desolation Wilderness

West of Lake Tahoe, jaunt to Eagle Lake and points beyond from Emerald Bay, or do a longer day hike to scale the pinnacle of Mt Tallac. The glacially polished landscape of this easy-to-reach wilderness makes it well worth the crowds.

Petra's Bistro & Wine Bar CALIFORNIAN $$$
(Map p412; ☑760-934-3500; www.petrasbistro.com; 6080 Minaret Rd; mains $18-34; ☺5-9:30pm Tue-Sun) Settle in here for seasonal cuisine and wines recommended by the staff sommeliers. In wintertime the best seats in the house are the cozy fireside couches. Start the evening with a cheese course and choose from 36 wines available by the glass (250 vintages by the bottle), or the excellent cocktail menu. Reservations recommended.

Mammoth Rock Brasserie NEW AMERICAN $$$
(Map p412; 3029 Chateau Rd; mains $19-34; ☺5:30-9pm Mon-Thu, to 10pm Fri-Sun) This swanky brasserie at the Mammoth Rock 'n' Bowl serves tasty small plates and meaty main courses with breathtaking views of the Sherwin Range.

🍷 Drinking

Clocktower Cellar PUB
(Map p412; www.clocktowercellar.com; 6080 Minaret Rd; ☺4-11pm) In the winter especially, locals throng this half-hidden basement of the Alpenhof Lodge. The ceiling is tiled with a swirl of bottle caps, and the bar stocks 150 whiskies, 26 beers on tap and about 50 bottled varieties.

Mammoth Brewing Company Tasting Room BREWERY
(Map p412; www.mammothbrewingco.com; 18 Lake Mary Rd; ☺10am-6pm; 🍴) Now located in a large new space, try some of the dozen brews on tap (flights $5 to $7) – including special seasonal varieties not found elsewhere – then pick up some IPA 395 or Double Nut Brown to go.

🛍 Shopping

For outdoor equipment sales and rentals, in-town shops are usually cheaper than at Mammoth Mountain.

Footloose OUTDOOR EQUIPMENT
(Map p412; ☑760-934-2400; www.footloosesports.com; cnr Main St & Old Mammoth Rd; ☺8am-8pm) Full range of footwear and seasonal equipment; local biking info.

Mammoth Mountaineering Supply OUTDOOR EQUIPMENT
(Map p412; ☑760-934-4191; www.mammoth-gear.com; 3189 Main St; ☺8am-8pm) Offers friendly advice, topo maps and all-season equipment rentals.

Wave Rave OUTDOOR EQUIPMENT
(Map p412; ☑760-934-2471; www.waveravesnowboardshop.com; 3203 Main St; ☺7:30am-9pm Sun-Thu, 7:30am-10pm Fri & Sat, shorter hours off-season) Snowboarders worship here.

Mammoth Outdoor Sports OUTDOOR EQUIPMENT
(Map p412; ☑760-934-3239; www.mammothoutdoorsports.com; 452 Old Mammoth Rd, Sierra Center Mall; ☺8am-8pm Sun-Thu, to 9pm Fri & Sat) Bikes, boards and skis; across from Von's supermarket.

❶ Information

Mammoth Lakes Welcome Center (Map p412; ☑760-924-5500, 888-466-2666; www.visitmammoth.com; ☺8am-5pm) and the **Mammoth Lakes Ranger Station** (☑760-924-5500; www.fs.fed.us/r5/inyo; ☺8am-5pm) share a building on the north side of Hwy 203. This one-stop information center issues wilderness permits and rents bear canisters, helps find accommodations and campgrounds, and provides road and trail condition updates. From May through October, when trail quotas are in effect, walk-in wilderness permits are released at 11am the day before; permits are self-issue the rest of the year.

Two weekly newspapers, the *Mammoth Times* (www.mammothtimes.com) and the free *Sheet* (www.thesheetnews.com), carry local news and events listings.

Mammoth Hospital (☑760-934-3311; 85 Sierra Park Rd; ☺24hr) Emergency room.

❶ Getting There & Around

Mammoth's updated airport **Mammoth Yosemite** (MMH; www.visitmammoth.com/airport; 1300 Airport Rd, Mammoth Lakes) has a daily nonstop flight to San Francisco, operating winter through to spring on **United** (www.united.com). **Alaska Airlines** (www.alaskaair.com) runs year-round service to Los Angeles, and ski season service to San Diego. All flights are about an hour. Taxis meet incoming flights, and some lodgings provide free transfers. **Mammoth Taxi** (☑760-934-8294; www.mammoth-taxi.com) does airport runs as well as hiker shuttles throughout the Sierra Nevada.

Mammoth is a snap to navigate by public transportation year-round. In the summertime **YARTS** (☑877-989-2787; www.yarts.com) runs buses to and from Yosemite Valley, and the **Eastern Sierra Transit Authority** (☑800-922-1930; www.estransit.com) has year-round service along Hwy 395, north to Reno and south to Lone Pine.

Within Mammoth a year-round system of free and frequent **bus shuttles** connects the whole town with the Mammoth Mountain lodges; in summer, routes with bicycle trailers service the Lakes Basin and Mammoth Mountain Bike Park.

Around Mammoth Lakes

Reds Meadow

One of the beautiful and varied landscapes near Mammoth is the Reds Meadow Valley, west of Mammoth Mountain. Drive on Hwy 203 as far as Minaret Vista (Map p410) for eye-popping views (best at sunset) of the Ritter Range, the serrated Minarets and the remote reaches of Yosemite National Park.

The road to Reds Meadow is only accessible from about June until September, weather permitting. To minimize impact when it's open, the road is closed to private vehicles beyond Minaret Vista unless you are camping, have lodge reservations or are disabled, in which case you must pay a $10 per car fee. Otherwise you must use a mandatory shuttle bus (per adult/child $7/4). It leaves from a lot in front of the Adventure Center (next to the mammoth statue) approximately every 30 minutes between 7:15am and 7pm (last bus out leaves Reds Meadow at 7:45pm), and you must buy tickets inside before joining the queue. There are also three direct departures from the Village (on Canyon Blvd, under the gondola) before 9am, plus the option of using the free mountain-bike shuttle between the Village and the Adventure Center. The bus stops at trailheads, viewpoints and campgrounds before completing the one-way trip to Reds Meadow (45 minutes to an hour).

The valley road provides access to six campgrounds along the San Joaquin River. Tranquil willow-shaded Minaret Falls Campground (Map p410) is a popular fishing spot where the best riverside sites have views of its namesake cascade.

Hot Creek Geological Site

For a graphic view of the area's geothermal power, journey a few miles south of Mammoth to where chilly Mammoth Creek blends with hot springs and continues its journey as Hot Creek. It eventually enters a small gorge and forms a series of steaming, bubbling cauldrons, with water shimmering in shades of blue and green reminiscent of the tropics. Until recently, soakers reveled in the blissful but somewhat scary temperate zones where the hot springs mixed with frigid creek water. But in 2006 a significant increase in geothermal activity began sending violent geysers of boiling water into the air, and the site is off-limits for swimming until the danger has subsided.

To reach the site, turn off Hwy 395 about 5 miles south of town and follow signs to the Hot Creek Fish Hatchery. From here it's another 2 miles on gravel road to the parking area, and a short hike down into the canyon and creek.

For a soak that *won't* cook your goose, take Hwy 395 about 9 miles south of Mammoth to Benton Crossing Rd, which accesses a trove of primitive hot spring pools. Locals call this 'Green Church Rd,' because of the road's unmistakable marker. For detailed directions and maps, pick up the bible – Matt Bischoff's excellent *Touring California & Nevada Hot Springs*. And keep in mind these three golden rules: no glass, no additives to the water and, if you can, no bathing suit.

Convict Lake

Located just southeast of Mammoth, Convict Lake is one of the area's prettiest lakes, with emerald water embraced by massive peaks. A hike along the gentle trail skirting the lake, through aspen and cottonwood trees, is great if you're still adjusting to the altitude. A trailhead on the southeastern shore gives access to Genevieve, Edith, Dorothy and Mildred Lakes in the John Muir Wilderness. To reach the lake, turn south from Hwy 395 on Convict Lake Rd (across from the Mammoth airport) and go 2 miles.

In 1871 Convict Lake was the site of a bloody shoot-out between a band of escaped convicts and a posse that had given chase. Posse leader, Sheriff Robert Morrison, was killed during the gunfight and the taller peak, Mt Morrison (12,268ft), was later named in his honor. The bad guys got away only to be apprehended later near Bishop.

The campground (☎877-444-6777; www.recreation.gov; tent & RV sites $20; ◷mid-Apr–Oct) has flush toilets and nicely terraced sites. Otherwise your only option is Convict Lake Resort (☎760-934-3800; www.convictlake.com; 2000 Convict Lake Rd; cabins from $189; 🛜🐾), whose three houses and 28 cabins with kitchens sleep from two to 34 and range from rustic to ritzy. Foodies with deep pockets flock to the elegant restaurant (☎760-934-3803; lunch $10-15, dinner $24-38; ◷5:30-9pm daily, plus 11am-2:30pm Jul &

DEVILS POSTPILE

The most fascinating attraction in Reds Meadow is the surreal volcanic formation of **Devils Postpile National Monument** (Map p410; ☑ 760-934-2289; www.nps.gov/depo; shuttle day pass adult/child $7/4; ☺ late-May–Oct). The 60ft curtains of near-vertical, six-sided basalt columns formed when rivers of molten lava slowed, cooled and cracked with perplexing symmetry. This honeycomb design is best appreciated from atop the columns, reached by a short trail. The columns are an easy, half-mile hike from the Devils Postpile Ranger Station (Map p410).

From the monument, a 2.5-mile hike passing through fire-scarred forest leads to the spectacular **Rainbow Falls** (Map p410), where the San Joaquin River gushes over a 101ft basalt cliff. Chances of actually seeing a rainbow forming in the billowing mist are greatest at midday. The falls can also be reached via an easy 1.5-mile walk from the Reds Meadow area, which also has a cafe, store, the **Reds Meadow campground** (Map p410) and a pack station. Shuttle services run to the Reds Meadow area in season (p417).

Aug), which many consider the best within a 100-mile radius.

McGee Creek

Eight miles south of Mammoth Lakes, off Hwy 395, McGee Creek Rd rises into the mountains and dead-ends in a dramatic aspen-lined canyon, a particularly beautiful spot for autumn foliage. From here, the **McGee Pass Trail** enters the John Muir Wilderness, with day hikes to **Steelhead Lake** (10 miles round-trip) via an easy walk to subtle **Horsetail Falls** (four miles round-trip).

On the drive up, the **McGee Creek Pack Station** (☑ 760-935-4324; www.mcgeecreekpackstation.com) offers trail rides, and spacious **McGee Creek campground** (www.recreation.gov; McGee Creek Rd; tent & RV sites $20; ☺ late Apr–Oct; ☒) has 28 reservable sites at 7600ft with sun-shaded picnic tables along the creek and stunning mountain vistas.

At the intersection after you leave the highway, don't miss the coffee and home-baked goodies at the cute **East Side Bake Shop** (☑ 760-914-2696; www.facebook.com/EastSideBakeShop; 1561 Crowley Lake Dr; mains $8-15; ☺ 6:30am-3pm Wed-Sun, to 9pm Fri & Sat); check its calendar for fun local music on the weekends.

Rock Creek

South off Hwy 395 and roughly equidistant between Mammoth Lakes and Bishop, Rock Creek Rd travels 11 miles into some of the dreamiest landscapes in the Sierra. At roads' end, the Mosquito Flat trailhead into the **Little Lakes Valley** (part of the John Muir Wilderness) clocks in at a whopping

10,300ft of elevation. Mountaintops seem to be everywhere, with the 13,000ft peaks of Bear Creek Spire, Mt Dade, Mt Abbot and Mt Mills bursting out along the southwestern horizon and lush canyon meadows popping with scores of clear blue lakes. Ecstatic hikers and climbers fan out to explore, though most anglers and hikers just go as far as the first few lakes. An excellent day-hike destination is the second of the **Gem Lakes** (7 miles round-trip), a lovely aquamarine bowl and five-star lunch spot.

At the Rock Creek Lakes Resort, nine miles from the highway, don't put off a visit to tiny **Pie in the Sky Cafe** (☑ 760-935-4311; www.rockcreeklakesresort.com; pie $7; ☺ 7am-7pm late-May–mid-Oct, shorter hours early & late season). Its scratch-baked confections go on sale at 10:30am and usually sell out by 2pm. The slices of chocolate mud pie are gargantuan.

A dozen popular **USFS campgrounds** (☑ 877-444-6777; www.recreation.gov; tent & RV sites $20) line the road; most are along Rock Creek and a few are reservable. In wintertime there's a Sno-Park seven miles in, and during summer, the **Rock Creek Pack Station** (☑ 760-872-8331; www.rockcreekpackstation.com; Rock Creek Rd; trail rides from $45) offers trail rides from its location just before the trailhead.

The area is deservedly popular, and trailhead parking can be challenging; be prepared to trek an extra half mile from the overflow lot.

Bishop

The second-largest town in the Eastern Sierra, Bishop is about two hours from

Yosemite's Tioga Pass entrance. A major recreation hub, Bishop offers access to excellent fishing in nearby lakes, climbing in the Buttermilks just west of town, and hiking in the John Muir Wilderness via Bishop Creek Canyon and the Rock Creek drainage. The area is especially lovely in fall when dropping temperatures cloak aspen, willow and cottonwood in myriad glowing shades.

The earliest inhabitants of the Owens Valley were Paiute and Shoshone Native Americans, who today live on four reservations. White settlers came on the scene in the 1860s and began raising cattle to sell to nearby mining settlements.

⊙ Sights

★**Laws Railroad Museum**   MUSEUM
(📞 760-873-5950; www.lawsmuseum.org; Silver Canyon Rd; donation $5; ⊙10am-4pm; 🅿) Railroad and Old West aficionados should make the 6-mile detour north on Hwy 6 to this museum. It re-creates the village of Laws, an important stop on the route of the *Slim Princess,* a narrow-gauge train that hauled freight and passengers across the Owens Valley for nearly 80 years. You'll see the original 1883 train depot, a post office, a schoolhouse and other rickety old buildings. Many contain funky and eclectic displays (dolls, fire equipment, antique stoves etc) from the pioneer days.

Mountain Light Gallery   GALLERY
(📞 760-873-7700; www.mountainlight.com; 106 S Main St; ⊙10am-5pm Mon-Sat) FREE To see the Sierra on display in all its majesty, pop into this gallery, which features the stunning outdoor images of the late Galen Rowell. His work bursts with color, and the High Sierra photographs are some of the best in existence.

🏃 Activities

Fishing is good in the high-altitude lakes of Bishop Creek Canyon (west of town along Hwy 168). Other fine spots include the Owens River (northeast) and the Pleasant Valley Reservoir (Pleasant Valley Rd, north of town).

Eastside Sports   OUTFITTER
(📞 760-873-7520; www.eastsidesports.com; 224 N Main St; ⊙9am-9pm) Rents climbing and backpacking equipment and sells maps and guidebooks.

Mammoth Mountaineering Supply   OUTFITTER
(📞 760-873-4300; www.mammothgear.com; 298 N Main St; ⊙9am-7pm) Sells lots of used gear and clothing, including shoes.

Climbing

Bishop is prime bouldering and rock-climbing territory, with terrain to match any level of fitness, experience and climbing style. The main areas are the granite **Buttermilk Country**, west of town on Buttermilk Rd, and the stark **Volcanic Tablelands** and **Owens River Valley** to the north. The tablelands are also a wellspring of Native American petroglyphs – tread lightly.

Hiking

Hikers will want to head to the high country by following Line St (Hwy 168) west along Bishop Creek Canyon, past Buttermilk Country and on to several lakes, including Lake Sabrina and South Lake. Trailheads lead into the John Muir Wilderness and on into Kings Canyon National Park. Check with the White Mountain Ranger Station (p420) for suggestions, maps and wilderness permits for overnight stays.

Swimming

Keough's Hot Springs   SWIMMING
(📞 760-872-4670; www.keoughshotsprings.com; 800 Keough Hot Springs Rd; adult/child 3-12 $10/6; ⊙11am-7pm Wed-Fri & Mon, 9am-8pm Sat & Sun, longer summer hours) About 8 miles south of Bishop, this historic institutional-green outdoor pool (dating from 1919) is filled with bath-warm water from local mineral springs and doused with spray at one end. A smaller and sheltered 104°F (40°C) soaking pool sits beside it. Camping and tent cabins are also available.

🛏 Sleeping

Bishop has lots of economically priced motels, mostly chains.

USFS Campgrounds   CAMPGROUND $
(www.recreation.gov; tent & RV sites $21; ⊙May-Sep; 🐾) For a scenic night, stretch out your sleeping bag beneath the stars. The closest USFS campgrounds, all but one first-come, first-served, are between 9 miles and 15 miles west of town on Bishop Creek along Hwy 168, at elevations between 7500ft and 9000ft.

DON'T MISS

BENTON HOT SPRINGS

Soak in your own hot springs tub and snooze beneath the moonlight at Benton Hot Springs (☎866-466-2824, 760-933-2287; www.historicbentonhotsprings.com; Hwy 120, Benton; tent & RV sites for 2 people $40-50, d with/without bath incl breakfast $129/109; ☀), a small historic resort in a 150-year-old former silver-mining town nestled along the White Mountains. Choose from nine well-spaced campsites with private tubs or one of the themed antique-filled B&B rooms with semi-private tubs. Daytime dips ($10 hourly per person) are also available, and reservations are essential for all visits.

It's reachable from Mono Lake via Hwy 120 (in summer), Mammoth Lakes by way of Benton Crossing Rd, or Hwy 6 from Bishop; the first two options are undulating drives with sweeping red-rock vistas that glow at sunset, and all take approximately one hour. An Eastern Sierra Transit Authority (☎800-922-1930; www.estransit.com) bus connects Bishop and Benton ($6, one hour) on Tuesday and Friday, stopping right at the resort.

If you have time, ask for directions to the Volcanic Tablelands petroglyphs off Hwy 6, where ancient drawings decorate scenic rock walls.

Joseph House Inn Bed & Breakfast B&B $$
(☎760-872-3389; www.josephhouseinn.com; 376 W Yaney St; r incl breakfast $143-178; ❄☎☀) A beautiful restored ranch-style home, this place has a patio overlooking a tranquil 3-acre garden, and six nicely furnished rooms, some with fireplaces, all with TV and VCR. Guests enjoy a complimentary gourmet breakfast and afternoon wine.

Hostel California HOSTEL $
(☎760-399-6316; www.hostelbishop.com; 213 Academy Ave; dm $20, r $60-80; ❄@☎) A historic Victorian house located right in the center of town, this new hostel traded in the fussy doilies of the former B&B for climbing photos and gear displays. Hikers, anglers and climbers love the six-bed dorms, full kitchen and laundry-time loaner clothes, as well as the homey outdoors-loving atmosphere. Adults only.

🍴 Eating

Great Basin Bakery BAKERY, CAFE $
(www.greatbasinbakerybishop.com; 275-d S Main St, entrance on Lagoon St; salads & sandwiches $5-7; ☻6am-4pm Mon-Sat, 6:30am-4pm Sun; ☛) ✎ On a side street in the southern part of town, this excellent bakery serves locally roasted coffee, breakfast sandwiches on freshly baked bagels with local eggs, scratch-made soups and lots of delectable baked goods (with vegan and gluten-free options).

Erick Schat's Bakkery BAKERY $
(☎760-873-7156; www.erickschatsbakery.com; 763 N Main St; sandwiches $5-8.50; ☻6am-6pm Sun-Thu, to 7pm Fri) A much-hyped tourist mecca filled to the rafters with racks of fresh bread, it has been making its signature shepherd bread and other baked goodies since 1938. The bakery also features a popular sandwich bar.

Back Alley AMERICAN $$
(www.thebackalleybowlandgrill.com; 649 N Main St, behind Yamatani's Resturant; mains $13-23; ☻11:30am-9pm) Tucked off the main drag, this busy bowling-alley bar and grill (with bowling pin carpeting!) earns the locals' love with huge portions of fresh fish, rib eye steak, burgers and homemade desserts. Tiki-meets-televisions surf decor.

❶ Information

Public showers are available in town at **Wash Tub** (☎760-873-6627; 236 Warren St; ☻approx 5pm & 8-10pm), and near South Lake at **Bishop Creek Lodge** (☎760-873-4484; www.bishop-creekresort.com; 2100 South Lake Rd; ☻May-Oct) and **Parchers Resort** (☎760-873-4177; www.parchersresort.net; 5001 South Lake Rd; ☻late-May–mid-Oct).

Bishop Area Visitors Bureau (☎760-873-8405; www.bishopvisitor.com; 690 N Main St; ☻10am-5pm Mon-Fri, to 4pm Sat & Sun)

Inyo County Free Library (☎760-873-5115; 210 Academy Ave; ☻10am-6pm Mon, Wed & Fri, noon-8pm Tue & Thu, 10am-4pm Sat; ☎) Free internet access.

Northern Inyo Hospital (☎760-873-5811; www.nih.org; 150 Pioneer Ln; ☻24hr)

Spellbinder Books (☎760-873-4511; 124 S Main St; ☻10am-5:30pm Mon-Sat; ☎) Great indie bookstore with attached cafe and wi-fi.

White Mountain Ranger Station (☎760-873-2500; www.fs.usda.gov/inyo; 798 N Main

St; ⏰8am-5pm daily May-Oct, Mon-Fri rest of year) Wilderness permits, trail and campground information for the entire area.

Big Pine

This blink-and-you-missed-it town has a few motels and basic eateries. It mainly functions as a launch pad for the Ancient Bristlecone Pine Forest and to the granite Palisades in the John Muir Wilderness, a rugged cluster of peaks including six above 14,000ft. Stretching beneath the pinnacles is Palisades Glacier, the southernmost in the USA and the largest in the Sierra.

To get to the trailhead, turn onto Glacier Lodge Rd (Crocker Ave in town), which follows trout-rich Big Pine Creek up Big Pine Canyon, 10 miles west into a bowl-shaped valley. The strenuous 9-mile hike to Palisades Glacier via the North Fork Trail skirts several lakes – turned a milky turquoise color by glacial runoff – and a stone cabin built by horror-film actor Lon Chaney in 1925.

An ear-popping ascent up Glacier Lodge Rd passes by a trio of USFS campgrounds (☑877-444-6777; www.recreation.gov; tent & RV sites $20; ⏰May–mid-Oct) – Big Pine Creek, Sage Flat and Upper Sage Flat. Showers are available for $5 at Glacier Lodge (☑760-938-2837; www.jewelofthesierra.com; tent sites $25, RV sites $35, d cabins $135; ⏰mid-Apr–mid-Nov; 🐾), a bunch of rustic cabins with kitchens, as well as a campground, with a two-night minimum stay; though the original building no longer exists, it was one of the earliest Sierra getaways when built in 1917.

Independence

This sleepy highway town has been a county seat since 1866 and is home to the Eastern California Museum (www.inyocounty.us/ecmuseum; 155 N Grant St; donation requested; ⏰10am-5pm). It contains one of the most complete collections of Paiute and Shoshone baskets in the country, as well as artifacts from the Manzanar relocation camp and historic photographs of primitively equipped local rock climbers scaling Sierra peaks, including Mt Whitney.

Fans of Mary Austin (1868–1934), renowned author of *The Land of Little Rain* and vocal foe of the desertification of the Owens Valley, can follow signs leading to her former house at 253 Market St.

West of town via Onion Valley Rd (Market St in town), pretty Onion Valley harbors the trailhead for the Kearsage Pass (9.4 miles round-trip), an old Paiute trade route. This is also the quickest eastside access to the Pacific Crest Trail and Kings Canyon National Park.

In addition to a few small motels in town, Onion Valley has a couple of campgrounds (☑877-444-6777; www.recreation.gov; tent & RV sites $16; ⏰May-Sep) along Independence Creek. At 9200ft the Onion Valley campground is right at the Kearsage Pass trailhead and popular with backpackers.

Inexplicably located in a town otherwise inhabited by greasy spoon diners, Still Life Cafe (☑760-878-2555; 135 S Edward St; lunch $9-16, dinner $16-24; ⏰11am-3pm & 6-9:30pm Wed-Mon), a French gourmet bistro, pops out like an orchid in a salt flat. Escargot, duck-liver mousse, steak au poivre and other French delectables are served with Gallic charm in this bright, artistic dining room.

In the historic Masonic lodge next to the courthouse, bustling Jenny's Cafe (246 N Edwards St; mains $8-11; ⏰7am-2pm Sat-Tue, 7am-8pm Thu & Fri) serves rib-sticking fare like burgers, sandwiches and steaks in a country kitchen setting of rooster-print curtains and old teapots.

Manzanar National Historic Site

A stark wooden guard tower alerts drivers to one of the darkest chapters in US history, which unfolded on a barren and windy sweep of land some 5 miles south of Independence. Little remains of the infamous war concentration camp, a dusty square mile where more than 10,000 people of Japanese ancestry were corralled during WWII following the attack on Pearl Harbor. The camp's lone remaining building, the former high-school auditorium, houses a superb interpretive center (☑760-878-2194; www.nps.gov/manz; ⏰9am-4:30pm Nov-Mar, to 5:30pm Apr-Oct; 🐾) FREE. A visit here is one of the historical highlights of the state and should not be missed.

Watch the 20-minute documentary, then explore the thought-provoking exhibits chronicling the stories of the families that languished here yet built a vibrant community. Afterwards, take a self-guided 3.2-mile

HIKING MT WHITNEY

The mystique of Mt Whitney captures the imagination, and conquering its hulking bulk becomes a sort of obsession for many. The main **Mt Whitney Trail** (the easiest and busiest one) leaves from Whitney Portal, about 13 miles west of Lone Pine via the Whitney Portal Rd (closed in winter), and climbs about 6000ft over 11 miles. It's a super strenuous, really, *really* long walk that'll wear out even experienced mountaineers, but doesn't require technical skills if attempted in summer or early fall. Earlier or later in the season, you'll likely need an ice axe and crampons, and to overnight.

Many people in good physical condition make it to the top, although only superbly conditioned, previously acclimatized hikers should attempt this as a day hike. Breathing becomes difficult at these elevations and altitude sickness is a common problem. Rangers recommend spending a night camping at the trailhead and another at one of the two camps along the route: **Outpost Camp** at 3.5 miles or **Trail Camp** at 6 miles up the trail.

When you pick up your permit and pack-out kits (hikers must pack out their poop) at the Eastern Sierra Interagency Visitor Center in Lone Pine, get the latest info on weather and trail conditions. Near the trailhead, the **Whitney Portal Store** (www.whitneyportalstore.com) sells groceries and snacks. It also has public showers ($5) and a cafe with enormous burgers and pancakes. Its excellent website is a comprehensive starting point for Whitney research.

The biggest obstacle in getting to the peak may be to obtain a **wilderness permit** (per group $6 plus per person $15), which is required for all overnight trips and for day hikes past Lone Pine Lake (about 2.8 miles from the trailhead). A quota system limits daily access to 60 overnight and 100 day hikers from May through October. Because of the huge demand, permits are distributed via the online **Mt Whitney lottery** (www.fs.usda.gov/inyo), with applications accepted from February through mid-March.

Want to avoid the hassle of getting a permit for the main Mt Whitney Trail? Consider ascending this popular pinnacle from the west, using the backdoor route from Sequoia & Kings Canyon National Parks. It takes about six days from Crescent Meadow via the High Sierra Trail to the John Muir Trail – with no Whitney Zone permit required – and wilderness permits are much easier to secure.

driving tour around the grounds, which includes a re-created mess hall and barracks, vestiges of buildings and gardens, as well as the haunting camp cemetery.

Lone Pine

A tiny town, Lone Pine is the gateway to big things, most notably Mt Whitney (14,505ft), the loftiest peak in the contiguous USA, and Hollywood. In the 1920s cinematographers discovered that nearby Alabama Hills were a picture-perfect movie set for Westerns, and stars from Gary Cooper to Gregory Peck could often be spotted swaggering about town.

◉ Sights & Activities

A few basic motels, a supermarket, restaurants and stores (including gear and equipment shops) flank Hwy 395 (Main St in town). Whitney Portal Rd heads west at the lone stoplight, while Hwy 136 to Death Valley veers away about 2 miles south of town.

Mt Whitney   MOUNTAIN
(www.fs.usda.gov/inyo) West of Lone Pine, the jagged incisors of the Sierra surge skyward in all their raw and fierce glory. Cradled by scores of smaller pinnacles, Mt Whitney is a bit hard to pick out from Hwy 395, so for the best views, take a drive along Whitney Portal Rd through the Alabama Hills.

As you get a fix on this majestic megalith, remember that the country's lowest point is only 80 miles (as the crow flies) east of here: Badwater in Death Valley. Climbing to Mt Whitney's summit is among the most popular hikes in the entire country.

★ Alabama Hills   NATURAL FEATURE
Located on Whitney Portal Rd, the warm colors and rounded contours of the Alabama Hills stand in contrast to the jagged snowy Sierras just behind. The setting for count-

less ride-'em-out movies, the popular *Lone Ranger* TV series, and more recently, parts of Quentin Tarantino's *Django Unchained*, the stunning orange rock formations are a beautiful place to experience sunrise or sunset.

You can drive, walk or mountain bike along dirt roads rambling through the boulders, and along Tuttle and Lone Pine creeks. A number of graceful rock arches are within easy hiking distance of the roads. Head west on Whitney Portal Rd and either turn left at Tuttle Creek Rd, after a half-mile, or north on Movie Rd, after about 3 miles. The websites of the Lone Pine Chamber of Commerce and the Museum of Lone Pine Film History have excellent movie location maps.

Museum of Lone Pine Film History MUSEUM
(📞 760-876-9909; www.lonepinefilmhistorymuseum.org; 701 S Main St; adult/child $5/free; ⊙10am-5pm Mon-Sat, to 4pm Sun, longer summer hours) Hundreds of movies have been shot in the area, and this museum contains exhibits of paraphernalia from locally set films. It hosts screenings in its theater twice a month.

🛏 Sleeping & Eating

Whitney Portal Hostel & Hotel HOSTEL, MOTEL $
(📞 760-876-0030; www.whitneyportalstore.com; 238 S Main St; dm/r $25/100; 🅿🌐🐾) A popular launching pad for Whitney trips and for post-hike wash-ups (public showers available), its hostel rooms are the cheapest beds in town – reserve them months ahead for July and August. There's no common space for the carpeted single-sex bunk-bed rooms, though amenities include towels, TVs, in-room kitchenettes and stocked coffeemakers. New management has converted most of the establishment into plush and modern new motel rooms, and many look out toward Whitney and its neighbors.

Lone Pine Campground CAMPGROUND $
(📞 877-444-6777, 518-885-3639; www.recreation.gov; Whitney Portal Rd; tent & RV sites $19; ⊙mid-Apr–Oct; 🐾) About midway between Lone Pine and Whitney Portal, this popular creekside USFS campground (elevation 6000ft) offers flush toilets and potable water.

Dow Hotel & Dow Villa Motel HOTEL, MOTEL $$
(📞 760-876-5521; www.dowvillamotel.com; 310 S Main St; hotel r with/without bath $87/69, motel r $113-155; 🅿🌐🐾) John Wayne and Errol Flynn are among the stars who have stayed at this venerable hotel. Built in 1922, the place has been restored but retains much of its rustic charm. The rooms in the newer motel section have air-con and are more comfortable and bright, but also more generic.

Alabama Hills Cafe DINER $
(111 W Post St; mains $8-14; ⊙7am-2pm; 🐾) Everyone's favorite breakfast joint, the portions here are big, the bread fresh-baked, and the hearty soups and scratch-made fruit pies make lunch an attractive option, too.

Seasons NEW AMERICAN $$
(📞 760-876-8927; 206 N Main St; mains $17-30; ⊙5-9pm daily Apr-Oct, Tue-Sun Nov-Mar) Seasons has everything you fantasized about the last time you choked down freeze-dried rations. Sauteed trout, roasted duck, filet mignon and plates of carb-replenishing pasta will revitalize your appetite, and nice and naughty desserts will leave you purring. Reservations recommended.

ℹ Information

Eastern Sierra Interagency Visitor Center (📞 760-876-6222; www.fs.fed.us/r5/inyo; Hwys 395 & 136; ⊙8am-5pm) USFS information central for the Sierra, Death Valley and Mt Whitney; about 1.5 miles south of town at the junction of Hwys 395 and 136.

Lone Pine Chamber of Commerce (📞 760-876-4444; www.lonepinechamber.org; 120 S Main St; ⊙8:30am-4:30pm Mon-Fri)

Central Coast

Best Places to Eat

➜ Passionfish (p447)
➜ Ember (p481)
➜ Cracked Crab (p481)
➜ San Luis Obispo Farmers Market (p473)
➜ Penny Ice Creamery (p431)

Best Places to Stay

➜ Post Ranch Inn (p455)
➜ Dream Inn (p430)
➜ Cass House Inn (p462)
➜ HI Santa Cruz Hostel (p430)
➜ Pfeiffer Big Sur State Park Campground (p454)

Why Go?

Too often forgotten or dismissed as 'flyover' country between San Francisco and LA, this stretch of California coast is packed with wild beaches, misty redwood forests, and rolling golden hills of fertile vineyards and farm fields.

Coastal Hwy 1 pulls out all the stops, scenery-wise. Flower-power Santa Cruz and the historic port town of Monterey are gateways to the rugged wilderness of the bohemian Big Sur coast. It's an epic journey snaking down to vainglorious Hearst Castle, past lighthouses and edgy cliffs atop which endangered condors soar.

Get acquainted with California's agricultural heartland along inland Hwy 101, called El Camino Real (the King's Highway) by Spanish conquistadors and Franciscan friars. Colonial missions still line the route, which passes through Paso Robles' flourishing wine country. Then soothe your nature-loving soul in collegiate San Luis Obispo, ringed by sunny beach towns and volcanic peaks.

When to Go
Santa Cruz

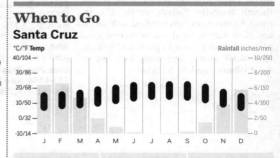

| Apr–May Balmy temperatures, but fewer tourists than summer; wildflowers bloom. | Jul–Aug Fog disappears as ocean waters warm up for beach season. | Sep–Oct Sunny blue skies, smaller crowds and wine country harvest festivals. |

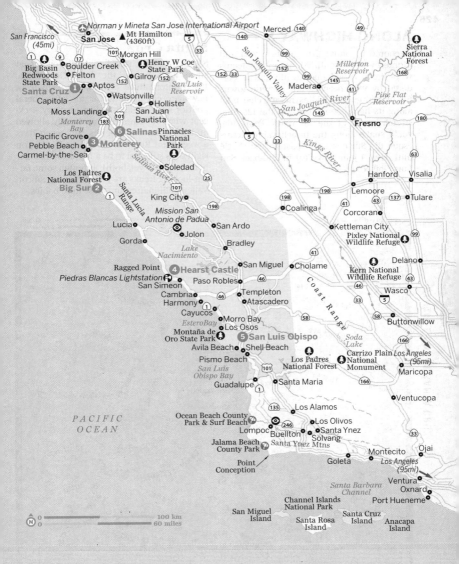

Central Coast Highlights

1 Screaming your head off aboard the Giant Dipper on the beach boardwalk, then learning to surf in **Santa Cruz** (p426).

2 Cruising Hwy 1, where the sky touches the sea, along the rocky coastline of mystical **Big Sur** (p449).

3 Being mesmerized by aquatic denizens of the 'indoor ocean' at the kid-friendly **aquarium** (p436) in Monterey.

4 Marveling in disbelief at the grandiosity of **Hearst Castle** (p458) after meeting the neighbors: ginormous elephant seals.

5 Hanging loose in college-town **San Luis Obispo** (p471), surrounded by beaches, vineyards and mountains.

6 Exploring down-to-earth novelist John Steinbeck's blue-collar world in the agricultural small town of **Salinas** (p466).

ALONG HIGHWAY 1

Anchored by Santa Cruz to the north and Monterey to the south, Monterey Bay teems with richly varied marine life and is bordered by wild beaches and seaside towns full of character and idiosyncratic charm all along its half-moon shore. On the 125-mile stretch south of the Monterey Peninsula, you'll snake along the unbelievably picturesque Big Sur coast and past Hearst Castle until Hwy 1 joins Hwy 101 in laid-back San Luis Obispo.

Santa Cruz

Santa Cruz has marched to its own beat since long before the Beat Generation. It's counterculture central, a touchy-feely, new-agey city famous for its leftie-liberal politics and live-and-let-live ideology – except when it comes to dogs (rarely allowed off-leash), parking (meters run seven days a week) and Republicans (allegedly shot on sight). It's still cool to be a hippie or a stoner here (or better yet, both), although some far-out-looking freaks are just slumming Silicon Valley millionaires and trust-fund babies.

Santa Cruz

Santa Cruz is a city of madcap fun, with a vibrant but chaotic downtown. On the waterfront is the famous beach boardwalk, and in the hills redwood groves embrace the University of California, Santa Cruz (UCSC) campus. Plan to spend at least half a day here, but to appreciate the aesthetic of jangly skirts, crystal pendants and Rastafarian dreadlocks, stay longer and plunge headlong into the rich local brew of surfers, students, punks and eccentric characters.

◉ Sights

One of the best things to do in Santa Cruz is simply stroll, shop and watch the sideshow along **Pacific Ave** downtown. A 15-minute walk away is the beach and **Municipal Wharf** (Map p426), where seafood restaurants, gift shops and barking sea lions compete for attention. Ocean-view **West Cliff Dr** follows the waterfront southwest of the wharf, paralleled by a paved recreational path.

★ Santa Cruz Beach Boardwalk
AMUSEMENT PARK

(Map p426; ☑ 831-423-5590; www.beachboardwalk.com; 400 Beach St; per ride $3-6, all-day pass $32-40; ☺ daily Apr-early Sep, seasonal hours vary; ⊕) The West Coast's oldest beachfront amusement park, this 1907 boardwalk has a glorious old-school Americana vibe. The smell of cotton candy mixes with the salt air, punctuated by the squeals of kids hang-ing upside down on carnival rides. Famous thrills include the Giant Dipper, a 1924 wooden roller coaster, and the 1911 Looff carousel, both National Historic Landmarks. During summer, catch free mid-week movies and Friday night concerts by rock veterans you may have thought were already dead.

Closing times and off-season hours vary. All-day parking costs $6 to $15.

★ Seymour Marine Discovery Center
MUSEUM

(Map p434; ☑ 831-459-3800; http://seymourcenter.ucsc.edu; 100 Shaffer Rd; adult/child 3-16yr $8/6; ☺ 10am-5pm Tue-Sun year-round, also 10am-5pm Mon Jul & Aug; ⊕) ◢ By Natural Bridges State Beach, this kids' educational center is part of UCSC's Long Marine Laboratory. Interactive natural-science exhibits include tidal touch pools and aquariums, while outside you can gawk at the world's largest blue-whale skeleton. Guided one-hour tours happen at 1pm, 2pm and 3pm daily, with a special 30-minute tour for families with younger children at 11am; sign up for tours in person an hour in advance (no reservations).

Sanctuary Exploration Center
MUSEUM

(Map p426; ☑ 831-421-9993; http://montereybay.noaa.gov; 35 Pacific Ave; ☺ 10am-5pm Wed-Sun; ⊕) ◢ **FREE** Operated by the Monterey Bay National Marine Sanctuary, this educational museum near the beach boardwalk is an interactive multimedia experience that teaches kids

CENTRAL COAST SANTA CRUZ

---

and adults about the bay's marine treasures, watershed conservation and high-tech underwater exploration for scientific research.

Santa Cruz Surfing Museum
MUSEUM

(Map p434; www.santacruzsurfingmuseum.org; 701 W Cliff Dr; admission by donation; ⊙10am-5pm Wed-Mon Jul 4-early Sep, noon-4pm Thu-Mon early Sep-Jul 3) A mile southwest of the wharf along the coast, this museum inside an old lighthouse is packed with memorabilia, including vintage redwood surfboards. Fittingly, Lighthouse Point overlooks two popular surf breaks.

University of California, Santa Cruz
UNIVERSITY

(Map p434; UCSC; www.ucsc.edu) Check it: the school mascot is a banana slug! Established in 1965 in the hills above town, UCSC is known for its creative, liberal bent. The rural campus has fine stands of redwoods and architecturally interesting buildings – some made with recycled materials – designed to blend in with rolling pastureland. Amble around the peaceful arboretum (http://arboretum.ucsc.edu; cnr High St & Arboretum Rd; adult/child 6-17yr $5/2, free 1st Tue of each month; ⊙9am-5pm) and picturesquely decaying 19th-century structures from Cowell Ranch, upon which the campus was built.

Santa Cruz Museum of Natural History
MUSEUM

(Map p434; ☑831-420-6115; www.santacruzmuseum.org; 1305 E Cliff Dr; adult/child under 18yr $4/free, free 1st Fri of each month; ⊙10am-5pm Tue-Sun;) The collections at this pint-sized museum include stuffed animal mounts, Native Californian cultural artifacts and a touch-friendly tide pool that shows off sea critters living by the beach right across the street.

Museum of Art & History
MUSEUM

(Map p426; ☑831-429-1964; www.santacruzmah.org; McPherson Center, 705 Front St; adult/child 12-17yr $5/2, free 1st Fri of each month; ⊙11am-5pm Tue-Thu, Sat & Sun, to 9pm Fri) Rotating displays by contemporary California artists and exhibits on local history are worth a quick look.

🏃 Activities

DeLaveaga Disc Golf Club
GOLF

(Map p434; www.delaveagadiscgolf.com; Upper Park Rd) FREE Touring pros and families with kids toss discs across this challenging hillside layout that peaks at Hole No 27, nicknamed 'Top of the World.' It's a couple of miles northeast of downtown, off Branciforte Dr.

Surfing

Year-round, water temperatures average under 60°F, meaning that without a wetsuit, body parts quickly turn blue. Surfing is incredibly popular, especially at experts-only Steamer Lane and beginners' Cowell's, both off West Cliff Dr. Other favorite surf spots include Pleasure Point Beach, on East Cliff Dr toward Capitola, and Manresa State Beach off Hwy 1 southbound.

Santa Cruz Surf School
SURFING

(Map p426; ☑831-345-8875, 831-426-7072; www.santacruzsurfschool.com; 131 Center St; 2hr group/1hr private lesson $90/120;) Wanna learn to surf? Near the wharf, friendly male and female instructors will have you standing and surfing on your first day out.

Richard Schmidt Surf School
SURFING

(Map p434; ☑831-423-0928; www.richardschmidt.com; 849 Almar Ave; 2hr group/1hr private lesson $90/120) Award-winning surf school can get you out there, all equipment included. Summer surf camps hook adults and kids alike.

O'Neill Surf Shop
SURFING

(Map p434; ☑831-475-4151; www.oneill.com; 1115 41st Ave; wetsuit/surfboard rental from $10/20; ⊙9am-8pm Mon-Fri, from 8am Sat & Sun) Head east toward Pleasure Point to worship at this internationally renowned surfboard maker's flagship store, with branches on the beach boardwalk and downtown.

Cowell's Beach Surf Shop
SURFING

(Map p426; ☑831-427-2355; www.cowellssurfshop.com; 30 Front St; 2hr group lesson $90; ⊙8am-6pm, to 5pm Nov-Mar;) Rent surfboards, boogie boards, wetsuits and other beach gear near the wharf, where veteran staff offer local tips and lessons.

Kayaking

Kayaking lets you discover the craggy coastline and kelp beds where sea otters float.

Venture Quest
KAYAKING

(Map p426; ☑831-425-8445, 831-427-2267; www.kayaksantacruz.com; Municipal Wharf; kayak rental/tour from $30/55; ⊙10am-7pm Mon-Fri, from 9am Sat & Sun late-May–late-Sep, hours vary late-Sep–mid-May) Convenient rentals on the wharf, plus whale-watching and coastal sea-cave tours, moonlight paddles and kayak-sailing trips. Book ahead for kayak-surfing lessons.

Kayak Connection
WATER SPORTS

(Map p434; ☑831-479-1121; www.kayakconnection.com; Santa Cruz Harbor, 413 Lake Ave; kayak

DON'T MISS

TOP SANTA CRUZ BEACHES

Sun-kissed Santa Cruz has warmer beaches than San Francisco or Monterey. *Baywatch* it isn't, but 29 miles of coastline reveal a few Hawaii-worthy beaches, craggy coves, some primo surf spots and big sandy stretches where your kids will have a blast. Fog may ruin many a summer morning; it often burns off by the afternoon.

West Cliff Dr is lined with scramble-down-to coves and plentiful parking. If you don't want sand in your shoes, park yourself on a bench and watch enormous pelicans dive for fish. You'll find bathrooms and showers at the lighthouse parking lot.

Locals favor less-trampled **East Cliff Dr** beaches, which are bigger and more protected from the wind, meaning calmer waters. Except at a small metered lot at 26th Ave, parking is by permit only on weekends (buy a $8 per day permit at 9th Ave).

Main Beach *The* scene, with a huge sandy stretch, volleyball courts and swarms of people. Park on East Cliff Dr and walk across the Lost Boys trestle to the beach boardwalk.

Its Beach (Map p434; 🐾) The only official off-leash beach for dogs (before 10am and after 4pm) is just west of the lighthouse.

Natural Bridges State Beach (Map p434; www.parks.ca.gov; 2531 W Cliff Dr; per car $10; ⊗8am-sunset; 🦶) Best for sunsets, this family favorite has lots of sand, tide pools and monarch butterflies from mid-October through mid-February. It's at the far end of W Cliff Dr.

Twin Lakes State Beach (Map p434; www.parks.ca.gov; E Cliff Dr & 9th Ave; ⊗8am-sunset; 🦶) Big beach with bonfire pits and a lagoon, good for kids and often fairly empty. It's off E Cliff Dr.

Moran Lake County Park (Map p434; www.scparks.com; E Cliff Dr; ⊗8am-sunset) With a good surf break and bathrooms, this pretty all-around sandy spot is further east of 26th Ave off E Cliff Dr.

New Brighton State Beach (Map p434; ☎831-464-6330; www.parks.ca.gov; 500 Park Rd, Capitola; per car $10; ⊗8am-sunset) Heading east of Santa Cruz to Capitola, New Brighton State Beach is a quieter place for a swim, paddleboarding or camping on a forested bluff.

Seacliff State Beach (☎831-685-6442; www.parks.ca.gov; State Park Rd, Aptos; per car $10; ⊗8am-sunset) Seacliff State Beach harbors a 'cement boat,' a quixotic freighter built of concrete that floated OK, but ended up here as a coastal fishing pier.

Manresa State Beach (☎831-761-1975; www.parks.ca.gov; San Andreas Rd, Watsonville; per car $10; ⊗8am-sunset) Near Watsonville, the La Selva Beach exit off Hwy 1 leads here to this sparsely populated beach.

Sunset State Beach (☎831-763-7062; www.parks.ca.gov; San Andreas Rd, Watsonville; per car $10; ⊗8am-sunset) The La Selva Beach exit off Hwy 1, near Watsonville, brings you here, where you can have miles of sand and surf almost all to yourself.

CENTRAL COAST SANTA CRUZ

rental/tour from $35/45; 🦶) Rents kayaks and offers lessons and tours, including whale-watching, sunrise, sunset and full-moon trips. Also rents stand-up paddleboarding (SUP) sets (from $25), wetsuits ($10) and boogie boards ($10).

Whale-Watching & Fishing

Winter whale-watching trips run from December through April, though there's plenty of marine life to see on a summer bay cruise. Many fishing trips depart from the wharf, where a few shops rent fishing tackle and poles.

Stagnaro's   BOAT TOUR
(Map p434; ☎info 831-427-0230, reservations 888-237-7084; www.stagnaros.com; 2896 Soquel Ave; adult/child under 14yr cruise from $20/13, whale-watching tour from $47/33) Longstanding tour operator offers scenic and sunset cruises around Monterey Bay and whale-watching tours year-round.

🎉 Festivals & Events

Woodies on the Wharf   CULTURE
(www.santacruzwoodies.com) Classic car show features vintage surf-style station wagons on Santa Cruz's Municipal Wharf in late June.

MYSTERY SPOT

A kitschy, old-fashioned tourist trap, Santa Cruz's **Mystery Spot** (☑831-423-8897; www.mysteryspot.com; 465 Mystery Spot Rd; admission $6; ☺10am-4pm Mon-Fri, to 5pm Sat & Sun Sep-May, 10am-6pm Mon-Fri, 9am-7pm Sat & Sun Jun-Aug) has scarcely changed since it opened in 1940. On a steeply sloping hillside, compasses seem to point crazily, mysterious forces push you around and buildings lean at silly angles. Make reservations, or risk getting stuck waiting for a tour. It's about 4 miles northeast of downtown, up into the hills via Branciforte Dr. Parking costs $5. Don't forget your bumper sticker!

Wharf to Wharf Race　　　　　SPORTS
(www.wharftowharf.com) More than 15,000 runners cruise from Santa Cruz to Capitola accompanied by 50 different live-entertainment acts in late July.

Open Studio Art Tour　　　　　CULTURE
(www.ccscc.org) Step inside local artists' creative workshops over three weekends in October. The arts council also sponsors 'First Friday' art exhibitions on the first Friday of each month.

🛏 Sleeping

Santa Cruz does not have enough beds to satisfy demand: expect outrageous prices at peak times for nothing-special rooms. Places near the beach boardwalk run the gamut from friendly to frightening. If you're looking for a straightforward motel, cruise Ocean St inland or Mission St (Hwy 1) near the UCSC campus.

★HI Santa Cruz Hostel　　　HOSTEL **$**
(Map p426; ☑831-423-8304; www.hi-santacruz.org; 321 Main St; dm $26-29, r $60-110, all with shared bath; ☺check-in 5-10pm; @) Budget overnighters dig this hostel at the century-old Carmelita Cottages surrounded by flowering gardens, just two blocks from the beach. Cons: midnight curfew, daytime lockout (10am to 5pm) and three-night maximum stay. Reservations are essential. Street parking costs $2.

California State Park Campgrounds　　　　CAMPGROUND **$**
(☑reservations 800-444-7275; www.reserveamerica.com; tent & RV sites $35-65; ☎) Book well

ahead to camp at state beaches off Hwy 1 south of Santa Cruz or up in the foggy Santa Cruz Mountains off Hwy 9. Family-friendly campgrounds include Henry Cowell Redwoods State Park in Felton and New Brighton State Beach in Capitola.

★Adobe on Green B&B　　　　B&B **$$**
(Map p426; ☑831-469-9866; www.adobeongreen.com; 103 Green St; r incl breakfast $169-219; ☎) 🍃 Peace and quiet are the mantras at this place, a short walk from Pacific Ave. The hosts are practically invisible, but their thoughtful touches are everywhere, from boutique-hotel amenities in spacious, stylish and solar-powered rooms to breakfast spreads from their organic gardens.

Pelican Point Inn　　　　　　INN **$$**
(Map p434; ☑831-475-3381; www.pelicanpointinn-santacruz.com; 21345 E Cliff Dr; ste $139-219; ☎☎❄) Ideal for families, these roomy apartments near a kid-friendly beach come with everything you'll need for a lazy vacation, including kitchenettes. Weekly rates available. Pet fee $20.

Mission Inn　　　　　　　　MOTEL **$$**
(Map p434; ☑800-895-5455, 831-425-5455; www.mission-inn.com; 2250 Mission St; r incl breakfast $130-220; ❄☎) Perfectly serviceable two-story motel with a garden courtyard, hot tub and complimentary continental breakfast. It's on busy Hwy 1 near the UCSC campus, away from the beach.

Sunny Cove Motel　　　　　MOTEL **$$**
(Map p434; ☑831-475-1741; www.sunnycovemotel.com; 21610 E Cliff Dr; r $90-250; ☎❄) No-frills retro hideaway east of downtown is a staunch surfers' fave. The long-time Santa Cruzian owner rents well-worn rooms and kitchenette suites.

Dream Inn　　　　　　　　HOTEL **$$$**
(Map p426; ☑866-774-7735, 831-426-4330; www.dreaminnsantacruz.com; 175 W Cliff Dr; r $249-479; ❄@☎❄) Overlooking the wharf from a spectacular hillside perch, this chic boutique hotel is as stylish as Santa Cruz gets. Rooms have all mod cons, while the beach is just steps away. Don't miss happy hour at Aquarius restaurant's ocean-view bar. Parking is $25.

Pacific Blue Inn　　　　　　B&B **$$$**
(Map p426; ☑831-600-8880; www.pacificblueinn.com; 636 Pacific Ave; r incl breakfast $189-289; ☎) 🍃 This downtown courtyard B&B is an eco-conscious gem, with water-saving fixtures

and renewable and recycled building materials. Refreshingly elemental rooms have pillowtop beds, electric fireplaces and flat-screen TVs with DVD players. Free loaner bikes.

West Cliff Inn
INN $$$

(Map p426; ☑800-979-0910, 831-457-2200; www.westcliffinn.com; 174 W Cliff Dr; r incl breakfast $195-325; ☎) In a classy Victorian house west of the wharf, this boutique inn's quaint rooms mix sea-grass wicker, dark wood and jaunty striped curtains. The most romantic suites have gas fireplaces and let you spy on the breaking surf. Rates include a breakfast buffet and afternoon wine, tea and snacks.

Sea & Sand Inn
MOTEL $$$

(Map p426; ☑831-427-3400; www.santacruzmotels.com; 201 W Cliff Dr; r $199-419; ☎) With a grassy lawn at the cliff's edge, this spiffy, if seriously overpriced motel overlooks Main Beach and the wharf. Fall asleep to braying sea lions! Rooms are smallish, but ocean views can be stellar. Rates include complimentary afternoon refreshments. Their contempo sister property, Carousel Beach Inn, is cheaper and closer to the beach boardwalk.

Babbling Brook Inn
B&B $$$

(Map p434; ☑831-427-2437, 800-866-1131; www.babblingbrookinn.com; 1025 Laurel St; r incl breakfast $229-309; ☎) Built around a running stream with meandering gardens, the inn has cozy rooms decorated in French-provincial style. Most have gas fireplaces, some have whirlpool tubs and all have featherbeds. There's afternoon wine and hors d'oeuvres, plus a full breakfast.

Hotel Paradox
HOTEL $$$

(Map p434; ☑855-425-7200, 831-425-7100; www.thehotelparadox.com; 611 Ocean St; r from $189; @☎☒) Downtown boutique hotel brings the great outdoors inside, with nature prints on the walls, textured wood panels and earth-toned furnishings. Relax in a cabana by the pool or next to an outdoor fire pit. Weekday rates can be reasonable, but summer weekends are high-priced. Parking is $10.

✗ Eating

Downtown is chockablock with casual cafes. If you're looking for seafood, wander the wharf's takeout counter joints. Mission St, near UCSC, and 41st Ave offer cheaper eats.

★ Penny Ice Creamery
ICE CREAM $

(Map p426; www.thepennyicecreamery.com; 913 Cedar St; snacks $2-4; ⊙noon-11pm; ▣) ✔ With a cult following, this artisan ice-cream shop crafts zany flavors like bourbon candied ginger, lemon verbena blueberry and ricotta apricot all from scratch using local, organic and wild-harvested ingredients. Even vanilla is special: it's made using Thomas Jefferson's original recipe. Also at a **downtown kiosk** (1520 Pacific Ave; ⊙noon-6pm Sun-Thu, to 9pm Fri & Sat; ▣) ✔ and near **Pleasure Point** (820 41st Ave; ⊙noon-9pm Sun-Thu, to 11pm Fri & Sat; ▣) ✔.

Picnic Basket
DELI $

(Map p426; http://thepicnicbasketsc.com; 125 Beach St; dishes $3-10; ⊙7am-4pm Mon-Thu, to 9pm Fri-Sun; ▣) Across the street from the beach boardwalk, this locavarian kitchen puts together creative sandwiches such as beet with lemony couscous or 'fancy pants' grilled cheese with fruit chutney, plus homemade soups, breakfast burritos and baked goods. Ice-cream treats are sweet.

Walnut Ave Cafe
BREAKFAST $

(Map p426; www.walnutavecafe.com; 106 Walnut Ave; mains $7-11; ⊙7am-3pm Mon-Fri, 8am-4pm Sat & Sun; ☑▣☒) Line up at this clean, well-lit breakfast spot for fluffy Belgian waffles, blackened ahi tuna eggs benny, Mexican huevos rancheros with pulled pork and all kinds of veggie scrambles. Lunch brings less-exciting sandwiches, salads and soups. Dogs are welcome on the outdoor patio.

Bagelry
DELI $

(Map p426; www.bagelrysantacruz.com; 320a Cedar St; dishes $1-9; ⊙6:30am-5:30pm Mon-Fri, 7am-4:30pm Sat, 7:30am-4pm Sun; ☑▣) The bagels here are twice-cooked (boiled, then baked), and come with fantastic spreads like crunchy 'Tofu del Fuego' or hummus with sprouts.

Tacos Moreno
MEXICAN $

(Map p434; www.tacosmoreno.com; 1053 Water St; dishes $2-6; ⊙10am-10pm Mon-Fri, 11am-7pm Sat & Sun) Who cares how long the line is at lunchtime? Find taquería heaven with these marinated pork, chicken or beef soft tacos. Also on 41st Ave in Capitola.

New Leaf Community Market
SUPERMARKET $

(Map p426; www.newleaf.com; 1134 Pacific Ave; ⊙8am-9pm; ☑) ✔ Organic and local produce, natural-foods groceries and deli take-out meals downtown and also off Hwy 1 near the UCSC campus. The 41st Ave branch has a healthy-minded Beet Cafe.

Santa Cruz Farmers Market
MARKET $

(Map p426; www.santacruzfarmersmarket.org; cnr Lincoln & Center Sts; ⊙1:30-6:30pm Wed; ☑▣)

🌱 Organic produce, baked goods and arts-and-crafts and food booths all give you an authentic taste of the local vibe. Shorter fall and winter hours.

Pono Hawaiian Grill
FUSION **$$**

(Map p426; www.ponohawaiiangrill.com; 120 Union St; mains $7-15; ⏱11am-10pm Sun-Wed, to 11pm Thu-Sat) Inside the Reef bar, this kitchen runs on 'island time' as it mixes up your fresh ahi tuna, salmon, shellfish or veggie *poke* (cubed raw salad) in a bowl or ladled on a plate with two-scoop rice and creamy macaroni or tossed green salad. The *loco moco* burrito with spicy gravy is a huge hit.

Engfer Pizza Works
PIZZERIA **$$**

(Map p434; www.engferpizzaworks.com; 537 Seabright Ave; pizzas $8-23; ⏱usually 4-9:30pm Tue-Sun; 🖉🚼) Detour to find this old factory, where wood-fired oven pizzas are made from scratch – the no-name specialty is like a giant salad on roasted bread. Play ping-pong and down draft microbrews while you wait.

Soif
BISTRO **$$$**

(Map p426; ☎831-423-2020; www.soifwine.com; 105 Walnut Ave; small plates $5-17, mains $19-25; ⏱5-9pm Sun-Thu, to 10pm Fri & Sat) Bon vivants swoon over a heady selection of three dozen international wines by the glass, paired with a sophisticated, seasonally driven Euro-Cal menu. Expect tastebud-ticklers like roasted beet salad with fava beans and maple vinaigrette or squid-ink linguini with spicy chorizo.

Laili
AFGHANI **$$$**

(Map p426; ☎831-423-4545; www.lailirestaurant.com; 101b Cooper St; mains $13-28; ⏱11:30am-2:30pm Tue-Sun, 5-9pm Tue-Thu & Sun, to 10pm Fri & Sat) A chic downtown dining oasis, family-owned Laili invites diners in with an elegant high-ceilinged dining room and garden patio. Share apricot-chicken flatbread, tart pomegranate eggplant, roasted cauliflower with saffron, succulent lamb kebabs and more. Service is spotty. Reservations advised.

🍷 Drinking & Nightlife

Downtown overflows with bars, lounges and coffee shops. Heading west on Mission St (Hwy 1), several Santa Cruz Mountains winery tasting rooms hide out along Ingalls St.

★ Verve Coffee Roasters
CAFE

(Map p426; www.vervecoffeeroasters.com; 1540 Pacific Ave; ⏱6:30am-9pm; 📶) To sip finely roasted artisan espresso or a cup of rich pour-over coffee, join the surfers and hipsters at this industrial-zen cafe. Single-origin brews and house blends rule.

Caffe Pergolesi
CAFE

(Map p426; www.theperg.com; 418 Cedar St; ⏱7am-11pm; 📶) Discuss conspiracy theories over stalwart coffee, tea or beer at this landmark Victorian house with a big ol' tree-shaded verandah. There's live music some evenings.

Vino Prima
WINE BAR

(Map p426; www.vinoprimawines.com; 55 Municipal Wharf; ⏱2-8pm Mon-Tue, 2-10pm Wed-Fri, noon-

---

LOCAL KNOWLEDGE

TOP SANTA CRUZ COUNTY BREWERIES

We asked Derek Wolfgram, home brewer and local beer columnist, to share with us his favorite places for a pint:

Boulder Creek Brewery (p434) High up in the mountains, these guys brew amber 'Redwood Ale' and 'Dragon's Breath' American IPA.

Sante Adairius Rustic Ales (Map p434; www.rusticales.com; 103 Kennedy Dr; ⏱3-8pm Tue-Fri, from noon Sat & Sun) Off Hwy 1 east of Santa Cruz, Belgian-inspired and barrel-aged beers are a beer geek's dream.

Discretion Brewing (Map p434; www.discretionbrewing.com; 2703 41st Ave, Soquel; ⏱11:30am-9pm) Rye IPA, English ales and traditional Belgian and German brews are always on tap, off Hwy 1.

Santa Cruz Mountain Brewing (Map p434; www.scmbrew.com; 402 Ingalls St; ⏱11:30am-10pm) Bold organic beers make this tiny locals' tasting room crowded. Oddest flavor? Lavender IPA.

Santa Cruz Ale Works (Map p434; www.santacruzaleworks.com; 150 Dubois St; ⏱11am-6pm; 🚼📶) Hefeweizen and 'Dark Night' oatmeal stout are commendable at this dog-friendly brewpub with a deli.

10pm Sat, noon-8pm Sun) With dreamy ocean views, this spot pours California boutique wines, including hard-to-find bottles from around Santa Cruz and Monterey Counties.

Surf City Billiards & Café   BAR
(Map p426; www.surfcitybilliardscafe.com; 931 Pacific Ave; ⊙5pm-midnight Sun-Thu, to 2am Fri & Sat) An escape from downtown's dives, this upstairs pool hall has Brunswick Gold Crown tables for shooting stick, darts, shuffleboard and big-screen sports TVs.

Hula's Island Grill   BAR
(Map p426; www.hulastiki.com; 221 Cathcart St; ⊙4:30-9:30pm Mon-Thu, 11:30am-11pm Fri & Sat, 11:30am-9:30pm Sun) Pull up a seat at this Hawaii-themed tiki bar for mai tais, *lilikoi* (passion fruit) margaritas, zombie cocktails and happy-hour *pupus* (appetizers).

☆ Entertainment

Free tabloid *Santa Cruz Weekly* (www.santacruzweekly.com) and *Good Times* (www.gtweekly.com) cover music, arts and nightlife scenes.

Catalyst   LIVE MUSIC
(Map p426; ☑831-423-1338; www.catalystclub.com; 1011 Pacific Ave) Over the years, this stage for local bands has seen big-time national acts perform, from Queens of the Stone Age to Snoop Dogg. Expect loads of punk attitude.

Kuumbwa Jazz Center   LIVE MUSIC
(Map p426; ☑831-427-2227; www.kuumbwajazz.org; 320 Cedar St) Hosting jazz luminaries since 1975, this nonprofit theater is for serious jazz cats snapping their fingers for famous-name performers in an intimate room.

Moe's Alley   LIVE MUSIC
(Map p434; ☑831-479-1854; www.moesalley.com; 1535 Commercial Way) In a way-out industrial wasteland, this joint puts on live sounds almost every night: jazz, blues, reggae, roots, salsa and acoustic world-music jams.

🔒 Shopping

Stroll Pacific Ave and downtown side streets to find one-of-a-kind, locally owned boutiques (not just smoke shops, dude). For vintage clothing and surf shops, amble 41st Ave around Portola Dr.

Annieglass   HOMEWARES
(Map p426; www.annieglass.com; 110 Cooper St; ⊙10:30am-6pm Mon-Sat, to 5pm Sun) Handcrafted sculptural glassware by an artist whose work is displayed at the Smithsonian American Art Museum is made right here in wackadoodle Santa Cruz.

Bookshop Santa Cruz   BOOKS
(Map p426; ☑831-423-0900; www.bookshopsantacruz.com; 1520 Pacific Ave; ⊙9am-10pm Sun-Thu, to 11pm Fri & Sat) Vast selection of new books, a few used ones, and 'Keep Santa Cruz Weird' bumper stickers.

Donnelly Fine Chocolates   FOOD
(Map p434; www.donnellychocolates.com; 1509 Mission St; ⊙10:30am-6pm Mon-Fri, from noon Sat & Sun) The Willy Wonka of Santa Cruz makes stratospherically priced chocolates on par with the big city. Try the cardamom or chipotle truffles.

ℹ Information

FedEx Office (www.fedex.com; 712 Front St; per min 30-40¢; ⊙6am-midnight Mon-Fri, 8am-9pm Sat, 9am-9pm Sun; 🖥) Pay-as-you-go internet workstations and photo-printing kiosks.

KPIG 107.5 FM (www.kpig.com) Streams the classic Santa Cruz soundtrack – think Bob Marley, Janis Joplin and Willie Nelson.

Public Library (www.santacruzpl.org; 224 Church St; ⊙10am-7pm Mon-Thu, 10am-5pm Fri & Sat, 1-5pm Sun; 🖥) Free wi-fi and public internet terminals for California public library cardholders (out-of-state visitors $10).

Santa Cruz Visitor Center (☑800-833-3494, 831-429-7281; www.santacruzca.org; 303 Water St; ⊙9am-noon & 1-4pm Mon-Fri, 11am-3pm Sat & Sun) Free public internet terminal, maps and brochures.

ℹ Getting There & Around

Santa Cruz is 75 miles south of San Francisco via coastal Hwy 1 or Hwy 17, a nail-bitingly narrow, winding mountain road. Monterey is about an hour's drive further south via Hwy 1.

Santa Cruz Airport Shuttles (☑831-421-9883; www.santacruzshuttles.com) runs shared shuttles to/from the airports at San Jose ($50), San Francisco ($80) and Oakland ($80), with a $5 cash discount; the second passenger pays $10.

Greyhound (☑800-231-2222; www.greyhound.com; Metro Center, 920 Pacific Ave) has a few daily buses to San Francisco ($16.50, three hours), Salinas ($14, one hour), Santa Barbara ($53, six hours) and Los Angeles ($59, nine hours).

Santa Cruz Metro (☑831-425-8600; www.scmtd.com; single-ride/day pass $2/6) operates local and countywide bus routes that converge on downtown's **Metro Center** (920 Pacific

Ave). Hwy 17 express buses link Santa Cruz with San Jose's Amtrak/CalTrain station ($5, 50 minutes, once or twice hourly).

From late May through early September, the **Santa Cruz Trolley** (www.santacruztrolley.com; per ride 25¢) shuttles between downtown and the beach from 11am until 9pm daily.

Around Santa Cruz

Santa Cruz Mountains

Winding between Santa Cruz and Silicon Valley, Hwy 9 is a 40-mile backwoods byway through the Santa Cruz Mountains, passing tiny towns, towering redwood forests and fog-kissed vineyards. Many wineries are only open for 'Passport Days' on the third Saturday of January, April, July and November. The Santa Cruz Mountains Winegrowers Association (www.scmwa.com) publishes a free winery map, available at tasting rooms, including those that have opened more convenient tasting rooms in Santa Cruz, mostly west of downtown off Hwy 1.

Heading north from Santa Cruz, it's 7 miles to Felton, passing Henry Cowell Redwoods State Park (☎info 831-335-4598, reservations 800-444-7275; www.parks.ca.gov; 101 N Big Trees Park Rd, Felton; entry per car $10, campsites $35; ☺sun-

rise-sunset; ♿), which has miles of hiking trails through old-growth redwood groves along the San Lorenzo River and camping. In Felton, Roaring Camp Railroads (☎831-335-4484; www.roaringcamp.com; 5401 Graham Hill Rd, Felton; tours adult/child 2-12yr from $26/19, parking $8; ☺call for schedules; ♿)operates narrow-gauge steam trains up into the redwoods and a standard-gauge train down to the Santa Cruz Beach Boardwalk. Seven miles further north on Hwy 9, you'll drive through the rustic town of Boulder Creek, a decent place to grab a bite or a pint at Boulder Creek Brewery & Cafe (☎831-338-7882; www.bouldercreekbrewery.net; 13040 Hwy 9, Boulder Creek; mains $9-18; ☺11:30am-10pm Sun-Thu, to 10:30pm Fri & Sat).

Follow Hwy 236 northwest for nine miles to Big Basin Redwoods State Park (☎831-338-8860; www.bigbasin.org; 21600 Big Basin Way, Boulder Creek; entry per car $10, campsites $35; ☺sunrise-sunset), where nature trails loop past giant old-growth redwoods and beside shady campgrounds. A 12.5-mile one-way section of the Skyline to the Sea Trail ends at Waddell Beach, almost 20 miles northwest of Santa Cruz on Hwy 1. On weekends between mid-March and mid-December, you can usually ride Santa Cruz Metro (☎831-425-8600; www.scmtd.com) bus 35A up to Big Basin in the morning and get picked up by bus 40 at the beach in the afternoon.

Around Santa Cruz

Capitola

Six miles east of Santa Cruz, the diminutive beach town of Capitola nestles quaintly between ocean bluffs. Show up for mid-September's Capitola Art & Wine Festival, or the famous Begonia Festival (www.begoniafestival.com), held over Labor Day weekend, with a flotilla of floral floats along Soquel Creek.

By the beach, downtown is laid out for strolling, where cutesy shops and touristy restaurants inhabit seaside houses. Drop by family-friendly Capitola Beach Company (Map p434; 831-462-5222; www.capitolabeachcompany.com; 131 Monterey Ave; 10am-6pm;) or Capitola Surf & Paddle (Map p434; 831-435-6503; www.capitolasurfandpaddle.com; 208 San Jose Ave; 10am-6pm) to rent water-sports gear or, if you book ahead, take surfing and stand-up paddleboarding lessons.

Catch an organic, fair-trade java buzz at Mr Toots Coffeehouse (Map p434; www.tootscoffee.com; 2nd fl, 231 Esplanade; 7am-10pm;), which has an art gallery, live music and ocean-view deck. Head inland to Gayle's Bakery & Rosticceria (Map p434; www.gaylesbakery.com; 504 Bay Ave; dishes $4-10; 6:30am-8:30pm;), which has a deli for assembling beach picnics. A few miles farther east in Aptos, Aptos St BBQ (www.aptosstbbq.com; 8059

Aptos St, Aptos; mains $5-23; 11:30am-9pm) pairs smoked tri-tip beef and pulled pork with California craft beers and live music.

The Capitola Chamber of Commerce (800-474-6522; www.capitolachamber.com; 716g Capitola Ave; 10am-4pm) offers travel tips. Driving downtown can be a nightmare in summer and on weekends; use the parking lot behind City Hall, off Capitola Ave by Riverview Dr.

Moss Landing & Elkhorn Slough

Hwy 1 swings back toward the coast at Moss Landing, just south of the Santa Cruz County line, almost 20 miles north of Monterey. From the working fishing harbor, Sanctuary Cruises (831-917-1042; www.sanctuarycruises.com; 7881 Sandholdt Rd; adult/child 12yr & under $50/40;) operates whale-watching and dolphin-spotting cruises year-round aboard biodiesel-fueled boats (reservations essential). Devour dock-fresh seafood at warehouse-sized Phil's Fish Market (831-633-2152; www.philsfishmarket.com; 7600 Sandholdt Rd; mains $11-21; 10am-8pm Sun-Thu, to 9pm Fri & Sat;) or, after browsing the antiques shops, lunch at Haute Enchilada (831-633-5483; www.hauteenchilada.com; 7902 Moss Landing Rd; mains $13-26; 11am-9pm Mon-Thu, from 9am Fri-Sun) , an inspired Mexican restaurant inside a Frida Kahlo–esque art gallery.

On the east side of Hwy 1, Elkhorn Slough National Estuarine Research Reserve (831-728-2822; www.elkhornslough.org; 1700 Elkhorn Rd, Watsonville; adult/child 16yr & under $4/free; 9am-5pm Wed-Sun) is popular with bird-watchers and hikers. Docent-led tours typically depart at 10am and 1pm on Saturdays and Sundays, or sign up for an electric-boat cruise with Whisper Charters (800-979-3370; www.whispercharters.com; 2370 Hwy 1, Moss Landing; 2hr tour adult/child 12yr & under $49/39;) . Kayaking is a fantastic way to see the slough, though not on a windy day or when the tides are against you. Reserve ahead for kayak or SUP rentals, guided tours and paddling instruction with Kayak Connection (831-724-5692; www.kayakconnection.com; 2370 Hwy 1, Moss Landing; kayak rental $35-65, tours adult/child from $45/35; 9am-5pm Mon-Fri, to 6pm Sat & Sun) or Monterey Bay Kayaks (800-649-5357, 831-373-5357; www.montereybaykayaks.com; 2390 Hwy 1, Moss Landing; kayak rental/tour from $30/55).

Around Santa Cruz

Monterey

Working-class Monterey is all about the sea. What draws many visitors is a world-class aquarium overlooking **Monterey Bay National Marine Sanctuary**, which protects dense kelp forests and a sublime variety of marine life, including seals and sea lions, dolphins and whales. The city itself possesses the best-preserved historical evidence of California's Spanish and Mexican periods, with many restored adobe buildings. An afternoon's wander through downtown's historic quarter promises to be more edifying than time spent in the tourist ghettos of Fisherman's Wharf and Cannery Row.

◉ Sights

★**Monterey Bay Aquarium**   AQUARIUM
(☑info 831-648-4800, tickets 866-963-9645; www.montereybayaquarium.org; 886 Cannery Row; adult/child 3-12yr/youth 13-17yr $40/25/30; ☺9:30am-6pm daily Jun, 9:30am-6pm Mon-Fri, to 8pm Sat & Sun Jul-Aug, 10am-5pm or 6pm daily Sep-May; ♿) ✐ Monterey's most mesmerizing experience is its enormous aquarium, built on the former site of the city's largest sardine cannery. All kinds of aquatic creatures are featured, from kid-tolerant sea stars and slimy sea slugs to animated sea otters and surprisingly nimble 800lb tuna.

The aquarium is much more than an impressive collection of glass tanks – thoughtful placards underscore the bay's cultural and historical contexts.

Every minute, up to 2000 gallons of seawater is pumped into the three-story **kelp forest**, re-creating as closely as possible the natural conditions you see out the windows to the east. The large fish of prey are at their charismatic best during mealtimes; divers hand-feed at 11:30am and 4pm. More entertaining are the sea otters, which may be seen basking in the **Great Tide Pool** outside the aquarium, where they are readied for reintroduction to the wild.

Even new-agey music and the occasional infinity-mirror illusion don't detract from the astounding beauty of jellyfish in the **Jellies Gallery**. To see marine creatures – including hammerhead sharks, ocean sunfish and green sea turtles – that outweigh kids many times over, ponder the awesome **Open Sea** tank. Upstairs and downstairs you'll find **touch pools**, where you can get close to sea cucumbers, bat rays and tidepool creatures. Younger kids love the interactive **Splash Zone**, with interactive bilingual exhibits and penguin feedings at 10:30am and 3pm.

To avoid long lines in summer and on weekends and holidays, buy tickets in advance. A visit can easily become a full-day affair, so get your hand stamped and break for lunch. Metered on-street parking is limited. Parking lots offering daily rates are plentiful just uphill from Cannery Row.

Cannery Row   HISTORIC SITE

(🏠) John Steinbeck's novel *Cannery Row* immortalized the sardine-canning business that was Monterey's lifeblood for the first half of the 20th century. A bronze bust of the Pulitzer Prize–winning writer sits at the bottom of Prescott Ave, just steps from the unabashedly touristy experience that the famous row has devolved into. The historical Cannery Workers Shacks at the base of flowery Bruce Ariss Way provide a sobering reminder of the hard lives led by Filipino, Japanese, Spanish and other immigrant laborers.

Back in Steinbeck's day, Cannery Row was a stinky, hardscrabble, working-class melting pot, which the novelist described as 'a poem, a stink, a grating noise, a quality of light, a tone, a habit, a nostalgia, a dream.' Sadly, there's precious little evidence of that era now, as overfishing and climatic changes caused the sardine industry's collapse in the 1950s.

★ Monterey State Historic Park   HISTORIC SITE

(🗐 audio tour 831-998-9458, info 831-649-7118; www.parks.ca.gov) 🖉 FREE Old Monterey is home to an extraordinary assemblage of 19th-century brick and adobe buildings, administered as Monterey State Historic Park, all found along a 2-mile self-guided walking tour portentously called the 'Path of History.' You can inspect dozens of buildings, many with charming gardens; expect some to be open while others aren't, according to a capricious schedule dictated by unfortunate state-park budget cutbacks.

➡ Pacific House

(🗐 831-649-7118; www.parks.ca.gov; 20 Custom House Plaza; admission incl Custom House $3, incl walking tour $5; ⊙ 10am-4pm Fri-Sun) Find out what's currently open at Monterey State Historic Park, grab a free map and buy tickets for guided walking tours inside this 1847 adobe building, which has fascinatingly in-depth exhibits covering the state's early Spanish, Mexican and American eras.

Nearby are some of the state park's historical highlights, including an old whaling station and California's first theater. A 10-minute walk south is the old Monterey

jail featured in John Steinbeck's novel *Tortilla Flat*.

➡ Custom House

(Custom House Plaza; admission incl Pacific House Museum $3, incl walking tour $5; ⊙ 10am-4pm Fri-Sun) In 1822, a newly independent Mexico ended the Spanish trade monopoly and stipulated that any traders bringing goods to Alta (Upper) California must first unload their cargoes here for duty to be assessed. In 1846 when the US flag was raised over the Custom House, *voilà!* California was formally annexed from Mexico. Restored to its 1840s appearance, today this adobe building displays an exotic selection of goods that traders once brought to exchange for California cowhides.

➡ Stevenson House

(www.parks.ca.gov; 530 Houston St; ⊙ 1-4pm Sat Apr-early Sep) FREE Scottish writer Robert Louis Stevenson came to Monterey in 1879 to court his wife-to-be, Fanny Osbourne. This building, then the French Hotel, was where he stayed while reputedly devising his novel *Treasure Island*. The boarding-house rooms were primitive and Stevenson was still a penniless unknown. Today the house displays a superb collection of the writer's memorabilia.

Cooper-Molera Adobe   HISTORIC BUILDING

(🗐 tour reservations 831-649-7172; 525 Polk St; ⊙ shop 10am-4pm, gardens from 9am, tours by appointment only) This stately early-19th-century adobe home was built by John Rogers Cooper, a New England sea captain, and three generations of his family resided here. Over time, the original adobe buildings were partitioned and expanded, gardens were added and later everything was willed to the National Trust for Historic Preservation. Worth a browse, the bookshop sells nostalgic toys and household goods.

Museum of Monterey   MUSEUM

(🗐 831-372-2608;   www.museumofmonterey.org; 5 Custom House Plaza; adult/child under 13yr $8/ free, free 1st Wed of each month; ⊙ 10am-7pm Tue-Sat & noon-5pm Sun late-May–early Sep, 10am-5pm Wed-Sat & noon-5pm Sun early Sep–late-May; 🏠) Near the waterfront, this voluminous modern exhibition hall illuminates Monterey's salty past, from early Spanish explorers to the roller-coaster-like rise and fall of the local sardine industry that brought Cannery Row to life in the mid-20th century. Highlights include a ship-in-a-bottle collection and the

Monterey

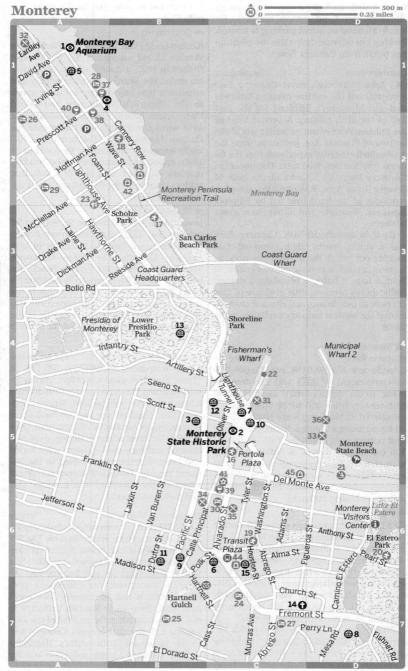

Monterey

historic Fresnel lens from Point Sur's lighthouse.

Monterey Museum of Art   MUSEUM
(MMA; www.montereyart.org; adult/child 18yr & under $10/free; ☉11am-5pm Thu-Mon) Downtown, **MMA Pacific Street** (☏831-372-5477; 559 Pacific St) is particularly strong in California contemporary art and modern landscape painters and photographers, including Ansel Adams and Edward Weston. Temporary exhibits fill **MMA La Mirada** (☏831-372-3689; 720 Via Mirada), a silent-film star's villa, whose humble adobe origins are exquisitely concealed. You can visit both locations on the same admission ticket.

Royal Presidio Chapel
& Heritage Center Museum   CHURCH
(☏831-373-2628; www.sancarloscathedral.org; 500 Church St; admission by donation; ☉10am-noon Wed, to 3pm Fri, to 2pm Sat, 1-3pm Sun, also 10am-12pm 2nd & 4th Mon of each month) Built

of sandstone in 1794, this graceful chapel is California's oldest continuously functioning church and first stone building. The original 1770 mission church stood here before being moved to Carmel. As Monterey expanded under Mexican rule in the 1820s, older buildings were gradually destroyed, leaving behind this National Historic Landmark as the strongest reminder of the defeated Spanish colonial presence.

Presidio of Monterey Museum   MUSEUM
(www.monterey.org/museums; Bldg 113, Corporal Ewing Rd; ☉10am-1pm Mon, to 4pm Thu-Sat, 1-4pm Sun) **FREE** On the grounds of the original Spanish fort, this museum of interest only to history buffs looks at Monterey's history from a military perspective through the Native American, Mexican and American periods.

🏃 Activities

Like its larger namesake in San Francisco, Monterey's **Fisherman's Wharf** is a tacky tourist trap, but also a jumping-off point for deep-sea fishing trips and whale-watching cruises. A short walk east at workaday **Municipal Wharf 2**, fishing boats bob and sway in the bay.

Dennis the Menace Park
PLAYGROUND

(www.monterey.org; 777 Pearl St; ⊙10am-dusk, closed Tue Sep-May; ⊞) `FREE` The brainchild of Hank Ketcham, the creator of the classic *Dennis the Menace* comic strip, this ain't your standard dumbed-down playground suffocated by Big Brother's safety regulations. With lightning-fast slides, a hedge maze, a suspension bridge and towering climbing walls, even some adults can't resist playing here.

Cycling & Mountain Biking

Along an old railway line, the **Monterey Peninsula Recreational Trail** travels for 18 car-free miles along the waterfront, passing Cannery Row en route to Lovers Point in Pacific Grove. Road-cycling enthusiasts can make the round trip to Carmel along the **17-Mile Drive**. Mountain bikers head to **Fort Ord National Monument** to pedal more than 80 miles of single-track and fire roads; the **Sea Otter Classic** (www.seaotterclassic. com) races there in mid-April.

Adventures by the Sea
CYCLING, KAYAKING

(✍831-372-1807; www.adventuresbythesea.com; 299 Cannery Row; rental per day kayak or bicycle $30, SUP set $50, tours from $60; ⊞) Beach cruisers, electric bike and water-sports gear rentals and tours available at multiple locations on Cannery Row and **downtown** (✍831-372-1807; www.adventuresbythesea.com; 210 Alvarado St; ⊞).

Bay Bikes
CYCLING

(✍831-655-2453; www.baybikes.com; 585 Cannery Row; bicycle rental per hour/day from $8/32) Cruiser, tandem, hybrid and road-bike rentals near the aquarium and also **downtown** (✍831-655-2453; www.baybikes.com; 486 Washington St).

Whale-Watching

You can spot whales off the coast of Monterey Bay year-round. The season for blue and humpback whales runs from April to early December, while gray whales pass by from mid-December through March. Tour boats depart from Fisherman's Wharf and Moss Landing (p435). Reserve trips at least a day in advance; be prepared for a bumpy, cold ride.

Monterey Whale Watching
BOAT TOUR

(✍831-205-2370, 888-223-9153; www.montereywhalewatching.com; 96 Fisherman's Wharf; 2½hr tour adult/child 5-11yr $45/35; ⌘) Several daily departures; no children under age five or pregnant women allowed.

Monterey Bay Whale Watch
BOAT TOUR

(✍831-375-4658; www.montereybaywhalewatch. com; 84 Fisherman's Wharf; 3hr tour adult/child 4-12yr from $40/27; ⌘) Morning and afternoon departures; young children are welcome on board.

Diving & Snorkeling

Monterey Bay offers world-renowned diving and snorkeling, including off **Lovers Point** in Pacific Grove and at Point Lobos State Natural Reserve (p447) south of Carmel-by-the-Sea. You'll want a wetsuit year-round. In summer upwelling currents carry cold water from the deep canyon below the bay, sending a rich supply of nutrients up toward the surface level to feed the bay's diverse marine life. These frigid currents also account for the bay's chilly water temperatures and the summer fog that blankets the peninsula.

Aquarius Dive Shop
DIVING

(✍831-375-1933; www.aquariusdivers.com; 2040 Del Monte Ave; snorkel/scuba-gear rental $35/65, dive tours from $65) Talk to this five-star PADI operation for gear rentals, classes and guided dives into Monterey Bay.

Monterey Bay Dive Charters
DIVING

(✍831-383-9276; www.mbdcscuba.com; scuba-gear rental $75, shore/boat dive from $65/85) Arrange shore or boat dives and rent a full scuba kit with wetsuit from this well-reviewed outfitter.

Kayaking & Surfing

Monterey Bay Kayaks
KAYAKING

(✍831-373-5357, 800-649-5357; www.montereybaykayaks.com; 693 Del Monte Ave; kayak or SUP set rental per day from $30, tours from $55) Rents kayaks and SUP equipment, offers paddling lessons and leads guided tours of Monterey Bay, including full-moon and sunrise trips.

Sunshine Freestyle Surf & Sport
SURFING

(✍831-375-5015; www.sunshinefreestyle.com; 443 Lighthouse Ave; rental surfboard/wetsuit/boogie board from $20/10/7) Monterey's oldest surf shop rents and sells all the surfing gear you'll need. Staff grudgingly dole out local tips.

⛲ Festivals & Events

Castroville Artichoke Festival
FOOD

(www.artichoke-festival.org) Head north of Monterey for 3D 'agro art' sculptures, cooking demos, a farmers market and field tours in May or June.

Blues, Brews & BBQ   FOOD, MUSIC
(www.bluesbrewsandbarbecue.com) Rockin' bands, California craft beers and barbecue-pit masters at the county fairgrounds in late July.

Strawberry Festival at Monterey Bay   FOOD
(www.mbsf.com) Berry-licious pie-eating contests and live bands in Watsonville, north of Monterey, in early August.

Monterey County Fair   CARNIVAL, FOOD
(www.montereycountyfair.com) Old-fashioned fun, carnival rides, horse-riding and live-stock competitions, wine tasting and live music in late August and early September.

★ Monterey Jazz Festival   MUSIC
(www.montereyjazzfestival.org) One of the world's longest-running jazz festivals (since 1958) showcases big-name headliners over a long weekend in mid-September.

Monterey Bay Birding Festival   OUTDOORS
(www.montereybaybirding.org) Enthusiastic birders and naturalists gather for field trips, workshops and lectures in Monterey and surrounding counties in late September.

🛏 Sleeping

Book ahead for special events, on weekends and in summer. To avoid the tourist congestion and jacked-up prices of Cannery Row, look to Pacific Grove. Cheaper motels line Munras Ave, south of downtown, and N Fremont St, east of Hwy 1.

HI Monterey Hostel   HOSTEL $
(☑831-649-0375; www.montereyhostel.org; 778 Hawthorne St; dm with shared bath $26-35; ⊙check-in 4-10pm; @🛜) Four blocks from Cannery Row and the aquarium, this simple, clean hostel houses single-sex and mixed dorms, as well as private rooms (call for rates). Budget backpackers stuff themselves silly with make-your-own pancake breakfasts. Reservations strongly recommended. Take MST bus 1 from downtown's Transit Plaza.

Veterans Memorial Park
Campground   CAMPGROUND $
(☑831-646-3865; www.monterey.org; tent & RV sites $27) Tucked into the forest, this municipal campground has 40 grassy, nonreservable sites near a nature preserve's hiking trails. Amenities include coin-op hot showers, flush toilets, drinking water and barbecue fire pits. Three-night maximum stay.

Casa Munras   BOUTIQUE HOTEL $$
(☑800-222-2446, 831-375-2411; www.hotelcasamunras.com; 700 Munras Ave; r from $120; @🛜🏊🐾) Built around an adobe hacienda once owned by a 19th-century Spanish colonial don, chic modern rooms come with lofty beds and some gas fireplaces, all inside two-story motel-esque buildings. Splash in a heated outdoor pool, unwind at the tapas bar or take a sea-salt scrub in the tiny spa. Pet fee $50.

Hotel Abrego   BOUTIQUE HOTEL $$
(☑800-982-1986, 831-372-7551; www.hotelabrego.com; 755 Abrego St; r from $140; 🛜🏊🐾) At this downtown boutique hotel, most of the spacious, clean-lined contemporary rooms have gas fireplaces and chaise longues. Work out in the fitness studio, take a dip in the outdoor pool or warm up in the hot tub. Pet fee $30.

Monterey Hotel   HISTORIC HOTEL $$
(☑800-966-6490, 831-375-3184; www.montereyhotel.com; 406 Alvarado St; r $80-220; 🛜) In the heart of downtown and a short walk from Fisherman's Wharf, this 1904 edifice harbors five-dozen small, somewhat noisy, but freshly renovated rooms with Victorian-styled furniture and plantation shutters. No elevator. Parking $17.

Colton Inn   MOTEL $$
(☑800-848-7007, 831-649-6500; www.coltoninn.com; 707 Pacific St; r incl breakfast $119-209; 🛜) Downtown, this dated two-story motel prides itself on cleanliness and friendliness. There's no pool and zero view, but staff loan out DVDs, some rooms have real log-burning fireplaces, hot tubs or kitchenettes, and there's even a dry sauna.

★ InterContinental–Clement   HOTEL $$$
(☑866-781-2406, 831-375-4500; www.ictheclementmonterey.com; 750 Cannery Row; r from $200; 🌀@🛜🏊) Like an upscale version of a New England millionaire's seaside mansion, this all-encompassing resort presides over Cannery Row. For the utmost luxury and romance, book an ocean-view suite with a balcony and private fireplace, then breakfast in bayfront C Restaurant downstairs. Parking is $23.

Sanctuary Beach Resort   HOTEL $$$
(☑877-944-3863, 831-883-9478; www.thesanctuarybeachresort.com; 3295 Dunes Dr, Marina;

r $179-329; ▨@奈▨▨) Be lulled to sleep by the surf at this low-lying retreat hidden in the sand dunes north of Monterey. Reached via golf carts, townhouses harbor petite rooms with gas fireplaces and binoculars for whale-watching. Sunset bonfires bring out s'mores. The beach is an off-limits nature preserve, but there are public beaches and walking trails nearby. Pet fee $40.

Jabberwock
B&B $$$

(☑888-428-7253, 831-372-4777; www.jabberwock-inn.com; 598 Laine St; r incl breakfast $169-309; @奈) High atop a hill and barely visible through a shroud of foliage, this 1911 arts-and-crafts house hums a playful *Alice in Wonderland* tune through its seven immaculate rooms, a few with fireplaces and whirlpool tubs. Over afternoon tea and cookies or evening wine and hors d'oeuvres, ask the genial hosts about the house's many salvaged architectural elements.

✖ Eating

Uphill from Cannery Row, Lighthouse Ave is chock-a-block with casual, budget-friendly eateries, from Hawaiian barbecue to Middle Eastern kebabs.

Old Monterey Marketplace
MARKET $

(www.oldmonterey.org; Alvarado St, btwn Del Monte Ave & Pearl St; ⊙4-7pm Tue Sep-May, to 8pm Jun-Aug; ▣) 🍴 Rain or shine, head downtown on Tuesdays for farm-fresh fruit and veggies, artisan cheeses, international food stalls and a scrumptious 'baker's alley.'

Crêpes of Brittany
FRENCH $

(www.crepesofbrittany.com; 6 Fisherman's Wharf; crepes $5-10; ⊙8am-3pm Mon-Fri, to 4pm Sat & Sun Sep-May, 8am-6:30pm Mon-Fri, to 8pm Sat & Sun Jun-Aug; ☑▣) Authentic savory and sweet crepes are swirled by a French expat – the homemade caramel is a treat. Expect long lines on weekends. Cash only.

First Awakenings
AMERICAN $$

(www.firstawakenings.net; American Tin Cannery, 125 Oceanview Blvd; mains $8-12; ⊙7am-2pm Mon-Fri, to 2:30pm Sat & Sun; ▣) Sweet and savory, all-American breakfasts and lunches and bottomless pitchers of coffee merrily weigh down outdoor tables at this cafe uphill from the aquarium. Try the unusual 'bluegerm' pancakes or a spicy Sonoran frittata.

LouLou's Griddle in the Middle
AMERICAN $$

(www.loulousgriddle.com; Municipal Wharf 2; mains $8-16; ⊙usually 7:30am-3pm & 5-8:30pm Wed-Mon; ▣▨) Stroll down the municipal wharf to this zany diner, best for breakfasts of ginormous pancakes and omelets with Mexican pico de gallo salsa or fresh seafood for lunch. Breezy outdoor tables are dog-friendly.

Montrio Bistro
CALIFORNIAN $$$

(☑831-648-8880; www.montrio.com; 414 Calle Principal; mains $17-29; ⊙5-10pm Sun-Thu, to 11pm Fri & Sat; ▣) Inside a 1910 firehouse, Montrio looks dolled up with leather walls and iron trellises, but the tables have butcher paper and crayons for kids. The eclectic seasonal menu mixes local, organic fare with Californian, Asian and European flair, including tapas-style small bites and mini desserts.

Monterey's Fish House
SEAFOOD $$$

(☑831-373-4647; 2114 Del Monte Ave; mains $9-28; ⊙11:30am-2:30pm Mon-Fri, 5-9:30pm daily; ▣) Watched over by photos of Sicilian fishermen, dig into oak-grilled or blackened swordfish, barbecued oysters or, for those stout of heart, the Mexican squid steak. Reservations are essential (it's *so* crowded), but the vibe is island-casual: Hawaiian shirts seem to be de rigueur for men.

Sandbar & Grill
SEAFOOD $$$

(☑831-373-2818; www.sandbarandgrillmonterey.com; Municipal Wharf 2; mains $18-30; ⊙11am-9pm; ▣) Watch otters play outside the bay-view windows at this floating seafood kitchen on the wharf. Stick with the classics such as creamy clam chowder, grilled sand dabs and jumbo crab club sandwiches. Reservations strongly recommended. Ring the bell to let them know you've arrived.

▼ Drinking & Nightlife

Prowl downtown's Alvarado St, touristy Cannery Row and locals-only Lighthouse Ave for more watering holes.

A Taste of Monterey
WINE BAR

(www.atasteofmonterey.com; 700 Cannery Row; tasting fee $10-20; ⊙11am-7pm Sun-Wed, to 8pm Thu-Sat) Sample medal-winning Monterey County wines from as far away as the Santa Lucia Highlands while soaking up dreamy sea views, then peruse thoughtful exhibits on barrel-making and cork production.

East Village Coffee Lounge
CAFE, LOUNGE

(www.eastvillagecoffeelounge.com; 498 Washington St; ⊙6am-late Mon-Fri, from 7am Sat & Sun; 奈) Downtown coffee shop on a busy corner brews with fair-trade, organic beans. At night, it pulls off a big-city lounge vibe with film, open-mic and live-music nights and an all-important booze license.

Crown & Anchor
PUB
(www.crownandanchor.net; 150 W Franklin St; ⏰11am-1:30am) At this basement British pub, the first thing you'll notice is the red plaid carpeting, then the plentiful draft beers and single-malt scotches, not to mention damn fine fish-and-chips.

Cannery Row Brewing Co
BAR
(www.canneryrowbrewingcompany.com; 95 Prescott Ave; ⏰11am-midnight Sun-Thu, to 2am Fri & Sat) Dozens of craft beers from around the world bring folks into this Cannery Row bar-and-grill, as does an outdoor deck with roaring fire pits.

Sardine Factory Lounge
LOUNGE
(www.sardinefactory.com; 701 Wave St; ⏰5pm-midnight) The legendary restaurant's fireplace lounge pours wines by the glass, delivers filling appetizers to your table and has a live piano player most nights.

☆ Entertainment

For comprehensive entertainment listings, browse the free tabloid *Monterey County Weekly* (www.montereycountyweekly.com).

Sly McFly's Fueling Station
LIVE MUSIC
(☎831-649-8050; www.slymcflys.net; 700 Cannery Row; ⏰11:30am-midnight Sun-Thu, to 2am Fri & Sat) Waterfront dive showcases live local blues, jazz and rock bands nightly after 8:30pm or 9pm. Skip the food, though.

Osio Cinemas
CINEMA
(☎831-644-8171; www.osiocinemas.com; 350 Alvarado St; adult $10, before 6pm $6.50) Downtown cinema screens indie dramas, cutting-edge documentaries and offbeat Hollywood films. Drop by its Cafe Lumiere for locally roasted coffee, loose-leaf tea, decadent cheesecake and wi-fi.

🔒 Shopping

Cannery Row is jammed with claptrap shops, while downtown's side streets hide more one-of-a-kind finds.

Wharf Marketplace
FOOD & DRINK
(www.thewharfmarketplace.com; 290 Figueroa St; ⏰7am-7pm Wed-Mon, to 2pm Tue) 🍴 Inside an old railway station, this gourmet-food emporium carries bountiful farm goodness and artisanal products from Monterey County and beyond.

Monterey Peninsula Art Foundation Gallery
ART
(www.mpaf.org; 425 Cannery Row; ⏰11am-5pm) Taking over a cozy sea-view house, more than 30 local artists sell plein-air paintings and sketches alongside contemporary works in all media.

Cannery Row Antique Mall
ANTIQUES
(www.canneryrowantiquemall.com; 471 Wave St; ⏰10am-5:30pm Mon-Fri, to 6pm Sat, to 5pm Sun) Inside a historic 1920s cannery building, two floors are stacked high with beguiling flotsam and jetsam from decades past.

Old Capitol Books
BOOKS
(559 Tyler St; ⏰10am-6pm Wed-Mon, to 7pm Tue) Tall shelves of new, used and antiquarian books, including rare first editions, California titles and John Steinbeck's works.

ℹ Information

Doctors on Duty (☎831-649-0770; www.doctorsonduty.com; 501 Lighthouse Ave; ⏰8am-8pm Mon-Sat, 8am-6pm Sun) Walk-in, nonemergency medical clinic.

FedEx Office (www.fedex.com; 799 Lighthouse Ave; per min 30-40¢; ⏰7am-10pm Mon-Fri, 8am-9pm Sat, 9am-9pm Sun; 🛜) Pay-as-you-go internet computer workstations.

Monterey Public Library (www.monterey.org; 625 Pacific St; ⏰noon-8pm Mon-Wed, 10am-6pm Thu-Sat, 1-5pm Sun; 🛜) Free wi-fi and public internet terminals.

Monterey Visitors Center (☎877-666-8373, 831-657-6400; www.seemonterey.com; 401 Camino El Estero; ⏰9am-6pm Mon-Sat, to 5pm Sun, closing 1hr earlier Nov-Mar) Free tourist brochures; ask for a *Monterey County Literary & Film Map*.

ℹ Getting There & Around

A few miles east of downtown off Hwy 68, Monterey Peninsula Airport has flights with United (LA, San Francisco and Denver), American (LA), Alaska (San Diego), Allegiant Air (Las Vegas) and US Airways (Phoenix).

Monterey Airbus (☎831-373-7777; www.montereyairbus.com; 🛜) links Monterey with international airports in San Jose ($40, 1½ hours) and San Francisco ($50, 2½ hours) almost a dozen times daily; book online for discounts.

To get here on public transportation, first take a Greyhound bus or Amtrak train to Salinas, then catch a Thruway bus (for Amtrak train passengers only) or MST bus 20 to Monterey ($3.50, one hour, every 30 to 60 minutes).

Monterey Peninsula

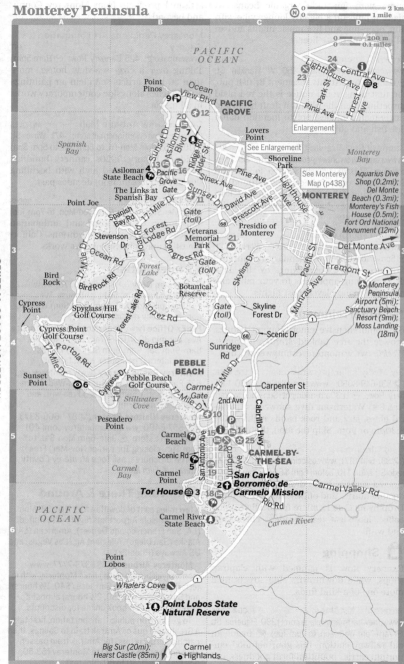

CENTRAL COAST MONTEREY

PACIFIC OCEAN

Point Pinos

9

12

Ocean View Blvd

PACIFIC GROVE

20

7

Lovers Point

See Enlargement

Spanish Bay

Sunset Dr

Asilomar Blvd

Ridge Rd

Alder St

13

16

Asilomar State Beach

Pacific Grove

Gate

Sinex Ave

Pine Ave

Shoreline Park

See Monterey Map (p438)

Monterey Bay

Aquarius Dive Shop (0.2mi); Del Monte Beach (0.3mi); Monterey's Fish House (0.5mi); Fort Ord National Monument (12mi)

Point Joe

The Links at Spanish Bay

Sunset Dr

David Ave

MONTEREY

11

Spanish Bay Rd

17-Mile Dr

Forest Lodge Rd

Gate (toll)

Veterans Memorial Park

Prescott Ave

Presidio of Monterey

21

Lighthouse Ave

Pacific St

Stevenson Dr

Ocean Rd

Bird Rock Rd

Slough Rd

Forest Lake Rd

Congress Rd

Gate (toll)

Skyline Dr

Del Monte Ave

Fremont St

Bird Rock

Forest Lake

Botanical Reserve

Lopez Rd

Gate (toll)

Skyline Forest Dr

Murras Ave

Monterey Peninsula Airport (5mi); Sanctuary Beach Resort (9mi); Moss Landing (18mi)

Cypress Point

Spyglass Hill Golf Course

Ronda Rd

Scenic Dr

Sunridge Rd

Cypress Point Golf Course

Portola Rd

PEBBLE BEACH

17-Mile Dr

Carpenter St

Sunset Point

Cypress Dr

Pebble Beach Golf Course

6

17

Stillwater Cove

Carmel Gate

2nd Ave

Cabrillo Hwy

Pescadero Point

10

15

14

25

Carmel Beach

San Antonio Ave

Scenic Rd

5

22

Juniper Ave

CARMEL-BY-THE-SEA

Carmel Bay

Carmel Point

19

2

San Carlos Borroméo de Carmelo Mission

Carmel Valley Rd

PACIFIC OCEAN

Tor House 3

18

Rio Rd

Carmel River

Carmel River State Beach

Point Lobos

Whalers Cove

1 **Point Lobos State Natural Reserve**

Big Sur (20mi); Hearst Castle (85mi)

Carmel Highlands

Enlargement

24

23

Central Ave

Lighthouse Ave

Park St

Pine Ave

Forest Ave

8

Monterey Peninsula

Monterey-Salinas Transit (MST; ☎ 888-678-2871; www.mst.org; single-ride $1.50-3.50, day pass $10) operates local and regional buses; routes converge on downtown's **Transit Plaza** (cnr Pearl & Alvarado Sts). From late May until early September, MST's free **trolley** loops around downtown, Fisherman's Wharf and Cannery Row between 10am and 7pm or 8pm daily.

Pacific Grove

Founded as a tranquil Methodist summer retreat in 1875, PG maintained its quaint, holier-than-thou attitude well into the 20th century. The selling of liquor was illegal up until 1969, making it California's last 'dry' town. Today, leafy streets are lined by stately Victorian homes and a charming, compact downtown orbits Lighthouse Ave.

◎ Sights & Activities

Aptly named Ocean View Blvd affords views from Lovers Point Park west to Point Pinos, where it becomes Sunset Dr, offering tempting turnouts where you can stroll by pounding surf, rocky outcrops and teeming tide pools all the way to Asilomar State Beach. This seaside route is great for cycling too – some say it rivals the famous 17-Mile Drive for beauty, and even better, it's free.

Point Pinos Lighthouse   LIGHTHOUSE
(☎ 831-648-3176; www.pointpinos.org; 90 Asilomar Ave; suggested donation adult/child 6-17yr $2/1; ⊙ 1-4pm Thu-Mon) The West Coast's oldest continuously operating lighthouse has been warning ships off the hazardous tip of the Monterey Peninsula since 1855. Inside are modest exhibits on the lighthouse's history and alas, its failures – local shipwrecks.

Monarch Grove Sanctuary   PARK
(www.ci.pg.ca.us; off Ridge Rd, btwn Lighthouse Ave & Short St; ⊙ dawn-dusk; 🚻) 🅿 FREE Between October and February, more than 25,000 migratory monarch butterflies cluster in this thicket of tall eucalyptus trees, secreted inland. During peak season, volunteer guides answer all of your questions.

Pacific Grove Museum of Natural History   MUSEUM
(☎ 831-648-5716; www.pgmuseum.org; 165 Forest Ave; admission by donation; ⊙ 10am-5pm Tue-Sat; 🚻) With a gray-whale sculpture out front, this small kid-oriented museum has old-fashioned exhibits about sea otters, coastal bird life, butterflies, the Big Sur coast and Native Californian tribes.

Pacific Grove Golf Links   GOLF
(☎ 831-648-5775; www.pggolflinks.com; 77 Asilomar Blvd; green fees $25-65) Can't afford to play at famous Pebble Beach? This historic

18-hole municipal course, where deer freely range, has impressive sea views, and it's a lot easier (not to mention cheaper) to book a tee time here.

🛏 Sleeping

Antique-filled B&Bs have taken over many stately Victorian homes around downtown and by the beach. Motels cluster at the peninsula's western end, off Lighthouse and Asilomar Aves.

Asilomar Conference Grounds　　LODGE $$
(☑888-635-5310, 831-372-8016; www.visitasilomar.com; 800 Asilomar Ave; r incl breakfast from $145; @🐾🛜🏊) This state-park lodge sprawls by sand dunes in pine forest. Skip ho-hum motel rooms and opt for historic houses designed by early-20th-century architect Julia Morgan (of Hearst Castle fame) – the thin-walled, hardwood-floored rooms may be small, but share a fireplace lounge. Head to the lodge lobby for ping-pong and pool tables and wi-fi. Bike rentals available.

Sunset Inn　　MOTEL $$
(☑831-375-3529; www.gosunsetinn.com; 133 Asilomar Blvd; r $90-235; 🐾) At this small motor lodge near the golf course and the beach, attentive staff hand out keys to crisply redesigned rooms that have hardwood floors, king-sized beds with cheery floral-print comforters and sometimes a hot tub and a fireplace.

Deer Haven Inn　　MOTEL $$
(☑831-373-7784; www.deerhaveninn.com; 750 Crocker Ave; r incl breakfast $109-209; 🐾) Stylish renovations have brought this two-story motel into the modern age. Every room has a gas fireplace, and it's a quick walk to the beach.

🍴 Eating

Downtown PG teems with European-style bakeries, coffee shops and neighborhood cafes.

Red House Cafe　　CAFE $$
(☑831-643-1060; www.redhousecafe.com; 662 Lighthouse Ave; mains breakfast & lunch $8-

---

SCENIC DRIVE: 17-MILE DRIVE

What to See

Pacific Grove and Carmel are linked by the spectacularly scenic, if overhyped, 17-Mile Drive, which meanders through Pebble Beach, a wealthy private resort. It's no chore staying within the 25mph limit – every curve in the road reveals another postcard vista, especially when wildflowers are in bloom. Cycling the drive is enormously popular: try to do it during the week, when traffic isn't as heavy, and ride with the flow of traffic from north to south.

Using the self-guided touring map you'll receive at the toll gate, you can easily pick out landmarks such as Spanish Bay, where explorer Gaspar de Portolá dropped anchor in 1769; treacherously rocky Point Joe, which was often mistaken for the entrance to Monterey Bay and thus became the site of shipwrecks; and Bird Rock, also a haven for harbor seals and sea lions. The ostensible pièce de résistance is the trademarked Lone Cypress, which has perched on a seaward rock for possibly more than 250 years.

Besides the coastal scenery, star attractions at Pebble Beach include world-famous golf courses, where a celebrity and pro tournament happens every February. The luxurious Lodge at Pebble Beach (☑800-654-9300, 831-624-3811; www.pebblebeach.com; 1700 17-Mile Drive; r from $765; 🏢@🛜🏊) embraces a spa and designer shops where the most demanding of tastes are catered to. Even if you're not a trust-fund baby, you can still soak up the rich atmosphere in the resort's art-filled public spaces and bay views from the cocktail lounge.

The Route

Operated as a toll road by the Pebble Beach Company, the 17-Mile Drive (www.pebblebeach.com; per car/bicycle $10/free) is open from sunrise to sunset. The toll can be refunded later as a discount on a $30 minimum food purchase at Pebble Beach restaurants.

Time & Mileage

There are five separate gates for the 17-Mile Drive; how far you drive and how long you take is up to you. To take advantage of the most scenery, enter off Sunset Dr in Pacific Grove and exit onto San Antonio Ave in Carmel-by-the-Sea.

14, dinner $12-23; ⊙8am-2:30pm daily, 5-9pm Tue-Sun; ♠) Crowded with locals, this shingled late-19th-century house dishes up comfort food with haute touches, including cinnamon-brioche French toast, grilled eggplant-fontina sandwiches or spinach-cheese ravioli in lemon beurre blanc sauce. Oatmeal-apricot-pecan cookies are what's for dessert. Reservations helpful.

★ **Passionfish** SEAFOOD $$$
(☑831-655-3311; www.passionfish.net; 701 Lighthouse Ave; mains $16-32; ⊙5-9pm Sun-Thu, to 10pm Fri & Sat) ⌔ Fresh, sustainable seafood is artfully presented in any number of inventive ways, and a seasonally inspired menu also carries slow-cooked meats and vegetarian dishes spotlighting local farms. The earth-tone decor is spare, with tables squeezed conversationally close together. An ambitious world-ranging wine list is priced near retail, and there are twice as many Chinese teas as wines by the glass.

Reservations strongly recommended.

ℹ Information

Pacific Grove Chamber of Commerce
(☑800-656-6650, 831-373-3304; www.pacificgrove.org; 584 Central Ave; ⊙9:30am-5pm Mon-Fri, 10am-3pm Sat) Free maps and brochures.

ℹ Getting There & Around

MST (☑888-678-2871; www.mst.org) bus 1 connects downtown Monterey and Cannery Row with Pacific Grove, continuing to Asilomar ($2.50, every 30 to 60 minutes).

Carmel-by-the-Sea

With borderline fanatical devotion to its canine citizens, quaint Carmel has the well-manicured feel of a country club. Watch the parade of behatted ladies toting fancy-label shopping bags to lunch and dapper gents driving top-down convertibles along Ocean Ave, the village's slow-mo main drag.

Founded as a seaside resort in the 1880s – fairly odd, given that its beach is often blanketed in fog – Carmel quickly attracted famous artists and writers, such as Sinclair Lewis and Jack London, and their hangers-on. Artistic flavor survives in more than 100 galleries that line downtown's immaculate streets, but sky-high property values have long obliterated any salt-of-the-earth bohemia.

Dating from the 1920s, Comstock cottages, with their characteristic stone chimneys and pitched gable roofs, still dot the town, making it look vaguely reminiscent of the English countryside. Even payphones, garbage cans and newspaper vending boxes are quaintly shingled.

◉ Sights & Activities

Escape downtown's harried shopping streets and stroll tree-lined neighborhoods on the lookout for domiciles charming and peculiar. The Hansel and Gretel houses on Torres St, between 5th and 6th Avenues, are just how you'd imagine them. Another eye-catching house in the shape of a ship, made from local river rocks and salvaged ship parts, is on Guadalupe St near 6th Ave.

★ **Point Lobos State Natural Reserve** PARK
(☑831-624-4909; www.pointlobos.org; Hwy 1; per car $10; ⊙8am-7pm, closing 30min after sunset early Nov–mid-Mar; ♠) They bark, they bathe and they're fun to watch – sea lions are the stars here at Punta de los Lobos Marinos (Point of the Sea Wolves), almost 4 miles south of Carmel, where a dramatically rocky coastline offers excellent tide-pooling. The full perimeter hike is 6 miles, but shorter walks take in wild scenery too, including Bird Island, shady cypress groves, and the historical Whaler's Cabin and Devil's Cauldron, a whirlpool that gets splashy at high tide.

The kelp forest at Whalers Cove is popular with snorkelers and scuba divers; without donning a wetsuit, you can still get an idea of the underwater terrain with a 3D model located by the parking lot. Reserve snorkeling, scuba-diving, kayaking and SUP permits (per person $5 to $10) up to 60 days in advance online.

Arrive early on weekends; parking is limited. Don't skip paying the entry fee by parking outside the park gates on the highway shoulder – California's state parks are chronically underfunded and need your help.

★ **San Carlos Borroméo de Carmelo Mission** CHURCH
(www.carmelmission.org; 3080 Rio Rd; adult/child 7-17yr $6.50/2; ⊙9:30am-7pm) Monterey's original mission was established by Franciscan friar Junípero Serra in 1770, but poor soil and the corrupting influence of Spanish soldiers forced the move to Carmel two years later. Today this is one of California's most strikingly beautiful missions, an oasis of solemnity bathed in flowering gardens. The

CARMEL VALLEY

Where sun-kissed vineyards rustle beside farm fields, Carmel Valley is a peaceful side trip, just a 20-minute drive east of Hwy 1 along eastbound Carmel Valley Rd. At organic **Earthbound Farm Stand** (☎805-625-6219; www.ebfarm.com; 7250 Carmel Valley Rd; ☺8am-6:30pm Mon-Sat, 9am-6pm Sun; ⊞) ✐, sample homemade soups and salads or harvest your own herbs from the garden. Several wineries further east offer tastings – don't miss the Pinot Noir bottled by **Boekenoogen** (www.boekenoogenwines.com; 24 W Carmel Valley Rd; tasting fee $8-10; ☺11am-5pm). Afterwards, stretch your legs in the village of Carmel Valley, chock-a-block with genteel shops and bistros.

mission's adobe chapel was later replaced with an arched basilica made of stone quarried in the Santa Lucia Mountains. Museum exhibits are scattered throughout the meditative complex.

The spartan cell attributed to Serra looks like something out of *The Good, the Bad and the Ugly,* while a separate chapel houses his memorial tomb. Don't overlook the gravestone of 'Old Gabriel,' a Native American convert whom Serra baptized, and whose dates put him at 151 years old when he died. People say he smoked like a chimney and outlived seven wives. There's a lesson in there somewhere.

★ **Tor House**   HISTORIC BUILDING
(☎831-624-1813; www.torhouse.org; 26304 Ocean View Ave; adult/child 12-17yr $10/5; ☺tours hourly 10am-3pm Fri & Sat) Even if you've never heard of 20th-century poet Robinson Jeffers, a pilgrimage to this house built with his own hands offers fascinating insights into both the man and the bohemian ethos of Old Carmel. A porthole in the Celtic-inspired **Hawk Tower** reputedly came from the wrecked ship that carried Napoleon from Elba. The only way to visit the property is to reserve a tour (children under 12 years old not allowed), although the tower can be glimpsed from the street.

Carmel Beach City Park   BEACH
(off Scenic Rd; ⊞) **FREE** Not always sunny, Carmel Beach is a gorgeous blanket of white

sand, where pampered pups excitedly run off-leash. South of 10th Ave, bonfires crackle after sunset.

☆ Festivals & Events

Carmel Art Festival   CULTURE
(www.carmelartfestival.org) Meet plein-air painters and sculptors in Devendorf Park over a long weekend in mid-May.

Carmel Bach Festival   MUSIC
(www.bachfestival.org) Classical and chamber-music performances are staged around town in July.

Pebble Beach Concours d'Elegance PARADE
(www.pebblebeachconcours.net) Rare vintage and classic cars roll onto the fairways at Pebble Beach in mid-August.

Carmel Art & Film Festival   CULTURE, FILM
(www.carmelartandfilm.com) Contemporary fine art, live music and more than 100 independent film screenings in mid-October.

🛏 Sleeping

Shockingly overpriced boutique hotels, inns and B&Bs fill up quickly, especially in summer. Ask the chamber of commerce about last-minute deals. For better-value lodgings, head north to Monterey.

Carmel Village Inn   MOTEL $$
(☎800-346-3864, 831-624-3864; www.carmel-villageinn.com; cnr Ocean & Junípero Aves; d incl breakfast buffet from $129; ☎) With cheerful flowers decorating its exterior, this well-located motel across from Devendorf Park has cheapish rooms, some with gas fireplaces, and nightly quiet hours.

Cypress Inn   BOUTIQUE HOTEL $$$
(☎831-624-3871, 800-443-7443; www.cypress-inn.com; Lincoln St, at 7th Ave; r incl breakfast from $245; ☎❀) Done up in Spanish Colonial style, this 1929 inn is co-owned by movie star Doris Day. Airy terra-cotta hallways with colorful tiles give it a Mediterranean feel, while sunny rooms face the courtyard. Pet fee $30.

Sea View Inn   B&B $$$
(☎831-624-8778; www.seaviewinncarmel.com; El Camino Real, btwn 11th & 12th Aves; r incl breakfast $145-295; ☎) Retreat from downtown's hustle to fireside nooks tailor-made for reading. The cheapest rooms with slanted ceilings are short on cat-swinging space. Rates in-

clude afternoon wine and noshes on the front porch.

Mission Ranch   INN $$$
(☎800-538-8221, 831-624-6436; www.mission-ranchcarmel.com; 26270 Dolores St; r incl breakfast $135-300; 🐾) If woolly sheep grazing on green fields by the beach doesn't convince you to stay here, maybe knowing Hollywood icon Clint Eastwood restored this historic ranch will. Accommodations are shabby-chic, even a tad rustic.

🍴 Eating

Carmel's staid dining scene is more about old-world atmosphere than value.

Bruno's Market & Deli   DELI, MARKET $
(www.brunosmarket.com; cnr 6th & Junípero Aves; sandwiches $6-9; ⏲7am-8pm) Small supermarket deli counter makes a saucy sandwich of oakwood-grilled tri-tip beef and stocks all the accoutrements for a beach picnic, including Sparkys root beer from Pacific Grove.

Mundaka   SPANISH, TAPAS $$
(☎831-624-7400; www.mundakacarmel.com; San Carlos St, btwn Ocean & 7th Aves; small plates $6-25; ⏲5:30-10pm Sun-Wed, to 11pm Thu-Sat) This stone courtyard hideaway is a svelte escape from Carmel's stuffy 'newly wed and nearly dead' crowd. Taste Spanish tapas and housemade sangria while world beats spin.

Katy's Place   BREAKFAST $$
(www.katysplacecarmel.com; Mission St, btwn 5th & 6th Aves; mains $8-16; ⏲7am-2pm) It's pricey, but what isn't in Carmel? Start your day with an apple-cinnamon Belgian waffle, Swedish pancakes or one of 16 Californicized variations on eggs benedict.

🍷 Drinking & Entertainment

Scheid Vineyards   WINE BAR
(www.scheidvineyards.com; San Carlos St, at 7th Ave; tasting fee $10-20; ⏲noon-6pm Sun-Thu, to 7pm Fri & Sat) Wine-tasting rooms abound downtown. Pop into Scheid Vineyards to sip a prodigious variety of grape varietals, all grown in Monterey County.

Forest Theater   THEATER
(☎831-626-1681; www.foresttheatercarmel.org; cnr Mountain View Ave & Santa Rita St) At this 1910 venue, community-theater musicals, dramas and comedies and film screenings take place under the stars by flickering fire pits.

ℹ Information

Downtown buildings have no street numbers, so addresses specify the street and nearest intersection only.

Carmel Chamber of Commerce (☎800-550-4333, 831-624-2522; www.carmelcalifornia.org; San Carlos St, btwn 5th & 6th Aves; ⏲10am-5pm) Free maps and brochures, including local art gallery guides.

Carmel Pine Cone (www.pineconearchive.com) Free weekly newspaper packed with local personality and color – the police log is a comedy of manners.

ℹ Getting There & Around

Carmel is about 5 miles south of Monterey via Hwy 1. There's free parking (no time limit) in a **municipal lot** (cnr 3rd & Junípero Aves) behind the Vista Lobos building.

MST (☎888-678-2871; www.mst.org) 'Grapevine Express' bus 24 ($2.50, hourly) connects Monterey's Transit Plaza with downtown Carmel, the mission and Carmel Valley. Bus 22 ($3.50) stops in downtown Carmel and at the mission en route to/from Point Lobos and Big Sur three times daily between late May and early September, and twice daily on Saturday and Sunday only the rest of the year.

Big Sur

Big Sur is more a state of mind than a place you can pinpoint on a map. There are no traffic lights, banks or strip malls, and when the sun goes down, the moon and the stars are the only streetlights – if summer's dense fog hasn't extinguished them, that is. Much ink has been spilled extolling the raw beauty and energy of this precious piece of land shoehorned between the Santa Lucia Range and the Pacific Ocean, but nothing quite prepares you for your first glimpse of the craggy, unspoiled coastline.

In the 1950s and '60s, Big Sur – so named by Spanish settlers living on the Monterey Peninsula, who referred to the wilderness as *el país grande del sur* ('the big country to the south') – became a retreat for artists and writers, including Henry Miller and Beat Generation visionaries such as Lawrence Ferlinghetti. Today Big Sur attracts self-proclaimed artists, new-age mystics, latter-day hippies and city slickers seeking to unplug and reflect more deeply on this emerald-green edge of the continent.

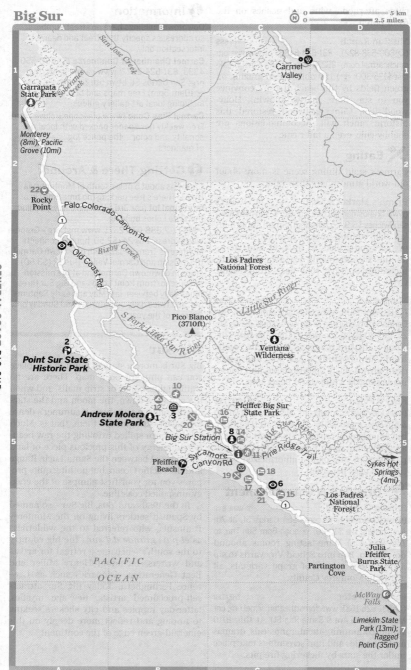

Big Sur

0 — 5 km
0 — 2.5 miles

San Jose Creek

Garrapata
State Park

Soberanes Creek

Monterey
(8mi); Pacific
Grove (10mi)

Carmel
Valley **5**

22
Rocky
Point

Palo Colorado Canyon Rd

4
Old Coast Rd

Bixby Creek

Los Padres
National Forest

Little Sur River

S Fork Little Sur River

Pico Blanco
(3710ft)

9
Ventana
Wilderness

2
Point Sur State
Historic Park

10

12
3

**Andrew Molera
State Park** **1**

16

Pfeiffer Big Sur
State Park

20

8 **14**

Big Sur Station

11 Pine Ridge Trail

Sykes Hot
Springs
(4mi)

Pfeiffer
Beach **7**

Sycamore
Canyon Rd

19

17
21

18

6
15
1

Los Padres
National Forest

PACIFIC

OCEAN

Julia
Pfeiffer
Burns State
Park

Partington
Cove

McWay
Falls

Limekiln State
Park (13mi);
Ragged
Point (35mi)

Big Sur

CENTRAL COAST BIG SUR

⊙ Sights

At Big Sur's state parks, your parking fee ($10) receipt is valid for same-day entry to all except Limekiln. Please don't skip paying the entry fee by parking illegally outside the parks along Hwy 1 – California's state parks have suffered severe budget cutbacks, and every dollar helps.

Garrapata State Park PARK
(☏831-624-4909; www.parks.ca.gov; off Hwy 1; 🅿) FREE Over 4 miles south of Point Lobos on Hwy 1, pull over to hike coastal headlands, where you might spot whales cruising by offshore during winter, or into canyons of wildflowers and redwood trees. *Garrapata* is Spanish for tick, of which there are many in the canyon and woods, so wearing long sleeves and pants is smart. Leashed dogs are allowed on the beach only.

Bixby Bridge LANDMARK
Less than 15 miles south of Carmel, this landmark spanning Rainbow Canyon is one of the world's highest single-span bridges. Completed in 1932, it was built by prisoners eager to lop time off their sentences. There's a perfect photo-op pull-off on the bridge's north side. Before Bixby Bridge was constructed, travelers had to trek inland on what's now called the Old Coast Rd, a rough

dirt route that reconnects after 11 miles with Hwy 1 near Andrew Molera State Park.

When the weather is dry enough, the old road is usually navigable by 4WD or a mountain bike.

★**Point Sur State Historic Park** LIGHTHOUSE
(☏831-625-4419; www.pointsur.org; off Hwy 1; adult/child 6-17yr from $12/5; ⊙tours usually at 1pm Wed, 10am Sat & Sun Nov-Mar, 10am & 2pm Wed & Sat, 10am Sun Apr-Oct, also 10am Thu Jul & Aug) A little more than 6 miles south of Bixby Bridge, Point Sur rises like a velvety green fortress out of the sea. It looks like an island, but is actually connected to land by a sandbar. Atop the volcanic rock sits an 1889 stone lightstation, which was staffed until 1974. During three-hour guided tours, ocean views and tales of the lighthouse keepers' family lives are engrossing. Meet your tour guide at the locked farm gate ¼-mile north of Point Sur Naval Facility.

Special monthly moonlight tours are given between April and October. Call ahead to confirm all tour schedules. Show up early because space is limited (no reservations, some credit cards accepted).

★**Andrew Molera State Park** PARK
(☏831-667-2315; www.parks.ca.gov; Hwy 1; per car $10; ⊙30min before sunrise-30min after

sunset; ⊞) Named after the farmer who first planted artichokes in California, this oft-overlooked park is a trail-laced pastiche of grassy meadows, ocean bluffs and rugged sandy beaches offering excellent wildlife watching. Look for the entrance just a little more than 8 miles south of Bixby Bridge.

South of the parking lot, you can learn all about endangered California condors inside the **Big Sur Discovery Center** (☑831-624-1202; www.ventanaws.org/discovery_center/; ☉10am-4pm Sat & Sun late-May–early Sep; ⊞) **FREE**. At the bird-banding lab inside a small shed, naturalists carry out long-term species monitoring programs.

From the main parking lot, a short walk along the beach-bound trail passes through a first-come, first-served campground, from where a gentle spur trail leads to the 1861 redwood **Cooper Cabin**, Big Sur's oldest building. Keep hiking on the main trail out toward a wild beach where the Big Sur River runs into the ocean; condors may be spotted circling overhead and migrating whales sometimes cruise by offshore.

Pfeiffer Big Sur State Park   PARK

(☑831-667-2315; www.parks.ca.gov; 47225 Hwy 1; per car $10; ☉30min before sunrise-30min after sunset; ⊞) Named after Big Sur's first European settlers who arrived in 1869, this is Big Sur's largest state park, where hiking trails loop through stately redwood groves. The most popular hike – to 60ft-high **Pfeiffer Falls**, a delicate cascade hidden in the forest, which usually runs from December to May – is a 2-mile round-trip. Built in the 1930s by the Civilian Conservation Corps (CCC), rustic Big Sur Lodge stands near the park entrance, about 13 miles south of Bixby Bridge.

Pfeiffer Beach   BEACH

(www.fs.usda.gov/lpnf; end of Sycamore Canyon Rd; per car $10; ☉9am-8pm; ☒) This phenomenal, crescent-shaped and dog-friendly beach is known for its huge double rock formation, through which waves crash with life-affirming power. It's often windy, and the surf is too dangerous for swimming. But dig down into the wet sand – it's purple! That's because manganese garnet washes down from the craggy hillsides above. To get here from Hwy 1, make a sharp right onto Sycamore Canyon Rd, marked by a small yellow sign that says 'narrow road' at the top.

From the turnoff, which is a half-mile south of Big Sur Station on the ocean side of Hwy 1, it's two narrow, twisting miles down to the beach (RVs and trailers prohibited).

Henry Miller Memorial Library   ARTS CENTER

(☑831-667-2574; www.henrymiller.org; 48603 Hwy 1; ☉11am-6pm) 'It was here in Big Sur I first learned to say Amen!' wrote novelist Henry Miller, a Big Sur denizen from 1944 to 1962. More of a beatnik memorial, alt-cultural venue and bookshop, this community gathering spot was never Miller's home. The house belonged to Miller's friend, painter Emil White, until his death and is now run by a nonprofit group. Stop by to browse and hang out on the front deck. It's about 0.4 miles south of Nepenthe restaurant.

Inside are copies of all of Miller's written works, many of his paintings and a collection of Big Sur and Beat Generation material, including copies of the top 100 books Miller said most influenced him. Check the online calendar for upcoming events.

Partington Cove   BEACH

(off Hwy 1) **FREE** It's a raw, breathtaking spot where crashing surf salts your skin. On the steep, half-mile dirt hike down to the cove, you'll cross a cool bridge and go through an even cooler tunnel. The cove's water is unbelievably aqua and within it grow tangled kelp forests. Look for the unmarked trailhead turnoff inside a hairpin turn on the ocean side of Hwy 1, about 6 miles south of Nepenthe restaurant and 2 miles north of Julia Pfeiffer Burns State Park.

The trail starts just beyond the locked vehicle gate. There's no real beach access and ocean swimming isn't safe, but some people scamper on the rocks and look for tide pools as waves splash ominously. Originally used for loading freight, Partington Cove allegedly became a landing spot for Prohibition-era bootleggers.

★ Julia Pfeiffer Burns State Park   PARK

(☑831-667-2315; www.parks.ca.gov; Hwy 1; per car $10; ☉30min before sunrise-30min after sunset; ⊞) If you're chasing waterfalls, swing into this state park named for a Big Sur pioneer. From the parking lot, the 1.3-mile round-trip Overlook Trail rushes downhill toward the ocean, passing through a tunnel underneath Hwy 1. Everyone comes to photograph 80ft-high **McWay Falls**, which tumbles year-round over granite cliffs and freefalls into the sea – or the beach, depending on the tide. The park entrance is on the east side of Hwy 1, about 8 miles south of Nepenthe restaurant.

McWay Falls is the classic Big Sur postcard shot, with tree-topped rocks jutting above a golden beach next to swirling blue pools and crashing white surf. From trailside benches, you might spot migrating whales during winter.

Limekiln State Park   PARK
(☑831-434-1996; www.parks.ca.gov; 63025 Hwy 1; per car $8; ☉8am-sunset) Two miles south of Lucia, this park gets its name from the four remaining wood-fired kilns originally built here in the 1880s to smelt quarried limestone into powder, a key ingredient in cement building construction from Monterey to San Francisco. Tragically, pioneers chopped down most of the steep canyon's old-growth redwoods to fuel the kilns' fires. A one-mile round-trip trail leads through a redwood grove to the historic site, passing a creekside spur trail to a delightful 100ft-high waterfall.

Los Padres National Forest   FOREST
(☑831-667-2315; www.fs.usda.gov/lpnf; 🐾) The tortuously winding 40-mile stretch of Hwy 1 south of Lucia to Hearst Castle is even more sparsely populated, rugged and remote, mostly running through national forest lands. Around 5 miles south of Kirk Creek Campground and Nacimiento-Fergusson Rd, almost opposite Plaskett Creek Campground, is **Sand Dollar Beach** (http://campone.com; Hwy 1; per car $10, free with paid local USFS campground fee; ☉9am-8pm; 🐾). From the picnic area, it's a five-minute walk to

southern Big Sur's longest sandy beach, a crescent-shaped strip of sand protected from winds by high bluffs.

In 1971, in the waters of nearby **Jade Cove** (http://campone.com; Hwy 1; ☉sunrise-sunset; 🐾) **FREE**, local divers recovered a 9000lb jade boulder that measured 8ft long and was valued at $180,000. People still comb the beach today. The best time to find jade, which is black or blue-green and looks dull until you dip it in water, is during low tide or after a big storm. Keep an eye out for hang gliders flying in for a movie-worthy landing on the beach. Trails down to the water start from several mostly unmarked roadside pulloffs immediately south of Plaskett Creek Campground.

If you have any sunlight left, keep trucking down the highway to **Salmon Creek Falls** (www.fs.usda.gov/lpnf; Hwy 1; 🚻 🐾) **FREE**, which usually flows from December through May. Tucked up in a forested canyon, this double-drop waterfall can be glimpsed from the hairpin turn on Hwy 1, about 8 miles south of Gorda. Roadside parking gets very crowded, as everyone takes the 0.3-mile walk up to the falls to splash around in the pools, where kids shriek and dogs happily bark.

Before leaving Lucia, make sure you've got at least enough fuel in the tank to reach the expensive gas stations at Gorda, about 11 miles south of Limekiln State Park, or Ragged Point, another 12 miles further south.

Ragged Point   LANDMARK
(19019 Hwy 1) Your last – or first – taste of Big Sur's rocky grandeur comes at this craggy

---

CALIFORNIA'S COMEBACK CONDORS

When it comes to endangered species, one of the state's biggest success stories is the California condor. These gigantic, prehistoric birds weigh over 20lb with a wingspan of up to 10ft, letting them fly great distances in search of carrion. They're easily recognized by their naked pink head and large white patches on the underside of each wing.

This big bird became so rare that in 1987 there were only 27 left in the world, and all were removed from the wild to special captive-breeding facilities. Read the whole gripping story in journalist John Moir's book *Return of the Condor: The Race to Save Our Largest Bird from Extinction*.

There are more than 400 California condors alive today, with increasing numbers of captive birds being released back into the wild, where it's hoped they will begin breeding naturally, although it's an uphill battle. Wild condors are still dying of lead poisoning caused by hunter's bullets in the game carcasses that the birds feed on.

The Big Sur coast and Pinnacles National Park (p468) offer excellent opportunities to view this majestic bird. In Big Sur, the **Ventana Wildlife Society** (www.ventanaws.org) occasionally leads two-hour guided condor-watching tours ($50) using radio telemetry to track the birds; for sign-up details, check the website or ask inside the Big Sur Discovery Center.

WORTH A TRIP

VENTANA WILDERNESS

The 240,000-acre Ventana Wilderness is Big Sur's wild backcountry. It lies within the northern Los Padres National Forest, which straddles the Santa Lucia Range running parallel to the coast. Most of this wilderness is covered with oak and chaparral, though canyons cut by the Big Sur and Little Sur Rivers support virgin stands of coast redwoods and the rare endemic Santa Lucia fir, which grows on steep, rocky slopes too.

Partly reopened after devastating wildfires in 2008, Ventana Wilderness remains popular with adventurous backpackers. A much-trammeled overnight destination is Sykes Hot Springs, natural 100°F (35°C) mineral pools framed by redwoods. It's a moderately strenuous 10-mile one-way hike along the Pine Ridge Trail, starting from Big Sur Station (☎831-667-2315; www.parks.ca.gov; Hwy 1; ⊗8am-4pm, closed Mon & Tue Nov-Mar), where you can get free campfire permits and pay for overnight trailhead parking ($5). Don't expect solitude on weekends during peak season (April through September) and always follow Leave No Trace (www.lnt.org) principles.

cliff outcropping with fabulous views of the coastline in both directions, about 15 miles north of Hearst Castle. Once part of the Hearst empire, it's now taken over by a sprawling, ho-hum lodge with a pricey gas station. Heading south, the land grows increasingly wind-swept as Hwy 1 rolls gently down to the water's edge.

🏃 Activities

Molera Horseback Tours HORSEBACK RIDING
(☎831-625-5486; www.molerahorsebacktours.com; Hwy 1; per person $48-74; 🚻) Across Hwy 1 from Andrew Molera State Park, Molera offers guided trail rides on the beach and through redwood forest. Walk-ins and novices are welcome; children must be at least six years old, with most rides recommended for ages 12 and up.

Esalen Institute RETREAT CENTER
(☎888-837-2536; www.esalen.org; 55000 Hwy 1) Marked only by a lit sign reading 'Esalen Institute – By Reservation Only,' this spot is like a new-age hippie camp for adults. Esoteric workshops treat anything 'relating to our greater human capacity,' from shapeshifting to Thai massage. Esalen's famous baths (☎831-667-3047; per person $25, credit cards only; ⊗ public entry 1am-3am nightly, reservations accepted 8am-8pm Mon-Thu & Sat, 8am-noon Fri & Sun), fed by a natural hot spring, sit on a ledge above the ocean. The entrance is on the ocean side of Hwy 1, a little more than 11 miles south of Nepenthe restaurant and 10 miles north of Lucia.

Dollars to donuts you'll never take another dip that compares panorama-wise with the one here, especially on stormy winter nights. Only two small outdoor pools perch

directly over the waves, so once you've stripped down (bathing is clothing-optional) and taken a quick shower, head outside immediately to score the best views. Otherwise, you'll be stuck with a tepid, no-view pool or even worse, a rickety bathtub.

Things have sure changed a lot since Hunter S Thompson was the gun-toting caretaker here in the 1960s.

🛏 Sleeping

With few exceptions, Big Sur's lodgings do not have TVs and rarely have telephones. This is where you come to escape the world. There aren't a lot of rooms overall, so demand often exceeds supply and prices can be steep. Bigger price tags don't necessarily buy you more amenities either. In summer and on weekends, reservations are essential everywhere from campgrounds to deluxe resorts.

★ Pfeiffer Big Sur State Park Campground CAMPGROUND $
(☎reservations 800-444-7275; www.reserveamerica.com; 47225 Hwy 1; tent & RV sites $35-50; 🚻) Best for novice campers and families with young kids, here more than 200 campsites nestle in a redwood-shaded valley. Facilities include drinking water, fire pits and coin-op hot showers and laundry.

Andrew Molera State Park Campground CAMPGROUND $
(www.parks.ca.gov; Hwy 1; tent sites $25) Two-dozen primitive tent sites (no reservations) in a grassy meadow come with fire pits and drinking water, but no ocean views. The campground is a 0.3-mile walk from the parking lot.

Limekiln State Park
Campground   CAMPGROUND $
(www.parks.ca.gov; 63025 Hwy 1; tent & RV sites $35; ⚐) In southern Big Sur, this quiet state park has two-dozen campsites huddled under a bridge next to the ocean. Drinking water, fire pits and coin-op hot showers are available.

Julia Pfeiffer Burns State
Park Campground   CAMPGROUND $
(www.parks.ca.gov; Hwy 1; tent sites $30) Two small walk-in campsites sit up on a semi-shaded ocean bluff, with fire pits and vault toilets but no water. All campers must check in first at Pfeiffer Big Sur State Park, 11 miles north.

USFS Plaskett Creek
Campground   CAMPGROUND $
(✉ reservations 877-477-6777; www.recreation.gov; Hwy 1; tent & RV sites $25) Nearly 40 spacious, shady campsites with drinking water and vault toilets circle a forested meadow near Sand Dollar Beach in southern Big Sur.

USFS Kirk Creek Campground   CAMPGROUND $
(✉ reservations 877-444-6777; www.recreation.gov; Hwy 1; tent & RV sites $25) More than 30 exposed ocean-view blufftop campsites with drinking water and fire pits cluster close together, nearly 2 miles south of Limekiln State Park.

Big Sur Campground & Cabins   CABIN,
CAMPGROUND $$
(✉ 831-667-2322; www.bigsurcamp.com; 47000 Hwy 1; tent/RV sites from $50/60, cabins $120-345; ⚐) On the Big Sur River and shaded by redwoods, cozy housekeeping cabins sport full kitchens and fireplaces, while canvas-sided tent cabins are dog-friendly (pet fee $20). The riverside campground, where neighboring sites have little privacy, is popular with RVs. There are hot showers, a coin-op laundry, playground and general store.

Ripplewood Resort   CABIN $$
(✉ 831-667-2242; www.ripplewoodresort.com; 47047 Hwy 1; cabins $105-225; ⚐) North of Pfeiffer Big Sur State Park, Ripplewood has struck a blow for fiscal equality by charging the same rates year-round. Throwback Americana cabins mostly have kitchens and sometimes even wood-burning fireplaces. Quiet riverside cabins are surrounded by redwoods, but roadside cabins can be noisy. Wi-fi in restaurant only.

Deetjen's Big Sur Inn   LODGE $$
(✉ 831-667-2377; www.deetjens.com; 48865 Hwy 1; d $90-260) Nestled among redwoods and wisteria, this creekside conglomeration of rustic, thin-walled rooms and cottages was built by Norwegian immigrant Helmuth Deetjen in the 1930s. Some antiques-furnished rooms are warmed by wood-burning fireplaces, while cheaper ones share bathrooms. This timeless escape isn't for everyone.

Ragged Point Inn   MOTEL $$
(✉ 805-927-4502; www.raggedpointinn.net; 19019 Hwy 1; r $169-319; ⚐⚐) At Big Sur's southern edge, split-level motel rooms are nothing special, except for those with ocean horizon views. Pet fee $50.

★ Post Ranch Inn   RESORT $$$
(✉ 831-667-2200; www.postranchinn.com; 47900 Hwy 1; d incl breakfast from $675; ⚐⚐) The last word in luxurious coastal getaways, the exclusive Post Ranch pampers demanding guests with slate spa tubs, wood-burning fireplaces, private decks and walking sticks for coastal hikes. Ocean-view rooms celebrate the sea, while treehouses lack views and have a bit of sway. Paddle around the clifftop infinity pool after a shamanic-healing session or yoga class in the spa. No children allowed.

Panoramic sea-view Sierra Mar restaurant has mostly disappointing food, except for the gourmet breakfast buffet served to guests only.

Ventana Inn & Spa   RESORT $$$
(✉ 800-628-6500, 831-667-2331; www.ventanainn.com; 48123 Hwy 1; d incl breakfast from $510; ⚐⚐) Almost at odds with Big Sur's hippie-alternative vibe, Ventana injects a little soul into its deluxe digs. Honeymooning couples and paparazzi-fleeing celebs pad from tai chi class to the Japanese baths and outdoor pools (one is famously clothing-optional), or hole up all day next to the wood-burning fireplace in their own private villa, hot-tub suite or ocean-view cottage.

Treebones Resort   LODGE $$$
(✉ 877-424-4787, 805-927-2390; www.treebonesresort.com; 71895 Hwy 1; d with shared bath incl breakfast from $215; ⚐⚐) Don't let the word 'resort' throw you. Yes, they've got an ocean-view hot tub, heated pool and massage treatments. But a unique woven 'human nest' and canvas-sided yurts with polished pine floors, quilt-covered beds, sink vanities and redwood decks are more like glamping, with little privacy. Communal bathrooms

and showers are a short stroll away. Wi-fi in main lodge only.

Children must be at least six years old. Look for the signposted turnoff a mile north of Gorda, at the southern end of Big Sur.

Glen Oaks Motel
MOTEL, CABIN $$$

(☎831-667-2105; www.glenoaksbigsur.com; 47080 Hwy 1; d $225-390; 🐾) 🍃 At this 1950s redwood-and-adobe motor lodge, rustic rooms and cabins seem effortlessly chic. Dramatically transformed by eco-conscious design, snug romantic hideaway rooms all have gas fireplaces. Woodsy cabins in a redwood grove have kitchenettes and share outdoor fire pits, or retreat to the one-bedroom house with a full kitchen.

Big Sur Lodge
LODGE $$$

(☎800-424-4787, 831-667-3100; www.bigsurlodge.com; 47225 Hwy 1; d $205-365; 🏊) What you're really paying for is a peaceful location, right inside Pfeiffer Big Sur State Park. Fairly rustic duplexes each have a deck or balcony looking out into the redwood forest, while family-sized rooms may have a kitchenette or wood-burning fireplace. The outdoor swimming pool is closed in winter.

Lucia Lodge
MOTEL $$$

(☎831-667-2718, 866-424-4787; www.lucialodge.com; 62400 Hwy 1; d $195-275) Vertiginous clifftop views from an ocean-view deck, but tired 1930s cabin rooms.

✕ Eating

Like Big Sur's lodgings, restaurants and cafes alongside Hwy 1 are often overpriced, overcrowded and underwhelming.

Big Sur Deli & General Store
DELI, MARKET $

(www.bigsurdeli.com; 47520 Hwy 1; dishes $2-7; ⏲7am-8pm) With the most reasonable prices in Big Sur, this family-owned deli slices custom-made deli sandwiches and piles up tortillas with carne asada, pork *carnitas,* veggies or beans and cheese. The small market carries camping food, snacks and beer and wine.

Big Sur Burrito Bar & General Store
DELI, MARKET $

(www.bigsurriverinn.com; 46840 Hwy 1; mains $8-10; ⏲11am-7pm; 🐾) Order a San Francisco–sized burrito or wrap sandwich with a fresh-fruit smoothie from the back of the Big Sur River Inn's well-stocked general store, which carries snacks, drinks and camping supplies.

Big Sur Lodge Restaurant & General Store
CALIFORNIAN $$

(☎831-667-3100; www.bigsurlodge.com/dining; 47225 Hwy 1; mains $10-30; ⏲8am-9:30pm; 🐾) Inside Pfeiffer Big Sur State Park, pull up a wooden table in the cabin-esque dining room or on an outdoor riverside deck to fill up on wild salmon, roasted veggie pasta and generous salads, all made with hungry hikers in mind. The lodge's small general store stocks camping groceries, snacks, drinks and ice-cream treats.

★ Restaurant at Ventana
CALIFORNIAN $$$

(☎831-667-4242; www.ventanainn.com; Ventana Inn & Spa, 48123 Hwy 1; lunch $16-26, 4-course dinner menu $75; ⏲7-10:30am, 11:30am-4:30pm & 6-9pm; 🐾) The old truism about the better the views, the worse the food just doesn't seem to apply here. The resort's clifftop terrace restaurant and cocktail bar are Big Sur's gathering spot for foodies and bon vivants. Feast on grilled swordfish with lemony couscous, a house-smoked pork sandwich or salads flavored with herbs grown in the garden right outside. Reservations essential.

Nepenthe
CALIFORNIAN $$$

(☎831-667-2345; www.nepenthebigsur.com; 48510 Hwy 1; mains $15-42; ⏲11:30am-4:30pm & 5-10pm) Nepenthe comes from a Greek word meaning 'isle of no sorrow,' and indeed, it's hard to feel blue while sitting by the fire pit on this aerial terrace. Just-okay California cuisine (try the renowned Ambrosia burger) takes a backseat to the views and Nepenthe's history – Orson Welles and Rita Hayworth briefly owned a cabin here in the 1940s. Reservations essential.

Downstairs, cheaper but still expensive Café Kevah delivers coffee, baked goods, light brunches and head-spinning ocean views on its outdoor deck (closed during winter and bad weather).

Big Sur Roadhouse
CALIFORNIAN, CAJUN $$$

(☎831-667-2370; www.bigsurroadhouse.com; 47080 Hwy 1; breakfast & lunch $6-12, dinner $19-30; ⏲7:30am-9pm) This Southern-spiced roadhouse glows with color-splashed artwork and an outdoor fire pit. At riverside tables, fork into a New Orleans–born chef's hearty fried chicken, white grits with serrano peppers, po' boy sandwiches and blackened locally caught fish with a dollop of fresh herb aioli. Reservations advised for dinner, or just stop by for drinks and small bites such as buttermilk biscuits.

Big Sur Bakery & Restaurant CALIFORNIAN $$$
(☑831-667-0520; www.bigsurbakery.com; 47540
Hwy 1; bakery items $3-14, mains $14-36; ☺bakery
from 8am daily, restaurant 9:30am-3:30pm Mon-Fri,
10:30am-2:30pm Sat & Sun, 5:30pm-close Tue-Sat)
Behind the Shell station, this warmly lit,
funky house has seasonally changing menus,
on which wood-fired pizzas share space with
more refined dishes such as butter-braised
halibut. Fronted by a pretty patio, the bakery
makes addictive fruit-and-ginger scones and
super-stuffed sandwiches. Expect long waits
and standoffish service. Dinner reservations
essential.

Deetjen's Restaurant AMERICAN $$$
(☑831-667-2378; www.deetjens.com; Deetjen's Big
Sur Inn, 48865 Hwy 1; mains $26-38; ☺breakfast
8am-noon Mon-Fri, to 12:30pm Sat & Sun, dinner
6-9pm daily) 🖋 At a quaint yesteryear lodge,
the cozy, candle-lit dining room has a daily changing menu of steaks, cassoulets and
other hearty country fare, primarily sourced
from organic local produce, hormone-free
meat and sustainable seafood. Breakfast is a
much better bet than dinner.

Big Sur River Inn AMERICAN $$$
(☑831-667-2700; www.bigsurriverinn.com; 46840
Hwy 1; breakfast & lunch $9-18, dinner $15-32; ☺8-
11am, 11:30am-4:30pm & 5-9pm; 🛜🏨) Woodsy
supper club with a deck overlooks a creek
teeming with throaty frogs. The wedding-
reception-quality food is mostly classic
American seafood, grilled meats and pastas,
but diner-style breakfasts and lunches – like
berry pancakes and BLT sandwiches – satisfy.

🍷 Drinking & Entertainment

Big Sur Taphouse BAR
(www.bigsurtaphouse.com; 47520 Hwy 1; ☺noon-
10pm Mon-Thu, to midnight Fri & Sat, 10am-10pm
Sun; 🛜) Down California craft beers and
regional wines on the back deck or by the
fireplace inside this high-ceilinged wooden
bar with board games, sports TVs and pub
grub from the next-door deli.

Maiden Publick House PUB
(☑831-667-2355; Village Center Shops, Hwy 1;
☺noon-2am) Just south of the Big Sur River
Inn, this dive has an encyclopedic beer bible
and motley local musicians jamming, most-
ly on weekends.

Rocky Point BAR
(www.rocky-point.com; 36700 Hwy 1; ☺11:30am-
8pm) Come for the hillside ocean-view ter-
race, where cocktails are served all day long.
It's about 2.5 miles north of Bixby Bridge.

Henry Miller Memorial Library PERFORMING ARTS
(☑831-667-2574; www.henrymiller.org; 48603 Hwy
1; 🛜) Just south of Nepenthe, this nonprofit
alternative space hosts a bohemian carni-
val of live-music concerts, author readings,
open-mic nights and indie film screenings
outdoors, especially during summer.

ℹ️ Information

Visitors often wander into businesses along
Hwy 1 and ask, 'How much further to Big Sur?' In
fact, there is no town of Big Sur as such, though
you may see the name on maps. Commercial
activity is concentrated along the stretch north
of Pfeiffer Big Sur State Park. Sometimes called
'the Village,' this is where you'll find most of the
lodging, restaurants and shops, some of which
offer free wi-fi. Cellphone reception is spotty to
non-existent.

Big Sur Chamber of Commerce (☑831-667-
2100; www.bigsurcalifornia.org; ☺9am-1pm
Mon, Wed & Fri) Pick up the free *Big Sur Guide*
newspaper at local businesses; it's also availa-
ble online as a free PDF download.

Big Sur Station (☑831-667-2315; www.
fs.usda.gov/lpnf; 47555 Hwy 1; ☺8am-4pm,
closed Mon & Tue Nov-Mar) About 1.5 miles
south of Pfeiffer Big Sur State Park, this
multiagency ranger station has information and
maps for state parks, the Los Padres National
Forest and Ventana Wilderness.

Henry Miller Memorial Library (www.henry-
miller.org; 48603 Hwy 1; ☺11am-6pm; 🛜) Free
wi-fi and public internet terminals (donation
requested).

Post Office (☑800-275-8777; www.usps.com;
47500 Hwy 1; ☺8:30-11am & 1-4pm Mon-Fri)
Just north of Big Sur Bakery.

ℹ️ DRIVING HWY 1 IN BIG SUR

Driving this narrow two-lane highway
through Big Sur and beyond is very slow
going. Allow about three hours to cover
the distance between the Monterey Pen-
insula and San Luis Obispo, much more
if you want to explore the coast. Trav-
eling after dark can be risky and more
to the point, it's futile, because you'll
miss out on the seascapes. Watch out
for cyclists and make use of signposted
roadside pullouts to let faster-moving
traffic pass.

ⓘ Getting There & Around

Big Sur is best explored by car, since you'll be itching to stop frequently and take in the rugged beauty and vistas that reveal themselves after every hairpin turn. Even if your driving skills are up to these narrow switchbacks, others' aren't: expect to average 35mph or less along the route. Parts of Hwy 1 are battle-scarred, evidence of a continual struggle to keep them open after landslides and washouts. Check current highway conditions with **CalTrans** (www.dot.ca.gov) and fill up your gas tank beforehand.

MST (☏ 888-678-2871; www.mst.org) bus 22 ($3.50, 1¼ hours) travels from Monterey via Carmel and Point Lobos as far south as Nepenthe restaurant, stopping en route at Andrew Molera State Park and the Big Sur River Inn. Buses run three times daily between late May and early September, and twice daily on Saturdays and Sundays only the rest of the year.

Point Piedras Blancas

Many lighthouses still stand along California's coast, but few offer such a historically evocative seascape. Federally designated an outstanding natural area, the jutting, wind-blown grounds of this 1875 light station (☏ 805-927-7361; www.piedrasblancas.gov; adult/child 6-17yr $10/5; ☉ tours usually 9:45am Mon-Sat mid-Jun–Aug, 9:45am Tue, Thu & Sat Sep–mid-Jun) have been laboriously replanted with native flora. Picturesquely, everything looks much the way it did when the first lighthouse keepers helped ships find safe harbor at the whaling station at San Simeon Bay. Guided tours meet at the old Piedras Blancas Motel, 1.5 miles north of the lighthouse gate on Hwy 1. No reservations are taken; call ahead to check tour schedules.

At a signposted vista point, around 4.5 miles north of Hearst Castle, you can observe a colony of northern elephant seals bigger than the one at Año Nuevo State Reserve near Santa Cruz. During peak winter season, about 18,000 seals seek shelter in the coves and beaches along this stretch of coast. On sunny days the seals usually 'lie around like banana slugs,' in the words of one volunteer. Interpretative panels along a beach boardwalk and blue-jacketed Friends of the Elephant Seal (www.elephantseal.org) guides demystify the behavior of these giant beasts.

Hearst Castle

The most important thing to know about William Randolph Hearst (1863–1951) is that he did not live like *Citizen Kane*. Not that Hearst wasn't bombastic, conniving and larger than life, but the moody recluse of Orson Welles' movie? Definitely not. Hearst also didn't call his 165-room estate a castle, preferring its official name, *La Cuesta Encantada* ('The Enchanted Hill'), or more often calling it simply 'the ranch.' From the 1920s into the '40s, Hearst and Marion Davies, his longtime mistress (Hearst's wife refused to grant him a divorce), entertained a steady stream of the era's biggest movers and shakers. Invitations were highly coveted, but Hearst had his quirks – he despised drunkenness, and guests were forbidden to speak of death.

Hearst Castle is a wondrous, historic (Winston Churchill penned anti-Nazi essays here in the 1930s), over-the-top homage to material excess, perched high on a hill. California's first licensed woman architect Julia Morgan based the main building, Casa Grande, on the design of a Spanish cathedral, and over the decades she catered to Hearst's every design whim, deftly integrating the spoils of his fabled European shopping sprees including artifacts from antiquity and pieces of medieval monasteries. The estate sprawls across acres of lushly landscaped gardens, accentuated by shimmering pools and fountains, statues from ancient Greece and Moorish Spain and the ruins of what was in Hearst's day the world's largest private zoo (drivers on Hwy 1 can sometimes spot the remnant zebra herd grazing on the hillsides of adjacent Hearst Ranch).

Much like Hearst's construction budget, the castle will devour as much of your time and money as you let it. To see anything of this state historic monument (☏ info 805-927-2020, reservations 800-444-4445; www.hearstcastle.org; 750 Hearst Castle Rd, San Simeon; tours adult/child 5-12yr from $25/12; ☉ from 9am daily except Thanksgiving, Christmas & New Year's Day, closing time varies), you must take a tour. In peak summer months, show up early enough and you might be able to get a same-day ticket. For holiday and evening tours, book at least two weeks in advance. Dress in plenty of layers: gloomy fog at the sea-level visitors center can turn into sunny skies at the castle's hilltop location, and vice versa.

Tours usually depart starting at 9am daily, with the last tour leaving the visitor center for the 10-minute ride to the hilltop by 4pm (later in summer). There are four main tours: the guided portion of each lasts about

EYEING ELEPHANT SEALS

The elephant seals that visit coastal California each year follow a precise calendar. In November and December, bulls (adult males) return to their colony's favorite California beaches and start the ritual struggles to assert superiority. Only the largest, strongest and most aggressive 'alpha' males gather a harem of nubile females. In January and February, adult females, already pregnant from last year's beach antics, give birth to pups and soon mate with the dominant males, who promptly depart on their next feeding migration. The bulls' motto is 'love 'em and leave 'em.'

At birth an elephant seal pup weighs about 75lb; while being fed by its mother, it puts on about 10lb a day. Female seals leave the beach in March, abandoning their offspring. For up to two months the young seals, now known as 'weaners,' lounge around in groups, gradually learning to swim, first in tidal pools, then in the ocean. The weaners depart by May, having lost 20% to 30% of their weight during a prolonged fast.

Between June and October, elephant seals of all ages and both sexes return in smaller numbers to the beaches to molt. Always observe elephant seals from a safe distance (minimum 25ft) and do not approach or otherwise harass these unpredictable wild animals, who surprisingly can move faster on the sand than you can!

45 minutes, after which you're free to wander the gardens and terraces, photograph the iconic Neptune Pool and soak up views. Best of all are Christmas holiday and springtime evening tours, featuring living-history reenactors who escort you back in time to the castle's 1930s heyday.

At the visitor center, a five-story-high theater shows a 40-minute historical film (free admission included with most tour tickets) about the castle and the Hearst family. Other visitor-center facilities are geared for industrial-sized mobs; it's better to grab lunch at Sebastian's General Store (p460) across Hwy 1. Before you leave, take a moment to visit the often-overlooked museum area at the back of the visitor center.

RTA (☑ 805-541-2228; www.slorta.org) bus 15 makes a few daily round-trips to Hearst Castle via Cambria and Cayucos from Morro Bay ($2, 55 minutes), where you can transfer to bus 12 to San Luis Obispo.

San Simeon

Little San Simeon Bay sprang to life as a whaling station in 1852, by which time California sea otters had been hunted almost to extinction by Russian fur traders. Shoreline whaling was practiced to catch gray whales migrating between Alaskan feeding grounds and birthing waters in Baja California. In 1865 Senator George Hearst purchased 45,000 acres of ranch land and established a small settlement beside the sea. Designed by architect Julia Morgan, the historic 19th-century houses today are rented to employees of the Hearst Corporation's 82,000-acre free-range cattle ranch.

◉ Sights & Activities

William Randolph Hearst Memorial State Beach   BEACH
(www.parks.ca.gov; Hwy 1; ⊙dawn-dusk) **FREE** Across from Hearst Castle, this bayfront beach is a pleasantly sandy stretch punctuated by rock outcroppings, kelp forests, a wooden pier (fishing permitted) and picnic areas with barbecue grills.

Coastal Discovery Center   MUSEUM
(☑ 805-927-6575; www.montereybay.noaa.gov; Hwy 1; ⊙11am-5pm Fri-Sun mid-Mar–Oct, 10am-4pm Fri-Sun Nov–mid-Mar; ⊞) **FREE** Educational displays include a talking artificial tide pool that kids can touch and videos of deep-sea diving and a WWII-era shipwreck just offshore.

Kayak Outfitters   KAYAKING
(☑ 800-717-5225, 805-927-1787; www.kayakcambria.com; Hwy 1; single/double kayak rentals from $10/20, tours $50-110; ⊙10am-4pm or later mid-Jun–early Sep, call for off-season hours) Right on the beach, you can rent sea kayaks, wetsuits, stand-up paddleboarding (SUP) sets, bodyboards and surfboards, or take a kayak-fishing trip or a guided paddle around San Simeon Cove.

🛏 Sleeping & Eating

A few miles south of Hearst Castle, the modern town of San Simeon is nothing more than a strip of unexciting motels and lack-luster restaurants. There are better-value places to stay and eat in Cambria and beach towns further south, such as Cayucos and Morro Bay.

San Simeon State Park
Campground
CAMPGROUND $

(☑ reservations 800-444-7275; www.reserveamerica.com; Hwy 1; tent & RV sites $20-25) About 5 miles south of Hearst Castle are two state-park campgrounds: San Simeon Creek, with coin-op hot showers and flush toilets; and undeveloped Washburn, located along a dirt road. Drinking water is available at both.

Morgan
MOTEL $$

(☑ 800-451-9900, 805-927-3828; www.hotel-morgan.com; 9135 Hearst Dr; r incl breakfast $139-235; ☎ ☒ ☜) Although rates are high for these revamped motel-style accommodations, the oceanfront setting makes up for a lot, as do gas fireplaces in deluxe rooms. Complimentary continental breakfast and board games to borrow. Pet fee $25.

Sebastian's General Store
DELI, GROCERIES $

(442 SLO-San Simeon Rd; mains $7-12; ⊙ 11am-5pm, kitchen closes at 4pm) Down a side road across Hwy 1 from Hearst Castle, this tiny historic market sells cold drinks, Hearst Ranch beef burgers, giant deli sandwiches and salads for beach picnics at San Simeon Cove. Hearst Ranch Winery tastings are available at the copper-top bar.

Cambria

With a whopping dose of natural beauty, the coastal idyll of Cambria is a lone pearl cast along the coast. Built on lands that once belonged to Mission San Miguel, one of the village's first nicknames was Slabtown, after the rough pieces of wood that pioneer buildings were constructed from. Today, just like at neighboring Hearst Castle, money is no object in this wealthy community, whose motto 'Pines by the Sea' is affixed to the back of BMWs that toodle around town.

◎ Sights & Activities

Although its milky-white moonstones are long gone, Moonstone Beach still attracts romantics to its oceanfront boardwalk and truly picturesque rocky shoreline. For more solitude, take the Windsor Blvd exit off Hwy 1 and drive down to where the road

dead-ends, then follow a 2-mile round-trip blufftop hiking trail across East West Ranch, where Outback Trail Rides (☑ 805-286-8772; www.outbacktrailrides.com; tours $65-95; ⊙ Wed-Mon May-Sep, by reservation only) offers horseback rides (reserve in advance).

A 10-minute drive south of Cambria, past the Hwy 46 turnoff to Paso Robles' wine country, tiny Harmony is a slice of rural Americana. An 1865 creamery now houses artists' workshops and a charming cafe (2177 Old Creamery Rd, Harmony; dishes $3-10; ⊙ usually 10am-4pm) run by an Italian chef, or visit the hillside winery, Harmony Cellars (www.harmonycellars.com; 3255 Harmony Valley Rd, Harmony; tasting fee $5; ⊙ 10am-5pm, to 5:30pm Jul & Aug). A few miles further south inside peaceful Harmony Headlands State Park (www.parks.ca.gov; Hwy 1; ⊙ 6am-sunset) FREE, a 4.5-mile round-trip hiking trail winds out to coastal bluffs with inspiring sea views.

🛏 Sleeping

Cambria's choicest motels and hotels line Moonstone Beach Dr, while quaint B&Bs cluster around the village.

HI Cambria Bridge Street Inn
HOSTEL $

(☑ 805-927-7653; www.bridgestreetinncambria.com; 4314 Bridge St; dm from $28, r $49-84, all with shared bath; ⊙ check-in 5-9pm; ☜) Inside a 19th-century parsonage, this tiny hostel seems more like a grandmotherly B&B. It has floral charm and a communal kitchen, but the shabby-chic rooms are thin-walled. Book ahead.

Bluebird Inn
MOTEL $$

(☑ 805-927-5215, 800-552-5434; www.bluebirdmotel.com; 1880 Main St; r $80-180; ☜) Surrounded by peaceful gardens, this friendly East Village motel offers basic, tidy rooms, some with fireplaces and private creekside patios or balconies. Wi-fi can be erratic.

Cambria Palms Motel
MOTEL $$

(☑ 805-927-4485; www.cambriapalmsmotel.com; 2662 Main St; r $109-149; ⊙ check-in 3-9pm; ☜) A 1950s motor lodge at the east edge of town, here simple wooden-floored rooms are spruced up by colorful wall art and above-average beds. The outdoor fire pit crackles after dark.

Blue Dolphin Inn
MOTEL $$$

(☑ 800-222-9157, 805-927-3300; www.cambriainns.com; 6470 Moonstone Beach Dr; r incl breakfast from $199; ☎ ☒) This sand-colored two-story, slat-sided building may not look as upscale as other oceanfront motels, but rooms have romantic fireplaces, pillowtop mattresses and to-go breakfast picnics to take to the beach. If it's full, try its sister property, the Sand Pebbles Inn. Pet fee $25.

Fogcatcher Inn　　　　　　　　HOTEL **$$$**
(☑800-425-4121, 805-927-1400; www.fogcatcher-inn.com; 6400 Moonstone Beach Dr; r incl breakfast from $220; 🛜🐾🏊) Moonstone Beach Dr hotels are nearly identical, but this one stands out with its pool and hot tub. Faux English Tudor–style cottages harboring quietly luxurious modern rooms, some with fireplaces and ocean views. Pet fee $75.

Cambria Shores Inn　　　　　　MOTEL **$$$**
(☑800-433-9179, 805-927-8644; www.cambri-ashores.com; 6276 Moonstone Beach Dr; r incl breakfast from $219; 🛜🐾) A stone's throw from Moonstone Beach, this ocean-view motel offers pampering amenities for pooches, including a welcome doggie basket. Rates include a breakfast basket delivered to your door. Pet fee $15.

✖️ Eating & Drinking

It's a short walk between cutesy cafes in the East Village.

Linn's Easy as Pie Cafe　　　AMERICAN **$**
(www.linnsfruitbin.com; 4251 Bridge St; dishes $4-9; ⏱10am-6pm Oct-Apr, to 7pm May-Sep; 🚸) If you don't have time to visit Linn's original farm stand out on Santa Rosa Creek Rd (a 20-minute drive east via Main St), you can fork into their famous olallieberry pie at this take-out counter that delivers soups, salads, sandwiches and comfort fare such as chicken pot pie to a sunny deck.

Boni's Tacos　　　　　　　　　MEXICAN **$**
(www.bonistacos.com; 2253 Main St; dishes $2-9; ⏱10am-4pm Sat & Sun) Honest Mexican food is slung from this family-owned taco trailer parked in the East Village. Fiery tacos, taquitos, quesadillas and burritos all fly out of the busy window.

★ Indigo Moon　　　　　　　CALIFORNIAN **$$$**
(☑805-927-2911; www.indigomooncafe.com; 1980 Main St; lunch $9-14, dinner $14-33; ⏱10am-9pm) Inside this artisan cheese-and-wine shop, breezy bistro tables complement superb salads and toasty sandwiches served with sweet-potato fries. Locals gossip over lunch on the back patio, where dinner dates order wild-mushroom risotto or crab-stuffed trout.

Cambria Pub & Steakhouse　　AMERICAN **$$$**
(☑805-927-0782; www.thecambriapub.com; 4090 Burton Dr; pub mains $9-12, steakhouse mains $20-35; ⏱11am-9pm Thu & Sun-Tue, to 10pm Fri & Sat; 🐾) Over in the East Village, pull up a barstool and order a burger while you watch big-screen sports TVs, or reserve a table in the contemporary-casual steakhouse to dig into Angus beef steaks (regrettably not from Hearst Ranch). The outdoor patio is dog-friendly.

❶ Information

Cambria has three distinct parts. In the tourist-choked East Village, antiques shops, art galleries and cafes hug Main St. The newer West Village, along Main St closer to Hwy 1, is where you'll find the **chamber of commerce** (☑805-927-3624; www.cambriachamber.org; 767 Main St; ⏱9am-5pm Mon-Fri, noon-4pm Sat & Sun). Hotel-lined Moonstone Beach Dr is west of Hwy 1.

❶ Getting There & Around

From San Luis Obispo, **RTA** (☑805-541-2228; www.slorta.org) bus 15 makes a few daily trips from Morro Bay via Cayucos to Cambria ($2, 35 minutes), stopping along Main St and Moonstone Beach Dr. Most buses continue north to Hearst Castle.

Cayucos

With its historic storefronts housing antiques shops and eateries, the main drag of amiable, slow-paced Cayucos recalls an Old West frontier town. Just one block west of Ocean Ave, surf's up by the pier.

◉ Sights & Activities

Fronting a broad white-sand beach, Cayucos' long wooden pier is popular with fishers. It's also a sheltered spot for beginner surfers.

Estero Bluffs State Park　　　　PARK
(www.parks.ca.gov; Hwy 1; ⏱sunrise-sunset) **FREE** Ramble along coastal grasslands and pocket beaches at this small state park, accessed from unmarked roadside pulloffs north of Cayucos. Look among the scenic sea stacks to spot harbor seals hauled out on tide-splashed rocks.

Good Clean Fun　　　　　　WATER SPORTS
(☑805-995-1993; www.goodcleanfuncalifornia.com; 136 Ocean Front Ln; group surfing lesson or kayak tour from $75) By the beach, this friendly surf shop has all kinds of rental gear –

wetsuits, boogie boards, surfboards, SUP sets and kayaks. Book in advance for surfing lessons and kayak (or kayak-fishing) tours.

Cayucos Surf Company   SURFING
(✆805-995-1000; www.cayucossurfcompany.com; 95 Cayucos Dr; 1hr private/2hr group lesson $90/100; ⊙10am-5pm Sun-Thu, to 6pm Fri & Sat) Near the pier, this landmark local surf shop rents surfboards, boogie boards and wetsuits. Call ahead for learn-to-surf lessons.

🛏 Sleeping

Cayucos doesn't lack for motels or beach-front inns. If there's no vacancy or prices look too high, head 6 miles south to Morro Bay.

Shoreline Inn on the Beach   HOTEL $$
(✆800-549-2244, 805-995-3681; www.cayucosshorelineinn.com; 1 N Ocean Ave; r $139-199; 🐾) There are few beachside lodgings on Hwy 1 where you can listen to the surf from your balcony for such a reasonable price tag. Standard-issue rooms are spacious, perked up by sea-foam painted walls, and also dog-friendly (pet fee $35).

Seaside Motel   MOTEL $$
(✆800-549-0900, 805-995-3809; www.seaside-motel.com; 42 S Ocean Ave; d $80-160; 🛜) Expect a warm welcome from the hands-on owners of this vintage motel with a pretty garden. Country-kitsch rooms may be on the small side, though some have kitchenettes. Cross your fingers for quiet neighbors.

Cypress Tree Motel   MOTEL $$
(✆805-995-3917; www.cypresstreemotel.com; 125 S Ocean Ave; d $80-120; 🛜🐾) Retro motor court has lovingly cared-for, but kinda hokey theme rooms, such as 'Nautical Nellie' with a net of seashells suspended behind the bed, plus a shared barbecue grill on the lawn. Pet fee $10.

Cayucos Beach Inn   MOTEL $$
(✆800-482-0555, 805-995-2828; www.cayucosbeachinn.com; 333 S Ocean Ave; d incl breakfast $99-215; 🐾🛜🐾) At this remarkably dog-friendly motel, even the doors have special peepholes for canine companions. Big rooms look bland, but grassy picnic areas and barbecue grills await out front. Rates include continental breakfast. Pet fee $10.

Cass House Inn   INN $$$
(✆805-995-3669; www.casshouseinn.com; 222 N Ocean Ave; d incl breakfast $195-365; 🛜) Inside a charmingly renovated 1867 Victorian inn, five boutique rooms beckon, some with ocean views, deep-soaking tubs and antique fireplaces to ward off chilly coastal fog. All rooms have plush beds, flat-screen TVs with DVD players and tasteful, romantic accents, while the beachy cottage comes with a full kitchen. Reservations essential.

🍴 Eating & Drinking

Ruddell's Smokehouse   SEAFOOD $
(www.smokerjim.com; 101 D St; dishes $4-13; ⊙11am-6pm; 🐾🛜) 'Smoker Jim' transforms fresh-off-the-boat seafood into succulently smoked slabs, sandwiches topped with spicy mustard and fish tacos slathered in a unique apple-celery relish. Squeeze yourself in the door to order. Dogs allowed at sidewalk tables.

Brown Butter Cookie Co   BAKERY $
(www.brownbuttercookies.com; 98 N Ocean Ave; snacks from $2; ⊙9am-6pm; 🐾) Seriously addictive, dearly priced cookies baked in all sorts of flavors – almond, citrus, cocoa, coconut-lime and original butter. Also in Paso Robles.

★Cass House Restaurant   CALIFORNIAN, FRENCH $$$
(✆805-995-3669; www.casshouseinn.com; Cass House Inn, 222 N Ocean Ave; tasting menu without/with wine pairings $85/125; ⊙5:30-7:30pm Thu-Mon) 🍴 The inn's chef-driven restaurant defies expectations. Linger over a locally sourced, seasonally inspired menu that ambitiously ranges from stone-fruit salad with whipped homemade ricotta and crispy abalone fritters to milk-and-honey almond cake, all paired with top-notch regional wines. Some diners lament portions are so modestly sized. Reservations essential.

Schooners Wharf   BAR
(www.schoonerswharf.com; 171 N Ocean Ave; ⊙11am-midnight) Come for drinks on the ocean-view deck, rather than the fried seafood.

❶ Getting There & Away

RTA (✆805-541-2228; www.slorta.org) bus 15 travels three to five times daily from Morro Bay ($2, 15 minutes) to Cayucos, continuing north to Cambria ($2, 20 minutes) and Hearst Castle ($2, 35 minutes).

Morro Bay

Home to a commercial fishing fleet, Morro Bay's biggest claim to fame is Morro Rock, a volcanic peak jutting dramatically from the ocean floor. It's one of the Nine Sisters, a 21-million-year-old chain of rocks stretching all the way south to San Luis Obispo. The town's less boast-worthy landmark comes courtesy of the power plant, whose three cigarette-shaped smokestacks mar the bay views. Along this humble, working-class stretch of coast you'll find fantastic opportunities for kayaking, hiking and camping.

◉ Sights & Activities

This town harbors natural riches that are easily worth a half day's exploration. The bay itself is a deep inlet separated from the ocean by a 5-mile-long sand spit. South of Morro Rock is the Embarcadero, a small waterfront boulevard jam-packed with souvenir shops and eateries.

Morro Rock   LANDMARK

Chumash tribespeople are the only people legally allowed to climb this volcanic rock, now the protected nesting ground of peregrine falcons. You can laze at the small beach on the rock's north side, but you can't drive all the way around it. Instead, rent a kayak to paddle the giant estuary, inhabited by two-dozen threatened and endangered species, including brown pelicans, snowy plovers and sea otters.

Morro Bay State Park   PARK

(☏805-772-2694; www.parks.ca.gov; park entry free, museum admission adult/child under 17yr $3/free; ☉museum 10am-5pm) This woodsy waterfront park is strewn with hillside hiking trails. A small natural history museum has interactive exhibits geared toward kids that demonstrate how the forces of nature affect us all. North of the museum, a eucalyptus grove harbors one of California's last remaining great blue heron rookeries.

Kayak Horizons   WATER SPORTS

(☏805-772-6444; www.kayakhorizons.com; 551 Embarcadero; kayak or SUP rental from $12, 3hr kayak tour $59; ☉9am-5pm) One of several places on the Embarcadero offering kayak rentals and tours for novices, as well as SUP set and canoes rentals. When paddling out on your own, be aware of the tide schedules: ideally, you'll want to ride the tide out and then back in. Winds are generally calmest in the mornings.

Kayak Shack   WATER SPORTS

(☏805-772-8796; www.morrobaykayakshack.com; 10 State Park Rd; kayak or SUP rental from $12;

☉usually 9am-4pm late-May–Jun, to 5pm Jul-early Sep, 9am-4pm Fri-Sun early-Sep–late-May) No one gets you out on the water faster than this laid-back kayak, canoe and SUP rental spot by the marina in Morro Bay State Park. A no-frills DIY operation, this is a calmer place to start paddling than the Embarcadero.

Cerro Alto   HIKING

(www.fs.usda.gov/lpnf; Cerro Alto Rd, Atascadero; per car $5; ☙) A 7-mile drive inland from Morro Bay on Hwy 41, a USFS campground is the start of a challengingly steep 4-mile round-trip trail up Cerro Alto (2624ft). From the summit, 360° views sweep from mountains to the sea. With more gradual switchbacks, an alternative route (5.5 miles round trip) also begins near campsite No 18. Leashed dogs allowed.

Morro Bay Golf Course   GOLF

(☏805-782-8060; www.slocountyparks.com; 201 State Park Rd; green fees $13-49) South of the Embarcadero, adjacent to the state park, this 18-hole golf course boasts tree-lined fairways and ocean views. A driving range and rental clubs and carts are available.

☞ Tours

Sub-Sea Tours   BOAT TOUR

(☏805-772-9463; www.subseatours.com; 699 Embarcadero; 45min tour adult/child 3-12yr $14/7; ☉hourly departures usually 11am-5pm; ☙) For pint-sized views of kelp forests and schools of fish, take the kids on a spin around the bay in a yellow semi-submersible with underwater viewing windows.

Virg's Landing   FISHING

(☏800-762-5263, 805-772-1222; www.morrobaysportfishing.com; 1169 Market Ave; tours from $59) Salty dogs ready for a little sportfishing can book half-day or all-day trips between May and December with this long-running local outfit.

Central Coast Outdoors   GUIDED TOUR

(☏888-873-5610, 805-528-1080; www.central-coastoutdoors.com; tours $65-150) Leads kayaking tours (including sunset and full-moon paddles), guided hikes and cycling trips along the coast and to Paso Robles and Edna Valley vineyards.

★ Festivals & Events

Morro Bay Winter Bird Festival   OUTDOORS

(www.morrobaybirdfestival.org) Every January, bird-watchers flock here for guided hikes, kayaking tours and naturalist-led field trips, during which more than 200 species can be spotted along the Pacific Flyway.

🛏 Sleeping

Dozens of motels cluster along Hwy 1 and around Harbor and Main Sts, between downtown and the Embarcadero.

California State Park Campgrounds
CAMPGROUND $

(☑reservations 800-444-7275; www.reserveamerica.com; tent & RV sites $35-50; 🐾) In Morro Bay State Park, more than 240 campsites are fringed by eucalyptus and cypress trees; amenities include coin-op hot showers and an RV dump station. At the north end of town off Hwy 1, Morro Strand State Beach has 75 simpler oceanfront campsites.

Pleasant Inn Motel
MOTEL $$

(☑805-772-8521; www.pleasantinnmotel.com; 235 Harbor St; r $75-209; 🛜🐾) Two blocks uphill from the Embarcadero, this spiffy motel has nautical-esque rooms (some with full kitchens) sporting sailboat photos on the walls, open-beam wooden ceilings and blue-and-white rugs underfoot. Pet fee $20.

Beach Bungalow Inn & Suites
MOTEL $$

(☑805-772-9700; www.morrobaybeachbungalow.com; 1050 Morro Ave; d $149-250; 🛜🐾) This motor court's chic, contemporary rooms are dressed up with hardwood floors, with rugs, pillowtop mattresses and down comforters for foggy nights. Pet fee $20.

Anderson Inn
INN $$$

(☑866-950-3434, 805-772-3434; www.andersoninnmorrobay.com; 897 Embarcadero; d $239-299; 🛜) Like a small boutique hotel, this waterfront inn has just a handful of spacious, soothingly earth-toned rooms. If you're lucky, you'll get a gas fireplace, spa tub and harbor views.

Inn at Morro Bay
MOTEL $$$

(☑800-321-9566, 805-772-5651; www.innatmorrobay.com; 60 State Park Rd; d $119-289; 🛜🐾) Dated two-story waterfront lodge with a kidney-shaped pool has an enviable waterfront setting inside the state park. Bicycle rentals available for guests.

🍴 Eating & Drinking

Predictably touristy seafood shacks line the Embarcadero.

Taco Temple
CALIFORNIAN, SEAFOOD $$

(2680 Main St; mains $8-20; ⏰11am-9pm Wed-Mon; 🐾) Overlook the Hwy 1 frontage-road location for huge helpings of Cal-Mex fusion flavor. At the next table, there might be fishers talking about the good ol' days or starving surfers. Try one of the specials – they deserve the name. Cash only.

Giovanni's Fish Market & Galley
SEAFOOD $$

(www.giovannisfishmarket.com; 1001 Front St; mains $6-15; ⏰9am-6pm; 🐾) At this family-run joint on the Embarcadero, folks line up for batter-fried fish and chips and killer garlic fries. You'll have to dodge beggar birds on the outdoor deck. Inside there's a market with all the fixin's for a beach campground fish-fry.

Stax Wine Bar
WINE BAR

(www.staxwine.com; 1099 Embarcadero; ⏰noon-8pm Sun-Thu, to 10pm Fri & Sat) Perch on barstools in front of the harbor-view windows for a hand-selected tasting flight of California wines. Toasted panini, salads and artisan cheese and cured-meat plates keep sippers fueled.

Libertine Pub
PUB

(www.thelibertinepub.com; 801 Embarcadero; ⏰noon-11pm Mon-Wed, to midnight Thu-Sun) Stroll down to the Embarcadero for barrel-aged house beer and sour cider or to try one of the almost 50 American craft beers on tap.

ℹ Information

Morro Bay Visitor Center (☑805-225-1633, 800-231-0592; www.morrobay.org; 255 Morro Bay Blvd; ⏰9am-5pm) A few blocks uphill from the Embarcadero, in the less touristy downtown area.

ℹ Getting There & Around

From San Luis Obispo, **RTA** (☑805-541-2228; www.slorta.org) bus 12 travels hourly on weekdays and a few times daily on weekends along Hwy 1 to Morro Bay ($2.50, 25 minutes). Three to five times daily, bus 15 heads north to Cayucos ($2, 15 minutes), Cambria ($2, 35 minutes) and Hearst Castle ($2, 55 minutes).

From late May through early October, a **trolley** (single-ride $1, day pass $3) loops around the waterfront, downtown and north Morro Bay, operating varying hours (no service Tuesday to Thursday).

Montaña de Oro State Park

In spring the hillsides are blanketed by bright California native poppies, wild mustard and other wildflowers, giving this park (☎805-772-7434; www.parks.ca.gov; 3550 Pecho Valley Rd, Los Osos; ◷6am-10pm) FREE its Spanish name, meaning 'mountain of gold.' Wind-tossed coastal bluffs with wild, wide-open sea views make it a favorite spot with hikers, mountain bikers and horseback riders. The northern half of the park features sand dunes and an ancient marine terrace visible due to seismic uplifting.

Once used by smugglers, Spooner's Cove is now a postcard-perfect sandy beach and picnic area. If you go tidepooling, only touch the marine creatures such as sea stars, limpets and crabs with the back of one hand to avoid disturbing them, and never remove them from their aquatic homes. You can hike along the grassy ocean bluffs, or drive uphill past the visitor center inside a historic ranch house to the start of the exhilarating 7-mile loop trail tackling Valencia Peak (1346ft) and Oats Peak (1347ft).

⏚ Sleeping

**Montaña de Oro State Park
Campground**　　　　　CAMPGROUND $
(☎reservations 800-444-7275; www.reserveamerica.com; tent & RV sites $20-25) Tucked into a small canyon, this minimally developed campground has pleasantly cool drive-up and environmental walk-in sites. Limited amenities include vault toilets, drinking water and fire pits.

❶ Getting There & Away

From the north, exit Hwy 1 in Morro Bay at South Bay Blvd; after 4 miles, turn right onto Los Osos Valley Rd (which runs into Pecho Valley Rd) for 6 miles. From the south, exit Hwy 101 in San Luis Obispo at Los Osos Valley Rd, then drive northwest around 16 miles.

ALONG HIGHWAY 101

Driving inland along Hwy 101 is a quicker way to travel between the Bay Area and Southern California. Although it lacks the striking scenery of coastal Hwy 1, the historic El Camino Real (King's Highway), established by Spanish conquistadors and missionaries, has a beauty of its own, from the fertile fields of Salinas, immortalized by novelist John Steinbeck, to the oak-dappled golden hills of San Luis Obispo and beaches beyond. Along the way are ghostly missions,

jaw-dropping Pinnacles National Park and wineries worth stopping for.

Gilroy

About 30 miles south of San Jose, the self-proclaimed 'garlic capital of the world' hosts the jam-packed Gilroy Garlic Festival (www.gilroygarlicfestival.com) over the last full weekend in July. Show up for the chow – garlicky fries, garlic-flavored ice cream and more – and cooking contests under the blazing-hot sun.

Unusual Gilroy Gardens (☎408-840-7100; www.gilroygardens.org; 3050 Hecker Pass Hwy; adult/child 3-10yr $50/40; ◷11am-5pm Mon-Fri early Jun–mid-Aug, plus 10am-6pm Sat & Sun late Mar-Nov; ⛲) is a nonprofit family-oriented theme park focused on food and plants rather than Disney-esque cartoon characters. You've got to really love flowers, fruit and veggies to get your money's worth, though. Most rides such as the 'Mushroom Swing' are tame. Buy tickets online to save. From Hwy 101, follow Hwy 152 west; parking is $12.

Heading east on Hwy 152 toward I-5, Casa de Fruta (☎408-842-7282; www.casadefruta.com; 10021 Pacheco Pass Hwy, Hollister; per ride $2.50-4; ◷seasonal hours vary; ⛲) FREE is a commercialized farm stand with an old-fashioned carousel and choo-choo train rides for youngsters.

San Juan Bautista

In atmospheric old San Juan Bautista, where you can practically hear the whispers of the past, California's 15th mission is fronted by the state's only original Spanish plaza remaining. In 1876 the railroad bypassed the town, which has been a sleepy backwater ever since. Along 3rd St, evocative historic buildings mostly shelter antiques shops and petite garden restaurants. Hark! That cock you hear crowing is one of the town's roosters, which are allowed by tradition to stroll the streets at will.

◎ Sights

Mission San Juan Bautista　　　CHURCH
(☎831-623-4528; www.oldmissionsjb.org; 406 2nd St; adult/child 5-17yr $4/2; ◷9:30am-4:30pm) Founded in 1797, this mission claims the largest church among California's original 21 missions. Unknowingly built directly atop the San Andreas Fault, the mission has been rocked by earthquakes. Bells hanging

in the tower today include chimes that were salvaged after the 1906 San Francisco earthquake toppled the original mission. Scenes from Alfred Hitchcock's thriller *Vertigo* were shot here, although the bell tower in the movie's climactic scene was just a special effect.

Below the mission cemetery, you can spy a section of El Camino Real, the Spanish colonial road built to link California's first missions.

San Juan Bautista State Historic Park

PARK

(☑831-623-4881; www.parks.ca.gov; 2nd St, btwn Mariposa & Washington Sts; museum entry adult/child $3/free; ⊙10am-4:30pm Tue-Sun) Buildings around the old Spanish plaza opposite the mission anchor this small historical park. Cavernous stables hint at San Juan Bautista in its 1860s heyday as a stagecoach stop. The 1859 Plaza Hotel, which started life as a single-story adobe building, now houses a little historical museum. Next door to the hotel, the Castro-Breen Adobe once belonged to Mexican general and governor José Castro. In 1848 it was bought by the Breen family, survivors of the Donner Party disaster.

Fremont Peak State Park

PARK

(☑observatory 831-623-2465; www.parks.ca.gov; San Juan Canyon Rd; per car $6; 🚻) Equipped with a 30in telescope, Fremont Peak's astronomical observatory (www.fpoa.net) is usually open to the public on many Saturday nights between April and October, starting at 8pm or 8:30pm. Afternoon solar viewing happens monthly between March and October. It's about 11 miles south of town.

🛌 Sleeping

Fremont Peak State Park Campground

CAMPGROUND $

(☑reservations 800-444-7275; www.reserveamerica.com; San Juan Canyon Rd; tent & RV sites $25) A pretty, but primitive 25-site campground with vault toilets (no water) is shaded by oak trees on a hilltop with distant views of Monterey Bay.

🍴 Eating

On 3rd St, you'll find a long line-up of Mexican American restaurants; none are especially memorable.

San Juan Bakery

BAKERY $

(319 3rd St; snacks $2-4; ⊙usually 7am-5pm Wed-Mon) Get there early for fresh loaves of cin-

namon bread, hot-cross buns and guava or apricot turnovers, as they often sell out.

Vertigo Coffee

CAFE $

(www.vertigocoffee.com; 81 4th St; dishes $3-10; ⊙7am-7pm Tue-Fri, from 8am Sat & Sun) Rich espresso and pour-over brews, wood-fired pizzas and garden salads make this coffee roaster's shop a find.

❶ Getting There & Away

San Juan Bautista is on Hwy 156, a few miles east of Hwy 101, about a 20-minute drive south of Gilroy. Further south, Hwy 101 enters the sun-dappled eucalyptus grove that James Stewart and Kim Novak drove through in *Vertigo*.

Salinas

Best known as the birthplace of John Steinbeck and nicknamed the 'Salad Bowl of the World,' Salinas is a working-class agricultural center with down-and-out streets. It makes a thought-provoking contrast with the affluence of the Monterey Peninsula, a fact of life that helped shape Steinbeck's novel *East of Eden*. Historic downtown stretches along Main St, with the National Steinbeck Center capping off its northern end.

◎ Sights

National Steinbeck Center

MUSEUM

(☑831-775-4721; www.steinbeck.org; 1 Main St; adult/child 6-12yr/youth 13-17yr $15/6/8; ⊙10am-5pm; 🚻) This museum will interest almost anyone, even if you don't know a lick about Salinas' Nobel Prize–winning native son, John Steinbeck (1902–68), a Stanford University dropout. Tough, funny and brash, he portrayed the troubled spirit of rural, working-class Americans in novels such as *The Grapes of Wrath*. Interactive, kid-accessible exhibits and short video clips chronicle the writer's life and works in an engaging way. Gems include Rocinante, the camper in which Steinbeck traveled around the USA while researching *Travels with Charley*.

Take a moment and listen to Steinbeck's Nobel acceptance speech – it's grace and power combined. Temporary exhibitions cover anything from agricultural history and political activism to California landscape photography.

Steinbeck House

HISTORIC BUILDING

(☑831-424-2735; www.steinbeckhouse.com; 132 Central Ave; tour $10; ⊙restaurant 11:30am-2pm

Tue-Sat, gift shop 11am-3pm Tue-Sat) Steinbeck was born and spent much of his boyhood in this house, four blocks west of the museum. It's now a twee lunch cafe, which we're not sure he'd approve of. Guided tours are given on select summer Sundays; check online for details.

Garden of Memories Memorial Park   CEMETERY

(850 Abbott St) Steinbeck is buried in the family plot at this cemetery, less than 2 miles southeast of downtown.

Tours

Farm   GUIDED TOUR

(☑ 831-455-2575; www.thefarm-salinasvalley.com; 7 Foster Rd; call for tour prices; ☺ usually 10am-5pm or 6pm May-Dec, tours by reservation only) This family-owned organic fruit-and-veggie stand offers educational walking tours of its fields. On the drive in, watch for the giant sculptures of farm workers by local artist John Cerney, which also stand along Hwy 101. The farm is off Hwy 68 at Spreckels Blvd, about 3 miles southwest of downtown.

Ag Venture Tours   GUIDED TOUR

(☑ 831-761-8463; www.agventuretours.com; tours adult/child 5-16yr from $70/60) Take an in-depth look at commercial and organic farm fields around the Salinas Valley.

Festivals & Events

California Rodeo Salinas   RODEO

(www.carodeo.com) Bull riding, calf roping, cowboy poetry and carnival rides in late July.

Steinbeck Festival   CULTURE

(www.steinbeck.org) Three-day festival in early May features films, lectures, live music and guided bus and walking tours.

California International Airshow   OUTDOORS

(www.salinasairshow.com) Professional stunt flying and vintage and military aircraft take wing in late September.

Sleeping

Salinas has plenty of motels off Hwy 101, including at the Market St exit.

Super 8 Salinas   MOTEL $

(☑ 800-454-3213, 831-758-4693; www.super8.com; 131 Kern St; r incl breakfast from $79; ❋ @ ⊛ ☒) Revamped rooms have surprisingly stylish accents, from geometric patterned bedspreads to vanity mirrors. Complimentary breakfast buffet.

Laurel Inn   MOTEL $

(☑ 831-449-2474; www.laurelinnmotel.com; 801 W Laurel Dr; r from $80; ❋ ⊛ ☒) If chain motels don't do it for you, this sprawling, family-owned cheapie has predictably worn rooms that are nevertheless spacious.

Eating & Drinking

Bakery Station   BAKERY, DELI $

(www.thebakerystation.com; 202 Monterey St; dishes $3-9; ☺ 6am-4pm Mon-Fri, 7am-2pm Sat; ☗) Inside a converted gas station one block east of Main St, the breads, pastries and cookies are baked fresh daily. Tasty sandwiches are stuffed full of farm-fresh goodness.

Pica Fresh Mex   MEXICAN $$

(157 Main St; mains $6-12; ☺ 11am-9pm Mon-Thu, to 10pm Fri & Sat, 2-9pm Sun; ☗) Just south of the National Steinbeck Center, this storefront Mexican kitchen gets a stamp of approval for handmade tortillas, smoky chipotle salsa, carne asada tacos, burritos and *brochetas* (meat kebabs).

First Awakenings   AMERICAN $$

(www.firstawakenings.net; 171 Main St; mains $8-12; ☺ 7am-2pm; ☗) Fork into diner-style breakfasts of fruity pancakes, crepes and egg skillets, or turn up later in the day for hand-crafted sandwiches and market-fresh salads.

XL Public House   BAR

(www.facebook.com/XLPublichouse; 127 Main St; tasting fee $5; ☺ noon-10pm) Stumble into this brick-walled bottle shop for craft beers on tap, board games and retro video arcade consoles.

Monterey Coast Brewing Co   BREWERY

(165 Main St; ☺ 11am-11pm Tue-Sun, to 4pm Mon) At this lively downtown microbrewery, an eight-beer tasting sampler costs just 10 bucks. The pub grub is bland.

Information

Salinas 411 (☑ 831-435-4636; www.oldtown-salinas.com; 222 Main St; ☺ 9am-7pm) Free information, maps and self-guided walking-tour brochures.

Getting There & Away

Amtrak (☑ 800-872-7245; www.amtrak.com; 11 Station Pl) runs daily *Coast Starlight* trains north to Oakland ($16, three hours) and south to Paso

Robles ($19, two hours), San Luis Obispo ($27, 3¼ hours), Santa Barbara ($39, 6¼ hours) and LA ($56, 9¼ hours).

Greyhound (☎ 800-231-2222; www.greyhound.com; 19 W Gabilan St) has a few daily buses north to Santa Cruz ($15, 65 minutes) and San Francisco ($27, 3½ to five hours) and south to San Luis Obispo ($32, 2½ hours) and Santa Barbara ($53, 4¾ hours). From the nearby **Salinas Transit Center** (110 Salinas St), **MST** (☎ 888-678-2871; www.mst.org) bus 20 goes to Monterey ($3.50, one hour, every 30 to 60 minutes).

Pinnacles National Park

Named for the towering spires that rise abruptly out of the chaparral-covered hills east of Salinas Valley, this off-the-beaten-path **park** (☎ 831-389-4486; www.nps.gov/pinn; per car $5) protects the remains of an ancient volcano. A study in geological drama, its craggy monoliths, sheer-walled canyons and twisting caves are the result of millions of years of erosion.

Sights & Activities

Besides **rock climbing** (for route information, click to www.pinnacles.org), the park's biggest attractions are its two talus caves, formed by piles of boulders. **Balconies Cave** is almost always open for exploration. Scrambling through it is not an exercise recommended for claustrophobes, as it's pitch-black inside, making a flashlight essential. Be prepared to get lost a bit too. The cave is found along a 2.5-mile hiking loop from the west entrance. Nearer the east entrance, **Bear Gulch Cave** is closed seasonally, so as not to disturb a resident colony of Townsend's big-eared bats.

To really appreciate Pinnacles' stark beauty, you need to hike. Moderate loops of varying lengths and difficulty ascend into the **High Peaks** and include thrillingly narrow clifftop sections. In the early morning or late afternoon, you may spot endangered California condors soaring overhead. Get an early start to tackle the 9-mile round-trip trail to the top of **Chalone Peak**, granting panoramic views.

Rangers lead guided full-moon hikes and star-gazing programs on some weekend nights, usually in spring or fall. Reservations are required: call ☎ 831-389-4485 in advance or check for last-minute vacancies at the visitor center.

Sleeping

Pinnacles National Park Campground CAMPGROUND $
(☎ 877-444-6777; www.recreation.gov; tent/RV sites $23/36) On the park's east side, this popular family-oriented campground has more than 130 sites (some with shade), drinking water, coin-op hot showers, fire pits and an outdoor pool (usually closed from October to March).

Information

The best time to visit Pinnacles National Park is during spring or fall; summer heat is extreme. Information, maps and books are available on the park's east side from the small **NPS visitor center** (☎ 831-389-4485; 9:30am-5pm daily, to 8pm Fri late Mar-early Sep) inside the **campground store** (☎ 831-389-4538; 3-4pm Mon-Thu, noon-6pm Fri, 9am-6pm Sat & Sun), which sells bottled water, snacks and sundries.

Getting There & Away

There is no road connecting the two sides of the park. To reach the less-developed **west entrance** (7:30am-8pm), exit Hwy 101 at Soledad and follow Hwy 146 northeast for 14 miles. The **east entrance** (24hr), where you'll find the visitor center and campground, is accessed via lonely Hwy 25 in San Benito County, southeast of Hollister and northeast of King City.

Mission San Antonio De Padua

Remote, tranquil and evocative, this historical **mission** (☎ 831-385-4478; www.missionsanantonio.net; end of Mission Rd, Jolon; adult/child 12yr & under $5/3; usually 10am-4pm) sits in the Valley of the Oaks, once part of Hearst Ranch's sprawling land holdings. Today it's inside the boundaries of the US Army's Fort Hunter Liggett.

The mission was founded in 1771 by Franciscan priest Junípero Serra. Built with Native American labor, the church has been restored to its early-19th-century appearance, with a wooden pulpit, canopied altar and decorative flourishes on whitewashed walls. A creaky door leads to a cloistered garden anchored by a fountain. The museum has a small collection of such utilitarian items as an olive press and a weaving loom once used in the mission's workshops. Around the grounds, you can inspect the remains of a mill and irrigation system with aqueducts.

It's seldom crowded here, and you may have the vast site all to yourself, except during **Mission Days** in early April and **La Fiesta** on the second Sunday of June. Pick up a visitor's pass from a military checkpoint on the way in; bring photo ID and proof of your vehicle's registration. From the north, take the Jolon Rd exit off Hwy 101 before King City and follow Jolon Rd (County Rte G14) about 18 miles south to Mission Rd. From the south, take the Jolon Rd (County Rte G18) exit off Hwy 101 and drive 22 miles northwest to Mission Rd.

San Miguel

San Miguel is a small farming town off Hwy 101, where life seems to have remained almost unchanged for decades. Founded in 1797, **Mission San Miguel Arcángel** (☎805-467-3256; www.missionsanmiguel.org; 775 Mission St; adult/child 5-17yr $3/2; ☉10am-4:30pm) suffered heart-breaking damage during a 2003 earthquake. Although repairs are still underway, the church, cemetery, museum and gardens are open. An enormous cactus out front was planted during the early days of the mission.

Hungry? Inside a converted retro gas station downtown, **San Miguel Coffee Station** (www.sanmiguelcoffeestation.com; 1199 Mission St; dishes $3-8; ☉6:30am-5pm Mon-Wed, to 8pm Thu-Sat) vends live-wire cups o' coffee, sweet baked goods, pulled-pork sandwiches and stuffed Cal-Mex burritos.

Paso Robles

In northern San Luis Obispo County, Paso Robles is the heart of a historic agricultural region where grapes are now the biggest money-making crop. Scores of wineries along Hwy 46 produce a brave new world of more-than-respectable bottles. The Mediterranean climate is yielding another bounty too: olive oil. Paso's historic downtown centers on Park and 12th Sts, where boutique shops and wine-tasting rooms await.

◎ Sights & Activities

You could spend days wandering country back roads off Hwy 46, running east and west of Hwy 101. Most wineries have tasting rooms and a few offer vineyard tours. For dozens more wineries and olive-oil farms to visit, browse www.pasowine.com.

Eastside

J Lohr Vineyards & Wines   WINERY
(www.jlohr.com; 6169 Airport Rd; tasting fee free-$10; ☉10am-5pm) A Central Coast wine pioneer, J Lohr owns vineyards in Napa Valley, Monterey's Santa Lucia Highlands and Paso's pastoral countryside. Knowledgeable staff guide you through a far-reaching wine list.

Tobin James Cellars   WINERY
(www.tobinjames.com; 8950 Union Rd; ☉10am-6pm) Anti-serious Old West saloon pours bold reds, including an outlaw 'Ballistic' Zinfandel and 'Liquid Love' dessert wine. No tasting fee.

Eberle Winery   WINERY
(www.eberlewinery.com; 3810 E Hwy 46; tasting fee free-$10; ☉10am-5pm Oct-Mar, 10am-6pm Apr-Sep) Offers lofty vineyard views and hourly tours of its wine caves. Sociable tastings run the gamut of white and red varietals and Rhône blends.

Cass Winery   WINERY
(www.casswines.com; 7350 Linne Rd; tasting fee $10; ☉11am-5pm) All that rich Rhône varietal wine-tasting, from Roussanne to Syrah, going straight to your head? An epicurean market cafe here serves lunch until 5pm daily.

Westside

Tablas Creek Vineyard   WINERY
(www.tablascreek.com; 9339 Adelaida Rd; tasting fee from $10; ☉10am-5pm) ✈ Breathe easy at this organic estate vineyard reached via a pretty winding drive up into the hills. Known for Rhône varietals, the signature blends also rate highly. Free tours at 10:30am and 2pm daily (reservations advised).

Castoro Cellars   WINERY
(www.castorocellars.com; 1315 N Bethel Rd; tasting fee $5; ☉10am-5:30pm) Husband-and-wife team produces 'dam fine wine' (the mascot is a beaver, get it?), including from custom-crushed and organic grapes. Outdoor vineyard concerts happen during summer.

Chronic Cellars   WINERY
(www.chroniccellars.com; 2020 Nacimiento Lake Dr; tasting fee $10; ☉11:30am-5:30pm) Everyone's favorite irreverent winery, where Día de Los Muertos designs cover bottles of bold blends. Play billiards in the tasting room or a game of horseshoes outside on the grass.

Re:Find Distillery & Villicana Winery   WINERY
(www.villicanawinery.com; 2725 Adelaida Rd; tasting fee $10; ☉11am-5pm) Paso Robles' first

micro-distillery makes clean-tasting botanical brandy (read: gin), which you can taste along with dry rosé in the adjoining wine-tasting room.

Thacher Winery
WINERY

(www.thacherwinery.com; 8355 Vineyard Rd; tasting fee $10; ⏰ 11am-5pm Thu-Mon) Breathe deeply as you drive up the dirt road to this historic ranch that makes memorable Rhône blends – 'Controlled Chaos' is a perennial fave.

✷ Festivals & Events

Wine Festival
WINE, FOOD

(www.pasowine.com) Oenophiles come for Paso's premier Wine Festival in mid-May, but the Vintage Paso weekend, focusing on Zinfandel wines, in mid-March and the Harvest Wine Weekend in mid-October are just as fun.

California Mid-State Fair
CARNIVAL, MUSIC

(www.midstatefair.com) In mid-July, 12 days of live rock and country-and-western concerts, farm exhibits, carnival rides and a rodeo draw huge crowds.

🛏 Sleeping

Chain motels and hotels line Hwy 101. B&Bs and vacation rentals are scattered among the vineyards outside town.

Melody Ranch Motel
MOTEL $

(☏ 800-909-3911, 805-238-3911; 939 Spring St; r $70-100; ❋ 🐾 🛜 ⛱) At this small, family-owned, 1950s motor court downtown, ultra-basic rooms mean prices that are almost as small as the outdoor pool.

Adelaide Inn
MOTEL $$

(☏ 800-549-7276, 805-238-2770; www.adelaide-inn.com; 1215 Ysabel Ave; r incl breakfast $115-165; ❋ @ 🛜 ⛱) Fresh-baked cookies, muffins for breakfast, mini golf and a fitness room keep families happy at this motel just off Hwy 101.

Summerwood Inn
B&B $$$

(www.summerwoodwine.com; 2175 Arbor Rd; d incl breakfast from $275) 🐾 Along Hwy 46 within an easy drive of dozens of wineries, this gorgeously renovated inn mixes vintage and modern elements. Each room has a gas fireplace and balcony overlooking the vineyards. Indulge with the chef's gourmet breakfast, afternoon hors d'oeuvres and evening desserts.

Inn Paradiso
B&B $$$

(☏ 805-239-2800; www.innparadiso.com; 975 Mojave Ln; ste incl breakfast $350; 🛜 ⛱) An intimate B&B pulls off no-fuss luxury with three suites decorated with art and antiques, and perhaps a fireplace, a deep soaking tub, a canopy king-sized bed or French balcony doors. Pet fee $50.

Zenaida Cellars
B&B $$$

(☏ 866-936-5638; www.zenaidacellars.com; 1550 W Hwy 46; ste $250-375; 🐾) Steal yourself away among the pastoral vineyards of Paso Robles' westside. The winemaker's loft above the tasting room sleeps four adults and has a full kitchen.

🍴 Eating & Drinking

Restaurants and wine-tasting rooms surround downtown's grassy central square, off Spring St between 11th and 12th Sts.

La Reyna Market
MEXICAN $

(www.lareynamarket.com; 532 24th St; dishes $2-8; ⏰ 8am-9pm Mon-Thu, to 9:30pm Fri-Sun) Off Hwy 101, this authentic Mexican grocery store and butcher's deli makes savory *tortas* (sandwiches), wet burritos and street-food tacos (the *al pastor* edges out the carne asada) on hot, homemade tortillas.

★ Artisan
CALIFORNIAN $$$

(☏ 805-237-8084; www.artisanpasorobles.com; 843 12th St; shared plates $11-19, mains $30-38; ⏰ 11:30am-9pm Mon-Thu, to 10pm Fri & Sat, 10am-9pm Sun) 🐾 Chef Chris Kobayashi often ducks out of the kitchen just to make sure you're loving his impeccable contemporary renditions of modern American cuisine, featuring sustainably farmed meats, wild-caught seafood and artisan California cheeses. Impressive wine, beer and cocktail menus. Reservations essential.

Fish Gaucho
MEXICAN, SEAFOOD $$$

(www.fishgaucho.com; 1244 Spring St; mains $17-26; ⏰ kitchen 3-9:30pm, from 11:30am Fri-Sun, bar till midnight daily) Hand-made furnishings, antiques and decor imported from Mexico fill this Baja-style seafood joint and tequila bar. Smoky, spicy and fruity cocktails wash down stuffed poblano chiles, braised short-rib tacos and oyster shooters with chorizo and cotija crumbles. Reservations recommended.

Firestone Walker Brewing Company
BREWERY

(☏ 805-225-5911; www.firestonebeer.com; 1400 Ramada Dr; ⏰ noon-7pm) Bring your buddies to the taproom to sample the famous Double Barrel Ale or seasonal Velvet Merlin oatmeal stout, plus barrel-aged vintages and experimental brews. Book ahead for free brewery tours.

BarrelHouse Brewing Co BREWERY
(www.barrelhousebrewing.com; 3055 Limestone Way; ⊙2-8pm Wed-Thu, 11am-9pm Fri & Sat, 11am-8pm Sun) Detour south of downtown, where locals chill outside at picnic tables with pints of ales, stout and fruity Belgian-style beers, while live bands frequently play.

🛍 Shopping

Around the downtown square, side streets are full of wine-country boutiques.

Paso Robles General Store FOOD, GIFTS
(www.generalstorepr.com; 841 12th St; ⊙10am-7pm) Stock up on picnic provisions including California-made pistachio butter, fresh local baguettes, fruit jams and more, plus home goods such as lavender soap.

We Olive FOOD
(www.weolive.com/paso-robles; 1311 Park St; ⊙10am-6pm Mon-Sat, 11am-4pm Sun) Step right up to the tasting bar to sample local growers' olive oils and fruit-infused balsamic vinegars. Also in downtown San Luis Obispo.

ℹ Information

Paso Robles Chamber of Commerce (☑805-238-0506; www.pasorobleschamber.com; 1225 Park St; ⊙8:30am-4:30pm, closed Sun Sep-May) Information and free winery maps.

ℹ Getting There & Away

From an unstaffed **Amtrak** (☑800-872-7245; www.amtrak.com; 800 Pine St) station, daily *Coast Starlight* trains head north to Salinas ($19, two hours) and Oakland ($30, 4¾ hours) and south to Santa Barbara ($28, 4¼ hours) and LA ($41, 7½ hours). Several daily Thruway buses link to more-frequent regional trains, including the *Pacific Surfliner*.

From the train station, **Greyhound** (☑800-231-2222; www.greyhound.com; 800 Pine St) runs a few daily buses along Hwy 101 south to Santa Barbara ($57, 2¾ hours) and LA ($81, six hours) and north to San Francisco ($74, six hours) via Santa Cruz ($57, 3¼ hours).

RTA (☑805-541-2228; www.slorta.org) bus 9 travels between San Luis Obispo and Paso Robles ($2.50, 70 minutes) hourly Monday to Friday, and a few times daily on weekends.

San Luis Obispo

Almost midway between LA and San Francisco, at the junction of Hwys 101 and 1, San Luis Obispo is a popular overnight stop for road trippers. With no must-see attractions, SLO might not seem to warrant much of your time. Even so, this low-key town has an enviably high quality of life – in fact, it has been named America's happiest city. CalPoly university students inject a healthy dose of hubbub into the city's streets, bars and cafes throughout the school year. Nestled at the base of the Santa Lucia foothills, SLO is just a grape's throw from Edna Valley wineries too.

👁 Sights

San Luis Obispo Creek, once used to irrigate mission orchards, flows through downtown. Uphill from Higuera St, Mission Plaza is a shady oasis with restored adobe buildings and fountains overlooking the creek. Look for the Moon Tree, a coast redwood grown from a seed that journeyed on board Apollo 14's lunar mission.

Mission San Luis Obispo de Tolosa CHURCH
(☑805-543-6850; www.missionsanluisobispo.org; 751 Palm St; donation $2; ⊙9am-5pm late Mar-Oct, to 4pm Nov–mid-Mar) Those satisfyingly reverberatory bells heard around downtown emanate from this active parish dating from 1772. The fifth California mission founded by Junípero Serra, it was named for a 13th-century French saint. The modest church has an unusual L-shape and whitewashed walls decorated with Stations of the Cross. An adjacent building contains an old-fashioned museum about daily life during the Chumash tribal and Spanish colonial periods.

San Luis Obispo Museum of Art MUSEUM
(www.sloma.org; 1010 Broad St; ⊙11am-5pm, closed Tue early Sep-early Jul) FREE By the creek, this small gallery showcases the work of local painters, sculptors, printmakers and fine-art photographers, as well as traveling California art exhibitions.

Bubblegum Alley STREET
(off 700 block of Higuera St) SLO's weirdest sight is colorfully plastered with thousands of wads of ABC ('already been chewed') gum. Watch where you step!

🏃 Activities

For more hiking with ocean views, head to Montaña de Oro State Park (p465), not far away.

Bishop Peak HIKING
SLO's most popular hike summits Bishop Peak (1546ft), the tallest of the Nine Sisters,

San Luis Obispo

a chain of volcanic peaks that stretches north to Morro Bay. The 2.2-mile one-way trail starts in a grove of live oaks (watch out for poison oak) and heads uphill along rocky, mostly exposed switchbacks. Carefully scramble up boulders at the tippy-top for panoramic views.

To get to the trailhead, drive northwest from downtown on Santa Rosa St (Hwy 1), turn left onto Foothill Dr, then right onto Patricia Dr; after 0.8 miles, look for three black posts and a trailhead sign on your left.

Margarita Adventures   ZIP LINING, KAYAKING
(☏ 805-438-3120; www.margarita-adventures.com; 22719 El Camino Real, Santa Margarita; adult/child zip-line tour $99/79, kayak tour $79/59; ⊘ closed Tue & Wed; ⏺) Whoosh down five zip lines across the vineyards or paddle around a lake beneath the Santa Lucia Mountains at this historic ranch, about a 10-mile drive northeast of SLO via Hwy 101. Reservations required.

★ Festivals & Events

Concerts in the Plaza   MUSIC, FOOD
(www.downtownslo.com) Every Friday night from early June through early September, downtown's Mission Plaza rocks out with local bands and food vendors.

Savor the Central Coast   FOOD, WINE
(www.savorcentralcoast.com) Behind-the-scenes farm, aquaculture and ranch tours, wine-tasting competitions and celebrity chefs' dinners in late September or early October.

⌘ Sleeping

Motels cluster off Hwy 101, especially off Monterey St northeast of downtown and around Santa Rosa St (Hwy 1).

HI Hostel Obispo   HOSTEL $
(☏ 805-544-4678; www.hostelobispo.com; 1617 Santa Rosa St; dm $27-31, r from $60, all with shared bath; ⊘ check-in 4:30-10pm; @ ☎) ⏺ On a tree-lined street near the train station, this

San Luis Obispo

solar-empowered, avocado-colored hostel inhabits a converted Victorian, which gives it a bit of a B&B feel. Amenities include a kitchen, bike rentals (from $10 per day) and complimentary sourdough pancakes and coffee for breakfast. BYOT (bring your own towel).

Peach Tree Inn MOTEL $$
(✆ 800-227-6396, 805-543-3170; www.peachtree-inn.com; 2001 Monterey St; r incl breakfast $89-140; ⊙ office 7am-11pm; @🐾) The folksy, nothing-fancy motel rooms here are inviting, especially those right by the creek or with rocking chairs on wooden porches overlooking grassy lawns, eucalyptus trees and rose gardens. Continental breakfast features homemade breads.

San Luis Creek Lodge HOTEL $$$
(✆ 800-593-0333, 805-541-1122; www.sanluis-creeklodge.com; 1941 Monterey St; r incl breakfast $149-269; ✴@🐾) Rubbing shoulders with

neighboring motels, this boutique inn has fresh, spacious rooms with divine beds (and some have gas fireplaces and jetted tubs) inside three whimsically mismatched buildings built in Tudor, California arts-and-crafts and Southern plantation styles. DVDs, chess sets and board games are free to borrow.

Petit Soleil INN $$$
(✆ 800-676-1588, 805-549-0321; www.petitsoleilslo.com; 1473 Monterey St; d incl breakfast $169-299; ⊙ office 7am-10pm; 🐾🐾) This French-themed, gay-friendly 'bed et breakfast' is a mostly charming retrofit of a courtyard motel. Each room is tastefully decorated with Provençal flair, and breakfast is a gourmet feast. The front rooms catch some street noise. Pet fee $25.

✗ Eating

★ **San Luis Obispo Farmers Market** MARKET
(www.downtownslo.com; ⊙ 6-9pm Thu) The county's biggest and best weekly farmers market turns downtown SLO's Higuera St into a giant street party, with smokin' barbecues, overflowing fruit and veggie stands, live music and free sidewalk entertainment, from salvation peddlers to wackadoodle political activists. Rain cancels it.

Firestone Grill BARBECUE $
(www.firestonegrill.com; 1001 Higuera St; dishes $4-10; ⊙ 11am-10pm Sun-Wed, to 11pm Thu-Sat; 🚸) If you can stomach huge lines, long waits for a table, and sports-bar-style service, you'll get to sink your teeth into an authentic Santa Maria–style tri-tip steak sandwich on a toasted garlic roll and a basket of super-crispy fries.

SLO Donut Company SNACKS $
(www.slodoco.com; 793 E Foothill Blvd; snacks from $2; ⊙ 24hr; 🐾) Home of unusually good flavor combos like bacon-maple and mint-chip donuts, served with cups of organic, fair-trade, locally roasted coffee. It's northwest of downtown off Santa Rosa St (Hwy 1).

Whole Foods GROCERY, FAST FOOD $
(www.wholefoodsmarket.com; 1531 Froom Ranch Way; ⊙ 8am-9pm) 🍃 For organic groceries, deli picnic meals and a hot-and-cold salad bar. It's 4 miles southwest of downtown via Hwy 101 (exit Los Osos Valley Rd).

Meze Wine Bar & Bistro MEDITERRANEAN $$
(www.mezewinebar.com; 1880 Santa Barbara Ave; mains $10-20; ⊙ 11am-9pm Mon-Wed, to 10pm

MADONNA INN

'Oh, my!' is one of the more printable exclamations overheard from visitors at the Madonna Inn (☑805-543-3000, 800-543-9666; www.madonnainn.com; 100 Madonna Rd; r $189-309; ❄@🛜🏊), a garish confection visible from Hwy 101. You'd expect outrageous kitsch like this in Las Vegas, not SLO, but here it is, in all its campy extravagance. Japanese tourists, vacationing Midwesterners and hipster, irony-loving urbanites all adore the 110 themed rooms – including Yosemite Rock, Caveman and hot-pink Floral Fantasy. Check out photos of the different rooms online, or wander the halls and spy into the ones being cleaned. The urinal in the men's room is a bizarre waterfall. But the most irresistible reason to stop here? Old-fashioned cookies from the storybook-esque bakery.

Thu-Sat) Hidden downhill from the Amtrak station, this tiny wine shop, gourmet market and tapas-style bar is an eclectic gem. Gather with friends around the cheese and charcuterie board, or stop in for a hand-crafted sandwich with a quinoa salad.

Big Sky Café   CALIFORNIAN $$
(www.bigskycafe.com; 1121 Broad St; dinner mains $11-22; ⊙7am-9pm Mon-Thu, to 10pm Fri, 8am-10pm Sat, to 9pm Sun; 🖋) 🍃 Big Sky is a big room, and still the wait can be long – its tagline is 'analog food for a digital world.' Vegetarians have almost as many options as carnivores, and many of the ingredients are sourced locally. Big-plate dinners can be a bit bland, but breakfast (served until 1pm daily) gets top marks.

★Luna Red   FUSION $$$
(☑805-540-5243; www.lunaredslo.com; 1023 Chorro St; shared plates $6-20, mains $20-39; ⊙11am-9pm Mon-Wed, to 11:30pm Thu-Fri, 9:30am-11:30pm Sat, to 9pm Sun; 🖋) 🍃 Local bounty from the land and sea, artisan cheeses and farmers-market produce pervade the chef's Californian, Asian and Mediterranean small-plates menu. Cocktails and glowing lanterns enhance a sophisticated ambience indoors, or linger over brunch on the mission-view garden patio. Reservations recommended.

Novo   FUSION $$$
(☑805-543-3986; www.novorestaurant.com; 726 Higuera St; mains $15-34; ⊙11am-9pm Mon-Thu, to 1am Fri & Sat, 10am-9pm Sun) Novo spins out hit-and-miss European, Latin and Asian-inspired tapas, but with an artistic eye towards presentation. Pick from dozens of international beers, wines or sakes, then savor the view from tables on the creekside deck.

Sidecar   CALIFORNIAN $$$
(☑805-540-5340; www.sidecarslo.com; 1127 Broad St; mains $14-28; ⊙11am-10pm Mon-Fri, from 10am Sat & Sun) 🍃 A long saloon-style bar where locals mingle with serious cocktails, and a casual Californian menu – try the fried brussels sprouts or the signature house burger with smoked mozzarella – make this downtown eatery a social spot.

🍷 Drinking & Nightlife

Downtown, Higuera St is littered with college-student-jammed bars.

Downtown Brewing Co   BREWERY
(☑805-543-1843; www.slobrew.com; 1119 Garden St) Nicknamed SLO Brew, this study in rafters and exposed brick has plenty of craft beers to go, along with filling pub grub. Downstairs, you'll find DJs or live bands (including some surprisingly famous acts) on many nights.

Tap It Brewing   BREWERY
(☑805-545-7702; www.tapitbrewing.com; 675 Clarion St; ⊙noon-6pm Sun-Wed, to 8pm Thu-Sat) Head toward the airport to this brewery's tap room, where cacti grow inside an old Jeep and live bands sometimes rock on the patio.

Mother's Tavern   PUB
(www.motherstavern.com; 725 Higuera St; ⊙11am-1:30am; 🛜) Cavernous two-story 'MoTav' draws in writhing CalPoly student masses with a no-cover dance floor, DJ and karaoke nights, and big-screen sports TVs.

Kreuzberg   CAFE
(www.kreuzbergcalifornia.com; 685 Higuera St; ⊙7:30am-10pm; 🛜) Shabby-chic coffeehouse and roaster has earned a fervent following with its comfy couches, sprawling bookshelves, local art and occasional live music.

Granada Bistro   COCKTAIL BAR
(www.granadahotelandbistro.com; 1126 Morro St; ⊙5-10pm Sun-Thu, to 11pm Fri & Sat) A swank indoor/outdoor hotel cocktail lounge, adorned with wrought-iron candelabras and outdoor fire pits, classes up SLO's downtown scene.

Luis Wine Bar
WINE BAR

(www.luiswinebar.com; 1021 Higuera St; ⏰3-11pm Mon-Thu, to midnight Fri, noon-midnight Sat, noon-11pm Sun) Evincing urbane style and unpretentious sophistication, this downtown wine bar has wide-open seating, a strong craft beer list and small noshes.

Creekside Brewing Co
BREWERY

(www.creeksidebrewingcom.ipage.com; 1040 Broad St; ⏰4pm-close Mon-Thu, from noon Fri-Sun) On the tiny patio overhanging a bubbling creek, you can sample respectable homemade and imported craft beers and ciders.

☆ Entertainment

Palm Theatre
CINEMA

(📞805-541-5161; www.thepalmtheatre.com; 817 Palm St; tickets $5-8) 🎫 This small-scale movie house showing foreign and indie flicks just happens to be the USA's first solar-powered cinema. Look for the SLO International Film Festival (www.slofilmfest.org) in March.

Performing Arts Center
PERFORMING ARTS

(PAC; 📞805-756-4849, 888-233-2787; www.pacslo. org; 1 Grand Ave) On the CalPoly campus, SLO's biggest cultural venue presents an internationally spiced variety of concerts, theater, dance recitals, stand-up comedy and other shows, including by big-name performers.

Sunset Drive-In
CINEMA

(📞805-544-4475; www.facebook.com/sunset-drivein; 255 Elks Ln; ♿) Recline your seat, put your feet up on the dash and munch on bottomless bags of popcorn at this classic Americana drive-in. Sticking around for the second feature (usually a B-list Hollywood blockbuster) doesn't cost extra. It's 2 miles southwest of downtown off Higuera St.

🔒 Shopping

Downtown Higuera and Marsh Sts, along with all of the arcades and cross streets in between, are full of unique boutiques. Just take a wander.

CENTRAL COAST SAN LUIS OBISPO

DON'T MISS

EDNA VALLEY WINERIES

A gorgeous bicycle ride into the rolling hills southeast of downtown SLO, Edna Valley wineries are best known for producing crisp Chardonnay and subtle Pinot Noir, as well as spicy and smoky Syrah. Annual events worth showing up for include 'Roll Out the Barrels' in mid-June and harvest celebrations in mid-November. For a winery map and more information, visit www.slowine.com.

Tolosa Winery (www.tolosawinery.com; 4910 Edna Rd; tasting fee $12-25; ⏰11am-4:45pm) No-oak Chardonnay, barrel-selected Pinot Noir and bold estate Syrah, with artisanal cheese, charcuterie and chocolate pairings on weekends.

Edna Valley Vineyard (www.ednavalleyvineyard.com; 2585 Biddle Ranch Rd; tasting fee $10-15; ⏰10am-5pm) Sip Paragon Vineyard estate Chardonnay by panoramic windows overlooking fields of grapes.

Baileyana (Niven Family Wine Estates; www.baileyana.com; 5828 Orcutt Rd; tasting fee $8-12; ⏰10am-5pm) Samples from six different labels inside an early-20th-century wooden schoolhouse, with a bocce ball court outside.

Talley Vineyards (www.talleyvineyards.com; 3031 Lopez Dr, Arroyo Grande; tasting fee $8-15; ⏰10:30am-4:30pm) Unpretentious, value-priced wines set among rolling hillsides, with vineyard tours ($10, including wine-tasting flight $15) by appointment.

Kynsi Winery (www.kynsi.com; 2212 Corbett Canyon Rd, Arroyo Grande; tasting fee $10; ⏰11am-5pm, closed Tue & Wed Nov-Jan) Small, family-run vineyard pours cult-worthy Pinot Noir inside a cozy brick tasting room.

Chamisal Vineyards (www.chamisalvineyards.com; 7525 Orcutt Rd; tasting fee $15; ⏰11am-5pm) In a rust-colored barn tasting room, tipple hand-crafted, small-lot wines grown mostly organically.

Sextant Wines (www.sextantwines.com; 1653 Old Price Canyon Rd; tasting fee $10; ⏰10am-4pm Mon-Fri, to 5pm Sat & Sun) Boisterous tasting room pours different varietals from Edna Valley and Paso Robles, with a tiny gourmet deli.

Hands Gallery
ARTS & CRAFTS

(www.handsgallery.com; 777 Higuera St; ⊙10am-6pm Mon-Wed, to 9pm Thu, to 8pm Fri & Sat, 11am-5pm Sun) Brightly lit downtown shop sells vibrant contemporary pieces by California artisans, including jewelry, fiber arts, sculptures, ceramics and blown glass.

Mountain Air Sports
OUTDOOR EQUIPMENT

(www.mountainairsports.com; 667 Marsh St; ⊙10am-6pm Mon-Sat, to 8pm Thu, 11am-4pm Sun) At this local outdoor outfitter, pick up anything from campstove fuel and tents to brand-name clothing and hiking boots.

Finders Keepers
CLOTHING

(www.finderskeepersconsignment.com; 1124 Garden St; ⊙10am-5pm Mon-Sat) Seriously stylish secondhand women's fashions that match SLO's breezy, laid-back coastal lifestyle, plus hand-picked handbags, coats and jewelry.

ℹ Information

SLO's compact downtown is bisected by the parallel one-way arteries Higuera St and Marsh St. Banks with 24-hour ATMs are off Marsh St, near the post office. Most downtown coffee shops offer free wi-fi.

FedEx Office (www.fedex.com; 1127 Chorro St; per min 30-40¢; ⊙7am-11pm Mon-Fri, 8am-9pm Sat, 9am-9pm Sun; 🖥) Pay-as-you-go internet workstations.

French Hospital (☑805-543-5353; www.frenchmedicalcenter.org; 1911 Johnson Ave; ⊙24hr) Emergency-room services.

San Luis Obispo Library (☑805-781-5991; www.slolibrary.org; 995 Palm St; ⊙10am-5pm Wed-Sat, to 8pm Tue; 🖥) Free wi-fi and public internet terminals.

San Luis Obispo Visitor Center (☑805-781-2777; www.visitslo.com; 895 Monterey St; ⊙10am-5pm Sun-Wed, to 7pm Thu-Sat) Free maps and tourist brochures.

ℹ Getting There & Around

Off Broad St, a little more than 3 miles southeast of downtown, San Luis Obispo County Regional Airport has scheduled flights with United (San Francisco and LA) and US Airways (Phoenix).

Amtrak (☑800-872-7245; www.amtrak.com; 1011 Railroad Ave) runs daily Seattle–LA *Coast Starlight* and twice-daily SLO–San Diego *Pacific Surfliner* trains. Both routes head south to Santa Barbara ($27, 2¾ hours) and Los Angeles ($41, 5½ hours). The *Coast Starlight* connects north via Paso Robles to Salinas ($27, three hours) and Oakland ($39, six hours). Several daily Thruway buses link to more regional trains.

Inconveniently stopping off Hwy 101, nearly 4 miles southwest of downtown, **Greyhound** (☑800-231-2222; www.greyhound.com; 1460 Calle Joaquin) operates a few daily buses south to Los Angeles ($30, five hours) via Santa Barbara ($28, 2¼ hours) and north to San Francisco ($53, seven hours) via Santa Cruz ($42, four hours).

San Luis Obispo Regional Transit Authority (RTA; ☑805-541-2228; www.slorta.org; single-ride fares $1.50-3, day pass $5) operates daily county-wide buses with limited weekend services. All buses are equipped with bicycle racks. Lines converge on downtown's **transit center** (cnr Palm & Osos Sts).

SLO Transit (☑805-541-2877; www.slocity.org) runs local city buses ($1.25) and a trolley (50¢) that loops around downtown every 20 minutes between 5pm and 9pm on Thursdays year-round, on Fridays from June to early September and on Saturdays from April through October.

Avila Beach

Quaint, sunny Avila Beach lures crowds with its strand of golden sand and a shiny seafront commercial district of restaurants, cafes and shops. Two miles west of downtown, Port San Luis is a working fishing harbor with a rickety old pier.

◉ Sights & Activities

For a lazy summer day at the beach, you can rent beach chairs and umbrellas, surfboards, boogie boards and wetsuits underneath Avila Pier, off downtown's waterfront promenade. Over by the port, the beach has bonfire pits and the barking of sea lions accompanies your stroll atop Harford Pier, one of the Central Coast's most authentic fishing piers.

Point San Luis Lighthouse
LIGHTHOUSE

(☑guided hike reservations 805-541-8735, trolley tour reservations 855-533-7843; www.sanluislighthouse.org; lighthouse admission adult/child under 12yr $5/free, trolley tour incl admission per adult/child 3-12yr $20/15; ⊙guided hikes usually 8:45am-1pm Wed & Sat, trolley tours usually noon & 2pm Wed & Sat, also 1pm Sat) Just getting to this scenic 1890 lighthouse, overshadowed by Diablo Canyon nuclear power plant, is an adventure. The cheapest way to reach the lighthouse is via a rocky, crumbling, 3.75-mile round-trip hiking trail, for which guided hike reservations are required. If you'd rather take it easy and ride out to the lighthouse, join an afternoon trolley tour, for which reservations are also required. Inside the lighthouse you can inspect an original Fresnel lens and authentic Victorian period furnishings.

The Pecho Coast Trail to the lighthouse is open only for guided hikes led by Pacific Gas & Electric (PG&E) docents, weather permitting. These guided hikes are free; children under nine years old are not allowed. Call for reservations at least two weeks in advance and bring plenty of water.

Avila Valley Barn FARM
(www.avilavalleybarn.com; 560 Avila Beach Dr; ☺ usually 9am-6pm mid-Mar–late Dec; 🅟) At this rural farmstand and pick-your-own berry farm, park alongside the sheep and goat pens, lick an ice-cream cone, then grab a basket and walk out into the fields to harvest jammy olallieberries in late spring and early summer, mid-summer peaches and nectarines, or autumn apples and pumpkins.

Sycamore Mineral Springs SPA
(☑ 805-595-7302; www.sycamoresprings.com; 1215 Avila Beach Dr; 1hr per person $13.50-17.50; ☺ 8am-midnight, last reservation 10:45pm) Make time for a therapeutic soak in one of these private redwood hot tubs discreetly laddered up a woodsy hillside. Call in advance for reservations, especially during summer and after dark on weekends.

Central Coast Kayaks KAYAKING
(☑ 805-773-3500; www.centralcoastkayaks.com; 1879 Shell Beach Rd, Shell Beach; kayak or SUP set rental $20-60, classes $50-105, tours $60-120) Paddle out among sea otters and seals and through mesmerizing sea caves, rock grottos, arches and kelp forests. Wetsuits, paddle jackets and booties available (small surcharge applies) with kayak rentals.

Patriot Sportfishing BOAT TOUR
(☑ 805-595-7200; www.patriotsportfishing.com; Harford Pier, off Avila Beach Dr; 2hr whale-watching tour adult/child under 13yr $35/25) Long-running local biz organizes deep-sea fishing trips and tournaments, as well as whale-spotting cruises between December and April.

Avila Hot Springs HOT SPRINGS
(☑ 805-595-2359; www.avilahotsprings.com; 250 Avila Beach Dr; adult/child under 16yr $10/8; ☺ usually 8am-9pm Sun-Tue & Thu, to 10pm Wed, Fri & Sat) Slightly sulfuric, lukewarm public swimming pool has kiddie waterslides that are usually open from noon to 5pm on Saturday and Sunday.

🛏 Sleeping

Port San Luis Campground CAMPGROUND $
(☑ 805-903-3395; www.portsanluis.com; RV sites without/with hookups from $40/65) First-come, first-served roadside parking spaces by the harbor have ocean views, but are for RVs only (no tents allowed).

Avila Lighthouse Suites HOTEL $$$
(☑ 800-372-8452, 805-627-1900; www.avilalighthousesuites.com; 550 Front St; ste incl breakfast from $289; ❉ @ 🛜 ▣) Any closer to the ocean, and your bed would actually be sitting on the sand. With families in mind, this apartment-style hotel offers suites and villas with kitchenettes. But it's the giant heated outdoor pool, ping-pong tables, putting green and life-sized checkers board that keeps kids amused. Ask about steep off-season discounts.

Avila La Fonda INN $$$
(☑ 805-595-1700; www.avilalafonda.com; 101 San Miguel St; d from $329; @ 🛜) Downtown, this small boutique hotel is a harmonious mix of Mexican and Spanish colonial styles, with hand-painted tiles, stained-glass windows, wrought iron and rich wood. Gather around the fireplace for nightly wine and hors d'oeuvres. Complimentary beach gear to borrow for guests.

🍴 Eating

At Port San Luis, Harford Pier is home to shops that sell fresh catch right off the boats.

Avila Beach Farmers Market MARKET $
(www.avilabeachpier.com; ☺ 4-8pm Fri early Apr-late Sep) 🥘 With local farmers, food booths and rockin' live music, this outdoor street party takes over downtown's oceanfront promenade weekly from spring to fall.

Olde Port Inn SEAFOOD $$$
(☑ 805-595-2515; www.oldeportinn.com; Harford Pier, off Avila Beach Dr; mains $14-46; ☺ 11:30am-9pm Sun-Thu, to 10pm Fri & Sat; 🅟) Clam chowder and cioppino are standouts at this seriously old-school seafood restaurant at the tip of Harford Pier. A few tables have see-through glass tops and floors, so lucky diners can peer down into the ocean. Reservations recommended.

ℹ Getting There & Around

Between 10am and 4pm on Saturdays and Sundays from late March until mid-October, a free **trolley** (SCT; ☑ 805-781-4472; www.slorta.org) loops from Pismo Beach around downtown Avila

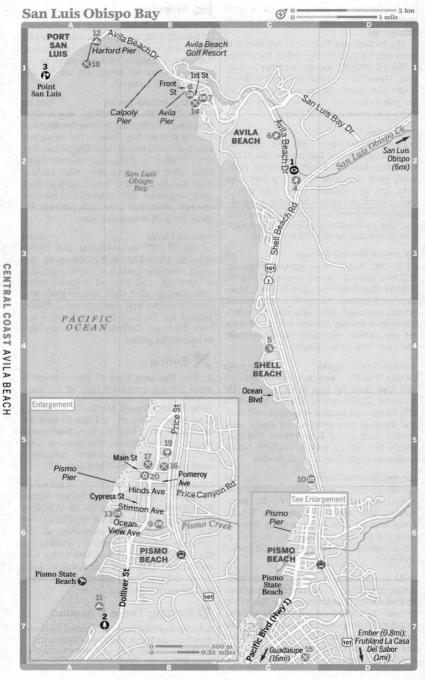

San Luis Obispo Bay

San Luis Obispo Bay

Beach to Port San Luis; from early June to early September, extended hours are 10am to 6pm Thursday through Sunday.

Pismo Beach

Backed by a wooden pier that stretches toward the setting sun, Pismo Beach is where James Dean once trysted with Pier Angeli. Fronted by an invitingly wide, sandy beach, this 1950s-retro town feels like somewhere straight out of *Rebel Without a Cause* or *American Graffiti*. If you're looking for a sand-and-surf respite from coastal road tripping, break your journey here.

◉ Sights & Activities

Pismo likes to call itself the 'Clam Capital of the World,' but these days the beach is pretty much clammed out. You'll have better luck catching something fishy off the pier, where you can rent rods. To rent a wetsuit, boogie board or surfboard, cruise nearby surf shops.

Pismo Beach Monarch Butterfly Grove   PARK
(www.monarchbutterfly.org; ☉ sunrise-sunset; ⊕) FREE From late October until February, more than 25,000 black-and-orange monarchs make their winter home here. Forming dense clusters in the tops of eucalyptus trees, they might easily be mistaken for leaves. Between 10am and 4pm during the roosting season, volunteers can tell you all about the insects' incredible journey, which outlasts any single generation of butterflies. Look for a gravel parking pull-out on the ocean side

of Pacific Blvd (Hwy 1), just south of Pismo State Beach's North Beach Campground.

✯ Festivals & Events

Wine, Waves & Beyond   CULTURE, FOOD
(www.winewavesandbeyond.com) Surfing competitions, surf-themed movies, wine tasting and a big bash on the beach with live music and food in late April or early May.

Classic at Pismo Beach   CULTURE
(www.theclassicatpismobeach.com) Show up in mid-June when hot rods and muscle cars roar off Hwy 1.

Clam Festival   FOOD
(www.pismochamber.com) In mid-October, celebrate the formerly abundant and still tasty mollusk with a clam dig, chowder cookoff, food vendors and live music.

⛌ Sleeping

Pismo Beach has dozens of motels, but rooms fill up quickly and prices skyrocket in summer, especially on weekends. Resorts and hotels roost on cliffs north of town via Price St and Shell Beach Rd, while motels cluster near the beach and along Hwy 101.

Pismo State Beach – North Beach Campground   CAMPGROUND $
(☏ reservations 800-444-7275; www.reserveamerica.com; 399 S Dolliver St; tent & RV sites $35; ⊛) About a mile south of downtown, off Hwy 1, the state park's North Beach Campground is shaded by eucalyptus trees and has more than 170 well-spaced, grassy sites with fire pits. The campground offers easy beach access, flush toilets and coin-op hot showers.

SCENIC DRIVE: HWY 1 SOUTH OF PISMO BEACH

What to See

Hwy 1 ends its fling with Hwy 101 at Pismo Beach, veering off toward the coast. Some truly wild, hidden beaches beckon along this back-door route to Santa Barbara.

Guadalupe Dunes

You almost expect to have to dodge tumbleweeds as you drive into the agricultural town of Guadalupe. Five miles further west at Rancho Guadalupe Dunes Preserve (www.countyofsb.org/parks; off Hwy 166; ⊘7am-sunset) FREE, enormous Egyptian-esque film sets from Cecil B DeMille's 1923 Hollywood epic The Ten Commandments still lie buried in the sand. Learn more about the 'Lost City of DeMille,' the ecology of North America's largest coastal dunes, and the mystical Dunites who lived here during the 1930s back at downtown's small Dunes Center (www.dunescenter.org; 1055 Guadalupe St; donation requested; ⊘10am-4pm Wed-Sun) museum.

Surf & Ocean Beaches

These wind-whipped beaches, one with a lonely Amtrak train whistlestop platform station, sidle up to Vandenberg Air Force Base. On the 10-mile drive west of Lompoc and Hwy 1 (take Hwy 246/W Ocean Ave), you'll pass odd-looking structures supporting spy and commerical satellite launches. Between March and September, Ocean Beach County Park (www.countyofsb.org/parks; Ocean Park Rd, off Hwy 246; ⊘8am-sunset, closed Mar-Sep) FREE is closed to the public and Surf Beach (www.vandenberg.af.mil/ploverupdate.asp; off Hwy 246; ⊘8am-6pm, subject to closure Mar-Oct) is also often closed to protect endangered snowy plovers during their nesting season.

Jalama Beach

Leaving Hwy 1 about 5 miles east of Lompoc, Jalama Rd follows 14 miles of twisting tarmac across ranch and farm lands before arriving at utterly isolated Jalama Beach County Park (📞recorded info 805-736-3616; www.countyofsb.org/parks; 9999 Jalama Rd, Lompoc; per car $10). As you soak up the views, munch on a grilled seafood or beef burger from the Jalama Beach Store (www.jalamabeachstore.net; dishes $4-12; ⊘usually 8am-7pm in summer). To stay overnight, reserve a cabin in advance or arrive by 8am to get on the waiting list for a campsite in the crazily popular campground (www.sbparks.org/reservations; tent/RV sites from $23/38, cabins $110-210) – look for the 'campground full' sign back near Hwy 1 to avoid a wasted trip.

The Route

Heading south of Pismo Beach, Hwy 1 slowly winds along, passing through Guadalupe and Lompoc, where you can detour to La Purísima Mission State Historic Park. Past Lompoc, Hwy 1 curves east to rejoin Hwy 101 south of Santa Barbara's wine country, near Gaviota.

Time & Mileage

With all of the detours described above, it's a 165-mile drive from Pismo Beach to Santa Barbara. The drive takes at least 3½ hours without any stops or traffic delays.

Beachwalker Inn & Suites   MOTEL **$$**
(📞805-773-2725; www.pismobeachwalkerinn.com; 490 Dolliver St; r from $120; 🕸🐾) Two blocks uphill from the beach, this renovated motel with a small outdoor heated pool lets you sleep peacefully atop deluxe mattresses. Suites have kitchenettes. Rates include morning coffee and pastries.

Pismo Lighthouse Suites   HOTEL **$$$**
(📞800-245-2411, 805-773-2411; www.pismolighthousesuites.com; 2411 Price St; ste incl breakfast from $275; @🕸🐾) With everything a vacationing family needs – from kitchenettes to a life-sized outdoor chessboard, a putting green, table tennis and badminton courts – this contemporary all-suites hotel right on the beach is hard to tear yourself away from. Ask about off-season discounts. Pet fee $30.

Sandcastle Inn
HOTEL $$$

(☎800-822-6606, 805-773-2422; www.sand-castleinn.com; 100 Stimson Ave; r incl breakfast $169-435; ☜☺) Many of these Eastern Seaboard–styled rooms are mere steps from the sand. The top-floor ocean-view patio is perfect for cracking open a bottle of wine at sunset or after dark by the fireplace. One-time pet fee $75.

Eating

Doc Burnstein's Ice Cream Lab
ICE CREAM $

(www.docburnsteins.com; 114 W Branch St, Arroyo Grande; snacks $3-8; ⏱11am-9:30pm Sun-Thu, to 10:30pm Fri & Sat; 🖫) In neighboring Arroyo Grande, Doc's scoops up fantastical flavors such as Merlot raspberry truffle and the 'Elvis Special' (peanut butter with banana swirls). Live ice-cream lab shows start at 7pm sharp on Wednesday. From Hwy 101 southbound, exit at Grand Ave.

Old West Cinnamon Rolls
BAKERY $

(www.oldwestcinnamon.com; 861 Dolliver St; snacks $2-5; ⏱6:30am-5:30pm) The name says it all at this gobsmacking bakery by the beach.

Bunn Thai Bistro
THAI $$

(☎805-473-2824; www.bunnthaibistro.com; 968 W Grand Ave, Grover Beach; mains $10-18; ⏱11am-3pm & 4-9pm Thu-Tue; 🖉) In the next-door town of Grover Beach, this nouveau Thai restaurant is splashed with tropical colors. Making side trips into Asian fusion, it caters to omnivores, vegans, vegetarians and gluten-free folks. Lunch specials are a steal. Follow Hwy 1 south from Pismo Beach, turning left onto Grand Ave.

Frutiland La Casa Del Sabor
MEXICAN $$

(803 E Grand Ave, Arroyo Grande; mains $7-13; ⏱9:30am-7pm Mon & Wed, to 3:30pm Thu, to 8pm Fri & Sat, 10am-6pm Sun; 🖫) Oversized, overstuffed Mexican *tortas* (sandwiches) will feed two, and there are two dozen varieties to choose from. Or order a platter of blue-corn-tortilla fish tacos with a mango or papaya *agua fresca* (fruit drink). To find this taco shack in Arroyo Grande, exit Hwy 101 southbound at Halcyon Rd.

★Ember
CALIFORNIAN $$$

(☎805-474-7700; 1200 E Grand Ave, Arroyo Grande; shared dishes $8-20, mains $16-30; ⏱4-9pm Wed-Thu & Sun, to 10pm Fri & Sat; 🖫) 🖉 Chef Brian Collins, who once cooked at Alice Waters' revered Chez Panisse, has returned to his roots in SLO County. Out of this heart-warming restaurant's wood-burning oven come savory flatbreads, artfully charred squid and hearty red-wine-smoked short ribs. No reservations, so show up at 4pm or after 7:30pm, or be prepared for a very long wait for a table.

Sociable seating in the bar, where you can order off the full menu, is first-come, first-served. The restaurant is west of Hwy 101 (southbound exit Halcyon Rd) in Arroyo Grande.

★Cracked Crab
SEAFOOD $$$

(☎805-773-2722; www.crackedcrab.com; 751 Price St; mains $12-45; ⏱11am-9pm Sun-Thu, to 10pm Fri & Sat; 🖫) Fresh seafood and regional wines are the staples at this super-casual, family-owned grill. When the famous bucket o'seafood, full of flying bits of fish, Cajun sausage, red potatoes and cob corn, gets dumped on your butcher-paper-covered table, make sure you're wearing one of those silly-looking plastic bibs. No reservations, but the wait is worth it.

Drinking & Entertainment

Taste of the Valleys
WINE BAR

(www.pismowineshop.com; 911 Price St; ⏱noon-9pm Mon-Thu, to 10pm Fri & Sat, to 8pm Sun) Inside a wine shop stacked floor to ceiling with hand-picked vintages from around California and beyond, ask for a taste of anything they've got open, or sample from an astounding list of 500 wines poured by the glass.

Pismo Bowl
BOWLING ALLEY

(www.pismobeachbowl.com; 277 Pomeroy Ave; game per person $4, shoe rental $3; ⏱noon-10pm Sun-Thu, to midnight Fri & Sat; 🖫) Epitomizing Pismo Beach's retro vibe, this old-fashioned bowling alley is just a short walk uphill from the pier. Blacklight 'cosmic' and karaoke bowling rule Friday and Saturday nights.

Information

Pismo Beach Visitors Information Center
(☎800-443-7778, 805-773-4382; www.classiccalifornia.com; 581 Dolliver St; ⏱9am-5pm Mon-Fri, 11am-4pm Sat) Free maps and brochures. Smaller kiosk on the pier is open from 11am to 4pm on Sunday.

Getting There & Around

Hourly from Monday to Friday, and a few times daily on weekends, **RTA** (☎805-541-2228; www.slorta.org) bus 10 links San Luis Obispo with Pismo's Premium Outlets mall ($2, 30 minutes), a mile from the beach, before continuing to downtown Arroyo Grande ($1.50, 15 minutes).

Sacramento & Central Valley

Why Go?

The Central Valley is a vast swath of golden fields, rolling hills and scenic waterways that span 400 miles from Chico to Bakersfield. Its rich soil feeds the nation. Half the produce in the US — and nearly every carrot, almond and asparagus spear — was grown here.

In spring, the rivers swell and the orchards bloom. In summer, vast vineyards thrive under the relentless sunshine, and produce comes to market still warm from the fields. By fall and winter, the skies mellow and migratory ducks and geese fly in for a visit. The birds stay longer than most travelers, who tend to zip through on their way to more popular parts, but the shady streets and stately mansions of the region's Victorian-era towns and the uniquely scenic communities dotting the Sacramento Delta and Hwy 99, warrant more than a glimpse through the window.

Best Places to Eat

➜ Noriega's (p510)
➜ Kitchen Restaurant (p490)
➜ Peeve's Public House & Local Market (p506)
➜ Diane's Village Bakery & Cafe (p510)

Best Places to Stay

➜ Padre Hotel (p509)
➜ Citizen Hotel (p489)
➜ Lake Oroville State Recreation Area (p496)

When to Go
Sacramento

Feb–Mar Stop for pie and hot cider in the valley's technicolor Blossom Trail orchards.

Nov–Feb Catch the spectacular return of millions of migratory waterfowl in Sacramento.

May–Sep The peak of harvest time brings farmers markets and food festivals aplenty.

Sacramento & Central Valley Highlights

1 Tubing the cool rivers of **Chico** (p496).

2 Uncorking the emerging wine scene in **Lodi** (p501).

3 Tasting the Valley's produce in Sacramento's **farmers markets** (p488).

4 Discovering the legacy of people who built the Chinese Temple and lake at **Oroville** (p494).

5 Grooving in a **Bakersfield** (p508) honkytonk to the sounds of musical icons.

6 Bumping down world-class rapids on **Kern River** (p511).

7 Circling the maypole during Kingsburg's **Swedish festival** (p510).

8 Exploring the levees and farms of the **Sacramento River Delta** (p491).

SACRAMENTO VALLEY

The labyrinth of waterways that makes up the Sacramento–San Joaquin River Delta feeds the San Francisco Bay and divides the Central Valley in half, with the Sacramento Valley in the north and the San Joaquin Valley in the south.

The Sacramento River, California's largest, rushes out of the northern mountains from Shasta Lake before hitting the Sacramento Valley basin above Red Bluff. It then snakes south across grassy plains and orchards before lazily skirting the state capital, fanning across the Delta and draining into the San Francisco Bay. The valley is at its most beautiful in the bloom of spring. The shaded gardens and stately homes of Sacramento, the state capital, and its progressive neighbor, the college town of Davis, offer friendly respites from the sun in the summer.

Sacramento

Sacramento is a city of contrasts. It's a former cow town where state legislators' SUVs go bumper-to-bumper with farmers' muddy, half-ton pickups at rush hour. It has sprawling suburbs, but also new lofts and upscale boutiques squeezed between aging mid-century storefronts.

The people of 'Sac' are a resourceful lot that have fostered small but thriving food, art and nightlife scenes. They rightfully crow about Second Saturday, the monthly Midtown gallery hop that is the symbol of the city's cultural awakening. Their ubiquitous farmers markets, farm-to-fork fare and craft beers are another point of pride.

History

The history of the state is contained in this city. Paleo-era peoples fished the rivers and thrived before colonists and the scourge of smallpox arrived in the 1800s. Control changed from Spanish to Mexican to finally American hands, when in 1847, a Swiss named John Sutter came seeking fortune. Recognizing the strategic importance of controlling the major rivers, Sutter built an outpost at a confluence and raised a private militia. Soon the outpost became a safe haven for traders, and Sutter expanded his business operations in all directions.

It was at his lumber mill near Coloma that something glittered in the river in 1848. Eureka! Gold rushers stampeded to the trading post, which was eventually christened the newly sprung town 'Sacramento.' Though plagued by fires and relentless flooding, the riverfront settlement prospered and became the state capital in 1850.

The Transcontinental Railroad was soon after conceived in Sacramento by the 'Big Four' – Leland Stanford, Mark Hopkins, Collis P Huntington and Charles Crocker. A fresco of them hangs in Sac's Amtrak station. They founded Central Pacific Railroad, which began construction here in 1863, and connected to the Union Pacific in Promontory, Utah, in 1869.

Sights

Sacramento is roughly halfway between San Francisco and Lake Tahoe. The city is boxed in by four main highways: Hwy 99, which is the best route through the Central Valley, and I-5, which runs along its west side; I-80 skirts downtown on the city's northern edge, heading west to the Bay Area and east to Reno; and Hwy 50 runs along downtown's southern edge (where it's also called Business Route 80) before heading east to Tahoe.

In the middle is the Grid, where numbered streets run north–south and lettered streets run east–west (Capitol Ave replaces M). One-way J St is a main drag east from Downtown to Midtown.

The Grid

It's easy finding sights along the Grid, but everything is spread out.

DON'T MISS

CALIFORNIA STATE FAIR

For two weeks in late July, the **California State Fair** (☏916-263-3247; www.bigfun.org; 1600 Exposition Blvd; adult/child $12/8) fills the Cal Expo, east of I-80 on the north side of the American River, with a small city of cows and carnival rides. It's likely the only place on earth where you can plant a redwood tree, watch a pig give birth, ride a roller coaster, catch some barrel racing and taste exquisite Napa vintages within one (exhausting) afternoon. Make time to see some of the auctions ($500 for a dozen eggs!) and the interactive ag-exhibits run by the University of California Davis. Hotels near Cal Expo run regular shuttles to the event.

Downtown Sacramento

★ **California Museum** MUSEUM
(www.californiamuseum.org; 1020 O St; adult/child
$9/6.50; ⏰10am-5pm Mon-Sat, from noon Sun)
This modern museum is home to the California Hall Of Fame and so the only place
to simultaneously encounter César Chávez,
Mark Zuckerberg and Amelia Earhart. The
California Indians exhibit is a highlight,
with artifacts and oral histories of more than
100 distinct tribes.

★ **California State Capitol** HISTORIC BUILDING
(capitolmuseum.ca.gov; 1315 10th St; ⏰8am-5pm
Mon-Fri, from 9am Sat & Sun) **FREE** The gleaming dome of the California State Capitol is
Sacramento's most recognizable structure. A
painting of the Terminator in a suit hangs in
the west wing with the other governors' portraits. Some will find Capitol Park, the 40
acres of gardens and memorials surrounding the building, more interesting than
what's inside. Tours run hourly until 4pm.

**Sutter's Fort State
Historic Park** HISTORIC SITE
(www.suttersfort.org; 2701 L St; adult/child $5/3;
⏰10am-5pm) Originally built by John Sutter,
this park was once the only trace of white
settlement for hundreds of miles. Reserve a
couple hours to stroll within its walls, where
furniture, medical equipment and a blacksmith shop are straight out of the 1850s.

State Indian Museum MUSEUM
(www.parks.ca.gov; 2618 K St; adult/child $3/2;
⏰10am-5pm) It's with some irony that the Indian Museum sits in the shadow of Sutter's
Fort. The excellent exhibits and tribal handicrafts on display are traces of cultures nearly
stamped out by the fervor Sutter ignited.

◉ Old Sacramento

This historic river port by Downtown remains the city's stalwart tourist draw. The
pervasive aroma of salt-water taffy and

pean masters. The contemporary collection is most enthusiastically presented.

California State Railroad Museum MUSEUM
(www.csrmf.org; 125 I St; adult/child $10/5, incl train ride $20/10; ⊙10am-5pm; ⊕) At Old Sac's north end is this impressive collection of railcars and locomotives from miniature to true scale. While the candy-coated recounting of the struggles of those who laid the track is unsettling, the fully outfitted Pullman sleeper and vintage diner cars will thrill rail fans. Board a restored passenger train (adult/child $10/5) from the Sacramento Southern Railroad ticket office, across the plaza on Front St, for a 40-minute jaunt along the river. Train rides run hourly on weekends from April to September.

Sacramento History Museum MUSEUM
(www.historicoldsac.org/museum; 101 I St; adult/child $6/4, Underground Tour Mar-Dec $15/10; ⊙10am-5pm; ⊕) Exhibits stories and artifacts of some of Sacramento's most fascinating citizens, though much of the information is focused on the Gold Rush. Get tickets here for the **Underground Tour**, a 45-minute look at what's under Old Sac's streets.

◉ Tower District

South of Midtown, at the corner of Broadway and 16th St, the Tower District is dominated by Tower Theatre (p491), a beautiful 1938 art-deco movie palace easy to spot on the way into town. From the theater, head east on Broadway to a stretch of the city's most eclectic and affordable ethnic eateries. The **Tower Records** chain started here in 1960 and closed in 2006, a digital music casualty, but the original neon sign survives.

🏃 Activities

The **American River Parkway** (north bank of American River), a 4600-acre river system, is surely Sacramento's most appealing natural feature. It's one of the most extensive riparian habitats in the continental US, scored by a network of trails and picnic areas. It's accessible from Old Sac by taking Front St north until it becomes Jiboom St and crosses the river, or by the Jiboom St exit off I-5/Hwy 99. The lovely, paved **Jedediah Smith Memorial Trail** (American River Bike Trail), stretches over 30 miles from Old Sac to Folsom Reservoir. Rent wheels from **City Bicycle Works** (www.citybicycleworks.com; 2419 K

somewhat garish restoration give Old Sac the vibe of a second-rate Frontierland, but it's good for a stroll on summer evenings, when boomers on Harleys rumble through the brick streets, and tourists and natty legislative aides stroll the promenade. California's largest concentration of buildings on the National Register of Historic Places is here. Most now peddle Gold Rush trinkets and fudge. There are a few quality attractions, but the restaurant scene is a bust – head to Midtown.

Crocker Art Museum MUSEUM
(https://crockerartmuseum.org; 216 O St; adult/child $10/5; ⊙10am-5pm Tue, Wed & Fri-Sun, to 9pm Thu) Housed in the Crocker family's ornate Victorian mansion (and sprawling additions), this museum is stunning as much for its striking architecture (old and new) as its collections. There are some very fine works by both California painters and Euro-

Downtown Sacramento

St; per hr/day from $5/20; ⊙10am-7pm Mon-Fri, to 6pm Sat, 11am-5pm Sun).

✷ Festivals & Events

Sacramento Central Farmers Market   MARKET
(www.california-grown.com; cnr 8th & W St, under Hwy 80 overpass; ⊙8am-noon Sun; ⊛) Sacramento has excellent farmers markets, with food trucks and often live music, year-round, and every day in the summer and fall.

Second Saturday   CULTURE
(www.2ndsaturdaysacramento.com) Every second Saturday the galleries and shops in Midtown draw people of all ages to the streets, with open-air music and cultural events.

Sacramento Music Festival & Jubilee   MUSIC
(www.sacmusicfest.com) Forty years old and running strong, this festival of jazz, rockabilly, Latin, swing, blues, zydeco, and anything with a beat takes over Memorial Day weekend (late May).

Gold Rush Days   CULTURE
(www.sacramentogoldrushdays.com; ⊛) Horse races, period costumes, music and kids' events make Old Sacramento particularly festive on Labor Day weekend (early September).

⊨ Sleeping

The capital is a magnet for business travelers, so Sacramento doesn't lack in hotels. Many have good deals during legislative recesses. Unless you're in town for something at Cal Expo, stay Downtown or Midtown, where there's plenty to do within walking distance. If you're into kitschy motor lodges from the 1950s, cross the river into West Sac for the last-standing members of **Motel Row** on Rte 40.

HI Sacramento Hostel   HOSTEL $
(☏916-443-1691; http://norcalhostels.org/sac; 925 H St; dm $29-33, r with shared/private bath from $58/99; ⊙check-in 2-10pm; @⊛) In a grand Victorian mansion, this hostel offers impressive trimmings at rock-bottom prices. It's within walking distance of the capitol, Old Sac and the train station and has a piano in the parlor and large dining room. It attracts an international crowd often open to sharing a ride to San Francisco or Lake Tahoe.

Folsom Lake State Recreation Area   CAMPGROUND $
(☏916-988-0205; www.parks.ca.gov; 7806 Folsom-Auburn Rd; tent & RV sites without/with hookups $33/58; ⊙office 6am-9pm summer, 7am-6pm winter) Sacramento is a good place for a final gear check before heading into the Sierras. This campground is not ideal – the lake

can be overrun by powerboats – but the only camping is a KOA west of town on I-80.

Delta King B&B $$
(☑800-825-5464, 916-444-5464; www.deltaking.com; 1000 Front St; d incl breakfast from $139; ✽🛜) It's a treat to sleep aboard the *Delta King*, a 1927 paddlewheeler docked in Old Sac that lights up like a Christmas tree at night.

★**Citizen Hotel** BOUTIQUE HOTEL $$$
(☑916-492-4460; www.jdvhotels.com; 926 J St; r/ste $169/269; ✽@🛜✽) With an elegant, ultra-hip upgrade by the Joie de Vivre group, the long-vacant Citizen has suddenly become one of the coolest stays in these parts. Rooms are sleek, with luxe linen and bold-patterned decor. The front desk has loaner bikes. There's an upscale farm-to-fork restaurant on the ground floor (mains from $28).

Amber House B&B $$$
(☑800-755-6526, 916-444-8085; www.amberhouse.com; 1315 22nd St; r $199-279; ✽@🛜) This Dutch Colonial home in Midtown has been transformed into an elegant bed and breakfast, where rooms have spa baths and fireplaces. The Mozart and Vivaldi rooms have private balconies perfect for enjoying breakfast.

✖ Eating

Skip the overpriced fare in Old Sacramento or by the capitol and head Midtown or to the Tower District. A cruise up J St or Broadway passes a number of hip, affordable restaurants where tables spill onto the sidewalks in the summer. Many source farm-fresh ingredients, even when they don't advertise.

Shoki II Ramen House JAPANESE $
(☑916-441-0011; 1201 R St; meals $8-16; ☉11am-10pm Mon-Fri, from noon Sat, 11am-8pm Sun) In their tiny original location on 24th St, diners cram in cheek-to-jowl, but this newer Midtown location offers elbow room and the same amazing housemade noodles. The fresh spinach and shiitake adorning your bowl are, of course, organic and local.

Gunther's ICE CREAM $
(www.gunthersicecream.com; 2801 Franklin Blvd; sundaes $4; ☉10am-10pm) A popular vintage soda fountain that makes its own ice cream.

Plum Cafe VEGAN $
(www.plumcafebakery.com; 2315 K St; dishes $8-12; ☉8am-8pm Mon-Thu, to 9pm Fri & Sat, 10am-8pm Sun; ✏) ❂ This brunch hotspot and bakery serves vegan and gluten-free fare in a restored Victorian with a tented back garden. Savory options are straightforward. The surprising desserts, such as the Entertainer (styled after a Hostess Cupcake) will satisfy sugar fiends.

La Bonne Soupe Cafe DELI $
(☑916-492-9506; 920 8th St; items $5-8; ☉11am-3pm Mon-Wed, to 8pm Thu & Fri) Divine soup and sandwiches assembled with such care that the line of downtown lunchers snakes out the door. If you're in a hurry, skip it. This humble lunch counter is focused on quality that predates drive-through haste.

DON'T MISS

THE GREAT MIGRATION

The Sacramento Valley serves as a rest stop for countless migrating species that arrive in such great numbers, they are a spectacle even without binoculars.

October to February Four million waterbirds winter in the warm tules (marshes) on their way along the Great Pacific Flyway. Tours at Sacramento National Wildlife Refuge (p495).

October to January Endangered chinook and steelhead fight their way upstream to spawn. Spot them along the American River Parkway (p487) and the **Nimbus Fish Hatchery** (☑916-358-2884; www.dfg.ca.gov; 2001 Nimbus Rd, Gold River; ☉8am-3pm Mon-Fri, from 9am Sat-Sun) FREE.

March to June Cabbage white, painted lady, and Western tiger swallowtail butterflies come to party. Their offspring will gorge and then grow wings to fly north. Sacramento National Wildlife Refuge (p495) has details.

June to August Hundreds of thousands of Mexican free-tailed bats shelter under the Yolo Causeway. Tours (www.yolobasin.org) catch them alighting at twilight.

Tank House BBQ and Bar
BARBECUE $$

(tankhousebbq.com; 1925 J St; pork butt sando $10; ⏱11:30am-2am Mon-Fri, from 11am Sat & Sun) The overwhelming hipster vibe – from the greasy 'dos to canned beer (six for $10) – may be hard to swallow, but the legit BBQ is not. Sidle up to the bar to order and start a tab. The smoker goes all day, so if you sit outside, position upwind.

Pizza Rock
PIZZERIA $$

(www.pizzarocksacramento.com; 1020 K St; pizzas $14-30; ⏱11am-10pm Sun-Thu, to 3am Fri & Sat; 🛜) An anchor of the K St Mall area, this loud, enormous pizza joint has a great Margherita, a rock 'n' roll theme and a well-tattooed staff.

Andy Nguyen's
VIETNAMESE, VEGETARIAN $$

(www.andynguyenvegetarian.com; 2007 Broadway; meals $9-16; ⏱11:30am-9pm Sun & Mon, to 9:30pm Tue-Thu, to 10pm Fri & Sat; 🖊) 🖉 Great meat-free fare is served at this tranquil Buddhist diner. Try the steaming claypots and artful fake meat dishes (the 'chicken' leg has a little wooden bone).

Waterboy
CALIFORNIAN $$

(☎916-498-9891; www.waterboyrestaurant.com; 2000 Capitol Ave; mains $13-29; ⏱11:30am-2:30pm Mon-Fri, 5-9:30pm Sun-Thu, to 10:30pm Fri & Sat) The wicker and palm in the windowed dining room offer a preview of the chef's style – a French-Italian spin on Central Valley ingredients. The ambitious menu soars from the start. The day's catch is always stellar.

Lucca
ITALIAN $$

(luccarestaurant.com; 1615 J St; meals $13-20; ⏱11:30am-10pm Mon-Thu, to 11pm Fri, noon-11pm Sat, 4-9pm Sun) Within a stroll of the convention center is this quality Italian eatery. Parmesan frites with truffle aioli are the way to start.

★Kitchen Restaurant
CALIFORNIAN $$$

(www.thekitchenrestaurant.com; No 101, 2225 Hurley Way; prix-fixe dinner $125; ⏱5-10pm Wed-Sun) Husband-and-wife team Randall Selland and Nancy Zimmer's cozy dining room in the northeast 'burbs is the pinnacle of Sacramento's food experience. Their demonstration dinners focus on – what else? – local, seasonal, organic food, immaculately prepared before your eyes. Reservations are essential.

Mulvaney's B&L
MODERN AMERICAN $$$

(☎916-441-6022; mulvaneysbl.com; 1215 19th St; mains $32-40; ⏱11:30am-2:30pm Tue-Fri, 5-10pm Tue-Sun) 🖉 With an obsessive commitment to seasonality, the menu at this swank, converted firehouse includes delicate pastas and grilled meats that change every day.

🍷 Drinking & Nightlife

Sacramento has a split personality when it comes to drinking – upscale joints where mustachioed bartenders shake cocktails, and sans-bullshit dive bars with vintage neons and menus that begin and end with a-shot-ana-beer. Both options dot the Grid.

Temple Coffee Roasters
COFFEE SHOP

(www.templecoffee.com; 1010 9th St; ⏱6am-11pm; 🛜) 🖉 Hip young patrons nurse organic free-trade coffee and chai morning to night in this steel and concrete space.

Mercantile Saloon
GAY

(☎916-447-0792; 1928 L St; ⏱10am-2am) Down an alley in a yellow Victorian, stiff drinks go for less than $4. Personal space is nil in this rowdy dive. Start here before touring the four-block radius of gay bars and clubs that locals call 'Lavender Heights.'

Pour House
PUB

(www.pourhousesacramento.com; 1910 Q St; ⏱11am-11pm Tue-Wed, to 12:30am Thu, to 1am Fri, 10am-1:30am Sat, 9am-10pm Sun) If the walls shake in this upscale watering hole, it's probably a train – not the whiskey or moonshine you've downed. But if your booth starts feeling like a soft bed, it's definitely the beer you've been pulling from the tap, so conveniently built into your table.

Rubicon Brewing Company
BREWERY

(www.rubiconbrewing.com; 2004 Capitol Ave; ⏱11am-11:30pm Mon-Thu, to 12:30am Fri & Sat, to 10pm Sun) These people take their hops *seriously*. Their heady selection is brewed on-site. Monkey Knife Fight Pale Ale is ideal for washing back platters of hot wings ($12.49 per dozen).

Old Tavern Bar & Grill
PUB

(1510 20th St; ⏱6pm-2am) This friendly dive stands out from Sac's many workaday joints with its huge beer selection, tall pours and '80s-loaded jukebox.

58 Degrees and Holding Co
WINE BAR

(www.58degrees.com; 1217 18th St; ⏱11am-10pm Mon, Wed & Thu, to 11pm Fri & Sat, to 9pm Sun) A wide selection of California and European reds and a refined bistro menu make this a favorite for young professionals on the prowl.

☆ Entertainment

Pick up a copy of the free weekly *Sacramento News & Review* (www.newsandreview.com) for a list of current happenings around town.

Harlow's   LIVE MUSIC
(www.harlows.com; 2708 J St) Quality jazz, R&B and the occasional salsa or indie act in a classy joint...if you don't go crazy with the potent martinis.

Old Ironsides   LIVE MUSIC
(www.theoldironsides.com; 1901 10th St; cover $5-10; ⊙8am-2am Tue-Fri & Sun, from 6pm Sat) The tiny back room of this cool, somewhat crusty, venue hosts some of the best indie bands that come through town.

California Musical Theatre   PERFORMING ARTS
(www.californiamusicaltheatre.com; 1419 H St) This top-notch company holds court at the Community Center Theater and the Wells Fargo Pavilion in town.

Sacramento River Cats   SPORTS
(www.milb.com; Raley Field, 400 Ballpark Dr; tickets $8-60; ⊙Apr-Sep) Sacramento's minor-league baseball team plays across the river at Raley Field, with views of the art-deco Tower Bridge.

Tower Theatre   CINEMA
(☑916-442-4700; www.ReadingCinemasUS.com; 2508 Landpark Dr) Classic, foreign and indie films screen at this historic movie house with a digital upgrade.

Crest Theatre   CINEMA
(www.thecrest.com; 1013 K St) A classic old movie house that's been restored to its 1949 splendor. Hosts indie and foreign films and the annual Trash Film Orgy (trashfilmorgy.com) on Saturdays in July and August.

ⓘ Information

Convention & Visitors Bureau (www.visitsacramento.com; 1608 I St; ⊙8am-5pm Mon-Fri) Local information, including event and bus schedules. The helpful folks at the Visitor Center (☑916.442.7644; www.visitsacramento.com; 1002 2nd St; ⊙10am-5pm) in Old Sacramento can also point you in the right direction.

ⓘ Getting There & Away

Amtrak Station (☑877-974-3322; www.capitolcorridor.org; 401 I St at 5th St) This station between downtown and Old Sac is the major hub for connecting trains to all points east and west, as well as regional bus lines serving the Central Valley. One way to San Francisco is very convenient ($32, two hours).

Greyhound (www.greyhound.com; 420 Richards Blvd) The station is 2 miles north of Downtown off I-5 or N 7th St. Services run to Colfax in Gold Country ($30, 1½ hours), San Francisco ($24, two hours), Bakersfield ($51, 6½ hours), Los Angeles ($86, nine hours) and other major towns.

Sacramento International Airport (SMF; www.sacairports.org; 6900 Airport Blvd) Twelve miles north of Downtown off I-5; SMF is served by major US airlines and has flights to Mexico.

ⓘ Getting Around

The regional **Yolobus** (☑530-666-2877; www.yolobus.com) route 42B costs $2 and runs hourly between the airport and Downtown and also goes to West Sacramento, Woodland and Davis. Local **Sacramento Regional Transit** (RT; www.sacrt.com; fare/day pass $2.50/6) buses run around town and RT also runs a trolley between Old Sacramento and Downtown, as well as Sacramento's light-rail system, which is best for commuting from outlying communities. Sacramento is also a fantastic city to cruise around by bike, rent them from City Bicycle Works (p487).

Sacramento–San Joaquin River Delta

The Sacramento Delta is a sprawling web of waterways and one-stoplight towns plucked out of the 1930s. On weekends, locals gun powerboats on glassy waterways and cruise the winding levy roads. This wetland area encompasses a huge swath of the state – from the San Francisco Bay to Sacramento, and all the way south to Stockton. Here the Sacramento and San Joaquin Rivers converge to drain into the San Francisco Bay. If you have the time to smell the grassy Delta breezes on the slow route between San Francisco and Sacramento, travel the iron bridges of winding Hwy 160, which lazily makes its way past rice fields, vast orchards, sandy swimming banks and little towns with long histories.

The town of Locke is the most fascinating, built by the Chinese who also built the

ⓘ GETTING AROUND THE CENTRAL VALLEY

Although the Central Valley's main artery is connected by bus and Amtrak, much of the region is best traveled by car. The main routes through are Hwy 99 and I-5. I-80 meets Hwy 99 in Sacramento, and I-5 meets Hwy 99 south of Bakersfield. Amtrak (p491) also intersects the state with two lines – the *San Joaquin* route through the Central Valley and the *Pacific Surfliner* between the Central Coast and San Diego. The *San Joaquin* service stops in just about every tourist destination. Greyhound (p491) stops in most Central Valley towns and cities.

The Central Valley has lots of long, straight byways for those making the trip on bikes, and the American River Parkway (p487) is a veritable human-powered expressway for commuters between Downtown Sacramento and Auburn.

Still, the transportation talk in the Central Valley these days is all about the high-speed rail. California voters gave the green light to build a network of super-fast trains connecting San Francisco and Los Angeles at speeds of up to 220 miles per hour (making the trip just over 2½ hours) by 2029.

The total price tag is a whopping $68 billion, and there are legal hurdles yet, but if everything clears, the first stage will be very humble – a 29-mile track connecting two tiny farm towns on either side of Fresno by 2017.

levees that ended perpetual flooding and allowed agriculture to flourish here. After a malicious fire wiped out the settlement in 1912, a group approached land baron George Locke for a leasehold (California barred Chinese from owning property). Locke became the only freestanding town built and managed by Chinese in the US; its unincorporated status kept it free of pesky lawmen, allowing for gambling houses and bootleg gin joints. Tucked below the highway and the levee, Locke's main street still has a few residents though the feel is of a ghost town, with weather-beaten buildings protected on the National Register of Historic Places that take an afternoon to explore.

The colorful Dai Loy Museum (www.locketown.com/museum.htm; 5 Main St, Locke; admission $1.25; ⊙noon-4pm Fri-Sun; 🚹), an old gambling hall filled with photos and relics of gaming operations, including *pai gow* tables and an antique safe, is a popular stop. Nearby is Al the Wop's (☑916-776-1800; 13943 Main St, Locke; mains $8-15; ⊙11am-9pm), a saloon that's been pouring since 1915 and serves peanut-butter-slathered Texas toast. Below are creaking floorboards; above, the ceiling's covered in crusty dollar bills and more than one pair of erstwhile undies. Check in at the visitors center (☑916-776-1661; www.locketown.com; 13920 Main St, Walnut Grove; tours adult/student $5/3; ⊙visitors center noon-4pm Tue & Fri, 11am-3pm Sat-Sun) for maps and tours.

Hwy 160 also passes through Isleton, so-called Crawdad Town USA, whose main street has more shops, restaurants, bars and buildings hinting at the region's Chinese heritage. Isleton's Cajun Festival, at the end of June, draws folks from across the state, but you can get very lively crawdads year-round at Bob's Bait Shop (www.isletonjoes.com; 212 Second St, Isleton; mains $5-17; ⊙8am-9pm).

Further west on Hwy 160 you'll see signs for the Delta Loop, a drive that passes boater bars and marinas where you can rent something to take on the water. At the end is the Brannan Island State Recreation Area (☑916-777-6671; www.parks.ca.gov; 17645 California 160; campsites $28; 🅿🛜), a tidy facility with boat-in, drive-in and walk-in campsites and picnic facilities.

In the 1930s the Bureau of Reclamation issued an aggressive water-redirection program – the Central Valley and California State Water Projects – that dammed California's major rivers and directed 75% of their supply through the Central Valley for agriculture and Southern California. The siphoning affected the Delta, its wetlands and estuaries, and kicked off neverending debate. Learn about the area's unique legacy by bus or on a self-guided tour with Delta Heartbeat Tours (☑916-776-4010; http://deltaheartbeattours.com; Deckhands Marina, 14090 Hwy 160, Walnut Grove), which also has leads on boat rides. If you have a car, taste the fruits of the delta on the Delta Grown Farm Trail (☑916-775-1166; http://sacriverdeltagrown.org) FREE.

Davis

Davis, home to a University of California school with the nation's leading viticulture department, is a sunny town where bikes outnumber cars two-to-one (it has more bikes per capita than any other American city). With students comprising about half of the population, it's a progressive outpost amid the conservative towns of Sacramento Valley that comes alive during the school year.

Dodging the bikes on a walk through downtown Davis you will pass a number of cute small businesses (city council has forbidden any store over 50,000 sq ft – sorry, Wal-Mart).

I-80 skirts the south edge of town, and you can reach downtown via the Richards Blvd exit. University of California, Davis (UCD) is southwest of downtown, bordered by A St, 1st St and Russell Blvd.

Sights & Activities

Everyone rides here in 'Bike City USA,' probably because the only hill around is the bridge that crosses over the freeway. Lake Berryessa, 30 miles west, is a favorite destination.

UC Davis Arboretum PARK
(http://arboretum.ucdavis.edu; 1 Shields Ave) FREE Stroll through the peaceful 'Arb' along the paved 3.5-mile loop. It follows one of the state's oldest reservoirs, dug in the 1860s.

Pence Gallery GALLERY
(www.pencegallery.org; 212 D St; ⊙11:30am-5pm Tue-Sun) This community-centric gallery exhibits contemporary California art and hosts classes, lectures and art films. It hosts a free reception 7pm to 9pm on the second Friday of each month.

Davis Transmedia Art Walk WALKING TOUR
(http://davisartwalk.com) FREE This two-hour walking tour winds through Davis' public art collection, mostly clustered on D and G Sts. Some works interact with your phone – you can hear an audio tour or record your own impressions for others after you. Maps at the Yolo County Visitors Bureau (p494) or John Natsoulas Center for the Arts (www.natsoulas.com; 521 1st St; ⊙11am-5pm Wed & Thu, to 10pm Fri, noon-5pm Sat & Sun) FREE.

Sleeping

As with most university towns, Davis' hotel rates are stable until graduation or special campus events, when they skyrocket and sell out fast. Worse, the trains that roll though the middle of town will infuriate a light sleeper. For a utilitarian (if bland) stay, look for chains along the highway.

University Park Inn & Suites HOTEL $$
(530-756-0910; www.universityparkinn.com; 1111 Richards Blvd; r $90-140; P❀@❈❂) Right off the highway and a short walk from campus and downtown, this independently operated hotel is not the Ritz but is clean, has spacious suites, and serves waffles for breakfast.

Aggie Inn HOTEL $$
(530-756-0352; www.aggieinn.com; 245 1st St; r from $139; ❈❂) Across from UCD's east entrance, the Aggie is neat, modern and unassuming. Cottages are not much more than regular rooms and have kitchenettes and spa baths.

Eating & Drinking

College students love to eat and drink cheap, and downtown has no short supply of lively ethnic eateries gunning for the student dollar. The Davis farmers market (www.davisfarmersmarket.org; cnr 4th & C Sts; ⊙8am-1pm Sat year-round, 2-6pm Wed winter) features food vendors, street performers and live bands. There are a number of good options for self-catering including the Co-op (http://davisfood.coop; 620 G St; ⊙7am-10pm).

Sam's Mediterranean Cuisine MIDDLE EASTERN $
(530-758-2855; 247 3rd St; shawarma $6.39; ⊙11am-8pm Mon-Fri, from noon Sat) Delicious and cheap shawarma and falafel made this little house with a green awning a university institution.

Woodstock's PIZZERIA $
(www.woodstocksdavis.com; 219 G St; slice $2.50, pizzas $7-25; ⊙11am-1am Mon-Wed, to 2am Thu-Sat, 9:30-midnight Sun; ✍) Woodstock's has Davis' most popular pizza, which is also sold by the slice for lunch. Besides the usual, the toppings get a touch more sophisticated with a variety of gourmet and veggie options all on a chewy wheat crust.

Delta of Venus Cafe & Pub CAFE $
(www.deltaofvenus.org; 122b St; mains $7-11; ⊙7:30am-10pm Mon-Wed, to midnight Thu & Fri, to 2am Sat & Sun; ✍) This converted Arts and Crafts bungalow has a very social, shaded front patio. The breakfast items, salads, soups and sandwiches include vegetarian

and vegan options. Dinner time you can order jerk-seasoned Caribbean dishes and enjoy the hip folk scene.

Davis Noodle City   ASIAN $
(129 E St; mains $7-10; ⊙11am-9:30pm Mon-Sat, to 8:30pm Sun) A starving student favorite, the best offerings involve the homemade noodles and scallion pancakes.

Redrum   BURGERS $
(✆530-756-2142; 978 Olive Dr; burgers $6.25; ⊙10am-11pm Mon-Thu, to midnight Fri-Sun) Formerly known as Murder Burger, Redrum serves made-to-order beef and turkey burgers, thick espresso shakes and crispy curly fries. The ZOOM – a gnarled, deep-fried pile of zucchini, onion rings and mushrooms – is to die for.

Davis Beer Shop   BEER HALL
(Bottle Shop; ✆530-756-5212; 211 G St; bottle from $3; ⊙11am-11pm Mon-Wed, to 12:30am Thu-Sat, to 9pm Sun) This mellow beer hall and shop stocks 650 varieties of craft beer, bottled and on tap, import and brewed down the block. Pull any bottle from the back, or order one of their daily changing draft flights. BYO food.

☆ Entertainment

For tickets and information to UC Davis' arts events, call the Mondavi Center. For athletic events, call the UC Davis Ticket office (✆530-752-2471; http://campusrecreation.ucdavis.edu; Aggie Stadium, off La Rue Rd).

ℹ TULE FOG

As thick as the proverbial pea soup, tule (too-lee) fog causes chain collisions each year on area roads. In 2007, more than 100 cars and big-rigs collided on a stretch of Hwy 99. At its worst, these dense, immobile clouds can limit visibility to a foot.

Tule fog, named after a marsh grass common here, is thickest from November to March, when cold mountain air settles on the warm valley floor and condenses. The fog burns off for a few afternoon hours, just long enough for the ground to warm again and perpetuate the cycle.

If you find yourself driving in fog, turn on your low beams, give other cars extra distance, and maintain an easy, constant speed. Avoid passing.

Mondavi Center for the Performing Arts   CONCERT VENUE
(www.mondaviarts.org; 1 Shields Ave) Major theater, music, dance and other performances take place at this state-of-the-art venue on the UCD campus.

Varsity Theatre   CONCERT VENUE
(www.davisvarsity.net; 616 2nd St) Davis' beloved arthouse movie theater began as a performance stage back in 1950.

Palms Playhouse   PERFORMING ARTS
(www.palmsplayhouse.com; 13 Main St, Winters) For rhythm 'n' blues and cover bands, just up the road in Winters.

ℹ Information

The exhaustive www.daviswiki.org is fascinating reading.

Yolo County Visitors Bureau (✆530-297-1900; www.yolocvb.net; suite 200, 132 E St; ⊙8:30am-4:30pm Mon-Fri) Free bike maps, travel brochures and transit info.

ℹ Getting There & Away

Amtrak (✆530-758-4220; 840 2nd St) Davis' station is on the southern edge of downtown. There are trains bound for Sacramento ($9, 26 minutes) or San Francisco ($30, two hours) throughout the day.

Yolobus (✆530-666-2877; ⊙5am-11pm) Routes 42A and B ($2) loop between Davis and the Sacramento airport. The route also connects Davis with Woodland and Downtown Sacramento.

ℹ Getting Around

Be aware of bike traffic when driving (especially backing out of a parking space or opening your door). Two wheels are the primary mode of transportation here.

Ken's Bike, Ski, Board (www.kensbikeski.com; 650 G St; ⊙9am-8pm Mon-Fri, to 7pm Sat, noon-5pm Sun) Rents basic bikes (from $19 per day) as well as serious road and mountain bikes.

Unitrans (✆530-752-2877; http://unitrans.ucdavis.edu; one-way $1) If you're not biking, this student-run outfit shuttles people around town and campus in red double-deckers.

Oroville

North of Sacramento's bustle, the quiet town of Oroville has seen quite a reversal. Then: the lust for gold brought a crush of white settlers, who drove out the native

LAKE OROVILLE

Lake Oroville (www.parks.ca.gov; 917 Kelly Ridge Rd; ⊗8am-night), a popular summertime destination, sits 9 miles northeast of town behind Oroville Dam, the largest earthen dam in the US. The surrounding Lake Oroville State Recreation Area attracts campers, boaters, and fishing folk. The lake's visitor center (☑530-538-2219; www.parks.ca.gov; 917 Kelly Ridge Rd; ⊗9am-5pm) has exhibits on the California State Water Project and local tribe history, plus a viewing tower and loads of recreational information.

The area surrounding Lake Oroville is also full of hiking trails, and a favorite is the 7-mile round-trip walk to 640ft Feather Falls. To get off your feet, Lazy T Trailrides (☑530-518-4052; http://lazyttrailrides.com; Saddle Dam parking lot, opp 283 Kelly Ridge Rd; per person $75; ⊗rides at 10am & 5pm) offers four-hour horseback rides on dedicated trails around the lake. The Brad Freeman Bicycle Trail is a 41-mile, off-road loop that takes cyclists to the top of 770ft Oroville Dam, then follows the Feather River back to the Thermalito Forebay and Afterbay storage reservoirs, east of Hwy 70. The ride is mostly flat, but the dam ascent is steep. Get a free map of the ride from the Oroville Area Chamber of Commerce (www.orovillechamber.net; 1789 Montgomery St). The Forebay Aquatic Center (www.forebayaquaticcenter.com; 930 Garden Dr; kayaks per day from $35; ⊗10am-6pm Wed-Sun May-Sep) rents non-motorized watercraft to get out on the water.

Stay overnight in rustic campsites (p496) on land or even on water.

tribes. Now: crowds flock to the thriving tribal casinos, on the outskirts of town, seeking riches. Aside from the slots, the economy leans on the local hospital, the tourists who mill though the throng of antique stores around Montgomery St, and an annual festival to celebrate the salmon run in September.

Oroville's most enduring attraction, aside from the nearby lake, is an excellent museum established by the descendants of a long-dispersed Chinese community. Its other preserved legacies relate to the pioneers who arrived after gold was discovered near here in 1848 by John Bidwell, and to a mysterious man who stumbled into town in 1911, and came to be known as the 'last wild Indian' (p496). Oroville is also a gateway to the rugged northern reaches of the Sierra Nevada.

Hwys 162 and 70 head northeast from Oroville into the mountains and on to Quincy. Hwy 70 snakes along the magnificent Feather River Canyon, an especially captivating drive in fall.

◉ Sights & Activities

Chinese Temple   MUSEUM
(☑530-538-2496; 1500 Broderick St; adult/child $3/free; ⊗noon-4pm) This restored temple and museum offers a fascinating glimpse into Oroville's Chinese legacy well worth exploring. Built in 1863, it served the Chinese

community, which built the area's levees and at its peak numbered 10,000. Inside is an unrivaled collection of 19th-century stage finery, religious shrines and a small garden with fine Qing-era relics throughout.

This temple's fascinating history includes its role as the last stop for touring Cantonese theater troupes. To lighten the shipload back across the Pacific, they left behind elaborate sets, costumes, and puppets, which are on rotating display.

Sacramento National
Wildlife Refuge   BIRD-WATCHING
(www.fws.gov; admission $6; ⊗1hr before sunset-1hr after sunset) Serious bird-watchers sojourn here in winter, when millions of migratory waterfowl make a spectacular sight. The visitor center (☑530-934-2801; 752 County Rd, Willows; ⊗9am-4pm, closed Mon Nov-Feb, closed Sat & Sun Mar-Oct) is off I-5 near Willows; a splendid 6-mile driving trail and walking trails are open daily. The peak season to see birds is between October and late February, with the largest skein of geese arriving in December and January.

⌘ Sleeping & Eating

Oroville is a launch pad for outdoorsy trips and there's plenty of camping in the area, which you can arrange through the Chamber of Commerce, the USFS office (p496), or the Lake Oroville visitor center. A strip of decent budget motels – mostly chains and some humble mid-century cheapies – are clustered on Feather River Blvd, between Hwy 162 to the south and Montgomery St to the north.

In terms of dining options, there's not much chance you'll be thrilled, but aside from the fast-food chains, there is decent pub grub and Vietnamese in the small downtown.

★ **Lake Oroville State Recreation Area**   CAMPING **$**
(☑800-444-7275, 530-538-2219; www.parks.ca.gov; 917 Kelly Ridge Rd; tent/RV sites $25/45; ☎) The wi-fi might be the first clue that this isn't the most rustic choice, but there are good primitive sites if you're willing to hike, and – perhaps the coolest feature of the park – boat. There's a cove of floating platform campsites ($175 per night).

❶ Information

The office of the **Feather River Ranger District** (US Forest Service Office; ☑530-534-6500; 875 Mitchell Ave; ☺8am-4:30pm Mon-Fri) has maps and brochures. For road conditions, phone ☑800-427-7623.

❶ Getting There & Away

Although Greyhound (p491) buses stop near the **Valero gas station** (☑530-533-2328; 555 Oro Dam Blvd E) a few blocks east of Hwy 70, a car is far and away the simplest and most cost effective way to reach the area. There are two buses daily between Oroville and Sacramento ($35, 1½ hours).

Chico

With its huge population of students, Chico has the devil-may-care energy of a college kegger during the school year, and a lazy, lethargic hangover during the summertime. Its oak-shaded downtown and university attractions makes it one of Sacramento Valley's more attractive social hubs, where easygoing folks mingle late in the restaurants and bars, which open onto patios in the balmy summer evenings.

Though Chico wilts in the heat of the summer, the swimming holes in Bidwell Park take the edge off, as does floating down the gentle Sacramento River. The fine pale ales produced at the Sierra Nevada Brewing Company, near downtown, are another of Chico's refreshing blessings.

There's a bit of irony in the fact a town so widely celebrated for its brews was founded by John Bidwell, the illustrious California pioneer who made a bid for US president with the Prohibitionist party. In 1868, Bidwell and his philanthropist wife, Annie Ellicott Kennedy, moved to the new mansion

---

ISHI, THE 'LAST WILD INDIAN'

At daybreak on August 28, 1911, frantic dogs woke the workers sleeping inside a slaughterhouse outside Oroville. The dogs were holding a man at bay – a Native American, disoriented and clad in a loincloth.

The 'wild man' became a media sensation, and soon Berkeley anthropologists traveled to Oroville to meet him. Testing out snippets of nearly lost vocabulary from native languages, they determined the man belonged to the Yahi, the southernmost tribe of the Yana (also known as the Deer Creek tribe), believed to be extinct.

The man never revealed his true name but adopted the name 'Ishi,' meaning 'man' in the Yana language. The anthropologists took Ishi to the museum at the university, where he was installed as a living exhibit, sharing his story and culture until he died from tuberculosis on March 25, 1916, just five years after he was 'discovered.'

By Ishi's accounts, in 1870, when he was a child, there had been only 12 or 15 Yahi people left, hiding in remote areas in the foothills east of Red Bluff. By 1908 Ishi, his mother, sister and uncle were all who were left. His family died that last year, leaving Ishi alone. With Ishi's death, newspapers pronounced the Yahi gone forever.

Anthropologists recently postulated that while Ishi's tribe had been virtually exterminated by settlers by the time he was born, a few found refuge with other tribes, so some of Ishi's kin do live on.

The site where Ishi was captured is east of Oroville along Oro-Quincy Hwy at Oak Ave, marked by a small monument. Part of the Lassen National Forest where Ishi and the Yahi people lived, is now called the Ishi Wilderness.

he had built, now the Bidwell Mansion State Historic Park.

⊙ Sights

Nearly all the sights are downtown, west of Hwy 99, easily reached via Hwy 32 (8th St). Main St and Broadway are the central downtown streets; from there, Park Ave stretches southward and the tree-lined Esplanade heads north.

Sierra Nevada Brewing Company BREWERY
(☑530-899-4776; www.sierranevada.com; 1075 E 20th St; Brewery tour free, Beer Geek tour $25; ⊗tours 11am-4pm Sun-Thu, to 5:30pm Fri & Sat) ✿ Hordes of beer snobs gather at the birthplace of the internationally distributed Sierra Nevada Pale Ale and Schwarber, a Chico-only black ale. Also for sale are the 'Beer Camp' collaborations (www.beercamp.sierranevada.com), short-run craft beers brewed by uber-beer nerds at invitation-only summer seminars. Free brewhouse tours are given regularly. True beerheads will want to book the three-hour tour ($25).

There's also a tour of the brewery's cutting-edge sustainable practices – their rooftop solar fields are among the largest privately owned solar fields in the US, and they extended a spur of local railroad to increase transportation efficiency. Recharge in the pub and restaurant (p498).

Chico Creek Nature Center SCIENCE CENTER
(www.bidwellpark.org; 1968 East 8th St; suggested donation adult/child $4/2; ⊗11am-4pm Wed-Sun; ⏷) If you plan on spending the afternoon in Bidwell Park, first stop at this sparkling nature center, with displays on local plants and animals and excellent hands-on science programs for families. The exhibit hall is closed on Wednesday.

Chico State University UNIVERSITY
Ask for a free map of the Chico State University campus, or about campus events and tours at the **CSU Information Center** (☑530-898-4636; www.csuchico.edu; cnr 2nd & Normal Sts; ⊗7am-11pm Mon-Thu, to 10pm Fri, 11am-10pm Sat, noon-11pm Sun school year), on the main floor of Bell Memorial Union. The attractive campus is infused with sweet floral fragrances in spring, and there's a rose garden at its center.

Bidwell Mansion State
Historic Park HISTORIC BUILDING
(☑530-895-6144; parks.ca.gov; 525 Esplanade; adult/child $6/3; ⊗noon-5pm Mon, 11am-5pm Sat

& Sun) Chico's most prominent landmark, the opulent Victorian home was built for Chico's founders John and Annie Bidwell. The 26-room mansion was built between 1865 and 1868 and hosted many US presidents. Tours start every hour from 11am to 4pm.

Honey Run Covered Bridge HISTORIC SITE
(www.honeyruncoveredbridge.com; parking $3) The historic 1894 bridge is an unusual style this side of the country and a favorite spot for engagement photos. Take the Skyway exit off Hwy 99 on the southern outskirts of Chico, head east and go left on Honey Run-Humbug Rd; the bridge is 5 miles along, in a small park.

✦ Activities

In summer you'll want to cool off by tubing the Sacramento. Inner tubes can be rented at grocery stores and other shops along Nord Ave (Hwy 32) for $7 to $10. Tubers enter at the Irvine Finch Launch Ramp on Hwy 32, a few miles west of Chico, and come out at Washout Beach, off River Rd.

Bidwell Park PARK
(www.bidwellpark.org) Growing out of downtown, the 3670-acre Bidwell Park is the nation's third-largest municipal park. It stretches 10 miles northwest along Chico Creek with lush groves and miles of trails. The upper part of the park is fairly untamed, rather refreshing to find smack in the middle of a city. Several classic movies have been shot here, including parts of *Gone with the Wind* and *The Adventures of Robin Hood*.

The park is full of swimming spots. You'll find pools at One-Mile and Five-Mile recreation areas and swimming holes (including Bear Hole, Salmon Hole and Brown Hole) in Upper Bidwell Park, north of Manzanita Ave (don't be surprised if some opt for birthday – rather than swim – suits).

Adventure Outing OUTDOORS
(☑530-898-4011; www.aschico.com/adventure-outings; 2nd & Chestnut Sts, Bell Memorial Union basement; life jackets $4-8; ⊗9am-5pm Mon-Fri) The CSU-student run outfitter rents equipment such as life jackets, rafts, and even coolers at very reasonable prices by the weekend or week. They also lead popular trips further afield.

✦ Festivals & Events

With the students out of town, family-friendly outdoor events take over the town each summer. The Thursday Night Market fills several blocks of Broadway from April to September. At City Plaza (Main and W 4th Sts), you'll find free Friday Night Concerts starting in May.

🛏 Sleeping

There's an abundance of decent independent motels with sparkling swimming pools, some of them along the shaded Esplanade north of downtown. Be aware that Chico State's graduation and homecoming mania (May and October, respectively) send prices skyward.

Woodson Bridge State Recreation Area   CAMPGROUND $

(☎530-839-2112; www.parks.ca.gov; South Ave; tent sites $25) This shaded campground on the banks of the Sacramento is popular with anglers. Its surrounded by a dense riparian forest preserve home to bald eagles and rare birds. The drive-in tent sites are first-come, first-served fall through spring – call for availability. Book online in summer.

The Grateful Bed   B&B $$

(☎530-342-2464; www.thegratefulbed.net; 1462 Arcadian Ave; r incl breakfast $140-180; ❄@) Well, obviously you're a bedhead if you stay here. Tucked in a residential neighborhood near downtown, it's a stately 1905 Victorian home with four sweetly decorated rooms and warm hosts.

★Hotel Diamond   HISTORIC HOTEL $$$

(☎866-993-3100; www.hoteldiamondchico.com; 220 W 4th St; r $120-349; ❄@🖥) This whitewashed 1904 building is the most luxurious place to lay your head in Chico, with high-thread counts and responsive room service. The Diamond Suite, with its balcony, original furnishings and spacious top-floor balcony, is a-*maz*-ing.

🍴 Eating

Downtown Chico is packed with fun places to eat, many of them catering to a student budget. The outdoor farmers market (☎530-893-3276; www.chicofarmersmarket.com; 305 Wall St, Chico Municipal parking lot; ⏰7:30am-1pm Sat May-Sep) draws from the plentiful surrounding valley.

Nobby's   BURGERS $

(☎530-342-2285; 1444 Park Ave; burgers $4.25-6.25; ⏰10:30am-9pm Tue-Sat) Simply put, the Nobby Burger, topped with a crispy fried blanket of cheese and crispier, thick bacon, is a heart attack. Worth it? Probably. This place is so tiny, you'll likely have to stand. Cash only.

Celestino's Live from New York Pizza   PIZZERIA $

(101 Salem St; pizzas from $14; ⏰10:30am-10pm Sun-Thu, to 11pm Fri & Sat) One of the best imitations of 'real' New York pizza in Northern California, they serve thin-crust pies and playfully themed variations such as the meaty Godfather. The slice-n-a-soda lunch special for $4 is a good deal.

Sin of Cortez   CAFE $

(www.sinofcortez.com; 2290 Esplanade; mains $6-16; ⏰7am-2pm; 🖊) The service won't win awards for speed, but this local favorite draws both vegetarian and omnivorous mobs with its burly breakfast plates. Order anything with the soy chorizo.

Shubert's Ice Cream & Candy   ICE CREAM $

(www.shuberts.com; 178 E 7th St; ⏰9:30am-10pm Mon-Fri, from 11am Sat & Sun) Five generations of Shuberts have produced delicious homemade ice cream and chocolates for more than 75 years at this beloved Chico landmark.

El Paisa Taco Truck   MEXICAN $

(cnr 8th & Pine Sts; mains $1.50-5; ⏰11am-8pm) Debate about which of Chico's taco trucks is best can quickly lead to fisticuffs, but the smoky *carnitas* (braised pork) tacos are most certainly a broke college kid's dream.

Sierra Nevada Taproom & Restaurant   BREWPUB $$

(www.sierranevada.com; 1075 E 20th St; mains $10-32; ⏰11am-9pm Sun-Thu, to 10pm Fri & Sat; 🖊) What's on tap is the main draw at the on-site restaurant of the Sierra Nevada Brewery (p497). This genuine Chico destination is great for downing brews but lacks ambience – the huge, loud dining room is basically a factory cafeteria. Still, it has better-than-average pub food and superbly fresh ales and lagers, some not available elsewhere.

Leon Bistro   CALIFORNIAN $$$

(http://leonbistro.com; 817 Main St; mains $18-35; ⏰from 5pm Wed-Sat) When the most ordinary thing on the menu is a wagyu beef burger with bacon-onion marmalade, you know you're in for something nice. Chef Ann Leon cooked in several fine kitchens before opening her namesake restaurant, a go-to among

Chico tastemakers. She regularly shares her skills in cooking classes.

5th Street Steakhouse AMERICAN $$$
(www.5thstreetsteakhouse.com; 345 W 5th St; steaks from $26; ⊙11:30am-2:30pm Fri, from 4:30pm daily) This is the joint where college kids take their visiting parents. It features crisp white tablecloths, steaks tender enough to cut with a reproachful look, and occasional live jazz loud enough to drown out any disapproval.

Red Tavern AMERICAN $$$
(www.redtavern.com; 1250 Esplanade; mains $17-28; ⊙from 5pm Tue-Sat, 10am-2pm Sun) 🍷 Slightly swanky, the Red Tavern is one of Chico's favorite fine-dining experiences, with a sophisticated menu that uses local, seasonal and organic ingredients, naturally.

🍸 Drinking & Nightlife

As you might have guessed from Chico's party-school rep, you're unlikely to go thirsty. There's a strip of bars on Main St if you want to go hopping.

Empire Coffee CAFE
(http://empirecoffeechico.com; 434 Orange St; ⊙7am-7pm; 🖥) It's not just that this coffee shop is housed in an orange-and-blue 1947 Empire Builder train car or that the baristas draw elaborate images in the foam and host Sunday crochet nights. It's all the fair-trade, organic coffees and creative specials such as macca root and matcha that make this the hippest stop in Chico.

Madison Bear Garden BAR
(www.madisonbeargarden.com; 316 W 2nd St; ⊙11am-1:45am Mon-Sat, from 10am Sun; 🖥) This whimsically decorated campus hangout is housed in a spacious brick building. It's the place to chat with students over thick burgers and cold drafts. The boozy action happens late night in the big beer garden.

Panama Bar & Cafe BAR
(http://panamabarcafeinchico.com; 177 E 2nd St; from $3; ⊙11:30am-1:30am Tue-Sat, 11am-9pm Sun) The house specializes in 31 variations of Long Island iced teas (most of which are around $3), so brace yourself. The only way to take in alcohol any faster would be by IV drip.

LaSalle's CLUB
(www.lasallesbar.com; 229 Broadway; patio cover $5; ⊙7pm-2am Wed-Sun) This venue puts on hip-hop, Top 40 and retro dance nights, and hosts live bands that play anything to pack people in – from reggae to hard rock.

☆ Entertainment

For entertainment options, pick up the free weekly *Chico News & Review* (www.newsandreview.com). For theater, films, concerts, art exhibits and other cultural events at the CSU campus, contact the **CSU Box Office** (☑530-898-6333; http://www.csuchico.edu; cnr 3rd & Chestnut, Sierra Hall; ⊙11am-6pm Mon-Fri) or the CSU Information Center (p497).

Pageant Theatre CINEMA
(www.pageantchico.com; 351 E 6th St; tickets $7.50) Screens international and alternative films. Monday is 'cheap skate night,' with all seats just $3.

1078 Gallery PERFORMING ARTS
(☑530-343-1973; www.1078gallery.org; 820 Broadway; ⊙12:30pm-5:30pm) Chico's contemporary gallery exhibits artworks, and hosts boundary-pushing literary readings, music and theater.

ℹ Information

Chico Chamber of Commerce & Visitor Center (☑800-852-8570, 530-891-5556; www.chicochamber.com; 441 Main St; ⊙10am-4pm Mon-Fri) Local information including bike maps.

ℹ Getting There & Around

Greyhound (www.greyhound.com) buses stop at 11.20am and 7.15pm at the **Amtrak station** (www.amtrak.com; 450 Orange St) heading to San Francisco ($60, five hours 40 minutes), Reno ($74, 10 hours), Los Angeles ($109, 11 hours) and cities in between. The platform is unattended so purchase tickets in advance or on board from the driver. Amtrak trains on the *Coast Starlight* line depart Chico at very inconvenient hours – at 1:47am for Redding ($20, one hour) and at 3:50am for Sacramento ($26, 2½ hours). Amtrak's connecting buses head to Oroville, Sacramento, Stockton, Fresno and Bakersfield, departing at reasonable hours four times daily, but require booking a connecting train.

B-Line (Butte Regional Transit; ☑530-342-0221; www.blinetransit.com; 326 Huss Lane; adult/child $1.40/1) handles all buses throughout Butte County, and can get you around Chico and down to Oroville in 50 minutes.

Car is the easiest way to get around, but Chico is one of the best biking towns in the country.

Rent from **Campus Bicycles** (www.campusbicycles.com; 330 Main St; half/full day $20/35).

Red Bluff

The smoldering streets of Red Bluff – one of California's hottest towns due to the hot-air trap of the Shasta Cascades – are of marginal interest in themselves, but a glimpse towards the mountain-dominated horizon reveals what brings most travelers this way.

Peter Lassen laid out the town site in 1847 and it grew into a key port along the Sacramento River. Now it's a pit stop on the way to the national park that bears his name.

Cowboy culture is alive and well here. Catch it in action the third weekend of April at the Red Bluff Round-Up (www.redbluffroundup.com; tickets $10-27), a major rodeo event dating back to 1918, or in any of the dive bars where the jukeboxes are stocked with Nashville, and plenty of big-buckled cowboys belly up to the bar. Or stock up on your own Western wear from one of several historic storefronts in the business district.

Sights & Activities

Red Bluff Recreation Area PARK
(www.fs.usda.gov) On the east bank of the Sacramento River this sprawling park of meadows has interpretive trails, bicycle paths, boat ramps, a wildlife-viewing area with excellent bird-watching, and a salmon and steelhead ladder (most active July to September).

William B Ide Adobe State Historic Park HISTORIC SITE
(530-529-8599; 21659 Adobe Rd; per car $6; 10am-4pm Fri-Sun) Set on a beautiful, shaded piece of land overlooking a languorous section of the Sacramento River, this park preserves the original one-room adobe house, old forge, and grounds of pioneer William B Ide, who 'fought' in the 1846 Bear Flag Revolt at Sonoma and became president of the California Bear Republic (it lasted 25 days).

Head about a mile north on Main St, turn east onto Adobe Rd and go another mile, following the signs.

Sacramento River Discovery Center SCIENCE CENTER
(www.srdc.tehama.k12.ca.us; 1000 Sale Lane; admission by donation; 11am-4pm Tue-Sat;) This kid-friendly center has exhibits on the river and the Diversion Dam just outside its doors, which has been permanently opened to allow endangered chinook and green and white sturgeon to migrate. Though the fish aren't visible, 120 species of birds are. Bird walks along the 4.2 miles of wheelchair-accessible trails start the first Saturday of each month at 8am.

Sleeping & Eating

More than a dozen motels are by I-5 and south of town along Main St. The historic residential neighborhood has some bed and breakfasts. The restaurant scene isn't thrilling – a lot of cheap take-out, pizza and stick-to-the-ribs grub straight from a can.

Sycamore Grove Camping Area CAMPGROUND $
(530-824-5196; www.recreation.gov; tent sites $16-25, RV sites $32.50) Beside the river in the Red Bluff Recreation Area is this quiet USFS campground. Campsites for tents and RVs are first-come, first-served, and offer new, shared showers and flush toilets. You can reserve a large group campground, Camp Discovery, with cabins you must book as a block ($175 for all 11 cabins per night).

Los Mariachis MEXICAN $
(www.redblufflosmariachis.com; 604 S Main St; mains $5-14; 9am-9pm Mon-Fri, to 9:30 Sat & Sun;) This bright, family-run Mexican spot overlooks the central junction of Red Bluff. They have great salsa and *molcajetes* (meat or seafood stew, served in a stone bowl) big enough to satisfy hungry campers.

Thai House THAI $
(www.newthaihouse.com; 248 S Main St; mains $5-14; 11am-3pm & 4-8:30pm Mon-Fri, 11am-8:30pm Sat, from noon Sun;) A solid Thai restaurant with excellent curries and soups.

Palomino Room AMERICAN, BARBECUE $$
(http://palominoroom.com; 723 Main St; mains from $11; from 11am Tue-Fri, from 4pm Sat;) Genuine Texas BBQ in a saloon that's been operating since 1946. Previously known for bar brawls, it's been overhauled and dressed up with signs dating back to Red Bluff's pioneer days. Go for the brisket or ribs with a side of green beans, wrapped in bacon and drizzled with maple glaze. And maybe a salad? Kids eat free on Tuesday.

Information

Red Bluff Chamber of Commerce (530-527-6220; www.redbluffchamber.com; 100 Main St; 8:30am-4pm Mon, to 5pm Tue-Thu, to 4:30pm Fri) To get your bearings and a stack of brochures, find this white building just south of downtown.

ℹ️ Getting There & Away

Most visitors pull into Red Bluff to take a break from the busy I-5. By highway, the town is three hours north of San Francisco and 15 minutes north of Sacramento. **Amtrak** (amtrak.com; cnr Rio & Walnut Sts) and **Greyhound** (www.greyhound.com; 22700 Antelope Blvd) connect it with other California cities via bus.

SAN JOAQUIN VALLEY

The southern half of California's Central Valley – named for the San Joaquin River – sprawls from Stockton to the turbine-covered Tehachapi Mountains, southeast of Bakersfield. Everything stretches to the horizon in straight lines – railroad tracks, two-lane blacktop and long irrigation channels.

Through the elaborate politics and machinery of water management, this once-arid region ranks among the most agriculturally productive places in the world, though the profits often go to agribusiness shareholders, not the increasingly disenfranchised family farmer. Some of the tiny towns scattering the region, such as Gustine and Reedley, retain their Main Street Americana appeal while slowly embracing the influence of the Latino labor force that work these fields.

This is a place of seismic, often contentious, development. Arrivals from the coastal cities have resulted in unchecked eastward sprawl – some half a million acres of prime farmland have been paved over as subdivisions in the last decade. What were once actual cattle ranches and vineyards are now nostalgically named developments: a big-box shopping complex named Indian Ranch, a tidy row of McMansions named Vineyard Estates. More green lawns appear as the irrigation systems drain dry. Water rights is *the* issue on everyone's minds.

To really see the region, skip I-5 and travel on Hwy 99 – a road with nearly as long a history as the famous Route 66. It'll be hot – very hot – so roll the windows down and crank up the twangy country or the booming *norteño* (an accordion-driven genre of Mexican folk music). If you have the time, exit often for bushels of the freshest produce on earth and brushes with California's nearly forgotten past.

Many San Joaquin Valley towns are excellent launching points for Yosemite National Park, and Hwy 99 is lined with classic, affordable motor lodges and hotel chains.

Lodi

Although Lodi was once the 'Watermelon capital of the world,' today, full-bodied wine rules this patch of the valley. Breezes from the Sacramento River Delta soothe the area's hot vineyards, where some of the world's oldest Zinfandel vines grow. Lodi's diverse soil is sometimes rocky, sometimes fine sandy loam, giving its grapes a range of distinctive characteristics that allow for experimentation with some less common varietals.

Lodi also hosts a slew of festivals dedicated to their famous export, including the Wine & Chocolate Weekend in February and ZinFest in May.

◉ Sights

Lodi Wine & Visitor Center　　TASTING ROOM
(www.lodiwine.com; 2545 W Turner Rd; tasting $5; ⏲10am-5pm) Get your first taste of Lodi's powerful, sun-soaked Zins and Petite Sirahs at the Lodi Wine & Visitor Center, where 100 local vintages are sold by the glass at the wood–tasting bar. They also provide maps to wineries of the region. Find them on the grounds of Wine & Roses hotel.

Micke Grove Regional Park and Zoo　　ZOO
(☎209-331-2010; www.mgzoo.com; 11793 N Micke Grove Rd; adult/child $5/3, parking $5; ⏲10am-5pm; ▣) For the seriously underage, Lodi's Micke Grove Regional Park and Zoo is a good stop, with a water play area, hissing cockroaches and some barking sea lions. There are also kiddie rides in a section called Fun Town. The park also houses an exceptional Japanese Garden (www.sjparks.com; 11793 N Micke Grove Rd; ⏲9am-2pm Mon-Thu, to 1pm Fri-Sun) FREE.

🛏️ Sleeping & Eating

Along Hwy 99, Lodi hosts a string of budget chain hotels. Though the rooms are bland, the competition ensures that they are all very clean, often at a real bargain.

Wine & Roses　　B&B $$$
(☎209-334-6968; www.winerose.com; 2505 W Turner Rd; r $179-240, ste from $335; 🖥️) Surrounded by a vast rose garden, this is the most luxurious offering to spring up amid

Lodi's vineyards. Tasteful and romantic, the rooms have slate bathrooms, high-quality toiletries and lots of square footage. The suites are grand, some open to private terraces, but there are significant discounts for long-term stays. There's an acclaimed spa and restaurant too.

Cheese Central
MARKET $

(cheesecentrallodi.com; 11 N School St; ⊗10am-6pm Mon-Sat, 1pm to 5pm Sun) Ask Cindy the cheesemonger for thoughtful pairings with Lodi wines. If you want to make a weekend out of Lodi's wine region, the cooking classes here get raves.

Crush Kitchen & Bar
ITALIAN $$

(☑209-369-5400; www.crushkitchen.com; 115 S School St, Woolworth bldg; mains $18-27; ⊗from 11:30am Thu-Mon, 5-9pm Wed) With an excellent, extremely long wine list of Lodi and imported wines plus an Italian-leaning menu to match, Crush is several notches of sophistication ahead of anything else in town. The plates of fresh tomato salad, gnocchi and duck confit are expert, simple and rustic.

Dancing Fox Winery & Bakery
AMERICAN, BAKERY $$

(☑209-366-2634; www.dancingfoxwinery.com; 203 S School St; mains from $11; ⊗7:30am-9pm Tue-Sat, 9am-3pm Sun) Everything here celebrates grapes — from the Lewis Family Estate's own wines to the bread cultures created from the vineyard's Petite Sirah grapes. The best selections from the overly broad menu involve the wood-burning oven.

Stockton

Stockton has had more than its share of ups and downs. Hit hard by housing foreclosures and almost a billion dollars in debt, in 2012, it became the largest US city to file for bankruptcy.

What remains of its proud past as a major inland port, the main supply hub for gold rushers, and a leading player in shipbuilding

TOP LODI WINERIES

Lodi's underrated wineries make an easy escape from the Bay Area, and the quality of grapes will delight true oenophiles. This is the source of many master blenders' secret weapons.

The region is easily accessed from I-5 or Hwy 99 and just as easy to navigate, as roads are well marked. For maps, check the Lodi Wine & Visitor Center (p501).

Jesse's Grove (www.jessiesgrovewinery.com; 1973 W Turner Rd; ⊗noon-5pm) With its summer concert series and very long history, this is an anchor of Lodi wine producers. There's a new tasting room downtown on E Locust St.

Harney Lane (www.harneylane.com; 9010 E Harney Lane; tasting $5; ⊗11am-5pm Thu-Mon) A sweet family outfit that's been around Lodi forever; their Tempranillo is an overachiever. Tasting fee refunded with purchase.

d'Art (www.dartwines.com; 13299 N Curry Ave; tasting $5; ⊗noon-5pm Thu-Mon) Helen and Dave Dart's bold Cab is as fun and inviting as the tasting room. Tasting fee refunded with purchase.

LangeTwins (www.langetwins.com; 1525 East Jahant Rd, Acampo; tasting $5-10; ⊗11am-4pm Thu-Sun) The Viognier and reserve blends are worth the 7-mile drive north of town to this state-of-the-art steel-and-redwood winery.

Riaza Wines (www.riazawines.com; 20 W Elm; ⊗1-6pm Fri-Sat, to 5pm Sun) The downtown tasting room pours Spanish varietals that only recently were discovered to grow like mad in the Lodi sun.

Jeremy Wine Co (www.jeremywineco.com; 6 W Pine St; ⊗1-5pm Wed-Sun) Friendly folk in this brass- and wood-fitted tasting room downtown pour a bright fruit-forward Sangiovese.

Michael David (www.michaeldavidwinery.com; 4580 W Hwy 12; tasting $5; ⊗10am-5pm) These brothers built an enthusiastic following with their oaky, fruity wines. Their renowned Zinfandel, 7 Deadly Zins, is a standout. The cafe and old-timey dry goods store make this tasting room a perfect lunch stop. Tasting fee refunded with purchase.

and modern transport, is today blighted by crime-ridden streets and crumbling facades. Still, the downtown and waterfront redevelopment is one of the valley's more promising grassroots efforts and warrants a brief detour.

A block east of Weber Point, the **Department of Tourism** (209-938-1555; www.visitstockton.org; 125 Bridge Pl; 9am-5pm Mon-Fri) has complete information about the goings-on in town.

◉ Sights & Activities

Weber Point Events Center   LANDMARK
(www.stocktongov.com; 221 N Center St) Downtown on the McLeod Lake waterfront, the modern white edifice standing in the middle of a grassy park looking rather like a pile of sailboats is the Weber Point Events Center and marks the center of the action. This is also the site of the huge April Asparagus Festival, a series of open-air concerts, and fountains where squealing kids cool off.

Banner Island Ballpark   BASEBALL
(209-644-1900; www.stocktonports.com; 404 W Fremont St) The beautiful Banner Island Ballpark is where the minor-league Stockton Ports play ball April to September.

Haggin Museum   MUSEUM
(www.hagginmuseum.org; 1201 N Pershing Ave; adult/child $8/5; 1:30-5pm Wed-Fri, noon-5pm Sat-Sun) This city gem houses a 26ft boat by Stockton's own Stephens Bros company, and an excellent collection of American landscape and 'Golden Age' paintings.

Opportunity Cruises   BOAT TOUR
(http://opportunitycruises.com; 445 W Weber Ave, Stockton Marina; cruises without/with meal $37/$55) Cruises around the Sacramento Delta in open-sided river boats depart from the Marina.

🛏 Sleeping & Eating

University Plaza Waterfront Hotel HOTEL $$
(209-944-1140; www.universityplazawaterfronthotel.com; 110 W Fremont St; r from $125; 🖥) If you're spending the night here, a nice option is the University Plaza Waterfront Hotel, a place where business travelers mingle with University of the Pacific students and the mayor, who all live in the lofts on the upper floors. The very modern building overlooking the harbor and historic park, unlike the highway chains, is walkable from other locations in the city center.

STOCKTON ASPARAGUS FESTIVAL

Of all the Central Valley food celebrations, perhaps none pay such creative respect to the main ingredient as the **Stockton Asparagus Festival** (http://asparagusfest.com; N Center St btwn Oak St & W Weber Av; adult/child $13/free), which brings together more than 500 vendors to serve these green stalks – more than 10 tons of them! – every way imaginable. It sprouts along the waterfront at the end of April.

Manny's California Fresh Café   AMERICAN $
(209-463-6415; www.mannyscaliforniafresh.com; 1612 Pacific Ave; mains $4.95-7.95; 10am-9:45pm) Get lunch at Manny's, which serves flavorful rotisserie meats and fried-chicken sandwiches. It's at the edge of the Miracle Mile district, a developing shopping stretch on Pacific Ave, north of downtown.

On Lok Sam   CANTONESE $
(http://newonlocksam.com; 333 S Sutter St; 11am-9pm) Venture south of the Crosstown Freeway (Hwy 4) to (New) On Lok Sam, established in 1895 in the center of Stockton's lively Chinese settlement.

Modesto

Cruising was banned in Modesto in 1993, but the town still touts itself as the 'cruising capital of the world.' The past time's notoriety stems mostly from homegrown George Lucas' 1973 film *American Graffiti*. You'll still see hot rods and flashy wheels around town, but they no longer clog thoroughfares on Friday nights.

This is a good spot for getting off the dusty highway. Old oaks arch over the city's streets and you can eat well in the compact downtown. The **Ernest & Julio Gallo Winery**, makers of America's best-selling jug wines, is among the town's biggest businesses.

Downtown sits just east of Hwy 99 (avoid the area west of the freeway), centering on 10th and J Sts. From downtown, Yosemite Blvd (Hwy 132) runs east toward Yosemite National Park.

Many historic buildings have survived revitalization, including the 1934 **State Theatre** (www.thestate.org; 1307 J St), which hosts films and live music, and the **Southern**

Pacific depot, a Mission-style beauty at J and 9th Sts that still serves as the transit hub. The famous Modesto Arch, on the corner of 9th and I Sts, stands at what was once the city's main entry point. The town's slogan on it, 'Water, Wealth, Contentment, Health,' came from a 1912 contest and remains as relevant today as when it went up. Ironically, the pithy little poem didn't actually win the contest. Judges chose the folksy, if less eloquent, 'Nobody's Got Modesto's Goat' but were overruled by the city government.

Classic car shows and rock 'n' roll fill the streets every June for Graffiti Summer (http://visitmodesto.com). Amid all the '50s charm, the sparkling Gallo Center for the Arts (☑ 209-338-2100; www.galloarts.org; 1000 I St; ☺ 10am-6pm Mon-Fri, from noon Sat) brings huge acts to the Valley. For details, check the Convention & Visitors Bureau (☑ 888-640-8467; http://visitmodesto.com; 1150 9th St).

✖ Eating

Brighter Side
SANDWICHES $

(www.brighter-side.com; 1125 K St, cnr 13th & K Sts; mains $5-6; ☺ 11am-3:30pm Mon-Fri; ☑) An earthy little sandwich shop housed in a wood-shingled, former gas station, serves up sandwiches including the Larry (polish sausage, mushrooms, green onions on rye) and the veggie Christine on the sunny patio.

A&W Drive-In
AMERICAN $

(www.awrestaurants.com; 1404 G St, cnr 14th & G Sts; cheeseburger $3, float $4; ☺ 10am-9pm, to 8pm Oct-Mar) A vintage burger stand (part of a chain founded in nearby Lodi), where roller-skating carhops and classic cars on display move a lot of root beer floats. George Lucas supposedly cruised here as a youth.

Minnie's
CHINESE $

(http://minnies.58-s.com; 107 McHenry Ave; mains from $7.50) On the north end of town, Minnie's is a mid-century Polynesian pop institution, one of the last-standing tiki restaurants of its era. Opened in 1954, the Mah family has kept the original carvings, rattan, and menu favorites including chow mein and deep-fried asparagus. Look for the oil-on-velvet paintings of nippled beauties by the celebrated Ralph Burke Tyree.

Merced

You can jog over to Yosemite from many of the small towns in this part of the valley, but this is a convenient staging area, right on Hwy 140. The machine of progress has not been kind to Merced, as it suffers more than its share of strip malls, but at its core are still tree-lined streets, historic Victorian homes and a magnificent 1875 courthouse. The downtown business district is a work-in-progress, with 1930s movie theaters, antique stores and a few casual eateries undergoing constant renovation.

Merced is right in the midst of a population makeover, thanks to the newest University of California campus, opened in 2005. UC Merced's first freshman class numbered just 1000 students, but the school continues to grow with a diverse student body and has begun to dramatically shape the city.

Downtown Merced is east of Hwy 99 along Main St, between R St and Martin Luther King Jr Way. The California Welcome Center (☑ 209-724-8104; http://visitmerced. travel; 710 W 16th St; ☺ 8:30am-5pm Mon-Sat, 10am-4pm Sun), adjacent to the bus depot, has local maps and information on Merced and Yosemite.

The big attraction is the Castle Air Museum (☑ 209-723-2178; www.castleairmuseum. org; 5050 Santa Fe Dr, Atwater; adult/child $10/8; ☺ 9am-5pm Apr-Sep, 10am-4pm Oct-Mar) in Atwater, about 6 miles northwest. A squadron of restored military aircrafts from WWII, the Korean War and the Vietnam War sit in repose across from a large hangar. Even the most conscientious of objectors will stand agape at these feats of engineering.

🛏 Sleeping & Eating

HI Merced Home Hostel
HOSTEL $

(☑ 209-725-0407; www.hiusa.org; dm $20-23; ☺ reception 5:30-10pm) A night in this six-bed homestay in the northeast part of town feels like staying with your long-lost Aunt Jan and Uncle Larry, the kind of folks happy to lend advice about Yosemite at the kitchen table. Beds fill quickly and must be reserved in advance (call between 5:30pm and 10pm). They can shuttle you to/from the bus and train stations.

Hooper House Bear Creek Inn
B&B $$

(☑ 209-723-3991; www.hooperhouse.com; 575 W North Bear Creek Dr; r $139-169; ❋ 🐾) In a grand old Colonial-style mansion, Hooper House Bear Creek Inn is a leisurely retreat. Rooms are large and beautifully furnished with hardwood furniture, soft beds and tiled bathrooms. A full breakfast is included, which you can have sent to your room.

Branding Iron
STEAKHOUSE **$$**

(www.thebrandingiron-merced.com; 640 W 16th St; lunch mains $9-11, dinner $10-27; 11:30am-2pm Mon-Fri, 5-10pm Sun-Thu, to 9:30 Fri & Sat) The Branding Iron roadhouse, a favorite of ranchers in the area, has been spruced up a bit for the tour buses, but locals still dig the hearty steak platters and Western atmosphere. Presiding over the dining room is 'Old Blue,' a massive stuffed bull's head from a local dairy farm.

Getting There & Away

YARTS (Yosemite Area Regional Transportation System; 209-388-9589; www.yarts.com) buses depart three (winter) to five (summer) times daily for Yosemite Valley from several Merced locations, including the **Merced Transpo Center** (www.mercedthebus.com; cnr 16th & N Sts) and the **Amtrak station** (www.amtrak.com; 324 W 24th St, cnr 24th & K Sts). The trip takes about 2½ hours and stops include Mariposa, Midpines and the Yosemite Bug Lodge & Hostel. Round-trip adult/child costs $25/18 and includes park entry (quite a bargain!). There's limited space for bicycles, so show up early.

Greyhound (710 W 16th St) also operates from the Transpo Center (Los Angeles four times daily, 6½ hours, $43).

Fresno

Smack in the arid center of the state, Fresno is the biggest city in the Central Valley. It may not be scenic (it's a testing ground for every new chain store), but it is beautifully situated, an hour's drive from four national parks (Yosemite, Sierra, Kings Canyon and Sequoia), making it an ideal last stop for expeditions.

Unfortunately, in recent years, Fresno's agriculture-based economy has been hit hard by catastrophic droughts and plummeting food prices, while unemployment has risen. A local farm movement to regain footing seeks to revolutionize food production through organic, sustainable practices and fair wages. Fresno's proximity to these progressive farms means it's experiencing a food and cultural renaissance. The produce and meat is the freshest you'll find anywhere. Fresno? Oh, Fresyes.

Like many valley towns, Fresno is home to diverse Mexican, Chinese and Basque communities, which arrived in successive waves. More recently thousands of Hmong people have put down roots in the area. The long-standing Armenian community is famously represented by author and playwright William Saroyan, who was born, lived and died in this city he loved dearly.

Sights & Activities

One hopping side of town is the Tower District, north of downtown, an oasis of gay-friendly, alterna-culture, book and record stores, music clubs and a handful of stylish restaurants. Many of the historic buildings are along the Sante Fe railroad tracks and downtown, including the 1894 Fresno Water Tower and the 1928 Pantages (Warnors) Theatre. The crowds gather at the sprawling Convention Center and Chukchansi Park, home of Fresno's Triple-A baseball team, the Grizzlies.

Downtown lies between Divisadero St, Hwy 41 and Hwy 99. Two miles north, the Tower District sits around the corner of E Olive Ave and N Fulton Ave.

Forestiere Underground Gardens
GARDENS

(559-271-0734; www.undergroundgardens.info; 5021 W Shaw Ave; adult/child $15/7; tours 10am-4pm hourly Wed-Sun May-Sep, reduced hr Oct-Apr) If you see only one thing in Fresno, make it this intriguing historic landmark, two blocks east of Hwy 99. The gardens are the singular result of Sicilian immigrant Baldassare Forestiere, who dug out some 70 acres beneath the hardpan soil to plant citrus trees, starting in 1906. This utterly fantastical accomplishment took him 40 years to complete.

With a unique skylight system, Forestiere created a beautiful subterranean space for commercial crops and his own living quarters. The tunnel system includes bedrooms, a library, patios, grottos and a fish pond. Check the website for tour times.

Tower Theatre
HISTORIC BUILDING

(559-485-9050; www.towertheaterfresno.com; 815 E Olive Ave) Fresno's Tower District began as a shopping mecca during the 1920s, gaining its name from the Tower Theatre, a beautiful 1939 art-deco movie house. The theater is now a center for the performing arts. Surrounding it are bookstores, boutiques, trendy restaurants and coffeehouses, and hipsters.

Fresno Art Museum
MUSEUM

(559-441-4221; www.fresnoartmuseum.org; 2233 N 1st St; admission $5; 11am-5pm Fri-Sun, to 8pm Thu) This museum has rotating exhibits of contemporary art – including work by local artists – that are among the most intriguing in the valley.

BLOODLESS BULLFIGHTS

Bullfighting has been illegal in the US since 1957, but there are exceptions to the rule. Portuguese communities in the Central Valley are permitted to stage bloodless bullfights at *festas*, huge cultural events that draw as many as 25,000 to honor St Anthony or Our Lady of Fátima. Portuguese fishermen and farmers, mostly from the Azores, began settling in California during the late 19th century.

Candlelight processions, folk dancing, blessing of the cows, *pezinho* singing (melodies accompanied by violin) and unbridled eating are all part of the experience. Major events happen in summer in Hanford, Gustine and Stevinson. They're not well publicized. Search 'festas california' and see what comes up in English.

Woodward Park　PARK
(www.fresno.gov; 7775 Friant Rd; per vehicle $5; ⊙6am-10pm Apr-Oct, to 7pm Nov-Mar) The city's largest park has 300 acres of barbecue facilities, lakes and ponds, a **Japanese garden** (adult/child $3/50¢) and a huge amphitheater for Shakespeare and other performances. A 6-mile network of bike trails connects to the **Lewis S Eaton Trail**, which runs 22 miles from the northeast corner along Friant Rd to Friant Dam.

Roeding Park　PARK
(www.fresno.gov; 890 Belmont Ave; per vehicle $5; ⊙6am-10pm Apr-Oct, to 7pm Nov-Mar) Just east of Hwy 99, this large and shady park is home to the small **Chaffee Zoological Gardens** (☑559-498-2671; www.fresnochaffeezoo.com; adult/child $7/3.50; ⊙9am-4pm Mon-Fri, to 6pm Sat & Sun; ⊛). Adjacent to it are **Storyland** (☑559-264-2235; storylandplayland.com; 890 W Belmont Ave; adult/child $5/3.50; ⊙10am-4pm Sat & Sun; ⊛), a kitschy children's fairytale world dating from 1962, and **Playland** (storylandplayland.com; 890 W Belmont Ave; adult/child $5/3.50; ⊙10am-4pm Sat & Sun; ⊛), which has kiddie rides and games.

🛏 Sleeping & Eating

Fresno has room to grow when it comes to world-class accommodations, but those using it as a launch pad for visiting Sequoia and Kings Canyon National Parks have plenty of options in the cluster of chains near the airport or a couple of high-rise offerings downtown.

For food, the best stuff is scattered around town – making this, most definitely, a driving town. Trendy eateries and breweries are in the Tower District and hidden among abandoned storefronts downtown. **Food trucks** (carthopfresno.com; Fulton Mall; ⊙10am-2pm Thu) circle up every Thursday accompanied by live music in front of Fresno Brewing Company. For fantastic raw ingredients, Fresno's excellent **farmers markets** (playfresno.org) are abundant year-round.

Piccadilly Inn Shaw　HOTEL $$
(☑559-348-5520; www.picadillyinn.com; 2305 W Shaw Ave; r $89-159; ⊛@⊠) This is Fresno's nicest option, with a lovely pool, big rooms and tons of amenities. Ask for a room with a fireplace to cuddle by in winter. If they are full, try one of the other properties, both by the airport: the Piccadilly Inn Express and the Piccadilly Inn Airport.

Dusty Buns Bistro　AMERICAN $
(www.dustybuns.com; 608 E Weldon Ave; mains $6-7; ⊙11am-9pm Mon-Sat) This restaurant began as a food truck dishing out sandwiches on buns, made from local ingredients, single handedly actualizing Fresno's modern foodie culture. The young couple in the drivers' seat still makes the rounds in the truck. Try the Dusty Bun, a brilliant little number of chipotle roast chicken and slaw.

Sam's Italian Deli & Market　DELI $
(www.samsitaliandeli.com; 2415 N First St; mains $5-9; ⊙9am-6pm Mon-Sat) This Italian market and deli is the real deal, stacking up the 'New Yorker' pastrami and some mean prosciutto and mozzarella.

Chicken Pie Shop　AMERICAN $
(Grandmarie's Chicken Pie Shop; ☑559-237-5042; 861 E Olive Ave; mains $8-8.45; ⊙7am-7pm Mon-Fri, 8am-2pm Sat & Sun) With a ladle of gravy and a flaky crust, the beautiful chicken-stuffed pies at this Tower District institution bear no resemblance to the frozen, soggy mess of your childhood, though the nostalgic decor might.

★Peeve's Public House & Local Market　AMERICAN $$
(peevespub.com; 1243 Fulton Mall; mains $10; ⊙11am-11pm Mon-Thu, to 1am Fri, 9am-1am Sat, 9am-9pm Sun) Located in the desolate Fulton

Mall in downtown, Peeve's is leading Fresno's new wave of urban-rural revitalization by celebrating hyper-local food. Every ingredient in their three daily offerings (burgers and salads, usually), the dozen microbrews ($5 to $6), and the extensive wine list are pure Fresno County. A small market next door offers some local producers' best.

☆ Entertainment

Check the Fresno Bee (http://calendar.fresnobee.com) for what's happening when.

Tower Theatre for the Performing Arts   PERFORMING ARTS
(www.towertheatrefresno.com; 815 E Olive Ave) In the center of Fresno's hippest neighborhood, it's hard to miss the neon deco palace that opens its stage to touring rock and jazz acts and seasonal cultural events.

ⓘ Information

Fresno/Clovis Convention & Visitors Bureau (☑559-981-5500, 800-788-0836; www.playfresno.org; 1550 E Shaw Ave, suite 101; ☺8am-5pm Mon-Fri) Visitor information in a non-descript office complex. Brochures are also stocked in the Water Tower and airport.

ⓘ Getting There & Around

Amtrak (Sante Fe station; ☑559-486-7651; 2650 Tulare St; ☺5:30am-9:45pm) The most scenic way to travel these parts, the San Joaquin service stops in a white Mission building smack in downtown Fresno on its way to other tourist destinations including Yosemite ($40, four hours, twice daily) and San Francisco ($55, four hours).

Fresno Area Express (FAX; ☑559-621-7433; www.fresno.gov; one-way $1.25) The local service that has daily bus services to the Tower District (bus 22 or 28) and Forestiere Underground Gardens (bus 20) from the downtown transit center at Van Ness Ave and Fresno St.

Fresno Yosemite International Airport (FAT; www.flyfresno.com; 5175 E Clinton Way) In the Central Valley.

Greyhound (☑559-268-1829; 1033 H St) Stops downtown near the Chukchansi ballpark. Multiple regular/express rides daily to Los Angeles ($31/32.50, five/four hours) and San Francisco ($45/47, six/four hours).

Visalia

Its agricultural prosperity and well-maintained downtown make Visalia one of the valley's convenient stops en route to Sequoia and Kings Canyon National Parks or

---

DOWN ON THE FARM

There's no better way to get a taste of this agricultural region than on its farms. Many offer tours and seasonal opportunities to pick your own. Central Valley visitor's bureaus can point you to popular stops. Here are a few family farms paving the way with progressive practices.

Riverdance Farm (☑209-394-1420; http://riverdancefarms.com; 12230 Livingston-Cressey Rd, Livingston) Permaculture farming produces delectable blueberries and cherries May to June at this fruit and nut farm, which also hosts a pick-and-gather festival the weekend after Memorial Day (late May).

Squaw Valley Herb Garden (www.squawvalleyherbgardens.com; 31765 E Kings Canyon Rd, Squaw Valley; tours Apr-Oct from $15) Pick your way through aromatic herb beds and fields of lavender on this stunning farm in the Sierra foothills.

T&D Willey Farm (http://tdwilleyfarms.com; 13886 Road 20, Madera) In between their work running a popular CSA (community-sourced agriculture program) and leading the regional small-farm movement, Tom and Denesse grow everything from organic arugula to rutabagas. Tours in October.

Page River Bottom Farms (17780 E Vino Ave, Reedley; ☺8am-5pm Mon-Sat) Heritage chickens and pasture-raised cattle, sheep and pigs roam this happy farm. Call for open house dates.

Organic Pastures (www.organicpastures.com; 7221 S Jameson Ave, Fresno; ☺8am-5pm Mon-Fri) This dairy offers raw milk and raw milk products – sweet, creamy and totally unlike anything in the supermarket. Regular tours and a chance to camp with the cows every Memorial Day weekend.

SCENIC DRIVE: THE BLOSSOM TRAIL

When the Central Valley fruit and nut trees are in bloom, the winding roads around Visalia make for a lovely, leisurely afternoon drive (just pack your antihistamines). The 62-mile Fresno County Blossom Trail (www.gofresnocounty. com) is especially stunning between February and March, when the orchards are awash in the pastel petals of apricot, almond, peach, nectarine, apple and citrus. Come back starting in May to taste the results.

Route maps are available online and at the Fresno/Clovis Convention & Visitors Bureau (p507), though DIY is possible if you don't mind taking occasional detours on the back roads between Sanger, Reedley, Orange Cove, Selma, Fowler and Kingsburg.

the Sierra Peaks. Bypassed a century ago by the railroad, the city is 5 miles east of Hwy 99, along Hwy 198. Its downtown has oldtown charm and makes for a nice stroll.

The original Victorian and Arts and Crafts–style homes in Visalia are architectural gems worth viewing on foot. Maps for many interesting self-guided tours are available via the website of the Visalia Convention and Visitor's Bureau (☑559-334-0141; www.visitvisalia.org; 303 E Acequia Av; ◷8:30am-5pm Mon-Fri).

The main draw in the area is the Kaweah Oak Preserve (www.sequoiariverlands.org; 29979 Rd 182, Exeter; donation adult/child $3/1; ◷8am-sunset), about 7 miles east of town. With 324 acres of majestic oak trees, the kind that once stretched from the Sierras to (long-gone) Tulare Lake in the valley, it is a gorgeous setting for easy hikes. From Hwy 198, turn north onto Rd 182; the park is about a half-mile along on your left.

🛏 Sleeping & Eating

If you stay for grub, there are plenty of choices, including a spread of ethnic food, down Main St between Floral and Bridge Sts.

Spalding House   B&B $
(☑559-739-7877; www.thespaldinghouse.com; 631 N Encina St; s/d $85/95; ❄) Spalding House offers a charming B&B experience for overnights.

★Brewbaker's Brewing
Company   BREWPUB $
(www.brewbakersbrewingco.com; 219 E Main St; mains from $8; ◷11:30am-10pm; 🐾) Brewbaker's Brewing Company serves up good pub grub and microbrews such as its smooth Sequoia Red for the crowds.

❶ Getting There & Around

Visalia's transit options, including direct access to Sequoia National Park (p391), all funnel through the **Transit Center** (www.ci.visalia. ca.us; 425 E Oak Ave; ◷6am-9:30pm Mon-Fri, 8am-6:30pm Sat & Sun). **Amtrak** (www.amtrak. com; 425 E Oak Ave) shuttles run between the Transit Center and Hanford station a half hour away by reservation only (use local buses as an alternative). From Hanford, you can connect to all other Amtrak routes in the state, including the San Joaquin, which travels north to Sacramento ($32, four hours, two direct daily) or south to Bakersfield ($22.50, 1½ hours, six daily).

The convenient, bike-rack equipped **Sequoia Shuttle** (☑877-287-4453; www.sequoiashuttle. com; 425 E Oak Ave; adult/child return incl park entry $15/7; ◷late May-Sep) picks up from major hotels and takes two hours to reach the Giant Forest Museum (p397) in Sequoia National Park. The **Visalia Towne Trolley** (425 East Oak Ave; ticket 25¢; ◷7:30am-5:30pm Mon-Thu, to 11pm Fri, 9:30am-11pm Sat) hits most downtown sights over two circuits and costs just a quarter.

Bakersfield

Nearing Bakersfield, the landscape has evidence of California's other gold rush: rusting rigs alongside the route burrow into Southern California's vast oil fields. Black gold was discovered here in the late 1800s, and Kern County, the southernmost along Hwy 99, still pumps more than some OPEC countries.

This is the setting of Upton Sinclair's Oil!, which was adapted into the 2007 Academy Award–winning film, There Will Be Blood. In the 1930s the oil attracted a stream of 'Okies' – farmers who migrated out of the dusty Great Plains – to work the derricks. The children of these tough-as-nails roughnecks put the 'western' in country western by creating the 'Bakersfield Sound' in the mid-1950s, with heroes Buck Owens and Merle Haggard waving a defiant middle finger at the silky Nashville establishment.

Bakersfield is making moves to fancy-up like some of its valley neighbors, but downtown holds some real surprises in its upbeat mix of restored buildings and new restaurants, theaters and clubs.

◉ Sights

The Kern River flows along Bakersfield's northern edge, separating it from its blue-collar neighbor, Oildale, and a host of oil fields. Truxtun and Chester Aves are the main downtown thoroughfares. Though currently suffering from some neglect, Old Town Kern, located east of downtown around Baker and Sumner Sts, still has character underneath the decay. Bakersfield Historic Preservation Commission (www.bakersfieldcity.us/edcd/historic) has downloadable maps of walking tours covering Old Town Kern and Bakersfield's historic downtown.

Five & Dime Antique Mall   LANDMARK
(☑ 661-321-0061; 1400 19th St, Woolworth bldg; ◷ 10am-5pm Mon-Sat, from noon Sun) Three stories hold vintage wares that date back to at least the same era as the Woolworth building they're housed in. Try to go when the diner (p510) is open.

Kern County Museum & Lori Brock Children's Discovery Center   MUSEUM
(www.kcmuseum.org; 3801 Chester Ave; adult/child $10/$7-9; ◷ 10am-5pm Tue-Sat, from noon Sun; ℗ ☻) ✎ This museum covers black and yellow gold with a pioneer village of more than 50 restored and replicated buildings. The musty main structure has a large (and fairly disturbing) display of taxidermied local wildlife. On the 2nd floor waits a collection of pristine memorabilia from Bakersfield's musical heyday.

California Living Museum   ZOO
(www.calmzoo.org; 10500 Alfred Harrell Hwy; adult/child $9/5; ◷ 9am-4pm; ☻) The zoo and botanical gardens have a menagerie of native animals and a rattlesnake house, which has every type of rattler in the state. It's about a 20-minute drive northeast from downtown Bakersfield.

Cesar E Chavez National Monument   HISTORIC SITE
(☑ 661-823-6134; http://chavezfoundation.org; 29700 Woodford-Tehachapi Rd, Keene; admission $3; ◷ 10am-4pm) This newly designated national monument, Nuestra Señora Reina de la Paz, is the national headquarters of the United Farmworkers of America and was the home of civil rights leader César Chávez from 1971 until his death in 1993. On view are exhibits on Chávez's work, his office, and

grave. Keene is 27 miles southeast of Bakersfield down Hwy 58.

Chávez was born near Yuma, Arizona in 1927, and was 11 when his family lost their farm and became migrant farm workers in California. At 14, he left school to labor in the fields. Eventually, he became a champion of nonviolent social change, negotiating for better wages and access to water and bathrooms in the fields. His work resulted in numerous precedents including the first union contracts requiring safe use of pesticides and the abolition of short-handled tools that had crippled generations of farm workers.

🛏 Sleeping & Eating

Chain motels sprout like weeds off the highways near Bakersfield. Old-school budget motels, starting from about $47, line Union Ave south heading south from Hwy 178, but can be shady. Great meals though are easy to find. Bakersfield is blessed with a Basque culinary tradition, where food is served family-style in a procession of courses including soup, salad, beans, thin slices of tangy beef tongue and cottage cheese, which all come *before* the main course.

★ Padre Hotel   BOUTIQUE HOTEL $$
(☑ 661-427-4900; www.thepadrehotel.com; 1702 18th St; r $119-229, ste from $459) After standing vacant for years, this historic tower

KINGSBURG: A LITTLE SWEDEN IN THE VALLEY

The quiet hamlet of Kingsburg has a vibrant ethnic heritage. Around 1873, when it was established as a rail stop called 'Kings River Switch,' two Swedes arrived. Their countrymen soon followed, and by 1921, 94% of Kingsburg's residents, as it had become known, were of Swedish heritage.

Draper St, the main drag, is decked out in vibrant Swedish Dala horses, a holy symbol. Inside the cutesy Tudor buildings are gift shops and little bakeries stocked with buttery pastries. The restaurants serve Swedish pancakes, Swedish meatballs and Swedish lingonberry soda, just eat early, because many close after lunch. Diane at **Diane's Village Bakery & Cafe** (559-897-7460; 1332 Draper St, Kingsburg Village Mall; mains less than $8.25; 8am-2:30pm Mon-Sat) in the back of the Village Mall cooks with her grandmother's recipes. **Dala Horse** (559-897-7762; 1531 Draper St; mains $7.25-10.25; 6am-2:30pm, to 2pm Sat, to 1pm Sun) is liberal with their lingonberry jam. Pick up Nordic decor and insight on the town from June, town icon and proprietor of **Svensk Butik**. Sure the town plays up its heritage for the crowds, but there is genuine pride in every 'Valkommen!'

The town has also gone through pains to preserve its oldest structures. Under the coffee-pot water tower, the **city jail** (http://www.kingsburghistoricalpark.org; 1400 Marion St; 24hr) FREE is a quick stop. On the east end of town, a general store, schoolhouse and windmill, as well as artifacts and farm equipment make up **Kingsburg Historical Park** (www.kingsburghistoricalpark.org; 2321 Sierra St; 1-4pm Fri).

Good times to visit are during the holiday explosion that is the **Santa Lucia Festival** (first Saturday of December) and the **Swedish Festival** (parades, maypole dancing, and a real smorgasbord) in May. The **Chamber of Commerce** (559-897-1111; www.kingsburg-chamber-of-commerce.org; 1475 Draper St; 9am-5pm) keeps a calendar.

reopened after a stylish facelift that added an upscale restaurant and two bars that instantly became *the* places for cocktails in Bakersfield. The standard rooms have lavish details: thick mattresses, plush sheets and designer furniture. The two themed suites – the 'Oil Baron' and 'Farmer's Daughter' – have sexy showers for two.

Woolworth Diner   DINER $
(661-321-0061; 1400 19th St, Five & Dime Antique Mall; burgers $5.95; 11am-4pm Mon-Sat, noon-4pm Sun) The white capped soda jerks flip fantastic cheeseburgers and pour great shakes at the store's original soda counter, buffed to its former glory.

Wool Growers   BASQUE $
(661-327-9584; www.woolgrowers.net; 620 E 19th St; lunch $12.50, dinner mains $16.40-27; 11:30am-2pm & 6-9pm Mon-Sat) A simple Basque eating hall loaded with character. You can order the nine – yes nine – sides without the main, or loosen your belt and get it all.

Luigi's   ITALIAN $
(www.shopluigis.com; 725 E 19th St; mains $7.75-11.95; 11am-2:30pm Tue-Sat;) Lined with black-and-white photos of sporting legends, this amazing lunch spot has been around

more than 100 years. The stuffed chicken melts in your mouth and the excellent bakery turns out soft, buttery rolls and an exceedingly rich Butterfinger Pie. The adjacent bar and deli stay open until 4pm.

Dewar's Candy Shop   ICE CREAM $
(661-322-0933; 1120 Eye St; sundaes from $4.50; 10am-9pm Mon-Sun;) Perched on the pink stools at the counter, families dig into homemade ice cream with ingredients sourced from surrounding farms since 1930. Dreamy flavors such as lemon flake and cotton candy change seasonally.

Jake's Original Tex Mex Cafe SOUTHWESTERN $
(www.jakestexmex.com; 1710 Oak E St; mains $7.95-13.29; 11am-8pm Mon-Sat) More Tex than Mex, this excellent cafeteria packs in city workers for smoky, slow-roasted pit beef. The chili fries are a messy delight, and the combination plates decadent.

★**Noriega's**   BASQUE $$
(661-322-8419; www.noriegahotel.com; 525 Sumner St; breakfast $10, lunch $17, dinner $22; 7am-9am, from noon, from 7pm Tue-Sun) Surly Basque gentlemen still pass the communal wine carafes at Bakersfield's last family-style Basque institution. Join them at a commu-

nal table for a procession of dishes leading to silky oxtail stew, ribs and every other possible protein (check online for the day's main course). The magical ambience and the food earned a prestigious James Beard award. Reserve in advance, seating hours are strict.

The Mark   AMERICAN **$$**
(atthemark.com; 1623 19th St; mains from $17; ⊙11am-10pm Mon-Fri, 4-11.30pm Sat, 7:30-11:30pm Sun) One of downtown Bakersfield's swanky new additions has red banquettes and big city classics such as cioppino and pistachio-crusted lamb chops.

☆ Entertainment

★ **Buck Owens' Crystal Palace**   LIVE MUSIC
(☑661-328-7560; www.buckowens.com; 2800 Buck Owens Blvd) For fans of the city's plucky musical heritage, this is the first stop – hard to miss thanks to the huge neon homage to Buck's famous red, white and blue guitar. Part music museum (gift shop open from 11am), honky-tonk, and steakhouse (dinner from 5pm, brunch 9:30pm to 2pm Sunday), the Palace has top-drawer country acts nearly nightly. Locals in sharp, snap-button shirts, shiny boots and pressed jeans tear up the dance floor.

Trout's & the Blackboard Stage   LIVE MUSIC
(therockwellopry.webs.com; 805 N Chester Ave at Decatur St, Oildale; ⊙11am-late Mon-Sat) The legendary Trout's, north of town, is the only remaining honky-tonk in these parts, hobbling along after half a century as a testament to hell-raisin' days past. This ain't no disco – the only thing glistening is broken glass – but the live music comes from Bakersfield legends and their disciples.

Fox Theater   CONCERT VENUE
(www.foxtheateronline.com; 2001 H St) This gorgeous Gilded Age theater hosts artists of today – from Merle Haggard to the Pixies.

❶ Information

Greater Bakersfield Convention & Visitors Bureau (☑661-852-7282; www.bakersfieldcvb.org; 515 Truxtun Ave; ⊙8am-5pm Mon-Fri) A spacious building with maps and brochures.

❶ Getting There & Around

Airport Valet Express (☑661-363-5000; www.airportvaletexpress.com; 201 New Stine, suite 120; one way/roundtrip $49/89; ⊙to LAX 3am, 8am, 3pm, 8pm) Large orange and white buses run between Bakersfield (from the north

side of the San Joaquin Valley College campus) and LAX (2½ hours, eight daily).

Amtrak Station (☑800-872-7245; 601 Truxtun Ave at S St) Trains head north from here to Sacramento ($45 to $65, five hours, two direct trains). Buses head to LA, but tickets must be purchased in combination with a train ticket.

Golden Empire Transit (GET; www.getbus.org; 1830 Golden State Ave, Transit Center; fares from $1.25) The efficient local bus system's Route 22 runs north on Chester Ave to the Kern County Museum (p509) and Oildale (22 minutes).

Greyhound (☑661-327-5617; 1820 18th St at G St) Cheap rides from downtown Bakersfield to Los Angeles ($9, two hours).

Kern River Area

A half-century ago the Kern River originated on the slopes of Mt Whitney and journeyed close to 170 miles before finally settling into Buena Vista Lake in the Central Valley. The lake is long dry. Now, after its wild descent from the high country – 60ft per mile – the Kern is dammed in several places and almost entirely tapped for agricultural use.

Its pristine upper reaches, declared wild and scenic by the Secretary of the Interior, is nicknamed the 'Killer Kern' for its occasionally lethal force and makes for world-class rafting.

Hwy 178 follows the dramatic Kern River Canyon and offers a stunning drive through the lower reaches of Sequoia National Forest. East of the lake, Hwy 178 winds another 50 miles through a picturesque mixture of pine and Joshua trees before reaching Hwy 395.

There are two USFS Ranger Stations in the area, one in Kernville (☑760-376-3781; www.fs.usda.gov; ⊙8am-4:30pm Mon-Fri) and another in Lake Isabella (☑760-379-5646; ⊙8am-4:30pm Mon-Fri). Both have hiking and camping information, maps and wilderness permits.

🏃 Activities

This part of the state is all about white water, and rafting is the banner attraction. The town of Lake Isabella is a dreary strip of local businesses on the south end of the lake, but Hwy 155 runs north to Kernville, a cute little town straddling the Kern River that is *the* hub for local water sports. While the lake is popular for cooling off, note that the river's currents can be extremely dangerous.

The Upper Kern and Forks of the Kern (both sections of the river north of Kernville)

WEEDPATCH CAMP

In the Depression era, more than a million poor, white laborers from the Dust Bowl states in the South and the Great Plains arrived in the Central Valley with dreams of opportunity. Branded 'Okies' by the locals (whether from Oklahoma or not), the majority found only more hardship in the Golden State.

Weedpatch Camp (Arvin Farm Labor Camp; ☑ 661-832-1299; www.weedpatchcamp.com; 8701 Sunset Blvd, Bakersfield; ⊙ by appointment) is one of about 16 Farm Security Administration camps built in the US during the 1930s to aid migrant workers, and today it is the only one with original buildings still standing (as of press time, they were undergoing renovation). A reporter named John Steinbeck researched the people in this camp and their lives inspired *The Grapes of Wrath*. Nearby tract housing still shelters migrant workers for the six-month grape harvest.

From Bakersfield, take Hwy 58 east to Weedpatch Hwy; head south for about 7 miles, past Lamont; then turn left on Sunset Blvd, driving another half mile. Look for the 'Arvin Farm Labor Center' sign on your right. The Dust Bowl Festival is a free celebration of Okie history held here the third Saturday of October.

---

yield Class IV and V rapids during spring runoff and offer some of the most awe-inspiring white-water trips in the country. You'll need experience before tackling these sections, though there are still opportunities for novices. Below Lake Isabella, the Kern is tamer and steadier.

Currently seven rafting companies are licensed to operate out of Kernville; all offer competitive prices and run trips from May to August, depending on conditions. Excursions include popular one-hour runs (from $37) and day-long Lower Kern trips (from $119) and multiday Wild Forks of the Kern experiences (from $600). Walk-ins are welcome and experience is not necessary. Kids ages six and up can usually participate.

Kern River Outfitters RAFTING
(☑ 800-323-4234; http://kernrafting.com; 6602 Wofford Heights Blvd; ⊙ 8:30am-5:30pm Mon-Fri) Offers the staple menu of trips plus an adults-only Pub & Grub trip, which includes beer tastings from the Kern River Brewery.

Mountain & River Adventures RAFTING, OUTDOORS
(☑ 760-376-6553, 800-861-6553; www.mtnriver.com; 11113 Kernville Rd) Besides rafting, this outfit offers combo-kayak and rafting, mountain biking and winter excursions.

Sierra South RAFTING
(☑ 800-457-2082, 760-376-3745; www.sierra-south.com; 11300 Kernville Rd) Rafting or for

something calmer, paddleboarding on Lake Isabella.

Whitewater Voyages RAFTING
(☑ 660-376-8806, 800-400-7238; www.whitewatervoyages.com; 11006 Kernville Rd) The first outfitter to dare to guide clients down the entire Wild and Scenic Forks of the Kern back in 1980.

🛏 Sleeping

Lake Isabella has motels, but Kernville is a nicer location with still reasonable rates. Many require two-day minimum stays on weekends.

USFS Campgrounds CAMPGROUND $
(☑ 877-444-6777; www.fs.usda.gov; developed/undeveloped sites $24/20) These campgrounds line the 10-mile stretch between Lake Isabella and Kernville, and several more lie north of Kernville on Mountain Hwy 99. Rangers recommend the Fairview and Limestone sites for their seclusion. Campgrounds without running water and electricity are free.

Whispering Pines Lodge B&B $$$
(☑ 760-376-3733; http://pineskernville.com; 13745 Sierra Way; r $189-219, house incl breakfast $359; ❄) This secluded B&B, blending rustic character with luxurious comfort, is just north of town. Rooms with kitchens book up quickly in the summer.

Understand Northern California

Northern California Today

Water is on everyone's mind. At the time of writing, the state was in the third year of its worst-ever drought. Wells are going dry, fields fallow and lawns brown. Another Brown, Jerry, famous governor from the 1970s, is again governor, and, for the first time in years, the state has a balanced budget and surplus of cash. But that doesn't stop everyone from arguing over his legacy plan – a high-speed rail line, already under way from San Francisco to Los Angeles.

Best NorCal Films

Maltese Falcon (Houston, 1941) Humphrey Bogart as a San Francisco private eye.
Vertigo (Hitchcock, 1958) Alfred Hitchcock's noir thriller, set in SF and San Juan Batista.
Dirty Harry (Siegel, 1971) Clint Eastwood as an SFPD inspector, investigating murder.
The Joy Luck Club (Wang, 1993) Intergenerational struggles between mother and daughter, in and around San Francisco.
Blue Jasmine (Allen, 2013) New York socialite disappears to Northern California.

Best NorCal Albums

Workingman's Dead The Grateful Dead
Green River Creedence Clearwater Revival
My Ghetto Report Card E-40
Time Out Dave Brubeck Quartet
Stand! Sly and the Family Stone
Dookie Green Day
Crooked Rain, Crooked Rain Pavement
Mama Tried Merle Haggard

NorCal in a Nutshell

The story of California has always been a story of water, now more than ever. With the state in the middle of its worst-ever drought, local officials are sounding the alarm, setting limitations on usage, but stopping short of rationing, which nobody wants. Reservoirs are dangerously low, and many creeks and wells have gone dry. Dowsers and well-drillers are in high demand. Portions of the agricultural Central Valley have gone unplanted, farmers are slaughtering cattle because they've nothing to feed them, and food prices have begun to climb. Even the honey bees are swarming because flowers aren't blooming and there's no pollen for them. Nobody knows what's going to happen, but this being California, expect creative solutions.

But even in this (mostly) forward-thinking state, not all creative solutions to ongoing problems are met with open arms. To wit, the governor's legacy plan to build a high-speed rail link from San Francisco to LA in under half the time it takes to drive, with the goal of improving air quality and getting Californians out of their cars. Though the voter-approved project began preliminary construction in August 2014, opponents have fought vigorously to defeat it, with a series of seemingly endless lawsuits. It's slated for completion in 2029. Stay tuned.

Roots of Environmentalism

Californians originally kick-started the world's conservation movement in the midst of the 19th-century's industrial revolution, with laws curbing industrial dumping, and protections for pristine wildernesses that helped establish the national parks system. In the 1970s, the modern-day environmental movement was born, when then-President Nixon established the Environmental Protection Agency, following an oil spill off the Santa Barbara coast. Today Northern Californians continue to lead the nation with new ideas about sustainable food and low-impact lifestyles – often with smug self-satisfaction. Locals know they have it good. Some towns even dub themselves nuclear-free zones. No surprise NorCal has the USA's highest demand for hybrid vehicles.

Fast Companies, Slow Food

The technology boom has changed the cultural DNA of Northern California, with cutting-edge biotech research, online social media like Facebook and Twitter, and of course Google. Tech gazillionaires have driven up housing prices in San Francisco, transforming the city into a bedroom community for Silicon Valley. Longtime locals aren't pleased, and blame the giant tech shuttlebuses – which everyone calls the 'Google Bus' – for the city's gentrification.

If talking tech is straying into dangerous social territory, change the subject to food. Northern Californians are obsessed by what they eat, fetishizing seasonal foods, like heirloom peaches and heritage cuts of pork, like a bodybuilder fetishizes protein supplements. But nowhere else in America can lay claim to such incredible bounty. Even in urban San Francisco, farmers markets offer still-warm-from-the-sun fruit, picked that very morning. 'Locavore' eating began here, and after you've gotten your own taste, chances are you too will be asking the provenance of your fried green tomatoes.

NORCAL POPULATION: **AROUND 14 MILLION**

CALIFORNIA'S PROPORTION OF US GDP: **13%**

ANNUAL TAXES EARNED FROM MEDICAL MARIJUANA SALES IN CALIFORNIA: **$105 MILLION**

if California were 100 people

40 would be Caucasian
38 would be Latino
14 would be Asian American
7 would be African American
1 would be other

belief systems
(% of population)

36 — Protestant

2 — Mormon

3 — Jewish

2 — Buddhist

1 — Muslim

31 — Catholic

24 — other

1 — Hindu

population per sq mile

California   Los Angeles   San Francisco

 = 240 people

History

When European explorers first arrived in the 16th century, over 100,000 Native Americans called this land home. Spanish conquistadors, and priests determined to convert the natives, marched through in search of a fabled 'city of gold' before establishing Catholic missions and *presidios* (military forts). After winning independence from Spain, Mexico briefly ruled the land, but got trounced by the fledgling USA, just before gold's discovery in 1848. Immigrant waves of star-struck dreamers haven't stopped washing up on these Pacific shores ever since.

In some Central Californian Native American communities, mothers-in-law were traditionally so revered that you dared not speak to yours, and obeyed her without question.

Native Californians

Speaking some 100 distinct languages, Native Californians mostly lived in small communities and a few migrated with the seasons. Their diet was largely dependent on acorn meal, supplemented by small game, such as rabbit and deer, and fish and shellfish. They were skilled craftspeople, making earthenware pots, fishing nets, bows, arrows and spears with chipped-stone points. Many tribes developed a knack for weaving baskets of local grasses and plant fibers, decorating them with geometric designs – some baskets were so tightly woven that they could even hold water.

Northern coastal fishing communities, such as Ohlone, Miwok and Pomo, built subterranean roundhouses and sweat lodges, where they held ceremonies, told stories and gambled for fun. Northern hunting communities, including the Hupa, Karok and Wiyot, constructed big houses and redwood dugout canoes, while the Modoc lived in summer tepees and winter dugouts; all chased salmon during their seasonal runs. Kumeyaay and Chumash villages dotted the central coast, where tribespeople fished and paddled canoes.

When English sea captain Sir Francis Drake harbored briefly in 1579 on Miwok land north of San Francisco, the English were taken to be the dead returned from the afterworld, and shamans saw the arrival as a warning of apocalypse. The omens weren't far wrong: within a century of the 1769 arrival of Spanish colonists, Northern California's indigenous

TIMELINE	10,000 BC	1542–43 AD	1769
	Native American communities settle across the state – the Yurok in gabled redwood houses in the north, the Tipai-Ipai in thatched domed dwellings in the south.	Juan Rodríguez Cabrillo becomes the first European explorer to navigate the California coast. His journey ends in the Channel Islands, when a gangrenous wound kills him.	Franciscan friar Junípero Serra and Captain Gaspar de Portolá lead a Spanish expedition to establish missions, rounding up Native Americans as converts and conscripted labor.

population was decimated to 20,000 by European diseases, conscripted labor, violence and famine.

The Spanish Missions

When 18th-century Russian and English trappers began trading valuable otter pelts along the California coast, Spain concocted a plan for colonization. For the glory of God and the tax coffers of Spain, missions would be built across the state. This 'Sacred Expedition' was approved by Spain's quixotic visitor general, José de Gálvez of Mexico, who was full of grand schemes – including controlling Sonora province with a trained army of apes.

Almost immediately after Spain's missionizing plan was approved in 1769, it began to fail. When Franciscan friar Junípero Serra and Captain Gaspar de Portolá made the overland journey to establish Mission San Diego de Alcalá in 1769, only half the sailors on their supply ships survived. Portolá had heard of a fabled cove to the north, but failing to recognize Monterey Bay in the fog, he gave up and turned back.

Portolá reported to Gálvez that if the Russians or English wanted California, they were welcome to it. But Serra wouldn't give up, and secured support to set up *presidios* alongside missions. When soldiers weren't paid regularly, they looted and pillaged local communities. Clergy objected to this treatment of potential converts, but still relied on soldiers to round up conscripts to build missions. In exchange for their forced labor, Native Californians were allowed one meal a day and a place in God's kingdom – which came much sooner than expected, due to diseases like smallpox and syphilis that the Spanish brought.

It's no surprise that California's indigenous tribes often rebelled against the Spanish colonists. However, the missions did achieve modest success at farming and just barely managed to become self-sufficient. But as a way of colonizing California and converting the indigenous people to Christianity, they were an abject failure. The Spanish population remained small, foreign intruders were not greatly deterred and ultimately, more Native Californians died than were converted.

California Under Mexican Rule

Spain wasn't sorry to lose California to Mexico in the 1810–21 Mexican War for Independence. As long as missions had the best grazing land, *rancheros* (ranchers) couldn't compete in the growing market for cowhides and tallow (for use in soap). Yet Spanish, Mexican and American settlers who intermarried with Native Americans were now a sizable constituency, and together these 'Californios' convinced Mexico to secularize the missions in 1834.

Traces of a Native American culture dating from the 1st century remain at Chumash Painted Cave State Historic Park, which features the most elaborate indigenous rock designs outside of the deserts of the Southwest.

HISTORY THE SPANISH MISSIONS

1821	1835	1846	1848
Mexican independence ends Spanish colonization of California. Mexico inherits 21 missions in various states of disrepair, along with unruly Californio cowboys and a decimated Native American population.	An emissary of President Andrew Jackson makes a formal offer to buy Alta California, but Mexico tries unsuccessfully to sell it off to England instead.	Sierra Nevada blizzards strand the Donner Party of settlers, some of whom avoid starvation by eating their dead companions. Five women and two men snowshoe 100 miles for help.	Gold is discovered near present-day Placerville by mill employees. San Francisco newspaper publisher, vigilante and bigmouth Sam Brannan spills the secret, and the Gold Rush is on.

Californios quickly snapped up deeds to privatized mission property. Only a few dozen Californios were literate, so the boundary disputes that arose were settled with muscle, not paper. By law, half the lands were supposed to go to Native Californians who worked at the missions, but few actually received their entitlements.

In her bestselling novel *The Joy Luck Club*, Amy Tan weaves the stories of four Chinese-born women and their American-born daughters into a textured history of immigration and aspiration in San Francisco's Chinatown.

Through marriage and mergers, by 1846 most of the land and wealth in California was held by just 46 *ranchero* families. The average *rancho* (ranch) was now 16,000 acres, having grown from cramped shanties to elegant haciendas where women were supposedly confined to quarters at night. But *rancheras* (ranch women) weren't so easily bossed around: women owned some Californian ranches, rode horses as hard as men and caused romantic scandals worthy of *telenovelas* (soap operas).

Meanwhile, land fever and dreams of westward migration swept America, and settlers from the east began walking across the continent to California. There was no easy route. Some arrived via the dangerous and hot Santa Fe and Old Spanish Trails into the dusty backwater that was Los Angeles. Most came via the straighter Oregon and California Trails, arriving at Sutter's Fort in Sacramento, but this necessitated crossing the Sierra Nevada, which you had to time just right, lest you get trapped by snow – as happened to the infamous Donner Party, tragically stranded at the summit, near Truckee, and forced into cannibalism to survive.

Despite distance and terrain, the US saw potential in California, but when US President Andrew Jackson offered financially strapped Mexico $500,000 for the territory, the offer was tersely rejected. After the USA annexed the Mexican territory of Texas in 1845, Mexico broke off diplomatic relations and ordered all foreigners without proper papers to be deported from California. The Mexican–American War was declared in 1846 and lasted two years, with very little fighting in California. Hostilities ended with the Treaty of Guadalupe Hidalgo, which ceded California and the present-day Southwest to the USA. The timing was fortuitous: a few weeks after the US took possession of California, gold was discovered.

California's Gold Rush

The Gold Rush began with a bluff. Real-estate speculator, lapsed Mormon and tabloid publisher Sam Brannan was looking to unload some California swampland in 1848 when he heard rumors of gold flakes found near Sutter's Mill, 120 miles east of San Francisco in the Sierra Nevada foothills. Figuring this news should sell some newspapers and raise real-estate values, Brannan published the rumor as fact. Initially the story didn't generate excitement so Brannan ran another story, this time verified by Mormon employees at Sutter's Mill who had sworn him to secrecy. Brannan kept his word by running through San Francisco's

1850	1851	1869	1882
With hopes of solid-gold tax revenues, the US dubs California the 31st state. When miners find tax loopholes, SoCal ranchers are left carrying the tax burden, creating early north–south rivalries.	The discovery of gold in Australia means cheering in the streets of Melbourne and panic in the streets of San Francisco, as the price of California gold plummets.	On May 10, the 'Golden Spike' is nailed in place at Promontory, UT, completing the first transcontinental railroad, which connects California to the East Coast.	The US Chinese Exclusion Act suspends new immigration from China, denies citizenship to those already in the country and sanctions racially targeted laws that stay on the books until 1943.

streets, brandishing gold entrusted to him as tithes for the Mormon church, shouting, 'Gold on the American River!'

Newspapers around the world ran stories of 'gold mountains' near San Francisco, and by 1850, the year California was fast-tracked for admission to become the 31st US state, California's non-native population had ballooned from 15,000 to 93,000. Early arrivals from across the country and around the world panned for gold side by side, slept in close quarters, drank locally made wine and ate wok-fired Chinese food; when they struck it rich, they ordered 'Hangtown Fry' (an omelet with bacon and oysters).

With each wave of new arrivals, profits dropped and gold became harder to find. In 1848 each prospector earned an average of about $300,000 in today's terms; by 1849, earnings were less than half that, and by 1865 they had dipped to $35,000. When surface gold became scarce, miners picked, shoveled and dynamited through mountains. The work was grueling and dangerous; the cost of living in cold, filthy mining camps was sky-high; and with few doctors around, injuries often proved lethal. With only one woman for every 400 men in some camps, many turned to paid company, booze and opium for consolation.

Vigilantes, Robber Barons & Railroads

Prospectors who did best arrived early and got out quick; those who stayed too long either lost fortunes searching for the next nugget or became targets for resentment. Successful Peruvians and Chileans were harassed and denied renewals to their mining claims, and most left California by 1855. Native American laborers who helped the '49ers strike it rich were denied the right to hold claims. Also at the receiving end of hostilities were the Chinese, the most populous minority group in California by 1860. Frozen out of mining claims, many Chinese opened service-based businesses that survived when mining ventures went bust. Meanwhile, criminal wrongdoing was sometimes hastily pinned on Australians – starting in 1851, San Francisco's self-appointed Committee of Vigilance tried, convicted, lynched and deported the 'Sydney Ducks' gang, so when another gold rush began in Australia that same year, many were ready to head home.

Inter-ethnic rivalries obscured the real competitive threat posed not by fellow miners or service workers, but by those who controlled the means of production: California's 'robber barons.' These speculators hoarded the capital and industrial machinery necessary for deep-mining operations. As mining became industrialized, fewer miners were needed, and jobless prospectors turned their anger toward a convenient target: Chinese workers, who by 1860 had become, after Mexicans, the second-most populous group in California. Discriminatory Californian

1886	1906	1927	1934
The Supreme Court decision in 'Santa Clara County versus Southern Pacific Railroad' establishes 'personhood' for American corporations, citing equal protection under the 14th Amendment.	An earthquake levels entire blocks of San Francisco in one long minute, setting off fires that rage for three days. Survivors start rebuilding immediately.	After a year of tinkering, San Francisco inventor Philo Farnsworth transmits the first successful TV broadcast of...a straight line.	A longshoremen's strike ends with 34 San Francisco strikers shot and 40 gassed or beaten by police. After mass funeral processions and citywide strikes, shipping magnates meet union demands.

laws restricting housing, employment and citizenship for anyone born in China were reinforced in the 1882 US Chinese Exclusion Act, which remained law until 1943.

Laws limiting work options for Chinese arrivals served the needs of robber barons, who needed cheap labor to build railroads to their claims and reach East Coast markets. To blast tunnels through the Sierra Nevada, workers were lowered down sheer mountain faces in wicker baskets, planted lit sticks of dynamite in rock crevices, then urgently tugged the rope to be hoisted out of harm's way. Those who survived the day's work were confined to bunkhouses under armed guard in cold, remote mountain regions. With little other choice of legitimate employment, an estimated 12,000 Chinese laborers blasted through the Sierra Nevada, meeting the westbound end of the railroad in 1869.

Fighting for Water

During the American Civil War (1861–65), California couldn't rely on food shipments from the East Coast, and started growing its own. California recruited Midwestern homesteaders to farm the Central Valley, with shameless propaganda. 'Acres of Untaken Government Land...for a Million Farmers...Health and Wealth without Cyclones or Blizzards,' trumpeted one California-boosting poster, neglecting to mention earthquakes or ongoing land disputes with *rancheros* and Native Californians. It worked: more than 120,000 homesteaders came to California in the 1870s and '80s.

These homesteaders soon discovered that California's gold rush had left the land badly scarred. Hills had been stripped bare, vegetation wiped out, streams silted up and mercury washed into water supplies. Cholera spread through the open sewers in camps and claimed many lives. Because mining claims leased by the US government had been granted significant tax exemptions, there were insufficient public funds for clean-up programs or public water works.

Frustrated farmers south of Big Sur voted to secede from California in 1859, but appeals for secession were shelved during the Civil War. In 1884 Southern Californians passed a pioneering law preventing dumping into California's rivers and, with the support of budding agribusiness and real-estate concerns, passed bond measures to build aqueducts and dams that made large-scale farming and real-estate development possible. By the 20th century, the lower one-third of the state took two-thirds of available water supplies, inspiring Northern California's own calls for secession.

While Southern California was urbanizing following the discovery of oil, Northern Californians – who had witnessed firsthand the environmental devastation of mining and logging – were jump-starting the

1935	1941	1942	1957
The Central Valley Project establishes dams and canals throughout central California, constructed from the 1930s to 1970s, forever changing Northern California geography and wildlife migration.	Five timber- and mineral-rich counties in Northern California and Southern Oregon begin a secession effort to form the State of Jefferson. Plans are halted when Japan bombs Pearl Harbor.	Executive Order 9066 sends 120,000 Japanese Americans to internment camps. The Japanese American Citizens' League files lawsuits, providing legal support for the 1964 Civil Rights Act.	At the height of McCarthyism, City Lights in San Francisco wins a landmark ruling against book-banning over the publication of Allen Ginsberg's *Howl*.

nation's first conservation movement. Sierra Nevada naturalist, lyrical writer and San Francisco Bay Area farmer John Muir founded the Sierra Club in 1892, and became California's greatest environmental champion. Pipelines and dams – including Hetch Hetchy Reservoir in Yosemite, which still supplies Bay Area water – were constructed to provide water to communities in California's deserts and coastal cities, despite Muir's strenuous objections. In drought-prone California, tensions still regularly come to a boil between land developers and conservationists.

Reforming the Wild West

When the great earthquake and fire hit San Francisco in 1906, it signaled change for California. With public funds for citywide water mains and fire hydrants siphoned off by corrupt political bosses, there was only one functioning water source in San Francisco. When the smoke lifted, one thing was clear: it was time for the Wild West to change its ways.

While San Francisco was rebuilt at a rate of 15 buildings per day, political reformers set to work on improving city, state and national policies, one plank at a time. Californians concerned about public health and the trafficking of women pushed for passage of the 1914 Red Light Abatement Act, which shut down brothels statewide. Mexico's revolution from 1910 to 1921 brought a new wave of migrants and revolutionary ideas, including ethnic pride and worker solidarity. As California's ports grew, in 1934 longshoremen's unions coordinated a historic 83-day strike along the entire West Coast, which forced concessions for safer working conditions and fair pay.

At the height of the Depression in 1935, some 200,000 farming families fleeing the drought-struck Dust Bowl in Texas and Oklahoma arrived in California, where they found scant pay and deplorable working conditions. California's artists alerted America to the migrants' plight, and the nation rallied around Dorothea Lange's haunting documentary photos of famine-struck families and John Steinbeck's harrowing fictionalized account in his 1939 novel *The Grapes of Wrath*. The book was widely banned and Steinbeck was accused of harboring Communist sympathies, but he still won both the Pulitzer and Nobel Prizes for his masterwork. The public support he generated for farm workers helped launch the United Farm Workers.

California's workforce permanently changed in WWII, when women and African Americans were recruited for wartime industries and Mexican workers were brought in to fill labor shortages. Contracts in military communications and aviation attracted an international elite of engineers, who would launch California's high-tech industry. Within a decade after WWII, California's population grew by 40%, surpassing 13 million.

Roman Polanski's film *Chinatown* (1974) is the fictionalized yet surprisingly accurate account of the brutal water wars that were waged to build both San Francisco and Los Angeles. For the real story, told in racing prose, of how LA swindled Eastern Sierra farmers to secure its future water rights, read *Cadillac Desert: The American West and Its Disappearing Water*, by Marc Reisner (1986).

1967	1969	1977	1989
The Summer of Love kicks off on January 14 at the Human Be-In in Golden Gate Park with blown conch shells and brain cells, and draft cards used as rolling papers.	Native American activists symbolically reclaim Alcatraz as native land until ousted by the FBI in 1971. Public support for protesters strengthens self-rule concessions for Native American tribes.	San Francisco Supervisor Harvey Milk becomes the first openly gay man elected to California public office. Milk sponsors a gay-rights bill before being murdered by political opponent Dan White.	On October 17, the Loma Prieta earthquake hits 6.9 on the Richter scale near Santa Cruz, destroying a two-level section of Interstate 880 and resulting in 63 deaths and almost 4000 injuries.

NORTHERN CALIFORNIA'S FIGHT FOR CIVIL RIGHTS

Before the 1963 march on Washington, DC, the civil rights movement was well under way in California. When 120,000 Japanese Americans along the West Coast were ordered into internment camps by President Roosevelt in 1942, the San Francisco–based Japanese American Citizens' League immediately filed suits that eventually made their way to the Supreme Court. These lawsuits established groundbreaking civil rights legal precedents; in 1992 internees received reparations and an official letter of apology for internment signed by George W Bush.

Adopting the nonviolent resistance practices of Mahatma Gandhi and Martin Luther King Jr, labor leaders César Chávez and Dolores Huerta formed United Farm Workers in 1962 to champion the rights of underrepresented immigrant laborers. While civil-rights leaders marched on Washington, Chávez and Californian grape pickers marched on Sacramento, bringing the issue of fair wages and the health risks of pesticides to the nation's attention. When Bobby Kennedy was sent to investigate, he sided with Chávez, bringing Latinos into the US political fold.

The Seeds of Counterculture

It's only fitting that San Francisco sits at the far left edge of the country, mirroring the city's political inclinations. WWII sailors discharged in San Francisco for insubordination and homosexuality found themselves at home in North Beach's bebop jazz clubs, Bohemian coffeehouses and City Lights bookstore. San Francisco was home to free speech and free spirits, and soon everyone who was anyone was getting arrested: Beat poet Lawrence Ferlinghetti for publishing Allen Ginsberg's epic poem *Howl,* comedian Lenny Bruce for uttering the F-word onstage, and Carol Doda for going topless.

When the CIA made the mistake of using writer and willing test subject Ken Kesey to test psychoactive drugs intended to create the ultimate soldier, it inadvertently kicked off the psychedelic era. At the January 14, 1967 Human Be-In at Golden Gate Park, trip-master Timothy Leary urged a crowd of 20,000 hippies to dream a new American dream and 'turn on, tune in, drop out.' When Flower Power faded, other Bay Area rebellions grew in its place: Black Power, Gay Pride and medical marijuana clubs.

California is America's top technology hub, accounting for one-third of all US venture capital, half of biotech employment and half of all FDA-approved medical therapies since 1985.

Geeking Out

When Silicon Valley introduced the first personal computer in 1968, advertisements breathlessly gushed that Hewlett-Packard's 'light' (40lb) machine could 'take on roots of a fifth-degree polynomial, Bessel functions, elliptic integrals and regression analysis' – all for just $4900 (over

$33,000 today). Consumers didn't know quite what to do with computers, but in his 1969 *Whole Earth Catalog,* author (and former LSD tester for the CIA) Stewart Brand explained that the technology governments used to run countries could empower ordinary people. Hoping to bring computer power to the people, Steve Jobs and Steve Wozniak, both in their 20s at the time, introduced the Apple II at the 1977 West Coast Computer Faire, with unfathomable memory (4KB of RAM) and microprocessor speed (1MHz).

Still, the question remained: what would ordinary people do with all that computing power? By the mid-1990s an entire dot-com industry boomed in Silicon Valley with online start-ups, and suddenly people were getting everything – their mail, news, politics, pet food and, yes, sex – online. But when dot-com profits weren't forthcoming, venture-capital funding dried up and fortunes in stock options disappeared when the dot-com bubble burst and the Nasdaq plummeted on March 10, 2000. Overnight, 26-year-old vice-presidents and Bay Area service-sector employees alike found themselves jobless. But as online users continued to look for useful information – and one another – in those billions of web pages, search engines and social media boomed.

Meanwhile, California's biotech industry had started to take off. In 1976 an upstart company called Genentech was founded in the San Francisco Bay Area, and quickly got to work cloning human insulin and introducing the hepatitis B vaccine. In 2004 California voters approved a $3 billion bond measure for stem-cell research. By 2008 California had become the USA's biggest funder of stem-cell research, as well as the focus of Nasdaq's new Biotechnology Index. Now all that's missing is another biotech boom – but if history is any indication, California will make good on its big talk, no matter how outlandish it might at first sound.

To read more about the garage-workshop culture of Silicon Valley go to www.folklore.org, which covers the crashes and personality clashes that made geek history.

2008	**2008**	**2013**	**2014**
California voters pass Proposition 8, defining legal marriage as between a man and a woman. Courts eventually rule the law unconstitutional, and same-sex marriages resume in 2013.	California voters approve the sale of bonds to fund California's High-Speed Rail Project, which by 2029 will link San Francisco and Los Angeles in under three hours.	The eastern span of the Bay Bridge opens, after 24 years of planning and construction, sparked by the 1989 Loma Prieta earthquake. It cost $6 billion, the state's costliest-ever public-works project.	The California Legislature passes a bill banning single-use plastic grocery bags – the nation's first such statewide ban – citing degradation of the state's waterways and environment.

The People: Tree Huggers to Techies

Believe (most of) what you've heard – Northern Californians are a different breed. Typically they espouse a live-and-let-live sensibility, which explains how ultra-left hippies and ultra-right libertarians coexist throughout the region. And although it may seem absurd to ponder the similarities between young tech execs from Silicon Valley and grizzled old lumberjacks from the far north, both pride themselves on fiercely independent thinking, the linchpin of NorCal culture.

There's truth in at least one outdoorsy stereotype: over 60% of Californians admit to having hugged a tree.

Regional Identity

In the Bay Area the politics are liberal and the people are generally open-minded, with a strong sense of social justice and a passionate devotion to the outdoors. Over the years, the tech boom has caused a wild rise in real-estate prices, changing the demographics of many San Francisco neighborhoods, which lately are starting to resemble the demographics of overwhelmingly wealthy and white Marin County, just over the Golden Gate Bridge. Both have a tremendous sense of self-satisfied civic pride. San Francisco, despite its all-embracing image, lately suffers from a loss of diversity. The East Bay and Alameda County, which include Oakland and Berkeley, have more ethnic diversity and middle-class blending, but because of unaffordable real-estate prices in San Francisco, these counties are also seeing prices skyrocket.

Far north of San Francisco, it's a different scene altogether. The counties of Mendocino, Humboldt and Del Norte are where people go to get away from other people, making for a small, self-selecting population. There aren't a lot of people in the far north – and there's not a lot of money either. At least not legal money.

Despite the fact that medical marijuana is legal in California, the remote woods of the far north still harbor enormous illegal marijuana farms, bringing with them an underground culture of growers and itinerant pickers. Some are on the up and up, growing 'medicine' (or 'flowers') for legal urban cannabis clubs, but since pot remains against federal law, even if legal by state law, the DEA flies in every year and destroys many farms (it doesn't usually seize the land, just the pot). Other operations are shadier, fly-by-nighters run by drug cartels, which set up for a season on public land that gets trashed by the grow. This pot goes out of the state. When in the far north, don't ever jump fences marked 'private property,' lest you hear rifle fire.

The state's more progressive liberals also live up north, and have fostered a strong and innovative culture of sustainability. (If you spot a beat-up old diesel Mercedes-Benz chugging along the highway, chances are it's running on biodiesel or recycled French-fry grease.) This faction is firmly entrenched against another sizable voting block: the conservative contingent in the northeast, who are still largely dependent on logging and mining.

The Central Coast, with its smaller pockets of population, starts below left-of-center Santa Cruz, and stretches all the way south to the laid-back, liberal college town of San Luis Obispo. Along the way, Hwy 1 winds past working-class Monterey, made famous in John Steinbeck's novels; the bohemian Big Sur coast; the conservative upper-crust village of Carmel-by-the-Sea; and Cambria, where the 'newly wed and nearly dead' have multimillion-dollar homes.

The Central Valley is the most socially conservative part of the state, with a largely agricultural economy. This is the land of cowboys, farmers, fruit barons and migrant workers. The identity of the region is also dramatically impacted by the presence of a Latino workforce that harvests the vast agricultural plains, and the echoes of the so-called 'Okies,' who fled the Oklahoma dust bowl generations ago. Highway billboards warn you to get right with God, and AM radio plays mariachi music.

The foothills of the Sierra Nevada include the small towns of the Gold Country, which are socially conservative; many locals are retirees. Further east, the high mountains of the Sierra have fewer towns because of winter's deep snows. Locals in the high mountains likewise skew conservative, but they are offset by the hordes of Bay Area families who have weekend houses in the areas around Lake Tahoe and Truckee, where skiing and hiking are the major draws.

California is defined as a 'minority majority' state, with no ethnic population in the majority. In March 2014, Latinos surpassed non-Hispanic whites as the state's largest ethnic group, comprising 39% of the population.

Lifestyle

Creativity, imagination and intellectualism are defining characteristics of Northern Californians, who are proud of their 'green' reputation and sensitive to environmental issues. On the whole, Californians have zoomed ahead of the national energy-use curve, buying more hybrid and fuel-efficient cars than any other state. San Francisco has gone so far as

MARRIAGE: EQUAL RIGHTS FOR ALL

Forty thousand Californians were already registered as domestic partners when, on Valentine's Day weekend in 2004, San Francisco Mayor Gavin Newsom issued marriage licenses to same-sex couples. This was in defiance of a statewide same-sex marriage ban, making San Francisco the first place in America to legally recognize gay marriage. City Hall remained open all weekend, and couples waited in the rain for hours in lines that snaked around the block, while other lovestruck San Franciscans arrived with umbrellas, trays of cookies and champagne, and musical instruments to serenade the waiting couples.

In the subsequent month, 4000 same-sex couples married, until courts blocked the issuance of any more licenses, pending legislative review. In November of that same year, the California Supreme Court deemed that the mayor hadn't had the authority to bypass state law, and voided the marriages. Subsequent lawsuits were brought by the couples whose marriages had been voided, and in May 2008 the state Supreme Court overturned the statewide ban, deeming it unconstitutional. For six months, couples once again came from around the world to marry in California, until in November 2008 voters passed – by slim margins (48% to 52%) – Proposition 8, which amended the state's constitution to prohibit same-sex marriage. This left those couples who held legally binding marriage certificates in legal limbo.

Meanwhile, over a dozen other states had begun to allow same-sex marriage, either by court decision, state legislation or popular vote. Then, in 2013, the US Supreme Court overturned Proposition 8, and maintained the validity of the licenses issued prior to the ban. Now some legally married couples hold two licenses: one from 2004 and one from 2008. Nationally, the debate continues to rage. The final outcome rests with the Supreme Court, which (as of this writing) had yet to decide which of the many pending cases from around the country it would hear.

WHO'S UP IN THAT TREE?

Although many people in Northern California are active defenders of the environment, few demonstrate the zeal of Julia Butterfly Hill, who protested the deforestation of Northern California's redwood forests by climbing into a 180ft tree near Scotia on December 10, 1997. And then she stayed there. Hill's tree, a 1500-year-old coast redwood that she named 'Luna,' was under threat from the Pacific Lumber Company. In an astonishing act of civil disobedience, Hill lived on a 6ft-by-6ft platform, weathering cold, rain and persistent harassment from lumberjacks, for 738 days – over two full years.

Hill's actions captured the nation's imagination, and she became both the face of radical environmental action and a punch line for late-night talk-show hosts. In the end, Luna was spared, and a $50,000 deal was brokered with the Pacific Lumber Company. Not that the campaign to protect old-growth redwood is over – a proposition to widen and straighten Hwy 101 by CalTrans threatened to bring chainsaws to over 40 trees in Richardson Grove State Park until, in 2014, courts ruled that the state highway agency hadn't followed the law in its assessment of impacts on the trees. Stay tuned.

to set the goal of 'zero waste,' going beyond mere recycling to city-wide composting of leftover food scraps.

With a median household income of $61,400, few Californians can afford a beachfront dream house. Many people rent their homes, as buying has become prohibitive in recent years: eight of the 10 most expensive US housing markets are in California. Almost half of all Californians reside in cities, but much of the other half lives in the suburbs, where the cost of living is just as high, if not higher; Marin County, outside San Francisco, is among the most costly places to live in America. San Francisco consistently tops national quality-of-life indices, and is right behind New York City as one of the nation's most expensive cities.

Among adult Californians, one in four lives alone, and almost 50% are unmarried. Of those who are currently married, 33% won't be in 10 years. Increasingly, Californians are shacking up: the number of unmarried cohabiting couples has increased 40% since 1990.

Politically, Northern California is among the most liberal places in the US, particularly in the coastal areas. Voters favored Barack Obama in the 2012 presidential election with a 23% margin of victory. In San Francisco County, Obama won 83% of the vote.

Self-help, fitness and body modification are major industries throughout California, successfully marketed since the 1970s as 'lite' versions of religious experience – all the agony and ecstasy of the major religious brands, without those heavy commandments. Exercise and good food help keep Californians among the fittest in the nation. Yet over 572,000 Californians are apparently ill enough to merit prescriptions for medical marijuana.

In 2002, Sacramento was cited by *Time* magazine and the Civil Rights Project at Harvard University as America's most diverse and integrated city. According to the *Sacramento Bee*, this still held true 10 years later.

The Homeless

Homelessness is not part of the California dream, but it is a reality for at least 160,000 Californians. With the additional impacts of the global economic crisis, the housing boom and recent unemployment numbers, some suggest that the numbers are much higher. The sheer visibility of homeless people in Northern California, particularly in San Francisco, is a shock for many visitors.

Understanding the causes and demographics of Northern California's homeless is not easy. Some are teens who have run away or been kicked out by their families, but the largest contingent of homeless Californians are US military veterans – almost 30,000 in all. Some say the problem started in the 1960s, when Ronald Reagan slashed funding to mental-health facilities, drug-rehab programs and low-income housing programs, both as governor of California and later as president. Over the following decades, this left few to no options for many Californians suffering from mental illness and drug addiction.

Also standing in line at homeless shelters and food banks are the working poor, unable to cover rent and expenses on minimum-wage salaries, despite recent increases to the latter. Rather than addressing the underlying causes of homelessness, some California cities have criminalized loitering, panhandling and even sitting on sidewalks, further marginalizing the homeless.

The bottom line is nobody knows how to address the issue, and until they do, panhandlers will be part of the experience of visiting Northern California cities – especially San Francisco. Whether you offer money or food is obviously up to you, but in general a polite 'no, thank you' will suffice if you'd rather not.

Sports

California has more professional sports teams than any other state, and loyalties to local NFL football, NBA basketball and major-league baseball teams run deep. Still, San Francisco doesn't necessarily have the sports nuts in large numbers like other American cities. That said, people in the Bay Area do get worked up before a big game – just go ahead and try to find tickets to see the San Francisco 49ers. After a dizzying season in 2010, the San Francisco Giants won the baseball World Series and transformed San Francisco's typically apathetic population into rabid fans in orange and black; they swarmed the streets again in 2012, after another World Series win.

A recent study found Californians are less likely to be couch potatoes than other Americans, but when one Californian team plays another, the streets are deserted, bars full and all eyes glued to the tube. The biggest grudge matches are between the San Francisco 49ers and the Oakland Raiders, the San Francisco Giants and the LA Dodgers, and baseball's Oakland A's and Anaheim's Angels. Sometimes tensions explode at these games. In August 2011, at a match between San Francisco's 49ers and the Oakland Raiders, an enormous brawl broke out in the parking lot and three people were shot.

To see small but dedicated crowds of hometown fans (and easily score cheaper tickets), watch pro men's or women's (WNBA) basketball in Sacramento, or pro hockey or soccer in San Jose. Or catch minor league baseball teams up and down the state, especially the winning San Jose Giants.

Except for championship play-offs, the regular season for major-league baseball runs from April to September, soccer from April to October, WNBA basketball from late May to mid-September, NFL football from September to early January, NHL ice hockey from October to March, and NBA basketball from November to April.

Surfing is the coastal spectator sport of choice, with waves reaching 100ft at the annual Mavericks competition near Half Moon Bay.

Southern California is *totally* known for its surfer drawl, but Northern California, too, has its own mix of idiosyncratic slang. The most iconic examples? 'Hella' and 'hecka,' which are technically defined by linguists as intensifiers.

The Land & Sustainability

Northern California has stunning landscapes. Its Mediterranean climate – characterized by dry summers and mild, wet winters with snow only at high elevations – makes it an easy year-round destination. Though the north is more sparsely populated than the south, together they comprise the largest population of any US state, and have the nation's highest projected growth rate. This puts tremendous strain on the natural environment, which is under constant threat from logging, water diversion and urban sprawl.

According to the US Geological Survey, the odds of a magnitude 6.7 or greater earthquake hitting California in the next 30 years are 99.7%.

Lay of the Land

The third-largest state after Alaska and Texas, California covers more than 155,000 sq miles, making it larger than 85 of the world's smallest nations. Northern California is bordered to the north by Oregon, to the east by Nevada, to the south by Mexico, and to the west by 3427 miles of Pacific coastline.

Geology & Earthquakes

As a whole, California is a complex geologic landscape formed from fragments of rock and earth crust scraped together as the North American continent drifted westward over hundreds of millions of years. Northern California has crumpled coastal ranges, the downward-bowing Central Valley and the still-rising Sierra Nevada; all provide evidence of the gigantic forces exerted as the continental and ocean plates crushed together.

Everything changed about 25 million years ago, when the ocean plates stopped colliding and instead started sliding against each other, creating the massive San Andreas Fault, which today moves an average of 2in per year. Because this contact zone doesn't slide smoothly, but catches and slips irregularly, it rattles California with an ongoing succession of tremors and earthquakes.

The San Andreas Fault is where the Pacific Plate (which runs under the Pacific Ocean floor and much of California's coastline) meets the continental North American Plate. The fault runs for over 650 miles and has spawned numerous smaller faults that extend toward the shoreline. Earthquakes are common, although most are too small or too remote to be detected without sensors. Fear not: small earthquakes are good news, evidence that the plates are moving along their paths, rather than storing kinetic energy and later causing bigger quakes.

The state's most famous earthquake, in 1906, measured 7.8 on the Richter scale and demolished San Francisco, leaving more than 3000 people dead. Walk the Earthquake Trail at Point Reyes National Seashore for an up-close lesson in plate tectonics: a broken fence line reveals how the 1906 quake moved the earth nearly 20ft in under a minute. The Bay Area made headlines again in 1989, when the Loma Prieta earthquake (6.9) caused a section of the Bay Bridge to collapse, and in 2014 when the Napa earthquake (6.0) caused an estimated $300 million in damage and loss. The last 'big one' occurred in 1994, in Southern California, when the Northridge quake (6.7) caused parts of the Santa Monica Fwy to fall down, making it the most costly quake in US history – so far.

The Coast to the Central Valley

Much of Northern California's coast is fronted by rugged coastal mountains that capture winter's water-laden storms and block passage of summertime fog, except at the Golden Gate, where fog slips inland over San Francisco Bay. San Francisco divides the Coast Ranges roughly in half. The foggy North Coast remains sparsely populated, while the Central Coast and lower regions of the Bay Area have a balmier climate and many more people.

Over 120in of rain falls each year in the northernmost reaches of the Coast Ranges and, in some places, persistent summer fog contributes another 12in of precipitation. Nutrient-rich soils and abundant moisture foster forests of giant trees, including stands of towering redwoods growing as far south as Big Sur and north all the way to the Oregon border, where their habitat abruptly stops. Because of this unique arrangement of mountains and weather, the most reliably sunny time to visit the North Coast is in the fall, when moisture (in the form of fog) isn't being sucked in by the blisteringly hot Central Valley's rising air currents.

On their eastern flanks, the Coast Ranges subside into gently rolling hills that give way to the sprawling Central Valley. Once an inland sea, this flat inland basin is now an agricultural powerhouse producing about half of America's fruits, nuts and vegetables, valued at over $14 billion a year. Its bounty is evident when driving through the region – large fields of edibles stretch horizon to horizon. The productivity of the region is a modern agricultural feat: about 450 miles long and 50 miles wide, the Central Valley gets about as much rainfall as a desert, but receives huge volumes of water running off the Sierra Nevada. Before the arrival of Europeans the valley was a natural wonderland – a region of vast marshes, flocks of geese that blackened the sky, and grasslands carpeted with countless flowers and plants where millions of antelopes, elk and grizzly bears grazed. Virtually this entire landscape has been plowed and replaced with alien weeds (including agricultural crops) and livestock.

Mountain Highs

Bordering the Central Valley on its eastern side looms California's most prominent topographic feature: the world-famous ridges of the Sierra Nevada mountain range. At 400 miles long and 50 miles wide, this is not only one of the largest mountain ranges in the world, it is also home to vast wilderness areas and 13 peaks over 14,000ft. The entire 150-mile region from Sonora Pass south to Mt Whitney lies mostly above 9000ft and is known as the High Sierra; this is a stunning and remote landscape of glaciers, sculpted granite peaks and lonely canyons. It's beautiful to see from a distance, but difficult to access, and crossing it posed the greatest challenge to settlers attempting to reach California in the 1800s.

Browse over 1200 aerial photos covering almost every mile of California's gorgeously rugged coastline, from Oregon to the Mexican border, at www.california-coastline.org.

THE LAND & SUSTAINABILITY LAY OF THE LAND

ALMOST AN ISLAND

Much of California is a biological island, cut off from the rest of North America by the soaring wall of mountains that is the Sierra Nevada. As on other 'islands' in the world, evolution has created unique plants and animals under these biologically isolated conditions. As a result, California ranks first in the nation for its number of endemic plants, amphibians, reptiles, freshwater fish and mammals. Even more impressive, 30% of all the plant species found in the USA, 50% of all bird species and 50% of all mammal species occur in California.

THE BIG ONES

Although the San Andreas Fault has apparently been rumbling for millennia, the earliest recorded earthquake in California dates to 1769, when it shook members of the Spanish Portolá Expedition near LA. Here are some of the largest rattlers in Northern California since then:

➡ 1868 Hayward earthquake – Mentioned by Mark Twain in *Roughing It,* this 7.0 magnitude quake destroyed every building in the Bay Area suburb of Hayward.

➡ 1872 Lone Pine earthquake – Although it was unmeasured, scientists think that this earthquake in the Owens Valley rivaled the intensity of the 1906 event. It apparently woke John Muir, who ran out of his Yosemite cabin shouting 'A noble quake!'

➡ 1906 San Francisco earthquake – The granddaddy of them all, this quake and the subsequent fires leveled San Francisco, leaving almost 75% of the city homeless. It was felt as far north as Oregon.

➡ 1964 Good Friday earthquake – Although the epicenter of this quake was near Anchorage, Alaska, it sent tsunami waves down the coast and destroyed much of downtown Crescent City.

➡ 1989 Loma Prieta earthquake – Centered in the Santa Cruz mountains, this shook players warming up for the 1989 World Series and caused the collapse of a section of the bridge connecting Oakland and San Francisco.

The soaring Sierra Nevada captures wintertime storm systems and drains them of their water. Most of the precipitation over 5000ft falls as snow. Snowfalls average 38ft at mid-elevations on the west slope, with a record of 73.5ft at one location, making the Sierra a premier skiing and winter-sports destination. These waters eventually flow into 11 major river systems down the west slope, and several on the east slope, providing the vast majority of water for agriculture in the Central Valley and meeting the needs of major metropolitan areas from San Francisco to Los Angeles.

Most of the Sierra Nevada is cloaked in dense conifer forests, with stands of oak in the lower foothills and chaparral zones. Twenty-three species of conifer occur in the Sierra Nevada, ranging from the stately incense cedars of the western foothills to tiny wind-sculpted whitebark and foxtail pines at 12,000ft. In between, mid-elevation forests are home to massive Douglas firs, ponderosa, sugar and Jeffrey pines, and biggest of all, the giant sequoia.

At its northern end the Sierra Nevada lowers in elevation and merges imperceptibly into the southern tip of the volcanic Cascade Mountains that continue north into Oregon and Washington. This wet mountainous region extends westward to the coast through a tangle of ancient and geologically complex ranges that are sparsely populated and also heavily cloaked with conifer forests.

California claims both the highest point in contiguous US (Mt Whitney, 14,497ft) and the lowest elevation in North America (Badwater, Death Valley, 282ft below sea level) – plus they're only 90 miles apart, as the condor flies.

National & State Parks

The majority of Californians rank outdoor recreation as vital to their quality of life, and the number of preserved lands has steadily grown due to important pieces of legislation passed since the 1960s, including the landmark 1976 California Coastal Act, which saved the coastline from further development. Today, **California State Parks** (www.parks.ca.gov) protect nearly a third of the state's coastline, along with redwood forests, mountain lakes, desert canyons, waterfalls, wildlife preserves and historical sites.

In recent years, both federal and state budget shortfalls and chronic underfunding have been partly responsible for widespread park closures, more limited visitor services and steadily rising park-entry and outdoor recreation fees. In May 2011, the State of California announced that it planned to close 70 state parks – about 25% of the system – but in the months following, nonprofit organizations, environmentalists and park advocates scrambled to save them, and miraculously $20 million appeared to spare them. In his 2014 budget, Governor Jerry Brown allocated $40 million for the estimated backlog of $1 billion in overdue maintenance, and all parks currently remain open. Many believe that it's in California's economic interests to protect the wilderness, since recreational tourism consistently outpaces competing 'resource extraction' industries, such as mining and logging.

Unfortunately, some of Northern California's parks are also being loved to death. Overcrowding severely impacts the environment, and it's increasingly difficult to balance public access with the principles of conservation. If possible, try visiting big-name parks like Yosemite in the shoulder seasons (ie not summer) to avoid the biggest crowds. Alternatively, lesser-known natural areas managed by the **National Park Service** (www.nps.gov/state/ca) may go relatively untouched most of the year, which means you won't have to reserve permits, campsites or accommodations months in advance.

There are 18 national forests in California run by the **US Forest Service** (USFS; www.fs.fed.us/r5), including lands around Mt Whitney, Mt Shasta and Big Bear Lake, and many other areas worth exploring. National wildlife refuges (NWR), favored by bird-watchers, are managed by the **US Fish & Wildlife Service** (USFWS; www.fws.gov/refuges). More wilderness tracts are overseen by the **Bureau of Land Management** (BLM; www.blm.gov/ca/st/en.html).

Take a virtual field trip courtesy of the myriad links put together by the California Geological Survey at www.conservation.ca.gov/cgs/geotour.

Northern California Water

Understanding California geography demands an understanding of how water moves – both physically and politically. Spring through fall are dry; almost all of the precipitation falls in the winter, when weather off the Pacific zips across the state, then gets hung up on the ridges of the Sierra Nevada, where snowstorms can last for days and dump up to 10ft of snow at a time. Come spring, all that snow begins to melt and drains down the river courses that support white-water rafting, through irrigation systems that provide water for California's famous crops, and through giant aqueducts and webs of pipes that provide fresh water to the densely populated urban Bay Area. Water has a profound effect on all aspects of culture in Northern California. And since the 2011 start of the state's worst drought in history, water is an especially hot topic, one that pits developers against conservationists, and farmers against city dwellers.

Moving through the inland territory of Northern California, you'll almost certainly encounter one or both of the region's two major rivers, the Sacramento and the San Joaquin. These are the aquatic highways into which so many other river systems feed – rivers such as the Kern, which runs through Bakersfield; the Tuolumne, which rushes through Yosemite's High Country; and the American, which crosses the Gold Country. For these rivers, the end of the line is San Francisco Bay, where 65% of the fresh water in all California drains into the Pacific. In the far north, another six rivers are popular for recreation – the Trinity, Smith, Klamath, Mad, Eel and Van Duzen.

Lakes are likewise a major draw for travelers. Lake Tahoe, the second-deepest lake in the US, and Clear Lake, north of Wine Country,

CALIFORNIA'S CAP & TRADE

In October 2011, California lawmakers adopted a cap-and-trade system for air emissions, in order to help the state achieve its ambitious goals to reduce greenhouse gas by 2020. The complex market system fixes a price on heat-trapping pollution by California's dirtiest industries – coal, oil and manufacturing – and allows them to trade carbon credits. Beginning in 2012, the state's largest carbon emitters were required by law to meet the caps or buy credits. The legislation, originally endorsed by former governor Arnold Schwarzenegger, had to overcome a number of legal challenges and a 2010 ballot initiative that aimed to suspend it. Current governor Jerry Brown is a big supporter. In 2013, the plan raised $850 million, most of which went toward public transit and affordable housing. Governor Brown allocated a third of these funds to go toward financing California's high-speed rail, which by 2029 will connect San Francisco and Los Angeles in under three hours.

are two of the region's most popular natural lakes, but reservoirs, such as Shasta Lake and Whiskeytown Lake, are also hugely popular destinations for recreation.

Northern California's water policies have major environmental, political and social consequences. An example is Hetch Hetchy reservoir, in Yosemite National Park. Once a deep natural gorge described by California's greatest environmental champion John Muir as 'one of nature's rarest and most precious mountain temples,' Hetch Hetchy was dammed and flooded in 1923 to create a pristine source of water for the city of San Francisco. (Some say Muir died of heartbreak afterward.) Lately a small, but vocal, minority has called for the draining of the reservoir to restore Hetch Hetchy Valley to its natural state. Opponents argue that not only is the valley's pristine state now irretrievable, but that un-damming it would undermine San Francisco's supply of clean water. Voters agreed, and with 77% of the vote, soundly defeated a 2012 ballot measure to tear down the dam.

Conserving California

Although California is in many ways a success story, development and growth have come at great environmental cost. Starting in 1849, Gold Rush miners tore apart the land in their frenzied quest for the 'big strike,' ultimately sending more than 1.5 billion tons of debris, and uncalculated amounts of poisonous mercury, downstream into the Central Valley where rivers and streams became clogged and polluted.

The San Francisco airport introduced green 'hydration stations' at its state-of-the-art terminal to decrease waste from bottled water. The stations came with a snappy slogan, offering a drink from the 'pristine Sierra snowmelt.'

Water, or the lack thereof, has long been at the heart of California's epic environmental struggles and catastrophes. The diversion of water to LA has contributed to the destruction of Owens Lake and its fertile wetlands, and to the degradation of Mono Lake. Statewide, the damming of rivers and capture of water for houses and farms has destroyed countless salmon runs and drained marshlands. The Central Valley, for example, today resembles a dust bowl, and its underground aquifer is in poor shape.

Altered and compromised habitats, both on land and water, make easy targets for invasive species, including highly aggressive ones that wreak havoc on California's economy and ecosystems. In San Francisco Bay, one of the most important estuaries in the world, there are now over 230 alien species choking the aquatic ecosystem, and in some areas they already comprise as much as 95% of the total biomass.

Although air quality in California has improved markedly in past decades, it's still among the worst in the country. Auto exhaust and fine particulates generated by the wearing down of vehicle tires, along with industrial emissions, are the chief culprits. An even greater health hazard is ozone, the principal ingredient in smog, which makes sunny days around the Central Valley look hazy.

But there's hope. Low-emission vehicles are becoming one of the most sought-after types of car in the state, and rapidly rising fuel costs are keeping more gas-guzzling SUVs off the road. Californians recently voted to fund construction of solar-power plants, and there's even talk of harnessing the tremendous tidal flows of the Pacific to generate more 'clean' energy. By law California's utilities must get 33% of their energy from renewable resources by 2020, the most ambitious target yet set by any US state.

Also, some of the most visionary sustainability practices in the world are unfolding throughout Northern California. The wine regions north of San Francisco are the greenest in the world, maximizing their water and energy usage and pioneering techniques that have all but eliminated the use of pesticides. The city government of Arcata has world-leading sustainability practices. The city purchased tracts of forest land to protect the integrity of its water supply and developed a revolutionary marsh-based sewer treatment system. Built on a solid waste, the marsh processes wastewater through a series of oxidation ponds and wetlands that also serve as a wildlife sanctuary. Additionally, citizens in towns of the far north, such as McCloud and Shasta, have brought landmark civic actions to protect their natural resources. In 2009, they blocked multinational Nestlé from tapping the Shasta watershed for a water-bottling facility.

NorCal Wildlife

With five distinct climatic zones, Northern California has an overwhelming variety of plant and animal species. These different zones lie within a short drive of one another. If you wanted, you could see sunrise on a beach, spend midday under the canopy of redwoods, and catch sunset from a snowcapped mountain. Even if you don't intend to spot wildlife, you will: herds of Roosevelt elk stop traffic, curious deer graze in meadows, and flocks of migratory birds fly constantly overhead.

Pick up one of the excellent *California Natural History Guides* published by the University of California Press (www.ucpress.edu), which are compact enough to carry in a day pack.

Wild Things

Much of California is a biological island cut off from the rest of North America by the soaring heights of the Sierra Nevada and, as on other 'islands' in the world, evolution created unique plants and animals under these conditions. As a result, California ranks first in the nation for its number of endemic plants, amphibians, reptiles, freshwater fish and mammals.

Although the staggering numbers of animals that greeted the first European settlers are now extinct, you'll still see wildlife thriving in Northern California, provided you go to the right places at the right times of year. During your travels, you're likely to spot at least a few iconic species, such as coyotes, bobcats and eagles. Unfortunately, some of these are but shadow populations, hovering at the edge of survival, marginalized by the burgeoning human population.

Whales & Other Marine Animals

Spend even one day along Northern California's coast and you'll get a crash course in marine wildlife – from the gulls overhead (or eyeing your picnic) to tide pools of starfish. Still, the king of the Northern California coast is much, much bigger: the magnificent gray whale. Gray whales migrate in growing numbers along California's coast, and visitors to coastal bluffs in the north should scan the horizons for their clouds of spray. Adult whales live up to 70 years, are longer than a city bus and can weigh up to 40 tons, making quite a splash when they dive below or leap out of the water.

In summer, the whales feed in the Arctic waters between Alaska and Siberia. In the fall, they move south down the Pacific coast of Canada and the USA to sheltered lagoons in the Gulf of California, by the Mexican state of Baja California. During this 6000-mile migration, the whales pass by California between December and April. Traveling night and day at a clip of about 3mph, this is thought to be the longest migration of any mammal. (Sooty shearwaters, seabirds that resemble a dark gray seagull, hold the record for the longest migration of anything in the animal kingdom, and they also can be seen in Northern California.)

Peak mating season for northern elephant seals along the Pacific coast just happens to coincide with Valentine's Day (February 14).

The best way to see whales is by getting right out on the water. During the season of their migration, visitors can depart from many cities along the North Coast on whale-watching expeditions, which often last two hours. These have no guarantees, but visitors can ask the boat operators about recent sightings to get an idea of what to expect.

Even if you don't spot the big guys, you'll likely see other charming little creatures, including playful sea otters and harbor seals. These species especially like to crowd around public piers and protected bays. Since the 1989 earthquake, the air of San Francisco's Pier 39 has been filled by the distinct sound (and distinct odor) of barking sea lions, much to the delight of ogling tourists. Another place to see wild pinnipeds is Point Lobos State Natural Reserve near Monterey.

Almost hunted to extinction by the late 19th century, northern elephant seals have made a remarkable comeback along California's coast. Año Nuevo State Park, north of Santa Cruz, is a major breeding ground for northern elephant seals. But California's biggest elephant seal colony is found at Piedras Blancas near Hearst Castle, south of Big Sur. There's a smaller rookery at Point Reyes National Seashore.

Mountain Kings

There's some irony in the fact that California's most symbolic animal is the grizzly bear. The brown beast that graces the state flag is long gone. Extirpated in the early 1900s, grizzlies once roamed California's beaches and grasslands in large numbers, eating everything from whale carcasses to acorns. Grizzlies were particularly abundant in the Central Valley, but retreated upslope into the mountains as they were hunted out. There's occasionally chatter from conservationists about reintroducing the grizzly population to California, but it seems unlikely.

All that remains now are the grizzlies' relatively diminutive cousins, black bears, which typically weigh under 400lb. These burly omnivores feed on berries, nuts, roots, grasses, insects, eggs, small mammals and fish, but can become a nuisance around campgrounds and mountain cabins where food is not stored properly. Remember the old adage that 'a fed bear is a dead bear' – people invite the destruction of these beautiful animals by carelessly leaving food unattended in their cars and at campsites. It's a wonderful complement to a trip in the woods to see a black bear foraging in a high mountain meadow, but sadly they're most often seen scrounging around in the campground dumpster.

Northern California's other fearsome mammal is the mountain lion. Sometimes called cougars, they hunt throughout the mountains and forests of Northern California, especially in areas teeming with deer. Solitary lions, which can grow to 8ft in length and weigh 175lb, are formidable predators, but they are very, very seldom seen. Although they incite a panic in many urbanites (and you'll see warning signs at many trailheads), these large cats are very skittish and attacks on humans are

California's mountain forests are home to an estimated 25,000 to 35,000 black bears, whose fur actually ranges in color from black to dark brown, cinnamon or even blond.

EYEING ELEPHANT SEALS

Northern elephant seals follow a precise calendar. In November and December, adult male 'bull seals' return to their colony's favorite California beaches and start the ritual struggles to assert superiority; only the largest, strongest and most aggressive 'alpha' males gather a harem. In January and February, adult females, already pregnant from last year's beach antics, give birth to their pups and soon mate with the dominant males, who promptly depart on their next feeding migration. The bull seals' motto seems to be 'love 'em and leave 'em'!

At birth an elephant seal pup weighs about 75lb, and while being fed by its mother it puts on about 10lb a day. Female seals leave the beach in March, abandoning their offspring. For up to two months the young seals, now known as 'weaners,' lounge around in groups, gradually learning to swim, first in tidal pools, then in the sea. Then they, too, depart by May, having lost 20% to 30% of their weight during this prolonged fast.

Between June and October, elephant seals of all ages and both sexes return in smaller numbers to the beaches to molt.

extremely rare. Most human encounters have occurred where encroachment has pushed hungry lions to their limits – for example, at the boundaries between wilderness and rapidly developing suburbs.

Feathered Friends & Butterflies

Northern California lies on major migratory routes for over 350 species of birds, which either pass through the state or linger through the winter. This is one of the top birding destinations in North America. Witness, for example, the congregation of one million ducks, geese and swans at the Klamath Basin National Wildlife Refuges every November. During winter, these waterbirds head south into the refuges of the Central Valley, another area to observe huge numbers of native and migratory species.

Year round you can see birds at California's beaches, estuaries and bays, where herons, cormorants, shorebirds and gulls gather at places such as Point Reyes National Seashore and the shores near Redwood National and State Parks. Monarch butterflies are gorgeous orange creatures that follow long-distance migration patterns in search of milkweed, their only source of food. They winter in California by the tens of thousands, mostly on the Central Coast, including at Santa Cruz, Pacific Grove and Pismo Beach.

As you drive along the Big Sur coast, look skyward to spot endangered California condors, which also soar over inland Pinnacles National Monument. Condors are the largest flying birds in the hemisphere, with a wingspan that can reach 9ft. They're easy to mistake with the wobbly, and common, turkey vulture, who are also frequent guests above the shorelines. You can tell the difference by their coasting pattern: turkey vultures are poorly balanced and seem to soar drunkenly, whereas condors glide much more smoothly. Also keep an eye out for regal bald eagles, which can be seen in the Sierra Nevada and along the North Coast.

The Audubon Society's free California chapter website (http://ca.audubon.org) has helpful birding checklists, a newsy blog, and descriptions of key species and important birding areas statewide.

Going Native: Wildflowers & Trees

Plant life in Northern California is both flamboyant and subtle. Many species are so obscure and similar that only a dedicated botanist could tell them apart, but add them all together in the spring and you end up with riotous carpets of wildflowers that can take your breath away. The state flower is the orange-yellow native California poppy.

California is also a land of superlative trees: the tallest (coast redwoods approaching 380ft), the largest (giant sequoias of the Sierra Nevada over 36ft across at the base) and the oldest (bristlecone pines of the White Mountains that are almost 5000 years old). The giant sequoia, which is unique to California, survives in isolated groves scattered on the Sierra Nevada's western slopes, including in Yosemite, Sequoia and Kings Canyon National Parks.

An astounding 20 native species of oak grow in California, including live, or evergreen, oaks with hollylike leaves and scaly acorns, which thrive in coastal ranges. More rare native species include the Monterey

WILDFLOWER WATCHING

The famous 'golden hills' of California are actually the result of European grasses drying up in preparation for the long dry summer. Originally, before these invasive species took root, the hills of California remained green year round with native bunch grass. Other plants have adapted to long periods of almost no rain by growing prolifically during California's mild wet winters, springing to life with the first rains of autumn and blooming as early as January. As snows melt later at higher elevations in the Sierra Nevada, Yosemite National Park's Tuolumne Meadows is a prime spot for wildflower walks and photography, with peak blooms usually in late June or early July.

pine, gnarly trees that have adapted to harsh coastal conditions such as high winds, sparse rainfall and sandy, stony soils. You can find groves of them near Monterey.

Heading inland, the Sierra Nevada has three distinct ecozones: the dry western foothills covered with oak and chaparral, conifer forests starting from about 2000ft, and an alpine zone above 8000ft. Twenty-three species of conifer occur in the Sierra Nevada, with mid-elevation forests home to massive Douglas firs, ponderosa pines and, biggest of all, the giant sequoia. Deciduous trees include the delightful quaking aspen, a white-trunked tree whose shimmering leaves brighten many mountain meadow edges. Its large, rounded leaves turn pale yellow in the early fall, creating some of the most spectacular scenery you'll see, notably around June Lake in the Eastern Sierra and Monitor Pass (Hwy 4) in the High Sierra.

In 2006 the world's tallest tree was discovered in Redwood National Park (its location is being kept secret). It's named Hyperion and stands at a whopping 379ft tall.

Arts & Architecture

You'll be sitting in a San Francisco taqueria (Mexican fast-food restaurant) minding your own business when suddenly a posse of mariachis arrives and breaks into a brassy ballad. *This* is the essence of Northern California's relationship with the arts: deeply woven into everyday life, unexpected and unavoidable. Northern California has been a bastion for creative thinkers, performance artists, contrarians and crackpots since its beginning. Expect to encounter the thriving culture they've created: broadly independent, highly spirited and marching to its own beat.

Music

When the 1906 earthquake hit San Francisco, the visiting Metropolitan Opera lost all its costumes, and tenor Enrico Caruso was thrown from his bed. Caruso never returned, but the Met played free shows in the rubble-choked streets.

The essential sounds of Northern California would be a schizophrenic playlist. It would lead with a track from Summer of Love icons like Jefferson Airplane, Janis Joplin or the Grateful Dead, include a few choice cuts from twanging, heartbroken country heroes from the Central Valley, and eventually make its way to the distinctive thump of the East Bay's 'hyphy' hip-hop movement. You'd also have to have a sample of haute folk nuevo acts like Joanna Newsom and a couple of lilting *norteño* ballads, which dominate the region's AM radio, and round things out with the San Francisco Symphony, now one of the nation's most exciting orchestral bodies, under the baton of Michael Tilson Thomas.

San Francisco is where most of the musical action happens. But even outside the city, you'll find fantastic outdoor festivals and spunky music scenes in college towns such as Arcata and Chico. Look for events listings online and also at coffeehouses, where bulletin boards often have posters for upcoming out-of-town events as diverse as the Queer Music Festival and Reggae on the River.

Golden Oldies

The guy crooning in the corner of the taco shop represents one of California's longest musical traditions – Mexican folk music. This sound arrived even before the Gold Rush introduced Western bluegrass, bawdy dance-hall ragtime and Chinese classical music and is still an essential sound of the region. Still, by the turn of the 20th century, opera had become California's favorite sound. San Francisco alone had 20 concert and opera halls before the 1906 earthquake literally brought down the houses. Among San Francisco's first public buildings to be completed was the War Memorial Opera House, now home to the second-largest US opera company after New York's Metropolitan. Although the San Francisco Opera still rolls out the same chestnuts that entertained fans after the quake, today its program includes a number of visionary modern works, including recent premieres *The Bonesetter's Daughter,* with a libretto written by Bay Area author Amy Tan, and *Dolores Claiborne,* adapted from the story by Stephen King.

It Don't Mean a Thing...

Swing – imported from black neighborhoods in the East and dance halls of the South – swept Northern California in the 1930s and '40s. Big bands packed houses in the Bay Area and Western Swing (the country kind) filled Central Valley dance halls. Swing's arty edge flourished on the stages of San Francisco's underground, integrated jazz clubs. These scenes might sound like estranged cousins, but swing's essential feel – lilting, often up-tempo rhythmic underpinnings – was the colorblind common thread.

Still, the era swung in two distinctly segregated ways in Northern California: the African American communities that arrived via the 'Great Migration' to work in the Bay Area's WWII shipping and manufacturing industries, and satin-clad Western Swing outfits that modeled themselves after Texas fiddler Bob Wills. While both San Francisco and Oakland fostered working-class blues scenes throughout the 1940s and '50s, championed by guitarists Pee Wee Crayton from Texas and Oklahoma-born Lowell Fulson, the most happening scene was in San Francisco's Fillmore district, known as the 'Harlem of the West' – which is rumored to have hosted the only gig where jazz icons Charlie Parker and Louis Armstrong ever played together. By marrying Western Swing and a rural working-class aesthetic, the Central Valley minted the Bakersfield Sound, a hard-edged, honky-tonk genre that would see the rise of Buck Owens and Merle Haggard.

While Beat poets riffed over improvised bass lines and audiences snapped their fingers along in San Francisco's North Beach neighborhood, the cool West Coast Jazz movement emerged from the 1950s, with champions in trumpeter Chet Baker and pianist Dave Brubeck. In the 1950s and '60s, doo-wop, rhythm and blues, and soul music were all in steady rotation at nightclubs in San Francisco, while the nexus of pop music became firmly established in the studios of Los Angeles.

The San Francisco Sound & Summer of Love

No tune captures the psychedelic San Francisco sound better than the brilliant, twisted, totally bizarre trip of Jefferson Airplane's musical take of Lewis Carroll's *Alice's Adventures in Wonderland*, 'White Rabbit.' After the building waves of musical rebellion manifested in the form of a sassy, sultry, salty singer named Janis Joplin, all ears were on San Francisco during the '60s. The Grateful Dead would emerge as the most enduring Bay Area ambassadors, but they were only a sliver of the scene. A seething, psychedelic mess of musical exploration, sexual liberation and mind-altering expression, it was a sound presented in vivid Technicolor by groups like Moby Grape, Quicksilver Messenger Service and Santana. This movement was cranked up to 11 during 1967, when the Summer of Love brought 10,000 pilgrims to San Francisco's Haight-Ashbury neighborhood. Golden Gate Park's 'Human Be-In' in January of that year kicked things off with a free-form festival of good vibes, LSD and live music. At the end of the '60s, Sly and the Family Stone – a funky, interracial group lead by the so-called 'Black Prince of Woodstock,' Sly Stone – perfectly captured the all-embracing, edgy, revolutionary spirit of the times with their hit 'I Want to Take You Higher.'

Wider social tensions, civic unrest and an increasingly volatile discourse on the Civil Rights movement later boiled over and changed the vanguard players of San Francisco's sound, and many musicians instrumental in the Summer of Love entered a period of decline hastened by over exposure and overdoses. Those who survived cleaned up and cashed out (lookin' at you, Mr Santana), though the Grateful Dead soldiered on until Jerry Garcia's passing in a Marin County rehabilitation clinic in 1995.

The Monterey Jazz Festival is among the longest-running jazz festivals in the world and has been swinging along on the Central Coast since 1958. Its organizers have included pianist Dave Brubeck and actor, former Carmel mayor (and occasional composer) Clint Eastwood. It is held annually at the end of September.

PUNKS OF THE NORTH

In the 1970s, when American airwaves were jammed with commercial arena rock, California rock critics like Lester Bangs and Greil Marcus formed the cultural front line to fight back. Sick of the prepackaged anthems, teenagers across the US and Northern California plugged secondhand guitars into crappy, distorted amplifiers and articulated their fury with three chords and unvarnished rage. Punk was born.

San Francisco's punk scene was arty and absurdist, in rare form with Dead Kennedys singer (and future San Francisco mayoral candidate) Jello Biafra howling 'Holiday in Cambodia.' The Avengers opened for the Sex Pistols' 1978 San Francisco show, which Sid Vicious celebrated with an OD in the Haight that broke up the band.

In the mid-'90s a fresh wave of influential punks grew out of all-ages, DIY venues like Berkeley's (now defunct) Gillman Street Project, including bands like Operation Ivy and Rancid. Of these, none had more sustained success than the Berkeley trio Green Day, who churned out catchy pop-punk hooks about suburban doldrums, masturbation and teen ennui. While Green Day grew into arena-sized audiences through the next decade, their 2004 LP *American Idiot* was a mainstream success with Bay Area ideals: its songs derided war, capitalism and conservative politics.

Alternative NorCal

Forget the '80s, the spandex, the commercial synth pop and hair metal. While these trends wafted north from LA like a noxious cloud of Aqua Net hair spray, Northern California's music scene slumbered. Aside from a couple of marginal mainstream acts, like Huey Lewis & the News, Tesla and MC Hammer, Northern California was relatively quiet and its influence relatively minor. But there's something in the cultural DNA of Northern California that delights in swimming against the stream, so when the cultural backlash against mainstream movements began in earnest with college radio, late-night MTV programming and the emergence of arty, post-punk underground, Northern California was back in the action.

As so-called 'alternative music' found larger and larger audiences, well-packaged Bay Area folk rockers like Counting Crows, Chris Isaak and 4 Non Blondes crossed over and enjoyed a moment of Top 40 success. Still, the most interesting music of the '90s was produced by a group of quietly influential, genre-bending groups like Jawbreaker, Pavement, Primus and Faith No More.

The dot-com boom was the death knell of San Francisco's underground music in the 2000s; escalating rents were bankrolled by venture-capital firms, and artists watched their venues and rehearsal spaces transformed into offices, sushi restaurants and boutiques.

Over the last decade, Northern California's music has flourished across the bay in Oakland, where there are plucky scenes of underground rock and hip-hop. Even further afield, unlikely musical centers have flourished – like Nevada City, home to harp-playing indie darling Joanna Newsom.

Rap & Hip-Hop Rhythms

Los Angeles' Compton neighborhood was the epicenter of the West Coast rap and hip-hop movements throughout the 1980s and '90s, but Northern California maintained a healthy grassroots hip-hop scene in the heart of the black-power movement in Oakland. One of the primary figures of West Coast rap, Tupac Shakur, spent his high-school years on the not-so-mean streets of Marin County. It wasn't until the 1990s that the Bay Area sound came into its own with the 'hyphy movement.' Like the Bay Area's punk and rock movements, its roots were also contrarian –

a reaction against the increasing commercialization of hip-hop. Its most enduring and influential players were underground Oakland artists like Keak Da Sneak, Mac Dre and E-40.

Also from Oakland, Michael Franti & Spearhead blended hip-hop with funk, reggae, folk, jazz and rock stylings into messages for social justice and peace in 2010's *The Sound of Sunshine*. Meanwhile, Korn from Bakersfield combined hip-hop with rap and metal to popularize 'nu metal.'

Architecture

There's more to Northern California than bungalows and boardwalks, and buildings here have often adapted imported styles to the climate and available materials – just look at the fog-resistant redwood-shingle houses in Mendocino. But after a century and a half of grafting on inspired influences and eccentric details as the mood strikes, the element of the unexpected is everywhere: tiled Maya deco facades in Oakland, English thatched roofs in Carmel, chinoiserie streetlamps in San Francisco. California's architecture was postmodern before the word even existed.

In 1915, newspaper magnate William Randolph Hearst commissioned California's first licensed female architect, Julia Morgan, to build his Hearst Castle. The commission would take decades to complete.

Spanish Missions & Victorian Queens

The first Spanish missions were built around courtyards, using materials that Native Californians and colonists found on hand: adobe, limestone and grass. Many missions crumbled into disrepair as the church's influence waned, but the style remained practical for the climate. Early California settlers later adapted it into the *rancho* (ranch) adobe style, as in the San Carlos Borroméo de Carmelo Mission in Monterey.

Once the mid-19th-century Gold Rush was on, Northern California's nouveau riche imported materials to construct grand mansions matching European fashions, and raised the stakes with ornamental excess. Many millionaires favored the gilded Queen Anne style. Outrageous examples of Victorian architecture, including 'Painted Ladies' and 'gingerbread' houses, can be found in such Northern California cities and towns as San Francisco, Ferndale and Eureka.

Art Deco & Arts & Crafts

Like much of the rest of the state, simplicity was the hallmark of Northern California's arts-and-crafts style. Influenced by both Japanese design principles and England's arts-and-crafts movement, its woodwork and handmade touches marked a deliberate departure from the Industrial Revolution. SoCal architects Charles and Henry Greene and Bernard Maybeck popularized the versatile one-story bungalow in Northern California, which became trendy at the turn of the 20th century. Today you'll spot these bungalows all over Sacramento and Berkeley with their overhanging eaves, terraces and sleeping porches, harmonizing indoors and outdoors.

California was cosmopolitan from the start, and couldn't be limited to any one set of international influences. In the 1920s, the international art-deco style took elements from the ancient world – Mayan glyphs, Egyptian pillars, Babylonian ziggurats – and flattened them into modern motifs to cap stark facades and outline streamlined skyscrapers, most notably in downtown Oakland and Sacramento. Streamline moderne kept decoration to a minimum and mimicked the aerodynamic look of ocean liners and airplanes, as seen at San Francisco's Maritime Museum at Fisherman's Wharf.

In the North Coast community of Sea Ranch, buildings are subject to rigorous zoning guidelines that require simple timber-frame structures clad in wooden siding or shingles and a harmonious relationship with the surroundings.

Postmodern Evolutions

True to its mythic nature, California can't help wanting to embellish the facts a little, veering away from strict high modernism to add unlikely postmodern shapes to the local landscape. Following in the footsteps of Southern California buildings like Richard Meier's Getty Center, and Frank Gehry's Walt Disney Concert Hall in Los Angeles, San Francisco has become home to a brave new crop of buildings in the new millennium.

San Francisco's brand of postmodernism is emblematic in Pritzker Prize–winning architects that magnify and mimic California's great outdoors, especially in Golden Gate Park. Swiss architects Herzog & de Meuron clad the MH de Young Memorial Museum in copper, which will eventually oxidize green to match its park setting. Nearby, Renzo Piano literally raised the roof on sustainable design at the LEED platinum-certified California Academy of Sciences, capped by a living garden.

Literature

For a traveler, there's much to love about Northern California's duo of great early literary icons, Jack London and Mark Twain. After all, it was Twain whose thoughts on travel are just so quotable: 'The World is a book, and those who do not travel read only a page.' Both men were avid adventurers, vivid storytellers and iconic literary stylists.

Timeless, rare Ansel Adams photographs are paired with excerpts from ca-nonical California writers, such as Jack Kerouac and Joan Didion, in *California: With Classic California Writings,* edited by Andrea Gray Stillman.

Long before Huck Finn, Twain got his break with a story called *The Celebrated Jumping Frog of Calaveras County,* which he wrote while living in a cabin in the California foothills. Every year the central event of Twain's story still sees the competition of little green contestants at the Calaveras County Fair in Angels Camp. Jack London was also a restless vagabond. Born in San Francisco, London shipped in and out of the ports of Oakland, which informed seafaring stories and adventure novels like *White Fang, The Call of the Wild* and *Sea Wolf.* London's old neighborhood isn't the turf of salty dogs any more; the waterfront area in Oakland is now a dining and entertainment district that bears his name.

A generation later came the Beats, a collection of poets, novelists and alternative thinkers who populated San Francisco's North Beach neighborhood. The cast of characters who drifted in and out of the scene are household names in American literature: Jack Kerouac, Allen Ginsberg and Lawrence Ferlinghetti. Ferlinghetti's City Lights bookstore published many of the generation's most definitive titles, including Ginsberg's *Howl and Other Poems,* which won a landmark 1957 obscenity case during the oppressive era of McCarthyism.

More recently, a number of Northern California authors have enjoyed attention on the international stage. Chinese American novelist Amy Tan's *Joy Luck Club* was a celebrated work about the dynamics of families in San Francisco's Chinatown. Writer, editor and publisher Dave Eggers was a Pulitzer Prize finalist for his 2000 memoir *A Heartbreaking Work of Staggering Genius,* and two literary ventures have earned national attention: a literary magazine *The Believer* and a nonprofit literary advocacy program, 826 Valencia, which is named for its Mission District address.

Some of the most eloquent modern writing on Northern California, the Summer of Love, the Central Valley and the California political circus is by the hand of Sacramento native essayist Joan Didion. Didion's *White Album* is a collection of essays that goes deep into the psyche of California in the late '60s, and discussion of the Central Valley in *Where I Was From* takes a thoughtful look at Ronald Reagan's governor mansion, water wars and the odysseys of California's mythmakers.

Visual Arts & Theater

Although the earliest European artists were trained cartographers accompanying Western explorers, their images of California as an island show more imagination than scientific rigor. This exaggerated, mythologizing tendency of depicting California continued throughout the Gold Rush era, as Western artists alternated between caricatures of Wild West debauchery and manifest-destiny propaganda that urged pioneers to settle in the gold-

FILM IN SAN FRANCISCO

Although San Francisco can't hold a candle to the cinematic clout of its neighbor to the south, the city hosts a number of internationally renowned film festivals. The annual San Francisco International Film Festival, held each spring, is the oldest continuously running film festival in the Americas and the city also hosts several other notable film festivals each year, including the Asian American Film Festival in March and the International LGBT Film Festival in June as part of the city's Pride Month. Film fans who come at other times of the year should look into UC Berkeley's Pacific Film Archive.

The Bay Area is also home to some notable film houses, including animation giant Pixar and George Lucas' Skywalker Ranch.

en West. The completion of the Transcontinental Railroad in 1869 brought an influx of romantic painters, who produced epic California wilderness landscapes. In the early 1900s, homegrown colonies of California impressionist plein-air painters emerged, particularly at Carmel-by-the-Sea.

With the invention of photography, the improbable truth of California's landscape and its inhabitants was revealed. Pirkle Jones saw expressive potential in California landscape photography after WWII, while San Francisco native Ansel Adams' sublime photographs had already started doing justice to Yosemite. Adams founded Group f/64 with Edward Weston from Carmel and Imogen Cunningham in San Francisco. Berkeley-based Dorothea Lange turned her unflinching lens on the plight of Californian migrant workers in the Great Depression and Japanese Americans forced to enter internment camps in WWII, producing poignant documentary photos.

As the postwar American West became crisscrossed with freeways and divided into planned communities, Californian painters captured the abstract forms of manufactured landscapes on canvas. In San Francisco Richard Diebenkorn and David Park became leading proponents of Bay Area Figurative Art, while San Francisco sculptor Richard Serra captured urban aesthetics in massive, rusting monoliths resembling ship prows and industrial Stonehenges. San Francisco also developed its own brand of pop art, with the rough-and-ready-made 1950s Beat collage, 1960s psychedelic Fillmore posters, earthy '70s funk and beautiful-mess punk, and '80s graffiti and skate culture. This tradition remains alive at the Fillmore Auditorium, which distributes show posters after most of its concerts.

The contemporary art scene in Northern California is a blend of all these influences, informed by the international community and augmented by muralist-led social commentary. There's also an obsessive dedication to craft and a new-media milieu pierced by Silicon Valley's cutting-edge technology. To see California-made art at its most experimental, check out independent NorCal art spaces in San Francisco's Mission District and the laboratory-like galleries of SoMa's Yerba Buena Arts District. The Yerba Buena Center for the Arts is at the center of it all.

San Francisco's priorities have been obvious since the great earthquake of 1906, when survivors were entertained in tents set up amid the smoldering ruins, and its famous theaters were rebuilt well before City Hall. Major productions destined for the lights of Broadway and London premiere at the American Conservatory Theater, and San Francisco's answer to Edinburgh is the annual SF Fringe Festival at the Exit Theatre. The Magic Theatre gained a national reputation in the 1970s, when Sam Shepard was the theater's resident playwright, and still today it premieres innovative California playwrights. Across the Bay, the Berkeley Repertory Theatre has launched acclaimed productions based on such unlikely subjects as the rise and fall of Jim Jones' People's Temple.

Due to cuts in the California Arts Council budget, Californians now invest only about 3¢ per capita in the arts – a minuscule amount compared with Canadians, who each contribute over $5 annually toward their arts.

Survival Guide

Directory A–Z

Accommodations

→ Budget-conscious accommodations include campgrounds, hostels and motels. Because midrange properties generally offer better value, most of our accommodations fall into this category.

→ At midrange motels and hotels, expect clean, comfortable and decent-sized double rooms with private bathroom and amenities including cable TV, direct-dial telephone, a coffeemaker and perhaps a microwave and minifridge.

→ Top-end lodgings offer more amenities, and perhaps a scenic location, designer decor and/or a historical building. Pools, fitness rooms, business centers, full-service restaurants and bars and other convenient facilities are standard.

→ In Northern California, where it rarely gets hot, air con is not often provided; ask when you book.

→ Some accommodations offer online computer terminals for guests, sometimes for an additional fee; others offer only wi-fi.

→ When wireless internet access is offered, there may be a fee, especially for in-room access. Look for free wi-fi hot spots in hotel public areas (eg lobby, poolside).

→ Many lodgings are now exclusively nonsmoking. Where they still exist, smoking rooms are often left unrenovated and in less desirable locations. Expect a hefty 'cleaning fee' ($100 or more) if you light up in designated nonsmoking rooms.

Rates & Reservations

→ Reservations are recommended for weekend and holiday travel year round, and every day during high season.

→ Generally, midweek rates are lower, except in hotels geared toward weekday business travelers. Unless noted, rates do not include taxes, which exceed 10%.

→ If you plan to arrive late in the evening, call ahead on the day of your stay. Hotels overbook, but if you've guaranteed the reservation with your credit card, the hotel should accommodate you.

→ Discount cards and auto-club membership (eg AARP or AAA) may yield an additional 10% off standard rates at participating hotels and motels.

→ Look for free ad magazines with hotel and motel discount coupons at gas stations, highway rest areas, tourist offices and online at HotelCoupons (http://hotelcoupons.com).

→ Bargaining may be possible for walk-in guests without reservations, especially during off-peak times.

B&Bs & Vacation Rentals

If you want an atmospheric or perhaps romantic alternative to impersonal motels and hotels, bed-and-breakfast inns typically inhabit fine old Victorian houses or other heritage buildings, bedecked with floral wallpaper and antique furnishings. People who like privacy may find them too intimate.

Rates often include a home-cooked breakfast, but occasionally breakfast is *not* included (never mind what 'B&B' suggests). Amenities vary widely. Rooms with TV and telephone are the exception; the cheapest rooms may share bathrooms. Standards are high at places certified by the **California**

BOOK YOUR STAY ONLINE

For more accommodations reviews by Lonely Planet authors, check out http://lonelyplanet.com/hotels/. You'll find independent reviews, as well as recommendations on the best places to stay. Best of all, you can book online.

Association of Boutique & Breakfast Inns (www.cabbi.com). Quality varies wildly at hosted and DIY-style vacation rental properties listed with **Airbnb** (www.airbnb.com) and **Vacation Rentals by Owner** (VRBO; www.vrbo.com).

Most B&Bs require advance reservations, although some will accommodate the occasional drop-in guest. Minimum-stay requirements are common, especially on weekends and in high season.

Camping

In California, camping is much more than a cheap sleep. The best campgrounds will have you bedding down by the beach, underneath pine trees at an alpine lake, or beside sand dunes in the desert. The website of **California State Parks** (www.parks.ca.gov) is a good starting place.

Hostels

Northern California has 14 hostels affiliated with **Hostelling International USA** (HI-USA; ☏888-464-4872; www.hiusa.org). Dorms in HI hostels are typically gender-segregated; alcohol and smoking are prohibited. HI-USA membership cards (adult/senior per year $28/18, under-18s free) save $3 per night.

There are scores of independent hostels, particularly in coastal cities. They generally have more relaxed rules, often no curfew and frequent parties and activities. Some hostels include a light breakfast, arrange tours or offer pick-ups at transportation hubs. No two are alike, but facilities typically include mixed dorms, semiprivate rooms with shared bathrooms, communal kitchens, lockers, internet access, laundry and TV lounges. The latest amenity is a lockable cabinet with electrical outlet, so you can charge electronics while they're stored; ask when you book.

Some hostels say they only accept international visitors (basically to keep out homeless locals), but Americans who look like travelers (eg you're in possession of a plane ticket) may be admitted, especially during slow periods.

Dorm-bed rates average $25 to $55 per night, including tax. Reservations are always recommended, especially in high season. Most accept reservations online or by phone. Booking services like www.hostels.com, www.hostelz.com and www.hostelworld.com sometimes offer lower rates.

Hotels & Motels

➡ Rooms are often priced by the size and number of beds, rather than number of occupants. Those with a double or queen-size bed usually cost the same for one or two people; rooms with a king-size bed or two double beds cost more.

➡ In America, a double room means double occupancy – as in two people, *not* two beds; you must specifically request two beds.

➡ There is often a surcharge for the third and fourth person, but children under a certain age (this varies) may stay free. Cribs or roll-away cots sometimes cost extra.

➡ Beware that suites or 'junior suites' may simply be oversized rooms; ask about the layout when booking. Proper suites have two (or

---

---

more) rooms, separated by doors.

➤ Recently renovated or larger rooms, or those with views, usually cost more. Descriptors like 'oceanfront' and 'ocean view' are too liberally used; rooms described as such may require a periscope to spot the surf.

➤ You can reserve chains by calling their central-reservations line, but to learn about specific amenities and promotions, call the property directly.

➤ If you arrive without reservations, ask to see a room before paying, especially at motels.

➤ Rates may include breakfast, which could be just a stale doughnut and wimpy coffee, an all-you-can-eat buffet, or anything in between.

Customs Regulations

Currently, non-US citizens and permanent residents may import:

➤ 1L of alcohol (if you're over 21 years old)

➤ 200 cigarettes (one carton) or 100 (non-Cuban) cigars (if you're over 18)

➤ $100 worth of gifts Amounts higher than $10,000 in cash, traveler's checks, money orders and other cash equivalents must be declared. Don't even consider bringing illegal drugs.

For more complete, up-to-date information, check the website of **US Customs & Border Protection** (www.cbp.gov).

Discount Cards

'America the Beautiful' Annual Pass (http://store.usgs.gov/pass; 12-month pass $80) Admits four adults and all children under 16 years for free to all national parks and federal recreational lands (eg USFS, BLM) for 12 months from the date of purchase. US citizens and permanent residents aged 62 years and older are eligible for a lifetime Senior Pass ($10), which grants free entry and 50% off some recreational-use fees such as camping.

American Association of Retired Persons (AARP; ☑800-566-0242; www.aarp.org; annual membership $16) This advocacy group for Americans 50 years and older offers member discounts (usually 10%) on hotels, car rentals and more.

American Automobile Association (AAA; ☑877-428-2277; www.aaa.com; annual membership from $57) Members of AAA and its foreign affiliates (eg CAA) qualify for small discounts (usually 10%) on Amtrak trains, car rentals, motels and hotels, chain restaurants and shopping, tours and theme parks.

International Student Identity & Youth Travel Cards (www.isic.org; 12-month card $25) Offers savings on airline fares, travel insurance and local attractions for full-time students (ISIC) and for nonstudents under 26 years of age (IYTC). Cards are issued by student unions, hosteling organizations and youth-oriented budget travel agencies.

Senior Discounts People over the age of 65 (sometimes 55, 60 or 62) often qualify for the same discounts as students; any ID showing your birth date should suffice as proof.

Go San Francisco Card (www.smarterdestinations.com; 1-day pass adult/child 3-12yr from $58/50) Covers museums, bicycle rental and bay cruises. You've got to do a lot of sightseeing over multiple days to make the pass pay off. For discounts, buy online.

Student Advantage Card (☑800-333-2920; www.studentadvantage.com; 12-month card $22.50) For international and US students, offers 15% savings on Amtrak trains and 20% on Greyhound buses, plus discounts of 10% to 20% on some rental cars and shopping.

Electricity

120V/60Hz

Food

➤ Lunch is generally served between 11:30am and 2:30pm, and dinner between 5pm and 9pm daily, though some restaurants stay open later, especially on Friday and Saturday nights.

➤ If breakfast is served, it's usually between 7:30am and 10:30am; some diners and coffee shops keep serving breakfast into the afternoon, or all day. Weekend brunch is a laid-back affair, usually available from 11am until 3pm on Saturdays and Sundays.

➤ Like all things Northern Californian, restaurant etiquette tends to be informal. Only a handful of restaurants require more than a dressy shirt, slacks and decent shoes.

➤ Tipping 15% to 20% above the pre-tax total is expected anywhere you receive table service.

EATING PRICE RANGES

The following restaurant prices refer to an average main course at dinner. These prices don't include drinks, appetizers, desserts, taxes or tip. Note the same dishes at lunch will usually be cheaper, even half-price.

Budget ($) Less than $10

Midrange ($$) $10–20

Top End ($$$) More than $20

➜ Smoking is illegal indoors. Some restaurants have patios or sidewalk tables where smoking is tolerated (ask first or look around for ashtrays), but don't expect your neighbors to be happy about secondhand smoke.

➜ You can bring your own wine to most restaurants, but expect a 'corkage' fee of $15 to $30. Lunches rarely include booze, though a glass of wine or beer, while not common everywhere, is socially acceptable.

➜ If you ask the kitchen to divide a plate between two (or more) people, there may be a small split-plate surcharge.

➜ Vegetarians, vegans and travelers with food allergies are in luck – many restaurants are used to catering to specific dietary needs.

Gay & Lesbian Travelers

Northern California is a magnet for lesbian, gay, bisexual and transgender travelers. Hot spots include San Francisco's Castro District, and Guerneville and Calistoga, both in Wine Country. Same-sex marriage is legal in California. Despite widespread tolerance, homophobic bigotry still exists. In small towns, especially away from the coast, tolerance often comes down to 'don't ask, don't tell.'

Helpful Resources

Advocate (www.advocate.com/travel) Online news, travel features and destination guides.

Damron (www.damron.com) Classic, advertiser-driven gay travel guides and 'Gay Scout' mobile app.

Gay & Lesbian National Hotline (☏888-843-4564; www.glnh.org; ⊗1-9pm Mon-Fri, 9am-2pm Sat) For counseling and referrals of any kind.

Gay.net Travel (www.gay.net/travel) City guides, travel news and pride events.

Out Traveler (www.outtraveler.com) Free online magazine with travel tips, destination guides and hotel reviews.

Purple Roofs (www.purpleroofs.com) Online directory of LGBTQ accommodations.

Health

➜ Medical treatment in the USA is of the highest caliber, but the expense could kill you. Many health-care professionals demand payment at time of service, especially from out-of-towners or international visitors.

➜ For medical emergencies, call ☏911 or go to the nearest 24-hour hospital emergency room, or ER.

➜ For nonemergency medical treatment, phone around to find a doctor who will accept your insurance.

➜ For sexually transmitted diseases, emergency contraception, or post-exposure prevention of HIV, contact **San Francisco City Clinic** (☏415-487-5500; www.sfcityclinic.org; 356 7th St; ⊗8am-4pm Mon, Wed & Fri, 1-6pm Tue, 1-4pm Thu).

➜ Some policies require you get pre-authorization for nonemergency medical treatment before seeking help.

➜ Overseas visitors with travel health-insurance policies may need to contact a call center for an assessment by phone before getting medical treatment.

Hypothermia

➜ Skiers and hikers will find that temperatures in the mountains and desert can quickly drop below freezing, especially during winter. Even a sudden spring shower or high winds can lower your body temperature dangerously fast.

➜ Instead of cotton, wear synthetic or woolen clothing that retains warmth even when wet. Carry waterproof layers (eg Gore-Tex jacket, plastic poncho, rain pants) and high-energy, easily digestible snacks like chocolate, nuts and dried fruit.

➜ Symptoms of hypothermia include exhaustion, numbness, shivering, stumbling, slurred speech, dizzy spells, muscle cramps and irrational or even violent behavior.

➜ To treat mild hypothermia, get out of bad weather and change into dry, warm clothing. Drink hot liquids (no caffeine or alcohol) and snack on high-calorie food.

➜ For more advanced hypothermia, seek immediate medical attention. Do not rub victims, who must be handled gently.

Insurance

Getting travel insurance to cover theft, loss and medical problems is highly

PRACTICALITIES

→ **Newspapers** *San Francisco Chronicle* (www.sfgate. com), *San Jose Mercury News* (www.mercurynews. com), *Sacramento Bee* (www.sacbee.com), *Oakland Tribune* (www.insidebayarea.com)

→ **Radio** National Public Radio (NPR), lower end of FM dial

→ **DVDs** NTSC standard (incompatible with PAL or SECAM); DVDs coded region 1 (USA and Canada only)

→ **Weights & Measures** Imperial

recommended. Some policies do not cover 'risky' activities such as scuba diving, motorcycling and skiing: read the fine print! Make sure the policy at least covers hospital stays and an emergency flight home.

Paying for your airline ticket or rental car with a credit card may provide limited travel accident insurance. If you already have private health insurance, or a homeowner's or renter's policy, find out what those policies cover and only get supplemental insurance. If you have prepaid a large portion of your vacation, trip cancellation insurance may be a worthwhile expense.

Worldwide travel insurance is available at www. lonelyplanet.com/travel-insurance. You can buy, extend and claim online anytime – even if you're already on the road.

Internet Access

→ Internet cafes typically charge $6 to $12 per hour for online access.

→ With branches in most cities and towns, **FedEx** (✆800-463-3339; www. fedex.com/us) offers internet access at self-service computer workstations (30¢ to 40¢ per minute) and sometimes free wi-fi, plus digital-photo printing and CD-burning stations.

→ Plenty of accommodations, cafes, restaurants and bars provide wireless access; some have online computer kiosks. There may be a charge for either.

→ Wi-fi hot spots (free or fee-based) can be found at major airports; many hotels, motels and coffee shops (eg Starbucks); and some tourist information centers, campgrounds (eg KOA), stores (eg Apple), bars and restaurants (including fast-food chains such as McDonald's).

→ Free public wi-fi is proliferating (for a list, visit http://ca.gov/wifi). Even some state parks are now wi-fi enabled (get details at www.parks.ca.gov).

→ Public libraries have internet terminals, although online time may be limited, advance sign-up may be required and a nominal fee for out-of-network visitors may apply. Libraries also increasingly have free wi-fi access.

Legal Matters

Drugs & Alcohol

→ Possession of under 1oz of marijuana is no longer a misdemeanor in California, but an infraction; over an ounce is a misdemeanor. Possession of any other drug is a felony punishable by lengthy jail time. For foreigners, conviction of any

drug offense is grounds for deportation.

→ Police can make roadside sobriety checks to assess if you've been drinking or using drugs. If you fail, they'll require you to take a breath, urine or blood test to determine if your blood-alcohol is over the legal limit (0.08%). Refusing to be tested is treated as failing the test.

→ Penalties for driving under the influence (DUI) can include license suspension, fines and jail time.

→ It's illegal to carry open containers of alcohol inside vehicles. Unless they're full and sealed, store them in the trunk.

→ Consuming alcohol anywhere other than at private residences or licensed premises is illegal, which puts most parks and beaches off limits (although many campgrounds allow it).

→ Bars, clubs and liquor stores often ask for photo ID as proof of age – even if you're well over 21.

Police & Security

→ For police, fire and ambulance emergencies, dial ✆911. For nonemergency police assistance, call directory assistance (✆411) for the number of the nearest local police station.

→ If you're stopped by the police, be courteous. Don't get out of the car unless asked. Keep your hands where the officer can see them (eg on the steering wheel). You have the right to refuse a search of your possessions or vehicle. Simply say, 'I do not consent to a search.'

→ There is no system of paying fines on the spot. Attempting to do so may result in attempted-bribery charges.

→ For traffic violations, the ticketing officer will explain your options. Most matters can be handled by mail.

➡ If you are arrested, you have the right to remain silent and are presumed innocent until proven guilty. Everyone has the right to make one phone call. Immediately ask to see a lawyer. If you don't have one, one will be appointed to you free of charge. Foreign travelers should call their embassy or consulate.

➡ Due to security concerns over terrorism, never leave your bags unattended, especially not at airports or bus and train stations.

➡ Carrying Mace or cayenne-pepper spray is legal in California, as long as the spray bottle contains no more than 2.5oz of active product. Federal law prohibits it from being carried on planes.

➡ In cases of sexual assault, rape-crisis center and hospital staff can advocate on your behalf and act as a liaison to community services, including the police. Telephone books have listings of local crisis centers, or call the 24-hour **National Sexual Assault Hotline** (📞800-656-4673; www.rainn. org).

Smoking

➡ Smoking is generally prohibited inside public buildings, including airports, shopping malls and train and bus stations.

➡ Smoking is prohibited inside restaurants.

➡ At hotels, you must specifically request a smoking room; some hotels are entirely nonsmoking.

Money
ATMs

➡ ATMs are available 24/7 at most banks, shopping malls, airports, and grocery and convenience stores.

➡ Expect a surcharge of $2 to $3 per transaction, in addition to fees from your home bank.

➡ Most ATMs are connected to international networks and offer decent foreign-exchange rates.

➡ Withdrawing cash from an ATM using a credit card incurs hefty fees and high interest rates.

Cash

Most people do not carry large amounts of cash for everyday use, relying instead on credit cards, ATMs and debit cards. Some businesses refuse bills over $20.

Credit Cards

Major credit cards are almost universally accepted. You'll need one to rent a car, book a room or buy tickets over the phone. Visa, MasterCard and American Express are the most widely accepted.

Moneychangers

➡ You can exchange money at major airports, some banks and all currency-exchange offices such as **American Express** (www. americanexpress.com) or **Travelex** (www.travelex.com). Always inquire about rates and fees.

➡ Outside cities, exchanging money may be impossible. Carry sufficient cash and/or a credit card.

Taxes

➡ The California state sales tax of 7.5% is added to the price of most goods and services (but *not* gasoline).

➡ Local and city sales taxes may add 1.5% or more.

➡ Hotel taxes vary statewide, but currently average over 12%.

Traveler's Checks

➡ Traveler's checks have pretty much fallen out of use.

➡ Larger restaurants, hotels and department stores will often accept traveler's checks (in US dollars only),

TIPPING

Tipping is *not* optional. Only withhold tips in cases of outrageously bad service.

Airport skycaps & hotel bellhops	$2 per bag, minimum per cart $5
Bartenders	10% to 15% per round, minimum $1 per drink
Concierges	Nothing for simple information, but up to $20 for securing last-minute restaurant reservations, sold-out show tickets etc
Housekeeping staff	$2 to $4 daily, left on the pillow; more if you're messy
Parking valets	At least $2 when handed back your car keys
Restaurant & room-service waiters, hairdressers & massage therapists	15% to 20%, unless a gratuity is already charged
Taxi drivers	10% to 15% of metered fare, rounded up to the next dollar

but small businesses, markets and fast-food chains may refuse them.

➡ Visa and American Express are the most widely accepted issuers of traveler's checks.

Opening Hours

Standard opening hours:

Banks 9am-5pm Mon-Thu, to 6pm Fri, some 9am-12:30pm Sat

Bars 5pm-2am daily

Business hours (general) 9am-5pm Mon-Fri

Nightclubs 9pm-2am Thu-Sat

Pharmacies 8am-9pm Mon-Fri, 9am-5pm Sat & Sun, some 24hr

Post offices 9am-5pm Mon-Fri, some 9am-noon Sat

Restaurants 7am-10:30am, 11:30am-2:30pm & 5-9:30pm daily, some later Fri & Sat

Shops 10am-6pm or 7pm Mon-Sat, noon-5pm Sun (malls open later)

Supermarkets 8am-9pm or 10pm, some 24hr

Post

➡ The **US Postal Service** (USPS; ☎800-275-8777; www.usps.com) is inexpensive and reliable.

➡ For sending important letters or packages, also consider **Federal Express** (FedEx; ☎800-463-3339; www.fedex.com) or **UPS** (UPS; ☎800-742-5877; www.ups.com).

Public Holidays

On national holidays, banks, schools and government offices (including post offices) are closed, and transportation, museums and other services operate on a Sunday schedule. Holidays falling on a weekend are usually observed the following Monday.

New Year's Day January 1

Martin Luther King Jr Day Third Monday in January

Presidents' Day Third Monday in February

Good Friday Friday before Easter in March/April

Memorial Day Last Monday in May

Independence Day July 4

Labor Day First Monday in September

Columbus Day Second Monday in October

Veterans' Day November 11

Thanksgiving Day Fourth Thursday in November

Christmas Day December 25

School Holidays

➡ Colleges take a one- or two-week 'spring break' around Easter, some time in March or April. Some hotels and resorts, especially on the coast and in the mountains, increase their rates during this time.

➡ Summer vacations run from early June to late August, making July and August the busiest travel months.

Safe Travel

Despite its seemingly apocalyptic list of dangers – guns, violent crime, riots, earthquakes – California is a reasonably safe place to visit. The greatest danger is posed by car accidents (buckle up – it's the law), while the biggest annoyances are city traffic and crowds. Wildlife poses some small threats, and, of course, there is the dramatic, albeit unlikely, possibility of a natural disaster.

Earthquakes

Earthquakes happen all the time but most are so tiny they are detectable only by sensitive seismological instruments. If you're caught in a serious shaker:

➡ Get under a desk or table or stand in a doorway if you're indoors.

➡ Protect your head and stay clear of windows, mirrors or anything that might fall.

➡ Don't head for elevators or go running into the street.

➡ If you're in a shopping mall or large public building, expect the alarm and/or sprinkler systems to come on.

➡ If outdoors, get away from buildings, trees and power lines.

➡ If you're driving, pull over to the side of the road away from bridges, overpasses and power lines. Stay inside the car until the shaking stops.

➡ If you're on a sidewalk near buildings, duck into a doorway to protect yourself from falling bricks, glass and debris.

➡ Prepare for aftershocks.

➡ Turn on the radio and listen for bulletins.

➡ Use the telephone only if absolutely necessary.

Riptides

If you find yourself being carried offshore by a dangerous ocean current called a riptide, the important thing is to just keep afloat. Don't panic or try to swim against the current, as this will quickly exhaust you and you could drown. Instead, swim parallel to the shoreline and once the current stops pulling you out, swim back to shore.

Wildlife

➡ Never feed or approach wild animals – it causes them to lose their innate fear of humans, which in turn makes them more aggressive.

➡ Disturbing or harassing specially protected species (eg many marine mammals) is a crime, subject to enormous fines.

➡ Black bears are often attracted to campsites, where they may find food, trash and any scented items left on picnic tables or stashed in tents and cars. Always use bear-proof containers where provided. For more bear-country travel tips, see the website of **SierraWild** (http://sierrawild. gov/bears).

➡ If you encounter a bear, don't run. Stay together; keep small children near you and pick up little ones. Keep back at least 100yd. If the bear approaches, face forward, back away slowly and let it pass, being careful not to block any of the bear's escape routes or get caught between mother and cub. Sometimes a black bear will 'bluff charge' to test your dominance. Stand your ground by making yourself look as big as possible (eg waving your arms above your head) and shouting menacingly.

➡ Mountain lion attacks on humans are rare. If you encounter one, stay calm, pick up small children, face the animal and retreat slowly. Try to appear larger by raising your arms or grabbing a stick. If the lion becomes aggressive, shout or throw rocks at it. If attacked, fight back aggressively.

➡ Snakes and spiders are common throughout California, including rattlesnakes. Always check your shoes before putting them back on outdoors, especially when camping. Snake bites are rare, but occur most often when a snake is stepped on or provoked (eg picked up or poked with a stick). Antivenin is available at most hospitals.

Telephone

Cell Phones

➡ You'll need a multiband GSM phone in order to make calls in the US.

➡ SIM cards are sold at telecommunications and electronics stores. These stores also sell inexpensive prepaid phones.

➡ You can rent a cell phone at San Francisco airport from **TripTel** (☑877-874-7835; www.triptel.com); pricing plans vary, but typically are expensive.

Phone Codes

➡ US phone numbers consist of a three-digit area code followed by a seven-digit local number.

➡ When dialing a number within the same area code, use the seven-digit number.

➡ If you are calling outside your area code, dial ☑1 plus the area code plus the phone number.

➡ Toll-free numbers begin with ☑800, ☑855, ☑866, ☑877 or ☑888 and must be preceded by ☑1.

➡ For direct international calls, dial ☑011, plus the country code, plus the city code (without the initial '0'), plus the local phone number.

➡ For international call assistance, dial ☑00 – but if the operator places the call it will be very expensive.

➡ If you're calling from abroad, the US country code is ☑1 – the same as Canada, but beware international rates apply between the two countries.

Payphones & Phonecards

➡ Where payphones still exist, they are usually coin-operated, although some may only accept credit cards (eg in national parks).

➡ Local calls usually cost 50¢ minimum.

➡ For long-distance calls, you're usually better off buying a prepaid phonecard, sold at convenience stores, supermarkets, newsstands and electronics stores.

Tourist Information

➡ For pre-trip planning, peruse the information-packed website of the

California Travel & Tourism Commission (www. visitcalifornia.com).

➡ The California Travel & Tourism Commission operates nearly 20 **California Welcome Centers** (www.visitcwc.com) around the state, where staff dispense maps and brochures and help find accommodations.

➡ Almost every city and town has a local visitor center or a chamber of commerce where you can pick up maps, brochures and information.

Travelers with Disabilities

Northern California is reasonably well-equipped for travelers with disabilities.

Mobility & Accessibility

➡ Most intersections have dropped curbs and sometimes audible crossing signals.

➡ The Americans with Disabilities Act (ADA) requires public buildings built after 1993 to be wheelchair-accessible, including restrooms.

➡ Motels and hotels built after 1993 must have at least one ADA-compliant accessible room; state your specific needs when making reservations.

➡ For nonpublic buildings built prior to 1993, including hotels, restaurants, museums and theaters, there are no accessibility guarantees; call ahead to find out what to expect.

➡ Most national and many state parks and some other outdoor recreation areas offer paved or boardwalk-style nature trails accessible by wheelchairs.

➡ US citizens and permanent residents with a permanent disability qualify for a free lifetime **'America the Beautiful' Access Pass** (http://store.usgs.gov/pass/access.html), which waives entry fees to all national parks and federal recreational lands and offers 50% discounts on some recreation fees (eg camping).

➡ California State Parks' disabled discount pass ($3.50) entitles those with permanent disabilities to 50% off day-use parking and camping fees; for an application, go to www.parks.ca.gov.

Communications

➡ Telephone companies provide relay operators (dial ☑711) for the hearing impaired.

➡ Many banks provide ATM instructions in braille.

Helpful Resources

➡ www.wheelingcalscoast.org – Free accessibility information for beaches, parks and trails, plus downloadable PDF guides.

➡ www.accessnca.com – Extensive links to accessible-travel resources, publications, tours and transportation, including outdoor recreation opportunities, plus a searchable lodgings database and an events calendar.

➡ http://access.parks.ca.gov – Online map and database of accessible features at state parks.

➡ http://disabledsports easternsierra.org – Offers summer and winter activities around Mammoth Lakes (annual membership $40).

➡ www.dsusafw.org – Organizes summer and winter sports, 4WD adventures and adaptive-ski rental around Lake Tahoe in the Sierra Nevada (annual membership $30).

➡ www.mossresourcenet.org/travel.htm – Useful links and general advice for accessible travel.

➡ www.sanfrancisco.travel/accessibility/san-francisco-access-guide.html – Free downloadable accessible travel info – dated, but useful.

➡ www.scaccessguide.com – Dated but still-handy bilingual (English/Spanish) accessible travel guide (US shipping $3).

➡ www.nps.gov/yose/planyourvisit/accessibility.htm – Detailed, downloadable accessibility information for Yosemite National Park, including American Sign Language (ASL) interpretation.

➡ www.wheelchairtraveling.com – Travel tips, lodging and helpful California destination info.

Flying Wheels Travel

(☑507-451-5005; www.flying-wheelstravel.com; 143 W Bridge St, Owatonna, MN 55060) is a full-service travel agency for travelers with disabilities, mobility issues and chronic illness.

Transportation

➡ All major airlines, Greyhound buses and Amtrak trains can accommodate people with disabilities, usually with 48 hours' advance notice.

➡ Major car-rental agencies offer hand-controlled vehicles and vans with wheelchair lifts at no extra charge, but you must reserve these well in advance.

➡ For wheelchair-accessible van rentals, try **Wheelchair Getaways** (☑800-642-2042; www.wheelchairgetaways.com) in San Francisco, or **Mobility Works** (☑877-275-4915; www.mobilityworks.com) in San Francisco, Oakland, San Jose, Sacramento, Fresno and Chico.

➡ Local buses, trains and subways usually have wheelchair lifts.

➡ Seeing-eye dogs are permitted to accompany passengers on public transportation.

➡ Taxi companies should have at least one wheelchair-accessible van, but you'll need to call ahead.

Visas

➡ Visa information is highly subject to change. Double-check current visa requirements *before* coming to the USA.

➡ Currently, under the US Visa Waiver Program (VWP), visas are not required for citizens of 36 countries for stays of up to 90 days (no extensions), as long as your passport meets current US standards. See the website of **US Customs & Border Protection** (www.cbp.gov/xp/cgov/travel).

➡ Citizens of VWP countries must still register online with the **Electronic System for Travel Authorization** (ESTA; https://esta.cbp.dhs.gov) at least 72 hours before travel. Once approved, ESTA registration ($14) is valid up to two years or your passport's expiration date, whichever comes first.

➡ For most Canadian citizens traveling with Canadian passports that meet current US standards, a visa for short-term visits (usually up to six months) and ESTA registration aren't required.

➡ Citizens from all other non-VWP countries, or whose passports don't meet US standards, should apply for visas in their home country. The process costs a nonrefundable $160, involves a personal interview and can take several weeks. Apply as early as possible.

→ For more information, consult http://travel.state.gov/content/visas/english.html.

Volunteering

Casual drop-in volunteer opportunities are most common in cities, where you can socialize with locals while helping out nonprofit organizations. Browse upcoming projects and sign up online with local organizations such as San Francisco's **One Brick** (www.onebrick.org) or **HandsOn Bay Area** (www.handsonbayarea.org). For more opportunities, check local alternative weekly newspapers and **Craigslist** (www.craigslist.org).

Helpful Resources
California Volunteers (www.californiavolunteers.org) State-run volunteer directory and matching service, with links to national service days and long-term programs.

Habitat for Humanity (www.habitat.org) Nonprofit organization that helps build homes for impoverished families across California; has day, weekend and week-long projects.

Idealist.org (www.idealist.org) Free searchable database that includes both short- and long-term volunteer opportunities.

Sierra Club (www.sierraclub.org) Day or weekend projects and longer volunteer vacations (including for families) that focus on environmental conservation (annual membership $25).

Wilderness Volunteers (www.wildernessvolunteers.org) Week-long trips that help maintain national parks, preserves, forests, seashores and other wilderness conservation and outdoor recreation areas.

Worldwide Opportunities on Organic Farms (www.wwoofusa.org) Long-term volunteering opportunities on local organic farms (annual membership from $30).

Transportation

GETTING THERE & AWAY

Getting to Northern California by air, bus, car or train is easy, but not always cheap. Flights, tours and train tickets can be booked online at www.lonelyplanet.com/bookings.

GETTING AROUND

Most people drive around California, but you can also fly (if time is limited and your budget isn't) or save money by taking buses or more-scenic trains.

Air

Several major US carriers fly within Northern California, including low-cost Southwest. Flights are often operated by regional subsidiaries, such as Alaska Airlines/Horizon Air, American Eagle, Delta Connection and United Express.

Bicycle

Although bicycle is a nonpolluting 'green' way to travel, the distances involved in cycling around Northern California demand a high level of fitness and make it hard to cover much ground. Forget the mountains in winter.

Davis, San Francisco, San Luis Obispo, Santa Barbara and Santa Cruz are among California's most bike-friendly communities, as rated by the **League of American Bicyclists** (www.bikeleague.org).

Some helpful resources:

Adventure Cycling Association (www.adventurecycling.org) Online resource for purchasing bicycle-friendly maps and long-distance route guides.

Better World Club (☑866-238-1137; www.betterworldclub.com) Annual membership (from $40) gets you two 24-hour emergency roadside pickups and transport within a 30-mile radius.

California Bicycle Coalition (http://calbike.org) Links to cycling route maps, events, safety tips, laws, bike-sharing programs and community nonprofit bicycle shops.

Road Rules

➡ Cycling is allowed on all roads – and some freeways where there's no suitable alternative; mandatory exits are clearly marked.

➡ Some cities, including San Francisco, Oakland and Sacramento, have designated bicycle lanes, but urban biking is not for the fainthearted.

➡ Cyclists must follow the same road rules as vehicles. Don't expect drivers to always yield right of way.

CLIMATE CHANGE & TRAVEL

Every form of transport that relies on carbon-based fuel generates CO_2, the main cause of human-induced climate change. Modern travel is dependent on airplanes, which might use less fuel pe kilometer per person than most cars but travel much greater distances. The altitude at which aircraft emit gases (including CO_2) and particles also contributes to their climate change impact. Many websites offer 'carbon calculators' that allow people to estimate the carbon emissions generated by their journey and, for those who wish to do so, to offset the impact of the greenhouse gases emitted with contributions to portfolios of climate-friendly initiatives throughout the world. Lonely Planet offsets the carbon footprint of all staff and author travel.

→ Bike helmets are mandatory for riders under 18 years old.

→ Ensure you have proper lights and reflective gear, especially if riding at night or in fog.

Rental & Purchase

→ You can rent bikes by the hour, day or week in most cities and major towns.

→ Rentals start at around $10 per day for beach cruisers and up to $45 or more for mountain bikes; ask about multiday and weekly discounts.

→ Most rental companies require a big credit-card security deposit.

→ To buy or sell used bikes, check online bulletin boards like **Craigslist** (www.craigslist.org) – but beware of scams.

Transporting Bicycles

→ Greyhound transports bicycles as luggage (surcharge $30 to $40), provided the bicycle is disassembled and placed in a rigid container ($10 boxes are available at some terminals).

→ Amtrak's *Capitol Corridor* and *San Joaquin* trains have onboard bike racks; space is more limited aboard the latter and is first-come, first-served.

→ On Amtrak trains without racks, bikes must be put in a box ($15 at most staffed terminals) then checked as luggage (fee $10). Not all stations or trains offer checked-baggage service.

→ Bicycles may be transported on many local trains (ie CalTrain and BART), sometimes only during off-peak, noncommuter hours; for rules, check the railroad's website.

→ Some urban and suburban buses have first-come, first-served pull-down racks for two bikes, but beware of theft in certain San Francisco neighborhoods, notably the Mission.

Boat

In San Francisco Bay, regular ferry routes operate between San Francisco and Sausalito, Larkspur, Tiburon, Angel Island, Oakland, Alameda and Vallejo.

Bus

Greyhound (www.greyhound.com) buses are an economical way to travel between major cities and points along the coast, but won't get you off the beaten path or to national parks. Frequency varies, but main routes have service several times daily.

Greyhound buses are usually clean, comfortable and reliable. The best seats are generally near the front, away from the bathroom. Limited onboard amenities include freezing air con (bring a sweater) and slightly reclining seats; select buses have electrical outlets and wi-fi. Long-distance buses stop for meal breaks and driver changes.

Bus stations are typically dreary places, often in dodgy areas. If you arrive at night, take a taxi into town or directly to your lodgings. In small towns where there's no station, know exactly where and when the bus arrives, be obvious as you flag it down, and pay the driver with exact change.

Costs

→ Save money by purchasing tickets seven to 14 days in advance, and by traveling Monday through Thursday.

→ Discounts (on unrestricted fares only) are available for seniors over 62 (5% off), students with a Student Advantage Card (20%) and children aged two to 11 (25%). Tots under two ride free.

→ Special promotional discounts, such as 50% off companion fares, are often available on the Greyhound website, but come with restrictions and blackout periods.

Tickets & Reservations

It's easy to buy tickets online with a credit card, then pick them up (be sure to bring photo ID) at the terminal. You can also buy tickets over the phone or in person from a ticket agent. Greyhound-terminal ticket agents also accept debit cards, traveler's checks (in US dollars) and cash.

Most boarding is first-come, first-served. Buying tickets in advance does not guarantee you a seat on any particular bus unless you also purchase priority

SAMPLE GREYHOUND FARES

ROUTE	FARE ($)	DURATION (HR)	FREQUENCY
San Francisco–Los Angeles	55	7½-12¼	14 daily
San Francisco–Sacramento	11	2-2¾	7 daily
San Francisco–San Luis Obispo	61	6½-7¼	3 daily
San Francisco–Arcata	69	7	1 daily

boarding (fee $5), available only at some terminals. Otherwise, arrive at least one hour before the departure to secure a spot in the line; allow extra time at weekends.

Travelers with disabilities who need special assistance should call ☑800-752-4841 (TDD/TTY 800-345-3109) at least 48 hours before traveling. Wheelchairs are accepted as checked baggage, and guide dogs are allowed on board.

Car, Motorcycle & Recreational Vehicle (RV)

For flexibility and convenience, you'll probably want a car, but rental rates and gas prices can eat up a good chunk of your trip budget.

Automobile Associations

For 24-hour emergency roadside assistance, free maps and discounts on lodging, attractions, entertainment, car rentals and more, consider joining an auto club.

American Automobile Association (AAA; ☑877-428-2277; www.aaa.com) Walk-in offices throughout California, add-on coverage for RVs and motorcycles, and

reciprocal agreements with some international auto clubs (eg CAA in Canada, AA in the UK) – bring your membership card from home.

Better World Club (☑866-238-1137; www.betterworldclub.com) Ecofriendly alternative auto club that supports environmental causes and offers optional emergency roadside assistance for cyclists.

Driver's License

➡ Visitors may legally drive a car in California for up to 12 months with their home driver's license.

➡ If you're from overseas, an International Driving Permit (IDP) will have more credibility with traffic police and simplify the car-rental process, especially if your license doesn't have a photo or isn't in English.

➡ To drive a motorcycle, you'll need a valid US-state motorcycle license or a specially endorsed IDP.

➡ International automobile associations can issue IDPs, valid for one year, for a fee. Always carry your home license with the IDP.

Fuel

➡ Gas stations in Northern California, nearly all of which are self-service, are

ubiquitous near cities, but not in national parks and sparsely populated mountain areas.

➡ Gas is sold in gallons (one US gallon equals 3.78L). At press time, the cost for mid-grade fuel hovered around $4.

Insurance

California law requires a minimum of $15,000 liability insurance for all vehicles. When renting a car, check your auto-insurance policy from home or your travel-insurance policy to see if you're already covered. If not, expect to pay about $10 to $20 per day, depending on coverage maximums. Sometimes the minimum liability insurance is included in the rate, but to protect your assets, make sure you have appropriate coverage.

Insurance against damage to the car itself, called Collision Damage Waiver (CDW) or Loss Damage Waiver (LDW), costs another $10 to $15 per day; you may be required to pay the first $100 to $500 – or more – for repairs (this is called the 'deductible'; ask if your specific policy has one). Some credit cards cover this, provided you charge the entire cost of the rental to the card. If there's an accident you may have to pay the rental-car company first, then seek reimbursement from the credit-card company. Carefully check your card's policy before renting.

Parking

➡ Parking is usually plentiful and free in small towns and rural areas, but scarce and expensive in cities.

➡ You can use coins (eg quarters) in municipal parking meters, and sometimes credit or debit cards.

➡ Expect to pay $30 to $50 to park overnight in a garage.

➡ When parking on the street, read all posted

FURTHER AFIELD: LOS ANGELES & LAS VEGAS

For muscle beaches, celebrity sightings and camera-ready wackiness, head south from San Francisco on coastal Hwy 1 to Los Angeles. It'll take 12 hours depending on traffic and how often you stop. A quicker jaunt is less-scenic Hwy 101 (nine hours); the fastest route is boring inland I-5, which takes about six hours.

Las Vegas, NV, is a nine-hour nonstop drive from San Francisco. Cross the Bay Bridge to I-580 east, then take I-5 south; veer off toward Hwy 99 south (at exit 278), to Hwy 58 east, then take I-15 the last 160 miles. A slower, gloriously scenic option is to go east through Yosemite National Park on Hwy 120 (summer only; verify by calling ☑800-427-7623), then south on Hwy 395, east on Hwy 190 through Death Valley National Park, then south on Hwy 95 straight into Sin City.

regulations and restrictions, and pay attention to colored curbs, or you may be ticketed or towed – which costs a fortune in San Francisco. Red curbs mean no parking or stopping; yellow have posted restrictions, usually limited to loading by commercial vehicles; green have posted time limits; white zones are for loading and unloading only; blue curbs are exclusively for disabled parking and require a placard.

Rental
CARS

To rent, you'll typically need to be at least 25 years old, hold a valid driver's license and have a major credit card, *not* a check or debit card. A few companies may rent to drivers under 25 (but over 21) for hefty surcharges. If you don't have a credit card, you may be able to make a large cash deposit instead.

With advance reservations, you can often get an economy-size vehicle with unlimited mileage from around $30 per day, plus insurance, taxes and fees, which typically double the rate. Weekend and weekly rates are usually more economical. Airport locations may have cheaper rates but higher fees. City-center branches may offer free pickups and drop-offs.

Rental rates generally include unlimited mileage, but expect surcharges for additional drivers and one-way rentals. Some companies let you pre-pay your last tank of gas; this is rarely a good deal, as prices are higher than at gas stations and you'd need to bring the car back almost empty. Child or infant safety seats are compulsory (reserve when booking); they're sometimes free, or $10 per day (with a capped maximum of about $65).

If you'd like to minimize your carbon footprint, some car-rental companies offer 'green' fleets of hybrid or biofueled rental cars, but they're in short supply. Reserve well ahead and expect to pay more for these models – but you'll save on gasoline.

Alamo (877-222-9075; www.alamo.com)

Avis (800-633-3469; www.avis.com)

Budget (800-218-7992; www.budget.com)

Enterprise (800-261-7331; www.enterprise.com)

Fox (800-225-4369; www.foxrentacar.com) Locations near LA, Burbank, San Diego, Orange County and San Francisco Bay Area airports.

Hertz (800-654-3131; www.hertz.com)

National (877-222-9058; www.nationalcar.com)

Rent-a-Wreck (877-877-0700; www.rentawreck.com) Minimum rental age and under-25 driver surcharges vary at a dozen locations, mostly around LA and the San Francisco Bay Area.

Super Cheap! Car Rental (www.supercheapcar.com) No surcharge for drivers aged 21 to 24; nominal daily fee applies for drivers aged 18 to 21 (full-coverage insurance required). Locations in the San Francisco Bay Area, LA and Orange County.

Thrifty (800-847-4389; www.thrifty.com)

Zipcar (866-494-7227; www.zipcar.com) Currently available in the San Francisco Bay Area, LA, San Diego, Sacramento, Santa Barbara and Santa Cruz, this car-sharing club charges usage fees (per hour or day), including free gas, insurance (a damage fee of up to $750 may apply) and limited mileage. Apply online (foreign drivers accepted); application fee $25, annual membership from $60.

MOTORCYCLES

Motorcycle rentals and insurance are not cheap, especially if you've got your eye on a Harley. Depending on models, renting a motorcycle costs $100 to $200 per day, plus taxes and fees. Discounts may be available for multiday and weekly rentals. Security deposits range from $1000 to $3000 (credit card required).

Motorcycle and scooter rental agencies include:

California Motorcycle Adventures (650-969-6198; www.californiamotorcycleadventures.com; 2554 W Middlefield Rd, Mountain View; 9am-6pm Mon-Fri, to 5pm Sat, 10am-5pm Sun) Harley-Davidson rentals in Silicon Valley.

Dubbelju (415-495-2774, 866-495-2774; www.dubbelju.com; 689a Bryant St, San Francisco; 9am-6pm Mon-Sat) Rents Harley-Davidson, BMW and Japanese and Italian imported motorcycles, as well as scooters.

Eagle Rider (310-536-6777, 888-900-9901; www.eaglerider.com) Nationwide company with 10 locations in California, as well as Las Vegas, NV.

RVS

It's easy to find campgrounds throughout Northern California with electricity and water hookups for RVs, but in big cities RVs are a nuisance, since there are few places to park or plug them in. RVs are cumbersome to drive and they burn fuel at an alarming rate (you only get a measly seven to 13 miles per gallon). But they do solve transportation, accommodations and cooking needs in one fell swoop. Even so, there are many places in national and state parks and in the mountains that RVs can't go. Book RV rentals as far ahead as possible. Rental costs vary by size and model, but expect to pay over $100 per day. Rates often don't include mileage, taxes, vehicle-prep fees and bedding or kitchen kits. If pets are even allowed, expect a surcharge.

Cruise America (480-464-7300, 800-671-8042; www.cruiseamerica.com) Nationwide RV rental company with almost two dozen locations statewide.

El Monte (562-483-4956, 888-337-2214; www.elmonterv.

com) With 15 locations across California, this national RV rental agency offers AAA discounts.

Escape Campervans

(☑310-672-9909, 877-270-8267; www.escapecampervans.com) Awesomely painted campervans at economical rates in LA and San Francisco.

Happy Travel Campers

(☑855-754-6555, 310-929-5666; www.camperusa.com) Campervan rentals in the San Francisco Bay Area, LA and Las Vegas, NV.

Jucy Rentals

(☑800-650-4180; www.jucyrentals.com) Campervan rentals in San Francisco, LA and Las Vegas, NV.

Road Conditions & Hazards

For up-to-date highway conditions in Northern California, including road closures and construction updates, dial ☑800-427-7623 or visit www.dot.ca.gov. For Nevada highways, call ☑877-687-6237 or check www.nvroads.com.

In mountain areas where winter driving is an issue, tire chains and snow tires may be required on two-wheel-drive vehicles. Four-wheel-drive vehicles with snow tires are usually excluded. The speed limit with chains is 25mph. Ideally, carry your own chains and learn how to use them before you hit the road. Otherwise, you can buy chains (but not cheaply) on the highway, at gas stations or in nearby towns; the best prices are at automotive stores. State-regulated chain installers operate on major highways, such as I-80 or US-50; expect to pay $30 for installation, $20 for removal (note that it's far easier to remove than install them; consider paying only for installation). In rural areas, you're on your own. Most car-rental companies don't permit the use of chains, and also prohibit driving off-road.

In rural areas, livestock sometimes graze next to unfenced roads. These areas are typically signed as 'Open Range,' with the silhouette of a steer. Where deer and other wild animals frequently appear roadside, you'll see signs with the silhouette of a leaping deer. Take these signs seriously, particularly at night.

In coastal areas thick fog may impede driving – slow down and if it's too soupy, get off the road. Along coastal cliffs and in the mountains, watch for falling rocks, mudslides and avalanches that could damage or disable your car.

Road Rules

➡ Drive on the right-hand side of the road.

➡ Talking or texting on a cell phone without a hands-free device is illegal – even when stopped at a light.

➡ The use of seatbelts is required for drivers, front-seat passengers and children under age 16. Drivers are responsible for compliance.

➡ Infant and child-safety seats are required for children under six years old or weighing under 60lb.

➡ All motorcyclists must wear a helmet. Scooters are not allowed on freeways.

➡ High-occupancy vehicle (HOV) lanes marked with a diamond symbol are reserved for cars with multiple occupants (minimum two or three, depending on the road), sometimes only during morning and afternoon rush hours.

➡ Unless otherwise posted, the speed limit is 65mph on freeways, 55mph on two-lane undivided highways, 35mph on major city streets and 25mph in business and residential districts and near schools.

➡ It's forbidden to pass a school bus – from either direction – when its red lights are flashing.

➡ Except where a sign says that it's illegal to do so, turning right at red lights, after coming to a full stop, is permitted; intersecting traffic has the right of way. Likewise, turning left on red between two intersecting one-way streets is also permitted, unless otherwise indicated.

➡ At four-way stop signs, cars proceed in the order they arrived. If two cars arrive simultaneously, the one on the right has the right of way. When in doubt, politely wave the other driver ahead.

➡ When emergency vehicles (ie police, fire or ambulance) approach from either direction, carefully pull over to the side of the road.

➡ California has strict anti-littering laws; throwing trash from a vehicle may incur a $1000 fine.

➡ Driving under the influence of alcohol or drugs is illegal.

➡ It's illegal to carry open containers of alcohol inside a vehicle – even empty ones. Unless containers are full and still sealed, store them in the trunk.

Local Transportation

Except in cities, public transportation is rarely the most convenient option, and coverage to outlying towns and suburbs can be sparse. However, it is usually cheap, safe and reliable.

Bus, Cable Car & Streetcar

➡ Most cities and larger towns have reliable local bus systems (average $1 to $3 per ride), but may be designed for commuters and provide only limited evening and weekend service.

➡ San Francisco's extensive Municipal Railway (MUNI) network includes not only buses and trains, but also historic streetcars and those famous cable cars.

Train

To get around the San Francisco Bay Area, hop aboard Bay Area Rapid Transit (BART) or Caltrain. Sacramento and San Jose also have limited light-rail systems.

Taxi

➡ Taxis are metered, with flag-drop fees of $2.50 to $3.50 to start, plus $2 to $3 per mile. Credit cards may be accepted; check before embarking.

➡ Taxis may charge extra for baggage (but not in San Francisco) and/or airport pickups.

➡ Drivers expect a 10% to 15% tip, rounded up to the next dollar.

➡ Taxis cruise the busiest areas in large cities, but elsewhere you may need to phone for one.

➡ For quickest service in San Francisco, download the Flywheel app for smartphones, which dispatches the nearest taxi. The following are large companies in San Francisco:

DeSoto Cab (☎415-970-1300; www.desotogo.com)

Luxor (☎415-282-4141; www.luxorcab.com)

Yellow Cab (☎415-333-3333; www.yellowcabsf.com)

Train

Amtrak (www.amtrak.com) runs comfortable, if occasionally tardy, trains and buses to major California cities and limited towns. At some stations Thruway buses provide onward connections – or replace trains (read schedules carefully). Smoking is prohibited on board.

Amtrak routes within California:

SAMPLE AMTRAK FARES

ROUTE	FARE ($)	DURATION (HR)
Oakland/San Francisco–LA	59	12
San Luis Obispo–LA	41	5½
San Francisco/Emeryville–Sacramento	32	2¼
San Francisco/Emeryville–Truckee	59	5½

California Zephyr Daily service from Emeryville (near San Francisco) via Davis and Sacramento to Truckee (near Lake Tahoe) and Reno, NV.

Capitol Corridor Links San Francisco's East Bay (including Oakland, Emeryville and Berkeley) and San Jose with Davis and Sacramento several times daily. Thruway buses connect west to San Francisco, north to Auburn in the Gold Country and east to Truckee and Reno, NV. Transfer to BART trains in Richmond for faster rush-hour connections to San Francisco from Sacramento. Wi-fi available.

Coast Starlight Chugs north–south almost the entire length of the state. Daily stops include LA, Santa Barbara, San Luis Obispo, Paso Robles, Salinas, San Jose, Oakland, Emeryville, Davis, Sacramento, Chico, Redding and Dunsmuir. Limited wi-fi only for sleeping-car passengers.

San Joaquin Several daily trains with onboard wi-fi between Bakersfield and Oakland or Sacramento. Thruway bus connections include San Francisco, LA, Palm Springs and Yosemite National Park.

Costs

Purchase tickets at train stations, by phone or online. Fares depend on day of travel, advance booking, route, seating etc. Fares may increase during peak travel times (eg summer). Round-trip tickets cost the same as two one-way tickets.

Usually seniors over 62 and students with an ISIC or Student Advantage Card receive a 15% discount. Up to two children, aged two to 12, accompanied by an adult, get 50% off. AAA members save 10%. Special promotions can become available any time: check Amtrak's website.

Reservations

Reservations can be made from 11 months in advance to day of departure. In summer and around holidays, trains sell out, so book tickets as early as possible. The cheapest coach fares are usually for unreserved seats; business-class fares come with guaranteed seats.

Travelers with disabilities who need special assistance, wheelchair space, transfer seats or accessible accommodations should call ☎800-872-7245 (TDD/TTY 800-523-6590), and also inquire about discounted fares when booking.

Train Passes

Amtrak's California Rail Pass costs $159 ($80 for children aged two to 12). The pass is valid on all trains (except certain long-distance routes) and most connecting Thruway buses for seven days of travel within a 21-day period. Passholders must make advance reservations for each leg of travel and obtain hard-copy tickets prior to boarding.

Behind the Scenes

SEND US YOUR FEEDBACK

We love to hear from travelers – your comments keep us on our toes and help make our books better. Our well-traveled team reads every word on what you loved or loathed about this book. Although we cannot reply individually to your submissions, we always guarantee that your feedback goes straight to the appropriate authors, in time for the next edition. Each person who sends us information is thanked in the next edition – the most useful submissions are rewarded with a selection of digital PDF chapters.

Visit **lonelyplanet.com/contact** to submit your updates and suggestions or to ask for help. Our award-winning website also features inspirational travel stories, news and discussions.

Note: We may edit, reproduce and incorporate your comments in Lonely Planet products such as guidebooks, websites and digital products, so let us know if you don't want your comments reproduced or your name acknowledged. For a copy of our privacy policy visit lonelyplanet.com/privacy.

OUR READERS

Many thanks for the travelers who used the last edition and wrote to us with helpful hints, useful advice and interesting anecdotes:
Steen Ballegaard, Tom Bates, William Dilworth, Alan Humason, Marc Negri, Janet Noonan, Luke Patterson, Megan Soderberg, Juliane von Akerman

AUTHOR THANKS

John A Vlahides

I owe great thanks to my commissioning editor, Suki Gear, whom I miss; to my co-author, Sara Benson, for her always-sunny disposition; and to my editor Clifton Wilkinson for giving me free reign – I'm grateful. And to you, dear readers: please accept my most heartfelt gratitude for letting me be your guide to Wine Country. Have fun. I know you will!

Sara Benson

Thanks to Suki Gear, Cliff Wilkinson, Alison Lyall and the entire Lonely Planet team, including my co-authors. Family and friends all over California generously gave me insider tips, good company on road trips and, most importantly, spare rooms to crash in. Special thanks to my Golden Gate Bridge running partners Beth

Kohn (also my Sierra Nevada trail guru) and Derek Wolfgram (home brewer and an expert advisor on Bay Area craft beer).

Alison Bing

Thanks to Suki Gear, Rana Freedman, Cliff Wilkinson, Katie O'Connell, Melissa Wong, and above all, Marco Flavio Marinucci, for making a Muni bus ride into the adventure of a lifetime.

Celeste Brash

Thanks first to my road trip buddies on this trip, Heather Griggs and Tevai Humbert (who is also my son). On the road I was given all the scoop by local heroes Grant Roden, Audie Theole, Freda Moon, John Vlahides, Kem Pence and Ken Pence. Thanks to Sara Benson for being so passionate about the region and the great Suki Gear for getting me on her last book.

Tienlon Ho

Thanks to Cliff Wilkinson, Suki Gear, Dianne and the SPP team, and Sara Benson for the opportunity and support along the way. Thanks to Ken Ho, Wenhuei Ho, Tienchin Ho, Richard Winters, Anli Winters, Mayli Winters, Alison Shinsato and, of course, Jon Adams for inspiration and everything else. Most importantly, thanks to the truly weary travelers who came before me, recorded or forgotten, who built the Central Valley, Gold Country and so, California.

Beth Kohn

Brava to Suki Gear for all her years of work on so many fantastic editions of this guide, and to Sara B, my running, hiking, baking and writing heroine! Thanks to Visit Oakland, Lisa Cesaro of DNC, Kari Cobb in Yosemite National Park and Lara Kaylor at Mammoth Lakes Tourism for their excellent on-the-ground assistance. Jen and Dillon provided worthy campfire s'mores and Claude kept me (reasonably) sane throughout.

ACKNOWLEDGEMENTS

Climate map data adapted from Peel MC, Finlayson BL & McMahon TA (2007) 'Updated World Map of the Köppen-Geiger Climate Classification', Hydrology and Earth System Sciences, 11, 1633¬44.

Illustration pp74–5 by Michael Weldon.

Cover photograph: Giant sequoia trees in the forest, Sequoia and Kings Canyon National Park, Danita Delimont Stock/AWL.

THIS BOOK

This 2nd edition of *Northern California* was researched and written by John A Vlahides, Sara Benson, Alison Bing, Celeste Brash, Tienlon Ho and Beth Kohn. Sara, Alison, Beth and John also worked on the previous edition, which was coordinated by Nate

Cavalieri. This guidebook was commissioned in Lonely Planet's Oakland office, and produced by the following:

Commissioning Editor Suki Gear

Destination Editor Clifton Wilkinson

Product Editor Katie O'Connell

Senior Cartographer Alison Lyall

Assisting Editors Michelle Bennett, Anne Mulvaney

Book Designer Cam Ashley

Cover Image Researcher Naomi Parker

Thanks to Ryan Evans, Larissa Frost, Elizabeth Jones

Index

Map Legend

Sights

- Beach
- Bird Sanctuary
- Buddhist
- Castle/Palace
- Christian
- Confucian
- Hindu
- Islamic
- Jain
- Jewish
- Monument
- Museum/Gallery/Historic Building
- Ruin
- Sento Hot Baths/Onsen
- Shinto
- Sikh
- Taoist
- Winery/Vineyard
- Zoo/Wildlife Sanctuary
- Other Sight

Activities, Courses & Tours

- Bodysurfing
- Diving
- Canoeing/Kayaking
- Course/Tour
- Skiing
- Snorkeling
- Surfing
- Swimming/Pool
- Walking
- Windsurfing
- Other Activity

Sleeping

- Sleeping
- Camping

Eating

- Eating

Drinking & Nightlife

- Drinking & Nightlife
- Cafe

Entertainment

- Entertainment

Shopping

- Shopping

Information

- Bank
- Embassy/Consulate
- Hospital/Medical
- Internet
- Police
- Post Office
- Telephone
- Toilet
- Tourist Information
- Other Information

Geographic

- Beach
- Hut/Shelter
- Lighthouse
- Lookout
- Mountain/Volcano
- Oasis
- Park
- Pass
- Picnic Area
- Waterfall

Population

- Capital (National)
- Capital (State/Province)
- City/Large Town
- Town/Village

Transport

- Airport
- BART station
- Border crossing
- Boston T station
- Bus
- Cable car/Funicular
- Cycling
- Ferry
- Metro/Muni station
- Monorail
- Parking
- Petrol station
- Subway/SkyTrain station
- Taxi
- Train station/Railway
- Tram
- Underground station
- Other Transport

Note: Not all symbols displayed above appear on the maps in this book

Routes

- Tollway
- Freeway
- Primary
- Secondary
- Tertiary
- Lane
- Unsealed road
- Road under construction
- Plaza/Mall
- Steps
- Tunnel
- Pedestrian overpass
- Walking Tour
- Walking Tour detour
- Path/Walking Trail

Boundaries

- International
- State/Province
- Disputed
- Regional/Suburb
- Marine Park
- Cliff
- Wall

Hydrography

- River, Creek
- Intermittent River
- Canal
- Water
- Dry/Salt/Intermittent Lake
- Reef

Areas

- Airport/Runway
- Beach/Desert
- Cemetery (Christian)
- Cemetery (Other)
- Glacier
- Mudflat
- Park/Forest
- Sight (Building)
- Sportsground
- Swamp/Mangrove

grounds, hike snowy peaks, find petroglyphs in caves, be awed by redwoods and seduced by the wild coast. Find out more about Celeste at www.celestebrash.com.

Tienlon Ho
Sacramento & Central Valley, Gold Country An Ohioan by birth but a Californian at stomach, Tienlon Ho has walked, run, climbed, crawled, tumbled, fished, swam, and eaten her way around the state enough times to say California is huge, and spectacular. Besides writing guides and books for Lonely Planet, she writes about food, environment, and technology for a number of publications. Follow her travels and more at tienlon.com and @tienlonho.

Beth Kohn
Marin County & the Bay Area, Lake Tahoe, Yosemite & the Sierra Nevada, California Wildlife, Best Hikes of the Sierra Nevada A lucky long-time resident of San Francisco, Beth lives to be playing outside or splashing in big puddles of water. For this guide, she hiked and biked Bay Area byways, backpacked Yosemite and Lake Tahoe in winter and soaked in myriad mountain view hot springs. An author of Lonely Planet's *Yosemite, Sequoia & Kings Canyon National Parks* and *Mexico* guides, you can see more of her work at www.bethkohn.com.

OUR STORY

A beat-up old car, a few dollars in the pocket and a sense of adventure. In 1972 that's all Tony and Maureen Wheeler needed for the trip of a lifetime – across Europe and Asia overland to Australia. It took several months, and at the end – broke but inspired – they sat at their kitchen table writing and stapling together their first travel guide, *Across Asia on the Cheap*. Within a week they'd sold 1500 copies. Lonely Planet was born.

Today, Lonely Planet has offices in Franklin, London, Melbourne, Oakland, Beijing and Delhi, with more than 600 staff and writers. We share Tony's belief that 'a great guidebook should do three things: inform, educate and amuse'.

OUR WRITERS

John A Vlahides

Coordinating Author, Napa & Sonoma Wine Country John A Vlahides co-hosts the TV series *Lonely Planet: Roads Less Travelled*, screening on National Geographic Channels International. John studied cooking in Paris, with the same chefs who trained Julia Child, and is also a former luxury-hotel concierge and member of Les Clefs d'Or, the international union of the world's elite concierges. He lives in San Francisco, sings tenor with the Grammy-winning San Francisco Symphony, and spends free time biking SF and skiing the Sierra. For more, see JohnVlahides.com, twitter.com/JohnVlahides.

Read more about John at:
lonelyplanet.com/members/johnvlahides

Sara Benson

Central Coast After graduating from college, Sara jumped on a plane to California with just one suitcase and $100 in her pocket. After driving tens of thousands of miles to every corner of this state, she settled in a little beach town halfway between San Francisco and LA. She's an avid hiker, backpacker, cyclist and all-seasons outdoor enthusiast who has worked for the National Park Service in the Sierra Nevada Mountains. The author of more than 65 travel and nonfiction books, Sara is the lead writer for Lonely Planet's *California, California's Best Trips, Coastal California* and *Los Angeles, San Diego & Southern California* guides. Follow her latest adventures online at www.indietraveler.blogspot.com, www.indietraveler.net, @indie_traveler on Twitter and indietraveler on Instagram.

Read more about Sara at:
lonelyplanet.com/members/Sara_Benson

Alison Bing

San Francisco Over 10 guidebooks and 20 years in San Francisco, author Alison Bing has spent more time on Alcatraz than some inmates, become an aficionado of drag and burritos, and willfully ignored Muni signs warning that "safety requires avoiding unnecessary conversation."

Celeste Brash

North Coast & Redwoods, Northern Mountains Celeste's ancestors moved to Northern California in 1906 and this is the region she will always consider home. After 15 years in French Polynesia she now lives in the Pacific Northwest and was thrilled to head south to explore and imbibe the treasures of her old stomping

OVER PAGE MORE WRITERS

Published by Lonely Planet Publications Pty Ltd
ABN 36 005 607 983
2nd edition – March 2015
ISBN 978 1 74220 731 5
© Lonely Planet 2015   Photographs © as indicated 2015
10 9 8 7 6 5 4 3 2 1
Printed in China